# PARKER AND MELLOWS:

# THE MODERN LAW OF TRUSTS

AUSTRALIA
Law Book Co.
Sydney

CANADA and USA
Carswell
Toronto

HONG KONG
Sweet and Maxwell Asia

NEW ZEALAND
Brookers
Wellington

SINGAPORE and MALAYSIA
Sweet and Maxwell Asia
Singapore and Kuala Lumpur

# PARKER AND MELLOWS:
# THE MODERN LAW OF TRUSTS

*Eighth Edition*

by

**A. J. OAKLEY, M.A., LL.B., T.E.P.,**
*of Lincoln's Inn, Barrister-at-Law,*
*Sometime Fellow of Trinity Hall, Cambridge*

LONDON
SWEET & MAXWELL
2003

| | |
|---|---|
| *First Edition by Profs D. B. Parker & A. R. Mellows* | 1966 |
| *Second Edition* " | 1970 |
| *Third Edition* " | 1975 |
| *Fourth Edition* " | 1979 |
| *Fifth Edition* " | 1983 |
| *Sixth Edition by A. J. Oakley* | 1994 |
| *Second Impression* | 1995 |
| *Third Impression* | 1997 |
| *Seventh Edition by A. J. Oakley* | 1998 |
| *Second Impression* | 2000 |
| *Eighth edition* | 2003 |

*Published in 2003 by*
*Sweet & Maxwell Ltd of*
*100 Avenue Road, Swiss Cottage,*
*London NW3 3PF*
*http://www.sweetandmaxwell.co.uk*
*Computerset by Interactive Sciences Ltd,*
*Gloucester*
*Printed in England by*
*William Clowes Ltd, Beccles and London*

*A CIP catalogue record for this book is available*
*from the British Library*
*ISBN–0421 781807*

# PREFACE

In the preface to the first edition of this work in 1966, its authors stated that the law of trusts "is a branch of the law which is developing at a rapid pace and which is highly relevant to modern conditions, not merely to a bygone age". The accuracy of this statement was demonstrated by the fact that four further editions rapidly followed, culminating in the fifth edition in 1983. The unexpected and untimely death of Professor Parker in 1987, just when the authors might have been expected to have been thinking about a further edition, delayed the production of the sixth edition until 1994. That edition, the seventh edition, and this eighth edition have been entrusted to me. However, while it is now twenty years since an edition was produced by Professor Parker and Professor Mellows and while the work has somehow since almost doubled in length, the debt which this edition owes to their erudition and scholarship will be apparent to anyone familiar with the editions produced by them and will continue to be apparent for many editions to come.

This edition generally follows the same order as its predecessor, save that I have reversed the order of two of the chapters on express private trusts so that the chapter on "The Essential Ingredients of a Trust" now precedes the chapter on "The Formal Requirements for the Creation of a Trust". However, the rationalisation in the Trustee Act 2000 of a number of different pre-existing standards by which the conduct of trustees was judged has meant that the contents of the three separate chapters which previously dealt with different aspects of the administration of trusts have been able to be incorporated into a single chapter. The chapters on "Pensions Trusts" and "Trusts in the Conflict of Laws", both of which appeared for the first time in the last edition, have been considerably expanded. All the remaining chapters have been brought fully up to date.

The most important legislative development since the last edition has been the enactment of the Trustee Act 2000, which has substantially amended the powers of trustees as well as the standards by which their conduct is to be judged. The most important judicial developments have both been provided by the decision of the House of Lords in *Twinsectra v. Yardley* which has restated both the law governing the nature and extent of *Quistclose* Trusts and the definition of dishonesty for the purposes of the imposition of "liability for dishonest assistance". However, many other significant judgments have been handed down at all levels.

The Law Commission and the Trust Law Committee have both remained active. The former has produced proposals for a new Perpetuities and Accumulations Act which is expected to be enacted during the lifetime of this edition; its provisions are already largely known and have therefore been able to be discussed in detail. Both have collaborated in proposals for legislation dealing with Trustee Exemption Clauses, which was still at the consultation stage when this edition had to go to press. However, more significant for trust law in general is likely to prove a report on charitable trusts published in 2002 by the Government's Strategy Unit. This consultation document, entitled

"Private Action, Public Benefit", envisaged a new statutory definition of charity as an organisation which provides public benefit and which has one or more of ten listed purposes; it was hoped that this definition would provide a clearer framework while retaining existing case law and the flexibility to evolve as society changes. The relevant consultation period concluded at the end of 2002 but no further developments had occurred by the time that this edition had to go to press; nevertheless some form of legislation is obviously likely during the lifetime of this edition.

This edition has been produced at the end of a period during which I progressively retired from my academic positions at Cambridge in order to concentrate on practice at the Chancery Bar. During this period I also had for four years the advantage of teaching an LL.M. course on Advanced Trust Law at Cambridge and this edition has benefited greatly from the contributions of both the students and the visiting lecturers on that course. More generally, I hope not only that this work is no less academic for now being written by a full time practitioner but also that it has benefited from the insights which I have acquired as a result of my practice.

I would like to thank Professor Mellows for continuing to repose his confidence in me by entrusting me with this further edition, for which I alone am responsible. Among the many friends and colleagues to whom I am grateful for the benefit of their ideas and criticisms over the years, I would on this occasion particularly like to mention Mr. Nicholas Davidson Q.C., Mr. Romie Tager Q.C., and Mr. Hodge Malek Q.C., all of whom have led me in cases which are discussed in this edition. I would also like to thank my wife, Margaret Halliwell, Reader in Law at City University, for her help and support and for the fact that, despite being the author of a rival textbook, she was prepared to tolerate the disruption of her weekends while this edition was being prepared. Finally, I would like to thank the publishers for producing the Index and the Tables of Cases, Statutes, and Statutory Instruments and for their general efficiency.

The law has been stated from the sources which were available to me on May 31, 2003.

A. J. Oakley

11 Old Square
Lincoln's Inn

July 16, 2003

# CONTENTS

### 13. THE APPOINTMENT, RETIREMENT AND REMOVAL OF TRUSTEES

# TABLE OF CASES

# Table of Statutes

# TABLE OF STATUTORY INSTRUMENTS

# CHAPTER 1

# INTRODUCTION

## I. THE TRUST TODAY

THE modern trust is the direct successor of the medieval use. Ever since the use was first invented, it has been impossible for any property lawyer to give a comprehensive service to his client unless he has had a thorough grasp of the law governing the creation, operation and determination of uses and, later on, of trusts. This is as true today as it has ever been; indeed, it is arguably more so. This is the case because lawyers have employed the use and the trust as devices to circumvent inconvenient rules of law throughout their history.

### 1. *The Historical Background*

It was during the early medieval period that the practice first arose of owners of property transferring it to third parties[1] to the use[2] either of themselves or of some other beneficiary. The effect of such a transfer was that the third parties became the owners of the property in the eyes of the law but held their legal title to the property for the benefit of the transferor and/or any other nominated beneficiary.

The fact that the law regarded the third parties as the owners of the property meant that, in the event that they failed to comply with the terms of the use, neither the transferor nor the other beneficiaries had any remedy in the Royal Courts which had been established up to then.[3] However, in such circumstances a complaint could be made by way of petition to the King in Council. At first the practice of the Council was to instruct its principal officer, the Chancellor, who was at that time also the King's principal minister, to

---

[1] Property transferred by way of use was virtually always put in the name of more than one third party so that on the death of any one of them the other(s) would take the property by survivorship; this avoided difficulties, principally in relation to the incidence of taxation but also in relation to enforceability, which would otherwise have arisen if a sole trustee had died. It is still the almost inevitable practice to have more than one trustee, although today the death of a sole trustee will only cause any difficulties in the relatively unlikely event that there is no documentary evidence of the terms on which he is holding the trust property.

[2] The expression comes from the Latin *ad opus*.

[3] By early in the thirteenth century, three courts had been established to deal with specific distinct areas of the Royal jurisdiction. These courts became known as the Court of King's Bench, the Court of Common Pleas, and the Court of Exchequer; they were collectively known as the Courts of Common Law and the body of rules which they enforced was known as the Common Law. They continued in existence until 1875 when they were abolished and their jurisdiction was transferred to the Supreme Court of Judicature.

investigate the matter and recommend an appropriate remedy, which the Council then put into effect. In due course,[4] however, the quantity of petitions of this and other types which reached the hands of the Chancellor brought about the establishment of what eventually became known as the Court of Chancery, a jurisdiction of the Chancellor quite separate from, although complementary to, that of the original Royal Courts.[5]

The Court of Chancery habitually protected those beneficially entitled under uses (and later on those beneficially entitled under trusts). This was one of the first, and remains the best, examples of the Chancellor developing rules of law distinct from those which had been developed by the original Royal Courts. Later on[6] the different rules developed by successive Chancellors were formulated and became known as the rules of Equity, of which the trust has always been the principal institution.

The earliest situations in which uses were employed were generally of a temporary nature. Until 1290, a freeholder who wished to alienate land in the modern sense, that is to say transfer his entire interest therein to the transferee, had to surrender the land in question to his feudal lord so that the latter could make the appropriate feudal grant to the transferee.[7] Between surrender and re-grant the lord held the land to the use of the transferee.[8] Uses also had to be employed, both before and after 1290, by anyone who wished to transfer his land into the name of himself and another; he had to put the land into the name of a third party who would hold it to his use pending a transfer back into joint names (this was necessary because until as recently as 1926 it was not possible for anyone to convey land to himself).[9] Further, there are examples of Crusaders about to depart for the Holy Land[10] transferring their lands to third

---

[4] Probably before the end of the fourteenth century.

[5] Initially the jurisdiction of the Chancellor was of an extraordinary nature. However, towards the end of the fifteenth century the number of petitions was increasing steadily and the sixteenth century saw such a dramatic increase that the Chancellor could scarcely cope. A substantial part of this increase consisted of petitions from defrauded beneficiaries of uses, making the rise of the use both a cause and an effect of the establishment of this separate jurisdiction. By the end of the sixteenth century, what can by then be described as the Court of Chancery had to all intents and purposes ceased to be an extraordinary court. It continued in existence alongside the Courts of Common Law until 1875 when, like them, it was abolished and its jurisdiction was transferred to the Supreme Court of Judicature.

[6] Towards the end of the seventeenth century, principally by Lord Nottingham who was Chancellor from 1675 to 1682.

[7] For this reason such an alienation (technically known as an alienation by substitution) required the consent of the feudal lord. The transferor could alternatively make the appropriate feudal grant himself but this did not transfer his entire interest in the land to the transferee; instead this created a fresh rung in the feudal ladder and the transferor became the feudal lord of the transferee. This did not affect his existing responsibilities to his own feudal lord and, consequently, this form of alienation (technically known as subinfeudation) could be carried out as of right. The Statute Quia Emptores 1290 changed the situation completely by prohibiting subinfeudation and permitting substitution without the consent of the feudal lord, thus establishing the right of free alienability which has ever since been enjoyed by all those absolutely entitled to freehold land.

[8] This remained the method of conveying copyhold land until the abolition of that tenure in 1925.

[9] It is now possible by virtue of Law of Property Act 1925, s.72(3).

[10] And others about to embark on hazardous journeys.

parties to hold for them until they returned or for their rightful heirs in the event that they did not do so.[11]

However, it soon came to be realised that uses could equally be employed on a permanent basis. An early example is provided by grants of land made to the Franciscan Friars, who were forbidden by their Order from owning land, shortly after they arrived in England in 1224.[12] Other permanent situations quickly followed.

During the thirteenth century the Crown made strenuous attempts to avoid land being given to corporations (the usual donees being the ever increasing number of ecclesiastical foundations). A series of statutes known collectively as the Statutes of Mortmain[13] purported to impose prohibitions on such gifts with a view to preventing land being taken out of circulation more or less indefinitely, something which had the effect of depriving feudal lords of most, if not all, of their revenue from the lands in question.[14] The effect of these statutes was for over a century able to be avoided by the employment of a use; until 1391,[15] a transfer of the land in question to third parties to the use of the corporation which was the intended donee was effective to circumvent these prohibitions.

More significantly, until 1540,[16] all freehold land automatically descended to the heir of a deceased person; it was simply not possible for the latter to make any alternative disposition of such land by will. However, this inability could be circumvented by a landowner transferring any land which he wished to leave away from his heir to third parties during his lifetime; they would hold the land to the use of the transferor for the remainder of his life and thereafter to the use of the intended beneficiary. This enabled the landowner to continue to derive the whole of the benefit from his land for as long as he lived; following his death, the third parties would automatically hold the land for and would normally convey it to the intended beneficiary.

However, the reason why uses were most frequently employed in the medieval period was for the purpose of avoiding feudal inheritance taxes; such uses were one of the earliest examples of what are now known as "tax avoidance schemes". These taxes principally affected the heirs of anyone who held land from his feudal lord as a tenant in knight service (by the fourteenth century[17] this had become and until 1661 remained the basic tenure by means of which land was held by persons other than subsistence farmers and agricultural labourers).[18] These feudal inheritance taxes differed depending on

---

[11] Since the odds were substantially against the Crusader returning and he was in any event likely to be absent for many years, such transfers were in practice more likely to be permanent than temporary.

[12] Such a grant was made to the municipal corporation of Oxford to the use of the Friars in 1225.

[13] Culminating in the Statute De Viris Religiosis 1279.

[14] By this time most of the feudal taxes worth collecting were levied on inheritances. Corporations die much more infrequently than natural persons and medieval ecclesiastical foundations never died at all (at least not until Henry VIII decided to dissolve the Monasteries in the sixteenth century) — hence the name "Mortmain" ("dead hand").

[15] When the device was prohibited by statute (15 Ric. II (1391), c.5).

[16] Prior to the enactment of the Statute of Wills 1540.

[17] Originally this had been the tenure of the aristocratic military class, the descendants of the leaders of the army which had come to England with King William the Conqueror in 1066.

[18] The impact of feudal inheritance taxes on the latter was much less significant.

whether the heir of the tenant in knight service in question was an adult or a minor.

An heir who was an adult could not claim his inheritance until he had paid a fixed sum and, originally, a year's profits of the land in question to his future feudal lord. By the fourteenth century, the former liability had ceased to have much significance due to the effects of inflation and the latter liability which, because it was related to the annual value of the land, kept pace with inflation, only arose where the feudal lord in question was the King.[19] This obviously meant that the latter liability became an increasingly important source of income for the King.

The position of an heir who was a minor, a situation which, due to the very limited life expectancy which then prevailed, was likely to occur at least every other generation, was considerably worse. The future feudal lord would be entitled to use the land for his own exclusive benefit[20] until the minor reached the age of majority.[21] This liability had originally been not unreasonable since it compensated the feudal lord for the inability of the minor heir to render the services in exchange for which the land had originally been granted; however, by the fourteenth century, as a result of inflation these services were no longer worth collecting, rendering the liability increasingly unreasonable. To make matters worse, the minor heir also had either to submit to the feudal lord's choice of a spouse or, if he or she could not endure the thought of spending a lifetime locked in the arms of the person chosen, to compensate the lord for the value of the marriage to him.[22] Further, if the feudal lord in question was the King, the minor also had to make a payment of half a year's profits of the land on attaining his or her majority.[23] Although these liabilities benefited all feudal lords, they again principally benefited the King because, apart from the additional payment payable to him, he alone was always feudal lord and never tenant.

All these potential liabilities could be avoided if a tenant in knight service conveyed his land to third parties during his lifetime to the use of himself during the remainder of his life and thereafter to the use of his heir. He would continue to derive the whole of the benefits from his land for as long as he lived and, following his death, the third parties would transfer the land to the heir — in the case of an adult heir, straightaway; in the case of a minor heir, when he or she came of age. The heir thus received the land as surely as if the tenant in knight service had retained legal title to that land until his death; however, because the heir had not actually received the land by way of inheritance, the feudal lord was not entitled to any of the payments or other rights set out above.

---

[19] As a result of the Statute of Marlborough 1267, c.16.

[20] This right was formally recognised in the Assize of Northampton 1176, c.4. However, Magna Carta 1215, cc.4, 5 subsequently prohibited feudal lords from destroying the capital value of the inheritance but they remained entitled to the whole of the income which it produced.

[21] 21 for males and 14 for females (unless the death occurred when the female was already over 14 and unmarried, in which case she came of age at 16 or upon earlier marriage).

[22] The lord could not put forward the most unattractive girl he could find in the hope that the infant would refuse and so give the lord a right to compensation. Magna Carta 1215, c.3 contained a list of defects in a potential spouse which prevented her from being put forward.

[23] Prior to Magna Carta 1215, c.3, this payment had had to be made to all feudal lords.

Because uses therefore had the effect of depriving feudal lords in general and the King in particular[24] of a substantial proportion of their feudal revenues, the existence of uses understandably became increasingly unpopular with the Crown. Henry VIII consequently attempted to take away the advantages conferred on the heirs of tenants in knight service by the employment of uses by enacting the Statute of Uses 1536.[25] Although the effects of this Statute were draconian,[26] its effects were relatively short-lived.[27] The right to leave freehold land by will was progressively re-established by Statute[28] and all the feudal taxes which uses had been employed to avoid were subsequently abolished.[29] Further by the eighteenth century the use had been re-established under the name of the trust.[30] The lawyers then found a number of further situations in which trusts could be usefully employed.

In the eighteenth and nineteenth centuries trusts were employed by wealthy

---

[24] Both because of his additional rights and because of the fact that he alone was always lord and never tenant (the benefits to other feudal lords were over time largely cancelled out by the liabilities of their own heirs to their own feudal lords, particularly where the latter was the King).

[25] This legislation "executed" the use by transferring the legal title to its subject matter from the third parties in which the latter had been vested to the beneficiary. As a result, the last two devices described in the text ceased to work because the effect of the Statute was that the transferor remained entitled to the land on his death.

[26] The Statute obviously re-imposed all the feudal taxes discussed in the text. This was of course the whole object of the exercise but the Statute also had the effect of preventing anyone from leaving freehold land, not just land held in knight service, away from his heir. This took away powers which had been regarded as a common right for more than a century and left freeholders unable to leave any of their freehold land to their younger children, thus preventing them from meeting some of the most serious obligations which morality and natural affection placed on them. This caused great unrest and a step back had to be taken almost immediately by the enactment of the Statute of Wills in 1540. This enabled two-thirds of land held in knight service and all land held in any other tenures to be left by will but did not, however, enable the beneficiaries of the will to escape the feudal taxes.

[27] Its most controversial effect was removed by the Statute of Wills 1540 (see the previous footnote) and the feudal taxes which it re-imposed disappeared when tenure in knight service was abolished by the Tenures Abolition Act 1661. Although the remaining effects of its provisions were, as will be seen below, rapidly circumvented by the ingenuity of lawyers, the Statute of Uses nevertheless remained in force until the end of 1925 and during this period considerable care had to be taken in drafting in order to avoid its provisions.

[28] By the Statute of Wills 1540 (see fn. 26 above) subject to restrictions in the case of tenure in knight service which were removed by the latter's abolition by the Tenures Abolition Act 1661.

[29] By the Tenures Abolition Act 1661.

[30] The Statute of Uses was held only to "execute" the first of two or more successive uses; second and subsequent uses were neither executed by the Statute nor valid at common law. Consequently, if land was transferred "unto and to the use of" third parties (to the third parties to their own use) "to the use of" the intended beneficiary, the third parties retained the legal title to the land in question and were regarded by the common law as its absolute owners. The intended beneficiary under the second or subsequent use was consequently as unprotected at common law as the beneficiaries of all uses had been before the Statute of Uses. The Chancellor therefore once again intervened to protect the beneficiaries of second or subsequent uses. Such uses were subsequently renamed trusts to distinguish them from the uses which were "executed" by the Statute of Uses. The result of all this was that the third parties held the legal title to the land in question on trust for the intended beneficiaries in exactly the same way as they had done before the Statute of Uses. The Statute of Uses had thus been avoided by the simple expedient of adding the words "and to the use of". This was acknowledged by Lord Hardwicke L.C. in *Hopkins v. Hopkins* (1738) 1 Atk. 581 at 591, where he said "by this means a Statute made upon great consideration … has had no other effect than to add at most three words to a conveyance" (a statement which not only overlooks the other very significant consequences of the Statute of Uses but also puts into question the ability of Lord Hardwicke to count).

landowners in order to tie up their wealth for the benefit of succeeding generations of their families and also in order to make provision for all their dependants. Under the traditional form of settlement which developed,[31] the land in question was vested successively in the eldest son of each generation, generally only for his lifetime, but the trustees of the settlement were given overriding powers to raise capital for the benefit of all the other members of the family.[32]

Trusts were also employed in order to avoid another rule of the common law, which was in principle of general application, that a married woman could not hold property in her own right during the marriage;[33] this rule could also be overcome by vesting her property in trustees to hold on trust for her. Further, during the nineteenth century, trusts paid a significant role in the development of unincorporated associations such as clubs, friendly societies and trade unions; because such bodies are not themselves legal entities and so cannot hold property, they would not have developed in the way that they have had it not been possible for their property to be held by trustees on their behalf.[34] Finally, in the twentieth century, trusts once again came to be used as a means of creating "tax avoidance schemes", a role which they continue to retain, subject to the ever-increasing attacks of the legislature, in this new century.[35]

## 2. The Principal Uses of the Trust Today

The many and varied purposes for which trusts are employed today will now be summarised. They may be classified as family, commercial or social purposes, although the majority fall within more than one category. The first six purposes set out below are primarily, but not exclusively, family purposes, the next three are virtually entirely commercial purposes, and the final three, particularly the last one of all, the provision of pensions for retired persons and their dependants, have elements of all three classifications.

1.  To enable property, particularly land, to be held for persons who cannot themselves hold it. Although the legal title to land cannot be vested in a minor, there is no objection to land being held on trust for

---

[31] A succinct description of settlements of this kind (generally known as "strict settlements") can be found in *Megarry's Manual of the Law of Real Property* (8th ed., 2002), pp. 247–249.

[32] This system however prevented the land from being developed since no one person had the power to dispose of or deal with the land in order to do and the son with the interest in possession for the time being had no interest in utilising its income for the purpose either. The end result was consequently often a situation of total sterility. During the nineteenth century, when land became necessary for development following the industrial revolution, the powers of the eldest son (or other beneficiary in possession) for the time being were therefore very considerably extended and full powers of disposal and management were finally conferred by the Settled Land Act 1882, which formed the basis of the Settled Land Act 1925.

[33] This restriction seems to date from the beginning of the thirteenth century. In its final form, all the personalty owned by a wife on marriage, or acquired by her thereafter, became the absolute property of her husband; he was also entitled to manage and to take the profits of her freehold land, which by law became vested in both of them. However, the property of the married woman nevertheless passed in accordance with her will or the appropriate intestacy rules on her death. The restriction was finally taken away by the Married Women's Property Act 1882.

[34] See *post*, p. 88.

[35] See *post*, pp. 8, 193–201.

such a person. Indeed the legislature has adopted this particular route, providing that a purported conveyance of a legal estate in land to a minor operates as a declaration that the land is held in trust for that person.[36]

2. To enable a person to make provision for dependants privately. The most obvious examples are any provision made by a man for his mistress or his illegitimate child. During his lifetime he can make such provision without publicity but an express testamentary gift in favour of a mistress or an illegitimate child by will may well become public knowledge. Once probate has been obtained, a will becomes a public document and is therefore open to public inspection — indeed tabloid journalists routinely inspect the wills of famous persons in the hope of finding embarrassing information of this type. A trust created other than by will, on the other hand, escapes publicity of this type provided that the person making such provision either settles property on the intended beneficiaries during his lifetime or creates what is known as a secret trust[37] in their favour in his will.

3. To tie up property so that it can benefit persons in succession. It is of course always possible to make an outright gift of property to a parent in the hope and expectation that on the parent's death that property will go to his children, but there is no guarantee that it will actually do so. On the other hand, a gift of property to trustees to hold on trust for the parent for life and, subject to that, for the children will ensure[38] that the children derive a benefit. It is admittedly not normally possible to ensure that the person ultimately entitled will receive the actual property which is settled, since the trustees will almost always have the power to sell it and re-invest the proceeds. But it is possible to ensure that the person ultimately entitled does at the very least receive whatever assets are derived from that property.

4. To protect family property from wastrels. A person may feel that an outright gift of money to a surviving spouse or child will lead to the money being rapidly dissipated. On the other hand, a gift of that money to trustees to hold on trust to pay either the income or only a limited proportion of the capital to the surviving spouse or child will probably prevent this happening. Flexibility can be preserved by giving the trustees a discretion as to the amount (if any) of income or capital which they may pay over at any one time; another possibility is for property to be given to trustees to hold on trust for a beneficiary in such a way that the property will be preserved from the beneficiary's creditors in the event that he becomes bankrupt.[39]

---

[36] Trusts of Land and Appointment of Trustees Act 1996, Sched. 1, para. 1. Before this Act came into force on January 1, 1997, such a conveyance operated as an agreement for valuable consideration to create a settlement of that land on the minor and in the meantime to hold the land on trust for him (Settled Land Act 1925, s.27); any conveyances so operating on January 1, 1997 thereafter also take effect as declarations of trust.

[37] See *post*, p. 114.

[38] Unless the parent and children agree, after all the children have reached the age of majority, to bring the trust to an end prematurely.

[39] This device is known as a protective trust; see *post*, pp. 264–270.

5. To make a gift to take effect in the future in the light of circumstances which have not yet arisen and so cannot yet be known. A person who has three young daughters may choose to set up a trust in his will whereby a sum of money is given to trustees for them to distribute among the daughters, either as they think fit or having regard to certain stated factors. They might, for example, in due course decide to give one-quarter each to two of the daughters who had married well and one-half to the poorer unmarried daughter.

6. To minimise the incidence of income tax, capital gains tax and inheritance tax. A high proportion of the numerous possible "tax avoidance schemes" which have been devised involve a trust in one way or another.[40] One example will suffice for the moment. At present a person with a high income[41] will pay income tax at the higher rate of 40 per cent on any investment income. However, substantial tax savings can be made if the higher rate taxpayer transfers an investment to trustees to be held on trust for other members of his family who are of more modest means and so either pay no income tax at all or pay income tax at lower rates (either at the starting rate of, at present, 10 per cent[42] or the basic rate of, at present, 22 per cent).[43] The potential saving varies depending on the nature of the investment.[44] Only rarely[45] is the minimum saving less than 18 per cent of the income (the difference between the 40 per cent tax otherwise payable and the 22 per cent basic rate of tax) and no income tax will ultimately be paid at all in respect of income other than income from shares[46] paid to any member of the family who does not have enough other income to use up his annual personal allowance.[47] However, it must be noted these figures do not take into account the administration expenses of the trust which have to be borne out of the taxed income of the trust before any income is distributed to any of the beneficiaries.

7. To enable two or more persons to own land. One of the more curious features of English land law is that, if two or more persons wish to own land jointly, they cannot be the absolute legal and beneficial

---

[40] Such schemes "involve" trusts because in the majority of cases they will necessitate either the setting up of a trust or the breaking of an existing trust or a combination of the two.

[41] In 2003–2004, income tax is payable at 40 per cent on any taxable income (that is on the balance of the taxpayer's income after the deduction of any personal allowances to which he is entitled) over £30,500.

[42] In 2003–2004, payable on the first £1,960 of taxable income.

[43] In 2003–2004, payable on taxable income between £1,961 and £30,500.

[44] Income from shares, bank interest, and other sorts of income such as rental income are now taxed at different rates.

[45] Where dividend income arising under a discretionary trust is paid to a basic rate taxpayer, in which case the total tax payable is, in 2003–2004, 29.8%.

[46] Income from shares necessarily bears tax of at least 10%.

[47] In 2003–2004, £4,615

owners of that land; up to four of them can be the legal owners but all beneficial interests have to take effect behind a trust.[48] Since the Second World War, it has become increasingly common for married couples (and for that matter unmarried couples living in a *de facto* relationship) to have the family home vested in their joint names — indeed, building societies and banks normally make any mortgage advance by means of which the property is to be acquired conditional on this being done. Substantially more than half the residential property in the country must now be owned jointly in this way; this means that, technically, well over half the houses in the country are now held on trust, a fact which would probably surprise most of their occupants.[49]

8. To facilitate investment through unit trusts and investment trusts. The objective of such trusts is to enable the small investor to acquire a small stake in a large portfolio of investments and thus to spread his risk across a substantial range of stocks and shares. Further, such portfolios are sufficiently large for their investments to be supervised on a full-time basis. The importance of investment vehicles of this kind for the small investor cannot be overestimated.[50] In the case of a unit trust, the promoter, usually the future manager, of the unit trust invites the public to subscribe for units of a fixed initial value. The funds so obtained are invested in the stock market, either entirely generally or with at least the majority of the holdings in a particular nominated sphere, such as in oil companies, or in a particular geographical location, such as the Far East. The investments so purchased are vested in trustees, usually in a trust corporation. The trustees receive the dividends on the investments which, after payment of their administration expenses and the remuneration of the manager (usually a percentage of the value of the fund), are distributed among the investors in proportion to the number of units held or reinvested to increase the total value of the fund and so of the individual units in it. The manager, who is responsible for selecting the original investments and changing them when he feels this to be appropriate, is obliged to buy back the units at any time at a price fixed by reference to the total value of the fund at any one time. He will offer for sale any units so bought back at a slightly higher price. There are consequently at any one time two different prices at which units are respectively bought back and sold. An investment trust

---

[48] This will be a trust of land under the Trusts of Land and Appointment of Trustees Act 1996. Before this Act came into force on January 1, 1977, the trust in question would either have been a trust for sale or a settlement under the Settled Land Act 1925. All pre-existing trusts for sale have been converted into trusts of land but pre-existing settlements under the Settled Land Act 1925 continue, although no new ones can be created.

[49] This has come to be so much a matter of course that some solicitors are now thought to have given up explaining the provisions of conveyances of land which declare the trusts upon which the property is to be held; if this is indeed the case, the fact that the property is to be held on trust may never even have been mentioned to its purchasers.

[50] Many unit trusts and investment trusts are incorporated in which case they are governed not by trust law but by the Companies Acts 1985 and 1989. All such investment vehicles are in any event subject, in addition to the normal provisions of trust law and company law, to special legislation designed to protect the public against fraud.

works in a broadly similar way with two important distinctions. First, the fund is not divided into units so that the capital subscribed can be of any amount which the manager is prepared to accept. Secondly, the individual investors can only deal with their investments on the stock exchange (the manager is not under any obligation to buy them back); this consequently means that the price paid will depend on market forces rather than being directly related to the total value of the fund at any one time.

9. To enable companies to raise finance from investors on the security of debentures and bonds. The principal assets of trading companies are their stock in trade, which is continuously bought and sold and so, unlike retained property such as their premises or plant, is not susceptible of being the subject matter of a fixed mortgage or charge.[51] Stock in trade can instead be used as security for funds advanced under what is known as a debenture, or floating charge, which attaches itself to whatever relevant assets the trading company holds at any one time. The interests of the debenture holders, the persons who advance the funds in exchange for the appropriate interest in the debenture stock in question, are often protected by having any substantial assets which are subject to those debentures transferred to trustees, usually a trust corporation, on trust for them. In the same sort of way, funds subscribed to United Kingdom financial institutions, against the issue of what are known as Eurobonds, for investment throughout Europe and the assets in which the funds raised are subsequently invested are held by the financial institution in question on trust for the subscribers.

10. To make provision, particularly by will, for causes or for non-human objects. By means of a trust, money can be donated for the furtherance of education or for the purpose of maintaining a beloved animal such as a favourite dog or cat.

11. In other jurisdictions, to protect the environment.[52] Canada has developed what is known as "the 'trusteed' environmental fund" in order to provide some form of assurance for the state that, following the termination of some environmentally harmful activity such as mining or logging, the post closure land reclamation will be adequately financed. The party carrying out the activity makes periodic payments to trustees who invest these payments for return; and the accumulated fund is the primary or immediate source for meeting the costs of land reclamation. This interesting use of the trust concept in a field which is today of such enormous international importance and interest could undoubtedly be adopted in this jurisdiction in appropriate circumstances. However, English law has no obvious need for

---

[51] The subject matter of fixed mortgages and charges, which also includes residential property mortgaged to the bank or building society which advanced funds for its purchase or improvement, cannot in practice be sold without the mortgage or charge first being paid off.

[52] See Waters, *Equity, Fiduciaries and Trusts 1993* (ed. Waters, 1993), p. 383.

the analogous "public trust doctrine" developed in the United States of America.[53]

12. Last, but by no means least, to provide pensions for retired persons and their dependants. This is today by far the most significant purpose of all, both because of the scale of funds which are now devoted to it[54] and because of its immense importance for every member of society other than the fortunate few who have never needed to work. Nothing shows this importance more clearly than the repeated, and so far not very successful, efforts made by the present government to persuade the populace as a whole that it is necessary for everyone to make some provision for his or her retirement in addition to the increasingly inadequate pension paid by the state. Since the Second World War pension schemes have increasingly been regarded as an essential part of virtually every contract of employment. Pension schemes for employees are either non-contributory, in which case the whole of the money is provided by the employer, or contributory, in which case both the employer and the employee pay into the fund. Their importance for employees is demonstrated by the furore which has accompanied the recent increasing tendency by employers to reduce pension provision because of its ever-increasing cost.[55] In the vast majority of cases, pension funds provided for employees are held by trustees with the objective, usually but sadly not always[56] achieved, of assuring the employee that his pension will in fact be forthcoming and that in the meantime his employer cannot in any way dispose of the money. Pensions are also an important factor for the self-employed, who take out personal pension schemes, facilitated by generous tax concessions (such schemes are also available to employees who either are not members of a pension scheme by virtue of their employment or wish to "top-up" the pension provision made by their employer's scheme). The funds contributed towards such pension schemes are typically paid to insurance companies for investment in insurance policies but can also be held in the form of investments by trustees, in such cases usually by trust corporations.

---

[53] In the United States of America, under the so-called "public trust doctrine", each State has a fiduciary obligation to ensure that the public lands which constitute the coastline, the bays of the sea, and the tidal rivers and their beds are made continuously available for the members of the public at large. No such doctrine could operate in England and Wales since all such lands are already vested in the Crown.

[54] In 1995 United Kingdom pension funds were estimated to be worth in excess of £500 billion and growing. Growth peaked at about £715 billion in 1999 but had fallen back to about £525 billion by the end of 2002 as a result of persistent falls in the value of the shares in which a large proportion of pension funds have habitually been invested.

[55] Fuelled by the falls in the value of shares referred to above and the ever-increasing longevity of the members of pension schemes.

[56] The systematic looting by the late Robert Maxwell of the pension fund established to provide pensions for ex-employees of *The Daily Mirror* caused great concern among employees in general; pension fund administration then became the subject of a Committee of Inquiry, the Pensions Law Reform Committee, which reported in the autumn of 1993 and came down on the side of continuing to utilise the trust vehicle.

All the illustrations which have just been given concern trusts which have been deliberately created in order to achieve the purpose in question. However, trusts can also arise in other ways. The court will in certain circumstances infer the existence of a relationship of trustee and beneficiary where the owner of property has intentionally carried out some other transaction (such trusts are known as "resulting trusts"). And the court is able to impose a relationship of trustee and beneficiary as a result of misconduct by the person held to be a trustee (such trusts are known as "constructive trusts").

The multiple purposes for which trusts can be and are employed today emphasise the importance of the trust in modern law and society. They also make it apparent that one of the greatest advantages of trusts is the flexibility of purpose for which they can be used. Another is the fact that the rules which govern trusts are by and large the same whatever the purpose for which they are employed. The remainder of this book attempts to explain those rules.

## II. THE DEFINITION OF A TRUST

### 1. Suggested Definitions

Considerable difficulty has been found in providing a comprehensive definition of a trust, but various attempts have been made. The following definitions deserve consideration.

#### (A) Lord Coke's Definition

Lord Coke defined a trust as "a confidence reposed in some other, not issuing out of the land but as a thing collateral thereto, annexed in privity to the estate of the land, and to the person touching the land, for which *cestui que* trust has no remedy but by subpoena in the Chancery".[57] Some of this language may require elucidation. When Coke says that a trust is collateral to land, not issuing out of it, he means that a trust differs from a legal proprietary interest. Traditionally, a legal proprietary interest has continued to subsist even after a purchase for value without notice of that interest, whereas an equitable proprietary interest such as that of a beneficiary under a trust does not do so and is, for that reason, collateral (this remains accurate save in the case of interests in registered land whose continued existence does not normally depend on whether they are legal or equitable). When Coke says that a trust is annexed in privity to the estate, he means that the trust will only continue so long as the estate continues. And when Coke says that a trust is annexed in privity to the person, he means that a purchaser for value of the legal estate without notice of the trust will (subject to the same exception) take free from its provisions.

It has, however, to be said that some objections can be made to Coke's formulation. First, what is a "confidence"? This expression does not explain precisely the meaning of "trust". Secondly, the definition imports the idea of a reliance placed by one person on another. This may not be universally correct. The *cestui que* trust (or "beneficiary") may be a babe-in-arms or unborn or for some other reason wholly ignorant of the trust. The trust in such cases may still be effective (and normally will be) but the *cestui que* trust will place no

---

[57] Co. Litt. 272b.

"reliance" whatever on the trustee. Thirdly, Coke's definition applies only to land, whereas the subject-matter of a trust has always also been able to be personal chattels. And, fourthly, his definition is procedurally out of date, although he can hardly be blamed for that! The Court of Chancery no longer exists and the entire Supreme Court of Judicature now has jurisdiction in equity matters.[58] Nevertheless this early definition is undoubtedly worth a mention subject to the criticisms which have been made, it is at least as useful as most of the modern definitions.

### (B) Sir Arthur Underhill's Definition

Sir Arthur Underhill, the original author of the leading practitioners' work which is now known as Underhill and Hayton, *Law of Trusts and Trustees*, described a trust as "an equitable obligation binding a person (who is called a trustee) to deal with property over which he has control (which is called trust property), for the benefit of persons (who are called beneficiaries or *cestuis que trust*),[59] of whom he may himself be one and any one of whom may enforce the obligation".[60]

As a comprehensive definition of all kinds of trusts, it may be objected that this one does not in terms cover charitable trusts and, further, makes no provision for the so-called "trusts of imperfect obligation",[61] such as a trust "for the maintenance and support of my dog Tigger" — this may well amount to a valid trust but is a trust of imperfect obligation because Tigger cannot enforce it. The successive editors of what is now Underhill and Hayton have, however, pointed out that, even though charitable trusts are outside the scope of the work, they are in any event covered by the definition, simply because such a trust is for the benefit of persons, namely the public, on whose behalf the Attorney-General may intervene.[62] They have also stated that trusts of imperfect obligation are not referred to because they are acknowledged to be "anomalous and exceptional".[63]

### (C) A Judicial Definition

*Lewin on Trusts*,[64] the other main practitioners' work, refers to a rather more comprehensive definition given in Australia by Mayo J. in *Re Scott*.[65] According to this formulation:

> "the word 'trust' refers to the duty or aggregate accumulation of obligations that rest upon a person described as trustee. The responsibilities are in relation to property held by him, or under his control. That property he will be compelled by a court in its equitable jurisdiction to administer in the manner lawfully prescribed by the trust instrument, or where there be no specific provision written or oral, or to the extent that such provision is

---

[58] Supreme Court of Judicature (Consolidation) Act 1925, s.4(4).
[59] This is the plural: "*Cestuis que trustent*" is "hopelessly wrong": Sweet (1910) 26 L.Q.R. 196.
[60] Underhill & Hayton, *Law of Trusts and Trustees* (16th ed.), p. 1. The definition was approved by Cohen J. in *Re Marshall's Will Trusts* [1945] Ch. 217 at 219 and by Romer L.J. in *Green v. Russell* [1959] 2 Q.B. 226 at 241.
[61] See *post*, p. 82.
[62] See *post*, p. 442.
[63] See *post*, p. 82.
[64] (17th ed.), p. 1.
[65] [1948] S.A.S.R. 193 at 196.

invalid or lacking, in accordance with equitable principles. As a consequence the administration will be in such a manner that the consequential benefits and advantages accrue, not to the trustee, but to the persons called *cestuis que trust*, or beneficiaries, if there be any, if not, for some purpose which the law will recognise and enforce. A trustee may be a beneficiary, in which case advantages will accrue in his favour to the extent of his beneficial interest."

## (D) The Definition in the Recognition of Trusts Act 1987

The Recognition of Trusts Act 1987 incorporates into English law The Hague Convention on the Law Applicable to Trusts and on their Recognition. This international convention contains the following definition of a trust in Article 2:

"For the purposes of this Convention, the term 'trust' refers to the legal relationships created — *inter vivos* or on death — by a person, the settlor, when assets have been placed under the control of a trustee for the benefit of a beneficiary or for a specified purpose. A trust has the following characteristics—

    (a) the assets constitute a separate fund and are not part of the trustee's own estate;

    (b) title to the trust assets stands in the name of the trustee or in the name of another person on behalf of the trustee;

    (c) the trustee has the power and the duty, in respect of which he is accountable, to manage, employ or dispose of the assets in accordance with the terms of the trust and the special duties imposed upon him by law.

The reservation by the settlor of certain rights and powers, and the fact that the trustee may himself have rights as a beneficiary, are not necessarily inconsistent with the existence of a trust."

    The purpose of the Convention was twofold: first, to provide rules by which the courts of signatory states can uniformly determine the jurisdiction by whose laws trusts with international dimensions are governed (this aspect of the Convention will be considered in detail in Chapter 23) and, secondly, to provide some means of dealing with trusts in jurisdictions where the trust concept is unknown. When property situated in such jurisdictions becomes the subject matter of a trust, problems potentially arise because it can be extremely difficult to convince the authorities of the jurisdiction in question that the trustees are not the beneficial owners of the trust property.

    In commercial terms, the principal potential difficulty relates to the issue of Eurobonds by United Kingdom financial institutions to raise funds for the purpose of investment throughout Europe. The funds subscribed and the assets in which they are invested are held on trust for the subscribers. This can cause problems where the funds are invested in those jurisdictions in mainland Europe where the trust concept is unknown. The insolvency of the trustees may cause the authorities in any of these jurisdictions in which trust assets are situated to attempt to take the trust assets for the benefit of the trustees' creditors. Alternatively, where the trustees lend the funds subscribed to organisations situated in any of these jurisdictions, doubts may be cast on the ability of the trustees to sue those organisations if the latter default on the loans.

In non-commercial terms, the principal difficulty relates to testamentary dispositions by the increasingly large number of English people who own holiday homes in jurisdictions where the trust concept is unknown. Such owners are quite likely to deal with those homes in the same way as with the rest of their property and leave them by will to their executors and trustees on trust for their surviving spouses and/or their children. The immediate reaction of the authorities of the jurisdiction in question will unquestionably be to treat the trustees as the beneficial owners of the property, something which has potentially adverse fiscal consequences; this is because in many of the jurisdictions of this type the rate of Inheritance Tax payable is determined by how closely the beneficiary is related to the testator[66] and many trustees will inevitably not be in any way related to their testator. Other difficulties can also arise.[67]

The definition set out above is therefore intended to provide the necessary explanation of the nature of a trust in a form which is capable of being applied to and being comprehensible in a large number of different legal systems. For this reason, its format inevitably not only has to include references to a number of features of a trust which are not mentioned in the definitions already considered but also cannot include specific references to features which apply only to English law, such as the fact that the trustee is compellable by a court acting under its equitable jurisdiction. This definition, like that referred to in *Lewin on Trusts*, does not roll off the tongue as easily as the one propounded by Sir Arthur Underhill. Nevertheless, its comprehensive nature cannot be disputed no trust recognised by English law falls outside the four corners of this most recent of the many attempts to define a trust.[68]

## 2. The Essential Elements of a Trust

All the definitions which have just been considered point to a number of

---

[66] In Spain, probably the country which contains the largest number of holiday homes owned by English people, this factor determines both the tax free allowance and the rate of tax charged. If the tax free sum to which spouses, ascendants and descendants are entitled is treated as 2X and the rate of tax payable by them is treated as 2Y, then the tax free sum to which more distant relatives are entitled is X and the rate of tax payable by them is 3Y, while beneficiaries who are not related in any way to the testator have no tax free sum whatever and pay tax at the rate of 4Y. The situation is broadly similar, although less extreme, in France.

[67] There may be other adverse fiscal consequences. If the trustees are beneficially entitled to other property in the same jurisdiction, the local Revenue may well try to aggregate the income and capital taxes payable on the trust property with that payable on their own property, thus producing a higher marginal rate of tax (most European countries have many more different rates of tax than the United Kingdom and the top rate is usually substantially higher; in Spain in 2003 it was 58%, which applied to both income tax and capital gains tax). Further, such jurisdictions never recognise the existence of the beneficiaries' equitable interests because there is no way in which they can be protected on the relevant Property Register. This can prejudice the beneficiaries in the event of a dispute between them and the trustees, particularly if the trustees are resident in the jurisdiction in question.

[68] For judicial definitions, see *Sturt v. Mellish* (1743) 2 Atk. 610 at 612, *per* Lord Hardwicke L.C.; *Burgess v. Wheate* (1759) 1 Eden 177 at 223, *per* Lord Mansfield C.J.; *Re Williams* [1897] 2 Ch. 12 at 19 (CA), *per* Lindley L.J. As to the meaning of "trust" and "trustee" in Trustee Act 1925, see *ibid.* s.68(17).

essential elements, all of which must be present in order for a trust to be effectively constituted.

## (A) Property Subject to the Trust

No valid trust can be created unless there is some identifiable property subject to the trust over which the trustees have control. Any property whatever can form the subject matter of a trust, whether that property be tangible, that is to say property such as a freehold or leasehold estate in land or a collection of books or silver (English law calls such property "a chose in possession"), or intangible, that is to say property such as a share or the benefit of a covenant or simple contract (English law calls such property "a chose in action").

It is evident from these illustrations that it makes no difference whether the property in question is realty or personalty. Furthermore, it makes no difference whether the interest subject to the trust is a legal estate or an equitable interest. If the legal estate in property is held by trustees on trust, the interests of the beneficiaries are necessarily equitable. If any beneficiary assigns his equitable interest to a third party to hold on quite different trusts, that equitable interest will constitute the subject matter of the second trust (technically a sub-trust and therefore subject to certain special rules which will be considered later)[69]; the legal estate will remain vested in the original trustees.[70]

However, property subject to a trust must be capable of being identified. Consequently a liability cannot, without more, be the subject matter of a trust. If a creditor suggests to his debtor and the debtor agrees that, instead of repaying the loan, the debtor should hold the sum in question on trust for a third party, a valid trust will only arise if the debtor segregates the appropriate sum from his other assets by, for example, opening a new bank account for the purpose. If he does so, the trust will then be of the segregated assets, not of the liability. If, on the other hand, he fails to do so, something which in practice is highly likely since if the debtor had the assets to segregate he could equally easily have repaid the loan on the spot, the third party will be unable to point to any property subject to any trust and so will have no remedy.[71]

## (B) One or More Trustees

There must be one or more trustees in whom title to the trust property is vested. In principle, any number of persons may be trustees but this basic rule is now subject to a number of statutory restrictions which will be discussed in detail later on.[72] Briefly, there can be no more than four trustees of either a

---

[69] See *post*, p. 101.

[70] See *Gilbert v. Overton* (1804) 2 H. & M. 110.

[71] Exactly this situation arose in *M'Fadden v. Jenkyns* (1842) 1 Ph. 153; however, despite the fact that all three parties had clearly intended the debtor to be the trustee, Lord Lyndhurst L.C. generously found that the effect of the agreement was that the creditor held his right to sue the debtor on trust for the third party, thus providing her with a remedy against his personal representatives. The creditor can of course create such a situation intentionally; in *Barclays Bank v. Willowbrook International* (1987) 1 F.T.L.R. 386, a creditor charged to the bank a debt which was due to be repaid and the Court of Appeal held that any repayments made by the debtor were held by the creditor on constructive trust for the bank.

[72] See *post*, p. 560.

non-charitable trust of land[73] or a trust *mortis causa* of any property for a minor where no trustees are appointed by any will.[74]

If a trust is created by a person during his lifetime (in which case it is said to have been created "inter vivos"), there may well be no trustee other than the person who has created the trust, who is known as its settlor; in such circumstances, he will have created the trust by declaration, by simply declaring that from then on he is holding the property in question on trust for the objects in question. Alternatively, and necessarily if a trust is created as the result of a death (in which case it is said to have been created "post mortem"), the trust may be created by transfer; in this case the trustees will be those persons (normally more than one in order to avoid the problems which might arise if a sole trustee died) to whom the settlor or the deceased has transferred the property in question; in the case of an inter vivos trust, the settlor will frequently be one of the initial trustees. If a settlor attempts to create an inter vivos trust by purporting to transfer property to trustees who are neither named nor identified or to persons who are already dead, no valid trust will have been created. If, on the other hand, a testator fails to nominate any trustees in his will, his personal representatives will hold the property as trustees until other trustees are appointed.

Once a trust has been validly constituted, it cannot thereafter fail for want of a trustee since anyone in whom the trust property comes to be vested, other than a bona fide purchaser for value of a legal estate in the property without notice of the interests of the beneficiaries[75] (or, in the case of registered land, the statutory equivalent),[76] will be bound by that trust and so will be a trustee of the property.

### (C) An Equitable Obligation

The trustees must be under an equitable obligation, often described as a fiduciary duty, to deal with the trust property for the persons, purposes or objects defined by the settlor or testator — if they are not under any duty to do anything at all, there cannot be a trust (this does not prevent trustees being given completely unfettered discretions as to whether and, if so, how to deal with the trust property; their duty in such cases consists of being obliged to consider from time to time what, if anything, they should do).[77] This equitable obligation not only imposes on the trustees potential personal liabilities to the beneficiaries, liabilities which can be both penal and extremely stringent;[78] it also binds the trust property itself in the hands of anyone who has not taken free of the interests of the beneficiaries therein for the reasons stated above.

---

[73] Trustee Act 1925, s.34(3).

[74] Administration of Estates Act 1925, s.42.

[75] The one person whose interests are always preferred to those of the beneficiaries of a trust (see *Basset v. Nosworthy* (1673) Rep.Temp.Finch 102, where this time honoured rule was laid down by Lord Nottingham L.C.). For this reason, such a person has traditionally been known as "equity's darling".

[76] A bona fide purchaser for valuable consideration (other than marriage consideration) claiming under a registered disposition (Land Registration Act 2002, ss.28–31, 129(1), 132(1)); some commentators jocularly refer to such a person as "the Registrar's darling".

[77] See *post*, pp. 177–235.

[78] See *post*, pp. 330–369.

## (D) One or More Beneficiaries

No trust can exist without one or more beneficiaries (or *cestuis que trust*) for whose benefit the property is held. The trustees may also be some or all of the beneficiaries (most co-owners of land hold the land in question as trustees on trust for themselves)[79] but a sole trustee cannot also be the sole beneficiary — in this event, there would simply be no trust.

The precise nature of the interest of a beneficiary in the trust property has always been difficult to define.[80] On the one hand, the beneficiary has a proprietary interest in the subject matter of the trust because he can recover it from anyone into whose hands it passes other than a bona fide purchaser for value of a legal estate therein without notice of the interest of the beneficiary (or, in the case of registered land, the statutory equivalent). On the other hand, given that, if the property does reach the hands of such a person, it cannot be recovered by the beneficiary, whose only option will then be to bring a personal action against his trustees for breach of trust, his interest is certainly not a right *in rem*. The best view is that the interest of a beneficiary is a true hybrid — substantially more than a right *in personam* but substantially less than a right *in rem*. This is reflected by the decided cases, which regard the beneficiary as owner of the trust property for some purposes but not for others. Thus in *Baker v. Archer-Shee*,[81] the beneficiary was held to be the real owner of the trust assets for income tax purposes. On the other hand, in *Schalit v. Joseph Nadler*,[82] a beneficiary was held unable to distrain for rent due under a lease of the trust property granted by the trustee. The Divisional Court stated that "[t]he right of the *cestui que trust* whose trustee has demised property subject to the trust is not to the rent, but to an account from the trustees of the profits received from the trust".[83] Both these decisions appear to be in accordance with principle.

### 3. *"Trusts in the Higher Sense" and "Trusts in the Lower Sense"*

As Lord O'Hagan once said,[84] there is no magic in the word "trust", which can mean different things in different contexts. For example, a person may be in a position of trust without being a trustee in the equitable sense and terms such as "anti-trust" or "trust territories" are not intended to relate to a trust enforceable in a court of equity. By the same token, a trust in the conventional legal sense may be created without actually using the word "trust".[85] In each case it is necessary to consider whether the latter type of trust was or was not intended.[86]

This is exactly what had to be decided in *Tito v. Waddell (No. 2)*,[87] a case

---

[79] Law of Property Act 1925, ss.34, 36 as amended by Trusts of Land and Appointment of Trustees Act 1996, Sched. 2, paras. 3, 4.
[80] See Latham (1954) 32 Can B.R. 520 on the question generally.
[81] [1927] A.C. 844.
[82] [1933] 2 K.B. 79.
[83] *ibid.* at 83.
[84] In *Kinloch v. Secretary of State for India in Council* (1882) 7 App. Cas. 619 at 630.
[85] *Tito v. Waddell (No. 2)* [1977] Ch. 106 at 211, *per* Megarry V.-C.
[86] See *post*, p. 46.
[87] [1977] Ch. 106.

which Megarry V.-C. aptly described as "litigation on a grand scale".[88] The case involved Ocean Island, a small island in the Pacific, called Banaba by its inhabitants, who were unsurprisingly known as Banabans. The island had formerly been part of the Gilbert and Ellice Islands Protectorate and subsequently became a Crown Colony. At the beginning of the twentieth century, phosphate was discovered on the island and royalties for mining the phosphate were duly paid to the islanders. As time passed, the Banabans understandably sought increases in the royalty payments. Some increases were paid but they were considerably less than what had been claimed. The Banabans continued to make various claims both politically and internationally but, when those claims finally failed, they brought these proceedings, claiming that the rates of royalties payable in respect of certain transactions had been less than the proper rates and that accordingly the Crown, as the responsible authority, was subject to a trust or fiduciary duty for the benefit of the Banabans or their predecessors and was liable for breach thereof.

The question as to whether there was indeed such a trust or fiduciary duty involved the construction of various agreements and ordinances as well as other documents. In the event, it was held that there was neither a trust nor a fiduciary duty. The essential elements of the decision for the purposes of any definition of a trust[89] appear to be as follows:

1. Although the word "trust" had occasionally been used with reference to the Crown or its agents, that did not create a trust which was enforceable in the courts (what Megarry V.-C. described as a "trust in the lower sense" or "true trust") but rather a trust "in the higher sense", by which was meant a governmental obligation which was not enforceable in the courts.[90]

2. Such a trust "in the higher sense" could only be discharged under the direction of the Crown.[91] There might be many means available of persuading the Crown to honour its governmental obligations for example, by means of international pressure, but even if its obligations were higher than normal obligations they were not enforceable by the court.[92]

3. Although some of the ordinances imposed statutory duties on the Crown, they did not also impose fiduciary obligations. As will be seen later on,[93] in some cases a person may be in a fiduciary position even though he is not a fiduciary in the proper sense of the word (for example, a trustee, an agent, a company director or a partner) and such a person will be liable if he is in breach of his fiduciary obligations. A relationship giving rise to fiduciary obligations may be either legal or equitable or purely statutory but it must be a rela-

---

[88] *ibid.* at 123. The report of the judgment of Megarry V.-C. runs to 241 pages. The Vice-Chancellor also held a view of the *locus in quo* (the Pacific island in question).

[89] For other aspects of the decision, see *post*, pp. 346, 780.

[90] Adopting the language of Lord Selborne L.C. in *Kinloch v. Secretary of State for India in Council* (1882) 7 App. Cas. 619 at 625.

[91] *Tito v. Waddell (No. 2)* [1977] Ch. 106 at 216.

[92] *ibid.* at 217.

[93] See *post*, pp. 330 *et seq.*

tionship with enforceable legal consequences.[94] However, as Megarry V.-C. specifically held, "a trust in the higher sense or governmental obligation lacks this characteristic and where the primary obligation itself is one which the courts will not enforce, then it [cannot] of itself give rise to a secondary obligation which is enforceable by the courts".[95]

4.   If a duty is imposed by statute (such as the ordinances in this case) to perform certain functions, that statute will not, as a general rule, also impose fiduciary obligations nor is it to be presumed that it does so. It has to be affirmatively shown that such obligations are indeed imposed.[96]

Suffice it to say that this book is concerned with "trusts in the lower sense" or "true trusts" and with those situations which give rise to enforceable fiduciary obligations.

## 4. Sources of the Law of Trusts

It has already been seen[97] that trusts emerged as a re-establishment of uses some 150 years after the enactment of the Statute of Uses 1536 and that those beneficially entitled under uses and, later, under trusts were only ever protected in the Court of Chancery. The early Chancellors were usually bishops rather than lawyers and, in exercising the residue of judicial power left in the hands of the King after the establishment of the Courts of Common Law, they acted as keepers of the King's conscience, giving or withholding a remedy to the persons who petitioned them on the basis of their view of what the conscience of the petitioner and the respondent in question demanded. At that stage it could fairly be said that, in so far as the Court of Chancery had any rules at all, they varied according to the views of each Chancellor. Indeed, decisions of the Court of Chancery were not even formally recorded until the middle of the sixteenth century — the earlier activities of the Chancellors can only be reviewed on the basis of the petitions received by them and any decrees endorsed on those petitions.

Even so, however, it is clear from other records that successive Chancellors gradually extended the protection given to those beneficially entitled under uses. Initially a use was enforceable only as against the third parties to whom the property had been originally transferred subject to that use; however, in 1465 it was laid down that a use would also be enforced against any transferee of the property in question who had notice of the use,[98] in 1483 the Chancellor stated that a use would also be enforced against any heir of the third parties who inherited the property in question,[99] and in 1522 it was said that a use would also be enforced against anyone to whom the third parties had given

---

[94] [1997] Ch. 106 at 224.
[95] ibid. at 225.
[96] ibid. at 235. See also Swain v. The Law Society [1983] A.C. 598 (in exercising a statutory power the Law Society was performing not a private duty but a public duty for breach of which there was no remedy in breach of trust or equitable account); see further post, p. 330.
[97] See ante, pp. 1–6.
[98] Y.B. 5 Edw. IV, Mich., Pl. 16.
[99] Y.B. 22 Edw. IV, Pasch., Pl. 18.

the property in question whether or not that person had notice of the use[1] (later on, Lord Nottingham was to consolidate these developments by enunciating[2] the time honoured rule to which reference has already been made[3] that the interests of the beneficiaries of a trust bind the whole world other than a bona fide purchase for value of a legal estate in the property without notice of the interest of the beneficiaries).

These extensions of the protection given to those beneficially entitled under uses constituted some of the earliest substantive principles of what later came to be known as the rules of equity. By the middle of the sixteenth century, the typical Chancellor was a lawyer rather than a bishop. At about the same time the decisions of the Court of Chancery began to be formally recorded and, in due course, to be the subject matter of law reports. Consequently, at the beginning of the seventeenth century, Lord Ellesmere (1596–1617) was able to begin to develop the rules of equity into a code of principles and the later work of Lord Nottingham (1673–1682) in systematising those rules earned him the title of "the father of equity". The rules of equity were therefore developed by the Chancellors rather than by the legislature and even today the rules of equity are principally derived from decided cases rather than from statute — in this jurisdiction the law of trusts has never been codified.[4]

Nevertheless, as early as 1677 the legislature intervened to establish mandatory formal requirements for the creation of inter vivos trusts of land and of interests under pre-existing trusts[5] and in 1837 similarly intervened to establish mandatory formal requirements for wills which obviously applied to all post mortem trusts.[6] Provisions of this type, in an amended form, still exist today.[7]

The legislature has also, during the last 150 years, increasingly intervened in relation to such matters as the appointment and removal of trustees and the administrative duties and powers of trustees. The pattern of these legislative interventions is typified by the provisions of the Trustee Act 1925 and the Trustee Act 2000. Provisions governing the appointment and removal of trustees[8] are mandatory; the provisions of the trust deed or will in question are relevant only to the extent that the statutory provisions specifically so pro-

---

[1] Y.B. 14 Hen. VIII, Mich. Pl. 5, fol. 7.
[2] In *Basset v. Nosworthy* (1673) Rep.Temp.Finch 102.
[3] See *ante*, p. 17.
[4] This is also true of the vast majority of the jurisdictions where the law of trusts has been established as part of the common law, such as the common law jurisdictions of the United States of America, Canada and the Caribbean and the remaining jurisdictions of the old Commonwealth such as Australia, New Zealand and Hong Kong. It is only where the law of trusts has been introduced into Commonwealth jurisdictions whose pre-existing law was not common law, such as India, Jersey, and Guernsey, or into jurisdictions which have never had anything to do with the common law, such as Liechtenstein, The Netherlands and the non-common law Caribbean jurisdictions, that it has been necessary for that law to be codified (a few off-shore jurisdictions, such as Belize and the Turks & Caicos Islands, have also codified their law of trusts for marketing purposes).
[5] Statute of Frauds 1677, ss.3, 7 & 9.
[6] Wills Act 1837, s.9. see *post*, p. 97.
[7] See, *post*, pp. 97–121.
[8] Trustee Act 1925, ss.34–40. See *post*, pp. 549–570.

vide.[9] Provisions imposing specific duties on trustees[10] are also mandatory, although the trustees in question may nevertheless escape liability for any breach of these provisions if the trust deed or will in question contains a valid exemption clause on which they can rely.[11] On the other hand, provisions conferring powers on trustees[12] generally[13] apply only to the extent that a contrary intention is not expressed in the trust deed or will in question;[14] such contrary intentions can either enlarge or reduce the statutory powers in question.

These are the sources of the law of trusts with which this book has to deal.

## III. THE DISTINCTION BETWEEN TRUSTS AND OTHER LEGAL CONCEPTS

### 1. *Contract*

English law recognises two types of contract, the simple contract (a contract constituted as a result of the existence of an offer and acceptance, intention to create legal relations, and consideration) and the specialty contract (a contract constituted by virtue of being in a deed), often also described as a covenant.

Until the enactment of the Contracts (Rights of Third Parties) Act 1999 on November 11, 1999, the general rule, to which there were exceptions, was that neither a simple contract[15] nor a specialty contract[16] was enforceable by a person who was not a party to that contract. These rules were in stark contrast with the rule that a trust has always been able to be enforced by a beneficiary who was not a party to the instrument creating the trust (indeed, it is very unusual for beneficiaries to be parties to such instruments save in the case where the settlor is also a beneficiary). However, the rigidity of the general rule was mitigated by the possibility of creating a trust of the benefit of the contract in question.

It has always been (and remains) the law that, if one of the parties to either form of contract expressly or impliedly contracts as trustee for a third party, that third party is entitled to the benefit of the contract by virtue of being the

---

[9] In that, for example, the settlor or testator can nominate who is to appoint new or additional trustees (see Trustee Act 1925, s.36(1)(a)).

[10] Such as the duty of care imposed by Trustee Act 2000, ss. 1–2 and Sched. 1; see *post*, p. 573 *et seq.*

[11] See *post*, pp. 785–793.

[12] Such as the powers of maintenance and advancement contained in Trustee Act 1925, ss.31–32; see *post*, pp. 682–688, 700–707.

[13] There are some exceptions; see for example Trustee Act 1925, s.14 (power of trustees to give receipts).

[14] Trustee Act 1925, s.69(2), which applies to all the relevant remaining provisions of that Act. Trustee Act 2000 so provides in respect of each relevant Part (see ss.6, 9, 26 governing respectively Parts II, III and IV) and some further sections (see ss.28(1), 29(5)).

[15] The general rule seems to have been firmly established as a result of the decisions of the House of Lords in *Midland Silicones v. Scruttons* [1962] A.C. 446 and *Beswick v. Beswick* [1968] A.C. 58; it was subject to a number of recognised exceptions founded in statute but, apart from Law of Property Act 1925, s.56 (which applies only to land), they had (and have) no particular relevance to the law of trusts.

[16] *Cannon v. Hartley* [1949] Ch. 213, *Beswick v. Beswick* [1968] A.C. 98 at 102–105. The same statutory exceptions applied (and apply). However, a deed poll, a deed to which only the covenantor is named as a party, could and can be enforced by anyone with whom he purports to make that deed.

beneficiary of a trust. The party who contracted as trustee can obviously enforce the contract on behalf of the third party anyway[17] but, in the event that he does not do so, the third party can sue as *cestui que trust* joining the trustee as co-claimant or, if he declines to be joined in that capacity, as co-defendant.[18]

It has also always been (and still is) possible for a person who has not originally contracted as a trustee subsequently to create a trust of the benefit of a contract for a third party either by declaring a trust of its benefit or by assigning the contract to trustees to hold on trust. Such a trust may be created either gratuitously or pursuant to the provisions of a contract between the original contracting party and the third party (whether or not a trust has actually been created is a question of construction).[19] Even where the contract in question is incapable of being assigned because for example, it is a contract for the provision of personal services, a trust can nevertheless be declared of its benefit unless this is specifically prohibited by the contract;[20] but in such a case the third party would not be permitted to put the subject matter of the trust, the non-assignable contract, at risk by attempting himself to enforce it against the other original party in the ways indicated in the previous paragraph.[21]

However, section 1 of the Contracts (Rights of Third Parties) Act 1999 provides that a third party to a contract who is identifiable may enforce any term of that contract in his own right provided that either the contract so provides or the term in question purports to confer a benefit on him and it does not appear, on a proper construction of that term, that the parties did not intend him to be able to do so. A third party will be identifiable if he is expressly identified by name, or is a member of an identified class, or answers a specific description; there is no requirement that he should have been in existence at the date of the contract.[22] The Act applies automatically to both simple contracts and specialty contracts entered into on or after May 11, 2000, six months after the Act was passed; however, the Act will apply to contracts entered into during that six-month period if the contracts in question contain an express provision to that effect.[23]

The enactment of this legislation does not of course prevent a party to a contract either from expressly or implied contracting as a trustee, or from making a declaration of trust of the benefit of a contract, or from assigning that benefit to trustees on trust. Contracting expressly as a trustee or subsequently

---

[17] In which case he can recover on behalf of the third party beneficiary the damages suffered by the latter as well as the nominal damages suffered by himself (see *Lloyd's v. Harper* (1880) 16 Ch. D. 290).

[18] *Vandepitte v. Preferred Accident Insurance Corporation of New York* [1933] A.C. 70 at 79. This principle does not entitle a beneficiary to institute proceedings in tort for negligence on behalf of his trust by joining the trustees in this way (see *Bradstock Trustee Services v. Nabarro Nathanson* [1995] 1 W.L.R. 1405 at 1411); outside the contractual area, the right of a beneficiary to intervene in proceedings is limited to cases where the position of the trustees has been compromised by virtue of a breach of trust, a conflict of interest and duty, or some other exceptional circumstances (see *Hayim v. Citibank* [1987] A.C. 730 at 747–748).

[19] *Don King Productions v. Warren* [2000] Ch. 291.

[20] *Ibid.* at 320–322 (Lightman J.), 335 (C.A.).

[21] *Ibid.*

[22] This is particularly important in the case of specialty contracts because the beneficiaries of trusts of after acquired property which are the subject matter of a covenant to settle are more often than not unborn at the time when the covenant is entered into; see *post*, pp. 163 *et seq.*

[23] Contracts (Rights of Third Parties) Act 1999, s.10.

creating a trust of the benefit of a contract has never given rise to any difficulties. The real difficulty before the legislation was to know when a trust of the benefit of a contract was to be implied; this difficulty obviously survives in the case of those contracts to which the legislation does not apply. In this respect, simple contracts and specialty contracts require separate consideration.

The series of decisions in which the courts have considered whether or not a trust of the benefit of a simple contract is to be implied,[24] which were examined in detail in previous editions of this book,[25] are not particularly easy to reconcile. However, it appears from the later decisions such as *Re Schebsman*[26] (now almost sixty years ago) and *Swain v. The Law Society*[27] (now over twenty years ago), which are summarised in the footnotes, that the courts have increasingly turned their backs on the earlier authorities and are now most reluctant to interpret a contract as creating a trust in the absence of the clearest possible evidence that a trust was intended. This view derives further support from the significant fact that no reliance was placed on the trust concept by the

---

[24] *Re Flavell* (1883) 25 Ch. D. 89 (trust implied of the benefit of a provision in articles of partnership whereby the surviving partner was to pay an annuity to the widow of his co-partner); *Les Affreteurs Reunis S.A. v. Leopold Walford (London)* [1919] A.C. 801 (similar decision reached where there was an express agreement enabling the third party to sue); *Harmer v. Armstrong* [1934] Ch. 65 (specific performance ordered of a contract for the sale of the copyright in certain periodicals which had been entered into for the benefit of the plaintiff); *Vandepitte v. Preferred Accident Insurance Corporation of New York* [1933] A.C. 70 (third party motor insurance policy issued by the defendant which covered all persons driving the car with the consent of the owner not enforceable by his daughter, while so doing, having injured the plaintiff while driving negligently; had it been enforceable, the plaintiff would have been subrogated to her rights under the relevant British Columbian legislation); *Re Schebsman* [1944] Ch. 83 (see below); *Swain v. The Law Society* [1983] A.C. 598 (see below).

[25] See the 7th (1998) edition, pp.19–23.

[26] [1944] Ch. 83. A company agreed with one of its employees that, in consideration of his retirement, it would pay certain sums to him during his lifetime and after his death to his wife and child. He subsequently became bankrupt and died soon afterwards. The question then arose as to whether his trustee in bankruptcy could "intercept" the money which the employers were willing to pay to the wife and child. The Court of Appeal held that the employee had not entered into the contract as a trustee for his wife and child. Du Parcq L.J. said (at 104) that, unless an intention to create a trust was clearly to be collected from the language used and the circumstances of the case, the court ought not to be "astute" to discover implications of any such intention. The wife and child therefore could not enforce the contract against the company (however, the court went on to hold that the trustee in bankruptcy could not intercept the payments because the employee would not have been able to do so; consequently, the company was free to comply with the terms of the contract and make the required payments).

[27] [1983] A.C. 598. The Law Society had under its statutory powers arranged a master policy for the provision of indemnity insurance, something which was compulsory for all practising solicitors. It had been agreed that a proportion of the commission earned by the insurance brokers should be paid to The Law Society, which would apply it for the benefit of the profession as a whole. Two solicitors claimed that The Law Society was a trustee of the benefit of the master policy contract for the benefit of all individual solicitors and was therefore accountable for the proportion of the commission which it received. Reliance was placed on the fact that the policy contract stated that the policy was being entered into "on behalf of" solicitors and former solicitors, words which, it was claimed, imputed an intention to create a trust. The House of Lords held that these words were clearly insufficient to express a trust and did not necessarily imply one. Lord Brightman said (at 621): "it would indeed, be surprising if a society of lawyers, who above all might be expected to make their intention clear in a document they compose, should have failed to express the existence of a trust if that was what they intended to create."

members of the House of Lords when they were deciding *Beswick v. Beswick*,[28] also summarised in the footnotes.

These decisions will be directly applicable in the relatively unlikely event that an action is now brought to enforce a simple contract entered into before May 11, 2000; only contracts of option entered into before that date are likely still to be executory and few if any of those are likely to be in favour of third parties. However, they will also be applicable to later contracts in any situations in which the provisions of the Contracts (Rights of Third Parties) Act 1999 do not apply.

Section 1 of that Act does not apply in two situations: first, where, in the absence of an express provision providing that the third party may enforce the contract, it does not, on a proper construction of a term of the contract purporting to confer a benefit on him, appear that the parties intended him to be able to enforce it; and, secondly, where the third party in question is not identifiable. In none of the authorities referred to above was there the slightest doubt that the third parties were intended to benefit from the contract and in all of them the third parties were clearly identifiable. Given that the trend of the recent authorities is against implying trusts of the benefit of a simple contract, it seems inconceivable that such a trust would be implied where it was decided as a matter of construction that the parties to a contract did not intend a third party to be able to enforce a term of the contract purporting to confer a benefit on him or where the third party in question was not identifiable.

However, section 2 of the Act provides that, where a third party has rights under section 1, the parties to a contract may not rescind it without his consent where he has communicated his assent to the term in question to the person bound by that term. It must follow as a necessary corollary of this provision that, at least so far as the Act is concerned, they can rescind the contract where he has not so communicated his consent. But any such rescission by a person who held the benefit of the term in question on trust would be a breach of trust by him. Consequently, if the third party only finds out about the existence of the term in question after the parties have purported to rescind the contract, it will be highly relevant whether or not there is such a trust.[29] Such a situation may appear somewhat far-fetched in respect of simple contracts but, as will be seen below, it certainly is not in relation to specialty contracts. However, it nevertheless remains as unlikely as it was before the enactment of the Contracts (Rights of Third Parties) Act 1999 that any trust of the benefit of a simple contract will now be implied.

Specialty covenants for the benefit of the third parties are, typically, covenants between a settlor and his trustees to settle on trust what is known as after-acquired property, property which had not yet come into existence when

---

[28] [1968] A.C. 58. A nephew was employed by his uncle in the latter's business as a coal merchant. An agreement was made between them whereby the uncle assigned the business to the nephew in return for the nephew's promise to pay the uncle £6/10/- a week for the rest of his life and, after his death, to pay an annuity of £5 a week to his widow. The nephew complied with this agreement during his uncle's lifetime but after his death made only one payment to the widow. The House of Lords held that the widow had no claim against him in her personal capacity because she was not a party to the contract; however, she was held to be entitled to obtain specific performance of the contract as her husband's administratrix.

[29] See Halliwell [2003] Conveyancer 192.

the covenant was entered into. While there is in principle no reason why the intended beneficiaries of the trust should not also be parties to the covenant in question, in which case it has always been clear that they can enforce that covenant as against the settlor,[30] in practice those beneficiaries will almost always be third parties to the covenant.

Prior to the enactment of the Contracts (Rights of Third Parties) Act 1999, it was accepted and established that the beneficiaries could enforce the covenant against the settlor by joining the trustees as co-claimants or co-defendants if there was an express or implied trust of the benefit of the specialty contract;[31] however, there was a great deal of controversy as to when such a trust could be implied. In the absence of such a trust, it was accepted and established that the beneficiaries were unable to compel the trustees to enforce the covenant against the settlor.[32] It was also established that the trustees would be directed not to enforce the covenant against the settlor if they sought the directions of the court.[33] Although it has been argued that the courts were wrong to restrain the parties to a covenant from exercising their legal rights to sue under that covenant if they wished to do so,[34] the likely consequences of such an exercise suggested that the established state of the law should be upheld.[35] However, the effect of the enactment of the Contracts (Rights of Third Parties) Act 1999 has unquestionably been to permit such beneficiaries to enforce the covenant directly against the settlor where that Act is applicable. To what extent does the pre-existing law remain relevant following the enactment of the Contracts (Rights of Third Parties) Act 1999?

It is of course much more likely than in the case of simple contracts that specialty contracts entered into before May 11, 2000 are still outstanding; it is obviously possible for after-acquired property which such specialty contracts covenanted to settle on trust to be acquired by the settlor only after that date. In such circumstances, it will obviously remain crucial whether or not there is a trust of the benefit of the specialty contract.

In respect of such contracts entered into on or after that date, the position seems to be as follows. No trust could arise where the beneficiaries were unidentifiable, since any such trust would be void for uncertainty of objects.[36] On the other hand, it could certainly be decided as a matter of construction that the settlor did not intend the beneficiaries to be able to enforce the term of the covenant purporting to confer a benefit on them. However, in such circumstances, it would be wholly inconsistent with such a decision to uphold the existence of an implied trust of the benefit of the specialty contract and the existence of such a trust is therefore inconceivable.

However, it is certainly possible for a beneficiary only to find out about the existence of the specialty contract after the settlor has purported to rescind it under section 2 of the Contracts (Rights of Third Parties) Act 1999. The settlor may initially conceal the existence of the covenant (as happened in the leading

---

[30] *Cannon v. Hartley* [1949] Ch. 213.
[31] As in *Fletcher v. Fletcher* (1844) 4 Hare 67.
[32] *Re d'Angibau* (1880) 15 Ch.D. 228.
[33] *Re Pryce* [1917] 1 Ch. 234; *Re Kay* [1939] Ch. 329; *Re Cook's Settlement Trusts* [1965] Ch. 92.
[34] Particularly by Elliott (1960) 76 L.Q.R. 100.
[35] See *post*, pp. 170–173.
[36] See *post*, pp. 59–74.

case,[37] where he concealed it until after his death)[38] and later purport to rescind it. Another possibility is that the beneficiary may not be born or may not attain the age of majority until after the settlor has purported to rescind the covenant. In such circumstances, it will obviously continue to be highly relevant whether or not there is a trust of its benefit.

Further, even where the Contracts (Rights of Third Parties) Act 1999 is applicable to a specialty contract, there are some circumstances in which the existence or non-existence of a trust of the benefit of that contract may determine precisely who is beneficially entitled to the property to be settled.[39]

Consequently, the pre-existing law remains relevant in a number of circumstances even where the specialty contract in question was entered into after May 11, 2000 and obviously remains relevant where it was entered into before that date. That pre-existing law is best considered in the context of the general rules governing the ways in which a trust can be completely constituted.[40]

## 2. Debt

It has already been seen that a liability cannot, without more, be the subject matter of a trust and that a debtor will only be able to create a valid trust of the sum owed in favour of his creditor or of a third party if he segregates the appropriate amount from his other assets.[41] Such a trust will clearly come into existence where the debtor makes an express declaration of trust in respect of duly segregated assets. The effect of the creation of such a trust will be to give its beneficiary an advantage over the other creditors of the debtor in the event of his bankruptcy — this is because the proprietary right of the beneficiary will enjoy priority over the purely personal rights of any unsecured general creditors. For this reason, in the event that the debtor does subsequently become insolvent, such a trust will be vulnerable to challenge under the Insolvency Act 1986[42] on the grounds that it amounts to preferential treatment (technically known as a "preference") of the beneficiary vis-à-vis the general creditors. However, if consideration is given to the possibility of the debtor's insolvency at the time when the debt is first created, it is sometimes possible for the creditor to obtain a priority which cannot be successfully challenged.

There is in principle no reason why the same transaction should not give rise to both a trust and a debt; a loan for a specific purpose can be made in such a way that the sum advanced will be held on trust for the lender unless and until that purpose is carried out. This was specifically held by the House of Lords in *Barclays Bank v. Quistclose Investments*.[43] Quistclose Investments advanced money to a company for the purpose of paying a dividend on its shares. The advance was made on the basis that the money was to be used only for this purpose but the company became insolvent before the dividend

---

[37] *Fletcher v. Fletcher* (1844) 4 Hare 67.

[38] The beneficiaries were the settlor's illegitimate sons and it seems tolerably clear that the settlor did not wish anyone to become aware of their existence until after his death.

[39] See Halliwell [2003] Conveyancer 192.

[40] See *post*, pp. 170–176.

[41] See *ante*, p. 16.

[42] s.239 in the case of companies, s.340 in the case of individuals. See *post*, pp. 255–262.

[43] [1970] A.C. 567.

had been paid. The House of Lords held that arrangements for the payment of a debtor's creditors by a third person were capable of giving rise to a trust unless and until the creditors were paid.[44] Once they were paid, the third person would become no more than an unsecured creditor of the debtor. However, there was "no difficulty in recognising the co-existence in one transaction of legal and equitable rights and remedies".[45] If instead the creditors were not paid and the purpose for which the money had been advanced therefore failed, the money would, as between the debtor and the third party, still be held on trust by the debtor for the third party.

The potential advantages of such a trust for the person advancing the money are demonstrated by the facts of the two leading cases. In *Barclays Bank v. Quistclose Investments*, the principal creditor of the company was the bank with whom the money advanced by Quistclose Investments had been deposited. If Quistclose Investments was merely an unsecured creditor of the company, it would enjoy no priority over any other creditors, the money in the bank would belong to the company, and the bank would be entitled to set off the credit balance of the account against the much larger amount owed to it by the company.[46] If, on the other hand, the money was held on trust for Quistclose Investments, its proprietary interest in that money would be capable of enjoying priority over the rights of the bank. In *Twinsectra v. Yardley*[47] the claimant had made a loan on the basis that the sum advanced was paid to the borrower's solicitors, who gave an undertaking to the claimant to utilise the loan money solely for the acquisition of property on behalf of the borrower and for no other purpose. In breach of that undertaking, the solicitors transferred most of that money to another solicitor; he disbursed the funds transferred to him in accordance with the instructions of the borrower but not all of those funds were spent on the acquisition of property. If the arrangement between the parties had given rise to a trust, the claimant would be able both to recover the product of the disbursements made by the other solicitor[48] and to seek to impeach the conduct of that solicitor because of his involvement in what would then amount to a breach of trust.[49] In each of these two cases, the House of Lords upheld the existence of a trust and the creditor obtained the consequential advantages.

It is theoretically possible for the parties to an arrangement of this type to have expressly agreed that, in the event that the specific purpose fails, the recipient of the money will hold it on trust for the person who paid it; in that event, the trust in his favour will obviously be an express trust. In practice, however, there is unlikely to have been any such express agreement; there was not in either of the two cases considered above. In that event, *Twinsectra v. Yardley* establishes that any failure of the purpose will give rise to a resulting trust of the money in favour of the person who paid it. Since this is generally the way in which what have become known as *Quistclose* trusts take effect, the

---

[44] [1970] A.C. 567 at 580.
[45] *ibid.* at 581.
[46] Banks have a statutory right to amalgamate the balances of the different accounts held with them.
[47] [2002] 2 A.C. 164.
[48] The claimant would have an equitable proprietary interest in that product by virtue of the trust; see *post*, p. 812.
[49] This aspect of the case is discussed *post*, p. 382.

various situations in which such trusts have been found to exist are best considered in the context of the general rules governing resulting trusts.[50]

Where no *Quistclose* trust has arisen, the liability of a debtor, whether the debt in question is contractual or non-contractual, is of course only a personal liability and does not confer any proprietary rights on the creditor. In *Re Sharpe (a Bankrupt)*[51] the bankrupt purchased a property with the help of a sum lent to him by his aunt as part of an arrangement whereby the aunt was to live in the property for the rest of her life. Browne-Wilkinson J., while finding in her favour on another ground, rejected her claim to a beneficial interest in the property by virtue of her loan advance, holding that where "moneys are advanced by loan there can be no question of the lender being entitled to an interest in the property".[52] He distinguished on the grounds of its "very special" facts the earlier decision in *Hussey v. Palmer*[53] where, in a similar situation, the Court of Appeal had been unable to agree as to whether the payment in question had been made by way of loan or by way of direct contribution to the building of an extension and had, by a majority, imposed a constructive trust on the basis of a principle[54] which is no longer regarded as good law.[55] While it is sometimes difficult to decide, in the context of family arrangements, whether a particular payment has been made by way of loan or by way of contribution to the acquisition of the property in question, once the intention of the parties has actually been established the two possibilities are mutually exclusive.

### 3. *Estates of Deceased Persons*

**(A) Personal Representatives and Trustees Compared**
In one sense it can indeed be said that the legal personal representative — an executor in the case of a person nominated as such in a will, otherwise an administrator — of a deceased person is a trustee for the creditors and beneficiaries claiming under the deceased; after all, he holds the real and personal estate for their benefit and not for his own. Further, by virtue of section 69 of the Trustee Act 1925, the provisions of that Act also apply to personal representatives.[56] However, it would be an error to equate the legal position of personal representatives with that of trustees because certain differences still persist, primarily as the result of other statutory provisions.

Thus, while an action by a beneficiary to recover trust property or in respect of any breach of trust cannot, in the absence of fraud or the retention of the property by the trustee,[57] be brought after six years[58], personal representatives are subject to a different period of limitation, namely twelve years for a claim to personal estate[59] and six years for actions to recover arrears of interest in

---

[50] See *post*, pp. 291–300.
[51] [1980] 1 W.L.R. 219.
[52] *ibid.* at 223.
[53] [1972] 1 W.L.R. 1286.
[54] That a constructive trust is a general equitable remedy which can be invoked in order to do justice in the individual case. See *post*, pp. 325, 429.
[55] See *post*, p. 429.
[56] See also Administration of Estates Act 1925, ss.33, 39, Trustee Act 2000, s.35(1).
[57] Limitation Act 1980, s.21(1).
[58] *ibid.* s.21(3) and see *post*, p. 778.
[59] *ibid.* s.22.

respect of legacies.[60] However, the exception relating to fraud and to property retained by the trustee applies just as much to personal representatives as it does to trustees.[61] The authority of personal representatives in handling pure personalty is several, whereas that of trustees is joint.[62] Consequently, one of a number of personal representatives can give a valid title to a purchaser or pledgee of pure personalty whereas one of a number of co-trustees cannot, the intervention of all the trustees being necessary. However, the authority of personal representatives over realty (which since 1925 for this purpose been defined as including leasehold land[63]) is, like that of trustees, joint.[64] Since July 1, 1995, this applies just as much to contracts as to conveyances[65] (previously one of a number of personal representatives could enter into a valid contract for the sale of land).

The functions of personal representatives are also different from those of trustees. The duty of trustees is to administer a trust on behalf of beneficiaries, some of whom may be minors or unborn, and this may be a long continuing process since many years may elapse before a trust is brought to an end. On the other hand, the primary duty of personal representatives is to wind up the estate by, after payment of debts and any inheritance tax, transferring the net assets to the persons beneficially entitled to them under the will or intestacy[66] or to any nominated trustees, who more often than not will be the personal representatives themselves, to hold on trust. Furthermore, whereas a beneficiary has an equitable interest in the trust property as soon as a trust takes effect,[67] a legatee or devisee or intestate successor has neither a legal nor an equitable proprietary interest whilst the assets of the estate remain in course of administration. At that stage such persons have only the right to require the deceased's estate to be duly administered by the personal representatives.[68]

It follows that, although a personal representative has, like a trustee, fiduciary duties to perform, those duties are owed to the estate as a whole; it does not, therefore, necessarily follow that the duty of an executor in the course of administering an estate is subject to the trustee's duty to hold an even balance as between the different beneficiaries.[69] It was accordingly held in *Re Hayes's Will Trusts*[70] that, where executors had exercised a testamentary power of sale in favour of one of the children of the testator at the price at which the

---

[60] *ibid.*

[61] *ibid.* See also *post*, p. 778.

[62] *Jacomb v. Harwood* (1751) 2 Ves. Sen. 265; *Attenborough v. Solomon* [1913] A.C. 76. It has been recommended that the power should also be joint in the case of personal representatives (Law Reform Committee on the Powers and Duties of Trustees (23rd Report, Cmnd. 8733 (1982)). For the historical reasons for the existing rule, see 1 *Spence's Equitable Jurisdiction* (1846), p. 578 and *Collier v. Hollinshead* (1984) 272 E.G. 941.

[63] Administration of Estates Act 1925, ss.3(1), 54.

[64] *ibid.* s.2(2).

[65] Law of Property (Miscellaneous Provisions) Act 1994, s.16.

[66] Considered in more detail *post*, p. 550.

[67] At any rate, in the case of a "fixed trust", but not in the case of a "discretionary trust"; see *post*, p. 230.

[68] *Commissioner of Stamp Duties (Queensland) v. Livingston* [1965] A.C. 694; *Eastbourne Mutual B.S. v. Hastings Corporation* [1965] 1 W.L.R. 861; *Lall v. Lall* [1965] 1 W.L.R. 1249; *Re Leigh's Will Trusts* [1970] Ch. 277.

[69] *Re Hayes's Will Trusts* [1971] 1 W.L.R. 758 at 764 and see *post*, p. 653 for discussion of the duties of trustees in this respect.

[70] [1971] 1 W.L.R. 758.

property had been valued for the purposes of estate duty,[71] his other children could not attack the valuation on the ground that the executors had not considered the question of holding an even balance between him and them.

## (B) When Personal Representatives Become Trustees

Personal representatives remain personal representatives indefinitely unless the grant to them is limited or is revoked by the court.[72] However, where a will nominates the persons who are acting as personal representatives also to be the trustees of all or part of the assets comprised in the estate, it is sometimes far from easy to determine the precise moment when, and the circumstances in which, they cease to hold the assets in question as personal representatives and instead hold them as trustees. What has to be determined is whether or not the personal representatives have exhausted all their duties and functions as such and have consequently taken on themselves the character of trustees.

Where trusts of land are designed to continue after the administration of an estate has been completed, no problems will arise if the technically correct procedure is followed and the personal representatives vest the land in question in themselves as trustees[73] by means of a document known as an assent[74] (the situation is exactly the same where the personal representatives are also beneficially entitled to the property under the will or intestacy in question). Where such a written assent is made, it is clear that the character of the personal representatives changes thereafter and that they become trustees (or beneficial owners) of the land in question, even though their liability as personal representatives may in other respects still persist. However, until 1964 it was generally accepted that such a written assent was not actually necessary in such circumstances and that, when the estate had been fully administered in the sense that all funeral and testamentary expenses and all debts and liabilities had been discharged and the net assets ascertained, the personal representatives became trustees[75] or, alternatively, could exercise their statutory powers to appoint new trustees in their place[76] (or, in the event that they were themselves absolutely beneficially entitled, became beneficial owners). However, this generally accepted practice was first doubted[77] and subsequently in 1964 was rejected in *Re King's Will Trusts*,[78] where it was held that an express written assent is necessary in every case. Although this decision is a little difficult to reconcile with the wording of the appropriate statutory provision,[79] such an express assent is clearly in practice more desirable because it admits of no doubt as to the precise capacity in which the land in question is being held. However, at the time the decision in *Re King's Will Trusts* was extremely inconvenient since it had the effect of rendering tech-

---

[71] One of the predecessors of inheritance tax. Such valuations tend to be lower than the open market value.

[72] See *Attenborough v. Solomon* [1913] A.C. 76 and see generally *post, infra*.

[73] *ibid.* at 83.

[74] As in *Re Bowden* (1890) 45 Ch.D. 444; *Re Swain* [1891] 3 Ch. 233; *Re Timmis* [1902] 1 Ch. 176; *Re Oliver* [1927] 2 Ch. 323 (where property was to be held for persons in succession) and as in *Re Claremont* [1923] 2 K.B. 718 (where property was to be held on trust for sale).

[75] *Re Ponder* [1921] 2 Ch. 59; *Re Pitt* (1928) 44 T.L.R. 371.

[76] *Re Cockburn's Will Trusts* [1957] Ch. 438.

[77] In *Harvell v. Foster* [1954] 2 Q.B. 367.

[78] [1964] Ch. 542.

[79] Administration of Estates Act 1925, s.36(4).

nically defective the title to any land which had been administered in accordance with what had since 1925 been regarded as the accepted practice; consequently, many of these defective titles had to be put in order by the time-consuming and expensive process of obtaining the necessary written assent, sometimes many years after the estate in question had been administered. Now that almost forty years have passed since 1964, virtually all the defective titles which have not already been rectified must now be hidden behind the present root of title to the land in question[80] and so are in practice completely irrelevant. Whether or not the decision in *Re King's Will Trusts* is actually correct,[81] any assent relating to a legal estate in land is now invariably made in writing. However, the Court of Appeal has since established that an assent to the vesting of an equitable interest need not be in writing but can be inferred by conduct[82] and it has always been clear that assents in writing are not necessary in the case of pure personalty.[83] Assents by the personal representatives to the vesting of both equitable interests in land and pure personalty in themselves, whether as trustees or as beneficial owners, can therefore still be implied and can be taken to have occurred as soon as the administration of the estate in question has been completed.

### 4. *Agency*

The relationship between principal and agent has some resemblances to the relationship between trustee and beneficiary. For example, agents are liable to their principals, as are trustees to their beneficiaries, for any secret profits made out of the property or business entrusted to them and in such circumstances their respective positions may coincide.[84] The main difference, from which various other consequences follow, is that the relationship between principal and agent is primarily that of creditor and debtor. Consequently, while a trustee has full title to the property vested in him,[85] an agent has not; while an agent acts on behalf of his principal and subject to his control, a trustee does not;[86] and, while agency is based on agreement, it is not necessary that there should be — and indeed there is usually not — any agreement between a trustee and his beneficiary.

### 5. *Equitable Charges*

An equitable charge is created where specific property is appropriated to the discharge of some debt or other obligation without there being any change in ownership either at law or in equity.[87]

---

[80] Only where the title to the land in question is still unregistered and where there has been no disposition for value since 1964 is it likely that any technical defect in title created by the decision in *Re King's Will Trusts* will still cause any problems.

[81] The Court of Appeal assumed that *Re King's Will Trusts* had been correctly decided (but in fact distinguished it) in *Re Edwards's Will Trusts* [1982] Ch. 30.

[82] *Re Edwards's Will Trusts* [1982] Ch. 30.

[83] Because Administration of Estates Act 1925, s.36 applies only to realty (defined, for this purpose, as including leasehold land).

[84] See *post*, pp. 330, 336.

[85] See *ante*, p. 16.

[86] See *post*, p. 618.

[87] *London County and Westminster Bank v. Tompkins* [1918] 1 K.B. 515 at 528.

The distinction between an equitable charge and a trust is that an equitable charge merely imposes a liability on the property which is subject to it whereas a trust imposes a fiduciary character on the owner of the property.[88] This has a number of consequences. If property is held subject to an equitable charge and the chargee satisfies the charge, he will hold the property beneficially,[89] whereas a trustee will, on the termination of the trust, hold the property on resulting trust.[90] Again, a chargee is not accountable for rents and profits during the subsistence of the charge,[91] whereas a trustee is.[92] On the other hand, there is a basic similarity in that both an equitable charge and a trust are equitable interests and may therefore be overridden, that is to say destroyed, by a bona fide purchaser for value of the legal estate without notice[93] or, in the case of registered land, the statutory equivalent.[94]

## 6. Conditions

A condition may, in certain carefully defined circumstances, operate as a trust. Property may be given to a person on condition that he does something or confers a benefit on somebody. But it is only if that condition can, or must necessarily, be fulfilled or satisfied out of the property that it will take effect as a trust.[95] This will not be its effect if the duty is merely collateral.[96]

## 7. Powers

The basic distinction between a trust and a power is that a trust is imperative whereas a power is discretionary. Almost all trusts involve the exercise of powers or discretions by the trustees. In many cases this does not affect beneficial entitlement. So, depending on the circumstances of the particular trust, the trustees will often have a number of powers of an administrative nature; examples are powers to vary the investments of the trust,[97] to grant a lease of property which is subject to the trust,[98] to settle claims,[99] to apply income for the support of a minor beneficiary or to accumulate it,[1] to apply to the court for guidance as to the execution of the trust,[2] and to insure trust

---

[88] *Cunningham v. Foot* (1878) 3 App. Cas. 974 at 992–993, *per* Lord O'Hagan.

[89] *Re Oliver* (1890) 62 L.T. 533.

[90] See *post*, p. 300.

[91] *Re Oliver* (1890) 62 L.T. 533.

[92] See *post*, p. 764.

[93] *Parker v. Judkin* [1931] 1 Ch. 475.

[94] A bona fide purchaser for valuable consideration (other than marriage consideration) claiming under a registered disposition (Land Registration Act 2002, ss.28–31, 129(1), 132(1)).

[95] *Att.-Gen. v. Wax Chandlers Co.* (1873) L.R. 6 H.L. 1; *Cunningham v. Foot* (1878) 3 App. Cas. 974 at 995, *per* Lord O'Hagan.

[96] See *Re Brace* [1954] 1 W.L.R. 955 (no trust was held to arise when a house was devised to a daughter on condition that "she provides a home" for another daughter); *Swain v. The Law Society* [1983] A.C. 598 (the words "on behalf of" were held not to express or imply a trust; see *ante*, p. 18 and *post*, p. 330). Compare *Re Frame* [1939] Ch. 700 (a condition in a will that a legatee should adopt the testator's daughter was held to constitute a trust); *Re Niyazi's Will Trusts* [1978] 1 W.L.R. 910 (the words "on condition that" were held apt to create a trust).

[97] See *post*, p. 592.

[98] Trusts of Land and Appointment of Trustees Act 1996, s.6(1)

[99] Trustee Act 1925, s.15.

[1] See *post*, p. 672.

[2] See *post*, p. 619.

property.[3] Administrative powers are also commonly given to other persons designated in the trust instrument; the power most commonly conferred on persons other than the trustees is the power to remove trustees and to appoint new ones in their place[4] (where a trust has what is known as a protector, a person nominated by, and usually a confidante of, the settlor in order to control the exercise of some or all of the powers which the trustees would otherwise have, such a power is normally granted to him instead). These, and other, administrative powers which can be conferred by the trust instrument on trustees and other persons will each be the subject of detailed discussion later on. It must be stressed at this stage, and cannot be stressed too often, that it is fundamental to the nature of a trust that its trustees should not be puppets dangling at the end of a string pulled by the settlor or the beneficiaries[5] but should instead be persons with the right and the ability to exercise an independent judgment in respect of a wide variety of issues.

The powers and discretions which can be conferred on trustees and other persons are not, however, limited to the type of administrative matters considered in the previous paragraph; they can also extend to beneficial entitlement to the trust property. Trustees (and other persons) can be given powers to select who will receive the benefit of the capital subject to the trust and/or the income produced by that capital. Such a power of selection can be exercisable either, first, in favour of anyone in the world or, secondly, in favour of specific persons or defined classes of persons to which the persons making the selection can additionally be given a power to add or, thirdly, in favour of anyone in the world except specific persons or defined classes of persons.[6] Alternatively, the beneficiaries or classes of beneficiaries may be determined once and for at the outset and the pre-trustees merely be given a discretion to determine how much each of them is actually to receive and/or, in relation to income, whether it is distributed or accumulated.[7] Where powers relating to the existence and extent of beneficial enjoyment are conferred on persons who are not themselves trustees, such persons are known as donees of a power (a protector is in principle no more than the donee of various powers; the difference in practice is that his powers are likely to be much more extensive,

---

[3] Trustee Act 1925, s.19. Until the Trustee Act 2000 (which amended the original Trustee Act 1925, s.19) came into force, not only were trustees under no duty to insure (*Re McEacharn* (1911) 103 L.T. 900) but were only entitled under the statutory power to insure for a sum up to three quarters of the value of the property. Express powers of insuring usually allowed (and allow) the cover to be effected in the full reinstatement value but the present provision, while not on its face obliging trustees to insure, subjects their power to insure to the duty of care introduced by Trustee Act 2000, ss.1, 2 & Sched. 1 and contains no restrictions as to the value of the cover.

[4] See *post*, p. 549.

[5] It is in this respect that the position of a normal trustee differs from that of a nominee trustee, who in the absence of contrary agreement is under an express or implied obligation to comply in all respects with the beneficiary's directions (there is only ever one beneficiary or two or more joint beneficiaries, which amounts to the same thing, in a nominee trust). As a result, the nominee trustee is entitled to a complete indemnity from the beneficiary not limited, as is the case with a normal trustee, to the value of the trust property.

[6] Such powers are known respectively as general powers, special powers, and intermediate (or hybrid) powers. The third category, the intermediate (or hybrid) power and the possibility of adding to the persons or classes of persons in whose favour a special power may be exercised have evolved relatively recently; neither was clearly established until the decision in *Re Manisty's Settlement* [1974] Ch. 17.

[7] See *post*, p. 177.

sometimes even more extensive than those of the trustees). In such circumstances, the trustees hold the property for whatever beneficiaries and to whatever extent the donee of the power in question indicates. The precise nature and interrelation of powers and discretions of this type are discussed fully later on.[8] For present purposes, all that is necessary is an outline of the different categories of trusts and powers which relate to beneficial entitlement.

Where a person not only has the right but is also under an obligation to make a selection relating to the beneficial enjoyment of property, he is said to hold a "trust power", an apparently contradictory term which indicates that, contrary to the basic distinction between trusts and powers, the power in question is imperative rather than discretionary. Rather confusingly, two quite distinct situations are now described as giving rise to the creation of a trust power: first, where a trustee is under a duty to make a selection relating to the beneficial enjoyment of property vested in him (this situation was traditionally and is still more usually described as a discretionary trust); and, secondly, where a person who is not a trustee is under a duty to make a selection relating to the beneficial enjoyment of property which is not vested in him (this situation was traditionally and is still sometimes described as a "power in the nature of a trust"). Given the very considerable differences between trusts and powers and, to a lesser extent, the differences between powers and discretions, it is most unfortunate that what were formerly described as discretionary trusts and powers in the nature of a trust can now both be described by the same name; the confusion thus potentially caused has often materialised and on at least one occasion has extended even to the members of the House of Lords.[9]

A trust power, whether it is what was formerly described as a discretionary trust or what was formerly described as a power in the nature of a trust, can only arise where the selection in question has to be made from an already defined class of persons; however, as a result of the decision of the House of Lords in *McPhail v. Doulton*,[10] it is no longer necessary for all the members of that class to be actually ascertainable. In this situation, it has always been held that, in the event that the person entitled to make the selection fails to do so, the court can and will step in to decide the beneficial enjoyment of the property in question; in other words, if a trust power is not exercised, the court can and will execute that power. Traditionally, the court has done so by dividing the capital or income in question equally between all the members of the class. However, now that it is no longer necessary for all the beneficiaries in whose favour a trust power can be exercised to be ascertainable, this is no longer always possible; in such circumstances, the court has to have recourse to three other possible methods of executing a trust power which were envisaged by the House of Lords in *McPhail v. Doulton*.[11] However, in the 30 years which have elapsed since the decision in that case, there has as yet been no reported case in which a court has actually had to do this.

Where, on the other hand, a person has the right, but is not under any obligation, to make a selection relating to the beneficial enjoyment of property,

---

[8] See *post*, p. 177.
[9] Particularly in *McPhail v. Doulton* [1971] A.C. 424.
[10] [1971] A.C. 424.
[11] [1971] A.C. 424 at 457; see *post*, p. 62.

he is said to hold a mere power. The traditional view was that, in the event that the person entitled to make the selection failed to do so, the court could not step in and decide the beneficial enjoyment of the property in question; in other words that, when a mere power was not exercised, that power could not be executed by the court. However, a distinction has more recently been drawn between mere powers held by trustees and, in some circumstances, by other persons in a fiduciary position[12] (described for this purpose as "fiduciary powers") and mere powers held by anyone else (described as "non-fiduciary powers" or "personal powers"). It has been stated[13] that, in the event that a fiduciary power is not exercised, the court will in appropriate circumstances step in and execute that power by having recourse to at least one and possibly all three of the additional methods of executing a trust power which were envisaged by the House of Lords in *McPhail v. Doulton*[14] (once again there has as yet been no reported case in which a court has had to do this). However, the court is still unable to step in and execute a non-fiduciary or personal power.

Precisely which of the various different kinds of trusts and powers outlined above has been created in any given case is a question of construction of the language of the deed or will in question. Such instruments should ideally be drafted in such a way as to leave no room for doubt. However, in the majority of the cases that have come before the courts, the wording of the instrument in question has given rise to considerable doubt and that doubt has consequently had to be resolved by the application of a number of rules of construction developed for the purpose. These rules and the other important distinctions between trusts and powers, particularly the different rights of the beneficiaries of a trust and the persons in whose favour a power is able to be exercised, will be discussed fully later on.[15]

---

[12] See *post*, pp. 201–203.
[13] In *Mettoy Pension Trustees v. Evans* [1990] 1 W.L.R. 1587; *post*, p. 210.
[14] [1971] A.C. 424 at 457.
[15] See *post*, p. 177.

CHAPTER 2

# THE CLASSIFICATION OF TRUSTS

## I. STATUTORY, EXPRESS, IMPLIED, RESULTING AND CONSTRUCTIVE TRUSTS

TRUSTS may be created either, first, by statute — these are statutory trusts; or, secondly, where a settlor or testator intentionally creates a relationship of trustee and beneficiary — these are express trusts; or, thirdly, where a settlor or testator carries out some intentional act other than the creation of a relationship of trustee and beneficiary from which the court infers a relationship of trustee and beneficiary — these are implied or resulting trusts; or, fourthly, by operation of law, where a relationship of trustee and beneficiary is imposed by the court as a result of the conduct of the trustee — these are constructive trusts.[1]

### 1. *Statutory Trusts*

A number of trusts have been created by statute, either expressly or by implication. A large number of these are set out in the Schedules 1 and 2 to the Trusts of Land and Appointment of Trustees Act 1996.[2] Those which are most likely to be relevant for the purposes of this book are as follows:

(a) Under section 34 of the Law of Property Act 1925, as amended by the Trusts of Land and Appointment of Trustees Act 1996,[3] whenever land is conveyed or devised to persons in undivided shares, it vests in the first four persons named in the conveyance or the personal representatives respectively on trust for all the grantees beneficially as tenants in common in equity.

(b) Under section 36 of the Law of Property Act 1925, as amended by the Trusts of Land and Appointment of Trustees Act 1996,[4] whenever

---

[1] For a well-known classification, see *Cook v. Fountain* (1676) 3 Swanst. 585, *per* Lord Nottingham L.C. Compare *Soar v. Ashwell* [1893] 2 Q.B. 390 and *Re Llanover Settled Estates* [1926] Ch. 626.
[2] These Schedules contain the amendments to the various statutes which comprise the Property Legislation of 1925 which are necessary to replace the trusts for sale imposed by that legislation by trusts of land. They also create wholly new statutory trusts, such as the bare trust imposed as the result of a purported grant of an entailed interest. Other statutory trusts may be found in the Settled Land Act 1925 (such as the trust for sale of land imposed by s.36 where undivided shares arise under a settlement subject to the Settled Land Act 1925); however, no new settlements of this kind can now be created.
[3] Sched. 2, para. 3.
[4] Sched. 2, para. 4.

land is conveyed or devised to persons as joint tenants, it vests in the first four named in the conveyance or the personal representatives respectively on trust for sale for all the grantees beneficially as joint tenants in equity.

(c)  Under section 33 of the Administration of Estates Act 1925, as amended by the Trusts of Land and Appointment of Trustees Act 1996,[5] on the death of a person intestate, his property vests in his personal representatives on trust to be divided between his surviving spouse, if any, and his issue or other relatives in the proportions specified by the legislation.[6]

### 2. Express Trusts

Express trusts arise where a settlor or testator intentionally creates a relationship of trustee and beneficiary; this may be done by deed, by writing, by parol or by will.[7] A trust will be regarded as express even where the settlor or testator has expressed himself ambiguously if the court concludes, upon a true construction of the instrument in question, that a trust was what was intended by the settlor; consequently, words of prayer, entreaty or expectation, collectively known as precatory words, may be held to have created an express trust.[8] Further, a power to distribute property among a class of persons may be construed as indicating an intention to create an express trust in favour of that class if there is no gift over in default of appointment. In each case the question is entirely one of construction of the relevant instrument.[9]

### 3. Implied or Resulting Trusts

Implied or resulting trusts arise where a settlor or testator carries out some intentional act other than the creation of a relationship of trustee and beneficiary from which the court infers a relationship of trustee and beneficiary. They consequently arise from the unexpressed but presumed intention of the settlor or testator. The two alternative names stem from the fact that not only are they implied by the court but also often cause the beneficial interest thereunder to "result" to the settlor, to his estate, or to the residuary beneficiaries or intestate successors of the testator. Implied or resulting trusts arise in two sets of circumstances. First, where one person transfers property to another or into the joint names of himself and that other or pays, wholly or in part, for the purchase of property which is vested either in the name of another or in the joint names of himself and that other, there is a presumption that no gift was intended; consequently, the property is held on trust for the payer or, in the case of a joint purchase, for the two of them in proportion to their contributions (this is, however, only a presumption and can be rebutted by the counter-presumption of advancement when the parties are in one of a number of established relationships or by affirmative evidence of the payer's intention

---

[5]  Sched. 2, para. 5.
[6]  See *post*, p. 550.
[7]  See *post*, p. 96 for cases where writing is necessary.
[8]  See *post*, p. 46.
[9]  See *post*, p. 203.

to make an outright beneficial transfer). Secondly, where a settlor or testator who creates an express trust fails to exhaust the whole of the beneficial interest in the property in question, the court will imply that so much of the beneficial interest as is undisposed of will be held on trust for the settlor himself, his estate, or the residuary beneficiaries or intestate successors of the testator.[10]

### 4. Constructive Trusts

Constructive trusts arise by operation of law. Unlike all other trusts, a constructive trust is imposed by the court as a result of the conduct of the trustee and therefore arises quite independently of the intention of any of the parties. To give a very well known illustration, where an express trustee of leasehold property used his position to induce the landlord, who had refused to renew the lease to the trust, to renew the lease in his own favour instead, a constructive trust was imposed on him whereby he held the new lease on the same trusts as he had held the old one—his attempt to obtain a personal advantage for himself was regarded as antagonistic to the interests of the beneficiaries and was therefore contrary to the duty of loyalty which he, as an express trustee, owed to them.[11]

## II. SIMPLE AND SPECIAL TRUSTS

### 1. Simple Trusts

A simple trust arises where a trustee is simply a repository of the trust property with no active duties to perform.[12] If a settlor or testator vests property in trustees to be held on trust for a nominated beneficiary absolutely, the trust is a simple trust. The only duty which the trustee has to perform is to transfer the whole or some part of the property to the beneficiary if the latter so directs.[13] In such a case, he is known as a bare trustee.

### 2. Special Trusts

A special trust arises where the trustee is appointed to carry out a purpose designated by the settlor or testator and is therefore obliged to exert himself actively in the performance of the trust.[14] Consequently, he is known as an active trustee. Therefore, if the trust created is for the trustee to collect the rents and profits of the trust property, to pay the cost of repairs to and insurance of that property out of these rents and profits, to pay whatever is left to a nominated beneficiary for his lifetime and then, on that person's death, to hold the property on trust for someone else absolutely, the trust will be a special one until the death of the life tenant because during that period the trustee has active duties to perform; however, on the death of the life tenant, the trust will

---

[10] *Westdeutsche Landesbank Girozentrale v. Islington L.B.C.* [1996] A.C. 669 at 708. See further *post*, p. 271.
[11] *Keech v. Sandford* (1726) Sel.Cas. Ch. 61 and see also generally *post*, p. 358.
[12] Underhill and Hayton, *Law of Trusts and Trustees* (16th ed., 2003), p. 57.
[13] See *Christie v. Ovington* (1875) 1 Ch.D. 279; *Re Cunningham and Frayling* [1891] 2 Ch. 567.
[14] Underhill and Hayton, *op. cit.*, p. 58.

become a simple trust and the trustee will become a bare trustee because the only duty still binding on him will be to transfer the trust property to the ultimate beneficiary in the manner and to the extent that he is directed by the latter.

Special trusts are subdivided into ministerial trusts and discretionary trusts. The former require for their performance no more than ordinary business intelligence on the part of the trustees, for example the collection of the rents and profits of the trust property and their distribution in accordance with the instructions of the settlor or testator. The latter require the exercise of a discretion on the part of the trustees. This will be the case and the trust in question will be discretionary where funds are transferred to the trustees for them to divide up at their absolute discretion between a number of local charities such as a Dogs' Home, a Cats' Home, and a Home for Distressed Gentlefolk. A trust will also be discretionary where the trustees have a discretion to determine whether and if so, how much, income should be paid to each of the members of a class of beneficiaries nominated by the settlor or testator.[15]

## III. EXECUTED AND EXECUTORY TRUSTS

In this context, the terms "executed" and "executory" are used in a particular technical sense. A trust is regarded as executed in this sense when all the terms of the trust are specified in the trust instrument or the declaration which has constituted it. A trust is, on the other hand, regarded as executory in this sense when, although the trust property is vested in the trustees or is the subject matter of an enforceable agreement to vest it in them, that instrument or declaration requires the execution of a further instrument setting out the detailed terms of the trust. The distinction between the two is that, in the case of an executed trust, the settlor has, in the language of the nineteenth century, been his own conveyancer[16] whereas, in the case of an executory trust, he has not. A conventional, if old-fashioned, example of an executory trust is marriage articles from which a formal marriage settlement is later to be prepared.[17] A modern example is an occupational pension scheme established, as most pension schemes are, by an interim deed of trust which provides for the subsequent execution of a definitive deed of trust. In one such case,[18] the definitive deed of trust was duly executed but its validity was challenged when questions arose as to the entitlement to surplus funds. Scott J. in fact found the definitive deed to be valid but stated that, had he not done so, the interim deed would nevertheless have been upheld as a valid executory trust capable of being executed by a court order; this would have had the effect of providing rules corresponding to those in the definitive deed by means of which the questions as to the surplus funds would have been able to have been resolved.

---

[15] See *post*, p. 177.
[16] *Egerton v. Brownlow* (1853) 4 H.L.C. 1 at 210, *per* Lord St Leonards.
[17] For further discussion, see *post*, p. 160.
[18] *Davis v. Richards & Wallington Industries* [1990] 1 W.L.R. 1511.

## IV. COMPLETELY AND INCOMPLETELY CONSTITUTED TRUSTS

A trust is described as completely constituted when it has been perfectly created by either the settlor declaring himself to be a trustee of the property in question or the settlor or testator vesting that property in the intended trustees by means of the appropriate formalities so that nothing more remains to be done by him. Both executed and executory trusts are inevitably completely constituted trusts. But if, on the other hand, something still remains to be done by the settlor or testator, the trust in question is imperfect and is said to be incompletely constituted; this is another way of saying that, because there is as yet no valid trust, no interest of a proprietary nature has yet vested in the beneficiary. This will be the case where the settlor has undertaken to vest title to the trust property in the intended trustees but has not actually transferred the property in question. In such circumstances, the only conceivable remedies of the beneficiaries will be a direct or indirect contractual action against the settlor; they will have no proprietary remedy against the trustees.[19]

## V. FIXED AND DISCRETIONARY TRUSTS

Discretionary trusts have already been mentioned as one of the two types of "special trusts". They must also be contrasted with fixed trusts, which are trusts in favour of pre-determined beneficiaries or classes of beneficiaries. In the case of a fixed trust, each of the beneficiaries is entitled in equity to a fixed pre-determined share of the trust property at the appropriate time and he may enforce his rights to that share against the trustees. In the case of a discretionary trust, on the other hand, the trustees will have to exercise one or more of the discretions vested in them by the settlor or testator before any individual beneficiary has a right to any part of the trust property. The discretion vested in the trustees may merely be that of deciding in what proportions, if any, the trust property is to be divided among the members of a pre-determined class; at the other extreme, the discretion vested in the trustees may be that of deciding the membership of the class itself. Whatever the discretion, unless and until it is exercised, no individual beneficiary or potential beneficiary has any proprietary rights.[20]

## VI. PRIVATE AND PUBLIC TRUSTS

A private trust aims to benefit one or more persons who have either been defined by the settlor or testator or are to be determined in the future in the manner which the settlor or testator has provided. A public or charitable trust, on the other hand, aims to bring about or to support some purpose which will be of benefit to society or to some considerable section of society. Because of their public nature, charitable trusts enjoy a number of privileges not shared by private trusts; in particular, they do not have to comply with the require-

---

[19] For further discussion, see *post*, p. 135.
[20] They do, however, have a right to compel the due administration of the trust and can share in the fund on a premature determination. See *post*, p. 230.

ments of certainty of objects or of the rule against perpetuity and, most important of all today, are exempt from payment of most local and national taxes.[21]


## VII. New Classifications?

The traditional classification of implied, resulting and constructive trusts, which has generally been thought to be workable, has been the subject of considerable judicial comment in the last 35 years. The effect of these comments on these types of trusts will be analysed in detail in due course in the appropriate chapters. However, these possible changes to the traditional classification of trusts merit some brief discussion here.

In the first place, it has been contended that the two recognised sets of circumstances in which implied or resulting trusts arise should respectively be classified as "presumed" and "automatic" resulting trusts. According to this distinction, suggested by Megarry J. in *Re Vandervell's Trusts (No.2)*,[22] a presumed resulting trust arises when a purchase or transfer is made in the name of another person but not on any express trust; in these circumstances, there is a presumption that that other holds the property in question on resulting trust for the purchaser or transferor but this implied or presumed intention can be rebutted either by other legal presumptions or by evidence to the contrary.[23] An automatic resulting trust, on the other hand, arises where a transfer has been made on trusts which has left the whole or some part of the beneficial interest undisposed of (because, for example those are in some way ineffective or incomplete); in this situation the transferee of the property in question automatically holds it on resulting trust for the transferor to the extent that the beneficial interest has not been disposed of. In such a case, according to Megarry J., the resulting trust "does not depend on any intentions or presumptions, but is the automatic consequence of [the transferor's] failure to dispose of what is vested in him".[24]

The distinction between "presumed" and "automatic" resulting trusts appears at first sight to accord with common sense; however, it is fair to say that, just as what Megarry J. described as a presumed resulting trust is said to be created by implication as the result of a purchase in or transfer into the name of another, so an intention can be said to be implied on the part of a settlor or testator that the settled property should result to him to the extent that he has failed to dispose of it. The implication of an intention in the second type of resulting trusts does not actually appear to be markedly more artificial than in the first type of resulting trusts. Precisely this argument was adopted in *Westdeutsche Landesbank Girozentrale v. Islington L.B.C.*[25] by Lord Browne-Wilkinson, who reasserted the traditional view that both types of resulting trusts are examples of trusts giving effect to the common intention of the parties; he said that he was not convinced that Megarry J. had been right to

---

[21] The distinctions are discussed *post*, p. 443.
[22] [1974] Ch. 269 at 294, 295. The actual decision of Megarry J. was reversed by the Court of Appeal at [1974] Ch. 269 but the Court of Appeal made no comment on the judge's formulation.
[23] See *post*, p. 279 for the ways in which it may be rebutted.
[24] [1974] Ch. 269 at 294.
[25] [1996] A.C. 669 at 708.

suggest that the second type of resulting trust does not depend on intention but operates automatically.[26]

Lord Browne-Wilkinson's view is certainly preferable to the view of Megarry J.[27] However, a further definition of resulting trusts has also been propounded,[28] namely that such trusts require nothing more and nothing less than a transfer of property in circumstances in which the provider of that property did not intend to benefit the recipient. This definition seems highly convincing,[29] at least so far as the two recognised categories of resulting trusts are concerned.[30] Its influence can be seen in the decision of the Privy Council in *Air Jamaica v. Charlton*,[31] where Lord Millett, while accepting that resulting trusts arise by operation of law and give effect to intention, emphasised that a resulting trust

"arises whether or not the transferor intended to retain a beneficial interest — he almost always does not — since it responds to the absence of any intention on his part to pass a beneficial interest to the recipient".

These observations seem successfully to blend the new definition into the view propounded by Lord Browne-Wilkinson, which of course unquestionably represents English law at present.

In the second place, there have been a number of attempts to bring the concepts of resulting and constructive trusts closer together with a view to changing the basic attitude of English law towards the constructive trust. These attempts were largely initiated by Lord Denning M.R. in a series of cases decided by the Court of Appeal in the years immediately before and after 1970. In *Cooke v. Head*[32] he stated that "whenever two parties by their joint efforts acquire property to be used for their joint benefit, the courts may impose or impute a constructive or resulting trust",[33] while in *Hussey v. Palmer*[34] he said this:

"the plaintiff alleged that there was a resulting trust. I should have thought that the trust in this case, if there was one, was more in the nature of a constructive trust: but this is more a matter of words than anything else. The two run together."[35]

---

[26] Lord Browne-Wilkinson went on to say that, if a settlor or testator has expressly, or by necessary implication, abandoned any beneficial interest in the trust property, there will be no resulting trust; the interest in question will instead vest in the Crown as *bona vacantia*.

[27] Birks [1996] R.L.R. 3 at 11 regards Lord Browne-Wilkinson's view as "correct", despite the fact that it led to the rejection of his own argument that a resulting trust should arise whenever money is paid under a mistake or under a condition which is not subsequently satisfied.

[28] By Chambers, *Resulting Trusts* (1997).

[29] His extrapolation of that definition dealing with the nature of *Quistclose* trusts was, however, reviewed and rejected by Lord Millett in *Twinsectra v. Yardley* [2002] 2 A.C. 164; see *ante*, p. 28 and *post*, p. 297.

[30] Chambers, *op.cit.*, also classifies as resulting trusts a large number of other situations which most commentators regard as having nothing whatever to do with resulting trusts.

[31] [1999] 1 W.L.R. 1399 at 1412.

[32] [1972] 1 W.L.R. 518.

[33] *ibid.* at 520.

[34] [1972] 1 W.L.R. 1286.

[35] *ibid.* at 1289.

The expressed intention of Lord Denning M.R. was to convert the constructive trust into a remedy for unjust enrichment, as it has long since been in the common law jurisdictions of the United States of America and is now also in the common law jurisdictions of Canada (constructive trusts of this type are generally known as remedial constructive trusts). Thus in *Hussey v. Palmer*, immediately following the passage which has just been cited, Lord Denning M.R. continued:

> "By whatever name it is described, it is a trust imposed by law whenever justice and good conscience require it. It is a liberal process, founded upon large principles of equity ... It is an equitable remedy by which the court can enable an aggrieved party to obtain restitution."[36]

English law had hitherto regarded the constructive trust as "an institutional obligation attaching to property in certain specified circumstances",[37] one of which was mentioned when constructive trusts were defined at the beginning of this chapter.[38] Despite the efforts of Lord Denning M.R., this remains the situation at present — his approach has been rejected in subsequent decisions in which the traditional approach towards the constructive trust has been reasserted.[39]

However, this traditional approach has not been universally adopted. In 1990 the Court of Appeal stated[40] that "there is a good arguable case" that circumstances may arise in which "the court will be prepared to impose a constructive trust *de novo* as a foundation for the grant of equitable remedy by way of account or otherwise", classifying such a trust as a "remedial constructive trust". Subsequently, in 1996, Lord Browne-Wilkinson said[41] that "the remedial constructive trust, if introduced into English law, may provide a more satisfactory road forward ... However, whether English law should follow the United States and Canada in adopting the remedial constructive trust will have to be decided in some future case where the point is directly in issue." It has been made abundantly clear by the Court of Appeal on a number of occasions[42] that the contention that English law should adopt the remedial constructive trust cannot be maintained other than in the House of Lords. In *Twinsectra v. Yardley*[43] counsel for the claimant[44] would have argued for its adoption, admittedly as an argument of last resort, had the House not accepted the existence of a *Quistclose* trust.[45] There can therefore be not the slightest doubt that the House of Lords will one day soon be called upon to decide whether to return to the trail blazed by the Court of Appeal immedi-

---

[36] *ibid.* at 1289–1290.

[37] Waters in *Equity and Contemporary Legal Developments* (ed. Goldstein, 1992) 457 at 463.

[38] See *ante*, p. 39.

[39] *Burns v. Burns* [1984] Ch. 317; *Grant v. Edwards* [1986] Ch. 638; *Ashburn Anstalt v. Arnold* [1989] Ch. 1; *Halifax Building Society v. Thomas* [1996] Ch. 217; *Re Polly Peck (No.2)* [1998] 3 All E.R. 812 at 827.

[40] In *Metall und Rohstoff A.G. v. Donaldson Lufkin & Jenrette* [1989] 1 Q.B. 391 at 473–474.

[41] In *Westdeutsche Landesbank Girozentrale v. Islington L.B.C.* [1996] 669 at 716.

[42] Most recently in *Twinsectra v. Yardley* [1999] Lloyd's Rep. Bank 438 and *Bank of Credit and Commerce International (Overseas) v. Akindele* [2001] Ch. 437.

[43] [2002] 2 A.C. 164.

[44] Who included the author of this edition.

[45] See *ante*, p. 28 and *post*, p. 297.

ately before and after 1970 or to retain the more traditional approach adopted before and after that period.

Whatever the fate of this possible new development, however, the series of decisions handed down immediately before and after 1970 has had a lasting influence on the law governing joint enterprises entered into by the members of a family unit. It is in this area of the law that the concepts of resulting and constructive trusts have been brought closer together as a result of the development of what has become known as "the common intention constructive trust", which contains elements of both resulting trusts and constructive trusts.

If two or more persons make direct contributions to the acquisition of a property, usually but not necessarily a property in which they intend to live together, the principles of resulting trusts will give each of them a beneficial interest in proportion to his respective contribution, provided that the contrary is not stated in the conveyance by means of which the property is conveyed to one or more of them. Additionally or alternatively, if a person is encouraged by another to believe that he will acquire a beneficial interest, or an enhanced beneficial interest, in a property, again usually but not necessarily[46] a property in which they are living together, as a result of making contributions of a less direct nature towards the repayment of the mortgage or the subsequent improvement of the property (a straightforward illustration is the payment by one of the parties of all the day-to-day household expenses so that the other can more easily make the repayments of the mortgage), any attempt subsequently to deprive that party of the enhanced beneficial interest which he or she has been encouraged to expect will be regarded as unconscionable and will lead either to the imposition of a constructive trust or to the invocation of the principle of equitable proprietary estoppel.[47]

This development has in no sense undermined the traditional categories of resulting and constructive trusts which have already been mentioned. What it has done is to produce a new type of trust which contains features of both types of trust and it is thought that this may in the end lead to the development of a general principle of unconscionability to replace both the "common intention constructive trust" and the principle of equitable proprietary estoppel (indeed it has now been held that an equitable proprietary estoppel will give rise to the imposition of a constructive trust where there has been unconscionable conduct[48]). For the moment, however, the "common intention constructive trust" has undoubtedly brought closer together certain aspects of resulting and constructive trusts which are now co-existing in a manner which, while clearly defined and wholly justifiable, could not possibly have been anticipated 50 years ago.

---

[46] An case where the joint enterprise was of a purely commercial nature was *Yaxley v. Gotts* [2000] Ch. 162.
[47] See particularly *Lloyds Bank v. Rosset* [1991] 1 A.C. 107, discussed *post*, p. 424.
[48] *Yaxley v. Gotts* [2000] Ch. 162.

CHAPTER 3

# THE ESSENTIAL INGREDIENTS OF A TRUST

## I. CERTAINTY

IN the leading case of *Knight v. Knight*[1] Lord Langdale laid down that three certainties are required for the creation of a trust: first, the words used must be so couched that, taken as a whole, they may be deemed to be imperative ("certainty of intention"); secondly, the subject matter of the trust must be certain ("certainty of subject matter"); and, thirdly, the persons or objects intended to be benefited must also be certain ("certainty of objects").

### 1. *Certainty of Intention*

Equity looks to the intent rather than the form. No particular form of words is required for the creation of a trust; the use of the word "trust" is not essential, though, of course, highly desirable. It is possible, therefore, that words expressing desire, belief, recommendation or hope (known as precatory words) may create a trust. And if an intention to create a trust can be clearly deduced from the expressions used by the settlor, even though these are in precatory form, the court will give effect to that intention.

**(A) The Changing Attitude of the Courts**
An important change in outlook has occurred towards this requirement. Before the middle of the nineteenth century, the courts tended to take the view that any expression of desire or hope or the like on the part of a testator was imperative and therefore created a binding trust. It may indeed be said that it is possible to see in the older cases on precatory trusts an intention attributed to a testator which had the effect of creating an artificial certainty where no such certainty really existed.

This practice derived from a rule relating to executors. Until the passing of the Executors Act 1830, an executor of a deceased person was permitted to take any part of the latter's estate which had not been disposed of by his will (at that time, and indeed thereafter until 1858, estates of deceased persons were administered by the ecclesiastical courts not by the royal courts). It was obviously unsatisfactory that executors were able to do this and the Court of Chancery therefore endeavoured to find some reason for intervening and making an executor in this position into a trustee of the property which had

---

[1] (1840) 3 Beav. 148 at 173. It is not normally possible to introduce extrinsic evidence in order to aid the process of construction (see *Rubin v. Gerson Berger Association* [1986] 1 W.L.R. 526).

not been disposed of. This had the unintended consequence that the rules relating to certainty of words became confused with the equitable practice in respect of executors. Because the Court of Chancery was anxious to make an executor in this position a trustee for the deceased's next-of-kin, that court would seize on any expression of hope or desire to negative the presumption that the executor was intended to take beneficially. But the court adopted the same attitude in the case of inter vivos trusts and regarded any precatory words in the same light; consequently, such words were regarded as sufficiently certain to create a trust even though the alleged trustee was not an executor and even though all the property in question had been disposed of.

However, the Executors Act 1830 provided for executors to hold any property which had not been disposed of for the next-of-kin unless the testator had shown an intention that the executor should take beneficially. Thereafter, it was no longer necessary or desirable for either post mortem or inter vivos trusts to be upheld in cases where only precatory words had been used. The necessary change of approach was confirmed later in the nineteenth century when expressions such as "desire", "wish", and "full confidence" received fresh consideration.[2] One of a number of illustrative decisions is *Re Adams and Kensington Vestry*,[3] where a testator gave all his real and personal estate to his wife "in full confidence that she would do what was right as to the disposal thereof between my children". The Court of Appeal held that, by virtue of these words, the widow took an absolute interest in the property unfettered by any trust in favour of the children. The court also stated that some of the previous cases had gone very far and had unjustifiably given words a meaning beyond that which they could possibly bear if looked at in isolation. This well-known authority was by no means the first decision of its type; by the time it was decided, the wind had already changed direction and beneficiaries were no longer being made into trustees unless this was clearly intended by the testator.

### (B) The Modern Test
By virtue of the change of approach referred to, the intention of the settlor or testator became all-important. While the use of precatory words can still be held to create a trust in appropriate circumstances, the intention to create a trust has to be established by construction of the instrument. However, the question of what are appropriate circumstances can be peculiarly difficult to establish in practice. This cannot be considered in a vacuum but can only be answered by examining carefully all the words used in the instrument in question.[4] This proposition, which to modern eyes appears somewhat self-

---

[2] Perhaps the earliest case which illustrates the new approach was *Lambe v. Eames* (1871) L.R. 6 Ch. 597 (property to be at disposal of widow "in any way she may think best for the benefit of herself and family").

[3] (1884) 27 Ch.D. 394.

[4] It has now been provided by Administration of Justice Act 1982, s.21, that extrinsic evidence, including evidence of the testator's intention, may be admitted to assist in the interpretation of a will: (a) in so far as any part of it is meaningless; (b) in so far as the language used in any part of it is ambiguous on the face of it; and (c) in so far as evidence, other than evidence of the testator's intention, shows that the language used in any part of it is ambiguous in the light of the surrounding circumstances. It is also provided (*ibid.* s.20) that the court has jurisdiction to rectify a will if satisfied that it is so expressed that it fails to carry out the testator's intention in consequence of a clerical error or of a failure to understand his instructions.

evident, was formulated by Lindley L.J. in *Re Hamilton*[5] in the following way: "You must take the will which you have to construe and see what it means, and if you come to the conclusion that no trust was intended you say so, although previous judges have said the contrary on some wills more or less similar to the one you have to construe."

Some doubt may perhaps have been cast on this impeccable principle by *Re Steele's Will Trusts*[6]; the judgment of Wynn-Parry J. in that case is capable of bearing the meaning that, where identical words to those before the court had been held in a previous case to create a trust, that case should be followed unless it was clearly wrongly decided. Such an approach is obviously rather different from construing the instrument in question on its merits, even when other earlier decisions are taken into account[7]; consequently, if this is indeed what Wynn-Parry J. meant to say, it is not easy to support his view.

### (C) Illustrations of the Modern Rule

It would be a difficult, and probably also a fruitless, exercise to consider even a small number of the many decided cases relating to this question. However, at the risk of making the subject seem rather easier than it actually is, two cases, one on each side of the line, may be considered. On the one hand, there is *Re Diggles*[8] where a testatrix gave all her property to her daughter and the latter's heirs and assigns, stating "And it is my *desire*[9] that she allows to A.G. an annuity of £25 during her life". The Court of Appeal held that no trust to pay this money had been imposed on the daughter.[10] On the other hand, in *Comiskey v. Bowring-Hanbury*[11] (which may also be usefully compared with the decision in *Re Adams and Kensington Vestry*[12]), the testator gave all his property to his wife "absolutely *in full confidence*[13] that she will make such use of it as I would have made myself and that at her death she will devise it to such one or more of my nieces as she may think fit". The House of Lords held that, on a true construction of the whole will, the words "in full confidence" created a trust. Whatever doubts there may be about the correctness of the actual decision, the significance of the preceding word "absolutely" perhaps not being fully appreciated and taken into account, as a decision of the highest authority it nevertheless underlines the rule that in the last analysis the question is one of construing the instrument as a whole.[14]

A much more recent illustration of some interest, involving the winding-up

---

[5] [1895] 2 Ch. 370 at 373. See also *Re Williams* [1897] 2 Ch. 12 at 14 and *Comiskey v. Bowring-Hanbury* [1905] A.C. 84 at 89.

[6] [1948] Ch. 603, following *Shelley v. Shelley* (1868) L.R. 6 Eq. 540.

[7] Compare *Langan* (1968) 32 Conv. (N.S.) 361.

[8] (1888) 39 Ch.D. 253.

[9] Emphasis added.

[10] No trust was held to have been created in the following cases: *Lambe v. Eames* (1871) L.R. 6 Ch. 597 ("in any way she may think best"); *Re Hutchinson and Tenant* (1878) 8 Ch.D. 540 ("have confidence"); *Mussoorie Bank v. Raynor* (1882) 7 App. Cas. 321 ("feeling confident"); *Re Hamilton* [1895] 2 Ch. 370 ("wish"); *Hill v. Hill* [1897] 1 Q.B. 483 ("request"); *Re Williams* [1897] 2 Ch. 12 ("fullest trust and confidence"); *Re Connolly* [1910] 1 Ch. 219 ("specially desire"); *Re Johnson* [1939] 2 All E.R. 458 ("request"); *Swain v. The Law Society* [1983] 1 A.C. 598 ("on behalf of").

[11] [1905] A.C. 84.

[12] (1884) 27 Ch.D. 394; see also *Re Williams* [1897] 2 Ch. 12.

[13] Emphasis added.

[14] A trust was held to have been created in the following cases: *Re Steele's Will Trusts* [1948] Ch. 603, ("request" but see above); *Re Endacott* [1960] Ch. 232 ("for the purpose of").

of a company, is *Re Kayford*.[15] This case involved rather different considerations. The company in question carried on a mail order business and its customers paid either the full price or a deposit on account. Difficulties arose over the supply and delivery of goods and so the company opened a separate bank account called a "Customers' Trust Deposit Account" into which all subsequent payments made by customers for goods were paid and only withdrawn when the goods ordered had been delivered; the idea of this was that, in the event that the company had to go into liquidation, the payments made by customers whose goods had not been delivered could be returned to them. When the company did subsequently go into liquidation, the question arose as to whether the money in the bank account was indeed held in trust for those customers or instead formed part of the general assets of the company available for all its creditors. Megarry J. had no doubt that the facts showed that there was a trust; consequently, the sums paid had remained in the beneficial ownership of those who sent them until the goods ordered were delivered.[16]

This first requirement therefore involves certainty of intention to create a trust appearing from the words in the instrument.[17] The words used are, however, relevant not simply for the purpose of deciding whether a trust or a mere moral obligation has been created; there are other possibilities, namely that a power of appointment has been created,[18] or that the Crown may be administering property in its hands in the exercise of its governmental functions without a trust having been created[19] (the mere fact that the word "trust" has been used in relation to the Crown is not decisive[20]).

All the examples referred to so far involved private trusts. Where, on the other hand, the intention discovered in the instrument is to create a charitable trust then, as the House of Lords confirmed in *I.R.C. v. McMullen*,[21] any ambiguity should receive a "benignant" construction if this is at all possible.[22] The House did not, however, find it necessary to resort to such a construction in that case.

### (D) The Effect of Uncertainty of Intention

If an intention to create a trust cannot be derived from the words used in the instrument but only at most some form of moral obligation, the effect of the consequential uncertainty of intention is that there is no trust. Consequently,

---

[15] [1975] 1 W.L.R. 279; see *post*, p. 295.

[16] Megarry J. emphasised that the general rule is that, if money is sent to a company for goods which are not delivered, the sender is merely a creditor of the company unless a trust has been created. In this case, however, he held at 282 that there was a trust whereupon "the obligations in respect of the money are transformed from contract to property, from debt to trust". He also indicated that a trust of this kind might not be effective in favour of trade creditors; however, in the case before him, the court was only concerned with the interests of members of the public.

[17] The question whether a trust or a power has been created is considered *post*, pp. 201–212.

[18] *ibid.*

[19] As a "trust in the higher sense"; see *Tito v. Waddell (No.2)* [1977] Ch. 106 at 216, *ante*, p. 18.

[20] *ibid.* at 212. The Crown can be a trustee but only if it deliberately chooses so to do: *ibid. Civilian War Claimants Association v. The King* [1932] A.C. 14 at 27; *Nissan v. Attorney-General* [1970] A.C. 179 at 223.

[21] [1981] A.C. 1. The facts are set out *post*, p. 472.

[22] *ibid.* at 14.

the donee will take the property beneficially[23] (unless of course the words are construed as having given rise to a power of appointment[24]).

## (E) Sham Trusts

Thus far it has been assumed that a conclusion that an instrument manifests sufficient certainty of intention will be conclusive. However, it is not impossible for the words of the instrument to be held to be a sham in the sense that the settlor never had the slightest intention of parting with his pre-existing beneficial interest in the property in question.[25] In such circumstances his intention will instead have been to prevent some third party, usually his creditors, his estranged or former spouse, or his dependants, from obtaining access to the settled assets. Where a trust is found to be a sham, the settled property will be held still to be vested beneficially in the settlor or his estate and will therefore be available to meet the claims of the creditors, spouse, or dependants in question.

### (1) Total shams

In *Midland Bank v. Wyatt*,[26] a husband and wife executed a declaration of trust, of whose precise effect the wife was unaware, in respect of their matrimonial home, which was mortgaged to the bank; this declared that the equity in the matrimonial home, in other words the value of the property after deducting the amount of the mortgage debt, was held as to one half for the wife and as to the other half for their daughters. The husband subsequently raised further loans from the bank secured on the matrimonial home on the basis that he was still entitled to one half of the equity; he was able to do so because he did not reveal the existence of the declaration of trust either to the bank or to his solicitors until the former sought to realise its security.

The judge[27] held that the husband had never had any intention of giving an interest in the property to his daughters but had declared the trust in order to safeguard his family from commercial risk. He therefore held that, irrelevant of whether the husband's motives were dishonest or fraudulent or simply based on mistaken advice, the declaration of trust was a pretence or sham in accordance with the definition of sham propounded by Diplock L.J. in *Snook v. London and West Riding Investments*:[28] "acts done or documents executed by the parties to the 'sham' which are intended by them to give to third parties or to the court the appearance of creating between the parties legal rights and obligations different from the actual legal rights and obligations (if any) which the parties intended to create". Although Diplock L.J. there required all parties to have been involved in the sham, unsurprisingly in the context of what was a bilateral transaction for value, the judge held that, in the context of a supposed settlement where only the settlor is in effect providing value, there is no requirement that all the parties to the transaction held to be a sham should have had a common interest or a common intention. Given that the

---

[23] See the cases cited *ante*, fn. 10.
[24] See *post*, pp. 201–212.
[25] See Hayton [1992] J.Int.P. 3; Mowbray 8 T.L.I. (1994) 68; Brownbill [1992] J.Int.P. 13; Birt (1992) 3 O.T.P.R. 81.
[26] [1995] 1 F.L.R. 696.
[27] D.E.M. Young, Q.C. sitting as a Deputy Judge of the High Court.
[28] [1967] 2 Q.B. 786 at 802.

unawareness of the wife was therefore irrelevant, the judge held that the declaration of trust was void and unenforceable;[29] the husband had consequently retained his beneficial interest in the house throughout and the bank was entitled to enforce its security over it.

In cases of this type the settlor is in effect held to have had no intention to create a trust at all. However, it is rare for a trust to be held to be a total sham in this way. The decision in *Midland Bank v. Wyatt*[30] was undoubtedly facilitated by the fact that the trust had been created by declaration rather than by transfer. Admittedly, the reasoning of the judge is in principle equally applicable to a trust created by a transfer of the purported trust property to trustees; in such circumstances the settlor will equally have been the only person providing value and so the unawareness of the trustees will also be irrelevant. But it is difficult to see how a transfer of property to trustees could be regarded as a total sham unless title to the property in question is capable of passing on delivery, in other words unless it is cash, bearer bonds, bearer shares, gold bars, or valuable personal chattels such as paintings. If the property in question is instead land or shares and title to that property has been transferred in accordance with the appropriate formal requirements, those formalities are likely to be conclusive, rendering a finding of total sham improbable. In such circumstances, any sham which is found to exist is likely to be held to be of a different type.

### (2) Partial shams

The other type of sham is generally known as a partial sham.[31] Such a sham occurs where a trust has been created and duly carried into effect but its provisions and *modus operandi* lead to the conclusion that it is a sham. A decision that a trust is a partial sham casts no doubt on the intention of the settlor to create a trust (and consequently has nothing to do with the requirement of certainty of intention at present under discussion); it is the beneficial interests supposedly vested in persons other than the settlor which are held to be shams. However, such a decision produces exactly the same result as a decision that a trust is a total sham in that it equally makes the trust property in question available to satisfy any claims which anyone may have against the settlor.

There is, in principle, no reason why the claims in question should not, as in *Midland Bank v. Wyatt*, be the claims of the settlor's creditors. However, for the first five years following the creation of the trust, his creditors are highly likely to be able to set aside the trust, whether or not it is a sham, under the Insolvency Act 1986[32]; only thereafter will creditors need to have recourse to the

---

[29] The trust was also held to be voidable under Insolvency Act 1986, s.423. See *post*, p. 255.
[30] [1995] 1 F.L.R. 696.
[31] Mowbray 8 T.L.I. (1994) 68 prefers the expression "illusory trust".
[32] See *post*, p. 255.

doctrine of partial sham and this is relatively unlikely. In all the claims which have been litigated to date in the trust context,[33] it has instead been the settlor's estranged or former spouses and/or children who have brought claims to the trust property on the basis that it is in reality still vested in the settlor or, if he is dead, in his testate or intestate successors. But in *R. v. Allen*[34] criminal sanctions were imposed on a settlor in respect of his failure to disclose to the Inland Revenue his beneficial interest in the subject matter of two trusts of which he was not formally a beneficiary but which the jury decided were shams of this type.

**(a) Effective retention of control by the settlor.** Allegations of partial sham are most likely where the trustees have slavishly followed the directions of the settlor and/or, contrary to the provisions of the trust, have continued to apply some or all of the trust property either directly or indirectly for his benefit. The trusts which were determined to be shams of this type in *R. v. Allen*[35] had only two beneficiaries, both charities, powers given to the trustees to add further beneficiaries having not been exercised. Nevertheless, the companies of which the trusts were the sole shareholders owned the settlor's house and paid all the living expenses of both him and his family and it was on this basis that he was convicted. The facts of the leading trust case of this type, the decision of the Royal Court of Jersey in *Rahman v. Chase Bank (C.I.) Trust Co.*,[36] are less extreme in that the settlor had expressly retained certain rights under the settlement in question but they are nevertheless comparable.

Under the provisions of a settlement set up in 1977, the settlor had retained during his lifetime a power of appointment over the whole of the trust property exercisable with the consent of the trustees and a power of appointment over a third of the current assets of the trust in each twelve-month period exercisable without their consent; the latter power thus enabled him to bring the trust to an end in any ten-year period. Although provision was made for the distribution of trust capital and income in default of any appointment by the settlor and on his death, in the interim the trustee was empowered to pay or apply the capital or income to, or for, the benefit of the settlor and was directed to have regard exclusively to his interests in determining whether or not to do so. Further, most of the trustee's administrative powers required the prior written consent of the settlor. The trustee made no

---

[33] *Rahman v. Chase Bank (CI) Trust Co.* 1991 J.L.R. 103 (Royal Court of Jersey); *Re Marriage of Ashton* (1986) 11 Fam.L.R. 457; *Re Marriage of Goodwin* (1990) 14 Fam.L.R. 801; *Re Marriage of Davidson* (1990) 14 Fam.L.R. 817 (all Family Court of Australia). At least one such claim has also been made in English proceedings in the Family Division heard in Chambers in which the author of this edition was Counsel. Similar reported claims relating to sham companies (also known as *alter ego* companies) have been made in such proceedings; see *Nicholas v. Nicholas* (1984) 5 F.L.R. 285; *Cruttenden v. Cruttenden* [1990] 2 F.L.R. 361; *Green v. Green* [1993] 1 F.L.R. 236.

[34] [2000] Q.B. 744, where the Criminal Division of the Court of Appeal rejected a challenge to the validity of the direction on the basis of which the jury had convicted (the challenge was not renewed on the subsequent unsuccessful appeal to the House of Lords, reported at [2002] 1 A.C. 509).

[35] [2000] Q.B. 744 (C.A.), [2002] 1 A.C. 509 (H.L.).

[36] 1991 J.L.R. 103. See also three decisions of the Family Court of Australia in *Re Marriage of Ashton* (1986) 11 Fam.L.R. 457; *Re Marriage of Goodwin* (1990) 14 Fam.L.R. 801; *Re Marriage of Davidson* (1990) 14 Fam.L.R. 817; *Hess v. Line Trust Corporation* (1998) 2 B.O.S. 385 (Court of Appeal of Gibraltar); *Re WKR Trust* (2000) unreported but see [2001] P.C.B. 111 (Zurich District Court, Switzerland).

independent investment decisions and invariably complied with the settlor's directions. Further, the settlor drew money and made distributions from the fund of which the trustee was only later informed and often directly instructed the trust banks in respect of investments.

Following the settlor's death intestate, his widow contended that the trust was void and that he had consequently died absolutely entitled to the trust property which therefore devolved according to the relevant intestacy rules.[37] One of the two grounds[38] on which this claim succeeded was the fact that the settlor had at all times remained in total control of the trust property, something which was held to show that he had never intended the trust to have legal effect.

The facts of this case may appear extreme to the uninitiated. However, although it must admittedly be rare for a settlor to be able to deal directly with the assets of a trust in this way, the actual provisions of the settlement were not at all unusual in the context of off-shore settlements, particularly where, as in this case, the settlor in question is not from a common law jurisdiction and is unlikely fully to understand the nature of a trust. This decision therefore caused great concern in many off-shore jurisdictions,[39] some of which have since attempted to prevent partial shams of this type from being upheld by enacting legislation providing that the retention, possession, or acquisition of a whole series of powers by settlors and the existence of provisions requiring their consent to any act or abstention will not invalidate a trust. Such legislation will clearly work in the courts of the jurisdictions in question; however, it cannot be guaranteed to do so if any attack on the validity of the trust is mounted elsewhere in a jurisdiction in which some or all of the trust property is actually situated.[40]

**(b) Disguised wills.** A different type of partial sham arises where a person purports to settle property on trust during his lifetime with the objective not of depriving anyone of anything but of avoiding the expense of a will and the subsequent administration of his estate. In *Re Pfrimmer*,[41] a settlor vested four properties in himself, his wife, their son and their son-in-law on immediate trusts, under which he and his wife were entitled to all the revenue from the properties until sale or other disposal, which they appeared to be able to initiate; in the event of sale, they also appeared to be entitled to the proceeds and whatever remained at the death of the survivor of the husband and wife was to be held on trust for their grandchildren. The deceased subsequently made a will disposing of one of the properties and the furniture in another one. The trust could probably have been held void for uncertainty of subject matter[42] but the Court of Appeal of Manitoba actually held that the deceased

---

[37] Both she and the various defendants to the action (basically his children by former marriages) were beneficiaries under the trust; however, she stood to do better under his intestacy than under the trust.

[38] The other was based on a rule of Norman Customary Law then (but not now) operable in Jersey.

[39] Such as The Bahamas, in (The Bahamas) Trustee Act 1998, s.3 and The Cook Islands, in (The Cooks Islands) International Trusts Act (1984), 13C.

[40] This is an endemic problem of creative trust legislation which is inherently vulnerable to being ignored in any other jurisdiction whose courts regard it as infringing what they regard as fundamental principles of trust law.

[41] [1936] 2 D.L.R. 460 (Court of Appeal of Manitoba, Canada).

[42] See *post*, p. 54.

had not absolutely parted with his interest in the property; consequently, this was not a trust and could only take effect if at all as a will. In the event, which seems highly unlikely, that it complied with the formal requirements for a will, it would be valid; otherwise, the later will would have effect according to its terms and the remaining properties would pass on a partial intestacy.

The problem here was not that the settlor had retained a life interest, which is not uncommon in some jurisdictions,[43] but that he had in reality not disposed of anything and so not only was in complete control of his property but, as the subsequent will showed, intended that he should be.[44] The off-shore legislation referred to above has also attempted to prevent partial shams being upheld on this ground.

(c) **Blind trusts**. The facts of *R. v. Allen*[45] demonstrate that a partial sham can also arise where a settlor has transferred property to trustees on trust intending that the persons who benefit from the trust should be quite different from the beneficiaries whose names appear in the trust instrument (the latter are, as in *R. v. Allen*, usually charities). In effect, the settlor is giving property to his trustees to hold for a discretionary class which is not closed; the original objects are charities who will in practice never receive a penny and the real objects are added later.[46] Unless and until they are added,[47] the trust is in effect a partial sham[48] and the trust property is consequently held on resulting trust for the settlor or his estate.[49] It is therefore not a pre-requisite of such a sham being upheld that the subject matter of the trust is, as in *R. v. Allen*, being applied for the benefit of the settlor, or his family, or indeed of anyone else; however, this fact will undoubtedly make that conclusion easier to reach.

Trusts of this type are often known as blind trusts (quite distinct from the type of blind trust that has recently become fashionable in political circles whereby the work of politicians is funded without them having any control of the assets in question) or "Red Cross" trusts (because the named charitable beneficiary has in practice often been the Red Cross, as indeed one of them was in *R. v. Allen*). The reasons for proceeding in this way, apart from the blatant and illegal tax evasion which was being practised in *R. v. Allen*, can either be to avoid the tax which would otherwise be payable on the creation of the settlement or to avoid a challenge to the trusts which are really intended.

## 2. *Certainty of Subject Matter*

Certainty of subject matter is also an essential ingredient for the effectual creation of a trust. The property subject to the trust must either be clearly

---

[43] It would be pointless today under English law since the entire settled property would fall into the estate of the settlor for inheritance tax purposes. See *post*, p. 639.

[44] This decision was applied by the Court of Appeal of Singapore in *Hiranand v. Harilela* (2000) 3 I.T.E.L.R. 297.

[45] [2000] Q.B. 744 (C.A.), [2002] 1 A.C. 509 (H.L.).

[46] See *Steele v. Paz* (1995) 1 B.O.S. 338 (Court of Appeal of the Isle of Man).

[47] In *Steele v. Paz* they were to be added not by the trustees but by the protector (see *post*, p. 190) and could not on the face of things be so added because no protector had been appointed.

[48] This argument does not appear to have occurred to anyone in *Steele v Paz*. Instead, the court appointed a protector who was then able to add the real beneficiaries.

[49] See *post*, p. 291.

defined or be capable of ascertainment. This requirement has a number of aspects.

## (A) The Property Subject to the Trust

It must be possible to establish exactly what property is subject to the trust. In *Palmer v. Simmonds*,[50] a testatrix left her residuary estate to her husband "for his own use and benefit" but subject to a trust on his death "to leave the bulk of my residuary estate" to four named relatives. This trust was held to fail for uncertainty of subject-matter and so the husband took the property absolutely. A similar result occurred in *Sprange v. Barnard*[51]; the testatrix left stock to her husband "for his sole use, and all that is remaining in the stock, that he has not necessary use for, to be equally divided between" her brothers and sisters. In both of these cases, the husband took the property in question absolutely by virtue of the rule generally known as the Rule in *Hancock v. Watson*[52]; this establishes that, where there is an absolute gift of property in the first instance and the necessary intention subsequently to impose trusts on that property can be established, then in the event that the trusts fail for any reason the property is not held on a resulting trust for the settlor or his estate but will vest absolutely in the person to whom the property was first given absolutely.

In both *Palmer v. Simmonds* and *Sprange v. Barnard* the conclusion was reached that the testator had intended the donee to receive an absolute interest on which the failed trusts were subsequently to be engrafted. However, apparently absolute gifts have sometimes been construed as conferring only a limited interest on the initial beneficiary; such a construction avoids uncertainty of subject matter in respect of the subsequent trusts. In *Re Last*[53] the testatrix left all her property to her brother, providing that "at his death anything that is left, that came from me" was to pass to certain other specified persons. This limitation is very similar to that in *Sprange v. Barnard* but it was in fact construed as conferring merely a life interest on the brother; consequently, on his death, all the property was held on the trusts specified by the testatrix. Similarly, in the earlier case of *Re Thomson's Estate*,[54] a testator left all his property to his widow "to be disposed of as she may think proper for her own use and benefit" but, "should there be anything remaining of the said property or any part thereof" on her death, it was to be held on various trusts. Hall V.-C. held that the widow had a life interest together with a power to dispose of the property *inter vivos* but no testamentary power so to do; consequently, any property not disposed of during her lifetime was held on the further specified trusts. These decisions are only justifiable on the basis that the intention of the testator was indeed to confer no more than a limited interest on the initial beneficiary.

Another method of avoiding uncertainty of subject matter is for the court to find some way of ascertaining what the subject matter of a potentially uncertain trust actually is. In *Re Golay's Will Trusts*[55] the testator directed his trustees to permit a beneficiary to "enjoy one of my flats during her lifetime

---

[50] (1854) 2 Drew 221; compare *Bromley v. Tryon* [1952] A.C. 265.
[51] (1789) 2 Bro.C.C. 585.
[52] [1902] A.C. 14 (formerly known as the Rule in *Lassence v. Tierney* (1849) 1 Mac. & G. 551).
[53] [1958] P. 137.
[54] (1879) 13 Ch.D. 144.
[55] [1965] 1 W.L.R. 969.

and to receive a reasonable income from my other properties". Ungoed-Thomas J. upheld the gift, holding that the yardstick of "reasonable income" indicated by the testator was not what he or some other person subjectively considered to be reasonable but what he identified objectively as "reasonable income", something which the court could therefore quantify. This conclusion was undoubtedly inconsistent with other contemporaneous decisions on certainty[56] but does seem to be consistent with the more recent practice of the courts in trying to avoid, if at all possible, holding dispositions to be void for uncertainty, particularly in respect of expressions such as "reasonable" or "satisfactory".[57]

### (B) The Part of the Property Subject to the Trust
Problems have also arisen in connection with attempts to declare trusts of some certain but unidentified part of a larger holding.

### (1) Tangible property
The situation with tangible property is relatively clear. In *Re London Wine Company*,[58] wine dealers sent letters to purchasers of wine confirming that they were the sole beneficial owners of the wine which they had bought and paid for; however, no steps were taken to segregate the wine in question from the general mass of stock held by the dealers. It was held that no trust had arisen so that the purchasers had no proprietary rights in the wine as against the holders of a floating charge which the dealers had granted over their entire assets. This decision remains a useful illustration of the general principle but, because it concerned a sale rather than a gift, its result would now be different because of the Sale of Goods (Amendment) Act 1995, which makes such purchasers tenants in common of the general mass of stock. However, this provision will not avail anyone in the position of the purchasers in *Re Goldcorp Exchange*.[59] They had purchased but had not taken delivery of unascertained bullion; save for a small group whose bullion had indeed been segregated, there was no identifiable property whatever to which any trust could attach and the remaining purchasers thus remained unsecured creditors in the bullion company's insolvency.

### (2) Intangible property
The position with intangibles is more controversial. In *Hunter v. Moss*,[60] a declaration of trust in respect of 50 shares in a company in which the settlor held 950 shares was upheld on the basis that any identification of the particular 50 shares held on trust was unnecessary and irrelevant. At first instance, the principle enunciated in *Re London Wine Company* was confined to tangible property since "ostensibly similar or identical assets may in fact have char-

---

[56] Such as *Re Kolb's Will Trusts* [1962] Ch. 531 (a reference to "blue-chip" securities was held to be uncertain and consequently an investment clause was held to be void for uncertainty).

[57] See particularly *McPhail v. Doulton* [1971] A.C. 424, *post*, pp. 62–74 and, in relation to expressions such as "reasonable" or "satisfactory'", *Sudbrook Trading Estates v. Eggleton* [1983] A.C. 444 and *Graham v. Pitkin* [1992] 1 W.L.R. 403.

[58] [1986] Palmer's Company Cases 123.

[59] [1995] 1 A.C. 74. (Privy Council on appeal from New Zealand).

[60] [1994] 1 W.L.R. 452.

acteristics which distinguish them from other assets in the class"[61] — as the judge[62] said, some of the wine might have become corked or might have deteriorated in some other way. He then went on to state that a declaration of trust in respect of £1,000 in a bank account with a current balance superior to £1,000 would also be effectual. Although the principle thus enunciated must clearly be confined to intangible property similar to the choses in action held by the settlor in respect of the shares and the imaginary bank account, it nevertheless caused some surprise. It had hitherto been thought that trusts of such choses in action would only be valid if the settlor declared a trust either of his entire interest in the chose in action or of a fixed proportion of it[63] (in other words, on the facts of *Hunter v. Moss*, a trust of one-nineteenth of the shares held in the company in question) so that thereafter they would be held on trust for the settlor and the beneficiary in the appropriate proportions.

The settlor appealed to the Court of Appeal where Dillon L.J.[64] simply held that *Re London Wine Company* was "a long way from the present" case and concluded that "[j]ust as a person can give by will a specified number of his shares in a certain company, so equally, in my judgment, he can declare himself a trustee of 50 of his ordinary shares and that is effective to give a beneficial proprietary interest to the beneficiary under the trust". This analogy between a bequest and a declaration of trust has been the subject of fierce criticism.[65] The effect of a will is to vest the whole estate of the testator in his executors to be administered; consequently, a legatee acquires merely an equitable chose in action until the administration has been completed, at which point he will receive whatever shares are allocated to him by the executors. The effect of a declaration of trust, on the other hand, is to vest an immediate proprietary interest in the beneficiary; this necessitates some immediate means of determining which shares are subject to the trust. How otherwise can it be determined, in the event that the trustee subsequently deals with the shares by, for example, selling 50 of them, with whose shares he has actually dealt — his own, those of the beneficiary, or a rateable proportion of the shares of each of them?

Whether or not these criticisms are actually justified, there can be no doubt that the decision in *Hunter v. Moss* is the law at present and it has since been applied in *Holland v. Newbury*[66] by Neuberger J., who upheld a trust where a dealer in securities was holding unidentified shares in identified companies as the nominee of various of its clients. This latter decision made it clear that the crucial distinction is indeed whether the property in question is tangible or intangible (this was the distinction which had been adopted at first instance in *Hunter v. Moss* but Dillon L.J. had made no reference whatever to it in the Court of Appeal). Thus it is apparently now possible to declare a trust of a fixed sum in a bank account with a balance superior to that amount.

Nevertheless it must be emphasised that, even in the case of intangible

---

[61] [1993] 1 W.L.R. 934 at 940.
[62] Colin Rimer, Q.C. sitting as a Deputy High Court Judge.
[63] See Underhill & Hayton, *Law of Trusts and Trustees* (16th ed., 2003), p. 78.
[64] [1994] 1 W.L.R. 452 at 458, 459. This was an unreserved judgment with which the other two members of the court simply agreed.
[65] By Hayton in 110 L.Q.R. (1994) 335 and in Underhill & Hayton, *Law of Trusts and Trustees* (16th ed., 2003), pp. 78–79.
[66] (1997) *The Times*, July 18, 1997.

property, where funds should have been segregated but have not been, there will still be no trust simply because there is no identifiable trust property at all. This occurred in *MacJordan Construction v. Brookmount Frostin*,[67] where under the provisions of a building contract 3 per cent of each stage payment was to be retained from but held on trust for the builder; however, the fund which it was envisaged should be constituted to hold these retentions was never set up and so there was nothing to form the subject matter of the intended trust. Similarly, in *Hemmens v. Wilson Browne*,[68] a document purporting to give one party the right to call on the other party for a payment of £110,000 at any time was held not to have created a trust either because there was no identifiable fund which could conceivably form its subject matter.

**(C) What Property is Held on Trust for Which Beneficiary**
Another aspect of uncertainty of subject matter arises where it is clear what property is intended to be subject to the trust but some or all of the beneficial interests are unascertained in the sense that it is not clear what property is held on trust for which beneficiary.

In *Curtis v. Rippon*,[69] the testator left all his property to his wife "trusting that she should, in fear of God, and in love of the children committed to her care, make such use of it as should be for her own and their spiritual and temporal good, remembering always, according to circumstances, the Church of God and the poor". There was no doubt what property was subject to the trust but the beneficial interest was to be taken by an ascertained beneficiary, subject to the right of others to unascertained portions of it. The rights of the latter were held to fail and the ascertained beneficiary took the entirety under the Rule in *Hancock v. Watson*.

Where, on the other hand, all the beneficial interests are unascertained, the trust will fail completely. Thus, in *Boyce v. Boyce*,[70] a testator devised two houses to trustees on trust to convey to Maria "whichever house she may think proper to choose or select" and to convey the other house to Charlotte. Maria died in the lifetime of the testator and was thus of course unable to make her choice. The court held that it was impossible to establish which house was held on trust for Charlotte (it is impossible to fault this decision as a matter of construction but it might have been easier to reach the opposite conclusion had there been more than two houses — the consequential direction to convey the "others" to Charlotte could have been construed as "the houses not chosen by Maria"). As a result the houses were held on resulting trust for the testator's residuary estate (the Rule in *Hancock v. Watson* did not apply since there had been no absolute gift of the houses to the trustees in the first instance). In contrast, in *Re Steel*,[71] the testator directed that his residue was to be divided between legatees who had only received "small amounts"; Megarry V.-C. rather generously held that this gift was valid on the basis that the words were merely explaining the testator's motives and ordered the residue to be divided between all the legatees equally whatever the size of their legacies.

---

[67] (1991) 56 B.L.R. 1.
[68] [1995] Ch. 223.
[69] (1820) 5 Madd. 434.
[70] (1849) 6 Sim. 476.
[71] [1979] 1 Ch. 218.

**(D) The Effect of Uncertainty of Subject Matter**
When a trust fails for uncertainty of subject matter then, assuming that there is certainty of intention, a trust will obviously have been intended; consequently, the basic rule is that the failure of the trust on the grounds of uncertainty of subject matter will not enable the potential trustees to take beneficially unless the Rule in *Hancock v. Watson* applies. As has already been seen,[72] this rule applies where there is an absolute gift of property in the first instance on which trusts are subsequently imposed; if the trusts fail for any reason, the property will vest absolutely in the person to whom the property was first given. In every other case, the property is in principle held on resulting trust for the settlor or (if he is dead) for the residuary legatee or devisee under his will, or, if there is no gift of residue, on trust for the persons entitled to his estate under the intestacy rules.

However, there is some authority for the proposition that the court may apply the maxim "equality is equity" and divide the entirety of the beneficial interest equally between the beneficiaries.[73] The best known mode of application of the maxim is to be found in cases involving joint bank accounts held by husband and wife where, after dissolution of the marriage, it is found impracticable to divide the fund meticulously between them.[74] However convenient and "equitable" this may be, it is somewhat difficult to justify in principle the application of the maxim in a case involving uncertainty as to the actual beneficial interest taken by the objects of a trust; it is therefore doubtful whether these decisions can actually be justified.

### 3. *Certainty of Objects*

It is also an essential ingredient for the effectual creation of a trust that its objects should be certain or be capable of being rendered certain. When this is not the case, the consequences are exactly the same as in the case of uncertainty of subject matter: unless the Rule in *Hancock v. Watson* applies, in which case the potential trustees will be entitled to take the trust property beneficially, that property will be held on resulting trust for the settlor or his estate. However, it should be observed that only private trusts are subject to the certainty of objects requirement. A charitable trust will be upheld despite the fact that its objects are uncertain provided that a paramount intention of charity can be upheld;[75] in such circumstances, what is known as a *cy-près* scheme can be made to enable the trust property to be devoted to defined charitable purposes.

Three possible tests for certainty of objects have been canvassed by the courts: first, that the objects of a private trust will only be certain if it is possible to draw up a complete list of the objects of the trust (this has become known as "the complete list test"); secondly, that the objects of a private trust will be certain if it is possible to say of any given person that he is, or is not, an object of the trust (this has become known as "the given postulant test"); and, thirdly, that the objects of a private trust will be certain if it is possible to show

---

[72] See *ante*, p. 55.
[73] See *Doyley v. Attorney-General* (1735) 2 Eq.Cas.Abr. 194.
[74] See *Jones v. Maynard* [1951] Ch. 572; *Rimmer v. Rimmer* [1953] 1 Q.B. 63.
[75] See *post*, p. 482.

that one identifiable person is clearly an object of the trust (this has become known as "the one person test").

## (A) The Position Prior to *McPhail v. Doulton*[76]

### (1) The scope of the complete list test

Prior to the decision of the House of Lords in *McPhail v. Doulton* in 1970, all private trusts had to comply with the complete list test; consequently, their objects were only certain if it was possible to draw up a complete list of them.

This requirement had originally been laid down in *Morice v. Bishop of Durham*[77] early in the nineteenth century. At this time virtually all trusts were fixed trusts, that is to say trusts in favour of pre-determined beneficiaries or classes of beneficiaries, each of whom is entitled to a fixed pre-determined share of the trust property.[78] However, following the subsequent development of discretionary trusts, whose trustees determine in what proportions, if any, the trust property is to be divided among members of a pre-determined class and sometimes even decide the membership of the class itself, the Court of Appeal confirmed in *I.R.C. v. Broadway Cottages Trust*[79] that such trusts were also subject to the same requirement.

In that case, trustees held funds on trust to apply the income for the benefit of all or any of a class of beneficiaries as they might think fit. It was held, as a matter of construction of the trust deed, that a trust had been created in favour of the specified class. That trust was consequently void for uncertainty on the ground that the whole of the class was at any given time unascertainable; the whole range of objects eligible for selection had to be ascertained or be capable of ascertainment at all times. The expressed principle underlying this decision was that the court, if called upon to execute the trust, could only do so on the basis of equal division, something which would not be possible unless the identity of all the members of the class could be ascertained.

### (2) The scope of the given postulant test

On the other hand, mere powers only had to comply with the given postulant test; consequently, their objects were certain if it was possible to say of any given person that he was, or was not, an object of the mere power (it will be remembered[80] that a person is said to hold a mere power if he has a right, but is not under any obligation, to make a selection relating to the beneficial enjoyment of property).

The given postulant test had originally been formulated by Harman J. in *Re Gestetner Settlement*.[81] In that case, capital was held on trust for such member or members of a specified class as the trustees might think fit. The specified class comprised certain named individuals; any person living or thereafter born who was a descendant of the settlor's father or uncle; any spouse, widow or widower of any such person; five charitable bodies; any former employee of the settlor or his wife; the widow or widower of any such employee; and any

---

[76] [1971] A.C. 424.
[77] (1804) 9 Ves.Jr. 399, affirmed (1805) 10 Ves.Jr. 522.
[78] See *ante*, p. 41.
[79] [1955] Ch. 20; see also *Re Sayer* [1957] Ch. 423.
[80] See *ante*, p.35.
[81] [1953] Ch. 673.

director or employee of a named company. Harman J. held that it was unnecessary in a power of this kind to establish that the objects were all capable of ascertainment. It was simply necessary to be able to say of any given person that he was, or was not, an object of the power. The trustees did not have "to worry their heads to survey the world from China to Peru"[82] to find out who was within the designated class. There was no difficulty in ascertaining whether or not any given postulant was a member of the class. Consequently, the mere power in question was held to be valid.

The combined effect of this decision and the slightly later decision in *I.R.C. v. Broadway Cottages Trust*,[83] was to establish a crucial difference between discretionary trusts and mere powers, since the former had to comply with the complete list test and the latter only had to comply with the given postulant test. Given the factual similarity between the two, this caused considerable problems when the courts had subsequently to consider the proper construction of gifts which would be void if they were construed as having created discretionary trusts but valid if they were construed as having created mere powers. These difficulties were undoubtedly the principal reason why the House of Lords eventually assimilated the position of discretionary trusts and mere powers in *McPhail v. Doulton*.[84]

### (3) The scope of the one person test

Gifts subject to the donee satisfying a condition precedent clearly had to comply only with the one person test; consequently, their objects were certain if it was possible to show that one identifiable person was clearly an object of the gift. Thus in *Re Allen*,[85] a testator left property to the eldest of his nephews "who shall be a member of the Church of England and an adherent to the doctrine of that Church"; this gift was held to be valid on the basis that, whatever the precise meaning of the conditions, it was perfectly possible for a claimant to show that he fell within them.

However, following the formulation of the given postulant test in *Re Gestetner Settlement*,[86] it was on a few occasions, most notably by Lord Denning M.R.,[87] contended that that test should be interpreted in the same way as the one person test. However, the more strict interpretation of the given postulant test, under which, if it was impossible to ascertain whether or not a given individual was within the class, the power would fail despite the fact that other classes of persons were clearly within it, was supported by the pre-

---

[82] *ibid.* at 688–689. This expression was incorrectly attributed by Harman J. to Alexander Pope (see *Re Baden's Trust Deeds* [1969] 2 Ch. 388 at 397, *per* Harman L.J.); the words are in fact those of Samuel Johnson.

[83] [1955] Ch. 20; see also *Re Sayer* [1957] Ch. 423.

[84] [1971] A.C. 424.

[85] [1953] Ch. 810.

[86] [1953] Ch. 673.

[87] In the Court of Appeal in *Re Gulbenkian's Settlement Trusts* [1968] 1 Ch. 126 at 34; see also, *per* Winn L.J. at 138 (the limitation is discussed *post* in the text). It was also used in *Re Gibbard* [1967] 1 W.L.R. 42 at 47–48, where Plowman J. upheld a power to appoint to "any of my old friends", and in *Re Leek* [1967] Ch. 1061 at 1073 where Buckley J. upheld a power to appoint to "such other person as the company may consider to have a moral claim upon you" (the Court of Appeal held ([1969] 1 Ch. 563) that the gift in question was a trust rather than a power and so was void because it was impossible to ascertain all the members of the class. The one person test still applies to individual gifts subject to the donee satisfying a condition precedent or answering a particular description; see *post*, p. 65.

ponderance of authority[88] and was finally confirmed definitively by the House of Lords in *Re Gulbenkian's Settlement Trusts*.[89]

That case involved the construction of a clause in a work of precedents then much used by the legal profession. The clause provided that a special power of appointment could be exercised for the maintenance and personal support of all or any one or more of the following persons as the trustees should in their absolute discretion think fit: the settlor's son; any wife, children or remoter issue of the son; and any persons in whose house or apartments or in whose company or under whose care and control or by whom the husband might from time to time be employed or residing.

The clause had been considered before in *Re Gresham's Settlement*,[90] where Harman J. had held it void for uncertainty on the grounds that there might be a number of persons of whom it could not be determined whether they were or were not within the dragnet of this unusually constructed clause; he had distinguished his own decision in *Re Gestetner Settlement* because there, despite the fact that not all the persons within the specified class were actually known, it could be said whether any given person was or was not within the class. But in *Re Gulbenkian's Settlement Trusts* the House of Lords overruled *Re Gresham's Settlement* and held that the clause before them was sufficiently certain to satisfy the test laid down in *Re Gestetner Settlement*. Lord Upjohn, in affirming the latter test, rejected the application of the one person test which had been advocated by Lord Denning M.R. in the Court of Appeal.[91]

**(B) The Effect of *McPhail v. Doulton*[92]**
In *McPhail v. Doulton*[93] in 1970, the majority of the House of Lords overruled the test laid down in *I.R.C. v. Broadway Cottages Trust* and held that discretionary trusts had to comply only with the given postulant test, not with the complete list test.

The case for rigid requirements for trusts which had been made in *I.R.C. v. Broadway Cottages Trust*, namely that their imperative nature necessarily required that all their objects should be known, was admittedly a persuasive one. Indeed it had been restated in the House of Lords by Lord Upjohn in the intervening decision of the House of Lords in *Re Gulbenkian's Settlement Trusts*.[94] However, Lord Wilberforce indicated in *McPhail v. Doulton* that the law should take account of practicalities, particularly the narrow distinction between discretionary trusts (often also known as trust powers) and mere powers.

Lord Wilberforce also rejected as inappropriate the theory specifically postulated in *I.R.C. v. Broadway Cottages Trust* that the court can only execute a

---

[88] *Re Coates* [1955] Ch. 495 (for any friends his wife might feel that he had forgotten); *Re Sayer Trust* [1957] Ch. 423 (power in favour of employees, ex-employees, widow, children and "dependants"); in both these cases the power was held to be valid despite the application of the stricter test.

[89] [1970] A.C. 508, applied in *Re Denley's Trust Deed* [1968] Ch. 373.

[90] [1956] 1 W.L.R. 573, followed in *Re Allan* [1958] 1 W.L.R. 220, where the same clause had been utilised.

[91] Lord Donovan reserved his opinion on this point.

[92] [1971] A.C. 424.

[93] [1971] A.C. 424.

[94] [1970] A.C. 508 The point was restated by Lord Hodson in his dissenting speech in *McPhail v. Doulton* [1971] A.C. 424 at 442.

trust by ordering equal distribution in which every beneficiary shares: "equal division among all may, probably would, produce a result beneficial to none", being "surely the last thing the settlor ever intended".[95] Lord Wilberforce stated that, if the trustees failed to execute the trust, the court would instead do so "in the manner best calculated to give effect to the settlor's ... intentions". He envisaged this being done in one of three ways: either by appointing new trustees, or by directing persons representative of the classes of beneficiaries to prepare a scheme of distribution, or, should the proper basis for distribution be apparent, by directing the trustees how to distribute the fund.[96] (This does not of course mean that equal distribution will never again be ordered; in the case of a small class of beneficiaries whose entire membership is known, it is almost inevitable that equal distribution will still be ordered. It is therefore likely that the novel powers of the court outlined by Lord Wilberforce will only in fact be used where it is not possible to ascertain the entire membership of the class of beneficiaries in question, that is to say in the case of discretionary trusts which would have been void for uncertainty but for the decision in *McPhail v. Doulton*). This fundamental change in judicial attitudes enabled the certainty of objects requirements for discretionary trusts and for powers to be equated — the criterion for both is whether or not it can be said of "any given postulant" that he is a member of the class of potential beneficiaries.

However, the fact that the test for certainty of objects in mere powers and discretionary trusts has now been assimilated does not mean that mere powers and discretionary trusts have themselves been assimilated. As will be seen in a later chapter,[97] the basic distinction between the two remains. The court will not normally compel the exercise of a mere power and, when it is exercised, will interfere only where that power is exercised improperly or, possibly, capriciously. On the other hand, in the event that the trustees do not exercise their discretion under a discretionary trust, the court will do so in the manner thought most appropriate to carry out the settlor's intentions. Moreover, as a result of this distinction, "a wider and more comprehensive range of inquiry"[98] as to the range of possible objects is called for in the case of discretionary trusts than in the case of mere powers.

## (C) Outstanding Questions
Despite the decision in *McPhail v. Doulton*, a number of aspects of certainty of objects have not yet been finally resolved.

### (1) The scope of the given postulant test
While *McPhail v. Doulton* has established that the given postulant test is the appropriate test for certainty of objects of both discretionary trusts and mere powers, there is, in other respects, still some room for debate as to the applicability of the test.

---

[95] [1971] A.C. 424 at 451.
[96] *ibid.* at 457.
[97] See *post*, p. 177.
[98] *McPhail v. Doulton* [1971] A.C. 424, *per* Lord Wilberforce at 457.

**(a) Fixed trusts.** The first question is whether the given postulant test only applies to the type of trust which was under consideration in that case, that is to say only to discretionary trusts, or also applies to fixed trusts.

In the editions of this work which were prepared by Professor Parker and Professor Mellows,[99] it was contended that there seems to be no reason in principle why the given postulant test should not also apply to fixed trusts. Just as an order for distribution (not necessarily, as has been seen, on the basis of equal division) can be made by the court in the case of a discretionary trust, so also, it might be thought, could such an order be made in the case of a fixed trust where one or more of the beneficiaries are not ascertainable.[1] (The point is conceded to be "more academic than real", arising only in the almost inconceivable case of a trust for objects which could not be fully ascertained also containing a provision for distribution to them in equal or some other definite shares.)

However, the more general view, which is shared by the author of this edition, is that the "given postulant" test does not apply to fixed trusts, in respect of which it is still necessary to be able to draw up a complete list of the objects.[2] It is generally thought, contrary to the view already considered, that, if the trust property is to be divided among a class of beneficiaries in fixed shares, it would be wholly contrary to the intention of the settlor for the court to order any other form of division; on this basis, it is essential that all the possible beneficiaries should be capable of being ascertained by the time at which any distribution of capital or income has to be made.

**(b) "Powers in the nature of a trust".** It has already been seen that discretionary trusts are today often known as trust powers. However, the same name is also used to denote powers whose donees are under an obligation to exercise them. Such powers are also known as "powers in the nature of a trust".[3] Where such a power is found to exist, the court will execute the power in the event that its donee fails to exercise it.

Such a case was *Burrough v. Philcox*.[4] The testator left property on trust for his two children for life and, subject thereto, to their issue but further declared that, if both his children should die without issue, the surviving child should have the power to dispose by will of the property "among my nephews and nieces or their children, either all to one of them or to as many as my surviving child shall think proper". The surviving child died without so appointing. Lord Cottenham L.C. held that, "when there appears a general intention in

---

[99] See, for example, the fifth and last of those editions (1983) at p. 79. See also Matthews [1984] Conv. 22.

[1] The authors' reading of Lord Wilberforce's speech was that the new test applies to all trusts. Furthermore, it was contended that it would be regrettable if this were not so, because a discretionary trust is a trust, despite the fact that such trusts have close affinities with powers.

[2] See, for example, Hanbury & Martin, *Modern Equity* (16th ed., 2001), pp. 102–103; Underhill & Hayton, *Law of Trusts and Trustees* (16th ed., 2003), p. 84.

[3] The terminological confusion caused by the fact that the expression "trust power" is now used to describe two factually similar but legally quite distinct types of gift has already been mentioned (see *ante*, p. 35). Hanbury & Martin, *Modern Equity* (16th ed., 2001), p. 114 suggests that it may have been the two meanings of "trust power" which caused the discrepancy between the majority and the minority in *McPhail v. Doulton*, the majority having in mind the modern discretionary trust and the minority the old style power in the nature of a trust.

[4] (1840) 5 Myl. & Cr. 72.

favour of a class, and a particular intention in favour of individuals of a class to be selected by another person, and the particular intention fails from that selection not being made, the Court will carry into effect the general intention in favour of the class".[5] He held that the words used evinced a general intention of this type consequently the court could execute the power on behalf of its donee by dividing the property equally among all the members of the class (had he not found a general intention of this type, the property would have passed on a resulting trust for those entitled to the residuary estate of the testator).

With which test for certainty of objects do such powers in the nature of a trust have to comply? If it is still the case that the court would automatically execute such a power by dividing the property equally between all the members of the class, then it ought to follow that the test is the same as that for fixed trusts; in this case, according to the general view that the appropriate test for dixed trusts is the complete list test,[6] it will be necessary for it to be possible to draw up a complete list of the members of the class at the appropriate time. If, on the other hand, the remarks of Lord Wilberforce in *McPhail v. Doulton* as to the ways in which the court can now execute a discretionary trust[7] also apply to powers in the nature of a trust, then there will be no need for the complete list test to apply and such limitations will presumably also be governed by the given postulant test.

This question is in fact somewhat academic since powers in the nature of a trust are almost invariably in favour of small groups of beneficiaries, usually, as in *Burrough v. Philcox*, the members of a family. Gifts of this type will inevitably satisfy either test for certainty of objects and in practice, the court would almost inevitably order equal distribution quite irrelevant of whether or not this was actually obligatory. It has admittedly been argued that powers in the nature of a trust should be regarded as fixed trusts subject to defeasance by exercise of the power of selection and, as a result, must still be governed by the test appropriate to fixed trusts.[8] However, because of the factual similarity between powers in the nature of a trust and discretionary trusts, it seems as a matter of principle to be more appropriate that such powers should today also be governed by the given postulant test on the already mentioned assumption that, whenever the entire membership of the class is known, equal division will in fact be ordered.

(c) **Gifts subject to a condition precedent and individual gifts.** The one person test clearly still applies to gifts subject to the donee satisfying a condition precedent. This is illustrated by *Re Tuck's Settlement Trusts*,[9] where requirements that the principal beneficiary for the time being under a settlement had to be of the Jewish faith and, if married, be married to an approved Jewish wife were held by the majority of the Court of Appeal[10] to be conditions precedent and consequently valid under the one person test.

---

[5] *ibid.*
[6] The contrary view was adopted in earlier editions of this work (see *ante*, p. 63).
[7] See *ante*, p. 62.
[8] In Hanbury & Martin, *Modern Equity* (16th ed., 2001), p. 114.
[9] [1978] Ch. 49.
[10] Lord Russell of Killowen and Eveleigh L.J.; Lord Denning M.R. adopted a different approach, discussed *post*, p. 70.

The one person test has now also been extended to gifts made to individuals who answer a particular description.[11] In *Re Barlow's Will Trust*,[12] the testatrix provided that "any friends of mine who may wish to do so" might purchase any of her paintings at their probate valuation. This limitation was not expressed in the form of a condition precedent; however, it nevertheless amounted to a series of gifts to any individuals who answered a particular specified description. Browne-Wilkinson J. held that, had this been a gift to a class and therefore had had to satisfy the given postulant test, it would have been void; it would obviously also have been void if it had had to satisfy the complete list test. However, he regarded the limitation as creating a series of individual gifts in the form of options exercisable by any person who qualified as a "friend"; since there might be persons who could, on any conceivable test, prove that they were friends, the limitation was valid.

While the applicability of the one person test to conditions precedent and other analogous gifts is clearly established, it would certainly not be easy for the court to decide whether any individual did in fact qualify in such circumstances; any doubts as to qualification would therefore presumably lead to the automatic disqualification of the claimant. However, this is not necessarily an objection to the existence of the test since, as will be seen in the next section, this is now arguably also the case with the given postulant test.

### (2) Conceptual and evidential certainty

In *Re Gulbenkian's Settlement Trusts*,[13] Lord Upjohn posed the distinction between conceptual certainty and evidential certainty; this distinction was also adopted in *McPhail v. Doulton*.[14] Objects will be conceptually uncertain if the exact meaning of the definition used contains any linguistic or semantic uncertainty, if in other words it is impossible to say what the words in question actually mean. If this is the case, the gift in question will be wholly void unless the court can resolve the conceptual uncertainty in some way. Only where objects are conceptually certain does any question of evidential certainty arise; this is the question of whether, on the facts, it can be established whether or not the objects satisfy the relevant test for certainty of objects; if it cannot be so established, the gift in question will also be rendered wholly void.

### (a) The complete list test

(a) **The complete list test**. The complete list test requires total certainty. Any form of conceptual or evidential uncertainty will render the gift in question void. On the assumption that fixed trusts are still governed by the complete list test, a fixed trust for the settlor's "old friends" in equal shares would be

---

[11] Conditions subsequent are subject to a stricter test; the situations in which such a condition will operate must be wholly clear from the outset. For a recent discussion, see *Re Tepper's Will Trusts* [1987] Ch. 49.
[12] [1978] 1 W.L.R. 278.
[13] [1970] A.C. 508 at 524.
[14] [1971] A.C. 424 at 457.

likely to be conceptually uncertain,[15] simply because the expression used is capable of so many different interpretations.[16] On the same assumption, the objects of a fixed trust will be evidentially uncertain if it is impossible to list all the members of the class at the appropriate time. However, there is never any difficulty about a trust for one person for life followed by a gift in remainder to his children in equal shares; even if the life tenant has no children at the time at which the trust is constituted, it will become clear whether or not he has any children and, if so, how many not later than nine months after the determination of his life interest upon his death.[17] But the sort of classes of beneficiaries which were established in *Re Gestetner Settlement*,[18] *Re Gulbenkian's Settlement*[19] and *McPhail v. Doulton*[20] cannot conceivably satisfy the "complete list" test because of the impossibility of determining between how many persons the capital or income has to be divided. Having said that, provided that it is possible to establish the maximum number of possible beneficiaries, it does not matter that the continued existence or present whereabouts of some of the possible members of the class cannot be discovered; the shares payable to any such beneficiaries can be paid into court to await either their appearance or definitive proof that they did not in fact qualify.[21] All that is necessary is that the list which is able to be drawn up at the appropriate time is, on a balance of probabilities, complete.

**(b) The one person test**. The one person test does not require any conceptual certainty whatever. This follows inexorably from *Re Barlow's Will Trust*[22] where Browne-Wilkinson J. held that, had the gift to "any friends of mine" been governed by either the complete list test or the given postulant test, it would have been void for conceptual uncertainty. That did not prevent him from upholding the gift.

The only evidential certainty required by the one person test is that it must be possible for that one person to show that he satisfies the criteria of the gift in question. Thus the gift in *Re Allen*[23] was upheld because, whatever the precise meaning of the words "a member of the Church of England and an adherent to the doctrine of that Church", it was perfectly possible for a claimant to show that he fell within them.

**(c) The given postulant test**. The effect of conceptual and evidential uncertainty in relation to the given postulant test had to be considered in *Re*

---

[15] This was stated by Browne-Wilkinson J. in *Re Barlow's Will Trusts* [1970] 1 W.L.R. 278 at 281–282.
[16] However, such an expression would satisfy the more diluted test advocated by Lord Denning M.R. (see *ante*, fn. 87), provided that one "old friend" of the settlor could be clearly identified — this was specifically held by Browne-Wilkinson J. in *Re Barlow's Will Trusts* [1979] 1 W.L.R. 278 in respect of a series of individual gifts with a condition precedent or description attached, to which the more diluted test was held to be applicable.
[17] The point at which the children's interest would vest in possession (each child having acquired a vested interest in interest on his birth); the nine-month extension is made so that any posthumous children can be included.
[18] [1953] Ch. 673.
[19] [1970] A.C. 508.
[20] [1971] A.C. 424.
[21] See Emery (1982) 98 L.Q.R. 551.
[22] [1978] 1 W.L.R. 278.
[23] [1953] Ch. 810.

*Baden's Deed Trusts (No.2),*[24] the sequel to *McPhail v. Doulton* in which the test laid down by the House of Lords had to be applied to the terms of the trust in question.

The trust deed in question directed the trustees to apply the net income of the fund in making at their absolute discretion grants to or for the benefit of any of the officers and employees or ex-officers or ex-employees of a specified company or to any relatives or dependants of any such persons. The Court of Appeal held that this class satisfied the given postulant test but the members of the court neither agreed as to the correct interpretation of the test nor, consequently, as to the conceptually certain meaning of the two problematic words, "relatives" and "dependants".

Of the three members of the Court of Appeal, Stamp L.J. alone interpreted the given postulant test strictly, holding that the test would only be satisfied if it was possible to say either "yes" or "no" to any person who could conceivably present himself to the trustees.[25] On the other hand, both Sachs L.J. and Megaw L.J. seemed to broaden the test laid down by the House of Lords. Sachs L.J. held that, provided that the class was conceptually certain, the gift could never fail for evidential uncertainty; the burden of proof was on the postulant and, if he could not positively prove that he was within the class, then he was outside it.[26] Megaw L.J. held that, if it could be said with certainty that a substantial number of objects did fall within the class, then it did not matter that, as regards a substantial number of other persons, the answer had to be that "it is not proven whether they are in or out".[27]

All three views are susceptible to criticism. The interpretation advocated by Stamp L.J. in practice does not fall far short of a return to the complete list test expressly rejected in *McPhail v. Doulton;* according to this interpretation, while there is no need for the trustees actually to draw up a list, it has to be admitted that those otherwise entitled to the property subject to a discretionary trust will be able to upset that trust whenever they can come up with one person whose claim to be a member of the class cannot be proven one way or the other. On the other hand, the interpretations adopted by both Sachs L.J. and Megaw L.J. move some considerable way towards the one person test specifically rejected in *Re Gulbenkian's Settlement Trusts.* The interpretation adopted by Sachs L.J. could undoubtedly lead to there being only one beneficiary within the class but only if the expression used was conceptually certain, something which is not actually required in the case of gifts subject to the one person test.[28] The interpretation adopted by Megaw L.J. would admittedly require a substantial number of persons rather than just one to fall within the class; however, it is unclear whether or not conceptual certainty would also be required.

Having expressed these differing views as to the interpretation of the given postulant test, the members of the Court of Appeal all accepted that, no matter what meaning was given to "dependants", the trust would be both conceptually and evidentially certain.[29] Sachs and Megaw L.JJ. held that the trust

[24] [1973] Ch. 9.
[25] *ibid.* at 28.
[26] *ibid.* at 19.
[27] *ibid.* at 24.
[28] See *ante,* p. 67.
[29] [1973] Ch. 9 at 20, 22, 30.

would also be conceptually certain even if the widest possible meaning, "descendants from a common ancestor", was attributed to "relatives" and that there was no evidential difficulty about ascertaining whether any given postulant was a relative.[30] Stamp L.J., on the other hand, held that, if such a meaning was given to "relatives", the trust would fail because of the impossibility of saying that any given postulant was not a relative of a past or present officer or employee of the company; he consequently interpreted "relatives" as meaning "statutory next-of-kin", an expression which is on any view both conceptually and evidentially certain.[31]

It is not easy to determine the precise effect of Re Baden's Deed Trusts (No.2) so far as conceptual certainty is concerned. There has been little or no subsequent judicial discussion of this aspect of the interpretation of the test laid down in Re Gulbenkian's Settlement Trusts and McPhail v. Doulton. The limitation in Re Baden's Deed Trusts (No.2) was of course complex and it must not be thought that problems of this kind will often arise; however, it must not be forgotten that, in Re Barlow's Will Trust,[32] Browne-Wilkinson J. held that, had the gift to "any friends of mine" been a gift to a class and therefore had had to satisfy the given postulant test, it would have been void for conceptual uncertainty. Other illustrations of conceptual uncertainty are to be found in cases prior to McPhail v. Doulton where it was plain that there was, and would still be, conceptual uncertainty of objects.

Thus in Re Astor's Settlement Trusts,[33] which concerned the newspaper The Observer, a settlement provided for income to be applied at the trustees' discretion among a number of non-charitable purposes including the "maintenance of good understanding, sympathy and co-operation between nations" and "the preservation of the independence and integrity of newspapers" and other such purposes for the protection of newspapers. Roxburgh J. held that the objects listed above were void for uncertainty and that for this, and other reasons, the trusts were void; he said that purposes must be stated in phrases which embody definite concepts and, moreover, the means by which the trustees are to attain them must be prescribed with a sufficient degree of certainty. Similarly, in Re Endacott,[34] the Court of Appeal held that a trust which was in effect for a purpose regarded by the trustees as "useful" was void for uncertainty because it was not clear what "utility" meant.

It is also generally thought that a discretionary trust in favour of "persons having a moral claim" on the settlor would also be void for conceptual uncertainty because of the impossibility of defining "moral claim". Admittedly, in Re Leek,[35] a limitation in favour of "such persons as the [donee of the power in question] may consider to have a moral claim" on the settlor was held by Buckley J. to be sufficiently certain, a view which was supported by

---

[30] ibid. at 21, 22.
[31] ibid. at 28–30. "Relatives" has traditionally been construed as "statutory next-of-kin" if this is necessary to save a gift; however, an appointment by the trustees in favour of relatives who are not statutory next-of-kin is nevertheless valid, which signifies that, in the event that the court were called upon to execute the trust because of a default by the trustees, distribution would necessarily be among a narrower class than that available to the trustees (see Re Poulton's Will Trusts [1987] 1 W.L.R. 795).
[32] [1978] 1 W.L.R. 278.
[33] [1952] Ch. 534. See also post, p. 76.
[34] [1960] Ch. 232.
[35] [1967] Ch. 1061 (Buckley J.) [1969] 1 Ch. 563 (C.A.).

Harman L.J. in the Court of Appeal by way of dictum.[36] However, it is arguable that the restriction of the class to such persons as a specified individual or individuals regards as having such a moral claim makes the issue more, rather than less, conceptually uncertain, unless that restriction is regarded as a valid delegation in the manner considered below.

**(d) Can conceptual uncertainty be cured by delegation?** *Re Leek*[37] raises a question of general importance, which can arise in all cases in which conceptual certainty is required, as to the extent to which conceptual uncertainty can be cured by a provision that the matter is to be settled by the decision of either the trustees or of some third party.

The orthodox view is that a question of fact can be delegated for resolution in this way[38] but not a question of law, since the jurisdiction of the court to decide matters of law cannot be ousted.[39] For present purposes, this suggests that, while an issue of evidential uncertainty could be delegated by the settlor to the trustees[40] or to some third party for resolution, an issue of conceptual uncertainty could not be so delegated.[41] However, in *Dundee General Hospital Board of Management v. Walker*,[42] the House of Lords held, on a Scottish appeal, that a proviso that a legacy was only to be paid to a hospital if the trustees of the will "were in their sole and absolute discretion" satisfied that the hospital had not been placed under state control made the trustees the sole judges of this question; therefore there could be no appeal to the courts from their decision unless they had considered the wrong question or failed to consider the right question in a proper manner. This decision suggests that a question of law can now be referred to a third party for decision, in which case there seems no reason why an issue of conceptual uncertainty should not similarly be delegated.

This impression is confirmed by some remarks of Lord Denning M.R. in *Re Tuck's Settlement Trusts*,[43] which concerned conditions precedent in a settlement that the principal beneficiary for the time being had to be of the Jewish faith and, if married, be married to an approved Jewish wife. The settlement provided that any dispute as to the conditions was to be referred to the Chief Rabbi for decision. The majority of the Court of Appeal found that these

---

[36] As the words in square brackets indicate, Buckley J. actually held that this limitation had created a mere power. At that time, only mere powers were subject to the given postulant test and, on appeal, the Court of Appeal instead found that the limitation had created a discretionary trust which, under the then law, was void for uncertainty because it was impossible to satisfy the complete list test (such a discretionary trust would of course now also be subject to the given postulant test).

[37] [1967] Ch. 1061 (Buckley J.) [1969] 1 Ch. 563 (C.A.).

[38] *Re Coxen* [1948] Ch. 747.

[39] *Re Wynn* [1952] Ch. 271.

[40] *Re Coxen* [1948] Ch. 747. This case concerned a condition subsequent; a provision that the trustees should be able to determine whether or not the testator's widow had "ceased permanently to reside" at a particular property was upheld. See also *Re Burton* [1955] Ch. 82 at 95.

[41] *Re Jones* [1953] Ch. 125. This case also concerned a condition subsequent; a provision that the "uncontrolled opinion" of the trustees should determine whether or not the testator's daughter had "social or other relationship" with a named person was held to be void for uncertainty.

[42] [1952] 1 All E.R. 896. This decision was considered in *Re Jones* [1953] Ch. 125 (see *ante*, fn. 41) but was distinguished on the grounds that it concerned a condition precedent whereas *Re Jones* concerned a condition subsequent.

[43] [1978] Ch. 49.

conditions were conditions precedent; consequently, they did not need to be conceptually certain anyway and so were valid.[44] Lord Denning M.R., however, held that, in the event that there was any conceptual uncertainty in the conditions, this was cured by the reference to the Chief Rabbi.[45] If this view is correct, the further question arises as to whether it is necessary for the person to whose decision the resolution is delegated to be someone who, like the Chief Rabbi, can be regarded as having some expertise in this respect or can be anyone at all. This may be relevant in any consideration of the question mentioned above as to whether the restriction of a class to such persons as a specified individual or individuals regards as having a moral claim on a settlor makes the gift in question more or less conceptually uncertain.

In any event, this matter cannot yet be regarded as settled, particularly in the light of the fact that Lord Denning's remarks were subsequently overlooked in the rather inadequately reported *Re Wright's Will Trusts*.[46] However, there is clearly considerably more possibility than hitherto that issues of conceptual uncertainty can now be cured in this way.

### (3) Administrative unworkability

In *McPhail v. Doulton*,[47] Lord Wilberforce added a third class of potential uncertainty, where "the meaning of the words used is clear but the definition of beneficiaries is so hopelessly wide as not to form 'anything like a class' so that the trust is administratively unworkable" (he gave as an example "all the residents of Greater London"). A discretionary trust was indeed struck down for this reason in *R. v. District Auditor, ex p. West Yorkshire Metropolitan County Council*,[48] where the local authority resolved to create a trust "for the benefit of any or all or some of the inhabitants of the County of West Yorkshire" for various specific purposes.[49] Given that there were 2,500,000 potential beneficiaries, the court, while prepared to assume without deciding that "inhabitant" was sufficiently conceptually certain, held that the trust was void for administrative unworkability on the grounds that the class was much too large.

While the concept of administrative unworkability thus clearly applies to discretionary trusts, there has been considerable debate over whether or not it also applies to mere powers. In *Blausten v. I.R.C.*,[50] the trustees had power to introduce to the class of beneficiaries any person other than the settlor. An argument that this power was void for administrative unworkability was rejected on the ground that, although the trustees had this admittedly wide power, it could only be exercised with the written consent of the settlor and hence only during his lifetime. Therefore, it could not be said that the settlor had failed to set "metes and bounds" to the beneficial interests which he intended to create or to permit to be created under the settlement. Buckley L.J. therefore clearly assumed, admittedly only by way of dictum, that the concept of administrative unworkability did apply to mere powers.

---

[44] *ibid., per* Lord Russell of Killowen at 63–64, *per* Eveleigh L.J. at 64–65.
[45] *ibid.* at 60, 62.
[46] [1981] Law Society Gazette Reports 841.
[47] [1971] A.C. 424 at 457.
[48] (1986) 26 R.V.R. 24. See Harpum (1986) 45 C.L.J. 391.
[49] See *post*, p. 77.
[50] [1972] Ch. 256.

However, this reasoning is difficult to reconcile with subsequent decisions. In *Re Manisty's Settlement*,[51] the trustees had a mere power to add beneficiaries and to benefit the persons so added and this power was exercisable in favour of anyone in the world except the settlor, his wife and some other persons. Templeman J. held that this power did not fail for administrative unworkability even though there were no expressed restrictions on its operation by the trustees; he preferred the view that a mere power could not be void on the grounds of breadth of numbers but only if its terms were capricious. Megarry V.-C. in *Re Hay's Settlement Trusts*[52] also took the view that a mere power would not be administratively unworkable on the grounds of mere numbers on the basis that this should not inhibit the trustees in its exercise and would not prevent the courts from controlling them. He did however, state that a discretionary trust as broad as the power in that case ("to or for the benefit of any person or persons whatsoever or to any charity" with only the settlor, her husband, and the trustees excluded) would have been void as administratively unworkable. Subsequently, in *Re Beatty's Will Trusts*[53] a mere power given to trustees in favour of "such person or persons as they think fit" was held valid, this time without any mention of the possibility of it being administratively unworkable at all.

At this stage, it seemed tolerably clear that the concept of administrative unworkability did not apply to mere powers. However, as will be seen in a later chapter,[54] the duties of the donee of a mere power and the remedies available to the objects of such a power have now been the subject of an important review in *Mettoy Pensions Trustees v. Evans*;[55] this decision envisages the adaption of the remedies available for the enforcement of discretionary trusts for the purpose of enforcing mere powers. It has therefore been suggested[56] that this may cause the concept of administrative unworkability to be applied to at least some types of mere powers. It obviously remains to be seen whether this is yet another consequence of this important decision.

### (4) Capriciousness

Another possible ground of potential uncertainty is capriciousness, a concept developed by Templeman J. in *Re Manisty's Settlement*,[57] in which he upheld a mere power of very considerable breadth. He held that the exercise of the process of selection by discretionary trustees and by the donees of powers may be rendered practically impossible if the terms of the discretionary trusts and powers in question are capricious. He gave as an example of a capricious power one in favour of "the residents of Greater London", not because of the number of objects of the power but "because the terms of the power negative any sensible intention on the part of the settlor" and any "sensible consideration by the trustees of the exercise of the power". "If the settlor intended and expected the trustees would have regard to persons with some claim on his bounty or some interest in an institution favoured by the settlor, or if the

---

[51] [1974] Ch. 17.
[52] [1982] 1 W.L.R. 202.
[53] [1990] 1 W.L.R. 1503.
[54] See *post*, p. 230.
[55] [1990] 1 W.L.R. 1587.
[56] By Gardner (1991) 107 L.Q.R. 214.
[57] [1974] Ch. 17.

settlor had any other sensible intention or expectation, he would not have required the trustees to consider only an accidental conglomeration of persons who have no discernible link with the settlor or with any institution."[58]

Because the example given by Templeman J. of a capricious power was exactly the same as the example given by Lord Wilberforce in *McPhail v. Doulton* of an administratively unworkable discretionary trust, it was originally thought that the two concepts were the same,[59] the former being applicable to mere powers and the latter being applicable to discretionary trusts. However, it is now clear that the concept of capriciousness applies both to discretionary trusts and to powers. In *R. v. District Auditor, ex p. West Yorkshire Metropolitan County Council*,[60] the discretionary trust held void for administrative unworkability because the 2,500,000 inhabitants of West Yorkshire constituted too large a class was held not to be capricious since the County Council had every reason for wishing to benefit the inhabitants of West Yorkshire. The concepts of administrative unworkability and capriciousness are therefore apparently distinct, the former but not the latter being limited to breadth of numbers. No discretionary trust or mere power has yet been set aside on the grounds of capriciousness; it will be interesting to see whether this ever occurs.

### (5) Duty to survey the field

Given that, save in the case of a fixed trust, the identity of all the objects of a trust or a power will not necessarily be known, the trustees of a discretionary trust and those entitled to exercise a power in the nature of a trust or a mere power cannot be obliged to consider the claims of every possible object. In *McPhail v. Doulton*,[61] Lord Wilberforce stated that the trustees of a discretionary trust "ought to make such a survey of the range of objects or possible beneficiaries as will enable them to carry out their fiduciary duty" and emphasised that a "wider and more comprehensive range of enquiry is called for" in the case of discretionary trusts than in the case of mere powers. Where the possible objects number thousands or hundreds of thousands, the trustees must assess "the size of the problem" in a businesslike manner.[62] A more detailed account of the duties of discretionary trustees was provided by Megarry V.-C. in *Re Hay's Settlement Trusts*[63] in the following passage.

> "The trustee must not simply proceed to exercise the power in favour of such of the objects as happen to be at hand or claim his attention. He must first consider what persons or classes of persons are objects of the power ...: what is needed is an appreciation of the width of the field, and thus whether a selection is to be made merely from a dozen or, instead, from thousands or millions. ... Only when the trustee has applied his mind to the 'size of the problem' should he then consider in individual cases whether, in relation to other possible claimants, a particular grant is appropriate. In doing this, no doubt he should not prefer the undeserving

---

[58] *ibid.* at 27.
[59] See Emery (1982) 98 L.Q.R. 551.
[60] (1986) 26 R.V.R. 24.
[61] [1971] A.C. 424.
[62] *Re Baden's Deed Trusts (No.2)* [1973] Ch. 9 at 20, *per* Sachs L.J.
[63] [1982] 1 W.L.R. 202 at 209–210.

to the deserving but he is not required to make an exact calculation whether, as between deserving claimants, A is more deserving than B."

This duty, considerably broader than had hitherto been thought,[64] has so far been applied only to trustees of discretionary trusts but would presumably also be applied to the donees of powers in the nature of a trust. The duties of a donee of a mere power "cannot be more stringent than those for a discretionary trust".[65] It will be remembered[66] that mere powers are divided into fiduciary powers (basically mere powers held by trustees) and non-fiduciary or personal powers (mere powers held by anyone else). A donee of a non-fiduciary mere power is under no obligation to do anything at all and so cannot possibly have any duty to survey the field. On the other hand, in *Mettoy Pension Trustees v. Evans*,[67] it was stated that a donee of a fiduciary mere power must consider periodically whether or not he should exercise the power, the range of objects of the power, and the appropriateness of individual appointments. As will be seen in a later chapter,[68] a donee of a fiduciary power is consequently "to some extent subject to the control of the courts in relation to its exercise"[69]; as a result, powers held by fiduciaries may well in some respects have been assimilated to discretionary trusts. However, the precise scope of the duties which were enunciated in *Mettoy Pension Trustees v. Evans* must await further clarification.

## II. THE BENEFICIARY PRINCIPLE

A further essential ingredient for the effectual creation of a trust is that there should be some beneficiary capable of enforcing it. As Grant M.R. stated in *Morice v. Bishop of Durham*,[70] "there must be someone in whose favour the court can decree performance". This requirement does not apply to charitable trusts, which can be enforced by the Attorney-General. However, private trusts which do not satisfy the beneficiary requirement will not generally be enforced; "a court of equity does not recognise as valid a trust which it cannot both enforce and control".[71]

The qualification "generally" is necessary for two reasons. First, some trusts which are on the face of things for some purpose rather than for the direct benefit of any beneficiary capable of enforcing them have in fact been construed as outright gifts to some person or persons, the purpose being construed merely as an expression of the motive for the gift. Trusts construed in such a way necessarily satisfy the beneficiary requirement; thus a trust for the planting of trees on an estate for shelter has been held to be for the benefit of

---

[64] In *Re Gestetner* [1953] Ch. 672 at 688, Harman J. had stated that "there is no obligation on the trustees to do more than consider from time to time the merits of such persons of the specified class as are known to them".

[65] *Re Hay's Settlement Trusts* [1982] 1 W.L.R. 202 at 209–210.

[66] See *ante*, p. 35.

[67] [1990] 1 W.L.R. 1587.

[68] See *post*, p. 230.

[69] *Mettoy Pension Trustees v. Evans* [1990] 1 W.L.R. 1587 at 1614.

[70] (1804) 9 Ves. 399 at 405.

[71] *Re Astor's Settlement Trusts* [1952] Ch. 534 at 549.

whoever was entitled to that estate,[72] and trusts for the education of children have been held to be a trust for their benefit.[73] Secondly, it has been held[74] that a trust which, despite the fact that it is expressed in the form of a purpose, is directly or indirectly for the benefit of one or more ascertainable individuals satisfies the beneficiary requirement, provided that all its terms comply with the relevant certainty requirements. This decision seems to have been the impetus for the enactment of legislation[75] in a large number of off-shore jurisdictions[76] permitting not only purpose trusts of this kind[77] but also purpose trusts where there are no such ascertainable individuals;[78] it is questionable whether the latter type of purpose trusts would be enforceable in this jurisdiction.

Further, there are a number of anomalous cases in which non-charitable purpose trusts have been upheld even though there has been no human beneficiary capable of enforcing them. Such trusts are often described as trusts of imperfect obligation on the grounds that, although they will not be enforced, the courts will not forbid their performance if the trustees wish to carry them out. In *Re Endacott*,[79] these cases were said to fall into the following categories: trusts for the erection or maintenance of monuments or graves; trusts for the saying of masses in jurisdictions where such trusts are not regarded as charitable; trusts for the maintenance of particular animals; trusts for the benefit of unincorporated associations (although, due to subsequent developments in the law, many trusts for the benefit of unincorporated associations are now valid anyway); and miscellaneous cases (a few further cases which do not fit into any of the other categories). The decisions which have established these anomalous exceptions have been described as "concessions to human weakness or sentiment"[80] and will not now be extended.[81]

## 1. *The General Rule*

Trusts for non-charitable purposes are generally void for two different reasons: first, because there is no one who can enforce them; and, secondly, because the courts are unable to control the execution of such trusts. This rule was originally established in *Morice v. Bishop of Durham*,[82] which concerned a gift of residue to the Bishop of Durham to be applied by him "for such objects of benevolence and liberality as [he] in his own discretion shall most approve

---

[72] *Re Bowes* [1896] 1 Ch. 507.
[73] *Re Andrew's Trust* [1905] 2 Ch. 48; *Re Osoba* [1979] 1 W.L.R. 247.
[74] In *Re Denley's Trust Deed* [1969] 1 Ch. 373.
[75] The trust legislation already enacted in Liechtenstein in 1928 and in Nauru in 1960 was in terms broad enough to permit the creation of purpose trusts, although this was probably unintentional, at least in the case of Liechtenstein.
[76] Although The Cook Islands introduced legislation of this type in 1984, this was not taken seriously; it was Bermuda which really set the ball rolling by enacting the widely copied Trusts (Special Provisions) Act 1989, subsequently redrafted and substantially amended in 1998; see *post*, p. 80.
[77] See Matthews in *Trends in Contemporary Trust Law* (ed. Oakley, 1996) 1.
[78] See Matthews, 12 T.L.I. (1998) 98 and in *Extending the Boundaries of Trusts* (ed. Hayton, 2002) 203; Duckworth, 13 T.L.I. (1999) 158; Hayton 117 L.Q.R. (2001) 96; Parkinson [2002] C.L.J. 657.
[79] [1960] Ch. 232.
[80] *Re Astor's Settlement Trusts* [1952] Ch. 534 at 547.
[81] *Re Endacott* [1960] Ch. 232 at 250–251.
[82] (1804) 9 Ves. 399 (1805) 10 Ves. 522.

of". Grant M.R. held that this gift failed, saying[83] that "there can be no trust, over the exercise of which this Court will not assume a control, for an uncontrollable power of disposition would be ownership, and not trust". On appeal, Lord Eldon L.C. added[84] that the court had to be in a position both to execute the trust if the trustees for any reason did not do so and to prevent maladministration of the trust. Both these reasons are eminently justifiable; since it is the lack of enforceability which in practice inhibits judicial control, they are also linked. However, whether the lack of enforceability or the lack of judicial control is the principal reason for the existence of the general rule is perceived as crucial to the debate about the potential validity in this jurisdiction of some of the types of purpose trusts recently created in off-shore jurisdictions.[85]

The first in a line of important decisions which reconsidered the whole question of trusts for non-charitable purposes was *Re Astor's Settlement Trusts*,[86] whose objects included "the establishment, maintenance and improvement of good understanding, sympathy and co-operation between nations", "the preservation of the independence and integrity of newspapers" and "the promotion of freedom of the press" (the trust was intended to facilitate the continued independence of the newspaper *The Observer*, which had been founded by the Astor family). This case has already been considered in relation to certainty of objects; the conclusion which was reached, that these objects were conceptually uncertain, was however only a secondary ground for the decision that the trusts were ineffectual. The primary question considered by the court was whether, irrespective of whether or not the objects were certain, the trusts would have been effective as non-charitable purpose trusts. Roxburgh J. concluded that the general principle was that gifts on trust must have a beneficiary or *cestui que trust*, to which principle the anomalous cases already referred to constituted exceptions. He suggested that these cases should, following the view of Underhill,[87] be regarded as concessions to human weakness or sentiment; however, he held that they could not be used to justify the proposition that a court of equity would recognise as an equitable obligation a direction to apply funds in furtherance of enumerated non-charitable purposes in a manner which no court could control.[88]

The views of Roxburgh J. were applied in *Re Shaw*,[89] another decision at first instance, where the main question was whether George Bernard Shaw's testamentary trusts whereby his residuary estate was to be used for 21 years in experimentation in the possible reform of the English alphabet of 26 letters by its substitution for a phonetic alphabet of 40 letters were valid charitable trusts. In the event it was held that they were not charitable trusts and the question then arose as to whether they could be valid as non-charitable

---

[83] (1804) 9 Ves. 399 at 404–405.
[84] (1805) 10 Ves. 522 at 539–540.
[85] See Matthews 12 T.L.I. (1998) 98 and Duckworth 13 T.L.I. (1999) 158. Matthews stresses the importance of the lack of enforceability and, in particular, the absence of any equitable ownership for the duration of the purpose trust, in other words the absence of anyone capable of exercising the Rule in *Saunders v. Vautier* (1841) Cr. & Ph. 240 so as to bring the trust to a premature end.
[86] [1952] Ch. 534.
[87] See now Underhill & Hayton, *Law of Trusts and Trustees* (16th ed. 2003), p. 111.
[88] [1952] Ch. 534 at 547.
[89] [1957] 1 W.L.R. 729.

purpose trusts. Harman J. held that they were invalid since they lacked any *cestui que trust*.

Subsequently, the compass of non-charitable purpose trusts seemed to have been firmly confined by the decision of the Court of Appeal in *Re Endacott*.[90] The testator had given his residuary estate to the North Tawton Parish Council "for the purpose of providing some useful memorial to myself". The court held that this trust did not fall within the "anomalous" classes of trusts of imperfect obligation since it was of too wide and uncertain a nature to qualify. Harman L.J. affirmed the views on this type of trusts which had been expressed by Roxburgh J. in *Re Astor's Settlement Trusts*. He said[91]: "I applaud the orthodox sentiments expressed by Roxburgh J. and I think, as I think he does, that though one knows there have been decisions which are not satisfactorily classified but are merely occasions when Homer has nodded, yet the cases stand by themselves and ought not to be increased in number nor indeed followed except where the one is exactly like the other." He added that he could not think that a case of this kind, that of providing outside a church an unspecified and unidentified memorial, was the kind of instance which should be added to these "troublesome, anomalous and aberrant" cases.

Similarly, one of the reasons why the Court of Appeal held in *R. v. District Auditor ex p. West Yorkshire Metropolitan Council*[92] that a discretionary trust to apply £400,000 for one of four purposes "for the benefit of any or some of the inhabitants of" West Yorkshire was void was because it was a non-charitable purpose trust.

As will be seen later on,[93] a number of trusts for unincorporated associations, where the subject matter of the gift was to be held on trust for the purposes of the association as a quasi-corporate entity, have been held void on the grounds of perpetuity. Such cases are primarily concerned with perpetuity and are best dealt with under that heading. However, in one of the leading cases, *Leahy v. Attorney-General for New South Wales*,[94] Viscount Simonds, although concluding that the gift in question was indeed void for perpetuity, was clearly of the opinion that such a purpose trust would be void in any event because of the lack of any cestui que trust to enforce it. He said:[95]

> "If the words 'for the general purposes of the association' were held to import a trust, the question would have to be asked, what is the trust and who are the beneficiaries? A gift can be made to persons (including a corporation) but it cannot be made to a purpose or to an object; so also a trust may be created for the benefit of persons as *cestuis que trust* but not for a purpose or object unless the purpose or object be charitable. For a purpose or object cannot sue but, if it be charitable, the Attorney-General can sue to enforce it."[96]

---

[90] [1960] Ch. 232.
[91] *ibid.* at 250–251.
[92] [1986] R.V.R. 24.
[93] See *post*, p. 85.
[94] [1959] A.C. 457.
[95] *ibid.* at 478.
[96] In *Re Lipinski's Will Trusts* [1976] Ch. 235, Oliver J. argued (at 246) that this was not intended as an exhaustive statement or to do more than indicate the broad division of trusts into those where there are ascertainable beneficiaries (whether for particular purposes or not) and trusts where there are none.

Thus, the question raised in cases such as *Re Astor's Settlement Trusts* and *Re Shaw*, namely whether the categories of the anomalous trusts of imperfect obligation could be extended to other non-charitable purposes which complied with the requirement for certainty of objects, was clearly answered in the negative both by the Court of Appeal in *Re Endacott* and by the Privy Council in *Leahy v. Attorney-General for New South Wales*.

The fact that the reasoning adopted, namely that the lack of a *cestui que trust* to enforce such trusts puts their execution outside the control of the courts, appears to be unimpeachable does not of course necessarily mean that the present position is entirely satisfactory. At present, the law permits a person to give his property to human beings, whether they are good or bad, to give that property to charity, and even to set up trusts for the various anomalous purposes recognised by the law, such as for his dogs and cats or for the promotion of foxhunting. But, as a general rule, it seems that a person cannot dedicate his property to a social experiment falling outside the confines of the law of charity if that experiment is defined in terms of purposes, no matter how certain those purposes may be[97] (this proposition of course assumes that it is only possible to construe the gift in terms of purposes; as was stated at the outset, if the gift can instead be construed as an outright gift to some person or persons, the purpose being construed merely as an expression of the motive for the gift, the beneficiary requirement will of course be satisfied[98]).

## 2. *The Qualification Established by* Re Denley's Trust Deed[99]

The qualification "as a general rule" had to be added because, according to the decision of Goff J. in *Re Denley's Trust Deed*,[1] there may in certain circumstances be a way out of this difficulty. He held that the basic rule laid down in *Morice v. Bishop of Durham* was confined to purpose trusts which were "abstract or impersonal"; consequently, he held that a trust which, despite the fact that it was expressed in the form of a purpose, was directly or indirectly for the benefit of one or more ascertainable individuals was nevertheless valid, provided that all its terms satisfied the relevant certainty requirements.

In *Re Denley's Trust Deed*,[2] the expressed purpose of the trust was the maintenance of a sports ground, primarily for the benefit of the employees of a company and secondarily for the benefit of such other persons as the trustees allowed to use it. Goff J. held the trust to be valid on the basis that it was an express private trust in favour of ascertainable human beneficiaries by whom it could necessarily be enforced. However commendable this approach may be as an attempt to "liberalise" the law, there must nevertheless be some doubt as to whether it is actually correct. The trust in *Re Denley's Trust Deeds* was, as a matter of construction, clearly framed as a purpose; it could not be construed as an outright gift to the employees of the company and any other persons whom the trustees allowed to use the sports ground. Consequently, despite

---

[97] See Marshall (1953) 6 C.L.P. 151; Kiralfy (1950) 14 Conv. (N.S.) 374; Sheridan (1953) 17 Conv. (N.S.) 46.

[98] See *Re Bowes* [1896] 1 Ch. 507; *Re Andrew's Trust* [1905] 2 Ch. 48; *Re Osoba* [1979] 1 W.L.R. 247. See also *Re Sanderson's Trust* (1857) 3 K. & J. 497 at 503.

[99] [1969] 1 Ch. 373.

[1] [1969] 1 Ch. 373.

[2] [1969] 1 Ch. 373.

the fact that the trust was for their benefit, the purpose of the trust was its dominant factor; consequently, if that purpose was non-charitable (which it clearly was), it should have failed unless it could be brought within the recognised anomalous exceptions.

*Re Denley's Trust Deed* was nevertheless followed in *Re Lipinski's Will Trusts*,[3] where the testator left his residuary estate to trustees for an unincorporated recreational association, which was not charitable, for the purpose of constructing and improving buildings for that association. Oliver J. held that this was a valid purpose trust, principally because the beneficiaries, the members of the association, were ascertainable and so could enforce the purpose. As a matter of construction, *Re Lipinski's Will Trusts* may well be a stronger case than *Re Denley's Trust Deed* because of the fact that it was a gift to an unincorporated association and thus also able to be upheld on that basis,[4] something which was not the case in *Re Denley's Trust Deed*. The conclusion arrived at in *Re Denley's Trust Deed* was also accepted by Megarry V.-C. in *Re Northern Developments (Holdings)*.[5] Subsequently, however, in *Re Grant's Will Trusts*,[6] Vinelott J. expressed the view that *Re Denley's Trust Deed* did not involve a purpose trust at all but rather a discretionary trust. This view is not really consistent either with the lengthy discussion of purpose trusts in *Re Denley's Trust Deed* or with the subsequent interpretation of that decision by Oliver J. and Megarry V.-C.; consequently, it does not appear to be an acceptable explanation of that decision.

If the view expressed in *Re Grant's Will Trusts* is for this reason discounted, the other three authorities, all first instance decisions, indicate that this type of non-charitable purpose trust may be treated as a valid express private trust for the incidental benefit of ascertainable beneficiaries, albeit for a particular purpose. It must be re-emphasised that, despite the fact that the rationale of such trusts being upheld is that they incidentally benefit identifiable persons, those persons have no right to call for the trust property; consequently, such trusts are quite distinct from those trusts which, despite the fact that they are on the face of things for some purpose, have in fact been construed as outright gifts to some person or persons, the purpose being construed merely as an expression of the motive for the gift.[7] It must also be emphasised that the rule that a valid power cannot be deduced from what is intended to be a trust applies just as much to non-charitable purpose trusts as to any other type of trust;[8] if a trust is intended, it cannot be treated as a power. That does not of course prevent the express creation of powers for non-charitable purposes but such powers impose no obligations on their donees to exercise them.

---

[3] [1976] Ch. 235.
[4] It was held that it was valid as a gift in favour of an unincorporated association with a superadded discretion; see *post*, p. 88.
[5] (1978) unreported; see (1985) 101 L.Q.R. 280.
[6] [1980] 1 W.L.R. 360.
[7] See *Re Bowes* [1896] 1 Ch. 507; *Re Andrew's Trust* [1905] 2 Ch. 48; *Re Osoba* [1979] 1 W.L.R. 247. See also *Re Sanderson's Trust* (1857) 3 K. & J. 497 at 503.
[8] See *I.R.C. v. Broadway Cottages Trust* [1955] Ch. 20 at 36; *Re Endacott* [1960] Ch. 232 at 246. This principle is not affected by *McPhail v. Doulton* [1971] A.C. 424 (see *ante*, pp. 62–63).

As has already been mentioned,[9] the decision in *Re Denley's Trust Deed* seems to have been the impetus for the enactment of purpose trust legislation[10] in a large number of off-shore jurisdictions;[11]; such trusts can be and have been employed for a wide variety of purposes.[12] The most influential legislation has been Bermudan, the Trusts (Special Provisions) Act 1989[13] whose original form[14] was widely copied elsewhere. Typically,[15] such legislation permits trusts to have specified types of non-charitable purposes[16] provided that a person known as an enforcer,[17] who generally cannot also be one of the trustees, is appointed to enforce the non-charitable purposes if this proves to be necessary (this obviously deals with the main traditional objection to the existence of non-charitable purpose trusts). Subsequent Bermudan legislation[18] has removed the need for an enforcer; instead the Supreme Court of Bermuda can make orders for the enforcement of the trust on the application of the settlor,[19] any enforcer there may be, any trustee, and any other else whom the court considers has a sufficient interest.[20] The Cayman Islands have gone considerably further than any other jurisdiction and now permit the creation of both purpose trusts and trusts with human beneficiaries which cannot be enforced in any way by anyone other than their enforcer.[21] It is somewhat questionable whether any of these types of trusts, particularly The Cayman

---

[9] See *ante*, p. 75.

[10] The trust legislation already enacted in Liechtenstein in 1928 and in Nauru in 1960 was in terms broad enough to permit the creation of purpose trusts, although this was probably unintentional, at least in the case of Liechtenstein.

[11] See Matthews in *Extending the Boundaries of Trusts* (ed. Hayton, 2002) 203; Hayton 117 L.Q.R. (2001) 96; Parkinson [2002] C.L.J. 657.

[12] See Matthews in *Trends in Contemporary Trust Law* (ed. Oakley, 1996) 1. The principal commercial purposes, off balance-sheet transactions and special purpose vehicles, are unlikely long to survive the crackdown on accounting standards which followed a number of spectacular corporate collapses in the United States of America in 2002 caused by the consequential inaccuracy of those corporations' on-shore balance sheets.

[13] See Anderson in *Equity, Trusts and Fiduciaries 1993* (ed. Waters, 1993) p. 99. Although The Cook Islands introduced legislation of this type in 1984, this was not taken seriously; it was Bermuda which really set the ball rolling by enacting this legislation.

[14] It was subsequently redrafted and substantially amended in 1998.

[15] See (Jersey) Trusts (Jersey) Law 1984 Articles 10A, 10B and 10C (added in 1996), which are similar to the original Bermudan legislation.

[16] The Jersey legislation permits any purposes other than those which are contrary to the law of Jersey; the original Bermudan legislation restricted permissible purposes to those which are "specific, reasonable and possible" and "not under the law immoral, contrary to public policy or unlawful"; the current Bermudan legislation merely requires them to be sufficiently certain to allow the trust to be carried out, lawful, and not contrary to public policy.

[17] Also one of the alternative names for a protector (see *post*, p.164); "enforcer" is presumably utilised in the context of purpose trusts to distinguish the role played in that context from that played by a protector in the normal sense of that expression.

[18] The (Bermuda) Trusts (Special Provisions) Act 1989 was subsequently redrafted and substantially amended in 1998; the current provisions are ss.12A–12D.

[19] In the absence of contrary provision in the trust instrument (something which is probably advisable).

[20] If the Attorney-General of Bermuda satisfies the court that none of these persons is able and willing to make an application, he may do so.

[21] (Cayman Islands) Special Trusts (Alternative Regime) Law 1997, now (Cayman Islands) Trusts Law 2001, ss.95–109 (because of the name of the original legislation, such trusts are known as STAR trusts). See Matthews 12 T.L.I. (1998) 98; Duckworth 13 T.L.I. (1999) 158.

Islands' trusts of this type for human beneficiaries, would be enforceable in this jurisdiction in the event that this proved to be necessary.[22]

It should be added that it is generally thought that any non-charitable purpose trusts which are upheld in accordance with the decision in Re Denley's Trust Deed,[23] must comply with the rule against inalienability, one of the aspects of the rule against perpetuties which restricts the duration of the anomalous trusts which take effect as exceptions to the beneficiary principle (this rule is referred to in the next section[24] and considered in detail in a later chapter[25]). However, whether such trusts are so restricted has not yet actually had to be decided since, both in Re Denley's Trust Deed and in the two reported cases in which that decision has been applied, the trusts in question were expressly limited so that they could take effect only within the relevant perpetuity period; those trusts therefore necessarily complied with the rule against inalienability.

Some of the off-shore jurisdictions which have enacted legislation permitting purpose trusts limit such trusts to a stated statutory perpetuity period.[26] It is thought that this would be acceptable to an English court since English law has long permitted such a period[27] for the purposes of the rule against remoteness, although admittedly not for the purposes of the rule under discussion, the rule against inalienability.[28] However, the current Bermudan legislation and The Cayman Islands' legislation permit purpose trusts to last for ever[29] and this is a further reason for questioning whether such purpose trusts would be acceptable to an English court.

Finally, it must be emphasised that, despite the decision in Re Denley's Trust Deed, it is nevertheless from a practical point of view, inadvisable in this jurisdiction to endeavour to provide expressly for the establishment of a non-charitable purpose trust, other than one falling within the existing anomalous exceptions; this will only cease to be the case in the event that legislation validating non-charitable purpose trusts is also enacted here. In the meantime, the simplest solution to the problem remains what it has always been: the formation of a company to carry out the non-charitable purpose in question (the permissible objects of companies are not subject to any of the restrictions which apply to non-charitable trusts) and the subsequent transfer of the relevant property to that company.[30]

---

[22] See the series of articles by Matthews and Duckworth summarised in Matthews 12 T.L.I. (1998) and Duckworth 13 T.L.I. (1999) 158. Enforceability here might become an issue if any assets of such a trust were within the jurisdiction.

[23] [1969] 1 Ch. 373.

[24] See post, p. 83.

[25] See post, p. 252.

[26] Jersey permits a period of up to 100 years.

[27] At present 80 years, although the Law Commission has recently proposed that this should be increased to 125 years.

[28] See post, p. 252.

[29] (Bermuda) Trusts (Special) Provisions) Act 1989, s.12A(2) (as amended in 1998); (Cayman Islands) Perpetuities Law (1999 Revision), s.13(1).

[30] The Goodman Committee on Charity and Law and Voluntary Organisations (see post, p. 450) recommended that trusts for non-charitable purposes should be valid but no steps have been taken to enact this part of their proposals.

## 3. *The Anomalous Cases*

As has already been mentioned, the situations in which non-charitable purpose trusts have been upheld even though there has been no human beneficiary capable of enforcing them have been said[31] to fall into the following categories: trusts for the erection or maintenance of monuments or graves; trusts for the saying of masses in jurisdictions where such trusts are not regarded as charitable; trusts for the maintenance of particular animals; trusts for the benefit of unincorporated associations; and miscellaneous cases (a few further cases which do not fit into any of the other categories).

It also seems that these exceptions will only be upheld if the trust in question is contained in a will. Indeed, it has also been said that the will must be drafted in such a way that any of the property not expended on the non-charitable purpose will fall into residue.[32] This is allegedly because in such circumstances an order can be made whereby the trustees undertake to carry out the non-charitable purpose with the residuary legatees being given leave to apply to the court if the trustees fail to do so; this of course makes the trust in question indirectly enforceable in that the trustees have a choice between carrying out the specified purpose and transferring the property to the residuary legatees. However, the residuary legatees or intestate successors can clearly be given such leave to apply even if the will is not drafted in this way; consequently, there seems no reason in principle why such a provision should be necessary or why the subject matter of the trust should not be the residue itself.[33]

The existence of these anomalous cases, particularly the miscellaneous cases, contrasts markedly with the willingness of the courts to strike down as capricious trusts for the management of property in a manner which confers no obvious benefit on anyone. Such a case was *Brown v. Burdett*,[34] where a gift of a house on trust to block up its windows and doors for twenty years was held to be void. There is no possible justification for this difference in attitude; its explanation may be that the anomalous exceptions are regarded as "concessions to human weakness or sentiment"[35]. The present state of the authorities really requires a review either by the House of Lords or by the legislature (such a review could usefully also encompass the decision in *Re Denley's Trust Deed*[36]).

These non-charitable purpose trusts are subject to a further requirement, namely that the property subject to the trust must not be rendered inalienable.[37] This principle is one of the aspects of the rule against perpetuities, which will be considered in detail in a later chapter.[38] If, at the time when the trust comes into effect, there is any possibility, no matter how remote, that it is

---

[31] *Re Endacott* [1960] Ch. 232; the Court of Appeal adopted the classification put forward in Morris & Leach, *The Rule against Perpetuities* (2nd ed.), p. 306.
[32] *Re Thompson* [1934] Ch. 342 at 344; *Re Astor's Settlement Trusts* [1952] Ch. 534 at 546.
[33] See *Re Endacott* [1960] Ch. 232 at 240.
[34] (1882) 21 Ch.D. 667.
[35] *Re Astor's Settlement Trusts* [1952] Ch. 534 at 547.
[36] [1969] 1 Ch. 373.
[37] *Carne v. Long* (1860) 2 De G.F. & J. 75 at 80.
[38] See *post*, p. 252.

capable of continuing for longer than the appropriate perpetuity period, then the trust will be void.

The testator may specify a perpetuity period consisting of one or more nominated lives in being plus 21 years or of any fixed period of years up to 21 years.[39] The nominated lives in question can be those of the persons related in some way to the trust or its purposes; alternatively, the testator can use what is known a "royal lives clause", specifying the perpetuity period by reference to the lives of the Royal Family — an example of such a clause is one specifying a period "ending at the expiration of 21 years from the death of the last survivor of all the lineal descendants of his late Majesty King George VI[40] who shall be living at the time" when the trust comes into effect. Only human lives can be specified[41] otherwise it would be open to an eccentric settlor to tie up property indefinitely by settling it on trusts limited by reference to the lives of tortoises or other animals noted for their longevity. Alternatively, the testator may prefer to specify "such period as the law allows" in which case, assuming that there are no relevant lives, the perpetuity period will be 21 years. If no period is specified at all, the trust will be void unless it must necessarily determine before the end of the perpetuity period, which in most cases will mean within 21 years.

## (A) Trusts for the Erection or Maintenance of Monuments or Graves

A trust for the erection of a particular monument or for the maintenance of a particular grave is not charitable but it has been held that such a trust may nevertheless be valid as a trust of imperfect obligation.

In *Trimmer v. Danby*,[42] a legacy of £1,000 left by the painter Turner to his executors "to erect a monument to my memory in St Paul's Cathedral" was upheld. There is no requirement that the monument or tombstone be for the testator himself. In *Musset v. Bingle*,[43] a somewhat bizarre gift for the erection of a monument to the testator's widow's first husband was also upheld. It does, however, seem that the monument must be of a funerary nature if it is to fall within the scope of this exception.[44] The question of perpetuity has not been raised in any of the cases involving the construction of monuments on the basis that it will inevitably be carried out as soon as is reasonably practicable after the testator's death and thus well within the perpetuity period.

However, perpetuity is an issue in relation to trusts for the maintenance of monuments and graves. Thus in *Re Hooper*,[45] a gift to trustees for the upkeep of

---

[39] *Re Dean* (1899) 41 Ch.D. 552 at 557.
[40] The father of the present Queen. Consequently, the royal lives in question are those of HM Queen Elizabeth II, her descendants, and the descendants of her late sister, HRH Princess Margaret. It is also probably just about possible still to use King George V (the grandfather of the present Queen), although the number of his descendants is now very considerable. It is certainly unsafe to specify the descendants of any previous sovereign. One potential difficulty about such clauses today is the fact that "descendants" now includes illegitimate descendants, who are not necessarily identifiable. But there seems no reason why future "royal lives clauses" should not be expressly restricted to legitimate descendants.
[41] *Re Kelly* [1932] I.R. 255.
[42] (1856) 25 L.J.Ch. 424.
[43] [1876] W.N. 171.
[44] See *Re Endacott* [1960] Ch. 232.
[45] [1932] 1 Ch. 38, following *Pirbright v. Salwey* [1896] W.N. 86 (a gift of consols for application "so long as law permitted" to keep up a burial enclosure was held valid for 21 years).

graves and monuments "so long as they can legally do so" was held to be valid for 21 years but would clearly have been void for perpetuity if it had not been so restricted. Indeed in *Musset v. Bingle*,[46] it had been agreed that a perpetual trust to maintain the monument which was to be erected was void for perpetuity. However, as will be seen in the next part of this section,[47] there are certain other methods whereby the maintenance of monuments and graves for longer periods can be achieved.

The courts made it clear in these authorities that the trustees could not be compelled to erect the monument or keep up the grave in question but that if they decided to do so they would not be prevented. On the other hand, if the trustees are unwilling to perform the trust, they will hold the trust property on resulting trust for the testator's estate. Any surplus left after the purpose has been carried out will be held in the same way. The trust property will also "result" to the testator's estate on the determination of the period stipulated in the instrument for the duration of the trust or of the relevant perpetuity period, as the case may be.

### (B) Trusts for the Saying of Masses

It was for a long time uncertain whether or not trusts for the saying of masses were charitable but this point was finally settled in *Re Hetherington*,[48] where such trusts were held to be charitable provided that the masses in question are open to the public. However, in the event that this condition is not satisfied in any individual case, as would be the case where the masses were to be celebrated either for the members of a cloistered and contemplative religious order and/or in a private chapel to which the public are not admitted,[49] the trust in question will clearly be valid as a non-charitable purpose trust provided that it complies with the rule against inalienability by being limited to take effect only within the perpetuity period.[50]

### (C) Trusts for the Maintenance of Particular Animals

Gifts for the maintenance of animals in general are charitable.[51] However, gifts for the maintenance of one or more particular animals are not; such gifts can only take effect, if at all, as trusts of imperfect obligation.

Thus in *Pettingall v. Pettingall*,[52] the testator bequeathed £50 a year to his executor to provide for the testator's favourite black mare. It was held that the executor could perform the testator's wishes and might keep the surplus for his own purposes. It was also indicated that, if the executor failed to look after the mare, the beneficiaries could apply to the court to reconsider the arrangement but that, subject to that possibility, the trust was to last for the animal's lifetime. Similarly, in *Re Dean*,[53] there was a bequest of an annual sum for the maintenance of the testator's horses and hounds for a period of 50 years, if any of the horses and hounds should so long live. This was also held

---

[46] [1876] W.N. 171.
[47] See *post*, p. 86.
[48] [1990] Ch. 1.
[49] Trusts for such orders are not regarded as charitable; *Gilmour v. Coats* [1949] A.C. 426.
[50] *Bourne v. Keane* [1919] A.C. 815 at 874–875.
[51] See *post*, p. 468.
[52] (1842) 11 L.J.Ch. 176.
[53] (1889) 41 Ch.D. 552.

to be valid; the trustees were clearly at liberty to carry out the terms of the gift although the beneficiaries, being dumb, could not compel them to do so. *Re Dean* is an explicit authority — not all the early cases in this area of the law are particularly explicit — that a trust of imperfect obligation for the upkeep of a given animal may be valid notwithstanding the fact that by its nature it is not enforceable by the beneficiary.

Few of the cases on animals deal adequately with the question of perpetuity. Judicial notice is sometimes taken of the fact that the expected life of the animal in question is less than the 21-year period.[54] In the large majority of cases, the animals will inevitably survive the testator for a time much shorter than 21 years and it seems convenient and not at all improper that, if a period is not stipulated in the trust instrument, the trust should not fail if the contemplated duration of the life of the animal in question falls short of the 21-year period. However, this does not justify either of the cases mentioned above. Horses can certainly live for more than 21 years and so the decision in *Pettingall v. Pettingall* that the trust was to last for the animal's lifetime, could undoubtedly have contravened the rule against inalienability, depending of course on how old the mare was at the time of the testator's death. Further, the fixed period of 50 years established in *Re Dean* certainly does not constitute one of the permissible perpetuity periods and the horses, if not the hounds, could certainly have survived for more than 21 years. The only correct and safe approach to follow with trusts of this kind is therefore to limit the duration of the trust by reference to nominated lives in being or alternatively to use some expression like "for such period as the law allows".

### (D) Trusts for the Benefit of Unincorporated Associations

The existence of this category has always been regarded as somewhat doubtful.[55] The view has been expressed in some quarters that some types of trusts for the benefit of unincorporated associations[56] depend for their validity on the existence of a further anomalous exception to the beneficiary principle. This was thought to be the case where such trusts were held to have been made by way of endowment (one of a number of ways in which gifts in favour of unincorporated associations can be construed) since such an endowment is likely to have been intended to be perpetual, the adoption of this construction will generally lead to the gift being held to be void for perpetuity.[57] But if a trust has been established which satisfies the rule against perpetuities (because, for example, it is held to have been intended to benefit only the existing members),[58] it will also have to satisfy the beneficiary principle. Prior to the decision in *Re Denley's Trust Deed*,[59] it was sometimes thought that such a trust could only do so by virtue of being a further anomalous exception to that principle. However, if the decision in *Re Denley's Trust Deed* is in fact correct, any need for the existence of this particular exception to the bene-

---

[54] *Re Haines* (1925), *The Times*, November 7, 1952 (life of cat approximately 16 years) but this may be wrong — see Morris & Leach, *The Rule against Perpetuities* (2nd ed.), p. 323 and compare *Re Kelly* [1932] I.R. 255 at 260–261.

[55] Morris & Leach, *op. cit.* in their classification comment that "this group is more doubtful".

[56] Discussed more fully *post*, p. 88.

[57] As in *Leahy v. Attorney-General for New South Wales* [1959] A.C. 457.

[58] As in *Re Drummond* [1914] 2 Ch. 90.

[59] [1969] 1 Ch. 393.

ficiary principle will now have disappeared. Only if that decision is rejected, therefore, will this exception have any further role to play.

### (E) Miscellaneous Cases
From time to time anomalous cases have cropped up which do not fit into any of the other categories. Of these cases, the Court of Appeal in *Re Endacott*[60] referred only to *Re Catherall*,[61] where Roxburgh J. had upheld a gift to a vicar and churchwardens for a suitable memorial to the testator's parents and sisters whether or not it was charitable. No doubt was cast on this decision in *Re Endacott*, although Lord Evershed M.R. said that the decision could in any event be justified on the grounds that the purposes in question were charitable.[62]. However, this certainly cannot be said of the best known of these miscellaneous cases, *Re Thompson*,[63] which concerned a gift of £1,000 to be applied towards the promotion and furtherance of fox-hunting. The residuary legatee, Trinity Hall Cambridge, wished to carry out the testator's wishes in so far as this was legally possible but, as a charity, felt obliged to object to the enforcement of this trust. The gift, which complied with the rule against inalienability, was nevertheless upheld by analogy with *Pettingall v. Pettingall*.[64]. Neither this decision nor the other authorities in which trusts of this type have been upheld[65] can be supported. Nor can the apparent preparedness of the courts to allow in principle a number of further trusts of this type which in the event were held void on the grounds of perpetuity.[66] None of these authorities is likely to be followed. In this respect, the miscellaneous cases are distinct from those in the other categories, which will be applied but not extended.[67]

### 4. *Maintenance of Monuments and Tombs for Longer than the Perpetuity Period*

It has already been seen that a trust for the maintenance of monuments and graves will be valid as a trust of imperfect obligation if its duration is limited to the perpetuity period. It may, however, be possible for a testator to ensure that a trust of perpetual duration for this purpose is valid.[68] However, the

---

[60] [1960] Ch. 232.
[61] (June 3, 1959) unreported.
[62] [1960] Ch. 232 at 249.
[63] [1934] Ch. 342.
[64] (1842) 11 L.J.Ch. 176.
[65] *Re Catherall* (June 3, 1959) unreported but referred to in *Re Endacott* [1960] Ch. 232 at 248–249, (discussed *ante*, p. 107); *Re Gibbons* [1917] 1 I.R. 448 (a trust for property to be disposed of "to [the testator's] best spiritual advantage as conscience and sense of duty may direct", which was upheld where the executors were Roman Catholic priests and were prepared to perform the trust by constructing a church and saying masses in it for the testator's soul).
[66] *Re Nottage* [1895] 2 Ch. 649 (trust to endow an annual cup for yacht racing); *Re Gassiott* (1901) 70 L.J.Ch. 242 (trust to keep a portrait in repair); *Re Lawlor* [1934] V.L.R. 22 (Supreme Court of Victoria, affirmed by the High Court of Australia *sub nom. Roman Catholic Archbishop of Melbourne v. Lawlor* (1934) 51 C.L.R. 1) (trust to found a Catholic newspaper).
[67] *Re Endacott* [1960] Ch. 232 at 250–251, *per* Harman L.J.
[68] It may also be possible to take advantage of Parish Councils and Burial Authorities (Miscellaneous Provisions) Act 1970, s.1, which authorises local authorities and burial authorities to make an agreement to maintain graves and so forth for a period not exceeding 99 years. The text is, however, only concerned with the use of trust machinery for this purpose.

ways in which this may be achieved are somewhat complex and heavy-handed.

The first possibility is to set up a trust for the maintenance of the whole of the churchyard containing the monument or tomb in question. This is a valid charitable trust[69] and so will succeed in bringing about the maintenance of the monument or tomb for ever.

The second possibility is to make a gift to one charity with a gift over to another if the monument or tomb is not kept in repair. This will be successful provided that a trust is actually imposed on the first charity for the upkeep of the monument or tomb. In Re Tyler,[70] a sum of stock was given to the trustees of the London Missionary Society with a gift over to the Blue Coat School if the Society failed to keep a tomb in repair. Since both the donees were charitable bodies, the perpetuity rule did not apply to them[71] but the question still remained as to whether the condition in question (that is to say, for the maintenance of the tomb) contravened the rule. It was held by the Court of Appeal that, since the testator had not actually required the Society to maintain the tomb, the condition was valid. On the other hand, in Re Dalzeil,[72] the testator gave to the governors of St. Bartholomew's Hospital the sum of £20,000 "upon and subject to the condition" that they should use the income so far as necessary for the upkeep of a certain mausoleum; if they failed to carry out this purpose, there was a gift over to such other charities as the trustees might select on the same conditions. In this case, the condition, on its true construction, amounted to a positive direction that the income was to be applied in the first instance to the maintenance of the mausoleum; it did not, as in Re Tyler, simply impose a moral obligation. Cohen J. accordingly held that the trust failed.

The third possibility, a highly controversial method which probably now no longer works, was to rely on the decision in Re Chardon.[73] In that case, the testator gave his trustees £200 to invest and to pay the income to a cemetery company "during such period as they shall continue to maintain and keep the graves of my great grandfather and Priscilla Navone in good order and condition". The will further provided that if the graves were not maintained the income was to fall into residue. Romer J. held this gift to be valid. Very great difficulty has been found in ascertaining the meaning of this case; perhaps the best view, even though it does not emerge at all clearly from the judgment, is that the decision could be justified at the time when it was made on the grounds that an interest of the type given to the cemetery company, a determinable interest capable of coming to an end at any time in the future, was not then subject to the rule against perpetuities.

Re Chardon was followed by Wynn-Parry J. on virtually identical facts in Re Chambers Will Trusts,[74] but was distinguished by the same judge in Re Wightwick's Will Trusts.[75] The distinction drawn in the latter case was that the gift there contained a trust of income for an indefinite period for a non-charitable

---

[69] Re Pardoe [1906] 2 Ch. 184.
[70] [1891] 3 Ch. 252.
[71] See post, p. 443.
[72] [1943] Ch. 277.
[73] [1928] Ch. 464.
[74] [1950] Ch. 267.
[75] [1950] Ch. 260.

purpose and was, therefore, void as tending to a perpetuity, whereas in *Re Chardon*, there was not actually a trust. In view of the uncertain state of the law, it was extremely risky to rely on *Re Chardon*,[76] even before the passing of the Perpetuities and Accumulations Act 1964. The enactment of this legislation appears to have rendered this discussion academic by providing that a determinable interest is now subject to the perpetuity rule anyway;[77] consequently, the determining event must now take place no later than the end of the perpetuity period. While this provision would not render the gift void *ab initio*, any disposition of the income, whether express or implied, to take effect on the occurrence of the determining event would become void at the end of the perpetuity period. Consequently, by maintaining the graves until the end of the perpetuity period, the cemetery company would then acquire an absolute interest in the fund without any further obligations.[78]

### 5. *Gifts for the Benefit of Unincorporated Associations*

An unincorporated association has been defined as "two or more persons bound together for one or more common purposes, not being business purposes, by mutual undertakings each having mutual duties and obligations, in an organisation which has rules which identify in whom control of it and its funds rests and on what terms and which can be joined or left at will".[79] Because an unincorporated association is not a legal person, its property necessarily has to be vested in some or all of its members as trustees. Where its purposes are charitable, such trusts do not give rise to any difficulties. Charitable trusts have to comply neither with the requirement of certainty of objects, nor with the beneficiary principle, nor with the rule against perpetuities. All these requirements have to be satisfied, however, when the purposes of an unincorporated association are not charitable, giving rise to very considerable theoretical difficulties.

It was formerly thought that a gift of property to a non-charitable unincorporated association could only be construed in two possible ways. Both these constructions are still possible but have become uncommon; virtually all such gifts are now construed in accordance with a third possible construction enunciated by Cross J. in *Neville Estates v. Madden*,[80] and considerably developed in subsequent decisions.

The first possible construction was and is that the gift has been made to the persons who were the members of the association on the date that it was made. Such a gift may be outright, in that title to the property in question passes immediately to the members as tenants in common or joint tenants, or may vest the property in trustees for the members as beneficial tenants in common or joint tenants. Either way, if they are tenants in common they can

---

[76] See generally Hart (1937) 53 L.Q.R. 24; Albery (1938) 54 L.Q.R. 258.
[77] Perpetuities and Accumulations Act 1964, s.12.
[78] See Underhill & Hayton, *Law of Trusts and Trustees* (16th ed., 2003), pp. 119–121.
[79] *Conservative and Unionist Central Office v. Burrell* [1982] 1 W.L.R. 522, *per* Lawton L.J. at 525. The case was concerned with the meaning of "unincorporated association" for the purposes of taxation legislation but this definition seems to be of general application. Underhill & Hayton, *Law of Trusts & Trustees* (16th ed., 2003), p. 123 questions whether it is in fact necessary that the association should be able to be joined and left at will on the basis that the existence of rules restricting membership should not negative the existence of an unincorporated association.
[80] [1962] Ch. 832.

take their share while, if they are joint tenants, any member can sever his share and then claim it, whether or not he remains a member. Where such a trust exists, its objects must be sufficiently certain but it will clearly comply with the beneficiary principle and will not offend the rule against perpetuities.[81] However, this construction is not without theoretical difficulties: any member who subsequently leaves will retain his share unless he assigns it to the other members with the appropriate formalities;[82] no member who subsequently joins will acquire any interest in the property in question; and, where the members are tenants in common, the share of any member who dies will devolve according to his will or intestacy. In practice, these theoretical difficulties have generally been ignored.

The second possible construction was and is that the gift has been made by way of endowment for the unincorporated association. Such a gift necessarily has to take effect by way of trust. Any such endowment is likely to have been intended to be perpetual; consequently, the adoption of this construction will generally lead to the gift being held to be void for perpetuity.[83] However, if a trust has been established which satisfies the rule against perpetuities, it will undoubtedly be valid provided that its objects are sufficiently certain. Such a trust will satisfy the beneficiary principle by virtue of the decision in *Re Denley's Trust Deed*,[84] assuming of course that that case was correctly decided (prior to that decision, it was sometimes thought that such trusts constituted one of the anomalous exceptions to the beneficiary principle).[85] Some trusts have been held to satisfy the rule against perpetuities on the grounds that they were intended to benefit only the existing members of the unincorporated association.[86] In principle, it must also be possible to satisfy the rule against perpetuities by expressly providing that the property is to be held on trust for the benefit of the unincorporated association until the end of the perpetuity period and then be held for some ascertained person (such as the estate of the donor) or some charitable purpose.

Apart from such exceptional cases, however, prior to the decision in *Neville Estates v. Madden*, gifts to unincorporated associations were in practice only valid if the first possible construction was adopted; consequently, there was a presumption in favour of this construction. Where there was a gift "for the general purposes of the association", then, although those words appeared to seek to impose a perpetual trust which would consequently be void, they could be disregarded by the court as having virtually no meaning; this would enable the first construction to be adopted. This was not, however, always

---

[81] It is not particularly likely that a trust will be utilised if the intention of the donor is really only to benefit the existing members. The intention to exclude future members has been far from clear in some of the decided cases such as *Re Drummond* [1914] 2 Ch. 90, *Re Prevost* [1930] 2 Ch. 383 and *Re Turkington* [1937] 4 All E.R. 501; such cases would today probably be regarded as falling within the more recently developed third possible construction.

[82] Where a trust exists, writing will be required by virtue of Law of Property Act 1925, s.53(1)(c); see *post*, pp. 97–101.

[83] *Re Macaulay's Estate* (1933) [1943] Ch. 435; *Leahy v. Att.-Gen. for New South Wales* [1959] A.C. 457.

[84] [1969] 1 Ch. 393.

[85] See *ante*, p. 85.

[86] *Re Drummond* [1914] 2 Ch. 90 was a case of this kind. These trusts might equally well have been classified as falling within the first possible construction and, like such trusts, would today probably be regarded as falling within the third possible construction.

possible. In *Leahy v. Attorney-General for New South Wales*,[87] a ranch was left "upon trust for such order of nuns of the Catholic Church or the Christian Brothers as my executors and trustees shall select". This gift was *prima facie* valid as a gift to the individual members of the order chosen. However, the Privy Council held that the presumption was rebutted: first, because of the improbability of a beneficial gift to the members of the order who happened to be alive at the date of the death of the testator; and, secondly, because of the nature of the property. As an intended endowment for the benefit of the order as a continuing society, the trust would therefore have been void for perpetuity but for a saving legislative provision in a New South Wales statute.

The absence of any effective method of making gifts for the present and future members of unincorporated associations was hardly satisfactory and was eventually remedied by the enunciation in *Neville Estates v. Madden*,[88] of a third possible construction. This is that there may be:

"a gift to the existing members not as joint tenants, but subject to their respective contractual rights and liabilities towards one another as members of the association. In such a case a member cannot sever his share. It will accrue to the other members on his death or resignation, even though such members include persons who became members after the gift took effect. If this is the effect of the gift, it will not now be open to objection on the score of perpetuity or uncertainty unless there is something in its terms or circumstances or in the rules of the association which precludes the members at any given time from dividing the subject of the gift between them on the footing that they are solely entitled to it in equity."[89]

Thus the members of an unincorporated association have the possibility of enjoying rights in property in a new manner distinct from the traditional joint tenancy and tenancy in common (whether this is, strictly speaking, a form of co-ownership is not entirely clear).

Where a gift to an unincorporated association is construed in this way, the property in question is held by some or all of the individual members (or, of course, by independent trustees) on trust to be applied in accordance with the contract between the members contained in the rules of the association. This apparently resolves the technical difficulties caused by the adoption of the first possible construction in that any member who leaves or dies will lose his share in the property of the association without any need for any formal disposition and any new member of the association will be able to enjoy the benefit of its property without any need for any transfer of any shareto him. Precisely how the statutory formal requirements of the Law of Property Act 1925 and the Wills Act 1837 are actually satisfied has never been made entirely clear; signed acceptance by each member of rules drafted in an appropriate form would presumably satisfy section 53(1)(c) of the Law of Property Act 1925 but certainly would not satisfy the Wills Act 1837. The answer may be that, by entering into the contract contained in the rules, each member estops himself

---

[87] [1959] A.C. 457.
[88] [1962] Ch. 832.
[89] *ibid.* at 849, *per* Cross J.

(and, after his death, his personal representatives) from relying on the absence of the statutory formalities to claim his proportion of the property of the association.

The objects of trusts of this type must of course be sufficiently certain.[90] However, such trusts will clearly satisfy the beneficiary principle. Further, it has been held that they will satisfy the rule against perpetuities provided that the members are entitled under the rules (if necessary as a result of exercising a power in the rules to change them) to bring the association to an end and to divide its property between themselves.

The third construction has been adopted and developed on a number of occasions; the combined effect of the decisions which have been reached means that there is now little chance of a gift of this type being void for perpetuity.

In *Re Recher's Will Trusts*,[91] the testatrix left part of her residuary estate to a specified "Anti-Vivisection Society" (a non-charitable unincorporated association). Had the society not ceased to exist before her death, the gift would have been upheld as a valid non-charitable purpose trust. Brightman J. stated that, where the subscriptions of the members of an unincorporated association are held as an accretion to its funds to be applied in accordance with its rules, any gifts or legacies to the association will, in the absence of any words purporting to impose a trust, be held on the same basis. The rules of the association could have been changed by the unanimous agreement of the members. Therefore, it would have been irrelevant that it existed for the promotion of some purpose rather than for the benefit of the members themselves, since they could nevertheless vote to change the rules in order to abandon this purpose and to divide the assets between themselves.

*Re Lipinski's Will Trusts*,[92] concerned a gift to an unincorporated association "in memory of my late wife to be used solely in the work of constructing the new buildings for the association and/or improvement to the said buildings". The purpose specified was within the powers of the association and, despite the fact that the gift was to be used "solely" for this purpose, Oliver J. held that the members would not thereby be prevented from abandoning the specified purpose and instead dividing the assets between themselves. Consequently, the gift was valid as a non-charitable purpose trust for the benefit of the members of the association.

In *News Group Newspapers v. SOGAT 82*,[93] the local branches of the union SOGAT 82 were held to be unincorporated associations capable of seceding from the union and dissolving themselves; consequently, a sequestration order issued against the union was held not to apply to funds held by its local branches.

Finally, in *Universe Tankships Inc. of Monrovia v. International Transport Workers' Federation*,[94] the House of Lords held that a payment by shipowners into the fund maintained by the Federation fund took effect as an accretion to that fund by way of outright gift rather than a contribution on trust (in which

---

[90] The trusts in question will almost inevitably be discretionary trusts and so will be governed by *McPhail v. Doulton* [1971] A.C. 424.
[91] [1972] Ch. 526.
[92] [1976] Ch. 235.
[93] [1986] I.C.R. 716.
[94] [1983] 1 A.C. 366.

case, it would have been void). In the Court of Appeal,[95] Megaw L.J. had emphasised that, even if there is no provision for the amendment of the rules of an association, they can nevertheless be "altered at will by the unanimous agreement of the contracting parties".

There is now a strong presumption that an unincorporated association holds its property in this way; gifts to unincorporated associations will therefore not now normally be construed either as gifts to the members of the association in question[96] or as gifts for the purposes of its endowment. However, the third possible construction is not actually all-embracing.

This construction cannot be applied unless there is a set of rules to provide the necessary contract between the members. This was emphasised by Lawton L.J. in *Conservative and Unionist Central Office v. Burrell*.[97] This was why the third possible construction could not have been adopted in *Leahy v. Attorney-General for New South Wales*;[98] no such contract existed between the members of the religious orders. Consequently, even on the basis of this construction, the gift would still have had to be held to be an intended endowment and, but for statute, void for perpetuity.

Nor can this construction be applied when the members are unable to divide the assets between themselves. In *Re Grant's Will Trusts*,[99] Vinelott J. held that a gift to "the Labour Party Property Committee for the benefit of the Chertsey Headquarters of the Chertsey and Walton Constituency Labour Party" could not be construed as a gift to the members of the Constituency Party. They did not have the power to alter their rules, which were under the control of the National Labour Party. Although this did not of itself give rise to any problems of perpetuity (because the rules provided, in the last resort, for a resulting trust for the original subscribers), the members were clearly unable to dispose of the property among themselves.[1] Vinelott J. held that, consequently and in any event, the gift amounted to a trust for the purposes specified and not, as in *Re Lipinski's Will Trusts*,[2] a gift for the members of the Constituency Party for those purposes; for this reason, the gift was void for perpetuity. It has admittedly been suggested that the requirement that the members should be able to divide the property between themselves is unnecessary provided that they have the right "to ensure that the funds are used to pay for general expenses benefitting them as members".[3] However, the requirement clearly exists at present.

It should be noted that the way in which a gift to an unincorporated association is construed can have some effect on what happens to the assets of the association in the event of its dissolution. In the highly unlikely event that the first possible construction is adopted, those assets will be the property of those who were the members of the association on the date that the gift was made. In the only slightly less unlikely event that the second possible construction is

---

[95] [1981] I.C.R. 129 at 159.

[96] *Re Grant's Will Trusts* [1980] 1 W.L.R. 360 at 365.

[97] [1982] 1 W.L.R. 522 at 525.

[98] [1959] A.C. 457.

[99] [1980] 1 W.L.R. 360.

[1] The National Labour Party was entitled to alter the rules so as to require the property to be transferred to itself.

[2] [1976] Ch. 235.

[3] Underhill & Hayton, *Law of Trusts and Trustees* (16th ed., 2003), p. 127.

adopted and the gift to the association has therefore taken effect as a valid trust by way of endowment, such a trust will necessarily be limited to take effect only within the perpetuity period; it will therefore inevitably contain some provisions as to what is to happen to the property thereafter and, in such circumstances, dissolution of the association will presumably mean that it will devolve in accordance with these provisions. In the highly likely event that the third possible construction is adopted, there are three possibilities: first, that each asset is held on resulting trust for whoever gave it to the association in the first place; secondly, that the assets are divided between those who were the members of the association on the date of its dissolution; and, thirdly, that the assets go to the Crown as *bona vacantia*. As will be seen in a later chapter,[4] although there is at present a conflict of authority between a number of first instance decisions, it is now generally accepted[5] that the resulting trust analysis is no longer appropriate, that the general rule is for equal division between the members of the association, and that *bona vacantia* is only relevant when the association in question has become moribund in that all, or all but one of the members have resigned or died.

Finally, where a gift is made to a body which does not satisfy the definition of an unincorporated association because of the absence of the necessary mutual obligations contained in its rules, the gift will take effect by way of mandate or agency. In *Conservative and Unionist Central Office v. Burrell*,[6] the Court of Appeal held that the Conservative Party was not an unincorporated association for the purposes of taxation legislation because of the absence of any contractual link between a contributor of funds and their recipient; Brightman L.J. correspondingly characterised the recipient of the funds as the agent of the contributor for the purpose of dealing with the funds in accordance with the object or mandate for which the contribution was made. He said this:[7]

"So far as the money is used within the scope of the mandate, the recipient discharges himself *vis-à-vis* the contributor. The contributor can at any time demand the return of his money so far as not spent, unless the mandate is irrevocable, as it might be or become in certain circumstances. But once the money is spent, the contributor can demand nothing back, only an account of the manner of expenditure. No trust arises, except the fiduciary relationship inherent in the relationship of principal and agent. If, however, the recipient were to apply the money for some purpose outside the scope of the mandate, clearly the recipient would not be discharged. The recipient could be restrained, like any other agent, from a threatened misapplication of the money entrusted to him, and like any other agent could be required to replace any money misapplied."

---

[4] See *post*, p. 300.
[5] As a result of the decision in *Re Bucks Constabulary Fund Friendly Society (No.2)* [1979] 1 W.L.R. 936. However, the view expressed by Walton J. in this case is inconsistent with, but generally regarded as preferable to, the view expressed by Goff J. in *Re West Sussex Constabulary's Benevolent Fund Trusts* [1971] Ch. 1. These and other authorities are discussed *post*, p. 300.
[6] [1982] 1 W.L.R. 522.
[7] *ibid.* at 529.

This analysis is not without difficulties. Precisely who is the beneficial owner of the money until it is spent? Presumably the contributor unless and until the mandate becomes irrevocable by, for example, the money being mixed in the larger fund administered by the recipient. What happens if the mandate thereafter cannot be carried out or is carried out leaving a surplus? At first instance,[8] Vinelott J. took the view that in such circumstances there would be an implied obligation to return the fund to the subscribers in proportion to their original contributions (anonymous gifts and contributions to raffles would devolve as *bona vacantia*). Do the rights of the contributor survive a change in the identity of the person administering the fund? And, finally, how can testamentary gifts be brought within the framework of mandate or agency when "no agency could be set up at the moment of death between a testator and his chosen agent"?[9]

Whatever the answers to these questions, it is at least clear that there are considerable differences between the mandate or agency analysis and the treatment of gifts to unincorporated associations. It has been suggested that it might be appropriate for the mandate or agency theory to be extended to those gifts to unincorporated associations which, according to the rules which have already been discussed, are void.[10] Whether that theory is extended in this, or indeed in any other, way obviously remains to be seen.

---

[8] [1980] 3 All E.R. 42 at 63–64.
[9] [1982] 1 W.L.R. 522 at 530. Brightman L.J. thought that the answer to this problem was not difficult to find but no one else has yet succeeded in finding it (see Smart [1987] Conv. 415).
[10] See Creighton [1983] Conv. 15.

CHAPTER 4

# THE FORMAL REQUIREMENTS FOR THE CREATION OF A TRUST

## I. CAPACITY TO CREATE A TRUST

ANY person who has a power of disposition over a particular type of property can generally create a trust of it. Accordingly, any person over the age of 18[1] who is not suffering from mental incapacity may create an express trust of any property which is capable of disposition and may also create a trust of certain types of property of which he cannot dispose — an example of the latter type of property is a pension granted by a company to a retired director on the basis that it is non-assignable; the director may nevertheless be able to create a valid trust of the benefit of that agreement. Full capacity is therefore required before a fully binding express trust can be created; however, any property validly transferred under a trust which is subsequently held to be void is generally held by its recipient on resulting trust for the incapable settlor.

The position governing mental incapacity depends on whether a receiver has been appointed under sections 94 and 99 of the Mental Health Act 1983 on the grounds that the settlor is incapable of managing his affairs. Where a receiver has been appointed, it is generally thought that any trust purportedly made by the mental patient would be void.[2] The court may, however, order the creation of a trust of a mental patient's property, either on the application of another person or on its own initiative.[3] Further, since January 1, 1970, the court has been able to make a will on behalf of the patient[4] and it is also able to vary any trust which has been made, whether by the patient or by its own order, at any time prior to the patient's death.[5] When exercising these powers, the court must principally consider what the patient would have been likely to have done if he had not been incapable.[6] However, even where no receiver has been appointed, a trust will nevertheless be set aside if it can be shown that the settlor did not understand the nature of the act in which he was engaged.[7] It appears that the burden of proof will, at the outset, always lie on the person

---

[1] Family Law Reform Act 1969, s.1(1).
[2] There is no authority under the 1983 Act; however, this is the effect of *Re Marshall* [1920] 1 Ch. 284, a decision on the Lunacy Act 1890.
[3] Mental Health Act 1983, s.96(1)(d).
[4] *ibid.* ss.96(1)(e), 97.
[5] *ibid.*
[6] *Re T.B.* [1967] Ch. 247; *Re D.(J.)* [1982] Ch. 237.
[7] *Re Beaney* [1978] 1 W.L.R 770; *Simpson v. Simpson* [1992] 1 F.L.R 601 (both cases in which *inter vivos* gifts which upset the balance of the settlor's estate were held to be void).

seeking to set the trust aside; however, where there is a long history of mental illness, this burden will easily be able to be discharged and will then effectively be reversed, since the court will then require evidence that the settlor created the trust during a lucid interval.[8] Where a trust is set aside for this reason, any property transferred will be held by the recipient on a resulting trust for the settlor. It must, however, be emphasised that no trust created for valuable consideration will be set aside where the person providing the consideration was unaware of the mental incapacity of the settlor at the time when the trust was made.[9]

A person under the age of 18 cannot hold land[10] although he can certainly hold an equitable interest in land and will do so in the event of a purported conveyance of a legal estate to him, since this takes effect as a declaration of trust in his favour.[11] Consequently, while a minor cannot create a settlement of a legal estate in land, for no such estate can be vested in him, he can create a trust of such property as he does hold, including a trust of an equitable interest in land. Any trust which he does create is voidable until shortly after he attains the age of 18; if he does not repudiate it then, the trust will become fully binding upon him.[12] However, in order to create even a voidable trust, a minor must be old enough to appreciate the nature of his act. If he is too young to do so, his act is void and property which has been transferred is held by the recipient on a resulting trust[13] for the minor (little does the unsuspecting adult who has a sticky bag of sweets pushed into his hand by a toddler appreciate that thereafter he holds them on resulting trust for him).[14] Finally, it should be noted that it was formerly possible for a minor female aged 17 or over to make a binding settlement (this was at the time when the age of majority was 21)[15] however, there was no obvious point in preserving this right when the age of majority was reduced to 18 and so it was abolished.[16]

## II. THE STATUTORY REQUIREMENT OF WRITING

It has already been seen that an express trust can be constituted *inter vivos* either by declaration, where the settlor declares that specific property vested in him is thereafter the subject matter of a trust, or by transfer, where a settlor transfers specific property to trustees for them to hold on trust, the latter method being the only way of constituting a testamentary trust. The creation of trusts by either of these methods is subject to certain statutory rules con-

---

[8] See *Cleare v. Cleare* (1869) 1 P. & D. 655; *Chambers and Yatman v. Queen's Proctor* (1840) 2 Curt. 415.
[9] *Price v. Berrington* (1851) 3 Mac. & G. 486.
[10] Law of Property Act 1925, s.1(6); Family Law Reform Act 1969, s.1.
[11] Trusts of Land and Appointment of Trustees Act 1996, Sched. 1, para. 1 (this replaced Settled Land Act 1925, s.27, under which such a conveyance operated as an agreement for valuable consideration to create a settlement of the land on the minor).
[12] *Edwards v. Carter* [1893] A.C. 360.
[13] See *post*, p. 291.
[14] Prior to the enactment of the Trustee Act 2000, he was presumably expected to sell them and convert them into authorised investments: see *post*, p. 592.
[15] Under the Infant Settlements Act 1855.
[16] By the Family Law Reform Act 1969, s.11(a), which repealed the Infant Settlements Act 1855.

cerning formalities, testamentary trusts being governed by the Wills Act 1837 and *inter vivos* trusts being governed by the Law of Property Act 1925.

### 1. *The Statutory Provisions Governing Testamentary Trusts*

Testamentary trusts are governed exclusively by the provisions of the Wills Act 1837 (all the relevant provisions of the Law of Property Act 1925 require the transaction in question to be made by will[17] rather than in accordance with the formal requirements of that Act).

Section 9 of the Wills Act 1837 (as substituted by section 17 of the Administration of Justice Act 1982) provides that no will is valid unless it satisfies the following conditions: first, it must be in writing and signed by the testator or by some other person in his presence and by his direction; secondly, it must appear that the testator intended by his signature to give effect to the will; thirdly, that signature must be made or acknowledged by the testator in the presence of two or more witnesses present at the same time; and, fourthly, each witness must either attest and sign the will or acknowledge his signature in the presence of the testator (but not necessarily in the presence of any other witness), no particular form of attestation being necessary.

The formal validity of any trust whose terms are entirely contained within a will is determined entirely by whether or not that will was executed in accordance with this provision; testamentary trusts of this type therefore do not require any further consideration in this section. It is, however, possible for a will executed in accordance with this provision to constitute a trust whose existence and/or terms are not revealed on the face of the will. The validity of such trusts is governed by the doctrine of secret trusts, which will be considered in detail at the end of this section.[18]

### 2. *The Statutory Provisions Governing Inter Vivos Trusts*

The principal statutory provision governing the creation of *inter vivos* trusts is section 53 of the Law of Property Act 1925. Its wording has been the subject of detailed analysis by the courts and therefore needs to be set out in full.

"(1) Subject to the provisions hereinafter contained with respect to the creation of interests in land by parol—

    (a) no interest in land can be created or disposed of except by writing signed by the person creating or conveying the same, or by his agent thereunto lawfully authorised in writing, or by will, or by operation of law;

    (b) a declaration of trust respecting any land or any interest therein must be manifested and proved by some writing signed by some person who is able to declare such trust or by his will;

---

[17] Law of Property Act 1925, s.55 provides, *inter alia*, that nothing in s.53 is to invalidate dispositions by will. It also provides that nothing in that section is to affect any interest validly created before the commencement of the Act, or the acquisition of title by adverse possession, or affect the law relating to part performance (now anyway abolished by the Law of Property (Miscellaneous Provisions) Act 1989).

[18] See *post*, pp. 114–134.

(c) a disposition of an equitable interest or trust subsisting at the time of the disposition, must be in writing signed by the person disposing of the same, or by his agent thereunto lawfully authorised in writing or by will.[18A]

(2) This section does not affect the creation or operation of resulting, implied or constructive trusts."

### (A) The Different Formal Requirements of this Provision

Paragraphs (a) and (c) of subsection (1) require the transaction in question to be in writing, therefore any failure to comply with this requirement makes the transaction in question wholly void. However, the writing need not in all cases contain every detail — if the assignee is to hold subject to some fiduciary duty, the writing need not comprise particulars of the trust.[19] Nor does it seem to be necessary that the writing should all be contained in one document; a number of documents may be joined together for the purpose of satisfying the statute, provided that they are sufficiently connected.[20]

On the other hand, paragraph (b) of subsection (1) requires only evidentiary writing so that any failure to comply with this requirement does not make the transaction in question wholly void but merely unenforceable. This has two consequences: first, that the transaction is and remains valid unless and until one of the parties specifically raises the absence of the writing;[21] secondly, the necessary evidentiary writing can take the most diverse forms[22] and be provided at any time and quite unintentionally, provided that it does contain all the terms of the trust.

A further difference is that the writing required by paragraphs (a) and (c) can be signed either by the grantor or by an agent of the grantor who has been duly authorised in writing, while the writing required by paragraph (b) can be signed only by the grantor.

### (B) The Scope of the Different Paragraphs

Paragraphs (a) and (b) of subsection (1) are expressed to apply only to interests in land; paragraph (c), on the other hand, is not expressly so restricted.

---

[18A] To be effective, such a disposition must be unconditional; *Chandler v. Clerk* [2003] 1 P.C.R. 239.
[19] *Re Tyler* [1967] 1 W.L.R. 1269.
[20] *Re Danish Bacon Company Staff Pension Fund Trusts* [1971] 1 W.L.R. 268. Megarry J. stated that this was a novel question on which there appeared to be no previous direct authority.
[21] This can presumably be done at any time, even long after the creation of the trust. In principle, this means that there is nothing to stop a settlor who has created an inter vivos trust of land without the necessary formalities (or, more realistically, his trustee in bankruptcy or the residuary beneficiaries of his estate) from recovering the land in question at any time. However, any beneficiary who had acted to his detriment would inevitably be able to resist such a claim by relying on an equitable proprietary estoppel (see *post*, pp. 154–160). Further, it may now follow from *Pennington v. Waine* [2002] 1 W.L.R. 2075 (see *post*, p. 145) that it would be regarded as unconscionable for the residuary beneficiaries so to do even if the beneficiary had not acted to his detriment; however, this decision actually concerned the complete constitution of trusts, not their formalities; see Halliwell [2003] Conveyancer 192.
[22] For example, it may be provided by correspondence (*Foster v. Hale* (1798) 3 Ves.Jun. 696), by a recital in an instrument (*Re Hoyle* [1893] 1 Ch. 84), by an answer to what used to be known as interrogatories, now known as requests for further information (*Hampton v. Spencer* (1693) 2 Vern. 288), or even by a telegram (*McBlain v. Cross* (1871) 25 L.T. 804). It remains to be seen whether it would today also be held capable of being provided by a fax, a type of document which it is notoriously easy to forge.

However, the definitions section of the Law of Property Act 1925,[23] provides that "equitable interests" means "all the other interests and charges in or over land", unless the context otherwise requires. The question of whether this definition does restrict the scope of paragraph (c) to interests in land or whether, on the other hand, the context does otherwise require, has not been specifically addressed by an English court (it was considered by the High Court of Australia in *Adamson v. Hayes*,[24] where the members of the court disagreed).[25] It is generally thought that the context does otherwise require; were this not the case, paragraph (c) would be superfluous since every situation falling within it would already have been caught by paragraph (a), something which cannot possibly have been the intention of the legislature. Moreover, the House of Lords applied paragraph (c) to a relevant disposition of pure personalty in *Grey v. Inland Revenue Commissioners*[26] without any objection being raised, a decision which must resolve the question in this jurisdiction unless and until it is specifically raised.

A further difficulty is the apparent overlaps between paragraphs (a), (b), and (c) of subsection (1), which respectively deal with the creation or disposition of any interest in land, any declaration of a trust of land, and any disposition of a subsisting equitable interest or trust. The distinction thus drawn between the creation and the disposition of interests must be applied in the light of the fact that, when property is owned legally and beneficially by the same person, he holds only a legal interest therein, not a separate equitable interest as well.[27] Consequently, when such a person confers an equitable interest in that property on someone else, he is not disposing of an existing equitable interest therein but creating a new one. This is capable of falling within paragraphs (a) and (b) but not within paragraph (c), which clearly relates only to the disposition of a "subsisting" equitable interest, that is to say one existing separately from the legal estate. This however only rules out any overlap between paragraph (b) and paragraph (c); there may nevertheless be overlaps between, on the one hand, paragraph (a) and, on the other hand, paragraphs (b) and (c).

The fact that, on the face of things, there seems to be a clear overlap between paragraph (a) and paragraph (c), in that a disposition of a subsisting equitable interest in or trust of land is caught by both of them, has no significance in this jurisdiction since the formal requirements of the two paragraphs are identical.[28]

---

[23] s.201(1)(x).

[24] (1973) 130 C.L.R. 276.

[25] Menzies J. held that the equivalent Western Australian provision was restricted to interests in land, whereas Gibbs J. held that it was not. The remaining judges did not specifically mention this point but, since Walsh and Stephen JJ. agreed with Gibbs J. in other respects, the Australian commentators have concluded that they also rejected the view of Menzies J. and that there was therefore a majority against the provision being so restricted.

[26] [1960] A.C. 1.

[27] *Commissioner of Stamp Duties (Queensland) v. Livingston* [1965] A.C. 694 (Privy Council on appeal from the High Court of Australia).

[28] This is undoubtedly why the question has never been raised. The only way of escaping from this conclusion is to hold that paragraph (a) is confined to legal interests in land. This was held by Menzies J. in *Adamson v. Hayes* (1973) 130 C.L.R. 276 but the majority of the High Court of Australia (Walsh, Gibbs and Stephen JJ.) took the opposite view. However, none of them specifically mentioned the possible overlap, which would be significant only in Queensland, whose equivalent of paragraph (c) unusually requires only evidentiary writing — the legislation in the remaining Australian jurisdictions is similar to s.53(1)(c).

Potentially more problematic is the fact that a declaration of trust respecting land appears to fall within both paragraph (a) and paragraph (b), which have different formal requirements; such a trust supported only by evidentiary writing signed by the settlor appears to be void under paragraph (a) and valid under paragraph (b). Once again there is no English authority and the Australian decisions are mutually inconsistent.[29] If this overlap exists, paragraph (b) is in effect superfluous, something which again cannot possibly have been the intention of the legislature. It is thought that the potential difficulty could and should be resolved by reading paragraph (a) as if it said "no interest in land can be created or disposed of *otherwise than by the declaration of a trust* except by writing ..." (the words italicised being interpolated). However, unless and until this matter is actually considered by a court, there must be a certain amount of doubt as to whether a declaration of trust of land which is not in writing and is supported only by evidentiary writing signed by the settlor is actually valid.

## (C) The Exception in Subsection (2)

The exception contained in section 53(2) qualifies the whole of section 53(1). Consequently, the creation or operation of implied, resulting or constructive trusts does not have to comply with the formal requirements of the section.

This provision is applied extremely literally. It clearly exempts such trusts from having to comply with section 53(1)(b). This is illustrated by *Hodgson v. Marks*,[30] where an elderly widow was persuaded by her lodger to convey her house into his name on the spurious grounds that this would prevent him from being turned out of it after her death. He subsequently sold and conveyed the property to third parties without revealing that he had no beneficial interest therein. The Court of Appeal decided that as he had held the property on resulting trust for the widow, such a trust arose without any need to comply with the statutory formalities required by section 53(1)(b) and so was capable of binding the third parties.[31] The equivalent provision in the Law of Property (Miscellaneous) Provisions Act 1989,[32] which exempts such trusts from having to comply with the formal requirements for contracts of the sale of land, has been held not to apply to equitable proprietary estoppel interests where it is unconscionable for their existence to be denied.[33]

However, although resulting, implied and constructive trusts can come into existence and operate without any need for writing, any disposition of an interest arising under such a trust must comply with section 53(1)(c) — this is

---

[29] In *Adamson v. Hayes* (1973) 130 C.L.R. 276, Gibbs and Stephen JJ. expressly and Walsh J. implicitly but not Menzies J., held that there was such an overlap but the opposite view was subsequently taken at first instance in *Secretary, Department of Social Security v. Jones* (1990) 95 A.J.R. 615 (Supreme Court of Western Australia), where a declaration of trust of land was held only to fall within paragraph (b).

[30] [1971] Ch. 892.

[31] It was in fact held to bind the third parties on the grounds that the widow had an overriding interest under s.70(1)(g) of the Land Registration Act 1925 by virtue of her actual occupation of the house. This remains the position under ss.29, 30 and Sched. 3, para. 2, of the Land Registration Act 2002, unless it is held that her occupation would not have been obvious on a reasonably careful inspection of the land and the purchasers had no actual knowledge of it.

[32] s.2(5).

[33] *Yaxley v. Gotts* [2000] Ch. 162.

demonstrated by the decision of the House of Lords in *Grey v. I.R.C.*,[34] where what was being disposed of by the settlor was an interest arising under a resulting trust.

### 3. *The Effect of the Statutory Provisions Governing Inter Vivos Trusts*

**(A) The Creation by Declaration of a Trust of Property Vested in the Settlor**
If the interest in the property in question held by the settlor is a legal interest, the effect of the statutory provisions depends on whether it is in land or in pure personalty. If it is an interest in land,[35] section 53(1)(b) applies on any view; consequently, the declaration of trust will require evidentiary writing signed by the settlor, in default of which the declaration will be unenforceable. Signature by an agent is insufficient.[36] The appropriate writing will still be required even if the land in question is situated out of the jurisdiction and no writing is necessary according to the *lex situs*; this is because this is a rule of evidence which must be complied with in an English court.[37] If, on the other hand, the property is an interest in pure personalty, none of the statutory provisions applies and so the declaration of trust will be able to be made entirely orally. It is indeed rather surprising that a declaration of trust requires the appropriate writing even if it relates to as little as a square foot of land while a declaration of trust of millions of pounds worth of cash or investments does not; however, that is what the statutory provisions provide.

If, on the other hand, the interest in the property in question held by the settlor is an equitable interest,[38] the result is exactly the same with one further complication. The equitable interest in question must necessarily be taking effect behind an existing trust so that what the settlor will in reality be declaring is a sub-trust.

The effect of this may depend on whether the sub-trust declared is passive or active.[39] If it is passive, there is binding authority[40] (although contrary views

---

[34] [1960] A.C. 1. See *post*, p. 103.

[35] This includes freehold and leasehold property: Law of Property Act 1925, s.205(1)(ix).

[36] If, contrary to what was suggested above, there is indeed an overlap between s.53(1)(a) and s.53(1)(b), the former provision will also apply, requiring the declaration of trust to be in writing signed by the settlor or by an agent of the settlor duly authorised in writing, in default of which the declaration will be void.

[37] *Rochefoucauld v. Boustead* [1897] 1 Ch. 196 at 207.

[38] This includes freehold and leasehold property (Law of Property Act 1925, s.205(1)(ix)) and also apparently a share in the proceeds of sale of land (Law of Property (Miscellaneous Provisions) Act 1989, s.2(6)).

[39] It will be regarded as passive where the settlor has declared that his entire interest under the existing trust is to be held for the intended beneficiary of the sub-trust; where, on the other hand, the settlor has either declared that only a part of his interest under the existing trust is to be held for that beneficiary or has reserved some duties which in effect restrict the nature of the interest being given to him (the example which is always given is a declaration of trust to pay the rents and profits of the trust property to the intended beneficiary, thus restricting his rights to call for the capital), it will be regarded as active. It is unclear whether an apparently passive sub-trust for persons by way of succession is passive or active; however, it is suggested that the better view is that of Fry L.J. in *Re Lashmar* [1891] 1 Ch. 258 (by way of dictum) that it is passive.

[40] This was stated in *Grainge v. Wilberforce* (1889) 5 T.L.R. 436 at 437 and held by the Court of Appeal in *Re Lashmar* [1891] 1 Ch. 258.

have been expressed[41]) that the settlor of the sub-trust will "disappear from the picture" and drop out so that his trustees will hold the property directly on trust for the intended beneficiary of the sub-trust; if it is active, there is further authority[42] (and it is generally agreed) that the settlor of the sub-trust will not drop out and will hold his own subsisting interest on trust for the intended beneficiary of the sub-trust.

So far as formalities are concerned, the conventional view[43] is that, if the settlor does drop out, his purported declaration of trust will be treated as amounting to a disposition of his subsisting equitable interest under the original trust; consequently, section 53(1)(c) will apply, requiring the declaration of sub-trust to be in writing signed by the settlor or by an agent of the settlor duly authorised in writing, in default of which the declaration will be void. According to this view, a declaration of a passive sub-trust (but not an active sub-trust) requires writing under section 53(1)(c). This is not particularly significant in the case of a sub-trust of land, where evidentiary writing under section 53(1)(b) is necessary on any view,[44] but it is immensely significant in the case of a sub-trust of pure personalty, which would otherwise require no formality whatever. An alternative view has been put forward[45] that all declarations of a sub-trust, whether active or passive, have to comply with section 53(1)(c) whether the settlor drops out or not; this view thus requires writing in even more cases than the conventional view. However, it is thought that the conventional view should be adopted until such time as the question is considered by a court (it has never had to be considered in relation to the Law of Property Act 1925).

### (B) The Creation by Transfer of a Trust of Property Vested in the Settlor
In this case, the settlor must vest the property in question in the trustees on the intended trusts by the appropriate formalities.

### (1) Legal interests
If the interest in the property in question held by the settlor is a legal interest, the formalities depend on the nature of the property.

Registered land or any interest therein must be transferred by the appropriate land transfer form and duly registered in the name of the trustees in the Land Register,[46] whereas unregistered land must be transferred by deed.[47] The transfer or deed in question will normally set out the trusts on which the interest in land in question is to be held; if it does not do so,[48] those trusts

---

[41] By Green in (1984) 37 M.L.R. 385. This view has also been expressed in some of the common law jurisdictions of the United States of America and seems to be supported in Australia by some remarks of Dixon J. in *Comptroller of Stamps (Victoria) v. Howard Smith* (1936) 54 C.L.R. 614 (High Court of Australia).

[42] *Onslow v. Wallis* (1849) 1 Mac. & G. 506.

[43] See Battersby [1979] Conv. 17.

[44] If, contrary to what was suggested above, there is indeed an overlap between s.53(1)(a) and s.53(1)(b), this will make no difference at all.

[45] By Green in (1984) 37 M.L.R. 385.

[46] Land Registration Rules 2003, (formerly Land Registration Rules 1925, r.98).

[47] Law of Property Act 1925, s.52.

[48] This will necessarily be the case where the trusts in question are secret (see *post*, pp. 114–134) and was formerly the case where what was being created was a settlement under the Settled Land Act 1925 (no further settlements of this type can now be created).

should have been set out in a separate document which complies with section 53(1)(b)[49] — in default, the trustees will hold the property on resulting trust for the settlor.

Choses in possession, that is to say personal chattels, can be transferred either by delivery of the chattel with the appropriate intention to give or by deed;[50] the trusts on which they are to be held can be communicated orally.

Choses in action must in principle be assigned in accordance with section 136 of the Law of Property Act 1925[51] but the assignment of some specific choses[52] in action is instead governed by their own specific legislative provisions.[53] However, a transfer which has not been made in accordance with these formal requirements may nevertheless take effect in equity by virtue of the Rule in *Re Rose*[54] where the settlor has done everything within his power to bring about the transfer; it may also, more controversially, take effect in equity where it would be unconscionable for the settlor to deny its existence.[55]

**(2) Equitable interests**
If the interest in the property in question held by the settlor is an equitable interest, then, no matter what the nature of the property, its transfer will constitute a disposition of a subsisting equitable interest; consequently, both the actual transfer and the trusts on which the equitable interest are to be held will have to be in writing complying with section 53(1)(c). An equitable interest can also be assigned under section 136 of the Law of Property Act 1925 on the basis that it is a chose in action.[56]

**(C) The Creation of a Trust by the Settlor Giving Instructions to his Trustees**
In all the examples considered so far the settlor in question has himself dealt with property vested in him. It is now necessary to consider the situation where a settlor who is beneficially entitled to property under a trust gives instructions to his trustees to deal with that property in some way in order to vest his interest in a third party.

**(1) Where the settlor directs his trustees to hold on trust for a third party**
This situation had to be considered by the House of Lords in *Grey v. I.R.C.*[57] Trustees were holding shares as the nominees of the settlor, who was therefore

---

[49] *Re Baillie* (1886) 2 T.L.R. 660 (half secret trust; the absence of writing has never been raised in respect of a fully secret trust). If there is indeed an overlap between s.53(1)(a) and s.53(1)(b), the writing in question will instead have to comply with s.53(1)(a).

[50] See *Cochrane v. Moore* (1890) 25 Q.B.D. 57. However, if the trust is being constituted pursuant to a contract for the sale of goods, the legal title will pass in accordance with the legislation governing sales of goods.

[51] This provision requires the assignment to be in writing signed by the assignor and for express notice in writing to be given to the debtor or other person from whom the assignor would have been able to claim the debt or other chose in action.

[52] Such as shares, copyrights, certain types of insurance policies, and bills of exchange.

[53] Most shares are transferred simply by filling in the appropriate share transfer form, sometimes printed on the back of the share certificate itself, and sending it to the Registrar of the company in question for entry on the Register of Shareholders.

[54] [1952] Ch. 499. See *post*, p. 143.

[55] *Pennington v. Waine* [2002] 1 W.L.R. 2075 (see *post*, p. 145 and Halliwell [2003] Conveyancer 192).

[56] This will require the assignment to be in writing signed by the assignor and for express notice in writing to be given to the trustee in question.

[57] [1960] A.C. 1.

beneficially entitled to them under a resulting trust. The settlor, having made six settlements in favour of his grandchildren, orally directed the trustees to hold the shares on the trusts of those settlements. The trustees then executed six written declarations of trust in similar form, each of which recited their legal ownership of the shares, the settlor's oral direction, and their acceptance of the trust reposed in them by that direction. This apparently pointless manoeuvre was in fact an ingenious scheme to avoid payment of the *ad valorem* stamp duty which was then normally chargeable on a transfer of shares into a settlement.[58] However, the Inland Revenue rejected this scheme and assessed the six written declarations to this duty. The House of Lords held that the directions given by the settlor to the trustees were in fact dispositions by him of his subsisting equitable interest in the shares and so were within section 53(1)(c); because they had not been made in writing as required by that paragraph, they were ineffective at the time but became effective later on the execution of the written declarations of trust by the trustees. It was held that the word "disposition" in section 53(1)(c) had to be given the wide meaning which it bears in normal usage and the declarations of trust had accordingly been rightly assessed.

It had been persuasively argued that section 53 was merely a consolidation of three provisions of the Statute of Frauds 1677, sections 3, 7 and 9. There is a general principle that consolidating statutes are not to be interpreted as changing the pre-existing law unless the words are too clear to admit of any other construction. On this basis, the term "disposition" had to be interpreted in the same way as the expression "grants and assignments" found in section 9 which, it was contended, would not cover the directions given by the settlor. It was, as Lord Radcliffe said, a "nice question" whether or not this type of direction would have been caught by section 9; the point had never been decided and perhaps never would be. But the question was only relevant if section 53 was indeed to be treated as a true consolidation of the three sections of the Statute of Frauds. The House of Lords actually held that this was not the case — the section could not be regarded as a consolidating enactment in that sense. The Law of Property Act 1925 was undoubtedly a consolidating statute

---

[58] Stamp duty has traditionally been a tax which is payable only on documents so that, when a transaction is properly effected orally, no duty is payable (this remains the law at present but reforms are now envisaged, and are clearly necessary, in order to deal with the types of electronic transfer already envisaged for registered land — see Land Registration Act 2002, ss.91–95 and Sched. 5). Some considerable time before *Grey v. I.R.C.*, a method of avoiding duty had been evolved whereby the settlor orally made a declaration of trust and some time later signed a document merely recording what he had done. As long as these two events were separate — see *Cohen and Moore v. I.R.C.* [1933] 2 K.B. 126, no duty was payable because the trust was effected by the oral declaration. *Grey v. I.R.C.* was an attempt to extend this principle by a three stage operation: first, a transfer by the settlor of the shares to the trustees to hold as nominees on his behalf (because this transfer made no change in the beneficial interest, this stage unquestionably involved the payment of the then nominal duty of only 50p — now £5); secondly, an oral direction by the settlor to the trustees to hold for a third party (because this direction was oral, this stage equally clearly involved no payment of duty at all); and, thirdly, a subsequent written declaration of trust by the trustees. It was hoped that the oral declaration by the settlor would be sufficient to pass the equitable interest already, in which case no duty would be payable on the subsequent written declaration by the trustees. However the Revenue contended that, by virtue of s.53(1)(c), any disposition by the settlor had to be in writing; consequently, no disposition had taken place until the written declaration of trust had been signed so that stamp duty was payable thereon.

but what it had consolidated was the Law of Property Act 1922 and the Law of Property (Amendment) Act 1924. While the relevant sections of the Statute of Frauds 1677 were untouched by the 1922 Act, they had been repealed and re-enacted in an altered form by the 1924 Act. Consequently, there was no direct link between section 53(1)(c) and section 9 of the Statute of Frauds 1677 — the link had been broken by the changes introduced by the 1924 Act and it was those changes, not the previous provisions, which section 53 must be taken as having consolidated. It was therefore inadmissible to allow the construction of the word "disposition" to be limited or controlled by any meaning which could conceivably be attached to "grants and assignments" in section 9 of the Statute of Frauds.[59]

The word "disposition" in section 53(1)(c) must therefore be given the wide meaning which it bears in normal usage; if at the start of a transaction a person has a subsisting equitable interest and at the end of that transaction no longer has that interest, there will have been a disposition and the paragraph will have to be complied with.[60] Only two exceptions to this rule have subsequently emerged.

First, it has been established that a disclaimer of an equitable interest is not caught by section 53(1)(c) and so does not have to be made in writing. This was held in *Re Paradise Motor Company*,[61] where a verbal disclaimer by a person to whom shares had been given in such a way as to give him an equitable interest therein was held to be effective and therefore disentitled him from claiming in the liquidation of the company in question.

Secondly, it has been stated that the paragraph does not apply to a right commonly given by pension schemes to employees who are not yet in receipt of their pensions to nominate a person to receive a payment in the event of their death. In *Re Danish Bacon Company Staff Pension Fund*,[62] Megarry J. held that such a right did not amount to a testamentary disposition and so did not have to comply with the formal requirements for wills.[63] He also stated that he "very much doubted" whether the right was caught by section 53(1)(c) in the first place, doubting not only whether such a nomination could properly be described as a disposition, given that it had no more than a mere possibility of disposing of anything, but also whether the interest of the person at the time of making the nomination could properly be described as "subsisting". This view seems entirely justified; however, given that he was able to hold that there was sufficient writing in any event, he did not actually have to decide the point.

**(2) Where the settlor directs his trustees to transfer the trust property to a third party beneficially**
This situation occurred in *Vandervell v. I.R.C.*,[64] the first of three cases which

---

[59] [1960] A.C. 1 at 17–18.
[60] If there is indeed an overlap between s.53(1)(a) and s.53(1)(c), paragraph a will also apply where the subject matter is land but this in practice makes no difference whatever.
[61] [1968] 1 W.L.R. 1125.
[62] [1971] 1 W.L.R. 248 at 256.
[63] See *ante*, p. 97. On this point, the decision of Megarry J. was confirmed and applied by the Privy Council in *Baird v. Baird* [1990] 2 A.C. 548.
[64] [1967] 2 A.C. 291.

arose out of an endowment in favour of the Royal College of Surgeons whose ramifications were insufficiently investigated in advance.[65]

Vandervell had during his lifetime been a very successful businessman. He was beneficially entitled to virtually all the shares in a private products company which he ran and he could declare dividends as and when he pleased. In 1949 he had formed a trust company for the benefit of his children and had transferred money and shares to it to be held on trust for them. In 1958 he decided to respond to an appeal for funds by the Royal College of Surgeons by founding a chair of pharmacology at a cost of £150,000.[66] In the hope of making this endowment in a tax efficient way,[67] he directed a bank, who held shares in his products company as his nominee, to transfer those shares to the College; however, the shares were not transferred as an outright gift but subject to the College granting to the trust company an option to re-purchase the shares for £5,000 (a figure considerably less than their market value) at any time within five years. It was intended that, once sufficient dividends had been declared and paid on the shares to provide £145,000, the trust company would exercise the option, pay the remaining £5,000 and reacquire the shares, which could then be used for other purposes. Between 1958 and 1961 the products company declared dividends on the shares which were more than sufficient to endow the chair at the College.[68]

Unfortunately, however, Vandervell had not by 1961 specifed the trusts on which the trust company was to hold the option (it appeared that he had not made up his mind whether the option should be held in trust for his children or for the employees of his company). The Revenue therefore argued that Vandervell was liable to surtax on the dividends[69] on the basis that he had throughout retained a beneficial interest in the shares. By a majority of three to two, the House of Lords held that, because no trusts of the option had yet been declared, the option was held on resulting trust for Vandervell himself and he had therefore been rightly assessed to surtax. This conclusion, which has nothing to do with formalities, was sufficient to dispose of the case.

However, for present purposes, what is important is the Revenue's alter-native argument, which was indeed argued first, that section 53(1)(c) had not

---

[65] An incisive statement of the facts can be found in the judgment of Lord Denning M.R. in *Re Vandervell's Trusts (No.2)* [1974] Ch. 269 at 316–318; this decision of the Court of Appeal was the final stage of the third of the three cases.

[66] Well over £2,000,000 when converted to 2003 values using the Retail Prices Index.

[67] Any dividends declared by the company would be subject to deduction at source of the tax payable on company distributions (then 6s.8d. in the pound — 33.33 per cent) and would then be subject to surtax (the name then given to what is now known as the higher rate of income tax) in the hands of the shareholders (in Vandervell's case at 50 per cent). The total tax payable by Vandervell on any dividends would thus have been 83.33 per cent. The purpose of vesting the shares in the Royal College of Surgeons was to remove any liability of Vandervell to surtax and to enable the College, as a charity, to recover the 33.33 per cent tax already paid on the company distributions. That way a third of the endowment would be being provided out of tax already paid. This scheme would have worked perfectly had Vandervell not failed fully to divest himself of his beneficial interest in the shares.

[68] The dividends amounted to over £266,000; after tax at source, the College received about £175,000 plus the £5,000 payable under the option and it was envisaged that it would also be able to reclaim the tax deducted at source.

[69] Amounting, ultimately, to the whole amount of the dividends. The initial demand was for £250,000 in respect of the first two years of assessment; a further assessment was no doubt made in respect of the third year. The surtax was payable by virtue of the Income Tax Act 1952, s.415.

been complied with. At the outset Vandervell had undoubtedly held the equitable beneficial interest in the shares which were in the name of his bank. According to the Revenue, he had never transferred that equitable interest to the College in the manner required by section 53(1)(c); consequently, the beneficial interest was still vested in him and he was for that reason liable to surtax on the dividends declared thereon. The House of Lords rejected this contention, holding that section 53(1)(c) has no application where the holder of the equitable interest also controls the legal interest and intends that both should be transferred to a third party beneficially. In other words, section 53(1)(c) only applies to the disposition of an existing equitable interest when that interest is both before and after the disposition vested in someone other than the holder of the legal interest. The House had little alternative but to reach this conclusion since otherwise nominees would no longer have been able to pass a beneficial interest to a third party in the absence of a written disposition by or on behalf of the beneficiary.[70] However, the reasons enunciated in support of this conclusion are less than wholly convincing.

Two of the speeches can be immediately dismissed. Lord Reid[71] simply refused to give any reasons whatever for his decision on this point. Lord Wilberforce[72] held that Vandervell had done everything in his power to transfer his beneficial interest and so could rely on the rule in Re Rose[73] which gives effect in equity to transfers which a settlor has done everything within his power to bring about; however, this argument in fact begged the question because Vandervell had only done everything in his power if he did not have to use writing — precisely the question in issue.[74]

The remaining argument, by Lord Upjohn,[75] merits more serious consideration. He had recourse to the mischief rule of statutory interpretation and held that section 53(1)(c) had been enacted to prevent fraud on those who were truly beneficially entitled; consequently, he held that it could not apply to an absolutely entitled beneficiary like Vandervell, who could control his trustees. Since the only person whom such a person could possibly defraud was himself, there could therefore be no grounds for invoking the section where such an absolute beneficial owner wanted to deal with the legal estate. Lord Pearce agreed with the speech of Lord Upjohn and Lord Donovan[76] reached the same conclusion without bothering to make any specific reference to the rules of statutory interpretation. Lord Upjohn's argument therefore found favour with at least three members of the House and is not wholly unconvincing. How-

---

[70] In particular, the practice whereby brokers who are holding shares on behalf of their clients can and do resell them on the strength of oral instructions would have required some reconsideration in the event that the House of Lords had reached the opposite conclusion.

[71] [1967] 2 A.C. 291 at 307.

[72] ibid. at 329–330.

[73] See post, p. 143.

[74] See Jones 24 C.L.J. (1968) 19.

[75] [1967] 2 A.C. 291 at 311.

[76] ibid. at 317–318.

ever, the mischief rule of statutory interpretation is only supposed to be invoked where there is some ambiguity or lacuna in the provision in question, something which is certainly not the case with section 53(1)(c).[77]

Thus far, it appeared that the decision of the House of Lords on the form-alities argument was best regarded as having been taken on policy grounds. Much more recently, it has instead been suggested that the decision can be justified by recourse to the doctrine of overreaching, in other words that the transfer of the shares by the bank to the Royal College of Surgeons for value (the option contract to retransfer them) overreached Vandervell's beneficial interest into the benefit of that option contract;[78] if this analysis is correct, neither Vandervell's instructions to the bank nor the subsequent overreaching of his interest when the bank complied with those instructions fell with sections 53(1)(c).[79] However, whatever the grounds for the decision, it has to be admitted that the conclusion reached does at least have the merit of being clear: where a settlor directs his trustees to transfer the trust property to a third party with the intention that that third party should take both the legal and the beneficial interest in the property, the settlor does not have to comply with section 53(1)(c).

### (3) Where the settlor directs his trustees to declare new trusts in favour of a third party

This situation occurred in *Re Vandervell's Trusts (No.2)*.[80] These proceedings were a direct consequence of the decision in *Vandervell v. I.R.C.* that the option was held on resulting trust for Vandervell between 1958 and 1961.

It will be recalled that during this period the trusts on which the option to repurchase was held had not been specified and the option itself had not been exercised. At the end of that period, in October 1961, the trust company exercised the option and paid the £5,000 payable thereunder to the Royal College of Surgeons from the funds of the children's settlement. The trust company therefore became the legal owners of the shares themselves, no longer merely of the option to re-purchase them. All subsequent dividends were paid to the trust company and held on the trusts of the children's set-tlement. But even at this stage Vandervell made no express declaration of the trusts on which the shares or the dividends should be held. It was not until March 1964 (when judgment was given at first instance in *Vandervell v. I.R.C.*[81]) that it occurred to anyone that he might have retained an interest under a

---

[77] Nor is this argument wholly consistent with the decision in *Grey v. I.R.C.* Lord Upjohn admittedly took great pains to confine his argument to the situation where the settlor intended to deal with the legal title and so the *rationes decidendi* of the two decisions are wholly distinct; however, that does not alter the fact that the settlor in *Grey v. I.R.C.* was also absolutely beneficially entitled to the subject matter of the trust and s.53(1)(c) was nevertheless held to apply.

[78] Nolan [2002] C.L.J. 169.

[79] Vandervell could also validly have revoked those instructions prior to the bank acting on them; however, a transfer by the bank without notice of any revocation would not have been a breach of trust and so would have been effective to overreach Vandervell's interest; *Leslie v. Baillie* (1843) 2 Y. & C.C.C. 91.

[80] [1974] Ch. 269.

[81] [1966] Ch. 261.

resulting trust.[82] Subsequently, in January 1965,[83] he did execute a deed transferring to the trust company such interest as he might have in the shares or dividends and expressly declaring that the trust company was to hold them on the trusts of the children's settlement. The Revenue accepted that this deed was effective to divest Vandervell of any interest in the shares or dividends.[84]

Re Vandervell's Trusts (No.2) concerned the period between October 1961 and January 1965. The Revenue, on the basis that Vandervell had not divested himself of his interest in the shares or the option until January 1965, assessed his estate to surtax in respect of the dividends received by the trust company during this period.[85] In order to be able to pay this tax, his executors therefore had to claim from the trust company all the dividends from the shares which had been paid to that company during this period (the children were not beneficiaries of Vandervell's will because he had thought that he had made sufficient provision for them under their settlement). The Revenue sought and failed to be joined to these proceedings (their unsuccessful attempt was also taken to the House of Lords[86]) but, pending their conclusion, the executors' appeal against the surtax assessment was stood over.

It has already been seen that the £5,000 payable under the option was provided out of the children's settlement and that thereafter all the dividends received by the trust company were transferred to the children's settlement and treated as part of its funds. Furthermore, during this period the solicitors for the trust company had written a letter to the Revenue stating that the shares which the company had purchased would be held on the trusts of the children's settlement.

The Revenue admitted that these dealings, all of which had been done with Vandervell's approval, showed that he and the trust company intended that the shares should be held on trust for the children's settlement; however, they argued that this intention was in fact unavailing and that the shares and dividends had in fact been held on trust for Vandervell until January 1965 for the following reasons: first, until October 1961, Vandervell had had an equitable interest under a resulting trust — this was indisputable since the House of Lords had so held in Vandervell v. I.R.C.;[87] secondly, he himself had never disposed of that interest until January 1965; and, thirdly and in any event, any disposition prior to January 1965 would necessarily have been an oral disposition of an equitable interest which, by virtue of section 53(1)(c), had to be in writing.

This argument succeeded before Megarry J. but the Court of Appeal rejected

---

[82] Plowman J. so held (the decision of the Special Commissioners which was under appeal to him had found Vandervell liable on a different ground).

[83] The first day of the hearing of the appeal to the Court of Appeal from the decision of Plowman J. (see [1966] Ch. 261).

[84] Vandervell subsequently died early in 1967, aware of the result of Vandervell v. I.R.C. (the House of Lords handed down its decision on November 24, 1966) but not of the subsequent proceedings which were to drag on for more than seven years after his death until the Court of Appeal gave judgment in Re Vandervell's Trusts (No.2) on July 3, 1974.

[85] Amounting to the frivolity of £628,229, not far short of £8,500,000 when converted to 2003 values using the Retail Prices Index.

[86] Re Vandervell's Trusts [1971] A.C. 912. This meant that, paradoxically, the executors had to fight the Revenue's battle on its behalf because they would be liable for the surtax if the Revenue ultimately succeeded.

[87] [1967] 2 A.C. 291. See ante, p. 105.

it as fallacious. The court held, *inter alia*,[88] that the dealings with the dividends during this period not only showed an intention to create but actually amounted to the declaration of a trust of the shares in favour of the children's settlement which, because its subject matter was pure personalty, could be created without writing.[89] Section 53(1)(c) was, therefore, irrelevant. Leave to appeal to the House of Lords against this decision was granted but in the end no appeal was in fact made. This was presumably a cause of great relief to the Vandervell trustees but was perhaps unfortunate for the development of the law since the decision of the Court of Appeal has given rise to the following difficulties.

Some of these difficulties concern other requirements for the creation of a valid express private trust each of which is considered elsewhere. First, it is questionable whether a valid trust of the shares could have been completely constituted.[90] Secondly, even if such a trust could have been constituted, it is not easy to find the certainty of intention which was a necessary prerequisite of its creation.[91] While there is no doubt that both Vandervell and the trust company intended that the shares should be held on trust for the children's settlement, it is difficult to infer that Vandervell could have intended to dispose or did dispose of his equitable interest under the resulting trust of the option in 1961 when he was totally unaware that he had such an interest until the first instance decision in *Vandervell v. I.R.C.* was handed down in March 1964.

It is the other difficulty which is relevant for present purposes. Even if a trust could have been completely constituted and the necessary intention can be inferred to have existed any time prior to January 1965,[92] why did the decision in *Grey v. I.R.C.*,[93] where the settlor had similarly been trying to dispose of an interest under a resulting trust, not oblige Vandervell to dispose of his equitable interest in writing in accordance with section 53(1)(c)?[94] The Court of Appeal actually held that Vandervell's interest under the resulting trust had been extinguished when the gap in the beneficial ownership which had given rise to it was filled by the creation or declaration of a valid trust. In other words, the gap in the beneficial ownership had only existed until the option was exercised; as soon as this had occurred, a valid trust of the shares was created in favour of the children's settlement.

This proposition can be interpreted in two ways. It is possible to confine its effect to the situation where an option is held on trust; in this case *Re Vandervell's Trusts (No.2)* merely decides that, where an option is held on resulting trust, a direction by the beneficiary to the trustees to declare new trusts of the property which they receive as a result of exercising the option does not require writing under section 53(1)(c).[95] However, the formulations of princi-

---

[88] Other aspects of their decision are discussed *post*, pp. 138, 140, 158.
[89] Law of Property Act 1925, s.53(1)(b) applies only to trusts of land. See *ante*, p. 101.
[90] See *post*, pp. 138, 140.
[91] See *ante*, p. 46.
[92] When Vandervell executed the deed which the Revenue accepted was effective to deprive him of any beneficial interest.
[93] [1960] A.C. 1. See *ante*, p. 103.
[94] See the summary of the argument by Stephenson L.J. in *Re Vandervell's Trusts (No.2)* [1974] Ch. 269 at 322–323. This particular point had not been argued before Megarry J. at first instance.
[95] Where the subject matter is land, s.53(1) (b) (or, in the event of an overlap, s.53(1)(a)) would apply to such a declaration of trust.

ple in the judgments are not actually restricted to options and so at least suggest that, where any property of any type is held on resulting trust, a direction by the beneficiary to the trustees to declare new trusts of that property does not require writing under section 53(1)(c); if this is indeed the case, then it is not easy to see any satisfactory distinction[96] between *Re Van-dervell's Trusts (No.2)* and *Grey v. I.R.C.*, where a similar direction by the beneficiary of a resulting trust to the trustees to hold the property on new trusts was held to require writing.

### (D) The Creation of a Trust as a result of a Specifically Enforceable Contract of Sale

This possibility depends on section 53(2) which provides that section 53 as a whole does not apply to the creation or operation of resulting, implied or constructive trusts.[97] It was contended in *Oughtred v. I.R.C.*[98] that this provision enables equitable interests to be disposed of without any need for writing where the disposition in question is by way of constructive sub-trust arising as the result of the formation of a specifically enforceable contract of sale.

In this case, shares in a private company had been settled on trust for a mother for life and subject to that for her son. In order to enable each of them to own shares in the company absolutely, they agreed to exchange other shares in the same company to which the mother was already absolutely entitled for the son's equitable remainder, thus enlarging her life interest into absolute ownership. A contract for the sale of shares in a private company, unlike the majority of contracts for the sale of pure personalty, is specifically enforceable; this is because damages would not be an adequate remedy for the loss of the shares. The effect of any specifically enforceable contract is that the vendor holds its subject matter on a constructive trust for the purchaser, who therefore acquires an immediate equitable interest therein.[99] So the contract between mother and son automatically gave rise to a constructive trust (strictly speaking, because its subject matter was a subsisting equitable interest, a constructive sub-trust) under which the son held his equitable remainder on trust for his mother.

It was argued that, as a result of the creation of this passive sub-trust, the son had "disappeared from the picture" and dropped out,[1] causing his equitable remainder to pass to his mother; since, by virtue of section 53(2), no writing was necessary for the creation of this constructive sub-trust, the mother had therefore acquired an absolute beneficial interest in the shares without the use of any instrument on which stamp duty could be levied. The trustees had admittedly subsequently transferred the legal title to the shares to her but it was argued that this had transferred only a bare legal title, in respect of which only a nominal duty of 50p was payable.

The majority of the House of Lords, however, accepted the Revenue's contention that the latter transfer had to be stamped *ad valorem*. The reasoning

---

[96] Unless there is some forensic difference between telling trustees "to hold on new trusts" and telling them "to declare new trusts".

[97] See *ante*, p. 98.

[98] [1960] A.C. 206.

[99] See *post*, p. 438.

[1] This was stated in *Grainge v. Wilberforce* (1889) 5 T.L.R. 436 at 437 and held by the Court of Appeal in *Re Lashmar* [1891] 1 Ch. 258. See *ante*, p. 101.

behind this decision was stated by Lord Jenkins, who held that, if the subject matter of a sale is such that the full title to it can only be transferred by an instrument, then any instrument executed by way of transfer ranks for the purposes of stamp duty as a conveyance upon sale. He stated that, in the case of a contract for the sale of land, "a constructive trust in favour of the purchaser arises on the conclusion of the contract for sale, but (so far as I know) it has never been held on this account that a conveyance subsequently executed in performance of the contract is not stampable *ad valorem* on a transfer on sale".[2]

The attempt to save stamp duty therefore failed without any need for the majority of the House of Lords to consider the scope of section 53(2). However Lord Radcliffe, who dissented, had to do so; he accepted the contention that the mother had acquired the equitable remainder without any writing having been used.[3] On the other hand, Lord Cohen (also dissenting) and Lord Denning (the only one of the majority to mention the point) both stated by way of dicta[4] that, although the constructive sub-trust had come into existence without any need for writing, the interest arising thereunder could not be transferred without complying with section 53(1)(c). This view, which at first sight appears consistent with *Grey v. I.R.C.*, in fact overlooks the point that authority,[5] admittedly not binding on the House of Lords, establishes that the son "disappeared from the picture", something which must have caused his interest to pass to his mother automatically by operation of law. Consequently, the view of Lord Radcliffe has always seemed preferable and has now been adopted definitively.

The first decision in which this view was subsequently adopted was in *Re Holt's Settlement*,[6] where Megarry J. held that, when beneficiaries of a trust agree for valuable consideration to a variation of the beneficial interests, their existing interests (which are necessarily equitable) are varied without any need for any writing. Further support was provided by the remarks of two members of the Court of Appeal in *D.H.N. Food Distributors v. Tower Hamlets L.B.C.*[7] and of Lord Wilberforce in *Chinn v. Collins*.[8] Lord Radcliffe's view was, however, definitively accepted by the Court of Appeal in *Neville v. Wilson*.[9] All the shares in a private company were owned beneficially by a second private company but in order to qualify the two directors for office each held the legal

---

[2] [1960] A.C. 206 at 240.
[3] *ibid.* at 228.
[4] *ibid.* at 230; at 233.
[5] *Grainge v. Wilberforce* (1889) 5 T.L.R. 436 at 437; *Re Lashmar* [1891] 1 Ch. 258. See *ante,* p. 101.
[6] [1976] 1 Ch. 100 at 116.
[7] [1976] 1 W.L.R. 852. Goff L.J. at 865 and Shaw L.J. at 867 accepted that, where the transaction in question is not a gift, an equitable interest in land could pass without writing.
[8] [1981] A.C. 533 at 548, where he stated that, as soon as there was an agreement for the sale of the equitable interest in shares in a public company held by nominees followed by payment of the price, "the equitable title passed at once to the purchaser". This contract was not even specifically enforceable so that this enunciation of principle is even wider than that of Lord Radcliffe. However, it had the effect of defeating a capital gains tax avoidance scheme and Hanbury & Martin: *Modern Equity* (16th ed., 2001) pp. 90–91 indicates that this may have been an important factor.
[9] [1997] Ch. 144. A contrary view had earlier been expressed by Chadwick J. by way of dictum in *United Bank of Kuwait v. Habib* [1997] Ch. 107 but the question was not raised on the subsequent appeal which was heard by a differently constituted Court of Appeal after argument but before judgment in *Neville v. Wilson*.

title to 60 shares as the second company's nominee. These shares were, as the result of an oral agreement, included in the subject matter of an agreement made by all the shareholders of the second company to distribute all the shares in the first company to them in proportion to their shareholdings; consequently, the two directors had entered into a specifically enforceable contract to assign the subsisting equitable interests in the shares. The Court of Appeal merely had to consider the validity of the contract; no issue arose as to the effect of sub-trusts. Nourse L.J.[10] analysed the speeches in *Oughtred v. I.R.C.* and held that the analysis of Lord Radcliffe was "unquestionably correct". Consequently, the oral contract was not rendered ineffectual by section 53(1)(c) due to the existence of the constructive sub-trust and the effect of section 53(2). This approval of Lord Radcliffe's view must therefore also establish that, where an equitable interest becomes subject to a constructive sub-trust as a result of the creation of a specifically enforceable contract of sale, that equitable interest will, by virtue of section 53(2), immediately vest in the purchaser without any need for writing.[11] However, since only specifically enforceable contracts have this effect, this possibility is now limited to contracts for the sale of shares in private companies and of rare chattels;[12] the only other specifically enforceable contracts, contracts for the sale of land, now have to be in writing anyway.[13]

### 4. *Equity will not Allow a Statute to be Used as an Instrument of Fraud*

The courts will not allow the statutory provisions which have just been considered (any more than they would allow their predecessor, the relevant sections of the Statute of Frauds 1677) to be applied in such a way as to achieve a fraudulent purpose. A basic equitable maxim is that equity will not allow a statute to be used as a "cloak" or "engine" for fraud. It of course cannot be doubted that a major, if not the major, objective of all the statutory provisions which have been reviewed is the prevention of fraud and was the primary reason for the enactment of the first of them — the Statute of Frauds. But it is easy to visualise a situation where an automatic application of the statutory provisions would have the unintended effect of allowing fraud by one party to succeed and in such circumstances the court will intervene in order to protect the other party under the umbrella of the equitable maxim set out above.

Thus in *Bannister v. Bannister*,[14] the defendant sold and conveyed two adjoining cottages to the plaintiff on the basis that she could continue to occupy one of them rent free for as long as she wished. When he subsequently sought to evict her on the basis that the conveyance did not mention her right of occupation, she successfully counterclaimed for a declaration that the plaintiff held the cottage on trust for her for her lifetime. The Court of Appeal

---

[10] At 157, giving the judgment of the court.
[11] However, this will cease to be the case if a different view is ever taken of the effect of a passive sub-trust. See *ante*, p. 101.
[12] The only type of contracts for the sale of pure personalty which are specifically enforceable; contracts for the sale of property which is readily available on the open market, such as shares in a public company and normal chattels, are not specifically enforceable because damages will always be an adequate remedy for the purchaser.
[13] Under the Law of Property (Miscellaneous Provisions) Act 1989, s.2.
[14] [1948] 2 All E.R. 133; [1948] W.N. 261.

classified as fraudulent the conduct of the plaintiff in attempting to rely on the absence of the writing which section 53(1)(b) of the Law of Property Act 1925 requires for the creation of the interest claimed by the defendant and imposed a constructive trust under which he held the property on trust for her for her lifetime. This and the other relevant authorities will be considered more fully in the chapter on Constructive Trusts.[15]

The principle that equity will not allow a statute to be used as an instrument of fraud has also been relied on by the courts as the justification for the existence of the doctrine of secret trusts. Such trusts arise when an intending settlor makes a gift of property in his will or leaves an existing will unrevoked or dies intestate on the strength of an undertaking by the person entitled under his will or intestacy to hold whatever property he receives on trust for a third party. In such circumstances, the court will enforce performance of the undertaking at the suit of the third party despite the fact that this involves admitting evidence which does not comply with section 9 of the Wills Act 1837. This has been justified on the basis that otherwise the person who made the undertaking would be being allowed to benefit from his own fraud. However, this work adopts the alternative view, which has been relied on by the courts in the majority of the more recent authorities, that the justification for the admission of such evidence is that secret trusts operate outside the will, so that the provisions of the Wills Act have nothing whatever to do with them. Nevertheless, this is a convenient moment to examine the rules governing secret trusts, which are discussed in detail in the next section.[16]

## III. SECRET TRUSTS

As was mentioned in the previous section, a secret trust arises when an intending settlor makes a gift of property in his will[17] or leaves an existing will unrevoked[18] or dies intestate[19] on the strength of an undertaking by the person entitled under his will or intestacy to hold whatever property he receives on trust for a third party. In such circumstances the court will enforce performance of the undertaking at the suit of the third party. There are two types of secret trusts, fully secret trusts and half secret trusts. A trust is fully secret when both the existence of the trust and its terms are concealed; such a trust therefore arises where the property which is the subject matter of the trust is, on the face of the will, left to the recipient absolutely or where the settlor has died intestate. On the other hand, a trust is half secret when the existence of a trust is revealed but its terms are concealed; such a trust therefore arises where

---

[15] See *post*, pp. 418–419.

[16] See *post*, pp. 114–134.

[17] This is what occurs in the overwhelming majority of cases of secret trusts. The earliest cases, *Crook v. Brooking* (1688) 2 Vern. 50 and *Pring v. Pring* (1689) 2 Vern. 99 were cases of this kind, as were *McCormick v. Grogan* (1869) L.R. 4 H.L. 82 and *Blackwell v. Blackwell* [1929] A.C. 318, which are respectively the leading cases on fully secret and half secret trusts.

[18] This occurred in *Tharp v. Tharp* [1916] 1 Ch. 142.

[19] This occurred in *Sellack v. Harris* (1708) 5 Vin.Abr. 512, p. 1.31. See also *Re Gardner* [1920] 2 Ch. 523, where there was a partial intestacy (a wife made a will which merely left her property to her husband for life; she died possessed only of personalty and he therefore also took the interest in remainder under the intestacy rules; both interests were held to be subject to a fully secret trust communicated and accepted after the date of the will).

the property which is the subject matter of the trust is, on the face of the will, left to the recipient as a trustee. The advantages of a secret trust are that a testator can conceal the true objects of his benevolence from public view — a will is, of course, a public document — and can also, in the case of a fully secret trust, alter those objects at any time before his death simply by communicating with the secret trustee.

Secret trusts depend for their efficacy on the intervention of equity. This intervention is, on the face of things, directly contrary to the important statement of principle contained in section 9 of the Wills Act 1837. This provision, which was summarised at the beginning of the previous section,[20] requires wills to be in writing signed by the testator, or some other person in his presence and by his direction, in the presence of two witnesses both present at the same time, who also sign. It was enacted for an obvious and important reason of policy — to ensure that false claims cannot be generated after the death of a testator when he is in no position to refute them. Such a policy can undoubtedly operate in an extremely harsh way but the courts have, rightly, always been reluctant to admit as evidence in proceedings concerning the administration of an estate any documents which fail to comply with these formal requirements.

It is almost inevitable that the existence of secret trusts will only be able to be proved by evidence which does not comply with these requirements; the whole object of the exercise is to exclude the identity of the beneficiary from the formally attested documents admitted to probate. Inevitably, therefore, the evidence of the communication, acceptance and terms of the secret trust in question will be either oral or contained in a document which has not been properly signed and attested. The existence of secret trusts therefore involves a departure both from the letter and the spirit of the Wills Act and consequently, as might be expected, various justifications for their existence have been suggested by the courts. Since several of the rules governing the operation of secret trusts stand or fall depending upon the justification which is adopted, it is necessary to discuss them before considering these rules.

1. *The Theoretical Justification for the Existence of the Doctrine of Secret Trusts*

**(A) Fraud**
It has often been stated that the justification for the existence of the doctrine of secret trusts is that, if evidence of the terms of the trust were not admitted contrary to the provisions of the Wills Act, the result would be fraud. However, there has been considerable judicial disagreement as to the nature of this fraud. Some judges have found this fraud in the ability of the intended trustee to take the property beneficially if evidence of the terms of the trust is not admitted. Others have instead found it in the consequential failure to observe the intentions of the testator and the consequential destruction of the beneficial interests arising under the trust.

**(1) By the legatee**
The view that the potential fraud stems from the ability of the intended trustee to take the property beneficially is normally expressed in this way. If evidence

---

[20] See *ante*, p. 97.

of the terms of the trust were not admitted contrary to the provisions of the Wills Act, the person who received the property under the will or intestacy in question would be able to disregard his undertaking to the intending settlor and take the property beneficially.

This was the argument adopted by the members of the House of Lords in *McCormick v. Grogan*.[21] The testator made a will leaving all his property to Grogan. When near to death, he summoned Grogan, told him of the will and said that a letter would be found with it. However, he did not seek to obtain any undertaking from him in respect of the letter, which named various persons to whom the testator wished Grogan to give money and the amount of the intended gift to each, concluding with these words: "I do not wish you to act strictly to the foregoing instructions, but leave it entirely to your own good judgment to do as you think I would if living and as the parties are deserving, and as it is not my wish that you should say anything about the document there cannot be any fault found with you by any of the parties should you not act in strict accordance with it."

One of the named persons whom Grogan decided to exclude brought an action claiming that Grogan held the property on secret trust to give effect to the provisions of the letter. This action failed on the grounds that the testator had imposed no legally binding obligation upon Grogan. The members of the House of Lords clearly stated that the doctrine of secret trusts was established so as to prevent any possibility of fraud by the secret trustee. Lord Hatherley L.C. said that the doctrine of secret trusts "involves a wide departure from the policy which induced the legislature to pass the Statute of Frauds,[22] and it is only in clear cases of fraud that this doctrine has been applied — cases in which the Court has been persuaded that there has been a fraudulent inducement held out on the part of the apparent beneficiary in order to lead the testator to confide to him the duty which he undertook to perform".[23]

This line of reasoning is a possible justification for the existence of the doctrine when, as in *McCormick v. Grogan*, the trust in question is fully secret. In such a case, unless evidence of the trust is admitted contrary to the provisions of the Wills Act, the intended trustee will be able to take the property beneficially and so will clearly profit from his own misconduct. But this line of reasoning cannot normally justify the existence of half secret trusts.

In such a trust, the intended trustee takes the property as a trustee on the face of the will. Therefore, if the court declined to admit evidence of the terms of the half-secret trust, he would not take the subject matter beneficially but would clearly hold the property in question on trust for whoever was entitled to the testator's residuary estate[24] or his statutory next-of-kin.[25] On the face of things, therefore, there is no way in which such an intended trustee could profit by failing to carry out his promise to the testator, unless of course he

---

[21] (1869) L.R. 4 H.L. 82. A similar view had been expressed over a century earlier in *Drakeford v. Wilks* [1747] 3 Atk. 539 and was subsequently repeated by Lord Davey in *Re French* [1902] 1 I.R. 172, 230 (an appeal to the House of Lords from the Court of Appeal of Ireland).

[22] Prior to the enactment of the Wills Act 1837, the formal requirements for wills were contained in the Statute of Frauds 1677.

[23] (1869) L.R. 4 H.L. 82 at 89.

[24] Whatever is left after payment of the testator's debts and after any specific gifts made in the will.

[25] *Re Pugh's Will Trusts* [1967] 1 W.L.R. 1262.

were himself the residuary beneficiary or intestate successor of the testator. It is not entirely clear whether he would in such circumstances be entitled to take the property as residuary beneficiary or intestate successor if the half secret trust failed but it is suggested that in principle he should be able to do so on the grounds that in such a situation he would be claiming the property not as a trustee but in a different capacity of which the testator must necessarily have been aware. On this assumption, an intended trustee holding property under a half secret trust would be enabled to profit by failing to carry out his undertaking to the testator and so the admission of evidence contrary to the terms of the Wills Act could be justified by the fraud argument. But this argument will obviously not apply to the vast majority of half secret trusts simply because the intended trustee will not normally be the appropriate residuary beneficiary or intestate successor. Consequently in such circumstances there would be no possibility whatsoever of the intended trustee taking the subject matter beneficially if evidence of the trust were not admitted contrary to the provisions of the Wills Act.

Thus in normal circumstances the fraud argument, while a possible justification for the existence of fully secret trusts, cannot justify the existence of half secret trusts.

## (2) On the testator and the beneficiaries

The alternative view is that the fraud in question is committed on the testator and the beneficiaries by reason respectively of the failure to observe the intentions of the former and of the destruction of the beneficial interests of the latter. This view is normally expressed in this way. If evidence of the terms of the trust were not admitted contrary to the provisions of the Wills Act, the testator would be defrauded in that, on the faith of the promise made by the secret trustee, he had either made or left unrevoked a disposition of his property. In the same sort of way, the beneficiaries of the secret trust would be defrauded in that they would be deprived of their beneficial interests.

This argument (which of course applies just as much to fully secret trusts as to half secret trusts) emerged as early as 1748 in *Reech v. Kennegal*,[26] where Lord Hardwicke L.C. admitted evidence contrary to the Statute of Frauds "in respect of the promise and of the fraud upon the testator in not performing it". This view was expressed even more clearly in the Irish case of *Riordan v. Banon*[27] in a passage which was subsequently cited with approval by Hall V.-C. in *Re Fleetwood*:[28] "The testator, at least when his purpose is communicated to and accepted by the proposed legatee, makes the disposition to him on the faith of his carrying out his promise and it would be a fraud in him to refuse to perform that promise."

While the authorities so far discussed all emphasised the fraud on the testator, Lord Buckmaster emphasised rather the fraud on the beneficiaries in the leading case of *Blackwell v. Blackwell*.[29] Blackwell left in his will £12,000 to five persons "upon trust ... to apply for the purposes indicated by me to them". In fact the money was to be used to maintain his mistress and illegitimate son.

---

[26] (1748) 1 Ves. 123. See also the review of the early authorities by Hargrave, *Juridical Arguments and Collections* (1801) Vol. II, p. 912.

[27] (1876) 10 Ir.Eq. 469 (Court of Chancery of Ireland).

[28] (1880) 15 Ch.D. 594 at 606–607.

[29] [1929] A.C. 318.

His deceived wife and child brought an action against the five legatees claiming that no valid trust for these purposes existed. Their counsel raised the argument that fraud could not justify the admission of evidence of the terms of a half secret trust contrary to the provisions of the Wills Act because there was no possibility of a half secret trustee taking the property beneficially. Counsel for the legatees relied not on principle but on the previous practice of the courts manifested in cases such as *Re Fleetwood*. The House of Lords upheld the existence of the doctrine of half secret trusts. Lord Buckmaster (with whose speech Lord Hailsham L.C. concurred) said that "a testator having been induced to make a gift on trust in his will in reliance on the clear promise by the trustee that such trust will be executed in favour of certain named persons, the trustee is not at liberty to suppress the evidence of the trust and thus destroy the whole object of its creation, in fraud of the beneficiaries".[30]

The emphasis placed in the authorities just discussed on the failure to observe the intentions of the testator and the destruction of the beneficial interests is deceptively simple and is, superficially, quite attractive. In fact, however, such arguments are completely circular. To refer to the terms of the secret trust as the "wishes of the testator" and to describe those entitled under the secret trust as "beneficiaries" begs the question; only if evidence of the terms of the trust is admitted contrary to the provisions of the Wills Act is it appropriate to describe the terms of the secret trust as the wishes of the testator and to refer to those entitled thereunder as its beneficiaries. It is not possible to use as a justification for admitting evidence contrary to the provisions of the Wills Act facts which can only be proven if such evidence is admitted. Consequently it is impossible to regard this argument as a valid justification for the existence of the doctrine of either fully secret trusts or half secret trusts.

### (B) That Secret Trusts Operate Outside the Will

Given that fraud can justify only the existence of fully secret trusts, if half secret trusts are to be accepted as valid some other possible justification must be sought. One does indeed exist in the totally different approach adopted by Viscount Sumner in *Blackwell v. Blackwell*. His lordship stated that the provisions of the Wills Act have nothing whatsoever to do with the doctrine of secret trusts and that it is inappropriate to state that evidence of their existence is adduced contrary to the provisions of the Wills Act. He said that it is "communication of the purpose to the legatee, coupled with acquiescence or promise on his part, that removes the matter from the provisions of the Wills Act and brings it within the law of trusts, as applied in this instance to trustees, who happen also to be legatees".[31] In other words, secret trusts operate wholly outside the will or intestacy in question and so are governed not by the rules of probate but by the rules of the law of trusts, which in no way prevent the introduction of oral evidence. This argument will obviously apply both to fully secret trusts and to half secret trusts.

The notion that secret trusts so operate wholly outside the will or intestacy had in fact been referred to many years earlier by Lord Westbury in *Cullen v.*

---

[30] *ibid.* at 328–329.
[31] [1929] A.C. 318 at 339.

*Attorney-General for Ireland*.[32] This notion suggests that the enforcement of secret trusts is dependant upon fraud only to the extent that the basic duty of trustees to carry out their obligations as such is dependant on general equitable principles. A similar conclusion may perhaps be drawn from one of the more recent case on secret trusts, *Re Snowden*,[33] where Megarry V.-C. held that the standard of proof necessary to establish the existence of a secret trust is the ordinary civil standard of proof required to establish an ordinary trust, not the higher standard necessary for rectification claims, on the grounds that "the whole basis of secret trusts ... is that they operate outside the will, changing nothing that is written in it, and allowing it to operate according to its tenor, but then fastening a trust on to the property in the hands of the recipient".[34] Thus, according to these authorities, the justification for the existence of secret trusts, whether fully secret or half secret, is that such trusts operate wholly outside the will or intestacy in question. This proposition requires close examination.

### (1) The problem

Clearly, a secret trust cannot operate completely independently of the will in question simply because the will alone can vest the subject matter of the trust in the secret trustee. To take an extreme example, if the will itself is invalid, the secret trust will fail with it for lack of subject matter. Therefore, the rules of probate clearly have some role to play. The crucial question is at what point the rules of probate cease to operate and are superseded by the rules of the law of trusts.

### (2) The crucial situations

This question can only be answered by an examination of the situations where the rules of probate and the rules of the law of trusts are in conflict. There are three such situations: when the secret trustee or secret beneficiary has attested the will, when the secret trustee or secret beneficiary has predeceased the testator or intestate, and where the secret trustee disclaims the gift in his favour. An examination of these situations suggests that the only possible answer is that the rules of probate govern the vesting of the subject matter of the secret trust in the secret trustee, while the rules of the law of trusts govern any matter concerning the operation of the secret trust.

**(a) Attestation.** Section 15 of the Wills Act 1837 provides that a legacy to an attesting witness is ineffective, whereas, as a matter of the law of trusts, there is no reason why the trust deed should not be signed by the trustees or beneficiaries. What happens if the secret trustee or the secret beneficiary attests the will?

In *Re Young*[35] one of the beneficiaries under a half secret trust attested the will. Danckwerts J. held that, since the trust arose outside the will, section 15 of the Wills Act 1837 was quite irrelevant and so the beneficiary could take his interest. This conclusion is consistent with the possible principle suggested

---

[32] (1866) L.R. 1 H.L. 190 at 198 (on appeal from the Court of Appeal in Chancery of Ireland).
[33] [1979] Ch. 528.
[34] *ibid.* at 535.
[35] [1951] Ch. 344.

above and presumably would also apply in the case of a fully secret trust (there is no authority on this point).

No case has yet been reported in which a secret trustee has attested the will. However, if the possible principle suggested above is correct, this matter should be governed by the rules of probate since it concerns the vesting of the legacy. A legatee who takes beneficially on the face of the will is clearly caught by section 15. Therefore, if a fully secret trustee attested the will, the legacy to him would be ineffective and so the secret trust would fail for lack of subject matter (unless, presumably, the property nevertheless vested in the secret trustee under the intestacy rules, in which case he would undoubtedly be bound to perform the trust). On the other hand, a legatee who takes as a trustee on the face of the will is not caught by section 15.[36] Therefore, if a half secret trustee attested the will, the legacy to him would be effective and so the half secret trust would not fail by reason of his attestation. This discrepancy between fully secret and half secret trusts is, admittedly, a little odd; however, there are in fact many examples of discrepancies of this kind.

**(b) Predecease.** Section 25 of the Wills Act 1837 provides that, subject to certain exceptions which are not here material, a gift in a will lapses if the recipient predeceases the testator. Similarly, no one who predeceases an intestate can possibly take any of his property under the intestacy rules. What therefore happens if the secret trustee or secret beneficiary predeceases the testator or intestate?

If the secret trustee predeceases the testator or intestate, the result once again seems to differ depending on whether the trust in question is fully secret or half secret. In *Re Maddock*[37] Cozens-Hardy L.J. stated, by way of dictum, that if a fully secret trustee predeceases the testator the legacy will lapse and the secret trust will fail for lack of subject matter. This conclusion is another example of probate principles being applied to the vesting of the legacy. On the other hand, it has always been clear that a gift to a person who takes as a trustee on the face of a will will not lapse by reason of his predecease.[38] Thus, if a half secret trustee predeceases the testator, this principle will presumably apply and the secret trust will therefore not fail.

Much more controversy surrounds the situation where the secret beneficiary predeceases the testator or intestate. This occurred in *Re Gardner (No.2)*.[39] Romer J. held that a beneficiary under a secret trust acquires an interest in the trust property as soon as the trust is communicated to and accepted by the secret trustee. Thus, the beneficiary had acquired an interest before his death and that interest naturally passed to his personal representatives for the benefit of those entitled under his will or intestacy.

This decision has been rightly criticised on the grounds that a beneficiary under a trust acquires no interest in the trust property until the trust has been completely constituted in accordance with the rules discussed in the next chapter.[40] Since this could not possibly have occurred until the trust property vested in the secret trustee at the death of the testatrix, the beneficiary could

---

[36] *Cresswell v. Cresswell* (1868) L.R. 6 Eq. 69.
[37] [1902] 2 Ch. 220.
[38] *Re Smirthwaite's Trusts* (1871) L.R. 11 Eq. 251.
[39] [1923] 2 Ch. 230.
[40] See *post*, pp. 136–159.

not have acquired an interest prior to his death. It is therefore generally accepted that this case was wrongly decided.[41]

It is of course quite impossible to justify the reasoning which led Romer J. to his conclusion. If, however, it is accepted that the trust became completely constituted at the death of the testator, what has to be considered is the effect of completely constituting a trust in favour of a person who is already dead — that is, after all, what actually happened in *Re Gardner (No.2)*.

If, as the authorities so far discussed suggest, the rules of probate govern the vesting of the legacy in the secret trustee while the rules of the law of trusts govern any matter concerning the operation of the secret trust, this issue falls to be determined by application of the rules of the law of trusts. Is, therefore, there any rule of the law of trusts which provides that it is not possible to constitute a trust in favour of a dead person? The authorities on the effect of constituting a trust in favour of someone whom the settlor knows to be dead are indecisive.[42]

However, that is not the situation under discussion; that question is what is the effect of constituting a trust in favour of someone whom the settlor thinks is alive but is in fact dead. This question is totally devoid of authority. If such a trust were valid, it would necessarily have to take effect in favour of those entitled under the dead beneficiary's will or intestacy; if this is the case, for this reason rather than the reasoning adopted by Romer J., *Re Gardner (No.2)* was correctly decided. However, the overwhelming view of the commentators is that such a trust would be wholly void;[43] if this is the case, then *Re Gardner (No.2)* was indeed wrongly decided. Whatever view is taken (and in the light of the weight of academic opinion, the second view seems almost inevitable), that view should clearly apply whether the trust in question is, as in *Re Gardner (No.2)*, fully secret or half secret.

**(c) Disclaimer.** Where a person who is nominated as a trustee declines to act, the court will appoint another to act in his stead.[44] Thus it seems that, if a half secret trustee declines to act, the court will appoint a replacement trustee and the secret trust will therefore not fail.

However, a disclaimer of a testamentary gift by a person who takes beneficially on the face of the will causes the legacy to fail;[45] on this basis a disclaimer by a fully secret trustee will necessarily have this effect.

This will not be a problem if the purpose of the disclaimer is to enable the secret trustee to take not under the disclaimed testamentary gift but rather as residuary beneficiary or intestate successor. Such clearly unconscionable conduct will inevitably lead to the imposition of a constructive trust on the

---

[41] See, for example, the views of Hayton in Hayton and Marshall, *Commentary and Cases on the Law of Trusts and Equitable Remedies* (11th ed., 2001), pp. 118–119.

[42] Prior to the enactment of the Property Legislation of 1925, there was some authority that it was not possible to constitute a trust in favour of a dead person (*Re Tilt* (1896) 74 L.T. 163, applying *Re Corbishley's Trusts* (1880) 14 Ch.D 846). However, it is questionable whether these authorities are still good law. Since 1925, a grantee is presumed to take the greatest interest that his grantor was able to give him (Law of Property Act 1925, s.60(1)) and so arguably will take an interest not only for himself but also for those entitled under his will or intestacy.

[43] See *ante*, fn. 41.

[44] The power of the court so to appoint trustees stems both from statute (Trustee Act 1925, s.41(1)) and from its inherent jurisdiction (see *Dodkin v. Brunt* (1868) L.R. 6 Eq. 580).

[45] *Townson v. Tickell* (1819) 3 B. & Ald. 31.

basis of the principle enunciated in *Bannister v. Bannister*,[46] which was discussed earlier on. Consequently the secret trustee will hold the property which passes to him under the residuary gift or intestacy on constructive trust to perform the secret trust.

However, where the disclaiming fully secret trustee takes no other benefit under the will or intestacy of the testator, such a disclaimer will produce a conflict between the rule of probate that a disclaimer of a legacy by a person who takes beneficially on the face of the will causes the legacy to fail and the rule of the law of trusts that equity will not permit a trust to fail for want of a trustee. This conflict has been the subject of opposing dicta: in *Re Maddock*,[47] Cozens-Hardy L.J. suggested that a fully secret trust would fail in such a situation, while in *Blackwell v. Blackwell*[48] Lord Buckmaster said that the court would intervene to prevent such a result. There is something to be said for each view: in favour of the view of Cozens-Hardy L.J. is the proposition that probate principles should govern the vesting of the legacy on the other hand, in favour of the view of Lord Buckmaster is the fact that a court would undoubtedly be extremely reluctant to permit a trustee who had agreed to act as such to destroy a completely constituted trust by disclaiming his office. It remains to be seen which view is finally adopted.

### (3) Conclusion

The discussion of these three difficult areas shows that it is perfectly possible to decide which rule to apply in situations where there is a conflict between the rules of probate and the rules of the law of trusts. It is therefore suggested that this view, as laid down by Viscount Sumner in *Blackwell v. Blackwell*,[49] is both correct and workable. Indeed, nearly all the authorities decided since *Blackwell v. Blackwell* which have just been discussed[50] support the view that secret trusts operate wholly outside the will or intestacy in question. As has already been seen, this view alone is a satisfactory justification for the existence both of fully secret and of half secret trusts. It is therefore suggested that the theoretical justification for the existence of the doctrine of secret trusts is that such trusts operate wholly outside the will or intestacy in question. The enforceability of such trusts in equity is therefore no more dependant upon fraud than is any other type of trust. For these and other reasons, it will later be suggested that secret trusts are in fact express trusts.

### 2. *The Prerequisites of Secret Trusts*

In *Kasperbauer v. Griffith*,[51] the Court of Appeal held that a secret trust will come into existence if the following three requirements are satisfied: an intention by the testator to create a trust, satisfying the traditional requirement of three certainties which have already been considered,[52] namely certain

---

[46] [1948] W.N. 261. See *ante*, p. 113.
[47] [1902] 2 Ch. 220.
[48] [1929] A.C. 318.
[49] [1929] A.C. 318
[50] The only decision clearly contrary to this conclusion is *Re Gardner (No.2)*, the reasoning of which is on any view clearly incorrect.
[51] (1997) [2000] W.T.L.R. 333.
[52] See *ante*, pp. 46–73.

language in imperative form, certain subject matter and certain objects or beneficiaries; secondly, the communication of the trust to the intended trustee; and, thirdly, acceptance of the trust by the intended trustee, an acceptance which can take the form of silent acquiescence. Secret trusts must also satisfy the other requirements for the creation of a valid private trust, in that there must be a beneficiary capable of enforcing the trust and that that trust must be completely constituted. The extent to which the formal requirements discussed earlier in this chapter apply to secret trusts is more debateable.

## (A) The Three Certainties

### (1) Certainty of intention
This was which was in issue in *Kasperbauer v. Griffith*.[53] The testator said at a family meeting attended by his wife and his children by a former marriage that he intended to leave his house and his lump sum pension benefit to his wife on the basis that the lump sum would pay off or reduce the mortgage; the house was to be sold within a year of his death and the proceeds divided between the children; his remaining property was to go to his children. A secret trust was alleged to have arisen as a result of the testator saying, in response to a suggestion from the son that this should be written down, that his wife "knew what she had to do". The wife said nothing whatever during the meeting. The testator subsequently changed his mind and made a will in a slightly different form as a result of which the wife received both the house and the lump sum without having to discharge the mortgage out of it and the children received effectively nothing. The judge held that it was not the intention of the testator to impose any binding obligation on his wife and so there was no secret trust. The Court of Appeal upheld his decision, holding that the testator's words were equivocal and were at least consistent with the belief and intention that only a moral obligation was being imposed on the wife. They added that his subsequent change of mind was also consistent with this conclusion.

The question of whether there was certainty of intention to create a trust is quite distinct from the question of whether a fully secret or a half secret trust has been created. Where a secret trust has arisen as the result of an intestacy, the trust in question is necesarily fully secret.[54] Where a secret trust has arisen as the result of a will, whether the trust in question is fully secret or half secret is determined entirely on the basis of the contents of the will.

Where the property in question vests beneficially in the intended trustee under the provisions of the will in question so that the legatee takes the property as beneficial owner on the face of the will, the trust in question will be a fully secret trust. This requirement is satisfied despite the presence of phrases such as "in the hope that he will use the property for certain purposes which I have communicated to him" or "imposing no trust upon him". Provided that such expressions are, as is highly likely, held to be insufficiently

---

[53] (1997) [2000] W.T.L.R. 333.
[54] *Sellack v. Harris* (1708) 5 Vin. Abr. 512, pl.31; *Re Gardner* [1920] 2 Ch. 523, where the intestacy in question was partial (a wife had made a will which merely left her property to her husband for life; she died possessed only of personalty and he therefore also took the interest in remainder under the intestacy rules; both interests were held to be subject to a fully secret trust).

certain to create a trust on the face of the will, any secret trust which is found to exist will, despite their presence, be fully secret.[55]

Where, on the other hand, the property in question vests non-beneficially in the intended trustee under the provisions of the will in question so that the legatee takes the property as a trustee on the face of the will, the trust in question will be a half secret trust.[56] For this requirement to be satisfied, the testator must use an expression which imposes an obligation to hold the property upon trust.

## (2) Certainty of subject matter

It is not entirely clear that the normal requirements for certainty of subject matter apply to secret trusts. In *Ottaway v. Norman*,[57] a testator devised his bungalow to his housekeeper and bequeathed her £1,500 and half his residuary estate. Before the death of the testator, she had agreed to leave the bungalow and whatever money was left at her own death to the testator's son.

---

[55] An interesting point which has yet to arise in a reported case is whether expressions of this type, although insufficiently certain to create a trust, may nevertheless have an effect upon the rules governing communication of the terms of the trust to the secret trustee. Communication of a fully secret trust may normally be made either before or after the execution of the will provided that it takes place during the lifetime of the testator and may normally be either written or oral. If the will contains some expression such as "in the hope that he will use the property for certain purposes which I have communicated to him in writing", do those words, although imposing no trust upon the face of the will, nevertheless invalidate any communication which is subsequent to the execution of the will and/or any communication which, whether before or after the communication of the will, is oral? (This would undoubtedly be the case if the trust in question were half secret (see *Re Keen* [1937] Ch. 236 and *Re Spence* [1949] W.N. 237, both discussed in the text, *post* p. 127, although such cases are readily distinguishable because in a half secret trust such expressions on the face of the will are necessarily effective to impose a trust and therefore must inevitably limit the trust so imposed). It is clear that a court will admit evidence of a fully secret trust despite the fact that the will in question expressly states that no trust is imposed on the legatee (*Re Spencer* (1887) 57 L.T. 519, where the will contained the words "relying but not by way of trust upon their applying the said sum in or towards the object or objects communicated to them" and a fully secret trust was upheld). In the light of such authorities and the fact that it has been suggested that fully secret trusts operate wholly outside the will in question, it is suggested that in a fully secret trust the presence of such expressions on the face of the will should not have the effect of limiting the permissible ways of communication of the terms of the trust. Nevertheless it would be extremely interesting to see how the courts dealt with this question.

[56] It is necessary to distinguish half secret trusts from the cases where the probate doctrine of incorporation by reference arises. If the testator on the face of his will makes a disposition of property for the purposes set out in a named existing and identifiable document, then that document is deemed to be incorporated into the will and is admitted to probate as part of the will even though it does not itself comply with the formal requirements of the Wills Act (see for example *In the goods of Smart* [1902] P. 238). In fact, this doctrine has on occasions been argued to be the theoretical justification for the doctrine of half secret trusts (see Matthews [1979] Conveyancer 360). Adoption of this argument would indeed explain the otherwise inexplicable and much criticised rule that in a half secret trust communication of the terms of the trust must be made before or contemporaneously with the making of the will in question. However, apart from the fact that there seems to be no authority whatsoever in support of such an argument, its acceptance would involve either extending the probate doctrine of incorporation by reference to oral communications or alternatively requiring communication of the terms of a half secret trust to be in writing (in which case *Blackwell v. Blackwell* was wrongly decided). Neither of these possibilities seems to be consistent either with principle or with precedent and it is therefore suggested that this argument is not an acceptable justification for the doctrine of half secret trusts.

[57] [1972] Ch. 698.

However, in the event she left all her property away from the son, who brought an action against her executor for a declaration that her estate was subject to a trust in his favour. Brightman J. duly held that the bungalow was subject to a fully secret trust in favour of the son. However, he held that there was no valid secret trust of the residue of the money. His lordship was prepared to assume, without deciding, that it was possible to impose a secret trust under which the secret trustee could deal as he liked with the subject matter during his lifetime and then leave anything that was left to a third party. However, even on that assumption, he held that the terms of the alleged trust were far too unclear. The housekeeper had not been placed under any obligation to keep the money subject to the alleged trust separate from her own funds and, in any event, it was unclear precisely what was meant by money in this context. This decision has several novel features.

It is unusual to find a secret trust where the obligation imposed on the trustee is to enjoy the property left to him for his lifetime, either as in this case by occupying it or by receiving the income therefrom, and then to leave it on in his will to a third party. However, there is no particular reason for objection to be made to this,[58] at least where the property which is subject to this obligation is clearly ascertainable (as the bungalow in *Ottaway v. Norman* clearly was).

The other novel feature of *Ottaway v. Norman* is that Brightman J. was prepared to assume, without deciding, that a secret trust is also feasible where the secret trustee is entitled to dispose of the property at will and need only leave anything that is left to a third party. If this is indeed the case, then secret trusts will have become exempt from complying with the rules governing certainty of subject matter which were considered in the previous chapter.[59] The only trusts which at present appear to be exempt from the requirement of certainty of subject matter are the constructive trusts which arise as a result of mutual wills when the first party to die has left a will made in accordance with the agreement between him and the survivor. As will be seen in the chapter on Constructive Trusts,[60] such trusts clearly embrace both the property left to the survivor by the first party to die and whatever property of the survivor is subject to the agreement.[61] Nevertheless, the survivor is entitled, in the absence of any agreement to the contrary,[62] to dispose freely of the property during his lifetime;[63] only whatever remains at his death has to be left to the ultimate beneficiary of the mutual wills.[64] The nature of such trusts has been considered

---

[58] At the time of the decision, objection could have been taken by reason of the fact that such a secret trust evaded the provisions of the Settled Land Act 1925. However, no further settlements subject to this Act can now be created as a result of the Trusts of Land and Appointment of Trustees Act 1996.

[59] See *ante*, pp. 54–59.

[60] See *post*, pp. 430–438. See also *Constructive Trusts* (3rd ed., 1997), pp. 263–272.

[61] *Re Hagger* [1930] 2 Ch. 190.

[62] As in *Re Green* [1951] Ch. 148.

[63] *Birmingham v. Renfrew* (1937) 57 C.L.R. 666 at 689, *per* Dixon J. (High Court of Australia); *Re Goodchild (decd.)* [1996] 1 W.L.R. 694 at 700, *per* Carnwath J.

[64] *Birmingham v. Renfrew, ibid.*, does admittedly envisage the possibility of the ultimate beneficiary restraining a disposition by the survivor which is calculated to defeat the mutual wills. However, in practice this will only be feasible where the subject matter of the mutual wills is or includes a specific asset and not where, as is normally the case, it is the residuary estate of both parties.

judicially on various occasions[65] but none of the explanations given is really satisfactory; the only answer seems to be to regard such trusts as an entrenched anomaly. The type of secret trust envisaged by Brightman J. would move secret trusts into the murky area which has caused such conceptual difficulties in the case of mutual wills. It is much to be hoped that no such secret trusts will ever be upheld so that the doctrine of secret trusts can be spared this sort of conceptual confusion. That does not alter the fact that the judgment in *Ottaway v. Norman* clearly envisages this possibility.

### (3) Certainty of objects

There does not actually appear to have been any secret trust case in which this has been an issue. However, it has never been doubted that this requirement is the same in secret trusts as in all other trusts; it therefore depends on whether the trust in question is fixed or discretionary.[66] All the secret trusts which have had to be considered in reported cases have in fact been fixed trusts.

### (B) The Communication of the Trust to the Intended Trustee

The rules governing the communication of a secret trust to the intended trustee differ depending on whether the trust in question is fully secret or half secret.

### (1) Fully secret trusts

The rules governing communication of a fully secret trust emerge from *Moss v. Cooper*[67] and *Re Boyes*.[68] Before his death, the testator must ask the legatee to hold the legacy on trust for a third party. It does not matter whether the communication of the trust to the legatee takes place before or after the execution of the will provided that it takes place during the lifetime of the testator — communication by a letter received after the death of the testator is not sufficient since the legatee then has no opportunity to refuse to act. Nor does it matter that the legatee does not know the precise terms of the trust — a testator may hand the legatee a sealed envelope to be opened after his death[69] or reserve the details of the trusts for future communication provided such communication occurs before his death. These rules equally apply in the case of a secret trust arising as the result of an intestacy (where no will has been made because the intestate has asked his intestate successor to hold the property which he receives on trust for a third party).

Problems sometimes arise where the testator leaves a legacy to two or more persons jointly and fails to communicate with all of them. Special rules have been developed to deal with this situation. These rules are generally stated in the form laid down by Farwell J. in *Re Stead*.[70]

Where the property is left to the legatees as tenants in common, only those

---

[65] *Birmingham v. Renfrew* (1937) 57 C.L.R. 666 at 689, *per* Dixon J. (High Court of Australia); *Re Goodchild (decd.)* [1996] 1 W.L.R. 694 at 700, *per* Carnwath J. (not considered on appeal at [1997] 1 W.L.R. 1216).

[66] See *ante*, pp. 59–74.

[67] (1861) 1 J. & H. 352.

[68] (1884) 26 Ch. D. 531.

[69] *Re Boyes* (1884) 26 Ch.D. 531 (where the letters were not in fact handed to the intended trustee before the death of the testator and so the communication was held to be unsuccessful); *Re Keen* [1937] Ch. 236 (actually a case of a half secret trust).

[70] [1900] 1 Ch. 237 at 241.

legatees with whom the testator has communicated are bound — the others take their shares in the property beneficially.

Where, on the other hand, the property is left to the legatees as joint tenants, then, if the testator has communicated with any of the legatees prior to the execution of the will, all the legatees are bound by the trust; on the other hand, if the testator does not communicate with any of the legatees until after the execution of the will, only those with whom he does communicate are bound — the others take their shares beneficially.

The cases which are alleged to establish these peculiar rules have been examined in detail recently by Perrins.[71] He argues convincingly that this formulation of the rules was based on a misunderstanding of the earlier cases, from which a different rule in fact emerges. In his view, the only question is whether the gift to all the legatees was induced by the agreement to act of any of them; if it was, all are bound but, if it was not, then only those who have agreed to act are bound — the others take their shares beneficially. In his opinion, neither the type of co-ownership nor the time of communication is decisive in determining whether or not the necessary inducement has occurred, although it will obviously be more difficult to show inducement where the legatees are tenants in common and well-nigh impossible to show it where communication is subsequent to the execution of the will. It is not possible to fault Perrins' analysis of the authorities. However, it remains to be seen whether the courts will adopt his rule in preference to the more traditional ones.

## (2) Half secret trusts

Before or contemporaneously with the making of the will, the testator must ask the legatee to hold the legacy on trust for a third party. This rule was established by dicta of the members of the House of Lords in *Blackwell v. Blackwell*,[72] was reiterated, also by way of dicta, by the Court of Appeal in *Re Keen*,[73] and was applied, apparently without any contrary argument from counsel, in *Re Bateman's Will Trusts*.[74] It is difficult to see any justification for making this distinction between half secret trusts and fully secret trusts (where, as has already been seen, communication and acceptance may occur at any time prior to the death of the testator); if there was going to be a difference between the two, the rule should arguably be the other way round because there is much more chance of something going wrong where the secret trustee is absolutely beneficially entitled on the face of the will than where he is named as a trustee on its face. It is therefore suggested that the rule governing fully secret trusts should be applied also to half secret trusts so as to permit communication and acceptance at any time prior to the death of the testator. This has been done in Ireland[75] and in most of the common law jurisdictions of the United States of America.[76] However, at present the rule of English law is quite clear — communication and acceptance must occur before or contemporaneously with the making of the will.

---

[71] 88 L.Q.R. (1972) 225.
[72] [1929] A.C. 318.
[73] [1937] Ch. 236.
[74] [1970] 1 W.L.R. 1463.
[75] *Re Browne* [1944] Ir.R. 90 (High Court of the Republic of Ireland).
[76] See *Scott on Trusts* (4th ed., 1989 & subsequent cumulative supplements), para. 55.8.

However, the form of communication made must not be contrary to the express provisions of the will. In *Re Keen*,[77] the testator left £10,000 to two persons "to be held upon trust and disposed of by them among such person, persons or charities as may be notified by me to them or either of them during my lifetime". Before the execution of the will, he had handed a sealed envelope containing the name of the intended beneficiary to one of the legatees. The Court of Appeal held that it did not matter that the testator had given the legatee his instructions in a sealed envelope which was not to be opened until after his death. However, the Court held that the express provisions of the will contemplated only a future communication and so the communication before the date of the will was contrary to the express provisions of the will and consequently ineffective. (Of course, any communication made after the date of the will in accordance with its provisions would also have been ineffective since communication after the date of the will is impermissible in the case of a half secret trust). Similarly, in *Re Spence*,[78] the testator left property to four persons "to be dealt with in accordance with my wishes which I have made known to them". In fact the testator had communicated only with some of the legatees and this communication was also held to be contrary to the express provisions of the will and therefore ineffective.

Problems can arise where the testator (without having made an express provision as in *Re Spence*) leaves a legacy to two or more persons jointly and fails to communicate with all of them. Of course all the legatees will quite clearly be trustees and so the only question which arises is whether those with whom the testator failed to communicate hold their share of the property on trust for the communicated purpose or for the residuary beneficiary or intestate successor. There seems to be no reported half secret trust case in which this problem has actually arisen. Presumably the issue would be determined by application of the rules which apply in this situation to fully secret trusts — the nature of these rules is at present uncertain since, as has already been seen,[79] Perrins has recently challenged the established formulation of the rules.

### (C) Acceptance of the Trust by the Intended Trustee

The requirement that a secret trust must be accepted by the intended trustee is the same for fully secret and half secret trusts. The legatee must agree to hold the legacy on trust for a third party but he will be deemed to have done so unless he positively refuses—silence constitutes assent for this purpose.[80] This was confirmed by the Court of Appeal in *Kasperbauer v. Griffith*;[81] consequently, had there been certainty of intention in that case, the wife would have been bound despite the fact that she had said nothing. However, knowledge that the testator intended to create a secret trust is not enough in the absence of any

---

[77] [1937] Ch. 236.
[78] [1949] W.N. 237.
[79] See *ante*, p. 127.
[80] *Paine v. Hall* (1812) 18 Ves. 475.
[81] (1997) [2000] W.T.L.R. 333.

agreement on the part of the alleged secret trustees to honour its terms. This was held by the Court of Appeal of Singapore in *Hiranand v. Harilela*.[82]

### (D) Satisfaction of the Beneficiary Principle

It has already been seen that no private trust can exist without one or more beneficiaries for whose benefit the trust property is held[83] and that, as a general rule, that beneficiary must be capable of enforcing the trust.[84] Although the Court of Appeal did not specifically refer to these requirements in *Kasperbauer v. Griffith*,[85] it undoubtedly applies to both fully secret and half secret trusts.

It is obviously not possible for the sole trustee of a fully secret trust also to be its sole beneficiary. However, where there is a plurality of fully secret trustees, there is nothing to stop one of them being the sole beneficiary nor, where there is a plurality of beneficiaries, is there anything to stop a sole fully secret trustee from being included among them. This latter proposition was upheld expressly in *Irvine v. Sullivan*,[86] where a legatee who took absolutely on the face of the will was held to be entitled to take whatever surplus remained after observing the testator's instructions to pay various pecuniary legacies. It also follows from *Ottaway v. Norman*,[87] where the question was not raised explicitly but a fully secret trust in favour of the secret trustee for life, with remainder over to the testator's son, was held to be valid.

It is equally obvious that it is not possible for the sole trustee of a half secret trust also to be its sole beneficiary. In principle, it might be thought that, where there is a plurality of half secret trustees, there is nothing to stop one of them being the sole beneficiary and that, where there is a plurality of beneficiaries, there is nothing to stop a sole half secret trustee from being included among them. However, this does not appear to be the law. According to the decision of the Court of Appeal in *Re Rees' Will Trusts*,[88] a half secret trustee cannot be one of the secret beneficiaries since such a beneficial interest would be contrary to the express provision of the will that he takes the property as a trustee[89]. On the basis that, as has already been suggested, secret trusts operate outside the will, it is not easy to justify this harsh rule, which must undoubtedly lead to the frustration of the intentions of the testator. Considerable doubts as to its validity were expressed by Pennycuick J. in *Re Tyler*,[90] although his lordship conceded that he would have been bound by *Re Rees' Will Trusts* if the point had arisen for decision.

---

[82] (2000) 3 I.T.E.L.R. 297, 3 B.O.S. 483. It had to be assumed that the executors and beneficiary of what turned out to be the testator's last will had known that he had intended to make a later will in favour of someone else which was in fact invalid for lack of formality. A claim by a beneficiary of the later invalid will that its provisions nevertheless took effect as a fully secret trust on the basis of this knowledge was rejected.

[83] See *ante*, p. 18.

[84] See *ante*, pp. 74–94.

[85] (1997) [2000] W.T.L.R. 333.

[86] (1869) L.R. 8 Eq. 673.

[87] [1972] Ch. 698.

[88] [1950] Ch. 204.

[89] This rule was also stated by way of dicta in *Irvine v. Sullivan* (1869) L.R. 8 Eq. 673, which actually concerned a fully secret trust.

[90] [1967] 1 W.L.R. 1269 at 1278.

## (E) Complete Constitution of the Secret Trust

Nor did the Court of Appeal specifically refer in *Kasperbauer v. Griffith*[91] to the requirement that a secret trust become completely constituted by the subject matter of the secret trust being vested in the secret trustee under the will or intestacy of the deceased. However, this requirement clearly applies to both fully secret and half secret trusts. If it were not complied with, as would be the case if the will were not executed in accordance with section 9 of the Wills Act and so was void, the secret trust, despite complying with the three requirements actually listed in *Kasperbauer v. Griffith*,[92] would have no subject matter and so would be completely ineffective. It has already been seen[93] that a secret trust may also not become completely constituted because the secret trustee or secret beneficiary has witnessed the will or has died before the testator, or because the secret trustee disclaims his interest under the will.

## (F) Formalities

It may also be necessary for the communication and acceptance of a secret trust to comply with the formal requirements of section 53(1) of the Law of Property Act 1925. This would mean that a secret trust of land would, under section 53(1)(b), have to be "manifested and proved by some writing signed by some person who is able to declare such trust", while a secret trust of a subsisting equitable interest would, under section 53(1)(c), have to be "in writing signed by the person disposing of the same, or by his agent thereunto lawfully authorised in writing". This question did not arise in *Kasperbauer v. Griffith*[94] but would have done had the necessary intention been held to exist. Whether section 53(1) has to be complied with depends on whether secret trusts are or are not express trusts (if they are not and are instead either implied, or resulting or constructive trusts, they would be exempt from the formal requirements of section 53(1) by virtue of section 53(2)).

The authorities are inconclusive. In *Re Baillie*,[95] a half secret trust of land was held to be ineffective because of the absence of the necessary writing. That decision suggests that half secret trusts, at least, are express trusts. On the other hand, fully secret trusts of land have been upheld in the absence of the necessary writing—most recently in *Ottaway v. Norman*,[96] although neither in this nor in any of the other reported cases has the absence of this writing actually been raised. At first sight, this might be thought to suggest, if only by virtue of the silence of the courts, that fully secret trusts are not express trusts. However, any such conclusion would in fact be unsound. The absence of evidentiary writing must be specifically pleaded; if it is not so pleaded, then

---

[91] (1997) [2000] W.T.L.R. 333.
[92] (1997) [2000] W.T.L.R. 333.
[93] See *ante*, pp. 119–122.
[94] (1997) [2000] W.T.L.R. 333.
[95] (1886) 2 T.L.R. 660 (this was of course a decision on the pre-existing provision, Statute of Frauds 1677, s.7).
[96] [1972] Ch. 698.

the absence of the writing will not be a bar to the success of the action.[97] Consequently, the fact that fully secret trusts have been upheld in the absence of the evidentiary writing required by section 53(1)(b) is totally irrelevant to the question of whether such writing is actually necessary because in none of the authorities was the absence of the necessary writing pleaded. And, although in *Gold v. Hill*[98] section 53(1)(c) was stated to be inapplicable to a secret trust of rights arising under a pension trust, that is not in fact relevant either; such rights are not within section 53(1) anyway.[99]

What then is the nature of secret trusts? Most commentators, on the strength of *Re Baillie* and the fact that half secret trusts, unlike fully secret trusts, appear on the face of the will, seem to accept that half secret trusts are express trusts. However, the general view seems to be that no fully secret trust can ever fail for lack of writing, simply because of the maxim that a statute cannot be used as an instrument of fraud; for this reason, many commentators have classified fully secret trusts as constructive trusts.[1] Indeed this classification was assumed by Nourse J. by way of dictum in *Re Cleaver*,[2] a case which actually concerned mutual wills, and was upheld by the Court of Appeal in *Kasperbauer v. Griffith*;[3] however, in neither case was there any argument to the contrary, nor did the issue arise, nor was there any reference to half secret trusts.

Apart from the fact that it seems contrary to principle to distinguish in this way between fully secret and half secret trusts,[4] the proposition that no fully secret trust can ever fail for lack of writing is in fact unsound. Obviously no fully secret trustee would be allowed to profit by raising the absence of the necessary writing as the basis of a claim to take the property beneficially. The clearly unconscionable conduct involved in any attempt to do this would inevitably lead to the imposition of a constructive trust on a quite different ground, namely the principle enunciated in *Bannister v. Bannister*.[5] But there remains the possibility that a fully secret trustee who admits that he is holding the property which he has received under the will or intestacy in question but cannot point to the writing required by section 53(1) will find himself confronted by opposing claims from the beneficiaries of the secret trust and the testator's residuary beneficiary or his statutory next-of-kin. In this situation,

---

[97] *North v. Loomes* [1919] 1 Ch. 378 (actually a decision on Statute of Frauds 1677, s.4 (subsequently Law of Property Act 1925, s.40, now repealed by Law of Property (Miscellaneous Provisions) Act 1989, s.2); however s.53(1)(b), like s.40 and Statute of Frauds 1677, s.4, requires only evidentiary writing and is generally thought to be governed by the same principles). A specific decision on the predecessor of s.53(1)(b), Statute of Frauds 1677, s.7, where the point presently under discussion did not arise, is *Foster v. Hale* (1798) 3 Ves.Jun. 696, which concerned the question of what type of writing would satisfy the provision.

[98] [1999] 1 F.L.R. 54.

[99] *Re Danish Bacon Company Staff Pension Fund* [1971] 1 W.L.R. 248 at 256; see *ante*, p. 105.

[1] See, for example, the view of Hayton in Hayton & Marshall, *Commentary and Cases on the Law of Trusts and Equitable Remedies* (11th ed., 2001) p. 121, repeated in the current edition of *Underhill and Hayton, Law of Trusts and Trustees* (16th ed., 2003), p. 257, where he states that "secret trusts should be categorised as constructive trusts".

[2] [1981] 1 W.L.R. 939 at 947.

[3] (1997) [2000] W.T.L.R. 333.

[4] This view was adopted by Hayton in Hayton and Marshall: *Cases and Commentary on the Law of Trusts* (9th ed.), p. 105, n. 31: "since the court is recognising and enforcing a testator's express trust why not call a spade a spade?" but this is no longer his view (see *ante*, fn. 1). A more ambivalent view is expressed by Martin in Hanbury & Martin: *Modern Equity* (16th ed.), pp. 168–169.

[5] [1948] 2 All E.R. 133, [1948] W.N. 261; discussed *ante*, pp. 113–114.

the maxim that a statute cannot be used as an instrument of fraud will be of no assistance whatever and the result will be determined by whether fully secret trusts are constructive trusts, in which case the property will go to the beneficiaries of the secret trust, or express trusts, in which case because of the absence of the necessary writing it will go to his residuary beneficiary or the statutory next-of-kin.

It is therefore necessary to decide as a matter of principle whether secret trusts are express trusts or constructive trusts. In the case of both fully secret and half secret trusts the testator clearly intends to create a relationship of trustee and beneficiary. This suggests that, as a matter of definition, both fully secret and half secret trusts should be classified as express trusts. This view is strengthened if, as has already been suggested, the theoretical justification for the existence of the doctrine of secret trusts is not fraud but the fact that such trusts operate wholly outside the will or intestacy in question. It is accordingly suggested that all secret trusts are express trusts and so must comply with section 53(1) of the Law of Property Act 1925. However, it has to be admitted that there is as yet no general agreement on this question, which must therefore await definitive resolution by the courts.

### (3) The Effect of the Creation of a Secret Trust

**(A) Fully Secret Trusts**
Where all the requirements for the creation of a fully secret trust are satisfied, the beneficiary will be able to enforce that trust in the same way as any other trust, not only against the fully secret trustee but also against any successor in title to the fully secret trustee who has not taken the property in question free of the equitable interest of the beneficiary. If no property vests beneficially in the intended trustee, the fully secret trust will simply fail for want of subject matter. If property vests under the will or intestacy in question but there is no trust because, for example, of a lack of certainty of intention or because the same person is sole trustee and sole beneficiary, the person in whom the property vests will take it absolutely under the will. However, where there has been a failure of communication, the situation is less straightforward. If the intended trustee does not hear of the existence of the secret trust until after the death of the testator, he will take the property beneficially even though it can be proved that the testator intended that a secret trust should be imposed upon him. This was held in *Wallgrave v. Tebbs*.[6] However, if the legatee agrees during the lifetime of the testator to hold the property on trust but is not informed of the beneficial interests before the death of the testator, then he will hold the property on trust for whoever is entitled to the testator's residuary estate or for his statutory next-of-kin. This was held in *Re Boyes*.[7] Although the question has never arisen, it is suggested that this would be the case even if the legatee were himself entitled to the residuary estate or were the intestate successor in question.

The effect of attestation by, or the predecease of, the beneficiary of a fully secret trustee was considered in an earlier part of this section.[8] If, as was

---

[6] (1855) 2 K. & J. 313.
[7] (1884) 26 Ch.D. 531.
[8] See *ante*, pp. 119–122.

suggested there, the theoretical justification for the existence of the doctrine of secret trusts is that such trusts operate wholly outside the will in question, then the effect of the occurrence of either of these events will be governed by the rules of the law of trusts. Attestation of the will by the beneficiary will therefore be irrelevant but the effect of the predecease of the beneficiary will depend on what the relevant rule of the law of trusts actually is. *Re Gardner (No.2)*[9] decided that in such circumstances the beneficial interest would devolve according to the beneficiary's will or intestacy; this decision undoubtedly constitutes the present law but has been universally condemned by the commentators.

If, on the other hand, the theoretical justification for the existence of secret trusts is fraud, any secret trust which can be proved to have been the subject of the necessary communication and acceptance will presumably be regarded as taking effect as part of the will in question; if this is indeed the case, the probate rules will presumably apply rather than the rules of the law of trusts. In this event, attestation of the will by the secret beneficiary will therefore prevent him from taking beneficially under the will while the predecease of the secret beneficiary will unquestionably bring the doctrine of lapse into play; in both cases, the fully secret trustee will therefore presumably hold whatever property he receives on trust for whoever is entitled to the testator's residuary estate or for his statutory next-of-kin.

### (B) Half Secret Trusts

Where all the requirements for the creation of a half secret trust are satisfied, the beneficiary will be able to enforce that trust in the same way as any other trust, not only against the half secret trustee but also against any successor in title to the fully secret trustee who has not taken the property in question free of the equitable interest of the beneficiary. However, if the testator asks the intended trustee to hold a particular sum on trust and in fact leaves him a larger sum, only the sum in respect of which the trustee undertook to act will be subject to the secret trust; the residue will be held by him on trust for whoever is entitled to the testator's residuary estate or for his statutory next-of-kin. This was held in *Re Cooper*.[10] More generally, if no property vests beneficially in the intended trustee under the will, the half secret trust will simply fail for want of subject matter. If the trust fails for any other reason, the intended trustee will not take the property beneficially but will hold it on trust for whoever is entitled to the testator's residue or for his statutory next-of-kin. This was held in *Re Pugh's Will Trusts*.[11] It is suggested that the half secret trustee should be able to take the property beneficially if he is himself entitled to the residuary estate or is the intestate successor in question, although this may be contrary to the spirit, if not the letter, of the already criticised decision of the Court of Appeal in *Re Rees' Will Trusts*.[12]

The effect of attestation by, predecease of, and disclaimer by a half secret trustee were considered in a previous part of this section.[13] If, as was suggested there, the theoretical justification for the existence of the doctrine of secret

---

[9] [1923] 2 Ch. 230.
[10] [1939] Ch. 580.
[11] [1967] 1 W.L.R. 1262.
[12] [1950] Ch. 204.
[13] See *ante*, pp. 119–122.

trusts is that such trusts operate wholly outside the will in question, then the effect of the occurrence of any one of these three events will be governed by the rules of probate and will therefore be irrelevant. If, on the other hand, the theoretical justification for the existence of secret trusts is fraud, any secret trust which can be proved to have been the subject of the necessary communication and acceptance will presumably be regarded as taking effect as part of the will in question; if this is indeed the case, the probate rules will presumably still apply with exactly the same results.

CHAPTER 5

# THE CONSTITUTION OF A TRUST

## I. INTRODUCTION

AN express trust is completely constituted either by an effective transfer of the trust property to trustees or by an effective declaration of trust. The implications of this principle were clearly brought out by Turner L.J. in his classic judgment in *Milroy v. Lord*[1] when he said:

"In order to render a voluntary settlement valid and effectual, the settlor must have done everything which according to the nature of the property comprised in the settlement was necessary to be done in order to render the settlement binding upon him. He may, of course, do this by actually transferring the property to the persons for whom he intends to provide and the provision will then be effectual and it will be equally effectual if he transfers the property to a trustee for the purposes of the settlement, or declares that he himself holds it on trust for those purposes and if the property is personal, the trust may, as I apprehend, be declared either in writing or parol but, in order to render the settlement binding, one or other of these modes must, as I understand the law of this court, be resorted to, for there is no equity in this court to perfect an imperfect gift."

The latter part of this passage emphasises the crucial difference between a completely constituted trust and an incompletely constituted trust. Only when a trust is completely constituted is it binding on the settlor; in other words, only in such circumstances is a trust enforceable by the beneficiaries, whose equitable proprietary interest in the trust property will then be binding not only upon the settlor but also against any third party into whose hands the trust property may come other than a bona fide purchaser of a legal interest therein for value without notice (or the statutory equivalent).

Trusts which are completely constituted are divided into executed and executory trusts; an executed trust arises when the settlor has defined in the trust instrument precisely what interests are to be taken by the beneficiaries, whereas an executory trust arises where the instrument or declaration requires the subsequent execution of a further instrument whose terms it does not itself define precisely.

When, on the other hand, a trust has not been completely constituted, there is in effect no trust enforceable by the beneficiaries, who therefore have no

---

[1] (1862) 4 De G.F. & J. 264 at 274.

equitable proprietary interest whatever. Their position is often illustrated by
reference to equitable maxims, a recourse which is at best unhelpful and at
worst potentially confusing. The straightforward proposition that, if the settlor
has failed completely to constitute the trust, equity will not do so for him is
often expressed by reference to the equitable maxim that "equity will not
perfect an imperfect gift" (however, this maxim is somewhat imprecise
because of the number of exceptions to the basic rule which equity has permitted). In such circumstances, the incompletely constituted trust can only be
enforced under the law of contract; the rights of the beneficiaries depend on
the existence of a binding contract enforceable either by them or on their
behalf. In the absence of such a contract, they have no rights whatsoever and
are therefore often described as volunteers. This is in accordance with another
equitable maxim that "equity will not assist a volunteer"; this maxim is not
merely imprecise but positively confusing because of the failure of equity
clearly to define precisely who is regarded as a volunteer for this purpose.

This chapter therefore involves the consideration of three questions: first,
the circumstances in which a trust will be held to be completely constituted;
secondly, the distinction between executed and executory trusts; and, thirdly,
the circumstances in which, where a trust is incompletely constituted, the
beneficiaries will have a contractual remedy.

## II. When Will a Trust be Completely Constituted?

### 1. By Transfer of the Trust Property To Trustees

**(A) Legal Interests**
If the subject matter of the proposed trust is a legal estate or interest, the
transfer of the trust property must be effective to vest that estate in the trustees. Consequently the basic rule, to which there are some exceptions,[2] is that
the settlor must comply with all the formalities required for a complete
transfer of the property in order to give the trustees full legal title thereto.
Exactly the same rule applies where the transfer is made with the intention of
making a gift; the donor must comply with all the formalities required for a
complete transfer of the property in order to give the donee may have full
legal title thereto.

So if the subject matter of the trust or gift is land, a deed is necessary[3]
followed, in the case of registered land, by registration of the transfer on the
Land Register[4]; if it is a copyright, then writing is necessary[5]; if it is a bill of
exchange or other negotiable instrument, then whether it is payable to the
bearer or to the holder, delivery and the appropriate form of indorsement are
necessary[6]; if it is shares in a company other than bearer shares,[7] the correct
form of transfer is necessary followed by registration of the transfer in the

---

[2] See *post*, pp. 147–160.
[3] Law of Property Act 1925, s.52.
[4] Land Registration Act 2002, ss. 29, 30.
[5] Copyright Act 1956, s.5(2).
[6] See *Antrobus v. Smith* (1806) 12 Ves. 39; *Jones v. Lock* (1865) 1 Ch. App. 25.
[7] The rights attached to bearer shares vest in whoever has physical possession of the share
certificates.

Share Register of the company in question;[8] if it is the benefit of a right of action, writing is necessary, followed by notice in writing to the other party;[9] and, finally, if it is a chattel, either a deed of gift[10] or an intention to give together with a delivery of possession is necessary, although any such personal delivery must be effectual.[11]

The requirement that the full legal title be transferred to the trustees is illustrated by a number of decisions involving the transfer of shares. In *Milroy v. Lord*[12] itself, the intending settlor had covenanted to transfer bank shares to the defendant on trust for the plaintiff. The defendant already had a general power to transfer the shares into his own name at any time but neither he nor the settlor actually did so prior to the settlor's death, which had the effect of revoking the power of attorney. Since neither the settlor nor the defendant was any longer in a position to make the necessary transfer, the shares therefore remained the settlor's property; consequently, they formed part of his residuary estate and could not successfully be claimed by the plaintiff. Similarly, in *Re Fry*,[13] the intending settlor, who was domiciled in the United States of America, executed transfers of shares in a limited company, partly by way of gift to his son and partly to a trust. The company was unable to register the transfers because the consent of the Treasury had not been obtained under the Defence Regulations then operative. The forms required for obtaining this consent were sent to the settlor, who signed and returned them but died before the consent was given. Romer J. held that the trust had not been completely constituted prior to the settlor's death; consequently the shares did not pass either to the son or to the trust but, as in *Milroy v. Lord*, formed part of the settlor's residuary estate. In order to perfect the transaction it would apparently have been necessary for the donor to have effected confirmatory transfers after the consent had been given.[14]

These two decisions establish that, as long as something remains to be done by a settlor in order to render a voluntary transfer effective, that transfer will remain abortive.[15] However, some subsequent decisions have established a number of glosses on that basic rule, at least some of which are extremely questionable. These glosses apparently enable an ineffective transfer nevertheless to take effect in equity and to bring about the complete constitution of a

---

[8] *Milroy v. Lord* (1862) 4 De G.F. & J. 264, see also *post*, p. 138. The relevant Act is the Stock Transfer Act 1963, s.1.

[9] Law of Property Act 1925, s.136.

[10] *Jaffa v. Taylor Gallery* (1990) *The Times*, March 21, 1990, where a trust of a painting was held to have been completely constituted without physical delivery to the trustees, one of whom was abroad, on the grounds that the formal declaration of trust contained in the deed transferred title to the painting to the trustees.

[11] See *Re Cole* [1964] Ch. 175, which concerned an alleged delivery of furniture by a husband to his wife when the two were living together in a common establishment. The Court of Appeal held that this did not unequivocally establish either a change in possession or a delivery of the furniture; accordingly, there was no effected or perfected gift to her, the court rejecting the contention that a perfect gift of chattels can be constituted simply by showing them to the donee and speaking the appropriate words of gift.

[12] (1862) 4 De G.F. & J. 264. The classic statement of the law made by Turner L.J. at 274 is set out: *ante*, p. 135 and *post*, p. 141.

[13] [1946] Ch. 312.

[14] *ibid*. at 316.

[15] See also *Letts v. I.R.C.* [1951] 1 W.L.R. 201, which concerned a direction by a father to a company to allot shares direct to his children.

trust in that way. These glosses will be considered in detail later in this section.[16]

Further, it is in any event questionable how far it is possible to reconcile the authorities already discussed with the decision in *Re Vandervell's Trusts (No.2)*,[17] whose facts have already been considered. Lord Denning M.R., as an alternative ground for his decision that the shares in the products company were held on trust for the children's settlement, was of the opinion[18] that Vandervell had made a perfect gift to the trust company of the dividends on the shares "so far as they were handed over or treated by him as belonging to the trust company for the benefit of the children". In reaching this conclusion, his Lordship purported to follow *Milroy v. Lord* itself.

It has already been seen that, in *Milroy v. Lord*, an attempt to create a trust of bank shares was held to have been ineffective because legal title to the shares had never been vested in the intended trustee and, as a result, the shares finished up in the hands of the settlor's residuary legatees. However, during the settlor's lifetime, the dividends payable on the shares had been paid by the bank to the intended trustee by virtue of the power of attorney which he held; he had paid these dividends on to the beneficiary who had in turn used them to purchase shares in a quite different company. It was held that the settlor should be treated as having made a perfect gift of the dividends to the beneficiary; the settlor's residuary legatees therefore had no claim to the shares in the other company which had been purchased with the dividends.

It is not easy to see how this decision can justify the conclusion reached by Lord Denning M.R. in *Re Vandervell's Trusts (No.2)*. The settlor in *Milroy v. Lord* had given the intended trustee a power of attorney to collect the dividends and so must inevitably have intended them to be held for the beneficiary, whereas Vandervell had not even been aware that he had still retained an equitable interest in the option relating to the shares of his products company at the time when he had made the supposedly perfect gift of the dividends to the trust company. The two decisions thus seem readily distinguishable.

## (B) Equitable Interests

The decisions already discussed are illustrations of the important principle that, if the subject matter of a trust or a gift is a legal interest, the transferor must vest the legal title to the property in the trustee or donee. The same principle applies to the transfer of an equitable interest. It is not, of course, necessary for the transferor to procure a conveyance of the legal interest (which will be held by the trustees); all that is necessary is that he should make a perfect assignment of his interest, which in this case will be necessarily and universally required to be in writing by virtue of section 53(1)(c) of the Law of Property Act 1925.[19] This assignment will, where a trust is being constituted, be followed by a direction to the trustees to hold it for the future upon trust for

---

[16] See *post*, pp. 141–147.
[17] [1974] Ch. 269. See *ante*, pp. 105–109.
[18] *ibid.* at 321.
[19] See *Kekewich v. Manning* (1851) De G.M. & G. 176 (assignment of an equitable reversionary interest in shares); *Gilbert v. Overton* (1864) 2 H. & M. 110 (assignment of an agreement for lease); and *ante*, pp. 97–98.

the assignee.[20] This is as much as the transferor of an equitable interest is able to do.

However, the fact that this at least must be done is shown by the decision of the Court of Appeal in *Re McArdle*.[21] In this case, some brothers and sisters were entitled under the will of their father to a house after the death of their mother, who lived in the house with one of the brothers and his wife. After the wife had effected various improvements to the house, all the brothers and sisters signed a document addressed to her, stating that "in consideration of your carrying out certain alterations to the property, we hereby agree that the executors shall repay to you from the estate when distributed the sum of £488" in settlement of the amount spent on improvements. The court held, in effect, that this document was neither one thing nor the other. If it was intended to create a contract, the contract lacked consideration since the only possible consideration was past. If, on the other hand, it was an attempted gift, that gift was imperfect because the donors had not done what was necessary to make the gift complete; it was still necessary for them to authorise the executors to make the necessary payment and, unless and until they did so, the gift remained ineffectual.

## 2. By Declaration of Trust

By far the most common method of completely constituting a trust is for the settlor to transfer the trust property to trustees in the manner just described. However, it is equally effectual for a settlor to make a declaration of trust that he is from the moment of the declaration a trustee of the property in question for the intended beneficiaries. Any words which clearly express the intention to create a present and irrevocable trust will give rise to the creation of a completely constituted trust — it is not necessary for an effective declaration of trust that the settlor should say in terms "I hereby declare myself to be a trustee".

That does not alter the fact that the necessary intention must be satisfactorily shown. In *Jones v. Lock*,[22] a father put a cheque, presumably payable to himself, into the hands of his infant son, saying: "Look you here, I give this to baby; it is for himself". He then took back the cheque and put it away but subsequently reiterated his intention of giving the amount of the cheque to his son. Shortly afterwards he died and the cheque was found among his effects. Lord Cranworth L.C. held that there was neither an effective transfer by way of gift nor a valid declaration of trust. It was quite impossible to regard the somewhat theatrical exercise enacted by the father as a delivery of the moneys represented by the cheque. To effect a perfect transfer, he should have paid the

---

[20] See *Grey v. I.R.C.* [1960] A.C. 1 (direction to trustees to hold on trust may take effect as an assignment), discussed *ante*, p. 103.
[21] [1951] Ch. 669.
[22] (1865) 1 Ch. App. 25.

cheque, presumably after the necessary endorsement,[23] into a bank account opened either in the name of his son or in the name of trustees on behalf of his son. Nor had he made a valid declaration of trust, since no inference that he had made himself a trustee could be deduced from his words and actions.

In all such cases, it is a question of construction whether the words used, taking into account the surrounding circumstances, amount to a clear declaration of trust. So in *Paul v. Constance*,[24] acknowledged[25] to be a "borderline case", the words used by the deceased were "[T]he money is as much yours as mine", words which he had often repeated to the plaintiff, a woman with whom he had lived for a number of years. He was referring to money in a bank account which had been opened to hold a sum paid to him by way of compensation for an industrial injury; however, the account also contained their joint bingo winnings and the only withdrawal ever made had been used for their joint benefit. The Court of Appeal held, distinguishing *Jones v. Lock*, that the words, taken with the use which had been made of the account during the deceased's lifetime, amounted to a present irrevocable declaration that the plaintiff was entitled to half the balance of the account.[26]

Thus far the law appears reasonably clear. However, the requirements established by the authorities discussed so far seem to have been relaxed materially in *Re Vandervell's Trusts (No.2)*.[27] The Court of Appeal managed to find an effective declaration of trust of the shares in question by the trust company in favour of a settlement for the benefit of Vandervell's children from the following facts: first, that the trust company had used £5,000 from the children's settlement for the purposes of exercising an option to re-purchase the shares; secondly, that thereafter all the dividends received by the trust company had been paid into the bank accounts of the children's settlement and subsequently treated as part of the funds of that settlement; and, thirdly, that the solicitors for the trustee company had written to the Inland Revenue stating that the shares would be held on the trusts of the settlement. None of these facts, least of all the third, seems to indicate a present irrevocable declaration of trust;[28] further, as Stephenson L.J. expressly indicated, it is not easy to see how a limited company such as the trust company could have declared a trust by parol or conduct or, for that matter, could have declared a trust at all without a resolution of its board of directors[29] (this need to find an effectual declaration of trust only of course arose because the Court of Appeal had resolved the question of how Vandervell could have disposed of the equitable interest which the House of Lords had held still to be vested in him[30]

---

[23] A cheque can, as a negotiable instrument, be endorsed by the holder (the person in whose favour it is drawn) either to bearer (by the holder signing the cheque on the back) or in favour of a specified person X (by the holder writing on the back of the cheque "Pay X" and signing it). However, modern personal cheques tend to bear the words "ACCOUNT PAYEE" which means that they are payable only to the original holder. Whether or not cheques have to be paid into a bank account depends on whether or not they are crossed (modern personal cheques invariably are).

[24] [1977] 1 W.L.R. 527.

[25] *ibid.* at 532, *per* Scarman L.J.

[26] See also T. *Choithram International S.A. v. Pagarani* [2001] 1 W.L.R. 1, discussed *post*, p. 142.

[27] [1974] Ch. 269. The facts are stated in detail *ante*, pp 105–109.

[28] The question was not argued before Megarry J. at first instance.

[29] *ibid.* at 323.

[30] In *Vandervell v. I.R.C.* [1967] 2 A.C. 291. See *ante*, pp. 105–107.

without using the writing required by section 53(1)(c) of the Law of Property Act 1925 in favour of the trust company in the equally questionable way which has already been considered.[31]) It is not considered that the courts are likely often to be so generous to settlors.

Finally, it should be recalled that, if the subject matter of a declaration of trust is land, the requirements of section 53(1) of the Law of Property Act 1925 will need to be complied with. This certainly requires evidentiary writing in accordance with section 53(1)(b), in default of which the trust in question will be valid but unenforceable. Further, if there is indeed an overlap between section 53(1)(b) and section 53(1)(a), the declaration of trust will actually have to be made in writing in accordance with the latter provision, in default of which the trust in question will be wholly void.[32]

### 3. By an Ineffective Transfer Taking Effect in Equity

**(A) The General Rule**
Where it is clear that the settlor intended to create a trust by transfer but has used an ineffectual method of transfer, the general rule is that this ineffectual transfer will not be interpreted as taking effect in equity as an effectual declaration of trust. In *Milroy v. Lord*[33] itself, Turner L.J., immediately after the passage from his judgment which has already been cited,[34] continued:[35]

> "The cases, I think, go further to this extent: that if the settlement is intended to be effectuated by one of the modes to which I have referred, the court will not give effect to it by applying another of these modes. If it is intended to take effect by transfer, the court will not hold the intended transfer to operate as a declaration of trust, for then every imperfect instrument would be made effectual by being converted into a perfect trust."

This principle was applied in *Richards v. Delbridge*.[36] The deceased, the owner of certain leasehold premises, indorsed and signed on the lease the following memorandum: "This deed and all thereto I give to [the intended transferee] from this time forth, with all the stock-in-trade". The Court of Appeal held that there was no perfected transfer, since the indorsement had not been made with the formalities necessary for a deed and so was ineffective to transfer the leasehold interest. Nor, in the circumstances, could the indorsement take effect as a declaration of trust.

The existence of this principle does not, however, mean that a settlor who intends to create a trust by transfer cannot expressly declare himself to be trustee of the subject matter pending that transfer. If he does so, he will himself be the trustee of a completely constituted trust of the subject matter unless and

---

[31] See *ante*, p. 107.
[32] See *ante*, pp. 98–101.
[33] (1862) 4 De G.F. & J. 264.
[34] See *ante*, p. 135.
[35] (1862) 4 De G.F. & J. 264 at 275.
[36] (1874) L.R. 18 Eq. 11.

until he transfers that property to the intended trustees. Thus in *Re Ralli's Will Trusts*,[37] a settlor entered into a covenant to transfer any existing or after-acquired property to the trustees of her marriage settlement; the deed of settlement stated that it was "the intention" of the parties that all such property "shall become subject in equity to the settlement". The settlor failed to transfer to the trustees certain property caught by the covenant which, although existing during the settlor's lifetime, did not vest in possession in her until after her death. Buckley J. held that, although no completely constituted trust of the property had arisen by transfer, the settlor had declared herself to be a trustee of any such property pending transfer; consequently this completely constituted trust arising by declaration of trust could be enforced by the beneficiaries of the marriage settlement against the settlor's personal representative.

**(B) Where a Settlor who is One of a Number of Trustees Declares a Trust**

In *T. Choithram International S.A. v. Pagarani*,[38] the settlor, who knew that he was dying of cancer, wished to create a philanthropic foundation before his death. To this end, one month before his death, he arranged a ceremony at his bedside in which he executed the requisite deed of trust, of which he and nine other persons, three of whom were present, were to be the trustees, and purported orally to make an immediate absolute gift to the foundation of his shareholdings and credit balances in four British Virgin Islands' companies. Although the minutes of a meeting of each of these companies held later that day recorded that the trustees of the foundation were now the holders of the assets in question, the settlor did not vest those assets in the other trustees prior to his death and it was therefore contended that the trust was incompletely constituted (in which case the assets would have devolved under the settlor's intestacy).

The Privy Council,[39] whose opinion was delivered by Lord Browne-Wilkinson, held that what the settlor had done satisfied the criteria for the creation of a trust by declaration (this decision is consistent with the authorities on creating trusts by declaration which have already been considered.[40]) However, on the face of things the settlor was instead purporting to create a trust of which he was one of a number of trustees by transfer. The Board held that there was in principle no distinction between a settlor declaring himself to be sole trustee and one of a number of trustees.[41] In both cases it would be equally unconconscionable for him subsequently to be able to resile from his declaration of trust (this statement, although unobjectionable in its context) has since unjustifiably been interpreted much more broadly.[42]) Consequently, the trust was completely constituted.

It was clearly crucial to this decision that the execution of the deed of trust and the oral gift formed part of one composite transaction; any special factors, such as any intention of the settlor, whether expressed or implied from the

---

[37] [1964] Ch. 288. See also *Middleton v. Pollock* (1876) 2 Ch.D. 194, where effective declarations of trust were made.

[38] [2001] 1 W.L.R. 1. See Halliwell [2003] Conveyancer 192.

[39] On appeal from the Court of Appeal of the British Virgin Islands.

[40] See *ante*, pp. 139–141.

[41] [2001] 1 W.L.R. 1 at 12.

[42] See *Pennington v. Waine* [2002] 1 W.L.R. 2075; *post*, p. 145.

circumstances, that no trust should arise until the moment of transfer of the subject matter to the other trustees, would have led to a different result. It must so be remembered that, if the subject matter had been land, the requirements of the equivalent of section 53(1) of the Law of Property Act 1925 would have had to be complied with. Since the members of the Privy Council can hardly be blamed for the wholly objectionable manner in which their decision has since been extended,[43] that decision is therefore supportable. This was anyway not a case in which an ineffectual transfer has been held to take effect as an effectual declaration of trust because it was held that there had been a declaration of trust by the settlor. However, it is obviously unlikely that similar circumstances will arise very often.

### (C) Where a Settlor has Done All in his Power to Transfer the Property

Where a settlor has done everything within his power in order to render a transfer effectual but something has yet to be done by a third party, the transfer will be immediately valid in equity; consequently, although it will remain ineffective to pass the legal title unless and until the third party does whatever remains to be done by him, the transferor will in the meantime hold the subject matter of the transfer on the trusts of the settlement.[44] This was established by the decision of the Court of Appeal in *Re Rose*[45] in which an earlier unconnected first instance decision, coincidentally also bearing the name *Re Rose*,[46] was applied and followed. Not surprisingly, the rule so established is known as the Rule in *Re Rose*.

In the first case named *Re Rose*,[47] a testator had made a specific bequest of shares but subsequently before his death executed a share transfer in respect of the same shares in favour of the legatee. Because these were shares in a private company, its directors had the right to refuse to register the transfer and did not actually register it until after the death of the testator. The question then arose as to whether the legatee had taken the shares inter vivos or could only take them, if at all, post mortem.[48] Jenkins J. held that, because the testator had done everything in his power to transfer the shares inter vivos, from that moment he held the shares on trust for the transferee; consequently, the legatee had taken the shares inter vivos.

This decision was followed and applied by the Court of Appeal in the second case named *Re Rose*.[49] Two transfers of shares in a private company, one by way of gift to the transferor's wife and the other to trustees on trust, were not registered until three months later. The transferor subsequently died

---

[43] See *post*, p. 145.

[44] Since this trust does not arise out of any express or implied intention of the transferor or the beneficiaries, it must therefore necessarily be brought into existence by operation of law and should therefore be classified as a constructive trust (see *post*, p. 440).

[45] [1952] Ch. 499.

[46] [1949] 1 Ch. 78.

[47] [1949] 1 Ch. 78.

[48] This mattered because the bequest was conditional on the shares not having been transferred to the legatee prior to the testator's death; it was therefore possible to argue that the transfer *inter vivos* was ineffective to pass any title but nevertheless sufficient to defeat the testamentary gift, thus preventing the legatee from receiving the shares at all.

[49] [1952] Ch. 499.

at a point when estate duty was payable if the transfers had only been effective on registration but not if they were effective on execution.[50] Were the transfers effective upon execution or upon registration? The Court of Appeal held that, once the transferor had executed the transfers in the appropriate form, the transferor had done everything in his power which was necessary to vest the legal interest in the shares in the transferees. Consequently, from that moment the transfers were effective in equity and the transferor consequently held the legal title to the shares on trust for the transferees until they subsequently acquired legal title thereto upon registration of the transfers. Therefore no estate duty was payable.

The conclusion reached in these two decisions is not easy to reconcile either with the passages from the judgment of Turner L.J. in *Milroy v. Lord*,[51] which have been set out above or with the decision in *Re Fry*[52] which has already been considered.[53] In the second case named *Re Rose*, the Court of Appeal held that the remarks of Turner L.J. only applied where the transfer in question had not been carried out in the appropriate way (this was admittedly the situation under consideration in *Milroy v. Lord*[54] but no such restriction was actually mentioned by Turner L.J.); on the other hand, *Re Fry* was distinguished on the basis that there the transferor had not done all in his power to vest the property in the transferees, apparently because in order to perfect the transaction he would have had to have effected confirmatory transfers after the consent had been given. Neither of these distinctions is particularly convincing.

Difficulties also arise in relation to the role of the third party. Some third parties have a merely formal role in that they have no effective discretion to refuse to act — those responsible for registering a transfer of registered land or the transfer of shares in a public company clearly fall within this category. Is the Rule in *Re Rose* limited to situations such as these or does it also operate where the third party in question is able to decline to act? In both the cases named *Re Rose*, the directors of the companies in question were indeed entitled to refuse to register the share transfers and in the first case actually refused to do so for over 18 months. Although the point was not specifically considered, the two decisions must therefore establish that the rule will indeed operate even where the third party in question is entitled to decline to act. However, in this respect, it is once again difficult to reconcile the Rule in *Re Rose* with the decision in *Re Fry*.

---

[50] A gift made inter vivos within a prescribed minimum period prior to death is treated as forming part of the estate of the deceased for the purpose of calculating the tax payable on his estate. Under the present system of Inheritance Tax, a gift is exempt if made inter vivos more than seven years before death; if made more than three years before death, the tax is progressively reduced. At the time of *Re Rose*, the relevant period for Estate Duty had just been increased to five years without any progressive reductions but the testator's estate was subject to transitional provisions which produced the result stated in the text.

[51] (1862) 4 De G.F. & J. 264 at 274–275.

[52] [1946] Ch. 312.

[53] See *ante*, p. 137.

[54] The settlor had covenanted to transfer bank shares to the defendant on trust for the plaintiff. The defendant already held a general Power of Attorney to transfer shares of the settlor so the settlor merely handed over the share certificates to him. However, neither he nor the settlor ever procured the entry in the books of the bank which was necessary for the transfer of the legal title.

Notwithstanding the doubts expressed in the previous two paragraphs, the Rule in *Re Rose* is undoubtedly English law at the present time. The rule was applied by Lord Wilberforce in *Vandervell v. I.R.C.*[55] in order to justify his conclusion as to the scope of section 53(1)(c) of the Law of Property Act 1925.[56] More recently in *Mascall v. Mascall*,[57] it was held that delivery by the transferor of registered land to the transferee of a duly executed transfer form and the land certificate will bring the rule into operation so that, pending the registration of the transferee's title, the transferor will hold the land in question on trust for the transferee.[58] And in *Brown & Root Technology v. Sun Alliance and London Assurance Co*[59] it was held that an assignment of a lease which had been duly executed with the consent of the landlord but had not even been stamped *ad valorem*, never mind presented to the Land Registry, had taken effect in equity under the rule.[60] The Rule in *Re Rose* therefore constitutes an established, although questionable, exception to the general rule that equity will not regard an ineffective transfer as taking effect in equity as a declaration of trust.

## (C) Where it is Unconscionable for the Transferor to Change his Mind
The wholly novel proposition that an ineffectual transfer will take effect in equity where it is unconscionable for the transferor to change his mind was established by the Court of Appeal in *Pennington v. Waine*.[61]

A donor intended to transfer 400 shares in a private company to her nephew. Having consulted the company's auditors, she duly signed the necessary transfer form but this was never delivered either to the company or to the nephew; had it been delivered to the company, the other shareholders would have had a right of pre-emption. She also wished him to become a director, which required him to hold at least one share, and they both signed a form agreeing to his appointment. After her death, the question arose as to whether the 400 shares formed part of the donor's residuary estate or were held on trust for the nephew. On the face of things, because of her failure to deliver the share transfer form, she had neither transferred the shares to him nor done all in her power to do so. However, the Court of Appeal held that the delivery of a share transfer form could be dispensed with in some circumstances. It would have been unconscionable for the donor to have recalled what she clearly intended to have been a gift once the nephew had signed the form agreeing to become a director. Consequently thereafter she, and after her death her estate, held the 400 shares on constructive trust for the nephew.

This decision seems to have been based on a complete misunderstanding of

---

[55] [1967] 2 A.C. 271. See *ante*, p. 105.
[56] This argument actually begged the question being considered by the House of Lords (see Jones (1966) 24 C.L.J. 19) but that does not alter the fact that Lord Wilberforce applied the Rule in *Re Rose*.
[57] (1984) 50 P. & C.R. 119.
[58] Consequently, it was too late for the transferor to revoke his gift of the land in question to his son, who at the time of the purported revocation had had the transfer stamped *ad valorem* but had not yet presented it to the Land Registry.
[59] [1996] Ch. 51. This question did not arise in the subsequent appeal: (1996) 75 P. & C.R. 223.
[60] This prevented the original tenant from exercising a right to bring the lease to an end which could not be exercised following an effective assignment.
[61] [2002] 1 W.L.R. 2075. See Halliwell [2003] Conveyancer 192.

the decision of the Privy Council in *T. Choithram International S.A. v. Pagarani*.[62] Lord Browne-Wilkinson had there held that it would be as unconscionable for a settlor who had declared a trust when he was one of a number of trustees subsequently to resile from his declaration of trust as it would be if he had declared himself to be sole trustee.[63] In this context he stated[64] that, although equity would not aid a volunteer, it would not strive officiously to defeat a gift. The Court of Appeal[65] seized on the latter statement as authority for upholding the gift in *Pennington v. Waine*, completely overlooking the fact that in *T. Choithram International S.A. v. Pagarani*, Lord Browne-Wilkinson had held that there had been a declaration of trust; in contrast, in *Pennington v. Waine*, the donor had neither declared a trust nor made a gift nor done everything in her power to make a gift. Further, in *T. Choithram International S.A. v. Pagarani* the Privy Council had upheld the declaration of an express trust, not as Arden L.J. suggested in *Pennington v. Waine*,[66] a constructive trust.

It is apparent that the result reached by the Court of Appeal in *Pennington v. Waine* is not supported by *T. Choithram International S.A. v. Pagarani*; in fact the Court of Appeal's decision contradicts every single previous authority, including all the cases in which the Rule in *Re Rose* has been applied.[67] Indeed Clarke L.J. acknowledged that hard cases make bad law.[68] It is therefore suggested that *Pennington v. Waine* was wrongly decided and should not be followed. However, at least for the moment, it constitutes a second exception to the general rule that equity will not regard an ineffective transfer as taking effect in equity as a declaration of trust.

If *Pennington v. Waine* is followed, it is conceivable that that decision could be interpreted in such a way as to affect the formalities rules which have already been discussed.[69] Failure to comply with section 53 (1) (b) of the Law of Property Act 1925, which requires a trust of land to be evidenced in writing, makes the transaction in question unenforceable rather than wholly void. While any beneficiary who had acted to his detriment on the basis of an oral declaration of trust would inevitably be able to uphold that trust by relying on an equitable proprietary estoppel,[70] until now a beneficiary who has not so acted has been unable to prevent the settlor (or, more realistically his trustee in bankruptcy or his residuary beneficiaries) from recovering the land in question at any time. But it may now follow from *Pennington v. Waine* that it would be regarded as unconscionable for such a person to do so even if the beneficiary had not acted to his detriment. It is to be hoped that this does not turn out to be a further consequence of this controversial decision. However, it does not seem that the decision could operate in a similar way in respect of a failure to comply with section 53(1)(c) of the Law of Property Act 1925, since such a failure renders the disposition in question wholly void and reliance on such a

---

[62] [2001] 1 W.L.R. 1. See Halliwell [2003] Conveyancer 192.
[63] *ibid.* at 12.
[64] *ibid.*
[65] [2002] 1 W.L.R. 2075 at 2089 (Arden L.J.), 2105 (Clarke L.J.).
[66] *ibid.* at 2088.
[67] Arden L.J. and Clarke L.J. both stated that it was not crucial to the decision in the second case named *Re Rose* that in that case the share transfers had been delivered (*ibid.* at 2091 and 2103) but these statements are entirely speculative and, it is suggested, wrong in principle.
[68] *ibid.* at 2093.
[69] See *ante*, pp. 101 *et seq.*
[70] See *post*, pp. 154–160.

provision in the absence of detriment does not appear to be capable of being classified as unconscionable.

### 4. By Virtue of Other Exceptions to the Rule in Milroy v. Lord

**(A) The Rule in Strong v. Bird[71]**

The decision in *Strong v. Bird* itself had nothing to do with the law of trusts; it established the relatively unobjectionable proposition that an intention to release a debt or to make a gift is manifested and effected by appointing the debtor or the donee as executor of the creditor's will. A complete gift basically involves two elements: intention to make the gift and transfer of legal title to the property in question to the donee. The developed Rule in *Strong v. Bird* establishes that, where a testator maintains up until the time of his death a continuing intention to make a gift, the requirement for the transfer of legal title can be fulfilled by the legal title vesting in the donee as executor by operation of law on the death of the donor. In other words, the appointment of the intended donee as executor perfects the intention of the donor and completes the gift, displacing by virtue of being first in time the equity of anyone else who is otherwise entitled to the property in question under the will.

The rule was originally limited to debts. In *Strong v. Bird* itself, the defendant had borrowed £1,000 from his stepmother, who lived in his house paying him £200 a quarter for board. They agreed that the debt should be paid off by the deduction of £100 from each quarter's payment. Deductions of this amount were duly made for two quarters but on the third quarter-day the stepmother generously refused to hold to the agreement any longer and paid the full £200 board on each subsequent quarter-day until her death four years later. She appointed the defendant as sole executor of her will, which he duly proved. Those otherwise entitled to the stepmother's estate then claimed that the defendant still owed the balance of the debt to her estate. At common law it had long been established that a debt owed to a deceased person was extinguished by the appointment of the debtor as executor.[72] *Strong v. Bird* decided that equity would in this respect follow the common law and deny any claim by the beneficiaries claiming under the will provided that there was evidence that, up until the moment of his death, the creditor had had a continuing intention to release the debt (this was easily demonstrated in *Strong v. Bird* by the fact that the stepmother had continued to pay £200 per quarter).

The rule has since been extended very considerably. In *Re Stewart*,[73] it was held that any ineffectual gift, not just the release of a debt, made inter vivos to a person who later became the donor's executor could be and was perfected by his appointment as such. On the other hand, it has been established that the rule is restricted to specific existing property;[74] thus a continuing unfulfilled intention to make a gift of a sum of money will not be perfected by the intended donee subsequently becoming the donor's executor. This restriction to specific existing property also makes it questionable whether the rule is applicable to a residuary gift.

---

[71] (1874) 18 Eq. 315.
[72] At least since *Wankford v. Wankford* (1704) 1 Salk. 299.
[73] [1908] 2 Ch. 251.
[74] *Re Innes* [1952] 1 Ch. 188.

Further, where the rule is applicable, it will still only be applied if it can be shown that, after making the ineffectual gift, the donor maintained a continuing intention to make an immediate gift *inter vivos*. In *Re Freeland*,[75] a testatrix promised to give the plaintiff a motorcar at a future date but never actually did so. On the testatrix's death, the plaintiff became her executrix and claimed that the imperfect gift had thereby been perfected. However, the Court of Appeal refused to apply the Rule in *Strong v. Bird* because no absolute gift had ever been made at all. Similarly, in *Re Wale*,[76] the testatrix, having overlooked the need to transfer part of the intended trust property to the trustees, subsequently forgot all about the trust and treated the part of the property which she had not transferred as her own. It was held that she lacked the necessary continuing intention for the Rule in *Strong v. Bird* to apply.

Thus far it is just about possible to justify the existence of the rule. Even though the vast majority of testators will necessarily be unaware of its existence, an executor is at least expressly nominated by his testator. However, it is less easy to justify the subsequent extension of the rule to administrators. This occurred in *Re James*,[77] where the deceased had, on the earlier death of his father, handed over the title deeds of his father's house to his father's housekeeper. This was of course insufficient to vest the legal title to the house in the housekeeper (which would have necessitated a deed) but she continued to live there until the son died and it was clear that he had at all times intended her to have the house. When he died intestate, she obtained appointment as his administratrix and so the legal title to the house became vested in her by operation of law. It was held that this fortuitous occurrence brought the Rule in *Strong v. Bird* into operation and thus perfected the incomplete gift to her.

No administrator is ever nominated by the deceased. Who becomes administrator depends, in principle, on the order of preference set out in the Non-Contentious Probate Rules and, as between relatives of the same degree or, in the absence of any relatives, other beneficiaries of a will, it is often a matter of pure chance which of them ends up as administrator. It therefore seems highly unreasonable that that person should obtain an advantage over the other beneficiaries by reason of his appointment. This was indeed precisely the reason why the original common law rule relating to the release of debts was never applied to administrators. Precisely these criticisms of *Re James* were forcefully made in *Re Gonin (deceased)*,[78] by Walton J., who doubted the decision in that case. However, since both counsel had accepted its correctness, Walton J. nevertheless applied it to an ineffectual gift inter vivos of a house and its furniture by a mother to the daughter who had devoted her life to caring for her parents; however, on the facts, he held that sufficient continuing intention had been made out in respect only of the furniture and not of the house.

Other uncertainties remain. It is probable that, like the original common law rule, the rule in *Strong v. Bird* gives the executor or administrator priority only

---

[75] [1952] Ch. 110.
[76] [1956] 1 W.L.R. 1346. See also *Re Eiser's Will Trusts* [1937] 1 All E.R. 244, where the donor subsequently took security for the debt given.
[77] [1935] Ch. 449.
[78] [1964] Ch. 288.

over those beneficially entitled to the estate and not over the creditors of the estate; however, this has never been the subject of judicial comment in this jurisdiction.[79] Nor does it appear to have been expressly decided whether the rule applies where the imperfect gift is in favour of the executor or administrator as trustee rather than beneficially. However in *Re Wale*,[80] where the rule was not in fact applied, no objection was made on the grounds that in that case the executors would have taken as trustees. Consequently, it appears highly likely that the Rule in *Strong v. Bird* does indeed apply in such circumstances. For present purposes, it should be emphasised that only if this is the case will the Rule in *Strong v. Bird* be capable of operating in such a way as to constitute an otherwise incompletely constituted trust.

## (B) The Principle Enunciated in Re Ralli's Will Trusts[81]

In this case, a settlor entered into a covenant to transfer any existing or after-acquired property to the trustees of her marriage settlement. At the time of this settlement, she already held existing property caught by this covenant, namely an interest in remainder in the residue of her father's estate subject to the prior life interest of her mother. She never assigned this interest to the trustees of the marriage settlement at any time prior to her death 32 years later. Her mother actually survived her so that it was over four years after her death before her interest in remainder vested in possession. At that point the sole trustee of her father's will was, fortuitously, also the sole trustee of the marriage settlement. He was therefore in the former capacity holding on trust for her an interest which she should have assigned to him in the latter capacity. The question therefore arose as to whether this fortuitous occurrence had the effect of completely constituting a trust of the interest in favour of the beneficiaries of the marriage settlement.

As has already been seen,[82] Buckley J. actually held, as a matter of construction, that the settlor had declared herself to be a trustee for her marriage settlement of any property caught by the covenant pending transfer of that property to the trustees. Thus her interest in remainder had, ever since the date of the marriage settlement, been subject to a completely constituted trust in favour of that settlement. Its beneficiaries could therefore obviously enforce this trust without any need to rely on the fact that the interest had fortuitously vested in their trustee in another capacity. This decision on construction was obviously enough to dispose of the case.

However, Buckley J. went on to held that, since the interest in question had fortuitously reached the hands of the person to whom the settlor should have transferred it, the trust of that property in favour of the beneficiaries of the marriage settlement had by this means also become completely constituted, this time by transfer rather than by declaration. He went on to say that it was totally irrelevant how the property had come into the hands of the person to whom it should have been transferred; the mere fact, fortuitous though it was, that the property had reached his hands was sufficient to have completely constituted the trust. Nor was it of any significance that the result of the case

---

[79] The question has been considered in Australia; see *Bone v. Stamp Duty Commissioner* (1974) 132 C.L.R. 38 at 53 (High Court of Australia).

[80] [1956] 1 W.L.R. 1346.

[81] [1964] Ch. 288.

[82] See *ante*, p. 141.

would, on this ground, have been different had anyone other than the trustee of the marriage settlement been the trustee of the will.

It does not seem appropriate to regard the statements of Buckley J. merely as a further extension of the Rule in *Strong v. Bird*. It is admittedly of no great significance that the person whose hands the property had reached had no beneficial interest therein — it has never been expressly held that the Rule in *Strong v. Bird* is limited to beneficial gifts to executors and administrators and, as has already been indicated, no objection was taken in *Re Wale*[83] to the applicability of the rule on this ground. But it is questionable whether the Rule in *Strong v. Bird* is applicable to a residuary gift, given its restriction to specific existing property.[84] Further, the trustee in question does not appear to have been either the executor or the administrator of the settlor and no evidence was either required or given that the settlor had had any continuing intention of transferring the property in question to the trustees of her marriage settlement at any time during the 32 years which had elapsed between the creation of the settlement and her death. It is therefore clear that virtually none of the established requirements of the Rule in *Strong v. Bird* was actually satisfied in *Re Ralli's Will Trusts*.

It therefore seems more appropriate to regard the statements of Buckley J. as authority for the existence of a wholly distinct principle which can be formulated in the following way: if property of any type reaches without impropriety[85] the hands of a person to whom it should already have been transferred as a trustee *inter vivos*, the trust in question will become completely constituted by transfer whether or not there is any continuing intention on the part of the settlor that this should occur. Since it seems from the judgment of Buckley J. that his statements were intended by him to amount to a second *ratio decidendi* rather than merely *obiter dicta*, this distinct principle may well represent the present law; if it does, it will therefore also be capable of operating so as to constitute an otherwise incompletely constituted trust.

Having said that, it must also be said that any such principle appears to be inconsistent with the earlier decision in *Re Brooks's Settlement Trusts*,[86] which was not cited to Buckley J. In this case, under the terms of a voluntary settlement the settlor had covenanted to transfer to the trustees any property which he might acquire under his parents' marriage settlement. A bank was trustee of both settlements so that, when a sum was subsequently appointed to the settlor as a result of the exercise of the powers contained in the marriage settlement, that sum was already in the hands of the trustees to whom he had covenanted to transfer it. At that time, for reasons which will be considered later in this section,[87] neither the trustees nor the beneficiaries of the voluntary settlement could have enforced against the settlor his covenant to transfer that sum. Consequently Farwell J. held that, despite the coincidence of trustees, the settlor was entitled to receive the sum appointed to him. In the light of this decision, it must therefore be questionable whether the novel principle

---

[83] [1957] 1 W.L.R. 1346.

[84] See *Re Innes* [1952] 1 Ch. 188, *ante*, p. 147.

[85] This point was particularly emphasised by Buckley J. His principle would therefore clearly not have applied in the event that the property had reached the hands of the trustee as the result of a disposition of property in breach of trust.

[86] [1939] 1 Ch. 993.

[87] See *post*, pp. 170–173.

enunciated by Buckley J. in *Re Ralli's Will Trusts* does indeed actually represent the law; it remains to be seen which of the two decisions is followed in future.

### (C) *Donationes Mortis Causa*

The rules governing *donationes mortis causa*, or death bed gifts, can also have the effect of constituting an otherwise incomplete transfer. In *Cain v. Moon*,[88] Lord Russell C.J. provided that an effectual *donatio mortis causa* requires the presence of the following three elements.

### (1) The gift must have been made in contemplation of death

All that is necessary is that the donor contemplated death at the time of the gift. Although the point has never been expressly decided in England,[89] the test seems to be subjective and not objective. It is the donor's own state of mind, not the actual circumstances, which is material. Moreover, the title of the donee will not be invalidated if the donor dies from some cause other than the disease from which he knew that he was suffering.[90] In *Wilkes v. Allington*[91] the donor was suffering from an incurable disease and made the gift knowing that he had not long to live. As things turned out, he lived an even shorter time than he thought, because he died two months later from pneumonia. The gift, however, remained valid.

### (2) The gift must have been conditional on the death of the donor

The gift must have been made under circumstances indicating that it was conditional on the death of the donor. In this respect it is different from a gift *inter vivos*; the latter is absolute whereas a *donatio mortis causa* is necessarily conditional on death. The condition is not usually expressed in so many words but an inference to this effect will usually be drawn from the fact of the illness of the donor.[92] This of course means not only that the subject matter of the gift will revert to the donor if he recovers from his illness but also that he can revoke his gift at any time during his lifetime.[93] The donor will be regarded as having expressly revoked his gift if he resumes dominion over it;[94] there is also some authority for the proposition that it will also be sufficient if the donor simply informs the donee of his intention to revoke.[95] However, a purported revocation by will will not suffice simply because the will does not take effect

---

[88] [1896] 2 Q.B. 283.

[89] It appears that an objective test has been adopted in Canada; see 81 L.Q.R. (1965) 21 and the Canadian cases cited *post*, fn. 90.

[90] It need not, perhaps, necessarily be illness, though it normally is. Nor apparently need the donor be *in extremis*. The contrary suggestion is made in *Thomson v. Meechan* [1958] D.L.R. 103, but this seems incorrect. For a similar suggestion, see *Canada Trust Co. v. Labrador* [1962] O.R. 151. See also 81 L.Q.R. (1965) 21.

[91] [1931] 2 Ch. 104. See also *Mills v. Shields* [1948] I.R. 367 (death from suicide). *Re Dudman* [1925] Ch. 553 held contemplation by the deceased of suicide to be insufficient but, since this case was decided before the Suicide Act 1961 provided that suicide was and is no longer a crime, it is arguable, but by no means certain, that a *donatio mortis causa* made in such circumstances may now be valid.

[92] *Re Lillingston* [1952] 2 All ER 184.

[93] *Staniland v. Willott* (1850) 3 Mac. & G. 664.

[94] *Bunn v. Markham* (1816) 7 Taunt. 224 at 231.

[95] *Jones v. Selby* (1710) Prec.Ch. 300 at 303. Resuming mere possession for the purpose of ensuring safe custody of the subject matter is not enough; *Re Hawkins* [1924] 2 Ch. 47.

until the death of the testator, by which time the donee will have become unconditionally entitled.[96]

However, the fact that the gift is conditional in the sense considered in the previous paragraph does not detract from the basic requirement that, for a *donatio mortis causa* to be effective, it must, like any other gift, be a present gift and not a gift to take effect at some time in the future.[97]

**(3) There must have been some form of delivery from donor to donee**

The donor must have delivered to the donee either the subject matter of the gift or the means or part of the means by which the subject matter can be obtained. The nature of this requirement varies according to the nature of the subject matter of the *donatio mortis causa* but it is in all cases a pre-condition that the donor intended to part with dominion,[98] a question which is ultimately a matter of fact.

No difficulties normally arise in the case of personal property which is capable of physical delivery. Handing the chattel itself to the donee will not only constitute delivery,[99] but will also pass the legal title. Sufficient delivery will also occur if the donee is given some means of obtaining the chattel such as the keys of a cupboard in which it is stored.[1] The circumstances of the delivery must also be sufficient to demonstrate that the donor can no longer interfere with the subject matter of the gift.[2]

However, some items of personal property, such as a bank account, are choses in action and so are incapable of physical delivery.[3] In such circumstances, the gift will be ineffective unless the donee can compel the personal representative of the deceased to complete the gift of the chose in action to him. The essential pre-condition which, according to the conventional formulation, must be satisfied is that the donor must have delivered to the donee whatever document constitutes the essential evidence of his title to the chose in action in question. This test was applied in *Re Weston*,[4] where a dying man had handed over to his fiancée his Post Office Savings Book; this action was held sufficient to constitute an effective *donatio mortis causa* of the savings

---

[96] *Jones v. Selby* (1710) Prec.Ch. 300.

[97] *Re Ward* [1946] 2 All E.R. 206.

[98] *Birch v. Treasury Solicitor* [1951] Ch. 298.

[99] See *Re Cole* [1964] Ch. 175.

[1] *Re Mustapha* (1891) 8 T.L.R. 160; see also *Re Lillingston* [1952] 2 All E.R. 184.

[2] *Re Craven's Estate* [1937] Ch. 423 at 427, where the delivery of one of two duplicate keys was held to be insufficient. However, the fact that a donor had possibly retained a second set of car keys which he was too ill to use was held to be insignificant in *Woodard v. Woodard* [1995] 3 All E.R. 980, as was the retention by a donor of a set of keys to a house to which he knew he would not return in *Sen v. Headley* [1991] Ch. 425.

[3] Some choses in action, such as bearer shares and bearer bonds, are of course transferable by delivery. Delivery of such choses in action will therefore be sufficient to constitute an effective *donatio mortis causa* and so also will delivery of the key of a box containing them; *Re Wasserberg* [1915] 1 Ch. 195.

[4] [1902] 1 Ch. 680. A similar conclusion was reached in *Darlow v. Sparks* [1938] 2 All E.R. 235 in respect of national savings certificates and, rather more unexpectedly, in *Re Mead* (1880) 15 Ch.D. 651, in respect of a cheque drawn by a third party in favour of the donor (unexpected because the cheque was capable of being endorsed; the decision would be unexceptionable in respect of a modern cheque stated to be "A/C Payee only" and so not endorsable). However, a cheque drawn by the donor in favour of the donee is not sufficient to take effect as a *donatio mortis causa* because such a cheque is simply a revocable order to the bank to make payment to the payee which will inevitably be revoked by the donor's death (*Re Leaper* [1916] 1 Ch. 579).

recorded in it. In the course of his judgment, Byrne J. expressed the view that the document in question must also contain all the essential terms on which the subject matter of the chose in action was held. However, it is easy to visualise circumstances in which a strict application of this rule would work injustice, although it did not do so in *Re Weston* itself. Consequently, the Court of Appeal was clearly right expressly to disapprove this view in *Birch v. Treasury Solicitor*,[5] which concerned a similar gift of a bank deposit pass-book. The correct approach to be followed is, in the words of Evershed M.R. in that case, that delivery must be made of the "essential indicia of title, possession or production of which entitles the possessor to the money or property purported to be given".[6] This principle was applied by the Court of Appeal in *Sen v. Headley*,[7] where the authorities on *donationes mortis causa* of choses in action were reviewed particularly fully.

However, *Sen v. Headley* actually concerned an attempted *donatio mortis causa* of land. In that case, three days before his death the deceased had, with the necessary intention, delivered to the donee the only key to the steel box which contained the title deeds to his unregistered house and land; she already had a set of keys to the house in question and after the deceased's death found the box in a cupboard. Land is, of course, if anything more incapable of physical delivery than a chose in action and in *Duffield v. Elwes*,[8] Lord Eldon L.C. had appeared to suggest that land cannot be the subject matter of a *donatio mortis causa*. However, in *Sen v. Headley* the Court of Appeal stated that anomalies do not justify anomalous exceptions, that to make a distinction in the case of land would be to make just such an exception, and that a *donatio mortis causa* of land was "neither more nor less anomalous than any other".[9] Consequently, since the Court of Appeal in *Birch v. Treasury Solicitor* had extended rather than restricted the operation of the doctrine of *donationes mortis causa*, the court held that land is indeed capable of passing by way of a *donatio mortis causa*. The court then went on to hold that the fact that the donor also had a set of keys to the house and had obviously retained the theoretical ability to deal with the title to it despite the delivery of the key to the donee did not, on the facts, amount to a retention of dominion. The *donatio mortis causa* was therefore upheld. However, it is obviously unlikely that anything less than delivery of the deeds (or, in the case of registered land, the

---

[5] [1951] Ch. 298.
[6] *ibid.* at 311.
[7] [1991] Ch. 425. See Halliwell [1991] Conv. 307.
[8] (1827) 1 Bli. (N.S.) 497.
[9] [1991] Ch. 425 at p. 440. Every *donatio mortis causa* circumvented the Wills Act 1837 and the fact that inter vivos transfers of land were subject to statutory formalities not applicable to pure personalty did not constitute a more substantial obstacle since any trust needed to give effect to any *donatio mortis causa* would be a resulting or constructive trust and so exempt from those formalities anyway (the trust would presumably be a resulting trust if the personal representatives of the donor agreed to be bound by the *donatio mortis causa* subject to proof of its constitutent elements but a constructive trust if they sought to rely on the provisions of the Wills Act 1837 to deny its existence).

Land Certificate[10]) or the means of obtaining them will ever be held to constitute an appropriate delivery in respect of land.

Finally, it must be emphasised that, in the case both of choses in action and of land, the legal title to the property in question will not be automatically acquired by the donee as a result of a delivery in the manner prescribed. The gift of whatever property is represented by whatever has been delivered will still be imperfect. The effect of establishing a *donatio mortis causa* is instead that the donor's personal representatives will be compelled to perfect the gift.[11] It is therefore in the case of *donationes mortis causa* of choses in action and of land that equity, contrary to the Rule in *Milroy v. Lord*, compels the completion of what would otherwise be an incomplete gift.

## (D) The Doctrine of Equitable Proprietary Estoppel[12]

### (1) The nature of the doctrine

If the doctrine of estoppel were still limited to the sense in which it has traditionally been generally applied, it would barely be worthy of mention here. Since the traditional form of the doctrine operated only defensively so as to prevent a party from asserting his rights which, but for that doctrine, he would have been able to assert, it obviously could not operate so as to perfect an imperfect gift or complete an incompletely constituted trust.[13] However, the modern principle of proprietary estoppel can be used offensively, "as a sword" as it is sometimes described, in order to perfect an imperfect gift if, for example, the donor has stood by and watched the donee improve property or do other acts to his detriment on the supposition that there has been or will be an effective gift.

The doctrine appears to be of early origin[14] but until relatively recently had evolved in the form of three separate overlapping categories of cases: first, cases concerning imperfect gifts; secondly, cases concerning common expectations, where parties have consistently dealt with one another in such a way as to cause one of them to rely on a shared supposition that he would acquire rights of some kind in the land of the other; and, thirdly, cases of unilateral

---

[10] This possibility was not specifically envisaged by the Court of Appeal but must follow from their finding that it did not matter that the donor had retained the theoretical ability to deal with his title. If the proprietor of registered land which is mortgaged has no more than a copy of the Charge Certificate and the Land Certificate is held by the Land Registry (this will be the case if the land was mortgaged under the Land Registration Act 1925 prior to the coming into force of the Land Registration Act 2002), delivery of the copy of the Charge Certificate will presumably suffice.

[11] *Re Dillon* (1890) 44 Ch.D. 76 at 82–83.

[12] See Gray & Gray, *Elements of Land Law* (3rd ed., 2001), 753–815; Pawlowski, *The Doctrine of Proprietary Estoppel* (1996); Halliwell, *Equity & Good Conscience in a Contemporary Context* (1997), pp. 19–38; Spence, *Protecting Reliance* (1999).

[13] This was predominantly so in a case of so-called promissory estoppel but the traditional distinctions between promissory estoppel and proprietary estoppel have been eroded by recent authorities. See particularly *Taylors Fashions v. Liverpool Victoria Trustees Company* (1976) [1982] Q.B. 133N; *Amalgamated Investment & Property Company v. Texas Commerce International Bank* [1982] Q.B. 84 (leave to appeal to the House of Lords was subsequently not granted [1982] 1 W.L.R. 1). One distinction which must nevertheless remain is that promissory estoppel, unlike proprietary estoppel, is not permanent in its effect. The promisor can resile from his position if he gives the promisee notice which provides him with a reasonable opportunity of resuming his former position; see *Re Vandervell's Trusts (No.2)* [1964] Ch. 269 at 301, *per* Megarry J.

[14] See *Foxcroft v. Lester* (1703) 2 Vern. 456.

mistake, where the owner of land has stood by and allowed another person to act to his detriment on a mistaken belief that he has a legally enforceable interest in the land in question. The principles established by these three groups of authorities have now been synthesised into the modern principle of proprietary estoppel. The key decision in this process seems to have been *Taylor Fashions v. Liverpool Victoria Trustees Company*.[15] In this case Oliver J. rejected the notion that the principle was narrowly confined to the three categories of cases already mentioned. Instead his Lordship found support in these three groups of cases for "a much wider jurisdiction to interfere in cases where the assertion of strict legal rights is found by the courts to be unconscionable".[16] He therefore held that the purchasers of a freehold reversion were estopped from claiming to have taken free for want of registration of options to renew leases which, at the time of their grant, were wrongly thought by conveyancers not to be registrable.

As a result of this synthesis, it is now clear that a successful claim of proprietary estoppel involves three elements: an assurance, a reliance and a detriment. Such an assurance will occur where the owner of land, expressly or by necessary implication, raises in another person an expectation that that person will obtain some interest or entitlement in land which he would not otherwise have. The assurance can range from an express request to incur expenditure through encouragement or incitement so to do, to silent abstention from the assertion of rights, although in the last case the owner of the land obviously has to be shown to have at least some knowledge of the mistaken belief of the other party. Where such an assurance has been made, the other person must then show that he has acted in reliance upon that assurance to his detriment. This involves him showing both that he has changed his position and that this change of position is a direct consequence of the assurance given.

Where such a proprietary estoppel has arisen, the court enjoys very considerable flexibility in that a remedy can be provided appropriate to the circumstances of each individual case. Such remedies range from the grant of an unqualified estate in fee simple or lesser interest in or over land such as a lease, or an easement through the grant of a right to occupy the land to the grant of monetary compensation; it is also possible for a grant of a right in or a right to occupy land to be combined with a grant of monetary compensation. The doctrine is of course still developing and not only is there an increasing overlap between the doctrine of proprietary estoppel and the "common intention constructive trust" (as will be seen later[17]) but also an equitable proprietary estoppel has been held itself to give rise to a constructive trust where it is unconscionable for the estopped party to deny its existence.[18] The terminology employed in the majority of the cases decided prior to *Taylor Fashions v. Liverpool Victoria Trustees Company* would be likely to be very different if those cases were to recur today. However, there is no doubt whatsoever that all the cases in which proprietary estoppels were upheld would still be decided in the same way and they consequently remain important as illustrations of the situations, formerly quite distinct, which today fall within

---

[15] (1976) [1982] Q.B. 133N.
[16] *ibid.* at 147.
[17] See *post*, p. 428.
[18] *Yaxley v. Gotts* [2000] Ch. 162.

the doctrine of proprietary estoppel. The difference today is that the enunciation of a broader general jurisdiction means that proprietary estoppels are now likely to be upheld in situations in which this would not formerly have been the case.

## (2) The relevance of the doctrine for the constitution of trusts

For the purposes of the complete constitution of trusts, what are important are the cases concerning imperfect gifts. A useful starting point is *Dillwyn v. Llewelyn*,[19] where a father put his son into possession of land without a conveyance. It was intended that the son should build a house on the land. The son successfully claimed that the land should be formally conveyed to him. Lord Westbury L.C. said: "If A puts B in possession of a piece of land and tells him 'I give it to you that you may build a house on it', and B, on the strength of that promise, with the knowledge of A, expends a large sum of money in building a house accordingly, I cannot doubt that the donee acquires a right from the subsequent transaction to call on the donor to perform that contract, and complete the imperfect donation which was made." In other words, the subsequent acts of the donor gave the donee a right which he did not acquire from the original gift. In the much more recent decision in *Pascoe v. Turner*,[20] the parties had lived together in a house as man and wife and the man had encouraged or acquiesced in the woman improving the house in the belief that it belonged to her. He was ordered to execute a conveyance of the house to her. In both these cases, the donee took an estate in fee simple. However, as has already been mentioned, the estate or interest of the donee depends on the circumstances of the case. Thus, in *Inwards v. Baker*,[21] the donee was held to be entitled to remain in occupation for as long as he wished.

All the cases discussed so far were cases between the donee and the donor (or the latter's estate). *E.R. Ives Investments v. High*,[22] on the other hand, was a case between the donee and a successor in title of the donor for value. In that case, the donee, the defendant, was allowed a right of way for as long as the plaintiff and his successors in title maintained the foundations of a building on the defendant's land; this was because the plaintiff's predecessors in title, by licensing the defendant to use the yard in question, had encouraged him to build a garage on his own adjoining land, something which had created an estoppel in his favour. It was also held that the equitable interest which had arisen as a result of this estoppel was not subject to the rules regarding the registration of land charges,[23] which of course only apply to unregistered land; consequently, the equitable interest was governed by the equitable doctrine of notice and bound the whole world other than a bona fide purchaser for value of a legal interest without notice. Interests protected by proprietary estoppel are also capable of binding the successors in title of the party originally estopped where the land in question is registered — this is specifically provided by the Land Registration Act 2002.[24] However, whether such an interest

---

[19] (1862) 4 De G.F. & J. 517.
[20] [1979] 1 W.L.R. 431.
[21] [1965] 2 Q.B. 29. See also *Ward v. Kirkland* [1967] Ch. 194, where a perpetual easement of drainage was granted.
[22] [1967] 2 Q.B. 289.
[23] Under what is now the Land Charges Act 1972.
[24] Land Registration Act 2002, s.114.

will be so binding depends on the general principles of registered conveyancing; it will therefore only be binding if it has been protected on the register unless its holder has an interest which overrides the registration of the title of the third party by virtue of his actual occupation of the land.[25]

These decisions were applied in *Crabb v. Arun District Council*,[26] where there was an agreement "in principle", not amounting to a binding contract, that the plaintiff should have a right of access, in reliance on which he sold the front portion of his land without reserving a right of way over it giving access to the back portion. The Court of Appeal held that this was a case of proprietary estoppel and that he was therefore entitled to an easement or licence;[27] he had been encouraged to act to his detriment by the defendant's conduct.[28] Similarly, in *Jones v. Jones*,[29] a father had led his son to believe that a house would be his home for the rest of his life, on the basis of which expectation the son had given up his job and moved in. It was held that he could pray in aid the doctrine of estoppel and that both the father and his administratrix were estopped from turning the son out during his lifetime. Again in *Re Sharpe*,[30] where an aged aunt had lent money for the purchase of a house by her nephew so that she could live there with him and his wife, it was held that an irrevocable licence to occupy the house had arisen in favour of the aunt until such time as the loan was repaid.

Moreover, the burden of proof is on the plaintiff to show that the defendant has not acted to his detriment or prejudice where the latter is relying upon an estoppel. So, in *Greasley v. Cooke*,[31] assurances had been given that the defendant could remain in a house, where she had not only been employed as a maid for more than 40 years but had also lived with one of the children of the family as man and wife. It was held that these assurances raised an equity in her favour and it was to be presumed that she had acted on the faith of those assurances. The plaintiffs failed to rebut the presumption.[32] However, the position of the burden of proof does not of course alter the fact that it is essential for a case of proprietary estoppel that a party acted as he did to his detriment in the expectation of acquiring a right to or over somebody else's land.

It used to be thought that the conduct of the owner of the property in question could only be held to give rise to the inequitable consequences which are a necessary ingredient of establishing a proprietary estoppel if he was aware of the true facts. This is certainly still a requirement for the type of cases traditionally classified as cases of unilateral mistake. However, it no longer

---

[25] Land Registration Act 2002, Sched. 1, para.3, Sched. 3, para.3.

[26] [1976] Ch. 179.

[27] An easement according to Lord Denning M.R. and Lawton L.J.; an easement or licence according to Scarman L.J.

[28] One of the acts to his detriment was the sale of land separate from the land over which the access was to be granted. Normally, the acts involve expenditure in relation to the actual land intended to be disposed of.

[29] [1977] 1 W.L.R. 438.

[30] [1980] 1 W.L.R. 219.

[31] [1980] 1 W.L.R. 1306.

[32] Lord Denning M.R. said (at 1311) that the incurring of expenditure of money or other prejudice was not a necessary element. However, this appears to be far too wide a generalization; see at 1313 *per* Dunn L.J.

appears to be essential for the type of cases under discussion at present, cases concerning imperfect gifts.[33]

Admittedly Megarry J. did uphold the existence of such a requirement at first instance in *Re Vandervell's Trusts (No.2)*.[34] He refused to find an estoppel, pointing out that, although Vandervell had concurred in the dealings with the moneys and shares carried out by the trust company[35] following the exercise of the option, the company had not been able to show that he even knew that he was the beneficial owner of the option at the time of its exercise. However, the question was not fully argued before Megarry J. and the opposite view was subsequently taken in the Court of Appeal. The court was of the opinion that, if Vandervell had been alive, his concurrence in these dealings would have estopped him from denying the existence of a beneficial interest vested in the children's settlement of which the trust company was trustee; consequently, his executors could be in no better position. This was admittedly not the only ground on which the Court of Appeal decided the case[36] and it might therefore be a mistake to read too much into these remarks about proprietary estoppel. In particular, knowledge cannot possibly be, as the Court of Appeal appeared to suggest, totally irrelevant.

The better view must therefore be the intermediate position adopted by Oliver J. in *Taylors Fashions v. Liverpool Victoria Trustees Company*[37] where he held that knowledge of the true position by the party alleged to be estopped was merely one of the relevant factors in the overall inquiry. He held that the essential question was whether, in the particular circumstances, it would be unconscionable for a party to be permitted to deny that which, knowingly or unknowingly, he had allowed or encouraged another to assume to his detriment.[38] Accordingly, the principle could apply where, at the time the expectation was encouraged, both parties (not just the representee) were acting under a mistake of law as to their rights. He therefore held that the purchasers of a freehold reversion were estopped from claiming to have taken free for want of registration of options to renew leases which, at the time of their grant, were wrongly thought by conveyancers not to be registrable.[39] This decision, which, as has already been seen, set the doctrine of proprietary estoppel on its present course, obviously did not involve the law of trusts but must nevertheless have had an effect on it.

### (3) The impact of the doctrine on the law of trusts

The doctrine of equitable proprietary estoppel gives rise to a number of potential difficulties for the law of trusts.

The first relates to cases involving the incidence of taxation such as the second case named *Re Rose*.[40] Were the gift or trust in such a case to have arisen as a result of the doctrine of equitable proprietary estoppel, it would have to be

---

[33] Nor is it for cases concerning common expectation.

[34] [1974] Ch. 269 at 301.

[35] These dealings are referred to *ante*, p. 140.

[36] See *ante*, p. 140.

[37] (1976) [1982] Q.B. 133N.

[38] See also *Amalgamated Investment & Property Company v. Texas Commerce International Bank* [1982] Q.B. 84 (leave to appeal to the House of Lords was subsequently not granted: [1982] 1 W.L.R. 1).

[39] See also *Thomas Bates & Son v. Wyndhams (Lingerie)* [1981] 1 W.L.R. 505; estoppel applied where the mistake was a unilateral rather than a common mistake.

[40] [1952] Ch. 499, discussed *ante*, p. 143.

determined whether the gift or trust in question was to be regarded as having been constituted at the time when the gift was made or the trust created or on the occurrence of the subsequent events which created the estoppel. In this case, the position is relatively straightfoward since the latter would certainly seem to be the correct approach.[41]

In other respects, however, the position is more doubtful. In *Williams v. Staite*,[42] Cumming-Bruce L.J. considered, without finding it necessary to decide, that the rights of an equitable licensee for life did not necessarily crystallise when his rights came into existence but only when the court came to determine what interest he had in the property, since the court might well decide that, as a result of his conduct, he had forfeited an interest to which he otherwise would have been entitled. Lord Denning M.R. shared the opinion that, in an extreme case an equitable licence might be revoked on the grounds of misconduct.[43] However, he actually held that the conduct of the licensees, which involved excessive user and bad behaviour, was not of a kind to bring the equity established in their favour to an end; their behaviour could instead be remedied by an award of damages. While it may be regarded as debatable whether or not an established equity can be forfeited in this way, it does at least seem clear that, when a person is asserting a right to an equity for the first time, his conduct may be taken into account in deciding whether to uphold such a right; this is no more than an application of the basic maxim that "he who comes to equity must come with clean hands".[44]

There can be no doubt that, when an equity is being so asserted for the first time, virtually everything must be dependant on the facts of the case. Having said that, however, in cases where the party with the benefit of the equity has not been in any way guilty of misconduct, such as *Re Sharpe*,[45] it is absolutely essential that his rights are held to have arisen at the time of the transaction in question. This is because it is only in this event that a subsequent breach of those rights by the other party caused by, for example, a disposition of the property in question to a third party will be able to be appropriately remedied; priority over that third party will only be able to be asserted if the equity was indeed in existence prior to any order of the courts.[46]

It therefore seems that there is a distinction between, on the one hand, the undeniable existence of an equity prior to any decision of the court which can be relied on in order to confer any necessary priority over third parties and, on the other hand, the manner in which the court may choose, in the exercise of its discretion in the light of all the facts, to implement that equity.

## (4) Conclusion

Some of the aspects of the scope of the doctrine of proprietary estoppel and the consequences of its utilisation in fiscal and conveyancing terms have still to be finally clarified. Nevertheless, the doctrine is clearly one of the most significant movements occurring in the contemporary law of real property. The extent to

---

[41] In this respect, see generally: Jackson (1965) 81 L.Q.R. 84; Poole (1968) 38 Conv. (N.S.) 96; Sunnucks (1968) 118 New L.J. 769.
[42] [1979] Ch. 291.
[43] *ibid.* at 297.
[44] Goff L.J. was of this opinion in *Williams v. Staite* [1979] Ch. 291 at 299.
[45] [1980] 1 W.L.R. 219. The facts were stated *ante*, p. 143.
[46] *ibid.* at 225.

which its development will increase the extent to which equity will constitute trusts which would otherwise be incompletely constituted remains to be seen. Nevertheless, there can be no doubt that the development of this doctrine has increased both the importance of this particular exception and the possibilities of a trust becoming completely constituted thereby.

## (E) Statutory Exceptions

Since January 1, 1997 there has only been one statutory exception to the rule that equity will not constitute a trust which would otherwise be incompletely constituted. A trust will be constituted by statute as a result of a purported conveyance of a legal estate in land to a minor. Because such an estate can only be held by an adult,[47] the conveyance will, by virtue of the Trusts of Land and Appointment of Trustees Act 1996,[48] operate as a declaration that the land is held in trust for the minor in question. Prior to January 1, 1997, there was also a second exception arising out of the fact that it was not possible to create a settlement of a legal estate in land pursuant to the Settled Land Act 1925 without the use of two documents — a trust instrument and a vesting document (either a deed or an assent).[49] The use of only one document did not pass the legal estate but, under section 9 of the Settled Land Act 1925, such a document operated as a trust instrument and therefore took effect as an enforceable trust pending the execution of the vesting deed by the trustees.[50] As a result of the Trusts of Land and Appointment of Trustees Act 1996, no further settlements under the Settled Land Act 1925 can now be created;[51] consequently, this exception only survives to the extent that any such settlement created before January 1, 1997 still has no vesting deed, a possibility which will become less and less likely with the passage of time.

## III. THE DISTINCTION BETWEEN EXECUTED AND EXECUTORY TRUSTS

Completely constituted trusts may be either executed or executory trusts and it is still in some circumstances important to distinguish not only between these two categories of trusts but also between the two of them and trusts which are incompletely constituted. An executed trust arises when the settlor has defined in the trust instrument precisely what interests are to be taken by the beneficiaries.[52] An executory trust, on the other hand, arises where the instrument or declaration requires the subsequent execution of a further instrument and does not itself precisely define the terms of that instrument.[53]

---

[47] Law of Property Act 1925, s.1(6).

[48] Sched. 1, para.1. Before this Act came into force on January 1, 1997, such a conveyance operated as an agreement for valuable consideration to create a settlement of that land on the minor and in the meantime to hold the land on trust for him (Settled Land Act 1925, s.27); any conveyances so operating on January 1, 1997 thereafter also take effect as declarations of trust.

[49] Settled Land Act 1925, s.4.

[50] The trustees were entitled to execute a vesting deed at any time and could be compelled to do so by the beneficiary who held the estate in possession for the time being (the person described in the Settled Land Act 1925 as the tenant for life).

[51] Sched. 1, para.1.

[52] See *Egerton v. Brownlow* (1853) 4 H.L.C. 1 at 210, *per* Lord St. Leonards.

[53] Nevertheless, the directions as to the trusts to be defined must not be too ambiguous; if they are, there will be no executory trust either. See *Re Flavel's Will Trusts* [1969] 1 W.L.R. 444.

## 1. *The Nature of the Distinction*

The practical importance of the distinction between executed and executory trusts relates to their construction although today the position is no longer of as much importance as it used to be.[54] The construction of an executed trust is governed by rules of law, whereas executory trusts are construed more liberally and always with a view to carrying out the true intention of the settlor. This may be illustrated by comparing two cases.

In *Re Bostock's Settlement*,[55] the settlor had omitted certain words of limitation which, had they been inserted, would have given an estate in fee simple to the beneficiaries. It was held that, in the absence of those words, the beneficiaries took only a life estate notwithstanding the fact that it was probably intended that they should have taken an estate in fee simple. This was a case of an executed trust and, in the absence of the necessary technical expressions, the limitation was construed according to strict rules of law.

On the other hand, in *Glenorchy v. Bosville*[56] the testator had devised real property to trustees upon trust to convey the estate, after the marriage of his grand-daughter, to her use for life, remainder to the use of her husband for life, remainder to the use of the issue of her body. Under the rule of construction known as the Rule in *Shelley's Case*,[57] the grand-daughter would, if this had been an executed trust, have taken an estate in fee tail (a now obsolete estate of freehold[58] which cannot as such be alienated[59] and can descend only to the heirs of the body of the original tenant). However, since this was an executory trust, the court was able to look at the true intention of the testator. His intention had clearly been to provide for the children of the marriage; consequently, it was held that the trustees should, regardless of the Rule in *Shelley's Case*, convey the property to the grand-daughter for life, with remainder to her first and other sons for an estate in fee tail and an ultimate remainder to her daughter for an estate in fee simple.

These cases illustrate the practical importance of the distinction between executed and executory trusts in matters of construction. One case, *Re Arden*,[60] does admittedly suggest that it could be argued that the distinction is not anything like as clear-cut. In that case it was held, in effect, that the use of an non-technical expression by the creator of an executed trust gave the court a loophole which enabled it to apply a construction which accorded with the real intentions of the settlor. The settlor had used the word "absolutely"; Clauson J. held that the use of this word entitled him to decide that the beneficiary in whose favour it had been used took an equitable fee simple even though, if that word had been omitted, it was acknowledged that he would only have taken a life interest. If this decision is correct, which is in fact somewhat questionable, the position may be somewhat different from that

---

[54] See *post*, p. 162.
[55] [1921] 2 Ch. 469.
[56] (1733) Cas. t. Talb. 3; see also *Papillon v. Voice* (1728) P. Wms. 471.
[57] (1581) 1 Co.Rep. 88B. This case does not apply to instruments taking effect after 1925; see *post*, p. 149.
[58] No estates in fee tail have been able to be created since 1996; pre-existing estates nevertheless continue. Trusts of Land and Appointment of Trustees Act 1996, Sched. 1, para. 5.
[59] A tenant for an estate in fee tail in possession can nevertheless generally convert his estate into an estate in fee simple.
[60] [1935] Ch. 326.

stated above, namely that a non-technical expression which is present in a document may be given a technical meaning even in an executed trust, while the absence of any such expression — as in *Re Bostock's Settlement*[61] — will still nevertheless produce the effect prescribed by strict rules of law.

## 2. *The Special Treatment of Marriage Articles*

One class of executory trusts has been given special treatment. These are executory trusts arising under marriage articles. In such cases the presumption is that the intention of the settlor was to provide for the issue of the marriage so that, despite any technical rules of construction, the husband and wife will normally take life interests,[62] a presumption which will apply unless it is clear that the parties intended to create some other type of interest. This presumption is a strong one and will only be rebutted by the clearest evidence to the contrary. It was particularly significant in the application of the Rule in *Shelley's Case*. In a limitation of land before 1926 for a person for life, remainder to the heirs of his body, that person would have taken an estate in fee tail by virtue of the rule of construction established in that case. But if an executory trust on these lines was contained in marriage articles, the court would strive to avoid this construction and would give that person only a life estate; had this not been done, that person would have been able immediately to bar the estate in fee tail, that is to say bar the interests of his successors in title including his own issue, by converting his own interest into an estate fee simple.

However, in the case of other types of executory trusts, which normally only arise under the provisions of wills, the court, while as always construing the instrument as a whole in order to ascertain the true intention of the settlor, would consider the question of construction on its merits. So, in the ancient case of *Sweetapple v. Bindon*,[63] a testator gave the then substantial sum of £300 to trustees upon trust to invest it in the purchase of land and to settle the land to "the only use of" a person and her children and, in the event that that person died without issue, "the land to be divided between her brothers and sisters then living". Since this was an executory trust under a will, the question of construction was approached on the basis that there was no overriding necessity to give that person a life interest; consequently, it was held that she took an estate in fee tail.

## 3. *The Modern Significance of the Distinction*

What has already been stated above is still applicable as a matter of principle but, along with the authorities cited, must now be read subject to the effect of the legislation of the twentieth century. The Property Legislation Act of 1925 had two effects on instruments taking effect on or after January 1, 1926: first, it abolished the rule in *Shelley's Case*;[64] and, secondly, it removed any necessity for the use of words of limitation for the purpose of creating an estate in fee

---

[61] [1921] Ch. 469.
[62] *Jervoise v. Duke of Northumberland* (1820) 1 Jac. & W. 559 at 574; *Trevor v. Trevor* (1720) 1 P. Wms. 622.
[63] (1706) 2 Vern. 536.
[64] Law of Property 1925, s.131.

simple.[65] The distinction still had to be borne in mind thereafter because of the continuing necessity for words of limitation for the creation of estates in fee tail;[66] however, this too has ceased to have any relevance since January 1, 1997, given that the Trusts of Land and Appointment of Trustees Act 1996 has prevented the creation of any further estates in fee tail on or after that date.[67]

The modern significance of the distinction is therefore little. Marriage articles are now rare, presumably because, in so far as marriage settlements are still created at all, they are highly likely to have been set up at least partly for the purpose of tax avoidance, something which requires all the documents involved to have been carefully thought out and prepared in advance. Nevertheless, modern examples of executory trusts still exist.

Where a settlor or testator has manifested an intention to create an immediate charitable trust but further steps may have to be taken in order to effectuate the charitable intention which he has expressed, the trust will amount to an executory trust and will be immediately established. This was specifically held by the Court of Appeal in *Harris v. Sharp*, [68] where a memorandum manifesting such an intention was signed by a settlor in respect of property already held by the intended trustees, the settlor's solicitors; the settlor subsequently seems to have changed his mind[69] but the Court of Appeal held that a valid charitable trust had been created.

An even more significant illustration, given the importance of pension trusts today, is that of a pension scheme established, as most pension schemes are, by an interim deed of trust which provides for the subsequent execution of a definitive deed of trust later on. In *Davis v. Richards & Wallington Industries*,[70] following the initial execution of an interim deed, the definitive deed was subsequently duly executed; however, the validity of the latter deed was challenged when questions arose as to the entitlement to surplus funds. Scott J. in fact found the definitive deed to have been valid. However, he stated that, had he not done so, he would have upheld the interim deed as a valid executory trust capable of being executed by a court order; this would have had the effect of providing rules corresponding to those in the definitive deed by means of which the questions relating to the surplus funds would have been able to have been resolved. The distinction between executed and executory trusts can therefore still be extremely important today in the field of construction.

## IV. WHEN A TRUST IS INCOMPLETELY CONSTITUTED, WHEN WILL THE BENEFICIARIES HAVE A CONTRACTUAL REMEDY?

Where no completely constituted trust has arisen either as a result of the effectual transfer of the intended trust property to the trustees or as a result of

---

[65] *ibid.* s.60.
[66] *ibid.* s.130.
[67] Sched. 1, para. 5.
[68] (1989) [2003] T.L.I. 41.
[69] He had signed the memorandum between his conviction and his subsequent sentencing for defrauding another charity; its execution was clearly intended to be and was used in mitigation but he was nevertheless sent to prison.
[70] [1990] 1 W.L.R. 1511.

a declaration of trust by the settlor and where the beneficiaries are unable to rely on any of the exceptions to the rule that equity will not perfect an imperfect gift, the only possibility open to them will be to rely on the law of contract. There are a number of situations where a contractual remedy will enable the beneficiaries either to bring about the complete constitution of the trust or, in default, obtain common law damages. The possibility that the beneficiaries will be able to do so has been considerably enhanced by the enactment of the Contracts (Rights of Third Parties) Act 1999.[71]

That obviously does not mean that a contractual remedy is always available to the beneficiaries. Where there is neither a completely constituted trust nor a contractual remedy, the trust in question is said to be voluntary and the beneficiaries are said to be volunteers. It is a long-established equitable maxim that "equity will not assist a volunteer".[72] Although this maxim is invariably relied on by the courts whenever a beneficiary is denied a remedy, its utilisation adds nothing and is a source of potential confusion. The maxim neither denies a remedy to a beneficiary who already has one nor provides a remedy to a beneficiary who does not have one. Consequently, it does no more than state the obvious, namely that, if a beneficiary can point neither to the existence of a completely constituted trust nor to the existence of any form of contract enforceable either by him or on his behalf, then equity will not assist him. More significantly, the existence of the maxim has hindered the development of the law since, unfortunately but predictably, the courts have tended to utilise it as a substitute for reasoned analysis of whether or not in any particular case any contractual remedy is actually available to the beneficiary.

The contractual remedies available to the beneficiaries of an incompletely constituted trust may arise either under a simple contract (a contract constituted as a result of the existence of offer and acceptance, intention to create legal relations, and consideration) or under a specialty contract (a contract constituted by virtue of being contained in a deed, often also described as a covenant).

The contract entered into by the settlor may be a straightforward contract to settle some of his existing property, that is to say property of which he is already able to dispose.[73] However, there is normally little reason for a settlor to enter into such a contract in respect of existing property.[74] Such property can be the subject of a valid assignment, of a valid declaration of a trust, and of a valid contract to assign or declare a trust. Consequently, if the subject matter of a proposed trust is existing property, the settlor can just as easily constitute the trust immediately by transfer to trustees or by declaration as enter into a contract so to do.

For this reason, most contracts of this type (and most of the cases which have come before the courts) have concerned property which has not yet come

---

[72] *Ellison v. Ellison* (1802) 6 Ves. 656 at 662, *per* Lord Eldon L.C.; see also *Jefferys v. Jefferys* (1841) Cr. & Ph. 138.

[73] Such cases were *Williamson v. Codrington* (1750) 1 Ves.Sen. 511 (covenant to settle a plantation); *Fletcher v. Fletcher* (1844) 4 Hare 167 (covenant to settle £60,000); and *Re Cavendish Browne's Settlement Trusts* [1916] W.N. 341 (covenant to settle property to which the settlor was entitled under the wills of persons who had already died).

[74] In both *Williamson v. Codrington* and *Fletcher v. Fletcher*, the reason was undoubtedly the fact that the beneficiaries were the illegitimate children of the settlors, who clearly wished to avoid embarrassing publicity until after their deaths.

into existence, generally known as after-acquired property. Such property cannot be the subject of a valid assignment, which is at law wholly void,[75] although equity will treat the assignment of after-acquired property made in exchange for valuable consideration as a contract to assign or declare a trust if and when the property is acquired.[76] Nor can after-acquired property be the subject of a valid declaration of trust[77] although equity will enforce this declaration of trust in favour of anyone who has provided valuable consideration if and when the property is acquired.[78] Further, an express contract to assign or declare a trust if and when the property is acquired will be enforced whether it is a simple contract and is consequently supported by valuable consideration or merely a speciality contract; a simple contract of this type will be enforced both in equity and at common law,[79] while a speciality contract of this type will be enforced at common law,[80] but not in equity.[81] All this means that, where the subject matter of a proposed trust is after-acquired property, the settlor will have no option but to enter into what either is or is deemed by equity to be a contract to settle the property in question if and when it is acquired.

Because of this significant distinction between existing and after-acquired property, it is important to note that, for this purpose, existing property is not confined to property which has already vested in possession and is thus available for the immediate enjoyment of the person entitled thereto. Existing property also includes property which has not yet come into possession, either because the interest is vested in interest, in other words awaiting the determination of some prior interest (an example is the interest of a person who is absolutely entitled in remainder during a preceding life tenancy) or contingent (an example is the interest of a person entitled to property at the age of 30 when he has not yet attained that age). Further, existing property includes existing choses in action (an example is the right to recover book-debts arising in the course of a business)[82] and the right to exercise an existing power of appointment only at some future time (an example is an already granted power of appointment which is exercisable only by will).

After-acquired property, on the other hand, is property in respect of which only the future will determine whether or not the person in question ever acquires any rights at all (examples are the possibility of receiving property

---

[75] *Holroyd v. Marshall* (1862) 10 H.L.C. 191 (assignment by way of mortgage of machinery which in the future might be substituted for existing machinery); *Re Tilt* (1896) 40 Sol.Jo. 224 (assignment of an expectancy under the intestacy of a person who was still alive); *Re Ellenborough* [1903] 1 Ch. 697 (assignment of an expectancy under the will of a person who was still alive).

[76] *Holroyd v. Marshall* (1862) 10 H.L.C. 191 at 211, 220.

[77] *Williams v. C.I.R.* [1965] N.Z.L.R. 395 (Court of Appeal of New Zealand) (declaration of trust of the first £500 of the net income arising under a life interest in each of four future years).

[78] *Ellison v. Ellison* (1802) 6 Ves.Jun. 656 at 662; *Williams v. C.I.R.* [1965] N.Z.L.R. 395 (Court of Appeal of New Zealand).

[79] The simple contract will not be enforceable at common law if the valuable consideration in question is marriage, which is not regarded as valuable consideration at law. However, a simple contract supported by marriage consideration will nevertheless be enforceable in equity; see *Pullan v. Koe* [1913] 1 Ch. 9, *post*, p. 168.

[80] *Cannon v. Hartley* [1949] Ch. 213. See *post*, p. 170.

[81] *Jefferys v. Jefferys* (1841) Cr. & P. 138.

[82] As in *Barclays Bank v. Willowbrook International* [1987] 1 F.T.L.R. 386.

(including the right to exercise a power of appointment)[83] under the will[84] or intestacy[85] of someone who is still alive or under an as yet unexercised power of appointment, the possibility of receiving future royalties payable in respect of a copyright or a mining operation,[86] and the possibility of acquiring future book-debts arising in the course of a business.[87])

Consequently, while a settlor may validly assign an equitable remainder to trustees on trust, declare a trust[88] of that interest, or enter into either a simple or a specialty contract to make such an assignment or declaration of trust, his possible courses of action in respect of the payments which he hopes to receive as the royalties on a book or a mine are much more restricted. He cannot validly either assign or declare a trust of such payments, although a purported assignment or declaration of trust will be regarded by equity as a contract to assign or declare a trust if and when the property is acquired; however, he can enter into either a simple contract (enforceable both at law[89] and in equity) or a specialty contract (enforceable only at law) to make such an assignment or declaration of trust.

### 1. A Simple Contract to Create the Trust

If the settlor and the beneficiary have entered into a simple contract for the creation by the settlor of a completely constituted trust in favour of the beneficiary, then both parties to the contract will be entitled to the appropriate contractual remedies. The beneficiary will also be so entitled if he is a third party to the contract in question who is entitled to enforce that contract under the Contracts (Rights of Third Parties) Act 1999.[90]

### (A) A Simple Contract Recognised both at Common Law and in Equity

Where the consideration provided by the beneficiary is money or money's worth, then the existence of the contract will be recognised both at common law and in equity. Consequently both settlor and beneficiary will be able to obtain damages for breach of contract or, if the contract in question is capable of being specifically enforced, a decree for specific performance.

Where specific performance is available, the property in question will in equity immediately become subject to the trust. Thus, if the settlor contracts with the beneficiary for money or money's worth to transfer land to trustees to hold on trust for him, in equity the land will immediately become subject to the trust and the beneficiary will be able to obtain a decree for specific per-

---

[83] *Re Ellenborough* [1903] 1 Ch. 697.
[84] *Re Tilt* (1896) 40 Sol.Jo. 224.
[85] *Re Parkin* [1892] 3 Ch. 510.
[86] *Coulls v. Bagot's Trustee* [1967] 40 A.L.J.R. 471.
[87] *Tailby v. Official Receiver* (1888) 13 App. Cas. 523. A further example which the author of this edition has encountered in practice is any new tenancy or monetary compensation given for the future surrender of a protected tenancy under the Rent Act 1977 (the right to remain in occupation under such a tenancy is not itself a proprietary interest but merely consists of the right to resist eviction and so cannot itself be the subject of an assignment or a declaration of trust); another example would be similar rights in relation to a business tenancy protected under Part II of the Landlord and Tenant Act 1954.
[88] Strictly speaking, a sub-trust. See *ante*, p. 101.
[89] Provided that the consideration is money or money's worth rather than marriage consideration.
[90] See *ante*, pp. 22–27.

formance of this contract; thus he will be able to oblige the settlor to transfer the land to the trustees in exchange for the money or money's worth in question. This remedy will also be available to the beneficiary where the subject matter of the intended trust is pure personalty for whose loss equity regards damages as an inadequate remedy; this will be the case where the subject matter is a chattel not readily available on the open market, such as a rare painting, a rare antique, a vintage motor vehicle, or shares in a private company.

Where, on the other hand, the contract in question is not capable of being specifically enforced because damages are an adequate remedy for the loss of the subject matter of the intended trust, the beneficiary will be limited to common law damages for breach of contract. These damages will be payable directly to the beneficiary rather than to the intended trustees, although there will obviously be nothing to prevent the beneficiary from himself paying the sum in question on to the trustees and thus creating a completely constituted trust of the money.

These principles apply not only to existing property but also to after-acquired property if and when it is acquired. In *Holroyd v. Marshall*,[91] following the sale of machinery in a mill, the purchaser assigned the machinery to a trustee on trust for the vendor if he should pay £5,000 to the purchaser and if not on trust for the purchaser. The deed of assignment included both the existing machinery and any after-acquired machinery which might be added to or substituted for the original machinery. The House of Lords held that, as soon as any further machinery was acquired, it vested immediately in equity in the trustee on these trusts and thus could not be the subject of execution by the creditors of the vendor. It has been established by subsequent authorities that this will occur even in the case of property in respect of which specific performance would not normally be decreed provided that the valuable consideration has already been furnished by the beneficiary.[92] Thus in *Re Gillott's Settlement*[93] debtors agreed with their creditors that any income which they received should within three days of receipt be paid to a trustee on various trusts for both debtors and creditors. It was held that an equitable interest in each payment received by the debtors vested immediately in the trustee so that the trust of each payment was immediately completely con-stituted. The majority of the decided cases, however, concern marriage con-sideration, a type of valuable consideration which is not recognised by the common law, and so will be discussed in the following section.[94]

## (B) A Simple Contract Recognised Only in Equity

In one particular situation not recognised by the common law, equity will imply both a contract for the creation by the settlor of a completely constituted trust in favour of the beneficiary and the consideration necessary for that contract on the part of the beneficiary. This occurs where the beneficiary can bring himself within a marriage consideration.

Where a settlement in consideration of marriage is made either before the

---

[91] (1862) 10 H.L.C. 191.
[92] Principally by the House of Lords in *Tailby v. Official Receiver* (1888) 13 App. Cas. 523 (a case concerning an assignment by way of mortgage rather than an assignment to trustees on trust).
[93] [1934] Ch. 97. See also *Re Lind* [1915] 2 Ch. 345 and *Re Haynes' Will Trusts* [1949] Ch. 5.
[94] See *post, infra*.

marriage or contemporaneously with the celebration of the marriage or sub-sequent to the marriage pursuant to an agreement made prior to the marriage, equity implies that the settlor, the spouses, and the children and more remote descendants of the marriage are parties to a contract in respect of which they have given consideration. Any of the persons thus deemed to be a party to this implied contract can enforce any of the obligations arising thereunder, not only the original obligation of the settlor to create the settlement in question but also any obligations of the spouses to transfer any of their existing or after-acquired property to the trustees to be held on the trusts of the settlement. Any such obligation is capable of being specifically enforced even where damages would normally be an adequate remedy for the loss of the property in ques-tion. In the case of a marriage settlement, common law damages are never an adequate remedy for the simple reason that they are not available in an action by the beneficiaries[95] — the common law does not recognise marriage consideration.

These principles are illustrated by the case of *Pullan v. Koe*.[96] A wife was given a sum of money which was caught by a covenant to settle after-acquired property into which both she and her husband had entered in their marriage settlement. The sum was never transferred to the trustees and part of the money was eventually invested in bonds which were held at a bank in the name of the husband. Following his death, the bonds came into the hands of his executor. Any action by the trustees on the covenants had by then become statute barred. However, it was held that the money received by the wife had been subject to the trusts of the marriage settlement from the moment of its receipt. Consequently, the children of the marriage could specifically enforce the simple contract implied by equity and thus bring about the transfer of the bonds by the executor to the trustees.

Normally the only persons within the marriage consideration are the spouses, the children and the more remote descendants of the marriage.[97] However, there is some authority that, in certain circumstances, illegitimate children and children of an earlier or subsequent marriage of one of the spouses may be brought within the marriage consideration if their interests are so "interwoven" with the interests of the children of the marriage in con-sideration of which the settlement was made that the interests of the latter cannot be enforced without also enforcing the interests of the former. This was suggested in *Attorney-General v. Jacobs-Smith*[98] and was supported by Buckley J. in *Re Cook's Settlement Trusts*.[99] The latter case, however, shows that this extension, which is in any case somewhat ambiguous, will apparently not be extended any further.

In that case,[1] an attempt was made to establish a similar principle to enable an intended beneficiary who is specially an object of the intended trust or is

---

[95] Common law damages will of course be available in an action by the trustees to enforce any covenants entered into by either the settlor or the spouses.

[96] [1913] 1 Ch. 9.

[97] *MacDonald v. Scott* [1893] A.C. 642 at 650 establishes that "issue" includes both children and more remote issue such as grandchildren and great-grandchildren.

[98] [1895] 2 Q.B. 341 at 354, *per* Kay L.J.

[99] [1965] Ch. 902. See also *Re D'Avigdor-Goldsmid* [1951] Ch. 1038 at 1053 (overruled on other grounds: [1953] A.C. 347).

[1] [1965] Ch. 902.

within the consideration of the deed of settlement to enforce any obligations contained therein. (This alleged principle bears some resemblance to the former doctrine of "meritorious consideration", a principle analogous to marriage consideration which existed at least until the end of the 18th century;[2] the latter principle was based on the natural love and affection between parent and child and consequently could be utilised by the latter to enforce settlements made by the former.) Sir Francis Cook had entered into a settlement which was not in consideration of marriage in which he had covenanted with his father and with the trustees that, in the event that he sold certain valuable paintings which had been transferred to him by his father, he would pay over the proceeds of sale to the trustees to be held on the trusts of the settlement, ultimately for the benefit of his children. He subsequently purported to give one of the paintings to his then wife who wished to sell it. Buckley J. refused to accept the alleged principle, holding that the equitable exception to the rule that equity will not assist a volunteer is confined to persons within the marriage consideration. Having consequently held that the children could not enforce the covenant against Sir Francis, he then went on to hold, for reasons that will be considered later but which no longer necessarily constitute the law,[3] that the trustees ought not to enforce the covenant against him either.

Because at the time when a marriage settlement is entered into, it is not normally known whether or not there will actually be any issue of the marriage, it is usual to insert an ultimate remainder in favour of the statutory next-of-kin of one of the spouses. Such persons are not within the marriage consideration and cannot enforce any of the obligations arising under the marriage settlement. This is illustrated by Re Plumptre's Settlement.[4] The husband and wife, on the occasion of their marriage, covenanted with their trustees to settle the wife's after-acquired property for the benefit of herself and her husband successively for life, then for the issue of the marriage, and then for the wife's next-of-kin. The husband bought certain stock in the wife's name and the wife afterwards sold it and invested the proceeds of sale in other stock. She then died without issue, leaving her husband as her administrator. It was held that the next-of-kin, because they were volunteers, could not enforce the wife's covenant against her husband as administrator. It was also held that the trustees could not sue for damages for breach of covenant because the claim was statute-barred.[5]

Finally, it should be noted that, if the settlement is made after marriage and not in pursuance of an ante-nuptial agreement, it will be wholly voluntary. This is because, although there may be consideration between husband and wife, that consideration would not be their marriage — such being past — but consideration of some other kind to which their children would be strangers.[6]

---

[2] This is generally thought to be the basis on which a covenant to settle a plantation on illegitimate children was enforced in Williamson v. Codrington (1750) 1 Ves.Sen. 511 and is one of the possible explanations of the decision in Fletcher v. Fletcher (1844) 6 Hare 67 (see Jones (1965) 24 C.L.J. 46 at 49).

[3] See post, p. 171.

[4] [1910] 1 Ch. 609. See also to a like effect Re D'Angibau (1880) 15 Ch.D. 228.

[5] Any such action subsequently appeared to have become impossible whether or not it was statute-barred because of the decisions in Re Pryce [1917] 1 Ch. 234, Re Kay's Settlement [1939] Ch. 329 and Re Cook's Settlement Trusts [1965] Ch. 902; however, those decisions now no longer represent the law so the issue of limitation has once again become relevant. See post, p. 171.

[6] Such as the consideration provided in Re Cook's Settlement Trusts.

This was expressly held in *Green v. Paterson*,[7] which was applied in *Re Cook's Settlement Trusts*.

## 2. A Specialty Contract or Covenant to Create the Trust

Specialty contracts or covenants to settle property on trust have traditionally played an important role in settlements of all types. Not only have settlors commonly entered into covenants to create entirely new trusts by transferring existing or after-acquired property to trustees on trust; trusts which have already been completely constituted have regularly included covenants by the beneficiaries to transfer their existing or after-acquired property to the trustees to be held on the trusts of the settlement. This is illustrated by the cases which have already been discussed in this section. When a covenant to create a trust is entered into in exchange for valuable consideration, it will be enforceable in accordance with the principles which were considered in the immediately preceding part of this section. This part of this section is concerned with the situation where a covenant has been entered into other than for valuable consideration. In such circumstances, the beneficiaries will inevitably be in a weaker position. Their only possibilities are to attempt to enforce the covenant themselves or to show that there is a completely constituted trust in their favour of its benefit.[8]

### (A) Enforcement of the Covenant by the Beneficiaries
The beneficiaries will be able to maintain an action at common law against the settlor on the covenant to settle if the covenant to settle purports to be made with them as covenantees and is either a deed poll (a deed to which only the settlor is a party) or a deed *inter partes* (a deed to which the settlor and others are parties) to which the beneficiaries are either parties or are made parties by section 56 of the Law of Property Act 1925 (which applies only where the subject matter is land).[9] In *Cannon v. Hartley*[10] a husband, wife and daughter were all parties to a deed of separation in which the father covenanted to settle on himself, the wife and the daughter one half of any property which he might receive under the will of either of his parents. Having received such property, he refused to settle it. The daughter was held to be entitled to maintain against him an action for damages for breach of covenant. Since she had given no value, she was clearly unable to obtain specific performance. However, the fact that, because she was a volunteer, equity declined to assist her did not mean that equity would frustrate her right at common law to enforce a covenant to which she was a party. She consequently recovered, by way of damages, the value of the interest which she should have received under the settlement. Thus, while this remedy will not enable the trust to be completely constituted, the beneficiaries will be able to recover compensation for the loss of the interest which they would have obtained thereunder.

---

[7] (1886) 32 Ch.D. 95.
[8] These possibilities have been the subject of an immense body of periodical literature, of which the principal articles are (in chronological order): Elliott (1960) 76 L.Q.R. 100; Hornby (1962) 78 L.Q.R. 228; Lee (1969) 85 L.Q.R. 213; Barton (1976) 92 L.Q.R. 236; Meagher & Lehane (1976) 92 L.Q.R. 427; Rickett (1979) 32 C.L.P. 1 and (1981) 34 C.L.P. 189; Friend [1982] Conv. 280.
[9] See the review of the authorities by Lord Upjohn in *Beswick v. Beswick* [1968] A.C. 98 at 102–105.
[10] [1949] Ch. 213.

The beneficiaries will also be able to maintain an action at common law against the settlor on the covenant to settle if they can bring themselves with the provisions of the Contracts (Rights of Third Parties) Act 1999. Section 1 of that Act provides that a third party to a contract who is identifiable may enforce any term of that contract in his own right provided that either the contract so provides or the term in question purports to confer a benefit on him and it does not appear, on a proper construction of that term, that the parties did not intend him to be able to do so. A third party will be identifiable if he is expressly identified by name, or is a member of an identified class, or answers a specific description. There is no requirement that he should have been in existence at the date of the contract; this is very important for present purposes because the beneficiaries of trusts of after acquired property which are the subject matter of a covenant to settle are more often than not unborn at the time when the covenant is entered into. The Act applies automatically to specialty contracts entered into on or after May 11, 2000, six months after the Act was passed; however, the Act will apply to contracts entered into during that six month period if the contracts in question contain an express provision to that effect.[11]

This provision will normally be applicable to covenants to settle property on trust. The beneficiaries will necessarily be identifiable, since otherwise the trust in question would be void for uncertainty of objects.[12] Consequently, those beneficiaries will normally be able to enforce the covenant against the settlor and obtain damages for breach of covenant.

However, there are a number of circumstances where this will not be possible. First, it could be decided as a matter of construction that the settlor did not intend the beneficiaries to be able to enforce the term of the covenant purporting to confer a benefit on them. Secondly, the covenant may have been entered into before May 11, 2000 (it is obviously possible for after-acquired property which was the subject matter of a covenant entered into before that date to be acquired by the settlor only after that date). Thirdly, the beneficiaries may only find out about the existence of the covenant after the settlor has purported to rescind it under section 2 of the Contracts (Rights of Third Parties) Act 1999[13] (this possibility is not as far-fetched as it might appear since the settlor may initially conceal the existence of the covenant[14] and later purport to rescind it; alternatively, he may purport to rescind the contract before a relevant beneficiary has been born or has attained the age of majority). In all these situations, the pre-existing law will remain relevant.

In such circumstances, the beneficiaries will nevertheless be able to enforce the covenant indirectly if there is a completely constituted trust of its benefit of the type considered in the next part of this section. In the absence of any such

---

[11] Contracts (Rights of Third Parties) Act 1999, s.10.

[12] See *ante*, pp. 59–74.

[13] This section provides that, where a third party has rights under s 1, the parties to a contract may not rescind it without his consent where he has communicated his assent to the term in question to the person bound by that term. It must follow as a necessary corollary of this provision that, at least so far as the Act is concerned, they can rescind the contract where he has not so communicated his consent.

[14] In *Fletcher v. Fletcher* (1844) 4 Hare 67, *post*, p. 173, the settlor concealed the existence of the covenant throughout his lifetime and it was only discovered among his papers some years after his death; the beneficiaries were his illegitimate sons and it seems tolerably clear that he did not wish anyone to become aware of their existence until after his death.

trust, they will clearly have no direct means of enforcing the covenant. This somewhat obvious proposition was confirmed by the Court of Appeal in *Re d'Angibau*,[15] where the eventual beneficiaries under a marriage settlement, the wife's next-of-kin, who were of course not within the marriage consideration, were held unable to enforce a covenant by the wife to transfer an equitable remainder to the trustees of the settlement. In such circumstances, the only remaining option of the beneficiaries will be to attempt to enforce the covenant indirectly by means of an action by the trustees on the covenant at law against the settlor.

It is clear that the beneficiaries cannot compel the trustees to bring such an action (in the absence of a trust of the benefit of the covenant and of any simple or specialty contract to which they are parties, they are clearly in no position to compel anyone to do anything and are undoubtedly volunteers). However, given that the trustees have an undoubted right of action at law against the settlor, it might be thought that they would be entitled to exercise that right of action if they so chose and hold any damages recovered from the settlor on trust for the beneficiaries. This is not in fact the case. It has long been established that, if the trustees seek the directions of the court,[16] they will be directed not to sue the settlor on the covenant. Indeed, this rule is so well established that there is now no need for the trustees to trouble to obtain any directions — the present authorities provide them with a complete defence to any action for breach of trust.[17]

The three relevant authorities are *Re Pryce*,[18] *Re Kay's Settlement*[19] and *Re Cook's Settlement Trusts*.[20] None of them contains any reasoned discussion of exactly why the trustees must not enforce the covenant. It has been argued[21] that there is no reason for equity thus to restrain parties to a covenant from exercising their legal rights thereunder if they wish to do so.[22] However, it seems that the consequences of such an action would not ultimately favour the

---

[15] (1880) 15 Ch.D. 228.

[16] Something which trustees habitually do before embarking on legal proceedings to avoid any risk of being made personally responsible for the costs in the event that they were subsequently held not to have been properly incurred.

[17] See *Re Ralli's Will Trusts* [1964] Ch. 288 at 301–302.

[18] [1917] 1 Ch. 234. The trustees of a marriage settlement sought directions from the court as to whether they were bound to enforce in favour of the wife's next-of-kin (who were the only persons beneficially entitled other than the wife) a covenant by the wife to settle after-acquired property. Eve J. held, correctly, that the next-of-kin could not obtain relief directly and that, consequently, there was no reason for equity to give them relief indirectly by an order to the trustees to enforce the covenant. He then went on to hold, without further discussion, that they were bound not to enforce the covenant (this conclusion was not in fact necessary, since the negative answer to the question which Eve J. was asked was, strictly speaking, 'the trustees are not bound to sue' rather than 'the trustees are bound not to sue'; this is one of the grounds on which the decision has been criticised by Elliott (1960) 76 L.Q.R. 100).

[19] [1939] Ch. 329. The trustees of a voluntary settlement sought directions whether they should or should not take proceedings in favour of the ultimate beneficiaries against the settlor on her covenant to settle after-acquired property and were directed by Simonds J. not to do so. The question put to him envisaged three possible answers: "the trustees must sue", "the trustees may sue", "the trustees must not sue"; consequently, his direction to the trustees not to sue clearly constitutes his *ratio decidendi*.

[20] [1965] Ch. 902.

[21] Particularly by Elliott (1960) 76 L.Q.R. 100.

[22] Because of the risk of being held personally liable for the costs, no trustee would be likely to do so unless the beneficiaries were members of his family or had agreed to indemnify him fully.

beneficiaries. Even on the assumption that the trustees would be able to obtain substantial damages for breach of covenant (an assumption which, although it has been doubted,[23] is in fact supported both by principle[24] and by precedent[25]), there is no reason why these damages should be held on the trusts of the settlement. In a situation where, as is being assumed, there is not a completely constituted trust of the benefit of the covenant, it appears that any damages arising from any action on the covenant would be held by the trustees not on trust for the beneficiaries but on resulting trust for the settlor.[26] Since any action brought by the trustees against the settlor would thus result in the damages payable being held on resulting trust for the person paying them, equity is clearly correct to prohibit such a circuitous action. Consequently, for this reason *Re Pryce, Re Kay's Settlement* and *Re Cook's Settlement Trusts* were, in this respect, correctly decided.

It thus follows that the beneficiaries will not be able to enforce a covenant to settle indirectly by means of an action by the trustees on the covenant at law against the settlor and thus, in the absence of a completely constituted trust and of any simple or specialty contract which they can enforce, they will have no means either of bringing about the complete constitution of the trust of the benefit of the covenant or of obtaining any compensation for the settlor's failure to comply with his covenant to settle.

**(B) A Completely Constituted Trust of the Benefit of the Covenant**
As has already been indicated, where the beneficiaries are unable to enforce a covenant to settle in any other way, they will nevertheless be able to enforce that covenant indirectly if there is a completely constituted trust of its benefit. There is no objection in principle to such a trust. Any chose in action can be the subject matter of a trust and so a settlor is certainly capable of declaring that the right which, by means of his covenant, he has conferred upon the trustees to enforce the covenant against him should be held on trust for the beneficiaries of the intended trust. If such a trust can be found to have been created, then, although the trust of the property which the settlor covenanted to settle will remain incompletely constituted unless and until he transfers that property to the trustees, the beneficiaries will nevertheless be entitled to enforce the completely constituted trust of the benefit of the covenant. This trust will be enforceable in the same way as any other completely constituted trust; the beneficiaries will be able to request the trustee to enforce the covenant against the settlor[27] and, if he declines so to do, they will be able either to bring an action to compel him to do so or to sue the settlor directly on the covenant joining the trustee as a co-defendant to the action.[28]

The existence or non-existence of such a trust will be crucial in the situations

---

[23] See Marshall (1950) 3 C.L.P. 30.

[24] The fact that a party to an action at law is a trustee cannot be a ground for limiting him to nominal damages for the simple reason that the common law does not recognise trusts. For this reason, it should not matter that the trust is in fact incompletely constituted or that the property to be settled is after-acquired.

[25] *Re Cavendish-Browne's Settlement Trusts* [1916] W.N. 341. An analogous authority involving a trust of the benefit of a simple contract is *Lloyd's v. Harper* (1880) 16 Ch.D. 290.

[26] See Underhill & Hayton, *Law of Trusts and Trustees* (16th ed., 2003), pp. 179–182.

[27] *Lloyd's v. Harper* (1880) 16 Ch.D. 290.

[28] *Les Affreteurs Reunis v. Leopold Walford* [1919] A.C. 801.

where the Contracts (Rights of Third Parties) Act 1999 is not applicable to a covenant.[29] Further, whether or not that legislation is applicable, there are some circumstances in which the existence or non-existence of a trust of the benefit of that covenant may determine precisely who is beneficially entitled to the property to be settled.[30] If, for example, the covenant is to settle after-acquired property on persons as joint tenants, even if the latter have a right of action on the covenant, they will not have a proprietary right which they are capable of severing unless and until the property is acquired and vested in the trustee. Consequently, if one of them dies before that time, the other will take the entire property by survivorship. If, on the other hand, the benefit of the covenant is the subject matter of a completely constituted trust, they will each have an immediate proprietary right which they will be able to sever so as to prevent the property passing by survivorship; it will instead devolve according to the will or intestacy of each of them.

The principal difficulty lies in determining exactly when a trust of the benefit of a contract will arise. In *Fletcher v. Fletcher*[31] a settlor covenanted with trustees that, if either or both of his two illegitimate sons survived him, his executors should, within 12 months of his death, pay to the trustees £60,000 which was to be held on trust for such of the two as reached the age of 21. The existence of the deed was never revealed by the settlor either to the trustees or to his sons; he retained the deed in his possession until his death and it was only discovered some years later among his papers. Only one of the sons both survived the settlor and reached the age of 21; he sought to enforce the covenant against the executors. Wigram V.-C. held that the settlor had clearly vested in the trustees the right to sue his executors for £60,000. He held that this was sufficient to produce a completely constituted trust of the benefit of the covenant, which could be enforced by the son.

This decision, which is supported by other contemporaneous authorities,[32] has been interpreted in a variety of ways. However, it has to be seen against the background of the rules which at that time governed certainty of intention (the question of when a settlor will be held to have had sufficient intention to constitute a trust.[33]) Until the middle of the nineteenth century, the courts tended to take the view that any expression of desire or hope or the like on the part of the settlor was imperative and therefore created a binding trust. Given that the settlor had clearly intended his sons to receive the benefit of the covenant after his death, it was perhaps not unreasonable, in the light of the view then habitually adopted as to certainty of intention, for Wigram V.-C. to have found a completely constituted trust of the benefit of the covenant.

---

[29] See *ante*, p. 171.
[30] See Halliwell [2003] Conveyancer 192.
[31] (1844) 4 Hare 67.
[32] None of these authorities contains as clear a statement of principle as that contained in *Fletcher v. Fletcher*; consequently, all have been the subject of different explanations. Wigram V.-C. himself relied on *Clough v. Lambert* (1839) 10 Sim. 74 and *Williamson v. Codrington* (1750) 1 Ves.Sen. 511 (although this decision is equally explicable as based on 'meritorious considera-tion' (see *ante*, fn. 2)). *Watson v. Barker* (1843) 6 Beav. 283 and *Cox v. Barnard* (1850) 8 Hare 310 have also been described as cases of this type, although the better explanation for the latter, as well as for the much later inadequately reported *Re Cavendish-Browne's Settlement Trusts* [1916] W.N. 341 may well be the presence of a covenant for further assurance.
[33] See *ante*, pp. 46–54.

However, following the modification of the rules governing certainty of intention which took place towards the end of the nineteenth century,[34] it is difficult to see how any such intention could today be deduced from the facts of *Fletcher v. Fletcher*. Certainly no such trust has been upheld in any of the cases subsequent to the change in the certainty of intention rule in which arguments based on *Fletcher v. Fletcher* have been raised. Admittedly in one of those cases, *Re Cook's Settlement Trusts*,[35] Buckley J. distinguished *Fletcher v. Fletcher* not on this ground but on the basis that the covenant which he was considering related to after-acquired property, something which was also the case in three other decisions in which *Fletcher v. Fletcher* was not applied.[36] Given that after-acquired property can undoubtedly form the subject matter of a covenant,[37] there seems no good reason for this distinction[38] nor is it consistent with other authorities. In *Davenport v. Bishopp*,[39] Knight-Bruce V.-C. indicated that it was possible for there to be a completely constituted trust of the benefit of a covenant to settle after-acquired property, a view which is confirmed by other authorities in which promises to pay uncertain sums on uncertain future dates arising under simple contracts have been held capable of forming the subject matter of a trust.[40]

Consequently, the distinction of *Fletcher v. Fletcher* on the grounds of lack of certainty of intention seems clearly preferable to the distinction adopted by Buckley J. in *Re Cook's Settlement Trusts*; the latter case is better explained on the grounds that there was no intention to create a trust of the benefit of Sir Francis Cook's covenant in favour of his children but merely an intention to create a trust if and when its subject matter came into existence and was duly transferred to the trustees. On this basis, a completely constituted trust of the benefit of a covenant to settle either existing or after-acquired property must certainly be capable of being found today if the settlor has clearly manifested the appropriate intention[41] by for example, stating expressly that, pending transfer of the intended trust property, "the benefit of the covenant to settle shall be held by the trustees on the trusts of the settlement".

While all the commentators would be likely to agree that the use of this wording would give rise to a completely constituted trust of the benefit of the covenant in question, there is no general agreement as to what, if any, other situations should be found to give rise to such a trust.

---

[34] *ibid.*

[35] [1965] Ch. 902. The facts were considered *ante*, p. 168.

[36] *Re Plumptre's Settlement* [1910] 1 Ch. 609; *Re Pryce* [1917] 1 Ch. 234; *Re Kay's Settlement* [1939] Ch. 329.

[37] See *ante*, p. 167.

[38] See Barton (1976) 92 L.Q.R. 236 and Meagher & Lehane (1976) 92 L.Q.R. 427.

[39] (1843) 2 Y. & C.C.C. 451 at 460.

[40] *Lloyd's v. Harper* (1880) 16 Ch.Div. 290 (Lloyd's was held to be entitled to sue as trustee for the benefit of all those with whom an underwriter had entered into contracts of insurance); *Royal Exchange Assurance v. Tomlin* [1928] Ch. 179 (trust of the benefit of a promise to pay a sum only in the event of a person's death before a certain date upheld).

[41] It has been questioned whether the relevant intention should be that of the settlor or of the trustees, since it is the latter who hold the chose in action which is the subject matter of the trust. However, in the case of a covenant to settle other than for value, the better view is that the relevant intention should be that of the settlor (see *The Restatement of Trusts* (2nd ed.), para. 26; Rickett (1979) 32 C.L.P. 1; Feltham (1982) 98 L.Q.R. 17).

On the one hand, it has been contended that such a trust should never be found in the absence of some clear indication of the type exemplified above that this was indeed the intention of the settlor.[42] This view has the merit of being consistent with the modern rule as to certainty of intention and with all the modern authorities; however, it involves distinguishing *Fletcher v. Fletcher* in one of the ways mentioned above and undoubtedly enables settlors to go back on voluntary covenants to settle where the beneficiaries cannot enforce those covenants directly.[43]

On the other hand, it has been contended that such a trust should be implied into every covenant to settle.[44] This view is clearly inconsistent with the vast majority of the decided cases[45] but does prevent voluntary covenants to settle from ever becoming unenforceable and, therefore, meaningless.[46]

Between these two extreme views, various intermediate positions have been suggested. It has been argued[47] that such a trust should be implied where the covenant in question gives rise to a debt[48] but not otherwise.[49] It has also been argued[50] that such a trust should be implied where the deed in question merely consists of one covenant, on the basis that, since the deed would otherwise be futile, this must be taken to be the intention of the settlor, but that, on the other hand, such a trust should not be implied in the case of lengthy settlements,[51] where the intention of the settlor in relation to individual covenants is necessarily unclear.[52]

However, despite the bewildering variety of views which have been expressed,[53] there is absolutely no doubt that at present, for whatever reason, a completely constituted trust of the benefit of a covenant will not be found in the absence of some clear manifestation of the appropriate intention of the settlor; it certainly has to be admitted that only this view seems to be consistent with the modern rule as to certainty of intention. Only in these circumstances will beneficiaries who are unable to enforce a covenant to settle in any other way nevertheless be able to enforce that covenant indirectly by relying on the existence of such a trust.

---

[42] This view has been adopted in successive editions of this work, of Hanbury & Martin, *Modern Equity* and of Pettit, *Equity and the Law of Trusts*.

[43] See Feltham (1982) 98 L.Q.R. 17.

[44] See Elliott (1960) 76 L.Q.R. 100; Hornby (1962) 78 L.Q.R. 228.

[45] Other than *Fletcher v. Fletcher* and the other cases referred to *ante*, fn. 32.

[46] See *The Restatement of Trusts* (2nd ed.), para. 26 and Feltham (1982) 98 L.Q.R. 17.

[47] By Friend [1982] Conv. 280.

[48] Which will be the case where the subject matter of the covenant is existing money.

[49] In other words, where the subject matter of the covenant is either specific and presently existing property other than money or after-acquired property.

[50] By Hayton in Hayton & Marshall, *Commentary and Cases on the Law of Trusts and Equitable Remedies* (11th ed., 2001) pp. 249–250.

[51] Such as marriage settlements, where covenants to settle are invariably made in favour both of persons within the marriage consideration and of persons outside it.

[52] The settlor cannot be taken to have intended to create such a trust in favour of persons outside the marriage consideration.

[53] Those mentioned in the text are only a sample.

CHAPTER 6

# DISCRETIONS AND POWERS

---

## I. THE NATURE OF DISCRETIONS AND POWERS

### 1. *Generally*

ALMOST all trusts[1] involve the exercise of powers of a largely administrative nature, either conferred expressly by the trust instrument or implied into it by statute; whether or not the powers are exercised is a matter of discretion. Such powers arise whether the trust in question is fixed or discretionary. Discretionary trusts, but not fixed trusts, additionally involve the exercise of discretions of a entirely dispositive nature. This follows from the basic distinction between fixed and discretionary trusts,[2] namely that each of the beneficiaries of a fixed trust is entitled in equity to a fixed pre-determined share of the trust property at the appropriate time and may enforce his rights to that share against the trustees; on the other hand, before any individual beneficiary of a discretionary trust has a right to any part of the trust property, the trustees have to exercise one or more of the discretions vested in them by the settlor or testator. The immense majority of discretionary trusts also confer powers of a dispositive nature exercisable by the trustees, by the settlor, by one or more of the beneficiaries or by some third party who is often described as the protector of the settlement in question;[3] the exercise of these powers is also capable of conferring proprietary rights on individual beneficiaries of the discretionary trust.

It is discretions and powers of a dispositive nature with which this chapter is principally concerned. However, a few words about powers of an administrative nature are also necessary. Such powers are normally conferred only on trustees, although their exercise is sometimes made subject to the control of the settlor, one or more of the beneficiaries or, in the case of discretionary trusts, of the protector of the settlement. Among the powers generally granted are the following: powers to deal with the investment of the trust property by making and transposing investments[4] (these powers now[5] confer all the

---

[1] Only nominee trusts do not do so. Trustees are nominees where they are bare trustees for a sole beneficiary and additionally have agreed with their beneficiary to follow his instructions in all respects; in return, they are entitled to be indemnified by the beneficiary against any liabilities which they may incur to third parties (see *Hardoon v. Belilios* [1901] A.C. 118).
[2] See *ante*, p. 41.
[3] See *post*, p. 189.
[4] See *post*, p. 592.
[5] Since the enactment of the Trustee Act 2000.

powers of an absolute owner;[6] this includes the power to make investments in land — until 2001 this power arose only in the case of trusts holding land or the proceeds of its sale);[7] powers to settle claims;[8] powers to apply to the court for guidance as to the execution of the trust;[9] powers to insure trust property;[10] powers during a minority either to advance income for the maintenance of the infant beneficiary or to accumulate that income;[11] and powers to apply advance capital for the benefit of any beneficiary.[12] All these powers, and many more, will be implied by statute into every trust instrument unless they are expressly excluded.

The last two powers mentioned, the powers of maintenance and advancement, although administrative in nature, are of course dispositive in effect and can be used to achieve the same results as purely dispositive discretions and powers. They are therefore much more relevant to the subject matter of this chapter than are the purely administrative powers. So are the vital powers to replace some or all of the existing trustees and appoint new ones which are generally conferred on the settlor of an inter vivos trust and, subject to that, on the existing trustees or indeed on anyone else at all — in the absence of any express provision, statute confers these powers on the existing trustees although, in such circumstances, beneficiaries of full age who are between them absolutely entitled to the trust property are now also entitled to exercise them.[13] These latter powers are important for the somewhat obvious reason that it is the persons appointed trustees as a result of their exercise who will normally be able to exercise the dispositive powers thereafter.

Two final points must be stressed. First, most of the principles discussed in this chapter are applicable to all the discretions and powers conferred by the trust instrument or by statute, whether those discretions and powers are administrative or dispositive in nature. Secondly, it is fundamental to the nature of a trust that a trustee, or for that matter anyone else who is exercising

---

[6] Trustee Act 2002. s.3(1).

[7] Trustee Act 2000, s.8; this Act has also amended Trusts of Land and Appointment of Trustees Act 1996, s.6(1). Similar powers are held by whoever has the power of investment under a settlement subject to the Settled Land Act 1925, which have not been able to arise since 1996; continuing settlements of this type are not trusts of land and their position is still governed by Settled Land Act 1925, s.41.

[8] Trustee Act 1925, s.15, as amended by Trustee Act 2000, s.40(1), Sched. 2, Pt. II, para. 20.

[9] See post, p. 619.

[10] Trustee Act 1925, s.19, as substituted by Trustee Act 2000, s.34(1). The substituted provision amends the much criticised former position under which trustees were under no duty to insure and had power only to insure for a sum up to three-quarters of the value of the property in question. Trustees who fail to exercise their power are now likely to be in breach of the duty of care imposed by Trustee Act 2000, ss.1, 2 and Sched. 1.

[11] See post, p. 682.

[12] See post, p. 694.

[13] See post, p. 549. The latter powers were conferred on absolutely entitled beneficiaries by Trusts of Land and Appointment of Trustees Act 1996, ss.19, 20. However, they may be (and in practice generally are) excluded by the trust instrument. Although they prima facie apply to trusts created prior to 1997, in the case of such trusts they can also be excluded by a deed executed thereafter by the settlor or by the surviving settlors of full capacity.

discretions and powers, should not be a puppet at the end of a string pulled by the settlor or by the beneficiaries;[14] he must instead be a person who can and will exercise an independent judgment over a wide field. In this respect, the fact that a trustee has been appointed by the settlor, by someone else who has been given an express power so to do such as a protector, or by beneficiaries of full age who are between them absolutely entitled to the trust property does not enable him to escape from liability for breach of trust if he fails to exercise his own independent judgment; however, while he will certainly be at risk if he blindly follows the instructions of the settlor or a protector, he will not be at any risk if he follows instructions given to him by beneficiaries of full age who are between them absolutely entitled to the trust property.

## 2. *Aspects of Discretions*

### (A) Generally

Discretions of a dispositive nature arise under discretionary trusts, trusts in favour of such of the members of a class, either pre-determined or selected by the trustees, as the trustees in their absolute discretion determine from time to time.

Where the class is pre-determined, there are two possibilities: the trustees may merely have the discretion to decide to whom and in what proportions the trust property, or more usually the income arising from that property in any particular year, is to be distributed (this type of trust is known as an exhaustive discretionary trust); alternatively, the trustees may have the discretion both whether to make any distribution at all and, in the event that they decide to do so, to whom and in what proportions (this type of trust is known as a non-exhaustive discretionary trust.[15]) Where the trustees also have the right to determine the membership of the class (or add to the membership of a pre-determined class), they obviously have yet a third discretion.

In all three cases, no individual beneficiary or potential beneficiary of the trust has any right to any part of the trust property unless and until the trustees have exercised in his favour one or more of the discretions vested in them by the settlor or testator. However, individual or potential beneficiaries do have the right to compel the trustees to administer the trust properly;[16] this includes a right to have their claims properly considered from time to time by the trustees.[17] They may also, under what is known as the Rule in *Saunders v.*

---

[14] It is in this respect that the position of a trustee differs from that of a nominee; a bare trustee who is often under an express or implied contractual obligation to comply in all respects with the directions of the beneficiaries. A bare trust is one where property is held directly on trust for a body corporate or one or more beneficiaries of full age absolutely. However, not all trustees whose beneficiaries are of full age and between them absolutely entitled to the trust property are bare trustees. A trustee who holds property by way of succession for persons who are between them absolutely beneficially entitled is certainly not a bare trustee and must act in such a way as to protect the interests both of the tenant for life and of the remainderman. However, both his beneficiaries and the beneficiaries of a bare trust have the right to terminate the trust at any time by calling for the transfer of the trust property to them.

[15] A discretionary trust can only be non-exhaustive during whatever accumulation periods are permitted.

[16] See *post*, p. 715.

[17] See *ante*, p. 73.

*Vautier*,[18] join together to wind up the trust although this is only possible if they are all ascertained and of full age and are between them absolutely entitled to the subject matter of the trust; if these requirements are satisfied, it does not matter that the interests of some of them are deferred or contingent or wholly dependant on the exercise of discretions by the trustees in their favour.

Whether a trust in fact confers a discretion on its trustees is a question of construction which is not always easy to resolve. Fixed, rather than discretionary, trusts were upheld in each of the following three cases.

In *Re Sanderson's Trust*,[19] the trustees were directed to apply the whole or any part of the income "for and towards maintenance, attendance and comfort" of a specified person. Page-Wood V.-C. held that the trustees had no discretion and must apply such part of the income as was necessary for his maintenance, attendance and comfort of that person. The author of this edition recently relied on this decision in order to compromise proceedings arising out of a gift on trust "to utilise a maximum of one-third of my residuary estate for the purposes of rehousing my father for the rest of his lifetime or for so long as he shall wish to reside in such accommodation". This was done on the basis that the trustees equally had no discretion and therefore had to use whatever part of a third of the residuary estate proved to be necessary in order to rehouse the father.[20]

In neither of these two cases was it relevant that the trust in question was for a purpose; this was because of the general rule that trusts of this type are regarded as absolute gifts to the person in question with the purpose being merely their motive.[21] However, this might perhaps have been regarded as relevant in the rather more controversial decision in *Re Bowes*[22] that a trust to expend funds "in planting trees for shelter" on an estate which, although held by the testator during his lifetime, had become vested in another on his death had created an absolute beneficial interest in favour of the latter; he was therefore held to be entitled to call for the money and spend it on whatever he liked. The only real justification for this decision appears to be the fact that, since he could not be compelled to plant trees on his own land, the only other option was to hold that the trust was void for lack of a beneficiary to enforce it so that, on balance, the conclusion reached appears closer to what the testator presumably intended.

### (B) For How Long are Discretions Exercisable?
Although the discretions vested in trustees obviously permit very considerable flexibility, they nevertheless cannot be exercised indefinitely but only within a reasonable time. What is reasonable depends on the facts of each case. In *Re Gulbenkian's Settlement Trusts (No.2)*,[23] the trustees learned in April 1957 of a

---

[18] (1841) Cr. & Ph. 240; see *post*, p. 717.
[19] (1857) 3 K. & J. 497
[20] In both cases, there are obvious difficulties about certainty of subject matter (see *ante*, p. 54); this point was not raised before Page-Wood V.-C. and was not particularly relevant to the issue before him, which was what was to happen to the surplus of the income not so expended. The possibility of it being raised in the more recent proceedings was one of the bases on which the proceedings were settled.
[21] See *Re Osoba* [1979] 1 W.L.R. 247.
[22] [1896] 1 Ch. 507.
[23] [1970] Ch. 408.

decision[24] which cast doubt on the validity of a provision of the trust instrument relating to the accumulation of income. They therefore retained the income without accumulating it. The doubt raised was not actually resolved until the decision of the House of Lords in *Re Gulbenkian's Settlement Trusts (No.1)*[25] in October 1968. The question then arose as to whether the trustees were still entitled to exercise their discretion in respect of income which had been accruing ever since 1957. Plowman J. held that in the circumstances the trustees' retention of the income was not unreasonable; consequently, they could still exercise their discretion in respect of the whole of the accrued income. It therefore follows that, provided the surrounding circumstances make it reasonable for them so to do, trustees can retain income as income for some time and only then decide whether or not to accumulate it.

On the other hand, if the trustees do not exercise their discretion within a reasonable time, the consequences differ depending on whether or not the trustees were obliged to exercise it, in other words whether the discretion in question arose by virtue of a trust power or mere power. In the former case, the trustees will have been under an obligation to exercise their discretion; consequently, it will not be extinguished by lapse of time. Accordingly, the trustees will be able to exercise it at any time, no matter how much later, and, if they fail to do so, the court will direct them so to do[26] or, in default, execute the trust in one of the ways laid down by Lord Wilberforce in *McPhail v. Doulton*.[27] In the latter case, on the other hand, while the trustees will have been under a duty to consider whether or not to exercise their discretion, they will not have been under any duty actually to exercise it; in such circumstances, any failure to exercise their discretion within a reasonable time will cause it to be lost and, consequently, no longer exercisable.[28] Any income which they could have distributed will therefore either have to be turned into capital by being accumulated or, if this is no longer possible,[29] will have to be given to whichever beneficiary is next entitled under the trust.

### (C) To What Extent can Discretions be Delegated?

While there is no restriction on the ability of settlors and testators to confer discretions on their trustees and on other persons, there are restrictions on the ability of the latter to delegate those discretions to others. The basic position is that matters involving a decision on a matter of policy, or importance, which would include a decision as to whether or not a person is to benefit and, if so, to what extent, cannot be delegated,[30] but that ancillary decisions taken in order to give effect to the trustees' decision can be delegated.[31] So, if the trustees in the exercise of their discretion decide to give a beneficiary £500, they are entitled to leave to their solicitor the decision as to whether to pay that sum by cheque or in cash. Otherwise impermissible delegation is of course

---

[24] *Re Gresham's Settlement* [1956] 1 W.L.R. 573, subsequently overruled.
[25] [1970] A.C. 508 and see *ante*, p. 62.
[26] *Re Locker's Settlement Trusts* [1978] 1 All E.R. 216.
[27] [1971] A.C. 424 at 457; *ante*, p. 62.
[28] *Re Gourju's Will Trusts* [1943] Ch. 24; *Re Wise* [1896] 1 Ch. 281; *Re Allen-Meyrick's Will Trusts* [1966] 1 W.L.R. 499.
[29] At present, accumulation is permitted only for limited periods; see *post*, p. 253.
[30] *Re May* [1926] 1 Ch. 136; *Re Mewburn* [1934] Ch. 112; *Re Wills' Will Trusts* [1959] Ch. 1.
[31] *Att.-Gen. v. Scott* (1750) 1 Ves.Sen. 413; *Re Hetling and Merton's Contract* [1893] 3 Ch. 269.

capable of being authorised by the terms of the trust instrument but in the case of discretions, as distinct from powers, this is not normally done.

### 3. Aspects of Powers

**(A) The Basic Definition of Powers**
While powers are most frequently found as provisions in trust instruments, they can exist outside a trust and it is therefore necessary to consider them as a separate concept. A power can be said to be the right to exercise, in respect of property belonging to another, one or more of the rights which are the normal incidents of ownership. Some differences between trusts and powers are immediately apparent. For example, a trust is necessarily equitable, while a power may or may not be. Thus a power of attorney to convey a legal estate and a power of sale over a legal estate exercisable by a mortgagee are both legal; on the other hand, a power affecting the beneficial entitlement to property is now necessarily equitable.[32] But the primary basis of the distinction is of course that a trust is imperative, whereas a power is not. The distinction may be shown by contrasting a trust for sale and a power of sale. Where land is given by deed *inter vivos* or by will to trustees on express trust for sale, then the trustees will be under a duty to sell the land, even though statute now implies a power to postpone sale in every case.[33] On the other hand, where there is merely a power of sale, whether in a deed *inter vivos* or a will, the person in whom the power is vested will not be compelled to exercise it.[34]

**(B) Powers in the Trust Context**
Concentrating on the dispositive powers which are the principal subject matter of this chapter rather than the administrative powers to which reference has already been made, there has been a general tendency to make trusts more and more flexible, which is of course one of the reasons why discretionary trusts have become more popular than fixed trusts. Two of the more recent developments have been to include what are generally known as overriding powers of appointment and powers to alter the class of beneficiaries.

**(1) Overriding powers of appointment**
Where property is settled on discretionary trusts, it necessarily follows that no one has an immediate interest in possession either as to income or as to capital; this is also the effect of a settlement on fixed trusts for persons who are not *sui juris*. In such circumstances, it has become the normal practice to vest in the trustees, or where appropriate the protector, a power, exercisable at any time before any beneficiary obtains an absolute interest in the capital of the trust, for

---

[32] LPA 1925, s.1(7).

[33] Trusts of Land and Appointment of Trustees Act 1996, s.4(1). Prior to this legislation, which came into force on January 1, 1997, the existence of a binding obligation to sell converted the land in the eyes of the law (even if not in fact converted) into money as soon as the will or deed took effect, despite the presence of a power to postpone sale in the instrument in question; however, the doctrine of conversion was, in this respect, abolished by Trusts of Land and Appointment of Trusts Act 1996, s.3 except where the trust in question was created by the will of a testator who died before January 1, 1997.

[34] In such circumstances, the land was not in the eyes of the law converted into money even prior to the Trusts of Land and Appointment of Trustees Act 1996.

the following purposes: first, to permit some or all of the existing trusts to be revoked and for new trusts to be declared in favour of the same, or sometimes slightly different, beneficiaries; and/or, secondly, to permit the trust property to be transferred to the trustees of other settlements under which the same, or sometimes slightly different, persons are beneficially entitled. Such powers are generally known as overriding powers of appointment.

The first of these powers enables the trusts of a settlement to be modified in the light of subsequent events with a view particularly to avoiding for as long as possible anyone obtaining an interest in possession and so giving rise to the deemed disposal for the purposes of capital gains tax which such an event inevitably brings with it.[35] The second of these powers enables the trust to be wound up without having to give any of the beneficiaries an interest in possession in the process, although in this case such a deemed disposal cannot be avoided.[36] Well drawn overriding powers of appointment[37] normally also contain a modified form of the statutory power of advancement (which would be implied anyway in the absence of contrary intention); this power will be exercised in order to vest property in one or more of the beneficiaries absolutely,[38] something which will also give rise to a deemed disposal.

Any trust which contains an overriding power of appointment will inevitably also contain an ultimate absolute beneficial gift in favour of some person or persons who is or are already *sui juris*. No one ever has the slightest intention that these persons, who are generally known as default beneficiaries, should ever obtain an interest in possession save in the unlikely event that all the other beneficiaries are wiped out by some unforeseen disaster such as an air crash or a terrorist bomb. They are there for two purposes: first, to forestall the sort of argument which succeeded in *Vandervell v. I.R.C.*,[39] that the ultimate beneficiary is in fact the settlor, something which can affect not only, as in that case, the incidence of income tax but also the incidence of inheritance tax[40] (for the same reason, the settlor and his present and future spouse also have to be excluded from the class of beneficiaries in whose favour the power can be exercised); and, secondly, to forestall any argument that the trustees have for any moment of time in effect, even though not on the face of things, been holding on trust for one of the earlier beneficiaries absolutely, something which would trigger an undesired deemed disposal.

It will be apparent from the contents of the previous two paragraphs that the utilisation of overriding powers of appointment is a complicated affair. The most elaborate precautions have to be taken: first, in order to ensure that what is being done is within the powers which have been conferred on the trustees, which are in turn subject to various overriding rules of law, such as the var-

---

[35] See *post*, pp. 199, 633.

[36] Because the trustees will be holding the property on trust for the trustees of the other settlement absolutely; see *post*, p. 638.

[37] An excellent example are the overriding powers of appointment which are explained and set out in the precedents included in Kessler, *Drafting Trusts and Will Trusts* (it is particularly important always to use the most recent edition of this work; the current one is the 6th (2002) edition).

[38] Powers of advancement can also be used to make resettlements (see *Pilkington v. I.R.C.* [1964] A.C. 612) but this is not necessary where the settlement in question also contains an overriding power of appointment.

[39] [1967] 2 A.C. 191; see *ante*, p. 105.

[40] See *post*, pp. 199, 639.

ious rules against perpetuities and accumulations which will be discussed in the next chapter;[41] and, secondly, to avoid any undesirable or unexpected fiscal consequences. These difficulties multiply when overriding powers of appointment are being used on a second or subsequent occasion because of the need to act in a way which is consistent not only with the provisions of the original settlement but also with the modifications which have already been made. Dealing with such clauses is therefore one of the most difficult and, therefore, one of the most stimulating aspects of modern discretionary trusts.

## (2) Powers to alter the class of beneficiaries

The decision in *Re Manisty's Settlement*,[42] established, resolving previous doubts in this respect, that there is in principle no objection to a settlor conferring powers on the trustees, or for that matter on any protector, which permit the alteration of the class of beneficiaries, either by addition to or by subtraction from the pre-existing class.

What was actually in issue in that case was a power to add persons to the existing class of beneficiaries. The settlement was a discretionary trust for the benefit of the children and remoter issue of the settlor. The trustees purported to exercise a power to bring other persons into that class by bringing in the settlor's mother and any person who in the future might become the settlor's widow. Templeman J. held that such a power could indeed be validly conferred on trustees and that their exercise of it was therefore valid.[43] Such powers provide a useful means of providing for people whose existence has been overlooked or whose financial situation suddenly changes for the worse.

However, the settlement also conferred a power on the trustees to exclude any individual members of the existing class of beneficiaries. Such a power is even more useful because it enables the settlor initially to declare a very wide class of beneficiaries and at the same time give his trustees power to exclude anyone within that class if this becomes necessary at any later stage (as it often does, usually as a result of the introduction of new legislation adversely affecting the fiscal liabilities of the settlor, the trust or the beneficiaries). Templeman J. was equally prepared to accept the validity of this sort of power.

Needless to say, exactly the same precautions have to be taken in the exercise of this type of power as in the exercise of overriding powers of appointment.

## (C) To What Extent can Powers be Delegated?

There is no doubt that a settlor or testator can give a power of appointment to a trustee or indeed to anyone else — even a general power of appointment given by a testator to his trustees cannot be impugned as a delegation of testamentary disposition.[44] The basic rule governing the extent to which trustees or others can delegate the powers which have been given to them is the same as in the case of discretions: matters involving a decision on a matter

---

[41] See *post*, pp. 238–255.

[42] [1974] Ch. 17; see also *Blausten v. I.R.C.* [1982] Ch. 256 and *Re Hay's Settlement Trusts* [1982] 1 W.L.R. 202, discussed *ante*, p. 71.

[43] The decision was consistent with the earlier approval by the House of Lords in *Pilkington v. I.R.C.* [1964] A.C. 612 of the exercise of a power of advancement which took effect by way of resettlement; see *post*, p. 704.

[44] *Re Beatty's Will Trusts* [1990] 1 W.L.R. 1503; see Davies 107 L.Q.R. (1991) 211.

of policy, or importance, which would include a decision as to whether or not a person is to benefit and, if so, to what extent, cannot be delegated,[45] but ancillary decisions taken in order to give effect to the trustees' decision can be delegated.[46]

However, the instrument by which a power is conferred can expressly authorise delegation of its exercise and modern overriding powers of appointment generally contain provisions to this effect.[47] Occasionally, powers can also be delegated by virtue of express statutory provisions.[48] Where there is no such express authority, it seems that delegation can still be made effectively where there is an implied power to this effect in the instrument creating the power but not otherwise.

So far as powers to determine beneficial entitlements are concerned, the question of delegation most often arises where there is a power to appoint a fund among a number of beneficiaries and the donee of the power wishes to make an appointment not in favour of a particular beneficiary absolutely but instead on trust for him. It is clear that the donee of the power cannot appoint the fund on discretionary trusts, even if all the beneficiaries of the discretionary trust in question are beneficiaries of the original settlement, unless this is expressly or impliedly authorised in the trust instrument (most modern overriding powers of appointment specifically so provide.[49]) This is because an unauthorised appointment on discretionary trusts amounts to the donee of the power delegating to the trustees of the new trust the power to decide what each beneficiary of the discretionary trust will in fact receive.[50] Similarly if, in the absence of such authorisation, an appointment is made on protective trusts[51] (which has the effect of conferring a life interest which, in the event of on the life tenant's bankruptcy, will determine and be replaced by discretionary trusts), the appointment of the life interest will be valid but the discretionary trusts will be void in the event that they replace the life interest.[52] However, it is accepted that any appointment on trust which is validly made in accordance with the terms of the power may also confer a power of advancement on the trustees, even if the trustees of the original settlement did not have one or did not have one as broad; to this extent at least, an appointment may confer an additional discretion on the trustees of a new settlement.[53]

---

[45] *Re May* [1926] 1 Ch. 136; *Re Mewburn* [1934] Ch. 112; *Re Wills' Will Trusts* [1959] Ch. 1.

[46] *Att.-Gen. v. Scott* (1750) 1 Ves.Sen. 413; *Re Hetling and Merton's Contract* [1893] 3 Ch. 269.

[47] See the overriding powers of appointment set out in Kessler, *Drafting Trusts and Will Trusts* (it is particularly important always to use the most recent edition of this work; the current one is the 6th (2002) edition).

[48] An example of statutory authority to delegate is that conferred by Trusts of Land and Appointment of Trustees Act 1996, s.9 (replacing Law of Property Act 1925, s.29), which enables trustees of land to delegate their powers of management see also *post*, pp. 493, 508.

[49] See the overriding powers of appointment set out in Kessler, *Drafting Trusts and Will Trusts* (it is particularly important always to use the most recent edition of this work; the current one is the 6th (2002) edition).

[50] *Re Morris' Settlement* [1951] 2 All E.R. 528; *Re Hay's Settlement Trusts* [1982] 1 W.L.R. 202.

[51] See *post*, p. 264.

[52] *Re Boulton's Settlement Trusts* [1928] Ch. 703; *Re Morris' Settlement* [1951] 2 All E.R. 528; *Re Hunter* [1963] Ch. 72.

[53] This was specifically held in *Re Morris' Settlement* [1951] 2 All E.R. 528, a decision which was accepted to be correct in *Re Wills' Will Trusts* [1959] Ch. 1 and in *Pilkington v. I.R.C.* [1964] A.C. 612.

The different question of the extent to which trustees can delegate their powers of management and administration and appoint agents to act on their behalf is considered in later chapters.[54]

### 4. Distinctions between Discretions and Powers of Appointment

It has already been seen that the practical effect of the exercise of discretions and of powers of appointment is very similar. Deciding which of the two has been created is often far from straightforward. In *Bond v. Pickford*,[55] the trustees were given the power to "apply capital for the benefit of any one or more of the beneficiaries by allocating or appropriating to such beneficiary such sum or sums out of or investments forming part of the capital of the trust fund" as they thought fit. Nourse J. held that this power of "allocation or appropriation" was akin to a limited special power of appointment. Conclusions of this type, however marginal they may be, may nevertheless be important because there are three significant practical differences between discretions and powers of appointment.

### (A) Payments from the Trust Fund

The first difference relates to payments from the trust fund. Strictly speaking, a discretion deals with funds which are already in hand, whereas a power of appointment governs money which will arise or become payable in the future. An analogy can usefully be drawn with the operation of a railway with each train representing a payment.

The exercise of a discretion in favour of a beneficiary takes place after a train or a number of trains have already reached the marshalling yard and are under the control of the marshaller (that is to say, after a payment of funds or a number of payments of funds have reached the hands of the trustees); in such circumstances, the marshaller has to decide down which of a number of possible tracks to send the individual wagons making up the train or trains (that is to say, the trustees have to decide which of the beneficiaries should receive the whole or some part of each payment received).

On the other hand, the exercise of a power of appointment in favour of a beneficiary amounts to setting the points towards a particular track. This action does not of course in itself cause a train to come along and go down that particular track (that is to say, the exercise of the power of appointment in favour of the beneficiary does not of itself cause any payment to be made to him). However, whenever a train comes along (that is to say, whenever funds become available for payment), that train will go down that track (that is to say, the funds will be paid to that particular beneficiary) without any further action or decision being taken for so long as the points remain set in that direction (that is to say, for so long as the appointment remains unrevoked).

This difference is particularly important when, as is generally the case, the funds subject to the power are the income of the trust fund. In the case of a discretion, a separate decision has to be taken on each occasion on which any income is available for distribution. This latter point may be illustrated by

---

[54] See *post*, pp. 570, 611.

[55] [1982] S.T.C. 403; the subsequent appeal to the Court of Appeal is reported only in *The Times*, May 24, 1983.

*Wilson v. Turner*.[56] In that case the trustees had a power to pay or apply income arising from the trust fund to or for the maintenance of an infant beneficiary.[57] They did not make a conscious decision on each occasion but merely handed over the income to the infant's father. The Court of Appeal held that the payments so made had to be repaid to the trust fund. Had the trustees instead from time to time actively considered the merits of the case and consciously decided to apply the income for the maintenance of that infant, their decision would have been valid.[58] If, on the other hand, income is subject to a power of appointment, then, once an appointment has been made, all income arising will go to the beneficiary to whom it has been appointed without any further decision having to be taken.

The applicability of the distinction to payments of income is of crucial importance in relation to the incidence of inheritance tax. As will be seen in a later chapter,[59] whether or not the death of a person with an interest under a settlement gives rise to a charge to inheritance tax on the value of the settled property depends on whether or not he has an interest in possession in that property. A beneficiary who is only entitled to any income from a trust in the event that the trustees decide to exercise a discretion in his favour does not have an interest in possession in the trust property and, in the event of his death, no charge to inheritance tax will arise in respect of the settled property. On the other hand, once there has been an appointment of income in favour of a beneficiary of a settlement, that beneficiary has an interest in possession in the settled property, even if the appointment is revocable; consequently, if he dies without the appointment having been revoked, the whole of the settled property whose income has been appointed to him will be subject to inheritance tax. The same distinction now seems also to apply to the situation where a beneficiary is in occupation of the trust property.[60]

## (B) Formalities

The second difference between a discretion and a power of appointment is in relation to formalities. No formality whatever is required for the exercise of a discretion, simply because the discretion is exercised at the moment when those exercising it reach their decision so to do.[61] On the other hand, although in principle no formality is necessary for the exercise of a power of appointment either, in practice some formality is almost always prescribed in the instrument by which the power is conferred. Where this is the case, the formal requirements in question have to be strictly complied with. Consequently, if a power of appointment is to be exercised by deed, it cannot be exercised by

---

[56] (1883) 22 Ch.D. 521.

[57] The statutory power of maintenance is considered *post*, p. 682.

[58] A further illustration of the same principle is *Re Greenwood* (1911) 105 L.T. 509.

[59] See *post*, p. 639.

[60] See *I.R.C. v. Lloyds Private Banking* [1999] S.T.C. 559, although in that case the beneficiary was held to have a determinable life interest and so clearly had an interest in possession in the property in question.

[61] It is theoretically possible for the donor of the power to prescribe some formal requirement for the exercise of any discretion arising thereunder but it is most unlikely that this would ever be done.

will[62] and a power which is to be exercised by will cannot be exercised by any instrument which is not a will.[63] Further, where a power has to be exercised within a particular time, it will only be validly exercised by will if the testator has died by then.[64] However, there are some exceptions to this basic rule.

If the donor of the power not only specifies the type of instrument by which the power is to be exercised, such as a deed or will, but also specifies particular formalities to be observed in the execution of that instrument, such as signature in the presence of witnesses, the requirements stipulated by him are sometimes modified by statute. Section 159 of the Law of Property Act 1925 provides that, in the case of a power which has to be exercised by deed, any exercise of it will be formally valid if the deed in question is executed in the presence of at least two witnesses; similarly, in the case of a power which has to be or is exercised by will, the exercise will be formally valid provided that the will in question complies with the provisions of the Wills Acts.[65]

A possible further exception to the general principle that formal requirements must be strictly observed is that equity has in certain cases perfected the imperfect exercise of a power in a somewhat similar way to that in which it will perfect an imperfect gift.[66] Broadly speaking, equity has done this where the donee of the power intended to exercise it and his exercise of the power was in order to satisfy a moral obligation.[67] There are, however, no recent examples of this exception and it cannot be assumed that it would necessarily be applied today.

It can therefore generally be said that the exercise of a discretion requires only a metaphysical act, whereas the exercise of a power of appointment requires a physical act by the appointor. It should, however, be stressed that questions of formality must not be confused with any requirement that the consent of any person must be obtained prior to exercise. The exercise of both a discretion and a power of appointment can be made subject to various consents being first obtained and any purported exercise made without those consents will be ineffective.

## (C) Revocability
The third difference between discretions and powers of appointment relates to revocability. When a discretion is exercised, its effect is to confer upon the beneficiary a right to a sum which is in hand. The beneficiary has the right to demand payment, and payment is in fact usually made to him promptly. It is then too late for the person exercising his discretion to seek to change his mind and to recall the money.[68] On the other hand, a power of appointment looks towards the future. It can therefore clearly be expressed to be revocable, and in

---

[62] *Lord Darlington v. Pulteney* (1797) 3 Ves.Jr. 384; *Lady Cavan v. Doe* (1795) 6 Bro.P.C. 175; *Re Phillips* (1884) 41 Ch.D. 417.

[63] *Reid v. Shergold* (1805) 10 Ves.Jr. 370; *Re Evered* [1910] 2 Ch. 147.

[64] *Cooper v. Martin* (1867) L.R. 3 Ch.App. 47. However, this will not actually prevent the power being exercised inter vivos by then where this is a permissible alternative.

[65] Wills Act 1837, s.10; Wills Act 1963, s.2.

[66] See *ante*, p. 141.

[67] *Chapman v. Gibson* (1791) 3 Bro.C.C. 229; *Garth v. Townsend* (1869) L.R. 7 Eq. 220; *Kennard v. Kennard* (1872) L.R. 8 Ch.App. 227.

[68] It is theoretically possible for the donor of the power to provide that the donees of the discretion could change their minds between the exercise of the discretion and the payment over of the sum to the beneficiary in question but it is most unlikely that this would ever be done.

this event, subject to the terms of the instrument by which it was conferred, the appointment can be revoked and a new appointment made without any limit.

It should first be noted that whether a power is actually revocable depends on the terms of the instrument by which it is created. Most modern overriding powers of appointment[69] deal with this question expressly, usually by providing that powers may be exercised either revocably or irrevocably; however, there is obviously nothing to stop a settlor or testator from providing that any particular power can only be exercised irrevocably. In the absence of any express or implied provision dealing with the matter, it seems to be assumed that a power can be exercised in either of the two ways. There does, however, seem to be a presumption that, if nothing is said as to whether a power is being exercised revocably or irrevocably, it is being exercised irrevocably.[70]

It is apparent that a discretion and revocable power of appointment can both be used to achieve the same general effect. For example, suppose the donor has at his disposal the income of a fund and wishes that for the year 2004 it should go to Charles; for the year 2005 it should go to Douglas; and for the year 2006 it should go to Edward. If what the donor has is a discretion, a decision can be made at or after the end of 2004 in favour of Charles; at or after the end of 2005, in favour of Douglas; and, at or after the end of 2006, in favour of Edward. If, on the other hand, what the donor has is a revocable power of appointment, at the beginning of 2004 the income can be revocably appointed to Charles; at the beginning of 2005, that appointment can be revoked and a new revocable appointment be made in favour of Douglas; and, at the beginning of 2006, the appointment can again be revoked and a new revocable appointment made in favour of Edward. The result so far as the beneficiaries in question are concerned is the same in both cases. If, as is likely in the case of modern trust instruments, the donors are trustees and have the option of taking either course of action, they are likely to be influenced in their choice as to how to proceed by fiscal considerations.

## 5. The Exercise of Discretions and Powers by Third Parties

It has already been seen that discretions and powers can be vested not only in the two parties whose existence is necessary to the existence of any trust,[71] namely one or more trustees and one or more beneficiaries (each of the two can be and very often is[72] both trustee and beneficiary) but also in the settlor, even though he is neither trustee nor beneficiary, and in third parties who have no other connection with the trust in question.

There has long been a tendency for certain powers to be vested in settlors and in individual beneficiaries. Traditional settlements for persons by way of succession have habitually given the settlor or the initial tenant for life a power

---

[69] See the overriding powers of appointment set out in Kessler, *Drafting Trusts and Will Trusts* (it is particularly important always to use the most recent edition of this work; the current one is the 6th (2002) edition).

[70] Assuming that this presumption does in fact exist, it must clearly be able to be rebutted by implication in appropriate circumstances.

[71] See *ante*, p. 18.

[72] Every property which is jointly owned will, under Law of Property Act 1925, ss.34, 36, be held by its co-owners as trustees at law on trust for themselves as either joint tenants or tenants in common in equity.

to choose which of a number of potential remaindermen will take at the end of the life interest — a typical formulation would be a gift "to trustees to hold on trust for my wife for life and subject to that for such of our children as I the settlor [or she my wife] may by will or by deed appoint and in default of appointment for all our children in equal shares absolutely". Powers of this type are also sometimes given to persons who are otherwise totally unconnected with the settlement.

However, in recent years it has become increasingly common, particularly in trusts created in off-shore jurisdictions, for much more substantial powers to be conferred on a person who has generally become known as "the protector" of the settlement in question; such a person is, however, just as much the donee of powers as a person with more restricted powers.[73] Initially substantial powers of this type tended to be of a negative, rather than a positive nature, in that they merely enabled protectors to veto the ways in which the trustees exercised the powers vested in them, although such powers were admittedly often backed up by a power to remove the existing trustees and appoint new ones in their place. However, it is now normal for a protector to be given positive, rather than merely negative, powers both to determine the beneficial interests and to direct the trustees how to exercise the administrative powers vested in them.[74]

The expression "protector of the settlement" is actually derived from the Fines and Recoveries Act 1833 and originally denoted a person who, in certain circumstances, had to give his approval to a now virtually obsolete estate in land known as an estate in fee tail being converted into an estate in fee simple.[75] However, none of the characteristics of a modern protector is derived from this statute. Further, there is not the slightest need for a person with the sort of substantial powers referred to in the previous paragraph to be given any specific name whatever by the trust instrument and, even if such a person is given some specific name, there is no requirement that he be described as a protector. Other names, such as an enforcer, a nominator or a committee,[76] are also commonly employed, the name enforcer being particularly common in respect of the novel types of purpose trusts which, as has already been seen,[77]

---

[73] See generally Waters in *Trends in Contemporary Trust Law* (ed. Oakley, 1996), p. 63.

[74] (The Bahamas) Trustee Act 1998, s.81 specifically envisages a whole series of such powers being given to protectors.

[75] An estate in fee tail devolves on the successive heirs of the body of the original tenant in fee tail. However, such an estate can be converted into an estate in fee simple, a process known as barring the entail; this has the effect of depriving the next person in line of his inheritance. A tenant in fee tail in possession has, since 1833, been able to bar his entail by an *inter vivos* conveyance of the land in fee simple or, since 1925, by his will. But a tenant in fee tail who does not have an interest in possession has only ever been able to do this inter vivos and then only with the consent of the person known as the protector of the settlement. That person will now always be the holder of the interest in possession for the time being or, in default, the court; however, until 1926, settlors were entitled to nominate up to three persons of their choice to act as protector of the settlement and that possibility is the basis of the modern usage of the expression. Estates in fee tail do still exist but sadly no more can now be created as a result of the Trusts of Land and Appointment of Trustees Act 1996, Sched. 1, para. 5.

[76] See the British Virgin Islands Trustee Ordinance 1994, s.86 ("protector, nominator, committee or any other name").

[77] See *ante*, p. 80.

have been the subject of legislative development in some of the offshore jurisdictions.[78] However, for present purposes, all such persons will be described as protectors.

Where an off-shore jurisdiction has made specific reference to protectors by that or any other name,[79] the legislation in question has tended also to regulate in certain respects their powers and potential liabilities and any such regulation is of course definitive in the jurisdiction in question. However, many jurisdictions, such as England and Wales, have no legislation which contains any reference to the rights and duties of protectors and the legislation of jurisdictions in off-shore jurisdictions which has provided for the novel types of purpose trusts is not generally applicable to other types of trusts either. In such circumstances, the position of protectors is governed exclusively by the contents of the trust instrument in question. This was specifically held in Bermuda, one of the jurisdictions which has never had any relevant legislation other than that concerning purpose trusts, in one of the very few cases in which the position of protectors has yet had to be considered, *Von Knieriem v. Bermuda Trust Company;*[80] the same approach was adopted, although not explicitly, in the other leading case, the decision of the Court of Appeal[81] of the Isle of Man in *Steele v. Paz.*[82]

No matter what the precise powers conferred on any particular protector actually are, however, his appointment is for one purpose and one purpose only, namely to enable the trustees to be directed and controlled in the exercise of their discretions in the way desired by the settlor. It is because the settlors of trusts subject to English law are likely to know, and consequently have confidence in, their chosen trustees, and because such trustees are anyway likely to be reasonably susceptible to the influence of the settlor and the beneficiaries, that protectors have not yet become particularly common in such trusts. The frequent utilisation of protectors in off-shore trusts is precisely because in practice such trusts have to have locally based trustees whom neither the settlor nor the beneficiaries is even likely to know, never mind trust. While it is usually inadvisable for either a resident settlor of an off-shore trust or resident beneficiaries to be among its trustees,[83] the same risks do not automatically

---

[78] The most influential legislation was (Bermuda) Trusts (Special Provisions) Act 1989, subsequently redrafted and substantially amended in 1998; see also (Jersey) Trusts (Jersey) Law 1984 Articles 10A, 10B & 10C (added in 1996), which are similar to the original Bermudan legislation. Much more revolutionary was (Cayman Islands) Special Trusts (Alternative Regime) Law 1997, now (Cayman Islands) Trusts Law 2001, ss.95–109 (because of the name of the original legislation, such trusts are known as STAR trusts). All these statutes use the expression "enforcer").

[79] Other examples are (Belize Trusts) Act 1992, s.16 ("protector"); (Cook Islands) International Trusts Act 1984, s.2 ("protector").

[80] (1994) 1 *Butterworths Offshore Cases and Materials* 116 (see Matthews, 9 *Trust Law International* (1995) 108).

[81] Technically known as "the Staff of Government Division".

[82] (1995) 1 *Butterworths Offshore Cases and Materials* 338.

[83] This is because the Inland Revenue may then contend that the person in question is in control of the trust and attempt to tax him on its income and its capital gains, thus defeating the whole object of the exercise. This happened in *I.R.C. v. Schroder* [1983] S.T.C. 480, where the Revenue unsuccessfully claimed that this was the result of the settlor having the power to appoint trustees and protectors. Further, under the present law, a majority of off-shore trustees is necessary even where the settlor was non-resident.

attach to having a resident settlor as protector; however, having the settlor as protector is still not generally recommended.[84] But there is no risk at all in having a third party protector from the settlor's "home" jurisdiction; indeed the settlor's local lawyer often fulfils this role in the same way as he would fulfil the role of an on-shore trustee.[85] Such a protector can readily be informed of the wishes of the person who will necessarily have appointed him (and who *in extremis* will often be able to remove and replace him); this will normally mean that the trustees' discretions are exercised in accordance with the settlor's wishes not only during the settlor's lifetime but more or less indefinitely since the protector will continue in office after the settlor's death and is likely to have the power to nominate a successor.

The presence of a protector will also generally be advantageous for the beneficiaries, at any rate after the settlor's death. But this will not necessarily be the case during the settlor's lifetime, whether the protector is the settlor or someone else. In *Von Knieriem v. Bermuda Trust Company*,[86] the trust property comprised a substantial minority holding in a company which was in turn the holding company of a major pharmaceutical group. The settlor was the moving spirit of this holding company but, due to a boardroom struggle, had to face the possibility that he would be voted off its board of directors. The protector, the settlor's lawyer and personal friend, sought assurances from the trustee, a Bermuda trust company, that it would delegate its votes to him and thus enable him to vote for the settlor. The trust company, apparently under some pressure from the beneficiaries who seem to have been less enthusiastic about the settlor, refused to do so. So the protector simply removed the trustee and appointed another Bermudan trust company as trustee in its place. The court held that both the removal and the appointment were valid and granted the protector an order[87] that the shares be transferred to the new trustee. The position of the settlor was therefore preserved contrary to the wishes of the beneficiaries, who were also deprived of any possibility of recourse against the original trust company.[88] However, in the light of a subsequent decision[89] that such powers are normally[90] fiduciary powers, beneficiaries in this position might well now be able to avoid any exercise of the powers which could be shown not to be in their interests.

In any event, the exercise by a protector of his powers is not wholly devoid of control. As will be seen later on,[91] the exercise of any power can be set aside in the event that the donee commits fraud on the power or makes a relevant

---

[84] Where the settlor is resident, the income of the trust will be taxable as his income if he as protector has the power to direct its application. Further, whatever his residence, there is a risk, particularly if the powers given to the protector are very extensive, that it may be contended that the level of control thus retained by the settlor makes the trust a sham; see *ante*, p. 50.

[85] This has been the case in the majority of the reported cases on protectors where the protector has been a third party.

[86] (1994) 1 *Butterworths Offshore Cases and Materials* 116 (see Matthews, 9 *Trust Law International* (1995) 108).

[87] Where, as in this case, the protector had no statutory authority to seek the aid of the court, the basis of his right to do so is not entirely clear but has not been questioned in any of the relevant authorities (see also *Re X's Settlement* (1994) 1 B.O.S. 600 (Jersey) and *Re Omar's Family Trust* [2000] W.T.L.R. 713 (The Cayman Islands)).

[88] Who could not possibly be held liable for breach of trust if it had been sacked against its will.

[89] *Re Osiris Trustees and Goodways* (1999) 3 *Butterworths Offshore Service* 257 (Isle of Man).

[90] This is not the case where the protector is also one of the beneficiaries.

[91] See *post*, p. 220.

mistake and these rules must apply as much to protectors as to other donees of powers. In this respect, it will be significant whether the power in question is a fiduciary power or a personal power; such authorities as there are[92] suggest that only powers which cannot be used for the personal benefit of the individual protector are fiduciary powers. However, in the absence of dishonesty,[93] it does not appear that a protector can be held liable to compensate the beneficiaries for his actions except where relevant legislation so provides.[94]

### 6. Reasons for Creating Discretions and Powers

**(A) Flexibility**

As was mentioned in Chapter 1,[95] a settlor or testator often wishes to make a present disposition but to confer a benefit at some time in the future in the light of the circumstances then pertaining, circumstances which have not yet arisen and which therefore necessarily cannot be known. A person who is creating a trust for his children or remoter issue may wish the amount, if any, which each receives to depend on his or her conduct financial need and/or success. A much larger payment may be justified in the case of a beneficiary who is a student or who is training for entry into a profession or vocation than in the case of a sibling of his who is already well established in business. Alternatively, a person may have definitively decided to devote funds to charitable purposes but may wish the particular recipients of his bounty to be selected according to the social or other needs which seem most pressing at the time in the future when the funds become available. However, it must not be thought that the fact that discretions have been vested in trustees necessarily means that the objects of the trust must be treated unequally. A father who creates a trust for his children or more remote issue leaves the trustees entirely free to treat them all alike if the trustees wish to do so; equally, the trustees are free to treat them unequally whether or not one of the special circumstances which the father may have had in mind occurs.

**(B) Continuing Control of the Property**

**(1) By the settlor as such**

A settlor of a trust has no formal legal right to any control over the trust property by virtue of the fact that he was the settlor; indeed, he does not as such even the right to have his wishes listened to. However, there is nothing to stop the settlor of an inter vivos trust appointing himself as one of the original trustees and this is extremely common in the case of on-shore trusts, although

---

[92] Apart from the authorities already referred to, see *Rawson Trust Co. v. Perlman* (1990) 1 Butterworths Offshore Service 31 at 50–52 (The Bahamas).

[93] In which case, he may be liable for "dishonest assistance"; see *post*, p. 374.

[94] Only the (United States of America) Restatement (Second) of Trusts (1959) s.185 specifically envisages such liability, although jurisdictions such as The Bahamas and The British Virgin Islands, which exonerate protectors when acting in good faith, may well be regarded as envisaging such liability in the absence of good faith.

[95] See *ante*, p. 8.

usually inadvisable in the case of off-shore trusts.[96] Further, even where the settlor is not one of the original trustees, he will generally able to direct and control the trustees in the exercise of their discretions during his lifetime. He will undoubtedly have been responsible for choosing the original trustees and they are obviously likely to listen to his views. Indeed, in the case of off-shore trusts, settlors generally have the power to remove the trustees and appoint new ones in their place without having to show cause; however, such powers have been held to be fiduciary powers[97] and so their exercise will be voidable if they are not exercised in the interests of the beneficiaries but, for example, in the interests of the settlor himself.

### (2) By the settlor as the donee of powers

As has just been seen, the settlor of an inter vivos trust may well have the power to remove the trustees and appoint new trustees in their place without having to show cause. It has also already been seen[98] that traditional settlements for persons by way of succession have habitually given the settlor a power to choose which of a number of potential remaindermen will take at the end of the initial life interest and that there is no reason in principle why the settlor should not appoint himself as the initial protector, although this is not usually recommended.[99] A further type of power which is occasionally vested in the settlor of an inter vivos trust is a power to revoke the settlement in question. The exercise of such a power will necessarily take away any fiscal advantages which the creation of the settlement was intended to achieve and so, where the settlor remains subject to the tax regime of his home jurisdiction, there are now fewer[1] circumstances where its exercise will have any point. However, the existence, as distinct from the exercise, of such a power cannot now[2] of itself adversely affect the existence of a settlement and there is therefore now no reason why such powers should not be included, as they often are in off-shore jurisdictions.

### (3) By means of the use of a third party protector

It has also already been seen[3] that the purpose of appointing a protector is to enable the trustees to be directed and controlled in the exercise of their discretions in the way desired by the settlor; where the protector is neither the

---

[96] This is because the Inland Revenue may then contend that the person in question is in control of the trust and attempt to tax him on its income and its capital gains, thus defeating the whole object of the exercise. This happened in *I.R.C. v. Schroder* [1983] S.T.C. 480, where the Revenue unsuccessfully claimed that this was the result of the settlor having the power to appoint trustees and protectors. Further, under the present law, a majority of off-shore trustees is necessary even where the settlor was non-resident.

[97] *Re Osiris Trustees and Goodways* (1999) 3 Butterworths Offshore Services 257 (Isle of Man).

[98] See *ante*, p. 190.

[99] Because of the risk that it may be contended, particularly if the powers given to the protector are very extensive, that the level of control thus retained by the settlor makes the trust a sham; see *ante*, p. 50.

[1] The decision in *Melville v. I.R.C.* [2000] S.T.C. 628 established that the exercise of a power of revocation could enable capital gains tax which would otherwise have arisen on the creation of a settlement to be held over; however, that decision was in this respect been reversed by legislation in 2002.

[2] It could conceivably have done so before the effect of the decision in *Melville v. I.R.C.* [2000] S.T.C. 628 was reversed.

[3] See *ante*, p. 190.

settlor nor a beneficiary of a settlement, his appointment will normally mean that the trustees' discretions are exercised in accordance with the settlor's wishes not only during the settlor's lifetime but more or less indefinitely since, once the settlor is dead, each protector is likely to have the power to nominate his successor.

### (4) By means of letters of wishes

A less direct means by which settlors can control the ultimate devolution of the trust property is by means of letters of wishes.[4] As their name suggests, these are documents which exist outside the formal trust documents. They set out the wishes of the settlor but are not binding on the trustees.[5] Further, as will be seen later on,[6] at present the beneficiaries are not normally entitled to see them.

A genuine letter of wishes, by which the settlor provides additional guidance for the trustees of a discretionary trust who have little contact with and may well not know all the members of a class of beneficiaries, is not only not objectionable; it can be extremely helpful. Such non-binding guidance can be very useful for both settlor and trustees, although less so for beneficiaries even in the event that they are actually allowed to see the document in question.

However, in off-shore jurisdictions, letters of wishes can play rather different roles. Deeds of trust tend to be standard form documents used in hundreds of cases and often take the form of a declaration of trust by the off-shore trustees stating that a nominal sum has been transferred to them to be held on the trusts in question rather than a deed of settlement executed by the settlor. In such circumstances, letters of wishes are often the only documents which reveal the identity of the true settlor and the true beneficiaries. They therefore enable the existence of the settlement and the interests of the beneficiaries thereunder to be concealed both from any creditors, and dependants and fiscal authorities who might be interested in discovering them.[7] This admittedly does not prejudice either the settlor or the beneficiaries.

Letters of wishes are also used off-shore for more sinister purposes. Tailored letters of wishes are sometimes used to convince settlors unfamiliar with the nature of discretionary trusts, usually but not always settlors from non common-law jurisdictions with a less than perfect command of English, that their wishes will in fact be followed when the reality is that those wishes are not binding. In these circumstances, if the trust deed were held to be a sham and the settlor were held to have intended the letter of wishes to have been binding on the trustees, the letter of wishes could be regarded as constituting the true trusts. This would admittedly only be likely to cause any immediate problems if the settlor had expressed the wish that income or capital should be paid to him or to his spouse (for settlors in most jurisdictions, this would effectively make all income and capital gains taxable in their hands on-shore). However, the consequential loss of secrecy could obviously also in the long term prejudice the interests of other beneficiaries.

---

[4] See Matthews [1995] Offshore Tax Planning Review 181.
[5] *Bank of Nova Scotia Trust Co. (Bahamas) v. Ricart de Barletta* (1985) 1 Butterworths Offshore Service 5, 8–9.
[6] See *post*, p. 581.
[7] See the description of a settlement of this type in *Re T.R. Technology Investment Trust* [1988] B.C.L.C. 256, 263–264.

Even worse, letters of wishes are occasionally pure shams, either because their terms have not been explained to the settlor or because they have been signed by dummy settlors who request the trustees to take into account the wishes of a settlor whose name has not even yet been inserted in the appropriate space on the standard form letter;[8] the latter type of sham letters of wishes obviously often accompany sham trusts.[9] If the trust deed were held to be a sham and a much less precise letter of wishes obliged the trustees to follow the instructions of the settlor, he could be regarded as having retained a life interest in the trust property; if, on the other hand, both the trust deed and the letter of wishes were held to be a sham, there would be no trust at all and the trust property would be deemed to have been held on resulting trust for the settlor at all times. Both results would, in addition to the income tax and capital gains tax consequences already mentioned, expose settlors in most jurisdictions to inheritance tax on the entire trust property on their deaths and, in civil law jurisdictions, would also expose the assets much more readily to attacks by their forcible heirs, the persons in such jurisdictions whom it is not possible to disinherit.

Nevertheless, these abusive uses of letters of wishes should not be allowed to detract from the extremely useful function of a genuine letter of wishes in enabling the settlor to provide non-binding guidance for the trustees and thus control, at least to some extent, the devolution of the trust property.[10]

### (C) Fiscal Considerations

Despite the obvious advantages already discussed, it is nevertheless fiscal considerations which are, at the present time, generally the principal reason for the creation of discretionary trusts.

In the United Kingdom, income tax and capital gains tax are so-called "progressive taxes" in that they are imposed on the "slices" of a person's taxable income or capital gains at a progressively increasing rate. Each person is entitled to receive the first "slice" of his income free of tax.[11] The next "slice" is taxable at what is known as "the starting rate" of, at present, 10 per cent; the next "slice" is taxable at what is known as "the basic rate" of, at present, 22 per cent; and the residue is taxable at what is known as "the higher rate" of, at present, 40 per cent.[12] Income tax is withheld at source on income from company distributions at, at present, 10 per cent which is deemed to satisfy the basic rate of tax; higher rate taxpayers have to pay further tax on company

---

[8] See the facts of *West v. Lazard Brothers & Co. (Jersey)* [1993] Jersey L.R. 165, 201–205.
[9] See *ante*, p. 50.
[10] See *ante*, p. 8.
[11] The amount of this "slice" is calculated by means of personal allowances, which vary according to the personal circumstances of the individual. For the year 2003–04, a single person is entitled to a personal allowance of £4,615; additional allowances are available to married persons, to single parents, to widows and widowers, and to pensioners, in respect of dependant relatives, and in certain other circumstances. The size of these allowances is reviewed annually in each Budget and listed in the Finance Act by means of which each Budget is brought into effect. Income tax is at present governed by the Income and Corporation Taxes Act 1988.
[12] In 2003–04, the first £1,960 of taxable income (that is the income which exceeds a person's total allowances) was taxed at 10 per cent, taxable income between £1,961 and £30,500 was taxed at 22 per cent, and taxable income in excess of £30,300 was taxed at 40 per cent. The width of the bands and their thresholds are also reviewed annually in each Budget and listed in each Finance Act.

distributions of, at present, 22.5 per cent; the 10 per cent so withheld can no longer be recovered. Income tax is also withheld at source on income from bank deposits but this time at what is known as "the lower rate" of, at present, 20 per cent which is equally deemed to satisfy the basic rate of tax; this 20 per cent can be recovered by non-tax-payers and taxpayers who are liable only to the starting rate, while higher rate taxpayers have to pay further tax of, at present, 20 per cent. Capital gains tax is imposed at the same rate as income tax on such part of a person's taxable capital gains in each year as exceeds his annual exemption.[13] Inheritance tax, on the other hand, is imposed at a fixed rate of 40 per cent on such part of a person's estate (which for this purpose includes any property disposed of other than for value during the seven years immediately prior to his death) as exceeds his lifetime allowance.[14]

In terms of tax planning, a discretionary trust has three main advantages. First, the terms of the trust instrument usually allow the trustees to decide whether to distribute or to withhold income. They can therefore distribute income to a beneficiary in a year when his total income is low, so that his total liability to tax is kept down, and withhold income when the beneficiary's total income is high. Secondly, the trust instrument usually allows the trustees to accumulate income, so that it becomes converted into capital, although this is at present only possible for the first 21 years of the trust and during subsequent minorities (however, if current proposals are enacted, the permissible periods will be increased to no less than 125 years).[15] Thirdly, a discretionary trust allows income and capital to be spread among members of a family, rather than being bunched in the hands of one member. To take a simple example, suppose that Andrew, Basil and Colin are brothers and suppose, also, that Andrew's top rate of income tax is 40 per cent, that Basil's top rate of income tax is 22 per cent and that Colin, as a student, has no taxable income whatsoever. In principle,[16] if Andrew receives £1,000 of investment income, income tax of £400 would ultimately be payable on it, leaving Andrew with £600 in his pocket. If, however, the investment income arises in a discretionary trust and the trustees elect to pay £400 to Basil and £600 to Colin, Basil will pay £88 income tax and Colin will pay nothing (assuming in each case, of course, that the investment income does not move his total taxable income into a higher "slice"). The family as a whole, therefore, will now in principle pay only £88 in tax, a reduction of £312.[17]

However, as a result of the widespread use of discretionary trusts in order

---

[13] In 2003–04, £7,900. There are many other exemptions, including the taxpayer's main residence, chattels worth less than £6,000, and certain securities. Capital gains tax is at present governed by the Taxation of Chargeable Gains Act 1992.

[14] In 2003–04, £255,000. Further exemptions include all gifts between spouses, small gifts of up to £3,000 per donor and £250 per donee per annum, gifts in consideration of marriage (£5,000 by each parent, £2,500 by each grandparent, and £1,000 by anyone else), gifts to charities, and gifts of agricultural property, business property, and woodlands. Inheritance Tax is at present governed by the Inheritance Tax Act 1984.

[15] See post, p. 254.

[16] This example is only given to illustrate the principle. In practice, the result is modified by a number of provisions of the income tax legislation.

[17] However, in practice, the administration expenses of the discretionary trust must also be taken into account; these will have to be paid out of income which has already been taxed in the hands of the trustees at the rates stated below and this will reduce the amount of tax actually saved.

to preserve income and capital for the benefit of the family, discretionary trusts in general have come under increasing attack from the legislature.

Dealing first with income tax, at present trusts other than discretionary trusts pay income tax at 10 per cent when the tax is withheld at source from income arising from company distributions, at 20 per cent when the tax is withheld at source from income arising from bank deposits, and at 22 per cent when the tax is payable by the trustees on income from other sources.[18] The beneficiary entitled to the income has to pay the same tax as he would have had to pay had there not been a trust. This means that non-taxpayers and starting rate taxpayers will be able to recover the excess tax paid, other than the 10 per cent withheld from company distributions; basic rate taxpayers will pay no further tax (the 10 per cent and 20 per cent withheld at source are regarded as satisfying the basic rate of taxation); and higher rate taxpayers will have to pay such tax as is necessary to bring the overall tax paid up to 40 per cent.

The rate of income tax paid by discretionary trusts, on the other hand, is at present in principle 34 per cent and this is indeed what is payable on income arising from all sources other than company distributions (credit being given for the 20 per cent withheld at source on income arising from bank deposits); if any part of that income is distributed to beneficiaries rather than being accumulated, non-taxpayers and starting rate taxpayers have the same rights to recover the excess tax paid while higher rate taxpayers will have to pay further tax.[19] But income arising from company distributions is instead taxed at 25 per cent (15 per cent in addition to the 10 per cent withheld at source). Any part of that income which is distributed is taxed again at 34 per cent in the hands of the trustees but credit is only given for the 15 per cent already paid by the trustees, not for the 10 per cent withheld at source; while non-taxpayers and starting rate taxpayers can recover any excess tax paid by the trustees (other of course than the 10 per cent withheld at source), higher rate tax payers still have to pay a further 6 per cent.[20] This means that income arising from company distributions which is received by basic rate taxpayers and higher rate taxpayers under a discretionary trust is subject to more income tax than would otherwise have been the case.

Turning now to capital gains tax, any transfer inter vivos of property (other than cash or the settlor's main residence) to any trust is deemed to be a disposal of that property by the settlor.[21] That property is therefore subject to capital gains tax (at whatever rate is payable by the settlor after taking into account his annual exemption) on the difference between its acquisition cost[22] and its market value at the date of the deemed disposal, with appropriate

---

[18] Income and Corporation Taxes Act 1988, s.686 (as amended by Finance Act 1999).

[19] This will not necessarily enable the recovery of all the income tax paid by the trust because any income expended on administration expenses will not be able to be distributed and so the tax paid in respect of these expenses will not be able to be recovered. However, all administration expenses now have to be set against the 20 per cent tax withheld on bank deposits and so bear tax at the lowest possible rate. See post, p. 629.

[20] Expenses can however be set against the 10 per cent so withheld so that they still bear tax at the lowest possible rate.

[21] Taxation of Chargeable Gains Act 1992, s.70.

[22] Its market value on March 31, 1982 or, if acquired subsequently, its original acquisition cost.

adjustments being made to the capital gain in order to take account of intervening inflation.[23] A settlor of property inter vivos can only escape this liability to capital gains tax in certain limited circumstances,[24] in which he can elect to have the capital gain held over; where this is possible, the trust takes over the property at its original acquisition cost, thus obviously increasing the capital gains tax which the trust will itself necessarily have to pay later when it comes to dispose of the property.

Such disposals are the other aspect of capital gains tax which affects trusts, this time whether they have been created inter vivos or by will; the trustees obviously dispose of the property if they sell it to a third party and are deemed to do so when one or more of the beneficiaries[25] becomes entitled to an interest in possession in any of the trust property as against them. In such circumstances, all trusts now[26] pay capital gains tax at 34 per cent,[27] discretionary trusts being additionally penalised by the fact that their annual exemption is only half that of individuals.[28] Even so, this rate of 34 per cent is still less than the rate of 40 per cent at which most settlors will almost inevitably have to pay capital gains tax; consequently, the transfer of property to a discretionary trust is more likely to reduce than to increase the total capital gains tax payable,[29] which can in fact be reduced even further if the settlor[30] and the trustees take full advantage of their annual exemptions.

Turning finally to inheritance tax, any transfer, whether inter vivos or testamentary, of any property to a discretionary trust is subject to inheritance tax[31] (paid at 20 per cent in respect of transfers inter vivos rather than the usual 40 per cent payable on death) if the total transfers of property in the previous seven years exceed the settlor's current lifetime allowance. Where any inheritance tax is initially payable, a further charge to inheritance tax is made on every 10th anniversary of the creation of the discretionary trust at 30 per cent of whatever inheritance tax would have been payable had the property been disposed of at that time[32] and the appropriate proportion of this 10-yearly charge is payable if any property is disposed of during a 10 year period.[33] On the other hand, normally no inheritance tax will be payable at all if the settlor

---

[23] Capital gains made in respect of the period between March 31, 1982 or, if later, the date of acquisition and April 5, 1998 are adjusted by notionally increasing the acquisition cost by reference to the intervening change in the Retail Price Index; capital gains made in respect of periods after April 6, 1998 are adjusted by reducing or "tapering" the gain made by a percentage which increases in accordance with the length of time that the settlor has owned the property being settled since April 5, 1998.

[24] If the assets settled comprise business property (Taxation of Chargeable Gains Act 1992, s.75) or if the creation of the trust involves a chargeable transfer for the purposes of inheritance tax.

[25] Or, for that matter, the trustees of another settlement.

[26] Since April 6, 1998.

[27] Taxation of Chargeable Gains Act 1992, s.1AA (previously trusts other than discretionary trusts paid at the basic rate of income tax).

[28] Thus £3,950 in 2003–04. Where the same settlor has created more than one discretionary trust, this exemption is divided between them.

[29] This of course assumes that the value of the property continues to move upwards throughout; if the value of the property falls after it has been transferred to a discretionary trust, the capital gains tax paid at the time of the settlement will obviously be greater than that which would have been paid had the settlor not settled the property.

[30] The settlor can of course do so by adding the appropriate amount to the settlement each year.

[31] Inheritance Tax Act 1984, ss.2, 3(1).

[32] ibid., ss.61, 64.

[33] ibid., s.65.

settles no more than the total amount of his lifetime allowance in each seven year period.

There is no doubt that discretionary trusts are treated more harshly than other types of trusts but the overall tax payable in respect of a discretionary trust is still less than that payable by a tax payer with a top rate of 40 per cent (and few, if any, settlors are likely to have a lower top rate); further, the overall tax will be considerably less if full advantage is taken of the annual capital gains tax exemption and the amount settled is limited to each settlor's lifetime allowance.

Further, the legislature has given privileged treatment to a special type of discretionary trust, known as an accumulation and maintenance settlement.[34] Such a settlement must be for the benefit of one or more persons under 25, usually but not necessarily the children or grandchildren of the settlor; at least one beneficiary must be alive at the outset. The beneficiaries must become entitled to the trust property or to an immediate vested interest in its income upon reaching an age not exceeding 25; in the meantime, the income can either be accumulated or be applied for their maintenance, education or benefit. Such trusts are not liable to any of the charges to inheritance tax outlined above; inheritance tax will therefore only be payable in the normal way on the death of the settlor to the extent that his estate exceeds his lifetime allowance.[35]

Accumulation and maintenance settlements also have other fiscal advantages. Although they are liable to income tax and capital gains tax at the higher rate of 34 per cent, no disposal for the purposes of capital gains tax is deemed to occur (as it would in the case of all other types of trusts) when the beneficiaries first become entitled to an interest in possession in the income or the capital of their share of the trust property at the age which has been specified. Further, save in the case of infant children of the settlor, income applied for the maintenance, education or benefit of the beneficiaries is taxed at the top rate applicable to each beneficiary rather than that applicable to his parents; consequently, such a beneficiary will be able to recover the 34 per cent tax already paid by the trustees (other than the 10 per cent withheld at source on company distributions) to the extent that that rate exceeds his own top rate. These advantages are substantial; they are however limited by the fact that accumulation and maintenance trusts can only last for 25 years unless all the beneficiaries have a common grandparent.

Men will go to considerable lengths to preserve their wealth and the creation of discretionary trusts remains a popular and successful way of so doing, particularly if full advantage is taken of all the available exemptions and allowances. Further, settlors are not obliged to create their discretionary trusts in this jurisdiction. Consequently, where the property to be settled very greatly exceeds the settlor's lifetime allowance,[36] there has been an increasing ten-

---

[34] *ibid.*, s.71.
[35] His estate will as usual include any property disposed of other than for value in the preceding seven years including, if appropriate, the property settled on the accumulation and maintenance trust.
[36] In such circumstances, the available exemptions and allowances are much less relevant; further such settlors (and only such settlors) can afford the exorbitant fees normally charged in the off-shore jurisdictions for setting-up and subsequently administering the trusts in question.

dency to use discretionary trusts set up not here but in other jurisdictions; the trust law of the majority of these jurisdictions was originally based on English law[37] but some of the others have enacted legislation specifically in order to adopt the English concept of a trust[38] while the remainder utilise quite different institutions including different concepts of trusts.[39] Since most of these jurisdictions do not tax discretionary trusts (or the equivalent institutions) at all, the fiscal advantages of such off-shore settlements are even greater. The legislature has therefore intervened with a view to discouraging the creation of such settlements; the problems which this has produced for a person who is domiciled and/or resident in some part of the United Kingdom who wishes to create an off-shore trust are discussed in a later chapter.[40] The same chapter also considers the increasingly stringent provisions which have been enacted in order to make the beneficial interests of those beneficiaries of off-shore trusts who are or are deemed to be domiciled and/or resident in some part of the United Kingdom liable to United Kingdom taxation.

## II. The Exercise of Discretions and Powers

### 1. *Generally*

Where it is left to the trustees, or for that matter to some other person, to decide either whether a particular individual will receive a benefit from the trust at all or the extent of the benefit of any particular beneficiary, the discretion or power vested in the trustees or other person will be one of two broad types, depending on whether or not there is any obligation to exercise it.

If the trustees, or other persons, are under an obligation to exercise their discretion or power, then they are said to hold a trust power, or a power in the nature of a trust. It is important to note that these terms have traditionally been used to denote two quite distinct situations. The first is where the person subject to the obligation has the property in question vested in him as a trustee; in this case the term trust power or power in the nature of a trust is virtually indistinguishable from the term discretionary trust — indeed in the leading case of *McPhail v. Doulton*,[41] the two terms were used interchangeably. The second is where the person subject to the obligation is not himself a trustee of the property in question so that his only role is that of exercising the discretion or power; in this case, although he may be described as the donee of a trust power or a power in the nature of a trust, he certainly cannot be described as a discretionary trustee since he is not a trustee of anything.

If a person is holding property on trust for such of the members of a defined class and in such proportions as he shall in his absolute discretion appoint,

---

[37] Such as the Channel Islands, the Isle of Man, Gibraltar, Hong Kong, Bermuda, The Bahamas, The Cayman Islands, The British Virgin Islands and a number of other Caribbean and Pacific tax havens (the most notable, and notorious, example of the latter is The Cook Islands).

[38] Such as Nauru and Malta.

[39] Such as Liechtenstein, where bodies corporate such as foundations and establishments are the usual vehicles despite the existence of a concept of trust law which has now been held to be based primarily on contract.

[40] See *post*, p. 867.

[41] [1971] A.C. 424.

then he is likely to be held to hold a trust power or a power in the nature of a trust in the former sense; he is in effect a discretionary trustee. If, on the other hand, a person is holding property on trust for such of the members of a defined class and in such proportions as a third party shall in his absolute discretion appoint, the third party is likely to be held to have a trust power or a power in the nature of a trust in the latter sense; he is not a trustee of anything and no discretion whatever is vested in the person who is actually holding the property on trust. However, while it is necessary to remember that there is no requirement that the holder of a trust power should himself be a trustee of the property in question, there is no practical significance in this distinction. In each of the two cases, the holder of the trust power is under an obligation to exercise it and, in the event that he fails to do so, the court will exercise it instead. Traditionally, this was always done by dividing the property in question equally between all the objects of the power but, where this is not possible,[42] it will have to be done in one of the three ways envisaged by Lord Wilberforce in *McPhail v. Doulton*,[43] namely by either appointing new trustees, or directing persons representative of the donees of the power to prepare a scheme of distribution or, should the proper basis for distribution be apparent, directing the trustees how to proceed.

If, on the other hand, no obligation has been imposed on the trustees, or the other person in question, to exercise whatever discretion or power is vested in them or in him, then they or he are said to hold a mere power or a bare power (or, less commonly, a power collateral).[44] Once again these terms cover two quite distinct situations, identified much more recently.[45] The first is where the donee of the mere power holds that power in his capacity as a trustee, either because he is actually trustee of the property which is to be appointed or where this is not the case but it is nevertheless apparent that the power has been given to him in a fiduciary capacity;[46] in this case, he is said to be a fiduciary donee. The second is where the donee of the mere power is not a trustee in any sense, in which case he is said to be a non-fiduciary donee.

If a person is holding property on trust for such of the members of a class and in such proportions as he may in his absolute discretion appoint and, in default of any such appointment, on trust for an identified beneficiary, he is likely to be held to be a fiduciary donee of a mere power. If, on the other hand, a person is holding property on trust for such of the members of a class and in such proportions as a third party may in his absolute discretion appoint and,

---

[42] As will be the case where the trust power in question is of the type validated by the decision of the House of Lords in *McPhail v. Doulton* [1971] A.C. 424 and a complete list of the objects of the power therefore cannot be drawn up.

[43] [1971] A.C. 424 at 457.

[44] See *Vestey v. I.R.C. (No.2)* [1979] Ch. 198, *per* Megarry J. at 206 (affirmed on other grounds in *Vestey v. I.R.C. (Nos. 1 & 2)* [1979] A.C. 1148) and *Re Hay's Settlement Trusts* [1982] 1 W.L.R. 202, *per* Megarry V.-C. at 210.

[45] In *Mettoy Pension Trustees v. Evans* [1990] 1 W.L.R. 1587 at 1614 (not the first enunciation of the distinction but the first fully developed statement of the remedies available against a fiduciary donee of a mere power). See generally Gardner 107 LQ.R. (1991) 214.

[46] In *Mettoy Pension Trustees v. Evans* [1990] 1 W.L.R. 1587, a company held a power to appoint any surplus in its pension fund, which was actually vested in a separate trustee company, in favour of the pensioners with a gift over in default of appointment to itself. The liquidators of the company wished to release this power and so enable the surplus in the pension fund to become available for its creditors. Warner J. held that the company held the power in a fiduciary capacity; consequently, it could not be released.

in default of any such appointment, on trust for an identified beneficiary, the third party is likely to be held to be a non-fiduciary donee of a mere power. This distinction is extremely significant. Although a fiduciary donee of a mere power is under no obligation to exercise it, he does owe certain obligations towards the objects of the power (as well as a duty to those entitled in default of appointment not to misuse the power) and is "to some extent subject to the control of the courts in relation to its exercise".[47] In particular, he must consider periodically whether or not he should exercise the power (in default, the court may direct him to do so and, in the last resort, may remove or replace him), must consider the range of objects of the power, must consider the appropriateness of individual appointments and, above all, is not entitled to release the power so as to cause the property to pass to those entitled in default of appointment. On the other hand, a non-fiduciary donee of a mere power owes no obligations whatever to the objects of the power (his only duty, owed to those entitled in default of appointment, is not to misuse the power). In particular, he does not even have to consider whether to exercise the power and may release it at any time and consequently cause the property to pass to those entitled in default of appointment.

Thus, the first and crucial question is whether or not there is any obligation to exercise the power in question. If the answer to that question is affirmative, then the only remaining matter is in whose favour it should be exercised, either by the donee of the power or, if he fails to do so, by the court. If, on the other hand, the answer to that question is negative, it is necessary to consider whether the donee of the power is a fiduciary or a non-fiduciary; only in the former case is there any possibility of the court intervening in the event that the donee himself fails to exercise his power and even then the role of the court is almost certainly limited to ensuring that the fiduciary has complied with his duty to consider periodically whether or not to exercise the power.

### 2. *The Distinction between Trust Powers and Mere Powers*

The distinction between trust powers and mere powers must now be considered more closely. The question whether or not a trust or a power has been created is essentially one of construction of the instrument. The distinction may be a fine one in any individual case, because what appears on the face of the trust instrument to be a trust power may in fact be a mere power and vice versa. Further, despite the fact that trust powers often appear in the form of powers, they are nevertheless construed and take effect as trusts. It is important to stress that, when what is in issue is whether a trust power or a mere power has been created, it does not matter whether what has been conferred on the donee of the power is a discretion or a power of appointment; although most of the discussion which follows refers to powers of appointment, it is equally applicable to discretions.

The question of construction is best approached by reference to the following questions. An affirmative answer to either of the first two questions is decisive and establishes that what has been created is a mere power. If both the first two questions are answered in the negative, then the matter generally has to be resolved by answering the third question; only if the matter remains

---

[47] *ibid.* at 1614.

very evenly balanced after the third questions has been answered can recourse ever be had to the fourth question.

## (A) Is the Discretion or Power General or Intermediate, as Distinct from Special?

A general power is by its nature incapable of being a trust power. A power is described as general when it confers on its donee a power to exercise it in favour of whoever he pleases, including the donee himself. Thus, the donee of a general power of appointment can exercise it by appointing the property to himself beneficially. Since he is entitled to do this, the court cannot compel him to appoint to any one else or indeed at all.

On the other hand, a special power is capable of taking effect as a trust power. A power is described as special when it confers on its donee the power to exercise it only in favour of one or more of a number of designated persons or classes of persons. Thus the donee of a special power of appointment can only appoint the property in question to the persons or classes of persons designated by the donor.

The position of the third type of power, the much more recently developed intermediate (or hybrid) power is not entirely clear. Such powers have been described as a power "betwixt and between",[48] neither strictly general nor strictly special. The feature of such a power is that it confers on its donee the power to exercise it in favour of anyone other than one or more designated persons or classes of persons. The persons usually excluded are the settlor and his present and future spouses; this is generally done in order to forestall any argument that he has retained a beneficial interest under the trust in question, something which could have negative fiscal consequences.[49] It is also common to exclude the donee,[50] whether or not he is also the settlor. Thus the donee of an intermediate power of appointment can appoint the property in question to anyone other than the excluded person or persons. Another common type of intermediate power is the power to add persons to a class of beneficiaries; for the same reasons as above, it is usually crucial to ensure that the settlor and his present and future spouses cannot be so added.

Intermediate powers are regarded as general powers for some purposes and as special powers for others.[51] It is, however, difficult to see how an intermediate power could possibly take effect as a trust power because, as in the case of a general power, there is no one in whose favour the court can compel appointment. It is therefore considered that such powers are, like general powers, necessarily mere powers.

## (B) Is there a Gift Over in Default of Exercise?

If the settlor has provided for a gift over, an alternative gift in the event that

---

[48] *Re Gestetner Settlement* [1953] Ch. 672 at 685.

[49] As will be seen *post*, p. 639, no inheritance tax is chargeable on the death of any person in respect of any property which he has transferred away more than seven years earlier. The retention of any benefit or potential benefit under the terms of any settlement to which the property has been transferred prevents the seven year period from starting or continuing.

[50] As in *Re Park* [1932] 1 Ch. 580. See also *Re Jones* [1945] Ch. 105 (power to appoint to anybody being a person and not a corporation); *Blausten v. I.R.C.* [1972] Ch. 256; *Re Manisty's Settlement* [1974] Ch. 17; *Re Hay's Settlement Trusts* [1982] 1 W.L.R. 202.

[51] Such a power is a special power for the purposes of the Wills Act 1837, s.21 and the Perpetuities and Accumulations Act 1964, s.7.

the donee of the power fails to exercise it, then that power cannot be a trust power. The existence of a gift over is incompatible with the imperative nature of a trust and necessarily therefore operates as a denial of one's existence. Thus in *Re Mills*,[52] a power was given to appoint among those children and remoter issue who in the opinion of the donee of the power should evidence a desire to maintain the family fortune. This limitation was followed by a gift elsewhere in default of appointment. The Court of Appeal held that because there was a gift over the power did not operate as a trust. It is not easy to think of any example of a gift over in default of exercise other than a gift which, like the gift in *Re Mills*, is a gift over in default of appointment. This second question therefore appears to relate exclusively to powers of appointment.

It is not always easy to decide whether any particular gift is indeed a gift over in default of exercise. Only if it actually is, will a trust power not be able to be upheld. Therefore, if the gift over is to take effect only in the event of a failure of the class in whose favour a power of appointment is to be exercised and/or their non-attainment of a specified age, it will operate only in those circumstances rather than as a result of any failure to make an appointment; consequently, such a power is capable of being held to be a trust power.[53]

However, it is clear that a residuary gift (a gift of that part of the property of a testator which has not been specifically devised or bequeathed) is not a gift over for present purposes; consequently, the presence of a residuary gift will not necessarily deprive a prior power of the character of a trust power. Thus in *Re Brierley*,[54] a testator gave his wife a life interest in £50,000 with the power to bequeath or appoint that sum among such of her relatives or next-of-kin as she thought proper. She was also given the residue of her husband's estate absolutely. The wife, having released and thereby purported to extinguish the power of appointment, claimed the whole £50,000 as her own beneficially by virtue of the gift of residue in her favour. The court held that this manoeuvre was not possible; a gift of residue was totally different from a gift over of specific property which is the subject of the power of appointment.

### (C) What was the Real Intention of the Settlor or Testator?

Where the matter has not been resolved by one of the first two questions, then whether or not there is a trust power is entirely a question of construction of the words used in the instrument[55] in order to establish the real intention of the settlor or testator.

It must first be observed that, if the settlor or testator has specifically provided that the discretion or power in question is not a trust power, then it will not be even if the remaining words used point clearly and inescapably towards a trust power. The House of Lords held in *Gisborne v. Gisborne*[56] that this was the effect of a gift "upon further trust that my said trustees in their discretion, and of their uncontrollable authority, pay and apply the whole, or such portion only, of the annual income of my real and personal estate . . . as

---

[52] [1930] 1 Ch. 654.
[53] *Re Llewellyn's Settlement* [1921] 2 Ch. 281.
[54] (1894) 43 W.R. 36.
[55] Extrinsic evidence, including evidence of the intentions of a testator, may in certain circumstances be admitted as an aid to the construction of a will; see Administration of Justice Act 1982, s.21 and see *ante*, p. 47, fn. 4.
[56] (1877) 2 App.Cas. 300.

they shall think expedient, to or for" the testator's widow. This was of course a discretion but it has been recognised that the same principle applies to powers.[57] However, in the absence of any such express provision, the question can be less straightforward.

In *Burrough v. Philcox*,[58] the testator directed that, after certain contingencies had been fulfilled, property was to be held in trust for his two children for life, with remainder to their issue, and declared that, if they should both die without issue, the survivor should have power to dispose by will of the property among his nephews and nieces and their children as he should think fit. The testator's children did in fact die without issue and without any appointment having been made by the survivor of them. It was held that a trust had been created in favour of the testator's nephews and nieces and their children; the trust in their favour was simply subject to a power of selection vested in the surviving child. Lord Cottenham L.C. stated the principle in these words: "Where there appears a general intention in favour of a class, and a particular intention in favour of individuals of a class to be selected by another person, and the particular intention fails from that selection not having been made, the court will carry into effect the general intention in favour of the class".[59] It should also be noted that, if the decision in *Burrough v. Philcox* is applied to a power in favour of the donor's relations generally which is not exercised and a trust is consequently deduced in their favour, the trust will take effect in favour of the settlor's statutory next-of-kin.[60]

However, it must be emphasised that the fact that there is, as in *Burrough v. Philcox*, no gift over in default of exercise of the power in question does not automatically lead to the conclusion that a trust should be implied. It is apparent from other decisions that a trust will not be implied unless there is, on the true construction of the instrument in question, an indication of a clear intention to benefit the designated person or class in any event with only a mere power of selection conferred on the donee of the power.

Thus in *Re Weekes' Settlement*[61] there was a gift of land to the testatrix's husband for life with "power to dispose of all such property by will amongst our children" but without any gift over in default of appointment. When the husband died without having exercised the power of appointment in favour of the children, Romer J. held that what the husband had been given was a mere power, not one coupled with a trust, and that accordingly no gift to the children as a whole arose by implication. The judge pointed out that there had been no express gift to such of the class as the husband might appoint — as there had been, in effect, in *Burrough v. Philcox* — but only a mere power to appoint among a class.

Similarly, in *Re Combe*[62] a life interest in property was given to the son of the testator and, after his death, the property was to be held "in trust for such person or persons as my said son shall appoint but such appointment must be

---

[57] See *Steele v. Paz* (1995) 1 Butterworths Offshore Service 338 at 405 (Court of Appeal of the Isle of Man).

[58] (1840) 5 Myl. & Cr. 72.

[59] *ibid.* at 92.

[60] *Re Scarisbrick's Will Trusts* [1951] Ch. 622; *Re Baden's Deed Trusts (No.2)* [1973] Ch. 9 at 30, *per* Stamp L.J.

[61] [1897] 1 Ch. 289.

[62] [1925] Ch. 210.

confined to any relation of mine of the whole blood"; there was again no express gift over in default of appointment. It was held that the words quoted had created a mere power and not a trust power; according to Tomlin J., there was nothing in the words of the will to justify importing into it something which was simply not there.

The principle laid down in both these decisions was applied in the somewhat more recent decision in *Re Perowne*.[63] In this case the testatrix gave all her estate to her husband for life, "knowing that he will make arrangements for the disposal of my estate, according to my wishes, for the benefit of my family". The husband did in fact purport to make an appointment but this turned out to be void; consequently, the question arose as to whether, since the power had not been effectively exercised, what had been created was a trust in favour of the family or a mere power to appoint in their favour. Harman J. declined to spell a trust out of the words which had been used and held they had given the husband a mere power to distribute the testatrix's estate among the large and indefinite class in question.

These decisions illustrate a number of propositions: first, that the question is purely one of construction, namely whether or not the settlor has shown an intention to benefit the objects of the power; secondly, that the absence of a gift over in default of appointment does not raise any necessary inference that a trust is intended — it is an argument, and nothing more than an argument, that that was the intention of the settlor or testator; and, thirdly, that because the question is one of construction, the resolution of the problem may depend on "a few words" and "mere straws in the wind".[64]

The fact that this is inevitable in relation to questions of construction is demonstrated by the leading case of *McPhail v. Doulton*.[65] The deed which had to be considered in this case provided that the trustees should apply the net income in making payments at their absolute discretion "to or for the benefit of any of the officers and employees or ex-officers or ex-employees of the company or to any relatives or dependants of any such persons in such amounts or on such conditions (if any) as they think fit". One of the questions which had to be decided was whether the clause had created a trust power or a mere power. At first instance, Goff J.[66] held that it had created a mere power; the Court of Appeal,[67] by a majority, reached the same conclusion; however, the House of Lords[68] unanimously held that it had created a trust power and therefore took effect as a trust — the clearly expressed scheme of the deed pointed to a mandatory construction. Lord Wilberforce, undoubtedly bearing in mind the differing judicial opinions expressed by the three different tribunals, said:[69]

"It is striking how narrow and in a sense artificial is the distinction, in cases such as the present, between trusts, or as the particular type of trust

---

[63] [1951] Ch. 785.
[64] *Re Baden's Deed Trusts* [1969] 2 Ch. 388 at 398, *per* Harman L.J. For a formulation of the relevant rules of construction, see *Re Leek* [1967] Ch. 1061 at 1073, *per* Buckley J.
[65] [1971] A.C. 424.
[66] [1967] 1 W.L.R. 1457.
[67] [1969] 2 Ch. 126. Russell L.J. dissented.
[68] [1971] A.C. 424.
[69] *ibid.* at 448.

is called, trust powers, and powers. It is only necessary to read the learned judgments in the Court of Appeal to see that what to one mind may appear as a power of distribution coupled with a trust to dispose of the undistributed surplus, by accumulation or otherwise, may to another appear as a trust for distribution coupled with a power to withhold a portion and accumulate or otherwise dispose of it. A layman and, I suspect, also a logician would find it hard to understand what difference there is."

### (D) Will the Construction Adopted Effectuate rather than Frustrate that Real Intention?

It is only where the decision reached is as marginal as the Court of Appeal apparently thought that it was in *McPhail v. Doulton* that recourse is ever had to this fourth rule. In that case,[70] the majority of the Court of Appeal held that, in cases where the considerations were very evenly balanced in arriving at one or other of the two possible constructions, the court was at liberty to lean towards the construction which would effectuate rather than frustrate the intentions of the settlor or testator.[71] In other words, the court could take account of the legal consequences of any given interpretation; in particular, the consequence that, if construed as a trust power, the gift would certainly be void for uncertainty of objects whereas, if construed as a mere power, it would be likely to be valid,[72] might cause the court to lean in favour of construing it as a mere power.

The fourth question was relevant in the Court of Appeal because, as has already been seen in a previous chapter,[73] at that time the test for certainty of objects was totally different for trust powers and for mere powers. But the House of Lords[74] subsequently held, by a bare majority, that the basic test for certainty of objects for trust powers and mere powers is in fact the same. Consequently, this fourth question did not arise in their lordships' house.

However, at least one[75] aspect of the test for certainty of objects may still differ depending on whether the limitation in question has created a trust power or a mere power. This is the question of whether the requirement of administrative workability, which clearly applies to trust powers, is or is not applicable to mere powers. Prior to the decision in *Mettoy Pension Trustees v. Evans*,[76] it seemed tolerably clear that this requirement did not apply to mere powers.[77] If this is indeed the case, then this fourth question may well be decisive in determining the validity of a limitation which does not satisfy this requirement.

However, now that *Mettoy Pension Trustees v. Evans* has upheld the adap-

---

[70] [1969] 2 Ch. 126 (*sub nom. Re Baden's Deed Trusts*).

[71] On the principle of *ut res magis valeat quam pereat*.

[72] As was indeed ultimately held by the Court of Appeal in *Re Baden's Deed Trusts (No.2)* [1973] Ch. 9; by then the test that the Court of Appeal had considered to be applicable to mere powers had been held by the House of Lords to apply to trust powers as well

[73] See *ante*, p. 59.

[74] [1971] A.C. 424.

[75] At least one commentator also thinks that the basic test is still different where what is in issue is an old fashioned power in the nature of a trust rather than a discretionary trust; see *ante*, pp. 64–65.

[76] [1990] 1 W.L.R. 1587.

[77] See *ante*, p. 71.

tation of the remedies available for the enforcement of discretionary trusts, trust powers and powers in the nature of a trust to mere powers held by fiduciaries, it has been suggested[78] that this may cause the requirement of administrative workability also to be applied to at least this type of mere power. If this indeed turns out to be yet another consequence of this important decision, the applicability of the fourth question will be reduced still further and will only be capable of being decisive in respect of mere powers which are non-fiduciary or personal; indeed, if the decision in *Mettoy Pension Trustees v. Evans* is extended still further, this question may well[79] cease to have any relevance at all in relation to private trusts.[80] However, for the moment it clearly remains relevant although the likelihood of it having to be considered is obviously extremely small.

### 3. The Distinction between Fiduciary and Non-Fiduciary Donees of Mere Powers

While the recently consolidated distinction between fiduciary and non-fiduciary donees of mere powers to which reference has already been made was certainly not new,[81] its initial enunciations did not receive universal judicial approval. As recently as 1969 Lord Upjohn, in *Re Gulbenkian's Settlement Trusts*,[82] felt able to deny that donees of mere powers of appointment ever owed any duties to the objects of those powers. However, in the following year, Lord Wilberforce, in *McPhail v. Doulton*,[83] foreshadowed the somewhat later decision in *Mettoy Pension Trustees v. Evans*[84] by remarking that a "trustee of an employees' benefit fund, whether given a power or a trust power, is still a trustee and he would surely consider in either case that he has a fiduciary duty"; he added that it would be "a complete misdescription of his position to say that, if what he has is a power unaccompanied by an imperative trust to distribute, he cannot be controlled by the court unless he exercised it capriciously, or outside the field permitted by the trust".

These remarks set the scene for the authoritative statement of the distinction made by Megarry V.-C. in *Re Hay's Settlement Trusts*.[85] Having stated that a trustee is not normally bound to exercise a mere power and that the court will not compel him to do so, he continued:

> "That, however, does not mean that he can simply fold his hands and ignore it, for normally he must from time to time consider whether or not to exercise the power, and the court may direct him to do this. Whereas a person who is not in a fiduciary position is free to exercise the power in any way that he wishes, unhampered by fiduciary duties, a trustee to whom, as such, a power is given is bound by the duties of his office in exercising that power to do so in a responsible manner according to its

---

[78] By Gardner, 107 L.Q.R. (1991) 214 at 218–219.
[79] This of course depends on whether the test for certainty of objects is indeed the same for all discretions and powers.
[80] It is clearly still applicable to public trusts; see *I.R.C. v. McMullen* [1981] A.C. 1 at 16; *I.R.C. v. Guild* [1992] A.C. 310; *post*, p. 444.
[81] See the authorities cited by Gardner, 107 L.Q.R. (1991) 214.
[82] [1970] A.C. 508 at 521, 524–525.
[83] [1971] A.C. 424 at 449.
[84] [1990] 1 W.L.R. 1587.
[85] [1982] 1 W.L.R. 202 at 209–210.

purpose. It is not enough for him to refrain from acting capriciously he must do more. He must 'make such a survey of the range of objects or possible beneficiaries' as will enable him to carry out his fiduciary duty. He must find out 'the permissible area of selection and then consider responsibly, in individual cases, whether a contemplated beneficiary was within the power and whether, in relation to the possible claimants, a particular grant was appropriate'."[86]

This statement established a clear distinction between a mere power held by the trustees of the property in question and a mere power held by a third party and classified all mere powers held by trustees as fiduciary powers.

However, this classification must be subject to at least one exception, namely where the settlor or testator has specifically provided that the power in question is a personal power. This qualification follows from the decision of the House of Lords in *Gisborne v. Gisborne*,[87] considered above which was cited as authority for precisely this proposition by Hegarty J.A. in the Court of Appeal of the Isle of Man in *Steele v. Paz*.[88] Hegarty J.A. admittedly did go on to say that in such circumstances the donee might not necessarily be entirely free from the duties set out in *Re Hay's Settlement Trusts*, presumably envisaging the situation where the trustees had declined to give any consideration whatever to the exercise of their powers (*Gisborne v. Gisborne* was a case where the trustees had given proper thought to the exercise of their powers and were willing to exercise them but not in the same way as the court would have done). However, a decision of the House of Lords of this antiquity would not be easy to circumvent.

The decision in *Re Hay's Settlement Trusts* also showed that there was some significance in the distinction which it had established in that the court could direct the trustees to consider whether or not to exercise their power; this in turn led to the further conclusion, already enunciated in two earlier judgments,[89] that a refusal to follow such a direction from the court might well lead to the replacement of the existing trustees.

It has subsequently been established that a donee of a mere power may be classified as a fiduciary even if he is not a trustee of the property in question. In *Mettoy Pension Trustees v. Evans*,[90] a company held the following power in respect of any surplus in its pension fund, which was actually vested in a quite separate trust company: "any surplus of the trust fund remaining ... may at the absolute discretion of the employer be applied to secure further benefits within the limits stated in the rules, and any further balance thereafter remaining ... shall be paid to" the employer. The company became insolvent and its liquidators sought to release this power of appointment so that the gift over in default of appointment could take effect and immediately vest the surplus in the company for the benefit of its general creditors. Warner J. held that the company held this mere power as a fiduciary (he consequently held,

---

[86] The quotations come from the speech of Lord Wilberforce in *McPhail v. Doulton* [1971] A.C. 424 at 449, 457.

[87] (1877) 2 App.Cas. 300.

[88] (1995) 1 Butterworths Offshore Service 338 at 405.

[89] *Re Gestetner* [1953] Ch. 672 at 688; *Re Manisty's Settlement* [1974] Ch. 17 at 25.

[90] [1990] 1 W.L.R. 1587.

as will be seen later in this chapter,[91] not only that the power could not be released but also that all the remedies available to the court for the purpose of enforcing discretionary trusts were also available to it in the case of mere powers held by fiduciary donees).

He adduced two main reasons for concluding that the company held this power as a fiduciary: first, that the inclusion of the power in the rules of the pension fund would have been quite pointless unless its donee were a fiduciary — since the company could have made such payments to its pensioners even if it had been absolutely entitled to the surplus, a non-fiduciary power would have added nothing; and, secondly, that the pensioners were not volunteers, in that it was unlikely that the surplus had arisen solely as a result of over-contribution on the part of the company and, in any event, the existence of the power and the expectation that its utilisation in their favour would be the subject of proper consideration had undoubtedly formed part of the overall scheme which the employees had contracted to obtain. It is undoubtedly significant that this conclusion was reached in the context of a pension fund, a context in which, as will be seen in a later chapter,[92] a large number of the recent developments in the law of trusts have been enunciated. Thus, one commentator[93] has described the conclusion as "perhaps swayed by a deeper-lying consideration", namely that, if such powers are not held to be fiduciary powers, "the surpluses to which they apply will in practice fall to companies' creditors and successful take-over predators"; whether he is right also to describe the conclusion as "not overwhelming" is rather more questionable.

Whether or not the basis of the classification adopted in *Mettoy Pension Trustees v. Evans* was indeed the special nature of pension funds and the public concern about the security of pension schemes at the time, there seemed little doubt, particularly in the light of the wholly novel remedies which that decision had made available to the court, that there would be many future attempts to classify as fiduciaries donees of mere powers who are not trustees of the property in question.

Such an attempt was made in The Cayman Islands in The *Cayman Islands* in *Re Z's Settlement Trusts*,[94] which concerned a provision that "this trust and any of its provisions may during the joint lives of the Grantor and E be altered or amended with the unanimous consent of the Grantor and the Management Committee, executed with the same formality as this trust and delivered to the Trustee". This power was exercised so as to confer an enhanced beneficial interest on one of the members of the Management Committee. Some of the beneficiaries contended that this power was a fiduciary power and that, consequently, the members of the Management Committee could not exercise it in such a way as to enhance the beneficial interests of any of them. It was held that the basic powers vested in the Management Committee were fiduciary powers, albeit of a qualified nature; however, the only natural and workable construction of the power to amend was that it conferred a personal or non-fiduciary power on the Man-

---

[91] See *post*, p. 503.
[92] See *post*, p. 225.
[93] Gardner, 107 L.Q.R. [1991] 214 at 215–216. He cites in support of this proposition *Re Courage Group's Pension Schemes* [1987] 1 W.L.R. 495 and *Imperial Group Pension Trust v. Imperial Tobacco* [1991] 1 W.L.R. 589 and would now undoubtedly also cite *Re William Makin & Sons* [1993] B.C.C. 435. All these authorities are considered *post*, pp. 503 *et seq.*
[94] [1997] Cayman Islands L.R. 298.

agement Committee and the Grantor together, subject only to the obligation to act in good faith. If viewed in any other way, the power would be potentially unenforceable since it would be impossible for the court to exercise such a fiduciary power on behalf of the Management Committee at the same time as complying with the Grantor's intentions.

This decision appears to confirm suggestions previously made,[95] that powers relating to pension funds of the type considered in *Mettoy Pension Trustees v. Evans* will come to be regarded as a special case and that the classification and the remedies adopted in that case will not be extended more generally. If this is the case, the traditional distinctions between trust powers and mere powers will not require any further reconsideration. However, confirmation that this is indeed the position must obviously await a decision to this effect in this jurisdiction.


## III. When will the Exercise of Discretions and Powers be Improper?

It will be recalled that the donees of a trust power, in any of the meanings of that expression, are, whether or not they are also trustees, obliged to exercise it, whereas the donees of a mere power are not obliged to exercise it, although if they are fiduciaries they must at the very least consider whether or not to do so. However, once a discretion or power has been exercised, the principles which determine whether or not its exercise was proper are the same whether the power in question was a trust power or a mere power and whether or not it was exercised by a trustee or other fiduciary.


### 1. *When will the Exercise of Discretions and Powers be Defective?*

The exercise of a discretion or power will be defective unless it is exercised with whatever formalities are required by the trust instrument. In principle the exercise of neither a discretion nor a power requires any formality but in practice, while trust instruments do not normally prescribe any formality for the exercise of discretions, they almost always prescribe some formality for the exercise of powers of appointment.[96]

A discretion or power can also only be exercised within the limits prescribed by law or by the trust instrument; consequently, if it can be exercised only with the consent of some person, that consent must be duly obtained. In *Breadner v. Granville-Grossman*,[97] a power of appointment was held to have been executed one day too late and its exercise was therefore ineffective; consequently, the interests of those entitled in default of exercise of the power took effect. The court rejected a somewhat optimistic argument that the trusts declared by the power nevertheless took effect in equity on the basis that it had no jurisdiction to deprive the default beneficiaries of their interests, even though no one had intended that they should ever obtain them. The court also rejected an argument that equity could relieve against the defective exercise of the power. As is

---

[95] In the 7th (1998) edition of this work at pp. 182–183.
[96] See *ante*, p. 201.
[97] [2001] Ch. 523.

shown by *Cooper v. Martin*,[98] there is indeed such a doctrine but Park J. held that it is confined to defects of form which are not of the essence of the power in question and to powers which are being exercised in discharge of some moral or natural obligation; further, and in any event, he held that, for this doctrine to apply, the power in question had to be in existence at the time of the defective exercise and the power in *Breadner v. Granville Grossman* no longer was, having expired the previous day.

Further, the person exercising the discretion or power must make a positive mental decision to do so rather than merely allowing a situation to arise as a result of his inaction. In *Turner v. Turner*,[99] the trustees left all the decisions to the settlor (who was not a trustee) and signed the necessary documents without actually reading them. A power of appointment which they signed in this manner was held to be defective. Similarly, in *Wilson v. Turner*,[1] the trustees had a power to pay or apply income arising from the trusts to or for the maintenance of an infant beneficiary. They did not make any conscious decision whether or not to do so but merely handed over the income to the infant's father. The Court of Appeal held that their payments had been ineffective and that they had to repay the money to the trust fund. However, had the trustees actively considered the merits of the case and consciously decided to apply the income for the maintenance of the infant, their decision would have been valid and would have been upheld. The test is therefore not the consequences of the action or inaction of the holder of the discretion or power in question but the nature of his own mental processes.

## 2. What is the Effect of a Mistake?

Where a discretion or power has been exercised as a result of a mistake by the person exercising it, different considerations arise. As was illustrated in the course of the reviews of this area of the law made by Lawrence Collins J. in *AMP (UK) v. Barker*,[2] and by Lightman J. in *Re Barr's Settlement Trusts*,[3] such mistakes can be of a number of types each of which leads to different consequences.

### (A) Rectifiable Mistakes

The first possibility is that the document by which the discretion or power was exercised may be able to be rectified as a result of the mistake. *AMP (UK) v. Barker*,[4] concerned the power of amendment which is normally given to trustees of pension trusts (as will be seen in Chapter 12,[5] this power is the equivalent in a pension trust of the overriding power of appointment normally given to the trustees of a voluntary settlement; its exercise is usually subject to the consent of the employer in question). The trustees had exercised the power with the consent of the employer in order to enhance the benefits of employees who were forced to give up employment on the grounds of incapacity; no one

---

[98] (1867) L.R. 3 Ch.App. 47.
[99] [1984] Ch. 100.
[1] (1883) 22 Ch.D. 521.
[2] [2001] W.T.L.R. 1237, [2001] P.L.R. 79, (2000) 3 I.T.E.L.R. 414.
[3] [2003] 2 W.L.R. 1362.
[4] [2001] W.T.L.R. 1237, [2001] P.L.R. 79, (2000) 3 I.T.E.L.R. 414.
[5] See *post*, p. 503.

had realised that, because their benefits were linked to the benefits of employees who left for any other reason, this would have the effect of enhancing the benefits of the latter as well. The trustees successfully sought rectification of the deed by which the amendment had been made.

There was no difficulty in establishing the convincing proof of what had been intended which is required for all rectification claims. Despite the fact that, in bilateral transactions, it is also necessary for all the relevant parties to have been under a common mistake as to the effect of the contract or document in question, it has long been established that a trust deed creating a voluntary settlement can be rectified where the mistaken belief of the settlor was not shared by some or all of the trustees who were, with the settlor, parties to it;[6] here, however, rectification was being sought not of an original trust deed but of a deed amending a valid original trust deed, which had obviously created proprietary rights. Lawrence Collins J. held that, in these circumstances, rectification would only be possible if the mistake was common both to the persons with the power to make the amendment and all the persons who had to consent to it. This was in fact the case so the deed by which the power of amendment had been exercised was duly rectified.

### (B) Mistakes as to the Effect of What has been Done

The second possibility is that the exercise of the discretion or power can be avoided because of a mistake as to its effect (this possibility does not extend to mistakes as to its consequences.[7]) Even before the general abrogation of the distinction between mistakes of fact and mistakes of law,[8] it was not in this respect necessary to distinguish between them[9] and it is certainly not necessary to do so now.[10]

A mistake as to the identity of the person in whose favour a discretion or power is being exercised clearly falls within this category. A mistaken belief that no previous appointment had been made in favour of the person to whom the appointment in question was being made was held to do so in *Lady Hood of Avalon v. MacKinnon*.[11] So will a mistake as to either the factual or the legal effect of the terms of what has been done. In *Anker-Peterson v. Christensen*,[12] the tenants for life of a settlement which was to be varied under the Variation of Trusts Act 1958[13] were ignorant of the factual effect of the proposed variation, under which the settled property was to be assigned to off-shore trustees and re-settled. They gave the consent to this variation which was a pre-requisite of its approval by the court and subsequently assigned their interests to the new trustees in ignorance of the fact that their life interests under the new settlements would no longer be indefeasible. The deeds of assignment were set aside. So too, in *Gibbon v. Mitchell*,[14] was a deed assigning a beneficial interest

---

[6] *Re Butlin's Settlement Trusts* [1976] Ch. 251.
[7] This limitation on this second possibility was imposed by Millett J. in *Gibbon v. Mitchell* [1990] 1 W.L.R. 1304.
[8] By the House of Lords in *Kleinworth Benson v. Lincoln City Council* [1999] 2 A.C. 349.
[9] See *Gibbon v. Mitchell* [1990] 1 W.L.R. 1304.
[10] Lawrence Collins J. so stated in *AMP (UK) v. Barker* [2001] W.T.L.R. 1237, [2001] P.L.R. 79.
[11] [1909] 1 Ch. 476.
[12] [2002] W.T.L.R. 313.
[13] See *post*, p. 747.
[14] [1990] 1 W.L.R. 1304.

under a protective trust[15] whose legal effect was not what had been intended; however, mistakes of law of this type will usually be as to the effect of some overriding rule of law, such as the various rules against perpetuities and accumulations.[16] Any mistake as to the factual or legal effect of the exercise of a discretion or power by the person exercising it would clearly lead to the same result. In *AMP (UK) v. Barker*,[17] Lawrence Collins J. stated that he would have invoked this principle to set aside the exercise of the power of amendment had he not already ordered rectification.

Where the mistaken exercise of a discretion or power falls within this category, whatever has been done will be wholly void *ab initio*. However, where the effect of only part of what has been done is mistaken and that part can be severed from the remainder of what has been done, only the former will be void; the latter will take effect. This indeed happened in *Walker v. Armstrong*.[18] Any property transferred will be recoverable by the trustees from the transferee. If for any reason it cannot be recovered, the trustees will be potentially liable for breach of trust; however, they may possibly be relieved from liability under section 61 of the Trustee Act 1925[19] and are highly likely to be so relieved if the mistaken exercise of the discretion or power was by a person other than themselves.

### (C) Mistakes within the Rule in Re Hastings-Bass (dec'd)[20]

The third possibility is that the exercise of the discretion or power may be held to have been vitiated because of the failure of the persons who exercised it to take into account all the correct considerations. This principle has become known as the Rule in *Re Hastings-Bass (dec'd)*.[21] In that case, trustees exercised a power of advancement to resettle property on trust but misunderstood the effect of the rule against perpetuities with the result that, while a valid life interest was conferred on the person principally intended to benefit, all the remainders over were void for perpetuity. The question before the court was whether the entire transaction failed or whether the life interest nevertheless survived (a result which would produce the saving of estate duty which had been the objective of the advancement). The Court of Appeal said this:

> "where a trustee is given a discretion as to some matter under which he acts in good faith, the court should not interfere with his action, notwithstanding that it does not have the full effect which he intended, unless (1) what he has achieved is unauthorised by the power conferred on him, or (2) it is clear that he would not have acted as he did (a) had he not taken into account considerations which he should not have taken into account or (b) had he not failed to take into account considerations which he ought to have taken into account."

---

[15] See *post*, p. 264.
[16] See *post*, p. 238.
[17] [2001] W.T.L.R. 1237, [2001] P.L.R. 79.
[18] (1856) 8 De G.M. & G. 531. The deed in question carried out the wishes of the appointors by confirming their life interests but also contained gifts over which had not been intended. The life interests were upheld; the gifts over were held to be void.
[19] See *post*, p. 789.
[20] [1975] Ch. 25. See Lord Walker [2002] P.C.B. 226; Hilliard [2002] T.L.I. 202.
[21] [1975] Ch. 25.

It is the second of these two grounds for interference which constitutes the Rule.[22]

Subsequently, in *Mettoy Pension Trustees v. Evans*,[23] Warner J. reformulated the Rule in positive terms, stating[24] that, "where a trustee acts under a discretion given to him by the terms of the trust, the court will interfere with his action if it is clear that he would not have acted as he did had he not failed to take into account considerations which he ought to have taken into account". Shortly afterwards, in *Stannard v. Fisons Pension Trust*,[25] the Court of Appeal held that the test is not whether the trustees *would* not have acted as they did but whether they *might* not have done so. In *AMP (UK) v. Barker*,[26] Lawrence Collins J., who would have set aside the defective exercise of the power of amendment under the Rule had he not already ordered rectification, regarded himself as bound[27] to hold that the test was "might" rather than "would", although he stated that this made no difference on the facts of that case. Lightman J. also stated that this made no difference on the facts in *Re Barr's Settlement Trusts*;[28] however, he instead expressed the view that the choice between the two criteria still remains open.[29]

It is not yet been established precisely what categories of mistakes will give rise to the application of the Rule. The facts of *Re Hastings-Bass (dec'd)* itself appear to have fallen within the second possibility anyway in that there had been a mistake as to the effect of the exercise of the power in question; however, at that time, prior to *Gibbon v. Mitchell*,[30] it was not generally appreciated that this possibility extended to mistakes of law. In any event, as was implicit in the negative formulation of the Rule which the Court of Appeal enunciated, the court declined to interfere in *Re Hastings-Bass (dec'd)* because what had been achieved was sufficient to bring about the saving of estate duty, in other words because, if the trustees had appreciated the true effect of the advancement, they would have acted broadly as they had done. Consequently, the advancement was held to take effect in so far as it could.

It has been contended that the Rule in *Re Hastings-Bass (dec'd)* should be confined to mistakes of this type,[31] in which case it would amount to little more than an alternative formulation of what was later decided in *Gibbon v. Mitchell*.[32] However, the Rule is clearly not so confined at present. It was specifically held in *Mettoy Pension Trustees v. Evans*,[33] that the Rule extends to *any* taking into account of inappropriate considerations or failure to take into account appropriate considerations.

In that case, it was contended that the grant by the trustees to the employer of the power to appoint the surplus in the pension scheme should be set aside

---

[22] The first ground is the subject matter of pp. 213–214 *ante*.
[23] [1990] 1 W.L.R. 1587.
[24] *ibid.* at 1621.
[25] [1991] P.L.R. 224, [1992] I.R.L.R. 27.
[26] [2001] W.T.L.R. 1237, [2001] P.L.R. 79.
[27] By *Stannard v. Fisons Pension Trust* [1991] P.L.R. 224, [1992] I.R.L.R. 27 and by earlier unreported statements of the Court of Appeal to the same effect in *Kerr v. British Leyland (Staff) Trustees Ltd.*
[28] [2003] 2 W.L.R. 1362.
[29] Relying on *Scott v. The National Trust* [1998] 2 All E.R. 705 at 718.
[30] [1990] 1 W.L.R. 1304.
[31] This is in effect the contention of Lord Walker [2002] P.C.B. 226.
[32] [1990] 1 W.L.R. 1304.
[33] [1990] 1 W.L.R. 1587.

because the trustees had not realised that they were depriving themselves of their pre-existing power so to do. However, Warner J. emphasised[34] that "it is not enough that it should be shown that the trustees did not have a proper understanding of the effect of their act. It must also be clear that, had they had a proper understanding of it, they would not have acted as they did." He therefore also declined to apply the Rule since, on the facts, he considered that the trustees would still have done the same thing anyway.

However, the Rule was applied in *Stannard v. Fisons Pension Trust*,[35] where the Court of Appeal set aside the deed by which the trustees of a pension trust had exercised a discretion on the basis of an out of date valuation of the pension fund.[36] It has to be admitted that, if the Rule is ever to be extended to mistakes which go beyond mistakes as to the effect of what has been done, this is an obvious case for its application; the discretion was exercised on the basis of a mistaken view of a factor which was clearly crucial to the decision taken by the trustees. The difficulty lies in formulating a rule which will permit the application of the Rule in these circumstances without also permitting its application whenever a discretion or power has been exercised on the basis of a mistake as to or failure to take into account the possible consequences.

In *Breadner v. Granville-Grossman*,[37] Park J. held that the decision in *Stannard v. Fisons Pension Trust* turned mainly on principles particularly applicable to pension trusts and not on what he described as the "general" Rule. He said that, although the limits to the Rule had not yet been established, it must have some; it could not be right that, whenever trustees did something which they later regretted and thought that they ought not to have done, they could say that they never did it in the first place. He also emphasised that he knew of no decision in which the principle had been applied to take away the beneficial interests of those properly entitled under the trust instrument[38] (presumably meaning the beneficial interests of those already entitled to interests in possession since the exercise of any dispositive power is bound to take away any default interests which have not yet vested in possession, something which the exercise of the power of advancement under consideration in *Re Hastings-Bass (dec'd)* itself undoubtedly did). However, these remarks were no more than dicta because what Park J. actually held was that the Rule is limited to undoing something which has been done; it was therefore not applicable to the case before him, where it was being invoked in order to do something which the trustees had not done.[39] This restriction on the application of the Rule seems wholly appropriate.

By then the Rule had already been applied in *Green v. Cobham*,[40] where the mistake by the trustees amounted merely to a failure to take into account the possible fiscal consequences of what they had done, and the Rule was sub-

---

[34] *Ibid.* at 1624.

[35] [1991] P.L.R. 224, [1992] I.R.L.R. 27.

[36] Such valuations normally have to be produced every three years but tend to appear some considerable time after the end of the three year period in question.

[37] [2001] Ch. 523.

[38] This would have been the consequence of the application of the Rule in the case before him since what he had earlier held to have been the failure of the trustees to exercise the power of appointment in time had caused the interests of those entitled in default to vest indefeasibly.

[39] They had failed to exercise the power of appointment in time and as a result their purported exercise of it was ineffective.

[40] [2000] W.T.L.R. 1101.

sequently applied again in similar circumstances in *Abacus Trust Co. (Isle of Man) v. N.S.P.C.C.*[41] In both these cases the exercise of the powers in question[42] had had exactly the intended effect but had the unforeseen consequences of imposing unintended substantial charges to capital gains tax,[43] which were saved as a result of the application of the Rule. In cases such as this, of course, it is in the interests of everyone involved with the settement in question that the Rule is applied and the only serious opposition to its application is therefore likely to come from the Inland Revenue in the event that they are invited and agree to appear.[44]

The most recent authority, *Re Barr's Settlement Trusts*,[45] has however restricted the categories of mistakes which will give rise to the application of the Rule. The trustees and the protector had exercised a power of appointment in respect of 60% of the trust property with the intention of giving effect to the wishes of the settlor. However, the relevant intermediary had misinformed them as to the wishes of the settlor, who only wanted 40 per cent to be so appointed. On this occasion there was serious opposition to the application of the Rule,[46] as there had also been in *Breadner v. Granville-Grossman*.[47] Lightman J. was therefore faced by competing contentions: on the one hand, that the Rule could be applied whenever there had been a mistake, no matter how that mistake arose; and, on the other hand, that the Rule could only be applied where the mistake in question was sufficiently fundamental (and that, on the facts, it was not). He rejected both contentions and instead held that the Rule was only applicable where the exercise of the discretion or power amounts to a breach of fiduciary duty by the person exercising it, in other words where the latter was under a duty to consider what he had failed to take into account or was under a duty not to consider what he had taken into account.

This conclusion enabled Lightman J. to apply the Rule on the basis that the intermediary had been acting as agent for the trustees when he misrepresented the wishes of the settlor to them. The view that this rendered the trustees' subsequent exercise of the power a breach of fiduciary duty is just about supportable on the basis that they had by then decided to act in accordance with the settlor's wishes and can therefore be regarded as having been under a duty to establish what those wishes actually were. However, Lightman J. made no reference to the fact that trustees are not as such under any duty whatever to act in accordance with the wishes of their settlor; indeed, any argument that they were in the case of any individual trust would point inevitably to the conclusion that the trust in question was a sham.[48] Nor does a

---

[41] [2001] W.T.L.R. 953.

[42] A power to appoint additional trustees in *Green v. Cobham*; a straightforward power of appointment in *Abacus Trust Co. (Isle of Man) v. N.S.P.C.C.*

[43] In *Green v Cobham* because of a subsequent reduction in the number of non-resident trustees; in *Abacus Trust Co. (Isle of Man) v. N.S.P.C.C.* because the power of appointment had been executed three days too early.

[44] The Revenue was apparently not informed in advance about the proceedings in *Green v. Cobham* but was informed about the proceedings in *Abacus Trust Co. (Isle of Man) v. N.S.P.C.C.* and declined either to be joined to or to be bound by them.

[45] [2003] 2 W.L.R. 1362.

[46] From the persons in whose favour the appointment had been made.

[47] [2001] Ch. 523. In that case, the opposition had been from the default beneficiaries who had taken as a result of the trustees' failure to exercise the power of appointment in time.

[48] See *ante*, p. 50.

failure effectively to exercise a discretion or power amount, without more, to a breach of fiduciary duty.

But if Lightman J. was correct to hold that the Rule can only be applied where there has been a breach of fiduciary duty, then it must follow that the Rule should not have been applied in *Stannard v. Fisons Pension Trust*;[49] it is not easy to see how the trustees could have been held to be in breach of fiduciary duty merely because they had acted on the basis of an out of date valuation for whose preparation they were not responsible. It is also at least arguable that on this basis the Rule should not have been applied in *Green v. Cobham*,[50] either; while trustees who fail to take fiscal consequences into account are at least arguably acting in breach of fiduciary duty, the negative fiscal consequences in that case arose out of events which could not possibly have been foreseen at the time when the powers were exercised. The question of precisely what types of mistake will give rise to the application of the Rule requires urgent review at appellate level, preferably by the House of Lords (the Court of Appeal could conceivably be hampered by its own decision in *Stannard v. Fisons Pension Trust*.)[51] The choice seems most likely to be between mistakes of any type whatever (the view adopted in *Green v. Cobham*,[52] and *Abacus Trust Co. (Isle of Man) v. N.S.P.C.C.*)[53]) and mistakes which amount to a breach of fiduciary duty (the view adopted in *Re Barr's Settlement Trusts*[54]).[55]

When the Rule can be and is applied, the effect of its application is also at present uncertain. In *AMP (UK) v. Barker*,[56] Lawrence Collins J. stated that its application makes the exercise of the discretion or power void rather than voidable. However, the exact opposite was held by Lightman J. in *Re Barr's Settlement Trusts*.[57] His conclusion that the appointment, which had been made 10 years earlier, was voidable rather than void was significant because substantial distributions of income and capital had been made pursuant to its provisions in the interim; whether the appointment was in fact to be avoided and, if so, on what terms was adjourned for further argument. In this respect, the view of Lightman J. seems preferable and, since it formed part of his ratio, must constitute the law at present; it also answers many of the criticisms which have been made of the Rule.[58] However, the last has certainly not yet been heard of this particular point either, particularly given that, in every other situation in which discretions and powers are exercised improperly, their exercise is wholly void, a point to which Lightman J. did not expressly advert.

Another analogous but less significant point which still awaits resolution is

---

[49] [1991] P.L.R. 224; [1992] I.R.L.R. 27.
[50] [2000] W.T.L.R. 1101.
[51] [1991] P.L.R. 224; [1992] I.R.L.R. 27.
[52] [2000] W.T.L.R. 1101.
[53] [2001] W.T.L.R. 953.
[54] [2003] 2 W.L.R. 1362.
[55] The author of this edition has suggested the adoption of the former view, provided that the mistakes in question are both mistakes as to the *existing* consequences of what has been done and mistakes but for which the discretion or power in question *would* not have been exercised (T.E.L.J. (April 2003) 4).
[56] [2001] W.T.L.R. 1237; [2001] P.L.R. 79.
[57] [2003] 2 W.L.R. 1362.
[58] Particularly by Lord Walker [2002] P.C.B. 226.

whether or not it is possible, as Warner J. stated in *Mettoy Pension Trustees v. Evans*,[59] for the court, where it concludes that the donee of the discretion or power would have acted in the same way but with the omission of one or more of the clauses of the deed in question, to uphold that deed with the deletion of the provisions in question. Since this is possible where there has been a mistake as to the effect of what has been done,[60] there is no obvious objection to this where the offending provisions are capable of being severed. However, it remains to be seen whether the flexible approach manifested by this statement is in fact carried into effect and, if so, exactly how.

### 3. When will the Exercise of a Discretion or Power be Dishonest?

#### (A) The Doctrine of Fraud on a Power

Different considerations arise where the discretion or power has not been exercised honestly. In such cases, there is said to have been a "fraud on a power" (this expression is used in connection with the exercise of both a power and a discretion). In equity the word "fraud" denotes nothing more than an improper motive. Various attempts have been made to categorise the circumstances in which there is a fraud on a power, the classic statement being found in the decision of the House of Lords in *Vatcher v. Paull*.[61] A number of propositions emerge from the decided cases.

First, where the donee of the discretion or power has exercised it bona fide, the court will not interfere even if it would itself have acted differently. In *Gisborne v. Gisborne*,[62] the trustees of a will had discretion to apply the whole or such portion of the income as they should think expedient for the benefit of the testator's wife, who was a person of unsound mind. The trustees refused to apply the whole of the income for her support and proposed to apply only so much of it as would be necessary to maintain her in care when the income from her own property was also taken into account. The House of Lords acknowledged that they would have ordered the trust fund to have been applied primarily for the benefit of the wife; however, in the light of their specific decision that the trustees had acted bona fide, they could not interfere with the exercise of the trustees' discretion.

Secondly, the fact that a discretion or power is exercised in such a way as to defeat the intention of the donor does not automatically make its exercise void.[63] This rule is comparable to the rule which permits beneficiaries who between them are absolutely beneficially entitled to join together and bring a trust to an end even though the intention of the settlor was that it should continue.[64] Once a discretion or power has been conferred, or a trust has been created, the donor or settlor ceases to have any control as such unless he has provided at the time when the discretion, power or trust was created that his consent (or the consent of the protector of the settlement) is a necessary precondition of any exercise.

---

[59] [1990] 1 W.L.R. 1587 at 1624–1625.

[60] See *Walker v. Armstrong* (1856) 8 De G.M. & G. 531; *ante*, p. 215.

[61] [1915] A.C. 372.

[62] (1877) 2 App.Cas. 628. See also *R. v. Archbishop of Canterbury and Bishop of London* [1903] 1 K.B. 289.

[63] *Lee v. Ferrie* (1839) 1 B. 483.

[64] See *post*, p. 717.

Thirdly, in every case it is necessary to identify who would be entitled in default of exercise of the discretion or power (these persons may be specified in the trust instrument; alternatively there may be a resulting trust in their favour). Since these are the persons who will lose as a result of any improper exercise of the discretion or power, in the event that they agree to that exercise with knowledge of all the relevant facts, the exercise will inevitably be valid.[65]

Fourthly, the essential feature which makes the exercise of a discretion or power improper is the intention of the person exercising it. If it is exercised with the intention of benefiting some non-object of the discretion or power, whether that person is the person exercising it or someone else, the exercise is void. Classic examples are where a discretion or power is exercised in favour of a beneficiary when he has already agreed that he will apply the property in question in whole or in part for the benefit of someone who is not one of its objects[66] and where, even though there has been no such prior agreement, the discretion or power is exercised with the intention of benefiting someone outside its scope.[67] So, in the case of a settlement to A for life, remainder to such of A's issue as A may appoint and, in default of appointment to A's children in equal shares, an appointment by A in favour of his children with a view to A and his children breaking the trust and dividing the capital between them (which they would be able to do once the issue of A other than his children had thus been excluded) will indirectly benefit A and so will unquestionably amount to a fraud on his power.[68]

If, on the other hand, there is no such intention, but the exercise does in fact benefit a non-object, it is valid. Thus, in the situation where a father has a discretion or power to appoint in favour of his child, an appointment in favour of that child is basically valid[69]; however, if it is made when the child is very ill, with the intention that the appointor will benefit by taking the child's estate on his or her death, the exercise will be invalid and will strictly be so even if the child subsequently recovers.[70] On the other hand, if a discretion or power is exercised with a view to bringing the trust to an end as part of a tax-saving scheme, and the appointment in question is made with the intention of benefiting its objects, the appointment is valid even though it confers an incidental benefit on the appointor or on other persons.[71] Further, it has been held[72] that it would not be a fraud on a power for trustees to add a father as a beneficiary of a settlement of which the principal beneficiaries were his infant children and then to appoint some of the trust property to him in order to enable him more easily to make the financial provision which he had been ordered to provide for the mother, not herself a beneficiary, in their divorce proceedings.

Fifthly, where a discretion or power is to be exercised in favour of one of its objects but in the hope that the recipient will benefit a non-object, the validity of the exercise will depend upon whether the recipient had legal and moral

---

[65] *Re Turner's Settled Estates* [1884] 28 Ch.D. 205; *Re Greaves* [1954] Ch. 434.
[66] *ibid.*
[67] *Portland v. Topham* (1867) 11 H.L.Cas. 32; *Vatcher v. Paull* [1915] A.C. 372.
[68] However, the same result can be achieved in a different way, by A releasing his power; see *post*, p. 225.
[69] *Henty v. Wrey* (1882) 21 Ch.D. 332.
[70] *Lord Hinchinbroke v. Seymour* (1789) 1 Bro.C.C. 395.
[71] *Re Merton* [1953] 1 W.L.R. 1096; *Re Robertson's Will Trusts* [1960] 1 W.L.R. 1050.
[72] *Netherton v. Netherton* [2000] W.T.L.R. 1171.

freedom of action.[73] Suppose a discretion or power is exercisable in favour of a person who makes it known that, if it is in fact exercised in his favour, he will give part of the fund to his parents, who are not objects. If the intention of the appointment is to benefit the parents, the exercise is invalid under the rule stated in the previous paragraph. If that is not the case but the recipient is under great pressure to benefit the parents, the exercise is also invalid.[74] However, if the recipient has genuine freedom of action but wishes to give his parents a benefit, the exercise of the power is good.[75]

## (B) The Reasons for Exercise

The donee of a discretion or power does not have to give the objects of that power or discretion the reasons for his decisions; however, as Robert Walker J. stated in *Scott v. The National Trust*,[76] if his decision is challenged in the courts he may be compelled to do so either through the process of disclosure if there are any relevant documents or, in practical terms, as the only way of avoiding an adverse inference being drawn.

In *Re Beloved Wilkes' Charity*,[77] trustees had a duty from time to time to select a candidate to be sent to the University of Oxford to be trained as a minister of the Church of England; they were obliged to select any suitable candidate who came forward from certain nominated parishes but in default had a more general discretion. They decided to nominate a candidate from outside those parishes rather than one from within them. Lord Truro L.C. declined to interfere with this decision, saying:

> "It is to the discretion of the trustees that the execution of the trust is confided, that discretion being exercised with an entire absence of indirect motive, with honesty of intention, and with a fair consideration of the subject. The duty of supervision on the part of this court will thus be confined to the question of the honesty, integrity and fairness with which the deliberation has been conducted, and will not be extended to the accuracy of the conclusion arrived at."

However, if the trustees do choose to state their reasons, the court will examine them in order to ascertain whether or not the trustees have acted in error. In *Klug v. Klug*,[78] a mother who was one of a number of trustees declined to concur in the exercise of a power in favour of her daughter on the grounds that she disapproved of the latter's marriage. The court held that this was an impermissible reason; consequently she had acted dishonestly and her refusal to concur was set aside. Trustees of pensions trusts also tend, quite understandably, to give reasons for their decisions. But, as Robert Walker J. stated in *Scott v. The National Trust*,[79] the principles on which the court must proceed are the same whether or not the trustees give their reasons; it simply becomes

---

[73] *Birley v. Birley* (1858) 25 B. 299.
[74] *Re Crawshay* [1948] Ch. 123; *Re Dick* [1953] Ch. 343.
[75] *Re Marsden's Trusts* (1859) 4 Drew. 594.
[76] [1998] 2 All E.R. 705 at 717–719.
[77] (1851) 3 Mac. & G. 440.
[78] [1918] 2 Ch. 67.
[79] [1998] 2 All E.R. 705 at 717–719.

easier for the court to examine a decision if the reasons for it have been disclosed.

In *Edge v. Pensions Ombudsman*,[80] a pension trust had a surplus which had to be reduced in order to preserve the tax advantages given to pension trusts. The trustees decided to use £20,000,000 of the surplus to credit additional service to those members in employment on a particular date and to reduce the contributions of both employers and employees from a date six months earlier; no additional service was credited either to those already receiving pensions or to a number of employees who were to be made redundant during the six-month period. The trustees explained to one of the latter that their decision had been taken in order to encourage all employees to become and remain members of the pension scheme and to support the employers in providing continued employment for their current employees. The Pensions Ombudsman set aside the trustees' decision on the grounds that the trustees had breached their duty of impartiality and had not acted in the best interests of all the beneficiaries. His decision was reversed by the Court of Appeal, who held that the duty to act impartially was no more than the ordinary duty imposed on any holder of a discretionary power, namely to exercise the power for the purposes for which it is given, giving proper consideration to the matters which are relevant and excluding from consideration matters which are irrelevant. Provided the trustees complied with that duty, they were entitled to reach a decision which appeared to prefer the claims of some beneficiaries over others.

### (C) The Effect of Fraud on a Power
In principle, where the exercise of a discretion or power is successfully impugned on the grounds of fraud on a power, its exercise is totally invalid.[81] However, this can in some circumstances work harshly on the objects of the discretion or power. If the person with the discretion or power reaches an agreement with one of the objects that he will appoint £1,000 to the object provided that the latter pays £500 to someone who is not an object, then in principle the whole appointment is invalid and the object will receive nothing. Accordingly, in an attempt to help objects, in some cases the court will try to sever the improper element in the appointment from the remainder of that appointment. [82] If there is no intent to benefit the object of the power at all, the exercise is clearly wholly invalid.[83] If, however, there is an intent to benefit the object to some extent, and the improper element is in the form of a condition attached to the appointment, the court will delete the condition to leave the object free to take unconditionally.[84]

As has already been seen,[85] the latter possibility has been held[86] to be open to the court where the exercise of a discretion or power is set aside under the Rule in *Re Hastings-Bass (dec'd)*,[87] although this has not yet actually been done. Thus far, the effect of the application of that Rule and of fraud on a power are

---

[80] [2000] Ch. 602.
[81] *Daubeney v. Cockburn* (1816) 1 Mer. 626.
[82] *Topham v. Duke of Portland* (1858) 1 D.J. & S. 517.
[83] *Re Cohen* [1911] 1 Ch. 37.
[84] *Hay v. Watkins* (1850) 3 Dr. & War. 339.
[85] See *ante*, p. 219.
[86] See *Mettoy Pension Trustees v. Evans* [1990] 1 W.L.R. 1587 at 1624–1625.
[87] [1975] Ch. 25.

therefore the same. However if, as Lightman J. held in *Re Barr's Settlement Trusts*,[88] the effect of the application of the Rule in *Re Hastings-Bass (dec'd)* is that the exercise of the discretion or power in question is voidable rather than void, the normal consequences of the application of the two doctrines will be completely different. It is arguable that Lightman J. should have considered this point when reaching his decision.

### 4. Can the Exercise of Powers and Discretions be Categorised as Unreasonable?

Quite apart from any of the possibilities which have been considered so far, beneficiaries of pension trusts appear to have the further possibility of being entitled to attack the exercise of a power or discretion on the grounds that it was in administrative law terms "unreasonable" in accordance with what is known as the *Wednesbury* test (laid down in *Associated Provincial Picture Houses v. Wednesbury Corporation*,[89] in the context of judicial review of administrative action). This possibility emerges from *Harris v. Lord Shuttleworth*[90] and *Wild v. Pensions Ombudsman*.[91] The applicability of this test was also reviewed in *Edge v. Pensions Ombudsman*,[92] where the Court of Appeal held that pension trustees are chosen to exercise discretions for very much the same reasons as the local authority in the *Wednesbury* case had been chosen to exercise a discretion, namely their knowledge and experience.

It is not generally thought that the *Wednesbury* test is in this jurisdiction applicable to voluntary settlements as such. However, it was applied to such a settlement in New Zealand in *Blair v. Vallely*,[93] where trustees were enjoined from carrying into effect what the court classified as an unreasonable decision as to how to attribute what the trustees described as intangible benefits to beneficiaries whom they wished to treat equally; however, this conclusion was undoubtedly facilitated by the fact that the trustees had explained their reasons to the court, something which they are not actually obliged to do.

Whether a similar approach is one day adopted in this jurisdiction remains to be seen. However, it appears that what is known as "legitimate expectation", which has an enormously important part to play in judicial review of administrative action, may have some part to play in the context of voluntary settlements. In *Scott v. The National Trust*,[94] which concerned a challenge to the decision of the National Trust to ban the hunting of deer with hounds on some of its lands, the claimants applied to bring both charity proceedings[95] (the National Trust being a charity) and proceedings for judicial review. Robert Walker J. allowed the former and not the latter but commented that no reasonable body of trustees who had for the last ten years paid £1,000 a quarter to an elderly impoverished beneficiary would discontinue the payment without any warning and without giving the beneficiary the opportunity of trying to persuade the trustees to continue the payment, at least temporarily. This is

---

[88] [2003] 2 W.L.R. 1362.
[89] [1948] 1 K.B. 223.
[90] [1994] I.C.R. 991.
[91] [1996] P.L.R. 275.
[92] [2000] Ch. 602.
[93] [2000] W.T.L.R. 1101.
[94] [1998] 2 All E.R. 705.
[95] See *post*, p. 501.

obviously a very extreme example and this comment was anyway no more than a dictum. However, it does indicate one route down which the law might one day go.

## IV. When can Discretions and Powers be Released?

### 1. *Reasons for the Release of Discretions and Powers*

Those entitled to exercise discretions and powers sometimes have to consider the possibility of releasing them. There are two overlapping reasons for releasing a discretion or power: first, in order to prevent the trust from being, or from continuing to be being, subject to some form of taxation and, secondly, in order to ensure that some particular beneficiary or class of beneficiaries will inevitably either become entitled to the trust property or be prevented from becoming entitled to the trust property.

A release solely for the first reason may be induced by the effect of changes in taxation law such as the one which occurred in 1973. Until April 5, 1973, all the income of a trust was taxable in the hands of the trustees at the same rate; however, thereafter an additional charge to tax was (and still is) imposed on income which could be accumulated.[96] In the case of a pre-existing trust under which the trustees had a power to accumulate but, subject thereto, could pay the income to a named person, one possible way of avoiding the additional charge to tax was for the trustees to release their power to accumulate so that the named beneficiary became entitled to the whole of the income. Taxation may also be saved as the result of a release which irrevocably fixes beneficial entitlement. Thus in *Re Wills' Trust Deeds*,[97] the trustees wished to release a power to appoint the trust property between charitable and non-charitable objects in order to convert the trust into one which was entirely charitable; although no comments as to their motives appear in the report of the decision, the only obvious one can have been a desire to obtain the exemption from most forms of taxation which is granted to all charitable trusts.[98]

A release made solely for the second reason is potentially, but not necessarily, more conflictive. A straightforward and non-controversial example of this type is where a release is made in order to ensure that a beneficiary will inevitably be entitled and so can deal with his beneficial interest; thus where trustees hold a fund on trust for such of three nominated beneficiaries as they may appoint and, in default of appointment, for all three equally, release of the power will give each of them a fixed interest which he can sell or mortgage. More controversially, a person with a right to appoint an interest in remainder away from himself may try to release that right in order himself to become absolutely beneficially entitled.[99] Further and, much more controversially, a release may be made to prevent one or more beneficiaries from becoming entitled and thus indirectly enable the only other beneficiaries to take (this was of course the objective of the proposed release in *Mettoy Pension Trustees v.*

---

[96] Finance Act 1973, s.16; see *ante*, p. 198.
[97] [1964] Ch. 219.
[98] See *post*, p. 444.
[99] See *Re Brierley* (1894) 43 W.R. 36, where the manoeuvre actually failed.

*Evans*;[1] a release of the power to use the surplus in the pension fund to enhance the benefits of the employees would, if it had been held to have been possible, enabled that surplus to have passed to the employer company and therefore to the latter's creditors).

In many of the situations where a release is being considered for the second reason, the same result could on the face of things be achieved by exercising the discretion or power in question. However, this will in practice often be impeded by the doctrine of fraud on a power.[2] The conventional view is that the doctrine of fraud on a power does not apply to the release of powers,[3] permitting the release of a power in circumstances where its exercise could be set aside. Thus, in the example already referred to[4] of a settlement to A for life, remainder to such of A's issue as A may appoint and, in default of appointment to A's children in equal shares, the inability of A to enable him and his children to break the trust by making an appointment A in favour of his children can be circumvented by A releasing his power which would equally produce the necessary exclusion of the issue of A other than his children.

However, in *Mettoy Pension Trustees v. Evans*,[5] Warner J., having stated that, where there is a gift over in default of appointment, the donee of a mere power owes no duty to the objects of that power but merely a duty to those interested in default of appointment not to misuse the power, held that "[the donee] may therefore release the power but he may not enter into any transaction that would amount to a fraud on the power, a fraud on the power being a wrong committed against the beneficiaries under the trust in default of appointment". This statement may well have produced a modification of the pre-existing law by making releases subject to the doctrine of fraud on a power but only in respect of fraud on those entitled in default of appointment, not as against the objects. However, this novel proposition, which is clearly no more than a dictum, would not have prevented the power in *Mettoy Pension Trustees v. Evans* from being released had that power been held to be a mere power rather than a fiduciary power since the liquidator would have owed no duties to the objects of the power other than the company; nor would it be applicable to the example set out above because all the default beneficiaries, A's children, would necessarily benefit from the release of the power. It remains to be seen whether this proposition is ever applied.

## 2. *The Propriety of a Release*

The traditional exposition of the circumstances in which a discretion or power can be effectively released is found in *Re Wills' Trust Deeds*,[6] where Buckley J. formulated five general propositions which have been set out in previous editions of this work.[7] However, these propositions are arguably defective in at least one respect and, although this is certainly not the fault of Buckley J., undoubtedly now require some modification in the light of the subsequent

---

[1] [1990] 1 W.L.R. 1587.
[2] See *ante*, p. 220.
[3] *Re Somes* [1896] 1 Ch. 250.
[4] See *ante*, p. 220.
[5] [1990] 1 W.L.R. 1587 at 1613.
[6] [1964] Ch. 219 at 236, 237.
[7] See the 7th (1998) ed., pp. 197–198.

evolution of the distinction between fiduciary and non-fiduciary donees of mere powers and of the rather different formulation which was adopted by Warner J. in *Mettoy Pensions Trustees v. Evans*.[8] The present position seems to be as follows.

## (A) Trust Powers of All Types

There is no possibility whatever of a trust power being released. The very essence of such a power is that the person entitled to exercise it is under an obligation so to do and, if he fails to do so, it will be exercised by the court. This was stated in *Re Wills' Trust Deeds*;[9] however, that case was decided before *McPhail v. Doulton*,[10] so Buckley J. must there have been using the expression "trust power" in its traditional sense, in other words as not including a discretionary trust. However, in *Mettoy Pensions Trustees v. Evans*,[11] Warner J. applied the same rule both to discretionary trusts and to discretions which have to be exercised and there certainly seems little point in drawing any distinction between the different categories of trust powers now.

## (B) Mere Discretions or Powers held by Fiduciary Donees

A mere discretion or power vested in a fiduciary donee which expressly authorises release can be released. This was specifically held in *Muir v. I.R.C.*,[12] where the wording of the relevant clause was held to authorise such a release. This was in effect also the position in *Blausten v. I.R.C.*,[13] where the Court of Appeal came to the conclusion that a resettlement of the trust fund upon trusts identical with the existing trusts, but excluding a particular power vested in the trustees, was a good exercise of the power of appointment (the immediate effect of the appointment was simply to exclude the wife of the settlor from the objects of the discretionary trusts of income and that was held to be within the terms of the power of appointment).

However, a mere discretion or power vested in a fiduciary donee which does not authorise release cannot be released. This has always been the law where the donees of the discretion or power are the trustees and it has been conferred upon them *virtute officii*; this is the case whether it is vested in the trustees as such or in named persons selected because they are the trustees. Despite the fact that the trustees cannot be obliged to exercise the discretion or power, they cannot ignore it since, as has already been seen,[14] they must consider periodically whether or not to exercise the discretion or power, its range and objects, and the appropriateness of individual appointments. Thus in *Re Courage Group's Pension Schemes*,[15] it was held that a committee which had been established to manage a pension scheme could not deprive their successors of the right to exercise their powers even if (which was not in fact decided) they were themselves entitled to release, fetter or agree not to exercise those powers.

---

[8] [1990] 1 W.L.R. 1587 at 1613–1614.
[9] [1964] Ch. 219.
[10] [1971] A.C. 424.
[11] [1990] 1 W.L.R. 1587 at 1613–1614.
[12] [1966] 1 W.L.R. 1269.
[13] [1972] Ch. 256.
[14] See *ante*, p. 209.
[15] [1987] 1 W.L.R. 495.

This principle was subsequently extended to fiduciary donees of mere powers who are not trustees by the decision in *Mettoy Pension Trustees v. Evans*.[16] Although doubts have been expressed as to whether the donee of that particular power was correctly classified as a fiduciary (as has already been seen, this conclusion has been described as "not overwhelming"[17]), there cannot be the slightest doubt that the extension of the principle to all fiduciary donees will be upheld.

### (C) Mere Discretions or Powers held by Non-Fiduciary Donees

Mere discretions or powers vested in non-fiduciary donees can certainly be released where there is no express or implied trust in favour of the members of the class in default of appointment. This was the situation and the decision reached in *Re Wills' Trust Deeds*.[18]

However, in that case, Buckley J. went on to state that, where there is an express or implied trust in favour of the members of the class in default of appointment, such powers cannot be released. Although he did not actually say so, Buckley J. may well have been thinking principally of gifts in default of appointment which are in favour of all rather than only some of the objects of the power in question. However, even if so restricted, his proposition is contrary to the much earlier decision of the Court of Appeal in *Re Radcliffe*,[19] which was not cited to him. In that case a father, who was not a trustee, released a mere power in order to enable the shares of his sons, who were entitled in default, to become absolute and the release was upheld even though it also benefited the father, in that he thereby received the share of a deceased son. Nor is the proposition of Buckley J., whether or not restricted in the way already mentioned, consistent with *Mettoy Pension Trustees v. Evans*.[20] Warner J. there specifically held that release was possible where the only person entitled in default was the donee of the power but also seemed prepared to permit such a release where persons other than the donee were entitled in default provided that the release did not amount to a fraud on them.[21] The mainstream of authority therefore seems to be in favour of permitting a release even where there is a gift over in default of appointment.

### 3. *The Effectiveness of a Release*

Some doubt has been cast on the effectiveness of releases by holders of discretions or powers who hold them not in their personal capacity but as the result of holding an office such as a trusteeship (no corresponding difficulty arises concerning releases by holders who are named as such, even if they happen also to be trustees). This is another possible adverse effect of the decision in *Re Wills' Trust Deeds*.[22] Buckley J. held that, although the current trustees had validly released the power in accordance with the authorisation

---

[16] [1990] 1 W.L.R. 1587.
[17] See *ante*, p. 211.
[18] [1964] Ch. 219.
[19] [1892] 1 Ch. 227.
[20] [ 1990] 1 W.L.R. 1587 at 1613–1614.
[21] This was the novel proposition to which reference has already been made (see *ante*, p. 226); its adoption would not affect the outcome of a case such as *Re Radcliffe*.
[22] [1964] Ch. 219.

given by the trust instrument and so had precluded themselves from exercising it, that release would not prevent their successor trustees from exercising the power. He said:[23]

"A power granted to successive holders of an office is unlike trust property, the entire ownership of which is vested in the trustees for the time being of the settlement and devolves on each change of trustee by succession. Where a power is granted to successive holders of an office all that is vested in the incumbent for the time being of the office is the capacity to exercise the power while he holds that office."

A similar view was taken in *Re Courage Group's Pension Scheme*,[24] although in that case it was not actually decided whether or not the existing donees were entitled to release their power anyway.

Whether this is indeed the law has been questioned. The remarks of Buckley J. certainly do not seem entirely consistent with the later decision of the Court of Appeal in *Muir v. I.R.C.*,[25] where the court implicitly treated the release of the fiduciary power which it held to have been authorised as both complete and binding. It is suggested that the better view is that, in the absence of provision to the contrary, office holders who can release should be able to bind their successors. However, until this point has been resolved, there must clearly be some doubt about the validity of some of the types of releases which have already been considered (particularly those made to enable a beneficiary to deal with his interest) where the holders of the discretion or power in question hold it by virtue of their appointment as trustees; this is obviously because of the possibility of the released power being exercised by later trustees. More is likely to be heard of this particular question. However, even if *Re Wills' Trust Deeds* and *Re Courage Group's Pension Schemes* are correct in this respect, their effect could undoubtedly be avoided by sufficiently sophisticated drafting since it would certainly be open to a settlor to provide that discretions or powers could be released in such a way as to bind successors to the original holders; many modern precedents so provide.

### 4. The Possibility of Surrender to the Court

Unless and until a discretion or power can be and is effectively released, it remains with its holder who alone can exercise it. Are there any circumstances in which the discretion or power in question can be surrendered to the court?

In *Re Allen-Meyrick's Will Trusts*,[26] the trustees of a will held the trust fund upon trust to pay so much of the income as they thought fit to the husband of the testatrix and, subject to the exercise of their discretion in his favour, upon trust for her god-daughters. The husband was an undischarged bankrupt and the trustees had, in the exercise of their discretion, paid the rent of the house in which he lived; however, apart from this, they could not agree as to whether or

---

[23] *Ibid.* at 238.
[24] [1987] 1 W.L.R. 495.
[25] [1966] 1 W.L.R. 1269.
[26] [1966] 1 W.L.R. 499.

not to make any further payments to him. They therefore asked the court to accept a surrender of their discretion but Buckley J. refused to do so.

As Buckley J. specifically held, it is of course open to the trustees of any trust to seek the directions of the court in any particular circumstances and the court was prepared to give directions as to what should be done with the income which had accrued; however, the court would not accept a surrender of the trustees' discretion for the future. This seems to have been largely due to difficulties as to how matters could proceed following surrender since, had the court accepted the surrender, there would have been no ready way in which it could have been informed of the actual circumstances of the beneficiaries each time that a decision had to be made. However, the decision actually reached opened up the possibility that, although this would certainly not have been welcomed by the court, the trustees could have sought the directions of the court on a new application each year or so.

It is also possible for the holders of a discretion or power to give the court the opportunity of deciding whether to abrogate or vary that discretion or power by making an application for this purpose under the Variation of Trusts Act 1958.[27]

## V. THE POSITION OF THE POTENTIAL BENEFICIARIES

### 1. *The Potential Beneficiaries Themselves*

What is the position of a person who is one of the objects of a power pending its exercise? Two aspects require consideration.

### (A) The Individual Rights of an Object of a Discretion or Power

#### (1) When can application be made to the court?
A person who is one of the objects of a discretion or power can require its holder to consider exercising it in his favour, or in favour of any of the other objects.[28] Accordingly, if he can show that the holder has refused to consider him as a possible object, he can apply to the court. This is, however, subject to any contrary provision in the instrument by which the discretion or power was created (some modern deeds authorise the holders of discretions and powers to exercise them in favour of some of their objects without even considering their other objects).

A person who is one of the objects of a discretion or power can also apply to the court if, despite giving due consideration to his own position, its holder has acted capriciously in other respects. In *Re Manisty's Settlement*,[29] Templeman J. stated that holders of a discretion or power would be acting capriciously if they acted "for reasons which I apprehend could be said to be irrational, perverse or irrelevant to any sensible expectation of the settlor for

---

[27] See *post*, p. 747.
[28] *Re Gestetner* [1953] Ch. 672, *per* Harman J. at 688; *Re Manisty's Settlement* [1974] Ch. 17, *per* Templeman J. at 25.
[29] [1974] Ch. 17 at 25.

example, if they chose a beneficiary by height or complexion or by the irrelevant fact that he was a resident of Greater London".

In other respects, a person who is one of the objects of a discretion or power is in a curious position. On the one hand, he may well not know that he is an object; only in the case of discretionary trusts in favour of relatively small groups of beneficiaries are the trustees obliged to inform those beneficiaries of the existence of their interests.[30] On the other hand, where he does know that he is an object of the discretion or power in question, it seems that he is entitled to apply to the court in the event that the trustees in whom the property subject to the power is vested are guilty of any acts of improper administration or in the event that the holder of the discretion or power improperly exercises it or purports to release it. However, whether he will ever realise that he is in a position to do so obviously depends on his rights to obtain information from his trustees. The position is discussed in detail in a later chapter.[31] The Privy Council has recently held, in *Schmidt v. Rosewood Trust*,[32] that in this respect there is no formal distinction between the beneficiaries of trusts and those who are merely a possible object of a discretion or power. It was held that "their right to seek disclosure of trust documents, although sometimes not inappropriately described as a proprietary right, is best approached as one aspect of the court's inherent jurisdiction to supervise (and where appropriate intervene in) the administration of trusts". However the Board went on to hold that "in many cases the court may have no difficulty in concluding that an applicant with no more than a theoretical possibility of benefit ought not to be granted any relief". The Privy Council did not have to apply their decision, which is bound to be followed by the English courts, to the facts but information is clearly likely to be restricted to those who in practical terms have a reasonable chance of receiving some part of the trust property at some point.

The persons entitled to the property in default of the exercise of a discretion or power will necessarily be beneficiaries of fixed trusts and will therefore be entitled to know about the existence of their beneficial interests. They are similarly entitled to apply to the court in the event that of any improper conduct by the trustees in whom the property in question is vested or by the holder of a discretion or power. But their rights to information may well now in practice be considerably restricted by the fact that they are even less likely ever to receive any part of the trust property than some of the possible objects of a discretion or power.

## (2) Remedies where the discretion or power is not exercised

**(a) Trust powers.** On the case of trust powers in any of the senses in which this expression is used, where, in other words, a mandatory discretion or power is vested in the trustees or in third parties (in the latter case it will in effect be an old fashioned power in the nature of a trust), the holder of the discretion or power will be under an obligation to exercise it; therefore, he can be directed to do so by the court.

---

[30] See *post*, pp. 499–501.
[31] See *post*, pp. 496–499.
[32] [2003] 2 W.L.R. 1442.

Where the power is vested in trustees, the court will additionally have all the powers enunciated by Lord Wilberforce in *McPhail v. Doulton*.[33] Prior to that decision, a trust power was only valid for certainty of objects if a complete list of all its objects could be drawn up; consequently, in the event that the power was not exercised, the court would invariably order that the property should be divided equally between all the objects of the power. However, the new test for certainty of objects established by *McPhail v. Doulton* inevitably means that, in the case of trust powers validated by that decision, not all the objects of the power will be known either to the trustees or to the court. Lord Wilberforce consequently held that, in such circumstances, the court can either appoint new trustees or direct persons representative of the classes of beneficiaries to prepare a scheme of distribution or, should the proper basis for distribution be apparent, direct the trustees how to distribute the fund (this does not, of course, mean that equal distribution will never again be ordered; in the case of a small class of beneficiaries whose entire membership is known, it is almost inevitable that equal distribution will still be ordered).

Where, on the other hand, the power is vested in third parties, there does not seem any obvious basis on which the court can replace those third parties. Consequently, the court can presumably only either direct persons representative of the classes of beneficiaries to prepare a scheme for distribution or, should the proper basis for distribution be apparent (normally the case in old fashioned powers in the nature of a trust, which tend to be in favour of reduced groups), direct the trustees how to distribute the fund (in the case of a reduced group, inevitably in equal shares).

**(b) Mere discretions or powers.** In the case of mere discretions or powers, the court is unable to direct their exercise.

Where such a discretion or power is held by a non-fiduciary donee, the court can do nothing at all.

Where, on the other hand, the discretion or power is held by a fiduciary donee, the court can direct him to consider whether or not to exercise it. It has been stated on several occasions,[34] that a refusal to follow such a direction from the court might well lead to the replacement of the fiduciary in question.

More controversially, it has now been held, in *Mettoy Pension Trustees v. Evans*,[35] that all the remedies available to the court to enforce trust powers are also available in the case of mere discretions and powers held by fiduciary donees. This was the case in which a company held a power to appoint any surplus in its pension fund, which was actually vested in a separate trustee company, in favour of the pensioners with a gift over in default of appointment to itself. Warner J. held that the company was unable to release the power and thus make the surplus available for its general creditors. It was obviously impossible to leave the liquidators of the company to exercise the power since their duty to the creditors would have conflicted with and presumably prevailed over their duty to consider the claims of the pensioners. No application had been made for the appointment of new fiduciaries (had there

---

[33] [1971] A.C. 424 at 457.
[34] *Re Gestetner* [1953] Ch. 672 at 688; *Re Manisty's Settlement* [1974] Ch. 17 at 25; *Rosewood Trust v. Schmidt* [2001] W.T.L.R. 1081 (Court of Appeal of the Isle of Man; the point was not mentioned in the subsequent opinion of the Privy Council ([2003] 2 W.L.R. 1442)).
[35] [1990] 1 W.L.R. 1587.

been, the obvious remedy would have been to vest the power in the trustee company, which had been the donee of the power at an earlier stage). Warner J. therefore held that he was entitled to approve or dictate a scheme himself and invited further argument as to what scheme was appropriate.[36]

This decision has been criticised[37] on the grounds that judicial exercise of fiduciary discretions is inappropriate, even "as regards quasi-public trusts such as pension funds" and that the judge should have confined himself to appointing suitable new fiduciaries. It remains to be seen whether the novel remedies enunciated in *Mettoy Pension Trustees v. Evans* for the non-exercise of a mere discretion or power by a fiduciary donee are ever actually put into effect.

### (3) Remedies where the power is exercised improperly

The general rule is that any improper exercise of any discretion power will be set aside, both where the donees "exceed their power, and possibly if they are proved to have exercised it capriciously."[38] To this basic rule there may be one exception, where the Rule in *Re Hastings-Bass (dec'd.),*[39] applies. Lightman J. held in *Re Barr's Settlement Trusts,*[40] that the effect of the application of this Rule was that the appointment in question was voidable rather than void. This view must constitute the law at present but, in the light of earlier judicial statements adopting the opposite view,[41] it is unlikely that the last has yet been heard of this particular point.

An example of the general rule is *Turner v. Turner,*[42] where the trustees had left all the decisions to the settlor (who was not a trustee) and had made a series of appointments without reading the necessary documents before signing them; all the appointments were held to be null and void other than one concerning land which had been effective to transfer the legal title, which the appointee therefore held on trust for the settlement.

If the person to whom the property was improperly appointed under a disposition which is avoided has dealt with that property in favour of a third party, the latter will not be able to claim to have taken free of the interests of those otherwise entitled under the discretion or power and so will be bound by their interests[43] except in the relatively unlikely situation in which the third party has acquired the legal title to the property in question (in which case he may be able to claim to be a bona fide purchaser for value without notice or, in the case of registered land, the statutory equivalent). The only other exception to this is the limited defence provided by section 157 of the Law of Property Act 1925, which rather curiously is available only when the appointee was at least 25 years old at the time of the transaction and only to the extent that he was presumptively entitled in default of appointment.

---

[36] This part of the case was adjourned pending an appeal. Both the appeal and the outstanding part of the case were subsequently settled.

[37] By Gardner 107 L.Q.R. (1991) 214 at 217–218.

[38] *McPhail v. Doulton* [1971] A.C. 424, *per* Lord Wilberforce at 456.

[39] [1975] Ch. 25; see *ante,* p. 215.

[40] [2003] 2 W.L.R. 1362.

[41] Particularly in *AMP (UK) v. Barker* [2001] W.T.L.R. 1237, [2001] P.L.R. 79.

[42] [1984] Ch. 100.

[43] *Cloutte v. Storey* [1911] 1 Ch. 18.

**(B) The Collective Rights of the Objects of a Discretion or Power**
There is one respect in which the objects of a power have a more direct interest in the property subject to the power. It will be seen later that, where a beneficiary of a trust is of full age and *sui juris* and he alone is entitled to the trust fund, he may bring the trust to an end.[44] Somewhat similarly, where all the possible objects of a discretion or power combine, then they together may deal with the beneficial interest in the property subject to it; however, if the discretion or power is limited to income, that is all that they will be able to deal with unless they also combine with whoever is entitled to the capital, including, if necessary, the default beneficiaries.

In *Re Smith*,[45] a fund was held on discretionary trust as to income and capital for Lilian and, after her death, for her children. Lilian and her three children, who were between them the only persons entitled to benefit under the trust, together assigned all their interest therein to an insurance company. The assignee was held entitled to demand the whole of the income. Romer J. said that in such a case "you treat all the people put together as though they formed one person, for whose benefit the trustees were directed to apply the whole of a particular fund".[46]

**(C) The Right to Release Interests**
Just as a man cannot be forced to accept a gift,[47] so a man cannot be forced to remain an object of a discretion or power and he can, if he so wishes, release his rights thereunder. In that event, the discretion or power is administered as if his name did not appear among the class of those entitled to be considered as objects of the exercise of the holder's discretion.[48]

### 2. *Assignees and Trustees in Bankruptcy*

An assignee or trustee in bankruptcy of a potential beneficiary is, in principle, in the same position as the potential beneficiary himself. Thus in *Re Coleman*,[49] the Court of Appeal held that, where a discretionary beneficiary had assigned his beneficial interest, the trustees were compelled to pay to the assignee the amount which they had allotted to the beneficiary. In principle, the position of a trustee in bankruptcy ought to be the same but this is subject to the general principle of bankruptcy law that a bankrupt is entitled to retain sufficient funds for his own support, the trustee in bankruptcy being entitled only to the balance. This principle was applied by Vaughan Williams J. in *Re Ashby*.[50] In that case a discretionary beneficiary became bankrupt and the trustees continued to make payments to him. The beneficiary was held to be entitled to retain what was necessary for his basic support and his trustee in bankruptcy was held to be able to claim the excess.

The terms of a trust instrument may require payment to be made to the beneficiary personally; alternatively, they may entitle the trustees either to pay

---

[44] See *post*, p. 717.
[45] [1928] Ch. 915.
[46] See also *Re Nelson* [1928] Ch. 920N.
[47] *Thompson v. Leach* (1690) 2 Vent. 198; *Re Stratton's Deed of Disclaimer* [1958] 2 Ch. 42.
[48] *Re Gulbenkian's Settlement Trusts (No.2)* [1970] Ch. 408.
[49] (1889) 39 Ch.D. 443. See also *Re Smith* [1928] Ch. 915.
[50] [1892] 1 Q.B. 872.

the beneficiary directly or to make payments to third parties for his benefit. In *Re Bullock*,[51] which was concerned with a discretionary trust containing the latter type of provision, Kekewich J. held that, when a discretionary beneficiary had become bankrupt, the trustees could continue to pay income to third parties for his benefit. The precise scope of this decision is a matter of some doubt and it has been suggested that such a discretion is restricted so that the trustees can only provide the bankrupt with sufficient funds to cover his necessaries. However, this is probably not correct. It seems that, so far as the trustees are concerned, they may continue to apply funds for the benefit of the beneficiary in the same way as they could have done before the bankruptcy. If as a result assets come into the hands of the beneficiary which are not required for his necessaries, as where the trustees apply the money in providing a luxury holiday for the beneficiary, it seems that the trustee in bankruptcy is powerless to intervene. However, the trustees must of course exercise their discretion in good faith and must make their decision with a view to benefiting the beneficiary rather than in order to spite his trustee in bankruptcy and creditors.

---

[51] [1891] 64 L.T. 736.

# CHAPTER 7

# LEGALITY OF A TRUST

## I. GENERALLY

IT is an elementary principle that a trust which is wholly illegal or contrary to public policy will not be enforced. Indeed the court will not only prevent the illegal trust from taking effect but will also generally go so far as to refuse its assistance to the settlor in recovering the property in question. "Those who violate the law", said Lord Truro L.C. "must not apply to the law for protection".[1] The principle will not, however, be stretched to its uttermost limit. A settlor is entitled to recover the property where the illegal purpose is merely contemplated; in these circumstances, there is what is described as a *locus poenitentiae*.[2]

The consequences of a trust which is partially unlawful can be rather different. Strictly speaking, it appears that, if part of the trust funds is to be devoted to an unlawful purpose and the remainder to a lawful purpose, then, where the part of the funds to be devoted cannot be ascertained, the whole trust will fail because it will be impossible to ascertain the residue.[3] However, it must be truly impossible to ascertain the relevant part and it appears that the court will, if practicable, endeavour to ascertain it in order to uphold the remainder of the gift.[4] Indeed there is some, admittedly indecisive, authority[5] for the proposition that, if the lawful purpose is charitable, the whole of the property will be devoted to that purpose and the trust for the illegal purpose will be completely disregarded. However, in view of the confused state of the case law, it is not by any means certain that this is indeed the law, notwithstanding the fact that this would be extremely convenient.

This chapter deals principally with the circumstances in which a trust will be void for perpetuity or will be set aside because of the settlor's bankruptcy; both of these topics are of the utmost importance in any discussion of the legality of a trust. However, it is beyond the scope of this work to deal exhaustively with the many other types of illegality known to the law, which

---

[1] *Benyon v. Nettlefold* (1850) 3 Mac. & G. 94 at 102. See also *Ayerst v. Jenkins* (1873) L.R. 16 Eq. 275 but compare *Phillips v. Probyn* [1899] 1 Ch. 811.
[2] *Symes v. Hughes* (1870) L.R. 9 Eq. 475.
[3] See *Chapman v. Brown* (1801) 6 Ves. 404.
[4] See *Mitford v. Reynolds* (1842) 1 Ph. 185.
[5] See *Fisk v. A.-G.* (1867) L.R. 4 Eq. 521; *Hunter v. Bullock* (1872) L.R. 14 Eq. 45; *Dawson v. Small* (1874) L.R. 18 Eq. 114; *Re Williams* (1877) 5 Ch.D. 735; *Re Birkett* (1878) 9 Ch.D. 576 (all trusts for maintenance of tombs with surplus for a charitable purpose); see also *Re Rogerson* [1901] 1 Ch. 715.

are as capable of vitiating a trust as of vitiating any other transaction; a few examples will be briefly considered.

1. Restraints on alienation. A restraint on the alienation of property given to a beneficiary absolutely is contrary to public policy and void.[6]

2. Trusts in favour of illegitimate children. In certain circumstances, trusts which took effect before 1970, whether created by deed[7] or by will[8], in favour of illegitimate children who were yet to be born were void on the ground that they promoted immorality and so were contrary to public policy. The test of public policy applied to determine validity was whether or not future immorality was in fact being promoted. However, this rule does not apply to trusts contained in deeds inter vivos or in the wills of persons dying after 1969.[9]

3. Restraints on marriage. If a condition and/or a gift over to take effect upon that condition is contained in a settlement and it amounts to a total restraint on marriage, the condition and any gifts over are wholly void.[10] However this rule does not apply to conditions or gifts restraining second or subsequent marriages[11] nor does it apply to a partial restraint operating against designated persons or designated categories of persons such as the members of a particular religious faith or everyone other than the members of a particular religious faith.[12] On the other hand, however, a gift of property until marriage — as opposed to a gift to a person on condition that he does not marry — is perfectly good;[13]; validity depends on whether the wording is construed as having given rise to a (valid) determinable interest or a (void) conditional interest; this distinction is perhaps an unnecessarily fine one (some would say unnecessarily perverse) but it is well established. Curiously enough, the same difficulties do not attach to a condition requiring the consent of a particular person to marriage; it is clearly established that such a condition will be valid despite the apparent illogicality that the withholding of consent will bar a marriage just as effectively as the void conditions already referred to.[14]

4. Trusts separating parent and child. If a trust is designed to separate a parent (even if he or she has been divorced)[15] from his or her child, that will be void as contrary to public policy.[16] Similarly, a trust will

---

[6] See for example *Floyer v. Bankes* (1869) L.R. 8 Eq. 115.
[7] *Blodwell v. Edwards* (1596) Cro.Eliz. 509; see also *Occleston v. Fullalove* (1874) 9 Ch. App. 147, *per* Mellish L.J.
[8] *Metham v. Duke of Devonshire* (1718) 1 P.Wms. 529.
[9] Family Law Reform Act 1969, s.15(7).
[10] *Lloyd v. Lloyd* (1852) 2 Sim.(N.S.) 255.
[11] *Allen v. Jackson* (1842) 1 Ch.D. 399.
[12] *Jenner v. Turner* (1880) 16 Ch.D. 188.
[13] *Re Lovell* [1920] 1 Ch. 122.
[14] *Re Whiting's Settlement* [1905] 1 Ch. 96.
[15] *Re Piper* [1946] 2 All E.R. 503.
[16] *Re Boulter* [1922] 1 Ch. 75; *Re Sandbrook* [1912] 2 Ch. 471.

fail if it tends to interfere with parental duties; such duties should be discharged solely with a view to the moral and spiritual welfare of the child and without being influenced by mercenary considerations.[17]

5.  Name and arms clauses. A number of decisions were overruled by the Court of Appeal in *Re Neeld*,[18] so as to produce the unexceptionable principle that a name and arms clause requiring any husband whom a particular woman or any member of a particular family marries to change his name (usually to hers) on marriage is neither contrary to public policy nor uncertain; such clauses may reasonably be regarded as harmless if anachronistic.

## II. PERPETUITIES AND ACCUMULATIONS

Since medieval times, English law has been subjected to the tension between two conflicting influences. Owners of land and of other types of property have generally wished to tie up their property indefinitely, usually for the benefit of their family or for some institution or cause, while the courts and the legislature have always felt that it is in the interest of the nation as a whole that property should not be made inalienable and that money should circulate freely and be spent. The result has been a compromise.

Property may be tied up indefinitely for one particular type of purpose which the law wishes to advance, namely for charitable purposes.[19] Otherwise property may be tied up only for a comparatively short period. The rule which enforces this restriction is known as the rule against perpetuities. There are in fact two rules: the rule against remoteness, which is of general application and determines how far in the future the identity of a person entitled to a gift of property can be established; and the rule against inalienability, which applies only to non-charitable purpose trusts and determines how long such trusts can last.

On the other hand, income can at present not be accumulated for more than a comparatively short period. The rule which enforces this restriction, which applies to both charitable and non-charitable trusts, is known as the rule against accumulations.

### 1. *The Rule Against Remoteness*

The rule against remoteness basically provides that every gift of property must vest in the recipient not later than the end of a finite, although not necessarily pre-established, period. At common law, the permissible period was that of a life or lives in being at the time when the gift in question took effect plus a further 21 years thereafter (with allowance being made, where appropriate, for up to two periods of gestation).[20] This was the only possible period until July 15, 1964 and still applies today in the event that the settlor or testator has not

---

[17] *Re Borwick* [1933] Ch. 657.
[18] [1962] Ch. 643.
[19] See *post*, p. 443.
[20] *Cadell v. Palmer* (1833) 1 Cl. & Fin. 372; *Re Wilmer's Trusts* [1903] 2 Ch. 411.

expressly elected to adopt an alternative period which has been available in respect of gifts contained in instruments coming into effect after July 15, 1964, namely any fixed period of up to 80 years.[21] Current proposals from the Law Commission,[22] which are apparently going to be enacted, now envisage the prospective total abolition of the common law period and its replacement by a universal fixed period of 125 years.

The rule has, however, been bedeviled by an excess of zeal on the part of the judges. On the basis that under the rule property must vest, if at all, within the perpetuity period, the judges have striven to find some possibility, no matter how remote, whereby it might not do so. Whenever, looking at matters from the point of time at which the instrument creating the gift in question came into effect, they have managed to envisage any such possibility, the gift in question has been held to be void at common law. Thus at common law a gift by a testator to such of his issue as should be living when some gravel pits should become exhausted is necessarily void as it stands unless the pits have already been worked out by the time of his death; the decision in *Re Wood*[23] shows this is the case not only if by then it is highly probable that the pits will be worked out in five or six years but also if they have actually been worked out by the time that the court has to rule on the matter. Although bizarre, this example is at least logically defensible. But the common law has produced other examples where common sense has gone straight out of the window and Alice has walked in the front door.

The almost unbelievable nonsense which has ensued in this respect is illustrated by *Re Dawson*.[24] There a testator gave property to trustees to hold upon trust for his daughter for life, with remainder to such of her children as should attain the age of 21, with a provision that if any of her children should die under the age of 21, but should themselves leave issue, such issue on attaining the age of 21 would take the share of their parent. When the will came into effect on the death of the testator, his daughter was aged over 60 and all her children were over 21. The court nevertheless managed to hold this gift to be void. With blithe disregard for the principles of biology, it was held that the daughter was still capable of giving birth to a child who might himself subsequently die before reaching the age of 21 leaving issue. Such a future child was obviously not alive at the time of the death of the testator so that the relevant life in being was the testator's daughter. In such circumstances the issue of the after-born child would not attain his vested interest within 21 years from the death of the daughter. Therefore, since it was thus possible that one of the persons entitled in remainder might not obtain a vested interest within the perpetuity period, the entire remainder was therefore void for perpetuity at common law. In the same sort of way, in *Re Gaite*,[25] the court solemnly proceeded on the basis that a girl aged less than five could give birth to a child. In the apt expression of Morris and Leach,[26] at common law the

---

[21] See *post*, p. 242.
[22] Law Comm. No.251 (1998); see Sparkes [1998] T.L.I. 148. Earlier and now abandoned proposals were made in Law Comm. No.133 (1993).
[23] [1894] 3 Ch. 381.
[24] (1888) 39 Ch.D. 155.
[25] [1949] 1 All E.R. 459.
[26] *The Rule Against Perpetuities* (2nd ed., 1964), p. 89.

judicial world would seem to be populated by fertile octogenarians, pre-cocious toddlers and various other freaks.

To overcome some of the traps and generally to restore some semblance of sanity, Parliament has so far intervened on two occasions and is expected shortly to do so for a third time. Small and relatively insignificent amendments were made by the Law of Property Act 1925; large-scale alterations were made by the Perpetuities and Accumulations Act 1964 ("the 1964 Act"), which, with only a few exceptions,[27] applies only to instruments coming into effect after July 15, 1964;[28] and the new legislation proposed by the Law Commission, which will build on, but simplify, the reforms introduced by the 1964 Act, will generally[29] also apply only to instruments coming into effect after the legis-lation comes into force.

The modified rule may be stated in the following way: where a gift is made to take effect in the future, it must be seen from the instrument by which it is created that, if it is to vest at all, it must necessarily vest within the period prescribed by law; however, in the case of instruments governed by the 1964 Act or by the proposed new legislation, if it appears that the gift may or may not vest within the prescribed period, the gift is treated as if it does not offend the rule against remoteness until such time, if at all, as it becomes clear that it cannot vest within that period. The elements of this definition must now be examined and expanded.

### (A) The Rule Concerns Vesting

The rule against remoteness requires only that gifts must *vest* within the perpetuity period. This rule — as opposed to the rule against inalienability which will be considered later[30] — has no application to the length of time during which property may be enjoyed once it has vested. Accordingly, if an outright gift is made to a limited company so that the gift vests in the company immediately, that company may hold the property for more than a thousand years without ever infringing the rule against remoteness.[31]

It is, therefore, essential to know what is meant by "vesting". A future gift may be either vested or contingent. A gift is vested if:

(a) the person or persons entitled to the gift are in existence and are ascertained;

(b) the size of the beneficiaries' interests is ascertained;[32] and

(c) any conditions attached to the gift are satisfied.

If, therefore, property is left upon trust for Romeo for life, with the remainder to Juliet, the interest of Juliet is vested even if Romeo is still alive. Juliet's interest is vested because she herself is alive and is an ascertained person; the

---

[27] See s.8(2).

[28] The date of the Royal Assent (s.15(5)).

[29] Wills which are made before but come into effect after the legislation comes into force will continue to be governed by the previous rules.

[30] See *post*, p. 252.

[31] See, however, *post*, p. 252.

[32] *Pearks v. Moseley* (1880) 5 App. Cas. 714. This requirement for vesting applies only to the rule against perpetuities.

extent of her interest, namely an interest in the whole fund, is ascertained and no conditions have to be satisfied before she becomes entitled. On the other hand, if the gift were to Romeo for life, with the remainder to Juliet provided she has danced on the moon, her gift does not become vested until that condition is fulfilled.

A vested interest therefore may or may not carry the right to present enjoyment of the property in question.[33] To connotate this distinction, vested interests are classified as being:

(a) vested in possession, in which case the interest does carry the right to present possession or enjoyment; or

(b) vested in interest, where the interest carries only the right to future possession or enjoyment of the property in question.

The relevance of this for the purpose of the rule against remoteness is that the rule is satisfied despite the fact that the gift is only vested in interest. Thus, it was held in *Re Hargreaves*[34] that a gift to a person for life, with remainder to any woman who might become his widow for life, with remainder to his children who attained the age of 21, was necessarily good at common law. It is true that the woman who may become that person's widow need not be alive at the date of the settlement; however, at the end of the common law perpetuity period (21 years after the death of the life tenant), it will be possible to say that his widow (if any) and his children, who must by then necessarily have attained the age of 21, are between them the absolute owners of the property.

## (B) The Scope of the Rule
The general principle is that the rule against remoteness applies to all future gifts. In particular, for the purposes of the law of trusts, it applies to all future gifts arising under an inter vivos settlement or trust and to all trusts created by will. To this general principle there are three exceptions:

(a) a gift to a charity is exempt from the rule if the immediately prior interest is also in favour of a charity[35] (this is considered in greater detail in a later chapter);[36]

(b) rights of redemption under mortgages are not within the rule, so that a mortgagor's right to redeem can be exercised outside the perpetuity

---

[33] It is a question of construction whether an interest is contingent or is vested liable to be divested: *Brotherton v. I.R.C.* [1978] 1 W.L.R. 610.

[34] (1889) 43 Ch.D. 401.

[35] *Re Tyler* [1891] 3 Ch. 252. The normal provisions of the rule against remoteness do however apply in the case of a gift from a non-charity to a charity and a gift from a charity to a non-charity.

[36] See *post*, p. 443.

period,[37] and certain provisions of leases, such as options to renew the lease[38] and options to purchase the freehold or leasehold reversion,[39] are not within the rule against remoteness; and

(c) future personal obligations are not within the rule so that a covenant to pay future mining royalties is not within the rule against remoteness.[40]

## (C) The Perpetuity Period

The maximum period for which vesting may be postponed is:

(a) the period of a life or lives in being and a further period of 21 years (together, where appropriate, with up to two periods of gestation); or

(b) where there are no lives in being, a period of 21 years; or

(c) in gifts governed by the 1964 Act in this respect, a fixed period up to and not exceeding 80 years provided that that period is specified as the relevant perpetuity period in the instrument creating the gift; but

(d) under the proposed new legislation, a fixed universal period of 125 years will replace all of the previous possibilities.

It should be noted that, in certain circumstances, the statutory period of 80 years may actually turn out to be shorter than the common law period although this is unlikely to be the case under the proposed new legislation when the statutory period becomes 125 years. Nevertheless, the use of any statutory period has the advantage of simplicity and certainty. Indeed, the principal reason and justification for the proposed abandonment of lives in being is the fact that it can no longer be guaranteed that children will be born no later than nine months after the death of their parents. Recent developments in genetics whereby peoples' sperm and eggs can be frozen enable their children to be born far in the future; in such circumstances, the link between lives in being and the next generation on which the rule against remoteness has so far been based is broken. This difficulty does not arise with a fixed period of years since a child or grandchild either will or will not be born by the end of it.

One of the more difficult questions affecting the current law governing perpetuities is how to identify the life or lives in being (this will of course cease to be necessary under the proposed new legislation). It is clear that the life or lives chosen do not need to take any benefit under the gift. Consequently, the use of what is known as a "royal lives clause" is not uncommon; this is a clause which specifies the perpetuity period by reference to the Royal Family. One of the forms of royal lives clauses in use at the present time is "the period ending at the expiration of 21 years from the death of the last survivor of all

---

[37] *Knightsbridge Estates Trust v. Byrne* [1939] Ch. 441.
[38] *Woodall v. Clifton* [1905] 2 Ch. 257 at 265, 268.
[39] Perpetuities and Accumulations Act 1964, s.9(1).
[40] *Witham v. Vane* (1883) Challis R.P. 440.

the lineal descendants of his late Majesty King George VI[41] who shall be living at the time when the gift comes into effect". There is in principle no reason why other persons should not be used provided that their lifespan and that of their children is sufficiently well documented; however, in practice, this would only be likely to work if the person in question was still alive, something which would substantially shorten the period. Nor is there in principle any limit to the number of lives that may be selected, provided they can all be identified. In *Re Moore*,[42] the settlor specified as the lives in being all persons then living; however, the gift was void on the ground that it was impossible to identify which of them would be the survivor.

In the case of royal lives clauses and their like, it is apparent from the wording of the instrument in question that they are intended to be the lives in being for the purposes of the rule against perpetuities. However, in other cases it may be far more difficult to decide whether or not a person is to be taken as a life in being. The basic principle (or a basic principle) is that every person who is living at the date of the gift and is mentioned in it or whose existence is implied by it is a life in being. Thus, a gift by a testator to "my grandchildren" necessarily presupposes the existence of his children; therefore those of his children who are alive at the date of his death will be taken to be lives in being in respect of this gift for the purpose of the rule against remoteness.

It should also be noted that a child *en ventre sa mère* is treated as a child who is alive if this is necessary to save a gift. Accordingly, a gift to the children of a child *en ventre sa mère* will necessarily be valid, for the unborn child will by implication be regarded as a life in being and his or her own children must necessarily be born within his or her own lifetime or within nine months thereafter.[43] So is a gift to the children of a child *en ventre sa mère* at the age of 21 because, even if the unborn child is male and he dies leaving a child *en ventre sa mère*, the latter child will reach the age of 21, if at all, within 21 years and nine months of the death of his father, who must himself be born, if at all, within nine months of the gift taking effect. Thus a perpetuity period based on lives in being can potentially include two periods of gestation; one before the life in being in question is born and the other after his death; so a perpetuity period based on lives in being can be up to nine months plus a life in being plus a further nine months plus 21 years. Similarly, the end of a fixed period may be extended in the case of a pregnancy. If a period of 80 years is pre-scribed and at the end of that time a woman is pregnant with a child who

---

[41] The father of the present Queen. Consequently, the royal lives in question are those of H.M. Queen Elizabeth II, her descendants, and the decendants of her deceased sister, H.R.H. Princess Margaret. It is also probably just about still possible to use King George V (the grandfather of the present Queen), although the number of his descendants is now very considerable. It is certainly unsafe to specify the descendants of any previous sovereign (see the doubts cast, as early as 1901, on the validity of using the lives of descendants of Queen Victoria (then still alive) in *Re Moore* [1901] 1 Ch. 936). One potential difficulty about such clauses today is the fact that "descendants" now includes illegitimate descendants, who are not necessarily identifiable. But there seems no reason why future "royal lives clauses" should not be expressly restricted to legitimate descendants. The proposed new legislation will permit trustees to switch to its new 125-year fixed period where it is not reasonably practicable to establish whether a period specified by reference to lives in being has ended. This is one of only two provisions of that legislation which will affect gifts which have already come into effect.

[42] [1901] 1 Ch. 936.

[43] *Long v. Blackall* (1797) 7 T.R. 100.

would, if alive, take the gift, then that child will in fact take provided he or she is born alive.[44]

The obvious and amusing proposition that any life selected must be human should also be noted; it is apparently not permissible to choose either a specified animal (because some animals, such as tortoises, are extremely long-lived) or a specified long-lived tree such as a Californian pine. Only in an Irish case has this point actually been pronounced upon; this was in *Re Kelly*,[45] where it was stated by way of dictum that the life chosen must be that of a human and not of an animal. A similar pronouncement on the subject of trees is awaited.

In the case of instruments governed by the 1964 Act in which advantage has not been taken of the possibility of specifying a fixed period of up to 80 years, section 3(4) of the 1964 Act prescribes rules for identifying the lives in being; however, as will be seen later,[46] these statutory lives in being only operate for the purpose of determining whether or not a gift does in fact satisfy the requirements of the rule against remoteness within the perpetuity period; they do not determine whether or not a gift is valid at common law and so whether or not it is necessary to wait and see in the way considered below.[47] The 1964 Act provides that such of the following as are alive and ascertainable at the date of the gift, and no other persons, shall constitute the lives in being for this purpose:

(a) the person who made the disposition (obviously only relevant in a gift inter vivos since a testator will necessarily be dead);

(b) in the case of a contingent gift to an individual or individuals, any person who may in time satisfy the conditions and that person's parents and grandparents;

(c) in the case of a class gift, any member or potential member of the class and that person's parents and grandparents;

(d) any person who is given any power, option, or other right in connection with the gift; and

(e) where the interest is to arise only in the event that the prior interest of some person determines, the person having that prior interest.

The principal addition to persons who will be lives in being at common law are the parents and grandparents included within the second and third categories (at common law, they are only included in the case of a gift to someone who is necessarily their child or grandchild, not more generally). The lives of persons in the second, third and fourth categories are disregarded if the number of those persons in any of those caetgories is so large as to render it impossible to ascertain the date of death of the survivor. Further provisions apply where there is a special power of appointment.[48]

---

[44] See *Cadell v. Palmer* (1833) 1 Cl. & F. 372, especially at 421, 422.
[45] [1932] I.R. 255 at 260, 261.
[46] See *post*, p. 245.
[47] *Ibid.*
[48] See *post*, p. 250.

### (D) "Possibilities not Probabilities"

The general principle is that *any* possibility, no matter how remote, of the gift not vesting within the perpetuity period will make it void. This principle can be expressed by saying that the rule is concerned with "possibilities not probabilities", subject in the case of gifts governed by the 1964 Act and by the proposed new legislation to the "wait and see" rule considered below.[49] Illustrations of this principle are provided by the decisions in *Re Wood*, *Re Dawson* and *Re Gaite* which have already been mentioned above.[50] However, the advances in biological knowledge made during the twentieth century now enable the court, when considering gifts governed by the 1964 Act, to make certain presumptions,[51] namely that a male cannot have a child at an age of less than 14 and that a female can have a child between the ages of 12 and 55 but not outside that age-span (these presumptions will obviously not be relevant under the proposed new legislation where lives in being will themselves become irrelevant).

### (E) "Wait and See"

In relation to gifts which came into effect prior to the 1964 Act, it is necessary to construe the instrument creating the gift at the date when it comes into operation and only at that date. Therefore if a gift is made on or before July 15, 1964 to a person for life, with remainder to the first of his sons who goes to Canada, and at the date when the gift comes into effect that person has no children, the gift to the son will be void for perpetuity at common law; the life tenant is the only life in being and no son of his may go to Canada within 21 years of his death. In respect of gifts from this era (a large number of which are still operating despite the fact that almost 40 years have passed since 1964), it is not possible to wait and see whether the life tenant does in fact have a son who goes to Canada within 21 years of his death.

However, section 3 of the 1964 Act provides that, in relation to gifts which are subject to that section, the court may in some cases "wait and see" whether or not any particular gift does in the event offend against the rule. The first and most important case is where a gift may or may not become vested within whichever of the common law perpetuity period or the statutory perpetuity period of up to 80 years is relevant; in such circumstances, the gift is to be treated as if it does not offend against the rule until it can be definitely shown that the gift will necessarily vest, if at all, after the end of the appropriate period. Thus, if an instrument coming into operation after July 15, 1964 contains a gift to a person who does not as yet have any children for life, with remainder to the first of his sons who goes to Canada, then it is possible to wait and see: first whether he has any sons and, secondly, whether any of his sons goes to Canada within 21 years of the death of the survivor of him and his parents.[52] If any does, the gift is valid. Otherwise, the gift becomes void for perpetuity (and the following remainder vests) as soon as it is clear that it cannot vest; this will be at the earliest of the following times: the life tenant's

---

[49] See *post, infra.*
[50] See *ante,* p. 239.
[51] Perpetuities and Accumulations Act 1964, s.2.
[52] For the purposes of wait and see, the life tenant's parents are also lives in being (under s.3) so it is possible to wait and see until 21 years after the death of the survivor of him and his parents.

death without sons, the death of all his sons, or the expiry of 21 years from the death of the last of him and his parents.

Wait and see will work in the same way under the proposed new legislation. If a gift which is void for perpetuity at common law does not vest by the end of thae 125-year period, it will become void and the provisions of the settlement dependant on its not vesting will then take effect (of course, in practice it will generally become clear long before the end of the 125 years that a gift is never going to vest, as where a person whose children are the beneficiaries of the gift dies childless; in such cases, the provisions of the settlement dependant on the gift in question not vesting will take effect at that point).

### (F) Age-Reducing Provisions

Prior to 1926, if a qualifying age was not certain to be attained within the perpetuity period, then of course necessarily the common law perpetuity period, the gift was wholly void. However, section 163(1) of the Law of Property Act 1925 provided that, where the vesting of property was made to depend on the attainment by the beneficiary of an age greater than 21 and by virtue of that condition the gift was void for perpetuity, the age of 21 was to be substituted for the age stated in the instrument. The section applies only when the gift would otherwise have been void for perpetuity and only to instruments coming into effect between January 1, 1926 and July 15, 1964 (both inclusive).

This provision was replaced by section 4 of the 1964 Act for instruments coming into effect after July 15, 1964. By this section the age substituted is not 21 but the age nearest to the age which would have prevented the disposition from being void. Under the 1964 Act, therefore, the instrument is altered only to the extent necessary to save the disposition from offending against the rule. Further, before applying this section, it is first necessary to apply the "wait and see" rule. Suppose, therefore, that there is a gift by will to the first child of William to attain the age of 30 and that William has no children when the testator dies. This gift is obviously void for perpetuity at common law. It is first necessary to wait and see until the death of the survivor of William and his parents, who are the statutory lives in being for the purposes of wait and see, and assess the position then. At that point there will still be 21 years to go. All William's children will be born or *en ventre sa mère* by then; if they have all reached the age of 10, the gift will necessarily vest, if at all, within the perpetuity period. If, however, his only child is then five, the vesting age will have to be reduced to save the gift; it will therefore be reduced to 26 so that the vesting takes place at the last possible moment prior to the end of the 21 years which are still left.[53]

The proposed new legislation will contain no provisions for age reduction. Either the intended beneficiary will reach the specified age by the end of the

---

[53] It is not entirely clear what will happen if William has two children aged five and three; is the age first reduced to 26 to enable the five-year old to take and, if he fails to do so, reduced again to 24 to enable the three-year old to take or is the age immediately reduced to the age which will enable the younger child to take? The principal difficulty about the former way of proceeding is deciding what happens if the five-year old dies at the age of 25 and the qualifying age is as a result reduced to 24, an age which the five-year old attained during his lifetime; does he or does he not take posthumously?

125-year period and take a vested interest or he will not do so and the gift will fail.

### (G) Gifts after the Death of a Surviving Spouse

A provision of the 1964 Act which had no equivalent in the Law of Property Act 1925 enables gifts to children to be saved in other situations. Suppose that there is a gift to such of the children of Andrew as are living at the date of death of the survivor of Andrew and his spouse. This gift is void at common law, because Andrew may subsequently marry a woman who was not born at the date of the gift. In this case, only Andrew, and not his wife, will be a life in being at common law; since she may survive him for more than 21 years, the interest of the children may vest outside the perpetuity period. Again the "wait and see" rule has to be applied first. If Andrew has no surviving spouse or his surviving spouse turns out to have been alive at the date of the gift or survives him and his parents for less than 21 years, the gift will have been saved by "wait and see". If this does not save the gift, which will mean that a surviving spouse of Andrew who was not alive at the date of the gift survives him and his parents[54] for 21 years, then by virtue of section 5 of the Act the gift vests in interest immediately before the end of the perpetuity period; thus the children alive then qualify and the gift will have vested in interest exactly 21 years after the death of Andrew and his parents. However, it should be noted that this does not terminate any interest held in possession at that time; the effect of section 5 is to vest the gift in interest not in possession. So if, as is quite likely, the surviving spouse has a prior life interest (so that the original gift was to Andrew for life, remainder to any surviving spouse of Andrew for life, remainder to the children of Andrew living at the death of Andrew and his spouse), her interest will continue until her death and only then will the interest of the children vest in possession.

The proposed new legislation does not contain any similar provision because lives in being will cease to be relevant. In practice, there is anyway no realistic possibility that a surviving spouse of someone who is alive when a gift comes into effect will still be alive 125 years later.

### (H) Class Gifts

Special provisions relate to gifts to the members of a class. For this purpose, a class is a number of persons who "come within a certain category or description defined by a general or collective formula, and who, if they take at all, are to take one divisible subject in certain proportionate shares".[55] The problem that such gifts pose is that it is possible that, at the moment when the gift vests in possession, some of the potential members may have qualified but others may not yet have been born or may not yet have satisfied some other qualifying condition.

Although for the purposes of the general law any member of the class who has fulfilled all the necessary conditions is regarded as having a vested interest while those who have not yet qualified obviously still have only contingent interests, for the purposes of the rule against remoteness the gift is not regarded as vesting in any member of the class until all the members of the

---

[54] His parents are also lives in being for the purposes of wait and see.
[55] *Pearkes v. Mosely* (1880) 5 App.Cas. 714 *per* Lord Selborne L.C. at 723.

class are definitely known. In other words, the rule against remoteness demands that all the members of the class must qualify if at all within the perpetuity period.[56] A gift to the children of Brian who attain the age of 21 is clearly valid for perpetuity at common law since all the members of the class will necessarily attain that age if at all within 21 years of Brian's death and therefore within the perpetuity period. On the other hand, a gift to the children of Brian who marry is potentially void for perpetuity since one or more of Brian's children may not marry within 21 years of Brian's death in which case that child or children will not have qualified by the end of the perpetuity period. This is also a problem where a fixed perpetuity period is used since some of the potential members of the class may not have qualified by the end of that period either.

Class gifts are further complicated by the existence of certain rules of construction known as the class-closing rules.[57] These rules, which can be excluded by contrary intention,[58] provide that a class whose size is not yet fixed will close when any member of the class becomes entitled to claim a vested interest in possession. The class so closed will include any potential members of the class who have been born by then but will exclude all potential members of the class who have not yet been born.[59] The fact that these rules reduce the size of classes means that they can operate to save a gift which would otherwise be void for perpetuity. Thus the gift to the children of Brian who marry will be saved from being void for perpetuity if any child of Brian has married when the gift takes effect since the class will immediately close on the children born by then, who can only marry in their own lifetimes and therefore will necessarily qualify if at all within the perpetuity period,[60] But the class-closing rules operate in exactly the same way in respect of gifts which are entirely valid for perpetuity. Thus in the case of the gift to the children of Brian who attain the age of 21, the class will close when the first child reaches 21 on the children born by then even though the presence of the excluded children would not cause the gift to be void for perpetuity.

For a class gift in a instrument which came into effect on or before July 15, 1964 to be valid, it had to be possible to establish at the moment when the gift took effect that every single member of the class would necessarily fulfil any necessary conditions, if at all, within the perpetuity period; the possibility that any member of the class would fail to do so rendered the entire gift void.[61]

---

[56] *Leake v. Robinson* (1817) 2 Mer. 363.

[57] These rules are often also known, not wholly accurately, as the Rule in *Andrews v. Partington* (1791) 3 Bro.C.C. 401. Relatively recent illustrations of the working of these rules can be found in *Re Chapman's Settlement Trusts* [1977] 1 W.L.R. 1163 and *Re Clifford's Settlement Trusts* [1981] Ch. 63.

[58] However, the contrary intention must be extremely clear: a gift "to the children of Brian who attain the age of 21 whenever born" would certainly contain a contrary intention but a gift "to all the children of Brian who attain the age of 21" would not.

[59] However, where the only requirement for membership of the class is birth, the class will close only if any member of the class has qualified when the gift vests in possession; if no member of the class has been born by then, the class can never close thereafter for the somewhat obvious reason that otherwise the first member's birth would cause the class to close on himself alone.

[60] If no child of Brian has married by then, the class will close whenever the first child of Brian marries thereafter but that will not necessarily save the gift from being void for perpetuity because someone included within the closed class may nevertheless not marry by the end of the perpetuity period.

[61] *Pearks v. Moseley* (1880) 5 App.Cas. 714; *Re Hooper's Settlement Trust* [1948] Ch. 586.

Thus a gift to the children of Brian who marry which was contained in such an instrument would be wholly void for perpetuity unless it was saved by the class-closing rules in the manner already described.

Where the 1964 Act applies, however, the vast majority of class gifts will be saved by the wait and see provisions. In the case of the gift to the children of Brian who marry, if any child marries during the wait and see period, the class-closing rules will operate to exclude any children born thereafter and by the end of that period all possible members of the class may either have married or died unmarried. The wait and see provisions will not, however, have saved the gift if at that point one or more members of the class have qualified but one or more other members of the closed class have not yet done so but are still capable of so doing so. At that point, what happens depends on the reason for the failure to qualify.

If the reason is an age requirement over 21, that age can be reduced to the extent necessary to save the gift under section 4(1) of the Act in the manner already described.[62] Where the reason is some failure to satisfy a requirement other than an age requirement, recourse can instead be had to section 4(4) of the Act to save the gift. Under this subsection, any members of the closed class who have not qualified by the end of the relevant perpetuity period are simply excluded. In the case of the gift to the children of Brian who marry, the wait and see period will end 21 years after the death of the last survivor of Brian, Brian's parents, and any wife or children of Brian who were ascertainable when the instrument in question took effect. If at that point any of the children of Brian who were alive when the first child married have not yet themselves married, they will simply be excluded from membership of the class.[63]

Under the proposed new legislation, as in the case of individual gifts age reduction will no longer be feasible but any potential members of the class who have neither been excluded by the class-closing rules nor have qualified by the end of the 125-year period will simply be excluded.

## (J) Dependent Limitations
Prior to the 1964 Act, where a gift followed and was dependent upon prior limitations which were void, that gift was necessarily also void.[64] Vested gifts are of course not subject to the rule against remoteness at all and so could not possibly be affected by the fact that they followed a prior void gift. Contingent gifts were, however, void if they not only followed but were also dependent

---

[62] See *ante*, p. 247, fn. 53. It is again not entirely clear whether the age is immediately reduced to the age which will enable the youngest potential member of the class to take or whether the age is reduced progressively as necessary to enable individual members of the class to take. As before, the difficulty which arises about the latter way of proceeding, much more starkly than in the case of individual gifts, is what will happen if a potential member of the class has died without qualifying but would have qualified had the qualifying age to which it is later reduced to accommodate a younger potential member of the class; does he or does he not qualify posthumously?

[63] Where two requirements have to be satisfied, one of which is an age requirement, such as a gift to the children of Brian who marry and attain the age of 40, then it is possible under s.4(3) of the Act both to age-reduce and to exclude if that will cause fewer members to be excluded. Thus, if at the end of the wait and see period, some members have married but are not yet 40, some members are 40 but have not yet married, and some are neither married nor 40, the members of the first group can be saved by age reduction but the other two groups will have to be excluded.

[64] *Re Buckton* [1964] Ch. 497; compare *Re Robinson* [1963] 1 W.L.R. 628.

upon a prior void gift.[65] The distinction between gifts which merely followed and gifts which both followed and were dependent on a prior void gift was not particularly easy to draw in practice;[66] in broad terms, a gift had to have its own independent date of vesting if it was not to be regarded as dependent.[67] Thus a gift for life to the first child of Charles who marries but, if none does, to the first child of David who attains the age of 21 for life was wholly void unless a child of Charles had already married — the gift to David's child, although it would have been valid if it had stood alone, is wholly dependent on the prior void gift. On the other hand, in the case of a gift to the first child of Charles who marries for life and, subject to that, to the first child of David who attains the age of 21, the gift to David's child is in no sense dependent on the prior gift and so was valid at common law.

However, section 6 of the 1964 Act provides that no gift governed by that Act can fail merely because it is dependent upon a prior void gift. This means that, where the 1964 Act applies, both the gifts to David's child are now valid for perpetuity; both the gifts to Charles' child both remain void at common law unless a child of his has already married but both are obviously now highly likely to be saved by the wait and see provisions. This will remain the position under the proposed new legislation.

## (K) Powers of Appointment

### (1) Classification of powers

The classification of powers has already been discussed.[68] It is doubtful whether, at common law, intermediate powers should for the purposes of the rule against remoteness be classified as general or special powers (intermediate powers were effectively unknown when the rules of the common law were formulated). However, it is suggested that the rules prescribed by the 1964 Act for instruments governed by that Act should also be followed for common law purposes. In any event, by virtue of section 7 of the 1964 Act, a general power for the purposes of that Act is a power exercisable by one person only which can be exercised by that person to transfer property to himself without the consent of any other person;[69] a power may be general for this purpose even if it is exercisable only by will and not also inter vivos.[70] For the purposes of the rule against remoteness, it therefore follows that an intermediate power may be either general or special, depending on its terms. Thus a power to appoint to anyone except Eric will for these purposes be a general power unless the donee of the power is Eric himself.

### (2) Validity of powers

Two questions have to be considered: first, whether the power is itself valid and, secondly, whether the appointment made under the power is valid.

---

[65] *Re Coleman* [1936] Ch. 528.
[66] *Re Backhouse* [1921] 2 Ch. 51.
[67] *Re Coleman* [1936] Ch. 528.
[68] See *ante*, p. 201.
[69] Except where any consent is required as to the mode of exercise of the power.
[70] This is also the position at common law; see *Rous v. Jackson* (1885) 29 Ch.D. 521.

## (a) Whether the power is itself valid

(i) *Special powers.* A special power is void at common law if it is capable of being exercised outside the perpetuity period.[71] However, for instruments governed by the 1964 Act, the wait and see provisions may be applied in order to establish whether the power is in fact fully exercised during the perpetuity period. Where it is exercised only partially within the period, the power is only void to the extent that it was not exercised during the perpetuity period.[72] This will also be the case for instruments governed by the proposed new legislation.

(ii) *General powers.* Because the donee of the power may appoint to himself, property subject to a general power is regarded for most purposes as property belonging to the donee. Therefore, so far as the validity of the power is concerned, it is necessary only that the power should be acquired by the donee within the perpetuity period; it is not necessary for it to be exercised within that period.[73] However, where the general power in question is exercisable by will, it is governed by the same rules as special powers.[74] No legislative reform of these rules has ever been necessary.

## (b) Whether the appointment is valid

(i) *Special powers.* Because the disposition of property subject to a special power is restricted, the perpetuity period has up until now commenced at the date when the power is created, not when it is exercised. In principle, therefore, at common law it is necessary to consider the position as at the date of creation of the power, assume that the appointment is then made, and then see whether the gift made by virtue of the appointment necessarily vests, if at all, within the perpetuity period. Even at common law, however, it is permissible to take into account the circumstances prevailing at the time when the power is exercised. Therefore, despite the fact that the terms of the appointment might theoretically enable the gift to vest outside the perpetuity period, if the circumstances existing at the time of the appointment establish that the gift must vest, if at all, within the period, the appointment will be valid.

This can be illustrated by considering a gift by will by Charles to Desmond for life giving Desmond a power to appoint the subject matter to his children, which Desmond subsequently exercises by making an appointment in favour of his son Fergus "as and when he attains the age of 30" at a time when Fergus, who was born after the death of Charles, has attained the age of 10. If this situation is examined only as at the time when the power was created, that is to say on the death of Charles, the gift and appointment have to be read together as if they provided: "to Desmond for life, with remainder to Fergus as and when he attains the age of 30"; since Fergus was not alive at that point, he could clearly take more than 21 years after the death of Desmond to attain the age of 30 and so the gift would prima facie be void at common law. However,

---

[71] *Re Abbot* [1893] 1 Ch. 54.
[72] Perpetuities and Accumulations Act 1964, s.3.
[73] *Re Fane* [1913] 1 Ch. 404.
[74] *Woolaston v. King* (1868) L.R. 8 Eq. 165.

since it is permissible to take into account the circumstances existing when the power is actually exercised, it can be seen that, since Fergus is already 10, the gift will necessarily vest, if at all, within 20 years of the death of Desmond and consequently the appointment is valid.

Quite apart from the limited form of wait and see which is therefore permissible at common law, the general wait and see provisions of the 1964 Act also apply to powers which are both created and exercised after July 15, 1964.[75]

Under the proposed new legislation, all special powers, whenever created, will be permitted the new 125-year fixed period measured from the date of the original creation of the power. This is one of only two provisions of that legislation which will affect gifts which have already come into effect.

(ii) *General powers.* In the case of general powers, the perpetuity period runs from the date of the exercise of the power, not from the date of its creation. Therefore rules in respect of property comprised in a general power are the same as for property comprised in an absolute gift. It must however be remembered that, if a power is general in its terms but is only exercisable by more than one donee, it is treated as a special power for the purposes of the Rule against Perpetuities.[76]

**(L) The Effect of Failure to Comply with the Rule against Remoteness**
If a limitation in a trust instrument infringes the rule against remoteness, then any subsequent limitation which is nevertheless valid will take effect; in default of any such limitation, the property in question will be held on resulting trust[77] for the settlor. Where the void limitation is contained in a will, that means that the property in question will fall into the testator's residuary estate or, if the void limitation is itself the residuary gift or there is no residuary gift, will be distributed according to the intestacy rules.

## 2. The Rule Against Inalienability

The corollary to the rule that a gift must vest, if at all, within the perpetuity period is the principle that property must not be rendered inalienable.[78] The basis of this principle is that land and, for that matter, all other property should be kept freely marketable and in circulation among the members of the community. A gift is inalienable if there is some provision which prevents the property being disposed of. This provision may be either a term of the gift itself,[79] or, in the case of a gift to a club or association, a rule of that club or association.[80]

To this general principle there are two exceptions: first, by analogy with the rule against remoteness, it seems that property may validly be made inalienable during the lifetime or lifetimes of persons in being at the time of the gift

---

[75] Perpetuities and Accumulations Act 1964, s.3 (compare s.8, which relates only to administrative powers of trustees).
[76] *Re the Earl of Coventry's Indentures* [1974] Ch. 77.
[77] See *post*, p. 291.
[78] *Carne v. Long* (1860) 2 De G.F. & J. 75 at 80.
[79] *Re Patten* [1929] 2 Ch. 276.
[80] *Rickard v. Robson* (1862) 31 Beav. 244; *Re Nottage* [1895] 2 Ch. 649; *Re Drummond* [1914] 2 Ch. 90.

and for 21 years thereafter,[81] or for any fixed statutory perpetuity period which has been substituted for that common law perpetuity period; and, secondly, property may be made inalienable in the hands of a charity.[82]

A gift to a body corporate which is not a charity is not in general capable of falling foul of the rule against inalienability. Even though the company may, if it so wishes, retain the property indefinitely for the benefit of its shareholders, it will not be under any obligation to retain the property if the gift is absolute. It is only where some condition is imposed on the gift prohibiting the company from disposing of the property that the gift will offend against the rule and be void.

The rule is principally applicable to non-charitable purpose trusts and to gifts to unincorporated associations.[83] These have already been considered in Chapter 3.[84] It should be noted that section 15(4) of the 1964 Act provides that a donor of property for these purposes cannot opt to use for the purposes of the rule against inalienability the statutory period of up to 80 years which section 1 makes available for the purposes of the rule against remoteness; in this respect, therefore, the position remains the same as it was before that Act.[85] The proposed new legislation will not affect the rule against inalienability either.

As will be seen later on,[86] a gift to a charity is not void even if the property in question is made inalienable.

### 3. The Rule Against Accumulations

Another consequence of the principle that property and wealth should generally be free to circulate has been the statutory control of accumulations.

At common law, the rule was that a direction to accumulate was valid if it was confined to the perpetuity period applicable to the rule against remoteness.[87] This rule was applied in *Thellusson v. Woodford*.[88] Thellusson had by his will directed that the income of his property should be accumulated during the lives of his sons, grandsons and their issue who were living at his death, and that on the death of the survivor, the accumulated fund should be divided among certain of his descendants. This direction, being confined to lives in being, was held valid (at that time this was generally regarded as the perpetuity period applicable to the rule against remoteness, the additional period of 21 years not yet having been firmly established).[89]

It was calculated that the fund accumulated under Thellusson's will would amount to many millions of pounds. Many of the members of Parliament did

---

[81] *Carne v. Long* (1860) 2 De G.F. & J. 75; *Re Dean* (1889) 41 Ch.D. 552 at 557.

[82] *Chamberlayne v. Brockett* (1872) 8 Ch.App. 206 at 211.

[83] A further reason for such trusts and gifts being void was that there was no person capable of enforcing the trust: *Morice v. Bishop of Durham* (1805) 10 Ves. 521 at 539; *Bowman v. The Secular Society* [1917] A.C. 406 at 441; *Re Wood* [1949] Ch. 498.

[84] See *ante*, pp. 74 *et seq.*

[85] The provision appears to be clearly to this effect but see Maudsley, *The Modern Law of Perpetuities*, p. 177, in which the opposite view is argued.

[86] See *post*, p. 443.

[87] *Wilson v. Wilson* (1851) 1 Sim. (N.S.) 288 at 298.

[88] (1799) 4 Ves. 227; (1805) 11 Ves. 112.

[89] This did not occur until the decision of the House of Lords in *Cadell v. Palmer* (1833) 1 Cl. & F. 372.

not relish either the prospect of Thelluson's descendants potentially becoming as wealthy as the Crown or the fact that the decision entitled their parents to keep them out of the capital which they expected to inherit for their entire lifetimes. Consequently, Parliament intervened to prevent further directions of this nature by enacting the ill–drafted Accumulations Act 1800 (hence the Act is often called "the Thellusson Act").

The position is now governed by sections 164 to 166 of the Law of Property Act 1925, as amended by section 13 of the Perpetuities and Accumulations Act 1964.[90] The proposed new legislation will restore the common law rule and permit accumulation throughout the perpetuity period; the applicable accumulation period will become the same 125-year period which is proposed for the rule against remoteness. The only exception will be in the case of charitable trusts, where accumulation will still be permitted for only 21 years on the basis that it is not consistent with the public benefit which charitable trusts are supposed to produce for income to be withdrawn from a charitable purpose for longer than that.

Section 164 of the Law of Property Act 1925 lays down the general rule that income may not be accumulated for longer than any one of the following periods (if none of them is selected, income cannot be accumulated at all except during minorities, where accumulation is in certain circumstances permitted under section 31 of the Trustee Act 1925):[91]

(a)   the life of the settlor (this is the period adopted in the case of gifts inter vivos where no other period is expressly specified); or

(b)   21 years from the death of the testator or settlor (this is the period adopted in the case of gifts by will where no other period is expressly specified); or

(c)   the duration of the minority or minorities of any persons living at the death of the testator or settlor (this period begins from the death of the settlor or testator); or

(d)   the duration of the minority or minorities of any persons entitled under the settlement (in this case the beneficiary need not be alive at the death of the testator or settlor and the accumulation period will commence at the birth of that beneficiary).

The 1964 Act added two further possible periods in respect of instruments coming into operation after July 15, 1964:

(e)   the period of 21 years from the date of making the disposition; or

(f)   the duration of the minority or minorities of any person in being at the date of the making of an inter vivos disposition.

Any direction to accumulate for a period longer than one of the foregoing makes the whole gift void if it is directed that the accumulation is to continue

---

[90] As further amended by Family Law Reform Act 1969, Sched. 3, para. 7.
[91] See *post*, p. 682.

for longer than the perpetuity period but is invalid only as to the excess over the longest authorised period if it is not so directed.[92]

Section 165 of the Law of Property Act 1925 expressly upholds the validity of successive periods of accumulation where a direction is given for income to be accumulated for one of the authorised periods and at the end of that period, or indeed at some time thereafter, the income has to be accumulated under the general law or under some other statutory provision. As will be seen later on,[93] when an infant is entitled to the income of property which is held on trust for him, any income which is not applied for his maintenance has, by virtue of section 31 of the Trustee Act 1925, to be accumulated until he reaches the age of majority. So if a testator gives property to a person for life, with remainder to his eldest son, the testator can direct that the income be accumulated for a period of 21 years from his death and, in the event that the eldest son is still an infant at the death of his father, the income can further be accumulated during any later period in which the eldest son is entitled to an interest in possession in the property but is an infant.[94] The existence of this rule is particularly important for one type of discretionary trust, known as an accumulation and maintenance trust.[95]

There are certain exceptions from the general restrictions on accumulations and in these cases any period of accumulation may be specified. These are:

(a) accumulations for the payment of the debts of any person;

(b) accumulations for the purpose of raising portions[96] for the children or more remote issue of the settlor, or any person entitled under the settlement; and

(c) accumulations of the produce of timber or wood.[97]

## III. SAFEGUARDING PROPERTY FROM CREDITORS

Ever since uses, the forerunners of trusts, were first invented, attempts have repeatedly been made by those who contemplate the actual or potential threat of financial ruin to employ uses and trusts in order to put their property beyond the reach of their creditors. Prima facie a transfer of property by a settlor to trustees on trust for his wife or some other relative or friend has the effect of removing that property from his assets and consequently of preventing his trustee in bankruptcy from claiming it on behalf of his creditors. Where the beneficiary of the trust is the settlor's wife, the effect and usually the objective is that the settlor can continue to enjoy the benefit of the settled property indirectly by living with her in property belonging to the trust and having his living expenses provided by her out of the income to which she is entitled. And even where a settlor does not act so blatantly as to derive indirect benefit from the property himself, there is no doubt whatever that he

---

[92] *Re Jefferies* [1936] 2 All E.R. 626.
[93] See *post*, p. 682.
[94] See also *Re Maber* [1928] Ch. 88.
[95] See *ante*, p. 200, *post*, p. 651.
[96] *Re Bourne* (1946) 115 L.J.Ch. 152.
[97] Law of Property Act, s.164(2).

will inevitably prefer his property to be enjoyed by his relatives and friends rather than by his creditors.

It is not surprising that both these results are looked on with disapproval by the legislature which has long placed statutory restrictions on the use of trusts for these purposes. These statutory restrictions are considered in this section; where they do not apply, trusts remain an effective means of preventing creditors from laying their hands on a person's property.[98] It should also be added that one of the principal reasons for the utilisation of off-shore trusts is in order to put property beyond the reach of these statutory restrictions,[99] something which is generally effective provided that the settlor is not already the subject of adverse claims at the time of the creation of the off-shore trusts,[1] and provided that the settled assets are also outside the settlor's home jurisdiction.[2]

Until relatively recently this area of the law was governed by two distinct statutory provisions: section 172 of the Law of Property Act 1925, which enabled dispositions of property made with intent to defraud creditors to be set aside, whether or not the person who made the disposition was bankrupt, and section 42 of the Bankruptcy Act 1914, which enabled various dispositions to be set aside when the person who had made them had become bankrupt. Both provisions were, however, repealed by the Insolvency Act 1985. The present law is contained in the Insolvency Act 1986.

### 1. Transactions Defrauding Creditors

The provisions of the Insolvency Act 1986 relating to dispositions of property made with intent to defraud creditors do not require that the person entering into the transaction should be bankrupt or even that he should be in debt. Previous provisions of this type have not done so either. As Jessel M.R. said in *Re Butterworth*,[3] where a settlement made by a prosperous baker immediately before purchasing a different type of business (that of a grocer) of which he had no experience was set aside under the predecessor of section 172 of the Law of Property Act 1925:

> "a man is not entitled to go into a hazardous business, and immediately before doing so, settle all his property voluntarily, the object being this: 'If I succeed in business, I make a fortune for myself. If I fail, I leave my creditors unpaid. They will bear the loss.' That is the very thing which the Statute of Elizabeth was meant to prevent."

It is admittedly somewhat ironic that, at about the time when this observation was made, legislation was being introduced permitting for the first time the incorporation of companies with limited liability, which makes it entirely

---

[98] See *post*, p. 264.

[99] See O'Sullivan, *Asset Protection Trusts* (2000); Jones in *The International Trust* (ed. Glasson, 2002).

[1] Off-shore jurisdictions will normally enforce adverse claims which pre-exist the creation of such a trust, although usually only for a short time.

[2] Assets within the settlor's home jurisdiction will generally be susceptible to execution there despite the fact that they are technically vested in an off-shore trust.

[3] (1882) 19 Ch.D. 588 at 598; see *Stileman v. Ashdown* (1742) 2 Atk. 477; *Mackay v. Douglas* (1872) L.R. 14 Eq. 106.

legitimate, subject to certain minimum requirements as to membership, for the shareholders to adopt exactly the policy so stringently condemned by Jessel M.R. But, despite the fact that the legislature has accepted that an appropriate way for an investor to limit his possible losses in hazardous ventures is to carry them out in the name of a limited company, it has continued to prohibit the use of trusts and settlements for the same purpose.

Section 423 of the Insolvency Act 1986 enables the court to intervene whenever it is satisfied that any person, whether a natural person or a body corporate,[4] has entered into a transaction at an undervalue for the purpose of putting assets beyond the reach of anyone who is making or may at some time make a claim against him or of otherwise prejudicing the interests of such a person in relation to the claim which he is making or may make. There is no requirement that that person should have acted dishonestly,[5] nor is it necessary for the purpose in question to be his sole purpose or even his dominant purpose. In *I.R.C. v. Hashmi*,[6] Arden L.J. held:

"It is sufficient if the statutory purpose can properly be described as a purpose and not merely as a consequence ... it will often be the case that the motive to defeat creditors and the motive to secure family protection will co-exist in such a way that even the transferor himself may be unable to say what was uppermost in his mind ... for something to be a purpose it must be a real substantial purpose; it is not sufficient to quote something which is a by-product of the transaction under consideration, or to show that it was simply a result of it, ... or an element which made no contribution of importance to the debtor's purpose in carrying out the transaction under consideration ... trivial purposes must be excluded."

The Court of Appeal therefore set aside a declaration of trust of a freehold property made on the occasion of its acquisition by its existing tenant in favour of his son. He had been under-declaring his profits to the Inland Revenue for many years and so was potentially liable for substantial arrears of tax, interest thereon and penalties; it was for this reason that he was held to have intended to put the property beyond the reach of his creditors. Section 423 was also successfully invoked in *Moon v. Franklin*[7] when a husband made substantial gifts to his wife at a time when he was threatened with legal proceedings which he knew might not be covered by sufficient insurance. Similarly, the Court of Appeal held in *Barclays Bank v. Eustice*,[8] that there was a strong prima facie case for the applicability of the section when a transfer of assets by a debtor left him with insufficient assets to meet an expected action by the bank.

A transaction will be at an undervalue in the following circumstances: first, if it is a gift or entered into on terms which provide for the transferor to receive no consideration; secondly, if it is made in the absence of consideration other than marriage consideration; or, thirdly, if it is entered into by the transferor for a consideration the value of which, measured in money or money's worth,

---

[4] See also Insolvency Act 1986 s.207.
[5] Hence the section can apply even where the transferor's legal advisers considered it proper; see *Arbuthnot Leasing International v. Havalet Leasing (No.2)* [1990] B.C.C. 636.
[6] [2002] W.T.L.R. 1027 at 1035.
[7] (1990) *The Independent*, June 22, 1990.
[8] [1995] 1 W.L.R. 1238.

is significantly less than the value, also measured in money or money's worth, of the consideration provided by the transferor.[9]

The creation of any trust other than for money or money's worth will obviously satisfy these requirements. This was the case in *I.R.C. v. Hashmi*[10] and would have been the case in *Midland Bank v. Wyatt*[11] had the trust in question not been held to be a sham, which of course meant that the property had at all times been vested in the settlor anyway. A less straightforward case was *Chohan v. Saggar*,[12] where a house was transferred into the name of its sitting tenant on the basis that she would declare a trust of it in favour of a specific creditor of the transferor; the trust so declared was set aside because his beneficial interest thereunder substantially exceeded the sum which he was owed by the transferor. An example of a transaction at an undervalue outside the trust context is *Barclays Bank v. Eustice*,[13] where a father granted an agricultural tenancy and sold agricultural assets to his sons on unusual terms as to payment;[14] however, in such circumstances whether a transaction is actually at an undervalue is sometimes not at all straightforward.[15] But when a transaction has been made for full value,[16] it cannot be impeached under this section even where there was a clear intention to prejudice creditors.[17]

Under section 424, an application to the court can be made by anyone prejudiced by a transaction; however, where the person entering into the transaction has become insolvent (bankrupt, in the case of a natural person,

---

[9] The latter formulation was approved by Lord Scott of Foscote in *Phillips v. Brewin Dolphin Bell Lawrie* [2001] 1 All E.R. 673 at 681–682, although this case actually concerned the analogous provision for setting aside transactions entered into by companies at an undervalue in the two years prior to going into liquidation.

[10] [2002] W.T.L.R. 1027.

[11] [1995] 1 F.L.R. 696; see *ante*, p. 50.

[12] [1992] B.C.C. 306.

[13] [1995] 1 W.L.R. 1238.

[14] The rent was payable substantially in arrears and the payment of the purchase price was deferred.

[15] In *Agricultural Mortgage Corporation v. Woodhead* (1995) 70 P. & C.R. 53, a mortgagor who was a farmer granted an agricultural tenancy to his wife at the full market rent which, if binding on the mortgagee, would have more than halved the value of its security. The Court of Appeal held that the wife had acquired not just the tenancy but also a number of additional benefits, the safeguarding of the family home, the ability to acquire and carry on the family business and a substantial surrender value, all of which enabled her to hold the mortgagee to ransom and for none of which she had given any value at all. However, the courts' preparedness to look in this way at the practical rather than the legal effects of what has been done does have limits; in *Pinewood Joinery v. Starelm Properties* [1994] 2 B.C.L.C. 412 at 418–419, the court declined to engage in speculative assessments of how the value of the property in question might increase as a result of a possible grant of planning permission and held that the transaction had been at the full market value.

[16] This would have been the case in *Re M.C. Bacon* [1991] Ch. 127 (actually a decision on preferences; see *post*, p. 261), where a company which created a floating charge over its assets in favour of a bank to secure its overdraft in consideration of the bank making further advances, continuing to honour cheques and, consequently, not calling in the overdraft was held not to have entered into a transaction at an undervalue. The assets of the company had not been reduced by the creation of the floating charge and so it had not provided any consideration in money or money's worth. Since no value in money or money's worth could be attributed to the consideration provided by the bank either, there was no imbalance between the consideration provided by the two parties. See also *Re Kumar (a Bankrupt)* [1993] 1 W.L.R. 224.

[17] This was not the case under Law of Property Act 1925, s.172; see *Lloyds Bank v. Marcan* [1973] 1 W.L.R. 1387.

wound up or the subject of an administration order in the case of a body corporate)[18], any such application requires the leave of the court — in such circumstances, it is the official receiver, the trustee in bankruptcy, or the liquidator who has the primary right to apply. Where a voluntary arrangement has been approved,[19] the supervisor of the voluntary arrangement can also apply. Any application made by any of these persons is treated as having been made on behalf of everyone prejudiced by the transaction.

On application, the court can, under section 423(2), make such order as it thinks fit for restoring the position to what it would have been if the transaction had not been entered into and protecting the interests of the persons prejudiced by the transaction. More specifically, section 425(1) enables the court to require the vesting in whoever it may direct, for the benefit of everyone in respect of whom the application is treated to be made, of the following: any property transferred, any property representing the application of the proceeds of sale of the property transferred or of any money transferred, and any sum which the court decides should be payable in respect of any benefit received as a result of the transaction. However, in the case of trusts, it will normally be sufficient for the trust in question to be set aside. An order of any of these types is obviously capable of prejudicing third parties; however, section 425(2) provides that no such order shall prejudice any interest in property acquired from a person other than the original transferor in good faith for value without notice nor require any person who was not a party to the original transaction to pay any sum in respect of any benefit received in good faith for value without notice.

## 2. Transactions Capable of being Impeached on Bankruptcy

The Insolvency Act 1986 has replaced section 42 of the Bankruptcy Act 1914 with a series of provisions which enable transactions at an undervalue and by way of preference entered into by natural persons and by bodies corporate to be set aside in the event that they occurred during stipulated periods of time prior to the bankruptcy.

### (A) Transactions Entered into by Natural Persons

### (1) Transactions at an undervalue

Section 339 enables the trustee in bankruptcy to apply to the court for an order where a natural person has entered into a transaction at an undervalue (which has the same meaning as in section 423)[20] within the periods of time set out in section 341. The court may make such order as it thinks fit to restore the position to what it would have been if the transaction had not been entered into. The available orders, set out in section 342, are similar to those which may be made under section 425[21]; no order may either prejudice any interest in property which was acquired from a person other than the bankrupt in good faith for value without notice of the relevant circumstances or require a person

---

[18] Under Pt II of the Insolvency Act 1986.
[19] Under Pt I of the Insolvency Act 1986 in the case of bodies corporate and under Pt VIII in the case of natural persons.
[20] See ante, p. 257.
[21] See ante, p. 257.

who was not a party to the transaction to make any payment in respect of any benefit which he received as a result of the transaction in good faith for value without notice of the relevant circumstances.

A trustee in bankruptcy can therefore claim a spouse's share in the matrimonial home to the extent that the beneficial interest held exceeds the contributions made to its acquisition during the appropriate period. The fact that that beneficial interest has been acquired as the result of a property adjustment order on divorce makes no difference since the order can be set aside;[22] particular problems may arise where the matrimonial proceedings were compromised since, if the compromise reached cannot be assessed in terms of money or money's worth, the section will apply.[23]

Section 341 provides that the basic period is two years prior to the date of the presentation of the bankruptcy petition but this period is increased to five years if the person later to become bankrupt was insolvent at the time of the transaction or became insolvent as a result of carrying it out. A person is insolvent for this purpose if at the time of the transaction he was unable to pay his debts as they fell due or if the value of his assets was less than the value of his liabilities, taking into account both contingent and prospective liabilities. There is a rebuttable presumption that a person was insolvent in this sense in the event that the other party to the transaction was an associate of his, defined by section 435 as including relatives of the bankrupt or of his spouse, his partners, his employers, his employees and any companies with which he was at the time related.

The length of this period, the rebuttable presumption of insolvency in the case of transactions between associates, and the very wide definition of associate pose very considerable potential problems, not only because of the difficulty of rebutting the presumption of insolvency, but also because of the difficulty of proving five years after the event that the transaction was not at an undervalue. Consequently, the only safe way to proceed when entering into a transaction between persons who fall within the definition of associates is to obtain affidavit evidence at the time from suitably qualified persons that the transaction was not at an undervalue and/or from the accountants of the parties that neither of them was insolvent at the time of or in consequence of the transaction. This will obviously involve a certain amount of expense but will avoid any possibility of future problems if any of the parties becomes bankrupt in the next five years.

At one time, even greater problems arose in the case of gifts of unregistered land. Since any subsequent purchaser would see the deed of gift in the course of his investigation of title, he would necessarily have notice of the relevant circumstance that the land was acquired at an undervalue. Thus, the enactment of section 339 had the effect of rendering the title of any donee of unregistered land bad for two years because of the possibility of the transferor becoming bankrupt during that period; the donee was thus effectively prevented from disposing of the land for value for that period. Matters were even worse in the highly likely event that the donor and donee fell within the definition of associates; in such circumstances, the period increased to five years unless the donee could affirmatively prove, presumably by affidavit

---

[22] Insolvency Act 1986, Sched 14.
[23] *Re Kumar (a Bankrupt)* [1993] 1 W.L.R. 224.

evidence from the donor's accountants, that the donor was not insolvent either at the time of or in consequence of the transaction. However, following the making of representations,[24] it was provided by the Insolvency (No. 2) Act 1994 that a transaction can be set aside against a purchaser of unregistered land only if he has notice both of the surrounding circumstances and of relevant bankruptcy proceedings. Thus a purchaser who knows as he necessarily will of a transaction at an undervalue will be protected provided, first, that he makes the normal conveyancing searches and enquiries and, secondly, that these do not reveal any bankruptcy proceedings being brought against the donor.

### (2) Transactions by way of preference
Section 340 enables the trustee in bankruptcy to apply to the court for an order where a natural person has given a preference to any person within the periods of time set out in section 341. The court may make such order as it thinks fit to restore the position to what it would have been if the preference had not been given — the available orders are set out in section 342.[25] Such a preference will have been given if the effect of the transaction is to improve the position of a creditor, surety or guarantor in the event of bankruptcy. An order can only be made if the transaction was influenced by a desire to bring about this result, although such a desire will be presumed where the other person is an associate. However, it has been held that, where the transaction has been entered into as a matter of commercial necessity, it was not influenced by any desire to give a preference.[26]

Section 341 provides that the basic period is six months prior to the date of presentation of the bankruptcy petition but this period is increased to two years if the person to whom the preference was given was an associate. However, if the transaction was not only by way of preference but also at an undervalue, the longer periods which apply to transactions at an undervalue will be applicable instead.

### (B) Transactions Entered into by Bodies Corporate
The provisions of the Insolvency Act 1986 which govern transactions entered into by bodies corporate are broadly similar to those which apply to natural persons; only the differences will be mentioned here.

Section 238 deals with transactions at an undervalue (defined in the same way but without any reference to marriage consideration); no order will be made if the court is satisfied that the company entered into the transaction in good faith for the purpose of carrying on its business and there were at the time reasonable grounds for believing that the company would be benefited thereby. The period of time is two years prior to the onset of insolvency but a transaction will only be set aside if the company was unable to pay its debts at the time of the transaction or became unable to do so as a result of it.

Section 239 deals with transactions by way of preference. In *Re M.C. Bacon*,[27] a company which could not have continued trading without its bank's support

[24] See (1992) 89/5 L.S.Gaz., p. 13.
[25] See *ante*, p. 261.
[26] *Re M.C. Bacon* [1990] B.C.L.C. 324.
[27] [1990] B.C.L.C. 324.

created a floating charge over its assets in favour of the bank to secure its overdraft shortly before becoming insolvent; it was held that, since the granting of the floating charge had been made for reasons of commercial necessity and not with any desire to improve the position of the bank in the event of insolvency, no preference had been given. The basic period is this time six months prior to the onset of insolvency but this period is increased to two years if the transaction by way of preference is in favour of a person connected with the company or at an undervalue. Once again, a transaction will only be set aside if the company was unable to pay its debts at the time of the transaction or became unable to do so as a result of it.

## IV. Safeguarding Property from Claims by Dependants

The development of statutory obligations to maintain dependants has inevitably led to attempts being made to avoid these obligations by the use of trusts and, equally inevitably, to the introduction of statutory restrictions on the use of trusts to defeat claims for maintenance and for financial provision out of estates.

### 1. Claims Made in the Course of Matrimonial Proceedings

Section 37 of the Matrimonial Causes Act 1973 enables a spouse to apply to the court for an order where the other spouse is about to make or has made some disposition of property with the intention of reducing the assets available for the provision of financial relief in matrimonial proceedings.[28] Such an intention is presumed if the disposition was made within the three-year period prior to the date of the application for financial relief; otherwise, intention must be proved affirmatively. If the disposition has not yet been made, the court may make such order as it thinks fit; if the disposition has already been made, it may be set aside.

### 2. Claims for Financial Provision out of Estates

English law does not contain any general restrictions on the ability of testators freely to dispose of their assets.[29] However, under the Inheritance (Provision for Family and Dependants) Act 1975,[30] a surviving spouse, a cohabitee,[31] children and other dependants are entitled to apply to the court for a share of the estate of any testator or intestate if reasonable financial provision for them

---

[28] Most of the recent reported cases have concerned surrenders by one spouse of jointly held tenancies which are prima facie effective to determine them; see *Newton Housing Trust v. Alsulaimen* [1999] 1 A.C. 313 and *Bater v. Bater* [1999] 4 All E.R. 944.

[29] The civil law systems of continental Europe and the Muslim legal systems require testators to leave to their descendants a substantial percentage (generally about 75%) of their assets and sometimes, in default of descendants, a lower percentage to any ascendants. Settlors from these jurisdictions often create trusts in off-shore jurisdictions in order to vary or exclude the rights of these "forcible heirs"; this is generally effective provided that the settled assets are also outside the settlor's home jurisdiction or jurisdictions with similar rules. See Duckworth [1995] P.C.B. 270, 334, 408; Matthews (2001) 5 Chase Journal 15.

[30] As amended by Law Reform (Succession) Act 1995.

[31] Cohabitees were added in respect of deaths on or after January 1, 1996.

has not been made. In order to prevent a testator from defeating such claims by disposing of all his property *inter vivos*, sections 10–13 of the Act provide that any person who, during the last six years of the deceased's life, has benefited from a disposition made other than for value "with the intention of defeating an application for financial provision under this Act" can be required to provide sums of money up to but not exceeding the value of the property received so that appropriate financial provision can be made. It should be noted that section 12 of the Act specifically provides that the necessary intention has to be determined on a balance of probabilities and does not have to constitute the only motive of the deceased for the making of the disposition.

# CHAPTER 8

# PROTECTIVE TRUSTS

---

It has already been seen that a trust which contravenes the policy of the insolvency legislation can be set aside.[1] This chapter discusses some indirect means by which this result can be avoided. However, before considering them, two fundamental points must be emphasised.

1.  A proviso or condition contained in a trust of property in favour of a third party that that property is not to be subject to the claims of his creditors will be void.[2]

2.  A trust set up by a person in favour of himself until bankruptcy, with remainders over, will generally also be ineffective. This is the well known Rule in *Re Burroughs-Fowler*,[3] which, usually but not actually always, prevents the type of trusts considered in this chapter from being created by the potential bankrupt, as distinct from any one else.[4] Where a trust is created in contravention of this rule and the person in question duly becomes bankrupt, the settled property will generally vest in his trustee in bankruptcy as if the settlement had never been created.

    However, this will not be the case if the interest which the potential bankrupt has conferred upon himself in fact determines prior to his bankruptcy. In *Re Detmold*,[5] a husband had settled his own property on trust for himself for life or until alienation, whether voluntary or involuntary by operation of law in favour of a particular creditor, and subject to that on trust for his wife and children. His interest was the subject of an involuntary alienation as the result of a judicial charge created by a judgment. He subsequently became bankrupt and his trustee in bankruptcy sought to set the settlement aside. North J. held that the gift over in favour of the wife and children was in such circumstances valid and effective; consequently, his trustee in bankruptcy could take nothing. This decision shows that a provision for

---

[1] See *ante*, p. 255.
[2] *Younghusband v. Gisborne* (1844) 1 Coll.C.C. 400, affirmed (1846) 15 L.J. Ch. 355; *Re Sanderson's Trust* (1857) 3 Kay & J. 497.
[3] [1916] 2 Ch. 251.
[4] The Rule in *Re Burroughs-Fowler* has been rejected by the legislature in certain off-shore jurisdictions such as The Cook Islands, thereby enabling such trusts to be created there.
[5] (1889) 40 Ch.D. 585; see also *Re Johnson* [1904] 1 K.B. 134.

determination will be effective if the determining event which first occurs is one other than the bankruptcy of the settlor.

Nevertheless, it is true to say that a settlor who wishes to achieve the objective of protecting the settled property against a spendthrift or reckless beneficiary by guarding against alienation or bankruptcy will need to use more sophisticated machinery than that already described. Essentially he will instead have to create a determinable interest in favour of a third party coupled, if necessary, with protective and discretionary trusts.

## I. DETERMINABLE INTERESTS

It has long been established that a settlor can validly grant an interest to any beneficiary (other, of course, than himself) which is determinable in the event of his bankruptcy.[6] At first sight, it appears somewhat surprising that such a grant is effective to whisk the property away from the beneficiary's creditors in the event of his bankruptcy when the same settlor cannot settle property on the same beneficiary subject to a condition or proviso that it will not be available to the latter's creditors in the event of his bankruptcy. The different result follows from the basic distinction between the nature of determinable interests and conditional interests, a distinction which, no matter how outmoded, is nevertheless fundamentally logical. A provision for a determining event does not deprive the beneficiary, or his creditors, of anything; it merely sets the limits of the interest which is being granted. On the other hand, a condition of this nature, like all other conditions, technically operates so as to cut down an interest which has already been granted. However, the existence of this admittedly fine distinction means that a draftsman must take special care not to create a conditional interest by accident and thereby defeat the intentions of the settlor.

## II. PROTECTIVE TRUSTS[7]

Protective trusts provide a highly effective means of restraining spendthrift beneficiaries. They combine a determinable life interest with a series of discretionary trusts. The beneficiary's life interest is normally made determinable in the event of alienation or bankruptcy and in this event will be replaced by a discretionary trust in favour of the former life tenant and the members of his family.

### 1. *Section 33 of the Trustee Act 1925*

At one time the normal practice was to set out the provisions of trusts of this kind *in extenso*. However, with the objective of shortening the length of settlements, section 33 of the Trustee Act 1925 was enacted to provide that the mere reference in a settlement to the fact that property is held "on protective

---

[6] *Billson v. Crofts* (1873) L.R. 15 Eq. 314; *Re Aylwin's Trusts* (1873) L.R. 16 Eq. 585.
[7] See Sheridan (1957) 21 Conv. (N.S.) 110.

trusts" will be sufficient to bring into play the protective trusts specifically set out in that section.

Section 33 provides that, where income, including an annuity or other periodical payment, is directed to be held on protective trusts for the benefit of any person for his life or for any less period[8] (such person being described in the section as "the principal beneficiary"), then during that period the income will be held on the following trusts (this is of course necessarily without prejudice to any prior interests arising under the settlement in question):

(a)  upon trust for the principal beneficiary during the trust period or until he does or attempts to do any act or thing, or any event happens (other than an advancement made under any statutory or express power) whereby, if the income were payable during the trust period to the principal beneficiary absolutely during that period, he would be deprived of the right to receive the same or any part thereof;

(b)  in the event that the trust fails or determines during the trust period, then for the residue of that period the income is to be held upon trust to be applied as the trustees in their absolute discretion (without being liable to account for the exercise of such discretion) think fit for the maintenance or support or otherwise for the benefit of all or any of the following persons, either for the principal beneficiary and his or her wife or husband, if any, and his or her children or more remote issue,[9] if any or, if there are no such persons other than the principal beneficiary, for him or her and the persons who would, if he or she were dead, be entitled to the trust property or to its income.[10]

Section 33 does not apply to trusts coming into operation before January 1, 1926 (hardly now likely to be a problem) and, more importantly, is subject to any variation of its provisions which may be made in the trust instrument in question.[11] The section also provides that none of its contents operates to validate any trust which, if contained in the trust instrument, would be liable to be set aside.[12]

### 2. "On protective trusts"

The purpose of the section is merely to avoid any need for the trusts in question to be set out expressly in the trust instrument. Quite apart from the provision just referred to whereby the statutory provisions can be modified to suit the circumstances of any individual settlement, protective trusts can also be (and often still are) expressly created by being set out *in extenso*. Further, irrelevant of whether the statutory form is used or its essence is set out in terms, its effect is confined to engrafting the trusts in question on the life

---

[8]  For an illustration of protective trusts designed to last until remarriage and the effect of a nullity decree on the second marriage, see *D'Altroy's Will Trusts* [1968] 1 W.L.R. 120. See also Matrimonial Causes Act 1973, ss.11, 12, 16.

[9]  Including illegitimate children and issue: Family Law Reform Act 1969, s.15(3).

[10]  s.33(1).

[11]  s.33(2).

[12]  s.33(3). Accordingly, a settlement made on the settlor himself until bankruptcy and then on discretionary trusts may be ineffective; *Re Burroughs-Fowler* [1916] 2 Ch. 251. See *ante*, p. 264.

interest granted. For this reason, it was held by Vaisey J. in *Re Allsopp's Marriage Settlement*[13] that, if the life interest is ever totally extinguished, as it was in that case by an order made by the court in divorce proceedings, the engrafted protective trusts are also extinguished on the basis that they are incapable of any separate existence.

### 3. Determining Events

The question of what events will be sufficient to produce a forfeiture of a protected life interest (as the interest of the principal beneficiary is described) and bring the discretionary trusts into operation has been considered in a large number of cases. This point is of importance, not only where the trusts contained in section 33 have been employed but also where there is an express protective trust. Indeed many of the cases which are about to be considered involved express protective trusts; however, the general view is that the principles laid down therein are equally applicable to the statutory trusts.

It is self-evident that the bankruptcy of or any alienation by the principal beneficiary will bring about the forfeiture of the protected life interest. But it is less obvious (although it was nevertheless so held to be the case by Luxmoore L.J. in *Re Walker*)[14] that the protected life interest will also be forfeited if the principal beneficiary has already become bankrupt by the time the protective trust first comes into operation. However, determining events have taken the most diverse forms.

In *Re Balfour's Settlement*,[15] various sums had in breach of trust been advanced by the trustees to the principal beneficiary. The trustees then asserted their right to retain the income of the fund in order to make good their own breach of trust. The principal beneficiary subsequently went bankrupt. Farwell J. held that, since the trustees had asserted their right to the income before the date of bankruptcy, the life interest had determined and the discretionary trust in question had come into operation; nothing therefore passed to the trustee in bankruptcy. Similarly, in *Re Baring's Settlement Trusts*,[16] the principal beneficiary had failed to comply with a court order to bring her children within the jurisdiction and a writ of sequestration was therefore issued empowering the sequestrators to take possession of all her real and personal estate until she did so. The sequestrators gave the trustees notice not to pay any further money to the principal beneficiary and required that all future income should be paid to them. Morton J. held that, since the trusts were designed to confer continuous enjoyment of the income on the principal beneficiary, the sequestration was effective to determine her life interest and bring the discretionary trusts into operation; the payment of income was therefore at the discretion of the trustees and could not be demanded by the sequestrators. Again, in *Re Dennis' Settlement Trusts*,[17] Farwell J. held that the execution of a deed of variation of the protective trusts set out in the principal deed of settlement, which had the effect of providing for the payment of part

---

[13] [1959] Ch. 81.
[14] [1939] Ch. 974.
[15] [1938] Ch. 928.
[16] [1940] Ch. 737.
[17] [1942] Ch. 283.

of the income to another person, equally brought the forfeiture clause into operation.

On the other hand, a wide variety of other events have been held not to have the effect of determining a protected life interest. In *Re Tancred's Settlement*,[18] the principal beneficiary appointed the trustees of the settlement as his attorneys to receive the income of the settled funds; not surprisingly Buckley J. held that this did not cause his life interest to be forfeited. The same conclusion was reached in *Re Oppenheim's Will Trusts*,[19] where a receiver had been appointed to a principal beneficiary who had been certified as a person of unsound mind. Similarly, it was held by the Court of Appeal in *Re Westby's Settlement*,[20] that a statutory charge on the settled property to secure the expenses incurred by a receiver appointed in such circumstances was not the kind of charge at which forfeiture clauses were intended to be directed. All these decisions show that, in the words of Farwell J., "we must bear in mind that the courts do not construe gifts on forfeitures so as to extend their limits beyond the fair meaning of the words unless they are actually driven to it. Forfeitures are not regarded with favour."[21]

Consideration has also had to be given as to the effect of a court order on a forfeiture clause. In *Re Mair*,[22] Farwell J. held that an order of the court under section 57 of the Trustee Act 1925[23] giving the trustees power to raise capital moneys for the benefit of life tenants would not cause a forfeiture of the protected life interests of those tenants; this was because he held that section 57 was an overriding provision which is deemed to be read into every single settlement. This decision must, however, be compared with that of Eve J. in *Re Salting*,[24] where the scheme sanctioned by the court under section 57 involved an agreement by the life tenant to pay the premiums on insurance policies on the basis of a promise that the trustees would pay them out of income if he failed to do so; the conclusion reached was that any failure by the life tenant to pay the premiums would produce a forfeiture. In cases of this type it is clear that what has produced the forfeiture is an act or omission of the life tenant, rather than the exercise by the court of its overriding power.

While the principles established by these two decisions discussed are perfectly clear enough, the position is otherwise by no means straightforward. Particular difficulty arises from cases involving orders in matrimonial proceedings varying protective trusts. In *General Accident, Fire and Life Assurance Corporation v. I.R.C.*,[25] the Court of Appeal had no doubt that an order in matrimonial proceedings for the principal beneficiary to pay an annual sum of

---

[18] [1903] 1 Ch. 715.

[19] [1950] Ch. 633.

[20] [1950] Ch. 296.

[21] *Re Greenwood* [1901] 1 Ch. 887, 891 (assignment of income accrued due in the hands of trustees: no forfeiture). See also *Re Longman* [1955] 1 W.L.R. 197 (authority given by beneficiary for payment of debts out of a future dividend where no dividend was ever declared: there was no forfeiture). For other cases involving the application of the Trading with the Enemy Act 1939, which may be relevant in the case of future wars, see *Re Gourju's Will Trusts* [1943] Ch. 24; *Re Hall* [1944] Ch. 46; *Re Wittke* [1944] 1 All E.R. 383; *Re Furness* [1944] 1 All E.R. 575; *Re Harris* [1945] Ch. 316; *Re Pozot's Settlement Trusts* [1952] Ch. 427.

[22] [1935] Ch. 562.

[23] See *post*, p. 742.

[24] [1932] 2 Ch. 57.

[25] [1963] 1 W.L.R. 1207.

money to his wife during her lifetime had not brought about a forfeiture of the protected life interest which he had under section 33; accordingly, the discretionary trusts set out in that section did not come into operation. This conclusion was reached because the court order in question overrode the trusts of the settlement. Not only was this an event to which both the life tenant and the trustee had to bow; it was moreover not an event of the type contemplated by the section, whose provisions were instead intended to protect spendthrift, improvident or weak life tenants.[26]

However, if the principle thus enunciated by the Court of Appeal is of general application, it is by no means easy to reconcile their decision with the earlier decision of Danckwerts J. in *Re Richardson's Will Trusts*.[27] In that case, an order had been made in matrimonial proceedings for the payment of an annual sum to the wife of the protected life tenant to be charged on the principal beneficiary's life interest and it was also ordered that a deed be settled to give effect to the charge. Danckwerts J. held that, because the order for the execution of a deed had not been complied with, the effect of that order was to create an equitable charge over the interest of the principal beneficiary; this in turn involved the forfeiture of his protected life interest and so the discretionary trusts set out in section 33 came into operation. This was in some ways undoubtedly a highly convenient result; the life tenant had subsequently been adjudicated bankrupt and the decision that a prior forfeiture had occurred meant that the income of the settlement did not fall into the hands of his trustee in bankruptcy. However, it does seem rather strange that a failure by the principal beneficiary to comply with an order of the court to settle a deed of variation will result in a forfeiture of his protected life interest while compliance with such an order will not do so.

While the policy behind the decision of the Court of Appeal in *General Accident, Fire and Life Assurance Corporation v. I.R.C.*,[28] is considered to have been desirable, it is somewhat doubtful whether the principle which the court applied was actually the correct one. The effect of an order of the Family Division — whether or not that order has to be implemented by a deed — is to deprive the life tenant of some or all of his income, an event which must surely constitute a forfeiture under section 33 and would probably also do so under the terms of most express protective trusts. On the other hand, quite different considerations may well be regarded as applying to an order of the court under section 57 of the Trustee Act 1925 simply because, as has already been seen, that provision is to be read into every settlement.

## 4. *Advances*

Section 33 expressly provides that advances under any express or statutory[29] power of advancement do not produce a forfeiture and bring the discretionary trusts set out therein into play.[30] This leaves open the question of whether the absence of words of exemption of this type in an express protective trust will

---

[26] *ibid., per* Donovan L.J. at 1218.
[27] [1958] Ch. 504.
[28] [1963] 1 W.L.R. 1207.
[29] Under Trustee Act 1925, s.32; see *post*, p. 694.
[30] s.33(1).

necessarily mean that the protected life interest granted thereby will determine if any advancement is in fact made.

The relevant authorities are not unanimous; however, they are in only slight disarray and the general consensus of judicial opinion is that no advancement made either under an express power or a statutory power will bring about a forfeiture. In *Re Hodgson*,[31] Neville J. specifically held that an advancement made under an express power did not bring about a forfeiture. His lordship found to be attractive and decisive an argument that the provision for forfeiture "should be read as though there had been inserted at the end of the clause 'But this provision is not to affect any steps taken by the husband to enable the advances by the trustees hereinafter provided for to take effect'." In *Re Shaw's Settlement*,[32] Harman J. came to exactly the same conclusion on similar facts. Further, in *Re Rees*,[33] Upjohn J. held that this conclusion also applied to the statutory power of advancement which is contained in section 32 of the Trustee Act 1925. It was only in *Re Stimpson's Trusts*,[34] where once again there was no express advancement clause so that reliance had to be put on the statutory power, that it was held that the principal beneficiary had forfeited his interest by consenting to an advancement under section 32.

There is, however, a factual distinction between the last two cases. In *Re Stimpson's Trusts* the will in question had been made in 1906, although it did not come into effect until 1929, and so its draftsman obviously could not have had in mind the provisions of section 32 of the Trustee Act 1925 not enacted until nearly 20 years later. In *Re Rees*, on the other hand, the will in question had been made in 1935 and so its draftsman had necessarily to be taken to have been aware of that provision. It is therefore a possibility, although admittedly a somewhat remote one, that in the almost inconceivable event that a case like *Re Stimpson's Trusts* came before the courts today, the court would view in the same way a situation where a will made before 1926 had contained no express advancement clause but the life tenant had after 1925 consented to an advancement being made under the statutory power. Consequently, although the validity of the decision in *Re Stimpson's Trusts* has been doubted,[35] it does appear to have applied the correct principle. The statutory power of advancement can undoubtedly be ousted by a contrary intention[36] and the fact that the will in question had been made before 1926 might well be held to constitute a sufficient contrary intention for this purpose.

---

[31] [1913] 1 Ch. 34 at 40.
[32] [1951] Ch. 833.
[33] [1954] Ch. 202.
[34] [1931] 2 Ch. 77.
[35] See *Re Rees* [1954] Ch. 202, *per* Upjohn J. at 209.
[36] Trustee Act 1925, s.69.

# Chapter 9

# IMPLIED OR RESULTING TRUSTS

## I. Introduction

THE vast majority of commentators regard the terms "implied trust" and "resulting trust" as synonymous;[1] this is also the view adopted in this edition of this work.[2] Such trusts arise where a settlor or testator carries out some intentional act other than the creation of a relationship of trustee and beneficiary from which the court infers a relationship of trustee and beneficiary. They consequently arise from the unexpressed but presumed intention of the settlor or testator. The two alternative names appear to stem from the fact that such a trust is not only implied by the court but also often causes the beneficial interest arising thereunder to "result" to the settlor or his estate, or to the testator's residuary beneficiaries or intestate successors. Trusts of this type are described as resulting trusts in this work.

### 1. Recognised Categories of Resulting Trusts

There are two sets of circumstances in which resulting trusts are universally recognised as arising. The first is where one person either pays, wholly or in part, for the purchase of property which is vested in the name of another (or in the joint names of himself and another) or gratuitously transfers property into the name of another (or into the joint names of himself and another); there is then generally[3] a rebuttable[4] presumption that no gift was intended, in accordance with which the property in question is presumed to be held on

---

[1] Other views exist. Some commentators consider that there are distinct categories of implied trusts and resulting trusts (for example, this view was adopted in the first five editions of this work (see 5th ed., p. 430) and the first seven editions of *Megarry's Manual of the Law of Real Property*, although not in the current (8th) edition at p. 292). Such commentators generally classify the subject matter of this chapter as resulting trusts and classify as implied trusts some of the trusts which the majority of commentators classify as constructive trusts (for example, earlier editions of this work have suggested that the trust which arises under mutual wills (see *post*, p. 430) should be classified as an "implied, though not a resulting" trust). Another variant is to use the term "implied trust" as a collective term for both resulting trusts and constructive trusts (see Lord Millett, 114 (1998) L.Q.R. 399, 406); this usage is more traditional than appropriate.

[2] As it has been in the two previous editions.

[3] It has now been established that this is not the case where land is the subject of such a transfer.

[4] The presumption can be rebutted by a counter-presumption known as the presumption of advancement when the parties are in one of a number of established relationships or by affirmative evidence that the payer or transferor intended to make an outright beneficial transfer.

trust for the payer or transferor (or, in the case of a joint purchase, on trust for the joint purchasers in proportion to their contributions). The second is where a settlor or testator who is creating an express trust fails to dispose of the whole of the beneficial interest in the property in question; the law then implies that so much of the beneficial interest as is undisposed of is held on trust for the settlor or his estate, or for the testator's residuary beneficiaries or intestate successors.[5]

It has been contended these two recognised categories of resulting trusts should respectively be classified as "presumed" resulting trusts and "automatic" resulting trusts. According to this distinction, suggested by Megarry J. in *Re Vandervell's Trusts (No.2)*,[6] a presumed resulting trust arises when a purchase is made in or a transfer is made into the name of another person without any express trust being constituted; in these circumstances, there is a presumption that that other holds the property in question on resulting trust for the real purchaser or the transferor but this implied or presumed intention can be rebutted either by other legal presumptions or by evidence to the contrary.[7] An automatic resulting trust, on the other hand, arises where a transfer has been made on trusts which have left the whole or some part of the beneficial interest undisposed of (because for example, those are in some way ineffective or incomplete); in this situation, the transferee of the property in question automatically holds it on resulting trust for the transferor to the extent that the beneficial interest has not been disposed of. In the latter case, according to Megarry J., the resulting trust "does not depend on any intentions or presumptions, but is the automatic consequence of [the transferor's] failure to dispose of what is vested in him".[8]

The distinction between "presumed" and "automatic" resulting trusts appears at first sight to accord with common sense; however, it is fair to say that, just as what Megarry J. described as a presumed resulting trust is said to be created by implication as the result of a purchase in or transfer into the name of another, so an intention can be said to be implied on the part of a settlor or testator that the settled property should result to him to the extent that he has failed to dispose of it. The implication of an intention in the second type of resulting trusts does not actually appear to be markedly more artificial than in the first type of resulting trusts. Precisely this argument was adopted in the House of Lords in *Westdeutsche Landesbank Girozentrale v. Islington L.B.C.*,[9] by Lord Browne-Wilkinson. He reasserted the traditional view that both types of resulting trusts are examples of trusts giving effect to the common intention of the parties and said that he was not convinced that Megarry J. had been right to suggest that the second type of resulting trust does not depend on intention but operates automatically. He also pointed out that resulting trusts of the second type are not, as the formulation of Megarry J. would appear to suggest, necessarily irrebuttable; if the settlor or testator has, expressly or by necessary implication, abandoned any beneficial interest in the

---

[5] *Westdeustche Landesbank Girozentrale v. Islington L.B.C.* [1996] A.C. 669 at 708.
[6] [1974] Ch. 269 at 294, 295. The actual decision of Megarry J. was reversed by the Court of Appeal at [1974] Ch. 269 but the Court of Appeal made no comment on the judge's formulation.
[7] See *post*, p. 279.
[8] [1974] Ch. 269 at 294.
[9] [1996] A.C. 669 at 708.

trust property, that property is held not on a resulting trust but for the Crown as *bona vacantia*.

Lord Browne-Wilkinson's view is certainly preferable to the view of Megarry J.[10] However, a further definition of resulting trusts has also been propounded,[11] namely that such trusts require nothing more and nothing less than a transfer of property in circumstances in which the provider of that property did not intend to benefit the recipient. This definition seems highly convincing,[12] at least so far as the two recognised categories of resulting trusts are concerned.[13] Its influence can be seen in the decision of the Privy Council in *Air Jamaica v. Charlton*,[14] where Lord Millett, while accepting that resulting trusts arise by operation of law and give effect to intention, emphasised that a resulting trust "arises whether or not the transferor intended to retain a beneficial interest — he almost always does not — since it responds to the absence of any intention on his part to pass a beneficial interest to the recipient". These observations seem successfully to blend the new definition into the view propounded by Lord Browne-Wilkinson, which of course unquestionably represents English law at present.

## 2. *Other Possible Categories of Resulting Trusts*

It has sometimes been contended[15] that resulting trusts can also arise as a result of a transfer of property which is either void *ab initio* or voidable. Such contentions have been made both in order to enhance the quantum of recovery[16] and to impose liabilities whose pre-requisites include the existence of a trust.[17] While the House of Lords has now rejected the contention that a resulting trust can arise as a result of a transfer of property which is void *ab initio*,[18] Lord Millett has stated, both judicially[19] and extra-judicially,[20] that a resulting trust will arise when property is transferred pursuant to a transaction which is voidable if and when that transaction is effectively avoided. However, when this issue arose in the Commercial Court in *Papamichael v. National Westminster Bank*,[21] the judge[22] held that the trusts which had arisen as a result of a transfer of property which was both mistaken and procured by fraud were

---

[10] Birks [1996] R.L.R. 3 at 11 regards Lord Browne-Wilkinson's view as "correct", despite the fact that it led to the rejection of his own argument that a resulting trust should arise whenever money is paid under a mistake or under a condition which is not subsequently satisfied.

[11] By Chambers, *Resulting Trusts* (1997).

[12] His extrapolation of that definition dealing with the nature of *Quistclose* trusts was, however, reviewed and rejected by Lord Millett in *Twinsectra v. Yardley* [2002] 2 A.C. 164; see *ante*, p. 27 and *post*, p. 291.

[13] Chambers, *op.cit.*, also classifies as resulting trusts a large number of other situations which most commentators regard as having nothing whatever to do with resulting trusts.

[14] [1999] 1 W.L.R. 1399 at 1412.

[15] See Chambers, *Resulting Trusts* (1997) *passim*.

[16] As a result of being able to obtain either priority over the general creditors of the transferee or an increase in the value of the property transferred or compound rather than simple interest.

[17] Such as liability for knowing receipt of property transferred as the result of a breach of trust or liability for dishonest assistance in a breach of trust; see *post*, pp. 370–406.

[18] *Westdeutsche Landesbank Girozentrale v. Islington L.B.C.* [1996] A.C. 669 at 715.

[19] In *El Ajou v. Dollar Land Holdings* [1993] 3 All E.R. 717 [1993] 3 All E.R. 717 at 734 (as Millett J.).

[20] 114 L.Q.R. (1998) 399.

[21] [2003] 1 Lloyd's Rep. 341.

[22] Judge Chambers Q.C., sitting as a Judge of the Commercial Court.

constructive trusts rather than resulting trusts, relying on what Lord Browne-Wilkinson had held in the House of Lords in *Westdeutsche Landesbank Girozentale v. Islington L.B.C.*[23] rather than what Lord Millett had said in the Chancery Division in *El Ajou v. Dollar Land Holdings*[24] (all these authorities are considered at the end of this chapter.[25]) While it is highly unlikely that the last has yet been heard of the views expressed by Lord Millett, it therefore seems, at least for the moment, more appropriate to regard any trusts which arise as a result of a voidable transfer of property as constructive trusts rather than as resulting trusts.

## II. PURCHASE IN THE NAME OF ANOTHER

### 1. *The Presumption of Resulting Trust*

One of the most important and the most common situations in which the presumption of resulting trust arises is where real[26] or personal[27] property is purchased in the name of another or in the name of the purchaser and another. In such circumstances, a resulting trust will be presumed to arise in favour of the person who is proved to have paid the purchase money; in other words, the beneficial interest in the property "results" to the true purchaser. This general principle was established as long ago as 1788 by Eyre C.B. in *Dyer v. Dyer.*[28] Such a presumption was recently held to arise in *Abrahams v. The Trustee of the Property of Abrahams*[29] in favour of a wife who had purchased in the name of her estranged husband a one-fifteenth share of a winning national lottery ticket bought by a syndicate of which they were both[30] members;[31] she was therefore held to be entitled to that proportion of the winnings as against his trustee in bankruptcy.

At one time this principle was particularly significant in establishing the ownership of matrimonial property, particularly the matrimonial home, on the breakdown of marriage; however, now that the courts have an unfettered discretion to reallocate property interests on divorce, this is no longer the case. However, the principle remains relevant in establishing the ownership of matrimonial property during marriage and is particularly important in relation to joint enterprises by members of a family unit, especially residential property occupied by unmarried partners. In this respect, the division between resulting and constructive trusts is somewhat blurred,[32] basically

---

[23] [1996] A.C. 669 at 715.

[24] [1993] 3 All E.R. 717, affirmed by the Court of Appeal without discussion of this particular point [1994] 2 All E.R. 685. See *post*, p. 393.

[25] *Post*, p. 308.

[26] *Dyer v. Dyer* (1788) 2 Cox Eq. 92.

[27] *Re Scottish Equitable Life Assurance Society* [1902] Ch. 282, in respect of personal property.

[28] (1788) 2 Cox Eq. 92 at 93.

[29] [2000] W.T.L.R. 593.

[30] She had also paid for her own one-fifteenth share of the ticket and had duly received that proportion of the winnings.

[31] The presumption of resulting trust was not rebutted by the presumption of advancement (see *post*, p. 245) and there was clear evidence that she did not intend to benefit him by herself paying the share of the price basically payable by him.

[32] See *Drake v. Whipp* [1996] 1 F.L.R. 826; *Collings v. Lee* [2001] 2 All E.R. 332.

because in the leading judgment, the speech of Lord Bridge in *Lloyds Bank v. Rosset*,[33] trusts of two different types which most commentators would classify respectively as resulting and constructive trusts were both described as constructive trusts. In any event, since what Lord Bridge described as "the first and fundamental question which must always be resolved" in such cases is whether the prerequisites of the imposition of what is on any view a constructive trust have been satisfied, it seems more appropriate to deal with this specific area in the chapter on constructive trusts.[34]

That remains the area which has been most often before the courts in recent decades. But both in that area and in joint purchases of any other type, everyone who has contributed directly to the purchase price is presumed to have a beneficial interest in the property in question; in this respect the identity of the person in whose favour that property is actually vested is irrelevant. In such circumstances, a question which always arises is the nature of the beneficial ownership, in other words whether the contributors are beneficial joint tenants, in which case, in the absence of any subsequent severance, their survivor will take the property absolutely, or beneficial tenants in common, in which case the share of each will devolve in accordance with his will or intestacy; in the latter case, the size of their respective shares will also have to be established.

Where the purchase money has been contributed in unequal shares, the position is straightforward. Irrelevant of the identity of the person in whom the property is vested, the beneficial interests will be held in common and will devolve in accordance with the will or intestacy of each beneficial owner in accordance with his respective contributions.[35] This is simply because, in many cases, equity leans against a joint tenancy because of the potential unfairness of its attendant consequence that the survivor is entitled to the whole of the property. Inequality in contributions to the purchase price is the clearest possible example of a situation which equity considers to be incompatible with the right of survivorship; consequently, even if the person in whom the legal title is vested happens to be the survivor, he will continue to hold the property on trust for himself and for those entitled to the estate of his co-proprietor in the same proportions as before.

Where, on the other hand, the purchase money has been contributed equally, the prima facie position is that the purchasers will be deemed to have purchased with a view to taking as joint tenants with the consequential applicability of the principle of survivorship.[36] However, equity regards the existence of a business relationship between the contributors as inconsistent with the existence of a right of survivorship, even if the contributions have been equal.[37] It is not enough that both parties happen to be in business with one another; the property must be acquired in the course of that business.[38]

---

[33] [1991] A.C. 107 at 132–133; the relevant passage is set out *post*, p. 425.

[34] See *post*, p. 423.

[35] *Wray v. Steele* (1814) 2 V. & B. 388.

[36] *Lake v. Gibson* (1732) 1 Eq.Cas.Abr. 290; *Lake v. Craddock* (1732) 3 P.Wms. 158 (seemingly reports of the same case under different names).

[37] *Lake v. Gibson* (1729) 1 Eq.Cas.Abr.290; *Lake v. Craddock* (1732) 3 P.Wms. 158; *Malayan Credit v. Jack Chia-MPH* [1986] A.C. 549.

[38] *Tan Chew Hoe Noe v. Chee Swee Cheng* (1928) L.R. 56 Ind.App. 112.

However, the matter is treated broadly. In *Malayan Credit v. Jack-Chia MPH*,[39] the parties had separate businesses and were not in any sense partners; they leased business premises as joint tenants on the basis that each would occupy a particular part of the premises and contribute towards the rent and out-goings in proportion to the area each occupied. The Privy Council held that the equitable presumptions should not be treated rigidly as closed categories; holding premises for separate business purposes was sufficient to give rise to a tenancy in common in equity.

The position with joint mortgages is, however, much more straightforward. If two persons advance money on the security of a mortgage, then, quite irrelevant of the identity of the person in whom the mortgage is vested and of the proportions in which the money was advanced, there is no right of survivorship and the interest of each mortgagee will devolve according to his will or intestacy. This is because a mortgage advance cannot possibly be regarded as anything other than a commercial undertaking; there therefore cannot conceivably have been any intention that an interest in a mortgage should be subject to any right of survivorship.[40] This is the case even if the mortgage in question incorporates, as it will in the absence of contrary intention, a statutory term[41] that the money is lent on a joint account;[42] the courts take the view that the purpose of this clause is to permit repayment to a surviving mortgagee rather than to affect the rights of the mortgagees *inter se*.

However, it must be emphasised that the general principle laid down in *Dyer v. Dyer* will not be applied arbitrarily. It is essential that a purchase is actually made. So, if a payment is made at the request of and by way of loan to the person in whose name the property is vested, there will be no resulting trust simply because in such circumstances the lender will not have advanced the purchase money as purchaser but merely as lender.[43] Further, there will be never be a resulting trust if it would be contrary to the law or to public policy to allow the presumption to arise. So, in an early case, it was decided that, if a person purchased an estate in the name of another so as to give the latter a vote at a parliamentary election, the latter will take beneficially even if there was no intention whatever to give the estate to him.[44]

Further, given that on any view this kind of resulting trust is based upon some form of presumed intention, no trust will arise where no such intention can be implied. Thus in *Savage v. Dunningham*,[45] it was held that, where there had been an informal flat-sharing arrangement under which the occupiers made contributions to the rent, the purchase of the flat by one of the flat-sharers did not give rise to a resulting trust in favour of the others. Plowman J. held that an income payment such as rent did not indicate any intention

---

[39] [1986] A.C. 549.
[40] *Morley v. Bird* (1798) 3 Ves. 628.
[41] Implied by Law of Property Act 1925, s.111.
[42] (1887) 34 Ch.D. 732.
[43] *Aveling v. Knipe* (1815) 19 Ves. 441. The opinion of Phillimore L.J. in *Hussey v. Palmer* [1972] 1 W.L.R. 1286 at 1291, which appears to be to the opposite effect, appears erroneous. Of course, completely different considerations apply where money is lent for a particular purpose which fails; in such circumstances, the borrower holds the money on trust for the lender: see *Barclays Bank v. Quistclose Investments* [1970] A.C. 567; *ante*, p. 27; *post*, p. 291.
[44] *Groves v. Groves* (1829) 3 Y. & J. 163 at 175; see also *Gascoigne v. Gascoigne* [1918] 1 K.B. 223; *Re Emery's Investment Trusts* [1959] Ch. 410; *Chettiar v. Chettiar (No.2)* [1962] A.C. 294.
[45] [1974] Ch. 181.

whatever in respect of the subsequent acquisition of the capital asset. However, the opposite result was reached in *Dewar v. Dewar*,[46] where the facts were admittedly very different. The plaintiff and the defendant, who were brothers, bought a house with their mother. The plaintiff and the mother each provided £500 and the defendant raised the remaining £3,250 on mortgage. The house was conveyed into the name of the defendant, as it presumably had to be in order to secure the mortgage advance. Goff J. held that the plaintiff's £500 had not been a loan; the presumption of a resulting trust applied and he was therefore entitled to a proportional share in the house. However, the mother's £500 was held on the facts to have been a gift and so there was no resulting trust in her favour.

## III. Voluntary Conveyance or Transfer

When there has been a gratuitous transfer of property into the name of another or into the joint names of the transferor and another, the question of whether there is a presumption of a resulting trust depends on the effect of section 60(3) of the Law of Property Act 1925. This subsection deals with transfers of this type taking effect after 1925 by providing that: "In a voluntary conveyance a resulting trust for the grantor shall not be implied merely by reason that the property is not expressed to be conveyed for the use or benefit of the grantee".

The first question which has to be considered is the scope of this provision. The definitions section of the Law of Property Act 1925, section 205, provides that, unless the context otherwise requires, "property" means "any interest in real or personal property". Is section 60(3) therefore applicable both to land and to pure personalty? The unanimous view of the commentators is that the context (and in particular the references to "conveyance" and "conveyed") does otherwise require and that, consequently, the effect of the subsection is confined to land. This appears to be confirmed by the fact that the subsection has never been referred to in any reported case concerning pure personalty.

Consequently, it appears that a gratuitous transfer of pure personalty is presumed to give rise to a resulting trust in favour of the transferor. This was certainly the case before 1926[47] and, if section 60(3) of the Law of Property Act 1925 does not apply to pure personalty, that must still be the position today. In any event, in *Re Vinogradoff*,[48] where war loan stock was transferred into the joint names of the transferor and her granddaughter, who was then four years of age but to whom she was not *in loco parentis*, Farwell J. held that a resulting trust had arisen; no reference was made to section 60(3).

However, section 60(3) undoubtedly applies to gratuitous transfers of land.

---

[46] [1975] 1 W.L.R. 1532.
[47] See also *Fowkes v. Pascoe* (1875) 10 Ch.App. 343 at 345–348.
[48] [1935] W.N. 68.

Its effect has long been controversial.[49] The majority view has always been that, "in the absence of evidence to the contrary, there will be no resulting trust on a voluntary conveyance to another, unless it has been expressly conveyed upon trusts which fail to dispose of the entire equitable interest".[50] It has to be said that, on the face of things, this view goes much farther than the subsection, which restricts itself to stating that no resulting trust will arise merely because of the absence of the words in question; it is also far from clear what words in the provision justify the existence of a resulting trust where there is evidence to the contrary and nowhere else.[51] But the majority view has now been accepted by the Court of Appeal. In *Khan v. Ali*,[52] Morritt V.-C. held that the earlier decision at first instance in *Lohia v. Lohia*[53] "establishes that the presumption of a resulting trust on a voluntary conveyance of land has been abolished by s.60(3) of the Law of Property Act 1925". The law therefore no longer presumes that a resulting trust arises as the result of a gratuitous transfer of land; consequently, in *Lohia v. Lohia* it was held that no such trust arose as a result of a voluntary conveyance by a son of his tenancy in common to the other joint tenant, his father. However, a resulting trust may nevertheless be inferred if the transferor is able to adduce evidence that he did not intend the transferee to take beneficially. The Court of Appeal upheld the existence of such a resulting trust in *Khan v. Ali* on the basis that the only purpose of the transfer on sale of a property worth £75,000 for £25,000 had been to enable the transferees to raise a mortgage advance of £25,000 on the strength of their incomes so that this sum could be utilised by the transferor, their father, who had no other means of raising the money.[54]

In effect, therefore, section 60(3) of the Law of Property Act 1925 affects the burden of proof. In the case of gratuitous transfers of land, where the subsection applies, there is no presumption of resulting trust and it is for the transferor to prove that he did not intend the transferee to take beneficially. In

---

[49] This was largely because of uncertainty as to what the position was before 1926, when the effect of transfers was governed by the Statute of Uses 1536. Where a transfer of property was intended to be voluntary and pass both legal and beneficial title to the transferee, the transfer would usually be expressed to be made "to the use of" or "for the benefit of" the grantee. The presence of these words undoubtedly passed legal title to the transferee in just the same way as a transfer "unto and to the use of" an intended trustee vested legal title in him (see *ante*, p. 5, fn. 28). Their presence was clearly also intended to pass the equitable title to him as well but, despite dicta that this was indeed their effect (in *Young v. Peachey* (1742) 2 Atk. 254 at 257; *Lloyd & Johnson v. Spillet* (1741) 2 Atk. 148 at 150; *Fowkes v. Pascoe* (1875) 10 Ch.App. 343, 348), some commentators thought that as a matter of principle the absence of any further express beneficial gift meant that the transferee held the property on resulting trust for the transferor (see Maitland, *Equity* (2nd ed.), p. 77; White and Tudor, *Leading Cases in Equity* (9th ed.), Vol. II, p. 762).

[50] Pettit, *Equity and the Law of Trusts* (8th ed., 1997), p. 161, citing *Snell's Principles of Equity* (29th ed.), p. 183. See also Hayton & Marshall, *Commentary and Cases on the Law of Trusts and Equitable Remedies* (11th ed., 2001), p. 327 and Underhill & Hayton, *Law of Trusts and Trustees* (16th ed., 2003), p. 367.

[51] Previous editions of this work have therefore consistently adopted the contrary view that there appears to be nothing in section 60(3) which prevents a resulting trust from being implied for reasons other than the absence of the words in question and, in particular, as a result of the operation of general equitable principles.

[52] (2002) 5 I.T.E.L.R. 232.

[53] [2001] W.T.L.R. 101 at 113.

[54] The presumption of advancement between father and child which would normally have rebutted the presumption of resulting trust in favour of the father was held to be have been rebutted by these facts.

the case of gratuitous transfers of pure personalty, where the subsection does not apply, there is a presumption of resulting trust and it is for the transferee to establish that he has taken beneficially.[55]

## IV. THE REBUTTABLE NATURE OF THE PRESUMPTIONS

The presumptions which arise on a purchase in or a transfer into the name of another are rebuttable by parol or, for that matter, any other evidence that the purchaser or transferor intended to confer a benefit on that other. Further, in certain circumstances, the presumption is actually reversed and it is instead presumed that there is no resulting trust. This is the case where the person in whom the property is vested is the lawful wife or child of the purchaser or is a person to whom he stood *in loco parentis* at the time of the purchase or transfer. In these cases, the donor is presumed to have intended to make an "advancement" to the donee and the presumption of resulting trusts is therefore said to have been rebutted by the presumption of advancement. It should also be remembered in this connection that section 53(1)(b) of the Law of Property Act 1925 (which provides that a declaration of trust as to land must be manifested and proved by writing) does not apply to implied, resulting or constructive trusts; consequently, oral evidence is admissible to show what the true nature of the transaction actually was.[56]

### (A) Intention to Confer a Benefit
This is entirely a matter of evidence. If it can be shown that there was an intention to confer a benefit on the donee, no resulting trust can arise. In *Standing v. Bowring*,[57] the plaintiff transferred £6,000 Consols into the joint names of herself and her godson. She did this with the express intention that the godson, in the event that he survived her, should take the Consols but that she herself should retain the right to the dividends during her lifetime; she had also been told that her act was irrevocable. The Court of Appeal held that the presumption of a resulting trust had been rebutted; there was ample evidence that, at the time of the transfer and for some time previously, the plaintiff had intended to confer a benefit on her godson by making the transfer. Similarly, in *Dewar v. Dewar*,[58] the presumption of a resulting trust in favour of a mother who had made a contribution to the purchase of property in the name of her son was rebutted by evidence that she had intended to make a gift.

### (1) Joint banking accounts
An intention to confer a benefit has been presumed in cases where a balance of a bank account has been put into joint names.[59] While this is generally

---

[55] Either by virtue of the counter-presumption known as the presumption of advancement when the parties are in one of a number of established relationships or by affirmative evidence that the transferor intended to make an outright beneficial transfer.

[56] Law of Property Act 1925, s.53(2).

[57] (1885) 31 Ch.D. 282.

[58] [1975] 1 W.L.R. 1532.

[59] See *Marshal v. Crutwell* (1875) L.R. 20 Eq. 328 at 330, *per* Jessel M.R. In that case the presumption (of advancement) was rebutted on the ground that the joint account had been merely for convenience. However, in *Re Figgis* [1969] 1 Ch. 123 it was held that the presumption was not rebutted by the available evidence: the "convenience" principle did not apply.

accepted to be the law, there is a potential difficulty where the donor subsequently maintains the right to use the substance of the gift during his lifetime; in such circumstances, the gift of the balance of the account to the other appears to be in the nature of a testamentary provision and, having not been made in accordance with the Wills Act 1837,[60] could be argued to be ineffective. This argument, which has been accepted in other jurisdictions,[61] appealed to Romer J. in *Young v. Sealey*,[62] but he declined to apply it because of the disturbing effect it would have on existing titles. The point remains open for adjudication by the Court of Appeal.

### (2) Joint banking accounts of husband and wife

A variant of the previous situation is where spouses have maintained a joint bank account in which their mutual resources have been pooled. In such circumstances it will be at the very least difficult, and in many cases quite impossible, to divide up the balance by ascertaining how much was paid in by each spouse. It has therefore been held that, in the event of dissolution of the marriage, each will be entitled to one half. The same principle will apply to investments which have been made by the husband in his own name out of money held in such a joint banking account.[63] However, it should be noted that, where such investments are instead made in the name of the wife, the situation may well be governed by the presumption of advancement, in which case she will prima facie take the investments beneficially.[64]

### (B) The Presumption of Advancement

The second situation where the presumption of a resulting trust does not operate is where its effect is reversed by a counter-presumption, the presumption of advancement. This is, however, only the case where the purchaser or transferor is the husband or father of or a person standing *in loco parentis* to the person in whose name the property is put. In these cases the presumption is that the purchaser or transferor intended to advance the property to the person in whose name it is put, in other words to give it to him; consequently, there is no resulting trust. Once the presumption has arisen (it is of course capable of being rebutted by contrary evidence), it cannot be upset by any subsequent event unless evidence of that event is admissible under the rules which will be discussed in the next section. This can be illustrated by the old case of *Crabb v. Crabb*,[65] where a father transferred stock from his own name into the name of his son and a broker. He also told the broker to carry the dividends to the son's account. Later, by a subsequent codicil to his will, the father bequeathed the stock to another person. It was held that the son had

---

[60] s.9 (as substituted by Administration of Justice Act 1982, s.17).

[61] By the Court of Appeal of Manitoba, Canada, in *Re Pfrimmer* [1936] 2 D.L.R. 460 and by the Court of Appeal of Singapore in *Hiranand v. Harilela* (2000) 3 I.T.E.L.R. 297. Neither decision actually concerned a joint bank account.

[62] [1949] Ch. 278.

[63] *Jones v. Maynard* [1951] Ch. 572; *Rimmer v. Rimmer* [1953] 1 Q.B. 63. Compare *Re Cohen* [1953] Ch. 88, where a bundle of notes found hidden in the matrimonial home after the death of both spouses, who died within a few months of each other, was held to be the property of the wife to whom the residue belonged.

[64] See *post, infra*.

[65] (1834) 1 Myl. & K. 511.

taken an absolute beneficial interest in the stock at the time of the transfer and so the father had nothing left to bequeath.

## (1) Husband and wife

The presumption of advancement by a husband in favour of his wife now has an extremely limited application, particularly when the marriage has broken down. This is a result of the following restatement of the law elaborated by Lord Diplock in *Pettitt v. Pettitt*.[66]

> "The consensus of judicial opinion which gave rise to the presumptions of 'advancement' and 'resulting trust' in transactions between husband and wife is to be found in cases relating to the propertied classes of the nineteenth century and the first quarter of the twentieth century among whom marriage settlements were common, and it was unusual for the wife to contribute her earnings to the family income. It was not until after World War II that the courts were required to consider the proprietary rights in family assets of a different social class. The advent of legal aid, the wider employment of married women in industry, commerce and the professions, and the emergence of a property-owning, particularly a real-property-mortgaged-to-a-building-society-owning democracy has compelled the courts to direct their attention to this during the last 20 years. It would, in my view, be an abuse of the legal technique for ascertaining or imputing intention to apply to transactions between the post-war generations of married couples 'presumptions' which are based on inferences of fact which an earlier generation of judges drew as to the most likely intentions of earlier generations of spouses belonging to the propertied classes of a different social era."

Notwithstanding these remarks of Lord Diplock, the doctrine of advancement between husband and wife can still have some application where for some reason, such as death, the evidence of one or both of the parties is unavailable. Where, on the other hand, both parties are available to give evidence, the court much prefers to hear them and to form its own view of their intention. Where this is done, it is highly unlikely that the presumption of advancement will ever have any effect as between husband and wife.

In so far, if at all, as the presumption may still be operative, it is immaterial that the marriage is later dissolved or is the subject matter of a decree of nullity on the grounds that the marriage was voidable.[67] However, if a marriage is held to have been void *ab initio*, the presumption of advancement does not appear to apply — this is simply because the marriage is treated as never having existed at all.[68] The essential requirement of the presumption is for the property to be purchased in the name of the lawful wife of the purchaser. For

---

[66] [1970] A.C. 777 at 783.

[67] *Dunbar v. Dunbar* [1909] 2 Ch. 639. A nullity decree in respect of a voidable marriage now has a prospective, not a retrospective effect. Accordingly the marriage is to be treated as if it had existed until the decree; Matrimonial Causes Act 1973, s.16. For the grounds on which a marriage is regarded as void or voidable, see *ibid.* ss.11, 12.

[68] See *Re Ames' Settlement* [1946] Ch. 217. See also *Re D'Altroy's Will Trusts* [1968] 1 W.L.R. 120.

this reason the presumption does not apply in favour of a purchaser's de facto wife or his mistress.[69]

Nor does the presumption of advancement apply where a wife purchases property in the name of her husband; in such circumstances, what is presumed to arise is a resulting trust in favour of the wife.[70] Thus, the presumption of advancement did not apply in *Abrahams v. The Trustee of the Property of Abrahams*[71] to rebut the presumption of resulting trust in favour of a wife who had purchased in the name of her estranged husband a one-fifteenth share of a winning national lottery ticket. At one time a resulting trust in favour of a wife only arose where the property in question had been purchased with her capital, not where it had been purchased with her income. However, in *Mercier v. Mercier*,[72] the Court of Appeal held that there was no fundamental distinction between capital and income except in degree, although Romer L.J. made it clear that the fact could still nevertheless be of importance when he said[73]: "No doubt in certain cases, in considering whether a gift was intended, the fact of the money having been income received by him with her consent may be material in respect of the weight of evidence but there is no other distinction, so far as I am aware, between capital and income". This decision certainly changed the pre-existing law; consequently, the fact that the wife used her income rather than her capital will now only be relevant as a matter of evidence as to whether or not any intention which she may have had to benefit the husband is sufficient to rebut the presumption of resulting trust in her favour.

### (2) Parent and child

"Child" here means "legitimate child". It is absolutely clear that if a father purchases property in the name of his legitimate child the presumption of advancement will apply.[74]

The traditional view is that if a mother does the same thing the presumption will not apply.[75] However, the authorities are not unanimous. In *Sayre v. Hughes*,[76] Stuart V.-C. appears to have held that what was most material was whether the mother's motivation was to confer a benefit on her child — a view which, if accepted, could clearly lead to the opposite conclusion and work an advancement in favour of the child, although Stuart V.-C. was specifically considering only the case of a widowed mother. Nor do the authorities in support of the traditional view agree as to the justification for it. In *Re De Visme*,[77] it was held that the presumption of advancement would not arise as

---

[69] *Soar v. Foster* (1858) 4 K. & J. 152.

[70] Although if the property is part of the matrimonial assets the court may apply the maxim that equality is equity: see, for example, *Jones v. Maynard* [1951] Ch. 572; *Rimmer v. Rimmer* [1953] 1 Q.B. 63 and *ante*, p. 280; *post*, p. 423.

[71] [2000] W.T.L.R. 593.

[72] [1903] 2 Ch. 98.

[73] *ibid.* at 101.

[74] *Dyer v. Dyer* (1788) 2 Cox Eq. 92.

[75] *Re De Visme* (1863) 2 De G.J. & S. 17; *Bennet v. Bennet* (1879) 10 Ch.D. 474. The same view was adopted much more recently in *Sekhon v. Alissa* [1989] 2 F.L.R. 94.

[76] (1868) L.R. 5 Eq. 376. See also *Garrett v. Wilkinson* (1848) 2 De G. & Sm. 244 at 246. The High Court of Australia upheld the existence of a presumption of advancement between mother and child in *Nelson v. Nelson* (1995) 132 A.L.R. 133.

[77] (1863) 2 De G.J. & S. 17.

between mother and child because a married woman was under no obligation to maintain her children. On the other hand, in *Bennet v. Bennet*,[78] Jessel M.R. held that the presumption of advancement essentially applied only to the father not because the mother was under no liability to maintain her children but because the father alone was under a moral obligation to make provision for his child, no such obligation being imposed on the mother. A quite different reason for rejecting *Re De Visme* in modern conditions is the fact that, since the enactment of the National Assistance Act 1948,[79] mothers have been under a statutory duty to care for their children. However, in *Sekhon v. Alissa*,[80] the most recent case in which the traditional view was adopted, Hoffmann J. chose simply to apply the older authorities without distinguishing between the different views expressed in them and therefore held that the presumption of resulting trust, and not the presumption of advancement, applied where a mother provided the majority of the price of a property purchased in the name of her daughter.

The traditional position is frankly, unsatisfactory. It is particularly difficult to see why a mother, especially if she has money, is not under the same moral obligation to maintain her children as their father is said to be. Having said that, however, it may not matter all that much in practice. If there is indeed no presumption of advancement between mother and child, the presumption of resulting trust in favour of the mother which consequently arises can be rebutted by any evidence of an intention on her part to benefit the child[81] and it is improbable that children will find this particularly difficult to achieve. The failure of the daughter to do so in *Sekhon v. Alissa*[82] admittedly shows that this cannot be assumed; however, that decision is perhaps best explained on the grounds that the mother was anyway able to rely on evidence in support of the presumption of resulting trust and in rebuttal of any presumption of advancement; although the transaction between the mother and the daughter had been entered into for an illegal purpose, with a view to evading capital gains tax, this evidence was nevertheless admissible.[83]

### (3) Person *in loco parentis* and child

A person *in loco parentis* is a person standing in the position of a parent, that is to say in the situation of the lawful father of the child. According to Jessel M.R. in *Bennet v. Bennet*,[84] such a person is one who takes upon himself the duty of the father of a child to make provision for that child. For example, an uncle or grandfather may, in the particular circumstances of the case, put himself *in loco parentis* to a child after, for example, the death of the latter's father.[85] Again, a father of an illegitimate child may, in the circumstances, be *in loco parentis* to that child.[86] However, for a person to be *in loco parentis* he must actually place

---

[78] (1879) 10 Ch.D. 474.
[79] ss.42(1), 64(1).
[80] [1989] 2 F.L.R. 94.
[81] See *Beecher v. Major* (1865) 2 Drew. & Sm. 431.
[82] [1989] 2 F.L.R. 94.
[83] Because the mother had withdrawn from the transaction in question before the purpose has been carried out; see *post*, p. 290).
[84] (1879) 10 Ch.D. 474 at 477.
[85] *Ebrand v. Dancer* (1680) 2 Ch. Cas. 26 (grandchild whose father was dead); *Currant v. Jago* (1844) 1 Coll.C.C. 261 (nephew of wife maintained by her husband).
[86] *Beckford v. Beckford* (1774) Lofft 490.

himself in the situation of the father; simply to pay an illegitimate child's school fees would not of itself be enough in itself to raise the presumption.[87]

### (4) The rebuttable nature of the presumption

When a presumption of advancement does arise, it is just as capable of being rebutted by evidence of actual intention as is a presumption of resulting trust. Thus in *McGrath v. Wallis*,[88] a father contributed about four-fifths of the purchase price of a house which was acquired for the occupation of father, mother, son and daughter but the property was put in the name of the son so that the balance of price could be raised by way of mortgage (the father was unemployed). A declaration of trust was indeed drawn up by means of which the beneficial interests were to be four-fifths to the father and one-fifth to the son but for some reason this was never executed. Following the death of his parents, the son claimed to be absolutely beneficially entitled. However, the need for an acceptable mortgagor, the absence of any evidence that the father had instructed the solicitors not to proceed with the declaration of trust, and the absence of any reason why the father should have wished to give the property to his son absolutely, were held sufficient to rebut any presumption of advancement. The presumption will also be rebutted if the mental state of the purchaser is such that he is incapable of any intention at all.[89]

### 3. *The Admissibility of Evidence to Rebut the Presumptions*

### (A) What Sort of Evidence is Admissible?

It is obviously important to determine exactly what sort of evidence is admissible for the purpose of rebutting the presumptions of resulting trust and advancement. The leading case on admissibility is *Shephard v. Cartwright*.[90]

The deceased had been a successful businessman. He had at various times formed a number of private companies which had been so successful that he had amalgamated them and turned them into a public company. At varying times he had shares in this company allotted to his three children but there was no evidence that any share certificates had been issued in their favour. In any case, the father continued to deal in these shares; at various times he sold them and received the proceeds of sale. However, at a later stage, he did place to the credit of the children in separate deposit accounts the exact amount of the cash consideration for the shares which he had sold. Later still, he obtained the children's signatures to documents (as to the contents of which they were wholly ignorant) authorising him to withdraw money from these deposit accounts and indeed in due course, unknown to them, his drawings exhausted those accounts. When he died, some 13 years after the accounts had been exhausted, his children brought an action against his executors claiming an account of money due to them. The executors contended that the presumption of advancement in favour of the children had been rebutted by the control which the father had continuously exercised over the shares. This argument succeeded in the Court of Appeal but the House of Lords held that the

---

[87] *Tucker v. Burrow* (1865) 2 Hem. & M. 515.
[88] [1995] 2 F.L.R. 114.
[89] *Simpson v. Simpson* [1992] 1 F.L.R. 601.
[90] [1955] A.C. 431.

registration of the shares in the names of the children gave rise to a presumption of advancement and that nothing had happened which was capable of rebutting that presumption. The law on the admissibility of evidence for the purposes of rebuttal was stated explicitly by Viscount Simonds. He adopted [91] the following passage from *Snell's Principles of Equity*.[92]

> "The acts and declarations of the parties before or at the time of the purchase, or so immediately after it as to constitute a part of the transaction, are admissible in evidence either for or against the party who did the act or made the declaration; subsequent acts and declarations are only admissible as evidence against the party who made them, and not in his favour."

As Viscount Simonds said, there are numerous cases of high authority[93] on which this passage is founded. Although its references to admissibility are no longer technically appropriate due to the subsequent enactment of section 2 of the Civil Evidence Act 1968, under which hearsay evidence, including evidence of subsequent declarations, is now formally admissible, there is no doubt that the principles stated in this passage still govern what evidence will be regarded as effective for the purpose of rebutting the presumptions. It is not too difficult to state the relevant principles in the abstract. They establish, in the context of the presumption of advancement between father and child, first that a father's declaration at the date of the transaction will be effective to enable him to rebut the presumption; secondly, that a father's declaration made after that date will not be effective to enable him to rebut the presumption but will be effective as against him to enable his child to support the presumption of advancement;[94] and, thirdly, that subsequent acts and declarations by the child will be effective as against him to enable his father to rebut the presumption.[95] However, difficulties may nevertheless arise in applying these principles in practice.

First, the question of whether or not a subsequent act is part of the same transaction as the original purchase or transfer is a potential cause of considerable difficulty — there is no universal criterion by which a link can, for this purpose, be found between one event and another but it is nevertheless essential that a link is able to be found.[96] In *Shephard v. Cartwright* itself, Viscount Simonds pointed out that the events which happened after the allotment of shares to the children did not form part of the original transaction, that is to say that allotment. All subsequent events were independent of that original transaction and, far from flowing inevitably from it, they would never have happened at all but for the phenomenal success of the testator's business.

Secondly, difficulties arise as to whether, and if so what, subsequent acts and declarations will rebut the relevant presumption. An early case which shows the difficulties that there may be in rebutting the presumption on this

---

[91] *ibid.* at 445.
[92] (28th ed.) p. 185; see now the current (30th) ed. p. 209.
[93] See, for example, the cases cited *post*, fnn. 94, 95.
[94] *Stock v. McAvoy* (1872) L.R. 15 Eq. 55; *Redington v. Redington* (1794) 3 Ridg.P.R. 106 at 177; *Sidmouth v. Sidmouth* (1840) 2 Beav. 447.
[95] *Scawin v. Scawin* (1841) 1 Y. & C.C.C. 65.
[96] [1955] A.C. 431 at 448–449, *per* Viscount Simonds.

basis is *Lord Grey v. Lady Grey*[97]; Lord Finch L.C., having considered the fact that the son had permitted his father to continue to receive the profits of the property in question, said that that fact was insufficient to rebut the presumption because it was an "act of reverence and good manners"![98] Of course, there are some circumstances which will obviously rebut the presumption. Thus, it was held in *Warren v. Gurney*,[99] that the fact that the father had retained the title deeds was, although not in itself conclusive, of great significance when coupled with certain contemporaneous declarations by the father. Another circumstance which assists in rebutting the presumption is the fact that the son is the father's solicitor.[1]

Yet, as Viscount Simonds said in *Shephard v. Cartwright*,[2] any such evidence of subsequent acts is regarded jealously. A question which arose in that case was whether, even though the events which happened after the allotments of the shares did not form part of the original transaction, they nevertheless amounted to an acknowledgment by the children that they had not in fact acquired any interest. However, for such an acknowledgment to be effective, it must have been made with full knowledge of the material facts. It was not disputed that the children had done whatever they had been told to do by their father without any inquiry of him or any knowledge of the consequences. This fact prevented their conduct from constituting an acknowledgment of anything which was contrary to their own interest and prevented evidence of that conduct from having any probative value.

### (B) Illegal and Fraudulent Conduct

There is a further restriction on the evidence which can be adduced in order to rebut the presumptions of resulting trust and advancement. Neither presumption can be rebutted by evidence that the reason for the transfer or purchase in question was an illegal or fraudulent purpose and that the transferor or purchaser nevertheless really intended to retain a beneficial interest in the subject matter. This basic rule has never been doubted; however, at least for the moment, it is subject to two exceptions. The first arises where the beneficial interest in question can be established independently; the existence of an illegal or fraudulent purpose will not prevent a beneficial interest being claimed where this can be done without any reliance being placed on any evidence of that purpose. The second arises where the illegal or fraudulent purpose has been abandoned; evidence of such a purpose is admissible if the person relying on that evidence withdrew from the purpose before it had been carried out in any way.[3]

It should be noted that in 1999 the Law Commission[4] produced a Consultation Paper as part of a general review of the effect of illegality on contracts and trusts. This criticises the existing law and tentatively proposes that illegality should be available only as a defence and then, unless any statute which rendered the conduct in question illegal made express provision as to the

---

[97] (1677) 2 Swans. 594.
[98] *ibid.* at 600.
[99] [1944] 2 All E.R. 472.
[1] *Garrett v. Wilkinson* (1848) 2 De G. & Sm. 244.
[2] [1955] A.C. 431 at 449.
[3] See Davies in *Trends in Contemporary Trust Law* (ed. Oakley, 1996), p. 31; Virgo [1996] C.L.J. 23.
[4] Law Com. C.P. No. 154 (1999).

consequences, only at the discretion of the courts, who would, in exercising their discretion, have to consider a series of factors.[5] No indication has as yet been given as to whether or not this Consultation Proposal is to be consolidated into a Report so any legislation must still be some years away.

## (1) The basic rule

The basic rule may be illustrated by *Gascoigne v. Gascoigne*,[6] where a husband who had put property into the name of his wife was held unable to adduce evidence to show that he had done so for the purpose of defeating his creditors; consequently, she was held to be beneficially entitled to that property. A similar result occurred in *Tinker v. Tinker*,[7] although in that case the husband's intention was apparently honest. In the words of Lord Denning M.R., he simply found himself on the horns of a dilemma in that, as between himself and his wife, he wanted to say that the property belonged to him whereas, as between himself and his creditors, he wished to say that it belonged to her. In such circumstances, the effect of the presumption of advancement was decisive. This was also the case in *Chettiar v. Chettiar (No.2)*,[8] where a father sought to evade regulations governing the holding of rubber plantations in Malaya which differed depending on whether more or less than 100 acres were held (in the former but not the latter case, the permissible production was controlled by an assessment committee). He acquired 40 acres at a time when he already owned 99 acres and, in order to avoid having to disclose to the authorities that he thereafter held more than 100 acres, he had the 40 acres put into the name of his son. He had not the slightest intention of making a gift of them and therefore subsequently claimed that the son held them on resulting trust for him. The Privy Council, in an opinion delivered by Lord Denning, held that the father could only rebut the presumption of advancement by disclosing his intention to deceive the authorities. The court was bound to take notice of this illegality and therefore would not lend him its aid; the legal and beneficial estate consequently lay where it had fallen, in the hands of the son.

## (2) Where the beneficial interest can be established independently

Prior to the decision of the House of Lords in *Tinsley v. Milligan*,[9] it was thought that the court would decline to intervene in favour of a participant in an illegal or fraudulent purpose whether or not evidence of the illegal or fraudulent conduct in question was necessary to his claim.[10] However, while this was indeed the view adopted by the minority in that case, the majority

---

[5] The seriousness of the illegal conduct; the knowledge and intention of the party seeking the enforcement of the transaction or the recognition of property rights; and the extent to which any refusal to assist would either deter illegality, and/or further the purpose of the rule making the transaction illegal and/or be proportionate to the illegality.

[6] [1918] 1 K.B. 223; see also *Re Emery's Investment Trusts* [1959] Ch. 410 (avoiding payment of taxes).

[7] [1970] P. 136. *Gascoigne v. Gascoigne* and *Tinker v. Tinker* were distinguished in *Griffiths v. Griffiths* [1973] 1 W.L.R. 1454, where a husband's false representation as to ownership formed no part of the legal proceedings between him and his wife (this decision was varied by the Court of Appeal on other grounds at [1974] 1 All E.R. 932).

[8] [1962] A.C. 294. See also *Collier v. Collier* [2003] W.T.L.R. 617.

[9] [1994] 1 A.C. 340.

[10] On the basis of the "clean hands" policy laid down by Lord Eldon L.C. in *Muckleston v. Brown* (1801) 6 Ves. 52.

instead held that the existence of an illegal or fraudulent purpose will not prevent a property right from being claimed if that right can be established without any reliance being placed on any evidence of that purpose.[11]

In *Tinsley v. Milligan*, two female lovers had agreed to put a house which they were purchasing into the sole name of the plaintiff in order to enable the defendant to make fraudulent claims for housing benefit. After this fraud had been practiced for a number of years, the two quarrelled and the plaintiff left. Subsequently, at a time when the defendant had discontinued her fraudulent claims and "made her peace" with the authorities, the plaintiff sought her eviction; the defendant counterclaimed for a declaration that the property was held on trust for both of them in equal shares. The Court of Appeal[12] held that a more flexible approach should be adopted in cases of illegal or fraudulent conduct on the basis that "the underlying principle is the so-called public conscience test. The court must weigh, or balance, the adverse consequences of granting relief against the adverse consequences of refusing relief. The ultimate decision calls for a value judgment."[13] This novel principle was unanimously rejected by the House of Lords, who confirmed the basic rule that evidence of an illegal or fraudulent purpose is not admissible to rebut a presumption of resulting trust or of advancement. However, the majority held[14] that the defendant did not need to rely on any such evidence to assert her claim. On its face, the transaction between the parties had given rise to a presumption of resulting trust in her favour. The relationship between the parties did not give rise to any presumption of advancement so as to rebut the presumption of resulting trust (had it done so, the basic rule would have prevented the defendant from introducing evidence of the illegal purpose in order to rebut the presumption of advancement). The defendant therefore had to be presumed to have an equitable proprietary interest in the property unless the plaintiff could rebut that presumption by contrary evidence. Thus the defendant could assert her claim to that interest without having to produce any evidence as to why the property had been conveyed into the sole name of the plaintiff and was consequently entitled to her beneficial interest.

The Court of Appeal has duly applied the decision in *Tinsley v. Milligan* but

---

[11] This has been the subject of considerable criticism; see Halliwell [1994] Conv. 62, Stowe 57 M.L.R. (1994) 441. Council in 143 N.L.J. (1993) 1577 says that the effect of the decision is that "he who comes to equity should keep unclean hands in his pockets", an amusing addition to the list of equitable maxims which will no doubt in due course prove to be as misleading as most of the others.

[12] [1992] Ch. 310.

[13] *ibid.* at 319, *per* Nicholls L.J. A different flexible public policy approach was subsequently adopted by the High Court of Australia in *Nelson v. Nelson* (1995) 132 A.L.R. 133, in which *Tinsley v. Milligan* was rejected. A mother was held able to rebut the presumption of advancement in favour of her children (which would probably not have arisen here anyway) by adducing evidence that she had purchased the property in their name in order to obtain housing subsidies which would not have been available had she purchased in her own name; she was therefore entitled to the property under a resulting trust but the majority went on to hold that as a condition of relief she was herself obliged to do equity by reimbursing the housing subsidies.

[14] It had long been established that the legal owner of property can rely on his title despite the fact that it was acquired as a result of an illegal transaction (*Bowmakers v. Barnet Instruments* [1945] K.B. 65). The disagreement between the members of the House of Lords was as to whether the "clean hands" policy to which courts of equity have always subscribed prevented this principle from also being applicable to an equitable owner.

not always uncritically. In *Silverwood v. Silverwood*,[15] Nourse L.J.[16] emphasised that, by virtue of *Tinsley v. Milligan*, a claimant is entitled to recover provided that he is not forced either to plead or to rely on any illegal or fraudulent conduct; however, he repeated his preference for the more flexible approach rejected by the House of Lords in *Tinsley v. Milligan*. In *Lowson v. Coombes*,[17] Robert Walker L.J. stated[18] that the importance which the decision in *Tinsley v. Milligan* attached to the presumption of advancement does "create difficulties because the presumption has been cogently criticised both as being out of date in modern social and economic conditions[19] ... and as being uncertain in its scope[20]".[21] As in *Tinsley v. Milligan*, there was no presumption of advancement in either of these cases and the absence of that presumption was admittedly crucial to the outcome of all three cases. But, as is shown by the more recent decision of the Court of Appeal in *Khan v. Ali*,[22] the presence of a presumption of advancement can be equally crucial in that it can similarly be relied on by a party to illegal or fraudulent conduct to rebut the presumption of resulting trust.

It is of course feasible to criticise the exception created by the majority in *Tinsley v. Milligan* as such and many have done so.[23] However, it does seem somewhat unreasonable to criticise that exception merely because of the impact on its application of the presumption of advancement. Even if that presumption has "fallen into disfavour", it is still part of English law and the House of Lords could not have overruled it in *Tinsley v. Milligan* even if the members of the House had wanted to do so. But, given that nearly all of the members of the Court of Appeal who have criticised *Tinsley v. Milligan* are

---

[15] (1997) 74 P. & C.R. 453. The majority of the testatrix's assets were placed in the names of two of her grandchildren and not declared to the Department of Social Security when she subsequently applied for income support. Her executor was held to be entitled to recover them on the basis that there was a presumption of resulting trust in her favour. Even on the assumption that the testatrix had been party to the illegal purpose (which was not held), she did not need to rely on any evidence of it since there was no presumption of advancement between her and her grandchildren which she needed to rebut.

[16] *ibid.* at 758–759.

[17] [1999] Ch. 373. A man and his mistress both contributed to the purchase price of a series of houses, all of which were transferred into the sole name of the mistress so as to prevent any claim to them being asserted by the man's estranged wife (this was an illegal purpose under Matrimonial Causes Act 1973, s.37; *ante,* p. 262). There was again no presumption of advancement so the man was able to rely on the presumption of resulting trust rather than on any evidence of the illegal purpose.

[18] *ibid.* at 385.

[19] Referring to the remarks of Lord Diplock in *Pettitt v. Pettitt* set out *ante,* p. 281.

[20] Referring to purchases and transfers by wives and mothers.

[21] See also *Tribe v. Tribe* [1996] Ch. 107 at 118 per Nourse L.J.; *Silverwood v. Silverwood* (1997) 74 P. & C.R. 453 at 458, per Nourse L.J.; Hanbury & Martin, *Modern Equity* (16th ed., 2001), p. 260.

[22] (2002) 5 I.T.E.L.R. 232. A father was asserting a beneficial interest in a house which he had transferred into the names of two of his daughters, on sale but only for about a third of its real value, to enable a mortgage for that amount to be raised on the strength of the daughters' income. At first instance, it was held that any presumption of resulting trust in favour of the father would have been rebutted by the presumption of advancement and that the father would not have been able to rely on evidence of what the judge regarded as a fraudulent purpose in order to rebut the presumption of advancement. The Court of Appeal cast no doubt on that analysis but held that on the facts the purpose had not involved any fraud. A resulting trust in favour of the father was upheld, subject to suitable arrangements being made in respect of the potential liability of the daughters under the mortgage.

[23] See Halliwell [1994] Conv. 62; Stowe, 57 M.L.R. (1994) 441; Council, 143 N.L.J. (1993) 1577.

now members of the House of Lords, it cannot be assumed that the exception created by that decision will survive a further review at the highest level.

### (3) Where the illegal or fraudulent purpose has been abandoned

The second exception to the basic rule was analysed, very considerably clarified, and applied by the Court of Appeal in *Tribe v. Tribe*,[24] and as a result it is no longer necessary to consider any of the earlier authorities. A father transferred shares in a family company to his son for a consideration which was not in fact paid in order to be able to deceive his landlord, to whom he was potentially liable for the cost of substantial works to the leased premises, as to his assets and consequently to safeguard them. In the event, the issue of the repairs was resolved without recourse to any deception.[25] The son subsequently claimed to be absolutely entitled to the shares by virtue of the presumption of advancement. The Court of Appeal held that, since the father's illegal purpose had not been carried out in any way, he could introduce evidence of it in order to rebut the presumption of advancement. Earlier authorities had required "repentance" from the illegal or fraudulent purpose, although it was far from clear whether or not this "repentance" had to be genuine (which it would not have been in *Tribe v. Tribe* because the father had not "repented" until the danger to his assets was past). The Court of Appeal rejected that requirement completely and held that evidence of an illegal or fraudulent purpose can be introduced by anyone who has withdrawn from the transaction in question before the purpose has been carried out. Although this undoubtedly broadened the scope of this second exception, the Court of Appeal felt that it was not inconsistent with the policy underlining the basic rule: "if the policy which underlines the [basic] rule is to discourage fraud, the policy which underlines the [exception] must be taken to be to encourage withdrawal from fraud before it is implemented, an end which is no less desirable".[26]

The decision actually reached in *Tribe v. Tribe* is certainly compatible with the decision in *Tinsley v. Milligan* and there is no doubt that the exceptions to the basic rule which the two decisions establish are mutually consistent. However, in *Tribe v. Tribe*, Millett L.J. said that a transferee cannot be prevented from rebutting a presumption by leading evidence of the transferor's subsequent conduct to show that it was inconsistent with any intention to retain a beneficial interest, giving the example of a transfer of property from uncle to nephew in order to conceal it from his creditors, with whom he subsequently settles on the basis that he has no interest in that property.[27] How can the admission of evidence of this illegal purpose in order to rebut the presumption of resulting trust possibly be consistent with the principle laid down in *Tinsley v. Milligan*, by virtue of which the uncle would undoubtedly be able to rely on the presumption of resulting trust? It may therefore be that any further review of *Tinsley v. Milligan* at the highest level may also have some effect on the nature and/or continued existence of this second exception.

---

[24] [1996] Ch. 107.
[25] The landlord agreed to take a surrender of one of the two leases and sold the father the reversion on the other one.
[26] [1996] Ch. 107, *per* Millett L.J. at 133. See also *Collier v. Collier* [2003] W.T.L.R. 617.
[27] *ibid.* at 130.

## V. FAILURE OF A TRUST OR ITS BENEFICIAL INTERESTS

Where a settlor or testator who is creating an express trust fails to dispose of the whole of the beneficial interest in the property in question; the law implies that so much of the beneficial interest as is undisposed of is held on trust for the settlor or his estate, or for the testator's residuary beneficiaries or intestate successors. Although the presumption which arises in this second category of resulting trusts is not rebuttable in the ways just considered, in *Westdeutsche Landesbank Girozentrale v. Islington L.B.C.*[28] Lord Browne-Wilkinson pointed out that resulting trusts of the second type are not[29] necessarily irrebuttable; if the settlor or testator has, expressly or by necessary implication, abandoned any beneficial interest in the trust property, that property is held not on a resulting trust but for the Crown as *bona vacantia*. However, the law is very reluctant to find that any such abandonment was intended; "it is only where it is absolutely clear that in no circumstances is a resulting trust to arise that it will be excluded".[30]

### 1. *Total Failure of a Trust*

Whenever the trusts of a settlement fail, there is a resulting trust of the trust property for the settlor or his estate. Thus in *Re Ames' Settlement*,[31] the funds of a marriage settlement were held to be subject to a resulting trust for the settlor's estate once the marriage had been declared void by a decree of nullity made by a Kenyan court. The settlement for which the marriage had constituted the consideration failed completely because, in that case, the legal effect of the decree was that the parties not only were no longer married to one another but had never been married at all.[32] Similarly, if property is transferred to a person to hold as a trustee without that person having any beneficial entitlement but no effective trusts are ever established, the property will also be held on a resulting trust for the transferor or his estate.[33]

### 2. *Failure of a Specified Purpose*

When a person pays money for a specified purpose on the basis it will be used only for that purpose, the recipient of the money will generally hold it on trust to use it only for that purpose. If the specified purpose fails, then, save in the wholly exceptional situation in which the parties have specifically provided

---

[28] [1996] A.C. 669 at 708.

[29] As the formulation adopted by Megarry J. in *Re Vandervell's Trusts (No.2)* [1974] Ch. 269 at 294, 295 would appear to suggest.

[30] *Jones v. Williams* (1988) unreported *per* Knox J., quoted in *Davis v. Richards & Wallington Industries* [1990] 1 W.L.R. 1511 at 1541.

[31] [1946] Ch. 217.

[32] In this case the marriage was merely voidable but the effect of the nullity decree was that the marriage was void *ab initio*. Since the Nullity of Marriage Act 1971, s.5 (now Matrimonial Causes Act 1973, s.16), this is no longer the position under English law; this section provides that a nullity decree in respect of a voidable marriage has only a prospective and not any retrospective effect. However, if the marriage is "void", it is treated as never having taken place. For a list of the grounds on which a marriage will be void or voidable, see Matrimonial Causes Act 1973, ss.11, 12.

[33] *Re Vandervell's Trusts (No.2)* [1974] Ch. 269.

for what is to happen in that event, there will be a resulting trust of the money for the person who paid it.

## (A) The Basic Principle

Trusts of this type were first upheld by the House of Lords in *Barclays Bank v. Quistclose Investments*[34] and for that reason are generally known as *Quistclose* trusts. Money was advanced to a company for the purpose of paying a dividend on its shares. The advance was made on the basis that the money was to be used only for this purpose but the company became insolvent before the dividend had been paid. Lord Wilberforce analysed this situation by reference to primary and secondary trusts, holding that the fact that "arrangements for the payment of a [debtor's] creditors by a third person give rise to a relationship of a fiduciary character or trust, in favour, as a primary trust, of the creditors, and secondarily, if the primary trust fails, of the third person has been recognised in a series of cases over some 150 years".[35]

The precise nature of the primary and secondary trusts so identified subsequently caused considerable controversy. As a result *Quistclose* trusts were variously classified as express trusts, resulting trusts and constructive trusts.[36] However, in the later decision of the House of Lords in *Twinsectra v. Yardley*[37] a different analysis of the effect of such trusts was adopted. The claimant made a loan on the basis that the sum advanced was paid to the borrower's solicitors, who gave an undertaking to the claimant to utilise the loan money solely for the acquisition of property on behalf of the borrower and for no other purpose. The House of Lords held that this undertaking had given rise to a trust and Lord Millett classified this trust as a *Quistclose* trust.[38] He went on to reach the conclusion, from which none of the other members of the House of Lords dissented, that in a *Quistclose* trust the person to whom the money is advanced holds it on trust for the person advancing it subject to a power to expend that money for the purpose designated by the latter and for no other purposes.

The different views which have been expressed will be considered in detail later on. However, Lord Millett's analysis in *Twinsectra v. Yardley* has unquestionably superseded the view expressed in *Barclays Bank v. Quistclose Investments* and leads inescapably to the conclusion that, save in the exceptional situation already referred to, *Quistclose* trusts are resulting trusts.[39]

## (B) The Scope of *Quistclose* Trusts

The full facts of *Barclays Bank v. Quistclose Investments*,[40] were that a company which was substantially indebted to its bankers needed money in order to pay a dividend on its shares. Quistclose Investments advanced the necessary

---

[34] [1970] A.C. 567.
[35] [1970] A.C. 567 at 580.
[36] See Lord Millett (pre-judicially) 101 L.Q.R. (1985) 269; Rickett 107 L.Q.R. (1991) 608 and in *Equity, Fiduciaries and Trusts 1993* (ed. Waters), p. 325; Chambers, *Resulting Trusts*, Chap. 3; Ho and Smart (2001) 21 O.J.L.S. 267.
[37] [2002] 2 A.C. 164.
[38] Lord Hoffmann, the only other law lord who specifically discussed the question of whether or not there was a trust, did not mention *Barclays Bank v. Quistclose Investments* at all and seems to have regarded the trust as a simple express trust.
[39] See Rickett [2002] R.L.R. 112; Yeo and Tho 119 L.Q.R. (2003) 13.
[40] [1970] A.C. 567.

money on the basis that it was only to be used for this purpose and it was paid into a separate account with the company's bankers, who were made aware of the arrangement. The company went into liquidation before the dividend had been paid. If Quistclose Investments was only an unsecured creditor of the company, it would enjoy no priority over any other creditors, the money in the bank would belong to the company, and the bank would be entitled to set off the credit balance of the account against the much larger amount owed to it by the company.[41] If, on the other hand, the money was held on trust for Quistclose Investments, its proprietary interest in that money would enjoy priority over the rights of the bank.[42] The House of Lords held that the common intention of Quistclose Investments and the company was such that the money had indeed been held on trust unless and until it was utilised for the purpose of paying the dividend. If that purpose had been fulfilled, Quistclose Investments would have become no more than an unsecured creditor of the company. However, that purpose had in fact failed.[43] Consequently, the money was, as between the company and Quistclose Investments, still held by the former on trust for the latter. Quistclose Investments was therefore able to recover from the bank the money which it had advanced.

There is no difficulty about upholding the existence of a *Quistclose* trust where, as in *Barclays Bank v. Quistclose Investments* itself, the payer and the recipient are held to have intended that the money in question should be held on trust. Such an intention will obviously be clearest where the parties have expressly provided in terms that this should be the case. In *Re Lewis's of Leicester*,[44] about half of the floor space of a department store was licensed to independent traders who were operating "shops within a shop". Some of these traders had agreements with the store whereby their takings, which had to pass through the store's till system, should be held by the store on trust for them subject to the deduction of the store's commission. When the store became insolvent, these traders were held able to recover such of their takings as were traceable into the store's bank accounts. But any intention that the money should be segregated is also likely to lead the court to infer that the parties intended to create a trust, even if that word was never actually used by anyone. In *Re Lewis's of Leicester*, other independent traders had agreements which merely provided for the segregation of their takings in a separate bank account and they were held to be entitled to such money as had actually been segregated.

However, *Quistclose* trusts have also been upheld where the payer and the recipient have merely agreed that there should be restrictions on the purposes for which the money advanced could be employed and, as a result, that money was not at the free disposal of the recipient. As has already been seen, in *Twinsectra v. Yardley*[45] the claimant made a loan on the basis that the sum

---

[41] Banks have a statutory right to amalgamate the balances of the different accounts held with them.

[42] Its beneficial interest would bind the bank because its officers had been aware of the basis on which the funds had been transferred.

[43] Although for present purposes all that matters is that the House of Lords so held, it has never been immediately obvious why the dividend could not have been paid despite the company's insolvency; see Lord Millett (pre-judicially) 101 L.Q.R. (1985) 269.

[44] [1995] 1 B.C.L.C. 428.

[45] [2002] 2 A.C. 164.

advanced was paid to the borrower's solicitors. Those solicitors made the following undertaking to the claimant: "1. The loan monies will be retained by us until such time as they are applied in the acquisition of property on behalf of [the borrower]. 2. The loan monies will be utilised solely for the acquisition of property on behalf of [the borrower] and for no other purpose." The claimant was not actually looking to the property acquired as security for repayment of the loan but rather to a further undertaking given by the solicitors personally to repay the sum advanced four months later together with interest at 24 per cent per annum. Nor had the claimant actually intended that the sum advanced should be held by the solicitors on any trust in its favour (solicitors hold funds in their client accounts on bare trust for the client in question but the client of the solicitors was the borrower not the claimant). But in the event the solicitors breached their undertaking by transferring most of the sum advanced to another solicitor; they also failed to repay the sum advanced. The other solicitor disbursed the funds transferred to him in accordance with the instructions of the borrower but not all of those funds were spent on the acquisition of property. Unexpectedly, it then became important whether or not the arrangement between the claimant, the borrower and the solicitors to whom the money had originally been paid had given rise to a trust.

This was because only if that arrangement had given rise to a trust would it be possible for the claimant either to recover the product of the disbursements made by the other solicitor,[46] or to seek to impeach the conduct of that solicitor because of his involvement in what would then amount to a breach of trust.[47] The House of Lords held that the restrictions on the purposes for which the money could be employed meant that the sum advanced was not at the free disposal of the solicitors who had received it; consequently, independent of the subjective intention of the claimant, the only possible construction of the terms of the undertaking was that they had been holding the sum advanced on trust for the claimant with power to apply it in the acquisition of property by the borrower. Lord Millett[48] classified that trust as a *Quistclose* trust.

It should also be noted that the fact that part of the money advanced has indeed been used for the specific purpose in question does not prevent a *Quistclose* trust arising in respect of whatever is left, enabling the payer to recover that amount.[49] Such a trust has also been held to arise where the money in question, although advanced for a specific purpose, had been paid not by way of loan but rather in satisfaction of a contractual debt.[50] In that respect Peter Gibson J. stated that "the principle in all these cases is that equity fastens on the conscience of the person who receives from another property transferred for a specific purpose only and not therefore for the recipient's

---

[46] The claimant would have an equitable proprietary interest in that product by virtue of the trust; see *post*, p. 812.

[47] This aspect of the case is discussed *post*, p. 382.

[48] Lord Hoffmann, the only other law lord who specifically discussed this issue, did not mention *Barclays Bank v. Quistclose Investments* at all and seems to have regarded the trust as a simple express trust.

[49] *Re EVTR* (1987) B.C.L.C. 647.

[50] *Carreras Rothmans v. Freeman Matthews Treasure* [1985] Ch. 207.

own purposes, so that such person will not be permitted to treat the property as his own or to use it for other than the stated purpose."[51]

Some common intention or agreed restriction of the type referred to above is necessary in order to prevent the general creditors of an insolvent recipient from successfully contending that the creation of the *Quistclose* trust has deprived them of assets which would otherwise have been divisible between them and so amounts to an unlawful preference.[52] In the absence of any such common intention or agreed restriction in the cases discussed above, the money would simply not have been paid over to the recipient at all; consequently, it could never possibly have become part of his general assets. This was specifically held in *Re Lewis's of Leicester*. Nor is such a contention feasible where, at the time when the payer remitted the money, he unilaterally specified that it was to remain his property in equity unless and until the recipient was able to carry out his side of the bargain by for example, providing goods which were being ordered and paid for in advance; money paid in such circumstances could not have become part of the general assets of the recipient either. However, while a reservation of this latter type will clearly bind the recipient and his trustee in bankruptcy, it will only bind any bank in which the recipient has deposited the funds if they are clearly segregated in what the bank knows to be an account maintained for this particular purpose.

The position of the general creditors of the recipient does, however, cause difficulties when the trust in question has been created as the result of a unilateral act by the recipient. The courts have held that it is possible for a *Quistclose* trust to be created, and for the same priority to be conferred, as the result of such an act. In *Re Kayford*,[53] a mail-order company in financial difficulties became concerned as to its ability to provide the goods for which its customers were paying in advance. It consequently opened a separate bank account called its "Customers' Trust Deposit Account" into which all purchase moneys subsequently received from customers were paid; they were withdrawn from this account only as and when the orders in question could be fulfilled. When the company went into liquidation shortly afterwards, Megarry J. held that the money in this account was held on trust for the customers; by paying the purchase moneys into a trust account, the company had prevented the customers from ever becoming its creditors and so no question of an unlawful preference arose.

*Re Kayford* was subsequently followed and applied by the Court of Appeal in *Re Chelsea Cloisters*,[54] where deposits paid to the landlord company by tenants which were to be credited to them at the end of their leases after making good any delapidations and damage caused had also been paid into a separate bank account. On the other hand, *Re Kayford* was distinguished in *Re Multi Guarantee Co.*,[55] where, despite the fact that the money in question had been paid into a separate account in the joint names of the solicitors of the two parties who had been designated, the party to whom it had originally been paid had continued to contemplate the possibility of making further drawings

---

[51] [1985] Ch. 207 at 222.
[52] See *ante*, p. 255.
[53] [1975] 1 W.L.R. 279.
[54] (1981) 41 P. & C.R. 98.
[55] [1987] B.C.L.C. 257.

for his own benefit; nor was *Re Kayford* applied in *Re Challoner Club*,[56] where donations to a club were paid into a separate account so that they would not become available to the creditors of the club but the circumstances in which the donations would become unconditional payments to the club had not been adequately defined.[57] The decision in *Re Kayford* has also on occasions been completely overlooked in circumstances where it would have been highly relevant.[58]

It has to be admitted that it is not easy to justify the existence of a *Quistclose* trust in cases of this kind. Those paying the money in question never had any intention of becoming anything other than general creditors of the recipient. Consequently, it is not easy to see why the unilateral creation of proprietary rights in their favour does not amount to an unlawful preference if the only reason why they did became beneficiaries of a trust rather than general creditors of the recipient is that unilateral act.[59] In *Re Kayford* itself the mail-order company could undoubtedly have rejected the orders and returned their customers' cheques, something which could not conceivably have been contended to have amounted to a preference; consequently the company's acceptance of the orders and segregation of the purchase moneys did not actually make the situation of the general creditors any worse. However, the decision in *Re Chelsea Cloisters* cannot possibly be justified in this way; the company clearly had to go on letting flats and had no realistic option of letting without taking deposits. What is more (and this was a point which clearly troubled Oliver L.J.), sums which had already been received as deposits and paid into the company's normal bank account were drawn out and paid into the segregated fund; the subsequent repayment of these sums to the tenants in question undoubtedly amounted to a preference of their interests at the expense of those of the general creditors. There can be little doubt that more will be heard of this particular point; however, it is only relevant where a *Quistclose* trust is created by a unilateral act of the recipient of the funds in question and does not in any way affect the validity of the types of *Quistclose* trusts upheld by the House of Lords in *Barclays Bank v. Quistclose Investments* and *Twinsectra v. Yardley*.

---

[56] (1997) *The Times*, November 4, 1997.

[57] The intended trust thus failed for uncertainty of objects (see *ante*, p. 59).

[58] In *Customs and Excise Commissioners v. Richmond Theatre Management* [1995] S.T.C. 257, a theatre had sold tickets in advance on the basis of its standard conditions which expressly imposed a trust on the money in favour of the purchasers until the performance in question had taken place. On the face of things, such a trust should have been binding in accordance with *Re Kayford*, indeed possibly in accordance with *Barclays Bank v. Quistclose Investments* as well. However, Dyson J. unexpectedly held that there was no trust because the standard conditions also provided that the theatre was "not accountable for interest or otherwise in respect of the use of the ticket money after its receipt"! As Hanbury & Martin, *Modern Equity* (16th ed., 2001) 51 observes, it is also far from obvious how this conclusion can be reconciled with the decision of the Court of Appeal in *R. v. Clowes (No.2)* [1994] 2 All E.R. 316, where it was said, in the context of theft, "that the requirement to keep money separately normally indicates a trust, and the absence of such a requirement normally negatives it if there were no other indicators of a trust the fact that the transaction contemplates the mingling of money is not necessarily fatal to a trust".

[59] See Goodhart and Jones 43 M.L.R. (1980) 489.

## (C) The Nature of *Quistclose* Trusts

It will be recalled that, in *Barclays Bank v. Quistclose Investments*,[60] Lord Wilberforce analysed the nature of *Quistclose* trusts by reference to primary and secondary trusts, holding that arrangements for the payment of a debtor's creditors by a third party give rise to a relationship of a fiduciary character or trust, in favour, as a primary trust, of the creditors, and secondarily, if the primary trust fails, of the third party. The precise nature of the trusts so identified subsequently caused very considerable controversy and they were variously classified as express trusts, resulting trusts and constructive trusts.[61]

The only normal practical significance of whether a trust is, on the one hand, express or, on the other hand, resulting or constructive is in relation to formal validity and then only in respect of trusts of land or subsisting equitable interests;[62] in this respect it is inconceivable that land could form the subject matter of a *Quistclose* trust and it seems highly unlikely, although not actually impossible, that a subsisting equitable interest could do so either. However, in the case of a *Quistclose* trust, the classification may also be relevant in identifying the location of the beneficial interest while what Lord Wilberforce classified as the primary trust is in existence (there is of course no doubt that the beneficial interest under what he classified as the secondary trust is in the person who advanced the money).

It is of course clear that the beneficial interest under what Lord Wilberforce classified as the primary trust cannot be in the recipient of the money advanced since this would defeat the whole object of the exercise by enabling that money to be claimed by his trustee in bankruptcy. The only other possibilities are that that beneficial interest is in the persons, if any, who will receive the benefit of any payments made pursuant to the specified purpose, that it is in suspense, or that it at all times remains in the person who advanced the money in the first place.

If the primary trust is an express trust, then it would appear to follow that the persons, if any, in whose favour payments can be made pursuant to the specified purpose (in *Barclays Bank v. Quistclose Investments*, the shareholders entitled to the dividend) have the right to call for payment of the sums due to them. In *Re Northern Development Holdings*,[63] Megarry V.-C. regarded the primary trust as an express trust but avoided this conclusion by classifying it as a purpose trust of the type recognised in *Re Denley's Trust Deed*.[64] Even if the decision in the latter case is acceptable in the first place, which is somewhat questionable, this conclusion has the effect of placing the beneficial interest under the primary trust in suspense until payment is either made or becomes impossible. This was indeed recognised in *Carreras Rothmans v. Freeman Matthews Treasure*,[65] by Peter Gibson J. who, although he reached the same conclusion, seems instead to have regarded the primary trust as a constructive trust. It is frankly, difficult to see how a trust which comes into existence

---

[60] [1970] A.C. 567 at 580.
[61] Lord Millett, pre-judicially, 101 L.Q.R. (1985) 269; Rickett 107 L.Q.R. (1991) 608 and in *Equity, Fiduciaries and Trusts 1993* (ed. Waters), p. 325; Chambers, *Resulting Trusts*, Chap. 3; Ho and Smart (2001) 21 O.J.L.S. 267.
[62] See *ante*, pp. 96 *et seq*.
[63] (1978) unreported but see (1985) 101 L.Q.R. 269 at 276–279.
[64] [1969] 1 Ch. 373; *ante*, p. 79.
[65] [1985] Ch. 207.

because of the express or implied intentions of its settlor and/or trustee can be classified as a constructive trust, since such a trust is imposed by the court as a result of the conduct of the trustee and therefore arises quite independently of the intentions of any of the parties.[66] The conclusion that the beneficial interest was in suspense was also one of two alternative views adopted by the Court of Appeal in *Twinsectra v. Yardley*.[67]

The other alternative view adopted by the Court of Appeal in *Twinsectra v. Yardley*,[68] was that there is no trust at all while what Lord Wilberforce classified as the primary trust is in existence; the recipient receives the entire beneficial ownership of the money advanced subject only to a contractual right vested in the person who has advanced it to prevent the recipient using it other than for the specified purpose. If that purpose fails, then, and only then, does a resulting trust in favour of the person who has advanced the money.[69] However, when *Twinsectra v. Yardley* reached the House of Lords, Lord Millett instead adopted the view which he had already advocated pre-judicially[70] and held that the recipient of the money advanced holds it on trust for the person who has advanced it subject to a power vested in the recipient to expend that money for the specified purpose and for no other purposes. He said this:[71]

> "I ... hold the *Quistclose* trust to be an entirely orthodox example of the kind of default trust known as a resulting trust. The lender pays the money to the [recipient] by way of loan, but he does not part with the entire beneficial interest in the money, and insofar as he does not it is held on a resulting trust for the lender from the outset. Contrary to the opinion of the Court of Appeal, it is the [recipient] who has a very limited use of the money, being obliged to apply it for the stated purpose or return it. He has no beneficial interest in the money, which remains throughout in the lender subject only to the [recipient's] power or duty to apply the money in accordance with the lender's instructions. When the purpose fails, the money is returnable to the lender, not under some new trust in his favour which only comes into being on the failure of the purpose, but because the resulting trust in his favour is no longer subject to any power on the part of the [recipient] to make use of the money. Whether the [recipient] is obliged to apply the money for the stated purpose or merely at liberty to do so, and whether the lender can countermand the [recipient's] mandate while it is still capable of being carried out must depend on the circumstances of the particular case."

It should be noted that Lord Millett envisaged that the power vested in the recipient could either be a trust power or a mere power (if the latter, it will clearly be a mere power of a fiduciary nature, given that the recipient is a

---

[66] See *post*, p. 312.
[67] [1999] Lloyd's Rep. Bank. 438 at 456.
[68] [1999] Lloyd's Rep. Bank. 438 at 456.
[69] This is the view of Chambers, *Resulting Trusts*, Chap. 3, based on *Re Drucker* [1902] 2 K.B. 53 at 57, where the property in question was said to be "impressed with a trust — not in the strict sense of the word — but in substance with a quasi-trust that it should be applied" only for the purpose agreed). Compare Ho and Smart: (2001) 21 O.J.L.S. 267.
[70] In 101 L.Q.R. (1985) 269.
[71] [2002] 2 A.C. 164 at 192.

trustee). The power in *Twinsectra v. Yardley* was, however, clearly a mere power and there is no obvious example among the earlier cases where the recipient would have been held to have had a trust power if this analysis had been adopted.

According to Lord Millett's analysis, successive primary and secondary trusts therefore do not arise. There is one trust throughout, a trust in favour of the person who advanced the funds. It has been said that this analysis leads inescapably to the conclusion that *Quistclose* trusts are resulting trusts.[72] This will indeed almost always be the case. If the person advancing the money expressly transferred it to the recipient on the basis that the latter held it on trust for him subject to a power to expend that money for the specified purpose and for no other purposes, the trust so created would obviously be an express trust and there would be no need or room for any resulting trust. In practice, however, it is highly unlikely that there will have been an express agreement in such specific terms and so it is virtually inevitable that the adoption of Lord Millett's analysis will mean that every *Quistclose* trust gives rise to a resulting trust.

### (D) Failure of the Specified Purpose

Almost all the examples of *Quistclose* trusts other than *Twinsectra v. Yardley* concern arrangements made in circumstances in which the recipient of the money advanced was known by the person paying it to be in financial difficulties. In the majority of those cases, the underlying objective of the arrangement was to try to stave off the recipient's bankruptcy while at the same time preventing the money advanced from passing to his creditors in the event of any bankruptcy. For this reason, it seems to have been assumed, without discussion, that in the event of the recipient's bankruptcy the specified purpose will necessarily have failed. However, bankruptcy does not actually prevent the recipient's pre-existing debts being paid with money which, because it is held on trust, does not form part of the bankrupt's assets and so is capable of being used for this purpose.

The reason why this issue has never been raised may be that in the first case to come before the courts, *Barclays Bank v. Quistclose Investments*,[73] the money was in an account with the recipient's bankers, who had purported to exercise their right to set off the credit balance of that account against the much larger amount owed to the bank by the company.[74] The money was therefore simply not available for payment to the company's shareholders at any stage prior to the decision of the House of Lords.

Before *Twinsectra v. Yardley*, the only way of dealing with this issue would presumably have been to have contended that the specified purpose of the primary trust was not only the payment of the recipient's debts but also the prevention of the recipient's bankruptcy. On the alternative view that there was no trust at all until the specified purpose failed, the contractual right vested in the person who advanced the money presumably extended to prevent the recipient from using it after bankruptcy.

---

[72] See Rickett [2002] R.L.R. 112; Yeo and Tho 119 L.Q.R. (2003) 13.
[73] [1970] A.C. 567 at 580.
[74] Banks have a statutory right to amalgamate the balances of the different accounts held with them.

Now, pursuant to Lord Millett's analysis, the recipient of the money advanced holds it on trust for the person who has advanced it subject to a power vested in the recipient to expend that money for the specified purpose and for no other purposes. It is therefore instead presumably necessary to say either that the intention of the parties was that the power should determine in the event of the recipient's bankruptcy or that, following his bankruptcy, as a power held by a fiduciary it cannot be either exercised or released by his trustee in bankruptcy.[75]

It should also be noted that, in the passage set out above, Lord Millett specifically envisaged the possibility of the person who advanced the money having the right to countermand the recipient's mandate, or more technically to revoke his power, in appropriate circumstances. Such an action, where permissible, will of course have exactly the same consequences as the failure of the specified purpose.

## 3. Unexhausted Beneficial Interests

### (A) Failure Wholly to Dispose of the Beneficial Interest

The same principle will be applied where the beneficial interest has not been wholly disposed of. However, it is not applied in all cases.

*Re Gillingham Bus Disaster Fund*[76] concerned an appeal set up in 1951 as a result of the deaths of 24 Cadets in the Royal Marines when a motor vehicle ran into them. The mayors of several boroughs in the area wrote the following letter to *The Daily Telegraph*: "The Mayors have decided to promote a Royal Marine Cadet Memorial Fund to be devoted to defraying funeral expenses, caring for the boys who may be disabled and then to such worthy cause or causes in memory of the boys who lost their lives as the Mayors may determine". This appeal resulted in subscriptions amounting to the then very substantial sum of nearly £9,000 contributed partly by identifiable persons but mainly anonymously as a result of street collections and the like. The trustees spent about £2,500 in fulfilling the objectives set out in the letter and then took out a summons for guidance as to what to do with the surplus.

Harman J. held that the trust could not be classified as charitable; consequently, the surplus had to be held on resulting trust for the donors, even though many of them were in fact anonymous. This conclusion followed naturally from the principle that where money was held upon trust and the trust declared did not exhaust the fund it would revert to the donor or settlor upon a resulting trust. The reasoning behind the application of the principle to these particular facts was that a donor did not part with the money out and out but only to a certain extent, namely with the intention that the wishes contained in his declaration of trust should be carried into effect. It must be emphasised, as Harman J. duly observed, that this doctrine does not rest on any evidence of the state of mind of the donor who in the vast majority of cases of this type will certainly not expect to get his money back under any circumstances. A resulting trust arises even where the donor's expectation has

---

[75] See *Mettoy Pension Trustees v. Evans* [1990] 1 W.L.R. 1587, *ante*, p. 227.

[76] [1958] Ch. 300 (affirmed on points not affecting this aspect of the decision by the Court of Appeal at [1959] Ch. 62; see also *post*, p. 479; Atiyah (1958) 74 L.Q.R. 190. For charitable gifts the position is otherwise; see *post*, p. 482.

been cheated of fruition for some reason which was totally unknown to him or anyone else at the time of the gift; this was indeed the case in *Re Gillingham Bus Disaster Fund*, where the donors' expectations failed because of an inference of law drawn only in the light of the knowledge of events which occurred after they had made their contributions to the fund.

It must be emphasised that the basis of the decision in *Re Gillingham Bus Disaster Fund* was that there was no intention on the part of the donors to part with their money out and out when they contributed it; in particular, such an intention could no more be attributed to the anonymous contributor who had made his gift in response to a street collection than it could to a contributor who was identifiable. As Harman J. said,[77] "I see no reason myself to suppose that the small giver who is anonymous has any wider intention than the large giver who is named. They all give for the one object. If they can be found by inquiry the resulting trust can be executed in their favour. If they cannot I do not see how the money could then change its destination and become *bona vacantia*."[78] Such part of the surplus whose donors could not be identified therefore had to be paid into court to await claims by them under the consequential resulting trusts;[79] most of it is probably still there today!

On the other hand, as the remarks of Harman J. indicate, if it could have been shown that each donor made his gift out and out with no intention of reclaiming it whatever the fate of the appeal might be, the surplus would have belonged to the Crown as *bona vacantia*. There is no doubt that this is a more practicable solution so far as the proceeds of collecting boxes are concerned because it is obviously likely to be a wholly fruitless exercise to try to establish who in fact contributed how many pounds or pence to the collection and is therefore entitled to have his contribution returned — this is of course precisely why most of the surplus had to be paid into court. Doubts have subsequently been expressed as to whether the decision of Harman J. in this respect was correct as a matter of law. In *Re West Sussex Constabulary's Benevolent Fund Trusts*,[80] Goff J. declined to follow *Re Gillingham Bus Disaster Fund*, at any rate so far as concerned the proceeds of collecting boxes. He held that persons who put money into collecting boxes should be taken to have intended to part with the money out and out absolutely in all circumstances; consequently, the Crown was entitled to that money as bona *vacantia* on the later failure of the trusts.

There are admittedly some dicta in other cases which support this view,[81] but they are not particularly weighty because they concerned a rather different question, namely whether the fact that contributions were made by unidentifiable donors to an appeal for charitable purposes indicated an intention to make the gifts outright so as to enable the funds to be applied *cy-près*, that is

---

[77] [1958] Ch. 300 at 314.
[78] In similar circumstances a resulting trust was held to arise in *Re Holbourn Aero Components Air Raid Distress Fund* [1946] Ch. 86 but in that case there was no argument about *bona vacantia*. Compare *Re Hillier's Trusts* [1954] 1 W.L.R. 9, where Upjohn J. held in these circumstances in favour of *bona vacantia* (when the Court of Appeal affirmed this decision at [1954] 1 W.L.R. 700, Denning L.J. approved the formulation of Upjohn J.).
[79] Under Trustee Act 1925, s.63.
[80] [1971] Ch. 1.
[81] *Re Hillier's Trusts* [1954] 1 W.L.R. 700 at 715, *per* Denning L.J.; *Re Welsh Hospital (Netley) Fund* [1921] 1 Ch. 655 at 659, 660, *per* P.O. Lawrence J.; *Re North Devon and Somerset Relief Fund Trusts* [1953] 1 W.L.R. 260 at 1266, 1267, *per* Wynn-Parry J.

to say to other analogous charitable purposes.[82] Neither *Re Gillingham Bus Disaster Fund* nor *Re West Sussex Constabulary's Benevolent Fund Trusts* can therefore be regarded as decisive in this respect and so the question of whether the proceeds of collecting boxes for non-charitable purposes which fail are held on resulting trust or are *bona vacantia* remains to be settled; while, on the one hand, it seems highly artificial to make a distinction between the intention of unidentified donors and that of identified donors, it is on the other hand equally true that the consequences of the existence of a resulting trust are highly inconvenient.

There is, in any event, another essential distinction between the facts of the two decisions. *Re Gillingham Bus Disaster Fund* concerned a fund raised to deal with one particular tragedy, a fund in which none of the contributors had any direct or indirect financial interest (other, of course, than the possibility of recovering any unspent surplus in the event that that surplus was indeed held on resulting trust); the contributors therefore paid their money on an outward looking basis. *Re West Sussex Constabulary's Benevolent Fund Trusts*, on the other hand, concerned a fund for the benefit of the dependants of the members of an unincorporated association and the contributors therefore largely paid their money on an inward looking basis. Further, the fund included not only the proceeds of collecting boxes, the proceeds of entertainments, raffles and sweepstakes, and donations and legacies but also the contributions of past and present members. Goff J. therefore had to deal with many types of contribution which were not present in *Re Gillingham Bus Disaster Fund*.

It has already been seen that he rejected the applicability of the doctrine of resulting trusts to the proceeds of street collections. He took a similar view in respect of the proceeds of entertainments, raffles and sweepstakes, holding that it was not appropriate to apply the doctrine of resulting trusts for two reasons: first, because the relationship was one of contract, not of trust (a contributor paid his money as the price of being entertained or of having his ticket put into the draw and that was precisely what he received); and, secondly, because there was no direct contribution to the fund at all — only the profit, if any, made out of the entertainment or the draw was ultimately received. The distinction thus made between trust and contract certainly seems sound in respect of these sources of funds. Goff J. consequently held that, since it was not appropriate to apply the doctrine of resulting trusts, the proceeds of these sources of funds must also be held for the Crown as *bona vacantia*. However, he held that the donations and legacies were indeed held on resulting trust.

That left the question of the contributions of past and present members, a question which arises whenever the funds of an unincorporated association contain a surplus on its dissolution. Such a surplus can clearly be dealt with in a number of ways. First, it can be regarded as being held on resulting trust for the members of the association in proportion to their contributions to its funds. This was the view taken in *Re Printers' and Transferrers' Society*,[83] where the surplus of the funds of a society which had collected weekly contributions from its members to provide defence and support, and in particular strike and lock-out benefits, for them was divided between those who were members at

---

[82] See *post*, p. 482.
[83] [1899] 2 Ch. 184.

the time of its dissolution in proportion to their contributions. Similarly, in *Re Holbourn Aero Components Air Raid Distress Fund*,[84] a fund established for employees who were on war service or who suffered loss in air raids which was financed by voluntary subscriptions from the employees was divided up between all contributors in proportion to the amount contributed. Secondly, and alternatively, the funds can be regarded as being subject to the contractual rights and liabilities of the members towards one another as members of the association. This was the view taken in *Cunnack v. Edwards*,[85] where it was held that the personal representatives of members of a society founded to provide funds for the widows of the members could not claim a share when the purposes of the society came to an end. The members, in making their contributions to the society, had received all that they had contracted for in the form of pensions for the widows. Consequently, the Crown took the surplus as *bona vacantia*. This was the decision which Goff J. chose to follow and apply in *Re West Sussex Constabulary's Benevolent Fund Trusts*. The therefore held that the contributions of the past and present members were also held for the Crown as *bona vacantia*.

However, it is now generally accepted that the resulting trust approach is normally no longer appropriate in respect of surpluses of the funds of unincorporated associations on their dissolution. It has already been seen[86] that there is now a strong presumption that the funds of an unincorporated association should be regarded as being subject to the contractual rights and liabilities of the members towards one another as members of the association. Consequently, in *Re Bucks Constabulary Fund Friendly Society (No.2)*,[87] Walton J. held that only where the association has become moribund, in that all or all but one of the members have resigned or died, will the assets of the association be held as *bona vacantia* and that in all other circumstances they will be divided equally between the existing members at the time of its dissolution, save where the rules of the association provide for division in some other way. He therefore divided equally between the members alive at the date of dissolution the surplus of a fund established to provide benefits for the members and the dependants of the members of a police force which had been amalgamated with other constabularies. Given that the association in question was a friendly society, this decision can technically be distinguished from that in *Re West Sussex Constabulary's Benevolent Fund Trusts*. However, Walton J. criticised that case and it is tolerably clear that he would have decided it differently, dividing all the funds held by Goff J. to be *bona vacantia* equally between the members of the association; indeed, it is possible that he might also have done the same with the donations and legacies which Goff J. had held to be subject to resulting trusts.

Ever since the decision in *Re Bucks Constabulary Fund Friendly Society (No.2)*, it has generally thought that the view adopted by Walton J., which has been followed and applied,[88] is the most appropriate of the various possibilities

---

[84] [1946] Ch. 86 & 194.
[85] [1896] 2 Ch. 679.
[86] See *ante*, pp. 88–94.
[87] [1979] 1 W.L.R. 936.
[88] In *Re G.K.N. Bolts & Nuts (Automotive Division) Birmingham Works, Sports and Social Club* [1982] 1 W.L.R. 774.

which have been discussed, principally because it is the view which fits most easily with the modern attitude to unincorporated associations in general.[89]

Doubt was, however, cast on the position by the decision in *Davis v. Richards & Wallington Industries*,[90] which concerned the hypothetical situation of a surplus arising in a pension fund whose rules contained no provision as to how that surplus should be dealt with. Scott J. took a view different from that of Walton J., opining that such part of the surplus as represented the employer's contributions would be held on resulting trust for the employer while such part as represented the employees' contributions would be held as *bona vacantia*. He accepted that neither the contractual relationship between employer and employees nor the fact that the employees had obtained everything for which they had contracted necessarily prevented there being a resulting trust in their favour as well. However, for two reasons he held that there was no such trust: first, because no intention could be imputed to the employees that they should receive a surplus greater than they were entitled to receive under the relevant tax legislation; and, secondly, because a resulting trust of their contributions would have been unworkable due to the need to value the benefits received by each employee in order to ascertain his entitlement to the surplus.

However, in *Air Jamaica v. Charlton*,[91] the Privy Council regarded the approach of Scott J. to the imputation of intention as erroneous, saying that it was not obvious that employees should ever be regarded as having no expectation of obtaining a return of excess contributions in the event of a surplus. However, this was no more than a dictum because the Privy Council was actually considering what was to happen to the subject matter of some of the trusts of the pension scheme in question which were void for perpetuity and in such circumstances it was impossible to say that the employees had received everything for which they had contracted anyway. The Privy Council therefore held that the subject matter of the trusts which were void for perpetuity was held on resulting trust for both the employers and the employees in proportion to their respective contributions. These resulting trusts arose by operation of law outside the provisions of the pension scheme and consequently outside the scope of the Jamaican tax legislation, which was therefore irrelevant. Nor did the valuation difficulty which Scott J. had identified apply in the light of the way in which the Privy Council had construed the provisions of the scheme which was before it.

As will be seen in the chapter on pensions trusts, such trusts are subject to many special rules and the treatment of surplus has been and remains a particular problem whose resolution has increasingly been regulated by statute; in any event, only rarely will such trusts not expressly provide what is to happen to any surplus. No provision of any approved pension trust can be void for perpetuity under English law anyway so, while the Privy Council's remarks as to the imputation of intention are clearly relevant to English pension trusts, an English court could not hold that any rights to surplus arose outside the pension scheme; it is therefore not clear whether the relevant English tax legislation could similarly be disregarded.

---

[89] See *ante*, pp. 88–94; see also Gardner [1992] Conv. 41.
[90] [1990] 1 W.L.R. 1511; see Gardner *op. cit.*
[91] [1999] 1 W.L.R. 1399.

Further, and in any event, it is questionable to what extent statutorily regulated pensions trusts can really be regarded as unincorporated associations in the normal sense of that expression. It is therefore unlikely that the decisions in *Davis v. Richards & Wallington Industries* and *Air Jamaica v. Charlton* will have a decisive impact on the earlier authorities. To the extent that they are regarded as relevant, the rejection of *bona vacantia* by the Privy Council is clearly preferable to its adoption by Scott J. It is anyway clear that, however *Air Jamaica v. Canada* is applied, the question of how surpluses in the funds of unincorporated associations should be treated is unlikely to be finally settled until the matter is considered by the Court of Appeal.

Two principal questions thus remain outstanding and both await review at appellate level. First, the question of whether surplus funds of the type considered in *Re Gillingham Bus Disaster Fund*, where no unincorporated association was involved, are held on resulting trust or as *bona vacantia* has still to be clarified in the light of the opposing attitudes adopted in that case and in *Re West Sussex Constabulary's Benevolent Fund Trusts* in this respect. And, secondly, the question of how surpluses in the funds of unincorporated associations on their dissolution should be treated awaits a final decision as to whether or not the resulting trust analysis preferred in the earlier authorities has been finally discredited by the decision in *Re Bucks Constabulary Fund Friendly Society (No.2)*.

## (B) Incomplete Trusts

A resulting trust solution will generally be adopted where the instrument is silent as to the way in which the beneficial interest is to be applied. Thus, if property is settled upon trust to pay the income to a life tenant and the instrument makes no provision for the destination of the property on the death of the life tenant, the trustee will prima facie hold the property on a resulting trust for the settlor or his estate. This occurred in *Re Cochrane*,[92] where, apparently as a result of a blunder by the draftsman, a provision was left out of the instrument so that the funds were not effectively disposed of. In such situations, there is no doubt that the nominated trustee cannot take beneficially moreover, it has been held that he cannot even adduce evidence to that effect.[93]

However, it must be emphasised that the implication of a resulting trust is merely the *prima facie* solution and may well be overridden as a matter of construction of the instrument; the court may be still able to construe the instrument in such a way that the trustee takes beneficially subject to the fulfilment of the trust in favour of the life tenant. So, in *Re Foord*,[94] property was given by will to the testator's sister absolutely on trust to pay his wife an annuity. The income was more than sufficient to meet the annuity and, upon a true construction of the will, the sister was held entitled to the balance. A similar conclusion was arrived at in *Re Andrew's Trust*,[95] where a fund had been subscribed for the education of the children of a distressed clergyman and "not for equal division between them". Kekewich J. held that there was no resulting trust; consequently, after their education had been completed, the

---

[92] [1955] Ch. 309.
[93] *Re Rees' Will Trusts* [1949] Ch. 541.
[94] [1922] 2 Ch. 519.
[95] [1905] 2 Ch. 48.

children were entitled to the balance equally. However, this latter decision is not particularly easy to reconcile with the decision in *Re The Trusts of the Abbott Fund*.[96] There a fund had been subscribed for the maintenance of two dis- tressed ladies and Stirling J. held that on the death of the survivor the balance was held on a resulting trust for the donors. Kekewich J. justified his decision in *Re Andrew's Trust* on the ground that the subscribers parted with their money once and for all when they gave it, the education of the children being merely the motive for their gifts.

While the distinction between these two cases is a very fine one, ultimately the question is one of construction in each case; it is therefore certainly pos- sible that both *Re Andrew's Trust* and *Re The Trusts of the Abbott Fund* may have been right on their particular facts. Precisely this point was made in *Re Osoba*,[97] where gifts had been made to the mother, wife, and daughter of the testator for various purposes which had failed or become exhausted. The Court of Appeal held, on a construction of the will, that these created trusts for the benefit of the beneficiaries and the respective purposes were to be disregarded as no more than expressions of the testator's motives in making the gifts.

## (C) Failure of a Common Purpose

In most cases the parties to a transaction have the same purpose but this is not necessarily so. The question therefore arises as to whether, when two or more persons acquire property each for a separate purpose and one of those pur- poses, previously uncommunicated to the other person(s) fails, a resulting trust arises. The answer appears to be that it does not.

In *Burgess v. Rawnsley*,[98] an elderly widowed couple met and became friendly.[99] The man was the tenant of a house in which he lived in the downstairs flat, the upstairs flat being vacant. Subsequently, they agreed to purchase the house, each of them providing half of the purchase price, and it was conveyed to them as joint tenants. The man bought the house as a matrimonial home in contemplation of marriage, but the woman said that she had intended to live in the upstairs flat and that he had never mentioned marriage to her. They did not in fact marry and she never moved into the house. Later she orally agreed to sell her share in the house to him but then refused to do so. Following his death, his daughter, as administratrix of his estate, claimed that there was a resulting trust of his share in favour of his estate or, alternatively, that the joint tenancy had been severed by the oral agreement to sell. The woman claimed that the house was hers by survivorship.

The Court of Appeal unanimously held that the joint tenancy had been severed. That was of course sufficient to dispose of the case but there was a difference of opinion as to whether there was also a resulting trust. Browne L.J. and Sir John Pennycuick held that, since the man alone had entered into the

---

[96] [1900] 2 Ch. 326. In *Re West Sussex Constabulary's Benevolent Fund Trusts* [1971] Ch. 1, it was held that *Re The Trusts of the Abbott Fund* was indistinguishable with regard to funds derived from donations and legacies from identified persons. For discussion of other aspects of *Re West Sussex Constabulary's Benevolent Fund Trusts*, see *ante*, p. 302.

[97] [1979] 1 W.L.R. 247.

[98] [1975] Ch. 429.

[99] Apparently despite the fact that, according to her evidence, "he looked like a tramp" and "had been picking up fag-ends".

conveyance in contemplation of marriage and he had not communicated that purpose to the woman, there was no common purpose which could fail so as to give rise to a resulting trust. On the other hand, Lord Denning M.R. considered that, where parties contemplate different objects both of which fail, the position is the same as where their common object fails; consequently, in such circumstances, the property is held on resulting trust for the parties in proportion to their payments. The view of the majority seems to be more logical.

## (D) Termination

It has been seen that a resulting trust comes into existence whenever there is a gap in the beneficial ownership. Accordingly, as was held in *Re Vandervell's Trusts (No.2)*,[1] when that gap is filled by someone becoming beneficially entitled, or where a trust is expressly declared, the resulting trust comes to an end.[2]

### 4. Bona Vacantia *Arising on Intestacy*

It has already been seen[3] that, where a beneficial interest has not been wholly disposed of, the property in question will in some circumstances be applied as *bona vacantia* rather than subject to a resulting trust. The doctrine of *bona vacantia* is also relevant where a beneficiary who is entitled to property dies wholly or partially intestate without any intestate successors. In these circumstances, it used to be necessary to distinguish between two classes of case: first, where the property is vested in trustees and, secondly, where it is vested in executors.

## (A) Trustees

If property is vested in trustees upon trust absolutely for a beneficiary who is living when the interest takes effect and the beneficiary then dies intestate leaving no one entitled to take as his intestate successor, there cannot possibly be a resulting trust because the beneficial interest will have effectively vested in the beneficiary during his lifetime.

Where the property in question is personalty, it is clearly established that in such circumstances the beneficial interest belongs to the Crown as *bona vacantia*; it has no owner and must devolve accordingly. This has always been the law.

Where, on the other hand, the property in question is realty, the position was at one time different. The law used to be that the trustee took it beneficially because the Court of Chancery did not apply the law of escheat to interests in real property. However, the law was changed first by the Intestates Estates Act 1884[4] and then by the Administration of Estates Act 1925; consequently, if a person dies after 1925 without testate or intestate successors, his real estate, like his personal estate, will go as *bona vacantia* to the Crown.[5]

---

[1] [1974] Ch. 269. The facts are stated *ante*, p. 108.
[2] *ibid.* at 320. No consideration was given as to the question of whether the equitable interest under the resulting trust should have been disposed of by writing in accordance with Law of Property Act 1925, s.53(1)(c); see *ante*, p. 96.
[3] See *ante*, pp. 300–305.
[4] ss.4, 7.
[5] Administration of Estates Act 1925, ss.45, 46.

## (B) Executors

So far as vesting of property in executors is concerned, the position at law at one time was that, if a testator died without having disposed of his residuary estate, his executors were entitled to it if the residue was personal estate or to the extent to which it consisted of personalty. Further, equity followed the rule of common law unless it was shown, on a true construction of the will, that the testator intended to exclude the executors from taking a benefit; if such an intention could be shown, they would of course hold as trustees for the testator's statutory next-of-kin.[6]

However, the law was changed by the Executors Act 1830, which provided that executors should hold as trustees for the next-of-kin unless it could be shown from the will that it was intended they should take beneficially. This statute had the effect of shifting the burden of proof from the next-of-kin to the executors. However, the executors nevertheless remained entitled to the residuary personalty beneficially if there were no next-of-kin. This last loophole was eventually closed by the Administration of Estates Act 1925, which provided that, even in the absence of persons entitled on intestacy, the executors will hold all the undisposed of property of their testator as *bona vacantia*; this rule will only be overridden if the will clearly shows that the executors are to take beneficially.[7]

## VI. RESULTING TRUSTS ARISING AS A RESULT OF VOID OR VOIDABLE TRANSACTIONS

It was mentioned in the introduction to this chapter that it has sometimes been contended[8] that resulting trusts can also arise as a result of a transfer of property which is either void *ab initio* or voidable and effectively avoided. Such contentions have been made in order to enable the transferor to assert that he has retained a sufficient equitable proprietary interest in the property transferred to be able to bring an equitable proprietary claim in respect of that property against the transferee or anyone claiming that property through him. A successful claim of this nature will enable the transferor to obtain an enhanced measure of recovery in one or more of the following ways: first, by obtaining priority over the general creditors of the transferee;[9] secondly, by recovering any increase in the value of the property transferred;[10] and, thirdly, by recovering compound rather than simple interest.[11] It will also enable the transferor to seek the imposition of personal liability on the transferee, his successors in title, or his agents by virtue of the fact that one or more of them has knowingly received property which has been transferred in breach of trust[12] or has dishonestly assisted in a breach of trust.[13]

Where a transfer of property is void *ab initio* for some reason such as

---

[6] See *ante*, p. 46.
[7] ss.46, 49.
[8] See Chambers, *Resulting Trusts* (1997) *passim*. The authorities are discussed *infra*.
[9] As in *Chase Manhattan Bank v. Israel-British Bank (London)* [1981] Ch. 105.
[10] As in *Papamichael v. National WestminsterBank* [2003] 1 Lloyd's Rep. 341.
[11] As in *Westdeutsche Landesbank Girozentrale v. Islington L.B.C.* [1996] A.C. 669.
[12] As in *El Ajou v. Dollar Land Holdings* [1993] 3 All E.R. 717 (Ch.D.), [1994] 2 All E.R. 685 (C.A.).
[13] As in *Papamichael v. National WestminsterBank* [2003] 1 Lloyd's Rep. 341.

illegality, mistake or lack of capacity of the transferor, no title will generally have passed to the transferee; in that case the transferor will not need any trust as a prerequisite of asserting his title. Only where title has nevertheless passed to the transferee because the property in question was or has subsequently been turned into money is a trust necessary and in such circumstances the fact that title has passed will mean that any trust will need to be imposed rather than implied; consequently, any trust which arises in such circumstances will necessarily be a constructive trust rather than a resulting trust. Further, neither type of trust can arise where title has passed to the transferee under a transaction which is within the capacity of the transferor but beyond the capacity of the transferee. This was specifically held by the House of Lords in *Westdeutsche Landesbank Girozentrale v. Islington L.B.C.*,[14] reversing the earlier decision of the House in *Sinclair v. Brougham*,[15] where the existence of such trusts in circumstances of this type had been upheld.[16]

Controversy therefore remains only in respect of transfers of property which are voidable. In *El Ajou v. Dollar Land Holdings*,[17] Millett J. held that persons who had been induced by fraudulent misrepresentations to purchase shares were "entitled to rescind the transaction and revest the equitable title to the purchase money in themselves, at least to the extent necessary to support an equitable tracing claim", stating that "the trust which is operating in these cases is not some new model remedial constructive trust, but an old fashioned institutional resulting trust".[18] The judge has confirmed this view extra-judicially,[19] stating that, "where the plaintiff pays away his money by a valid payment, fully intending to part with the beneficial interest to the recipient, but his intention is vitiated by some factor such as fraud, misrepresentation, mistake and so on ..., the beneficial interest passes, but the plaintiff has the right to elect whether to affirm the transaction or rescind it. If he elects to rescind it, it is usually assumed that the beneficial title revests in the plaintiff, and the authorities suggest that it does so retrospectively."

Earlier, in *Chase Manhattan Bank v. Israel-British Bank (London)*[20] Goulding J. had held that a New York bank which had, as the result of a clerical error, made twice rather than once a payment of US$2,000,000 to a London bank had at all times retained a beneficial interest in the sum overpaid under a trust, presumably a resulting trust. This decision was expressly applied by Cooke P. in the Court of Appeal of New Zealand in *Liggett v. Kensington*,[21] where he held that the mistaken belief of the purchasers of "non-allocated" bullion that they were acquiring gold, not merely contractual rights, from their gold-dealer meant that they had throughout retained an equitable proprietary interest in their purchase moneys. This point did not arise when the case reached the

---

[14] [1996] A.C. 669.
[15] [1914] A.C. 398.
[16] Viscount Haldane L.C. and Lord Atkinson held "a resulting trust, not of an active character" had arisen, while Lord Parker of Waddington instead held that a constructive trust had arisen. Lord Sumner held that there was a trust but did not specify its type. Lord Dunedin did not find a trust at all.
[17] [1993] 3 All E.R. 717, affirmed by the Court of Appeal without discussion of this particular point [1994] 2 All E.R. 685. See *post*, p. 393.
[18] [1993] 3 All E.R. 717 at 734.
[19] 114 L.Q.R. (1998) 399 at 416.
[20] [1981] Ch. 105.
[21] [1993] 1 N.Z.L.R. 257.

Privy Council under the name of *Re Goldcorp Exchange*,[22] but Lord Mustill declined to express an opinion as to whether or not *Chase Manhattan Bank v. Israel-British Bank* had been correctly decided.[23] His clear doubts in this respect were confirmed in *Westdeutsche Landesbank Girozentale v. Islington L.B.C.*[24] by Lord Browne-Wilkinson, who specifically stated that he did not accept the reasoning of Goulding J. He said that "the mere receipt of the moneys, in ignorance of the mistake, gives rise to no trust"; however, he went on to say that "the retention of the moneys after the recipient bank learned of the mistake may well have given rise to a constructive trust". Lord Millett has also stated, extra-judicially,[25] that he considers that *Chase Manhattan Bank v. Israel-British Bank* was wrongly decided.

All these issues arose in the Commercial Court in *Papamichael v. National Westminster Bank*.[26] The claimant's husband deposited 2 billion Greek drachmas of the claimant's money with the bank; it was, as intended by everyone involved, converted into dollars, producing about US$6.5 million. The claimant thought that the dollars had been placed on fixed term deposit with the bank. However, unknown to her, her husband had fraudulently arranged for the dollars to be used as security for the operation by the bank of a foreign exchange margin account for his benefit. This account traded unsuccessfully and most of the dollars were lost. It was held that the claimant was entitled to the recovery of the 2 billion drachmas from the bank on the basis that she had been under a mistake of fact as to what would happen to that sum once it had been paid to the bank. However, because the drachma had depreciated by about 20 per cent as against the dollar during what she thought was the term of the fixed deposit, she was interested in recovering the US$6.5 million instead. This was only possible if the bank held the dollars on some form of trust for her.

In this respect, the judge[27] held that such a trust arose for three different reasons, two of which are relevant for present purposes: first, because the bank had received the dollars with knowledge of the claimant's mistake (in this respect, he relied on the explanation given by Lord Browne-Wilkinson of the decision in *Chase Manhattan Bank v. Israel-British Bank* and therefore on a constructive trust); and, secondly, because the husband had obtained the dollars as a result of fraudulent conduct of which the bank was aware. In the latter respect, the judge held that Lord Millett's statement in *El Ajou v. Dollar Land Holdings*,[28] that "the trust which is operating in these cases is ... an old fashioned institutional resulting trust"[29] was "all very well, but Lord Browne-Wilkinson was specific in saying [in *Westdeutsche Landesbank Girozentale v. Islington L.B.C.*] that what was being imposed was an institutional constructive trust not a resulting trust". The judge therefore proceeded on the basis that both these trusts were constructive trusts rather than resulting trusts. He then

---

[22] [1995] 1 A.C. 74.
[23] *ibid.* at 103.
[24] [1996] A.C. 669.
[25] 114 L.Q.R. [1998] 399 at 412–413.
[26] [2003] 1 Lloyd's Rep. 341.
[27] Judge Chambers Q.C., sitting as a Judge of the Commercial Court.
[28] [1993] 3 All E.R. 717, affirmed by the Court of Appeal without discussion of this particular point [1994] 2 All E.R. 685. See *post*, p. 393.
[29] [1993] 3 All E.R. 717 at 734.

went on to hold that the bank was liable to account to the claimant for the whole of the dollars because it had dishonestly assisted in a breach of those trusts.[30]

This decision is contrary to, and therefore inconsistent with, the view expressed by Lord Millett that, where a transfer of property is voidable and is effectively avoided, beneficial title to that property revests in the transferor under a resulting trust. While it is obviously highly unlikely that the last has yet been heard of Lord Millett's views, it therefore seems, at least for the moment, more appropriate to regard any trusts which arise as a result of a voidable transfer of property as constructive trusts rather than as resulting trusts.

---

[30] See *post*, p. 374.

CHAPTER 10

# CONSTRUCTIVE TRUSTS[1]

## I. INTRODUCTION[2]

### 1. *The Nature of Constructive Trusts*

CONSTRUCTIVE trusts arise by operation of law. Unlike all other trusts, a constructive trust is imposed by the court as a result of the conduct of the trustee and therefore arises quite independently of the intention of any of the parties. Exactly which trusts fall within this definition cannot be stated with the same precision. As Edmund Davies L.J. remarked in *Carl-Zeiss Stiftung v. Herbert Smith (No.2)*,[3] "English law provides no clear and all-embracing definition of a constructive trust. Its boundaries have been left perhaps deliberately vague, so as not to restrict the court by technicalities in deciding what the justice of a particular case may demand." Judges have preferred to describe constructive trusts rather than to define them; thus Deane J. in *Muschinski v. Dodds*[4] described the constructive trust as "a remedial institution which equity imposes regardless of actual or presumed agreement or intention (and subsequently protects) to preclude the retention or assertion of beneficial ownership to property to the extent that such retention or assertion would be contrary to equitable principle". Lord Millett has stated that a constructive trust "arises by operation of law whenever the circumstances are such that it would be unconscionable for the owner of property (usually but not necessarily the legal estate) to assert his own beneficial interest in the property and deny the beneficial interest of another".[5]

The lack of a precise definition makes it difficult to determine precisely what trusts may properly be classified as constructive trusts. The line of distinction between express and constructive trusts has been blurred by the fact that, until the enactment of the Limitation Act 1939, express trustees were unable to rely

---

[1] Oakley, *Constructive Trusts* (3rd ed., 1997; 4th ed., 2004, forthcoming) deals specifically with this topic, as do Elias, *Explaining Constructive Trusts* (1990); Cope, *Constructive Trusts* (1992; 2nd ed. forthcoming); Wright, *The Remedial Constructive Trust* (1998).

[2] See, in addition to the introductory sections of the works cited above Scott (1955) 71 L.Q.R. 39; Waters in *Equity and Contemporary Legal Developments* (ed. Goldstein, 1992), p. 457; Goff & Jones, *The Law of Restitution* (6th ed., 2002), Chap. 2.

[3] [1969] 2 Ch. 276 at 300.

[4] (1985) 62 A.L.R. 429 at 451 (High Court of Australia).

[5] *Paragon Finance v. D.B. Thakerar & Co.* [1999] 1 All E.R. 400 at 408. Millett L.J., as he then was, accepted that a constructive trust will arise outside the scope of this description where "the defendant has assumed the duties of a trustee by a lawful transaction which was independent of and preceded the breach of trust and is not impeached by the plaintiff".

on the Statutes of Limitation as against the beneficiaries whereas the limitation period ran in favour of potential constructive trustees; this encouraged the courts to classify as express trusts certain trusts which were clearly nothing of the sort.[6] There has also been, historically, some confusion between resulting trusts and constructive trusts and, as has already been seen,[7] some judges have continued to use the terms almost interchangeably when endeavouring to establish the existence and extent of beneficial ownership of residential family property.[8]

However, some classifications are well established, long settled, and generally agreed. All the commentators accept that the following three situations give rise to the imposition of a constructive trust: first, where advantages have been obtained by fiduciaries breaching their duty of loyalty;[9] secondly, where there has been a disposition of trust property in breach of trust;[10] and, thirdly, where advantages have been obtained by fraudulent or unconscionable conduct.[11] However, there are certain other types of trust whose classification is more controversial. Such trusts include secret trusts,[12] mutual wills,[13] and the trusts which arise as a result of the creation of contracts of sale which are specifically enforceable,[14] as a result of the exercise by mortgagees of their powers under their mortgage,[15] and in order to give effect in equity to transfers of property which are at law incomplete.[16] These types of trust are extremely difficult to classify and have been classified in many different ways by different commentators. It is, however, suggested that all these types of trusts other than secret trusts should properly be classified as constructive trusts.

The imposition of a constructive trust potentially produces liabilities both of a proprietary and of a personal nature for the constructive trustee. Given the inherent nature of a trust as a relationship in respect of property, the imposition of a constructive trust necessarily confers on the beneficiary proprietary rights in the subject matter of the constructive trust, while the constructive trustee is necessarily subject to the liability which is imposed on every trustee to account personally to his beneficiary for his actions as trustee. However, the court is able to specify the precise moment at which the constructive trust takes effect and, consequently, the moment at which these proprietary rights and fiduciary obligations come into existence. As Millett J. observed in *Lonhro Plc v. Fayed (No.2)*,[17] "it is a mistake to suppose that in every situation in which a constructive trust arises the legal owner is necessarily subject to all the fiduciary obligations and disabilities of an express trustee".

It might be expected to follow from the inherent nature of a trust that a constructive trust can only be imposed if there is some identifiable property upon which to impose it, in other words that the property which is the subject

---

[6] See *Soar v. Ashwell* (1893) 2 Q.B. 390; *Paragon Finance v. D.B. Thakerar & Co.* [1999] 1 All E.R. 400.
[7] See *ante*, p. 43.
[8] See *Hussey v. Palmer* [1972] 1 W.L.R. 1286 at 1289.
[9] See Section II of this Chapter, *post*, p. 330.
[10] See Section III of this Chapter, *post*, p. 370.
[11] See Section IV of this Chapter, *post*, p. 407.
[12] See *ante*, p. 114.
[13] See Section V of this Chapter, *post*, p. 430.
[14] See Section VI of this Chapter, *post*, p. 438.
[15] See Section VII of this Chapter, *post*, p. 440.
[16] See *ante*, p. 143 and Section VIII of this Chapter, *post*, p. 440.
[17] [1992] 1 W.L.R. 1 at 12.

matter of the trust must be able to be identified in the hands of the constructive trustee, either at the time when the matter is brought before the courts or at some earlier stage. There has long been authority for this proposition[18] and it does indeed now seem to be accepted that it is inappropriate to use the expressions "constructive trust" or "constructive trustee" except in relation to identifiable property.[19]

However, when liability is imposed upon a person who has in one way or another dishonestly assisted in bringing about a disposition of trust property in breach of trust,[20] such a person is often said to be a constructive trustee whether or not any of the property disposed of in breach of trust has ever been in that person's hands. The existence of authorities in which this has been said has led some commentators to contend that there is a second type of constructive trust which can arise without any necessity for there to be any identifiable trust property;[21] indeed, in *Westdeutsche Landesbank Girozentrale v. Islington L.B.C.*,[22] Lord Browne-Wilkinson specifically said that the "only apparent exception" to the rule that there must be identifiable trust property "is a constructive trust imposed on a person who dishonestly assists in a breach of trust". No proprietary rights can conceivably be acquired by anyone beneficially entitled under a trust without identifiable property. Consequently, the existence of "this apparent exception" does not serve any obvious purpose; what is the point of creating an exception to the general rule requiring identifiable trust property if the exception so created does not enjoy the principal advantage conferred by the existence of a trust in the first place? The best which can be said for this alleged second type of constructive trust is that it is "a fiction which provides a useful remedy where no remedy is available in contract or in tort".[23]

In any event, the opposing view, that the imposition of this kind of liability does not give rise to the imposition of a constructive trust, is now increasingly prevalent. In *Dubai Aluminium Co. v. Salaam*,[24] Lord Millett, building on earlier observations which he had made both judicially[25] and extra-judicially,[26] said:

> "Equity gives relief against fraud by making any person sufficiently implicated in the fraud accountable in equity. In such a case he is traditionally (and I have suggested unfortunately) described as a 'constructive trustee' and is said to be 'liable to account as a constructive trustee'. But he is not in fact a trustee at all, even though he may be liable to account as if he were. He never claims to assume the position of trustee on behalf of others, and he may be liable without ever receiving or handling the trust property. ... In this second class of case the expressions 'constructive

---

[18] *Re Barney* [1892] 2 Ch. 265 at 273.
[19] See the remarks of Lord Millett in *Dubai Aluminium Co. v. Salaam* [2002] 3 W.L.R. 1913.
[20] See Section III of this Chapter, *post*, p. 319.
[21] See Ford & Lee, *op.cit.*, para. 22020 and previous editions of Hayton & Marshall, *op.cit.* (e.g. the 9th ed., 1991, pp. 440–441).
[22] [1996] A.C. 669 at 705.
[23] Hayton (1985) 27 Malaya Law Review 313, 314.
[24] [2002] 3 W.L.R. 1913 at 1946.
[25] As Millett J. in *Agip (Africa) v. Jackson* [1990] Ch. 265 at 291.
[26] In, among other places, 114 L.Q.R. (1998) 399 at 399–400.

trust' and 'constructive trustee' create a trap. ... The expressions are 'nothing more than a formula for equitable relief'[27] ... I think that we should now discard the words 'accountable as constructive trustee' in this context and substitute the words 'accountable in equity'."

Lord Millett's terminology is clearly preferable and it is to be hoped that it is universally adopted. That does not alter the fact that it is convenient to deal with the liability imposed upon a person who has dishonestly assisted in bringing about a disposition of trust property in breach of trust at the same time as other liabilities which on any view give rise to the imposition of a constructive trust;[28] this is because virtually all the authorities concern attempts to impose both types of liabilities, although not necessarily on the same defendants. For that reason, both are considered in this chapter.[29]

## 2. The Effect of the Imposition of a Constructive Trust[30]

### (A) When Does a Constructive Trust Take Effect?

It is important to know at precisely what moment a constructive trust takes effect for a number of reasons. The moment at which the constructive trust takes effect will determine the extent to which the rights of the constructive beneficiary will be binding upon third parties, whether the general creditors of the constructive trustee or any person to whom the property which forms the subject matter of the constructive trust has been transferred. Further, as from the moment at which the constructive trust takes effect, the constructive beneficiary will be entitled to any income or other fruits produced by the property which forms the subject matter of the constructive trust.

It seems to be generally accepted that, in the absence of any judicial order to the contrary, a constructive trust will take effect from the moment at which the conduct which has given rise to its imposition occurs. This was specifically held by Browne-Wilkinson J. in *Re Sharpe (a Bankrupt)*[31] and has been assumed without discussion on many other occasions. It is for this reason that the interest of a beneficiary under a constructive trust is binding on the trustee in bankruptcy of the constructive trustee and takes priority over the claims of his general creditors;[32] such an interest is also capable of taking priority over third party purchasers of the property or interests in that property[33] provided that the third party in question has not taken free of the beneficial interest in question.[34] Further, any order that the constructive trustee should account for

---

[27] Referring to *Selangor United Rubber Co. v. Cradock (No.3)* [1968] 1 W.L.R. 1555 at 1582, *per* Ungoed-Thomas J.

[28] In particular, liability for receiving trust property with knowledge that it was being transferred in breach of trust.

[29] See Section III of this Chapter, *post*, p. 370.

[30] See *Equity and Contemporary Legal Developments* (ed. Goldstein, 1992) p. 427.

[31] [1980] 1 W.L.R. 219 at 225.

[32] As was held in *Re Sharpe (a Bankrupt)* [1980] 1 W.L.R. 219 at 225. See particularly *Re Polly Peck (No.2)* [1998] 3 All E.R. 812 at 827, where the Court of Appeal specifically held that one particular type of constructive trust (a remedial constructive trust) cannot be imposed if the effect of its imposition is to modify the statutory scheme establishing the order in which the assets of a bankrupt or insolvent person are to be distributed to his creditors; see *post*, p. 325.

[33] As in *Belmont Finance Corporation v. Williams Furniture (No.2)* [1980] 1 All E.R. 393.

[34] As in *Thompson's Trustee v. Heaton* [1974] 1 W.L.R. 605.

income or profits has effect as from the date upon which the constructive trust took effect.[35] Since the vast majority of constructive trusts are imposed because of the circumstances in which the constructive trustee has acquired the property which forms the subject matter of the constructive trust, that trust will therefore normally take effect from the moment at which the constructive trustee acquires the property in question. However, this is not an absolute rule; there are circumstances in which the conduct which has given rise to the imposition of a constructive trust occurs only some time after the acquisition of the property by the constructive trustee.[36] In this case, consistent with the general rule, the constructive trust will obviously only take effect from the moment at which that conduct occurred.

It is anyway clear that the general rule is capable of being varied by the court in any individual case. The court is free to specify the precise moment at which the constructive trust takes effect and can therefore modify the effect of its imposition both on third parties and on the constructive trustee himself. Thus, in *Muschinski v. Dodds*,[37] the High Court of Australia imposed a constructive trust to give effect to a variation in the beneficial interests in property purchased by an unmarried couple but expressly held that, in order to avoid any possible prejudice to third parties, the constructive trust imposed in that case would take effect only as from the date of the publication of the judgments. In the same sort of way, in *Lonhro v. Fayed (No.2)*,[38] Millett J. stated that, in the event that the victim of a fraudulent misrepresentation elects to avoid the contract, the representor thereafter holds its subject matter on constructive trust for that victim but is not retrospectively subject to all the fiduciary obligations of an express trustee in respect of the period before the contract was avoided. These statements merely re-emphasise the universality of the general rule.

### (B) How Does a Constructive Trust Take Effect?

Whether or not a constructive trust can only take effect as the result of a court order providing for its imposition is a question. The question has not as yet had to be decided definitively in any English case and there is some disagreement between the commentators as to the effect of the decisions in other jurisdictions.[39]

This question was considered in *Chase Manhattan Bank v. Israel (British) Bank*[40] by Goulding J., who held that, at least under the law of the State of New York (with which the case was primarily concerned), a court order is not necessary. This view was also adopted by a bare majority of the Supreme Court of Canada in *Rawluk v. Rawluk*.[41] These decisions were unquestionably influenced by the fact that, as will be seen later in this section,[42] the common law jurisdictions of both the United States of America and Canada recognise

---

[35] As in *Boardman v. Phipps* [1967] 2 A.C. 46.
[36] As in *Bannister v. Bannister* [1948] W.N. 261; *Lyus v. Prowsa Developments* [1982] 2 All E.R. 953; *Ungurian v. Lesnoff* [1989] Ch. 206.
[37] (1986) 160 C.L.R. 583.
[38] [1992] 1 W.L.R. 1 at 11–12.
[39] The principal disagreement is between the two principal American practitioners works, *Scott on Trusts* and *Bogert: Trusts and Trustees*.
[40] [1981] Ch. 105 *passim*.
[41] (1990) 65 D.L.R. (4th) 161.
[42] See *post*, p. 322.

the constructive trust as a general equitable remedy, something which English law has so far declined to do. Further, doubt has now been cast on these decisions anyway by the subsequent highly controversial decision of the United States Federal Court of Appeals in *Re Omegas Group*,[43] also considered later in this section,[44] that the imposition of a constructive trust does not, as a matter of American bankruptcy law, give the beneficiary priority over the general creditors of a constructive trustee who is already bankrupt.

Consequently, it is suggested that, at least in this jurisdiction, the better view is that a constructive trust should be able to take effect only as the result of a court order. The manner in which this question is resolved does not in any way affect priorities as between the beneficiary and third parties but may affect the fiscal position of the beneficiary; if a constructive trust can take effect without any need for a court order, the beneficiary may find himself liable to income tax and capital gains tax on an interest arising under a constructive trust which he has never claimed and never enjoyed. It is therefore very much to the advantage of the beneficiary that a constructive trust should not be able to take effect without a court order.

### (C) The Position of the Constructive Beneficiary

As has already been seen,[45] the interest of a beneficiary under a constructive trust is binding on the trustee in bankruptcy of the constructive trustee and takes priority over the claims of his general creditors; this is the case whether the constructive trustee is already bankrupt at the relevant time or becomes bankrupt thereafter.[46]

### (1) The distinct proprietary and personal liabilities of the constructive trustee

The position of the constructive beneficiary who chooses to rely on his proprietary rights will obviously primarily depend on the precise nature of the constructive trust which has been imposed; he will clearly have the rights appropriate to the interest in the trust property to which he has been held to be entitled.

1.  In the event that the beneficiary is held to have an absolute interest in the property in question, he will obviously be entitled to call for the transfer of that property to him together with any income or other fruits which the property has produced since the moment at which the constructive trust took effect.[47]

2.  In the event that the beneficiary is held to have some lesser interest, his position, at least in relation to the property in question, will be exactly the same as if that interest had been expressly created. Thus,

---

[43] (1994) 16 Fed. 3d. 1443.
[44] See *post*, p. 324.
[45] See *ante*, p. 315.
[46] This may no longer be the position in the common law jurisdictions of the United States of America; see *Re Omega Group* (1994) 16 Fed. 3d. 1443, *supra* and *post*, p. 324.
[47] See *Re Duke of Marlborough* [1894] 2 Ch. 133; *Re Macadam* [1946] Ch. 73, discussed *post*, p. 736; *Williams v. Barton* [1927] 2 Ch. 9, discussed *post*, p. 343; *Lyell v. Kennedy* (1889) 14 App.Cas. 437, discussed *post*, p. 370; *Belmont Finance Corporation v. Williams Furniture (No.2)* [1980] 1 All E.R. 393, discussed *post*, p. 397.

where the beneficiary of a constructive trust is held to have a con-current interest in land,[48] his rights to enforce that interest against a third party or to obtain an order for sale of the property will be determined by exactly the same criteria as apply to a co-ownership which has arisen as the result of an express or statutory trust of land.[49] The position is similar where the beneficiary is held to have a limited interest in land; thus when a constructive trust is imposed to enforce lifetime occupancy rights, the life interest thus conferred on the beneficiary will equally take effect as if it had been expressly created.[50]

3.  It is also possible, although much less common in practice, for the beneficiary to be given an interest by way of lien or charge in order to secure his right to a payment; this has been done[51] to secure a profit made by agents of a trust who utilised confidential income acquired in the course of representing the trust to acquire with their own funds a majority shareholding in a private company of which the trust was a substantial minority shareholder — had the profit not been paid over, the beneficiary, like the holder of any other charge, could have forced a sale of the shares.

If the beneficiary chooses instead to rely on the personal liability of the constructive trustee to account, he will in effect be claiming equitable com-pensation for breach of trust from the constructive trustee. He will thus recover the value of whatever interest he is held to have in the subject matter of the constructive trust, valued as at the moment at which the constructive trust took effect, together with interest thereon. (This is also the remedy, and the only remedy, available where a person is accountable in equity for having dishonestly assisted in bringing about a disposition of trust property in breach of trust, a liability classified by some, it has already been suggested wrongly,[52] as arising under a constructive trust). Since such reliance on the personal lia-bility of the constructive trustee to account is normally[53] alternative to reliance on the beneficiary's proprietary rights, payment by the constructive trustee of the appropriate sum will have the effect of discharging those proprietary

---

[48] By virtue of having made direct or indirect financial or other contributions towards its acqui-sition. See *Burns v. Burns* [1984] Ch. 317 and *Grant v. Edwards* [1986] Ch. 638, discussed *post*, p. 424.

[49] These criteria are now contained in the Trusts of Land and Appointment of Trustees Act 1996.

[50] Under a trust of land pursuant to the Trusts of Land and Appointment of Trustees Act 1996. Prior to this legislation, such a beneficiary would usually become a tenant for life under the Settled Land Act 1925 which had the inconvenient result of conferring on him full adminis-trative powers to deal with the property (see *Ungurian v. Lesnoff* [1990] Ch. 206 and *Costello v. Costello* [1996] 1 F.L.R. 805). However, under the new legislation, these powers remain vested in the constructive trustee.

[51] In *Phipps v. Boardman* [1964] 1 W.L.R 993 (Ch. Div.) — this decision was subsequently affirmed by both appellate courts without any comments being made as to the nature of the constructive trust imposed.

[52] See *ante*, p. 314 and *post*, p. 374.

[53] Save in the unusual situation where the beneficiary seeks to rely on both the remedies available to him. See the next paragraph.

rights; consequently, the constructive trustee will thereafter be absolutely beneficially entitled to the property upon which the constructive trust was imposed.[54]

### (2) The choice of remedy when the property is still in the hands of the constructive trustee

When the property upon which the constructive trust is imposed is still identifiable in the hands of the constructive trustee, the beneficiary will be able to choose either to exercise his proprietary rights or to rely on the personal liability of the constructive trustee to account or, in rare circumstances, to exercise both of these remedies.

Where the constructive trustee is solvent, the election between these two remedies will not normally have any particularly significant effects on the measure of the recovery of the beneficiary.

1. As has already been seen, reliance on his proprietary rights will entitle the beneficiary to recover the appropriate interest in the property together with any income or other fruits which the property has produced since the moment at which the constructive trust took effect, while reliance on the personal liability of the constructive trustee to account will entitle the beneficiary to recover the value of the appropriate interest at the moment at which the constructive trust took effect together with interest thereon.

2. Consequently, if any increase in the value of the property plus the value of any income or other fruits which it has produced is more or less the same as the interest payable on the value of the property since the moment at which the constructive trust took effect, there will be no financial advantage in the beneficiary electing for one remedy rather than for the other. This is only likely not to be the case in the event of a substantial rise or a substantial fall in the value of the property, when it will obviously be to the advantage of the beneficiary to opt respectively for his proprietary rights or for the personal liability of the constructive trustee to account.

3. The only exception to this will be where it can be shown that any fall in the value of the property was the responsibility of the constructive trustee. In this event, there seems no reason why the beneficiary should not alternatively seek to rely on both the remedies available to him; if this is indeed possible, he will be able both to claim the appropriate interest in the property in question and, by relying on the personal liability of the constructive trustee to account, to obtain damages for the fall in value of the property. While this will not of course increase the total measure of recovery, it will enable the beneficiary to recover the property itself. There seems no reason

---

[54] Thus, once the agents of the trust referred to in the previous paragraph had paid their profit to the constructive beneficiary, they would have once again become absolute owners of the shares which they had purchased and could have retained them indefinitely. However, in such circumstances prudence would normally dictate an immediate sale of the shares at that point in order to forestall any possibility of the beneficiary coming back with a claim for future income or capital profits.

whatsoever why such a process should not be possible in an appropriate case.

Where, on the other hand, the constructive trustee is insolvent, the election between the two remedies will be immensely significant.

1.  If the beneficiary chooses to rely on his proprietary rights, he will take priority over the general creditors of the insolvent constructive trustee, whereas if he instead chooses to rely on the personal liability of the constructive trustee to account, he will rank with, rather than ahead of, the general creditors.

2.  Consequently, the only situation in which the beneficiary is likely to choose to rely on the personal liability of the constructive trustee to account will be where the property which is the subject matter of the constructive trust has fallen in value to a percentage of its original value smaller than the percentage which is likely to be paid out by the trustee in bankruptcy to the general creditors.

3.  In such circumstances, in the event that it can be shown that the constructive trustee was responsible for the fall in value of the property, it will always be in the interest of the beneficiary to take advantage of the possibility of relying on both the remedies available to him in order both to recover the appropriate interest in the property in question and to claim damages for the fall in its value; this is because such a double claim will give him both the property and the same percentage of the claim for damages as is paid out to the general creditors.

However, except in the extremely unlikely situation which has just been considered, the beneficiary will, in the event of the insolvency of the constructive trustee, inevitably choose to rely on his proprietary rights so as to obtain priority over the general creditors. This will in turn diminish the mass of general assets available for distribution among the general creditors of the insolvent trustee so that each general creditor will therefore obtain a smaller proportion of the sum owed to him. Thus, the imposition of a constructive trust upon a person who is, or subsequently becomes, bankrupt will almost inevitably prejudice the interests of his general creditors, who will *ex hypothesi* not be before the court to object to the imposition of the constructive trust in question. In such circumstances, the only possibility of avoiding the consequent prejudice to the interests of the general creditors will be for the trustee in bankruptcy of the constructive trustee to go to the court under section 340 of the Insolvency Act 1986[55] in order to seek an order setting aside the constructive trust on the grounds that its imposition has given a preference to the beneficiary. Such a claim was successfully made in *Re Densham (A Bankrupt)*,[56] but, as that case demonstrates, it is often a matter of pure chance whether the

---

[55] See *ante*, p. 255.
[56] [1975] 1 W.L.R. 1519 (this case concerned the previous statutory provision, Bankruptcy Act 1914, s.42).

legislation is applicable and so this possibility cannot be regarded as a substantial safeguard for the interests of the general creditors.

### (3) The choice of remedy when the property is no longer in the hands of the constructive trustee

When the property upon which the constructive trust is imposed is no longer identifiable in the hands of the constructive trustee, the property may nevertheless still be identifiable in the hands of a third party. In such circumstances, it will be possible for the beneficiary to recover the property by following it in equity into the hands of that third party, unless the latter is able to establish one of the accepted defences to the beneficiary's equitable proprietary claims; these include the defence of bona fide purchase for value of a legal interest in the property without notice of the beneficiary's adverse claim (or, in the case of property not subject to the equitable doctrine of notice, the statutory equivalent) and the defence of change of position. Such an equitable proprietary claim is possible because the imposition of a constructive trust gives rise to the relationship of trustee and beneficiary which, on any view, is sufficient to satisfy the prerequisites of such a claim.[57]

Where the trust property can be followed in this way into the hands of a third party, the situation will differ very little from that which has already been discussed. The beneficiary will have a choice between, on the one hand, exercising his proprietary rights in the subject matter of the constructive trust by following that property into the hands of the third party and, on the other hand, relying on the personal liability of the constructive trustee to account. The election between the two remedies will be dependant on exactly the same factors as have already been discussed. Where both the third party and the constructive trustee are solvent, the only relevant factors will be any changes in the value of the property, the presence or absence of income and other fruits, and the amount of interest payable by the constructive trustee. Where, on the other hand, the constructive trustee is insolvent, the beneficiary will almost always choose to rely on his proprietary rights and pursue his equitable proprietary claim against the third party.

It may, on the other hand, not be possible to recover the property upon which the constructive trust has been imposed. This will be the case where the property either has disappeared as the result of casual expenditure or dissipation by the constructive trustee or a third party, or has reached the hands of a third party against whom it is not possible to maintain an equitable proprietary claim because he is able to establish one of the accepted defences to such claims. In such circumstances, the only remedy available to the beneficiary will be to rely on the personal liability of the constructive trustee to account. Where the constructive trustee is solvent, this will not normally produce any particularly significant disadvantage. Where, on the other hand, the constructive trustee is insolvent, the absence of any proprietary rights will prevent the beneficiary from being able to claim priority over the general creditors of the constructive trustee since the liability of the constructive trustee to account will rank with, rather than ahead of, the claims of the general creditors.[58]

---

[57] See *post*, p. 807.
[58] See *Selangor United Rubber Estates v. Cradock (No.3)* [1968] 1 W.L.R. 1555.

**(4) The remedy where there has never been any identifiable property**
It has already been seen[59] that some commentators have contended that there is a second kind of constructive trust, which can arise without any necessity for there to be any identifiable trust property, a view which has received judicial support at the highest level.[60] Constructive trusts of this type allegedly arise where liability is imposed for having dishonestly assisted in a disposition of trust property in breach of trust. It has already been suggested[61] that it is preferable to adopt an alternative view which has also received judicial support at the highest level[62] and instead classify a person upon whom liability is imposed for this reason as being merely accountable in equity to the beneficiaries of the trust in question. However, no matter how this liability is classified, there is no doubt at all about its nature. The absence of any identifiable property prevents any proprietary claim from being available. Consequently, the beneficiaries in question will have no choice of remedy; all that they can do is to rely on the personal liability to account which has been imposed. Their rights will therefore enjoy no priority over the general creditors of the person on whom liability has been imposed and will rank with, rather than ahead of, the claims of those creditors in the event of his insolvency.

### 3. When and on what Grounds will a Constructive Trust be Imposed?

The most important single factor that will determine when, and on what grounds, a constructive trust will be imposed is the role which the courts consider that the constructive trust occupies in the legal system as a whole. Their perception of this role must inevitably take into account the various possible consequences of the imposition of a constructive trust which have just been considered. In this respect, the different common law jurisdictions adopt different approaches.

### (A) The Approach Adopted in the United States of America

**(1) When will a constructive trust be imposed?**
The common law jurisdictions of the United States of America have long regarded the constructive trust as an instrument for remedying unjust enrichment. Thus a constructive trust may be imposed whenever the constructive trustee has been unjustly enriched by receiving some item of property at the expense of the constructive beneficiary. In other words, all that has to be shown is that the constructive trustee has received some item of property which, as against the beneficiary, he cannot justly retain. This does not mean that a constructive trust will be imposed whenever unjust enrichment is found to exist; a constructive trust is merely one of a number of remedies available to the court and will be imposed when the court feels that it is appropriate to give the victim of the unjust enrichment a proprietary remedy. For this reason, this type of constructive trust is generally known as a remedial constructive trust.

---

[59] See *ante*, p. 314.
[60] From Lord Browne-Wilkinson in *Westdeutsche Landesbank Girozentrale v. Islington L.B.C.* [1996] A.C. 669 at 705.
[61] See *ante*, p. 314.
[62] From Lord Millett in *Dubai Aluminium Co. v. Salaam* [2002] 3 W.L.R. 1913 at 1946.

The origin of this view of the constructive trust was *The Restatement of the Law of Restitution* published by the American Law Institute in 1937; paragraph 160 provides: "Where a person holding title to property is subject to an equitable duty to convey it to another on the ground that he would be unjustly enriched if he were permitted to retain it, a constructive trust arises." This provision unquestionably represents the attitude of the judges. As Cardozo J. has remarked:[63] "A constructive trust is the formula through which the conscience of equity finds expression. When property has been acquired in such circumstances that the holder of the legal title may not in good conscience retain the beneficial interest, equity converts him into a trustee." The principle of unjust enrichment is the underlying basis of the "principal types of situations in which a constructive trust is imposed";[64] whether a constructive trust is imposed therefore depends on the presence or absence of unjust enrichment, not on whether the case can be brought within one of the distinct situations which English law recognises as giving rise to the imposition of a constructive trust.

However, the principle of unjust enrichment is not an absolute prerequisite of the imposition of a remedial constructive trust. Such trusts will also be imposed where property is obtained by mistake or by fraud or other wrong, whether or not the constructive trustee has been unjustly enriched.[65] The extent to which such constructive trusts are indeed remedies[66] and the extent to which they are distinguished from both express and resulting trusts is demonstrated by the fact that the constructive trust is not even included within the definition of a trust in *The Restatement of Trusts*; this is of course why constructive trusts are considered in *The Restatement of Restitution* rather than in *The Restatement of Trusts*.

### (2) The effect of the imposition of a constructive trust

In principle, as in this jurisdiction,[67] the imposition of a constructive trust in the common law jurisdictions of the United States of America gives the beneficiary priority over the general creditors of the constructive trustee. The courts of these jurisdictions have for many decades been much more ready than the English courts to interfere with existing third party rights. A claimant is permitted to bring an equitable proprietary claim whenever he can show that that property has been wrongfully disposed of with knowledge of the wrongful nature of the disposition[68] (the existence of a pre-existing equitable proprietary interest is not, as in English law, a prerequisite of such a claim[69]) and, when he is permitted so to do, will inevitably obtain priority over the third party creditors of the other party. The fact that the imposition of a remedial constructive trust brings about a similar alteration of priorities has therefore not been, of itself, a particularly significant consideration.

---

[63] In *Beatty v. Guggenheim Exploration Co.* (1919) 225 N.Y. 380 at 386, 122 N.E. 378 (New York Court of Appeals).

[64] Seavey and Scott (1938) 54 L.Q.R. 29, 42.

[65] *Scott on Trusts* (4th ed., 1989 with cumulative supplements), para. 461.

[66] The remedial theory of the constructive trust is considered in Cope, *op.cit.*, pp. 24–49; Wright, *op.cit. passim*; Rotherham, *Property and Proprietary Remedies* (2002) Chap. 1. See also Birks and Gardner in *Frontiers of Liability* (ed. Birks, 1994), Vol. II, pp. 214, 186.

[67] See *ante*, p. 315.

[68] *American Restatement of the Law of Restitution*, para. 202. See also Scott (1955) 71 L.Q.R. 39, 48.

[69] See *post*, p. 807.

However, in 1994 in *Re Omegas Group*,[70] the Federal Court of Appeals held that a mere entitlement to a beneficial interest under a constructive trust does not, as a matter of American bankruptcy law, give the person entitled to that interest priority over the general creditors of the constructive trustee; such priority only arises where the constructive trust in question has actually been imposed prior to his bankruptcy or insolvency. This decision has been criticised[71] as being contrary both to binding precedent[72] and to the intention of the Bankruptcy Code. However, unless and until it is reversed,[73] its effect is to prevent the general creditors of a bankrupt whom a state court declares to be a constructive trustee from being adversely affected by the imposition of that trust.[74] Consequently, at least for the moment, the imposition of a remedial constructive trust will only adversely affect the third party creditors of the constructive trustee if he is not yet bankrupt at the time; however, if that is the case, its imposition will adversely affect them even if he becomes bankrupt thereafter and even if his bankruptcy occurs as a direct result of the imposition of the constructive trust. This of course makes the effect of the imposition of a constructive trust in the United States of America even more random than it was before.

It obviously remains to be seen whether what has been described[75] as the "unravelling" of the remedial constructive trust in the United States of America as a result of the decision in *Re Omegas Group* is upheld or whether the law reverts to what it was formerly thought to be. However, the imposition of a remedial constructive trust is on any view still clearly capable of affecting the interests of third party creditors.

## (B) The Modified Approach Adopted Elsewhere

Canada and New Zealand have also recognised the possibility of imposing remedial constructive trusts. Some 20 years ago Canada recognised the possibility of doing so on the grounds of unjust enrichment[76] and, although this remains Canadian law, the stated prerequisites for the imposition of a constructive trust on this ground[77] now seem closer to the stricter prerequisite of unconscionability which has been adopted much more recently in New

---

[70] (1994) 16 Fed. 3d. 1443.

[71] Kull (1998) 72 American Bankruptcy L.J. 265.

[72] See the decision of the United States Supreme Court in *Cunningham v. Brown* (1923) 265 U.S. 1 at 11.

[73] In *Re Dow Corning Corp.* (1996) 192 B.R. 428, some of what were described as the "broad statements" in *Re Omegas Group* were said to be "clearly in error" but the bankruptcy judge held that he was bound by the decision in that case.

[74] Bankruptcy is a matter of federal law and will therefore prevail over state law in every bankruptcy court.

[75] By Rotherham, *op.cit.* p. 60.

[76] The Supreme Court of Canada recognized that remedial constructive trusts could be imposed on the grounds of unjust enrichment in *Pettkus v. Becker* (1980) 117 D.L.R. (3d) 257. However, the remedial constructive trust has been deployed principally in relation to joint enterprises by members of a family unit (see *Sorochan v. Sorochan* (1986) 29 D.L.R. (4th) 1; *Peter v. Beblow* (1993) 101 D.L.R. (4th) 621 (also decisions of the Supreme Court of Canada)) but not exclusively so (see *Lac Minerals v. International Corona Resources* (1989) 61 D.L.R. (4th) 14 (Supreme Court of Canada)).

[77] Set out in *Korkontzilas v. Soulas* (1997) 146 D.L.R. (4th) 214 at 231.

Zealand.[78] The difference is that these jurisdictions do not regard remedial constructive trusts as all-embracing; instead they regard remedial constructive trusts as existing side by side with the more traditional situations in which constructive trusts have been imposed.[79]

In none of the cases in which the courts of Canada and New Zealand have imposed remedial constructive trusts have there been genuine third party creditors, as distinct from persons claiming through the constructive trustee, who have been adversely affected by the imposition of the trust. It therefore remains to be seen how those jurisdictions will deal with the issue which the United States Federal Court of Appeals had to decide in *Re Omegas Group*.[80]

### (C) The Approach Adopted in this Jurisdiction

This jurisdiction, like Australia,[81] has not yet accepted the remedial constructive trust as such. The present law is illustrated by the decision of the Court of Appeal in *Halifax Building Society v. Thomas*.[82] The defendant obtained a mortgage advance from the plaintiff by fraudulently misrepresenting his identity and earnings. The plaintiff, having satisfied all sums due to it under the mortgage out of the proceeds of sale, sought to retain the surplus on the basis, *inter alia*, that it was beneficially entitled under a constructive trust imposed on the defendant in accordance with *The American Restatement of Restitution* to prevent what would otherwise be his unjust enrichment. The Court of Appeal specifically held that "English law has not followed other jurisdictions where the constructive trust has become a remedy for unjust enrichment" and declined "to extend the law of constructive trusts in order to prevent a fraudster benefiting from his wrong".[83]

Attempts to introduce the remedial constructive trust into English law had however been made with more success in the years immediately before and after 1970, when it did appear that English law might be moving towards an approach similar to that which was some years later adopted in Canada. At that time, a number of decisions emanating from the Court of Appeal suggested that a constructive trust "is a trust imposed by law whenever justice and good conscience require it ... it is an equitable remedy by which the court can enable an aggrieved party to obtain restitution".[84] However, subsequent

---

[78] The Court of Appeal of New Zealand recognized the possibility of imposing remedial constructive trusts on the grounds of unconscionability in *Fortex Group v. MacIntosh* [1998] 3 N.Z.L.R. 171 but this has so far seems only to have been done in one reported case, in *Commonwealth Reserves 1 v. Chodar* [2001] 2 N.Z.L.R. 374 where such a trust was imposed in order to frustrate attempts to prevent the enforcement of a judgment (see Richardson [2002] T.L.I. 53).

[79] *Korkontzilas v. Soulos* (1997) 146 D.L.R. (4th) 214. The present Canadian law is considered by Chambers in [2001] T.L.I. 214 & [2002] T.L.I. 2.

[80] (1994) 16 Fed. 3d. 1443.

[81] Although the possibility of remedial constructive trusts being accepted in Australia was envisaged by Deane J. in the High Court of Australia in *Muschinski v. Dodds* (1985) 160 C.L.R. 583 at 614–616, this has not yet been done.

[82] [1996] Ch. 217.

[83] At 229. The surplus had anyway been the subject of a confiscation order under Criminal Justice Act 1988, Pt. 6 in favour of the Crown Prosecution Service so the case was effectively between the plaintiff and the Crown Prosecution Service.

[84] *Hussey v. Palmer* [1972] 1 W.L.R. 1286 at 1290, *per* Lord Denning M.R., who was the principal advocate of this particular development.

decisions[85] rejected the approach manifested in this series of cases and English law therefore reverted, at least for the moment, to the traditional attitude towards constructive trusts which has already been described, an attitude which has perhaps been most accurately described by the statement that in England "the constructive trust continues to be seen as an institutional obligation attaching to property in certain specified circumstances".[86]

However, this attitude has not been universally adopted. In *Metall und Rohstoff A.G. v. Donaldson Lufkin & Jenrette*,[87] the Court of Appeal accepted that "there is a good arguable case" that circumstances may arise in which "the court will be prepared to impose a constructive trust *de novo* as a foundation for the grant of equitable remedy by way of account or otherwise", classifying such a trust as a "remedial constructive trust". This isolated remark was subsequently seized on by Lord Browne-Wilkinson in *Westdeutsche Landesbank Girozentrale v. Islington L.B.C.*[88] as a possible justification for a decision[89] that a bank which had received the same sum twice rather than once held the second payment on trust for the mistaken payer; he took the view that "the retention of the moneys after the recipient bank learned of the mistake may well have given rise to a constructive trust"[90] and opined that "the remedial constructive trust, if introduced into English law, may provide a more satisfactory road forward".[91] Similar sentiments have been voiced in Australia.[92]

However, Lord Browne-Wilkinson clearly stated that "whether English law should follow the United States and Canada in adopting the remedial constructive trust will have to be decided in some future case when the point is directly in issue".[93] It has been made abundantly clear by the Court of Appeal on a number of occasions[94] that the contention that English law should adopt the remedial constructive trust cannot be maintained other than in the House of Lords. In *Twinsectra v. Yardley*,[95] counsel for the claimant[96] would have argued for its adoption, admittedly as an argument of last resort, had the House not accepted the existence of a *Quistclose* trust.[97] There can therefore be

---

[85] See *Burns v. Burns* [1984] Ch. 317; *Grant v. Edwards* [1986] Ch. 638; *Ashburn Anstalt v. Arnold* [1989] Ch. 1. This followed earlier rejections by the Court of Appeal of New South Wales in *Allen v. Snyder* [1977] 2 N.S.W.L.R. 685 and by the High Court of New Zealand in *Avondale Printers and Stationers v. Haggie* [1979] 2 N.Z.L.R. 124.

[86] Waters in *Equity and Contemporary Legal Developments* (ed. Goldstein, 1992), pp. 457, 463.

[87] [1990] 1 Q.B. 391 at 479.

[88] [1996] A.C. 669 at 715.

[89] By Goulding J. in *Chase Manhattan Bank v. Israel-British Bank (London)* [1981] Ch. 105; see *ante*, p. 309, *post*, p. 815.

[90] [1996] A.C. 669 at 714. His lordship doubted the conclusion of Goulding J. that a mistaken payment is of itself sufficient to make the recipient a trustee of its subject matter. These remarks were applied and a constructive trust was imposed on this ground in the Commercial Court in *Papamichael v. National Westminster Bank* [2003] 1 Lloyd's Rep. 341. However, this decision is, as a matter of precedent, clearly wrong because of the repeated statements in the Court of Appeal that the remedial constructive trust does not form part of English law and that only the House of Lords can approve such a trust.

[91] [1996] A.C. 669 at 716.

[92] *Muschinski v. Dodds* (1985) 160 C.L.R. 583 at 615 (Deane J. in the High Court of Australia).

[93] [1996] A.C. 669 at 716.

[94] Most recently in *Twinsectra v. Yardley* [1999] Lloyd's Rep. Bank 438 and *Bank of Credit and Commerce International (Overseas) v. Akindele* [2001] Ch. 437.

[95] [2002] 2 A.C. 164.

[96] Who included the author of this edition.

[97] See *ante*, p. 291.

little doubt that the House of Lords will one day soon be called upon to decide whether to return to the trail blazed by the Court of Appeal immediately before and after 1970 or to retain the more traditional approach adopted before and after that period. However, the apparent preparedness of Lord Browne-Wilkinson to consider the adoption of the remedial constructive trust is markedly different from the sentiments which have been expressed by other senior judges. Lord Millett, writing extra-judicially,[98] has described the remedial constructive trust as "a counsel of despair which too readily concedes the impossibility of propounding a general rationale for the availability of proprietary remedies".

There can anyway be little doubt that the future deliberations of the House of Lords will be very heavily influenced by their perception of the effects of the imposition of a remedial constructive trust. All the commentators have thus far assumed that the imposition of such a trust will automatically give the constructive beneficiary priority over the general creditors of the constructive trustee. This was also the assumption of the Court of Appeal in *Re Polly Peck (No.2)*,[99] when it was specifically held that a remedial constructive trust cannot be imposed if the effect of its imposition is to modify the statutory scheme establishing the order in which the assets of a bankrupt or insolvent person are to be distributed to his creditors. This was of course another way of achieving the result arrived at by the United States Federal Court of Appeals in *Re Omegas Group*,[1] where it was actually held that the imposition of a constructive trust did not anyway give priority over the general creditors of a constructive trustee who was already bankrupt. However, Nourse L.J. also stated in *Re Polly Peck (No.2)*[2] that it was not seriously arguable that property rights can be varied by the imposition of a remedial constructive trust even if the potential constructive trustee is solvent; this is the opposite of the result of the decision in *Re Omegas Group*.[3]

As will be seen below, it is not suggested that English law should adopt the position that the effect of a constructive trust differs depending on whether or not the constructive trustee is already bankrupt. The House of Lords should either reject the remedial constructive trust or adopt it with all the usual consequences. However, the outcome of the future deliberations of the House of Lords is certainly not a foregone conclusion.

For the moment, pending the outcome of those deliberations, it is clear that the English courts, like those in Australia, continue to see the constructive trust "as an institutional obligation attaching to property in certain specified circumstances";[4] they have, generally speaking, only been prepared to impose a constructive trust when some cause of action against the constructive trustee has arisen independently. It is not enough to say, as in America, that a constructive trustee "is not compelled to convey the property because he is a constructive trustee; it is because he can be compelled to convey that he is a

---

[98] (1995–96) 6 King's College L.J. 1.
[99] [1998] 3 All E.R. 812 at 827.
[1] (1994) 16 Fed. 3d. 1443.
[2] [1998] 3 All E.R. 812 at 831.
[3] (1994) 16 Fed. 3d. 1443.
[4] Waters in *Equity and Contemporary Legal Developments* (ed. Goldstein, 1992), pp. 457, 463. See also *Re Polly Peck International (No.2)* [1998] 3 All E.R. 812.

constructive trustee".[5] In order to obtain the imposition of a constructive trust, the beneficiary must be able to demonstrate some legal or equitable wrong by the constructive trustee, be it breach of fiduciary duty, participation in a breach of trust, or fraudulent or unconscionable conduct. Such developments in the law as have occurred have been brought about by the enlargement of the concepts of fiduciary relationship[6] and unconscionable conduct rather than by recourse to the principle of unjust enrichment.[7] For the moment, therefore, the unjust enrichment of the constructive trustee is still not in itself sufficient.

### (D) What Should Be the Approach of English Law?

It has long been argued that the English courts should adopt the remedial constructive trust. "What English law needs", wrote Professor Donovan Waters in 1964, "is a practical, down to earth remedy, as vivid as specific performance and injunction, and within which the courts are brought immediately face to face with the policy decisions or the equities that the courts must and do already make or weigh".[8] The adoption of a remedial constructive trust based on the principle of unjust enrichment has, however, been rejected by other commentators.[9] As is implicit in some of the recent judicial observations already considered,[10] there is in principle no reason why the categories of situations in which English courts will impose a constructive trust should be regarded as closed. However, the liabilities which arise as the result of the imposition of a constructive trust provide a strong argument against its use as a general equitable remedy to do justice in the instant case in the way in which it is used in the United States of America.

The proprietary nature of the liabilities which arise as the result of the imposition of a constructive trust affects the existing property rights both of the constructive trustee and, in the event of his bankruptcy, of his general creditors. As a matter of principle, such alterations of existing property rights should not be able to ensue merely from the desire of a court to do justice in the instant case. It has never been the practice of English courts to alter existing property rights merely in order to do justice *inter partes*. The House of Lords has repeatedly stated that rights of property are not to be determined according to what is reasonable and fair or just in all the circumstances,[11] a principle which is crucial for the maintenance of that certainty which should be the hallmark of every system of law. The imposition of a constructive trust in the way that the Court of Appeal did immediately before and immediately after 1970 in order to resolve a dispute in a manner which appears to be just and equitable is inevitably contrary to such a principle. The consequences of

---

[5] *Scott on Trusts* (4th ed., 1987 with cumulative supplements), para. 462.
[6] See section II of this Chapter, *post*, p. 330.
[7] See section IV of this Chapter, *post*, p. 407.
[8] *The Constructive Trust* (1964), p. 73; also in *Frontiers of Liability II* (ed. Birks, 1994) Vol. II, p. 165. See also Wright, *op.cit. passim*; Rotherham, *op.cit.* Chap. 1
[9] See Cope, *op.cit.*, (1992), p. 48 who is, however, prepared to accept that the constructive trust is remedial in nature; Birks in *Frontiers of Liability* (ed. Birks, 1994), Vol. II, pp. 214, 223 who rejects the remedial constructive trust outright as "an object of suspicion" and in [1998] T.L.I. 202 writes of its "end" (compare Wright [1999] R.L.R. 128).
[10] See *ante*, p. 312.
[11] *Pettitt v. Pettitt* [1970] A.C. 777; *Gissing v. Gissing* [1971] A.C. 886; *Lloyds Bank v. Rosset* [1991] 1 A.C. 107.

the imposition of a constructive trust thus constitute powerful arguments against the use of the constructive trust as a means of doing justice *inter partes*.

It has already been seen[12] that in the United States of America these important considerations have until recently borne no weight because the courts of its common law jurisdictions have for many decades been much more ready than the English courts to interfere with existing third party rights. Since the rights of third party creditors are generally susceptible to random alteration by the courts, the fact that the imposition of a constructive trust brings about such an alteration of priorities has not been a particularly significant consideration; there has therefore been no reason why this should have been specifically taken into account in deciding whether or not a constructive trust should be imposed. However, the decision of the Federal Court of Appeals in *Re Omegas Group*[13] means that, at least for the moment, the imposition of a remedial constructive trust will only adversely affect the third party creditors of the constructive trustee if he has not yet become bankrupt at that time, thus making the effect of the imposition of a remedial constructive trust in the United States of America even more random than it was before.

Whether what has been described[14] as the "unravelling" of the remedial constructive trust in the United States of America as a result of this decision is upheld or whether the law reverts to what it was formerly thought to be, it is at any rate clear both that the English courts are reluctant to interfere with existing property rights whether or not their holder is bankrupt and that the imposition of a constructive trust here adversely affects the interests of the general creditors of the constructive trustee whether or not he is already bankrupt. On any view, therefore, the position is totally different in England. Consequently, the fact that the imposition of a constructive trust has these effects should be a much more significant consideration in England than it is in the United States of America. Its far-reaching ramifications not only for the person upon whom it is imposed but also for third parties mean that its indiscriminate invocation and imposition is, at least in England, therefore highly undesirable.

Remedial constructive trusts should therefore not be invoked and imposed in the way that the Court of Appeal did immediately before and immediately after 1970 as some sort of instant remedy to prevent what the court regards as an unjust result in an individual case. In this sense at least, constructive trusts should not be imposed merely in order to prevent unjust enrichment. This does not mean that the present process whereby the principle of unjust enrichment is gradually being incorporated into English law[15] should not continue, merely that the constructive trust is not an appropriate instrument for dealing out justice *inter partes*. It would not become an appropriate instrument even if it were to be held that its imposition did not affect the interests of third party creditors; the random alteration of the property inter-

---

[12] *Ante*, p. 322.
[13] (1994) 16 Fed. 3d. 1443.
[14] By Rotherham, *op.cit.* p. 60.
[15] Most recently in *Lipkin Gorman v. Karpnale* [1991] 2 A.C. 548 (in relation to the defence of change of position); see *post* p. 833 and in *Woolwich Equitable Building Society v. I.R.C.* [1993] A.C. 70 (in relation to the recovery of overpayments of taxes made under statutory instruments subsequently held to be *ultra vires*).

ests of the parties which would be produced by its imposition in order to deal out justice as between them would not be satisfactory either.

Although the categories of situations in which English courts will impose constructive trusts should not be regarded as closed, these categories should be extended only where the courts are prepared to lay down some new principle which will apply generally, as the House of Lords has done on occasions in the past;[16] the principle of unconscionability, so far applicable only in an admittedly increasing number of specific circumstances, could conceivably be converted into a general principle of this type. In any event, no such general principle should be established without the fullest consideration of its probable effects on the interests of third parties and of the possibility of reducing these effects by varying the normal consequences of the imposition of a constructive trust in the way which was done in *Muschinski v. Dodds*[17] and envisaged in *Lonhro v. Fayed (No.2)*;[18] in these respects, different types of constructive trusts should not be held to have different effects on the interests of third parties either generally or just where the constructive trustee happens to be already bankrupt. Finally, any principle laid down must above all be capable of being applied with sufficient certainty to enable litigants to be safely advised as to the probable outcome of legal proceedings.

## II. ADVANTAGES OBTAINED BY FIDUCIARIES BREACHING THEIR DUTY OF LOYALTY

One of the best known situations in which constructive trusts are imposed is where a fiduciary has obtained a benefit as a result of a breach of the duty of loyalty which he owes to his principal.[19]

### 1. *What Relationships will be Classified as Fiduciary?*

In *White v. Jones*,[20] Lord Browne-Wilkinson said that "the paradigm of the circumstances in which equity will find a fiduciary relationship is where one

---

[16] As in *Pettitt v. Pettitt* [1970] A.C. 777; *Gissing v. Gissing* [1971] A.C. 886 and *Lloyds Bank v. Rosset* [1991] 1 A.C. 107.

[17] (1985) 160 C.L.R. 583; see *ante*, p. 316.

[18] [1992] 1 W.L.R. 1.

[19] Of the vast literature on this subject, the most relevant work for present purposes is Goff & Jones, *op.cit.* pp. 707–739. Books include: Finn, *Fiduciary Obligations* (1977), supplemented by his articles in *Equity, Fiduciaries and Trusts* (ed. Youdan, 1989) p. 1, in *Commercial Aspects of Trusts and Fiduciary Obligations* (ed. McKendrick, 1992) p. 9, in (ed. Cope, 1995) p. 131, and in *Trends in Contemporary Trust Law* (ed. Oakley, 1996) 211; Shepherd, *The Law of Fiduciaries* (1981) (also in 97 L.Q.R. (1981) 51); Glover, *Commercial Equity: Fiduciary Relationships* (1995). Other materials include: Austin 6 O.J.L.S. (1986) 444, in *Equity and Commercial Relationships* (ed. Finn, 1987) 177, and in *Trends in Contemporary Trust Law* (ed. Oakley, 1996) 153; Birks, *An Introduction to the Law of Restitution* (1989) 338 & *passim* and [2002] T.L.I. 34; DeMott 30 Osgoode Hall L.J. (1992) 472; Flannigan 9 O.J.L.S. (1989) 285 and 54 Sask.L.R. (1990) 45; Frankel 71 Calif.L.Rev. 795 (1983) and in *Equity, Fiduciaries and Trusts 1993* (ed. Waters, 1993) 173; Maddaugh & McCamus, *The Law of Restitution* (1990) 575–621; Sealy [1962] C.L.J. 69, [1963] C.L.J. 83, [1967] C.L.J. 83, and 9 Journal of Contract Law (1995) 37; Weinrib 25 Univ.Toronto L.J. (1975) 1.

[20] [1995] 2 A.C. 706 at 728.

party, A, has assumed to act in relation to the property or affairs of another, B", while in *Bristol and West Building Society v. Mothew*,[21] Millett L.J. said:

"A fiduciary is someone who has undertaken to act for or on behalf of another in a particular matter in circumstances which give rise to a relationship of trust and confidence. The distinguishing obligation of a fiduciary is the obligation of loyalty. The principal is entitled to the single-minded loyalty of his fiduciary. The core liability has several facets. A fiduciary must act in good faith; he must not make a profit out of his trust; he must not place himself in a position where his duty and his interest may conflict; he may not act for his own benefit or the benefit of a third person without the informed consent of his principal. This is not intended to be an exhaustive list, but it is sufficient to indicate the nature of fiduciary obligations. They are the defining characteristics of the fiduciary."

Finn, on whose "classic work"[22] these statements were based, has emphasised that the fiduciary's undertaking "may be of a general character. It may be specific and limited. It is immaterial whether the undertaking is gratuitous. And the undertaking may be officiously assumed without request."[23] A fiduciary is expected "to act in the interests of the other — to act selflessly and with undivided loyalty".[24] This obligation to act selflessly is what distinguishes a person who owes fiduciary obligations from a person who owes merely contractual obligations; the latter is permitted to act in his own self interest, provided that he does not engage in conduct which the courts are prepared to classify as unconscionable.[25]

The "category of cases in which fiduciary obligations and duties arise from the circumstances of the case and the relationship of the parties is no more closed than the categories of negligence at common law".[26] Certain relationships are always classified as fiduciary. Traditionally there have been four: trustee and beneficiary; agent and principal; director and company; and partner and co-partner — the relationship in question may either have been expressly created or have arisen as a result of the officious conduct of the alleged fiduciary. It has also long been clear that the relationship between solicitor and client is fiduciary,[27] but only for as long as it lasts,[28] and in recent years the existence of two further fiduciary relationships, between senior management employee and company[29] and between member of the Security

---

[21] [1998] Ch. 1 at 18.
[22] *Fiduciary Obligations* (1977), so described in *Hooper v. Gorvin* [2001] W.T.L.R. 575 at 590.
[23] *ibid.* p. 201.
[24] Finn in *Equity, Fiduciaries and Trusts* (ed. Youdan, 1989), pp. 1, 4.
[25] *ibid.*
[26] *ibid.*
[27] This was implicit in *Nocton v. Lord Ashburton* [1914] A.C. 14 and was specifically held in *Brown v. I.R.C.* [1965] A.C. 244.
[28] In *Bolkiah (Prince Jefri) v. KPMG* [1999] 2 A.C. 222, Lord Millett said: "The fiduciary relationship which subsists between solicitor and client comes to an end with the termination of the retainer. ... The only duty to the former client which survives the termination of the client relationship is a continuing duty to preserve the confidentiality of information imparted during its subsistence."
[29] *Sybron Corporation v. Rochem* [1984] Ch. 112 at 127. But an employment relationship as such is not a fiduciary relationship: *Nottingham University v. Fishel* [2000] I.R.L.R. 471 where three differences between the two were identified.

Services and the Crown,[30] has been confirmed. Other additions are possible.[31] The full range of fiduciary obligations and prohibitions is normally imposed on fiduciaries within these categories, although this does not mean that the position of each is actually the same.[32] The relationships between accountant and client, broker and client, promoter and company, and guardian and ward have also been held, in certain circumstances and in respect of specific transactions, to be fiduciary and a member of the armed forces of the Crown has even been held to be a fiduciary in respect of his uniform and the opportunities and facilities attached to it,[33] On the other hand, as has already been seen,[34] it has been held that a duty imposed by statute to perform certain functions does not, as a general rule, impose fiduciary obligations and that the presumption is, in the absence of indications to the contrary in the statute, that no such obligations are imposed[35]; it has also been held that the Crown will not become a fiduciary unless it deliberately chooses so to do.[36]

To what extent should fiduciary obligations be imposed outside the traditional categories? This question is relevant because such obligations are capable of giving rise to the imposition of a constructive trust. Such a trust was indeed imposed in *Hooper v. Gorvin*,[37] where one of a number of leasehold tenants of a site had been nominated to act on their behalf in negotiations for the acquisition of the freehold. The statements of Lord Browne-Wilkinson, Millett L.J. and Finn set out above were relied on in support of the conclusion that, although the nominated person was not the agent of the other tenants, he had assumed fiduciary obligations towards them; he was therefore held to hold the freehold, which he had purchased in his sole name, on constructive trust for all of them.

This decision is an example of the question of whether a relationship is classified as fiduciary being resolved by a determination of the extent to which it has satisfied the characteristics of a fiduciary relationship (statements of the type set out above only purport to describe, rather than to define, a fiduciary relationship and none of the few comprehensive definitions which have been suggested has ever received any general approval). A number of different characteristics have been identified: the existence of an undertaking by the alleged fiduciary to the other party to the relationship; reliance placed on the alleged fiduciary by the other party to the relationship; property of the other

---

[30] *Att.-Gen. v. Guardian Newspapers (No.2)* [1990] 1 A.C. 109; *Att.-Gen. v. Blake* [1997] Ch. 84 (Ch.D.), [1998] Ch. 439 (C.A.), [2001] 1 A.C. 268 (H.L.).

[31] Other jurisdictions have added the relationships between doctor and patient (*McInerney v. MacDonald* (1992) 93 D.L.R. (4th) 415 (Supreme Court of Canada); *S.E.C. v. Willis* (1992) 787 Fed.Supp. 58 (U.S. District Court, New York) and the other authorities cited by Frankel in *Equity, Fiduciaries and Trusts 1993* (ed. Waters, 1993), p. 173) and between child-abuser and victim when the parties are parent and child (*M.(K.) v. M.(H.)* (1993) 96 D.L.R. (4th) 449 (Supreme Court of Canada)) but not otherwise (*H. v. R.* [1996] 1 N.Z.L.R. 299 (New Zealand High Court)). The relationship between priest and parishioner is another potential addition (see Frankel *op.cit.*).

[32] *Henderson v. Merrett Syndicates* [1995] 2 A.C. 145 at 205.

[33] *Reading v. Att.-Gen.* [1951] A.C. 507.

[34] See *ante*, p. 18.

[35] *Tito v. Waddell (No.2)* [1977] Ch. 106 at 235. See also *Swain v. The Law Society* [1983] A.C. 598, where The Law Society was held not to be in a fiduciary relationship with the members of the solicitors' profession.

[36] *Tito v. Waddell (No.2)* [1977] Ch. 106 at 212.

[37] [2001] W.T.L.R. 575 at 589–590.

party under the control of the alleged fiduciary; and vulnerability of the other party to the alleged fiduciary in that some power or discretion is vested in the latter which is capable of being used to affect the legal or practical interests of the former. None of these four characteristics is accepted to be of universal application (although the existence of an undertaking and, in particular, the existence of vulnerability are undoubtedly the most significant); however, each of them has, at one time or another, been held to be sufficient for the imposition of fiduciary obligations. Detailed consideration of these characteristics and the way in which they have been applied by the courts is, however, outside the scope of a book on the law of trusts.

It is, however, necessary to consider in detail the extent, if at all, to which fiduciary obligations should be upheld in commercial transactions. This is because proceedings instituted in order to establish the existence of such obligations in a commercial context generally have the same primary objective as in *Hooper v. Gorvin*: the imposition on one of the parties of a constructive trust in favour of the other in respect of the benefits which the alleged fiduciary has obtained by entering into some related transaction on his own behalf.[38] The proprietary claim which such a trust automatically makes available to the other party is obviously capable of stripping away a substantial proportion of the assets of the fiduciary, particularly if the constructive trust is imposed in such a way as to deprive him of both the past and future profits of the transaction in question. These will be profits to which the fiduciary will have appeared to be entitled and whose disappearance is capable of reducing very considerably the assets available for his general creditors,[39] who will necessarily not be before the court to defend their interests. This is why the extent to which commercial relationships entered into at arm's length and on an equal footing should be held to give rise to fiduciary obligations has been the subject of so much discussion in recent years.

Many commercial transactions expressly create fiduciary relationships; this will be the case where it is expressly provided that one or more of the parties is subject to fiduciary obligations or where the transaction has expressly created a relationship which is always classified as fiduciary, such as a partnership. Where this is not the case, the English courts have, generally speaking, been "mindful of the stern warnings uttered by Lindley L.J.[40] and Atkin L.J.[41] of the dangers of applying equitable doctrines to commercial transactions. To do so would paralyse the trade of the country and fundamentally affect the security of business transactions."[42]

Further, there "has been a natural reluctance to impose upon parties in a commercial relationship who are in a relatively equal position of strength the higher standards of conduct which equity prescribes. One manifestation of this reluctance is the disinclination of judges to find a fiduciary relationship

---

[38] This is the principal motive but not the only one. Others include more favourable limitation periods and more favourable rules governing the assessment of financial compensation.

[39] Indeed in *Re Goldcorp Exchange* [1995] 1 A.C. 74 (discussed *post*, p. 335), the objective was to obtain priority not only over the general creditors but also over a secured creditor, the holder of a floating charge (a charge over whatever assets a company may have at any one time).

[40] In *Manchester Trust v. Furness* [1895] 2 Q.B. 539 at 545.

[41] In *Re Wait* [1927] 1 Ch. 606 at 634 *et seq.*, especially at 639–640.

[42] Sir Anthony Mason (when Chief Justice of Australia) extra-judicially 110 L.Q.R. (1994) 238, p. 245.

when the arrangement between the parties is of a purely commercial kind and they have dealt with each other at arm's length and on an equal footing."[43] This was undoubtedly the attitude adopted by the Privy Council on an appeal from Bermuda in *Kelly v. Cooper*,[44] also in 1992, in relation to an estate agency contract. The Privy Council held that, despite the fact that it is normally a breach of an agent's duty to act for competing principals, it is the business of estate agents to act for numerous principals and to acquire information which is confidential to each principal;[45] that being so, the fiduciary duties owed by them to each principal were to be defined by the terms of the contract of agency.[46] [47]

While this attitude has also persisted in other jurisdictions,[48] their courts now appear to be much more ready to hold that the parties have not been dealing on an equal footing. In such cases, the "fiduciary relationship has been the spearhead of equity's incursions into the area of commerce".[49] In Australia and in New Zealand, joint venture arrangements have very readily been held to give rise to fiduciary obligations[50] and in 1994 the then Chief Justice of Australia stated, extra-judicially, that "a fiduciary relationship will arise out of a commercial arrangement when one party undertakes to act in the interests of the other party rather than in his or her own interests in relation to a particular matter or aspect of their arrangement and that other party, being unable to look after his or her interests in that matter or aspect of the arrangement, is basically dependent upon the first party acting in conformity with his or her undertaking".[51] However, his views have yet to be carried into effect by the Australian courts. In Canada, the courts have expressed a willingness to impose fiduciary obligations in favour of any party to a commercial transaction who is vulnerable to the other, even where the vulnerability has arisen only by virtue of the relative sizes and resources of the two commercial enterprises involved, but have emphasised that it is only rarely that such vulnerability will be found to exist.[52]

What are the possibilities of English law adopting similar attitudes? The consequences of the imposition of fiduciary obligations both for the fiduciary

---

[43] Mason C.J. *op.cit.*, p. 245.

[44] [1993] A.C. 205.

[45] This is also the case for auditors. See *Bolkiah (Prince Jefri) v. KPMG* [1999] 2 A.C. 222, where *Kelly v. Cooper* was explained; this case was an attempt to restrain alleged potential breaches of confidence — the auditors in question could not thereby have committed a breach of fiduciary duty after they had ceased to act as such (see *ante*, p. 331, fn. 28).

[46] An estate agent who had advised his principal to accept a price lower than that for which he knew that a similar adjoining property had already been sold was held liable to him in tort for having given negligent advice in *John D. Wood v. Knatchbull* [2003] T.L.R. 12.

[47] See also *Re Stapylton Fletcher* [1994] 1 W.L.R. 1181.

[48] *Jirna v. Master Donut of Canada* (1973) 40 D.L.R. (3d) 303 (Supreme Court of Canada); *United States Surgical Corporation v. Hospital Products International* (1984) 156 C.L.R. 41 (High Court of Australia).

[49] Mason C.J. *op.cit.*, p. 245.

[50] *United Dominion Corporation v. Brian* (1985) 157 C.L.R. 1.

[51] Mason C.J. *op.cit.*, pp. 245–246, citing *Liggett v. Kensington* [1993] 3 N.Z.L.R. 257, where the Court of Appeal of New Zealand imposed fiduciary obligations upon a gold trader who had offered purchasers the option of leaving their bullion in the custody of the trader on the purchasers' behalf as "non-allocated bullion". This decision was subsequently reversed by the Privy Council *sub. nom. Re Goldcorp Exchange* [1995] 1 A.C. 74; see *post*, p. 335.

[52] *Lac Minerals v. International Corona Resources* (1989) 61 D.L.R.(4th) 14; *Hodgkinson v. Simms* (1994) 117 D.L.R.(4th) 161 (both Supreme Court of Canada).

himself and for his general creditors constitute strong arguments against the adoption in England of the approach advocated in the Commonwealth and any thoughts that English law might have been about to develop along those lines were rapidly disabused by the opinion of the Privy Council in *Re Goldcorp Exchange* in 1994.[53] This, curiously enough, was an appeal from the decision which constituted the principal authority cited by the Chief Justice of Australia in support of the proposition set out in the previous paragraph. The Court of Appeal of New Zealand[54] had imposed fiduciary obligations on a gold-dealer which had offered its purchasers the option of leaving their bullion in its custody on the purchasers' behalf as "non-allocated bullion". Purchasers who did so were issued with a certificate of ownership and were entitled to take physical possession of their bullion on seven days' notice. The Court of Appeal's conclusion that the company was a fiduciary was based on two propositions: first, that it was bound to protect the interests of the purchasers; and, secondly, that it was, for all practical purposes, free from control and supervision by them.[55] The Privy Council, however, heeded the warnings of Lindley L.J. and Atkin L.J. to which reference has already been made. Lord Mustill said this:

> "But what kind of fiduciary duties did the company owe to the customer? None have been suggested beyond those which the company assumed under the contracts of sale read with the collateral promises; ... No doubt the fact that one person is placed in a particular position *vis-à-vis* another through the medium of a contract does not necessarily mean that he does not also owe fiduciary duties to that other by virtue of being in that position. But the essence of a fiduciary relationship is that it creates obligations of a different character from those deriving from the contract itself. ... Many commercial relationships involve just such a reliance by one party on the other, and to introduce the whole new dimension into such relationships which would flow from giving them a fiduciary character would (as it seems to their Lordships) have adverse consequences far exceeding those foreseen by Atkin L.J. in *Re Wait*.[56] It is possible without misuse of language to say that the customers put faith in the company, and that their trust has not been repaid. But the vocabulary is misleading; high expectations do not necessarily lead to equitable remedies."

These observations seem to rule out, at least for the present, any possibility of English law developing along the lines of the Australian and New Zealand decisions even in respect of joint venture arrangements, never mind in accordance with the wider principles enunciated in those jurisdictions and in Canada. The attitude manifested by the Privy Council does have the great advantage that the interests of third parties cannot be prejudiced by the conversion of a general creditor into a preferential creditor as the result of the imposition of fiduciary obligations on a bankrupt. For this reason, it is hoped

---

[53] [1995] 1 A.C. 74.
[54] [1993] 1 N.Z.L.R. 257.
[55] *ibid.* at 583, 584, *per* Cooke P. at 596, 597, *per* Gault J. Compare the view of the dissentient, McKay J. at pp. 604, 605.
[56] [1927] 1 Ch. 606 at 634 *et seq.*, especially at 639–640.

that, in the event that English law does one day develop along the lines advocated in the Commonwealth, the courts will not lose sight of the interests of third parties but will take them into account in the manner envisaged in the introductory section of this chapter.

## 2. The Nature of the Liability of Fiduciaries

In *Bray v. Ford*,[57] Lord Herschell laid down two overlapping principles: a fiduciary cannot be permitted to profit from his fiduciary position and a fiduciary must not allow his personal interest to prevail over his duty of loyalty to his principal. The precise relationship between these two rules has been expressed in a number of ways. In *Swain v. The Law Society*,[58] Stephenson L.J. regarded the first of these principles as merely one of the many examples of the second principle. However, it is clear that a fiduciary cannot profit from his fiduciary position even when there is no real conflict of interest and duty. Consequently, it is perhaps preferable to adopt the view of Deane J.[59] that the two principles "while overlapping, are distinct".

Within these principles, the attitude of English law towards fiduciaries is relatively consistent. Of course, as is only to be expected, the law differs from fiduciary relationship to fiduciary relationship.[60] This is the case even as between the traditional categories of fiduciary relationships; thus a director is in a more favourable position with regard to property transactions with his company than is a trustee with regard to property transactions with his trust. This apart, however, the attitude of English law towards fiduciaries is, generally speaking, a harsh one. As James L.J. remarked in *Parker v. McKenna*,[61] the rule that a fiduciary may not profit from his position without the knowledge and consent of his principal "is an inexorable rule, and must be applied inexorably by this court, which is not entitled, in my judgment, to receive evidence, or suggestion, or argument as to whether the principal did or did not suffer any injury in fact by reason of the dealing of the [fiduciary]". Not only is it thus irrelevant that the principal has suffered no loss; it is also irrelevant that the fiduciary acted in the utmost good faith and that his actions in fact benefitted his principal.

This inexorable rule exists for reasons of policy, namely to avoid the remotest risk of a fiduciary being swayed from his duty of loyalty to his principal by his own self interest. However, the decided cases provide innumerable examples of courts penalising fiduciaries (particularly trustees) totally irrespective of whether there was any serious conflict between their duty of loyalty and their self interest. A fiduciary is only allowed to retain a profit in very limited circumstances: first, when the conflict of interest which produced the profit must necessarily have been envisaged at the time when the fiduciary relationship was created;[62] secondly, when the making of the profit was spe-

---

[57] [1896] A.C. 44 at 51–52.
[58] [1982] 1 W.L.R. 17 at 29.
[59] In *Chan v. Zacharia* (1984) 53 A.L.R. 417 at 433 (High Court of Australia).
[60] See Millett J. in *Lonrho v. Fayed (No.2)* [1992] 1 W.L.R. 1 at 11–12.
[61] (1874) L.R. 10 Ch. 96.
[62] In cases where the fiduciary relationship has been created by the parties to it, the person who will have to have envisaged the conflict of interest in question is the principal; in the case of a voluntary settlement, it will instead be the settlor or testator.

cifically authorised in advance in the instrument by which the fiduciary relationship was created;[63] and, thirdly, when the fully informed prior consent or subsequent ratification of the principal to the making of the profit has been given.[64]

Lord Herschell remarked in *Bray v. Ford*[65] that this harsh rule "might be departed from in many cases, without any breach of morality, without any wrong being inflicted, and without any consciousness of wrongdoing". However, English law has never given much indication of being disposed to relax its strict penal rule in favour of a more flexible rule that fiduciaries should only be penalised where there has been a serious conflict of interest and duty. A rare example of flexibility some 35 years ago were the remarks of Danckwerts and Sachs L.JJ. in *Holder v. Holder*[66] to the effect that whether or not a transaction should be set aside because of an alleged conflict of interest and duty was a matter for the discretion of the judge.

However, greater signs of flexibility have recently been shown in relation to pension trusts. In *Re Drexel Lambert UK Pension Plan*,[67] Lindsay J., while acknowledging that the remarks of Lord Herschell were "not a licence for the rule to departed from when it can be seen that no breach of morality or wrongdoing would ensue", did hold that "the rule does not apply with such force as to deny the court even the jurisdiction to give directions";[68] he therefore approved an application made by the trustees of a pension scheme, all of whom were by virtue of being members of the scheme also beneficiaries and therefore had a conflict of interest and duty, for the distribution of the actuarial surplus of the pension fund in question. Scott V.-C. subsequently went even further in *Edge v. Pensions Ombudsman*,[69] where the trustees had had to make an amendment to the rules of a pension scheme in order to eliminate an excessive surplus. The effect of the amendment was to reduce employee contributions and to enhance pensions in payment, as a result of which some of the trustees benefitted. Scott V.-C. held that, given that statute[70] now requires pension schemes to have member-nominated trustees, it was "quite simply ridiculous" to contend that any trustees who were members had to be excluded from any new or enhanced benefits obtained by the exercise of their powers. His remarks were subsequently approved by the Court of Appeal.[71]

It remains to be seen whether this understandable, but nevertheless highly desirable, relaxation of the traditional position in the area of pension trusts is also applied outside that area. However, one important restriction on the potential liability of fiduciaries has now been made clear as a result of the decision of the Court of Appeal in *Bristol and West Building Society v. Mothew*.[72] This was one of many recent cases in which banks and building societies have endeavoured to recover shortfalls in the proceeds of their mortgage securities by imposing liability on the solicitors who acted both for them and for the

---

[63] *Sergeant v. National Westminster Bank* (1990) 61 P. & C.R. 518.
[64] *Holder v. Holder* [1968] Ch. 353.
[65] [1896] A.C. 44 at 51.
[66] [1968] Ch. 353; see *post*, pp. 348–349.
[67] [1995] 1 W.L.R. 32.
[68] *ibid.* at 41.
[69] [1998] Ch. 512 at 539.
[70] Pensions Act 1995, ss.16–21.
[71] [2000] Ch. 602.
[72] [1998] Ch. 1.

borrower at the time when the mortgage in question was created; in such circumstances the solicitors of course owe fiduciary duties both to the borrower and to the mortgagee. The Court of Appeal held that breaches of contract and acts of negligence committed by fiduciaries of this type will only give rise to the normal contractual and tortious remedies; such acts with therefore not give rise to the enhanced measures of compensation which can be recovered from fiduciaries[73] without the presence of some additional factor such as a clear conflict between the interests of the borrower and the interests of the mortgagee of which the solicitor has chosen not to inform the mortgagee.[74]

If English law ever does relax the strict rule which has traditionally been applied in the way that other jurisdictions have done, it will have to be decided whether the conflict of interest and duty is to be measured prospectively or retrospectively, whether, in other words, the question of whether there was a real sensible possibility of conflict has to be considered in the light of the facts existing at the time when the course of conduct complained of commenced or in the light of the facts existing at the time when that course of conduct ended. No clear answer to this question has been given in any of the decided cases, perhaps because the adoption of the strict penal rule has rendered it irrelevant. It is, however, suggested that the retrospective approach is preferable.

### 3. Remedies for Breach of Fiduciary Duty

The first and most significant remedy for breach of fiduciary duty, the one which is most favourable to the principal, and also the one with which this chapter is obviously mainly concerned, is the imposition of a constructive trust. It has already been seen[75] that this requires the identification of some specific property which either is or has been in the hands of the fiduciary on which the trust can be imposed and that the precise position of the principal depends on the nature of the constructive trust which has been imposed. When a constructive trust is not available, the principal can have recourse only to some form of personal remedy.

The second possible remedy is for the principal to seek an account. This remedy will be sought where the principal wishes to recover assets which have passed through the hands of a fiduciary who has committed a breach of fiduciary duty but cannot identify any specific property which either is or has been in the hands of the fiduciary which represents those assets or their product. In these circumstances, he will seek an account of whatever assets have reached the hands of the fiduciary. This involves the fiduciary rendering an account of what he has done with the property which has been in his hands. If the principal is dissatisfied with what the fiduciary has done, then he has the right to "surcharge" or "falsify" the account rendered. The effect of him opting to take either of these courses of action is considered in a later chapter.[76]

---

[73] See post, p. 764.
[74] A number of conflicts of this type were identified in Nationwide Building Society v. Balmer Radmore [1999] Lloyd's P.N. 241 and the mortgagee duly recovered the measure of compensation appropriate to a breach of fiduciary duty.
[75] See ante, p. 313.
[76] See post, pp. 764–766.

Any compensation which the principal recovers will be equitable compensation of the type which courts of equity have always been able to award; its continued availability was confirmed by the decision of the House of Lords in *Nocton v. Lord Ashburton.*[77] However, such an award will give him no priority over the fiduciary's general creditors — an account remains a personal remedy despite the fact that the person against whom it is sought is a fiduciary.

The third possible remedy, which is available only as an alternative and not in addition to the first two,[78] is for the principal to seek equitable compensation for breach of fiduciary duty; the availability of this type of compensation was established by the decision of the House of Lords in *Nocton v. Lord Ashburton.*[79] The purpose of such an award is, basically, to restore the principal to the position which he occupied prior to the breach of fiduciary duty in question. A number of examples of awards of equitable compensation of this type will be seen later on: first, where a fiduciary has failed to disclose a conflict of interest and duty and, in particular, has entered into some form of transaction with his principal without adequate disclosure[80]; secondly, where there has been a breach of an equitable obligation of confidence[81]; and, thirdly, where a fiduciary has disposed of trust property in breach of trust.[82] The precise measure of recovery is a matter of some controversy but the general view seems to be that common law principles of remoteness of damages should be applied to the assessment of equitable compensation.[83]

The fourth possible remedy, which is available only where the fiduciary has entered into some form of transaction with his principal without adequate disclosure, is for that transaction to be rescinded *ab initio*.[84] However, this is only possible for so long as *restitutio in integrum* is still possible, in other words while both fiduciary and principal are still able to restore the other to his initial position. This remedy is available only as an alternative to the three remedies already discussed.

Finally, there is obviously nothing to prevent the principal from seeking injunctive relief as a supplement to any of the remedies already discussed (usually in order to prevent a fiduciary from disposing of property which is claimed to be subject to a constructive trust or susceptible of *restitutio in integrum*); injunctive relief is also often sought independently in cases involving a breach of the equitable obligation of confidence. In theory, it is also possible for the principal to seek damages in lieu or in addition to an injunction under Lord Cairns' Act,[85] but in practice it is now almost inevitable that any monetary award for breach of fiduciary duty will instead be made pursuant to *Nocton v. Lord Ashburton.*

---

[77] [1914] A.C. 932.
[78] *Tang Man Sit v. Capacious Investments* [1996] 1 A.C. 514 (Privy Council on appeal from Hong Kong).
[79] [1914] A.C. 932.
[80] See *post*, pp. 351–353.
[81] See *post*, p. 368, fn. 10.
[82] See *post*, pp. 764–766.
[83] See *Constructive Trusts* (3rd ed., 1997), pp. 117–121 and the authorities there cited.
[84] See *post*, pp. 351–353.
[85] The name usually given to the Chancery Amendment Act 1858. This Act has long since been repealed but the jurisdiction conferred thereby is now contained in the Supreme Court Act 1981, s.50.

### 4. *The Classification of the Authorities*

The many authorities have been classified in a number of different ways. It is proposed to consider them in this order: first, cases where a fiduciary has as a result of his position obtained unauthorised remuneration secondly, cases where a fiduciary has entered into a transaction in a double capacity in that he has purported to represent the interests both of his principal and himself and, thirdly, cases where a fiduciary has as a result of his position obtained a benefit to the exclusion of his principal.

### 5. *Unauthorised Remuneration Obtained by a Fiduciary as a Result of his Position*

#### (A) When is a Fiduciary Entitled to Claim Remuneration?

The detailed rules governing the extent to which a trustee is entitled to claim and retain remuneration and benefits are discussed in a later chapter.[86] For present purposes, it is merely necessary to state that trustees have, historically, been under a duty to act without remuneration, even when they devote a considerable amount of time and trouble to managing the trust business, save to the extent that remuneration is permitted by the deed or will in question. This remains the position save to the extent that the Trustee Act 2000[87] provides the contrary in the case of trust corporations and trustees who are acting in a professional capacity.[88] This legislation has given both enhanced rights to charge whatever remuneration has been authorised and provides that, where no remuneration has been authorised at all, trust corporations and, if any other trustees agree, trustees who are acting in a professional capacity can charge such remuneration as is reasonable in the circumstances. The same rules apply to any remuneration received by a trustee by virtue of holding, as a result of his position as trustee, an office of profit such as a directorship in a company in which the trust has a shareholding.

The position of other express fiduciaries is more favourable. While they are in principle, like trustees, expected to act without remuneration,[89] it is in practice highly unlikely that they will have agreed to act without first having made provision for the payment of the appropriate remuneration. Thus the Articles of Association of a company generally provide for the payment of remuneration to its directors;[90] a partnership deed will normally provide for the payment of remuneration to the partners; and a contract of agency will normally make provision for the payment of the appropriate remuneration to the agent. Thus, in normal circumstances, a director of a company who is appointed by the board to a directorship of a subsidiary may undoubtedly retain both sets of directors' fees and a partner who is appointed by his partners to a directorship in a company in which the partnership holds shares may similarly retain his director's fees. However, in the event that the pay-

---

[86] See *post*, p. 721.

[87] ss. 28, 29.

[88] Defined as acting in the course of a profession or business which consists of or includes the provisions of services in connection with the management or administration of trusts generally or in some respect. See *post* p. 727.

[89] *Guinness v. Saunders* [1990] 2 A.C. 663 at 689–690.

[90] The Table A Articles of Association recommended by statute reserve to the company in general meeting the right to determine the remuneration of the directors of the company.

ment of remuneration has not been authorised, or the formula by which authorisation has to be obtained has not been complied with,[91] the fiduciary will not be entitled either to remuneration or to the benefits of any other office to which he has been appointed by virtue of his fiduciary position and will be liable to account to his principal for any sums received.[92] Further, the House of Lords has held that, where the formula by which authorisation has to be obtained has not been complied with, the court has no inherent jurisdiction to award remuneration to the fiduciary in question.[93]

### (B) Liability in respect of Unauthorised Remuneration

Where a fiduciary is liable to account for remuneration received as such, he will in principle clearly be liable as a constructive trustee in respect of the remuneration so obtained. However, only where the remuneration in question is still identifiable at the date of action (as will be the case where the remuneration takes the form of shares or, as is not uncommon today, share options) will there be any purpose in imposing such a trust. Where the remuneration has already passed into the general funds of the fiduciary (as will obviously be more usual), then the fiduciary will be liable merely to account to his principal for its value. In this situation there will obviously be no need for the imposition of a constructive trust since any fiduciary liable to account for remuneration of this kind will inevitably be an express fiduciary.

### (C) Liability in Respect of Secret Profits

A fiduciary will also be liable to account for any other payments which he may receive as a result of his position. Such payments are generally known as secret profits. It is clearly established that no fiduciary who receives a secret profit may retain it as against his principal unless its retention was either authorised in advance or subsequently ratified by the principal with full knowledge of all relevant facts.

### (1) Who is regarded as a fiduciary for these purposes?

For the purposes of the application of this principle, the courts take a particularly broad view of what constitutes a fiduciary relationship. In *Attorney-General v. Goddard*,[94] the principle was applied to a police officer who had been bribed not to report brothel keepers; in *Reading v. Attorney-General*,[95] it was applied to an ex-R.A.M.C Sergeant who had obtained large sums from smugglers for riding in his uniform through Cairo in lorries in which smuggled goods were being transported, thus enabling the lorries to pass the civil police without search; and, in modern conditions, it would presumably be

---

[91] In *Guinness v. Saunders* [1990] 2 A.C. 663, the remuneration of the director in question had not, as required by the Articles of Association, been approved by the board of directors.
[92] *ibid.*
[93] *ibid.*, at 693–694, 700–702.
[94] [1929] L.J.(K.B.) 743.
[95] [1951] A.C. 507.

applied to a security guard who was bribed to switch off the alarm system, thus facilitating the entrance of thieves.[96]

It is in fact arguable whether it is really appropriate for relationships of this kind to be classified as fiduciary. In *Reading v. Attorney-General*, the Sergeant was claiming by petition of right the return of some £19,000 which had been found in his possession and confiscated when he was eventually apprehended. For this action to fail, some basis for the Crown's right to confiscate the money had to be found. At first instance,[97] Denning J. held that there was no fiduciary relationship between the suppliant and the Crown but also held that no such relationship was in fact necessary. However, in the Court of Appeal,[98] Asquith L.J. took a different view, holding that, assuming a fiduciary relationship to be necessary, such a relationship arose from the use by the suppliant of his uniform and the opportunities attached to it. He admitted that this was using the concept of fiduciary relationship "in a very loose sense" but this did not stop the House of Lords from confirming his view. It is possible to criticise his reasoning on the grounds that the relationship between Sergeant Reading and the Crown does not appear to satisfy any of the criteria for the existence of a fiduciary relationship other than (possibly) the existence of property of the other party under the control of the alleged fiduciary property; in particular, it is not easy to see how the Crown was in any way vulnerable by virtue of some power or discretion vested in him which was capable of being used to affect its legal or practical interests. That is not to say that *Reading v. Attorney-General* was wrongly decided since its result can certainly be justified on other grounds.[99] However, the decision undoubtedly demonstrates how widely the courts are prepared to construe the concept of fiduciary relationship in order to permit the recovery of secret profits.[1] It is questionable whether the concept should be construed so widely for other purposes.[2]

### (2) For what profits will a fiduciary be liable?
It has already been stated that a fiduciary will be liable for any payments which he may receive as a result of his position. The vast majority of the reported cases have concerned bribes and commissions received by the fiduciary in order either to induce him to take a particular course of action or to reward him for having done so. A bribe may be defined as an undisclosed payment made to a person known by the payer to be a fiduciary in circumstances in which it could induce the fiduciary to favour the payer in some way

---

[96] This illustration was provided by Lord Millett extra-judicially in [1993] R.L.R. 7. In *Brinks v. Abu-Saleh (No.3)* [1996] C.L.C. 133, a security guard who provided both a key to, and information about, the security of a Heathrow warehouse was held to be a fiduciary but this was not for the purpose of imposing liability on him but for the rather more questionable purpose of imposing liability on third parties (see *post*, p. 378).

[97] [1948] 2 K.B. 268.

[98] [1949] 2 K.B. 232.

[99] By virtue of the principle that no criminal may benefit from his crime. See Section IV of this Chapter, *post*, p. 407.

[1] *Reading v. Att.-Gen.* was approved and applied in the equally extreme case of *Jersey City v. Hague* (1955) 155 At.(2d) 8, which concerned a successful attempt to recover from the Mayor of Jersey City the percentages of the salaries of each employee of the city which he had extorted over a period of 30 years in consideration of continued employment.

[2] See *post*, p. 378.

in his dealings with the fiduciary or with the fiduciary's principal.[3] In such

e of remedies. He can rescind any ribe,[4] provided of course that he can onally or alternatively, sue either the the bribe.

elevant for present purposes. In the nd *Attorney-General for Hong Kong v.* on the recipients of bribes. Such ility is imposed on the recipients of faith, something which is wholly ices. In *Williams v. Barton*,[9] a trustee alue trust securities. His action was ss held liable to account to the trust on which he had made out of the cision means that a solicitor who lient to a broker will be liable to n unless the latter has expressly question.

tually impossible for a fiduciary payment by way of secret profit position. However, it has recently to impose unreasonable restraints fiduciary or on his ability to earn during the fiduciary relationship. ich concerned an attempt by the respect of the autobiography of ret Intelligence Service who had ich he managed to escape after eral contended that Blake owed is position as a former member of e himself a profit; and, secondly, intangible property such as ori- it. Only the first of these alleged tt V.-C. held that both were for- le and went on to dismiss the

Crown's claim for the reasons stated above, both of which appear to relate principally to the second duty. No doubt was cast on this reasoning on appeal;[11] the Court of Appeal specifically held that Blake was not in breach of fiduciary duty but both there and in the House of Lords the Crown instead

---

[3] *Hovenden and Sons v. Milhoff* (1900) 83 L.T. 41 at 43; *Industries and General Mortgage Co. v. Lewis* [1949] 2 All E.R. 573 at 575.

[4] *Logicrose v. Southend United F.C.* [1988] 1 W.L.R. 1256.

[5] *Hovenden and Sons v. Milhoff* (1900) 83 L.T. 41; *Mahesan v. Malaysian Government Officers' Co-operative Housing Society* [1979] A.C. 374 at 383.

[6] These claims were held to be alternative rather than cumulative in *Mahesan v. Malaysian Government Officers' Co-operative Housing Society* [1979] A.C. 374.

[7] (1890) 45 Ch.D. 1.

[8] [1994] 1 A.C. 324 (Privy Council on appeal from New Zealand).

[9] [1927] 2 Ch. 9.

[10] [1997] Ch. 84.

[11] [1998] Ch. 439 (C.A.), [2001] 1 A.C. 268 (H.L.).

succeeded on public law and contractual arguments not raised at first instance. However, there seems little likelihood that the arguments which commended themselves to Scott V.-C. will often be invoked successfully; it is hardly likely that the courts would look very charitably on a trustee who deferred the receipt of bribes and commissions until after his retirement and then sought to retain them on that ground.

### (3) The nature of the liability

In principle, a fiduciary who is liable to account for secret profits will be liable as a constructive trustee in respect of the secret profit in question. This remedy was imposed in *Williams v. Barton*,[12] which of course meant that the principal was therefore entitled to follow the payment into its product in the admittedly unlikely event that it could be shown to have been invested in assets which had appreciated in value. However, until the decision of the Privy Council in *Attorney-General for Hong Kong v. Reid*,[13] the decided cases appeared to draw a distinction between bribes and other secret profits.

In *Lister & Co. v. Stubbs*,[14] the defendant was the plaintiff's foreman and was responsible for buying in whatever was needed in his employer's business. He regularly gave orders to a third party in return for a large commission. In an action to recover this bribe, the plaintiff sought an order restraining the defendant from dealing with certain investments purchased with the money received on the basis that the defendant was a constructive trustee of the bribes and the plaintiff would therefore be entitled to follow the money into its product and recover the investments. However, the Court of Appeal declined to grant this order, holding that the only obligation of the defendant was to pay over the sums received to the plaintiff; the relationship between them was held to be that of debtor-creditor rather than trustee-beneficiary. Although this decision was consistently followed,[15] it seemed quite extraordinary that the defendant in *Williams v. Barton* should have been held to have been a constructive trustee of a commission which he had earned in good faith if the defendant in *Lister & Co. v. Stubbs* was held not to have been a constructive trustee of an illicitly earned bribe. All the commentators agreed that both cases should have been decided in the same way. Some thought that a constructive trust should not have been imposed in either case on the grounds that proprietary remedies should be limited to situations where the claimant can show that he has lost property which, but for the conduct of the fiduciary, he would

---

[12] [1927] 2 Ch. 9.
[13] [1994] 1 A.C. 324.
[14] (1890) 45 Ch.D. 1.
[15] In *Att.-Gen. Ref. (No.1 of 1985)* [1986] 2 All E.R. 219 and in *Islamic Republic of Iran Shipping Line v. Denby* [1987] 1 F.T.L.R. 30. In Australia, the view had been expressed that the decision in *Lister & Co. v. Stubbs* was anomalous and should be confined to its own facts (*Consul Development v. D.P.C. Estates* [1974] 1 N.S.W.L.R. 443 (New South Wales Court of Appeal); the question was left open on the further appeal to the High Court of Australia ((1975) 132 C.L.R. 373)). Subsequently, the reasoning in *Lister & Co. v. Stubbs* was described as impeccable when applied to cases in which the person claiming the money had simply made what was described as an outright loan to the fiduciary (*Daly v. The Sydney Stock Exchange* (1986) 160 C.L.R. 371 (High Court of Australia)). This restricted the effect of *Lister & Co. v. Stubbs* in Australia to cases where a bribe was paid over to a fiduciary in the form of money.

have obtained.[16] Others thought that a constructive trust should have been imposed in both cases on the grounds that a fiduciary should never be allowed to retain any advantage from the violation of his fiduciary obligations, something which can only be achieved by the imposition of a proprietary remedy.[17] This issue was resolved by the Privy Council in *Attorney-General for Hong Kong v. Reid*.[18]

This case concerned a Hong Kong Public Prosecutor, who was convicted of having accepted bribes as an inducement to him to exploit his official position to obstruct the prosecution of certain criminals. He was ordered to pay the Crown the sum of HK$12,400,000, the value of assets then controlled by him which could only have been derived from the bribes. No payments having been made, the Attorney-General for Hong Kong brought proceedings in New Zealand claiming that three freehold houses which the bribes had been used to purchase were held on constructive trust for the Crown. The Court of Appeal of New Zealand applied *Lister & Co v. Stubbs* and dismissed this claim.[19] The Privy Council reversed this decision, holding that *Lister & Co. v. Stubbs* had been wrongly decided. Lord Templeman's opinion did not directly consider the important issue of policy on which the commentators were divided. He held that, as soon as any bribe is received, the fiduciary becomes in equity the debtor of his principal for the amount of the bribe, which should immediately be transferred to his principal. Because equity considers as done that which ought to have been done, the bribe therefore becomes subject to a constructive trust in favour of the principal as soon as it is received. Although this analysis is questionable in a number of respects,[20] it provided a basis for an examination of the case law, from which Lord Templeman concluded that *Lister & Co. v. Stubbs* was consistent neither with prior authority nor "with the principles that a fiduciary must not be allowed to benefit from his own breach of duty, that the fiduciary should account for the bribe as soon as he receives it and that equity regards as done that which ought to be done".[21]

Although the decision in *Attorney-General for Hong Kong v. Reid* is not, of course, formally binding on English courts, it will presumably be followed.[22] Whatever its shortcomings, it has removed a glaring inconsistency in the treatment of secret profits and has established that the liability of a fiduciary who receives a bribe will be exactly the same as that of a fiduciary who receives any other type of secret profit.

---

[16] Birks, *An Introduction to the Law of Restitution* (1989) 388; *Goode* (1987) 103 L.Q.R. 433, 422–445 and in *Essays on the Law of Restitution* (1991), p. 216.

[17] Lord Millett extra-judicially [1993] Restitution L.R. 7, citing Underhill & Hayton: *Law of Trusts and Trustees* (14th ed.), p. 305, *Constructive Trusts* (2nd ed.), p. 56, Goff & Jones: *op.cit.*, p. 657, Pettit: *Equity and the Law of Trusts* (6th ed.), p. 152, Meagher, Gummow & Lehane: *Equity — Doctrines and Remedies* (2nd ed.), para. 1323, Finn, *Fiduciary Obligations* (1977), para. 513, Sir Anthony Mason extra-judicially in *Essays in Equity* (ed. Finn, 1985), p. 246.

[18] [1994] 1 A.C. 324.

[19] [1992] 2 N.Z.L.R. 385.

[20] See [1994] C.L.J. 31.

[21] [1994] 1 A.C. 324 at 336.

[22] Although *Lister & Co. v. Stubbs* was said to be still binding on the High Court by Scott V.-C. in *Att.-Gen. v. Blake* [1997] Ch. 84 at 96.

## 6. *Transactions into which a Fiduciary has Entered in a Double Capacity*

This second group of cases concerns transactions in which a fiduciary has purported to represent the interests of both his principal and himself. Such situations produce an obvious conflict between the personal interest of the fiduciary in the transaction and his duty of loyalty towards his principal. Consequently, no matter how fair the transaction, the principal has the right to have the transaction set aside unless he was fully aware of the facts.

### (A) Purchases of Property by a Fiduciary from his Principal

Such purchases are regulated by two rules, which Megarry V.-C. in *Tito v. Waddell (No.2)*[23] described as the self-dealing rule and the fair-dealing rule, names which have been in general use ever since. The self-dealing rule applies to purchases by trustees of property belonging to their trust[24] and, at least in theory, to purchases by directors of property belonging to their companies[25] (although in practice the Articles of Association of virtually all companies expressly permit such purchases provided that appropriate disclosure is made). The fair-dealing rule applies to purchases by trustees of the beneficial interests of their beneficiaries[26] and to purchases by other fiduciaries (such as agents) of property belonging to their principals.[27]

### (1) The self-dealing rule

In *Tito v. Waddell (No.2)*,[28] Megarry V.-C. said that "if a trustee purchases trust property from himself, any beneficiary may have the sale set aside *ex debito justitiae*, however fair the transaction". The rationale of the self-dealing rule was laid down by Lord Eldon L.C. in *Ex parte Lacey*.[29] He applied the principle that a trustee must not place himself in a position where his interest and duty conflict, holding that, since in a purchase by a trustee of property belonging to his trust he is both vendor and purchaser, the sale is necessarily bad. In such circumstances it is impossible to determine from the evidence whether or not the purchase has been made on advantageous terms and so the court has no option but to set aside the sale at the instance of any beneficiary.

Most purchases which fall foul of these authorities are, as Megarry V.-C. said, not wholly void but only voidable at the instance of any beneficiary. However, this is not always the case since his formulation overlooks the fact that it is impossible for a person to contract with himself or for a trustee to exercise his power of sale in favour of himself.[30] Any transaction which falls foul of either of these rules is not merely voidable but wholly void. Since 1925,[31] this will admittedly only be the case when the same person is, or the

---

[23] [1977] Ch. 106 at 224–225.

[24] *Ex parte Lacey* (1802) 6 Ves. 625.

[25] *Aberdeen Railway Co. v. Blaikie Brothers* (1854) 1 Macq. 461 at 472; *Movitex v. Bullfield* [1988] B.C.L.C. 104.

[26] *Chalmer v. Bradley* (1819) 1 J. & W. 51.

[27] *Edwards v. Meyrick* [1842] 2 Hare 60.

[28] [1977] Ch. 106 at 224–225.

[29] (1802) 6 Ves. 625.

[30] See McPherson J. extra-judicially in *Trends in Contemporary Trust Law* (ed. Oakley, 1996), p. 135.

[31] Until 1926, prior to the enactment of Law of Property Act 1925, s.82, the rule applied if anyone either contracted with or conveyed to himself, even if someone else was also a party on one side or the other.

same persons are, both vendor and purchaser. Therefore a sole trustee cannot sell to himself and a plurality of trustees cannot sell to themselves (validity depends on there being at least one party who is not both vendor and purchaser) unless such a transaction is authorised by the trust instrument. Any breach of this rule will render both contract and conveyance wholly void;[32] there are only two ways out of such a situation: first, for the trustee to try to acquire the beneficial interests of the beneficiaries either as well[33] or instead (such a transaction will be governed by the fair-dealing rule); or, secondly, for the trustee to seek permission to purchase from the court.

Where, on the other hand, there is one party to the transaction who is not both vendor and purchaser, that transaction will indeed not be void but only voidable at the instance of any beneficiary. The many cases in which this rule has been applied have illustrated that it is quite irrelevant that the fiduciary was honest, the sale open and the price fair. In *Wright v. Morgan*[34] property was devised to two trustees on trust for sale for one of them. The will stated that the trustees were required to offer the trustee-beneficiary the land at a price to be fixed by independent valuers. The trustee-beneficiary assigned his beneficial interest to the other trustee, who bought the property at the price fixed by the independent valuers in accordance with the terms of the will. The Privy Council held that, since only a sale to the trustee-beneficiary had been authorised by the will, this sale had to be set aside. The fact that the price was to be fixed independently was not sufficient, for the trustees could themselves fix the time at which the property was to be sold and this could clearly have had a substantial effect on the price ultimately received. This seems to be a somewhat artificial conflict of interest. However, a similar attitude was taken in an eighteenth-century case,[35] in which it was held that a trustee must not purchase trust property which is put up for auction since he is in a position to discourage bidders.

*Wright v. Morgan* of course demonstrates that, just as in the case of potentially void transactions, the trust instrument can specifically authorise a transaction which is potentially voidable. Indeed this was specifically held in *Sargeant v. National Westminster Bank.*[36] As has already been mentioned, the Articles of Association of virtually all companies also expressly permit purchases by directors provided that disclosure of their interest is made in whatever way is required by the provision in question.[37] In the absence of such a provision, the trustee will have to do the same as in the case of a potentially

---

[32] Hence the decision in *Franks v. Bollans* (1868) 3 Ch.App. 717, where a trustee sold to himself, would still be the same today.

[33] This would have worked in *Williams v. Scott* [1900] A.C. 499 (Privy Council on appeal from New South Wales) had there been sufficient disclosure by the trustees to the beneficiaries.

[34] [1926] A.C. 788.

[35] *Whelpdale v. Cookson* (1747) 1 Ves.Sen. 9.

[36] (1990) 61 P. & C.R. 518.

[37] The Companies Acts have long contained a provision requiring directors who are in any way, whether directly or indirectly, interested in a contract or proposed contract with the company to declare the nature of their interest at a meeting of the directors of the company. The present provision is Companies Act 1985, s.317. The Table A Articles of Association recommended by statute provide that directors will not be liable to account for benefits resulting from transactions with the company which have been duly disclosed in accordance with the section. Many Articles of Association additionally provide that such directors should neither vote nor be counted in the quorum on any matter in which they are interested. See *Movitex v. Bullfield* [1988] B.C.L.C. 625.

void transaction, either try to acquire the beneficial interests of the beneficiaries or seek permission to purchase from the court. Such permission will only be granted on the basis of very clear evidence that the sale is in the interests of all the beneficiaries. Such leave is obviously necessary in cases where some of the beneficiaries are either unborn, unascertained or not *sui juris*. What is the situation if the beneficiaries are all *sui juris* and are between them absolutely entitled to the whole of the beneficial interest in the property in question?

In such circumstances, there seems in principle to be no reason why a trustee should not purchase property belonging to his trust without the permission of the court if all the beneficiaries do in fact agree; there is no reason for the court to upset a sale where the beneficiaries have genuinely agreed to it, although such an agreement would obviously only be effective if the trustees had disclosed to the beneficiaries all the information which they possessed relating to the property. Nevertheless, despite the theoretical possibility of an unimpeachable sale taking place in this way, there are in practice two serious objections: first, the onus on the trustee-purchaser of demonstrating that the beneficiaries were indeed given all the relevant information and that they all freely gave their consent is an extremely difficult burden of proof to discharge; and, secondly, even when the trustee-purchaser does acquire a valid title, the property will thereafter often be as unmarketable as if his purchase had been potentially voidable. A right to avoid a transaction is enforceable against successors in title with notice; consequently, if a purchaser becomes aware that his vendor previously held the property as a trustee, it will be most unlikely that he will complete the sale. Even where the former trustee of the property is able to produce a written agreement showing that his beneficiaries did indeed consent, his purchaser will never be able to be sure that those beneficiaries received all the information in the possession of their trustee before they entered into the agreement with him; consequently, it is only in quite exceptional circumstances that a subsequent purchaser will complete his purchase. For these reasons, a trustee-purchaser will be wise to obtain the permission of the court in every case.

Where a potentially voidable transaction has been entered into without any appropriate authorisation, only in most extraordinary circumstances will the court refuse to set aside a purchase of trust property by a trustee at the instance of the beneficiary, save where the trustee can successfully raise the defence of delay, usually known as "laches".[38] Exceptionally, however, the court did refuse to upset a transaction in *Holder v. Holder*.[39] One of the executors of a will renounced his executorship after carrying out certain acts which, it was conceded, amounted to intermeddling. He was the tenant of certain farms which the remaining executors offered for sale by auction subject to his tenancy. At the auction he purchased the farms at a good price, probably higher than would have been paid by anyone other than a sitting tenant and well above the reserve price, which had been fixed by an independent valuer. One of the beneficiaries subsequently sought to have the sale set aside. The Court of Appeal refused to do so.

Harman L.J. held that the rule in *Ex parte Lacey* was based on the principle

---

[38] See *Tito v. Waddell (No.2)* [1977] Ch. 106 at 249–250.
[39] [1968] Ch. 353.

that no man may be both vendor and purchaser. Here the purchaser had played no real part in the administration of the estate and had renounced his executorship long before the sale. All the beneficiaries were aware of this and so could not have been looking to him to protect their interests. Thus the mischief which the rule was intended to prevent did not arise and there was no reason to set aside the sale. Such an attitude, while quite different from that adopted in *Wright v. Morgan*, does not in any way affect the rule itself. But both the other members of the court declined to accept the underlying principle of that rule. Danckwerts L.J. said that Chancery judges were daily engaged in ascertaining the knowledge and intentions of parties to proceedings; the court could unquestionably sanction such a purchase and so the rule in *Ex parte Lacey* could be no more than a rule of practice. He therefore held that this type of issue was a matter for the discretion of the judge. Sachs L.J. took very much the same view. All three members of the court then went on to hold that, in any event, the beneficiaries had acquiesced in the purchase and could not now seek to set it aside.

The approach taken in *Holder v. Holder* by Danckwerts and Sachs L.JJ. suggested that the courts might be about to move away from the automatic application of the self-dealing rule and instead apply the fair-dealing rule to purchases by a trustee of the property belonging to his trust. This would have meant that such purchases would be set aside only where the trustee was unable to convince the court that he had obtained no advantage by virtue of his position, a flexible approach which would undoubtedly have been preferable. However, *Holder v. Holder* has not in fact been interpreted in this way. In *Re Thompson's Settlement*,[40] Vinelott J. took the view that the decision in *Holder v. Holder* had been reached for the reasons enunciated by Harman L.J. and held that the self-dealing rule "is applied stringently in cases where a trustee concurs in a transaction which cannot be carried into effect without his concurrence and who also has an interest in or holds a fiduciary duty to another in relation to the same transaction".[41] He therefore held that two leases in favour of a company and a partnership of which the two trustees were respectively a shareholder and a partner were not valid. Thus, at least for the moment, the self-dealing rule appears to retain its full force.

### (2) The fair-dealing rule

This rule, which is less stringent, applies to purchases by trustees of the beneficial interests of their beneficiaries and to purchases by other fiduciaries (such as agents) of property belonging to their principals.

Where a trustee purchases the beneficial interest of one of the beneficiaries under the trust, the mischief which the rule in *Ex parte Lacey* was intended to solve does not arise since the trustee is not both vendor and purchaser. Hence the courts have always been prepared to uphold such purchases provided that the trustee is able to establish that he obtained no advantage by reason of his position;[42] in particular, he must be able to show that he did not abuse his position as trustee, that he concealed no material facts, that the price was fair,

---

[40] [1986] Ch. 99.
[41] *ibid.* at p.115.
[42] *Chalmer v. Bradley* (1819) 1 J. & W. 51.

and that the beneficiary did not rely solely on his advice.[43] This will be an almost impossible burden of proof to discharge when the beneficiary is a minor;[44] in such circumstances, the trustee will again need to seek the permission of the court to purchase.

Similarly, where a fiduciary such as an agent purchases property belonging to his principal, he is again in practice unlikely to be both sole vendor and purchaser; even if he is, in comparison with the position of a trustee or a director who is purchasing property belonging to his principal, he will have far fewer possibilities of taking any unfair advantage. Consequently, such purchases will similarly be upheld provided that the fiduciary is able to show that he did not abuse his position in any way, that he paid a fair price, and that he has made full disclosure of his interest and of any information which he possesses about the property.[45]

## (3) The precise limits of the rules

The self-dealing rule and the fair-dealing rule cannot be evaded by selling to an associate of the fiduciary rather than to the fiduciary himself; the rules have proved strong enough to prevent evasion. Most of the decided cases concern purchases by associates of trustees. In the first place, although a sale to a relative of the trustee is not necessarily bad,[46] a purchase taken in the name of the trustee's children will usually be upset[47] and it is very risky to take a purchase in the name of the trustee's spouse,[48] at least if at the time the two "were living in perfect amity" rather than "separate and in emnity for a dozen years".[49] Nor can the rules be overcome by selling to a limited company of which the trustee is the majority shareholder,[50] or of which he has control.[51] It seems that a sale by a trustee to a company of which he is a member, but which he does not control, which is necessarily not void, is not *ipso facto* voidable either; however, if the beneficiaries seek to upset the transaction, the company may have to show that the trustee had taken all reasonable steps to find a purchaser and that the price paid by the company was at the time adequate.[52]

Similar rules presumably apply to partnerships; certainly, a sale by a trustee to a partnership comprising the trustee and his family will not be valid.[53] It is equally offensive to the rules to sell the property to a third person, with an agreement or understanding for its repurchase.[54] However, it has been held that, where there was no agreement or understanding for repurchase at the time of the sale to the third person, the fact that the trustee had sold the property to that person with the hope of being able to repurchase was not a

---

[43] *Coles v. Trescothick* (1804) 9 Ves. 234.
[44] See *Sanderson v. Walker* (1807) 13 Ves. 601.
[45] *Edwards v. Meyrick* (1842) 2 Hare 60.
[46] *Coles v. Trescothick* (1804) 9 Ves. 234.
[47] *Gregory v. Gregory* (1821) Jac. 631.
[48] *Ferraby v. Hobson* (1847) 2 Ph. 255; *Burrell v. Burrell's Trustee* 1915 S.C. 333.
[49] *Tito v. Waddell (No.2)* [1977] Ch. 106 at 240.
[50] *Silkstone and Haigh Moor Coal Co. v. Edey* [1900] 1 Ch. 167; *Movitex v. Bullfield* [1988] B.C.L.C. 104.
[51] *Re Thompson's Settlement* [1986] Ch. 99; *Movitex v. Bullfield* [1988] B.C.L.C. 104.
[52] *Farrar v. Farrar's* (1888) 40 Ch.D. 395.
[53] *Re Thompson's Settlement* [1986] Ch. 99.
[54] *Williams v. Scott* [1900] A.C. 499.

sufficient ground for setting the sale aside.[55] Finally, a sale may be upset if a trustee retires with the intention that the property will be conveyed to him after his retirement.[56] If, however, a sufficient length of time has elapsed between the retirement and the sale for the court to be satisfied that the ex-trustee has not taken any advantage of knowledge about the property gained while he was a trustee, the sale will be upheld. Such a transaction was upheld where there had been an interval of 12 years between the trustee's retirement and his purchase.[57]

### (4) The consequences of liability

When a transaction is void under the principles discussed above, it will simply have no effect. Thus in *Franks v. Bollans*,[58] a trustee contrived, by means of an extremely intricate deed, to sell to himself part of the land which he was holding on trust. One of the beneficiaries was subsequently held still to be beneficially entitled to it on the grounds that both contract and conveyance were wholly void. She was, however, fortunate that the trustee still held the property which he had purchased. Where this is not the case, the property will only be able to be recovered from a third party if the latter has not taken free of the beneficiary's interest.[59] If the third party has done so, then the only recourse of the beneficiary will be to attempt to follow the property into its product in the way (which will be discussed in a later chapter[60] or to attempt to obtain compensation for breach of trust.[61]

When on the other hand a transaction is not void but only voidable at the instance of the principal, the latter must avoid it within a reasonable time, otherwise his failure to do so will entitle the fiduciary to invoke the defence of laches.[62] If the sale is so avoided, the consequences will be as follows.

If the subject matter of the purchase is still in the hands of the fiduciary, then the principal will have a choice.

1.  He will be able to recover the property together with any income produced in the meantime provided that he is in a position to make *restitutio in integrum* by returning to the fiduciary the price which he paid for it. In the case of beneficiaries under a trust, this option will require the consent of all of them because of the risk that the property may not be able subsequently to be resold at a higher value, in which case "the beneficiaries would be worse off than if the claim had never been made".[63]

2.  Alternatively, the principal can require the property to be put up for

---

[55] *Re Postlethwaite* (1888) 37 W.R. 200, 60 L.T. 514.
[56] *Wright v. Morgan* [1926] A.C. 788; *Re Mullholland's Will Trusts* [1949] 1 All E.R. 460.
[57] *Re Boles and the British Land Company's Contract* [1902] 1 Ch. 244.
[58] (1868) 3 Ch.App. 717.
[59] Only likely if the third party has not purchased for value or if the property is unregistered land. A purchaser for value of registered land or pure personalty will almost inevitably have taken free.
[60] See *post*, pp. 807 *et seq.*
[61] This will only be possible if a breach of the self-dealing rule is itself a breach of trust, something which is not at present entirely clear. See *Constructive Trusts* (3rd ed., 1997), p. 147, fn. 70.
[62] See *Tito v. Waddell (No.2)* [1977] Ch. 106 at 249–250.
[63] *Holder v. Holder* [1968] Ch. 353 at 370–371 (Cross J.).

sale again under the direction of the court;[64] the fiduciary will not be allowed to bid at this resale if any of his principals objects to him so doing.[65] The reserve price will normally be the price originally paid by the fiduciary together with interest in respect of the time during which he has held the property, plus the value of any improvements which he has made to the property and interest on that amount, minus any income produced by the property or, if the fiduciary has himself been in occupation, the appropriate occupation rent.[66] If the sale "realises more than the reserve fixed by the court, the surplus belongs to the [principal], whereas if it realises less [the fiduciary] will be held to his bargain"[67] and so will lose the difference.

It will only be in the interests of the principal to use either of these remedies where the property is worth at least as much as the fiduciary paid for it. If it has fallen in value, avoiding the transaction will give the principal a property worth less than the sum which he has to return to the fiduciary; consequently, it will be in his interests to affirm the transaction.

If, on the other hand, the property is no longer in the hands of the principal, any third party to whom it has been transferred will have acquired legal title to that property because of the fact that the transaction was voidable rather than void. If the third party has not taken free of the right of the principal to have the purchase set aside (which is of course a mere equity), the third party will be in exactly the same position as the fiduciary. If, however, he has taken free of this mere equity because he is a bona fide purchaser for value without notice or a statutory equivalent, then the property will not be able to be recovered by the principal, whose position will be as follows.

1.   He will be entitled to recover any profit made by the fiduciary on the resale[68] with interest on that profit.[69]

2.   In the event of a resale at less than the true value, he will also be able to claim the difference between the price paid and the true value with interest thereon;[70] this will be recoverable by way of compensation for breach of fiduciary duty under *Nocton v. Lord Ashburton*[71] (such

---

[64] This was what was ordered at first instance in *Holder v. Holder, ibid.,* where the purchase was set aside.

[65] *Tennant v. Trenchard* (1869) 4 Ch.App. 537.

[66] This was the form of order made in *Holder v. Holder* at first instance; although the right to add to the reserve price the value of any improvements was conceded in that case, the existence of the right to do so emerges clearly from *O'Sullivan v. Management Agency and Music* [1985] Q.B. 428 at 466.

[67] *Holder v. Holder* [1968] Ch. 353 at 371 (Cross J.).

[68] *Hall v. Hallett* (1784) 1 Cox 134; *Ex parte James* (1803) 8 Ves. 337 at 351; *Silkstone and Haigh Moor Coal Co. v. Edey* [1900] 1 Ch. 167.

[69] Formerly 4% but, following *Bartlett v. Barclays Bank Trust Co.* [1980] Ch. 515 at 547, it seems that the rate will now be that of the court's short-term investment account (established under the Administration of Justice Act 1965, s.6 (1)).

[70] *Lord Hardwicke v. Vernon* (1800) 4 Ves. 411.

[71] [1914] A.C. 932. See Davidson (1982) 13 Melbourne U.L.R. 349.

compensation is also available as an alternative to an account of profits).[72]

3.  If, on the other hand, the price paid by the third party was less than the price paid by the fiduciary because the property had fallen in value, the fiduciary will have made no profit and the principal will have suffered no loss; consequently, in such circumstances, the principal will neither have nor be entitled to any remedy.

## (B) Sales of Property by a Fiduciary to his Principal

A sale by a fiduciary to his principal of property belonging to himself will be set aside at the instance of the principal unless the fiduciary has fully disclosed to the principal the nature of his interest in the transaction; this is the case no matter how honest the fiduciary or fair the price.[73] Such a sale may be set aside even where the fiduciary purchased the property in question before he entered into the fiduciary relationship. Thus, in *Armstrong v. Jackson*,[74] a stockbroker did not disclose to his client that he had owned the shares which he had been encouraging the client to buy ever since the company in question had originally been formed. Five years later, by which time the shares had fallen in value to less than a fifth of the purchase price which the client had paid, he discovered the true facts and successfully sought rescission of the sale. However, where the property has instead increased in value, it will not be in the interests of the principal to set aside the transaction. In the event that, for this or any other reason, the principal seeks not to set aside the sale but to recover the profit made by the fiduciary out of the transaction, his right to do so will depend on when the fiduciary oriiginally purchased the property.

In *Bentley v. Craven*,[75] the defendant was responsible for the purchase of sugar for a partnership of sugar refiners of which he was a member but also carried on an independent business as a sugar dealer. He purchased a quantity of sugar which he later resold to the partnership at a price which, although resulting in a profit to him, was the fair market price of the day. He was held liable to account for his profit to the partnership since he had been a fiduciary at the date of purchase and so should have purchased for the partnership rather than for himself. A similar decision was reached where an investment adviser purchased a property of a type which he knew that his client wished to purchase and subsequently sold it on to her at a substantial profit.[76]

On the other hand, in *Re Cape Breton Co.*,[77] a director acquiesced in the sale to his company of certain mining claims in which he had a beneficial interest. After discovering the facts, the company elected not to set aside the sale. Subsequently, after the property had been sold on at a loss, the company tried

---

[72] *McKenzie v. McDonald* [1927] V.L.R. 134 (Court of Appeal of Victoria). This is one of the possible explanations of *Coleman v. Myers* [1977] 2 N.Z.L.R. 225 (Court of Appeal of New Zealand), where minority shareholders recovered compensation from the directors of the company (held, unusually, to owe them fiduciary duties because of the family nature of the company) who had recommended the acceptance of an under-valued takeover bid without disclosing that the offeror was a company controlled by one of them.

[73] *Gillett v. Peppercone* (1840) 3 Beav. 78.

[74] [1917] 2 K.B. 822.

[75] (1853) 18 Beav. 75.

[76] *Cook v. Evatt (No.2)* [1992] 1 N.Z.L.R. 676 (High Court of New Zealand).

[77] (1885) 29 Ch.D. 795.

to claim the profit which the director had made on the original sale. This action failed because the director had acquired the property more than two years before the company in question had been formed. This conclusion is clearly correct when the fiduciary sold the property to his principal at the market value. The Court of Appeal actually held, by a majority, that it made no difference that the director had sold above the market value. However, the House of Lords[78] held that there was no evidence that the sale price was above market value. This point therefore did not have to be decided but Lord Herschell considered that an agent employed to purchase non-specific goods in the market would be liable for the excess if he sold his own goods to the company above market value.[79] Therefore, although the decision of the Court of Appeal clearly constitutes the law at present, this particular point cannot be regarded as finally settled.

These authorities show that, when the principal does not seek to rescind the sale or cannot do so because rescission is barred on the grounds of affirmation, laches or bona fide purchase, he will only have a remedy where the fiduciary acquired the property after he entered into the fiduciary relationship in question or, possibly, where the sale price was above the market value. All the authorities discussed deal with fiduciary relationships other than that of trustee and beneficiary. There appears to be no English authority dealing with a purchase by a trustee of his own property for his trust; however, an American decision[80] and dicta in *Bentley v. Craven* suggest that the same rules will also apply to such transactions.

### (C) Regular Trading between Fiduciary and Principal

Where a fiduciary engages in regular trading between his own business and a business which he is managing in a fiduciary capacity, the situation will be governed by exactly the same principles as where a fiduciary sells his own property to his principal.[81]

### (D) Loans from a Fiduciary to his Principal

This situation occurred in *Swindle v. Harrison*,[82] where a solicitor made a loan to his client to enable her to complete the purchase of a property and avoid the loss of the 20 per cent deposit which she had already paid. No other source of finance was available to her. The transaction did not ultimately prove profitable and she was unable to repay the advance, which was secured on the property. She had obviously been aware of the source of the funds but sought to prevent the solicitor from realising his security on the grounds that he had not explained to her exactly how much interest he would be making. The Court of Appeal accepted that his failure fully to explain this amounted to a breach of fiduciary duty. However, since *restitutio in integrum* was obviously impossible because of her inability to repay the sum advanced to the solicitor, her only conceivable remedy for his breach of fiduciary duty was equitable

---

[78] *Cavendish Bentinck v. Fenn* (1887) 12 App.Cas. 652.
[79] *ibid.* at 659. The remedy would presumably have been either an account of profits or compensation under *Nocton v. Lord Ashburton, post.*
[80] *Cornet v. Cornet* (1916) 269 No. 298.
[81] This situation is discussed by Finn, *Fiduciary Obligations* (1977), pp. 228–231.
[82] [1997] 4 All E.R. 705.

compensation under *Nocton v. Lord Ashburton*.[83] The Court of Appeal in fact also denied her any equitable compensation because her position would have been even worse if the loan had never been made.[84]

### 7. Benefits obtained by a Fiduciary as a result of his Position to the Exclusion of his Principal

This third group of cases has emerged as the result of the rigorous application by the courts of a decision in 1726,[85] which established what was, in the light of the prevailing legal rules and financial circumstances, a wholly under-standable prohibition on trustees renewing for their own benefit leases formerly held by their trusts. This decision has had two quite distinct effects. First, it has produced a line of authority concerning the extent to which this prohibition also applies to other fiduciaries and the associated question of whether a fiduciary may purchase for his own benefit the freehold reversion in property of which his principal is lessee. Secondly, and totally unconnected with any question of the renewal of leases or the purchase of reversions, the decision has also had a profound effect on the general question of what opportunities a fiduciary is entitled to utilise for his own benefit.

### (A) Speculation by a Fiduciary with the Property of his Principal
This is almost the only situation within this third group of cases which is wholly uncontroversial. Where a fiduciary engages in speculation with the property of his principal, the latter will be entitled to all the profits made by the fiduciary under a constructive trust.[86]

A somewhat extreme example of the operation of this principle is *Reid-Newfoundland Co. v. Anglo-American Telegraph Co.*[87] Under the terms of a contract, a telegraph company had erected a special telegraph wire for use in the operation of a railway. The contract provided that no commercial messages should be passed over this wire except for the account of the telegraph company. When this prohibition was directly contravened, the telegraph company successfully claimed that the profits made thereby were held subject to a constructive trust in its favour. The Privy Council appear to have regarded the company operating the railway as the agent of the telegraph company in respect of its use of the latter's telegraph wire. Thus, the former had in breach of fiduciary duty made a profit out of the use of the latter's property and so was clearly bound to account for that profit under a constructive trust.

However, a similar claim failed in *Attorney-General v. Blake*.[88] It has already been seen[89] that the Attorney-General contended that the Soviet spy Blake owed the Crown a fiduciary duty, *inter alia*, not to use the Crown's property, including intangible property such as originally confidential information, for his profit. Scott V.-C. held that this duty was formulated in terms too wide to be acceptable and went on to dismiss the Crown's claim on the grounds that

---

[83] [1914] A.C. 932.
[84] See *post*, pp. 764 *et seq.*
[85] *Keech v. Sandford* (1726) Sel.Cas.Ch. 61.
[86] *Brown v. I.R.C.* [1965] A.C. 264.
[87] [1912] A.C. 555.
[88] [1997] Ch. 84.
[89] See *ante*, p. 343.

the law will not go so far as to impose unreasonable restraints either on the freedom of speech of a former fiduciary or on his ability to earn his living by exploiting expertise acquired during the fiduciary relationship. No doubt was cast on this reasoning on appeal;[90] the Court of Appeal specifically held that Blake was not in breach of fiduciary duty but both there and in the House of Lords the Crown instead succeeded on public law and contractual arguments not raised at first instance. However, there seems little likelihood that the arguments which commended themselves to Scott V.-C. will often be invoked successfully; it is hardly likely that the courts would look very charitably on a trustee who deferred the receipt of bribes and commissions until after his retirement and then sought to retain them on that ground.

When liability is imposed in this type of case, the situation will be as follows. Where the principal has been owner of the property throughout, and also in cases where the fiduciary is already holding the property in question on trust for his principal, the constructive trust will be imposed merely on the profit. But if the property has instead reached the hands of the fiduciary in some other way, both the property and the fiduciary's profit will be subject to a constructive trust. If there is no profit, because the speculation has resulted in a loss, a constructive trust may still be imposed, if necessary, upon any of the property remaining in the hands of the fiduciary and, in the event that the value of the property has fallen as a result of the breach by the fiduciary of his duty of loyalty, the principal will be able to recover compensation for that loss under *Nocton v. Lord Ashburton*.[91] The latter actually occurred in *Tang Man Sit v. Capacious Investments*.[92] The defendant had made secret profits from letting certain houses on his land which he had agreed to assign to the plaintiff, who had financed their construction pursuant to a joint venture agreement. The plaintiff recovered not only those profits but also compensation for the diminution in value of the houses caused by their wrongful occupation.

## (B) Competition between a Fiduciary and the Business of his Principal

There are certain circumstances in which a fiduciary will not be able to compete with the business of his principal. Different rules apply to the different fiduciary relationships.

### (1) Trustees

Where the trust property includes a business, or the trustees carry on any income earning activity, a trustee must not commence a business or activity on his own account which will compete with that of the trust. Thus, in *Re Thomson*,[93] one of the assets of a trust was a yachtbroker's business, which was being carried on by the trustees. One of them sought to set up on his own a similar business in the same town, which would have competed with the trust business, but the court granted an injunction restraining him from doing so. The decision in *Re Thomson* appears to be at variance with that in the earlier Irish case of *Moore v. M'Glynn*.[94] There the court had refused an injunction, although it was thought that the setting up of a competing business would be a

---

[90] [1998] Ch. 439 (C.A.), [2001] 1 A.C. 268 (H.L.).
[91] [1914] A.C. 932.
[92] [1996] 1 A.C. 514 (Privy Council on appeal from Hong Kong).
[93] [1930] 1 Ch. 203.
[94] [1894] 1 Ir.R. 74.

good ground for removing the trustee from his trusteeship. It was said that a breach of trust would only be committed if in carrying on the new business the trustee practised deception, or solicited the customers from the old shop. It is sometimes suggested that this decision can be reconciled with that in *Re Thomson* on the basis that the yachtbroker's business was so specialised that any other yachtbroking business in the town was bound to compete with the trust business, even if the customers were not solicited. This is a possible solution, but it does not appear to have been the basis of the decision in *Re Thomson*.

*Re Thomson* seems clearly right in principle and it may well be that *Moore v. M'Glynn* would not now be followed. As has been shown, in other circumstances the court has been so astute to find a conflict of interest that it is doubtful if it would stop itself from finding a conflict where the same business was being carried on, at least if it were serving the same locality. Where, however, a person who is carrying on a business is then appointed to be a trustee, the position seems to depend on whether the person making the appointment knew of that business. If he did, the trustee will be entitled to continue his business, but if it then appears that there is an actual conflict of interest, he may be required to resign, or be removed.[95]

### (2) Other fiduciaries

It might be expected that, if an unpaid trustee may thus in appropriate circumstances be prevented from competing, the paid director and partner would necessarily be prohibited from so doing. Partners are indeed under a statutory duty not to compete with the partnership business,[96] but the position of directors is both obscure and anomalous.

At common law, a director is not under any obligation not to compete with his company; this emerges from *London and Mashonaland Exploration Co. v. New Mashonaland Exploration Co.*,[97] where it was held that a director cannot be restrained from acting as a director of a rival company, a decision which was approved in *Bell v. Lever Bros*,[98] by Lord Blanesburgh, who added that "[w]hat he could do for a rival company he could, of course, do for himself". However, in the light of authority that an employee may not compete with the business of his employer,[99] it seems likely that an executive director will be under a similar duty not to compete with his company.

This seems to have been recognised by Lord Denning in *Scottish Co-operative Wholesale Society v. Meyer*,[1] which concerned an application under what is now section 459 of the Companies Act 1985 to wind a company up on the grounds that the manner in which its affairs were being conducted was unfairly prejudicial to the applicant. In practice, the matter must often be dealt with in the Articles of Association or in the service contract of any individual director. Thus, in *Thomas Marshall Exports v. Guinle*,[2] a managing director had specifically agreed in his service contract not to engage in any other business without

---

[95] See, by analogy, *Peyton v. Robinson* (1823) 1 L.J.(O.S.)Ch. 191; *Moore v. M'Glynn* [1894] 1 Ir.R. 74.
[96] By virtue of the Partnership Act 1890, s.30.
[97] [1891] 1 W.N. 165.
[98] [1932] A.C. 161 at 165. See also *In Plus Group v. Pyke* [2002] 2 B.C.L.C. 201.
[99] *Hivac v. Park Royal Scientific Instruments* [1946] Ch. 169.
[1] [1959] A.C. 324 at 366–367.
[2] [1979] Ch. 227.

the company's consent or to disclose confidential information. It was alleged that he had done both as a means of diverting the company's business to himself and that, subsequently, he had repudiated his service contract by resigning half way through a fixed 10 year contract. Interim injunctions were granted restraining him from dealing with the company's customers and from disclosing any confidential information. This decision was based primarily on the express contractual stipulation but also, to a lesser extent, on his fiduciary obligations as a director. This suggests that, at least in the case of executive directors, competing with the business of the company will constitute a breach of fiduciary duty. However, it appears that merely to accept directorships in competing companies does not constitute a breach of the duty of loyalty owed by the director to the first company.

The authorities discussed establish that, where a fiduciary has breached his duty of loyalty by competing with the business of his principal, the latter can obtain an injunction restraining such competition. Further, although there does not seem to be any case in which this has actually been held,[3] the fiduciary should be liable to account to his principal for any profits which he has made out of this competition under a constructive trust.

## (C) Renewal by a Fiduciary for his own Benefit of a Lease Formerly Held by his Principal

In *Keech v. Sandford*,[4] a lease of a market was held on trust for an infant. The trustee sought, unsuccessfully, to renew the lease for the benefit of the trust. However, the landlord, although not prepared to renew the lease to the trust, was prepared to grant a renewal to the trustee in his personal capacity and the trustee duly took up the lease in his own right. Lord King L.C. held that any trustee who abuses his position by entering into a transaction with a third party must account for the benefit of the transaction as a constructive trustee. Consequently the trustee held the benefit of the lease on constructive trust for the infant. The rationale of the rule was stated both simply and cynically: if a trustee on the refusal of a lessor to renew a lease to the trust were permitted to take a lease himself, few leases would ever be renewed in favour of trusts.

This prohibition was wholly understandable at that time. Many ecclesiastical, charitable and public bodies were by law restricted as to the length of leases which they were able to grant and leases were therefore renewed more or less as a matter of right. By taking a renewal of a lease for himself, a trustee was therefore in practice depriving the trust of a grant which it had a right to expect. This was also the time of the South Sea Bubble, a period of extravagant financial speculation and even more extravagant financial collapses, when the existence of stringent controls on the activities of fiduciaries was unquestionably necessary. However, the rule laid down in *Keech v. Sandford* has continued to be applied despite the relaxation of the rules as to the length of leases; and the greater financial stability of the nineteenth and twentieth centuries indeed it has been extended so as to apply also to other fiduciaries.

The precise limits of the rule were discussed very fully in *Re Biss*.[5] The Court

---

[3] Such a claim was made, unsuccessfully, in *Moore v. M'Glynn* [1894] 1 Ir.R. 74 and in *In Plus Group v. Pyke* [2002] 2 B.C.L.C. 201 where the fiduciary was held to have been entitled to compete with his principal.
[4] (1726) Sel.Cas.Ch. 61.
[5] [1903] 2 Ch. 40.

of Appeal held that the rule applies with all its stringency to persons clearly occupying a fiduciary position such as trustees or agents; there is an irrebuttable presumption that such persons cannot retain the benefit of transactions entered into in their personal capacity. On the other hand, persons owing a special but non-fiduciary duty are subject only to a rebuttable presumption. Thus if such a person can show that he did not abuse his position, he can retain the benefit of the transaction. The court considered mortgagees, tenants for life, joint tenants, tenants in common and (rather unexpectedly) partners to be in this category. There seems no good reason why partners, who are quite clearly fiduciaries for all other purposes, should be in the latter rather than the former category and *Thompson's Trustee v. Heaton*[6] and *Popat v. Shonchintra*[7] (both of which actually concerned purchases of freehold reversions) may well have changed the law in this respect, although this question cannot yet be regarded as finally settled. On the other hand, it is clear that the rule in *Keech v. Sandford* does not apply to a person who owes neither fiduciary obligations nor a special non-fiduciary duty. Thus in *Savage v. Dunningham*,[8] where three persons were sharing an unfurnished flat and the rack rent payable therefor, it was held that one of them was perfectly entitled to purchase a long leasehold interest therein for his own benefit.

While the rule in *Keech v. Sandford* is certainly a stringent penal rule which it is impossible to justify in modern conditions, there is absolutely no doubt that it remains English law. Where the rule applies, the principal will be entitled to take over the lease but will obviously have to pay the rent due thereunder. There has never been a reported case where the fiduciary has paid a capital sum for the lease in question. In this event, the result would presumably be the same as where a fiduciary has purchased the reversion on a lease held by his principal, discussed below.

### (D) Purchase by a Fiduciary of the Reversion on a Lease Held by his Principal

The rule in *Keech v. Sandford* has been extended to cases where the fiduciary has acquired the reversion, normally but obviously not necessarily the freehold reversion, in property of which his principal is lessee.

When the fiduciary has acquired the reversion by means of an abuse of his fiduciary position, it is clearly in accordance with principle for a constructive trust to be imposed. A trust was imposed on this ground in *Hooper v. Gorvin*,[9] where one of a number of leasehold tenants of a site had been nominated to act on their behalf in negotiations for the acquisition of the freehold. As has already been seen,[10] he was held to have assumed fiduciary obligations towards them and therefore held the freehold, which he had purchased in his sole name, on constructive trust for all of them. This will also be the case where the fiduciary has only obtained the opportunity to purchase because, as fiduciary, he was the nominal lessee.[11] Similarly, when leases were renewable by custom, a fiduciary who purchased the reversion would also be held to

---

[6] [1974] 1 W.L.R. 605. See *post*, p. 360.
[7] [1995] 1 W.L.R. 908. See *post*, p. 360.
[8] [1974] Ch. 181.
[9] [2001] W.T.L.R. 575 at 589–590.
[10] See *ante*, p. 332.
[11] *Griffith v. Owen* [1907] 1 Ch. 105.

hold the reversion on constructive trust for his principal since, otherwise, he would be able to prejudice the interests of his principal by declining to renew the lease.[12]

On the other hand, where the lease in question is not renewable by custom or by right, the acquisition of the reversion by the fiduciary can hardly be said to prejudice his principal, and until relatively recently, it was held that in such circumstances a fiduciary who had not abused his position was entitled to retain the reversion for his own benefit.[13] This seemed wholly in accordance with principle. However, more recent cases have raised some doubt as to whether a fiduciary can ever purchase a reversion for his own benefit.

In *Protheroe v. Protheroe*,[14] a husband held a leasehold on trust for himself and his wife in equal shares. After they had separated, he acquired the freehold reversion. The Court of Appeal, in a short extempore judgment which did not refer to any of the authorities just discussed, held that a trustee of leasehold property can never acquire the freehold for himself and imposed a constructive trust. It seems highly likely that the husband only obtained the opportunity to acquire the reversion because he was, as trustee, the nominal lessee. If this was the case, discussion and application of the earlier authorities would have made no difference. However, the broad principle thus enunciated was subsequently applied in *Thompson's Trustee v. Heaton*.[15] After the dissolution of a partnership, one of the partners remained in possession of land of which the partners had been, and remained, joint lessees. After that partner's death 14 years later, his executors acquired the freehold reversion and subsequently resold the land. The trustee in bankruptcy of the other partner successfully claimed to be entitled to one half of the profit so obtained, Pennycuick V.-C. holding that on the facts the leasehold interest remained an undistributed asset of the partnership and thus, by virtue of *Protheroe v. Protheroe*, neither partner could acquire the reversion for his sole benefit.

This decision obviously casts doubt on the statement by the Court of Appeal in *Re Biss*,[16] that partners were only to be caught by the rule in *Keech v. Sandford* if it could be shown that an advantage had actually been obtained by virtue of their position (this dictum has admittedly already been criticised,[17] but should it not at the very least have been discussed?). More significantly, the broad statement in *Protheroe v. Protheroe* was applied without reference to the earlier authorities, the application of which might well have led to a different result. This would not, however, have been the case in *Popat v. Shonchintra*,[18] in which *Thompson's Trustee v. Heaton* was subsequently applied, where another former partner had only acquired the opportunity to purchase the freehold because he had continued to run the business and so was clearly a trustee of it. This decision also establishes that the beneficial interests in such reversions are divided in proportion to each partner's capital injections — an entirely justifiable extrapolation of the rule in *Keech v. Sandford*.

---

[12] *Phillips v. Phillips* (1885) 29 Ch.D. 673.
[13] *Randall v. Russell* (1817) 3 Mer. 190; *Bevan v. Webb* [1905] 1 Ch. 620.
[14] [1968] 1 W.L.R. 519.
[15] [1974] 1 W.L.R. 605.
[16] [1903] 2 Ch. 40.
[17] See *ante*, p. 359.
[18] [1995] 1 W.L.R. 908. On appeal ([1997] 1 W.L.R 1367), the case was decided on the basis of technical partnership rules.

It may therefore well be that *Protheroe v. Protheroe* has swept away all the earlier distinctions and has established that a fiduciary may never purchase for his own benefit a reversion in property of which his principal is lessee. If this is indeed the case, then only where, as in *Savage v. Dunningham*,[19] a purchaser of a reversion is not a fiduciary at all will he be able to acquire it for his own benefit. The principle enunciated in *Protheroe v. Protheroe* seems unnecessarily harsh and it is therefore suggested that the approach of the earlier authorities was preferable.

Where the purchase of a reversion by a fiduciary is successfully impugned, the imposition of a constructive trust does not mean that he will lose the money which he has paid for it. His principal is entitled to purchase the reversion from him for the price which he originally paid, so that he is only deprived of his profit. Where, as in *Hooper v. Gorvin*,[20] it was always intended that the fiduciary would acquire a share in the reversion, he will nevertheless be entitled to retain that share. However, the principal may be unable or unwilling to purchase the reversion; it is not unlikely that this will be the position of a trust. In that event, the principal can nevertheless insist on the reversion being sold and he will then take any profit; this was also held in *Hooper v. Gorvin*.

### (E) Utilisation by a Fiduciary for his own Benefit of an Opportunity of Profit

A fiduciary is obviously entitled to utilise for his own benefit opportunities which have nothing whatever to do with the fiduciary relationship in question. The mere fact that a person is a trustee of an investment fund does not prevent him from purchasing shares in his private capacity — were this not the case, it would be impossible to find anyone prepared to accept a trusteeship. Equally obviously, if such a trustee obtains the opportunity to take up a rights issue by virtue of the fact that the trust is a shareholder in the company in question, then he is not entitled to take up that rights issue in his personal capacity and if he does so the shares in question will be subject to a constructive trust in favour of the fund. A fiduciary will only be in breach of his duty of loyalty to his principal if the transactions into which he enters in his personal capacity fall within the scope of his fiduciary obligations. As Oliver L.J. stated in *Swain v. The Law Society*:[21]

> "What one has to do is ascertain first of all whether there was a fiduciary relationship and, if there was, from what it arose and what, if there was any, was the trust property and then to inquire whether that of which an account is claimed either arose, directly or indirectly, from the trust property itself or was acquired not only in the course of, but by reason of, the fiduciary relationship."

The question of whether a transaction falls within the scope of a fiduciary relationship will sometimes be capable of being resolved by reference to the terms of the agreement between the fiduciary and principal in question. Thus

---

[19] [1974] Ch. 181.
[20] [2001] W.T.L.R. 575 at 589–590.
[21] [1982] 1 W.L.R. 17 at 37. This approach was approved by Lord Brightman in the House of Lords at [1983] 1 A.C. 598 at 619.

in *Aas v. Benham*,[22] a member of a ship-broking partnership utilised information which he had received in his capacity as partner to help form a ship-building company of which he became a director. An action by his partners for an account of the benefits received from the company failed on the grounds that the business of the company was quite different from the business of the partnership, the Court of Appeal holding that there was nothing to prevent a partner utilising information obtained in his fiduciary capacity provided that he was not competing with the partnership business.[23] However, the scope of a fiduciary obligation is not often closely defined by the parties to it and, when it is not, rather more difficulties can be encountered.

### (1) Clear misconduct by the fiduciary

Cases of clear misconduct by a fiduciary are of course quite straightforward. In *Cook v. Deeks*,[24] three of the four directors and shareholders of a company, with the intention of excluding the fourth member, arranged for a contract which they had negotiated on behalf of the company to be made with them in their private capacities. The excluded member claimed successfully that the company was entitled to the benefit of this contract. The Privy Council held that the whole reputation of the three had been obtained with the company; they could have excluded the plaintiff quite legitimately by using their majority shareholding to wind up the company but instead had used their position as directors to deprive the company of any chance of obtaining the contract. This was a clear case of abuse of fiduciary position. However, an identical attitude has been adopted where the misconduct of the fiduciary has been much more questionable. The decided cases of this type have generally arisen when the principal in question has been unable or unwilling to utilise an opportunity and the fiduciary has subsequently utilised that opportunity for his own benefit.

### (2) Opportunities unutilised by the principal

(a) **The approach of the English authorities.** In *Regal (Hastings) v. Gulliver*,[25] the plaintiff company owned a cinema in Hastings and wished to acquire two other local cinemas with the intention of selling the whole enterprise as a package. A subsidiary, with a capital of 5,000 £1 shares, was formed to take leases of these two cinemas. The original scheme was for only 2,000 of these shares to be paid up but the owner of the cinemas declined to grant the leases on this basis. Since the company could not afford to put more than £2,000 into the subsidiary, four of the directors and the company solicitor each subscribed for 500 shares and the fifth director found some outsiders to take up the remaining 500. The combined concern was then sold not as a whole but by way of takeover and each holder of shares in the subsidiary obviously made a profit. The purchasers then brought an action against all five directors and the company solicitor claiming that this profit had been made out of a breach of their fiduciary duty and therefore had to be accounted for to the company (this

---

[22] [1891] 2 Ch. 244.
[23] See also *British American Oil Producing Co. v. Midway Oil Company* (1938) 82 P. (2d) 1049 (Supreme Court of Oklahoma).
[24] [1916] A.C. 554.
[25] [1942] 1 All E.R. 378 [1967] 2 A.C. 134N.

claim was wholly unmeritorious; its only objective was to recover part of the price which the purchasers had freely agreed to pay).

The action against the director who had not subscribed for any shares obviously failed, for he had made no profit.[26] So too did the action against the company solicitor, for he had subscribed for his shares with the consent of the board of directors as then constituted. But the actions against the other four directors succeeded in the House of Lords, whose decision was based fairly and squarely on *Keech v. Sandford*. Lord Russell of Killowen stated that the directors had unquestionably acquired their shares by virtue of their fiduciary position. It made no difference that the company could not itself have subscribed for the shares — the trust in *Keech v. Sandford* could not itself have obtained a new lease and that had made no difference. Thus the four directors had to surrender a profit which they would have been able to retain had the transaction been carried out in a different way and so were deprived of any return on their investment, while the purchasers finished up paying less for the cinemas than they had originally bargained to pay.

Given that the company could not afford to put more than £2,000 into the subsidiary, what alternative did the directors have? Lord Russell of Killowen thought that they should have obtained a resolution of the shareholders in general meeting approving the transaction.[27] This view seems to conflict with the decision in *Cook v. Deeks*,[28] where such a resolution had been obtained and was held to be ineffective. It was suggested in *Prudential Assurance Co. v. Newman Industries (No.2)*[29] that a ratification by a company in general meeting will only be effective if the directors in question do not control the majority of the votes. It is not clear whether or not the directors of Regal (Hastings) did in fact control the majority;[30] only if they did not is this a valid distinction between *Cook v. Deeks* and *Regal (Hastings) v. Gulliver*.

However, a very much more generous attitude to ratification was subsequently demonstrated by the Privy Council in *Queensland Mines v. Hudson*.[31] The board of the plaintiff company, having been fully informed of all relevant facts, decided to renounce all interest in the exploitation of certain mining exploration licences which it had obtained and assented to the venture being taken over by the defendant; he was still a director of the company and had earlier been its managing director until a shortage of finance had prevented the plaintiff from exploiting the licences itself. The plaintiff subsequently claimed to be entitled to the profit obtained by the defendant. The Privy Council held that the defendant had obtained the opportunity to make this profit by virtue of his position as managing director of the plaintiff and was therefore in principle liable under *Regal (Hastings) v. Gulliver* to account for his profit; however, the fully-informed decision of the board amounted to sufficient consent to enable him to retain his profit.

This conclusion is clearly inconsistent with the decision in *Regal (Hastings) v.*

---

[26] No claim was brought against the outsiders for their profit. Any such claim would have been governed by the principles to be discussed in the next section of this chapter (see *post*, p. 370).
[27] [1942] 1 All E.R. 378 at 389; [1967] 2 A.C. 134N at 150.
[28] [1916] A.C. 554.
[29] [1981] Ch. 257 at 308 (Vinelott J.).
[30] The Editorial Note in [1942] 1 All E.R. 378 at 379 assumed that they did; Vinelott J. in *Prudential Assurance Co. v. Newman Industries (No.2)* [1981] Ch. 257 at 308 disagreed.
[31] (1977) 18 A.L.R. 1.

*Gulliver*, where all the members of the board had taken part in the impeached transaction and so must necessarily have consented to it. The approach taken by the Privy Council may be able to be justified on the grounds that the plaintiff had only two shareholders, both of whom were represented on the board, and the shareholder represented by the defendant held only 49 per cent of the shares; the decision of the board can thus be regarded as a decision of the shareholders where the majority was not controlled by the defendant, which satisfies the test suggested in *Prudential Assurance Co. v. Newman Industries (No.2)*.

In any event, one commentator has argued that the approach of the Privy Council should now be followed so that "if the board has taken a bona fide decision that the company should reject the opportunity on its merits, it may then permit one (or more) of its members to take it up".[32] It is clear that "a court is likely to take a deal of persuading that the board's decision to reject the opportunity was taken bona fide in the interests of the company rather than in that of their fellow director — especially if he has a powerful personality".[33] In practice, for the moment the only safe option seems to be a decision of the shareholders in general meeting and even this can only be guaranteed to work if the directors in question do not control the majority of the votes.

Leaving on one side the question of ratification, there is however no doubt at all that the decisions in *Regal (Hastings) v. Gulliver* and *Queensland Mines v. Hudson* are entirely consistent on the question of the liability of the directors in question to account and certainly represent English law at present. In both cases it was assumed that, in the absence of the appropriate consent, any director who obtained an opportunity by virtue of his fiduciary position was liable to account to the company for this profit. Thus it is clear that the courts are not prepared to countenance a fiduciary exploiting an opportunity for his own benefit and are more concerned to penalise him for having taken up an opportunity of entering into a profitable transaction on his own behalf than to ascertain whether or not there has been a conflict between his duty of loyalty to his principal and his own self-interest.

**(b) The approach of other jurisdictions**. Other jurisdictions have felt able to adopt a more flexible approach and have permitted directors to take up opportunities for their own benefit without the prior consent or subsequent ratification of their companies where there was no serious conflict of duty and interest.

In *Peso Silvermines v. Cropper*,[34] the defendant was on the board of the plaintiff company at a time when the company geologist invited and advised that board to purchase certain mining claims, some of which were contiguous to claims already owned by the company. The board rejected this offer, partly for financial reasons and partly because some of the directors considered the claims to be an uninviting business risk. Subsequently, the geologist, with the defendant and two other directors of the plaintiff, formed a company to purchase and exploit these claims. In due course, the plaintiff was taken over

---

[32] Gower and Davies, *Principles of Modern Company Law* (7th ed., 2003), p. 421.

[33] *ibid.*

[34] (1966) 56 D.L.R.(2d) 1 (British Columbia Court of Appeal); 58 D.L.R.(2d) 1 (Supreme Court of Canada).

and its new board claimed that the defendant held his shares in the new company on constructive trust for the plaintiff.

This claim failed. The Court of Appeal of British Columbia rejected *Regal (Hastings) v. Gulliver* and held, by a majority, that the strict penal rules of equity had been carried far enough and were not appropriate for a modern country in a modern era. The Supreme Court of Canada took a rather narrower view and merely distinguished *Regal (Hastings) v. Gulliver* on the grounds that the defendant had acted entirely in good faith in participating in the initial decision of the board not to purchase the claims. He had not obtained any advantage at all as a result of participating in this decision and was therefore entitled to take up a subsequent offer in his private capacity without being liable to account for his profit. Even this narrower view seems preferable in every way to the approach adopted in *Regal (Hastings) v. Gulliver*. It is undoubtedly possible to criticise *Peso Silvermines v. Cropper* on the grounds that "[t]o allow directors to decide that the company shall not accept the opportunity and then to accept the opportunity themselves might impose too great a strain on their impartiality".[35] However, the sort of attitude adopted by the House of Lords in *Regal (Hastings) v. Gulliver* prevents such matters of policy being raised at all; this in itself is an argument for the adoption of a more flexible attitude, even if its adoption does not in the end alter the conclusion actually reached by the courts.

In *Consul Development v. D.P.C. Estates*,[36] the High Court of Australia adopted an attitude similar to that of the Supreme Court of Canada. The plaintiff was one of a group of property companies which employed a manager to find properties for purchase. He was under an express duty of confidentiality in respect of all group business and had undertaken not to engage in real estate business other than for the group. However, in breach of these obligations, he collaborated with another employee of the group, who was also the managing director of the defendant, by providing him with information about a number of properties which the defendant then acquired, telling him, for reasons which were entirely plausible, that the group was not interested in their acquisition. The plaintiff succeeded in recovering the manager's own profit on the grounds that he had breached his duty of loyalty but failed in its claim that the properties were subject to a constructive trust. A majority of the High Court held that the manager would have been entitled to purchase the properties for himself if the group had really declined to buy them. The defendant was entitled to believe that this was in fact the case and so was clearly entitled to purchase them for its own benefit and retain its entire profit. This approach also seems preferable to that adopted in *Regal (Hastings) v. Gulliver*.

**(c) The two approaches contrasted in *Boardman v. Phipps*[37].** The contrast between the two approaches emerges extremely clearly from the majority and minority speeches handed down in the controversial decision of the House of Lords in *Boardman v. Phipps*.

---

[35] Gower and Davies, *op.cit.*, 418. Similar sentiments have been expressed by Prentice in (1967) 30 M.L.R. 450 and by Swan J. in *Irving Trust Co. v. Deutsch* (1934) 73 Fed. (2d) 121, 124 (United States Circuit Court of Appeals).

[36] (1975) 132 C.L.R. 373.

[37] [1967] 2 A.C. 46.

A testator established a trust for the benefit of his widow and children. Some 12 years after his death, the trust solicitor, Boardman, became concerned about one of the principal assets of the fund — a 27 per cent holding in a private company. After an unsuccessful attempt to bring about the election of one of the testator's sons to the board of the company, Boardman reached the conclusion that the only way of protecting the trust investment was to acquire a majority holding in the company. He suggested this to the managing trustee, who said that it was entirely out of the question for the trust to acquire such a holding. Boardman and the son then decided to purchase the outstanding shares themselves. They duly obtained control of the company and by capitalising some of the assets, were able to make a distribution of capital without reducing the value of the shares. The trust benefitted by this distribution to the tune of £47,000 and Boardman and his colleague made a profit of about £75,000. However, in the course of negotiations leading up to the takeover, Boardman had purported to represent the trust and thereby had incontrovertibly obtained information which would not have been made available to the general public. One of the other sons of the testator, who had not been particularly fully consulted, therefore claimed that this profit of £75,000 had been made by the utilisation of information which had reached Boardman while acting on behalf of the trust and so in a fiduciary capacity.

This claim was upheld by the House of Lords, who held that the shares which had been acquired were subject to a constructive trust in favour of the trust. Thus the trust potentially[38] obtained the whole of the profit made on the takeover; the defendants in effect had a choice between paying this over to the trust and retaining their shares or having the shares sold and the profit deducted from the proceds of sale. However, the House awarded an allowance to Boardman under its inherent jurisdiction by way of remuneration for the work which he had done.[39] In reaching these conclusions, all the members of the House of Lords agreed that (as was clearly the case) the defendants had placed themselves in a fiduciary relationship by acting as representatives of the trust for a number of years and that out of this fiduciary relationship they had obtained the opportunity to make a profit and the knowledge that a profit was there to be made. The majority adduced two inter-connected reasons for going on to hold that the defendants were therefore liable as constructive trustees to account for their profit to the trust.

Two of the majority, Lord Hodson and Lord Guest, both held that, since the only basis on which the defendants had obtained their information was the fact that they had been purporting to represent the trust, this information was trust property. Therefore, the defendants had, in effect, made a profit out of speculating with trust property and thus were clearly liable. The third member of the majority, Lord Cohen, reached the same conclusion by a slightly different route. He held that information was not property in the strict sense of the word and that it did not necessarily follow that a fiduciary must account for any profit obtained by the use of information acquired in his fiduciary capacity. In this case, however, the information had been acquired while the

---

[38] In fact they only lost one-third of their profit since the son who brought the proceedings only had a one-third beneficial interest, the remaining two-thirds being held by his brother, Boardman's associate, and their sister, who made no claim.

[39] This aspect of the decision will be discussed *post*, pp. 369, 730.

defendants had been purporting to represent the trust. Thus, the defendants were liable to account for their profit under the principle in *Regal (Hastings) v. Gulliver*.

All three members of the majority also felt that Boardman had placed himself in a position where his duty and interest might conflict (such a conflict would have arisen, for example, had the trustees sought his advice as to the merits of the trust acquiring a majority holding in the company). No matter how remote the possibility of such a conflict arising, a fiduciary who placed himself in this position was bound to account to his principal for any profit he had made. Since the defendants had accepted that their positions were the same, both were thus liable to account for their profit. In the opinion of the majority, it was quite immaterial that the defendants had acted honestly and openly in a manner highly beneficial to the trust in a situation where the trust itself could not have utilised the information which they had received.

The dissentients, Viscount Dilhorne and Lord Upjohn, took the view that the remoteness of the possibility of any conflict of interest arising and the various factors just referred to which the majority had found irrelevant led inescapably to the conclusion that the defendants had not breached their duty of loyalty to the trust. Lord Upjohn said that a conflict of interest only arose where the reasonable man looking at all the relevant circumstances would think that there was a real sensible possibility of conflict and not where the only possibility of conflict arose from events not contemplated as real sensible probabilities by any reasonable person. Boardman knew when he decided to proceed on his own behalf that there was no possibility of the trustees seeking his advice as to the merits of a purchase by the trust — the managing trustee had already told him that this was quite out of the question. Further, Lord Upjohn doubted the classification of the information as trust property. He said that information was not in any sense property; equity would merely restrain its transmission to another in breach of confidence. This was not such a case.

If the information was indeed properly classifiable as trust property, then the defendants had of course made a profit out of speculating with property of the trust and were therefore clearly liable as constructive trustees under the principle laid down in *Reid-Newfoundland Co. v. Anglo-American Telegraph Co.*,[40] which was discussed at the beginning of this section.[41] However, it is clear that information cannot be trust property in any normal sense; if it were, it could presumably be followed into the hands of the whole world other than a bona fide purchaser thereof for value without notice. Given the essential nature of information, which can be divulged in its entirety to any number of persons, such a conclusion could lead to quite absurd results.[42]

That is not to say that a fiduciary should automatically be entitled to utilise for his own benefit information which has come to him in his fiduciary capacity. A fiduciary who by the utilisation of such information abuses his fiduciary position should clearly be liable as a constructive trustee, but as a result of the application of the principles which have already been discussed, not by the automatic classification of the information as the property of his

---

[40] [1891] 2 Ch. 244.
[41] See *ante*, p. 355.
[42] See Jones (1968) 84 L.Q.R. 472.

principal. Such a case was *Industrial Development Consultants v. Cooley*.[43] The defendant, who was managing director of the plaintiff company, had been attempting, on behalf of the plaintiff, to obtain a contract to design certain depots for the Eastern Gas Board. These attempts failed because the Gas Board did not like the plaintiff's organisation and were not prepared to deal with the plaintiff in any capacity. The following year, a representative of the Gas Board sought a meeting with the defendant in his private capacity and intimated to him that if he could free himself from his ties with the plaintiff he had a very good chance of obtaining the contract for himself. The defendant therefore secured his release from his contract with the plaintiff by a totally false representation that he was on the verge of a nervous breakdown and accepted an offer from the Gas Board to do substantially the same work which he had unsuccessfully attempted to obtain for the plaintiff the year before. The plaintiff claimed that the defendant was a trustee of that contract for the benefit of the plaintiff and successfully sought an account of the defendant's profits. At the time when the defendant first realised that he had an opportunity of obtaining the contract for himself, the only capacity in which he was carrying on business was as managing director of the plaintiff and as such he was under a fiduciary duty to pass on to the plaintiff any information which reached him while carrying on business in that capacity. His failure to do so and subsequent utilisation of the information for his own benefit was a clear breach of fiduciary duty which made him a trustee of the contract for the plaintiff, who was entitled to all the profit thereunder. Similar decisions have been reached in other jurisdictions.[44] It is thus clear that a constructive trust can be imposed on a fiduciary who has abused his position whether or not the information which he has utilised is classified as the property of his principal.[45] Therefore, given the absurd consequences of such a classification, there is no good reason why it should ever be adopted.

There has also been considerable criticism of the majority decision in *Boardman v. Phipps* that the fiduciaries were not entitled to exploit for their own benefit the opportunity of purchasing a controlling interest in the company.[46] Not only has reference been made to the fact that other jurisdictions have felt able to adopt a more flexible approach.[47] It has also been demonstrated that the conflict of interest found to exist by the House of Lords is in

---

[43] [1972] 1 W.L.R. 443.

[44] *Pre-Cam Exploration Co. v. McTavish* [1966] S.C.R. 551; *Canadian Aero Services v. O'Malley* (1973) 40 D.L.R.(3d) 371 (both decisions of the Supreme Court of Canada); *Consul Development v. D.P.C. Estates* (1975) 49 A.L.J.R. 74 (High Court of Australia).

[45] Quite apart from any question of the imposition of a constructive trust for breach of fiduciary duty, both fiduciaries and non-fiduciaries may be held liable for breach of the equitable obligation of confidence where a person who has received information in confidence takes unfair advantage of it to the prejudice of the person who disclosed it to him, the courts will consider the whole gamut of remedies open to them and award that which is most appropriate to the situation. See Goff & Jones, *op.cit.*, pp. 749–772; Hedley & Halliwell (ed), *op.cit.* 181; and F. Gurry, *Breach of Confidence* (1984).

[46] See particularly Jones (1968) 84 L.Q.R. 472 and Finn, *Fiduciary Obligations* pp. 244–246.

[47] In the authorities discussed *ante*, p. 364 and also in *Manufacturers Trust Co. v. Becker* (1949) 338 U.S. 304, where the Supreme Court of the United States of America held that directors of a company had been entitled to encourage their associates to purchase its debentures at a time when their market value was a fraction of their face value; not only had the directors acted in the best interests of the company, their associates' profits had been made at the expense not of the company but of the selling bond-holders, who had in no way been misled or deceived.

fact wholly illusory; given that it arose out of the mere possibility that Boardman might in the future have been asked to advise the trustees, in this eventuality he could, like any other solicitor, have declined to advise them or, if they insisted, have declared his interest.[48] There is much to be said for these criticisms but that does not alter the fact that the approach adopted by the majority in *Boardman v. Phipps* in relation to the rights of fiduciaries to utilise for their own benefit opportunities of profit is entirely consistent with the earlier authorities such as *Regal (Hastings) v. Gulliver* and is undoubtedly representative of the present state of English law.

**(d) Possible ways forward.** It has already been seen that the effects of the harsh attitude at present adopted under English law were alleviated in *Boardman v. Phipps* by the House of Lords awarding an allowance to Boardman under its inherent jurisdiction by way of remuneration for the work which he had done. This jurisdiction, which will be discussed in detail later on,[49] was considerably extended in *Badfinger Music v. Evans*,[50] where a former member of a rock group which had broken up in very acrimonious circumstances had retained some tapes of a live concert which, after a considerable amount of essential remixing and remastering, he succeeded in releasing in a form which achieved a commercial success. He did not dispute that he was in a fiduciary relationship with the other members of the group or that they were entitled to share in the profit. The question was whether he was entitled to remuneration for the work which he had done. This was not a case where a fiduciary had, as in *Boardman v. Phipps*, acted honestly and openly in the best interests of his principal, although there was no doubt that his work had ultimately benefitted the others. However, the judge[51] held that he could award remuneration despite a lack of honesty and openness[52] and did so because the work done was not only of a special character calling for the exercise of a particular kind of professional skill but also could realistically only have been done by the fiduciary. He added that, in appropriate circumstances, the court's jurisdiction might extend to an award of a share of the profits.

Such awards of remuneration, and possibly shares of profits, are available even where, as in all the decisions adverse to fiduciaries which have been discussed in this section, a constructive trust has been imposed. However, the High Court of Australia has demonstrated in *Warman International v. Dwyer*[53] that the other remedies available for breach of fiduciary duty which have already been discussed[54] can also be utilised in cases of this type. The plaintiffs had declined an opportunity to participate in a joint venture with a manufacturer whose products they distributed. The manufacturer therefore terminated the distributorship, as it was entitled to do at any time, and instead

---

[48] If it is indeed the law that a person cannot benefit himself in any matter in which he might in the future be asked to advise, it is difficult to see how any professional person can ever safely enter into a transaction on his own behalf in any area in which he habitually advises.

[49] See *post*, p. 730.

[50] [2001] W.T.L.R. 1.

[51] Lord Goldsmith Q.C., sitting as a Deputy Judge of the Chancery Division.

[52] He relied heavily on *O'Sullivan v. Managament Agency and Music* [1985] 1 Q.B. 428, where remuneration had been awarded to an agent who had exercised actual undue influence over his principal, the singer Gilbert O'Sullivan.

[53] (1995) 128 A.L.R. 201. See also *Kao Lee & Yip v. Koo Hoi Yan* (2003) to be reported in [2003] W.T.L.R.

[54] See *ante*, p. 338.

carried out the joint venture with the defendant, the employee of the plaintiffs most closely connected with the distributorship. He had clearly committed a technical breach of fiduciary duty,[55] but the court declined to hold that the goodwill of the joint venture was held on constructive trust for the plaintiffs, awarding instead an account of the first two years' profits of the joint venture less an appropriate allowance for the expenses, skill expertise, effort and resources contributed by the joint venturers. The High Court specifically distinguished between cases in which a fiduciary acquires an asset which was within the scope and ambit of his fiduciary responsibilities, where it will be appropriate to impose a constructive trust, and cases in which a business is acquired and operated, where it may well not be.

Adoption of this approach by the English courts would not necessarily alter the result of either *Regal (Hastings) v. Gulliver* or *Boardman v. Phipps*. This would only be the case if the shares acquired in those cases by the respective fiduciaries could be held not to fall within the scope and ambit of their fiduciary responsibilities; it is somewhat improbable that such a conclusion would ever be reached on the facts of *Regal (Hastings) v. Gulliver* although it has already been argued that it should have been in *Boardman v. Phipps*. However, the adoption of this approach would have a profound effect on the liability of fiduciaries who acquire and operate businesses as a result of a purely technical breach of fiduciary duty.

It should also be noted that, in *Target Holdings v. Redferns*,[56] Lord Browne-Wilkinson, in an entirely different context,[57] said that it is "wrong to lift wholesale the detailed rules developed in the context of traditional trusts and then seek to apply them to trusts of quite a different kind". No better example of this practice can be found than the utilisation by Lord Russell of Killowen in *Regal (Hastings) v. Gulliver* of the decision in *Keech v. Sandford* more than two centuries earlier: it made no difference in *Regal (Hastings) v. Gulliver* that the company could not itself have subscribed for the shares — the trust in *Keech v. Sandford* could not itself have obtained a new lease and that had made no difference there. If Lord Browne-Wilkinson's remarks cause judges to think twice before automatically applying conclusions reached in totally different legal and economic contexts to modern conditions, English law may indeed one day adopt the more flexible attitudes already manifested in other jurisdictions.

## III. DISPOSITIONS OF TRUST PROPERTY IN BREACH OF TRUST

### 1. *The Different Types of Liability*

When trust property has been disposed of in breach of trust, the courts will, in certain circumstances, impose equitable obligations on those responsible for the wrongful disposition. Equity has always been prepared to impose on any

---

[55] Although he had not participated in the plaintiffs' decision to reject the manufacturer's proposal, his conduct had probably caused the manufacturer to terminate its agency earlier than it might otherwise have done.

[56] [1996] 1 A.C. 421, see *post*, p. 767.

[57] That of the liability of trustees who have paid away trust property in breach of trust to reconstitute the trust fund.

person who has officiously chosen to act as a fiduciary the appropriate fiduciary obligations, by virtue of which he will hold any property which he has received in his assumed capacity on constructive trust for the person on whose behalf he has chosen to act. Such a person has obviously intermeddled with property which is subject to a trust but this is merely the most obvious example of equity imposing obligations as a result of a disposition of trust property in breach of trust. Equity is also prepared to do so in three other situations: first, on anyone who has dishonestly been accessory to, or assisted in, a disposition of property in breach of trust (this type of liability is now generally known as "liability for dishonest assistance", although until a change in the law in 1995 it was instead generally known as "liability for knowing assistance"); secondly, on anyone who, with the requisite level of knowledge, has received for this own benefit property which has been disposed of in breach of trust (this type of liability is generally known as "liability for knowing receipt"); and, thirdly, on anyone who has received lawfully and not for his own benefit property subject to a trust but who has subsequently either misappropriated it or dealt with it in some other manner which is inconsistent with the trust (this type of liability is generally known as "liability for inconsistent dealing"). It is important to distinguish between these different types of liability.

If solicitors or accountants invest trust funds in their hands without any instructions from the trustees, they will be potentially liable to be treated as trustees of the investments because of their officious conduct; if, in accordance with directions from the trustees, they transfer trust funds to a third party in breach of trust, they will be potentially liable for dishonest assistance; if, in accordance with directions from the trustees, they use trust funds to settle their professional fees, they will be potentially liable for knowing receipt; and, if they themselves debit the trust funds to settle their professional fees, they will be potentially liable for "inconsistent dealing".

Similarly, if a bank deals with funds in an account which it knows to be a trust account without any instructions from the trustees, it will be potentially liable to be treated as a trustee of those funds because of its officious conduct; if it permits a cheque drawn on that account to be credited in breach of trust to the account of a third party but acts merely as the conduit by means of which the funds are transferred from one account to the other, it will be potentially liable for dishonest assistance; if the account of the third party is overdrawn at the time of the transfer, the bank may additionally be potentially liable for knowing receipt to the extent that it has utilised the funds in reduction of the overdraft; and, if the bank itself debits the balance of the account to cover an overdraft created in another account held by the same person, it will potentially be liable for inconsistent dealing. However, it is not always particularly easy to determine whether debiting the fees and commissions which banks commonly charge for carrying out certain types of transactions to such an account potentially gives rise to liability for dishonest assistance or to liability for knowing receipt.

In this respect fees are normally charged for transactions such as issuing banker's drafts,[58] while commissions are normally charged for bank transfers,

---

[58] Fees are also often charged simply for keeping accounts open and for each cheque but it is hardly likely that the amounts involved would be sufficient to justify proceedings.

particularly those to other jurisdictions. In the event that such a transaction amounts to a breach of trust, the potential liability of the bank in respect of the value of the banker's draft or the sum transferred will clearly be for dishonest assistance; however, in principle, the bank should also be potentially liable for knowing receipt in respect of any fees or commissions which it has charged. Not only has this latter liability generally been ignored by the courts; a quite different distinction was adopted in *Polly Peck International v. Nadir (No.2)*.[59] In this case a bank effectively controlled by the plaintiff company made a number of transfers of the plaintiff's funds totalling about £45,000,000 to the London branch of the Central Bank of Northern Cyprus in exchange for a corresponding amount of either sterling or Turkish lire being credited to its account with the Central Bank in Northern Cyprus. Scott L.J. held that the potential liability of the Central Bank to the liquidators of the plaintiff company in respect of the sterling transfers was for dishonest assistance since it had "received the funds transferred not in its own right but as banker and, as a banker, credited the funds ... in Northern Cyprus" but that its potential liability in respect of the Turkish lire transfers was for knowing receipt because "it was exchanging Turkish lire for sterling and became entitled to the sterling not as banker ... but in its own right". Apart from any fees or commissions which the Central Bank may have charged, to which no reference was made, the bank became no more beneficially entitled to the Turkish lire than it did to the sterling. It is therefore difficult to justify the distinction made by Scott L.J.[60] and it is suggested that it should not be followed.

The growth of discovered corporate fraud in recent years has ensured that the courts have had to consider the availability and scope of these remedies on an ever-increasing number of occasions. The proceedings which have been brought have, however, generally involved not only one or more of the types of liability listed above but also a considerable number of other claims arising out of the same disposition of property in breach of trust; the possibilities include proprietary claims, both at law and in equity, to follow the property into the hands of its recipients, personal claims at law for money had and received, and personal claims in equity against whoever was responsible for initiating the disposition in question. (The interrelation of all these different claims has made some of the recent proceedings extremely complex and commentators have begun to question whether so many different remedies should continue to be available for the same disposition of property.)[61] However, there is no doubt at all that by far the most effective way to proceed is to seek the imposition of one or more the equitable obligations at present under discussion, particularly if anyone can be found who is potentially liable for dishonest assistance; potential defendants of the latter type tend to be

---

[59] [1992] 4 All E.R. 769 at 777.

[60] It has not been followed in New Zealand; see *Nimmo v. Westpac Banking Corporation* [1993] 3 N.Z.L.R. 218 and *Cigna Life Insurance New Zealand v. Westpac Securities* [1996] 1 N.Z.L.R. 80.

[61] See particularly Lord Millett extra-judicially (1991) 107 L.Q.R. 71; Lord Hoffmann extra-judicially in *Frontiers of Liability* (ed. Birks, 1994), p. 27; Harpum *ibid.*, at p. 9; Finn in *Equity, Fiuciaries and Trusts 1993* (ed. Waters) p. 195; Lord Nicholls of Birkenhead extra-judicially in *Restitution — Past, Present and Future* (ed. Cornish, 1998) p. 231.

either members of the professions with insurance against liability for professional negligence or financial institutions of virtually guaranteed solvency.[62] Such persons are far more likely to be able to satisfy any unfavourable judgment than the other potential defendants — the initiators of the offending disposition and the recipients of the property in question. Indeed the presumed solvency of persons who have been accessory to or dishonestly assisted in a disposition of property in breach of trust is the basic reason why this particular area of the law has become so important in recent years.

## 2. *Officiously Acting as a Fiduciary*

Any person who takes it upon himself to act as a fiduciary without having been appointed as such will in every respect be treated as if he had been expressly appointed to the office in question and will be held to be a constructive trustee of any property acquired by him in the course of his intervention.

In *Mara v. Browne*,[63] A.L. Smith L.J. stated that "if one, not being a trustee and not having authority from a trustee, takes upon himself to intermeddle with trust matters or to do acts characteristic of the office of trustee, he may therefore make himself what is called in law a trustee of his own wrong — i.e. a trustee *de son tort*, or, as it is also termed, a constructive trustee". However, in *Dubai Aluminium Co. v. Salaam*,[64] Lord Millett expressed a preference for alternative terminology, saying that "[s]ubstituting dog Latin for bastard French, we would do better today to describe such persons as de facto trustees". He went on to say: "In their relations with the beneficiaries they are treated in every respect as if they had been duly appointed. They are true trustees and are fully subject to fiduciary obligations. Their liability is strict; it does not depend on dishonesty." However it is classified, control of the property is a prerequisite of this type of liability, to which Kekewich J. was specifically referring when, in *Re Barney*,[65] he stated particularly clearly that "it is essential to the character of a trustee that he should have trust property actually vested in him or so far under his control that he has nothing to do but require that, perhaps by one process, perhaps by another, it should be vested in him".

A good illustration of the imposition of this type of liability is provided by

---

[62] Liability for dishonest assistance is potentially much more onerous than liability for knowing receipt or inconsistent dealing. The latter will generally merely restore the status quo; any order for repayment of the trust funds utilised will normally simply reconstitute the original potential loss in respect of the professional fees or overdraft in question. The only situation in which the position will be any worse than it was at the outset will be if the use of the trust funds to discharge the fees or overdraft has given a false impression of the financial position of the client and thus caused further fees to be run up or further advances to be made. The imposition of liability for dishonest assistance will, on the other hand, necessarily involve the payment of funds which have never been beneficially received by the member of the professions or advanced by the financial institution in question; what is more, the quantum of potential liability is not in any way restricted to the value of the fees and commissions which the services rendered could reasonably have been expected to bring in.

[63] [1896] 1 Ch. 199 at 209.

[64] [2002] 3 W.L.R. 1913 at 1946.

[65] [1892] 2 Ch. 265 at 273.

*Blyth v. Fladgate.*[66] Trust funds were, by direction of the sole trustee, paid to a firm of solicitors and invested in Exchequer Bills, which were deposited in the name of the firm. Subsequently, following the death of the sole trustee and before any new trustees had been appointed, the Exchequer Bills were sold and the proceeds of sale invested in a mortgage, the security for which proved to be insufficient. The partners of the firm were held liable to account to the trust for the sums so lost on the basis that they themselves had been carrying out the functions of the trustees; they were clearly constructive trustees of the proceeds of sale and, as such, responsible for any improper investment. It is entirely proper that the law should impose the office of trustee upon a person who purports to act as such without authority and that such a person should be burdened with all the same responsibilities and liabilities as an express trustee.[67] Thus, in addition to being a constructive trustee of any property which he receives, he will also be responsible for any diminution in its value and will be subject to all the rules discussed in the previous section of this chapter; if an intermeddler obtains a secret profit, he will be in exactly the same position as if he had been an express trustee.

Similar principles apply to fiduciaries other than trustees. Most of the cases have concerned persons who have taken it upon themselves to act as agents. In *Lyell v. Kennedy*,[68] during the 22 years which it took to determine the identity of the heir at law of a landowner, his manager continued to collect the rents from the tenants without telling them of the death of their landlord. The House of Lords held that, since he had taken it upon himself to receive the rents of property which he knew to belong to another, he held these sums (which had been placed in a separate bank account) on constructive trust for the heir. Lord Selborne emphasised that the motives which induce a person to intermeddle in the administration of a trust or other fiduciary relationship are totally irrelevant to the imposition of a constructive trust; thus it made no difference whether the manager had intervened with the intention of protecting the interests of the heir at law or with the intention of taking the benefit for himself. The latter was clearly the intention of the prospective purchaser in *English v. Dedham Vale Properties*,[69] who, purporting without authority to act as agent for the prospective vendors, submitted an application for planning permission in respect of part of the subject matter of the proposed sale; he was held liable to account to the vendors for the profits made thereby.[70]

### 3. *Dishonestly Assisting in a Disposition of Property in Breach of Trust*

**(A) Terminology**
The type of liability imposed upon a person who has in one way or another dishonestly assisted in bringing about a disposition of trust property in breach of trust is now generally known as "liability for dishonest assistance", although until a change in the law in 1995 it was instead generally known as

---

[66] [1891] 1 Ch. 337. The explanation of the decision given in the text is that adopted by Vinelott J. in *Re Bell's Indenture* [1980] 1 W.L.R. 1217. See also *James v. Williams* [2000] Ch. 1.

[67] See *Soar v. Ashwell* [1893] 2 Q.B. 390 at 394, *per* Lord Esher M.R.

[68] (1889) 14 App.Cas. 437.

[69] [1978] 1 W.L.R. 93.

[70] Had he waited until after exchange of contracts, the equitable interest thereby acquired would have entitled him to make the application for his own benefit.

"liability for knowing assistance". Until recently the vast majority of the relevant judgments have described persons held liable for what is now known as dishonest assistance as constructive trustees. However, it has already been seen that the essential feature of this type of liability is the fact that property subject to a trust has by virtue of the assistance provided reached the hands of a third party who may or may not himself be under some proprietary or personal obligation to restore it. What is more, it is only ever necessary to attempt to impose liability for dishonest assistance on persons who have not beneficially received the property in question (anyone who has actually taken the property beneficially will be subject to the different, and probably more stringent, heads of liability for knowing receipt or inconsistent dealing which will be discussed later on in this section). The classification of such persons as constructive trustees is as a matter of principle somewhat difficult to reconcile with the inherent nature of a trust — given that a trust is a relationship in respect of property, it might be expected to follow that a constructive trust can only be imposed if there is some identifiable property upon which to impose it. Yet liability for dishonest assistance has often been imposed when there has been no obviously identifiable property subject to the trust.

Where a person held liable for dishonest assistance has played an active part in the disposition of the property in question, as in the case of a solicitor or bank who, following the instructions of trustees, has actually made the disposition in question, it is just about possible to identify property subject to the alleged constructive trust. This is because the fact that the property in question passed through the hands of the person upon whom liability is imposed makes it possible to argue that a constructive trust in fact arose at the moment when the property was actually in his hands. However, quite apart from the fact that none of the judges has ever seemed to have regarded as important the question of what property was subject to the constructive trust said to be being imposed, there are other decisions in which it is, on any view, totally impossible to identify any such property. This is because in these cases liability for dishonest assistance was imposed on persons who had never received or in any way controlled the property in question. Thus in *Eaves v. Hickson*[71] what is now known as liability for dishonest assistance was imposed on a father who produced a forged marriage certificate to the trustees of a settlement in order to convince them that his children were legitimate and so entitled to the trust property, which was duly distributed to them. Liability was imposed on the basis that he had dishonestly induced the trustees to make the distribution in question and so was accessory to it.

The existence of authorities of this type has led some commentators to contend that there is a second type of constructive trust which can arise without any necessity for there to be any identifiable trust property;[72] indeed, in *Westdeutsche Landesbank Girozentrale v. Islington L.B.C.*,[73] Lord Browne-Wilkinson specifically said that the "only apparent exception" to the rule that there must be identifiable trust property "is a constructive trust imposed on a person who dishonestly assists in a breach of trust". No proprietary rights can

---

[71] (1861) 30 Beav. 136.
[72] See Ford & Lee: *op.cit.*, para. 22020 and previous editions of Hayton & Marshall: *op.cit.* (e.g. the 9th ed., 1991, pp. 440–441).
[73] [1996] A.C. 669 at 705.

conceivably be acquired by anyone beneficially entitled under a trust without identifiable property. Consequently, the existence of "this apparent exception" does not serve any obvious purpose; what is the point of creating an exception to the general rule requiring identifiable trust property if the exception so created does not enjoy the principal advantage conferred by the existence of a trust in the first place? The best which can be said for this alleged second type of constructive trust is that it is "a fiction which provides a useful remedy where no remedy is available in contract or in tort".[74]

In any event, the opposing view, that the explanation for the existence of authorities of this type is that the imposition of this kind of liability does not give rise to the imposition of a constructive trust anyway, is now increasingly prevalent. In *Dubai Aluminium Co. v. Salaam*,[75] Lord Millett, building on earlier observations which he had made both judicially[76] and extra-judicially,[77] said:

> "Equity gives relief against fraud by making any person sufficiently implicated in the fraud accountable in equity. In such a case he is traditionally (and I have suggested unfortunately) described as a 'constructive trustee' and is said to be 'liable to account as a constructive trustee'. But he is not in fact a trustee at all, even though he may be liable to account as if he were. He never claims to assume the position of trustee on behalf of others, and he may be liable without ever receiving or handling the trust property. ... In this second class of case the expressions 'constructive trust' and 'constructive trustee' create a trap. ... The expressions are 'nothing more than a formula for equitable relief'[78] ... I think that we should now discard the words 'accountable as constructive trustee' in this context and substitute the words 'accountable in equity'."

Lord Millett's terminology is clearly preferable. Although its adoption entails a recognition that the imposition of liability for dishonest assistance does not give rise to a constructive trust, that type of liability is nevertheless best dealt with in this chapter; this is because virtually all the relevant authorities also concern attempts to impose liability for knowing receipt or liability for inconsistent dealing, which on any view give rise to the imposition of a constructive trust.

## (B) The Elements of Liability for Dishonest Assistance

For some 120 years the starting point for every discussion of what is now known as liability for dishonest assistance was the statement of Lord Selbourne L.C. in *Barnes v. Addy*[79] in 1874 that "strangers are not to be made constructive trustees merely because they act as the agents of trustees in transactions within their legal powers, transactions, perhaps, of which a Court

---

[74] Hayton (1985) 27 Malaya Law Review 313, 314.
[75] [2002] 3 W.L.R. 1913 at 1945.
[76] As Millett J. in *Agip (Africa) v. Jackson* [1990] Ch. 265 at 291.
[77] In, among other places, 114 L.Q.R. (1998) 399 at 399–400.
[78] Referring to *Selangor United Rubber Co. v. Cradock (No.3)* [1968] 1 W.L.R. 1555 at 1582, *per* Ungoed-Thomas J.
[79] (1874) 9 Ch. App. 244 at 251–252.

of Equity may disapprove, unless ... they assist with knowledge in a dishonest and fraudulent design on the part of the trustees". Peter Gibson J. subsequently[80] identified four distinct elements of this type of liability: the existence of a trust; the existence of a dishonest and fraudulent design on the part of the trustee of the trust; the assistance by the stranger in that design; and the knowledge of the person potentially liable.

Neither formulation has survived the decision of the Privy Council in *Royal Brunei Airlines v. Tan*,[81] in 1994, subsequently definitively accepted as representing English law by the House of Lords in *Twinsectra v. Yardley*.[82] Lord Selborne's statement[83] remains important only because of its manifestation of a continuing policy, the need to protect from liability agents of trustees who are guilty only of following instructions which have given to them. The current requirements for the imposition of liability for dishonest assistance were instead identified by Mance L.J., sitting in the Commercial Court, in *Grupo Torras v. Al-Sabah*[84] as "(i) a breach of trust or fiduciary duty by someone other than the defendant, (ii) in which the defendant assisted (iii) dishonestly, together with (iv) resulting loss".

### (1) "A breach of trust or fiduciary duty by someone other than the defendant"[85]

Most of the older cases concerned the situation expressly envisaged by Lord Selborne, where agents of trustees have assisted in bringing about a misapplication of the trust property by following the instructions of the trustees.[86] Many modern cases have equally concerned express trusts, frequently the situation where a failure to segregate funds held on trust from the other funds

---

[80] In *Baden v. Société Générale* (1983) [1993] 1 W.L.R. 509N at 573 (the full name of this case is *Baden v. Société Générale pour Favoriser le Developpement du Commerce et de l'Industrie en France S.A.*).

[81] [1995] 2 A.C. 378.

[82] [2002] 2 A.C. 164.

[83] Which was anyway not wholly consistent with the pre-existing authorities; see Harpum *op.cit.*

[84] [1999] C.L.C. 1469.

[85] Until *Royal Brunei Airlines v. Tan* [1995] 2 A.C. 378, the breach of trust or fiduciary duty had to be, as Lord Selborne had stated in *Barnes v. Addy* (1874) 9 Ch. App. 244 at 252, "a dishonest and fraudulent design on the part of the trustees". Although it has since been demonstrated (by Harpum *op.cit.*) that this requirement "leapt forth fully formed from the brow of Lord Selborne", subsequent authorities regarded it as an essential prerequisite of liability and the Court of Appeal eventually decided in *Belmont Finance Corporation v. Williams Furniture* [1979] Ch. 250 at 267 that "dishonest" and "fraudulent" had the same meaning and signified something more than mere misfeasance or breach of trust. However, in *Royal Brunei Airlines v. Tan* [1995] 2 A.C. 378 at 385, 392, the Privy Council rejected *Belmont Finance Corporation v. Williams Furniture* and concluded that: "what matters is the state of mind of the third party sought to be made liable, not the state of mind of the trustee ... his state of mind is essentially irrelevant to the question whether the third party should be made liable to the beneficiaries for the breach of trust. If the liability of the third party is fault-based, what matters is the nature of his fault, not that of the trustee. In this regard dishonesty on the part of the third party would seem to be a sufficient basis for his liability, irrespective of the state of mind of the trustee who is in breach of trust ... it is not necessary that ... the trustee or fiduciary was acting dishonestly, although this will usually be so where the third party who is assisting him is acting dishonestly." The Privy Council has therefore reduced the pre-existing requirement for the existence of a dishonest and fraudulent design on the part of the trustee of the trust to a requirement for a misfeasance or breach of trust on his part, which will in practice be automatically satisfied whenever there has been a disposition of property in breach of trust.

[86] As in *Barnes v. Addy* (1874) 9 Ch.App. 214 itself; *Williams v. Williams* (1881) 17 Ch.D. 437; *Williams-Ashman v. Price & Williams* [1942] 1 Ch. 219.

of the trustee has permitted the funds to be taken in discharge of the trustee's overdraft.[87]

However, it is clear that "the trust need not be a formal trust. It is sufficient that there should be a fiduciary relationship between the 'trustee' and the property of another person."[88] Consequently, this first requirement is equally satisfied where the misapplication of property occurs as a result of agents following the instructions of any other express fiduciary. The "directors of a company are treated as if they were the trustees of the company's property under their control"[89] and many modern cases have concerned illegal or unauthorised transactions carried out in accordance with the instructions of company directors. There has been a whole series of cases resulting from successful attempts to use the funds of a company to finance its own acquisition,[90] while a number of cases have resulted from directors misapplying a company's funds for their own personal benefit.[91]

It is also sufficient if the trust in question is a resulting trust[92] or a constructive trust,[93] even if the latter only arose as a result of the misapplication of the property itself. Millett J. emphasised in *Agip (Africa) v. Jackson*[94] that "the embezzlement of a company's funds almost inevitably involves a breach of fiduciary duty on the part of one of the company's employees or agents" and he went on to hold that "there is a receipt of trust property when a company's funds are misapplied by a director and, in my judgment, this is equally the case where a company's funds are misapplied by any person whose fiduciary position gave him control of them or enabled him to misapply them". This principle is not of course confined to funds but applies to property of any type.[95] A glance at some of the authorities cited in the footnotes will emphasise the substantial sums which were at stake in them and the extent to which the victims of corporate fraud are increasingly looking towards members of the professions and financial institutions to compensate them for their losses.

Only rarely has there been any dispute as to whether or not this first requirement has been satisfied. However the unusual facts of *Brinks v. Abu-Saleh (No.3)*,[96] did produce a contention that the claim brought in that case failed because of the lack of any trust. The theft of over £26,000,000 from the plaintiff's Heathrow warehouse had been facilitated by one of the plaintiff's employees, a security guard who had provided both a key to the premises and information about its security arrangements to the other persons involved in the robbery. In proceedings seeking the imposition of liability for dishonest

---

[87] As in *Royal Brunei Airlines v. Tan* [1995] 2 A.C. 378.
[88] *Baden v. Société Générale* (1983) [1993] 1 W.L.R. 509N at 573.
[89] *ibid.*
[90] As in *Selangor United Rubber Estates v. Cradock (No.3)* [1968] 1 W.L.R. 1555; *Karak Rubber Company v. Burden (No.2)* [1972] 1 W.L.R. 602; *Belmont Finance Corporation v. Williams Furniture* [1979] Ch. 250, *(No.2)* [1980] 1 All E.R. 393; *Eagle Trust Co. v. S.B.C. Securities* (1991) [1993] 1 W.L.R. 484.
[91] *Baden v. Société Générale* (1983) [1993] 1 W.L.R. 509N; *Eagle Trust Co. v. S.B.C. Securities* (1991) [1993] 1 W.L.R. 484; *Cowan de Groot Properties v. Eagle Trust* (1991) [1992] 4 All E.R. 700; *Polly Peck International v. Nadir (No.2)* [1992] 4 All E.R. 769.
[92] *Twinsectra v. Yardley* [2002] 2 A.C. 164.
[93] *Competitive Insurance Company v. Davies Investments* [1975] 1 W.L.R. 1240.
[94] [1990] Ch. 265 at 290.
[95] Information in respect of which a manager owed a fiduciary duty to his company would have sufficed in *Consul Development v. D.P.C. Estates* (1975) 132 C.L.R. 373.
[96] [1996] C.L.C. 133.

assistance, the plaintiff contended that, because the robbery had taken place as a result of the actions of a dishonest fiduciary (the security guard) it "had an equity to trace into [the proceeds of the robbery] which were in the nature of trust moneys". It was conceded that the security guard was a fiduciary but it was argued that he did not owe a fiduciary duty which was sufficient to impress the proceeds of the robbery with a trust. Rimer J. predictably rejected this argument so the claim satisfied this first requirement. The defendant might have been better advised to have argued that, even though the security guard was a trustee of any property which reached his hands, that did not make him a trustee of the entire £26,000,000 at all, or at any rate not a sufficient trustee to lead to the imposition of liability for dishonest assistance on a third party; however, it is now clear from subsequent authority[97] that this first requirement was satisfied by virtue of the fact that the thieves were constructive trustees of the stolen property. In any event, Rimer J. went on to hold that the claim satisfied neither the second nor the third requirements.

## (2) "In which the defendant assisted"

It is "a simple question of fact"[98] whether someone has been accessory to, or assisted in, the misfeasance or breach of trust in question. It makes no difference whether the agent has previously advised against the course of conduct in question,[99] whether he has made the appropriate enquiries and reasonably come to what was in fact an incorrect conclusion,[1] or whether he has simply relied on the instructions given without checking relevant documents in his possession.[2] All that matters is the fact of having been accessory to, or assisted in, a misfeasance or breach of trust in a significant way.

In this connection, it should be noted that, although the vast majority of cases of this type inevitably involve agents of trustees or other fiduciaries, liability also extends to persons who have been in some other way accessory to a disposition of property in breach of trust. Thus, in *Eaves v. Hickson*,[3] liability was imposed on a person who had merely induced the disposition in question; he had produced a forged marriage certificate to the trustees of a settlement in order to convince them that his children were legitimate and so entitled to the trust property, which was duly paid to them. In *Royal Brunei Airlines v. Tan*,[4] liability was imposed on the managing director and therefore the person who was in physical control of a company which had misapplied money which was held on trust. Persons with such control are not "strangers" to the defaulting trustee in the way that its solicitors and bankers are but they are nevertheless its agents. They have immunity from direct liability as insiders (directors owe fiduciary duties only to their company, not to either its shareholders or beneficiaries) and it would be absurd if they could also claim immunity from liability for dishonest assistance on the grounds that they were not "outsiders". The possibility of imposing liability for dishonest assistance on the directors of a company which was acting as a corporate trustee has since been

---

[97] *Westdeutsche Landesbank Girozentrale v. Islington L.B.C.* [1996] A.C. 669 at 705.
[98] *Baden v. Société Générale* (1983) [1993] 1 W.L.R. 509N at 574–575.
[99] As in *Barnes v. Addy* (1874) 9 Ch.App. 214.
[1] As in *Williams v. Williams* (1881) 17 Ch.D. 437.
[2] As in *Williams-Ashman v. Price & Williams* [1942] 1 Ch. 219.
[3] (1861) 30 Beav. 136.
[4] [1995] 2 A.C. 378.

expressly confirmed by Lindsay J. in *H.R. v. J.A.P.T.*,[5] which concerned a claim against the corporate trustee of a pension scheme which had invested a high proportion of the assets of the scheme in purchases of property from the employer company at excessively high prices. However, liability for dishonest assistance will only actually be imposed if there is held to have been sufficient dishonesty to satisfy the third requirement discussed below.[6]

It is rare for the significance of the conduct of a person potentially liable for dishonest assistance to be challenged as a matter of fact but this was done successfully in *Brinks v. Abu-Saleh (No.3)*.[7] As has already been seen,[8] £26,000,000 had been stolen from the Heathrow warehouse of the plaintiff who, in these particular proceedings,[9] was seeking the imposition of liability for dishonest assistance on a defendant who had accompanied her husband on various trips by car in the course of which he had transported to Zurich over £3,000,000 of the proceeds of the robbery for one of the convicted robbers, thereby enabling this sum to be laundered. Rimer J. held that she had accompanied him merely in her spousal capacity; her presence therefore had not constituted relevant "assistance" in furtherance of the breach of trust complained of. Therefore, although the plaintiff's claim satisfied the first requirement considered above, this rather generous finding of fact meant that the plaintiff's claim failed to satisfy this second requirement (as will be seen later on,[10] Rimer J. then went on to state that the third requirement was not satisfied either). However, the facts of this case were extremely unusual and it is unlikely that the presence or absence of this requirement will often be the subject of dispute.

### (3) "Dishonestly"

This is the aspect of liability for dishonest assistance which has produced most judicial disagreement. In *Barnes v. Addy*,[11] Lord Selborne held that liability would only be imposed on persons who assisted "with knowledge". This caused Peter Gibson J. in *Baden v. Société Générale*[12] both to regard knowledge as the last of his four distinct elements and to identify five different categories of knowledge. These were: "(i) actual knowledge; (ii) wilfully shutting one's

---

[5] [1997] P.L.R. 99.
[6] *H.R. v. J.A.P.T.* also threw up a possible alternative means of imposing liability on the directors of a corporate trustee without any need to show dishonesty on their part. If their activities amount to breach of the fiduciary duty which they owe to the corporate trustee as its directors, a duty of strict liability not dependant on them having been dishonest or even negligent, Lindsay J. accepted that it was arguable that the members of the scheme were entitled to argue that such rights of action as the corporate trustee had against its directors were themselves part of the property of the pension trust, thus enabling the members of the scheme to force the trustee company to sue the directors and hold the fruits of that action on trust for them (by analogy with the decision in *Fletcher v. Fletcher* (1844) 4 Hare 67; see *ante*, pp. 173–176). Although this claim (described by Lindsay J. as a "dog-leg claim") is in itself nothing to do with liability for dishonest assistance, it is potentially an even more effective way of attacking the directors of corporate trustees; however, an appeal against his decision was subsequently compromised so it remains to be seen whether such a claim is indeed feasible.
[7] [1996] C.L.C. 133.
[8] See *ante*, p. 378.
[9] Proceedings had been brought against no fewer that 57 defendants.
[10] See *post*, p. 385.
[11] (1874) 9 Ch.App. 214.
[12] (1983) [1993] 1 W.L.R. 509N at 575–576.

eyes to the obvious; (iii) wilfully and recklessly failing to make such inquiries as an honest and reasonable man would make; (iv) knowledge of circumstances which would indicate the facts to an honest and reasonable man; (v) knowledge of circumstances which would put an honest and reasonable man on inquiry". Although these categories were justifiably described as "unhelpful"[13] and "unrememberable",[14] they were repeatedly referred to and eventually,[15] it became generally accepted that liability would only be imposed on persons whose knowledge fell within the first three categories. However, in *Royal Brunei Airlines v. Tan*,[16] the Privy Council specifically rejected knowledge as a prerequisite of the imposition of liability and replaced it by a requirement for dishonesty by the accessory or person assisting (this is why what used to be known as liability for knowing assistance has now been renamed liability for dishonest assistance).

In that case the airline was seeking to impose liability for what was then known as knowing assistance on the managing director and principal shareholder of an insolvent travel agency which had paid into its ordinary current account the ticket moneys which, according to I.A.T.A. regulations, it held on trust for the airline. The Court of Appeal of Brunei Darussalam had rejected this claim on the grounds that it had not been established that there had been, on the part of the travel agent, the fraudulent and dishonest design which English law then required.[17] However the Privy Council held that there was no such requirement and that it was only necessary to show a misfeasance or a breach of trust. This conclusion would in itself have been sufficient to dispose of the appeal; since it had been conceded that there had been a breach of trust in which the managing director had assisted with actual knowledge, all the requirements for the imposition of liability were clearly satisfied. However, the Privy Council did not restrict its observations to this particular aspect of accessory liability, holding that "[a] conclusion cannot be reached on the nature of the breach of trust which may trigger accessory liability without at the same time considering the other ingredients including, in particular, the

---

[13] By Millett J. in *Agip (Africa) v. Jackson* [1990] Ch. 265 at 293.

[14] By Blanchard J. in *Nimmo v. Westpac Banking Corporation* [1993] 3 N.Z.L.R. 218 at 228 (High Court of New Zealand).

[15] Consistent with the expressed primary concern of Lord Selborne in *Barnes v. Addy* to protect agents of a trust, the older cases such as *Barnes v. Addy* itself, *Williams v. Williams* (1881) 17 Ch.D. 437 and *Williams-Ashman v. Price & Williams* [1942] 1 Ch. 219 had restricted liability to strangers whose knowledge fell within what Peter Gibson J. would later classify as categories (i), (ii) and (iii). However, a different view was taken by Ungoed-Thomas J. in *Selangor United Rubber Estates v. Cradock (No.3)* [1968] 1 W.L.R. 1555; he held that liability would be imposed on an agent who had assisted in bringing about a misapplication of property subject to a trust who would be liable for knowing assistance if he either knew or ought to have known of that misapplication. This decision was subsequently followed at first instance (see *Karak Rubber Company v. Burden (No.2)* [1972] 1 W.L.R. 602 and *Rowlandson v. National Westminster Bank* [1978] 3 All E.R. 370) but the more traditional approach also continued to be adopted, most significantly by members of the Court of Appeal in *Carl-Zeiss Stiftung v. Herbert Smith (No.2)* [1969] 2 Ch. 276 and in *Belmont Finance Corporation v. Williams Furniture* [1979] 1 All E.R. 118. Despite the continued existence of these conflicting authorities, the general acceptance of the latter approach was manifested by Millett J. in *Agip (Africa) v. Jackson* [1990] Ch. 265 and, despite some alarums and excursions when that case went to the Court of Appeal ([1991] Ch. 547), by Scott L.J. in *Polly Peck International v. Nadir (No.2)* [1992] 4 All E.R. 769.

[16] [1995] 2 A.C. 378.

[17] See *ante*, p. 377, fn. 85.

state of mind of the third party".[18] Lord Nicholls considered and rejected the two extreme possibilities of imposing either no liability at all or strict liability on accessories to breaches of trust. Having thus necessarily opted for the imposition of some form of fault-based liability, he reviewed the existing authorities and the opinions of the commentators and concluded:[19]

> "Drawing the threads together, their Lordships' overall conclusion is that dishonesty is a necessary ingredient of accessory liability. It is also a sufficient ingredient. A liability in equity to make good resulting loss attaches to a person who dishonestly procures or assists in a breach of trust or fiduciary obligation. It is not necessary that, in addition, the trustee or fiduciary was acting dishonestly, although this will usually be so where the third party who is assisting him is acting dishonestly. 'Knowingly' is better avoided as a defining ingredient of the principle, and in the context of this principle the Baden scale of knowledge is best forgotten."

Despite one unsuccessful challenge[20] and the occasional contrary statement,[21] there is now no doubt that these observations of the Board constitute English law. However, considerable doubts were expressed as to whether the courts would adopt a wholly objective standard when considering whether or not any particular third party had been dishonest or would also take into account more subjective factors applicable only to the specific third party so as to impose either a higher or a lower standard of behaviour on him. Despite the fact that Lord Nicholls had clearly warned against over-categorisation, the members of the Court of Appeal were unable to resist developing categories of dishonesty in subsequent cases, particularly in *Grupo Torras v. Al-Sabah*.[22] This issue had to be resolved by the House of Lords in *Twinsectra v. Yardley*.[23]

The claimant had made a loan on the basis that the sum advanced was paid to the borrower's solicitors who gave an undertaking to the claimant to utilise the loan money solely for the acquisition of property on behalf of the borrower and for no other purpose. The solicitors breached their undertaking by

---

[18] [1995] 2 A.C. 378 at 386.

[19] *ibid.* at 392.

[20] In the Commercial Court in *Dubai Aluminium Company v. Salaam* [1999] 1 Lloyd's Rep. 387 at 452.

[21] Such as the remarks by Nourse L.J. in *Heinl v. Jyske Bank (Gibraltar)* [1999] Lloyd's Rep Bank. 511.

[22] [2001] Lloyd's Rep. Bank. 36. From this and other decisions, the following categories emerged: first, subjective dishonesty, where the accessory was liable because he knew exactly what was going on (*Royal Brunei Airlines v. Tan* itself); secondly, objective dishonesty, where the accessory was liable because he wilfully shut his eyes as to what was going on (*Grupo Torras v. Al-Sabah*, where this category was described as "blind eye dishonesty"); thirdly, another type of objective dishonesty, where the accessory was liable because, although he believed that he was doing nothing wrong, he nevertheless was by any objective standards (the pleaded facts in *Walker v. Stones* [2000] W.T.L.R. 79; this category was described in *Grupo Torras v. Al-Sabah* as "Robin Hood dishonesty", presumably a reference to Robin Hood taking money from the rich and giving it to the poor); fourthly, subjective honesty, where the accessory was not liable because he did not know of the misapplication in breach of trust and the transaction was in commercial terms of an ordinary nature (*Heinl v. Jyske Bank (Gibraltar)* [1999] Lloyd's Rep. Bank. 511); and, fifthly, another type of subjective honesty, where the accessory was not liable because he acted either innocently or, at worst, no more than negligently (the pleaded facts in *Houghton v. Fayers* [2000] Lloyd's Rep. Bank 145).

[23] [2002] 2 A.C. 162.

transferring most of the sum advanced to another solicitor, Leach; he disbursed the funds transferred to him in accordance with the instructions of the borrower but not all of those funds were spent on the acquisition of property; some of the funds were used on behalf of the borrower for other purposes, including the payment of Leach's own fees. The claimant contended that the arrangement between himself, the borrower and the original solicitors had given rise to a trust; if there was such a trust, the transfer by the original solicitors in breach of their undertaking would amount to a breach of trust; consequently, Leach would be potentially liable for dishonest assistance in that he had been an accessory to the disposition in breach of trust and had subsequently disbursed the funds transferred to him in ways which were inconsistent with the undertaking.[24]

At first instance, Carnwath J. held that the arrangement had not given rise to any trust; that in itself was enough to prevent Leach from being liable for dishonest assistance[25] but Carnwath J. held that, although Leach had not been dishonest, he had wilfully shut his eyes. The Court of Appeal held[26] that the arrangement had given rise to a trust and that Leach had been dishonest; he was consequently held liable for dishonest assistance.[27] Leach appealed to the House of Lords,[28] who confirmed the existence of a trust.[29] Was Leach liable for dishonest assistance?

Lord Hutton, with whose speech three of the other members of the House of Lords agreed, held that there were three possible interpretations of what Lord Nicholls had meant by "dishonesty":[30] first, "a purely subjective standard, whereby a person is only regarded as dishonest if he transgresses his own standard of honesty, even if that standard is contrary to that of reasonable and honest people"; secondly, "a purely objective standard whereby a person acts dishonestly if his conduct is dishonest by the ordinary standards of reasonable and honest people, even if he does not himself realise this"; and, thirdly, "a standard which combines an objective test and a subjective test, and which requires that before there can be a finding of dishonesty it must be established that the defendant's conduct was dishonest by the ordinary standards of reasonable and honest people and that he himself realised that by those standards his conduct was dishonest". His lordship opted for the third of these interpretations, which he described as "the combined test".

The dissentient, Lord Millett, held[31] that Lord Nicholls had been adopting a purely objective standard of dishonesty. However, he held that the issue

---

[24] Leach would also be potentially liable for knowing receipt of the sums used to pay his own fees. It would also be possible for the claimant to recover all the property which had been purchased on behalf of the borrower from the companies into whose names that property had been put (this would be by virtue of the equitable proprietary interest in that property which the claimant had because of the trust; see *post*, p. 807).

[25] Because the first requirement above was not satisfied.

[26] [1999] Lloyd's Rep. Bank. 438.

[27] And also for knowing receipt of the sums used to pay his own fees. The claimant also recovered all the property which had been purchased on behalf of the borrower from the companies into whose names that property had been put.

[28] The companies into whose names the property purchased had been put also obtained leave to appeal to the House of Lords but withdrew their appeal at the last minute for financial reasons.

[29] See *ante*, p. 293.

[30] [2002] A.C. 164 at 171–172.

[31] *ibid.* at 200–201.

before the House was not what Lord Nicholls had meant by dishonesty but whether it was necessary "to establish that an accessory to a breach of trust had a dishonest state of mind (so that he was subjectively dishonest ...); or whether it should be sufficient to establish that he acted with the requisite knowledge (so that his conduct was objectively dishonest)". He preferred the latter view, holding that "it should not be necessary that the accessory realised that his conduct was dishonest; it should be sufficient that it constituted intentional wrongdoing". He went on to comment that "the introduction of the criterion of dishonesty is an unnecessary distraction, and conducive to error" and advocated a return to the "traditional description of this head of equitable liability as arising from 'knowing assistance'". However, he did not go further into precisely what he meant by knowledge of intentional wrongdoing.

Applying these statements of the law to the facts, the majority had considerable difficulty with the apparent mutual inconsistency of the statements of Carnwath J. that Leach, on the one hand, had not been dishonest but, on the other hand, had wilfully shut his eyes; the difficulty arose because everyone else has always regarded a wilful shutting of eyes as amounting to dishonesty. However, the majority felt unable to do what the Court of Appeal had done and go behind the statement that Leach had not been dishonest. Faced with the consequential choice between ordering a new trial and allowing Leach's appeal, they opted for the latter. Lord Millett would, on the other hand, have held Leach liable because he had known every detail of the undertaking which the payment to him had breached (not only had he himself at an earlier stage been asked by the claimant and had refused to give a similar undertaking but the solicitor who had agreed to give the undertaking had, before doing so, faxed a copy of it to him for his comments); presumably it was due to the fact that Leach's knowledge of the breach of the undertaking was so clear cut that Lord Millett did not define what he meant by knowledge of intentional wrongdoing.

Lord Hutton's combined test, which now clearly constitutes English law, is not devoid of problems. Later in his speech,[32] he emphasised that an accessory "should not escape a finding of dishonesty because he sets his own standards of honesty and does not regard as dishonest what he knows would offend the normally accepted standards of honest conduct" (this is the sort of dishonesty which the Court of Appeal had described in *Grupo Torras v. Al-Sabah*[33] as "Robin Hood dishonesty"). This statement is wholly consistent with his combined test but overlooks the possibility that the accessory fails to realise that his conduct was dishonest by the ordinary standards of reasonable and honest people because of the fact that he wrongly but genuinely regards his own standards of dishonesty as the ordinary standards of reasonable and honest people. If such an accessory is regarded as liable (and it is highly unlikely that he would not be), then there must be limits beyond which a subjective belief that conduct is honest will not be accepted by the court. On this basis, subjectivity will clearly have to be subdivided in some way, possibly into reasonable subjectivity and unreasonable subjectivity.

The answer to this potential difficulty may simply be that the courts would

---

[32] *ibid.* at 174.
[33] [2001] Lloyd's Rep. Bank. 36.

never in practice accept that such an accessory genuinely believed that his own standards of dishonesty were the ordinary standards of reasonable and honest people. However, the existence of this difficulty does cast some doubt on the combined test. Further, any test based on dishonesty inevitably gives rise to a further potential difficulty, namely whether it is necessary for the imposition of liability that the accessory was actually aware of the existence of a trust.

This question did not arise in *Twinsectra v. Yardley* because, as has already been mentioned, Leach knew every detail of the facts which were held to have given rise to the trust of the funds lent by the claimant. However, it did arise in *Brinks v. Abu-Saleh (No.3)*[34] where, as has already been seen,[35] the attempt to impose liability for dishonest assistance on the defendant in question for having accompanied her husband on various trips by car to Zurich failed because it was held that she had not thereby assisted her husband to launder the money in question. Despite the fact that the claim against her therefore did not satisfy the second requirement for the imposition of liability, Rimer J. nevertheless went on to consider whether or not it would have satisfied the third requirement. She was clearly unaware of the source of the funds being transported and so was necessarily also unaware of the existence of any trust. Rimer J. stated that he did not consider that the Privy Council had in *Royal Brunei Airlines v. Tan* "intended to suggest that an accessory could be made liable regardless of whether he had any knowledge of the existence of the trust" in question. Consequently, even if the defendant had actually been an accessory, she would not have been held liable for dishonest assistance.

On the face of things, this conclusion seemed inconsistent with the earlier decision of Millett J. in *Agip (Africa) v. Jackson*,[36] where he held that: "it is no answer for a man charged with having knowingly assisted in a fraudulent and dishonest scheme to say that he thought that it was 'only' a breach of exchange control or 'only' a case of tax evasion. ... A man who consciously assists others by making arrangements which he knows are calculated to conceal what is happening from a third party, takes the risk that they are part of a fraud practised on that party." But, in *Grupo Torras v. Al-Sabah*,[37] at first instance, Mance L.J. purported to reconcile this conflict of authority by saying that "the answer to this problem seems to lie in recognising that, for dishonest assistance, the defendant's dishonesty must have been towards the plaintiff in relation to property held or potentially held on trust or constructive trust, rather than in the introduction of a separate criterion of knowledge of any such trust".

Although the Court of Appeal in *Grupo Torras v. Al-Sabah*,[38] seemed more inclined to adopt the view of Rimer J., in *Twinsectra v. Yardley*,[39] Lord Hoffmann adopted a view entirely consistent with that of Mance L.J. He did not "suggest that a person cannot be dishonest without a full appreciation of the legal analysis of the transaction". Instead, he said that someone "may dishonestly assist in the commission of a breach of trust without any idea of what a trust means. The necessary dishonest state of mind may be found to exist

---

[34] [1996] C.L.C. 133.
[35] See *ante*, p. 380.
[36] [1990] Ch. 265 at 295.
[37] [1999] C.L.C. 1469.
[38] [2001] Lloyd's Rep. Bank 36.
[39] [2002] 2 A.C. 164 at 171.

simply on the fact that he knew perfectly well that he was helping to pay away money to which the recipient was not entitled." However, he accepted that this was not the case in *Twinsectra v. Yardley*. Consequently, despite the consistency of the views expressed by Mance L.J. and Lord Hoffmann, this other potential difficulty caused by having a test based on dishonesty cannot yet be regarded as finally settled.

### (4) Resulting loss

Until the decision in *Grupo Torras v. Al-Sabah*,[40] it was generally thought that the quantum of recovery for dishonest assistance was the loss suffered as a result of the dishonest assistance in question and that it was for the claimant to prove what that loss actually was. However, in that case, the claimant submitted that a defendant who is guilty of dishonest assistance is liable for the whole loss resulting from the breach of trust in question, whether or not causally linked to his acts of specific assistance. At first instance, Mance L.J. said this:

> "The starting point in my view is that the requirement of dishonest assistance relates not to any loss which may be suffered, but to the breach of trust or fiduciary duty. The relevant enquiry is in my view what loss or damage has resulted from the breach of trust or fiduciary duty which has been dishonestly assisted. In this context, as in conspiracy, it is inappropriate to become involved in attempts to assess the precise causative significance of the dishonest assistance in respect of either the breach of trust or fiduciary duty or the resulting loss. ... But it is necessary to identify what breach of trust or duty was assisted and what loss may be said to have resulted from that breach of trust or duty. An allegation of a single and continuing conspiracy to commit and cover up a misappropriation is one thing. But it may involve a series of breaches of trust and fiduciary duty. The actual loss may have resulted at the early stage of misappropriation, rather than from the cover up. Dishonest assistance confined to the cover up stage may or may not necessarily attract liability for such previous loss."

This proposition unquestionably formed part of the ratio of Mance L.J. (the point did not arise on appeal). This effective acceptance of the claimant's contention, subject only to the exclusion of losses which occurred before the dishonest assister first became involved, obviously increases still further the potential burden of liability for dishonest assistance.

A further aspect of the quantum of this type of liability was considered in *Fyffes Group v. Templeman*,[41] where the shipping manager of the claimant had received secret commissions of 1.25 per cent on the lump sum freight paid by the defendant shipping company for transporting the claimant's bananas. The claimant now sought, among other heads of recovery, an account of the profits which the shipping company had made on the voyages as part of the compensation for its dishonest assistance in the breach of fiduciary duty by the shipping manager. Toulson J. held that in principle such relief should be

---

[40] [1999] C.L.C. 1469 (the point did not arise on appeal).
[41] [2000] 2 Lloyd's Rep. 643.

available in appropriate circumstances. However, he held that it should not be granted to the claimant in these circumstances so as to deprive the shipping company of the ordinary profit element of the freight charged; the extent to which the claimant had paid more than it would otherwise have done had already been compensated in damages and there was no justification for awarding any further relief. This decision seems clearly correct but more may well be heard of this particular head of liability in the future.

### (C) The Liability of Agents of Invalidly Appointed Trustees

The primary concern of Lord Selborne when he gave his judgment in *Barnes v. Addy* to protect agents of a trust who act in accordance with the instructions of the trustees. Is this protection available to an agent even if the trustee by whom he is instructed has not himself been validly appointed? This issue arose in *Mara v. Browne*,[42] where it was argued that an agent appointed by such a trustee must act as a principal and so would be deprived of the protection of *Barnes v. Addy* — this would of course mean that the agent in question would be treated as if he were officiously acting as a fiduciary and so, under the principles which have already been discussed,[43] would inevitably be liable no matter what his motives and his honesty. This argument succeeded at first instance before North J.,[44] but the Court of Appeal found that the trustee in question had been validly appointed and so the issue did not have to be decided. However, Lord Herschell stated that the protection of *Barnes v. Addy* would be available to such an agent. It is suggested that this latter view, although not clearly established, is preferable since it is unreasonable to expect an agent to carry out a detailed investigation into the status of his principal.

### (D) The Liability of Partners of Persons Liable for Dishonest Assistance

The answer to the question of whether the partners of a person who is held liable for dishonest assistance are vicariously liable for the acts or omissions which have caused this type of liability to be imposed upon him was far from clear prior to the decision of the House of Lords in *Dubai Aluminium Co. v. Salaam*.[45] However, as a result of that decision, the earlier authorities[46] can now, at least for the moment, be disregarded. The House of Lords held unanimously that liability for dishonest assistance fell within the scope of section 10 of the Partnership Act 1890 and that, consequently, the partners of a person held liable for dishonest assistance were vicariously liable for the wrongful acts or omissions which had led to the imposition of liability if "he was acting in the ordinary course of the business of the firm, or with the authority of his co-partners". The latter situation is self-evident; the former requires further consideration.

In *Dubai Aluminium Co. v. Salaam*, the senior partner of a firm of solicitors

---

[42] [1896] 1 Ch. 199.
[43] See *ante*, p. 373.
[44] [1895] 2 Ch. 69.
[45] [2002] 3 W.L.R. 1913.
[46] *Blythe v. Fladgate* [1891] 1 Q.B. 337; *Mara v. Browne* [1895] 2 Ch. 69 (North J.), [1896] 1 Ch. 199 (C.A.); *Re Bell's Indenture* [1980] 3 All E.R. 425; *Agip (Africa) v. Jackson* [1990] Ch. 265 (Millett J.), [1991] Ch. 547 (C.A.).

had to be assumed[47] to be liable for dishonest assistance by virtue of the fact that he had prepared the documentation by means of which the other defendants had succeeded in defrauding the claimant of some US$50,000,000 which had been paid out pursuant to a bogus consultancy agreement which was nothing more or less than a sham device for abstracting money from the claimant. He had purported to act for the other defendants as a member of his firm, which had charged and had been paid relatively modest fees for the work which he had done. The House of Lords held that, for liability to arise, the wrongful conduct of the partner in question had to be so closely connected with acts which he was authorised to do that, for the purpose of the liability of the firm to third parties, the wrongful conduct could fairly and properly be regarded as done while he had been acting in the ordinary course of the firm's business. This involved a factual conclusion based on primary facts rather than a simple question of fact. It was held that drafting the necessary agreements would have been within the ordinary course of the firm's business even though the documents were being drafted for a dishonest purpose. Consequently, on the facts as pleaded by the claimant, the senior partner would have been liable for dishonest assistance and so his partners would have been vicariously liable for his conduct.

In normal circumstances, this conclusion would have prejudiced the partners who would have been potentially liable for the entire US$50,000,000, in the same way as the partner of an accountancy firm was held, by Millett J. and the Court of Appeal in *Agip (Africa) v. Jackson*,[48] to be potentially liable for the whole of the money which his partner had, by acting as a director of a series of dummy companies, enabled a fraudster to launder. However, in *Dubai Aluminium Co. v. Salaam* the conclusion actually benefited the partners because it entitled them to claim contribution from the other defendants, who had actually benefited from the fraud. This result was not in itself objectionable but, controversially and probably wrongly,[49] the House of Lords went on to allow the firm of solicitors to recover their entire liability by way of contribution, thus enabling them to escape completely the liability imposed on them by the Partnership Act 1890.

*Dubai Aluminium Co. v. Salaam* does at least make clear the criteria for the imposition of vicarious liability on the partners of a person held liable for dishonest assistance; the latter at least now have the comfort of knowing that they cannot be held liable for the acts or omissions of one of their partners who goes off on a frolic of his own or, as Lord Millett specifically held, of one of their partners who is held to be a constructive trustee as a result of having decided officiously to act as a fiduciary or, as Lord Millett would prefer to describe him, as a "de facto trustee".[50] However, it will not be often that the partners who are vicariously liable for dishonest assistance will find anyone from whom to claim contribution (most fraudsters will have either disappeared or have become bankrupt); further, even if they do manage to find a

---

[47] His partners had settled the claim against him for US$10,000,000 on the basis that all allegations of dishonesty against him were withdrawn but, for the purpose of their claim for contribution against the defendants who had actually benefited from the fraud, it had to be assumed that he was liable.
[48] [1990] Ch. 265 (Millett J.), [1991] Ch. 547 (C.A.).
[49] See *post*, p. 776.
[50] That was held not to be conduct within the ordinary course of the business of anyone.

solvent potential contributary, they are unlikely often to encounter such judicial generosity in respect of their contribution claim. Their position is undoubtedly much more likely to be as in *Agip (Africa) v. Jackson*, where there was no one from whom either the accountant or his partner had the slightest chance of being able to obtain any contribution.

### (E) What Should a Suspicious Agent Do?
If an agent suspects that he may be assisting in a misapplication of property subject to a trust and it is too late for him to withdraw from the transaction (this would be the position of a solicitor or a bank who became suspicious about the provenance of funds being held to the order of a client), he is entitled to make an application to the High Court under Part 64 of the Civil Procedure Rules 1998[51] for administration directions. In the event that there are sufficient grounds for his suspicions, it was held in *Finers v. Miro*[52] that any directions given by the court can, if necessary, override any legal or other professional privilege of confidentiality to which the client would normally have been entitled.

However, *Finers v. Miro* was distinguished in *Moss v. Integro Trust B.V.I*,[53] where the beneficiaries were ascertainable, of full age, and between them absolutely beneficially entitled to the trust property and brought an action successfully claiming the trust property under the rule in *Saunders v. Vautier*.[54] Nor can an agent safely refuse to comply with his client's instructions merely because he has become suspicious; this can only safely be done where he has positive evidence of a misfeasance or breach of trust on the part of the client. In *T.T.S. International v. Cantrade Private Bank*,[55] the Royal Court of Jersey went so far as to enter summary judgment against a bank who had refused to comply with instructions to transfer the balance of an account out of the jurisdiction; the court found, first, that at the relevant time there was no evidence of a dishonest and fraudulent design (still necessary at that time); secondly, that there was no evidence that the funds would be paid to anyone other than their true owners; and, thirdly, that the bank had taken an overly cautious view of its duties, appearing more concerned to protect itself against possible claims than to look after the interests of its account holders. Refusing to comply with the instructions of clients therefore appears only to be feasible in very extreme cases.

However, if the funds do have to be paid out for one of the reasons set out above, it has been held in Hong Kong[56] that this fact will constitute a defence to any subsequent attempt to impose liability for dishonest assistance on the agent who has been obliged to pay them out. It was held in that case that this followed from the fact that a bank, in that case the Bank of China, is normally liable to comply with the instructions of its client. This decision suggests that a suspicious agent will be best advised to apply for administration directions in

---

[51] Part 64 replaced Order 85 of the Rules of the Supreme Court in December 2002.
[52] *Finers v. Miro* [1991] 1 All E.R. 182.
[53] (1997) 2 B.O.S. (British Virgin Islands High Court) 173.
[54] (1841) Cr. & Ph. 240; *post*, p. 637. It is of course not particularly likely that all the beneficiaries of an offshore trust will satisfy these requirements — this caused a similar action to fail in Barbados in *Bank of Nova Scotia Trust Company (Caribbean) v. Tremblay* (1998) 2 B.O.S. 89.
[55] (1995), unreported but see (1995) 4 J.Int.Tr. 60.
[56] In *Bardissy v. D'Souza* (1999) to be reported in [2003] W.T.L.R.

any event because, even if he is unsuccessful, his liability will be limited to the costs of that application since it is likely that he will thereafter be protected from being held liable to the principal of his client for dishonest assistance.

## 4. *Receiving Property Disposed of in Breach of Trust*

### (A) The Different Remedies Available Against the Recipient

The imposition of the obligations of trusteeship on the recipient of property disposed of in breach of trust is generally known as "liability for knowing receipt". The imposition of such liability is, however, only one of a number of claims which may be available to the person from whom the property has been abstracted. If the property or its product is still identifiable in the hands of the recipient or of any third party to whom it has been subsequently transferred, he will also have the possibility of bringing a proprietary claim, either at law or in equity, to enable him to follow the property into the hands of its present holder.[57] Additionally he may be able to bring a personal action at law for money had and received against the recipient, a personal action in equity against whoever was responsible for initiating the misapplication, and a claim to make accountable in equity anyone who has been guilty of dishonest assistance.[58]

For example, in *Agip (Africa) v. Jackson*,[59] an employee of the plaintiff company fraudulently altered the names of the payees on a number of payment orders to make them payable to one of a series of dummy companies operated by the defendant firm of accountants who, as soon as the funds were received, transferred the funds on to third parties and wound up the company in question. The plaintiff, having already obtained an unsatisfied judgment against the dummy company in question, sought the following relief against the defendants: at law, a proprietary claim to follow the funds into the hands of the defendants and a personal claim for money had and received and, in equity, a proprietary claim to follow the funds into the hands of the defendants and the imposition of liability for knowing receipt and dishonest assistance. In *Lipkin Gorman v. Karpnale*,[60] a member of a firm of solicitors had drawn from the firm's client accounts funds which he subsequently gambled away at a casino. The solicitors claimed that its bank was liable for conversion of cheques, for conversion of a draft, for breach of contract and for dishonest assistance; they also claimed that the casino was liable for money had and received, for negligence, for conversion of cheques, for conversion of a draft, and for knowing receipt and, additionally, was liable in equity to both proprietary and personal claims as a result of its receipt of the solicitors' funds.

It has already been observed[61] that the interrelation of these different claims makes proceedings of this type extremely complex. The principal difficulty is the existence of what have been described[62] as "arbitrary and anomalous distinctions" between the claims at law and the claims in equity. It is perhaps

---

[57] See *post*, p. 807.
[58] See *ante*, p. 374.
[59] [1990] Ch. 265 (Millett J.); [1991] Ch. 547 (Court of Appeal).
[60] [1987] 1 W.L.R. 987 (Alliott J.); [1989] 1 W.L.R. 1340, C.A.; [1991] 2 A.C. 548, H.L.
[61] See *ante*, p. 372.
[62] By Millett J. in *El Ajou v. Dollar Land Holdings* [1993] B.C.L.C. 735 at 757. Millett J. contended that these distinctions should not be insisted upon.

inevitable that, as will be seen in a later Chapter,[63] the prerequisites of and defences to proprietary claims differ depending on whether the claim is being brought at law or in equity. But there are also distinctions between the different personal claims. An action at law for money had and received will succeed quite irrelevant of the state of mind of the recipient of the money; the only defences available to him will be bona fide purchase for value without notice and change of position.[64] On the other hand, although there is some uncertainty as to precisely what mental element will lead to the imposition of liability for knowing receipt, that liability is certainly not at present strict (nor for that matter is liability for dishonest assistance). In other words, liability at law is strict, subject to defences, while liability in equity depends on the state of mind of the recipient.

This (and other) distinctions have led commentators to question whether so many different remedies should continue to be available for the same misapplication of property.[65] Indeed Millett J. once commented[66] that he did not see "how it would be possible to develop any logical and coherent system of restitution if there were different requirements in respect of knowledge for the common law claim for money had and received, the personal claim for an account in equity against a knowing recipient and the equitable proprietary claim". As a result of observations of this type, the Law Commission at one stage considered reviewing this whole area of the law with a view to rationalising all the available remedies. Despite the fact that this review has not taken place, an ever-increasing majority of the commentators, including at least two of the present Lords of Appeal in Ordinary writing extra-judicially, have expressed the view that the best way forward is to introduce a universal principle of strict liability subject to clearly defined defences.[67] For the moment, however, the existing distinctions between the different claims obviously continue.

For present purposes, it is important only to distinguish between, on the one hand, the possibility of following the property disposed of in breach of trust into the hands of its recipient by means of an equitable proprietary claim and, on the other hand, the imposition of liability for knowing receipt. Where property has been disposed of in breach of trust, the interests of the beneficiaries in that property are, in accordance with the basic principles of property law, enforceable against the whole world unless and until the property in question reaches the hands of someone who takes it free of their equitable proprietary interests therein.[68] Any recipient of property disposed of

---

[63] See *post*, pp. 800, 807.
[64] *Lipkin Gorman v. Karpnale* [1989] 1 W.L.R. 1340, CA [1991] 2 A.C. 548, HL. See Birks [1991] L.M.C.L.Q. 473.
[65] See the articles cited *ante*, p. 372, fn. 61.
[66] In *El Ajou v. Dollar Land Holdings* [1993] B.C.L.C. 735 at 759.
[67] See the articles cited *ante*, p. 372, fn. 61.
[68] When the property or its product is pure personalty or unregistered land, the interests of the beneficiaries will be enforceable against the whole world other than a bona fide purchaser for value of a legal interest therein without notice of those interests. When it is registered land, their interests will be enforceable against the whole world if they either override registration or have been protected by an entry on the Land Register but otherwise will not be enforceable against any bona fide purchaser for value claiming under a registered disposition. Further, whatever the nature of the property, any claim of the beneficiaries to enforce their interests will additionally be subject to the established defences to equitable proprietary claims considered *post*, pp. 832–838.

in breach of trust who is liable to an equitable proprietary claim will of course be a trustee of such property as is in his hands — this is simply because the equitable interests of the beneficiaries in that property must necessarily take effect behind a trust of the legal interest. However, the fact that it is possible to bring an equitable proprietary claim against the recipient does not necessarily mean that he will also be held liable for knowing receipt. This was stated particularly clearly by Megarry V.-C. in *Re Montagu's Settlement*.[69]

In fact in only three situations is it actually necessary to seek the imposition of liability for knowing receipt: first, where the recipient has dealt with some or all of the property in such a way that it can no longer be the subject of an equitable proprietary claim; secondly, where the property has depreciated in value while in the hands of the recipient; and, thirdly, where the recipient has obtained some incidental profit from the property.[70] In these circumstances, the equitable proprietary claim will enable the beneficiaries to recover only such property, if any, as remains in the hands of the recipient; the loss caused by any dealing with or reduction in the value of the property and any incidental profit obtained will only be recoverable if the recipient is held to have been a constructive trustee of the whole of the property originally transferred to him. In the overwhelming majority of the cases in which the imposition of liability for knowing receipt has been sought, the recipient has dealt with some or all of the property in such a way that it can no longer be the subject of an equitable proprietary claim.

### (B) The Elements of Liability for Knowing Receipt

Liability for knowing receipt has never been dependent on the existence of any dishonest or fraudulent design on the part of the person who disposed of the property in breach of trust; consequently the decision of the Privy Council in *Royal Brunei Airlines v. Tan*[71] to replace this requirement for the imposition of liability for dishonest assistance did not in any way affect liability for knowing receipt, which had never required more than the misfeasance or breach of trust preferred by the Privy Council. In *El Ajou v. Dollar Land Holdings*,[72] Hoffmann L.J. isolated three distinct elements of this type of liability: a disposition of property in breach of trust, beneficial receipt of the property disposed of in breach of trust or of its traceable product, and knowledge by the recipient.

### (1) A disposition of property in breach of trust

This first requirement is exactly the same as the first requirement for the imposition of liability for dishonest assistance. Thus, "the trust need not be a formal trust. It is sufficient that there should be a fiduciary relationship between the 'trustee' and the property of another person",[73] which can be either express or constructive, and that there should have been a disposition of property in breach of the appropriate fiduciary duty. In practice this requirement is likely to cause as few problems as the equivalent requirement for the imposition of liability for dishonest assistance.

---

[69] [1987] Ch. 264 at 272–273.
[70] Such as one of the types of secret profits discussed in the previous section of this chapter.
[71] [1995] 2 A.C. 378.
[72] [1994] 2 All E.R. 685.
[73] Peter Gibson J. in *Baden v. Société Générale* (1983) [1993] 1 W.L.R. 509N at 573, referring to liability for dishonest assistance.

It was because of the absence of such a disposition that the House of Lords did not impose any liability for knowing receipt in *Twinsectra v. Yardley*.[74] In the Court of Appeal liability for knowing receipt had been imposed on Leach, the solicitor to whom the majority of the funds had been transferred in breach of the undertaking given to the claimant, in respect of the funds which, in accordance with the instructions of the borrower, he had used to pay the fees which he had charged for carrying out a conveyancing transaction. But, in the course of argument in the House of Lords, the Appellate Committee decided that the expenditure on these conveyancing fees had been within the spirit of the undertaking on the strength of which the funds had been advanced.[75] This meant that Leach had not disbursed the sums in question in breach of trust and so could not be liable for knowing receipt.[76]

## (2) Beneficial receipt of the property disposed of in breach of trust or of its traceable product

Whether the property disposed of in breach of trust or its traceable product has been beneficially received by the person on whom it is sought to impose liability for knowing receipt is merely a question of fact. There are in fact two distinct elements of this second requirement: first, that the property should actually have reached the hands of that person; and, secondly, that he should have received that property beneficially.

As for the first element, the conventional view is that actual receipt is determined in the same way as in legal and equitable proprietary claims. However, some doubts were cast on this by the judgment of Millett J. at first instance in *El Ajou v Dollar Land Holdings*,[77] which seems to indicate that the rules for following property from one person to another are less strict in the case of liability for knowing receipt than in the case of equitable proprietary claims.

In this case,[78] a claim for the imposition of liability for knowing receipt was brought by and on behalf of the victims of a fraudulent share dealing operation carried out from Amsterdam on behalf of three Canadians. The latter had subsequently, through a Panamanian company, entered into a joint venture for the development of property in England with an English company which had not been involved in the fraud. They subsequently decided to withdraw from the joint venture and sold their interest in it to the English company. The plaintiff claimed that the Canadians' investment in the joint venture had been made with the funds of which he and the other victims had been defrauded. That in itself would not have made the English company liable in any way; at that stage the plaintiff's only conceivable claim would have been to attempt to attach the 50 per cent interest in the joint venture held by the Canadians' Panamanian company. But the plaintiff claimed that, as a result of the subsequent purchase of the Canadians' interest by the English company, that company had in effect received the funds of which he and the other victims had been defrauded and was therefore liable for knowing receipt.

---

[74] [2002] 2 A.C. 164.
[75] Contrary to what Lord Millett said in his speech, the claim in respect of those fees was never withdrawn.
[76] For this reason, no argument was called for in respect of liability for knowing receipt.
[77] [1993] 3 All E.R. 717.
[78] [1993] 3 All E.R. 717 (Millett J.); [1994] 2 All E.R. 685 (C.A.).

The problem about this claim which is relevant for present purposes was the fact that the victims' funds had, prior to their investment in the joint venture, been moved through several civil law jurisdictions which do not recognise the existence of trusts and that at one point a substantial sum had been sent from Geneva to Panama, where it had disappeared for a short time prior to the reappearance of a roughly similar sum in Geneva. Millett J. held that the property could be followed despite the passage of the funds through the civil law jurisdictions and that, notwithstanding their brief disappearance in Panama, there was sufficient evidence to conclude that the victims' funds had indeed been used to make this investment. Although Millett J. indicated the contrary, no equitable proprietary claim could possibly have survived the disappearance of the funds in Panama and it is not easy to see how such a claim could have survived the passage of the funds through the civil law jurisdictions either. If, for the purposes of knowing receipt, actual receipt is indeed determined in the same way as in legal and equitable proprietary claims, then this case was wrongly decided. Nor does it seem appropriate that actual receipt should be determined in any different way for the purposes of knowing receipt; only if it is can the decision of Millett J. in this respect be supported.

His decision that the funds of the victims had indeed been received by the English company as a result of the purchase of the Canadians' share was not of course in itself sufficient for the imposition of liability for knowing receipt. It was also necessary to satisfy the third requirement, knowledge by the recipient. The chairman of the English company, who had originally brought the joint venturers together, had had dealings with the Canadians prior to the joint venture and was unquestionably aware of the manner in which they had acquired their funds. The Court of Appeal held, reversing Millett J. in this respect, that knowledge of the fraud acquired by the chairman in a quite different capacity prior to any involvement with the English company could be attributed to that company once he became its chairman. The English company was therefore obliged to pay a second time for the Canadians' 50 per cent interest. To make matters still worse, they were held liable in subsequent proceedings[79] to account not for the sum actually paid to the Canadians but for 50 per cent of the substantially higher amount for which the joint venture property had eventually been sold on.

As for the second element of this requirement, it is (or at least ought to be) merely a question of fact whether the property disposed of in breach of trust or its traceable product has been beneficially received by the person on whom it is sought to impose liability for knowing receipt. When property disposed of in breach of trust is received by persons for them to hold on trust, the recipient trustees are for these purposes regarded as receiving it beneficially. A solicitor certainly receives his fees beneficially[80] and, in principle, a banker receives beneficially the fees normally charged for transactions such as issuing banker's drafts[81] and the commissions normally charged for bank transfers, particularly

---

[79] *El Ajou v. Dollar Land Holdings (No.2)* [1995] 2 All E.R. 213.

[80] This was the basis of the unsuccessful claim for knowing receipt in *Twinsectra v. Yardley* [2002] 2 A.C. 162.

[81] Fees are also often charged simply for keeping accounts open and for each cheque but it is hardly likely that the amounts involved would be sufficient to justify proceedings.

those to other jurisdictions. However, as has already been seen,[82] while the potential liability of banks for knowing receipt in respect of any fees or commissions which it has charged has generally been ignored by the courts, in *Polly Peck International v. Nadir (No.2)*,[83] Scott L.J. held that the potential liability of the Central Bank of Northern Cyprus in respect of Turkish lire which it had exchanged for sterling and transferred to Northern Cyprus was for knowing receipt because it "became entitled to the sterling not as banker … but in its own right". Apart from any fees or commissions which the Central Bank may have charged, to which no reference was made, the bank became no more beneficially entitled to the Turkish lire than it did to the sterling which it had also sent to Northern Cyprus (in respect of which its potential liability was held to be only for dishonest assistance). It is suggested that this potential liability for knowing receipt cannot be justified and that the decision of Scott L.J.[84] should not in this respect be followed.

### (3) Knowledge by the recipient

Where a recipient of property has no knowledge whatever that it has been disposed of in breach of trust, this third requirement will obviously not be satisfied and he will not be liable for knowing receipt (it is for the claimant to prove knowledge, not for the recipient to disprove it).[85] This is the case whether or not the recipient gave value for the property which he received.[86]

In *Carl-Zeiss Stiftung v. Herbert Smith (No.2)*,[87] an East German company sought to impose liability for knowing receipt on the firm of solicitors who were representing a West German company in proceedings in which the East German company was claiming that the property and the assets of the West German company either belonged to or were held on trust for them (both claimed to be the original Zeiss Foundation and hence to be entitled to use the Zeiss trademark — the company had become divided due to the division of Germany after the Second World War). The basis of the claim against the solicitors was that they had actual notice that the East German company claimed to be entitled to all the assets of the West German company including, obviously enough, any legal fees which they had paid out. The Court of Appeal dismissed this claim on the somewhat controversial ground[88] that notice of an adverse claim to the property of the West German company had not amounted to notice of a trust since difficult questions both of fact and law were involved in the claim; the solicitors therefore had had no effective knowledge whatever of any adverse claim to the funds which they had

---

[82] See *ante*, p. 371.

[83] [1992] 4 All E.R. 769 at 777.

[84] It has not been followed in New Zealand; see *Nimmo v. Westpac Banking Corporation* [1993] 3 N.Z.L.R. 218 and *Cigna Life Insurance New Zealand v. Westpac Securities* [1996] 1 N.Z.L.R. 80.

[85] *Polly Peck International v. Nadir (No.2)* [1992] 4 All E.R. 769 at 777.

[86] On the other hand, whether or not he gave value will of course be highly relevant in relation to an equitable proprietary claim, since only if he did will he be able to make out the defence of bona fide purchase for value without notice.

[87] [1969] 2 Ch. 276.

[88] See Gordon (1970) 44 A.L.J. 261.

received and therefore were, in effect, bona fide purchasers for value without notice of the fees which they had received.[89]

A more straightforward illustration is *Cowan de Groot Properties v. Eagle Trust*,[90] where an attempt was made to impose liability for knowing receipt on the purchaser of five properties sold at a gross undervalue by a company in urgent need of liquid funds in order to make an urgent payment needed to keep an important company project in existence. Knox J. held that the purchaser did not fall within any of the five categories of knowledge identified by Peter Gibson J. in *Baden v. Société Générale* and so was consequently not liable.

The courts have also declined to impose "the heavy obligations of trusteeship"[91] upon recipients of property disposed of in breach of trust who received that property in good faith without any knowledge of the breach of trust in question. In *Re Diplock*,[92] under the provisions of a will subsequently declared to be void for uncertainty, executors distributed large sums of money to various charities who received the property in good faith without the slightest idea that the House of Lords would at a later stage hold that the will was void.[93] The next of kin of the testator (who were entitled under the resulting intestacy) brought an action against the charities to recover the money. They were obviously entitled to bring an equitable proprietary claim in order to follow the sums so paid into their product.[94] But the Court of Appeal held that the charities were not liable for knowing receipt and so the sums which could not be recovered by means of the equitable proprietary claim could not be recovered by the imposition of a constructive trust. This decision was expressly approved by the House of Lords in *Westdeutsche Landesbank Girozentrale v. Islington L.B.C.*[95]

Where the situation is not so clear cut, the authorities conflict. Discussion of the position formerly focused principally around the five categories of knowledge identified by Peter Gibson J. in *Baden v. Société Générale*:[96] "(i) actual knowledge; (ii) wilfully shutting one's eyes to the obvious; (iii) wilfully and recklessly failing to make such inquiries as an honest and reasonable man would make; (iv) knowledge of circumstances which would indicate the facts to an honest and reasonable man; (v) knowledge of circumstances which would put an honest and reasonable man on inquiry". However, reference has more recently been made both to dishonesty and to unconscionability as criteria for the imposition of liability. At present, there is authority for the following conflicting propositions as to what will lead to the imposition of liability: first, that any of the five categories of knowledge identified in *Baden v. Société Générale* will suffice; secondly, that only the first three of these categories will suffice; thirdly, that the question of whether the fourth and fifth of

---

[89] Although the Court of Appeal did not specifically say so, it is thought by practitioners that this restrictive view of notice can be relied on only by solicitors and possibly only by solicitors engaged in litigation. Further, the courts will generally not make orders validating in advance the payment in any event of the costs of solicitors who are defending clients who are accused of involvement in dishonest breaches of trust (see *United Mizrahi Bank v. Docherty* [1998] Ch. 435).

[90] [1992] 4 All E.R. 700.

[91] This was the description utilised by Lord Greene M.R. in *Re Diplock* [1948] Ch. 465.

[92] [1948] Ch. 465.

[93] In *Chichester Diocesan Fund v. Simpson* [1944] A.C. 341.

[94] See *post*, p. 807.

[95] [1996] A.C. 669.

[96] (1983) [1993] 1 W.L.R. 509N at 575–576

these categories will suffice only arises in non-commercial transactions, only the first three of those categories being relevant in commercial transactions; fourthly, that the test for knowledge in knowing receipt is now the same as that for dishonesty in dishonest assistance; and, fifthly, that the state of the recipient's knowledge must make it unconscionable for him to retain the benefit of the receipt. It was hoped that the conflict between these lines of authority would be resolved by the House of Lords in *Twinsectra v. Yardley* but this did not occur because, as has already been seen, the claim for knowing receipt before the House failed to satisfy the first requirement.

(a) **The five categories of knowledge identified in** *Baden v. Société Générale*. Since the first three of the conflicting lines of authority all concern the five categories of knowledge identified by Peter Gibson J.[97] in *Baden v. Société Générale*, these are best considered together.

A recipient of property disposed of in breach of trust who has actual knowledge of the breach of trust will obviously be liable for knowing receipt. In *Belmont Finance Corporation v. Williams Furniture (No.2)*,[98] the directors of a company had had actual knowledge of a transaction whereby that company had permitted its wholly owned subsidiary to be purchased with its own money, a transaction which amounted to a breach of trust by the directors of the subsidiary. The purchase price for the subsidiary had of course been paid to the parent company which had therefore received property with actual knowledge that it had been disposed of in breach of trust. The Court of Appeal held that the parent company was therefore liable for knowing receipt and so was a constructive trustee of the purchase moneys received. Similarly, in *El Ajou v. Dollar Land Holdings*,[99] the Court of Appeal imposed liability for knowing receipt on a company because it had acquired the interest of a co-venturer at a time when, through its chairman, it was aware that the co-venturer had originally acquired its interest in the joint venture with the proceeds of fraud.

However, liability for knowing receipt is clearly not confined to cases of actual knowledge. In *Nelson v. Larholt*,[1] one of the executors of a will drew eight cheques on the estate's bank account, all of which were signed by him as executor of the testator, in favour of the defendant who cashed the cheques in good faith. The other executor and the beneficiaries claimed that the defendant held the proceeds of the cheques on constructive trust for the estate. Denning J. held that the defendant must be taken to know what any reasonable man would have known. Eight successive requests to cash cheques clearly drawn on the bank account of an estate would have placed a reasonable man on enquiry. Thus the defendant must be taken to have known of the executor's breach of trust and so, although he had obtained the cheques for value in good faith, he was held to be liable for knowing receipt and was a constructive trustee of their proceeds. The category of knowledge relied on by Denning J. as the basis for the imposition of this constructive trust appears to fall within the fifth category of knowledge which would later be identified by Peter Gibson J.

---

[97] Which were justifiably described as "unhelpful" and "unrememberable" by Blanchard J. in *Nimmo v. Westpac Banking Corporation* [1993] 3 N.Z.L.R. 218 at 228 (High Court of New Zealand).
[98] [1980] 1 All E.R. 393.
[99] [1994] 2 All E.R. 685.
[1] [1948] 1 K.B. 339.

(knowledge of circumstances which would put an honest and reasonable man on inquiry). Consequently, *Nelson v. Larholt*, together with dicta of the Court of Appeal in *Belmont Finance Corporation v. Williams Furniture (No.2)*[2] and in a number of first instance decisions,[3] was subsequently cited in *Cowan de Groot Properties v. Eagle Trust*[4] as authority for the proposition that liability for knowing receipt will be imposed if the recipient has any of the five categories of knowledge identified by Peter Gibson J.; and, much more recently, Lord Millett[5] stated in *Twinsectra v Yardley*[6] that "constructive notice is sufficient".

However, *Nelson v. Larholt* was explained in a different way in *Carl-Zeiss Stiftung v. Herbert Smith (No.2)*,[7] where Sachs L.J. described Nelson v. Larholt as a case where there had been an obvious shutting of eyes as opposed to a mere lack of prudence and suggested that a negligent, if innocent, failure to make inquiry was not sufficient to attract liability for knowing receipt. This interpretation of the decision appears to place the defendant in *Nelson v. Larholt* within the second category of knowledge which would later be identified by Peter Gibson J. (knowledge that he would have obtained but for wilfully shutting his eyes to the obvious).

This narrower view of liability for knowing receipt was adopted by Megarry V.-C. in *Re Montagu's Settlement*,[8] where he held that only the first three of the five categories of knowledge identified by Peter Gibson J. would give rise to liability for knowing receipt. This case concerned a settlement made in 1923 under one of the clauses of which certain chattels, largely comprising the furniture, plate, pictures and other heirlooms of the Montagu family, were assigned to the trustees who, in the events which happened, were under a fiduciary duty, after the death in 1947 of the ninth Duke of Manchester, to select and make an inventory of such of the chattels as they considered suitable for inclusion in the settlement and to hold the residue of the chattels on trust for the tenth Duke of Manchester absolutely. However, the trustees in fact made no such selection or inventory but instead treated all the chattels as being the absolute property of the tenth Duke. Many of the chattels were therefore sold by him in 1949 and the remainder were taken by him to Kenya where he was then living. Following his death in 1977, the eleventh Duke of Manchester sought to recover the chattels or their value from his step-mother, the tenth Duke's executrix. Megarry V.-C. ordered an inquiry in order to establish which of the chattels would have been selected had the trustees complied with their obligations in 1947. Such of the selected chattels as were still in the hands of the executrix could be recovered from her by means of an equitable proprietary claim but recovery of the value of those which had been sold required the imposition of liability for knowing receipt.

Megarry V.-C. held that the tenth Duke did not fall into any of the first three categories of knowledge identified by Peter Gibson J. and so his executrix was

---

[2] [1980] 1 All E.R. 393.
[3] *International Sales and Agencies v. Marcus* [1982] 3 All E.R. 551 at 558; *Agip (Africa) v. Jackson* [1990] Ch. 265 at 290; *Westpac Banking Corp v. Savin* [1985] 2 N.Z.L.R. 41 at 71 (High Court of New Zealand).
[4] [1969] 2 Ch. 276.
[5] Repeating what he had said in *Agip (Africa) v. Jackson* [1990] Ch. 265 at 290.
[6] [2002] 2 AC 164 at 194.
[7] [1969] 2 Ch. 276 at 298.
[8] [1987] Ch. 264.

not liable for knowing receipt. He held that the mistake as to the interpretation of the settlement had occurred as a result of what his lordship described as "an honest muddle". Admittedly the tenth Duke's solicitor, and possibly also the tenth Duke himself as one of the settlers of the 1923 settlement, had at one stage been aware of the true position. However, his lordship held that "a person is not to be taken to have knowledge of a fact that he once knew but has genuinely forgotten: the test (or a test) is whether the knowledge continues to operate on that person's mind at the time in question".[9] He also held that, where a person has received property as a result of a disposition in breach of trust, any knowledge which may be possessed by his solicitor will not be imputed to him, "at all events if the donee or beneficiary has not employed the solicitor to investigate his right to the bounty, and has done nothing else that can be treated as accepting that the solicitor's knowledge should be treated as his own". This narrower view of liability for knowing receipt was subsequently applied by Alliott J. at first instance in *Lipkin Gorman v. Karpnale*,[10] and by Steyn J. in *Barclays Bank v. Quincecare*.[11]

At this stage there were consequently two conflicting lines of authority based on the two different interpretations of the decision in *Nelson v. Larholt*. A further refinement was subsequently introduced by Vinelott J. in *Eagle Trust v. S.B.C. Securities*.[12] He held that the question of whether the fourth and fifth categories of knowledge identified by Peter Gibson J. suffice for the imposition of liability for knowing receipt only arises in non-commercial transactions.[13] In commercial transactions, on the other hand, "if, in the ordinary course of business, a payment is made in discharge of a liability to the [recipient], the [recipient] cannot be made liable as a constructive trustee merely upon the ground that he knew or had reason to suspect that there had been a breach of trust disentitling the trustee to make the payment. It must be shown that the circumstances are such that knowledge that the payment was improper can be imputed to him".[14] Thus in commercial transactions, liability for knowing receipt will be imposed if the recipient has any of the first three categories of knowledge identified by Peter Gibson J. or "if the circumstances are such that, in the absence of any evidence or explanation by the [recipient], that knowledge can be inferred" — it being inferred "if the circumstances are such that an honest and reasonable man would have inferred that the moneys were probably trust moneys and were being misapplied".[15]

This case concerned an attempt to impose liability for knowing receipt on

---

[9] *ibid.* at 285. In *El Ajou v. Dollar Land Holdings* [1993] 3 All E.R. 717 at 739–740, Millett J. held that, in the same way, "where the knowledge of a director is attributed to a company, but is not actually imparted to it, the company should not be treated as continuing to possess that knowledge after the director in question has died or left its service. In such circumstances, the company can properly be said to have 'lost its memory'." Although the Court of Appeal reversed Millett J., Nourse L.J. stated ([1994] 2 All E.R. 685) that, while this proposition did not assist the defendant, he "might agree" with it.

[10] [1987] 1 W.L.R. 987 (the question did not have to be decided in the Court of Appeal ([1989] 1 W.L.R. 1340) and did not arise in the House of Lords ([1991] 2 A.C. 548).

[11] (1988) [1992] 4 All E.R. 363.

[12] (1991) [1993] 1 W.L.R. 484.

[13] For such transactions, Vinelott J. appeared to favour the broader view of liability for knowing receipt rather than the view expressed in *Re Montagu's Settlement*.

[14] (1991) [1993] 1 W.L.R. 484 at 506.

[15] *ibid.*

the underwriter of a rights issue made by the plaintiff company in connection with a share exchange takeover; the underwriter had received in discharge of the sub-underwriting obligations of the plaintiff's chief executive what turned out to be the plaintiff's own funds. Because these funds had been received in a commercial context to discharge a debt, Vinelott J. struck out a claim alleging only knowledge within the fourth and fifth categories identified by Peter Gibson J. The Court of Appeal subsequently granted the plaintiff leave to amend the pleadings so as to allege knowledge within the first three categories as well. When the case came on for trial,[16] Arden J. followed and applied the statement of principle enunciated by Vinelott J. She held that, in a knowing receipt case "where the receipt occurs in the discharge of a lawful debt (at least one arising out of a transaction which does not itself constitute a breach of trust),[17] actual knowledge within categories (i), (ii) and (iii) in the Baden case is required". The underwriter was held to have had no such knowledge so the action failed. The principle enunciated by Vinelott J. had in the meantime also been applied with exactly the same consequences by Knox J. in Cowan de Groot Properties v. Eagle Trust.[18] While the further refinement introduced by these authorities is certainly consistent with the traditional reluctance of equity to extend the doctrine of constructive notice to commercial transactions,[19] to have distinct tests for different types of transactions may well only succeed in confusing the situation even further.

(b) Dishonesty. In Dubai Aluminium Co. v. Salaam,[20] both Rix J. and the Court of Appeal held that liability for knowing receipt will only be imposed if the defendant has been dishonest in the sense necessary for the imposition of liability for dishonest assistance, in other words that the test for knowledge in knowing receipt is now the same as that for dishonesty in dishonest assistance. Subsequently, in Bank of America v. Arnell,[21] Aikens J. held both that this was the test and that it had been established as such by the Court of Appeal in Twinsectra v. Yardley.[22] However, this was not in fact the basis on which liability for knowing receipt was imposed by the Court of Appeal in that case.[23]

Admittedly, prior to Royal Brunei Airlines v Tan,[24] many commentators had

---

[16] Eagle Trust v. S.B.C. Securities (No.2) (1994) [1996] 1 B.C.L.C. 121 at 152.

[17] Such as the transaction in Belmont Finance Corporation v. Williams Furniture (No.2) [1980] 1 All E.R. 393; this was the ground on which Arden J. distinguished this decision.

[18] (1991) [1992] 4 All E.R. 700. However, both Arden J. and Knox J. went on to state that, in the event that they were wrong as to the law, the respective recipients had had no knowledge within the fourth or fifth categories either, so both claims would actually have failed on any view of the law.

[19] See Manchester Trust v. Furness [1895] 2 Q.B. 539 at 545, discussed ante, p. 333.

[20] [1999] 1 Lloyd's Rep 415 at 453 (Rix J.); [2000] 2 Lloyd's Rep 168 at 172 (C.A.).

[21] [1999] Lloyd's Rep Bank 399 at 406.

[22] [1999] Lloyd's Rep. Bank. 438.

[23] The Court of Appeal in fact imposed liability for knowing receipt on some of the recipients of the funds which had been transferred to Leach in breach of trust on the basis that the borrower's knowledge of what was going on had to be attributed to them and imposed liability for knowing receipt on Leach himself on the grounds that he had notice of the breach of trust. Although it is therefore not clear which of the lines of authority discussed above the Court of Appeal was purporting to apply, it was certainly not applying liability on the basis of dishonesty.

[24] [1995] 2 A.C. 378.

thought that the better view was that the basis of liability for what was then called knowing assistance and knowing receipt should be the same. However, now that the House of Lords has so narrowed the scope of dishonesty for the purposes of dishonest assistance, it does not seem at all appropriate that that test should also apply to liability for knowing receipt and restrict the scope of that liability in the same way. In any event, the dishonesty test enunciated in *Dubai Aluminium Co. v. Salaam* has now been specifically rejected in the decision in which the Court of Appeal laid down the most recent test, which is discussed below.

**(c) The state of the recipient's knowledge makes receipt by him unconscionable.** In *B.C.C.I. (Overseas) v. Akindele*,[25] the Court of Appeal established a wholly new test, holding that liability for knowing receipt will only be imposed if the state of the recipient's knowledge makes it unconscionable for him to retain the benefit of the receipt. The case concerned an agreement into which the defendant had entered for the investment of US$10,000,000 in the shares of the holding company of a Cayman Islands bank; the other contracting party, a company associated with the group, was to provide the shares and to arrange for their repurchase between two and five years later if the defendant so wished at a price which would give him a profit of 15 per cent per annum, compounded annually. The agreement had been entered into at a time when no one had any reason to doubt the integrity of the management of the bank; in fact, however, the transaction enabled the other contracting party to conceal a number of dummy loans it had made to enable the holding company to acquire its own shares and thus boost its capital in the eyes of the world. But the defendant did have some suspicions about the way in which the bank was operating by the time that he realised his investment and recovered his capital and the guaranteed return; as a result of a breach of fiduciary duty, the relevant sum was paid to him by the Cayman Islands bank, which subsequently sought to hold him liable for his profit on the grounds of dishonest assistance and knowing receipt. Carnwath J. held that the defendant had not been dishonest (which was enough to dispose of the claim for dishonest assistance) and that he would have had no reason to question the form of the transaction and so was not liable for knowing receipt either.

After a full review of all the earlier authorities, Nourse L.J. specifically rejected dishonesty as the criterion for the imposition of liability for knowing receipt, holding:[26]

"I have come to the view that, just as there is now a single test of dishonesty for knowing assistance, so ought there to be a single test of knowledge for knowing receipt. The recipient's state of knowledge must be such as to make it unconscionable for him to retain the benefit of the receipt. A test in that form, though it cannot, any more than any other, avoid difficulties of application, ought to avoid those of definition and allocation to which the previous categorisations have led. Moreover, it should better enable the courts to give common-sense decisions in the

---

[25] [2000] Lloyd's Rep. Bank. 292.
[26] *ibid.* at 301.

commercial context in which claims in knowing receipt are now frequently made."

Nourse L.J. then went on to apply this test by holding that the defendant's state of knowledge was not such that it was unconscionable either for him to have entered into the transaction or for him to be entitled to retain the benefit of the profit which he received when he had enforced it; consequently, he was not liable for knowing receipt.

B.C.C.I. (Overseas) v. Akindele is both the most recent authority and the only one in which this third requirement for the imposition of liability for knowing receipt has received detailed consideration at Court of Appeal level; consequently, this new test must, at least as a matter of precedent, constitute the law at present. However, apart from reciting the findings of Carnwath J. and saying that the defendant would not have had actual or constructive knowledge of the breach of fiduciary duty, Nourse L.J. gave no specific indication as to why he held that there had been no unconscionability. It is therefore at present difficult to predict precisely when a recipient's state of knowledge will be held to be such as to make it unconscionable for him to retain the benefit of the receipt (there has as yet been no reported case in which liability for knowing receipt has been imposed on this somewhat amorphous basis). The application of the new test is bound, and was clearly intended to be, much more "broad brush" than the pre-existing law with its reliance on different categories of knowledge. Further, as the final sentence of the passage cited indicates, this test is going to require virtually every claim to impose liability for knowing receipt to be litigated, something which is far from an ideal state of affairs for potential litigants.

What is, however, clear is that, as a result of the adoption of this test, it has for the first time been clearly established that a person may have sufficient knowledge to be liable for knowing receipt while being insufficiently dishonest to be liable for dishonest assistance. As a result, the former and not the latter liability was imposed on a solicitor who had been involved in a pension trust fraud in a decision at first instance which had not yet been able to be reported by the time that this edition had to go to press.

## (C) Quantum
A person on whom liability for knowing receipt is imposed will be liable to return the value of the property which he has received together with compound interest thereon; in addition, the claimant can recover any fruits produced by the property while it has been in the hands of the recipient and any secret profits made by the recipient by virtue of his position as constructive trustee.

## (D) Defences
It follows from the fact that the constituents of liability for knowing receipt include a requirement of knowledge that neither a bona fide purchaser of a legal estate for value without notice (or the statutory equivalent) nor an innocent volunteer will be liable for knowing receipt. This is shown by the authorities which have already been discussed.[27]

---

[27] See ante, p. 395.

In principle, the defence of change of position established by the House of Lords in *Lipkin Gorman v Karpnale*,[28] should also be available as a defence to a claim in knowing receipt. However, there seems to be no scope for its operation under the present law since there is no obvious way in which anyone found liable for knowing receipt under any of the present views of the law could successfully show a change of position in good faith; that person will necessarily either have been dishonest or have some form of knowledge, either of the disposition of property in breach of trust itself or of something else which makes it unconscionable for him to retain the benefit of the receipt. However, this defence will become extremely relevant if the law is ever reformed in the way envisaged below.

## (E) Possible Law Reform

As has already been mentioned,[29] as a result of a number of judicial observations criticisng the present state of the law, the Law Commission at one stage considered reviewing this whole area of the law with a view to rationalising all the available remedies. Despite the fact that this review has not yet taken place, the reform of liability for knowing receipt has been canvassed by a large number of commentators. Although a number of other suggestions have been made,[30] an ever-increasing majority of the commentators have expressed the view that the best way forward is to sweep the existing law away completely and replace it with the introduction of a universal principle of strict liability subject only to specified defences, namely the defence of bona fide purchase for value without notice (or statutory equivalent) and the defence of change of position. The principal loser under such a reform would of course be an innocent volunteer, such as the charities in *Re Diplock*,[31] who was not able to show a change of position; such a person would for the first time become liable for knowing receipt.

The most significant advocate of this view has been Lord Nicholls of Birkenhead, writing extrajudicially.[32] Specific reference to his views was made by the Court of Appeal in *BCCI (Overseas) v. Akindele*,[33] although no argument was based on this suggestion and the court said that "at this level of decision, it would have been a fruitless exercise". The Court of Appeal then went on to doubt whether any such change in the law would be appropriate anyway. However, Lord Nicholls' views had been envisaged by Millett J. some years

---

[28] See *post*, p. 833.

[29] See *ante*, p. 391.

[30] Two other views deserve attention: Lord Hoffmann extra-judicially in *Frontiers of Liability* (ed. Birks, 1994), p. 27, has advocated that liability for knowing receipt should arise, if at all, under the law of tort and in particular the torts of negligence and deceit, and that all the forms of equitable liability should be abolished; Finn pre-judicially in *Equity, Fiduciaries and Trusts 1993* (ed. Waters, 1993), p. 195, has argued for the abandonment of much, if not all, of the existing law and its replacement by the following three questions, all of which need to be answered in the affirmative before what he denominates "participatory liability" can be imposed: (1) Has a fiduciary committed a breach of fiduciary duty or breach of trust? (2) Has the third party participated in the manner in which the breach has occurred? (3) In so doing, did that party know or have reason to know that a wrong was being committed by the fiduciary on his or her beneficiaries?

[31] [1948] Ch. 465, *ante*, p. 396.

[32] In *Restitution — Past, Present and Future* (ed. Cornish, 1998) 231. See also Birks [1993] L.M.C.L.Q. 218; Harpum in *Frontiers of Liability* (ed. Birks, 1993) 9.

[33] [2000] Lloyd's Rep. Bank. 399.

earlier in *El Ajou v Dollar Land Holdings*,[34] and were subsequently referred to by the same judge in the House of Lords in *Twinsectra v. Yardley*.[35] In that case Lord Millett, who had observed in the course of the argument that: "[i]f Leach succeeds on dishonest assistance, the House will have to consider knowing receipt in the light of his honesty, on which there are a number of irreconcilable authorities at first instance including some statements of my own", enunciated the following dictum. Having commenced by saying, uncontroversially, that a claim to impose liability for knowing receipt is a receipt based restitutionary claim, he continued:

> "There is no basis for requiring actual knowledge of the breach of trust, let alone dishonesty, as a condition of liability. Constructive notice is sufficient, and may not even be necessary. There is powerful academic support for the proposition that the liability of the recipient is the same as in other cases of restitution, that is to say strict but subject to a change of position defence."

Lord Millett's reference to constructive notice being sufficient was, of course, consistent with the earlier statements of his own to which he had referred in argument,[36] but completely overlooked *B.C.C.I. (Overseas) v. Akindele*,[37] a decision of the Court of Appeal which, although obviously not binding on the House of Lords, nevertheless as a matter of precedent must then have constituted (and, for that matter, must still constitute) English law. But, quite irrespective of this point, Lord Millett's apparent support for Lord Nicholls' proposal shows that a future reform of the law in accordance with that proposal certainly cannot be discounted.

Whether this reform could actually be effected by the judiciary or only by the legislature is unclear. Lord Nicholls appears to have envisaged the reform being made by the legislature and only by the legislature but some of the other potential members of any future Appellate Committee of the House of Lords may well adopt a less restrained approach if given the opportunity. If this reform is indeed effected, the scope of the defence of change of position will obviously become extremely important in relation to liability for knowing receipt, in particular the question of precisely what constitutes a change of position in good faith. It will then become significant that, in *Niru Battery Manufacturing Co. v Milestone Trading*,[38] Moore-Bick J. held that lack of good faith is not confined to dishonesty in the sense identified in *Twinsectra v. Yardley* "but is capable of embracing a failure to act in a commercially acceptable way and sharp practice of a kind that falls short of outright dishonesty as well as dishonesty itself".

However, the introduction of strict liability is not the preferred option of this work because of the impact which its introduction would have on innocent volunteers by potentially subjecting them to the burdens of constructive trusteeship. Leaving on one side the option of a test based on dishonesty,

---

[34] [1993] 3 All E.R. 717 at 739–740.
[35] [2002] 2 A.C. 164 at 194.
[36] In *Agip (Africa) v. Jackson* [1990] Ch. 265 at 290 and *El Ajou v. Dollar Land Holdings* [1993] 3 All E.R. 717 at 739–740.
[37] [2000] Lloyd's Rep. Bank. 292.
[38] [2002] 2 All E.R. (Comm.) 705, para. 135.

which has not been advocated by a single commentator and has been specifically rejected both by the Court of Appeal and by Lord Millett, the only effective choice therefore remains between, on the one hand, some or all of the categories of knowledge identified by Peter Gibson J. in *Baden v. Société Générale* and, on the other hand, the test substituted for them by the Court of Appeal in *B.C.C.I. (Overseas) v. Akindele*.

At the time when liability for both dishonest assistance and knowing receipt were governed by the categories of knowledge identified by Peter Gibson J., the principal justification for preferring the view expressed by Megarry V.-C. in *Re Montagu's Settlement*,[39] was that it achieved a much needed consistency between the circumstances in which liability to account would be imposed upon a person who had assisted in bringing about a disposition of trust property in breach of trust and the circumstances in which a constructive trust would be imposed on a person who had received property disposed of in breach of trust; on this basis this work used to contend that only the first three of these categories of knowledge should give rise to the imposition of liability for knowing receipt. This justification ceased to exist when the Privy Council specifically rejected these categories of knowledge in relation to liability for dishonest assistance in *Royal Brunei Airlines v. Tan*, a rejection which has of course now been definitively confirmed by the House of Lords in *Twinsectra v. Yardley*.

In the light of the similar rejection of these categories of knowledge in relation to liability for knowing receipt in *B.C.C.I. (Overseas) v. Akindele*, it might be thought to be both perverse and pointless to continue to advocate that the imposition of liability for knowing receipt should require the presence of one of these three categories of knowledge or, possibly, of some more felicitously worded equivalents. However, the application of these three categories of knowledge still seems considerably more predictable than the substitute based on unconscionability preferred by the Court of Appeal. For this reason, these categories of knowledge, or some equivalent, remain the preferred option of this work, although it is recognised that it can no longer realistically be contended that they constitute the present English law.

### 5. *Inconsistent Dealing with Property Subject to a Trust*

Any person who has received lawfully and not for his own benefit property subject to a trust will be liable to account for that property as a constructive trustee if he subsequently either misappropriates it or deals with it in some other manner which is inconsistent with the trust. The decided cases on what is generally known as "liability for inconsistent dealing" fall into two groups.

The first group of cases concerns agents. It has already been seen[40] that banks enjoy a right of set off between different accounts held by the same customer. If a bank manager has been duly notified that an account held at his branch in the name of an individual is in fact a trust account, the bank will be holding the credit balance of that account wholly lawfully and in no sense for its own benefit. If, however, the bank seeks to debit the credit balance of the trust account by way of set off against an overdraft created in another account

---

[39] [1987] Ch. 264.
[40] See *ante*, p. 28, fn. 46.

held in the name of the same individual, it will potentially be liable for inconsistent dealing.

In *Barclays Bank v. Quistclose Investments*,[41] Quistclose Investments made a loan to a company for the specific purpose of paying a dividend and the funds were paid into a new account at Barclays Bank opened by the company specifically for the purpose. When the company went into liquidation prior to the date on which the dividend was due to be paid, Barclays Bank claimed to offset the balance of this new account against the indebtedness of the company in other accounts. As has already been seen,[42] the House of Lords held that the company had been holding the funds in question on trust to pay the dividend and, subject to, for Quistclose Investments; since the bank had been made aware of the situation but had failed to draw the appropriate inference from facts known to it, it held the funds which it had sought to misapply on trust for Quistclose Investments.

Similarly in *Nesté Oy v. Lloyds Bank*,[43] the plaintiff shipowner was accustomed whenever one of its vessels entered a United Kingdom port to transfer to the bank account of its agent at Lloyds Bank sufficient funds to enable the agent to discharge all liabilities incurred by the vessel. A number of such payments were made immediately before and immediately after the agent appointed a receiver and therefore could not longer trade. Lloyds Bank set off all the payments so made against the agent's indebtedness to that bank. Bingham J. held that there was no express trust of any of the payments and that, even if there had been a trust in respect of any of the payments made before the appointment of the receiver, the bank would have taken free of that trust on the grounds that it did not fall within any of the categories of knowledge identified by Peter Gibson J. in *Baden v. Société Générale*. However, he held that the agent had become a trustee of the payment received after the appointment of the receiver; at the time of its arrival, the bank had already known of the appointment of the receiver and had therefore been placed upon enquiry. The bank was consequently bound by this trust and was not subsequently entitled to set off the payment.

An agent will thus clearly be liable for inconsistent dealing if he knowingly misapplies property subject to a trust; the criterion which in this respect suffices for the imposition of liability for knowing receipt, whether that criterion be knowledge, dishonesty or, as the law presently stands, unconscionability, should also apply to the imposition of liability for inconsistent dealing.

The second group of cases concerns strangers who receive property subject to a trust which has been misapplied without fulfilling whatever criterion is in this respect sufficient for the imposition of liability for knowing receipt. If such a stranger subsequently comes to fulfil that criterion, typically by acquiring the necessary knowledge of the misapplication of the property in breach of trust, that will not of itself render him liable as a constructive trustee. However, he will become so liable if he subsequently deals with the property in a manner inconsistent with the trust which has been breached.

In *Sheridan v. Joyce*,[44] a trustee lent out trust funds in breach of trust. The

---

[41] [1970] A.C. 567.
[42] See *ante*, p. 292.
[43] [1983] 2 Lloyd's Rep. 658.
[44] [1844] 1 Jo. & Lat. 41 (Court of Chancery of Ireland).

borrower originally had no knowledge whatever of this breach of trust and so was clearly not liable for knowing receipt. He subsequently discovered the true facts and thereafter made all the payments of interest to the beneficiary rather than to the trustee. Nevertheless, when the trustee subsequently sought repayment of part of the principal, the borrower made the repayment to him despite the contrary requests of the beneficiary and the money so repaid was lost. The borrower was held liable to repay the sum a second time on the grounds that he had dealt inconsistently with property which he knew to be subject to a trust.

Once again, the criterion which in this respect suffices for the imposition of liability for knowing receipt, whether that criterion be knowledge, dishonesty or, as the law presently stands, unconscionability, should also apply to the imposition of liability for inconsistent dealing.

## IV. Advantages Obtained by Fraudulent or Unconscionable Conduct

From its earliest days, equity has always been prepared to grant relief against fraudulent and unconscionable conduct and one aspect of this relief is the imposition of a constructive trust on any person who has obtained an advantage as the result of such conduct. The different situations which fall under this heading will be considered in descending order of moral turpitude.

### 1. *Obtaining Property as a Result of Crime*[45]

It has long[46] been clear that "no system of jurisprudence can with reason include among the rights which it enforces rights directly resulting to the person asserting them from the crime of that person".[47] There are two obvious areas where this principle might be expected to operate, where property has been acquired as a result of an unlawful killing and where property has been acquired by means of theft.

### (A) As a Result of an Unlawful Killing

The classic illustration of the operation of the principle as a result of an unlawful killing is *In the Estate of Crippen*.[48] Dr. Crippen was convicted of murdering his wife and was duly hanged. His residuary legatee, who was his mistress, was held not to be entitled to the property which Crippen would normally have received as the intestate successor of the wife whom he had murdered.

Some difficulties have arisen as to the precise scope of the operation of the principle. It clearly applies to anyone found to have committed murder, even

---

[45] See Goff & Jones, *op.cit.*, Chap. 37; Youdan (1973) 89 L.Q.R. 235; Earnshaw & Pace (1974) 37 M.L.R. 481.

[46] At least since *Bridgman v. Green* (1755) 2 Ves.Sen. 627.

[47] *Cleaver v. Mutual Reserve Fund Life Association* [1892] 1 Q.B. 147 at 156.

[48] [1911] P. 108.

unsuccessfully;[49] it is not necessary for a conviction to have been secured in criminal proceedings[50] nor are the results of any criminal proceedings decisive.[51] On the other hand, the principle does not apply to an insane killer (a person found not guilty of murder by reason of insanity or subsequently held by a civil court to have been insane[52] since a finding of insanity constitutes an acquittal.[53] The extent to which the principle should operate between these two extremes is a matter of some controversy. It has been contended[54] that its operation should be limited to intentional killing and should therefore not apply to a person convicted either of unintentional manslaughter (involuntary manslaughter or voluntary manslaughter on the ground of diminished responsibility) or of causing death by dangerous driving.[55] However, although it has been stated that there may be some types of unlawful killing to which the principle does not apply,[56] the courts have so far taken the view that it is not appropriate to draw any distinction between voluntary and involuntary manslaughter and have applied the principle to both[57]; it seems to follow from this approach that the principle would also be applied to the offence of causing death by dangerous driving. It has also been applied to the survivor of a suicide pact on the basis that she aided and abetted the suicide.[57A]

When applicable, the principle will deprive the unlawful killer of benefits received under his victim's will,[58] his victim's intestacy,[59] the proceeds of a life insurance policy maintained on the life of his victim,[60] and enhanced social security benefits arising out of the death of his victim.[61] In the unlikely event that the property has already reached the unlawful killer's hands (it will normally be intercepted), a constructive trust will be imposed for the benefit of those otherwise entitled. In *Re Sigsworth*,[62] a murderer was absolutely entitled under the will of his victim, his mother, and was also, together with his brother, her intestate successor; her entire estate went to the brother, who was undoubtedly otherwise entitled under her intestacy. Two specific difficulties have arisen in determining precisely who is otherwise entitled.

First, is someone who would have taken by substitution in the event that the

---

[49] In *Evans v. Evans* [1989] 1 F.L.R. 351, a wife convicted of inciting others to murder her former husband, who survived, was deprived of benefits payable under the divorce settlement.

[50] In *Re Sigsworth* [1935] 1 Ch. 89, the murderer committed suicide and so no criminal proceedings could be brought.

[51] *Gray v. Barr* [1971] 2 Q.B. 554 (principle applied where the defendant was acquitted of both murder and manslaughter); this is possible because of the different standards of proof, although according to *Halford v. Brookes* (1991) *The Times*, October 10, 1991 a finding of murder in civil proceedings requires the criminal standard of proof.

[52] *Re Holgate* (1971) (discussed by Earnshaw & Pace *op.cit.*).

[53] Criminal Procedure (Insanity) Act 1964, s.1.

[54] By Youdan *op.cit.*, pp. 237–238; Earnshaw & Pace *op.cit.*, pp. 492–496.

[55] A death in a motor accident can give rise to three distinct offences (see *R. v. Cooksley* [2003] 3 All E.R. 40; (*R. v. Seymour (Edward)* [1983] A.C. 493).

[56] In *Gray v. Barr* [1971] 2 Q.B. 554 at 581.

[57] *Re Giles* [1972] Ch. 544; *R. v. Chief National Insurance Commissioner, ex parte Connor* [1981] 1 Q.B. 758; *Re Royse (deceased)* [1985] Fam. 22; *Re K. (deceased)* [1986] Fam. 180.

[57A] An offence under the Suicide Act 1961, s.2(1); see *Dunbar v. Plant* [1998] Ch. 412.

[58] *Re Sigsworth* [1935] 1 Ch. 89.

[59] *In the Estate of Crippen* [1911] P. 108; *Re Sigsworth* [1935] 1 Ch. 89.

[60] *Cleaver v. Mutual Reserve Fund Life Association* [1892] 1 Q.B. 147; *Davitt v. Titcumb* [1990] Ch. 110.

[61] *R. v. Chief National Insurance Commissioner, ex parte Connor* [1981] 1 Q.B. 758 (murderess of husband deprived of widow's pension).

[62] [1935] 1 Ch. 89.

unlawful killer had predeceased his victim also disqualified or is the unlawful killer treated for this purpose as having predeceased his victim? This question would have arisen in *Re Sigsworth* if the murderer had had any issue. It did arise in *Re DWS*,[63] where an only child murdered both his parents, both of whom died intestate. Their only grandchild, the murderer's son, claimed to be entitled under the intestacy rules as the issue of a child who had predeceased the intestates.[64] The alternative claimants were the parents' more remote intestate successors,[65] on the basis that none of the issue of the intestates had obtained a vested interest, or, if they could not take either, the Crown. The Court of Appeal held unanimously that the grandchild could only take under the intestacy rules if his father had predeceased the intestates and that this was simply not the case. The court went on to hold, by a majority, that the fact that the grandchild could not take did indeed mean that none of the issue of the intestates had obtained a vested interest and so the more remote intestate successors had taken. Although it is virtually inconceivable that this decision can have coincided with the wishes of the murdered parents, it cannot possibly be faulted as a matter of statutory interpretation. Where, on the other hand, a victim has died testate, the result will be determined by the provisions of his will; standard substitutionary provisions seem likely to produce the same result.[66]

Secondly, what happens where the unlawful killer and his victim hold joint or successive interests? Where one of two joint tenants unlawfully kills the other, it has been held that the killer acquires the entire legal title to the property by virtue of the principle of survivorship but holds that legal title on constructive trust for himself and the representatives of his victim in equal shares as tenants in common.[67] Where a person entitled to property in remainder unlawfully kills the life tenant,[68] it has been suggested[69] that the killer's enjoyment should be postponed for as long as mortality tables predict that the victim would have lived, the latter's representatives receiving the income in the meantime under a constructive trust.

In any event, the court now has a discretion under the Forfeiture Act 1982 to grant relief against forfeiture to a person guilty of unlawful killing other than murder.[70] Where a court has determined that the principle has operated to bring about a forfeiture, it can modify the effect of the principle where it "is satisfied that, having regard to the conduct of the offender and of the deceased and to such other circumstances as appear to the court to be material, the justice of the case requires the effect of the rule to be so modified in that

---

[63] [2001] W.T.L.R. 445.

[64] This view had consistently been advocated in Goff & Jones, *op.cit.* (see 5th ed., p. 707) but contrast Ryder, 40 Conv. (1976) 86.

[65] The sister of the father and the nephews and nieces of the mother.

[66] It may well be that, in the light of *Re DWS*, the form of such substitutionary gifts may require reconsideration so as to envisage the possibility of a primary beneficiary being disqualified from taking for this or any other reason.

[67] *Re K. (deceased)* [1986] Fam. 180. This conclusion, supported by Commonwealth authority, is consistent with the view that the unlawful killer is not treated as having predeceased his victim (were he so treated, the representatives of the victim would of course be entitled to the property absolutely).

[68] The problem has not as yet arisen, although it was postulated in *Re Calloway* [1956] Ch. 559.

[69] By Youdan *op.cit.*, pp. 250–251.

[70] Excluded by Forfeiture Act 1982, s.5.

### 3. Obtaining Property as a Result of Undue Influence[85]

Since the eighteenth century, it has been a rule of equity that a person who obtains a manifest and unfair disadvantage as a result of undue influence will be unable to retain the benefit of the transaction in question. The equitable doctrine of undue influence which has been developed in the subsequent centuries applies only to inter vivos transactions.[86] The specific situations in which the doctrine is applicable have been recently reviewed on a number of occasions by the House of Lords.

#### (A) The Scope of the Doctrine

In *Barclays Bank v. O'Brien*,[87] Lord Browne-Wilkinson said: "A person who has been induced to enter into a transaction by the undue influence of another ("the wrongdoer") is entitled to set that transaction aside as against the wrongdoer. Such undue influence is either actual or presumed." His lordship went on to adopt the following classification.[88]

He stated that what he described as cases of "actual" undue influence fall into Class 1. A claimant who alleges this type of undue influence has "to prove affirmatively that the wrongdoer exerted undue influence on the complainant to enter into the particular transaction which is impugned".[89] If he can discharge this burden of proof, the wrongdoer will be unable to retain the benefit of the transaction in question whether or not it was to the manifest disadvantage of the claimant. This was held by the House of Lords in *C.I.B.C. Mortgages v. Pitt*.[90] A husband exerted actual undue influence on his wife in order to induce her to join with him in mortgaging their matrimonial home, ostensibly to raise funds for the purchase of a holiday home but in fact to enable the husband to raise funds for the purchase of shares. Although the transaction was not manifestly disadvantageous to her, she was held entitled to set aside the transaction as against him, although not as against the mortgagee. "Actual undue influence is a species of fraud. Like any other victim of fraud, a person who has been induced by undue influence to carry out a transaction which he did not freely and knowingly enter into is entitled to have that transaction set aside as of right."[91]

Lord Browne-Wilkinson went on to state that cases of what he described as "presumed" undue influence fall into Class 2:[92]

> "In these cases the complainant only has to show, in the first instance, that there was a relationship of trust and confidence between the complainant and the wrongdoer of such a nature that it is fair to presume that the wrongdoer abused that relationship in procuring the complainant to enter into the impugned transaction. In Class 2 cases therefore there is no need

---

[85] See generally Goff & Jones, *op.cit.*, Chap. 10; Hedley & Halliwell, *op.cit.*, Chap. 10.
[86] The analagous probate doctrine is much more rigid.
[87] [1994] 1 A.C. 180 at 196–197.
[88] Originally laid down by the Court of Appeal in *Bank of Credit and Commerce International v. Aboody* [1990] 1 Q.B. 923 at 953.
[89] [1994] 1 A.C. 180 at 196–197.
[90] [1994] 1 A.C. 200, overruling on this point the decision of the Court of Appeal in *Bank of Credit and Commerce International v. Aboody* [1990] 1 Q.B. 923 at 953.
[91] *ibid.* at 808.
[92] [1994] 1 A.C. 180 at 189.

to procure evidence that actual undue influence was exerted in relation to the particular transaction impugned: once a confidential relationship has been proved, the burden then shifts to the wrongdoer to prove that the complainant entered into the impugned transaction freely, for example by showing that the complainant had independent advice."[93]

He went on to hold that such a confidential relationship can be established in two ways, which he described as Class 2(A) and Class 2(B) cases. Class 2(A) comprises "[c]ertain relationships (for example solicitor and client, medical advisor and patient) [which] as a matter of law raise the presumption that undue influence has been exercised". Other relationships of this kind include parent-child, trustee-beneficiary and, particularly, spiritual adviser-religious devotee.[94] However, he specifically held that the relationship between husband and wife and between cohabitees does not fall within Class 2(A). He then went on to define Class 2(B) cases as follows:

"Even if there is no relationship falling within Class 2(A), if the complainant proves the de facto existence of a relationship under which the complainant generally reposed trust and confidence in the wrongdoer, the existence of such relationship raises the presumption of undue influence. In a Class 2(B) case therefore, in the absence of evidence disproving undue influence, the complainant will succeed in setting aside the impugned transaction merely by proof that the complainant reposed trust and confidence in the wrongdoer without having to prove that the wrongdoer exerted actual undue influence or otherwise abused such trust and confidence in relation to the particular transaction impugned."

The many cases in recent years in which the doctrine of undue influence has been relied on by spouses, or *de facto* partners, in order to challenge the validity of mortgages of their homes made in order to secure financial support for the business of the other spouse or partner are all examples of conduct falling within Lord Browne-Wilkinson's definition of Class 2(B). So was a relationship between son-in-law and trusting father-in-law in *Mahoney v. Purnell*,[95] and between a frail widow and her cleaner in *Re Morris*.[96]

However, in the more recent decision of the House of Lords in *Royal Bank of Scotland (No.2) v. Etridge*,[97] it was concluded that this sort of categorisation was not a useful tool. Lord Clyde said this:

"the attempt to build up classes or categories may lead to confusion. The confusion is aggravated if the names used to identify the classes do not bear their actual meaning. Thus on the face of it a division into cases of 'actual' and 'presumed' undue influence appears illogical. It appears to

---

[93] This was done in *Inche Noriah v. Shaik Allie Bin Omar* [1929] A.C. 127 at 135, (P.C.). See also *Banco Exterior Internacional v. Thomas* [1997] 1 W.L.R. 221.

[94] In *Allcard v. Skinner* (1887) 36 Ch.D. 145 at 183, Lindley L.J. stated that "the influence of one mind over another is very subtle, and of all influences religious influence is the most dangerous and the most powerful".

[95] [1996] 3 All E.R. 61.

[96] [2001] W.T.L.R. 1137.

[97] [2002] 2 A.C. 773.

414 THE MODERN LAW OF TRUSTS

confuse definition and proof. There is also room for uncertainty whether the presumption is of the existence of an influence or of its quality as being undue. I would also dispute the utility of the further sophistication of subdividing 'presumed undue influence' into further categories. All these classifications to my mind add mystery rather than illumination."

But this does not in any way detract from the utility of the descriptions of the different categories of undue influence made by Lord Browne-Wilkinson, irrelevant of the disputed question of how, if at all, they should have been described or labelled. Further, at least for the moment, some distinction between what Lord Browne-Wilkinson described as "actual" and "presumed" undue influence is undoubtedly necessary. This is because in the latter, but not in the former, case the person who exerted the undue influence will nevertheless be able to retain the benefit of the transaction unless it can be shown to have been wrongful in that, as the House of Lords held in *National Westminster Bank v. Morgan*,[98] it constituted "a disadvantage sufficiently serious to require evidence to rebut the presumption that in the circumstances of the relationship between the parties it was procured by the exercise of undue influence".

The existence of this restriction on the ability of the courts to set aside transactions on the grounds of undue influence has been consistently criticised. Its extension to "actual" undue influence was specifically rejected in *C.I.B.C. Mortgages v. Pitt*,[99] but in *Royal Bank of Scotland (No.2) v. Etridge*,[1] the House of Lords equally specifically declined to remove its effect in the case of "presumed" undue influence. Lord Nicholls instead advocated that the "manifest disadvantage" label should be removed and be replaced by a more direct adherence to the test outlined in *Allcard v. Skinner*.[2] In that case, Lindley L.J. had said: "But if the gift is so large as not to be reasonably accounted for on the ground of friendship, relationship, charity or other ordinary motives on which ordinary men act, the burden is upon the donee to support the gift." This is obviously the way in which the requirement will be satisfied in the case of a gift. In the case of a bilateral transaction, it will be satisfied by any inadequacy of consideration in favour of the person who has exerted the undue influence; a sale at an undervalue will satisfy this requirement,[3] but the transaction which was challenged in *National Westminster Bank v. Morgan*,[4] a short-term loan made at a commercial rate of interest to enable the borrower to prevent a mortgagee from going into possession of her home, did not do so.

### (B) The Effect of the Application of the Doctrine
Where the doctrine of undue influence applies, it is normally sufficient for the courts simply to set aside the transaction. If property has actually been transferred to the person who exerted the undue influence, the court will order its return; if, on the other hand, as is usually the case in bilateral transactions of the type which have been before the courts so often in recent years, the person

---

[98] [1985] A.C. 686 at 704.
[99] [1994] 1 A.C. 200, overruling on this point the decision of the Court of Appeal in *Bank of Credit and Commerce International v. Aboody* [1990] 1 Q.B. 923 at 953.
[1] [2002] 2 A.C. 773.
[2] (1887) 36 Ch.D. 145 at 185.
[3] *Possathurai v. Kannappa Chettiar* (1919) L.R. 47 I.A. 1 at 3–4 (P.C.).
[4] [1985] A.C. 686 at 703.

who exerted the undue influence has obtained some mortgage or charge by way of security for the liabilities of himself, the chargor (if different) or a third party, that security will be unenforceable. However, where the property in question has reached the hands of third parties who have taken it free of the right of the victim of the undue influence to set the transaction aside, it will obviously no longer be able to be set aside; in this situation the courts have power to award the victim fair compensation in equity[5] under *Nocton v. Lord Ashburton*.[6] In none of these circumstances is it necessary to classify the nature of the interest retained by the person upon whom the undue influence was exerted in any property which he has transferred away.

However, such a classification does become necessary as soon as any third party becomes involved. It is clear that the right to have a transaction set aside on the grounds of undue influence is capable of being assigned both *inter vivos*[7] and upon death[8] and so may be enforced by the successors of the person upon whom the undue influence was exerted. It also seems clear that, in the event of the death or insolvency of the person who exerted the undue influence, the interest of the person whom he influenced is regarded as analogous to an interest arising under a trust; thus in effect the person who exerted the undue influence holds any property transferred to him as a result of that undue influence on constructive trust. His personal representatives or trustee in bankruptcy will therefore obviously be bound by this constructive trust so that the person who transferred the property will be able to trace it in equity into their hands and, if necessary, claim priority over the general creditors of the transferee. But where, on the other hand, the person exerting the undue influence transfers property which he has received on to a third party or causes property to be transferred directly to a third party in the first place, the interest of the transferor seems to be regarded as a mere equity rather than a full equitable interest. Such a mere equity clearly binds a volunteer[9] and any third party who has notice of the undue influence, even if he has purchased the property for value.[10] Further, it seems to follow from the authorities that the transferor will be able to trace the property in equity into the hands of persons who are so bound by his interest.[11] However, it will not bind any bona fide purchaser for value of a legal or equitable interest in the property who has no notice of the undue influence.

### (C) Mortgages of Homes in order to Secure Business Debts

In recent years the doctrine of undue influence has been invoked on many occasions in relation to mortgages granted by married couples or *de facto* partners over their homes in order to secure financial support for the business of one of the mortgagors; the other mortgagor subsequently attempts to resist the mortgagee's action for possession by claiming that the mortgage was obtained by undue influence. Most of the examples of mortgages allegedly being obtained as a result of undue influence occurred in the late 1980s at a

---

[5] *Mahoney v. Purnell* [1996] 3 All E.R. 61.
[6] [1914] A.C. 932; see *ante*, p. 338.
[7] *Dickinson v. Burrell* (1866) L.R. 1 Eq. 337.
[8] *Stump v. Gaby* (1852) 2 De G.M. & G. 623.
[9] *Goddard v. Carlisle* (1821) 9 Price 169.
[10] *Lancashire Looms v. Black* [1934] 1 K.B. 380.
[11] *ibid.* at 417, *per* Lawrence L.J.

time when general financial difficulties produced a considerable fall in land values coupled with a substantial rise in interest rates. Many small businesses fell into financial difficulties and their owners came under pressure from their banks to secure their existing overdrafts and future facilities by guarantees secured on their matrimonial homes.

The facts of the first of a number of leading cases, *Barclays Bank v. O'Brien*,[12] were typical. The husband's company's bank manager agreed to an increased overdraft facility on the basis that the husband would guarantee the company's indebtedness and that this guarantee would be secured by a charge on the matrimonial home. The documents were sent by the bank to a branch near the matrimonial home with instructions fully to explain the transaction and the nature of the documentation and to advise the couple that if they were "in any doubt they should contact their solicitors before signing". The wife was told by the husband that liability under the charge was limited to £60,000 when it was in fact unlimited, the bank gave her neither explanation nor advice and she signed the documents without reading them. The mortgage was set aside as against her beneficial interest.

A much less typical variant was for an advance actually to be obtained on the security of the residential property ostensibly for the benefit of both husband and wife when it was in fact to be used for the purposes of only one of them. Thus in another leading case, *C.I.B.C. Mortgages v. Pitt*,[13] a couple obtained an advance on the security of their matrimonial home on the basis that its proceeds were to be used for the purchase of a holiday home. In fact the husband wished to purchase shares and had pressured his wife into signing the application and the charge, neither of which she read. Given that the mortgagee had no reason to think that both co-owners were not to benefit from the transaction, it was not placed on inquiry as to the possibility of any undue influence; the mortgage was consequently binding on the wife.

Precisely when will a mortgagee be affected by any undue influence which is found to have been exerted by the debtor? The mortgagee will clearly be affected by any such conduct by the debtor where the latter has been used as the agent of the former for the purposes of obtaining the signature of the surety. However, reliance on this agency argument is highly artificial since, in obtaining the signature of the surety, the debtor is acting for himself not for the mortgagee.[14] Therefore it is only in very unusual circumstances[15] that mortgagees will be adversely affected by this argument. It is also theoretically possible, where mortgagee and surety have used the same solicitor, for information communicated by the surety to the solicitor to be imputed to the mortgagee; however, because any information is likely to have been communicated to the solicitor before he was instructed by the mortgagee[16] and, even if it was communicated to him thereafter, probably could not be revealed by him to the mortgagee anyway,[17] this is highly unlikely in practice. Conse-

---

[12] [1994] 1 A.C. 180.
[13] [1994] 1 A.C. 200.
[14] *Barclays Bank v. O'Brien* [1994] 1 A.C. 180.
[15] An example was where the employees of the bank, its debtor and the guarantor were all members of the same religious sect; see *Shams v. United Bank* (May 24, 1994) on Lexis.
[16] *Halifax Mortgage Services v. Stepsky* [1996] Ch. 207 (C.A.).
[17] *Halifax Mortgage Services v. Stepsky* [1996] Ch. 1 (Ch.D.).

quently, in the normal case, a mortgagee will only be affected by any undue influence if he is held to have notice of it.

The effect of *Barclays Bank v. O'Brien*,[18] was only to put a mortgagee on inquiry as to the possibility of undue influence where the relationship between the debtor and surety was an emotional relationship between cohabitees,[19] or where the mortgagee was aware that the surety reposed trust and confidence in the debtor in relation to his or her financial affairs or was actually under the debtor's influence in other respects.[20] However, as a result of the later decision of the House of Lords in *Royal Bank of Scotland Plc v. Etridge (No.2)*,[21] a mortgagee is now put on inquiry in every case where the relationship between the debtor and the surety is non-commercial. In such circumstances, the mortgagee must always take reasonable steps to bring home to the individual surety the risks which he or more usually she is running by acting as such. A mortgagee who fails to take those steps will be deemed to have notice of any claim which the surety may have that the transaction was procured by undue influence on the part of the debtor.[22] This principle applies not only to co-owners who act as sureties but also to absolute owners of property who do so.[23]

A mortgagee who is put on inquiry need do no more than take reasonable steps to ensure that the practical implications of the proposed transaction have been brought home to the surety in a meaningful way, so that he or she enters into the transaction with her eyes open so far as its basic elements are concerned. After *Barclays Bank v. O'Brien*, any duty of inquiry could be satisfied by representatives of the mortgagees holding a private meeting with the surety in the absence of the debtor, informing him or her as to potential liability and risk, and urging him or her to take independent legal advice. Only in exceptional cases where the mortgagee knew further facts which made undue influence not only possible but probable was it necessary for the mortgagee to insist on independent advice. However, mortgagees came increasingly to rely on the confirmation of solicitors that such advice had been given and it was held in *Royal Bank of Scotland Plc v. Etridge (No.2)*[24] that such confirmation will ordinarily suffice in respect of past transactions.

For transactions after the decision in *Royal Bank of Scotland Plc v. Etridge (No.2)* in 2001,[25] the mortgagee is not required to satisfy any duty of inquiry by means of a personal meeting with the surety. Ordinarily it will be reasonable for the mortgagee to rely upon confirmation from a solicitor, acting for the surety, that he has advised him or her appropriately. Such a solicitor acts for the surety, not as the agent of the mortgagee, and any deficiencies in his advice are a matter between solicitor and surety. However, if the mortgagee knows that the solicitor has not duly advised the surety or knows facts from which it ought to have been realised that the surety has not received appropriate

---

[18] [1994] 1 A.C. 180.
[19] The requirement for cohabitation was not rigid; see *Massey v. Midland Bank* [1995] 1 All E.R. 929.
[20] *Credit Lyonnais Bank Nederland v. Burch* [1997] 1 All E.R. 144.
[21] [2002] 2 A.C. 773.
[22] *ibid.*; see also *Credit Lyonnais Bank Nederland v. Burch* [1997] 1 All E.R. 144.
[23] As in *Credit Lyonnais Bank Nederland v. Burch* [1997] 1 All E.R. 144 (the surety was the debtor's employee).
[24] [2002] 2 A.C. 773.
[25] [2002] 2 A.C. 773.

advice, the mortgage will be at risk if the mortgagee proceeds. The process of obtaining confirmation from the solicitor has been formalised as a series of requirements and detailed guidelines have also been provided for the solicitor advising the surety.

Although transactions entered into before the process was formalised in this way are likely to come before the courts for some years yet, the existence of all these guidelines makes it unlikely that any mortgagees will be adversely affected by any undue influence by the debtor in respect of future transactions; any remedy by the surety will instead be sought from the solicitor who advised him or her. The only remaining area of controversy relates to the precise nature of the right of the surety to have the transaction set aside when the mortgagee has in some way failed to comply with the requirements; is it a right to have the transaction set aside *in toto* or only subject to such of the terms of the transaction as the surety was aware of at the time it was entered into? The situation at present seems to be that the surety is entitled to have the transaction set aside *in toto*[26] unless he or she received a direct financial benefit from it.[27] However, this question still requires definitive resolution.

### 4. *Relying on the Absence of Statutory Formalities*

The courts have always been prepared to impose a constructive trust in order to prevent a transferee of property from going back on an undertaking or agreement made at the time of acquisition to respect an interest therein which has not been created or protected in the manner required by the law. Such cases are manifestations of the principle that equity will not permit the provisions of a statute to be used as an instrument of fraud.[28]

Of course it is not always fraudulent to rely on a failure to comply with the requirements of the law. Equity will not prevent a party to an oral contract for the sale of land from repudiating it on the grounds that it does not comply with the Law of Property (Miscellaneous Provisions) Act 1989[29] nor prevent a settlor who has made an oral declaration of trust respecting land from raising the absence of the writing required by the Law of Property Act 1925.[30] Similarly, if an incumbrancer has neglected to protect his interest in land by the appropriate registration, equity will not prevent a subsequent third party purchaser for value of the land from relying on a statutory right to take free of the interest in question.[31] Equity will only intervene in the event of an attempt to renege on an undertaking or agreement.

Sometimes the imposition of a constructive trust may prevent the relevant statutory provision from applying at all. This was controversially held to be the case in *Yaxley v. Gotts*,[32] where a person who had renovated a property in reliance on an oral agreement that he would become entitled to its ground floor was held to be entitled to rely on an equitable proprietary estoppel which, because of the unconscionable conduct of the other party, gave rise to a

---

[26] *TSB Bank v. Camfield* [1995] 1 W.L.R. 430.
[27] *Midland Bank v. Greene* [1994] 2 F.L.R. 827.
[28] *Rochefoucauld v. Boustead* [1897] 1 Ch. 196 at 206.
[29] s.2 requires that all the terms of such a contract must be in writing and signed by all the parties.
[30] s.53(1)(b). See *ante*, p. 96.
[31] *Midland Bank Trust Company v. Green* [1981] A.C. 513.
[32] [2000] Ch. 162.

constructive trust. As a matter of statutory interpretation, this trust was held to be sufficient to prevent the relevant provision of the Law of Property (Miscellaneous Provisions) Act 1989[33] from applying at all. But where the relevant statutory provision is *prima facie* applicable, equity can nevertheless impose a constructive trust on the grounds that that provision cannot be used as an instrument of fraud.

In *Bannister v. Bannister*,[34] the defendant sold and conveyed two adjoining cottages to the plaintiff on the basis that she could continue to occupy one of them rent free for as long as she wished. When he subsequently sought to evict her on the basis that the conveyance did not mention her right of occupation, she successfully counterclaimed for a declaration that the plaintiff held the cottage on trust for her for her lifetime. The Court of Appeal classified as fraudulent the conduct of the plaintiff in attempting to rely on the absence of the writing which the Law of Property Act 1925 then required for the creation of the interest claimed by the defendant and imposed a constructive trust under which he held the property on trust for her for her lifetime.[35] This was a case where the informal agreement in question was being enforced by the person in whose favour it had originally been made. However, equity is equally prepared to enforce agreements made for the benefit of third parties.

In *Binions v. Evans*,[36] a cottage was sold at a reduced price on the basis that the purchasers would honour the right of a widow of a former employee of the vendor to occupy the property rent-free for the rest of her life. When they sought to evict her, the majority of the Court of Appeal classified the conduct of the purchasers as unconscionable, applied *Bannister v. Bannister* and imposed a constructive trust on the purchasers to give effect to the interest of the widow.[37] Similarly, in *Lyus v. Prowsa Developments*,[38] a building plot was sold by mortgagees subject to and with the benefit of a building contract between the mortgagor and the plaintiffs. The purchaser subsequently claimed to have taken the land free of this contract because the plaintiffs had failed to protect it in the manner required by the Land Registration Act 1925. It was held that the provision in the contract of sale relating to the building contract had conferred new rights on the plaintiffs, which the purchaser had expressly agreed to honour. Consequently, because of the subsequent attempt to renege on this agreement, the purchaser held the plot on constructive trust to complete the house thereon and convey the plot to the plaintiffs for the price agreed in the original contract.

---

[33] S.2 did not apply because of s.2(5) which excludes resulting, implied and constructive trusts from its scope.

[34] [1948] W.N. 261.

[35] This caused the imposition of a settlement under the Settled Land Act 1925 and thus potentially involved the reconveyance of the cottage to the defendant, an admittedly odd result but one of which the plaintiff could hardly complain. However, this would no longer be the case today since no more settlements of this type can be created following the Trusts of Land and Appointment of Trustees Act 1996; the plaintiff would now simply hold the cottage in question on trust for the defendant.

[36] [1972] Ch. 359. See also *Neale v. Willis* (1968) 19 P. & C.R. 839.

[37] Lord Denning M.R. reached the same conclusion by a different route: see *post*, p. 422.

[38] [1982] 1 W.L.R. 1044. This decision has been criticised on the grounds that it casts doubt on the ability of a purchaser to rely on his statutory right to take free of incumbrances of which he is aware but which have not been protected in the appropriate way. However, the statements of the Court of Appeal in *IDC Group v. Clark* [1992] 1 E.G.L.R. 187 at 190 confirmed that the decision is explicable for the reasons stated in the text.

### 5. Informal Agreements for the Joint Acquisition of Property

In *Holiday Inns v. Broadhead*,[39] Megarry J. stated that "if A and B agree that A shall acquire some specific property for the joint benefit of A and B on terms yet to be agreed, and B, in reliance on A's agreement, is thereby induced to refrain from attempting to acquire the property, equity ought not to permit A, when he acquires the property, to insist on retaining the whole benefit for himself to the exclusion of B." Until recently, the principal reported authority in support of this proposition was the decision of Harman J. in *Pallant v. Morgan*.[40]

In that case, an agreement was made by the agents of two neighbouring landowners immediately prior to a land auction that the plaintiff's agent should refrain from bidding and that the defendant, if his agent was successful, would divide the land according to a formula agreed between the agents. Unfortunately, some details of the formula were left to be agreed later on and, although the defendant duly acquired the land at the auction, the parties were unable to agree those details. Harman J. held that, although the agreement for division was too uncertain to be specifically enforceable, the defendant was nevertheless not entitled to retain the whole of the property in the light of the agreement between the agents. He therefore held that the land was subject to a trust for the parties jointly and, in the event that they could not agree on a division, would have to be auctioned a second time. The principle so established was applied by Oliver J. in *Time Products v. Combined English Stores Group*,[41] on the following basis:

> "It is a fraud in the defendant to retain for himself the benefit of the bargain obtained with the plaintiff's assistance whether that assistance was obtained by the defendant through the plaintiff's erroneous belief in a given state of facts or through a promise, contractual or otherwise, given by the defendant. It is, in my judgment, equally unconscionable for the defendant, having reaped the benefit of the transaction, now to seek to retain the property and to disregard the rights which, under the agreement the plaintiff stipulated even though the agreement may lack certainty or be a mere gentlemen's agreement not enforceable as a contract."

In such circumstances, as Browne-Wilkinson V.-C. expressly held in *Frogmore Estates v. Berger*,[42] whichever person has acquired the property in question holds it on constructive trust to give effect to the agreement between the parties in so far as this is possible.[43]

The Court of Appeal considered this principle for the first time in *Banner Homes v. Luff Developments*.[44] The parties agreed that a site whose purchase and development neither felt able to finance alone would be purchased through a new single purpose company which they would own in equal shares. The

---

[39] (1969) Unreported, but quoted in *Banner Homes v. Luff Developments* [2000] Ch. 372.
[40] [1953] Ch. 43.
[41] (1974) Unreported but quoted in *Banner Homes v. Luff Developments* [2000] Ch. 372.
[42] (1989) 139 N.L.J. 1560).
[43] He also reiterated that if, as in *Pallant v. Morgan*, it is not possible to establish what benefit each was intended to take, they will take the property jointly.
[44] [2000] Ch. 372.

purchase, which both parties realised would precede any formal agreement, was duly made by a company acquired for the purpose by the defendant at a point when the plaintiff believed that the defendant had every intention of proceeding with the agreement; however, the defendant was by then having second thoughts and, shortly thereafter, withdrew from the agreement. Before the Court of Appeal it was accepted that the defendant was affected neither by any binding contract nor by any estoppel.

Chadwick L.J., who gave the only reasoned judgment, held that the following series of rather repetitive propositions will determine whether or not what he described as "The *Pallant v. Morgan* Equity" will arise, although he eschewed any attempt at an exhaustive classification: first, there must be an arrangement or understanding ("the deal") between A and B preceding the acquisition of property by A which colours that acquisition and leads to A being treated as a trustee if he acts inconsistently with the deal; secondly, the deal need not necessarily be contractually enforceable; thirdly, not only must the deal contemplate that A will take steps to acquire the property and that, if A does acquire it, B will obtain some interest in it but also A must not have informed B that A no longer intends to honour the deal before it is too late to restore both of them to a position in which there is neither advantage nor detriment; fourthly, in reliance on the deal, B must do or omit to do something which confers an advantage on A in relation to the acquisition of the property or is detrimental to B's ability to acquire the property on equal terms; and, fifthly, it is not necessary either that B agrees to keep out of the market or that there is both advantage to A and detriment to B.

At first instance the plaintiff was denied relief: first, because the fact that both parties had at all times had an implicit right to withdraw from the deal was inconsistent with the intervention of equity, which could not turn a deal which was qualified by a right to withdraw into an unqualified deal which denied any such right; and, secondly, because the plaintiff had failed to show that it had acted to its detriment in reliance on the deal. However, Chadwick L.J. disposed of the first ground by stating, very briefly, that what was required for equity to intervene was not a fully enforceable bargain but an acquisition of property in circumstances where it would be inequitable for the acquirer to treat the property as his own and rejected the second ground on the basis that detriment and advantage were alternative, not cumulative, requirements.[45] He therefore applied *Pallant v. Morgan* and held that the defendant held half the shares in the single purpose company on trust for the plaintiff.

While the reasoning of Chadwick L.J. is undoubtedly consistent with the relevant parts of the propositions which he had already enunciated, those propositions all required reliance on the deal by the plaintiff. It is extremely difficult to see how the plaintiff could conceivably have relied on the deal if, as Chadwick L.J. necessarily had to accept, the defendant had at all times had the right to withdraw. Therefore, while the propositions enunciated by Chadwick L.J. are both sound and workable and will undoubtedly be repeatedly applied, it has to be said that their application in *Banner Homes v. Luff Developments* is somewhat questionable; the plaintiff in that case must therefore be regarded as having been extremely fortunate.

---

[45] *ibid.*, p. 400.

## 6. *Contractual Licences*

Contractual licences have traditionally been regarded more as creatures of the law of contract than of the law of property. While it has long[46] been recognised that a contractual licensee may, in appropriate circumstances, be able to obtain the assistance of equity to force the licensor to perform his contract,[47] until 1952 it had never been suggested that he had any proprietary right in the subject matter of his licence capable of binding a third party, unless the latter had in some way estopped himself from revoking the licence.[48] However, in *Errington v. Errington and Woods*,[49] despite the existence of clear House of Lords authority to the contrary,[50–51] the Court of Appeal held that a contractual licence which could be enforced in this way against the licensor created an interest in land capable of binding third parties.

It has already been seen that, in the years immediately before and after 1970, a series of decisions emanating from the Court of Appeal imposed constructive trusts not only as a result of fraudulent or unconscionable conduct of the types which have just been considered but also as a result of conduct which the individual judges were prepared to classify merely as inequitable. The underlying and indeed often expressed objective of the judges in question was to prevent results which would otherwise have been inequitable. If application of the basic principles of property law led to a result which, in the view of the court in question, was contrary to good conscience, that court acted upon the conscience of the party who would otherwise have obtained this unjust benefit and imposed a constructive trust upon him to bring the result into line with the requirements of justice.

As part of this development, and despite the subsequent doubts[52] which had been expressed about the decision of the Court of Appeal in *Errington v. Errington and Woods*,[53] Lord Denning M.R. carried the novel proposition enunciated in that case a stage further in *Binions v. Evans*.[54] He there held that a contractual licence which was capable of binding a third party could be enforced by the imposition of a constructive trust if it was just and equitable so to do. This view was subsequently ratified by the whole of the Court of Appeal in *D.H.N. Food Distributors v. Tower Hamlets L.B.C.*[55]

However, the Court of Appeal subsequently "put the quietus to the heresy

---

[46] Since *Winter Garden Theatre (London) v. Millenium Productions* [1948] A.C. 173.

[47] *Foster v. Robinson* [1951] 1 K.B. 149 (injunction); *Verrall v. Great Yarmouth Borough Council* [1981] Q.B. 202 (specific performance).

[48] *Inwards v. Baker* [1965] 2 Q.B. 29; *Greasley v. Cooke* [1980] 1 W.L.R. 1306; *Hopgood v. Brown* [1955] 1 All E.R. 550; *E.R. Ives Investment v. High* [1967] 2 Q.B. 379. In *Re Basham* [1986] 1 W.L.R. 1498, the existence of a proprietary estoppel was held to give rise to the existence of a "floating" constructive trust similar to that which arises in the case of Mutual Wills (see *post*, p. 367) but this view is generally held to be misconceived.

[49] [1952] 1 K.B. 290.

[50–51] *King v. David Allen and Sons, Billposting* [1916] 2 A.C. 54.

[52] As a result of *National Provincial Bank v. Hastings Car Mart* [1965] A.C. 1175 at 1239, 1251 (matter left open for future discussion) and *Re Solomon (A Bankrupt)* [1967] Ch. 573 at 583 (contrary view preferred).

[53] [1952] 1 K.B. 290.

[54] [1972] Ch. 359; see *ante*, p. 418.

[55] [1976] 1 W.L.R. 852.

that a mere licence creates an interest in land"[56] in *Ashburn Anstalt v. Arnold*.[57] The court accepted that a third party who attempted to renege on an agreement or undertaking to honour a contractual licence would be liable as a constructive trustee in the manner which has already been discussed.[58] However, in the absence of any such agreement or undertaking, the court held that a contractual licence could bind no third party and that in such circumstances it would not be appropriate for a constructive trust to be imposed. Although the court obviously could not overrule *Errington v. Errington and Woods*, it stated that that decision had been made *per incuriam*, which makes it unlikely that anything further will be heard either of the principle enunciated therein or of its subsequent extension in *Binions v. Evans*. This legacy of the series of decisions emanating from the Court of Appeal in the years immediately before and after 1970 thus appears to have been nullified.

### 7. Joint Enterprises in a Non-Commercial Context

It has already been seen[59] that, where property has been purchased in the name of another, it will be presumed to result to whoever actually provided the purchase moneys, including if appropriate the person into whose name the property has been put, in proportion to their respective contributions. Such resulting trusts are just as applicable to joint enterprises entered into in a non-commercial or family context as to any other situation. However, during the last 40 years, the courts have had to grapple with an increasing variety of less direct contributions to the acquisition of property, usually contributions to the acquisition or improvement of residential property made by one of its occupiers; the interests of such contributors have often been protected by what have been described[60] as "common intention constructive trusts" and, rather more recently, also by the principle of equitable proprietary estoppel.

The first cases of this type concerned the devolution of matrimonial property on the breakdown of marriage. The law contained in these cases no longer applies where the marriage has been terminated since the courts have now acquired an absolute discretion to vary matrimonial property rights at the termination of marriage;[61] that law is however still applicable to disputes that arise during marriage concerning the property rights of the spouses, to analogous situations involving unmarried couples and to other types of joint enterprises.

The underlying principle applicable to cases of this type was originally laid down by the House of Lords in *Pettitt v. Pettitt*[62] and *Gissing v. Gissing*,[63] namely that property rights have to be determined in the light of the intentions of the parties at the time of acquisition of the property. However, in *Gissing v. Gissing*, Lord Diplock said this:[64]

---

[56] *I.D.C. Group v. Clark* [1992] 1 E.G.L.R. 187 at 190.
[57] [1988] Ch. 1.
[58] See *ante*, p. 418.
[59] See *ante*, p. 274.
[60] See, particularly, Hayton [1990] Conv. 370 and in Hayton & Marshall: *op.cit.* pp. 364–378.
[61] Under what is now Matrimonial Causes Act 1973, s.23.
[62] [1970] A.C. 777.
[63] [1971] A.C. 886.
[64] *ibid.* at 905.

"A resulting, implied or constructive trust — and it is unnecessary for present purposes to distinguish between these three classes of trust — is created by a transaction between the trustee and the cestui que trust in connection with the acquisition by the trustee of a legal estate in land, whenever the trustee has so conducted himself that it would be inequitable to deny to the cestui que trust a beneficial interest in the land acquired. And he will be held so to have conducted himself if by his words or conduct he has induced the cestui que trust to act to his own detriment in the reasonable belief that by so acting he was acquiring a beneficial interest in the land."

The first sentence of this passage, when isolated from the qualification subsequently placed upon it, appears to suggest that the courts may impose a constructive trust to do justice *inter partes* whenever the result would, otherwise, be inequitable. As part of the series of decisions emanating from the Court of Appeal in the years immediately before and after 1970, that sentence was cited as authority for that proposition in several subsequent cases in that court.[65] In one of these cases,[66] Lord Denning M.R. stated that "whenever two parties by their joint efforts acquire property to be used for their joint benefit, the courts may impose or impute a constructive or resulting trust".

The two different approaches can be seen side by side in *Eves v. Eves*.[67] The parties, who were living together as man and wife, purchased a dilapidated house as a home for themselves and their children, which was conveyed into the sole name of the man because he pretended to the woman that she was too young to acquire the legal title. All the purchase price was found by the man but the woman did a very considerable amount of work on the house. In the Court of Appeal she was granted a one-quarter share therein under a constructive trust. Lord Denning M.R. imposed a "new model" constructive trust on the strength of the first sentence of the passage cited above. But the majority applied *Pettitt v. Pettitt* and *Gissing v. Gissing* correctly, holding that it could be inferred from the circumstances that there had been an arrangement between the parties whereby the woman was to acquire a beneficial interest in the house in return for her labour in contributing to its repair and improvement; this entitled her to an interest under what has subsequently been called a "common intention constructive trust". Subsequent cases preferred this latter approach[68] and the scope of the "common intention constructive trust" has now been restated, if anything more narrowly, by the House of Lords in *Lloyds Bank v. Rosset*.[69]

In this case Lord Bridge, with whose speech the remaining members of the House of Lords agreed, said this:[70]

---

[65] *Heseltine v. Heseltine* [1971] 1 W.L.R. 342 (dispute during marriage concerning the property rights of the spouses); *Cooke v. Head* [1972] 1 W.L.R. 518 (unmarried couple); *Hussey v. Palmer* [1972] 1 W.L.R. 1286 (joint enterprise between married couple and parent).

[66] *Cooke v. Head* [1972] 1 W.L.R. 518 at 520.

[67] [1975] 1 W.L.R. 1338.

[68] *Midland Bank v. Dobson* [1986] 1 F.L.R. 171 (dispute during marriage concerning the property rights of the spouses); *Burns v. Burns* [1984] Ch. 317, *Grant v. Edwards* [1986] Ch. 638 (unmarried couples); *Re Sharpe (a Bankrupt)* [1980] 1 W.L.R. 219 (joint enterprise between nephew and aunt).

[69] [1991] 1 A.C. 107.

[70] *ibid.* at 132–133.

"The first and fundamental question which must always be resolved is whether, independently of any inference to be drawn from the conduct of the parties in the course of sharing the house as their home and managing their joint affairs, there has at any time prior to acquisition, or exceptionally at some later date, been any agreement, arrangement or understanding reached between them that the property is to be shared beneficially. The finding of an agreement or arrangement to share in this sense can only, I think, be based on evidence of express discussions between the partners, however, imperfectly remembered and however imprecise their terms may have been. Once a finding to this effect is made it will only be necessary for the partner asserting a claim to a beneficial interest against the partner entitled to the legal estate to show that he or she has acted to his or her detriment or significantly altered his or her position in reliance on the agreement in order to give rise to a constructive trust or a proprietary estoppel.

In sharp contrast with this situation is the very different one where there is no evidence to support a finding of an agreement or an arrangement to share, however reasonable it might have been for the parties to reach such an agreement if they had applied their minds to the question, and where the court must rely entirely on the conduct of the parties both as the basis from which to infer a common intention to share the property beneficially and as the conduct relied on to give rise to a constructive trust. In this situation direct contributions to the purchase price by the partner who is not the legal owner, whether initially or by payment of mortgage instalments, will readily justify the inference necessary to the creation of a constructive trust. But, as I read the authorities, it is at least extremely doubtful whether anything less will do."

This admirably succinct statement of the law establishes that, provided that there has been some express agreement, arrangement or understanding that the property is to be shared beneficially, then any act of detriment, whether or not actually envisaged by the agreement, will be sufficient to give rise to a constructive trust; on the other hand, where an agreement between the parties can only be inferred, only direct financial contributions to the purchase price[71] will justify the inference necessary to give rise to a constructive trust.[72]

The first limb of this test is, if anything, broader than the pre-existing law; where some express agreement can be found, not only the contribution

---

[71] The payment of mortgage instalments will give the payer the proportion of the value of the property secured by the mortgage in question whether or not he ultimately pays it off; the amount of the outstanding mortgage debt will be deducted from the value of his proportion of the overall value (*Huntingford v. Hobbs* [1993] 1 F.L.R. 736). On the other hand, someone who does not make any mortgage repayments at all and became a co-mortgagor merely so that sufficient income could be shown to justify the making of the mortgage advance will not thereby become entitled to any, or to any additional, beneficial interest (see *Carlton v. Goodman* [2002] 2 F.L.R. 259).

[72] Although Lord Bridge used the expression constructive trust, such contributions would anyway give rise to a presumption that the contributor had a beneficial interest under a resulting trust, in the absence of any contrary intention or any counter-presumption of advancement (see *ante*, p. 279) and it seems more satisfactory to regard the trust which arises in these circumstances as resulting rather than constructive.

envisaged in that agreement but also any other act of detriment, even if none was envisaged, will give rise to a constructive trust. Thus, if *Eves v. Eves* recurred, provided that there had indeed been an express agreement that the woman was to have an interest, it would now be irrelevant whether or not the parties had envisaged that she would do her very considerable amount of work on the house; all that would matter would be that she had actually done so.

On the other hand, the second limb of this test is considerably narrower than the pre-existing law. In the absence of an express agreement, no matter how much work the woman in *Eves v. Eves* had done she would not now obtain a beneficial interest simply because she had not made any direct financial contribution to the purchase price. Thus in *Lloyds Bank v. Rosset* itself, the wife had supervised builders who were renovating a delapidated building and had herself done a certain amount of preparatory cleaning and some painting and decorating but had made no direct contribution to the purchase price; this was held to be insufficient to justify the inference of any common intention that she should have a beneficial interest. It is of course highly desirable that unsolicited work on the property of another should not, in the absence of express subsequent ratification, lead to the creation of an interest therein. However, the requirement for a direct financial contribution to the purchase price may cause difficulties when substantial indirect financial contributions to, for example, household expenses have been necessary to enable the holder of the legal title to repay the mortgage. There will obviously be no difficulty where there is direct evidence of an express common intention that the contributor is to have a beneficial interest,[73] since this situation will fall within the first limb of the test. In the absence of any such express agreement, prior to *Lloyds Bank v. Rosset* such contributions would have caused such a common intention to be inferred.[74] However, it appears that such contributions will now be insufficient to justify the inference necessary to give rise to a constructive trust; the contributor will therefore presumably be limited to claiming what is likely to be a much smaller beneficial interest under a resulting trust proportional to the contributions actually made. This aspect of the decision in *Lloyds Bank v. Rosset* is clearly less than satisfactory.

The position in this respect has been to some extent ameliorated by the decision of the Court of Appeal in *Midland Bank v. Cooke*,[75] although this decision has also somewhat obscured the clear distinctions established by *Lloyds Bank v. Rosset*. The matrimonial home had been purchased, in part, with a sum provided by the husband's parents. This was held to have been a gift to both spouses so the wife had to this extent made a direct contribution to the purchase price and therefore had a beneficial interest of at least 6.47 per cent (half of the percentage provided by the parents). She had subsequently discharged household outgoings out of her earnings and contributed both physically and financially to the improvement of the house and garden. However, both spouses testified that there had been no discussion or agreement at the time of acquisition as to the beneficial ownership of the property. According to

---

[73] This was the situation in *Grant v. Edwards* [1986] Ch. 638, a decision which was expressly approved by Lord Bridge in *Lloyds Bank v. Rosset*.
[74] As in *Burns v. Burns* [1984] Ch. 317.
[75] [1995] 2 F.L.R. 915.

*Lloyds Bank v. Rosset*, the absence of any common intention meant that the wife's subsequent contributions could not be taken into account and that was what was held at first instance. Unexpectedly, however, the Court of Appeal took a wholly different view. Waite L.J. referred to the speech of Lord Diplock in *Gissing v. Gissing*[76] and held:[77]

"When the court is proceeding, in cases like the present where the partner without legal title has successfully asserted an equitable interest through direct contribution, to determine (in the absence of express evidence of intention) what proportions the parties must be assumed to have intended for their beneficial ownership, the duty of the judge is to undertake a survey of the whole course of dealing between the parties relevant to their ownership and occupation of the property and their sharing of its burdens and advantages. That scrutiny will not confine itself to the limited range of acts of direct contribution of the sort that are needed to found a beneficial interest in the first place. It will take into consideration all conduct which throws light on the question what shares were intended. Only if that search proves inconclusive does the court fall back on the maxim that 'equality is equity'."

He then assessed the wife's beneficial interest at 50 per cent on the basis that "[o]ne could hardly have a clearer example of a couple who had agreed to share everything",[78] a conclusion which it is not particularly easy to square with the spouses' own evidence that they had never considered the beneficial ownership of the house at all! Leave to appeal to the House of Lords was refused.

Where does this decision leave the law? The speech of Lord Diplock in *Gissing v. Gissing* does indeed provide support for the propositions enunciated by Waite L.J. in the passage cited. The difficulty is that this is precisely the respect in which *Lloyds Bank v. Rosset* narrowed the pre-existing law, a point which Waite L.J. does not appear to have taken into account. Consequently it now appears that, whenever some direct contribution to the purchase price can be shown, no matter how small provided, presumably, that it is not *de minimis*, the court can infer from the conduct of the parties not only a common intention that indirect contributions were to enhance that interest but also the amount by which that interest is to be enhanced. In contrast, the position of the indirect contributor who cannot show any direct contribution to the purchase price at all will still be wholly governed by *Lloyds Bank v. Rosset* and such a person will consequently be unable to establish any beneficial interest whatever. This revival, for some but not for all purposes, of those aspects of *Gissing v. Gissing* which were thought to have been abrogated by *Lloyds Bank v. Rosset* is scarcely satisfactory either. It is therefore almost inevitable that further changes in the law will follow, as the result either of another case reaching the

---

[76] [1971] A.C. 886 at 908: set out *ante*, p. 424.

[77] [1995] 2 F.L.R. 915 at 926.

[78] *ibid.* at 928. A similar "broad brush" approach to the quantification of beneficial interests was subsequently taken by the Court of Appeal in *Drake v. Whipp* [1996] 1 F.L.R. 826 although, in the light of concessions made by counsel at first instance, it might be a mistake to read too much into this decision.

House of Lords or of legislation (however, the only legislation at present envisaged[79] would affect only the rights of home-sharers who chose to register as such rather than the basic principles of law under discussion).

Under the present law further difficulties[80] potentially arise in quantifying the beneficial interests. Where the express common intention of the parties envisaged that the beneficial interest should be held in specific proportions, then this common intention should clearly be upheld provided that the parties have duly made whatever contribution was envisaged. But what is to happen where one of the parties has failed to provide the whole of the contribution which was envisaged?[81] The difficulties are even greater where a common intention envisaging a beneficial interest but no contribution is followed by acts of detriment in reliance on the existence of the beneficial interest. Are the beneficial interests to be quantified in the proportions envisaged quite irrelevant of the scale of the acts of detrimental reliance? These questions have yet to be considered by the courts but it has been suggested,[82] that they should adopt the flexible approach already utilised in the area of equitable proprietary estoppel and provide a remedy appropriate to the circumstances of each individual case.[83] There is no doubt that in this area of the law there is an increasing overlap between the "common intention constructive trust" and the doctrine of equitable proprietary estoppel;[84] indeed it has been suggested[85] that the distinction between the two is now quite illusory and that it is "time that the courts and counsel moved beyond pigeon-holing circumstances into common intention constructive trusts and equitable estoppels and concentrated upon the basic principle of unconscionability underlying both doctrines".

The principle of unconscionability certainly underlies "common intention constructive trusts"; it is only appropriate to classify them as constructive

---

[79] The Law Commission has for some time been carrying out a review of the property rights of home-sharers (this review, which was originally announced in the Programme published in July 1995, was welcomed in both *Midland Bank v. Cooke* and *Drake v. Whipp*). This review has so far only produced a tentative, and for that reason very disappointing, Discussion Paper published in July 2002 which inclines towards greater recognition of indirect contributions to mortgage payments and a broader approach to quantification in the light of the whole course of dealing between the parties and of all conduct which throws light on their intentions; however, the issues arising out of co-habitation are regarded as matters of social policy more appropriate for political debate than for a law reform body. This reluctance to express any clear view reflects the fact that the Discussion Paper was published a year after a private initiative, a Civil Partnerships Bill, was introduced into the House of Lords in 2001 by Lord Lester of Herne Hill; this envisaged co-habitants having the right to register civil partnerships which would, for present purposes, lead to their property devolving at the end of the partnership in accordance with any property agreement which they registered or, in default, in equal shares. This Bill was withdrawn pending a governmental review. The government has now proposed similar civil partnerships confined to co-habitants of the same sex. It is therefore unlikely that any legislation which is eventually enacted will have any effect on the general law discussed in the text.

[80] Highlighted by Hayton [1990] Conv. 370 and in Hayton & Marshall, *op.cit.*, pp. 393–395.

[81] Hayton & Marshall, *ibid.* envisages the situation where half of the potential contribution is withheld.

[82] *ibid.*

[83] Following suggestions made by Browne-Wilkinson V.-C. in *Grant v. Edwards* [1986] Ch. 638 at 656.

[84] See particularly *per* Browne-Wilkinson V.-C. in *Grant v. Edwards* [1986] Ch. 638 at 656 and *per* Lord Bridge in *Lloyds Bank v. Rosset* [1991] 1 A.C. 107 at 132.

[85] In Hayton & Marshall, *op.cit.*, (10th ed.) p. 373.

trusts at all because of the fact that in cases of this type the holder of the legal title will almost inevitably have attempted to go back on an express agreement or common intention. Indeed it is precisely for this reason that, when there is no such express agreement or common intention, only direct contributions to the purchase price will do, a proposition which is only another way of saying that in such circumstances the trust which arises is resulting rather than constructive. It is clear that this area of the law has yet to find its final form; however, unless and until the House of Lords chooses to go back on *Lloyds Bank v. Rosset* or the legislature intervenes, the principles enunciated in that decision constitute the framework within which the profession and the lower courts must attempt to operate. However, the decision of the Court of Appeal in *Midland Bank v. Cooke* demonstrates that this framework may be rather more flexible than the House of Lords (or for that matter anyone else) originally thought.

## 8. Possible Future Developments

The approach manifested in the series of decisions emanating from the Court of Appeal in the years immediately before and after 1970, to which reference has already been made, was of course much closer to the American attitude to the constructive trust[86] and was thought to be symptomatic of a general change of attitude towards the constructive trust. Even though, as has also been seen, subsequent decisions rejected the approach manifested in this series of cases and English law consequently appeared to have reverted to its traditional position, indications of a more remedial approach have continued to make their appearance.

In particular, in *Westdeutsche Landesbank Girozentrale v. Islington L.B.C.*,[87] Lord Browne-Wilkinson seized on an isolated remark of this kind by the Court of Appeal in *Metall und Rohstoff A.G. v. Donaldson Lufkin & Jenrette*[88] as a possible justification for the decision of Goulding J. in *Chase Manhattan Bank v. Israel-British Bank (London)*,[89] that a bank which had received the same sum twice rather than once held the second payment on trust for the mistaken payer. Lord Browne-Wilkinson took the view that "the retention of the moneys after the recipient bank learned of the mistake may well have given rise to a constructive trust"[90] and opined that "the remedial constructive trust, if introduced into English law, may provide a more satisfactory road forward".[91] These remarks were applied and a constructive trust was imposed on this ground in the Commercial Court in *Papamichael v. National Westminster*

---

[86] See *ante*, p. 322.

[87] [1996] A.C. 669 at 715.

[88] [1990] 1 Q.B. 391 at 479. The Court of Appeal accepted that "there is a good arguable case" that circumstances may arise in which "the court will be prepared to impose a constructive trust *de novo* as a foundation for the grant of equitable remedy by way of account or otherwise", classifying such a trust as a "remedial constructive trust".

[89] [1981] Ch. 105; see *post*, p. 815.

[90] [1996] A.C. 669 at 714. His lordship doubted the conclusion of Goulding J. that a mistaken payment is of itself sufficient to make the recipient a trustee of its subject matter.

[91] [1996] A.C. 669 at 716.

*Bank*.[92] However, this decision is, as a matter of precedent, clearly wrong because of the repeated statements in the Court of Appeal[93] that the remedial constructive trust does not form part of English law and that the contention that it should be adopted by English law can only be maintained in the House of Lords. For the moment, therefore, it is inappropriate to regard this possible justification for the decision in *Chase Manhattan Bank v. Israel-British Bank (London)* as part of English law.

That does not alter the fact that the House of Lords will undoubtedly one day soon be called upon to decide "whether English law should follow the United States and Canada by adopting the remedial constructive trust";[94] however, as has already been seen,[95] the outcome of the future deliberations of the House of Lords is certainly not a foregone conclusion, either in the context of mistaken payments or more generally.

## V. MUTUAL WILLS

Mutual wills arise where two or more persons enter into a legally binding agreement to make wills in a particular form with the intention that the provisions of such wills will be irrevocably binding. As soon as the first of the parties dies leaving a will made in accordance with the agreement, equity regards that agreement as irrevocable so far as the survivor is concerned and gives effect to it by the imposition of a trust. Thus if the survivor ultimately leaves his property other than in accordance with the agreement, his personal representatives will be deemed to hold it on trust for the agreed beneficiary.

This intervention of equity is, on the face of things, directly contrary to the Wills Act 1837 in that the agreement between the parties will normally[96] have to be proved by evidence which does not comply with the formal requirements for wills contained in section 9 of that Act. This provision was enacted for an obvious and important reason of policy — to ensure that false claims cannot be generated after the death of a testator when he is in no position to refute them. However, it has long been accepted that the intervention of equity can be justified by the fact that the survivor would otherwise be enabled to benefit by his own fraud.[97] As soon as one of the parties dies leaving a will made in accordance with the agreement, he will irrevocably have disposed of his property in reliance upon the agreement. Therefore any revocation of the mutual will at this stage will be a blatant fraud in that it will enable the survivor to take the benefit for which he contracted — the disposition by the other party of his property in accordance with that agreement — without the corresponding burden. This will be the case not only where the survivor takes some material benefit under the will but also where he disclaims any such

---

[92] [2003] 1 Lloyd's Rep. 341.

[93] Most recently in *Twinsectra v. Yardley* [1999] Lloyd's Rep. Bank 438 and *Bank of Credit and Commerce International (Overseas) v. Akindele* [2001] Ch. 437.

[94] [1996] A.C. 669 at 716.

[95] See *ante*, pp. 325–328.

[96] The agreement between the parties may be recited in one or both of the wills in question although this is not usually the case. It will certainly not be mentioned in any will executed in breach of the agreement.

[97] *Dufour v. Pereira* (1769) Dick 419, 421 (better reported in 2 Hargrave, *Jurisconsult Exercitations* 100, 104).

benefit and where the agreement gave him no such benefit; this is because in all three situations he will have obtained the benefit which he sought — the disposition of the property under the will. Consequently, equity imposes a trust to prevent the survivor from benefiting by his own fraud.

## 1. *The Prerequisites of Mutual Wills*

### (A) A Legally Binding Agreement Between the Parties

Evidence must be adduced that the parties intended that the provisions of their wills should be irrevocably binding.[97A] The best conceivable evidence is obviously recitals in the wills themselves. In *Re Hagger*,[98] a husband and wife made a joint will[99] which expressly stated that the parties had agreed to dispose of their property by that will and that there was to be no alteration or revocation except by agreement. Although the mere fact that the parties had made a joint will did not necessarily make it a mutual will, this recital clearly showed that the parties had agreed to bind themselves to make a mutual will. Equally convincing proof will be recitals of this type in the separate wills of the parties to the agreement.[99A] However, cases only tend to reach the courts where the survivor has revoked his mutual will in breach of the agreement and in such a situation there will obviously be no such recital in his later will. A recital in the sole will of the first party to die will be no more than *prima facie* evidence of an agreement.[1] In such a case, and also in situations where there is no mention of any agreement in either will, the agreement will have to be proved by some other form of evidence.

No agreement will be inferred merely because two parties make wills in substantially similar forms. In *Re Oldham*,[2] a husband and wife both made wills leaving their property to the other absolutely with the same alternative provisions in the event of the other's predecease. Although it was clear that they had agreed to make substantially identical wills, no evidence could be adduced of any agreement not to revoke and so the judge declined to infer such an agreement, particularly since both had left their property to the other absolutely (although this will clearly be a factor against the implication of such an agreement, there is nothing to prevent parties expressly agreeing to make mutual wills in this form, something which occurred both in *Re Green*[3] and in *Re Cleaver*[4]). Even the fact that both parties clearly intended that their assets should eventually go to the same third party in any event will not be enough, unless it can also be shown that they intended to enter into a legally binding obligation. Thus in *Re Goodchild (deceased)*,[5] a husband and wife, as part of a wider scheme dealing with the disposal of their business, each made wills in

---

[97A] Writing signed by both parties is in principle necessary where land is included but in practice it will be unconscionable for the survivor to rely on its absence; see *Healey v. Brown* [2002] W.T.L.R. 849.

[98] [1930] 2 Ch. 190.

[99] Such a document takes effect not as one will but as the separate wills of each party and is admitted to probate successively as the will of each testator.

[99A] As in *Healey v. Brown* [2002] W.T.L.R. 849.

[1] If it is finally found that there is insufficient evidence to prove the existence of mutual wills, it is possible that the equitable doctrine of election may apply.

[2] [1925] Ch. 75.

[3] [1951] Ch. 148.

[4] [1981] 1 W.L.R. 939.

[5] [1996] 1 W.L.R. 694 (Carnwath J.); [1998] 1 W.L.R. 1216, C.A.

favour of the other absolutely and, subject to that, in favour of their son. Evidence from their solicitor as to the advice which he habitually gave[6] led the court to conclude that the fact that the wife had understood that her intentions would be binding on the husband after her death, something which he would at that stage have taken for granted, did not mean that he had thought it necessary to bind himself to comply with those intentions; the wills were therefore not mutual.[7]

### (B) A Disposition of Property in Accordance with the Agreement

Equity will only intervene once one of the parties has died leaving a will made in accordance with the agreement. The vast majority of mutual wills involve the parties making a disposition in favour of the other with the same ultimate or substitutionary beneficiary; thus each party may leave property to the other for life and subject thereto to the same third party,[8] or to the other absolutely with the same substitutionary provisions in the event of predecease.[9] The property in question is most commonly the residuary estate of each but there is no reason why the agreement should not be for each to leave a specific sum of money or specific assets in this way with no restriction whatever on the disposition of the residue. Even where the agreement in question is for each party to dispose of his residue in this manner, it is common for each to make individual specific bequests or pecuniary legacies.[10]

Until recently, it has been unclear whether or not it is a prerequisite of the doctrine of mutual wills that the will of the first to die should, as in all the examples discussed so far, contain some disposition in favour of the survivor; but it has now been established that this is not actually necessary. In *Re Dale*,[11] spouses both made wills, which they had agreed should be irrevocable, in favour of their two children in equal shares. It was contended that the doctrine of mutual wills could only operate where the survivor obtained a personal financial benefit under the will of the first to die. Morritt J. rejected this argument, holding that it would be no less a fraud on the first to die if the agreement was that each party should leave his property to third parties rather than to the other; in both cases, the survivor would have obtained the benefit for which he had contracted — the agreed disposition of property in the will of the first to die. It must follow from this decision that the survivor will be equally bound to dispose of his property in accordance with the agreement if he disclaims any benefit to which he is entitled under the will of the first to die; in this case also, he will have obtained the benefit for which he has contracted but will have freely chosen to renounce it.[12]

All the examples discussed so far have related to agreements for the making

---

[6] He had never advised any of his clients to make mutual wills and had never had occasion to look into how such wills were drafted.

[7] However, the son was held entitled to make a claim under the Inheritance (Provision for Family and Dependants) Act 1975 in respect of the will of the wife (who had died first) on the grounds that it did not make reasonable provision for him; however, this claim could obviously only reach her property, not the property of the husband.

[8] As in *Re Haggar* [1930] 2 Ch. 190.

[9] As in *Re Green* [1951] Ch. 148 and *Re Cleaver* [1981] 1 W.L.R. 939.

[10] As in *Re Cleaver* [1981] 1 W.L.R. 939.

[11] [1994] Ch. 31.

[12] This was stated *obiter* in *Re Haggar* [1930] 2 Ch. 190 and must now clearly have been confirmed by *Re Dale* [1994] Ch. 31.

of wills in substantially similar form. However, there seems to be no reason in principle why the doctrine of mutual wills should be limited to agreements of this type and should not also extend to an agreement that, if A leaves property to B, B will leave that property and other property of his own[13] to C. Such an agreement is obviously subject to two pre-conditions: A must both die before B and leave the property in question to B; equally obviously, if either of these pre-conditions is not fulfilled, B will clearly be under no obligation to leave his own property to C. In *Birch v. Curtis*[14] a husband and wife agreed that the wife, who was terminally ill, should leave her interest in their matrimonial home to the husband and that he should leave the whole of his property to their respective children in equal shares. Both made wills in the form envisaged and the wife duly died first; however, the husband, having remarried, made a new will from which his former wife's children were excluded. The latter relied on the doctrine of mutual wills.[15] Rimer J. held that the nature of the agreement was not "a relevant difference" but did not find the necessary evidence that the husband had been legally bound. It is therefore clear that an agreement of this type is capable of falling within the doctrine of mutual wills; when it does so, once A has predeceased B having by his will made the appropriate disposition of property in B's favour, equity will intervene to prevent B from going back on the agreement.

## 2. *The Effect of Mutual Wills*

### (A) Before Either Party has Died

Equity will not intervene until one of the parties has died leaving a will made in accordance with the agreement. Consequently the position before either party has died will be governed by contractual principles. Like any other contract, the agreement between the parties can of course be revoked at any time by mutual agreement. If on the other hand, one party unilaterally revokes his mutual will in breach of the agreement during the lifetime of the other, the latter will be able to recover damages for breach of contract. However, since the only possible loss is loss of the right to receive an unascertained amount at an unascertained time in the future and since the other party still has unrestricted powers to dispose of his own property, it is relatively unlikely that any substantial damages could be recovered. A further bar to any successful action for damages in these circumstances is the fact that it seems that no such action will be available if the mutual will was revoked not by the act of the party but by operation of law (for example, by his marriage, divorce or

---

[13] If the agreement relates only to A's own property, C will not actually need to rely on the doctrine of mutual wills but will instead be able to claim, as in *Ottaway v. Norman* [1972] Ch. 698 (*ante*, p. 124), that B held that property on secret trust for C. Such a trust of course requires only an affirmative response from or the silent acquiescence of B to A's request that B should act in that way rather than the legally binding agreement between A and B which is necessary for there to be mutual wills. There is no obvious reason why an agreement of the type referred to in the text which is held not to be legally binding should not, insofar as it concerns A's property, nevertheless take effect as a secret trust.

[14] [2002] W.T.L.R. 965.

[15] No claim was made that the husband held the wife's share of the matrimonial home on what would have been a fully secret trust; on the evidence such a claim might well have been successful.

remarriage);[16] it appears that only intentional revocation will ground an action for damages.[17] Thus, while it is clear that revocation of the mutual will during the joint lives of the parties will determine the agreement and release the other party from his obligations thereunder,[18] no effective remedy is likely to result to the other party.

### (B) Where the First Party to Die Does Not Leave a Will Made in Accordance with the Agreement

If the other party does not discover that the first party to die has revoked his will until after the latter has died without leaving a will in accordance with the agreement, he will be able to claim damages from the latter's estate. However, although the loss suffered will certainly be able to be quantified in such a case, the other party will not have relinquished his powers over his own property and so may still find difficulty in obtaining substantial damages. The only exception to this seems to be the situation where he himself dies so soon after the first party to die that he does not have any opportunity of changing his own will and so dies leaving a will made in accordance with the agreement; in these circumstances, there seems no reason why his estate should not successfully bring an action for damages for breach of contract against the estate of the first to die for the value of the property which, according to the agreement, should have been disposed of in the will of the first to die. However, save in this exceptional situation, where the first party to die does not leave a will made in accordance with the agreement, the survivor is unlikely to have any effective remedy against the estate of the first to die; but it is of course clear that he will be released from his own obligations under the agreement.

### (C) Where the First Party to Die Leaves a Will Made in Accordance with the Agreement[19]

Once the first party to die has made the disposition of property envisaged by the agreement, a trust is immediately imposed upon the survivor for the benefit of those entitled under the agreement. This emerges most clearly from *Re Hagger*,[20] where one of the ultimate beneficiaries under the joint mutual will of a husband and wife survived the wife but predeceased the husband. Clauson J. held that her interest under the trust imposed by equity arose on the death of the first to die, the wife, and therefore did not lapse when she predeceased the husband.

The purpose of the imposition of the trust is to prevent the survivor from revoking his will in breach of the agreement. However, equity does not interfere with the fundamental probate principle that no will is irrevocable. If the survivor revokes his mutual will in breach of the agreement, his property will pass under his new will or his intestacy to his personal representatives,

---

[16] Wills Act 1837, ss.18, 18A.

[17] *Robinson v. Ommanney* (1883) 23 Ch.D. 285. See also *Re Marsland* [1939] Ch. 820, where the Court of Appeal reached a similar conclusion in respect of a covenant not to revoke a will contained in a deed of separation.

[18] *Stone v. Hoskins* [1905] P. 194.

[19] See Mitchell (1951) 14 M.L.R. 137.

[20] [1930] 2 Ch. 190.

who will hold it on trust to give effect to the agreement.[21] This will be the case even if the survivor's mutual will is revoked by operation of law upon a subsequent marriage, divorce or remarriage.[22]

However, whether or not the survivor revokes his will, difficulties arise in determining precisely what property is subject to the trust. Of course this will primarily be determined by the agreement. In *Re Green*,[23] the agreement specifically provided that each party would leave his property to the other absolutely and, on the death of the survivor, half his residuary estate was to be treated as the survivor's property and the other half was to be treated as property received by the survivor under the will of the first to die. Vaisey J. held that only the property which was to be treated as the property of the first to die was subject to the trust. This decision is justifiable as a matter of construction of the agreement in question but certainly cannot apply where an agreement contains no such provision. In such a case, there is absolutely no doubt that all the property received by the survivor under the mutual will is subject to a trust. If the survivor receives a limited interest, such as a life interest, that property will already be held on an express trust and so there is no scope for the trust imposed by equity. If, on the other hand, he receives an absolute interest, a trust will clearly be imposed but its precise nature is far from clear. In one sense, the survivor will be holding the property on trust for himself for his lifetime and then for the benefit of the ultimate beneficiary of the mutual will. But it is most unclear whether the interest of the survivor is a life interest in the technical sense (in which case he will have no right to resort to the capital) or whether the survivor has the right to dispose of the capital for his own benefit. This problem becomes even more acute when the survivor's own property is considered. Is this property subject to a trust from the time the first party dies and, if so, what is the nature of this trust?

It seems fairly clear from the decision in *Re Hagger*,[24] that the survivor's own property is also subject to a trust from the death of the first party to die since in that case the beneficiary was held to have an interest in property which was quite clearly vested in the survivor until his death. But if all the property owned by the survivor at the death of the first party becomes subject to a trust in favour of himself for life and thereafter for the ultimate beneficiary of the mutual will, the survivor will not be able to dispose of his own property for his own benefit without committing a breach of trust. Further, what happens to any property acquired by the survivor after the death of the first party? Does it immediately become subject to the same trust? If so, the effect of the death of the first party will be to make the survivor a life tenant not only of the property which he receives under the will but also of his own property, whether then existing or after acquired. The survivor will therefore have no power during the rest of his life to apply any capital for his own benefit. It could of course on the other hand be argued that the intention of the parties could reasonably be assumed to be that the survivor has the right to deal as he wishes with his own property and perhaps also with the property left to him absolutely under the terms of the agreement. The difficulty about this view is that the trust imposed

---

[21] *In the Estate of Heys* [1914] P. 192.
[22] *Re Green* [1951] Ch. 148.
[23] [1951] Ch. 148.
[24] [1930] 2 Ch. 190.

by equity then becomes so uncertain as to be virtually useless, since the survivor can destroy the subject matter of the agreement by alienation or dissipation.

This problem has only rarely had to be considered by the courts because most litigation involving mutual wills does not commence until after the death of the survivor — only then will the ultimate beneficiary discover whether or not the survivor has honoured his agreement. Where the subject matter of the agreement is a specific property,[25] the beneficiaries of the mutual will can clearly recover it or, if the survivor has in breach of trust sold it during his lifetime, its proceeds of sale and their product. But where the subject matter is, as is more usual, each party's residuary estate, litigation commenced after the death of the survivor can in practice only be concerned with the property owned by the survivor at his death; consequently, the English courts have generally been content to apply the terms of the agreement to this property. However, in the Australian case of *Birmingham v. Renfrew*,[26] Dixon J. considered the nature of the trust imposed during the life of the survivor and said this:

> "The purpose of an arrangement for corresponding wills must often be, as in this case, to enable the survivor during his life to deal as absolute owner with the property passing under the will of the party first dying. That is to say, the object of the transaction is to put the survivor in a position to enjoy for his own benefit the full ownership so that, for instance, he may convert it and expend the proceeds if he choose. But when he dies he is to bequeath what is left in the manner agreed upon. It is only by the special doctrines of equity that such a floating obligation, suspended, so to speak, during the lifetime of the survivor can descend upon the assets at his death and crystallise into a trust. No doubt gifts and settlements, inter vivos, if calculated to defeat the intention of the compact, could not be made by the survivor and his right of disposition, inter vivos, is, therefore, not unqualified. But, substantially, the purpose of the arrangement will often be to allow full enjoyment for the survivor's own benefit and advantage upon condition that at his death the residue shall pass as arranged."

This decision was cited with approval by Carnwath J. in *Re Goodchild (deceased)*,[27] where he held that: "the trust which is held binding in equity ... is an unusual form of trust, since it does not prevent the surviving testator using the assets during his lifetime. It is 'a kind of floating trust which finally attaches to such property as he leaves upon his death' ".[28] A somewhat similar view was expressed by Brightman J. in *Ottaway v. Norman*,[29] a case concerning secret trusts, where he said: "I am content to assume for present purposes but without so deciding that if property is given to the primary donee on the understanding that the primary donee will dispose by will of such assets, if any, as he may have at his command at his death in favour of the secondary

---

[25] As it was in *Re Newey (deceased)* [1994] 2 N.Z.L.R. 590 (High Court of New Zealand).

[26] (1937) 57 C.L.R. 666 at 689 (High Court of Australia).

[27] [1996] 1 W.L.R. 694 at 700.

[28] Citing *Birmingham v. Renfrew* (1937) 57 C.L.R. 666, *per* Latham C.J. at 675 (High Court of Australia).

[29] [1972] Ch. 698 at 713.

donee, a valid trust is created in favour of the secondary donee which is in suspense during the lifetime of the primary donee, but attaches to the estate of the primary donee at the moment of the latter's death."

These views undoubtedly recognise what actually happens in most mutual will cases. However, the passages from *Birmingham v. Renfrew* cited with approval by Carnwath J. seem to envisage the possibility of the ultimate beneficiary restraining an *inter vivos* disposition by the survivor (this would certainly be possible where the subject matter of the mutual will is a specific property and the beneficiaries of the will discover that the survivor intends to sell it). On the other hand, Brightman J. instead limits the scope of the trust to the property available to the survivor at this death (this difference may be because Brightman J. was actually dealing with a secret trust rather than with mutual wills).

It would be extremely interesting to see how, where the subject matter of mutual wills was each party's residue, a court reacted to an attempt to restrain an inter vivos disposition by the survivor and, in particular, whether any relief given was limited to the property received under the will of the first to die or also extended to the survivor's own property. It would also have been extremely interesting to see how the court dealt with the attempt which was made by the unsuccessful claimants in *Birch v. Curtis*[30] to recover part of the property subject to the alleged mutual will from someone to whom the survivor had given it during his lifetime — in this case the subject matter of the agreement had been the survivor's entire estate, although he only received a specific property under the will of the first to die, and he subsequently sold that property and purchased a property in the joint names of himself and a new wife.

No matter how the courts resolve difficulties of this type if and when the occasion arises, it must in any event be said that it seems hardly satisfactory to describe the suspended obligation referred to by the judges in the passages set out above as a trust; such an obligation clearly lacks the element of certainty of subject matter which is one of the principal requirements of a valid trust. The only answer to this conceptual difficulty may well be to regard the trust imposed to give effect to mutual wills as an entrenched historical anomaly.

### 3. *The Nature of the Trust Imposed by Equity*

It is quite clear that the trust imposed to give effect to mutual wills is not an express trust. However, there is a difference of opinion as to whether this trust is an implied or resulting trust or a constructive trust. Nothing turns on the classification adopted. Earlier editions of this work have suggested that it should be classified as an "implied, though not a resulting" trust.[31] However, in *Re Cleaver*,[32] Nourse J. took the view that it should be classified as a constructive trust. Both views are referred to with apparent approval in different sections of the judgment in *Re Dale*.[33] However, since the trust imposed to give effect to mutual wills is imposed to prevent the survivor obtaining a benefit by

---

[30] [2002] W.T.L.R. 965.
[31] (5th ed.), p. 154.
[32] [1981] 1 W.L.R. 939. See also *Healey v. Brown* [2002] W.T.L.R. 849.
[33] [1994] Ch. 31.

his own fraudulent conduct, it seems to the author of the present edition of this work that that trust is akin to the types of constructive trust described in the previous section of this chapter and should therefore be classified as a constructive trust.

## VI. THE VENDOR AS CONSTRUCTIVE TRUSTEE

When a vendor has entered into a contract of sale which is capable of being specifically enforced, equity regards as done that which ought to be done; this in accordance with one of its earliest maxims of equity. This is one of the situations in which the equitable doctrine of conversion still operates;[34] equity therefore regards the purchaser as owner of the subject matter of the contract and the vendor as owner of the purchase money. The operation of this equitable doctrine does not, of course, affect the legal title to the subject matter of the contract, which remains in the vendor pending performance of the contract. Thus the effect of the operation of the doctrine is to separate the legal and beneficial ownership of the property; it is therefore only to be expected that equity regards the vendor as a constructive trustee of the property pending performance of the contract. No corresponding trust of the purchase money will arise simply because such a trust would lack the necessary certainty of subject matter; however, the vendor acquires a lien or charge on the property for the unpaid purchase money.

The operation of the equitable doctrine of conversion and the consequential existence of a constructive trust are important because of the effect that can be produced both on the devolution of property and on the liabilities of the parties. Where a party to a contract dies after the equitable doctrine has operated, his property will devolve as if the contract has been performed. Thus, if a vendor or purchaser of freehold land dies after the doctrine of conversion has operated, the interest of the vendor devolves with his personalty and the interest of the purchaser devolves with his realty. However today,[35] this is important only in the relatively unlikely case of a testator leaving his realty and his personalty (or his land and his pure personalty) to different persons. But the effect of the operation of the doctrine of conversion on the liabilities of the parties remains as important today as it has ever been; this is precisely because of the fact that the vendor becomes a trustee of the subject matter of the contract. His liability to deal with the property as a trustee can be relied on by the purchaser not only in the event that the vendor fails to take reasonable care to preserve the property in a reasonable state of preservation,[36] but also to recover secret profits,[37] and to follow the subject matter of the trust into its product;[38] the corollary of this, however, is that the

---

[34] Since 1996, the doctrine has not operated when land is held on trust for sale (Trusts of Land and Appointment of Trustees Act 1996, s.3); until then this was the most significant example of the operation of the doctrine.

[35] Before 1926, when real and personal property devolved in different ways on intestacy, this effect was of much greater importance.

[36] *Clarke v. Ramuz* [1891] 2 Q.B. 456 at 459–460; see also *Michaels v. Harley (Marylebone)* [2000] Ch. 104.

[37] *English v. Dedham Vale Properties* [1978] 1 W.L.R. 95.

[38] *Lake v. Bayliss* [1974] 1 W.L.R. 1075.

purchaser becomes liable for all the risks attendant upon ownership, in particular that of accidental destruction.[39] Of course, this trusteeship of the vendor is of an extremely unusual nature; the vendor himself retains a substantial interest in the property for the simple reason that, in the event that the contract is not in the end completed, he will once again become absolute legal and beneficial owner; further, he is entitled to receive and retain any income produced by the property until the completion of the sale.[40] However, as soon as the purchase price has been paid in full, the qualified nature of the vendor's trusteeship will disappear since he no longer has any interest to protect; from that moment onwards he will be a bare trustee of the property for the purchaser.

Since the doctrine of conversion will only operate when a contract of sale is capable of being specifically enforced, it is a prerequisite of its operation that the failure of the vendor to transfer the subject matter of the contract to the purchaser is incapable of being adequately compensated by an award of damages. Little or no difficulties have been encountered in applying the equitable doctrine to the relatively few contracts for the sale of chattels which satisfy this requirement;[41] such contracts are capable of being specifically enforced from the moment at which they are entered into and so the vendor under such a contract will hold its subject matter on trust for the purchaser from the moment of contract. However, the vast majority of contracts that are capable of being specifically enforced are contracts for the sale of land; the application of the equitable doctrine to contracts of this type has encountered difficulties caused by the nature of title to land and, in particular, by the fact that a contract for the sale of land is not specifically enforceable until the vendor has made title in accordance with the contract or the purchaser has agreed to accept such other title as the vendor actually has. The constructive trusteeship of the vendor does not therefore arise until title has been so made or accepted,[42] when it is generally thought to have retrospective effect to the date of the contract. This is not an appropriate place to consider the various ways in which this basic principle has been developed in the light of the many different situations which can arise under the various types of contracts for the sale of land; these matters are fully discussed elsewhere.[43]

It has to be admitted that the inevitable self-interest of the vendor in the successful conclusion of the transaction does not sit very easily with his classification as a trustee. For this reason, many doubts have been expressed[44] as to whether it is appropriate for the relationship of vendor and purchaser to be classified as that of trustee and beneficiary. There is no doubt that the classification has led to the development of some anomalous rules but it is by no means certain that different anomalies would not have resulted from

---

[39] The Law Commission has proposed that this risk should pass only on completion (Law Commission No. 191 (1990), para. 2.25); although this proposal has not been enacted, it has been accepted by the draftsmen of standard form conveyancing contracts; see, for example, the provision to this effect which has been inserted in the Standard Conditions of Sale as Condition 5.1.1.

[40] *Cuddon v. Tite* (1858) 1 Giff. 395.

[41] Such as contracts to sell a rare antique, a rare book, or shares in a private company.

[42] *Lysaght v. Edwards* (1876) 2 Ch.D. 499 at 506–507, 510, 518.

[43] See *Constructive Trusts* (3rd ed., 1997), pp. 282–292 and Farrand, *Contract & Conveyance* (4th ed., 1983), pp. 167–173.

[44] Notably by Waters, *The Constructive Trust* (1964), pp. 141–142.

basing the relationship entirely on the law of contract. In any event, for the moment there seems little justification for or likelihood of any attempt to recast the relationship between the vendor and the purchaser under a specifically enforceable contract on any basis other than that of constructive trustee and beneficiary.

## VII. THE MORTGAGEE AS CONSTRUCTIVE TRUSTEE

At one time,[45] the majority of mortgages of land were effected by means of transfer of the subject matter of the mortgage to the mortgagee subject to a proviso for retransfer to the mortgagor upon discharge of the mortgage debt; many judges then saw fit to describe the mortgagee as a constructive trustee of the mortgaged property. Even when the courts came to recognise that the mortgagee, as such, was not a trustee at all,[46] it was still clearly established that he might nevertheless become a constructive trustee; first, he might be held to have become a constructive trustee as a result of the exercise of his powers under the mortgage; and, secondly, once the mortgage debt had been fully repaid, he did become a constructive trustee of the mortgaged property pending its retransfer to the mortgagor. But now[47] that mortgages of land cannot be created by the transfer of its subject matter to the mortgagee, the latter cannot possibly become a constructive trustee of the mortgaged property for the simple reason that it cannot now be vested in him; he can therefore only become a constructive trustee of property which reaches his hands as a result of the exercise of his powers under the mortgage.

After some initial uncertainty, it became clear that the mortgagee was not a trustee of his power of sale and therefore could exercise his express or implied contractual right of sale quite irrespective of the interests of the mortgagor;[48] but it became equally clear that any surplus produced by the exercise of this power of sale was held by the mortgagee on a constructive trust for the mortgagor.[49] However, this old constructive trust of the proceeds of sale seems now to have been totally superseded by the creation of a statutory trust.[50] Further, the better view is that a mortgagee in possession is not a constructive trustee of any rents and profits which he has or should have received but is merely under an obligation to account for them to the mortgagor.[51]

It consequently seems that, so far as the mortgagee is concerned, the constructive trust no longer has any role to play.

## VIII. TRANSFERS OF PROPERTY WHICH ARE AT LAW INCOMPLETE

As has already been seen,[52] the formalities necessary for the transfer of the legal title to certain kinds of property cannot all be carried out by the parties

---

[45] Prior to the enactment of the Property Legislation of 1925.
[46] See *Marquis Cholmondeley v. Lord Clinton* (1820) 2 Jac. & W. 1.
[47] Law of Property Act 1925, s.85.
[48] *Warner v. Jacob* (1882) 20 Ch.D. 220.
[49] *Banner v. Berridge* (1881) 18 Ch.D. 254.
[50] Law of Property Act 1925, s.105 (originally Conveyancing Act 1881, s.21(3)).
[51] *Kirkwood v. Thompson* (1865) 2 De G.J. & S. 613.
[52] See *ante*, p. 136.

themselves. A transfer of registered land is not effective to pass the legal title to that land until the duly executed transfer form is presented to the Land Registry and registered in the Register of Title. Similarly, a transfer of shares is not effective to pass the legal title to those shares until the transferor has complied with the procedure required by the Articles of Association of the company in question and the transfer is duly registered in the Register of Shareholders. In both these cases, the intervention of a third party is necessary to enable legal title to pass; consequently the transfer will not be effective at law until the third party in question acts. However, it has been held that once the parties have complied with all the formal requirements capable of being carried out by themselves, the transfer will become effective in equity and the transferor will hold the property in question on trust for the transferee pending the intervention of the third party. This rule was established in two unconnected cases both named *Re Rose*,[53] and for this reason is generally known as the Rule in *Re Rose*.

The precise scope of this Rule, which is clearly English law at the present time, has already been considered.[54] It is also clear that the trust which arises as a result of the operation of the Rule in *Re Rose* does not arise out of any intention of the parties to that trust; it must therefore necessarily be brought into existence by operation of law and should therefore be classified as a constructive trust.

---

[53] [1949] Ch. 78; [1952] Ch. 499.
[54] See *ante*, p. 143.

CHAPTER 11

# CHARITABLE TRUSTS

## I. INTRODUCTION

THE law and practice of charitable trusts was radically reformed by the Charities Act 1960.[1] This Act, which implemented, wholly or in part, many of the recommendations of the Report of the Nathan Committee on charitable trusts published in 1952,[2] achieved the arduous task of renovating what was then an appalling mass of statute law relating to charitable trusts. It cleared a great deal of dead wood from the statute book, especially that body of statutes known as the Charitable Trusts Acts 1853–1939. What was not obsolete was extracted from them and conveniently contained in the new statute. This Act therefore contained the whole of the statute law relating to charitable trusts from the sixteenth century to the present day and also added new provisions in keeping with modern circumstances. Subsequently, as a result of the Woodfield Report,[3] further reforms were enacted in the Charities Act 1992 with the intention of increasing the powers of the Charity Commissioners, a statutory governmental organisation which regulates charities subject to the supervision of the courts, to control abuse and maladministration by the trustees of charitable trusts. The Charities Act 1960 and much of the Charities Act 1992 have now been consolidated in the Charities Act 1993. The effect and scope of the current legislation, insofar as it is of relevance to this work, is considered later on in this chapter.

However, none of the legislation referred to so far was primarily concerned with the legal definition of charity. That continued, and for the moment continues, to be governed by the case law that has emerged down the centuries. However, in 2002, the Government's Strategy Unit published a Report entitled "Private Action, Public Benefit,"[4] a consultation document which envisaged not only further reforms of a regulatory nature but also a new statutory definition of charity as an organisation which provides public benefit and which has one or more of ten listed purposes; it was hoped that this definition would provide a clearer framework while retaining existing case law and the flexibility to evolve as society changes.[5] In July 2003, while the

---

[1] For accounts of the Act, see Nathan, *Charities Act 1960*; Maurice, *Charities Act 1960*.
[2] Cmd. 9538 (its full title is the "Committee on the Law and Practice relating to Charitable Trusts").
[3] "Efficiency Scrutiny of the Supervision of Charities" (1987 National Audit Office Report); House of Commons Paper 380, 1986–87.
[4] Available, along with much other useful information, on the Charity Commission's webSite.
[5] See *post*, p. 448.

proofs were being read, the Government published its response, which added three further purposes to the Strategy Unit's list. Some form of legislation is obviously likely during the lifetime of this edition.

## II. DISTINCTIONS FROM PRIVATE TRUSTS

A charitable trust aims to benefit society at large or an appreciable part of it. A private trust aims to benefit defined persons or defined classes of persons. In general, charitable trusts are subject to the same rules as private trusts, but because of their public nature they enjoy a number of advantages which are not shared by private trusts.

### 1. Perpetuity[6]

Charitable trusts are not subject to that aspect of the perpetuity rule commonly called the Rule against Inalienability. The objects of the charity may last for ever but a gift for such purposes will still be valid.[7]

However, charitable trusts are, generally, subject to the perpetuity rule in the sense that the interest must vest in the charity within the perpetuity period. Thus, in *Re Lord Stratheden and Campbell*,[8] an annuity of £100 was bequeathed for provision "for the Central London Rangers on the appointment of the next lieutenant-colonel". Since the next lieutenant-colonel might not be appointed within the perpetuity period, the limitation transgressed the rule and the gift was held by Romer J. to be invalid. However, even here there is an exception; provided that the trust in favour of one charity takes effect within the period, a gift over from that charity to another on the happening of an event which may be too remote will still be valid.[9] But this exception will not apply to a gift over to a charity after a gift to a non-charity;[10] in such a case, the normal rules as to vesting in the second charity within the perpetuity period must be observed. It is as if for this purpose the law regards "charity" as a unity — thus a gift from one charity to another charity is from or to this "unity" so that there is no scope for the operation of the perpetuity rule, while a gift from or to this unity is subject to it in the usual way.

At present, the Rule against Accumulations[11] applies to charitable trusts in the same way as it applies to private trusts. However, the proposed new legislation on perpetuities and accumulations, which will introduce a 125-year accumulation period, will for the first time treat private trusts and charitable trusts differently in this respect. The proposed 125-year period will not apply to charitable trusts, where accumulation will only be permitted for 21 years;

---

[6] See *ante*, p. 238.
[7] *Chamberlayne v. Brockett* (1872) L.R. 8 Ch.App. 206.
[8] [1894] 3 Ch. 265, applying *Chamberlayne v. Brockett* (1872) L.R. 8 Ch.App. 206. It is now possible to take advantage of the "wait and see" rule introduced by the Perpetuities and Accumulations Act 1964, s.3 in respect of instruments taking effect after the commencement of that Act. This will continue to be possible under the proposed new legislation governing perpetuities.
[9] *Re Tyler* [1891] 3 Ch. 252 but compare *Re Dalziel* [1943] Ch. 277; these cases are discussed *ante*, p. 86.
[10] *Re Bowen* [1893] 2 Ch. 491 at 494; *Re Peel's Release* [1921] 2 Ch. 218; *Re Wightwick's Will Trusts* [1950] Ch. 260; *Re Spensley's Will Trusts* [1954] Ch. 233.
[11] See *ante*, p. 253.

this has been proposed on the basis that it is not consistent with the public benefit which charitable trusts are supposed to produce for income to be withdrawn from a charitable purpose for any longer than that.

## 2. *Certainty*

A charity will not fail for uncertainty of objects provided that the settlor clearly intended the fund to go exclusively to charity.[12] If this is satisfied, the trust will not fail if the settlor omits to specify the objects with particularity.[13] In such circumstances a *cy-près* scheme[14] will be made to render the objects more precise. Again, for this purpose, it seems that the law regards charity as a unity so that, once the gift to this unity is established, it cannot fail.

## 3. *Construction*

In construing instruments in circumstances where the settlor or testator intended to set up a charitable trust but did so ambiguously, a "benignant" construction should be given if possible.[15] This was confirmed by the House of Lords in *I.R.C. v. McMullen*[16] (although it was not necessary to resort to such a construction in that case) and such a construction was subsequently adopted by the House of Lords in *Guild v. I.R.C.*[17]

## 4. *Taxation*

For taxation purposes, the distinction between a charitable trust and a private trust is seen both in the special taxation privileges which are afforded to a charitable trust and in the taxation inducements that are offered to individuals for them to confer benefits on charitable trusts.

## (A) Income Tax and Corporation Tax

### (1) A charity's liability to income tax and corporation tax
It is necessary to distinguish between the investment income and the trading income of a charity. The investment income of an unincorporated charity is exempt from income tax provided that it is applied for charitable purposes only.[18] If the charity carries on a trade, its profits from the trade are exempt from income tax only if first, they are applied solely for its charitable purpose and, secondly, either the purpose (or one of the primary purposes) of the charity is to carry on that particular trade or the work carried out in connection

---

[12] See *Moggridge v. Thackwell* (1803) 7 Ves. 36, affirmed (1807) 13 Ves. 416. Provided that the gift has a charitable object, it does not matter that the precise purposes specified are too vague and uncertain to be charitable themselves; *Re Koeppler's Will Trusts* [1986] Ch. 423.

[13] *Harris v. Sharp* (1986) [2003] T.L.I. 41, where the principle of executory trusts, *ante* p. 147, was relied on in this connection.

[14] See *post*, p. 482.

[15] See *ante*, p. 48 in relation to construction of private trusts.

[16] [1981] A.C. 1 at 16. The facts are stated *post*, p. 472. See also *Re Hetherington (deceased)* [1990] Ch. 1.

[17] [1992] 2 A.C. 310.

[18] Income and Corporation Taxes Act 1988, s.505.

with the trade is mainly done by the beneficiaries of the charity.[19] Where a charity is incorporated, the same principles apply to corporation tax.[20]

The question whether a body is established for charitable purposes is a question of law to be decided in accordance with the usual principles, but the question whether or to what extent income is applied to charitable purposes is one of fact.[21] However, in *I.R.C. v. Helen Slater Charitable Trust*,[22] the Court of Appeal held that one charity "applies" its income for charitable purposes if it pays that income to another charity, even if the terms of the instrument governing the second charity are almost identical to those of the instrument governing the first charity.

**2. *The treatment of donations***

Donations by an individual to charity can, in appropriate circumstances, be treated as donations of the amount in question after the deduction by the donor of income tax at the basic rate, in which case the charity is entitled to claim a refund of the income tax paid. In 2003/04 the basic rate of income tax is 22 per cent. Accordingly, where an individual is liable to income tax at this rate, he can enable the charity to receive a donation of £5,000 by making a net payment to it of £3,900. If the donor is a higher rate taxpayer, his threshold for the payment of higher rate tax at 40 per cent will also be increased by the gross cost of his donation, thereby effectively saving him a further 18 per cent of his donation. Consequently, where an individual who is liable to income tax at the higher rate has paid £3,900 to charity, he can save a further £900 which he would otherwise have had to pay in higher rate income tax; the net cost to him after income tax of paying £5,000 per annum to charity is therefore reduced still further to £3,000.

Before April 6, 2000, this system operated if an individual executed a deed of covenant by which he covenanted to pay a part of his income to a charity for a period which was capable of lasting for more than three years (four-year periods were habitually employed), but only in respect of basic rate tax. The charity was entitled to recover the basic rate income tax paid by the covenantor on the covenanted sum,[23] but the taxpayer was not entitled to set his donation off against higher rate tax. Charities entitled under covenants which were already in existence before that date continue to enjoy the same advantage and a covenantor who is a higher rate taxpayer can now also in effect save the higher rate tax payable in respect of the gross sum donated.

For donations made after April 5, 2000, the system operates only under what is known as Gift Aid, which until then was designed only for large one-off donations supported by a written certificate given by the donor to the charity.[24] All charitable donations can now be brought within the scope of Gift Aid and the only requirement is for a written or electronic declaration to be made by the donor (in the case of oral gifts, the charity still has to send the donor a written notification).[25]

---

[19] *ibid.*
[20] *ibid.* ss.505(1), 506(1).
[21] See *Williams' Trustees v. I.R.C.* [1947] A.C. 447.
[22] [1982] Ch. 49.
[23] Income and Corporation Taxes Act 1988, s.660. Finance Act 1989, s.56.
[24] Finance Act 1990, s.25.
[25] Finance Act 2000, s.39.

So far as corporate donors are concerned, the position before April 6, 2000 was broadly the same as for individuals. When they entered into a covenant, they could deduct the gross amount of the payments from their profits before these were assessed for corporation tax, provided that they deducted income tax at the basic rate from the gross amount before making the payment to the charity and accounted to the Revenue for the tax so deducted.[26] Corporate Gift Aid operated on a similar basis.[27] Since April 5, 2000, corporate donors can deduct the amount of charitable donations from their profits; consequently, charities no longer need to reclaim any tax and the full amount of the donation can therefore be paid directly to the charity by the donor.[28]

## (B) Capital Gains Tax

A capital gain accruing to a charity will not attract capital gains tax provided that it is both applicable and is in fact applied to the charitable purposes.[29] If the charity is incorporated, then it is entitled to exemption from corporation tax on its capital gains on the same basis.[30]

There is also a substantial inducement to make gifts to a charity. Normally, when a person makes a gift, capital gains tax is payable by him on, broadly, the difference between the value of the asset at the time of the gift, and its value at the time of acquisition.[31] However, no capital gains tax is payable where the disposal is to a charity.[32]

Gift Aid in respect of individuals can now also be set against any Capital Gains Tax payable by that individual in respect of other assets.[33] (This is of course not necessary in the case of corporations.)

## (C) Inheritance Tax

Compared with other private persons or bodies, charities enjoy important privileges with regard to inheritance tax:

    (a)   gifts made to charities, whether by will or inter vivos, are wholly exempt from the tax;[34]

    (b)   gifts made to nationally important institutions, such as the National Gallery, the British Museum or the National Trust, are wholly exempt from the tax, whether the gift takes effect on death or inter vivos;[35]

    (c)   gifts made to a charity by way of a payment from a discretionary trust are entitled to unlimited exemption;[36] and

    (d)   the Treasury is empowered to exempt, for example, a gift of land of

---

[26] Income and Corporation Taxes Act 1988, s.683. Finance Act 1989, s.59.
[27] Finance Act 1990, s.26.
[28] Finance Act 2000, s.40.
[29] Taxation of Chargeable Gains Act 1992, s.256.
[30] Capital gains tax applies only to capital gains made by individuals. Capital gains made by corporations are subject to corporation tax.
[31] Taxation of Chargeable Gains Act 1992, s.35.
[32] *ibid.* s.257.
[33] Finance Act 2000, s.39.
[34] Inheritance Tax Act 1984, s.23.
[35] *ibid.*
[36] *ibid.* s.76.

outstanding scenic or historical or scientific interest, gifts of buildings of outstanding historical or architectural or aesthetic interest, property given as a source of income for the upkeep of such land or buildings, and pictures, books, manuscripts, works of art, and so forth, of national or historic or scientific interest.[37]

It is, however, important to emphasise that, as a general rule, the exemptions apply only to gifts to charities which are immediate and absolute.[38] To this general rule, there is the qualification that, if the donor wishes a charity to benefit only after the death of himself and his spouse, he can leave a life interest in the property to the spouse, and on the latter's death, to the charity absolutely. Inheritance tax will not be payable on the death either of the donor or of his spouse.[39]

In addition to taking advantage of these immunities which are peculiar to charity, a donor may also take advantage of another exemption which applies generally, namely, that gifts to a total value of £3,000 in any one year are exempt.[40]

There is, therefore, considerable encouragement to make gifts to charity. Moreover, from the charity's point of view, any capital distributions made by it are also exempt.[41]

## (D) Stamp Duty[42]

Charities are exempt from stamp duty in relation to any conveyance, transfer or letting made or agreed to be made to them.[43]

## (E) Value Added Tax

Although there is no general exemption for charities from value added tax, certain medical charities are, in effect, exempt from the tax[44] and supplies to such charities are also exempt.[45]

## (F) Rating

The general law of rating is governed by the Local Government Finance Act 1933, section 43 of which provides for the rating relief (both mandatory and discretionary) given to charities.

Mandatory relief to the extent of 80 per cent[46] of the non-domestic rates which would otherwise be chargeable is available in respect of land occupied by or used by trustees for a charity and wholly or mainly used for charitable purposes.

---

[37] ibid. s.27.
[38] ibid. s.23.
[39] ibid. s.18.
[40] ibid. s.57.
[41] ibid. s.58(1)(a).
[42] See post, p. 624.
[43] Finance Act 1982, s.129.
[44] Value Added Tax Act 1983, Scheds. 5, 6.
[45] ibid.
[46] Special mandatory relief in the form of total exemption from rates is available in respect of places of public religious worship and buildings ancillary to them; Local Government Finance Act 1988, Sched. 5, para. 11 and see Broxtowe Borough Council v. Birch [1983] 1 W.L.R. 314 for the meaning of "public religious worship".

With regard to occupation, it is in most cases clear that the charity or the trustees of the charity are in occupation. More difficult questions may arise where the charity has provided a house or accommodation for servants or staff and whether mandatory relief can be claimed in respect of it. The test appears to be whether the occupation of the servant is required with a view to the more efficient performance of his duties so as to constitute occupation by the charity.[47]

With regard to the requirement that the land be wholly or mainly used for charitable purposes, it appears to be required that the charity's use of the property be wholly "ancillary to" or "directly facilitates" the carrying out of its main charitable purposes.[48] The meaning of these expressions was considered by the House of Lords in *Oxfam v. Birmingham City District Council*,[49] where Oxfam claimed relief from rates in respect of gift shops which it used for the sale of articles, mostly clothing, which had been donated to it, the profits being applied to Oxfam' objects. It was held that the charity gift shops did not "directly facilitate" the main object of the charity and that rating relief could not be claimed. Lord Cross held[50] that there was a distinction between user for the purpose of getting in, raising or earning money for the charity, as opposed to user for purposes directly related to the achievement of the objects of the charity. The charity gift shops simply raised money for Oxfam and were accordingly excluded from relief. The decision has been reversed by statute in respect of such shops so as to make them eligible for relief;[51] however, it remains intact in relation to other property owned by charities.

In addition to this relief, which is obtainable as of right, the rating authority has a discretion to reduce further, or remit entirely, the rates payable by a charity.[52]

## III. THE DEFINITION OF CHARITY

For the reasons implicit in the distinctions which have already been made between charitable and private trusts, it is essential to know when a trust is charitable and when it is not. The answer to this question is, at least for the moment, to be found, if at all, almost entirely in the decided cases, although that answer may in borderline cases be difficult to find. There are a vast number of cases and they certainly do not present an orderly picture.

In borderline cases, it is sometimes still necessary to go back to a statute dating from the reign of Elizabeth I,[53] which is generally known as the Charitable Uses Act 1601. In the Preamble of this statute, the following charitable objects are listed.

"The relief of aged, impotent and poor people, the maintenance of sick

---

[47] *Glasgow Corporation v. Johnstone* [1965] A.C. 609; *Northern Ireland Valuation Court v. Fermanagh Protestant Board of Education* [1969] 1 W.L.R. 1708.
[48] *Glasgow Corporation v. Johnstone* [1965] A.C. 609 at 622, *per* Lord Reid.
[49] [1976] A.C. 126. Compare *Aldous v. Southwark L.B.C.* [1968] 1 W.L.R. 1671.
[50] *ibid.* at 146.
[51] Rating (Charity Shops) Act 1976.
[52] Local Government Finance Act 1988, s.47.
[53] 43 Eliz. I (1601), c. 4.

and maimed soldiers and mariners, schools of learning, free schools and schools in universities, the repair of bridges, ports, havens, causeways, churches, sea-banks and highways, the education and preferment of orphans, the relief, stock or maintenance for houses of correction, the marriage of poor maids, the supportation, aid and help of young tradesmen, handicraftsmen and persons decayed, the relief or redemption of prisoners or captives and the aid or ease of any poor inhabitants concerning payment of fifteens, setting out of soldiers and other taxes."

The Charitable Uses Act 1601 was actually repealed by section 13(2) of the Mortmain and Charitable Uses Act 1888. However, its preamble has remained alive, arguably as a matter of statutory interpretation[54] and certainly as a result of the practice of the courts in continuing to ask whether or not a particular purpose is within the "spirit and intendment" or the "equity" or the "mischief" of the statute. Thus in *Scottish Burial Reform and Cremation Society v. Glasgow City Corporation*,[55] the House of Lords had to decide the novel question of whether or not cremation was a charitable purpose. In the course of deciding that it was, the House acknowledged that recourse to the Preamble was undoubtedly the accepted practice, although "in only a very wide and broad sense";[56] this meant, in the words of Lord Wilberforce, "that what must be regarded is not the wording of the preamble, but the effect of decisions given by the courts as to its scope, decisions which have endeavoured to keep the law as to charities moving according as new social needs arise or old ones become obsolete or satisfied".[57] Similarly, in *Incorporated Council of Law Reporting for England and Wales v. Attorney-General*,[58] when the Court of Appeal had to decide the equally novel question of whether law reporting was a charitable purpose, its decision that the publication or dissemination of law

---

[54] Section 13(2) of the Mortmain and Charitable Uses Act 1888 expressly preserved the Preamble, although not specifically for all purposes (its words seem to fall short of providing that the courts must in all cases continue to refer to the Preamble, since it refers specifically only to enactments and documents in which a reference to charity is made, a reference which does not *prima facie* include the reported judgments of the superior courts). Even if the effect of the Preamble thus survived the 1888 Act, section 13(2) was anyway itself repealed by the Charities Act 1960, s.38(1). In reality however, even if section 13(2) had been omitted from the 1888 Act, the courts would still have been bound to decide cases with the preamble in mind, simply because the practice of the courts referring to it had by then developed into a rule of law. And that rule of law — having, as it were, an independent existence irrespective of statute — also required an express statutory provision if it was to be extinguished. Anyway the Charities Act 1960 made it reasonably clear that no change in the law was intended. Although that Act repealed section 13(2) of the 1888 Act, it provided by way of substitution that a reference in any enactment or document to a charitable purpose within the scope of the Preamble should be construed as a reference to charity in the meaning which that expression bears as a legal term according to the law of England and Wales (s.38(4); see also the definition of "charity" in s.45(1) (now Charities Act 1993, s.96 as amended by Charities (Amendment) Act 1995) and of "charitable purposes" in s.46(1) (now Charities Act 1993, s.97)). Thus the Charities Act 1960 itself (and consequently also the subsequent legislation which has replaced it) seemed (and seems) to make it clear that the law of England and Wales, which has been based on the Preamble over a period of over 400 years, should remain intact.

[55] [1968] A.C. 138. The House of Lords had to decide whether cremation was a charitable purpose and held that it was.

[56] [1968] A.C. 138 at 151 *per* Lord Upjohn.

[57] *ibid.* at 154.

[58] [1972] Ch. 73.

reports was a purpose beneficial to the community and therefore charitable was specifically based on the conclusion that that purpose was within the spirit and intendment of the preamble to the Charitable Uses Act 1601.

While it is therefore still technically necessary today to decide whether a case falls within "the letter or the spirit and intendment" of the Preamble, in practice in most cases a reference to the pre-existing case law will be sufficient to dispose of the problem of whether or not any particular trust is charitable. It is only where, as in the two cases referred to above, novel facts have to be considered that the court is ever likely to feel compelled to refer back to the basic principles or indeed to the letter of the Preamble.

In any event, the Preamble was not, and was not intended to be, a definition of charity. It was simply a catalogue of purposes which in 1601 were regarded as charitable. There has never yet been a formal statutory definition, apart from the limited one provided for the purposes of the Recreational Charities Act 1958.[59] Naturally that has not prevented suggestions being made that there ought to be one. Such suggestions were made before the passing of the Charities Act 1960,[60] by the Expenditure Committee of the House of Commons in 1975,[61] and in the 1989 White Paper "Charities: A Framework For the Future".[62] And the suggestion has now been made again in the 2002 Report from the Government's Strategy Unit entitled "Private Action, Public Benefit". It is only fair to say that many laymen and some lawyers find it extraordinary that the question of whether a trust is charitable should, in the light of all the fiscal and other privileges which are enjoyed by charities today, still depend on a statutory provision of the early seventeenth century and the welter of case law which has grown up around it. Lord Upjohn once accepted that the Preamble had been "stretched almost to breaking-point"[63] while Lord Cross has expressed the view[64] that, given that the difficulties are undoubtedly exacerbated by the immunity from taxation which all English charities enjoy, one possible solution would be to separate the two and say that only some charities should enjoy fiscal privileges.

Past suggestions for a statutory definition were resisted because it was thought to be almost impossible to provide a foolproof definition applicable to all the cases which might arise. As Viscount Simonds once said, "There is no limit to the number and diversity of the ways in which man will seek to benefit his fellow men".[65] The problems of definition cannot be underestimated and Sachs L.J. appreciated "the wisdom of the legislature in refraining from providing a detailed definition of charitable purposes in the 1960 Act. Any statutory definition might well produce a fresh spate of litigation and provide a set of undesirable artificial distinctions."[66] It is noteworthy that in 1976 an independent committee which is generally known as the Goodman Commit-

---

[59] See post, p. 468.
[60] See for example the Nathan Report.
[61] 10th Report Session 1974–75.
[62] Cmd. 694.
[63] Scottish Burial Reform and Cremation Society v. Glasgow City Corporation [1968] A.C. 138 at 153.
[64] In Dingle v. Turner [1972] A.C. 601 at 624 (a case involving the relief of poverty, discussed post, p. 455).
[65] I.R.C. v. Baddeley [1955] A.C. 572 at 583.
[66] Incorporated Council of Law Reporting for England and Wales v. Att.-Gen. [1972] Ch. 73 at 94.

tee[67] found itself unable to devise a definition and instead recommended that the categorsies of charity set out in the Charitable Uses Act 1601 should be restated in simple and modern language and extended so as to include objects which are now considered to be charitable (so called "guide-lines");[68] it was envisaged that the case law would not be irrelevant but that the courts would have more freedom to reconsider the preamble in the light of the new categorisation.

The long-ignored proposals of the Goodman Committee bear a considerable resemblance to the contents of the 2002 Report from the Government's Strategy Unit, which envisage a new statutory definition of charity comprising ten charitable purposes[68A] which it is hoped will provide a clearer framework while retaining existing case law and the flexibility to evolve as society changes. It is, however, only fair to say that the new proposals do make a much greater effort to deal with one of the principal present difficulties of this area of the law, namely defining what is, and what is not, for the "public benefit".[69] These latest proposals have so far been more favourably received than their predecessors; it remains to be seen whether they will in the end be more successful.

## IV. THE CLASSIFICATION OF CHARITABLE TRUSTS

In *Commissioners for Special Purposes of Income Tax v. Pemsel ("Pemsel's* Case"),[70] Lord Macnaghten classified the trusts which have been held to be charitable under four heads: first, trusts for the relief of poverty; secondly, trusts for the advancement of education; thirdly, trusts for the advancement of religion; and, fourthly, trusts for other purposes beneficial to the community which do not fall under any of the other three heads.[71] The 2002 Report from the Government's Strategy Unit proposed renaming the first head "the prevention and relief of poverty" and adding a further six heads:[72] the advancement of health;[73] social and community advancement;[74] the advancement of culture, arts and heritage; the advancement of amateur sport; the promotion of human rights, conflict resolution and reconciliation; and the advancement of environmental protection and improvement.[74A] Some of the trusts which would fall within these new heads in the event that they were created are at present squeezed into the category of trusts for the advancement of education while

---

[67] An independent committee on Charity Law and Voluntary Organisations set up by the National Council of Social Service under the chairmanship of Lord Goodman which reported in 1976.

[68] At p. 16; these "guide-lines" are set out in Appendix 1 to the Report (p. 123).

[68A] Increased to 13 by the Government's response to the Report.

[69] See *post*, p. 456.

[70] [1891] A.C. 531 at 583.

[71] The classification was based on the argument of Sir Samuel Romilly in *Morice v. Bishop of Durham* (1805) 10 Ves. 522 at 532.

[72] Compare the classification in the American Restatement of Trusts which specifically refers also to two other purposes: (1) promotion of health; and (2) governmental and municipal purposes (Vol. II. p. 1140).

[73] Including the prevention and relief of sickness, disease or of human suffering.

[74] Including the care, support and protection of the aged, people with a disability, children and young people.

[74A] The Government has added: the promotion of animal welfare; the provision of social housing; and the advancement of science.

others at present fall into Lord Macnaghten's fourth head; the remainder are not at present charitable. All the heads envisaged by this Report and by the Government's response would be subject to the overriding requirement that the organisation in question must provide public benefit.

Lord Macnaghten's four heads are the nearest that there is to a definition in English law at present. The first three heads do not, generally, present too much difficulty. A case falling within any of those heads will be presumed to be for the benefit of the community and therefore charitable, unless the contrary is shown. As will be seen, the fourth head presents greater difficulty but it seems that the courts prefer the vague and undefined approach based on the "equity" or the "mischief" of the Preamble to the Charitable Uses Act 1601, rather than a "stepping-stones" approach based on analogy, when they have to determine the question of whether a trust falling under this head is or is not charitable.[75]

Before each of the four heads is considered, it is necessary first to emphasise the requirement, which is of general application and which was given even greater prominence in the Report from the Strategy Unit, that a charitable trust must have a public character.[76]

## 1. The Public Element in Charity

The fact that charitable trusts have to have a public character does not mean that all public trusts are charitable. This requirement means that a trust is incapable of being charitable in the legal sense unless it is for the benefit of the public, or some section of the public; under the present law, there is an exception in the case of trusts for the relief of poverty.[77] Whether or not the test is satisfied is decided by the court on the evidence,[78] not on the opinion of the settlor.

The Report from the Strategy Unit stated that there is a need to apply the public benefit test more consistently and proposed that all charities falling within the proposed heads should have to demonstrate public benefit, not just as at present at the time of registration but throughout their existence (the Charity Commission would undertake a rolling programme to monitor public benefit, particularly in the case of charities which charged fees for the provision of services). There would no longer, as at present, be a presumption that certain heads are for public benefit. On the other hand, the Report also stated that none of the objects currently recognised as charitable would be excluded. Precisely how all this would work in the case of trusts for the relief of poverty is not specified; it is likely that some of the existing trusts of this type discussed below would struggle to demonstrate sufficient public benefit even at the time when their registration as charities was first sought, never mind at later stages in their existence. Nor is it clear how the new law would actually be formulated and developed in the light of the expressed reluctance of the Report

---

[75] See *Scottish Burial Reform and Cremation Society v. Glasgow City Corporation* [1968] A.C. 138 and *Incorporated Council of Law Reporting for England and Wales v. Att.-Gen.* [1972] Ch. 73, both discussed above.

[76] It is also necessary that the trust is exclusively charitable; see *post*, p. 476.

[77] See *post*, p. 455.

[78] *Re Hummeltenberg* [1923] 1 Ch. 237; *National Anti-Vivisection Society v. I.R.C.* [1948] A.C. 31; *Re Wootton* [1968] 1 W.L.R. 681.

to envisage taking any case to court unless important issues of principle were evident.

## (A) The General Rule

A straightforward illustration of the general rule is *Re Compton*,[79] where a trust for the education of the descendants of three named persons was held not to be a valid charitable trust, because the beneficiaries were defined by reference to a personal relationship and the trust therefore lacked the quality of a public trust; the trust was a family trust and not one for the benefit of a section of the public. Similarly, in *Re Holbourn Aero Components Air Raid Distress Fund*,[80] an emergency fund which had been built up during the Second World War had been used partly for comforts for ex-employees serving in the Forces, and later for employees who had suffered distress from air-raids. It was held that, because of the absence of a public element, no charitable trust had been created and the surplus funds, in respect of which the application had been made to the court, should be returned to the contributors.[81]

But perhaps the most important illustration is to be found in the decision of the House of Lords in *Oppenheim v. Tobacco Securities Trust Co.*,[82] where *Re Compton* was applied to a trust for a much more extensive class of beneficiaries. The trustees were directed to apply funds in providing for the education of children of employees or ex-employees of British American Tobacco or any of its subsidiary or allied companies. The employees numbered over 110,000. A majority of the House of Lords held that, although the group of persons indicated was numerous, the nexus between them was employment by a particular employer and it therefore followed that the trust did not satisfy the test of public benefit which was required to establish it as charitable. The argument that the court should take into account the number of employees was rejected. As Lord Normand said,[83] if there is no public element to be found in the bare nexus of common employment, all attempts to build up the public element out of circumstances which had no necessary relation with it but were adventitious, accidental or variable must be unavailing where the settlor has chosen to define the selected class solely by the attribute of common employment. Putting this more generally, an aggregate of individuals ascertained by reference to some personal tie for example, blood or contract, such as the relations of a particular individual, the members of a particular family or the members of a particular association, does not amount to the public or a section of the public for the purpose of the general rule; a trust for that aggregate of individuals will not, accordingly, rank as legally charitable.[84]

Lord MacDermott dissented, saying[85] that he saw "much difficulty in dividing the qualities or attributes, which may serve to bind human beings into classes, into two mutually exclusive groups, the one involving individual

---

[79] [1945] Ch. 123.

[80] [1946] Ch. 194.

[81] On the basis that they were the members of an unincorporated association (see *ante*, p. 300).

[82] [1951] A.C. 297, in turn applied in *I.R.C. v. Educational Grants Association* [1967] Ch. 993 (up to 85 per cent of the income of an educational trust was paid to children of employees of Metal Box Ltd.; income tax was not recoverable because the income was not being applied only for charitable purposes).

[83] *ibid.* at 310–311.

[84] *Re Scarisbrick* [1951] Ch. 622 at 649, *per* Jenkins L.J.

[85] [1951] A.C. 297 at 317.

status and purely personal, the other disregarding such status and quite impersonal. As a task this seems to me no less baffling and elusive than the problem to which it is directed, namely the determination of what is and what is not a section of the public for the purposes of this branch of the law." Subsequently in *Dingle v. Turner*,[86] Lord Cross was of the same opinion. Moreover, he felt that whether or not the potential beneficiaries of a trust could fairly be said to constitute a section of the public was "a question of degree" and depended on the purpose of the trust. This sort of formulation, however, seems to be no more helpful, perhaps less helpful, in the present state of the law than the old formulation based on the distinction between personal and impersonal relationship.

On the other hand, if the trust is construed in such a way as to grant a mere preference to a limited class, such as employees or relations, the trust will succeed as a charity. This was the case, for example, in *Re Koettgen's Will Trusts*,[87] where a trust was established for the furtherance of the commercial education of British-born persons, with a direction that preference be given to employees of a particular firm. The essential question is whether or not there is anything more than an expression of preference. If the terms of the trust go beyond that and amount to a positive obligation, the trust will not be regarded as charitable because the obligation will vitiate the public character of the trust. Indeed, it is certainly possible to argue on this basis, and has been,[88] that *Re Koettgen's Will Trusts* was wrongly decided. Its validity was doubted both by Lord Radcliffe in *Caffoor v. Commission of Income Tax, Colombo*,[89] where the Privy Council held that the trust in question was no more than a family trust, and by Walton J. in *Re Martin*,[90] where a trust to establish a home for old people, with a right for either or both of the testator's daughters to reside there, was held not to be charitable. But in essence, the question will always come down to one of construction.

A number of major charities carry on part of their activities in foreign countries. In *Re Carapiet's Trusts*,[91] Jacob J. settled a long-standing controversy by holding that the correct approach to institutions operating abroad was as the Charity Commission had stated in 1993:[92] it should first be considered whether they would be regarded as charities if their operations were confined to the United Kingdom; if they would, then they should be presumed also to be charitable even though operating abroad unless it would be contrary to public policy to recognise them. Jacob J. held that the most important authority was *Camille and Henry Dreyfus Foundation v. I.R.C.*,[93] where the Court of Appeal had been invited to overruled the earlier decision in *Re Robinson*,[94] that the purpose of benefiting German soldiers injured in the First World War was charitable and had declined to do so, indicating that the key factor was not where the purpose was carried out but the public policy of the United King-

---

[86] [1972] A.C. 601 at 621.
[87] [1954] Ch. 252.
[88] See, for example, *I.R.C. v. Educational Grants Association* [1967] Ch. 123.
[89] [1961] A.C. 584 at 604. Compare *Re George Drexler Ofrex Foundation Trustees v. I.R.C.* [1966] Ch. 675.
[90] (1977) *The Times*, November 16, 1977.
[91] [2002] W.T.L.R. 989.
[92] In (1993) 1 C.Comm.Dec. 17
[93] [1954] Ch. 672.
[94] [1932] 2 Ch. 122.

dom. Jacob J. also held that in this respect there was no distinction between the different heads mentioned in *Pemsel's* Case.[95]

The normal requirements of public benefit, which of course differ from head to head, therefore apply to activities carried out abroad. This of course means that, where what is being provided abroad are public works or development projects such as roads and irrigation, these will only be charitable "if they are a reasonably direct means to the end of relieving poverty in observable cases". Nor will the courts ignore the probable results of the trust on the community of the country in question, which may of course have a wholly distinct history and social structure. One of the reasons why a trust to bring about the abolition of torture and other inhuman punishments was held not to be charitable in *McGovern v. Attorney-General,*[96] was that the court could not judge the probable effects of the necessary legislation on the local community in question.

On the other hand, foreign charities cannot acquire charitable status in the United Kingdom for the simple reason that the law of charity in the foreign country may be different from the equivalent English law.

## (B) The Poverty Exception

The principle that a trust should have a public element is, at least at present, not of absolutely universal application. There is, as indicated above, one important exception to it. This is that trusts for the relief of poverty have been held to be charitable even though they are not for the benefit of the public or a section of it. The exception may arise where the personal tie is one of blood or one of contract. In the case of blood, there are the so-called "poor relations" cases. The case of contract may be exemplified by a trust for the relief of poverty amongst employees of a particular firm or company.

This particular exception cannot be accounted for by reference to any principle,[97] but it was established by authorities of long standing which were binding on the Court of Appeal and which were reaffirmed by the House of Lords in *Dingle v. Turner.*[98] In that case there was a trust to apply income in paying pensions to poor employees of a company; it was held that the trust was charitable.

The class of persons within the expression "poor relations" is self-evident; however, while the older cases of this type[99] seem to have been approved more or less as a matter of course, some consideration has been given in the more recent cases as to the nature of the relief granted and the size of the class in

---

[95] [1891] A.C. 531 at 583. It had previously been thought that, while the first three heads mentioned in *Pemsel's* Case (the relief of poverty, the advancement of education and the advancement of religion) would be charitable purposes in whatever part of the world they were carried out, purposes within the fourth head of that classification (the advancement of other purposes beneficial to the community) would only be charitable if they were of benefit to the community of the United Kingdom.

[96] [1982] Ch. 321.

[97] It has been tentatively suggested that "the relief of poverty is of so altruistic a character that the public benefit may necessarily be inferred"; see *Re Scarisbrick* [1951] Ch. 622 at 639, *per* Evershed M.R. But this is not the basis of the case law and in any event seems highly debatable. In *Dingle v. Turner* [1972] A.C. 601 it was assumed that the law was anomalous.

[98] [1972] A.C. 601.

[99] See, for example, *Isaac v. Defriez* (1754) Amb. 595; *White v. White* (1802) 7 Ves. 423; *Att.-Gen. v. Price* (1810) 17 Ves. 371.

question. Trusts for such of the testator's relatives as shall be "in needy circumstances" and "in special need" were upheld in, respectively, *Re Scarisbrick*,[1] and *Re Cohen*,[2] while in *Re Segelman*,[3] a gift to "poor and needy"
members of a class of six named relatives and their issue, totalling 26 persons
at the date of the testator's death and likely to increase substantially in the
future, was also upheld.

Cases such as *Dingle v. Turner* and *Gibson v. South American Stores (Gath &
Chaves)*,[4] where a gift to employees of a particular company to whom a poverty
qualification was attached was upheld as a valid charitable gift, illustrate the
contractual tie. The principle also was applied in *Re Young*,[5] to members of a
club and in *Spiller v. Maude*,[6] to members of a society.

It was argued in *Dingle v. Turner* that the tests postulated in *Re Compton*,[7]
and *Oppenheim v. Tobacco Securities Trust*,[8] ought, in principle, to apply to all
charitable trusts and that the "poor relations" cases, the "poor members"
cases and the "poor employees" cases were all anomalous and should be
overruled; alternatively, that if it was not practicable to overrule the "poor
relations" cases because of their antiquity, the same could not be said of the
"poor employees" cases which dated only from 1900.[9] However, it was held
that the "poor members" and "poor employees" decisions were a natural
development of the "poor relations" cases and to draw a distinction between
them would be quite illogical; moreover, although not as old as "poor relations" trusts, "poor employees" trusts had been recognised for many years
and there would be a large number of such trusts in operation today. The
exception will not, however, be extended to other classes of trusts.[10]

It was also decided by the Court of Appeal in *Re Scarisbrick*,[11] — and this did
not appear to have been expressly decided before — that the exception was
not restricted to perpetual or continuing trusts (to which it will normally
apply) but even covered a trust for immediate distribution. Here a gift for poor
members of the class of relations of three children of the testatrix was upheld
as a valid charitable trust, even though the distribution of the property had to
be made within the perpetuity period.

## (C) The Limits of Public Benefit

It is important to notice that, although the general rule is (subject to the
exception just considered) that every charitable trust should have a public
element, it is not essential that everybody should be able to avail himself of its
benefits. As Viscount Simonds said in *I.R.C. v. Baddeley*,[12] there is a distinction

---

[1] [1951] Ch. 622. It was also held in this case that it does not matter that the trust fund can be
distributed to the "poor relations" in such a way as to exhaust the capital.
[2] [1973] 1 W.L.R. 415.
[3] [1996] Ch. 171.
[4] [1950] Ch. 177. See also *Re Coulthurst* [1951] Ch. 661 (officers and ex-officers of bank).
[5] [1955] 1 W.L.R. 1269.
[6] (1881) 32 Ch.D. 158N.
[7] [1945] Ch. 123.
[8] [1951] A.C. 297.
[9] *Re Gosling* [1900] 2 W.R. 300.
[10] *Re Compton* [1945] Ch. 123 (education); *Oppenheim v. Tobacco Securities Trust* [1951] A.C. 297,
*supra* (education); *Davies v. Perpetual Trustee Co.* [1959] A.C. 439 (religion).
[11] [1951] Ch. 622.
[12] [1955] A.C. 572 at 592. The case is considered *post*, p. 469.

"between a form of relief extended to the whole community, yet by its very nature advantageous only to the few and a form of relief accorded to a selected few out of a larger number equally willing and able to take advantage of it".

Thus, to illustrate the first class cited by Viscount Simonds, trusts which will be charitable, a gift for the benefit of New South Wales soldiers returning after the First World War was held by the Privy Council in *Verge v. Somerville*[13] to be valid; so also will a trust for the erection of a sea wall even though this is perhaps of benefit primarily to persons whose houses front the sea. On the other hand, in illustration of Viscount Simonds' second class, trusts which will fail as a charity, a gift to Presbyterians who could claim a particular descent was held by the Privy Council to fail for this reason in *Davies v. Perpetual Trustee Co.*[14] In *I.R.C. v. Baddeley*[15] itself, a trust in favour of the Methodists in West Ham and Leyton was also held by the House of Lords to fail.

## 2. *Lord Macnaghten's Classification*

### (A) Trusts for the Relief of Poverty

The Act of 1601 included among its objects the relief of "the aged, impotent and poor". But, despite the presence of the word "and", it has long been well-settled that the expression should be read disjunctively.[16] This rule was confirmed in *Re Robinson*,[17] where there was a gift to the old over 65 years of a certain district, and in *Re Lewis*,[18] where there was a gift for 20 blind children of another district; both gifts were upheld.

The question was most recently considered in *Joseph Rowntree Memorial Trust Housing Association v. Attorney-General;*[19] Peter Gibson J. confirmed the disjunctive reading but added a significant rider, which had not emerged from the cases previously cited, that in order to be charitable the gift to the aged or the impotent had to have as its purpose the relief of a need attributable to their condition. (It is hoped that this approach will finally scotch the theory that a trust for the relief of "aged peers" or "impotent millionaires" will be charitable;[20] a gift of money to such persons would not relieve a need of theirs as aged or impotent persons.) In the case itself, a charitable housing association wished to build small self-contained dwellings for sale to elderly people on long leases in consideration of a capital payment. It was held that, since the provision of special accommodation relieved a particular need of the elderly, whether poor or not, attributable to their aged condition, the proposed housing schemes were charitable. Peter Gibson J., in reaching this conclusion, applied the reasoning of Lord Wilberforce in *Re Resch's Will Trusts*,[21] where the

---

[13] [1924] A.C. 496.
[14] [1959] A.C. 439.
[15] [1955] A.C. 572.
[16] *Re Fraser* (1883) 22 Ch.D. 827; *Re Elliott* (1910) 102 LT. 528; *Re Glyn* (1950) 66 T.L.R. (Pt. 2) 510; *Re Cottam* [1955] 1 W.L.R. 1299 and the cases cited in the text.
[17] [1951] Ch. 198.
[18] [1955] Ch. 104.
[19] [1983] Ch. 159.
[20] (1955) 71 L.Q.R. 16 (R.E.M.).
[21] [1969] 1 A.C. 514 and see *Re Neal* (1966) 110 Sol. Jo. 549.

House of Lords held charitable a gift to a private hospital which charged substantial fees but was not run for the profit of individuals.

The meaning of "poverty" also requires consideration. It is unnecessary to show destitution; the degree of poverty need not be acute. Accordingly, gifts for such objects as "ladies of limited means"[22] or "decayed actors"[23] and similar purposes are well recognised as being charitable. All that seems to be required is that the individuals in question are in straitened circumstances and are unable to maintain a modest standard of living.[24] But it is essential that all the objects fall within the designation "poor" if a trust for the relief of poverty is to be upheld. If someone who is not poor is able to benefit, the gift will not qualify as a gift for the relief of poverty.

Thus, in Re Gwyon,[25] a fund was directed to be set aside to provide "knickers" (by which was meant a type of short trouser) for the boys of Farnham. The garments were unusual not only in their name but also because there were to be embroidered on the waistband the words "Gwyon's Present". Successful applicants were to be entitled to a new pair of knickers each year provided that on the subsequent application the legend "Gwyon's Present" was still decipherable on the old ones. Whatever may have been the testator's intention, none of these conditions necessarily imported poverty and the trust failed as a charity. Similarly, it was held in Re Sanders' Will Trusts,[26] that a gift for the "working classes" was not a gift for the relief of poverty because this expression did not necessarily indicate poor persons. It is possible, as Harman J. said, and as it has indeed been held,[27] that, if the gift had been made to members of the "working classes" who were aged or widows, then the object of relieving poverty might be implied. But, as Harman J. made plain, in Re Sanders Will Trusts there was nothing of this kind. The members of the working class were not old persons, they were not widows, they were simply men working in the docks and their families; it was therefore impossible to infer any element of poverty. On the other hand, Re Sanders Will Trusts was distinguished in Re Niyazi's Will Trusts,[28] where a trust for a working men's hostel in Famagusta, Cyprus, providing modest accommodation for persons of the lower income group was upheld as charitable, although, in the words of Megarry V.-C., the case was "desperately near the border-line".[29]

Nor is there any decisive definition of the terms "aged" or "impotent". It has been held that people who are not under the age of 50 are aged.[30] But in view of the advance in medical science this conclusion now seems very doubtful; a settlor who wished to specify an age might well be taking a risk today if the age specified were lower than 60. On the other hand, the word

---

[22] Re Gardom [1914] 1 Ch. 662.

[23] Spiller v. Maude (1881) 32 Ch.D. 158N.

[24] See Re Mary Clark Homes [1904] 2 K.B. 645; Re Gardom [1914] 1 Ch. 662; Shaw v. Halifax Corporation [1915] 2 K.B. 170; Re Clarke [1923] 2 Ch. 407; Re De Carteret [1933] Ch. 103. See also Cross (1956) 72 L.Q.R. 182 at 206.

[25] [1930] 1 Ch. 225.

[26] [1954] Ch. 265 (appeal settled; The Times, July 22, 1954).

[27] Re Glyn (1950) 66 T.L.R. (Pt. 2) 510; see also Re Cottam [1955] 1 W.L.R. 1299 (provision of flats for aged).

[28] [1978] 1 W.L.R. 910.

[29] ibid. at 915.

[30] Re Wall (1889) 42 Ch.D. 510. See also Re Payling's Will Trusts [1969] 1 W.L.R. 1595; Re Armitage [1972] Ch. 438.

"impotent", although generously construed, has never been precisely defined; it does however include pesons with a permanent disability[31] and the seriously ill or wounded[32] and also covers the prevention of cruelty to children.[33]

Whatever the words used, it is of course essential to establish that in trusts which fall under this head there is a trust for the relief of poverty in the proper sense of that expression. A trust for poor persons may take effect as a private rather than a charitable trust; the distinction is, as a matter of construction, whether the gift is for the relief of poverty amongst poor people of a particular description or merely a gift to particular poor persons for the purpose of relieving poverty among them. In the former case the trust will be charitable, in the latter it will be private.[34]

A related question involves housing associations which provide housing for the "aged, impotent and poor" and which enjoy charitable status because they are within the preamble to the Act of 1601. It is common to find such associations feeling the need to adopt a particular policy of tenant selection for example, selecting tenants who earn less than the national average wage, so as to preserve their charitable status. Such a policy may not only be inconvenient; it may actually fail if one of the residents is in fact not poor.[35] However, such difficulties now appear to have been alleviated to some extent by the decision in *Joseph Rowntree Memorial Trust Housing Association v. Attorney-General*.[36] It was held that it was not essential that a charitable gift was made solely by way of bounty and so, accordingly, the beneficiaries could be required to contribute to its cost. The fact that the housing schemes concerned made provision for special housing for the elderly on a contractual basis did not therefore prevent the schemes from being charitable. It was also held that the possibility that a beneficiary might profit by an increase in value of the property on a subsequent sale by him did not alter the fact that the trusts were charitable.

**(B) Trusts for the Advancement of Education**
Conventionally, the general rule governing this head is stated to be that the trust must manifest an intention that learning should be imparted, not simply that it should be accumulated. But this may now be a somewhat misleading yardstick, because the tendency in many of the cases is to widen the field of "education" in this context.

The conventional meaning does appear to have been adopted by Harman J. in *Re Shaw*.[37] George Bernard Shaw directed the trustees of his will to use his residuary estate for a number of designated purposes. These included: first, an inquiry into how much time per individual scribe would be saved by substituting for the established English alphabet one containing at least 40 letters; secondly, an inquiry into how many persons were speaking and writing English in the usual form at any moment in the world; thirdly, the ascer-

---

[31] *Re Fraser* (1883) 22 Ch.D. 827; *Re Lewis* [1955] Ch. 104.
[32] *Re Hillier* [1944] 1 All E.R. 486.
[33] *Pemsel's Case* [1891] A.C. 531 at 572; compare *Re Cole* [1958] Ch. 477; *Re Sahal's Will Trusts* [1958] 1 W.L.R. 1243.
[34] *Re Scarisbrick* [1951] Ch. 622 at 650, 651 *per* Jenkins L.J.; *Dingle v. Turner* [1972] A.C. 601 at 617, *per* Lord Cross; *Re Cohen* [1973] 1 W.L.R. 415 at 423, *per* Templeman J.
[35] *Over-Seventies Housing Association v. Westminster L.B.C.* (1974) 230 E.G. 1593.
[36] [1983] Ch. 159. The facts are stated *ante*, p. 457.
[37] [1957] 1 W.L.R. 729 (appeal dismissed by consent on terms that a sum of money should be devoted to these inquiries; [1958] 1 All E.R. 245N).

tainment of the time and labour wasted by the lack of at least 14 unequivocal syllables and an estimate of the loss of income in British and American currency caused thereby; and, fourthly, the employment of a phonetic expert to transliterate the testator's play *Androcles and the Lion* into the proposed new English alphabet. Harman J. held that the trusts were not charitable; they were merely intended to increase public knowledge in the advantages of the proposed alternative alphabet. Consequently, the research and propaganda directed by the testator would merely increase public knowledge in a particular respect, the saving of time and money achievable by the use of the proposed new alphabet; "no element of teaching or education" was combined with this. Harman J. also rejected an argument that the trusts were charitable as being in some way beneficial to the community (within the fourth head of Lord Macnaghten's classification) because it was highly controversial whether the proposals were in fact beneficial.

However, the question of the ambit of "education" was given fresh consideration by Wilberforce J. in *Re Hopkins' Will Trusts*.[38] The testatrix had given part of her residuary estate to "the Francis Bacon Society" to be applied towards finding the "Bacon-Shakespeare Manuscripts". One of the main objects of the society was "to encourage the general study of the evidence of Francis Bacon's authorship of plays commonly ascribed to Shakespeare". The terms of the will were therefore held to mean that the money was to be used to search for manuscripts of plays commonly ascribed to Shakespeare but believed by the testatrix and the society to have been written by Bacon. The judge held that the purposes of search or research for original manuscripts of England's greatest dramatist were within the law's conception of a charitable purpose on two grounds: first, as being for education; and, secondly, as being for other purposes beneficial to the community, within the fourth head of Lord Macnaghten's classification, as a gift for the improvement of this country's literary heritage. He duly considered the dictum of Harman J. in *Re Shaw*, that the increase of knowledge was not in itself a charitable object unless it was combined with teaching or education, but was unwilling to regard this as meaning that the promotion of academic research was not a charitable purpose unless the researchers were engaged in teaching or education in the conventional sense. He concluded (and many would agree) that the term "education" should be used in a wide sense and certainly extended beyond teaching.[39] Wilberforce J. valuably also spelt out the requirements that "research" must satisfy in order to be charitable, although he did not regard this formulation as exhaustive: first, it must be of educational value to the researcher; or, secondly, it must be so directed so as to produce something which will pass into the store of educational material; or, thirdly, it must improve the sum of communicable knowledge in an area which may be covered by education, which in this last context extends to the formation of literary taste and appreciation.[40]

This decision can be said to be part of a trend which has broadened the field

---

[38] [1965] Ch. 669. See also *Re Shakespeare Memorial Trust* [1923] 2 Ch. 398 (erection and endowment of a Shakespeare Memorial National Theatre with the object of performing Shakespeare's plays, reviving English classical drama and stimulating the art of acting held to be a good charitable trust).

[39] *ibid.* at 680.

[40] *ibid.*

of "education", a trend from which Re Shaw is arguably an aberration. Among the many cases which demonstrate how widely the idea of education has been extended,[41] in Re Dupree's Deed Trusts,[42] a trust for the encouragement of chess playing among the boys and youths of Portsmouth was upheld as charitable. In Re Delius,[43] the wife of the composer Delius gave her residuary estate for the advancement of her late husband's musical work by means of gramophone recordings, publication of his works and financing of public performances of his work; it was held that the purpose of the trust was to spread the knowledge and appreciation of Delius' work throughout the world and constituted an effective educational charity.[44] More conventionally, the promotion of "art" has also been held to be charitable.[45] But perhaps one of the most striking, if not startling, cases in which education was given an extremely and perhaps unjustifiably wide connotation was Re Shaw's Will Trusts,[46] where the testatrix, who was the wife of George Bernard Shaw and (it is necessary to add) herself of Irish origin, bequeathed the residue of her estate upon trusts for, among other things, the teaching, promotion and encouragement in Ireland of self-control, elocution, oratory, deportment, the arts of personal contact, of social intercourse and the other arts of public and private life. It was held that these somewhat eccentric trusts were wholly educational in character and constituted valid charitable trusts. Much less controversial was Re South Place Ethical Society,[47] where it was held that the cultivation of a rational religious sentiment was for the advancement of education because a rational sentiment could only be cultivated by educational methods.

As might be expected, trusts for the establishment and support of professorships and lectureships are educational in character,[48] but it should also be noticed that satellite purposes such as increasing the stipends of university teachers and fellows of colleges will also be upheld.[49] The same principles apply to schools,[50] colleges and universities,[51] and learned societies and institutions.[52]

---

[41] See also Re Mellody [1918] 1 Ch. 228 (annual school treat); Re Cranstoun [1932] 1 Ch. 537 (preservation of ancient buildings); Re Spence [1938] Ch. 96 (collection of arms and antiques); Re Webber [1954] 1 W.L.R. 1500 (Boy Scouts); Re Levien [1955] 1 W.L.R. 964 (raising musical standards); Re Koettgen's Will Trusts [1954] Ch. 252 (commercial education); Royal Choral Society v. I.R.C. (1943) 112 L.J.K.B. 648 (choral society); Re Royce [1940] Ch. 514 (church choir).

[42] [1945] Ch. 16.

[43] [1957] Ch. 299.

[44] It seems rather curious that it was found necessary to point out that the fact that pleasure was an incident of that appreciation or that the effect of the trust was to enhance the reputation of Delius did not prevent this result.

[45] Re The Town and Country Planning Act 1947 [1951] Ch. 132. But "artistic" is too vague to be charitable; see Associated Artists v. I.R.C. [1956] 1 W.L.R. 752.

[46] [1952] Ch. 163.

[47] [1980] 1 W.L.R. 1565. For other aspects of the case see post, pp. 464, 481.

[48] Att.-Gen. v. Margaret and Regius Professors at Cambridge (1682) 1 Vern. 55.

[49] Case of Christ's College, Cambridge (1751) 1 W.B.I. 90.

[50] See The Abbey Malvern Wells v. Ministry of Local Government and Planning [1951] Ch. 728, where a girls' school was carried on by a private company but under a trust deed all dividends were applied for school purposes. The school was held charitable. Danckwerts J. said (at 737) that all schools of learning are treated as charitable unless they exist purely as profit-making ventures. Compare Re Girls Public Day School Trust [1951] Ch. 400 where the school in question was not charitable because shareholders were beneficially interested. See also post, p. 468.

[51] Case of Christ's College, Cambridge (1751) 1 W.B.I. 90.

[52] For example, the Royal College of Surgeons: see Royal College of Surgeons v. National Provincial Bank [1952] A.C. 631.

It was also held in *Incorporated Council of Law Reporting for England and Wales v. Attorney-General*,[53] that the Council was an educational charity;[54] the preparation of law reports was for the advancement of education because their purpose was to record accurately the development and application of judge-made law and thereby disseminate knowledge of that law. The law, it was held by the Court of Appeal, was properly to be regarded as a science and therefore books which were produced for the purpose of enabling it to be studied were published for the advancement of education. It was also held that the fact that the reports were used by the legal profession for the purpose of earning fees did not make the purposes non-charitable. It may be observed that, despite the fact that the Council was carrying on a business, its profits could only be applied in the pursuit of the Council's objects; if the profits could have enured for the benefit of its individual members, it would not have achieved charitable status.[55]

Another case which may be thought to have given an equally robust interpretation to educational charity is *London Hospital Medical College v. I.R.C.*,[56] which involved the students' union of the London Hospital. The union was under the control of the medical college, an educational charity, and its objects were to "promote social, cultural and athletic activities amongst the members and to add to the comfort and enjoyment of the students". The question was whether the predominant object of the union was the furtherance of the purposes of the medical college as a school of learning (in which case it was charitable) or whether its objects were the private and personal benefit of those students who were members of the union (in which case it would not be).[57] Brightman J. held that it had no *raison d'être* except to further the educational purposes of the medical college and it was accordingly charitable. He said that what it did and was intended to do was to assist the teaching of medicine by providing those physical, cultural and social outlets which were needed, or at any rate highly desirable, if the art of teaching was to be efficiently performed at the College.[58]

But, although, generally speaking, education has been regarded as a conception of some width for the purposes of charity, there are limits beyond which the courts will not go. It is in the end a question of degree and it might be argued that the alphabet trust in *Re Shaw* fell on the wrong side of the line. But a case where the trusts were clearly out of order was *Re Pinion*.[59] A testator gave his studio and pictures, one of which he attributed to Lely and some of

---

[53] [1972] Ch. 73.
[54] Russell L.J. dissented, so far as the educational aspect was concerned, but all the members of the Court of Appeal agreed that it was also charitable as being for the benefit of the community within the fourth head of Lord Macnaghten's classification: see *post*, p. 467.
[55] Compare the cases cited *ante*, fn. 50.
[56] [1976] 1 W.L.R. 613; compare *Re Bushnell* [1975] 1 W.L.R. 1596 in which a trust for the advancement of "socialised medicine" was held not to be educational; see *post*, p. 475. In certain cases trusts for sport may be upheld as educational trusts; see *post*, p. 471.
[57] This was the result in *I.R.C. v. City of Glasgow Police Athletic Association* [1953] A.C. 380, discussed *post*, p. 472.
[58] *London Hospital Medical College v. I.R.C.* [1976] 1 W.L.R. 613 at 623, 624. It was apparently thought relevant that the London Hospital is on a site adjoining the Whitechapel and Commercial Roads in the East End of London; this was described as a "somewhat remote part of London" *ibid.* at 621.
[59] [1965] Ch. 85.

which were painted by himself, his antique furniture, silver, china and other things to be offered to the National Trust to be kept intact in the studio and maintained as a collection. In the event that the National Trust declined the trust, as in fact it did, he authorised the appointment of trustees to carry it out instead. It was acknowledged that a gift to found a public museum may be assumed to be charitable if no one questions that fact. But if the utility of the gift was brought into question, as it was here, it was essential to know something of the quality of the exhibits and for this purpose, expert evidence was admissible to assist the court in judging the educational value of the gift.[60] The evidence was to the effect that the collection was of low quality; the Lely was bogus and the testator's own paintings were bad. Among the furniture, there were some genuine English and Continental pieces of the seventeenth and eighteenth centuries which might have been acceptable as a gift to a minor provincial museum. But, according to the terms of the will, everything had to be exhibited together with the result that the good things would be stifled by the large number of absolutely valueless pictures and objects. Harman L.J. could conceive of no useful purpose in "foisting on the public this mass of junk",[61] and so the Court of Appeal, reversing Wilberforce J., held that the trust had neither public utility nor educational value and therefore failed as a charity.

It might be thought to be an elementary proposition that, if an institution is devoted to educational purposes (or indeed any other specific charitable purposes), its funds can only be applied to those purposes. Nevertheless the question arose for decision in *Baldry v. Feintuck*.[62] In this case the University of Sussex Students Union, which was conceded in argument[63] to be an educational charity, voted to authorise payments to "War on Want", a charitable but non-educational organisation, and to a campaign of protest against the Government's policy of ending the supply of free milk to schoolchildren, a political and therefore non-charitable purpose.[64] Brightman J. held that the moneys could not be applied for such purposes. A similar decision was reached in *Webb v. O'Doherty*,[65] where expenditure of student union funds on a campaign to end the First Gulf War was restrained.

One of the current more controversial questions in the field of education concerns the charitable status of independent schools;[66] there is no doubt whatever that many of them are registered charities. In practice, the vast majority of them ensure the continuance of their charitable status by utilising their income to provide free places and by enabling facilities such as playing fields to be utilised by their local community. The Report from the Strategy Unit envisaged this sort of practice being examined much more closely by proposing that the Charity Commission should undertake a rolling programme to monitor public benefit; independent schools are of course the classic example of charities which charge fees for the provision of services.

---

[60] For another example of expert evidence being admitted, see *Gilmour v. Coats* [1949] A.C. 426 and see *post*, p. 466.
[61] [1965] Ch. 85 at 107.
[62] [1972] 1 W.L.R. 552.
[63] On the basis of *London Hospital Medical College v. I.R.C.* [1976] 1 W.L.R. 613 at 624.
[64] See *post*, p. 474.
[65] (1991) *The Times*, February 11, 1991.
[66] See *ante*, p. 461.

## (C) Trusts for the Advancement of Religion

In equity there is a considerable measure of tolerance. This was recognised over almost 150 years ago in *Thornton v. Howe*,[67] where Romilly M.R. recognised as charitable a trust for the publication of the work of Joanna Southcott even though he evidently thought her doctrines to be ridiculous. This decision indicates that the advancement of all religions which are "not subversive of all morality"[68] will be held to be charitable. There is not actually a great deal of authority on non-Christian religions[69] but there seems no reason why all of them should not be recognised. Thus far the courts appear to have taken account only of monotheistic religion; in *Yeap Cheah Neo v. Ong Cheng Neo*,[70] the Privy Council held that a trust requiring ancestor worship was not charitable. However, this case is not actually decisive and could certainly be distinguished on the ground that the required religious observances were not for the public benefit, merely for the alleged advantage of the deceased and his family. The Report from the Strategy Unit confirms the general view of the commentators that the time has come to recognise formally the major religions of the world, whatever their forms. On the other hand, some of the "fringe" religious organisations which have increasingly been coming into existence[71] are so fanciful or freakish that charitable status can justifiably be denied to them on the basis that they lacking public benefit.

On the other hand, a gift for rationalist purposes designed to demonstrate that religious belief is erroneous clearly does not fall within the ambit of a trust for the advancement of religion.[72] Similarly, gifts for ethical or moral societies not founded on belief in a deity are not for the advancement of religion. But such gifts may nevertheless be held to be charitable on other grounds. This question arose in *Re South Place Ethical Society*,[73] which was established for the study and dissemination of "ethical principles" and for the cultivation of a rational religious sentiment eschewing all supernatural belief. "Ethical principles" were described by Dillon J. as belief in the excellence of truth, love and beauty, but not belief in anything supernatural. He held that the Society was not founded for the advancement of religion because "religion is concerned

---

[67] (1862) 31 Beav. 14.

[68] *ibid.* at 20. This principle was applied by Plowman J. in *Re Watson* [1973] 1 W.L.R. 1472 in upholding a trust for the publication and distribution of religious writings of no intrinsic merit but which displayed a religious tendency, and by Walton J. in *Holmes v. Att.-Gen.* [1981] Ch.Com.Rep. 10 in upholding a trust for the Exclusive Brethren. The correctness of the statement of principle of Romilly M.R. in *Thornton v. Howe* however still remains open to review by the court. See also *Bowman v. Secular Society* [1917] A.C. 406.

[69] But see *Straus v. Goldsmid* (1837) 8 Sim. 614 (trust for practice of Jewish religion valid); *Neville Estates v. Madden* [1962] Ch. 832 (trust for Catford synagogue valid); *Dawkins v. Gown Suppliers (PSA)* (1993) *The Times*, February 4, 1993 (Rastafarians).

[70] (1875) L.R. 381. See also *Re Hummeltenberg* [1923] 1 Ch. 237 (gift to college for training spiritualistic mediums); *Re Price* [1943] Ch. 422 (gift to the "Anthroposophical Society"). Neither of the cases fell within trusts for the advancement of religion and could only be considered under the fourth head of Lord Macnaghten's classification. The former was held invalid, the latter valid. On the other hand, in *Funnell v. Stewart* [1996] 1 W.L.R. 288, a gift to a group which engaged in faith healing but also held religious services some of which were open to the public was held to be charitable on the basis that the religious element contained sufficient public benefit.

[71] The Unification Church (The "Moonies") has been registered as a Charity (Annual Report 1982, paras 36–38).

[72] *Bowman v. Secular Society* [1917] A.C. 406.

[73] [1981] 1 W.L.R. 1565.

with man's relations with God, and ethics are concerned with man's relations with man".[74] However, the objects of the Society were upheld as charitable on other grounds: first, because they were for the mental and moral improvement of man and were therefore beneficial to the community within the fourth head of Lord Macnaghten's classification;[75] and, secondly, because they were for the advancement of education.[76]

Quite apart from gifts for the advancement of a religion or a religious sect as such, a number of satellite purposes have been recognised as charitable under this head, notably gifts for mission work. Thus in *Re Moon's Will Trusts*,[77] a bequest was made for "mission work". This expression was held on the evidence to connote "Christian mission work" which was held to be charitable. Similarly, trusts for the maintenance and repair of a church, a stained glass window,[78] or a vault[79] within a church have been held to be charitable; this will also apply to the churchyard and burial ground even if restricted to a particular religious sect[80] and also to the graves in it, provided that the object of the gift is the maintenance of all the graves.[81] Indeed, even cremation has also been held to be a charitable purpose.[82]

It is essential that the purpose of a trust should be exclusively charitable, a rule of general application subject to the Charitable Trusts (Validation) Act 1954.[83] In this context, therefore, the purpose of the trust should be exclusively religious. A draftsman may easily quite unwittingly say far too much, or just a word or two too much, in the trust instrument. Certainly the cases on the question of whether a trust is exclusively religious are difficult and present several fine distinctions. Gifts are normally made to a person holding a religious office, such as a bishop; the additional words that may permissibly be used to create a valid charitable trust appear to fall into two groups.

First, the words may confer an absolute discretion on the donee. In *Re Garrard*,[84] a gift was made "to the vicar and churchwardens of Kingston to be applied by them in such manner as they shall in their sole discretion think fit". Similarly, in *Re Rumball*,[85] a gift was made "to the bishop for the time being of the Windward Islands to be applied by him as he thinks fit in his diocese". In

---

[74] *ibid.* at 571. It was noted (at 573) that Buddhism was accepted as a religion although there was no belief in a god, but that question was not explored further.

[75] See *post*, p. 481.

[76] See *ante*, p. 459.

[77] [1948] 1 All E.R. 300.

[78] *Re King* [1923] 1 Ch. 243. See also *Re Royce* [1940] Ch. 514.

[79] *Hoare v. Osborne* (1886) L.R. 1 Eq. 585.

[80] *Re Manser* [1905] 1 Ch. 68 (Society of Friends).

[81] *Re Pardoe* [1906] 2 Ch. 184; in this case a gift for a peal of bells on the anniversary of the restoration of the monarchy also held to be charitable but this is questionable. Compare Brunyate (1946) 61 L.Q.R. 268, 274; *Re Eighmie* [1935] Ch. 524 (keeping in repair burial ground and monument to testator's late husband) and see *ante*, p. 86.

[82] *Scottish Burial Reform and Cremation Society v. Glasgow Corporation* [1968] A.C. 138.

[83] See *post*, p. 479.

[84] [1907] 1 Ch. 382.

[85] [1956] Ch. 105. The judgment of Jenkins L.J. is a notable exposition of the law.

both cases, as in several others[86] where an absolute discretion was conferred, the gift was upheld as charitable. The reason was that the gift was made to a person by his official name whose official status required charitable duties to be performed. Accordingly, the gift was assumed to be made for the charitable purposes inherent in that official status (this principle which arises *virtute officii* applies not merely to religious persons but to the holders of other offices).

Secondly, the words used may confine the object of the gift within the ambit of the donee's religious function. For example, in *Re Eastes*,[87] a gift "to the vicar and churchwardens, to be used by them for any purpose in connection with the Church which they shall select" was held to be charitable. But if the donor goes on to invite the donee to take into account the social as well as the religious functions of his office, the gift will fail; this is a respect in which the donor may unconsciously say too much. This apparent principle is illustrated by the leading case of *Dunne v. Byrne*,[88] where a gift was made to the Roman Catholic Archbishop of Brisbane and his successors to be used as they "may judge most conducive to the good of religion in the diocese". The words in inverted commas were held by the Privy Council to be too wide and the gift failed. Perhaps the most notorious words to induce fatality are "parish work"; a gift failed for this reason in the well known decision of the House of Lords in *Farley v. Westminster Bank*.[89]

Despite the attempts which have been made to rationalise some of the case law, it must be noted that these cases are not at all easy to reconcile and depend on an extremely close reading of the gift or trust in question. At times recognising the distinction between any two cases decided differently requires hair-splitting to an extent which frankly seems quite excessive.[90]

Like all charitable trusts other than trusts for the relief of poverty, a trust for the advancement of religion must be for the benefit of the public. Although it can be difficult to assess public benefit in a religious trust, the test nevertheless has to be satisfied. Thus, in the controversial decision in *Gilmour v. Coats*,[91] the trust fund was to be applied for the purposes of a Carmelite convent. The

---

[86] See *Re Simson* [1946] Ch. 299 ("to the Vicar of St. Luke's Ramsgate, to be used for work in the parish"; valid). Compare *Farley v. Westminster Bank* [1939] A.C. 430 ("for parish work"; bad) *Re Flinn* [1948] Ch. 241 (to the Archbishop of Westminster Cathedral to be used by him "for such purposes as he shall in his absolute discretion think fit"; valid). See also *Re Norman* [1947] Ch. 349 (to the editors of a missionary periodical who were also trustees of a missionary church, to be applied "for such objects as they may think fit"; valid).

[87] [1948] Ch. 257. See also *Re Bain* [1930] 1 Ch. 224 (to a vicar "for such objects connected with the church as he shall think fit") *Re Norton's Will Trusts* [1948] 2 All E.R. 842 ("for the benefit of the parish"). Compare *Farley v. Westminster Bank* [1939] A.C. 430.

[88] [1912] A.C. 407.

[89] [1939] A.C. 430. The words "parochial institutions or purposes" were also fatal in *Re Stratton* [1931] 1 Ch. 197.

[90] See cases cited *ante*, fnn. 86, 87.

[91] [1949] A.C. 426. Likewise see *Cocks v. Manners* (1871) L.R. 12 Eq. 574 (enclosed Roman Catholic convent); *Hoare v. Hoare* (1886) 56 L.T. 147 (private chapel); *Re Joy* (1889) 60 L.T. 175 (to suppress cruelty to animals by prayer); *Re Warre's Will Trusts* [1953] 1 W.L.R. 725 (retreat house but this case seems to have been wrongly decided; retreatants do mix in the world since they go into retreat only for a few days' contemplation and prayer). Compare *Neville Estates v. Madden* [1962] Ch. 832 discussed in the text and *Re Banfield* [1968] 1 W.L.R. 846, where the gift was to a religious community ("Pilsdon Community House") and was held to be a charitable trust because of its primarily religious character and also because it was for the general public benefit in providing a temporary home of rest for those who needed it.

convent comprised an association of strictly cloistered and purely contemplative nuns who did not engage in any activities for the benefit of people outside the convent. The House of Lords held, first, that the benefit of intercessory prayer could not be proved in law and, secondly, that the element of edification was too vague and intangible. It might be thought that far too stringent a test of public benefit was applied in this case. However, whether this is so or not, this case is distinguishable from cases such as *Neville Estates v. Madden*,[92] which concerned a synagogue in Catford which was not open to the public as of right. Cross J. nevertheless held that a trust in favour of the synagogue was charitable; the distinction was that the enclosed nuns lived apart from the world whereas the members of the synagogue lived in the world and a public benefit accrued as a result of their attendance at a place of religious worship.

Rather different considerations have been applied to trusts for the saying of masses for the dead.[93] In *Re Caus*,[94] Luxmoore J. held that a gift for such purposes was charitable. There was no provision in the testator's will that the masses should be said in public and the judge did not distinguish between masses said in public and those said in private; indeed he appeared to indicate that a gift for masses was in all cases charitable. This appeared erroneous in the light of *Gilmour v. Coats*, something which was duly confirmed in *Re Hetherington (deceased)*,[95] where a gift of £2,000 to the Roman Catholic Bishop of Westminster for "masses for the repose of the souls of my husband and my parents and my sisters and also myself when I die" was held to be charitable only on the grounds that sufficient public benefit was conferred by the public celebration of a religious rite and that the provision of stipends for the celebrants endowed the priesthood. It does not, however, seem likely that the latter reason would be sufficient to cause a gift for masses to be said in private to be charitable. Such trusts can however take effect as non-charitable purpose trusts.[96]

## (D) Trusts for Other Purposes Beneficial to the Community

This is the residuary class of Lord Macnaghten's classification in *Pemsel's* Case. It has been seen that the modern trend appears to be to look to the "equity" or the "mischief" of the preamble to the Statute of Charitable Uses 1601 in order to decide whether a given purpose falls within it, rather than to rely on the different approach based on analogy.[97] The class certainly presents a most variegated collection of decisions; what follows therefore does not profess to be an exhaustive account but merely an illustration of a number of the purposes which have been allowed admission into this head of charitable trusts.

---

[92] [1962] Ch. 832 and see *Holmes v. Att.-Gen.* (1981) Ch. Com. Rep. 10 (Exclusive Brethren).
[93] It is established that a gift for masses is not void as being for superstitious uses; *Bourne v. Keane* [1919] A.C. 815. The question remains however whether it is charitable.
[94] [1934] Ch. 162.
[95] [1990] Ch. 1.
[96] See *ante*, p. 84.
[97] See, for example, *Scottish Burial Reform and Cremation Society v. Glasgow City Corporation* [1968] A.C. 138; *Incorporated Council of Law Reporting for England and Wales v. Att.-Gen.* [1972] Ch. 73; see *ante*, p. 462.

## (1) Animals

It is clearly established that a trust for the protection of animals generally is a valid charitable trust.[98] It has been held that this is the case because it benefits humanity by promoting morality and curbing an inborn tendency to cruelty[99] — -a somewhat surprising process of reasoning even in an animal-loving country. But, however surprising, it indicates that the reason for the recognition of these trusts is that they promote the moral or spiritual welfare of the community (in contrast, the basis of most of the other examples of Lord Macnaghten's fourth head is "public utility").[1]

In contrast, the decision in *Re Grove-Grady*,[2] establishes that, if a donor establishes a trust to provide a sanctuary for all kinds of animals from human molestation with no safeguards against the destruction of the weaker animals by the stronger, the trust is not charitable. As Lord Hanworth M.R. pointed out,[3] the only characteristic of the trust was that the sanctuary was to be free from molestation by man, while all the fauna within it were to be free to molest and harry one another. Such a purpose did not afford any advantage to animals or any protection from cruelty to animals nor did it afford any elevating lesson to mankind.[4]

Further, in *National Anti-Vivisection Society v. I.R.C.*,[5] the House of Lords established the principle that a trust to abolish vivisection is not charitable for two reasons: first, that the advantages accruing from the abolition of vivisection did not equal those derived from its retention; and, secondly,[6] that anti-vivisection could not be achieved except by legislation and so the law could not stultify itself by holding that it was for the public benefit that the law itself should be changed.

Finally, it should be noted that, although an animal hospital is *prima facie* charitable,[7] it will not be if it is carried on for private profit as a profession, occupation or trade.[8]

## (2) Recreational trusts

The Recreational Charities Act 1958, which came into force on March 3, 1958, regulates recreational trusts. The Act was passed because of the highly

---

[98] *Re Wedgwood* [1915] 1 Ch. 113 (secret trust for protection and benefit of animals).

[99] *Re Wedgwood* [1915] 1 Ch. 113 at 117, *per* Lord Cozens-Hardy M.R.; *Re Moss* [1949] 1 All E.R. 415 at 497–498, *per* Romer J. (cats and kittens). Compare earlier cases: *London University v. Yarrow* (1857) 1 De G. & J. 72 (animal hospital) and *Re Douglas* (1887) 35 Ch.D. 472 (Home for Lost Dogs), where the court emphasised public utility but this is not the modern trend. See *ante*, p. 84.

[1] For other examples of "moral or spiritual improvement" see *Re Price* [1943] Ch. 422 (gift to the "Anthroposophical Society"); *Re South Place Ethical Society* [1980] 1 W.L.R. 1565 (society for the study and dissemination of "ethical principles" and the cultivation of a rational religious sentiment; see *ante*, p. 464).

[2] [1929] 1 Ch. 557, compromised on appeal *sub nom. Att.-Gen. v. Plowden* [1931] W.N. 89.

[3] [1929] 1 Ch. 557 at 573–574.

[4] This decision of course re-emphasises the importance of careful drafting of the trust instrument so that the "public benefit" requirement is satisfied. There is no doubt that a competently drawn trust for the preservation of wild life, taking due account of public benefit, will be charitable.

[5] [1948] A.C. 31, reversing *Re Foveaux* [1895] 2 Ch. 501. See also *Re Jenkins's Will Trusts* [1966] Ch. 249 (gift to the British Union for the Abolition of Vivisection).

[6] Adopting *Tyssen on Charitable Bequests* (1st ed., 1898), p. 176. See also *Bowman v. Secular Society* [1917] A.C. 406 at 442, *per* Lord Parker (political purposes) and see *post*, p. 474.

[7] *London University v. Yarrow* (1857) 1 De G. & J. 72.

[8] See *Re Satterthwaite's Will Trusts* [1966] 1 W.L.R. 277 at 284, *per* Russell L.J.

inconvenient decision of the House of Lords in *I.R.C. v. Baddeley*,[9] which concerned certain trusts "for the promotion of the moral, social and physical well-being of persons resident in West Ham and Leyton who for the time being are members or likely to become members of the Methodist Church by the provision of facilities for moral, social and physical training and recreation". It was held, by a majority, that the trusts failed because they were expressed in language so vague as to permit the property to be used for purposes which the law did not recognise as charitable and also because they did not satisfy the necessary test of public benefit. This case produced a situation where legislation of some kind was essential because, as a result of the decision, it appeared that there might be grave doubts as to the charitable status of many organisations and trusts, including women's institutes, boys' clubs, miners' welfare trusts and village halls, which had for a very long time been assumed to enjoy charitable status. The Recreational Charities Act 1958 was therefore enacted extremely promptly.

The Act provides that it shall be, and shall be deemed always to have been, charitable to provide, or assist in providing, facilities for recreation or other leisure-time occupations if the facilities are provided in the interest of social welfare.[10] This is subject to the overriding proviso that the trust will not be charitable unless it is for the public benefit.[11] Further, the requirement that facilities must be provided in the interest of social welfare is not satisfied unless: first, they are provided with the object of improving the conditions of life for the persons for whom the facilities are primarily intended; [12] and, secondly, either those persons have need of such facilities by reason of their youth, age, infirmity or disablement, poverty or social and economic circumstances,[13] or the facilities are to be available to the members or female members of the public at large.[14]

The composition of this part of the Recreational Charities Act 1958 is somewhat curious. In particular, the two final ingredients are alternative to one another. Accordingly, it appears that a recreational trust in favour of a limited class of the public will be within the Act if the beneficiaries are youthful, aged, infirm, disabled, or their "social and economic circumstances" are such that they have need of the facilities provided. But if the beneficiaries do not fall into these prescribed classes, the facilities must be available to the whole of the public and a trust in favour of a limited class will fail. There may well be a case for confining the objectives of the Act in this way. However, it is a little unfortunate that the position was not formulated with more precision.

The effect of these provisions, in particular the terms "social welfare" and "conditions of life") was considered by the Court of Appeal in *I.R.C. v. McMullen*,[15] which concerned the Football Association Youth Trust. The majority held, among other things, that the recreational facilities provided were primarily intended for pupils in schools and universities but that they

---

[9] [1955] A.C. 572.
[10] s.1.(1). The expression "social welfare" is used in the Local Government Finance Act 1988.
[11] s.1(1) proviso.
[12] s.1(2)(a).
[13] s.1(2)(b)(i).
[14] s.1(2)(b)(ii).
[15] [1979] 1 W.L.R. 130; for another aspect of the decision and the facts, see *post*, p. 472. See also Warburton [1980] Conv. 173.

were not provided with the object of improving the conditions of life of such pupils; they were instead provided for those of them who were persuaded to, or did, play football or some other game or sport irrespective of their conditions of life. Consequently, the trusts did not fall within the Recreational Charities Act 1958. Bridge L.J. dissented on the ground that the provision of recreational facilities for pupils unquestionably improved the pupils' conditions of life and met a social need of youth. This decision was reversed by the House of Lords on other grounds,[16] so the question of the effect of the Act did not fall to be considered. However, as a matter of statutory interpretation, the view of Bridge L.J. appeared highly persuasive and has now duly been approved by the House of Lords in *Guild v. I.R.C.*[17] This case concerned a gift of residue "to the town council of North Berwick for the use in connection with the sports centre in North Berwick or some similar purpose in connection with sport". This gift was held to fall within the Act on the grounds that "persons in all walks of life and all kinds of social circumstances may have their condition of life improved by the provision of recreational facilities of suitable character" and the facilities of the centre would have this effect.

Subject to the facilities being provided in the interests of social welfare, the Recreational Charities Act 1958 is specifically applied, in particular, to the "provision of facilities at village halls, community centres and women's institutes and to the provision and maintenance of grounds and buildings to be used for purposes of recreation or leisure-time occupation and extends to the provision of facilities for those purposes by the organising of any activity".[18] But these are simply well-known examples of recreational charities so this provision does not affect the generality of the statutory powers.

Miners' welfare trusts are specially provided for;[19] such trusts as had been declared before December 17, 1957[20] were validated retrospectively, although there were certain savings as to past transactions.[21] The provision so made seems entirely retrospective; consequently, all new miners' welfare trusts must fall within the statutory provisions already discussed.[22]

The Act left untouched the general law as to the meaning of charity.[23] It also seems to have left untouched the principle that charitable trusts must be for the public benefit which also came under consideration in *I.R.C. v. Baddeley*. Judging from the speech of Viscount Simonds,[24] it certainly seemed that the membership, whether actual or potential, of the Methodist Church, at least in a defined area, did not amount to a class sufficient to satisfy the test of public benefit.[25] If the view of Viscount Simonds prevails, trusts such as those which the House of Lords was actually considering in *I.R.C. v. Baddeley* would still fail. It was of course the other aspect of the decision, that the trusts were too

---

[16] [1981] A.C. 1; see *post*, p. 472.
[17] [1992] 2 A.C. 310 (a Scottish Appeal but the English definition of charity is incorporated into Scots law for tax purposes).
[18] s.1(3).
[19] s.2.
[20] This was the date of the first reading of the Bill in the House of Lords.
[21] s.3(2), (3), (4), (5).
[22] s.1.
[23] s.3(1).
[24] [1955] A.C. 572 at 589–593.
[25] Lord Somervell seemed to agree with Lord Simonds; Lord Reid, who dissented, took a different view. Lord Porter and Lord Tucker expressed no opinion on this point.

uncertain, which aroused apprehension among the women's institutes and other bodies which the Recreational Charities Act 1958 was designed to cure. This limited objective was probably successfully achieved, even though the material provisions are somewhat clumsily and ambiguously expressed. It was thought at the time that the Act would be difficult to apply and probably create more difficulties than it solved[26]; however, it has only occasionally had to be considered in decisions which have been reported.[27]

### (3) National and local defence
All trusts which promote the armed forces of the Crown are charitable[28] and this rule will apply even if the means of promotion are indirect.[29] Similarly, a trust for the benefit of the Mercantile Marine, which is not strictly part of the armed forces of the Crown, is charitable.[30] A more general purpose, that of promoting the defence of the United Kingdom from the attack of hostile aircraft, has also been upheld as charitable.[31]

The same applies to more mundane, but equally important, domestic protection. Thus in *Re Wokingham Fire Brigade Trusts*,[32] Danckwerts J. held that the provision and maintenance of a public fire brigade was a charitable purpose because it was designed to prevent damage to property and loss of life. The promotion of the efficiency of the police is also self-evidently charitable. This was stated in *I.R.C. v. City of Glasgow Police Athletic Association*,[33] but in that case the question was actually whether the association itself was charitable and it was held not to be because it was simply a sports club for the benefit of its members.

### (4) Trusts for sport
It appears to be settled that a gift for the promotion of a specific sport is not as such charitable. Accordingly, in *Re Nottage*,[34] where a trust was established to provide annually a cup for the most successful yacht of the season, with the expressed object of encouraging the sport of yacht racing, the Court of Appeal held that this was a gift for the encouragement of a mere sport which, although it might be beneficial to the public, was not charitable.[35] However, trusts for this purpose which are drawn so as to fall within the Recreational Charities

---

[26] See Maurice (1959) 23 Conv. (N.S.) 15.
[27] See *Wynn v. Skegness U.D.C.* [1967] 1 W.L.R. 52 where a seaside holiday home for Derbyshire miners was assumed to fall within the 1958 Act as a recreational charity; *I.R.C. v. McMullen* [1979] 1 W.L.R. 130, reversed on other grounds [1981] A.C. 1, see *post*, p. 472.
[28] *Re Stratheden and Campbell* [1894] 3 Ch. 265 (benefit of volunteer corps); *Re Stephens* (1892) 8 T.L.R. 792 (for teaching shooting); *Re Barker* (1909) 25 T.L.R. 753 (for prizes to be competed for by cadets).
[29] *Re Good* [1905] 2 Ch. 60 (providing a library for the officers' mess and providing plates for the mess); *Re Donald* [1909] 2 Ch. 410 (for the mess of the regiment and the poor of the regiment); *Re Gray* [1925] Ch. 362 (regimental fund for the promotion of sport).
[30] *Re Corbyn* [1941] Ch. 400.
[31] *Re Driffill* [1950] Ch. 92.
[32] [1951] Ch. 373.
[33] [1953] A.C. 380 at 391.
[34] [1895] 2 Ch. 649.
[35] See also to the same effect *Re Clifford* (1911) 106 L.T. 14 (angling); *Re Patten* [1929] 2 Ch. 276 at 289, 290 (cricket); *Re King* [1931] W.N. 232 (general sport); *I.R.C. v. City of Glasgow Police Athletic Association* [1953] A.C. 380 (athletic sports and general pastimes).

Act 1958[36] will now be effective. In any case, the provision of prizes for sport in a school was held in *Re Mariette*,[37] to be valid as advancing that part of the education of students which had to do with their bodily and physical development. The same result occurred in *Re Gray*,[38] where a gift for the promotion of a sport in an army regiment was held to be charitable because it increased the army's efficiency. Although the validity of this last decision was doubted in *I.R.C. v. City of Glasgow Police Athletic Association*,[39] the doubts appear to be unjustified since the army's efficiency will certainly be promoted if its soldiers are physically fit.

It is clear that whether a particular charitable purpose is in fact promoted by the prescribed sporting activity is a question of construction of the trust instrument. In *I.R.C. v. McMullen*,[40] the legal status of the Football Association Youth Trust had to be decided. Its object was to organise or provide or assist in the organisation and provision of facilities which would enable and encourage students at schools and universities to play Association Football or other games and sports and thereby to assist in ensuring that due attention was given to the physical education and development of such pupils as well as the occupation of their minds and, with a view to furthering this object, to provide such facilities as playing fields, equipment, and so forth. The House of Lords held, unanimously reversing Walton J. and the Court of Appeal, that the purpose of the deed was not merely to organise the playing of Association Football in schools and universities but also to promote the physical education and development of students as an addition to their formal education; therefore, it created a valid charitable trust for the advancement of education, the sporting activities contributing to a balanced education. Lord Hailsham of St Marylebone L.C. was at pains to reject any idea which would confine the education of the young to schools or university campuses, limit that education to formal instruction or render it devoid of pleasure in the exercise of skill.[41] The principle in *Re Mariette*[42] was held to apply.

### (5) Locality trusts
A gift to a locality, such as a town or village, will be charitable even if no charitable purposes are specified.[43] The Charity Commission will make a scheme[44] so that the funds can be devoted to such purposes within the locality as are charitable. It has also been decided that the same principle applies to a gift to "my country, England".[45] That such trusts should be valid as charities

---

[36] See *ante*, p. 468.
[37] [1915] 2 Ch. 284. See also *Re Dupree's Deed Trusts* [1945] Ch. 16 (chess; see *ante* p. 461).
[38] [1925] Ch. 362.
[39] [1953] A.C. 380 at 391, 401.
[40] [1981] A.C. 1.
[41] *ibid.* at 18.
[42] [1915] 2 Ch. 284.
[43] See *Goodman v. Saltash Corpn* (1882) 7 App.Cas. 633; *Re Allen* [1905] 2 Ch. 400; *Re Norton's Will Trusts* [1948] 2 All E.R. 842.
[44] See *post*, p. 482.
[45] *Re Smith* [1932] 1 Ch. 153. See also *Nightingale v. Goulbourne* (1847) 5 Hare 484 (gift to "the Queen's Chancellor of the Exchequer for the time being" to be used by him for the benefit of "my beloved country, Great Britain" valid. The case can also be justified on the ground that it was made *virtute officii*, see *ante*, p. 466).

seems curious,[46] but is now established beyond all possible doubt.[47] But if a locality trust is to be upheld, it is most important to ensure either that exclusively charitable purposes within the locality are specified in the trust instrument, or, alternatively, that no purposes whatsoever are specified. If the settlor uses words which demonstrate in terms that the subject-matter of the gift may be used for non-charitable purposes, it will fail. This was the case in *Houston v. Burns*,[48] where the trust was for "public, benevolent or charitable purposes" in a Scottish parish. If the purposes are not charitable *per se*, their localisation will not of itself make them charitable. [49] Nor can gifts to "organisations or institutions operating for the public good" be held charitable by analogy with the locality cases by being limited to those organisations operated for the public good by charitable means; this was specifically held by the Privy Council in *Attorney-General of the Cayman Islands v. Wahr-Hansen*.[50]

## (6) Institutional and other charities

A trust which is designed for a village hall, community centre, or other similar institutional purposes will, if drawn so as to fall within the Recreational Charities Act 1958,[51] create a valid charitable trust. Trusts for hospitals and other similar purposes have been upheld as charitable as a matter of the general law.[52]

The refinements which are all too evident in the law of charity were brought to the fore in the controversial and unfortunate decision of the Court of Appeal in *Re Cole*,[53] where the majority held that a gift for "the general benefit and general welfare" of the children for the time being in a children's home maintained by a local authority was not charitable. Romer L.J. in particular based his decision to this effect on a close reading of the preamble to the Charitable Uses Act 1601 and concluded that the conceivable provision of

---

[46] See Albery 21 L.Q.R. (1940) 49; *Williams' Trustees v. I.R.C.* [1947] A.C. 447 at 459, *per* Lord Simonds.

[47] So far as trusts for ethnic or national groups are concerned, there is a limited exception in favour of charities in the Race Relations Act 1976; it is provided (s.34) that any discrimination necessary to comply with the terms of the governing instrument of a charity which is established to confer a benefit on persons of a particular racial group shall not be unlawful, but it specifically excludes from the exception any provision which restricts the benefits by reference to race or colour. Accordingly, a school for the education of Pakistanis or Spaniards could lawfully be confined to such persons but any provision excepting persons on racial grounds would be in breach of the Act. There is also an exception in favour of charity under the Sex Discrimination Act 1975. It is provided (s.43) that where the trusts contain a provision for conferring benefits on one sex only, anything done by the charity trustees to comply with that provision is not unlawful. This safeguards the position of single sex charities, like the Y.M.C.A., the Y.W.C.A., the Boy Scouts and the Girl Guides and many small parochial charities restricted to one sex (such as elderly widows).

[48] [1918] A.C. 337; see also *Att.-Gen. v. National Provincial and Union Bank of England* [1924] A.C. 262 (patriotic purposes in the British Empire); *Re Strakosch* [1949] Ch. 529. The matter is discussed generally *post*, p. 476.

[49] *Williams' Trustees v. I.R.C.* [1947] A.C. 447 at 459–460, *per* Lord Simonds. This case involved an Institute of Welshmen in London which was not charitable because they were not an identifiable section of the community.

[50] [2001] 1 A.C. 75 (appeal from the Cayman Islands).

[51] See *ante*, p. 468.

[52] See *Re Dean's Will Trusts* [1950] 1 All E.R. 882; *Re White's Will Trusts* [1951] 1 All E.R. 528; *Re Smith's Will Trusts* [1962] 2 All E.R. 563; *Re Adams* [1967] 1 W.L.R. 162; *Le Cras v. Perpetual Trustee Co.* [1967] 1 All E.R. 915; *Re Resch's Will Trusts* [1969] A.C. 514.

[53] [1958] Ch. 877.

benefits, which could include such "new-fangled devices" as television sets, for the children in question, who might well be juvenile delinquents, were not within the express terms of the preamble or within its spirit and intendment. The decision was followed by Danckwerts J. in *Re Sahal's Will Trusts*[54] on similar facts. But the dissenting view of Lord Evershed M.R. in *Re Cole* seems the more commendable because of its wider outlook "that the inference to be drawn from the preamble is that the care and upbringing of children who for any reason have not got the advantage or opportunity of being looked after and brought up by responsible and competent persons, or who could by these or other reasons, properly be regarded as defenceless or 'deprived' are matters which *prima facie* qualify as charitable purposes".[55]

### (7) Political trusts

In *Bowman v. The Secular Society*,[56] Lord Parker of Waddington stated the general position as follows:

> "A trust for the attainment of political objects has always been held invalid, not because it is illegal, for everyone is at liberty to advocate or promote by any lawful means a change in the law, but because the court has no means of judging whether a proposed change in the law will or will not be for the public benefit, and therefore cannot say that a gift to secure the change is a charitable gift."

This most straightforward application of this principle is to trusts in favour of political parties, which are obviously not charitable. Trusts in favour respectively of the Conservative Party and the Labour Party failed for this reason in *Bonar Law Memorial Trust v. I.R.C.*,[57] and in *Re Hopkinson*.[58] Trusts whose objects necessarily involve a change in the law are also not charitable for this reason. As has been already seen,[59] the principle in *Bowman v. The Secular Society* was applied by the House of Lords in *National Anti-Vivisection Society v. I.R.C.*[60] when rejecting as charitable a trust to abolish vivisection on the grounds that its purposes would involve the promotion of legislation in bring about a change the law. However, most of the more recent cases have involved trusts which purport to be trusts for the advancement of education but are really intended to educate the public into the adoption of a particular political viewpoint aimed at bringing about an alteration in the law or governmental policy of the United Kingdom and/or of a foreign country.

*McGovern v. Attorney-General*[61] concerned the legal status of Amnesty International. The general object of this unincorporated non-profit making body was to secure throughout the world the observance of the provisions of the Universal Declaration of Human Rights in regard to various categories of persons referred to in its constitution as "prisoners of conscience", namely

---

[54] [1958] 1 W.L.R. 1243.
[55] 1958] Ch. 877 at 892.
[56] [1917] A.C. 406.
[57] (1933) 49 T.L.R. 220.
[58] [1949] 1 All E.R. 346.
[59] See *ante*, p. 468.
[60] [1948] A.C. 31.
[61] [1982] Ch. 321.

persons who were imprisoned, detained or restricted because of their political, religious or conscientiously held beliefs or because of their ethnic origin, sex, colour or language. The association also had various specific objects whose legal effect had to be considered: first, the release of prisoners of conscience, which was held to be a clear political purpose because it involved putting pressure on foreign governments to change their policies; secondly, the abolition of torture or inhumane treatment or punishment, which was similarly held not to be charitable because it would involve legislation requiring the abolition of corporal or capital punishment; and, thirdly, providing research into the observance of human rights and the dissemination of that research, which would have been charitable had it had stood alone but, because it did not, also failed because of the requirement that charitable trusts must be exclusively charitable. Slade J. therefore held that Amnesty International was not a charity.

This decision was applied in Re Bushnell,[62] where a testator had directed a fund to be used "for the advancement and propagation of the teaching of socialised medicine", with directions as to how the managers of the fund should carry out and foster this purpose. Goulding J. held that the trust could not be supported as an educational trust since the directions with regard to the principles of "socialised medicine" dominated the whole of the trust. Nor was the trust beneficial to the community since its validity had to be tested at the date of the testator's death in 1941, when the court could not have decided the question because it would have involved considering what would then have been a political question, the desirability or otherwise of legislation to bring into being a state health service.[63] Both decisions were confirmed and applied by the Court of Appeal in Southwood v. Attorney-General,[64] where it was held that the court could not determine whether or not it promoted the public benefit for the public to be educated into an acceptance of the belief that world peace would be best secured by "demilitarisation"; this belief was a political objective and the trust which had been set up to propagate it was therefore not charitable. The court rejected the contention of the settlors that their objective was instead to educate the public as to the differing means of securing a state of peace and avoiding a state of war, an objective which the court would have held to be charitable.

As the latter dictum demonstrates, the mere existence of some political motive is not necessarily fatal to the existence of a charitable trust. Thus in Re Koeppler's Will Trust,[65] the organisation of conferences with political themes but without any intention of furthering the interests of any particular political party was held to be an educational charitable purpose. The question is whether a trust's leading purpose is political by, for example promoting legislation with a view to changing the law, in which case it will fail, or whether that purpose is subsidiary. This may also be a way of justifying the much earlier decision of Stirling J. in Re Scowcroft,[66] which concerned a gift for the maintenance of a village club and reading-room "to be used for the further-

---

[62] [1975] 1 W.L.R. 1596.
[63] The fact that a state health service had subsequently been introduced was irrelevant; the trust had to stand or fall by the character of its objects as at the date of the testator's death.
[64] [2000] W.T.L.R. 1199.
[65] [1986] Ch. 423.
[66] [1898] 2 Ch. 638.

ance of Conservative principles and religious and mental improvement, and to be kept free from intoxicants and dancing". This was held to be charitable, apparently on the grounds that all the prescribed purposes were to be carried out simultaneously so that the clearly political purpose was not, in the event, predominant.

There is no doubt about the increasing desire of charities to become "involved" in the causes with which their work is connected, not just in the international arena as in *McGovern v. Attorney-General*, but in areas such as the provision of housing and other services for the under-privileged in society. The desire of organisations whose objectives are otherwise clearly charitable to draw to the attention of the public as forcefully as possible the need for action to remedy certain social conditions has led them to form pressure groups, action groups and lobbies for this purpose whose "political" nature is potentially capable of affecting their charitable status. In 1981, the Charity Commissioners suggested fairly detailed guidelines for charity trustees in these circumstances, which included the following:[67] first, a charity should undertake only those activities which can reasonably be said to be directed to achieving its purposes and which are within the powers conferred by its governing instrument; secondly, the governing instrument should not include powers to exert political pressure except in a way that is merely ancillary to a charitable purpose; thirdly, the powers and purposes of a charity should not include a power to bring pressure to bear on the Government to adopt, alter or maintain a particular line of action; fourthly, the charity should spend its money on the promotion of public general legislation only if in doing so it is exercising a power which is ancillary to, and in furtherance of, its charitable purposes; fifthly, if the objects include the advancement of education, care should be taken not to overstep the boundary between education and propaganda; sixthly, if the objects include research, the charity must aim for objectivity and balance; and, seventhly, charities, whether operating in this country or overseas, must neither seek to influence or remedy those causes of poverty which lie in the social, economic and political structures of countries or communities nor bring pressure to bear on a government to procure a change in policies or administrative practices, nor seek to eliminate social, economic, political or other injustice.

### (8) Trusts for the environment

Trusts for the protection of the environment and the conservation of the national heritage have become increasingly common. Such trusts are analogous to the public works referred to in the preamble to the Charitable Uses Act 1601.[68] While such trusts often appear to be involved in the political arena, they appear to be unobjectionable provided that the political activity carried on by the trustees is ancillary to and is not their main objective.

### 3. *The Exclusive Nature Of Charity*

It is essential, subject to the effect of the Charitable Trusts (Validation) Act 1954 when it applies, that the trustees of a charitable trust are bound to devote the

---

[67] For further details, see the Report for 1981, pp. 19–22 and the Annual Report 1986, App. A.
[68] The preamble refers to the repair of bridges, ports, havens, causeways, sea banks and highways.

funds to exclusively charitable purposes, even if these are expressed not specifically but in a general way. For example, the donor may join the word "charitable" with another adjective, such as "benevolent", "patriotic", "philanthropic". It might be thought that, if the word "and" is used, as in the case of a gift "for charitable and benevolent purposes", the gift will succeed because the property in question can only be applied to such benevolent purposes as are charitable. It might also be thought that if the word "or" is used, as in the case of a gift "for charitable or benevolent purposes", the gift will fail because the property in question can be applied to benevolent purposes which are not charitable. This is generally the case but this outcome cannot actually be assumed with any confidence because, as in every other case, it is entirely a question of construction. It is possible for the word "and" to have been used disjunctively and for the word "or" to have been used conjunctively.[69] There is also a great deal of authority on the expression "and/or".[70]

The basic principle that the subject matter of a charitable trust must be capable of being devoted exclusively to charitable purposes is demonstrated by two decisions of the House of Lords, in both of which the word "or" was given its normal disjunctive meaning. In *Houston v. Burns*,[71] a gift was made for "public benevolent or charitable" purposes in a Scottish parish. The gift was held not to be charitable because the words were wide enough to justify the trustees in disposing of the fund for non-charitable purposes. But the case which brought home the effect of this rule with a vengeance was *Chichester Diocesan Fund and Board of Finance v. Simpson*.[72] The words used there were "charitable or benevolent" and the same conclusion was reached as in *Houston v. Burns*.[73] Executors had paid the money in question, which was a very substantial sum, to some 139 charities, in advance of and not anticipating the litigation by the next-of-kin which in fact occurred. The latter's successful personal claim to recover the money from the charities also went to the House of Lords in *Ministry of Health v. Simpson*,[74] when no appeal was made against the equal success of their similar proprietary claim in the Court of Appeal,

---

[69] See *Re Sutton* (1885) 28 Ch.D. 464; *Re Best* [1904] 2 Ch. 354 ("charitable and deserving" and "charitable and benevolent" objects respectively were upheld). Contrast *Att.-Gen. of the Bahamas v. Royal Trust Co.* [1986] 1 W.L.R. 1001, where a gift for "education and welfare" was interpreted disjunctively and was held void.

[70] See, in addition to the cases mentioned in the text, *Morice v. Bishop of Durham* (1805) 10 Ves. 522; *Hunter v. Att.-Gen.* [1899] A.C. 309; *Blair v. Duncan* [1902] A.C. 37; *Re Davidson* [1909] 1 Ch. 567; *Re Da Costa* [1912] 1 Ch. 337; *Att.-Gen. for New Zealand v. Brown* [1917] A.C. 393; *Re Chapman* [1922] 2 Ch. 479; *Re Davis* [1923] 1 Ch. 225; *Att.-Gen. v. National Provincial and Union Bank of England* [1924] A.C. 262; *Att.-Gen. for New Zealand v. New Zealand Insurance Co.* [1936] 3 All E.R. 888; *Re Atkinson's Will Trusts* [1978] 1 W.L.R. 586 (evidence inadmissible to show that by "worthy" the testator meant "charitable").

[71] [1918] A.C. 337.

[72] [1944] A.C. 341.

[73] See also *Att.-Gen.of the Cayman Islands v. Wahr-Hansen* [2001] 1 A.C. 75, where the Privy Council held, on an appeal from the Cayman Islands, that a gift for "any one or more religious chartable or educational institution or institutions or any organisations or institutions operating for the public good" would not be charitable even if it created mandatory obligations. The Privy Council rejected arguments that the latter gifts were charitable by analogy with the locality cases by being limited to those organisations operated for the public good by charitable means (see *ante*, p. 472) and denied that there is a presumption that such gifts should be restricted to organisations which are operating in a charitable manner.

[74] [1951] A.C. 251.

under the name *Re Diplock*.[75] Both claims are considered in detail in a later chapter.[76]

## (A) Apportionment

It should, however, be remembered that a donor may direct an apportionment of his funds between charitable and non-charitable purposes. This class of gift will not fail, even if the trustees fail to make the apportionment, because in the last resort, the courts will apportion the funds equally between the objects. Consequently, if the non-charitable purposes are void for, for example, uncertainty, only the trust of the part of the funds devoted to those purposes will fail.[77]

## (B) Incidental Non-Charitable Purposes

It is also important to notice that the fact that a non-charitable purpose is incidental or ancillary to the achievement of a purpose which is, in fact, charitable will not destroy the gift. Thus, in *Royal College of Surgeons v. National Provincial Bank*,[78] the House of Lords held that the College was in law a charity since its object, as recited in the Charter, was "the due promotion and encouragement of the study and practice of surgery", the professional protection of its members provided for in its bye-laws being merely ancillary to that object. Similarly, in *Incorporated Council of Law Reporting for England and Wales v. Attorney-General*,[79] it was held that the fact that legal practitioners used law reports in order to earn their professional fees did not have the result that the objects of the Council were not charitable. The same result occurred in *Re Coxen*,[80] where Jenkins J. held that the provision made by the testator for a dinner to be held for the Aldermen of the City of London after their annual meeting to consider the management of a trust in favour of orthopaedic hospitals which he had also set up was purely ancillary to the primary charitable trust and procured its better administration. And in *London Hospital Medical College v. I.R.C.*,[81] once it had been held that the students' union in question existed to further the educational purposes of the College,[82] it was held to be immaterial that the union also provided personal benefits for the individual students who were elected members and chose to make use of its facilities.[83]

## (C) Subsidiary Purposes

Incidental purposes such as those just mentioned must be carefully distinguished from purposes which are subsidiary but not merely incidental. In *Oxford Group v. I.R.C.*,[84] the Court of Appeal held that one of the objects set out in the Group's memorandum of association, the support of "any charitable or

---

[75] [1948] Ch. 465.
[76] See *post*, p. 785.
[77] *Salusbury v. Denton* (1857) 3 K. & J. 529; *Re Clarke* [1923] 2 Ch. 407.
[78] [1952] A.C. 631.
[79] [1972] Ch. 73.
[80] [1948] Ch. 747.
[81] [1976] 1 W.L.R. 613.
[82] See *ante*, p. 462.
[83] See also, to a similar effect, *Neville Estates v. Madden* [1962] Ch. 852, in which it was held that the social activities of a synagogue were merely ancillary to the strictly religious activities of the synagogue; see *ante*, p. 467.
[84] [1949] 2 All E.R. 537. See also *Ellis v. I.R.C.* (1949) 31 Tax Cas. 178.

benevolent" associations, actually conferred powers that were so wide that they could not be regarded as charitable; they were not merely ancillary to the main, admittedly charitable, objects set out elsewhere in the memorandum. The Group did not therefore constitute a charity.

## (D) The Charitable Trusts (Validation) Act 1954

The decision in *Oxford Group v. I.R.C.* was thought to affect a large number of charities and the Nathan Committee therefore recommended some amendment to the law but not, however, the complete reversal of the decision.[85] The result was the Charitable Trusts (Validation) Act 1954, a short statute which has turned out to be exceptionally difficult to interpret.

Section 1(1) of the Act defines as an "imperfect trust provision" any provision declaring the objects and so describing them that, consistently with the terms of the provision of the property, they could be used exclusively for charitable purposes but could nevertheless be used for purposes which are not charitable. The instrument in which the "imperfect trust provision" is contained must have taken effect before December 16, 1952,[86] the date of the publication of the Nathan Report. The Act is to apply, by virtue of section 2(1), to any disposition or covenant to make such a disposition where, apart from the Act, the disposition or covenant would have been invalid[87] under the law of England and Wales, but would have been valid if the objects had been exclusively charitable.[88] Finally, in respect of the period before the Act came into force on July 30, 1954, the imperfect trust provision takes effect as if the whole of the declared objects had been charitable but, in respect of the period after the Act came into force, as if that provision required the property to be applied for the declared objects only in so far as they are charitable.[89]

Very real difficulty has been found in the interpretation of these provisions; indeed one judge confessed on two occasions[90] that he was "floored" by them. Particular difficulty has been found in reconciling section 1(1) and section 2(1). The definition of an imperfect trust provision in section 1(1) is limited to a provision declaring the objects for which the property is held, "objects" being synonymous with purposes. How then should section 2(1) be interpreted? It can be convincingly argued that the definition in section 1(1) includes certain gifts which are already valid, for example a gift for not longer than the perpetuity period for certain named purposes, some of which are charitable and some of which are not charitable (for example, a gift "for my dog Lassie") but nevertheless valid. According to this line of argument, section 2(1) then takes this class of gift outside the mischief of the Act into which section 1 has put it. It is hard to disagree with the observation that it is "an odd state of things if Acts of Parliament are passed in such a form that it is necessary to amend the effect of the first section by putting in a second".[91]

---

[85] 1952 Cmd. 8710, Chap. 12.
[86] s.1(2).
[87] For example, for perpetuity, uncertainty or other similar reason: *Vernon v. I.R.C.* [1956] 1 W.L.R. 1169.
[88] The Act will not however apply where the property or income from the trust has been paid or distributed on the basis that the imperfect trust provision was void (s.2(2)).
[89] s.1(2)(a), (b).
[90] *Re Harpur's Will Trusts* [1962] Ch. 78 at 95 (Harman L.J.); *Re Gillingham Bus Disaster Fund* [1958] 1 Ch. 300 (Harman J.).
[91] *Re Harpur's Will Trusts* [1962] Ch. 78 at 96, *per* Harman L.J.

Other difficulties have also arisen. One of them which arose in *Re Gillingham Bus Disaster Fund*[92] was whether the Act had validated an appeal launched in *The Daily Telegraph* by the mayors of several boroughs, after a number of cadets had been killed and injured in a road accident. The purpose of the appeal was "to promote a Royal Marine Cadet Memorial Fund to be devoted to defraying funeral expenses, caring for the boys who may be disabled and then to such worthy cause or causes in memory of the boys who lost their lives as the Mayors may determine". The majority of the Court of Appeal held that an imperfect trust provision was not validated unless the contributions to the fund were dispositions to which the Act applied, namely dispositions creating more than one interest in the same property.[93] A contribution was admittedly a disposition but, in view of the terms of the appeal, it did not create separate interests in the same property for funeral expenses, for the care of the disabled, and for worthy causes; accordingly, it was held not to have been validated by the Act.[94]

This is also what Harman J. had held at first instance and, despite a dissent, seems to be correct. However, Harman J. also stated that section 1(1) should be construed as applying only to trusts framed in such terms that the objects referred to included some express reference to charitable purposes as well as to other non-charitable purposes; on this basis, the Act therefore did not apply to a gift stating purposes in a general way, whose terms were capable of embracing charitable purposes but contained no express reference either to charity in general or to any specific charitable purpose. The majority of the Court of Appeal, having held that the Act was not applicable for the reasons already mentioned, did not have to decided this point and, while they expressed some sympathy with the view of Harman J., abstained from expressing any opinion on it. The point did however have to be decided by the dissentient, Ormerod L.J., who decided that section 1(1) should not be construed in the restricted manner favoured by Harman J. but more broadly in accordance with what he regarded as its unambiguous language.

In these circumstances, in *Re Wykes' Will Trusts*,[95] Buckley J. felt able to adopt the view favoured by Ormerod L.J. and declared that a trust for "benevolent or welfare" purposes was an imperfect trust provision to which the Act did indeed apply. Shortly afterwards, this decision was on two occasions reviewed by Cross J. In *Re Mead's Trust Deed*,[96] he said that a benevolent or welfare fund "is closely akin to a trust for the relief of poverty".[97] He therefore held that a trust to provide a convalescent home for members of a trades union and a home for its poor retired members was validated by the Act and that, as from the date of the Act, the property should be held for those members of the union who were poor persons and, in the case of the home for the aged, for its poor retired members. In *Re Saxone Shoe Co.'s Trust Deed*,[98] he actually held that the trust in question was essentially a private trust and therefore incapable of being validated. However, he nevertheless assumed *Re*

---

[92] [1959] Ch. 62.
[93] s.2(3).
[94] Compare *Re Chitty's Will Trusts* [1970] Ch. 254.
[95] [1961] Ch. 229.
[96] [1961] 1 W.L.R. 1244.
[97] *ibid.* at 1251.
[98] [1962] 1 W.L.R. 943.

*Wykes' Will Trusts* to have been correctly decided, while at the same time setting some limits on to the doctrine enunciated by Buckley J. Cross J said[99]:

> "In such a phrase as 'welfare purposes' there is at least some flavour of charity which may justify one in saying that the testator was seeking to benefit the public through the relief of a limited class. Here there is nothing of that kind, and if such a trust as this is validated by the Act, I do not see why one should stop short of turning any such invalid private trust into a trust for the relief of such beneficiaries as may from time to time be poor."

Nevertheless this problem, which is essentially one of construction of the Act, is still open for adjudication by the Court of Appeal. There seems no overwhelming reason why the restrictive application favoured by Harman J. should be adopted; all that seems to be essential is that the expression used has a charitable connotation. Indeed, in *Re South Place Ethical Society*,[1] Dillon J. held that the words "for such purposes either religious or civil" as the trustees might appoint did constitute an imperfect trust provision within the meaning of the Act; they were to be construed as "such purposes, either religious or civil, being charitable" and the provision was accordingly held to have been validated.

Another aspect of the effect of the Act had to be decided in *Re Harpur's Will Trusts*.[2] The Court of Appeal had to consider the question of whether the Act had validated a trust to divide a trust fund "between such institutions and associations having for their main objects the assistance and care of soldiers, sailors, airmen and other members of HM Forces who have been wounded or incapacitated during the recent [second] world war" as the trustees thought fit. It was held that this provision was not within the scope of section 1(1) because that was limited to provisions which declare the objects and describe them in such a ways as to enable effect to be given to them by an application for purposes which are exclusively charitable. This decision has the somewhat surprising result that a gift to an institution whose objects are not described in the trust instrument will not fall within the scope of the subsection.

The Act can only apply to instruments taking effect before December 16, 1952 and its importance is necessarily by now considerably reduced. However, it cannot yet be regarded as merely of academic interest; the validity of a provision may still arise for consideration on the determination of a life or other limited interest created before that date[3] and the charitable status of a trust which has been in existence since before that date may even today still be challenged.[4]

---

[99] *ibid.* at 958–959.

[1] [1980] 1 W.L.R. 1565.

[2] [1962] Ch. 78.

[3] If a person has a future interest in property the subject of the provision, he may challenge its validity within one year of the interest vesting in possession: s.3. *Re Chitty's Will Trusts* [1970] Ch. 254.

[4] In 2002 the author of this edition had to advise on a challenge made by the Charity Commissioners to the charitable status of a trust which had been in existence for over 70 years on grounds which might have been capable of being cured by the Act.

## V. THE *CY-PRÈS* DOCTRINE

It is possible that it may either from the outset be impossible, or may subsequently become impossible for a designated charitable purpose to be carried out. In these circumstances, the charitable purpose will not necessarily fail because of what is known as the *cy-près* doctrine[5] which, if it applies, will enable the funds to be applied for whatever charitable purposes are closest to the charitable purpose which was intended.

This issue only arises if the gift to charity is absolute. Such a gift will have been made where an absolute and perpetual gift that has been made to charity remains intact following the failure of a gift over for remoteness or for some other reason. It will not have been where a gift to charity is only for a limited period, in which case any interest which is undisposed of will result to the grantor. Which has occured is a question of construction.[6]

The *cy-près* doctrine is obviously only applicable where it is actually "impossible" for the designated charitable purpose to be carried out; whether or not this is the case is sometimes by no means straightforward. Where it is, then the doctrine is generally, but not always, only applicable where what is known as a general charitable intention can be shown to exist. The jurisdiction to apply property *cy-près* is exercisable by the courts or, in practice almost invariably, by the Charity Commissioners.[7]

### 1. *"Impossibility"*

It may be impossible to carry out a designated charitable purpose from the outset, either because it has never been possible at any stage or because it ceases to be possible during the interval between the making of a will and the death of the testator. It may be or become impossible because the specific charitable purpose has never existed or because a specific or general charitable purpose has become impracticable. It is also possible for a charitable trust which has initially taken effect to become impossible or impracticable,[8] or to become illegal,[9] or to fail, or to be satisfied without exhausting the whole of the trust fund.[10] Two specific situations require discussion: first, where the designated charitable object is an institution which does not exist, because it has either never existed or no longer exists in the form in which the donor described it; and, secondly, where section 13 of the Charities Act 1993 applies.

---

[5] For a full survey of the subject, see Sheridan and Delaney, *The Cy-près Doctrine; Tudor on Charities* (8th ed.), pp. 391 *et seq.*

[6] See *Re Cooper's Conveyance Trusts* [1956] 1 W.L.R. 1096 at 1102, *per* Upjohn J. Compare *Re Peel's Release* [1921] Ch. 218; *Re Bawden's Settlement* [1954] 1 W.L.R. 33N. The Rule in *Hancock v. Watson* [1902] A.C. 14, which was formerly known as the Rule in *Lassence v. Tierney* (1849) 1 Mac. & G., whereby a gift to donee with further directions which do not exhaust the funds is taken by the donee absolutely, also applies to charitable gifts: *Re Monk* [1927] 2 Ch. 197 at 211.

[7] See *post*, p. 493

[8] See the cases cited in the text and also *Att.-Gen. v. City of London* (1790) 3 Bro.C.C. 171 (promotion of Christianity among the infidels of Virginia); *Ironmongers Co. v. Att.-Gen.* (1844) 10 Cl. & F. 908 (redemption of British slaves in Turkey or Barbary).

[9] For example, where income is settled for a period which exceeds the permissible accumulation period; see *Re Monk* [1927] 2 Ch. 197; *Re Bradwell* [1952] Ch. 575.

[10] *Re King* [1923] 1 Ch. 243; *Re North Devon and West Somerset Relief Fund* [1953] 1 W.L.R. 1260; *Re Raine* [1956] Ch. 417.

## (A) Where the charitable object is an institution which does not exist.

### (1) Institutions which have never existed

It is possible for a donor to specify as his intended charitable object an institution which has never existed, either because the deed or will in question has described the intended institution by the wrong name or because he has simply invented one. In the former case, if there is convincing evidence of what the settlor or testator intended, the deed or will in question can be rectified to bring its provisions into line with that intention.[11] Even if there is insufficiently convincing evidence for rectification to be possible, the court can still decide as a matter of construction that the intended object was an existing institution; thus in *Re Spence*,[12] a gift to a particular Blind Home was held by Megarry V.-C. to be identifiable with a home for the blind of a different name and address and so was valid. In these cases, no "impossibility" will occur in the first place. If the gift cannot be saved in either of these two ways, the purpose will fail; this will necessarily also occur where an institution has simply been invented. However, in such circumstances, provided that the designated institution would have been charitable had it existed, the property will in practice almost always be applied *cy-près* because, as will be seen below, it appears to be relatively easy to infer the necessary general charitable intention.[13]

### (2) Institutions which formerly existed

Where the donor has specified as his intended charitable object an institution which formerly existed but no longer does in the form in which he described it, the question which arises is whether any continuing institution can be identified with the previous one. If this is possible, once again no "impossibility" will occur.

Institutions continue to exist where they have been amalgamated with others as a result of a scheme made by the court or by the Charity Commissioners. In *Re Faraker*,[14] a scheme had been made by the Commissioners consolidating the endowments of a number of charities with the general purpose of relief of the poor of Rotherhithe. A gift was subsequently made to one of these charities, "Hannah Bayley's Charity", whose original object was rather more limited; it was held that the gift took effect in favour of the amalgamated charity. Alterations to the constitution or objects of an institution may also be made by statute,[15] or improperly by the trustees under the terms of the trust deed without the necessary sanction of the court or the Charity Commissioners.[16] Subsequent gifts to the institution will similarly take effect. However, if an institution has the power to dissolve itself and formally does

---

[11] This has always been possible in the case of deeds; wills have only been able to be rectified since the enactment of Administration of Justice Act 1982, s.21.

[12] [1979] Ch. 483 at 491.

[13] *Re Harwood* [1936] Ch. 285. See *post*, p. 491.

[14] [1912] 2 Ch. 488.

[15] Many of the cases involved re-organisation of hospitals nationalised and re-organised under the National Health Services Act 1946; see *Re Morgan's Will Trusts* [1950] Ch. 137; *Re Glass* [1950] Ch. 643N; *Re Hutchinson's Will Trusts* [1953] Ch. 387.

[16] See *Re Bagshawe* [1954] 1 W.L.R. 238, where a scheme was made simply in accordance with the trust machinery, not by an outside body.

so, Plowman J. held in *Re Stemson's Will Trusts*[17] that a subsequent gift in its favour will not take effect; consequently, the gift will fail unless it can be applied *cy-près* as a result of the existence of a general charitable intention.

The effect of changes of these and other types was recently reviewed by the Court of Appeal in *Re Broadbent's Will*.[18] The resulting decision appears to have considerably simplified the law governing the question of whether or not there is "impossibility". The testatrix had left one-third of her residuary estate to the Vicar and Churchwardens of a Mission Church "for the general purposes of such Church but with the request that the money be used primaily for the upkeep of the fabric of the Church". There had never been a Vicar and Churchwardens. The Church was held pursuant to a deed of trust of 1913 of which the testatrix's deceased husband had been a trustee. This both envisaged both the sale of the church and provided that the proceeds of sale, if not invested in another church, were to be held for "such other religious or charitable purpose as the Trustees shall in their absolute discretion think proper". Between the date of the will and the testatrix's death, the trustees did sell the Church and it was demolished; no new church was purchased. Mummery L.J. said:

> "It appears ... that the court must ascertain whether the intention of the testator was to benefit a charitable purpose promoted in the work of the named institution, as distinct from an intention to benefit only the named institution in the carrying out of its charitable purpose at or in connection with particular premises. This problem commonly arises in the case of bequests to a named college, school, hospital, or Home which, prior to the death of the testator, has closed down, moved, amalgamated, expanded or undergone some other potentially significant change, such as a scheme altering its objects. If, on examination of all the relevant material, the court is satisfied that the gift is for a charitable purpose which the institution existed to promote and there are existing funds dedicated to that purpose (to which the bequest can be added), the gift will not be allowed to fail simply because the particular institution used as a means of attaining the charitable end has ceased to exist."

The Court of Appeal held that "the general purposes of the Church" included the trusts on which the proceeds of sale were to be held if not reinvested in another church. Consequently, the one-third was held on the trusts of the deed of 1913. A contrary decision would not have given rise to any issue of *cy-près* because the will provided that in that event there would be cross-accruer to the remaining gifts of residue.[19] However, that does not affect the value of this decision as an authority on when there is "impossibility".

## (B) Section 13 of the Charities Act 1993[20]

This section applies only where circumstances change after a charitable trust has come into existence and render some alteration of its original terms

---

[17] [1970] Ch. 16.
[18] [2001] W.T.L.R. 967.
[19] These were in favour of other charities, who contended that the gift to the Church had failed.
[20] Formerly Charities Act 1960, s.13.

desirable. The problem which it was enacted to resolve arose out of the fact that the wishes of a donor could not be, and for that matter still cannot be, disregarded simply because they are unpopular or because the funds in question could be applied for a more beneficial purpose. However, in *Re Dominion Students Hall Trust*,[21] the charity in question was restricted to Dominion students of European origin, yet the objects were stated to be the promotion of community interest in the Empire. An application was made to the court to delete the words "of European origin". Evershed J. held that the retention of these words amounted to a "colour bar" which would defeat the object of the charity; the word "impossibility" should be construed widely and therefore enabled the deletion to be made. In view of this dilution of "impossibility", it became desirable to provide a new test to clarify its nature. This was originally provided by section 13 of the Charities Act 1960, which has been reenacted as section 13 of the Charities Act 1993.

Under the section, *cy-près* is feasible, subject to the requirement for a general charitable intention, if the matter can be brought under one of the following heads:

1. Under paragraph (a), where the original purposes,[22] in whole or in part, have as far as may be been fulfilled, or cannot be carried out, or not according to the directions given and to the spirit of the gift.[23] This expression "spirit of the gift" appears in four of the five paragraphs. It is not a new phrase, being apparently borrowed from the Education (Scotland) Act 1946.[24] Although doubts about its meaning have been expressed,[25] it should not create any real difficulties. It has been said that "it is equivalent in meaning to the basic intention underlying the gift, as ascertained from its terms in the light of the admissible evidence".[26]

   The working of paragraph (a) is illustrated by *Re Lepton's Charity*.[27] This case concerned a gift by will in 1715 of land to be held on trust to pay out of the rents a sum of £3 a year to the minister of a chapel and the net surplus to the poor and aged of the town. The evidence was to the effect that at the date of the will the total income was £5 a year. The land had been sold and was represented by investments yielding £791 a year. Pennycuick V.-C. held that the basic intention had plainly been defeated when, in modern conditions, the minister took a derisory £3 out of the total of £791; he therefore made an order by way of a *cy-près* scheme to provide for the payment to the minister to be raised from £3 to £100 per annum.

2. Under paragraph (b), where the original purposes provide a use for

---

[21] [1947] Ch. 183.
[22] The words "original purposes" appear in all five paragraphs. They are applicable to the trusts of the disposition as a whole, and not severally in relation to its respective parts; *Re Lepton's Charity* [1972] Ch. 276 at 285.
[23] Charities Act 1993, s.13(1)(a).
[24] s.116(2).
[25] By Viscount Simonds, 221 HL Official Report 601 (March 1, 1960).
[26] *Re Lepton's Charity* [1972] 276 at 285, *per* Pennycuick V.-C. See also *Re Lysaght* [1966] Ch. 191; see *post*, p. 422.
[27] [1972] Ch. 276. See also *post*, p. 487.

only part of the property.[28] This paragraph can be illustrated by the facts of *Re North Devon and West Somerset Relief Fund*,[29] where a surplus remained out of funds subscribed for the relief of a flood disaster at Lynmouth.

3.  Under paragraph (c), where the property given and other property applicable for similar purposes can be more effectively used in conjunction and to that end can suitably, regard being had to the spirit of the gift, be made applicable for common purposes.[30] Strictly speaking, this paragraph does not involve a *cy-près* scheme at all since it has never been necessary to show "impossibility" to order to effect a consolidation of a number of charities.[31]

4.  Under paragraph (d), where the original purposes were laid down by reference to an area which was then, but has since ceased to be, a unit for some other purpose or by reference to a class of persons or to an area which has for any reason since ceased to be suitable, regard being had to the spirit of the gift, or practical for the purposes of administering the gift.[32] Common examples of the application of this paragraph are where the area in which the charity was originally to operate is, because of changes in local government boundaries or the class of beneficiaries, hard to identify or where the area or class of beneficiaries has dwindled or is otherwise provided for, so that no substantial public benefit is being conferred by the fulfilment of the original purposes. Thus in *Peggs v. Lamb*,[33] this paragraph was applied to a gift for the benefit of the freemen of the borough of Huntingdon, whose numbers had become substantially reduced; a scheme was directed so as to enlarge the class to cover the inhabitants of the borough as a whole.

5.  Under paragraph (e), where the original purposes have, in whole or in part, in the period since they were originally laid down either (i) been adequately provided for by other means, or (ii) ceased as being useless or harmful to the community or, for other reasons, to be in law charitable, or (iii) ceased in any other way to provide a suitable and effective method of using the property given, regard being had to the spirit of the gift.[34] The jurisdiction created by this paragraph, and in particular by sub-paragraphs (i) and (iii), affords the most important relaxation of the old *cy-près* rule and will probably be of the most practical use in enabling funds to be utilised for the maximum benefit of the public.

Sub-paragraph (i) may be illustrated by the situation where the original benefits of the charity are now provided for by the statutory services of public or local authorities. This would apply, for example,

---

[28] s.13(1)(b).
[29] [1953] 1 W.L.R. 1260; see also *Re King* [1923] 1 Ch. 243; *Re Raine* [1956] Ch. 417.
[30] s.13(1)(c).
[31] See *Re Faraker* [1912] 2 Ch. 488.
[32] s.13(1)(d).
[33] [1994] Ch. 172.
[34] s.13(1)(e).

to a charity for the upkeep of a road or bridge;[35] if the original purpose were kept on foot, its only real purpose would be to relieve the rates or the exchequer and it is therefore now possible to apply the funds *cy-près*.

Sub-paragraph (ii) will not often arise; indeed, there does not seem to have been a single reported case where a valid charitable trust has ceased to be charitable. But the principle may well in the future be applied more often than has hitherto been thought. This is because an institution registered by the Charity Commissioners is conclusively presumed to be a charity while on the register for all purposes other than rectification of the register.[36] This sub-paragraph will clearly be applicable if a charity is removed[37] from the register on the ground that its purposes have never been or are no longer charitable (the latter possibility is at present somewhat improbable but is likely to become not uncommon if the rolling programme monitoring public benefit envisaged by the Strategy Unit is put into effect). It will therefore be applicable to the endowments of charities such as independent schools if their charitable status is ever withdrawn.[38]

However, it is sub-paragraph (iii) which provides the widest relaxation of all. However, although its words are very general, it does not have a completely unlimited effect. It is still necessary to take into account the spirit of the gift, something which will prevent a *cy-près* scheme being made simply because the original purpose selected by the donor is less effective than some other application of the funds. It is still essential to establish that the mode of application which the donor selected has ceased to be suitable or effective. In *Re Lepton's Charity*,[39] it was held that the court had jurisdiction under this sub-paragraph (as well as under the wider terms of paragraph (a), where the original purposes, in whole or in part cannot be carried out, or not according to the directions given and to the spirit of the gift[40]) to direct an application of the property *cy-près*. More significantly, in *Varsani v. Jerwani*,[41] the Court of Appeal held that the sub-paragraph applied where a religious sect whose beliefs the charity had been set up to promote had split into two groups over a dispute as to whether its leader still had divine status. The need to consider the original purposes did not oblige the court to order an enquiry as to which of the groups was right; it was clear that the original purposes had ceased to be a suitable and effective means of using the available property. The court upheld the making of a scheme *cy-près* dividing the property between the two groups.

---

[35] See Charitable Uses Act 1601; *ante*, p. 448.
[36] Charities Act 1993, s.4(1).
[37] s.4(2).
[38] See Jaconelli [1996] Conv. 24.
[39] [1972] Ch. 276.
[40] See *ante*, p. 485. Pennycuick V.-C. was of opinion that this sub-paragraph was no more than "a final writing out at large" of paragraph (a); *ibid.* at 285.
[41] [1999] Ch. 219.

It must be emphasised that these provisions of section 13 of the Charities Act 1993 alter the law only so far as it previously required a failure of the original purposes of a charity before a *cy-près* application could be ordered.[42] *Cy-près* is therefore only possible if the requirement for a general charitable intention, discussed below, is satisfied.

### (2) A general charitable intention

Where it is indeed impossible for the designated charitable purpose to be carried out, the *cy-près* doctrine is generally, but not always, only applicable where it can also be shown that there was a general charitable intention. The two situations where this is not necessary will be considered first.

### (A) Subsequent Impossibility

A general charitable intention is only necessary where the charitable purpose of the donor has failed *ab initio*. Where a charitable trust has initially taken effect but at a later stage it becomes impossible for its purpose to continue to be carried out, the property subject to the charitable trust will always be applicable *cy-près*. Once property has been effectively and absolutely dedicated to charity, whether in pursuance of a general or a particular charitable intent, the donor and those claiming through him such as his residuary legatees or next-of-kin are excluded forever. It was held in *Re Wright*[43] that this is the case even if the failure occurs during the existence of a prior life interest before the charity is entitled in possession to the funds. The material date for the purpose of deciding whether the *cy-près* doctrine is applicable is therefore the date when the trust came into existence (the date of the relevant deed or, in the case of a will, the death of the testator). It is only if the trust has failed by then that the question of whether a general charitable intention has been shown becomes relevant.

This is also the case where an institution which is to carry out the charitable purpose in question ceases to exist after the charitable trust has come into effect. The Court of Appeal held in *Re Slevin*[44] that in such circumstances it is also unnecessary to show any general charitable intention in order for the gift to be upheld. The subject-matter of the gift will already have vested in the institution and, since the latter has ceased to exist, it will devolve on the Crown with the rest of the institution's property. The Crown will in practice allow the subject matter of the gift to be disposed of in favour of charity.

### (B) Unidentifiable Donors

A general charitable purpose is also not necessary even when it has from the outset been impossible for the designated charitable purpose to be carried out insofar as the donors of the property subscribed for that purpose cannot be identified. In this respect, section 14 of the Charities Act 1960, now section 14 of the Charities Act 1993, introduced reforms which were long overdue (until then, unless a general charitable intention could be shown in the usual way, the trustees were bound to refund the property and, if the donors could not be found, it had to be paid into court to await the usually remote possibility that

---

[42] s.13(2).
[43] *Re Wright* [1954] Ch. 347 at 363, *per* Romer L.J. See also *Re Wokingham Fire Brigade* [1951] Ch. 373.
[44] [1891] 2 Ch. 236.

they would reclaim it;[45] however, since the reform was retrospective,[46] any property which had not been reclaimed by the commencement of the Charities Act 1960 was able to be applied *cy-près* thereafter).

Section 14 provides that property given for specific charitable purposes which fail is to be applicable *cy-près* as though it had been given for charitable purposes generally, provided that it belongs, first, to any donors who, after such advertisements and inquiries as are prescribed by regulations made by the Charity Commissioners,[47] cannot be identified or found or, secondly, to any donor who has executed a written disclaimer of his right to have the property returned. [48] It is further provided that, for these purposes, property is to be conclusively presumed, without the necessity for advertisements or inquiries, to belong to donors who cannot be identified if it consists either of the proceeds of cash collections made by means of collecting boxes or other means not adapted for distinguishing one gift from another or of the proceeds of any lottery, competition, entertainment, sale or other such money-raising activity, although, as regards the latter, allowance must be made for prizes or articles for sale to enable the activity to be undertaken.[49] Donors who can be identified or who apply within six months of the making of a scheme are entitled to the return of their property or its proceeds of sale.[50] The court may, by order, direct that property be treated, without advertisement or inquiry, as belonging to donors who cannot be identified whenever it appears to the court either that it would be unreasonable, having regard to the amounts likely to be returned to the donor, to incur expense with a view to returning the property, or that it would be unreasonable, having regard to the nature, circumstances and amount of the gifts, and to the lapse of time since they were made, for the donors to expect the property to be returned.[51]

### (C) Where a General Charitable Intention is Necessary

#### (1) Gifts for charitable purposes
The question of whether or not a general charitable intention has been shown is entirely one of construction of the instrument in question. It is necessary to consider, as in all matters of construction, the whole scope and intent of that instrument. The essential question which has to be decided in this process is whether the paramount object of the settlor was to benefit a particular object *simpliciter* or whether it was instead to effect a particular mode of charity independently of the given object even though an object was specifically indicated.[52]

Bearing in mind the fact that the cases do not by any means present a consistent picture, the authorities may perhaps be divided into two classes.

The first class of case is where the gift is in form made for a particular charitable purpose but it is possible, taking the instrument as a whole, to say

---

[45] This was the result in *Re Ulverston* [1956] Ch. 622.
[46] Charities Act 1993, s.14(10); Charities Act 1960, s.14(7).
[47] Charities Act 1993, s.14(8).
[48] s.14(1).
[49] s.14(3).
[50] s.14(5), (6), (10).
[51] s.14(4).
[52] See *Re Taylor* (1888) 58 L.T. 538 at 543.

that, notwithstanding the form of the gift, the paramount intention is to give the property in the first instance for a general charitable purpose rather than a specified purpose; in such cases, a direction has in effect been engrafted onto the general gift as to the intention of the settlor which relates to the manner in which the general gift is to be carried into effect. In these circumstances, even though it may be impossible to carry out the specified directions, the gift for the general charitable purpose will remain perfectly good and the court or the Charity Commissioners will direct a scheme as to how it is to be carried out cy-près.

The second class of case is where, on the true construction of the instrument, the gift is not only in form but also in substance one for a particular purpose only; in such circumstances, if it proves impossible to carry out that particular purpose, the whole gift will fail and there is no room for the application of cy-près.[53]

The question as to the class in which a gift falls often raises serious problems of construction. The way in which the court sets about its task may be illustrated by the following cases. In *Biscoe v. Jackson*, [54] money was to be applied towards the establishment of a soup kitchen in Shoreditch and a cottage hospital there. It was not in fact possible to apply the fund in the manner indicated. The Court of Appeal held that there was a sufficient general intention of charity for the benefit of the poor of Shoreditch to entitle the court to execute the trust cy-près. It was in effect therefore decided that the direction to establish a soup kitchen and a cottage hospital were only two ways of benefiting the poor of Shoreditch whom there was a general intention to benefit. A more difficult example is *Re Lysaght*.[55] The testatrix gave a fund to the Royal College of Surgeons, for the establishment of studentships but provided that Jews and Roman Catholics should be excluded from them; the College would not accept the fund subject to these restrictions. Buckley J. held, first, that these discriminatory provisions did not form an essential part of the testatrix's intention; secondly, that her paramount intention was that the College should be the trustee of the fund; and, thirdly, that the impracticability of giving effect to this inessential part of her intention by virtue of the fact that the College had refused to accept her gift subject to the restrictions would not be allowed to defeat her paramount intention. Accordingly a scheme was directed under which the offending provision was deleted. Although the principle behind the decision is entirely clear, it is not at all easy, as a matter of construction of the will, to accept the judge's conclusion that the discriminatory provisions did not form part of the testatrix's paramount intention.

Another illustration, which is probably more straightforward from the point of view of construction, is *Re Woodhams*,[56] where the testator gave the residue of his estate to two colleges of music to found scholarships which were to be restricted to boys who were orphans from named children's homes. The colleges refused to accept the gift on these conditions, partly because of the

[53] The substance of this formulation is borrowed from *Re Wilson* [1913] 1 Ch. 314 at 320. For another formulation, see *Re Lysaght* [1966] Ch. 191 at 201, 202, *per* Buckley J.
[54] (1887) 35 Ch.D. 460.
[55] [1966] Ch. 191, applying *Re Robinson* [1923] 2 Ch. 332 (requirement of wearing a black gown in church held impracticable).
[56] [1981] 1 W.L.R. 493.

decrease in the number of orphans and partly because of the adequacy of public grants for education, but was prepared to accept it if the restrictions were deleted. Vinelott J. held that the testator had chosen orphans from these homes on the basis that they were the persons most likely to need assistance but that it was not an essential part of the scheme that the scholarships should be so restricted; accordingly, the trusts could be modified without frustrating his intention.

A case on the other side of the line is *Re Good*,[57] where there was a trust to provide rest homes in Hull. The testator had drawn up a detailed scheme of the types of home to be provided, the types of inmates to be admitted, and the management powers of the trustees. The scheme was in fact impracticable because the funds were insufficient. Wynn-Parry J. held that the language of the will and in particular the detailed instructions which had been given were inconsistent with the implication of a general charitable intention; therefore the *cy-près* doctrine did not apply. Similarly in *Re Spence*,[58] Megarry V.-C. held that, as a matter of the construction of the will, a gift to a specified old folk's home was one for a specific charitable purpose which, although possible when the will was made, had become impossible; it was not a gift to the old people of a particular district. Accordingly there was no general charitable intention and the gift failed.

### (2) Gifts to charitable institutions

Gifts to charitable institutions need to be dealt with separately since the circumstances of such institutions may vary considerably.

**(a) Institutions which have never existed**. It appears to be relatively easy to infer a general charitable intention where the charity named by the testator has never existed. In *Re Harwood*,[59] it was held that a gift to a "peace society" which had never existed indicated a general charitable intention; thus the fund could be applied *cy-près* to other existing similar organisations. Such a construction may, however, be rebutted by the circumstances of the gift. Thus, in *Re Goldschmidt*,[60] Harman J. held that the presence in the will of a residuary gift in favour of other charitable purposes into which lapsed funds would fall was a factor against deducing a general charitable intention.

**(b) Institutions which formerly existed**. Where the institution specified by the donor as his intended charitable object formerly existed but no longer does in the form in which he described it, it has already been seen that it is possible that no "impossibility" will have occurred. But the fact that "impossibility" has occured does not prevent a general charitable intention being found.

---

[57] [1950] 2 All E.R. 653. See also to the same effect *Re Packe* [1918] 1 Ch. 437 (holiday home for clergymen of Church of England and their wives); *Re White's Trusts* (1886) 33 Ch.D. 449 (almshouses); *Re Wilson* [1913] 1 Ch. 314 (school); *Re Harwood* [1936] Ch. 285. Compare *Re Finger's Will Trusts* [1972] Ch. 286.

[58] [1979] Ch. 483; another gift in the same will to a Blind Home was held to be identifiable with a home for the blind of a different name and address and so was valid.

[59] [1936] Ch. 285. See also *Re Davis* [1902] 1 Ch. 876 ("Homes for the Homeless"). See also *Re Satterthwaite's Will Trusts* [1966] 1 W.L.R. 277.

[60] [1957] 1 W.L.R. 524 (gift to "Fund for Relief of Distressed German Jews" and no fund of that name existed; failed).

None was found in *Re Rymer*,[61] where there was a gift by will to the Rector for the time being of St Thomas' Seminary for the education of priests in the diocese of Westminster for the purposes of such a seminary. The seminary ceased to exist during the testator's lifetime. It was held that the gift had been made to a particular institution; this meant that not only was there "impossibility" but there could be no general charitable intention either. It is of course much less likely that this question will arise when the institution in question is unincorporated than when it is incorporated. In the case of an unincorporated body, the gift is in itself a purpose trust; provided that the work is still being carried on, it is unlikely that the disappearance of the donee during the lifetime of the testator will amount to "impossibility" in the first place unless there is something positive to show that the continued existence of the donee was essential to the gift. In the case of a corporation, on the other hand, the position is different, since there has to be something positive in the will to create a purpose trust at all;[62] this is because a gift to a corporate body *prima facie* takes effect as a gift to that body beneficially.[63] The distinction is illustrated by *Re Finger's Will Trusts*.[64] There were gifts by will both to an unincorporated association, the National Radium Commission, and to an incorporated body, the National Council for Maternity and Child Welfare. Both had been dissolved before the testator's death. The gift to the Commission was held to be a purpose trust for the work of the Commission which was not dependent on its continuing existence; consequently, there was no "impossibility". There was however "impossibility" in respect of the gift to the Council because the testator could not be taken to have intended that the gift could be applied for its purposes. Goff J. however held that the share of the fund which had been intended for the Council could nevertheless be applied *cy-près* because the will as a whole showed a general charitable intention. A similar conclusion was reached in *Re Stemson's Will Trusts*.[65]

### (3) Gifts to a mixture of charitable and non-charitable purposes or institutions

The fact that one gift for a non-charitable purpose is found among a number of gifts for charitable purposes does not permit the inference that the testator intended the non-charitable gift to take effect as a charitable gift when in terms it is not charitable. This is so even though the non-charitable gift may have a close relation to the purposes for which the charitable gifts were made. This was held to be the position in *Re Jenkins's Will Trusts*,[66] where a gift made to an non-charitable anti-vivisection association was coupled with gifts for the charitable purpose of preventing cruelty to animals. As Buckley J. said, in rejecting a *cy-près* application: "If you meet seven men with black hair and one with red hair you are not entitled to say that there are eight men with black hair".[67] It is not entirely clear whether the previous case of *Re Satterthwaite's*

---

[61] [1895] 1 Ch. 19. See, for a similar result, *Re Goldney* (1946) 115 L.J.Ch. 337.
[62] [1972] Ch. 286 at 295.
[63] See *Re Stemson's Will Trusts* [1970] Ch. 16.
[64] [1972] Ch. 423.
[65] [1970] Ch. 16.
[66] [1966] Ch. 249.
[67] [1966] Ch. 249 at 256.

*Will Trusts*[68] is consistent with this decision. In this case a human-hating testatrix gave money to the "London Animal Hospital". No hospital of this name
could be identified but, because of other gifts in favour of established animal
charities, the gift was held by the Court of Appeal to be applicable *cy-près*. The
case is, however, probably distinguishable on the ground that a gift to an
admittedly unidentified animal hospital had a sufficient charitable "flavour"
about it to justify this result.

## VI. THE ADMINISTRATION OF CHARITIES

Some of the rules which are set out in this section will be amended in the event
that the proposals submitted for consultation by the Report of the Government's Strategy Unit in 2002 are enacted. However, a number of these proposals were the subject of adverse comment during the consultation period,
which ended on December 31, 2002, and, with a view to avoiding any pssible
confusion, it therefore seems preferable to confine this section to a discussion
of the existing law.

### 1. *Central Authorities*

There is now only one central authority exercising jurisdiction over charities,[69]
the Charity Commissioners for England and Wales.[70] Formerly, the Secretary
of State for Education and Science and the Secretary of State for Wales had
concurrent jurisdiction with the Charity Commissioners and exercised it in
relation to charities of an educational nature.[71] The reason for conferring the
exercise of functions under the Charities Act 1993 exclusively upon the
Commissioners is that these functions are primarily judicial and not, therefore,
appropriately to be exercised by Ministers of the Crown. As for the constitution of the Commission, it is provided that there are to be a Chief Charity
Commissioner and from two to four other Commissioners,[72] at least two of
whom must be barristers or solicitors.[73] They are appointed by the Home
Secretary,[74] but are quite independent of him in their day-to-day administration.[75] They cannot even be compelled to follow any general guidance which
he may care to give.[76]

### 2. *The Official Custodian for Charities*

Before the Charities Act 1960 there were two officers, the Official Trustee of
Charity Lands and the Official Trustee of Charitable Funds. They existed so
that the legal title to charity lands and to charity funds respectively could be

---

[68] [1966] 1 W.L.R. 277.
[69] This has been the case since the Education Act 1973, s.1(1)(a), which came into force on February 4, 1974.
[70] Charities Act 1993, s.1(1) and Sched. 1.
[71] Charities Act 1960, s.2(1), repealed by Education Act 1973, s.1(1)(a).
[72] Charities Act 1993, Sched. 1, paras 1(1), (5). At present there are three other Commissioners.
[73] Sched. 1, para. 1(2).
[74] *ibid.*, para. 1(3).
[75] s.1(3),(4).
[76] *ibid.*

vested in them. There seemed to be no good reason why there should be two such offices[77] and the Charities Act 1960 combined them into one under the title of the Official Custodian for Charities.[78] There are advantages in vesting property in such a custodian trustee: first, it may make the title to that property more straightforward and, secondly and more importantly, it makes the appointment of new trustees on deaths or retirements unnecessary, thus saving the expense of new appointments. The Official Custodian for Charities is an officer of the Charity Commissioners and ranks as a corporation sole, having perpetual succession and an official seal. Because he is simply a custodian trustee, the actual management and control of the property in question remains in the charity trustees, who can in their own name commence or defend proceedings relating to the property without seeking his permission or joining him as a party.[79]

However, by virtue of the Charities Act 1992, the future role of the Official Custodian is to be limited to land[80] and he is to progressively divest himself of other property by transferring it to the trustees, or to such other persons as they nominate. This reform, which originally involved the divesting of holdings in excess of £1.25 billion, was carried out in order to increase the responsibility of the trustees. The Official Custodian for Charities nevertheless may retain any property vested in him by virtue of an order of the Commissioners made under section 18 of the 1993 Act where they feel that this is necessary for the protection of the charity in question.[81]

### 3. Registration

Sections 3 and 4 of the Charities Act 1993[82] provide for a central register of charities. Before the Charities Act 1960 was passed, the alarming fact was that neither the actual number of charities nor the amount of money devoted to charitable purposes had ever been known with any sort of precision. These registration provisions must, since 1960, have gone a long way towards curing this palpable defect of charity administration. There is now a positive duty on all charity trustees to apply for registration enforceable by order of the Commissioners.[83] All charities are registrable[84] unless they are expressly

---

[77] See Nathan Report, para. 228.

[78] Charities Act 1960, s.3(1), now Charities Act 1993, s.2(1). See also Charities Act 1993, ss.21–22 for the vesting of property in the Official Custodian.

[79] *Muman v. Nagasena* [2000] 1 W.L.R. 299.

[80] s.29.

[81] See (1992) 142 N.L.J. 541.

[82] These provisions were in 1960 almost entirely new in their effect. Although a statutory obligation to register was imposed by the Charitable Donations Act 1812, this was not observed in practice.

[83] The Charity Commission's website stated that in March 2003, 163,167 charities were on the register.

[84] It is necessary that, in order to be a charity, the organisation in question be subject to control by the High Court in the exercise of the court's jurisdiction with respect to charities. If that jurisdiction is wholly ousted by statute in relation to the organisation, then the organisation is not a charity and cannot be registered; see *Construction Training Board v. Att.-Gen.* [1973] Ch. 173 (where, however, the Board was held to be a charity because the provisions of the Industrial Training Act 1964 did not oust the jurisdiction of the court; the court still had control over the Board's functions).

relieved from the requirement.[85] One example of the latter is to be found in the so-called "exempt charities"; these are not subject to any of the supervisory powers of the Commissioners because satisfactory arrangements have already been made for carrying out the objects of such trusts and safeguarding the trust property. Examples of exempt charities are certain universities and colleges, the Church Commissioners, industrial and provident societies and friendly societies.[86] Some charities are also entitled to relief from registration in addition to the so-called "exempt charities". These are charities without any permanent endowment, that is to say no property which must be retained as capital, without property bringing in an income of more than £1,000 a year, and without land in its use and occupation. [87] Furthermore, any charity excepted by order or regulation is not required to be registered;[88] a number of regulations to this effect covering, for example, voluntary schools,[89] and boy scouts and girl guides[90] have been made. A further exemption operates in favour of registered places of worship.[91]

Registration raises a conclusive presumption that the institution is a charity at any time while it is on the register.[92] This accordingly removes a great deal of uncertainty about the status of certain institutions. But provision is necessarily made for a person who is or may be affected by the registration of an institution or trust as a charity to object to its entry on the register or apply for its removal on the ground that it is not in fact a charity, something which is of course a question for the general law.[93] This provision is intended for the benefit of anyone, especially a donor's residuary legatees or next-of-kin, whose interests will be affected by the answer to the question of whether the institutions or trusts should be classified as charities. An appeal against any decision of the Commissioners may be made to the High Court.[94] The Commissioners also themselves have the positive duty to remove from the register any institution which no longer appears to them to be a charity and also to remove any charity because it has ceased to exist or is not operating.[95]

Any registered charity with a gross income of over £5,000 in its last financial year must state the fact of its registration in all documents soliciting donations and on all bills, invoices and receipts.

---

[85] Charities Act 1993, s.3.
[86] See Charities Act 1993, s.3(5)(a), Sched. 2.
[87] s.3(5)(c).
[88] s.3(5)(b).
[89] The Charities (Exception of Voluntary Schools from Registration) Regulations 1960 (S.I. 1960 No. 2366).
[90] The Charities (Exception of Certain Charities for Boy Scouts and Girl Guides from Registration) Regulations 1961 (S.I. 1961 No. 1044).
[91] Charities Act 1993, s.3(5)(c) and for definition of "Registered Place of Worship", see Places of Worship Registration Act 1855, s.9.
[92] s.4(1).
[93] s.4(2).
[94] s.4(3), (4).
[95] s.3(4). A charitable company incorporated under the Companies Acts may also be wound up on an application made by the Attorney-General under Charities Act 1993, s.63(1); see *Liverpool and District Hospital for Diseases of the Heart v. Att.-Gen.* [1981] Ch. 193.

### 4. Accounts

The Charities Act 1993[96] also imposed much more rigorous duties on the trustees of unincorporated charities (the duties in this respect of incorporated charities are the usual ones imposed on all companies by the Companies Act 1985) to keep proper accounts and to prepare annual accounts. These must be audited if income exceeds £100,000; on the other hand, if income is less than £25,000, all that is required is statements of income and expenditure and a balance sheet. The trustees must also send to the Charity Commissioners annual reports of their activities, enclosing the accounts and, where appropriate, their auditors' report.

### 5. Co-ordination of Charitable Activities

Sections 76 to 78 of the 1993 Act, which were entirely new in 1960,[97] have as their aim the formation of a basis for co-operation between charities and the statutory welfare services. They authorise local authorities to review the working of those charities with that of the statutory services.[98] However, no obligation is put on a charity actually to co-operate; the Act requires mutual agreement between the local authority and the charity.[99] It was obviously hoped that this would lead to rationalisation of charitable activities over the country as a whole but few reviews seem yet to have been put in hand. Moreover, the review powers relate only to local charities; there are no powers to ensure reviews or co-ordination of national charities.

### 6. Scheme-Making and Other Powers

Section 16 of the 1993 Act empowers the Commissioners to exercise a jurisdiction concurrent with that of the High Court to make schemes relating to the administration of the charity, or orders for the appointment and removal of trustees and with regard to the vesting or transfer of property.[1] Although the court has a scheme-making power, it should be emphasised that in practice the vast majority of such schemes will be made by the Commissioners.[2] A scheme can obviously take a wide variety of forms; it may for example, take the drastic form of rewriting the original user trusts or management trusts of the charity or both. Appointments and removals of trustees will not normally require a scheme; they will be made simply by order of the Commissioners. The same applies to any vesting of the property of a charity in the Official Custodian for Charities.[3] In the usual way, jurisdiction can only be exercised by the Commissioners on an application made by the charity or on a reference by the court[4] or, save in the case of an exempt charity, on the application of the Attorney-General. However, in the case of a non-exempt charity with an

---

[96] Charities Act 1993, s.5(1).
[97] As Charities Act 1960, ss.10–12.
[98] ss.41–49 and Charities (Accounts and Reports) Regulations (S.I. 1995 No. 2724).
[99] s.78(2).
[1] s.16(1).
[2] s.16(1), (4).
[3] s.18.
[4] s.16(4).

annual income of less than £500, they may exercise their jurisdiction on the application of any trustee, of any person interested in the charity, or of any two inhabitants in the locality where it operates.[5]

Power is also specifically given to the Commissioners to act for the protection of charities where there has been misconduct or mismanagement and where the property of the charity needs to be protected and properly applied.[6] In these circumstances they are empowered to remove or appoint trustees and to prevent the operation of any banking account.[7]

A number of miscellaneous powers are also conferred on the Commissioners. Perhaps most important of all is the power to make an order where it appears that the proposed action is in the interests of the charity, authorising dealings or other action to be made or taken, whether or not it is within the administrative powers of the trustees.[8] This power, which is primarily administrative, is akin to the powers conferred by section 57 of the Trustee Act 1925[9] and by section 64 of the Settled Land Act 1925.[10] It may for example, authorise any given transaction, compromise or application of property or may, more specifically, authorise a charity to use common premises, or employ a common staff or otherwise combine, for any administrative purposes, with any other charity, although these are purely examples and do not limit the generality of the statutory power.[11] Other powers include that of advising charity trustees if the latter apply for advice,[12] which is in practice a particularly convenient facility, and powers to preserve charity documents.[13]

### 7. Investment

The powers and duties of trustees of a charity in relation to the investment of the trust funds are generally governed, in the same way as in the case of non-charitable trusts, by the terms of the trust instrument, if any, and by the general law of trusts relating to investments.[14] Since the enactment of the Trustee Act 2000,[15] trustees, including the trustees of charitable trusts, have had what section 3 of that Act describes as "the general power of investment", enabling them to make any kind of investment that they could make if they were absolutely entitled to the assets of the trust, subject to having regard to standard investment criteria and to obtaining and considering proper advice.[16] But in order to make effective use of this general power of investment, and the more restricted power in the Trustee Investment Act 1961 which it replaced, a

---

[5] s.16(5).
[6] s.18(1).
[7] s.18(1). For the procedure on appeal against removal (see s.18(7)), see *Jones v. Att.-Gen.* [1974] Ch. 148.
[8] s.26(1).
[9] See *post*, pp. 622, 742.
[10] See *post*, p. 743.
[11] s.26(2).
[12] s.29.
[13] s.30.
[14] See *post*, p. 592 and see also *Soldiers', Sailors' and Airmen's Families Association v. Att.-Gen.* [1968] 1 W.L.R. 313, where it was held that a corporation incorporated by royal charter cannot, by the making of rules, confer upon itself powers wider than those conferred upon it by the general law or the royal charter.
[15] See *post*, p. 573.
[16] Trustee Act 2000, ss.3–5.

relatively substantial fund is necessary so that risk can be spread and management expenses assimilated without difficulty. Many charities have extremely small trust funds and, if special provision were not made, they would not always be able to invest those funds efficiently. At the time of the passing of the Charities Act 1960, it was therefore thought desirable to make general provision, by way of common investment schemes, for the joint administration of a number of charitable trust funds for the purposes of investment. Common investment schemes had been made before, but only in particular cases, by statute[17] and by the court,[18] and the Charity Commissioners have always had the power to make schemes of a similar nature; but the Charities Act 1960 contained the first general provisions of this type. These provisions are now contained in sections 24 and 25 of the Charities Act 1993, to which the provisions of the Trustee Act 2000 expressly do not apply.[19]

Section 24 of the Charities Act 1993 enables the court and the Charity Commissioners to make schemes, known as "common investment schemes", for the establishment of common investment funds. These provide for property transferred to the fund by or on behalf of a charity participating in the scheme to be invested under the control of trustees appointed to manage the fund; they also provide for the participating charities to be entitled, subject to the provisions of the scheme, to the capital and income of the fund in shares determined by reference to the amount or value of the property transferred to it by or on behalf of each of them and to the value of the fund at the time of the transfers.[20] The first common investment scheme, known as the Charities Official Investment Fund, in which all charities may participate, was made by the Commissioners in 1962 and in 1976 two further schemes were made.[21] Section 24 also provides that the court or the Charity Commissioners may make a common investment scheme on the application of any two or more charities.[22] In Re University of London Charitable Trusts,[23] Wilberforce J. held that this provision enabled an application to be made by the trustees of any two or more charitable trusts, notwithstanding the fact that, as in this case, the trustees of the trusts in question are the same. More recently, the creation of common deposit funds was also authorised so as to still any doubts as to whether, under the earlier schemes, it was only possible to deposit funds at interest. These common deposit funds are what are now governed by section 25 of the Charities Act 1993.

---

[17] See Universities and Colleges (Trusts) Act 1943, which enabled the Universities of Oxford and Cambridge and the Colleges in those universities and also Winchester College to make schemes providing for funds to be administered as a single fund. (See Re Freeston's Charity [1978] 1 W.L.R. 741.) Private Acts have established common investment schemes for other universities; see, e.g. Liverpool University Act 1931; Birmingham University Act 1948.

[18] See Royal Society's Charitable Trusts [1956] Ch. 87; Re University of London Charitable Trusts [1964] Ch. 282.

[19] Trustee Act 2000, s.38.

[20] Charities Act 1993, s.24(1).

[21] Charinco Charities Narrower-Range Common Investment Fund, and Charibond Charities Narrower-Range Common Investment Fund; see the Report of the Charity Commissioners for 1976.

[22] s.24(2).

[23] [1964] Ch. 282.

## 8. *Dealings with Property Belonging to Charities*

Section 29 of the Charities Act 1960 abolished the old restrictions on dealings with property belonging to charities, which were fraught with excessive complexity. It used to be necessary in the past to decide whether a charity was, in the language employed, a plain or an endowed or a mixed charity. Under this provision, which remained in force until the enactment of the Charities Act 1992, the question which had to be considered was instead which of the three possible kinds of land which could be owned by a charity the land in question actually was. First, it could be part of the "permanent endowment", which meant property held subject to a restriction which prevented it from being spent in the same way as income;[24] such property only existed if the trust instrument made a distinction between the expenditure of capital and the expenditure of income. Secondly, it could be "functional land", land whether or not it was part of the permanent endowment, was or had been in the use and occupation of the charity.[25] Thirdly, it might instead have been bought as an investment with funds which were expendable without distinction between capital and income. In the first two cases, the sanction of the court or the Charity Commissioners was required. In the third case, which was probably the least common of all, it was not,[26] presumably because in this case a sale would not indicate a radical change in the character of the charity in the way that a sale of land within the first two heads would. However, the different categories of charities and of land which were respectively relevant before and after the enactment of the Charities Act 1960 and their attendant difficulties can now be forgotten except in the increasingly unlikely event that a transaction from either of these periods appears as part of the title to property produced in a current transaction and so requires investigation.[27]

The modern law is contained in section 36 of the Charities Act 1993. No land may be sold, leased or otherwise disposed of without an order of the court or of the Charity Commissioners unless the trustees have obtained and considered a written report on the proposed disposition from a qualified surveyor, advertised the proposed disposition for such period and in such manner as the surveyor has advised, and are satisfied that the terms are the best reasonably obtainable. Leases for seven years are subject to less stringent requirements.[28] Where the land in question is expressly held on trust for the purposes of the charity, it is also required that public notice be given and any representations received within one month duly considered, unless the purpose of the transaction is to acquire replacement property. The instrument by which any disposition is effected must certify that these provisions have been complied with; the certificate is conclusive in favour of a purchaser for money or money's worth.[29] However, this does not help a purchaser under an uncompleted contract, since that is not a disposition.[30]

---

[24] Charities Act 1960, s.45(3).
[25] s.29(2).
[26] *ibid.*
[27] This is now only possible in the case of unregistered land which has not changed hands for value since before 1960.
[28] Comparable provisions apply to mortgages; see Charities Act 1993, s.38.
[29] s.37.
[30] *Bayoumi v. Women's Total Abstinence Educational Union* [2003] 1 All E.R. 864.

### 9. The Making of Ex Gratia Payments

The court and the Attorney-General have the power to authorise charity trustees to make *ex gratia* payments out of funds held on charitable trusts,[31] for example, in pursuance of a moral obligation to relatives of the deceased. But this jurisdiction is not exercised lightly; it is necessary to show that, if the charity were an individual, it would be morally wrong of him not to make the payment.[32]

### 10. The Appointment of Trustees of Charities[33]

Generally, the rules which apply to private trusts also govern the appointment trustees of charities.[34] A major exception is that the restriction on the number of trustees imposed by section 34 of the Trustee Act 1925,[35] does not apply to charities. But there were and still are certain other specific provisions.

Before the Charities Act 1960, a convenient mode of appointment was provided in respect of land held on religious or educational trusts where the method of appointment was not prescribed in the trust instrument or had lapsed; the appointment merely had to be made under the hand and seal of the chairman of a meeting of the charity at which the appointment could be made, executed in the presence of the meeting and attested by two witnesses. This was a "conclusive" act of appointment which vested the property in both the new and the continuing trustees.[36] But the Charities Act 1960 provided in what is now section 83 of the Charities Act 1993 that new trustees may be appointed at a meeting, if a memorandum of the appointment is signed at the meeting by the person presiding or in some other manner prescribed by the meeting, and attested by two witnesses; that is then "sufficient" evidence of the appointment. This provision applies to all charities (unlike the previous legislation) but it can be made use of only when the trusts permit it and, most importantly, it is only "sufficient" (as opposed to "conclusive") evidence of appointment, thus enabling its sufficiency to be checked on investigation of title by a purchaser.

The Charities Act 1992 in what is now section 73 of the Charities Act 1993 provided for the disqualification from holding the office of charitable trustee of anyone convicted of an offence involving dishonesty or deception, of undischarged bankrupts, and of those previously removed from such an office on the grounds of misconduct or mismanagement. Any one who acts while so disqualified is guilty of an offence carrying a maximum sentence of two years imprisonment and/or a fine. The Charity Commissioners may, subject to an appeal to the High Court to which they are not appropriate parties,[37] remove

---

[31] *Re Snowden* [1970] Ch. 700.

[32] *ibid.* at 710.

[33] For the powers of a receiver and manager appointed for a charity, see *Att.-Gen. v. Schonfeld* [1980] 1 W.L.R. 1182.

[34] See *post*, p. 543.

[35] See *post*, p. 560.

[36] The relevant legislation, the Trustees Appointment Acts 1850, 1869 and 1890, was repealed by the Charities Act 1960, s.35(6) but the provisions were nevertheless preserved in relation to land acquired by such trusts before January 1, 1961.

[37] *Weth v. Att-Gen.* [1999] 1 W.L.R. 686. The Attorney-General may be an appropriate party.

any trustee:[38] first, if they are satisfied that there has been misconduct or mismanagement and that this is necessary or desirable for the purpose of protecting the property of the charity; and, secondly, if a trustee has been discharged from bankruptcy during the last five years, is a corporation in liquidation, is mentally incapable, has not acted, is outside England and Wales, or cannot be found.

## 11. *Mortmain*

The law of mortmain was, rather belatedly, repealed by the Charities Act 1960.[39] This law, which dated from the thirteenth century,[40] prevented corporations from holding freehold land without a licence from the Crown. Its purpose was to prevent land being tied up in the dead hand ("mortmain") of such artificial persons indefinitely and it was aimed particularly at ecclesiastical foundations which were the principal type of corporations in existence at that time. Its underlying purpose was the protection of the feudal revenues of the Crown and other feudal lords, which largely arose as a result of freehold land passing by inheritance. The law of mortmain was extended to all gifts to charity by the Charitable Uses Act 1735. This Act, as well as the pre-existing law, was re-enacted by the Mortmain and Charitable Uses Act 1888. One of the principal provisions relating to charity in this Act was to require enrolment of every assurance of land in favour of a charity in the Central Office of the Supreme Court. This Act was later replaced by section 29(4) of the Settled Land Act 1925, which required in place of this the recording of any such assurance with the Charity Commissioners. This subsection was in turn repealed and replaced, so far as educational charities were concerned, by section 87(2) of the Education Act 1944, which required assurances of land in favour of educational charities to be recorded with the Minister of Education.

The registration provisions of what is now the Charities Act 1993 have rendered any such recording unnecessary and it has not been required since July 29, 1960.[41] But, since the whole of the law of mortmain has been abolished, it is not only the field of charity that is affected but the law generally. The repeal was retrospective so that the title to property cannot now be defeated as a result of a failure to comply with the mortmain legislation in the past.[42]

## 12. *Enforcement of Charitable Trusts*[43]

The Crown has the function of enforcing charitable trusts as *parens patriae* and the Attorney-General, on behalf of the Crown, will be joined as a party to any proceedings involving a charity. Where there is a bona fide dispute as to the existence of a charity, the Attorney-General should bring the proceedings or, where the existence of the charity is being challenged by those who would

---

[38] Charities Act 1993, s.18.
[39] s.38 & Sched. 7, Pt II.
[40] See *ante*, p.3.
[41] The date when the Charities Act 1960 came into force; Charities Act 1960, s.38(2).
[42] That is before July 29, 1960; s.38(2).
[43] For personal liability of charity trustees, see Hawkins (1979) 75 L.Q.R. 99.

otherwise be entitled to the property in question, defend them.[44] Proceedings for the enforcement of charitable trusts which do not challenge the existence of the charity in question can be brought not only by the Attorney-General, but also by the charity itself, by any of the trustees of the charity or by any persons interested in the charity or, if the charity in question is a local charity, by any two or more inhabitants from the area of the charity.[45] However, anyone who brings such proceedings other than the Attorney-General must first obtain an order from the Charity Commissioners or from a judge of the Chancery Division of the High Court authorising the institution of proceedings.[46] But this requirement does not apply where the trustees of a charity are bringing proceedings against an outsider, such as an action for possession against a commercial tenant of property owned by the charity; such proceedings are not for the enforcement of the charitable trusts.[47]

---

[44] *Re Belling* [1967] Ch. 425; *Hauxwell v. Barton-upon-Humber U.D.C.* [1974] Ch. 432; *Childs v. Att.-Gen.* [1973] 1 W.L.R. 497.

[45] Charities Act 1993, s.33(1).

[46] Charities Act 1993, s.33(2).

[47] See *Muman v. Nagasena* [2000] 1 W.L.R. 299, where permission was held to be necessary where the trustees' action for possession was against an insider, the patron or resident monk of the Buddhist charity in question.

CHAPTER 12

# PENSION TRUSTS[1]

ONE of the most important purposes for which trusts are employed today is to provide pensions for retired persons and their dependants. Since the Second World War, pension schemes have become increasingly important and are now regarded as an essential part of virtually every contract of employment and an important factor for the self-employed. About half the national work force are, by virtue of their employment, members of what are known as occupational pensions schemes; what are known as personal pension schemes have been taken out by about a quarter of the work force, either the self-employed or employees who are "topping-up" the pension provision made by their occupational pension scheme. However, these figures also meant that, at least until 2001, considerably more than a quarter of the work force had no pension other than their state pension; however, since April 6, 2001, every employer with more than five employees has had to offer those employees the right to join what is known as a stakeholder pension scheme (the terms of these schemes determine whether they take effect as occupational pension schemes or as personal pension schemes).

Pension provision is of enormous social significance, which is likely to become even more important in the light of the declared policy of the present government to move towards an increasing dependance on private rather than state pensions, a policy of which the introduction of stakeholder pensions formed merely the first stage. Further, the net value of the investment assets of pension schemes constitutes a very substantial proportion of the available investment capital of the country. In 1995 United Kingdom pension funds were estimated to be worth in excess of £500 billion and growing. Growth peaked at about £715 billion in 1999 but had fallen back to about £525 billion by the end of 2002 as a result of persistent falls in the value of the shares in which a large proportion of pension funds have habitually been invested.

Pension funds provided for employees are, in the vast majority of cases,

---

[1] Pensions law is considered in detail in *Tolley's Pensions Handbook* (4th ed., 2002). More detailed still are the two loose-leaf practitioner works: Ellison, *Pensions Law & Practice* and Sweet & Maxwell, *The Law of Pension Schemes*. The immense quantity of statutes, Statutory Instruments, and announcements by the Inland Revenue and the Occupational Pensions Regulatory Authority may be found in the loose-leaf *NAPF Pensions Legislation Service*. A useful summary of pensions law as it existed prior to the Pensions Act 1995 and the recommendations which led to that legislation may be found in *Pension Law Reform*: Pension Law Review Committee Report (1993) Cmd. 2342.

held by trustees with the objective, usually but sadly not always[2] achieved, of assuring the employee that his pension will in fact be forthcoming on his retirement and that in the meantime his employer cannot in any way dispose of the pension contributions which have been made. This objective has, at least in principle, been considerably enhanced by the recently enacted requirement that one-third of the trustees (or, where the trustee is a trust company, of its directors) must be nominated by the employees.[3] The funds contributed to personal pension schemes by both the self-employed and by employees are typically paid to insurance companies for investment in insurance policies but can also be held in the form of investments by trustees, in such cases usually trust corporations. The fact that the majority of the leading decisions in the last decade relating to the basic principles of trust law has involved a pension fund in one way or another demonstrates that litigation involving pension trusts has proliferated; it also means that a basic knowledge of the working of pension trusts is now essential for every trust lawyer.

## I. THE NATURE OF PENSION SCHEMES

This chapter is entirely concerned with occupational pension schemes and, more specifically, with those schemes in which payments are made to trustees to be invested and in due course, used for the provision of benefits for the employees. Occupational pension schemes may be either contributory, in which case both employer and employee pay into the fund, or non-contributory, in which case the whole of the necessary funding is provided by the employer (however, employers are not obliged to contribute to stakeholder pension schemes at all). Only occupational pension schemes are likely to give rise to litigation between the members and the trustees susceptible of affecting the basic principles of trust law. Even where the funds invested in a personal pension scheme are vested in trustees rather than, as is more usual, in insurance policies, there is no likelihood of any litigation of this type simply because the membership of the scheme is confined to the contributor and his dependants. All pension schemes are, of course, superimposed on the basic old age pension provided by the State. The way in which the State pension is calculated is relevant to the way in which occupational pension schemes work (and in particular the terminology employed in its calculation is often utilised in judgments); a brief consideration of this question is therefore necessary.

---

[2] The systematic looting by the late Robert Maxwell of about £450 million from the pension fund established to provide pensions for ex-employees of *The Daily Mirror* caused great concern among employees in general. Pension fund administration then became the subject of a Committee of Inquiry, the Pensions Law Reform Committee, which reported in the autumn of 1993 (*Pension Law Reform*: [1993] Cmd. 2342, generally known as "the Goode Report") and came down on the side of continuing to utilise the trust vehicle. However, the Committee proposed a substantial number of reforms, some of which were enacted in the Pensions Act 1995 (see Nobles (1996) 59 M.L.R. 241).

[3] Pensions Act 1995, ss.16–21. For the moment, this rule only operates where the employer cannot persuade the members to accept alternative arrangements more favourable to himself; see *post*, fn. 53.

## 1. *The State Pension*

The provision made by the State pension scheme for employees (Category A pensions) comprises a basic pension[4] and an additional element, related to the employee's earnings. The State also provides the same two elements by way of pension to the widow or widower of a deceased employee (Category B pensions) if the former's own State pension entitlement is lower.[5] To qualify for the basic pension, the employee must have paid National Insurance contributions for approximately 90% of his working life.[6] The State also provides non-contributory pensions to persons who retired before the State scheme started (Category C pensions) or are over 80, satisfy certain residence conditions, and have no other category of State pension (Category D pensions). All these pensions are increased annually in line with the Retail Prices Index.

The additional element related to the employee's earnings between April 6, 1978 (when entitlement to this element commenced) and April 5, 2002 came from the State earnings-related pension scheme, generally described by reference to the acronym "SERPS"; since April 6, 2002, SERPS has been replaced by the State Second Pension or "S2P". Both apply only to earnings between the lower and upper limits in respect of which basic[7] National Insurance Contributions are payable[8] and a percentage of those earnings, revalued each year to take account of inflation during the period prior to retirement, is what constitutes the additional element. The value of the SERPS element has been progressively reduced. Earnings during the first 10 years during which the system operated (until April 5, 1988) are averaged and multiplied by 25 per cent. Earnings thereafter are averaged during throughout a person's entire working life and multiplied by a figure which is being reduced from the former figure of 25 per cent[9] by ½ per cent each year until it reaches 20 per cent.[10] The value of the S2P element varies from 40% to 10% depending on which of three bands between the lower and upper limits is relevant. The principal change is that for the first time credits are being given to those caring for children under six and for sick and disabled persons and to sick and disabled persons themselves; they will be treated as if they had earned an interim figure known as the low earnings threshold. The pension payable is of one-eightieth of the total amount of the relevant earnings for each

---

[4] In the year 2003–2004, £77.45 per week for each person who qualifies, £46.35 extra per week for a non-qualifying spouse of a person who qualifies (after his or her death, the non-qualifier receives the higher amount).

[5] The State also provides non-contributory pensions at two-thirds of the above rates to persons who retired before the State scheme started (Category C pensions) or who are over 80, satisfy certain residence conditions, and have no other category of State pension (Category D pensions).

[6] 49 years for a man and for a woman born on or after April 6, 1955, both of whom retire at 65; 44 for a woman born before April 6, 1950 who retires at 60 (the working life and retirement age of women born between these two dates increases progressively in accordance with Pensions Act 1995, Sched. 4, para.1.).

[7] As from April 6, 2003, a further 1% has been payable on all earnings above the upper limit.

[8] In the year 2003–2004, the lower limit was £4,004 per annum and the upper limit was £30,940 per annum.

[9] Which applied up to April 5, 1999.

[10] For persons who reached retirement age before April 6, 1999, the average is instead the average of their best 20 years.

of the years during which SERPS or SUP has been earned or credited up to a maximum of forty-eightieths.

The two elements of the State pension are payable whether or not the person in question is a member of a private pension scheme. However, it is possible for an occupational pension scheme to contract out of SERPS and S2P. This means that its members agree not to take the additional element of their pension from the State and the private pension scheme then has to meet that liability instead. Financial incentives are provided to encourage contracting out in the form of reduced National Insurance Contributions by both employers and employees. Where the members of a scheme have elected to contract out, it is obviously essential that the pension provided to each member on retirement is at least as much as he would have obtained by way of the SERPS element. For service prior to April 6, 1997 this amount was known as the guaranteed minimum pension ("GMP") and was calculated by a formula similar, but not actually identical, to that by which the SERPS element itself is calculated. During this period, it was possible for schemes to cease to be contracted out, in which case its members had to be bought back into the SERPS scheme by the payment of what were known as "state scheme premiums".[11] Schemes which contracted out on or after April 6, 1997 (schemes which had already done so were obliged to re-elect so to do) have instead to meet a statutory standard (accumulated GMPs survive) and it is no longer possible to contract back into the SERPS scheme. The statutory benefits in respect of each year worked are basically one-eightieth of 90 per cent of the average earnings between the lower and upper limits in respect of which National Insurance Contributions are payable during the three years prior to termination of service, together with a spouse's pension of one-half, revaluation of the pension payable during any further period up to actual retirement, and limited indexation of pensions in payment. Obviously, if a person ceases to be employed by an employer with a contracted out scheme, he accrues entitlement to SERPS or, now, S2P in respect of non contracted out earnings.

## 2. Stakeholder Pension Schemes

Because stakeholder pension schemes straddle the normal division between occupational pension schemes and personal pension schemes, it is necessary to consider them briefly here. Since 2001, every employer with more than five employees has had to offer those employees the right to take out a stakeholder pension. Such pensions, which were introduced by the Welfare Reform and Pensions Act 1999, came into effect on April 6, 2001 and employers were obliged to have schemes in place by October 8, 2001. There are at present

---

[11] Where a member leaves a contracted out scheme prior to retirement, the pension to which he remains entitled to obtain on his retirement will include his GMP element, which will continue to grow by virtue of the process of revaluation. Originally only the GMP element of his pension was revalued (thereby gradually consuming any additional pension to which he was entitled) but by what is known as "anti-franking legislation", any excess in his pension over his GMP element was first preserved and eventually made subject to revaluation itself (see Pension Schemes Act 1993, ss. 83–86, 87–92 respectively). However, a member who leaves an occupational pension scheme is now entitled to transfer his pension rights to any other approved pension scheme which he joins (Pension Schemes Act 1993, Pt IV; Pensions Act 1995, s.95); if he chooses to do so, the sum transferred to his new scheme in respect of his accrued pension entitlements must include the GMP (or current equivalent) element of that entitlement.

exemptions for employers who offer membership of an occupational pension scheme to all employees within a year of the commencement of their employment, to employers who offer a group personal pension to which they contribute at least 3 per cent per annum of their employees' earnings, and to employers whose employees all earn less than the National Insurance Contributions lower earning limit.

The obligations of an employer who is obliged to offer his employees the right to take out a stakeholder pension are confined, first, to providing the scheme, either directly or through a pension provider, and, secondly, to enabling each employee's desired contributions to be deducted from his remuneration. It must be emphasised that employers are not obliged to make any contributions whatsoever. Employees cannot make contributions of less than £20 net of basic rate tax. Otherwise, they can contribute as much as they like,[12] subject to the fiscal limits which apply to all pension contributions,[13] as often as they like; there is no obligation to make regular contributions. No fees can be charged by the employer or anyone else for setting up the scheme and administration charges are limited to 1 per cent per annum of the value of the fund built up.

Stakeholder pension schemes can either be established on a trust basis or on a contract basis. If they are established on a trust basis, they take effect as occupational pension schemes and are governed by the vast majority of the rules considered in this chapter. If, instead, they are established on a contract basis, they take effect as personal pensions schemes and are outside the scope of this chapter. The choice is in principle that of the employer, although "industry-wide" schemes (schemes in which the definition of membership is by reference to employment in the industry, rather than by any particular employer)[14] must be established on a trust basis. Any existing occupational pension schemes which are converted to stakeholder pension schemes will also in practice have to be established on a trust basis, although such conversions are highly unlikely because of the low level of fees able to be charged under a stakeholder pension scheme. However, all stakeholder pensions which have been offered by pension providers have been offered on a contract basis. Consequently, apart from industry-wide schemes and any conversions, the only stakeholder pension schemes which are likely to have been set up on a trust basis are those schemes set up by employers alongside their existing occupational pension schemes; it is thought that such schemes would particularly assist employees who have an irregular working pattern or who have not been members of an occupational pension scheme throughout their working lives, but there is no evidence that this practice is at all widespread.

---

[12] There is an annual maximum figure for contributions by non-employees which in 2003–2004 was £3,600.

[13] Which is calculated in relation to the "pension cap"; see *post*, p. 513.

[14] An example is the Merchant Navy Pension Scheme.

The response so far to the offer of stakeholder pension schemes of both types seems to have been fairly poor.[15]

### 3. Occupational Pension Schemes

It should first be re-emphasised that no employer is under any legal obligation whatever to make any provision for his employees by way of pension; this remains the case despite the introduction of stakeholder pensions, since employers are obliged merely to provide such schemes, not to contribute to them. Employers who make no contributions to any pension scheme for their employees simply pay National Insurance Contributions at the higher contracted in rate so that the employees will receive both the basic and the additional elements of the State pension when they retire. Given the low level of pension produced by the State, most employees in this position need to give serious consideration to taking out a personal pension scheme or joining a stakeholder pension scheme.

### (A) Types of Schemes

Of the various types of occupational pension schemes which exist, this chapter is only concerned with those in which employees and/or employers make payments to trustees to be invested in assets, which will provide the payment of the benefits for which the scheme provides as they fall due. Brief mention should, however, be made of some of the other types of schemes.

The majority of schemes for employees in the public sector (the best example is the civil service) are established by legislation and are therefore backed by the revenue of the Government rather than by a segregated trust fund; in such circumstances, the employees have to rely on the certainty of the continuity of Government revenue to meet its statutory obligations rather than the performance of any fund.

Some non-statutory schemes are also, in the same sense, unfunded in that the employer does not segregate any assets for the purpose of providing for the payment of the benefits as they fall due; such schemes are known as "pay-as-you-go" schemes and are necessarily non-contributory. Employer and employees have to rely on the employer still having sufficient assets to fund the appropriate benefits at the appropriate time. The employees would certainly be most ill-advised so to rely in the case of a trading company, which

---

[15] The principal target of stakeholder pension schemes was obviously employees who had no existing pension provision, for whom the restriction on the level of administration costs is extremely beneficial since their only alternative, personal pension schemes, invariably have very much higher initial charges. The Government also hoped that holders of personal pension schemes who are "topping-up" their occupational pension schemes would convert to stakeholder pension schemes and that all such schemes would opt out of SERPS or S2P, thus saving the State a considerable amount of money. Neither objective was particularly realistic: the holders of existing personal pensions who converted would be prejudiced in that the charges under their personal pension schemes would in later years be likely to be considerably less than the 1% which stakeholder pension schemes will inevitably charge; nor is it in the interest of employees for their stakeholder pension schemes to opt out of SERPS or S2P except in the unlikely event that their employer is contributing. Further, because non-employees can also join a stakeholder pension scheme, these schemes have also become a means of enabling the adult children of the wealthy to build up pension provision at the expense of taxpayers. Reforms to the existing system are therefore obviously likely sooner rather than later.

could simply become insolvent or sell its business to a third party who was not bound by the contracts of employment in question, and the employer could find himself with the need to make a substantial payment before he expected to have to do so if any employee who left before retirement exercised his statutory right to an immediate[16] cash transfer of the value of his accrued benefits to another pension scheme.[17] Further, such schemes do not enjoy any of the taxation benefits of funded schemes so the employer will need to be satisfied that the net return which he can receive by leaving in his business the funds which would otherwise have provided the pension contributions will be at least as much as the gross returns which would be obtained by investing them in a funded scheme. However, employers such as the owners of large historic landed estates which they are, in practice, incapable of selling could certainly run "pay-as-you-go" schemes; their employees would presumably be content to rely on the underlying value of the estates in question while the benefits payable by way of pensions and lump sums in any one year could be charged by the employer as trading expenses against the income of the estate.

Even within the vast majority of private pension schemes which are funded by the segregation of assets in the hands of trustees, many of the smaller schemes operate as insured schemes, under which the trustees take out a contract with an insurance company in respect of each employee to provide the benefits which he has contracted to receive and use the pension contributions merely to pay the premiums on the policy. In such schemes, assuming that the policies in question provide whatever cover is appropriate from time to time, the only question which the trustees ever have to consider is whether the contributions are sufficient to pay the premiums.

### (B) Funded Schemes

The remaining schemes, where the trustees place the contributions paid to them in a fund which they then invest in order to provide in advance for the payment of pensions as they fall due, are known as funded schemes. They pose rather more problems.

Most schemes of this type are associated with groups of trading companies or a single trading company, where membership is dependent on being an employee of a company within the scheme. However, there are also what are known as "industry-wide" schemes, in which the definition of membership is by reference to employment in the industry, rather than by any particular employer.[18] One of the many ways in which schemes are classified is into "final salary schemes" and "money purchase schemes". Both may be either contributory or non-contributory.

### (1) "Final salary schemes"

A "final salary scheme", often also known as a "defined benefit scheme" provides benefit in accordance with length of service and salary. Such schemes are normally now contributory (except in the case of relatively low paid

---

[16] Early in 2003, schemes with substantial deficits were allowed temporarily to defer such transfers.

[17] Pension Schemes Act 1993, Pt IV; Pensions Act 1995, s.95. The sum transferred to the new scheme in respect of any member's accrued pension entitlements must include the GMP (or current equivalent) element of that entitlement.

[18] An example is the Merchant Navy Pension Scheme.

employment) and are usually on a "balance of cost" basis; the employee makes a fixed contribution of an established percentage of his salary and the employer has to make whatever contributions are from time to time actuarially necessary to provide the benefits for which the scheme is potentially liable as they fall due. In this type of scheme, it is the employer rather than the employee who runs the risk of a poor investment performance. The Pensions Act 1995 introduced a "minimum funding requirement" ("MFR") with effect from April 7, 1997.[19] Under MFR, periodic actuarial valuations must be obtained in order to determine whether the assets are sufficient to fund the minimum liabilities of the scheme; if they are not, the employer must eliminate the shortfall, originally within one year (now extended to three years) if it is greater than 10 per cent, and originally within five years (now extended to ten years) if it is less.[20] On the other hand, a good investment performance may enable the employer to take what is known as a "contributions holiday" by ceasing to pay any contributions whatever until an established surplus in the fund has been used up.

In its simplest form, "final salary" means the salary being earned by the employee at the date of his retirement but this is usually varied; the most common variants are the highest salary in the last three (or five) years of employment prior to retirement, or the average salary during one of those periods (however, not all the payments received by the employee will necessarily qualify for this purpose; allowances and bonuses are generally not pensionable, which means that they are excluded). The benefits provided by the scheme are determined, subject to limits imposed by the Inland Revenue as a condition of approval of the scheme, by length of service; a fairly standard percentage is one-sixtieth for each year of service, although many quasi-public employees, such as university lecturers, who have their own separately funded schemes, only receive a much more miserly one-eightieth for each year of service.

The benefits provided always include an annuity of the appropriate percentage of the relevant salary, usually guaranteed for five years (which means that the balance is payable to the pensioner's estate if he dies during this period). They also have to include, since April 6, 1973,[21] preservation rights, that is to say the right to what is known as a "deferred pension" by means of which the accumulated pension rights of any employee who leaves prior to retirement age are preserved and enhanced by revaluation and, since April 6, 1978[22] in the case of contracted-out schemes, provision for the payment in priority to all other liabilities of the scheme of the additional element of the State pension. The package of benefits usually also includes some or all of the following: an option to commute part of the annuity for the immediate payment of a lump sum — the annuity is then reduced by reference to a formula; an annuity, usually between a half and two-thirds of the pensioner's annuity, for a surviving widow (sometimes also extended to widowers) and/or any dependent children; and a death-in-service benefit, a lump sum which the trustees have the discretion to distribute, sometimes with a right of nomina-

---

[19] ss.56–59.
[20] The longer periods came into effect on March 19, 2002 but only prospectively.
[21] By virtue of Social Security Act 1973, now Pension Schemes Act 1993, ss.93–101.
[22] Social Security Pensions Act 1975, introducing SERPS and (for "defined benefit" schemes) contracting-out of SERPS with effect from April 1978, now Pensions Schemes Act 1993, s.14.

tion for the member.[23] All pensions in payment are now subject to "limited price indexation" ("LPI"), in that they are required to increase in line with the retail prices index or (if less) by 5 per cent per annum in respect of service on and after April 6, 1997.[24] Most schemes obviously endeavour also to increase pensions in payment in respect of earlier service but there are no statutory obligations in this respect.

### (2) "Money purchase schemes"

A "money purchase scheme" is also known as a "defined contribution scheme". Such schemes are usually, but not necessarily, contributory; where they are, the employer and the employee tend to contribute equal amounts, which for the employer will almost inevitably be less than he would have had to contribute to a final salary scheme.[25] The contributions made to the scheme are invested by the trustees and held by them for each member of the scheme and his dependants. Each member has in effect his own notional sub-fund comprising the contributions made by or on his behalf and the value of his benefits depends entirely on his share of the net return made by the investments in which the trustees invest the fund; his position is not unlike that of the holder of units in a unit trust. In such schemes, it is consequently the employee, not the employer, who assumes the risk of a poor investment performance. For this reason, the minimum funding requirement introduced by the Pensions Act 1995 does not apply to money purchase schemes. Because of the fact that employers do not have to contribute to stakeholder pension schemes, such schemes are necessarily money purchase schemes.

On retirement, or death in service, the notional sub-fund is realised and used to purchase an annuity, usually index-linked, for the benefit of the member and his dependants and to provide whatever other benefits are envisaged by the scheme (such as the right to commutation of part of the annuity for the payment of an immediate lump sum). The payments of the annuity are also now subject to limited price indexation in respect of service on or after April 7, 1997 and so must increase in line with the retail prices index or (if less) by 5 per cent per annum; the difference, of course, is that the employer is not obliged to pay for these increases — which must therefore be borne in mind when the annuity is being purchased.

### 3. *The Choice Between Final Salary and Money Purchase Schemes*

Given that no employer is under any legal obligation whatever to make any provision for his employees by way of pension, the choice of whether to implement a defined benefit or a defined contribution scheme and, for that matter, of whether whatever scheme is selected should be contributory or non-contributory is inevitably that of the employer. Final salary schemes predominated until the introduction of the minimum funding requirement with

---

[23] See Inheritance Tax Act 1984, s.151(5); in *Wild v. Smith* [1996] O.P.L.R. 129, Carnwath J. upheld the ruling of the Pensions Ombudsman that the member in question had not validly nominated his mistress as a dependant.

[24] Pensions Act 1995, s.51. The introduction of this requirement obviously makes more onerous the minimum funding requirement introduced by the same legislation.

[25] Because few employees would be enthusiastic about contributing as much of their emoluments as employees have to contribute to a final salary scheme.

effect from 1997. Once the legislation relating to this requirement had been enacted in 1995, employers introducing new occupational pension schemes tended instead to opt for money purchase schemes, to which that requirement does not of course apply, in order to be able to cap their own contributions. However, this did not initially have any impact on existing occupational pension schemes, other than raising the level of employer's contributions to them.

From 1999, however, many schemes became faced with actual or potential deficits as a result of the combination of the minimum funding requirement, the withdrawal from 1998, originally announced in 1997, of the tax credit previously given to pension schemes in respect of their dividend income, and the substantial falls in the value of shares which commenced in 1999. As early as 2000, the Government announced proposals for the eventual, but not immediate, abolition of the minimum funding requirement and, with effect from 2002, lengthened the periods for compliance with it. However, this proved to be too little too late in the light of the continued falls in the value of shares and it is now not likely that there will be all that many final salary schemes still open by the time that the minimum funding requirement is eventually abolished.

This is because from 2001 onwards an ever-increasing number of major companies closed their final salary schemes to new employees, offering the latter only membership of money purchase schemes. Admittedly, no one could justifiably complain about this, but some companies went further and closed their final salary schemes completely so that future service by both existing and new employees could only generate benefits under money purchase schemes. This did not of course affect benefits already earned but nevertheless altered the overall employment package of existing employees, producing some threats of industrial action. A few companies have provoked much more vociferous threats of this type by deciding to wind up their final salary schemes completely; this process tends also to reduce benefits already earned unless the scheme in question is extremely well funded.[26] It must however be emphasised that none of these courses of conduct is actually prohibited, or even frowned on, by the present law.

## (C) Fiscal Regulation
Substantial fiscal benefits are available to schemes which the Inland Revenue recognises as "exempt approved schemes";[27] such recognition and all other matters relating to the taxation of pension schemes are dealt with by one of the business streams of the Inland Revenue Capital and Savings organisation called IR SPSS. The main criteria are the Inland Revenue limits on benefits and, to a lesser extent, on contributions.

The limits on benefits restrict payments by way of pension to two-thirds of "final salary" and, in the case of employees joining after March 1987, only after 20 years' service (with the appropriate number of thirtieths until then).[28] Lump

---

[26] See post, p. 536.
[27] Under Income and Corporation Taxes Act 1988, ss.590–612. Approval is mandatory if the scheme fulfils the conditions in s.590, while discretionary approval can be granted under s.591 (the criteria are set out in the Inland Revenue "Practice Notes" IR12 (1991)).
[28] Employees who joined before March 1987 reached the two-thirds limit after 10 years' service, but until then could have only the appropriate number of sixtieths.

sum payments are restricted to 150 per cent of "final salary" and only then after 20 years' service (with the appropriate number of three-eightieths until then) with further restrictions to 225 per cent of the initial annuity for those joining after May 1989. Death in service lump sum benefits are restricted to four times the amount of remuneration at the time of death plus the return of all contributions paid with interest. A widow's (or, where relevant, widower's) pension is restricted to two-thirds of the maximum pension payable. The limits on contributions prevent more than 15 per cent of an employee's pensionable earnings from any employment being contributed, but he can make additional contributions to personal pension schemes up to a higher percentage, which increases in line with his age.[29] The total permissible benefits and contributions are the appropriate percentages of a figure known as "the pension cap", which is increased each year in line with inflation (it was £99,000 in 2003–2004).[30] These limits do not prevent further contributions being made to unapproved schemes but no fiscal benefits can be obtained thereby.

Under an "exempt approved scheme", the contributions of the employer are treated as trading expenses and thus are exempt from both income and corporation tax, while the employee is exempt from income tax both on his own contributions and on those of the employer. Lump sum payments are tax free in the hands of a pensioner, although his pension payments will be subject to income tax at his marginal rate. An approved funded scheme is liable neither to income tax nor to capital gains tax on its investments; however, the benefit of the income tax exemption was substantially reduced in 1998 when the exemption from what was then the 20 per cent tax retained by companies on their dividends was abolished (admittedly, the retention was subsequently reduced to 10 per cent anyway but, as has already been mentioned, the abolition of the exemption had the effect of placing many final salary schemes in actual or potential deficit and was a contributory factor in their closure). An approved insured scheme is entitled to equivalent benefits. Reform of the taxation of pensions has been promised with effect from April 6, 2004,[31] but it is not thought likely that this will affect any of the principles set out above.

Approval is available both to all types of funded schemes and to insured schemes. There seems no reason why the Inland Revenue should not in its discretion approve "pay-as-you-go" schemes as well if satisfied with their underlying assets and their limits on benefits; this would enable lump sum payments made under such schemes to be tax free in the hands of their beneficiaries.

However, approval will be withdrawn, with extremely adverse retrospective fiscal consequences, in the event that an approved scheme is found to have an excessive surplus of assets over liabilities which is not brought within the statutory limit of 105 per cent.[32] All schemes must have an actuarial

---

[29] A total of 17.5 per cent at the age of 35 or below, increasing to 40 per cent at the age of 61 or more.

[30] The increasing percentages and the pension cap also apply to the self-employed and determine their maximum contributions to approved personal pension schemes.

[31] Principally with a view to providing a common system for the taxation of all the different types of personal pensions.

[32] Income and Corporation Taxes Act 1988, Sched. 22; Pension Scheme Surpluses (Valuation) Regulations 1987 (S.I. 1987/412), referring to the previous legislation in Finance Act 1986, Sched. 12.

valuation at least every three years. However, in calculating the "statutory surplus", assets and liabilities have to be valued using prescribed actuarial assumptions which are generally regarded as rather "conservative". Consequently, it is perfectly possible for there to be a very substantial surplus in the fund when it is valued in accordance with the actuary's normal assumptions and criteria but no statutory surplus at all. The way in which surpluses are eradicated is one of the most conflictive questions and consequently the most litigated issue in contemporary pension law and will be the subject of specific consideration later in this chapter.[33]

## (D) Non-Fiscal Regulation

A considerable quantity of non-fiscal regulation is provided by the statutory provisions which have already been considered relating to preservation values, transfer values, contracting out, limited price indexation, and the minimum funding requirement. Further regulation has been provided by the decisions of the European Court of Justice relating to aspects of sex discrimination, where it has been held to be discriminatory to confer pension entitlements on women at any earlier age than on men[34] and to part-time employees.[35] A number of the other provisions of the Pensions Act 1995 which are discussed in the course of this chapter have also provided such regulation.

A quite different form of non-fiscal regulation is provided by tribunals. There are two tribunals specifically dealing with pension schemes: first, the Occupational Pensions Regulatory Authority (OPRA), set up by the Pensions Act 1995[36] in substitution for the previous Occupational Pensions Board, and, secondly, the Pensions Ombudsman, a one-man tribunal originally created in 1990 which is now regulated by the Pension Schemes Act 1993,[37] as amended by the Pensions Act 1995.[38] Additionally, there are a number of investment and financial regulatory bodies that are the appropriate tribunals for the investigation of matters such as complaints about the selling of personal pension schemes, which have been very frequent in recent years.

OPRA is the body primarily charged with the investigation of any complaint or dispute concerning non-compliance with the statutory rules relating to the requirement for member nominated trustees, the payment of surplus or excess assets to the employer, the restrictions on employer-related investments, the requirements to appoint professional advisers and to keep books and records, the minimum funding requirements and schedules of contributions thereto, and the requirement for money purchase schemes to keep schedules of payment. Once called in, OPRA has considerable powers, including the power to remove trustees from office, to impose fines and civil penalties for breach of statutory duty, and to wind up a scheme where it feels that this is in the interests of the members as a whole. However, it cannot otherwise order the payment of compensation for the benefit of the members of the scheme. Nor is it authorised to investigate breaches of the equal treatment or indexation

---

[33] See *post*, p. 527.
[34] *Barber v. Royal Exchange Assurance Group* [1991] 1 Q.B. 344; *Coloroll Pension Trustees v. Russell* [1995] I.C.R. 179.
[35] *Preston v. Wolverhampton NHS Trust* [2001] 2 A.C. 415.
[36] ss.1–15.
[37] ss.145–152.
[38] Which amends the relevant sections of the 1993 Act.

provisions or breaches of the general law of trusts. These excluded matters can only be dealt with by a complaint to the Pensions Ombudsman or by proceedings in the High Court.

The Pensions Ombudsman has no jurisdiction to deal with any of the matters with whose investigation OPRA is primarily charged. His jurisdiction is instead to investigate complaints made against past or present trustees, managers and employers that maladministration of their pension scheme has caused injustice to a member or deferred member[39] of that scheme or the widow, widower or surviving dependant of such a person. This original jurisdiction has now been extended to cover complaints by trustees of one pension scheme about the trustees of another scheme and complaints by the employers and trustees of a scheme about one another. Maladministration for this purpose has been said to involve "bias, neglect, inattention, delay, incompetence, ineptitude, perversity, turpitude, arbitrariness and so on".[40] Only this will do; it was held in *Hillsdown Holdings v. Pensions Ombudsman*,[41] that the Pensions Ombudsman cannot investigate breaches of trust unless they involve one of these types of act or omission. The essence of the complaint has to be that the complainant not only disagrees with the decision which has been made but also has reason to believe that it was not properly made or implemented. The Pensions Ombudsman also has jurisdiction to investigate and determine disputes of fact or of law which arise incidentally to a complaint of maladministration. Appeal from his determinations on a point of law now lies to the Chancery Division of the High Court.[42]

There have been a number of doubts about the jurisdiction of the Pensions Ombudsman. In procedural terms, he is an automatic party to appeals against his own adjudications and his right to appear if he so chooses to defend his own adjudication as a kind of *amicus curiae* is now accepted.[43] However, the Court of Appeal has now held[44] that leave should not be given to him to appeal to the Court of Appeal against a decision of the High Court adverse to his original adjudication on the grounds that it is inapproporate for him to appeal from the decisions of the tribunal authorised to review his own decisions except, perhaps, when he wishes to query an award of costs made against him by the High Court. As for his remedial powers, he can clearly direct apologies, order the holding of another meeting or election, and award compensation for financial loss. However, the Court of Appeal has held[45] that, where the act of maladministration consists of a breach of trust, he cannot order any remedy which could not have been ordered by the High Court. Whether he can order compensation of types which could not have been

---

[39] A former member of the scheme who left his employment before reaching retirement age and has still not done so.

[40] This is the famous "[Richard] Crossman Catalogue" of what constitutes maladministration.

[41] [1997] 1 All E.R. 862 at 884.

[42] Formerly it was to the Crown Office List of the Queen's Bench Division.

[43] *Dolphin Packaging Materials v. Pensions Ombudsman* (1993) unreported.

[44] *Edge v. The Pensions Ombudsman* [2000] Ch. 602.

[45] *ibid.*

ordered by the High Court is less clear.[46] Doubts have also been expressed[47] as to whether his jurisdiction extends to claims in tort. These and other aspects of the jurisdiction of the Pensions Ombudsman will doubtless be clarified in due course.

## II. SPECIAL FEATURES OF PENSION TRUSTS[48]

A pension trust has all the characteristics of a private trust, the employer being the settlor, the trustees being the trustees, and the members of the scheme and their dependants being the beneficiaries. There are further parallels with private trusts in that the remedies of a member are those of a beneficiary enforceable in equity against the trustees — there is no need for privity of contract — and in that the trustees have duties in relation to matters such as investment and discretionary powers which they can exercise. In particular, they normally have a power of amendment similar to the overriding powers of appointment given to the trustees of private trusts. However, these similarities with private trusts are in many ways less important than the differences; there is almost invariably an underlying contract of employment whose existence affects the construction of the trust documents and almost every aspect of the parallels between employer as settlor and member as beneficiary needs qualification. These differences are revealed, above all, when any question arises as to the destination of surplus.

### 1. The Position of the Employer

Because of the absence of any obligation on employers to make any financial provision for their employees by way of pension, the decision to set up a pension scheme other than a stakeholder pension scheme is necessarily that of the employer. In the case of stakeholder pension schemes to which the employer is not contributing, as the overwhelming majority are likely to be, the employer will merely provide the scheme by giving instructions for and

---

[46] This was in issue but was not finally decided in *Westminster City Council v. Hayward* [1998] Ch. 377. A jurisdiction to award compensation for distress was upheld in the High Court by Robert Walker J. (his decision was subsequently followed by Carnwath J. in *Wild v. Smith* [1996] O.P.L.R. 129 contrary to the latter's own earlier decision in *Miller v. Stapleton* [1996] 2 All E.R. 449). However, this specific issue was not considered by the Court of Appeal. Also in issue is the Pension Ombudsman's jurisdiction to award compensation for delay and for inconvenience.

[47] In *NHS Pensions Agency v. Beechier* [1997] P.L.R. 95.

[48] See Lord Walker, writing extra-judicially, in *Trends in Contemporary Trust Law* (ed. Oakley, 1996), p. 123.

financing the preparation of the necessary documentation.[49] In other cases, the employer will additionally need to initiate the necessary discussions with its employees and provide the (usually nominal) initial trust property. In all cases this clearly makes the employer the settlor. However, save in the case of stakeholder pension schemes to which the employer is not contributing, the employer will, unlike the settlor of a private trust, inevitably have a continuing obligation to make financial contributions to the scheme for so long as it continues to have employees who are members.

The employer may well also be the trustee of the scheme or appoint the members of its board of directors as the trustees or, in the not infrequent case where the trustee is a separate company, appoint its own directors as directors of the trustee company — small schemes almost invariably follow one of these practices, although it is now in principle necessary for at least one-third of the trustees, or the directors of a trustee company, to be nominated by the members of the scheme.[50] In any event the scheme will unquestionably vest powers in the employer. Some of these powers will clearly be fiduciary in the full sense of the term — an example is powers of the type considered in *Mettoy Pension Trustees v. Evans*[51] to appoint any surplus in the pension fund, which in that case was vested in a separate trustee company. Even where such powers are not actually fiduciary, the employer will nevertheless be subject to what has become known as the *"Imperial"* obligation of good faith,[52] by virtue of which a power cannot be exercised in such a way that it seriously damages the relationship of good faith between the employer and its employees and ex-employees.

Further, save in the case of stakeholder pension schemes to which the employer is not contributing, the employer will almost certainly also be a beneficiary of the scheme in that it is virtually bound to have a claim to at least

---

[49] Pension scheme documentation tends to be bulky. Because of the need for Inland Revenue approval, schemes tend to be created by an Interim Deed, which identifies the employer(s), the trustees, and the criteria for membership and also deals with contracting-out and priorities on the winding-up of the scheme. Following approval, this Interim Deed is replaced by a Definitive Deed, often containing little more than the appointment of the trustees and a power of amendment, to which extremely detailed Rules are appended; these set out the nature of the benefits provided, the rules as to contributions and transfers into and out of the scheme, and provisions relating to contracting-out, administrative powers, and the events which will trigger and the priorities on winding-up. The Deed and the Rules tend to be the subject of frequent amendment, usually in the form of an updated version of both incorporating all the amendments to date. An important role can also be played by the announcements and booklets issued to the members by the employer or the trustees; these have been known to give rise to an estoppel by convention even when they are not actually consistent with the Deed and Rules — see *Icarus (Hertford) v. Driscoll* [1990] P.L.R. 1; *ITN v. Ward* [1997] P.L.R. 131. Other scheme documentation includes the scheme accounts and the actuarial reports and three-yearly valuations.

[50] Pensions Act 1995, ss.16–21. Unfortunately, at present this rule only operates where the employer cannot persuade the members to accept alternative arrangements more favourable to himself. Changes to the existing rules which would have prevented this were enacted in the Child Support, Pensions and Social Security Act 2000, s.43 but the Government has decided not to introduce them pending a further review. In the meantime, matters have been made worse by new regulations that have extended the time limits for compliance with the original statutory provisions.

[51] [1990] 1 W.L.R. 1587; see *ante*, p. 210.

[52] Because it was laid down in *Imperial Group Pension Trust v. Imperial Tobacco* [1991] 1 W.L.R. 589.

some part of any surplus which arises while the scheme is still on-going or as a result of its being wound up.

## 2. The Position of the Trustees

### (A) The Composition of the Trustees
As has already been seen, the employer may well also be the trustee of the scheme or appoint the members of its board of directors as the trustees or, in the not infrequent case where the trustee is a separate company, appoint its own directors as directors of the trustee company — small schemes almost invariably follow one of these practices, although it is now in principle necessary for at least one-third of the trustees, or the directors of a trustee company, to be nominated by the members of the scheme.[53] However, in the case of small self-administered schemes containing 12 or fewer members, Inland Revenue approval is dependent on there being what is known as a "pensioneer trustee",[54] a non-member of the scheme, usually a body corporate, there to protect Inland Revenue interests and to prevent the disappearance of the assets if anything goes wrong.

Further, where the employer becomes insolvent, it is the responsibility of its liquidator to ensure that there is at least one "independent trustee" and, if there is not, to appoint one;[55] this is in order to deal with conflicts of interest which can become particularly acute on insolvency.[56] The appointment of an independent trustee does not displace the other trustees (unless the insolvent employer was the sole trustee) but all the discretionary powers conferred on the trustees, and all fiduciary powers conferred on the employer, become exercisable only by the independent trustee.[57]

### (B) Duties and Powers
The duties of the trustees are in principle the same as those of the trustees of any other private trust, namely to protect the trust funds and to administer them in accordance with the trusts on which they are held. In the pension trust context, the former duty is straightforward, merely obliging the trustees to ensure that the employer pays whatever contributions it is obliged to make and to inform OPRA and the members in the event of any failure to comply with the minimum funding requirement. The latter duty is complicated by a number of special factors.

The most important of these is the endemic conflicts of interest arising out of

---

[53] Pensions Act 1995, ss.16–21. Unfortunately, at present this rule only operates where the employer cannot persuade the members to accept alternative arrangements more favourable to himself. Changes to the existing rules which would have prevented this were enacted in the Child Support, Pensions and Social Security Act 2000, s.43 but the Government has decided not to introduce them pending a further review. In the meantime, matters have been made worse by new regulations that have extended the time limits for compliance with the original statutory provisions.

[54] Income and Corporation Taxes Act 1988, s.591(6).

[55] Pensions Act 1995, ss.22–26.

[56] See *Icarus (Hertford) v. Driscoll* [1990] P.L.R. 1 and *Mettoy Pensions Trustees v. Evans* [1990] 1 W.L.R. 1587, *ante*, p. 210.

[57] An independent trustee can automatically lose his independence, in which case, unless he is the sole trustee, he equally automatically ceases to be trustee even if he is unaware of the fact. See *Clark v. Hicks* [1992] P.L.R. 213.

the fact that a majority of the trustees are likely to be representatives of the employer and the remainder are likely to be members (or at the very least representatives of the members) of the scheme. These conflicts of interest become particularly acute whenever it is necessary to deal with surplus, whether on the winding-up of the scheme or while it is on-going. Indeed, it has been held that no member trustee can take any benefit under any augmentation of benefits arising out of the exercise of a discretion vested in him or which he has helped to negotiate.[58] However, it does not seem that this view can possibly survive the remarks of Scott V.-C. at first instance in *Edge v. Pensions Ombudsman*,[59] which were subsequently approved by the Court of Appeal,[60] where he held that it was "quite simply ridiculous" to contend that the member trustees had to be excluded from an augmentation of benefits made as the result of the exercise of their discretion as to how to deal with a surplus.

Other special factors include the fact that pension trusts are very long lasting — "exempt approved schemes" (and some others) are specifically exempted from the rule against perpetuities[61] — and the fact that pensions trusts are often extremely flexible and confer on the trustees considerable powers of amendment and augmentation of benefits. In exercising these powers, which are often exercisable by the trustees only with the prior consent of the employer, it appears that the trustees are not under any obligation to be impartial as between the different classes of beneficiaries or to adopt a starkly confrontational role with the employer or to ignore the latter's interests; all this was specifically held by the Court of Appeal in *Edge v. Pensions Ombudsman*.[62] However, the way in which the powers are exercised must be consistent with the purposes for which they were conferred and must of course not infringe any express or implied restrictions in the trust deed or affect any accrued rights of any class of beneficiaries.[63] Further, their exercise must be in the interests of the beneficiaries when all relevant considerations, including any corresponding benefits validly demanded by the employer as a condition of its consent,[64] are taken into account.

Other standard powers of trustees are also considerably modified in the case of pension trustees. In particular, the Pensions Act 1995[65] modifies the normal investment powers of trustees.[66] The Act both confers on the trustees unrestricted powers of investment and entitles them to delegate those powers to fund managers. It requires them to have a formal statement of investment principles and puts on a statutory basis their duties to diversify, to take advice, to select suitable investments, and to consider whether to retain them. Employer-related investments are limited by statute to 5 per cent of the assets

---

[58] By Vinelott J. in *Re William Makin & Sons* [1993] O.P.L.R. 171 at 179 and in *British Coal Corporation v. British Coal Staff Superannuation Scheme Trustees* [1994] O.P.L.R. 51 at 62.
[59] [1998] Ch. 512 at 539.
[60] [2000] Ch. 602.
[61] Pension Schemes Act 1993, s.163.
[62] [2000] Ch. 602.
[63] If it does, Pensions Act 1995, s.67 will have to be complied with.
[64] Some threats by employers not to consent other than on certain terms are quite legitimate; others fall foul of the "*Imperial*" duty of good faith; see *ante*, fn. 52.
[65] Pensions Act 1995, ss.33–36.
[66] See *post*, pp. 592 *et seq*.

of the scheme and loans to the employer are totally prohibited.[67] Liability for any breach of the trustees' duty of care or skill in the performance of any investment function cannot be excluded. Finally, the trustees are now required themselves to appoint their advisers, such as auditors and solicitors, in writing.[68]

## (C) Recovery of Lost Funds

Where pension funds have been lost, the trustees also have a duty to seek to recover them. This is sometimes necessary because of some fairly blatant intentional breach of trust, such as over-investment in the employer or the excessive augmentation of the benefits of its directors. However, this is more likely to be necessary when a scheme is being wound up, because at this point the liabilities of the scheme will for the first and only time be able to be assessed exactly. In any of these circumstances, recovery can potentially be sought from three groups of defendants: first, from past trustees; secondly, from those who have already received benefits under or from the scheme; and, thirdly, from professional advisers such as solicitors and actuaries. A case where recovery was sought from members of all three of these groups as a result of substantial purchases by the pension fund of assets from the employer at what were alleged to have been highly excessive prices and because of excessive augmentation of benefits for its chairman was *H.R. v. J.A.P.T.*,[69] although only some interlocutory proceedings were reported.

There are a number of difficulties about seeking recovery from past trustees. First, in the absence of fraud they are, like any other trustee,[70] at present[71] likely to be protected by the trustee exemption clauses which are absolutely standard in pension trusts deeds (although, as has just been seen, these cannot cover any breach in their duty of care or skill in the performance of any investment function). Secondly, save in the case of small pension schemes, there is little likelihood that any individual trustee will be able to make up a sufficient amount of any loss to be worth suing. And, thirdly, where (as is more often than not the case) the trustee is a £100 company without a single asset, its own directors will not owe direct fiduciary duties to the members of the scheme[72] and so cannot be sued directly unless they have actually acted dishonestly and so can be held liable for dishonest assistance.[73] However, a possibility has now been found of suing them indirectly where the conduct complained of is not dishonest but is nevertheless a breach of the fiduciary duty which as directors they owe to the corporate trustee. In *H.R. v. J.A.P.T.*,[74] it was contended, and Lindsay J. accepted as arguable and so declined to strike out a claim, that in such circumstances the members of the scheme were entitled to argue that such rights of action as the corporate trustee had against

---

[67] Pensions Act 1995, s.40.
[68] Pensions Act 1995, s.47. Previously actuaries and solicitors were generally appointed by the employer prior to the scheme being set up. Trustees now at the very least have to confirm these appointments however, whether this will make any difference depends on the effect of the provisions of the Act relating to the appointment of trustees already considered.
[69] [1997] P.L.R. 99 (an appeal was compromised).
[70] See *Armitage v. Nurse* [1998] 1 Ch. 241; see *post*, p. 787.
[71] The Law Commission is considering reform of the present law; see post, p. 788.
[72] *Bath v. Standard Land Co.* [1911] 1 Ch. 618.
[73] See *ante*, pp. 374 *et seq.*
[74] [1997] P.L.R. 99.

its directors were themselves part of the property of the pension trust, thus enabling the members of the scheme to force the trustee company to sue the directors and hold the fruits of that action on trust for them. However, an appeal against this decision was compromised so it remains to be seen whether this type of claim (which Lindsay J. described as a "dog-leg claim") is indeed feasible.

Seeking recovery from a pensioner who has simply received an overpayment of his pension is in principle relatively straightforward; the overpayment can either simply be recouped out of future payments or be the subject of an action for money paid under a mistake of fact. However, the payment of a pension must amount to at least some form of representation that the recipient is entitled to it and a series of overpayments may well therefore give rise to an estoppel. Sums paid away to anyone else in breach of trust are potentially recoverable by means of either an equitable proprietary claim[75] or a claim for knowing receipt.[76] Neither type of claim is likely to be particularly straightforward. Equitable proprietary claims depend on the ability to identify the sums paid and, quite apart from the continuing uncertainty as to precisely what knowledge will actually lead to the imposition of liability for knowing receipt, it is doubtful whether anyone other than a former trustee or the employer or their associates could be held to have any knowledge of any breach of trust at all. However, in *Hillsdown Holdings v. Pensions Ombudsman*,[77] liability for knowing receipt was imposed on an employer in respect of the part of a surplus of £18 million[78] which it had received as the result of an improper use of a power.

Finally, the difficulties of successfully maintaining proceedings for professional negligence against solicitors and actuaries are well known. Where pension funds have been lost, the principal problem is usually that of showing that the advice which the scheme's professional advisers either gave or failed to give actually caused the breach of trust complained of — paradoxically, the more blatant the breach of trust, the more difficult it becomes to demonstrate a causal connection with whatever professional advice was given.

Because of these difficulties, before bringing any such proceedings the trustees will inevitably make an application seeking the approval of the court in advance for their expenditure of the trust funds on the costs involved; this is in order to avoid any risk of them having to pay the costs themselves if they lose. Representative beneficiaries will be joined to any such application, which is generally known as an application for a *Beddoe* Order,[79] so that they can express their view as to whether the likelihood of success in the proceedings justifies the expenditure of part of what is left of the trust fund on an attempt to recover what has been lost. The decision of the court in this respect is

---

[75] See *post*, pp. 807 *et seq.*

[76] See *ante*, pp. 390 *et seq.*

[77] [1997] 1 All E.R. 862. An equitable proprietary claim was also held to lie against the employer as a matter of principle but no findings of fact had been made below as to what assets were still identifiable when it acquired notice of the members' adverse claim.

[78] The employer had only actually received 60% of the surplus because the remaining 40% of the surplus was payable and had been paid in tax. However, the pension fund also recovered the tax from the Inland Revenue (*Hillsdown Holdings v. I.R.C.* [1999] S.T.C. 566).

[79] After the decision in *Re Beddoe* [1893] 1 Ch. 547. Such proceedings were considered in *McDonald v. Horn* [1995] 1 All E.R. 961 and *Alsop Wilkinson v. Neary* [1996] 1 W.L.R. 1220 (which did not involve a pension trust). See *post*, p. 620.

further complicated by the fact that the costs of these beneficiaries, both in the application for the *Beddoe* Order and in the main proceedings, generally also have to be paid out of the trust fund.

### 3. *The Position of the Beneficiaries*

While a pension trust is on-going, its beneficiaries always include at least three classes: those persons at present in pensionable employment with the employer ("members"); those persons who have been but are no longer in pensionable employment with the employer but are not yet in receipt of pensions from the scheme ("deferred members"); and those persons who have retired and are in receipt of pensions from the scheme ("pensioners"). However, once the winding-up of a pension scheme has commenced, its trusts will have no beneficiaries of any of these types[80]; the assets will instead be held for whoever is entitled to them under the provisions for winding-up; as will be seen later on,[81] in this respect the relevant rules of the deed of trust now only operate to the extent that they are not overridden by statute.

The interests of the members, the deferred members and the pensioners are often quite different, particularly on a winding up where there is a shortfall in assets since in such circumstances the law at present provides that the pensioners are to be paid in full before the members and deferred members receive anything.[82] Further, the employer is likely also to be a beneficiary in that, save in the case of stakeholder pension schemes to which the employer is not contributing, it is virtually bound to have a claim to at least some part of any surplus which arises while the scheme is still on-going or as a result of its being wound up.

The essential difference[83] between the beneficiaries of a pension scheme and the beneficiaries of a family trust is that the former will inevitably have provided consideration for their beneficial interests by virtue of the contributions paid to the scheme on their behalf. This is as much the case in a non-contributory scheme as a contributory scheme since either way the payment of the contributions will be a term of their contract of employment. Thus, in the unlikely event that the pension trust does not become completely constituted, its beneficiaries will have a contractual remedy against the employer.[84] This is also the reason for the existence of the *"Imperial"* obligation of good faith to which reference has already been made,[85] by virtue of which the employer cannot exercise a power in such a way that it seriously damages the relationship of good faith between the employer and its employees and ex-employees.

However, this does not mean that the beneficiaries of a pension trust have any more rights than the beneficiaries of a family trust to be informed about the reasons for decisions made by the trustees as to the exercise of the dis-

---

[80] *Bus Employees Pension Trustees v. Harrod* [2000] Ch. 258.

[81] See *post*, p. 536.

[82] See *post*, p. 536.

[83] See *Imperial Group Pension Trust v. Imperial Tobacco* [1991] 1 W.L.R. 589; *Thrells v. Lomas* [1993] 1 W.L.R. 456; *McDonald v. Horn* [1995] 1 All E.R. 961.

[84] See *ante*, pp. 163 *et seq.* Such a claim was made in *Davis v. Richards & Wallington Industries* [1990] 1 W.L.R. 1511 but the trust was in fact held to be a valid executory trust (see *ante*, p. 160).

[85] Because it was laid down in *Imperial Group Pension Trust v. Imperial Tobacco* [1991] 1 W.L.R. 589.

cretions vested in them; this was specifically held in *Wilson v. Law Debenture Corporation*.[86] However, the beneficiaries (and prospective beneficiaries such as their spouses and dependants) do have a statutory right to see all the scheme documentation, including in particular accounts, actuarial reports and valuations, and documents relating to the minimum funding requirement.[87]

The remedies available to the beneficiaries of a pension trust against the trustees are also exactly the same as those available to the beneficiaries of a family trust. Where the only dispute is as to the proper construction of the trust deed, this will normally be resolved by the trustees taking out a construction summons, effectively "friendly" litigation in which all parties' costs will be paid out of the trust fund in any event.[88] "Hostile" litigation, on the other hand, is likely to be one of two kinds of dispute: either an individual dispute, where a particular beneficiary claims not to have been properly treated, or a collective dispute, where a complaint is made on behalf of the beneficiaries as a whole or of one of the classes of beneficiaries. In the event that an individual dispute of this type comes to court (as distinct from being dealt with by whatever internal dispute resolution procedure the pension scheme in question has[89] or as a result of the intervention of the Pensions Advisory Service[90] or, where appropriate, of the Pensions Ombudsman), costs will follow the event and do not come out of the assets of the pension trust.[91] Collective disputes pose rather greater problems of costs in the event that they come to court; this is because it is likely that the employer, the trustees, and the beneficiaries, either as a whole or in distinct classes where their interests are different, will need to be separately represented and expert evidence may well be necessary as well. In such circumstances, a representative beneficiary will be appointed to represent each class of beneficiaries which has a distinct interest; such representative beneficiaries will generally be able to obtain a what is now known as a prospective costs order,[92] whereby their own costs, and any costs which they may eventually be ordered to pay to any other party, will be paid out of the trust fund in any event.[93]

## 4. *The Power of Amendment*

The power of amendment is the equivalent in pension trusts of the overriding powers of appointment which are now invariably inserted in all private trusts whose provisions include some form of discretionary trust.[94] Like overriding powers of appointment, a power of amendment is not necessarily vested in the

---

[86] [1995] 2 All E.R. 337. These rights are discussed *post*, p. 581.
[87] Pensions Act 1995, s.41.
[88] *Re Buckton* [1907] 2 Ch. 406.
[89] Some such procedure is now obligatory under Pensions Act 1995, s.50(1).
[90] Formerly known as the Occupational Pensions Advisory Service, this is an independent voluntary organisation giving free help and advice to members of the public; since 1991, it has been a company limited by guarantee and is funded entirely by grants.
[91] *McDonald v. Horn* [1995] 1 All E.R. 961 (followed in *Alsop Wilkinson v. Neary* [1996] 1 W.L.R. 1220, which did not involve a pension trust).
[92] See the Practice Direction in [2001] 1 W.L.R. 1082.
[93] Orders of this type were made in *McDonald v. Horn* [1995] 1 All E.R. 961.
[94] See *ante*, p. 182.

trustees; it is frequently vested in the employer, although the trustees' consent to its exercise may nevertheless be necessary.[95] A power of amendment is even more essential than overriding powers of appointment because occupational pension schemes usually continue for many decades, during which their provisions are likely to need to be modified in the light of changes in circumstances which could not possibly have been foreseen at the outset.[96]

The exercise of an express power of amendment of this type is not the only way in which a pension scheme may be amended. An application can be made to the court for the rectification[97] or the variation[98] of a pension trust in exactly the same way as in the case of a private trust. It is also possible for a pension trust to become amended as a result of a contract entered into between the employer and some of its employees, under which those employees agree, for example, to accept lower pension benefits than those to which they are entitled under the provisions of their pension trust.[99] Conversely, the employer or the trustees may estop themselves from denying that the employees are entitled to higher pension benefits than those to which they are entitled under the provisions of their pension trust as a result of the making of announcements and the issuing of booklets to the members in which those higher benefits are set out.[1] OPRA has power[2] to order the amendment of a pension trust in three specified circumstances.[3] Finally, the trustees of a pension trust have a statutory power of amendment for a number of specific purposes,[4] principally[5] in order to bring the provisions of the trust into line with new statutory requirements, adoption of which is necessary in order to preserve the trust's status as an exempt approved scheme (recent examples are the requirement for equal treatment of men and women,[6] the requirement for the appointment of member nominated trustees,[7] and the requirement to permit pension sharing on divorce).[8]

Where an express power of amendment is utilised, that power, like a power

---

[95] Either as a result of express provision or because this is required by Pensions Act 1995, s.67 (see *infra*).

[96] If no power of amendment is included in the interim deed, it may still be possible to include one in the definitive deed (*Re Imperial Foods Ltd. Pension Scheme* [1986] 2 All E.R. 802); in default, the only possibility is to apply to the court for rectification (see the next footnote).

[97] See *ante*, p. 213 and *Re Butlin's Settlement Trusts* [1976] Ch. 251. Cases involving pension trusts will generally concern applications to rectify a deed exercising the power of amendment rather than the original trust deed; see *AMP (UK) v. Barker* [2001] W.T.L.R. 1237, [2001] P.L.R. 79, *ante* p. 213.

[98] See *post*, p. 747.

[99] *South West Trains v. Wightman* [1998] P.L.R. 113. In such circumstances, the employer is able to restrain the employees from claiming from the trustees the additional pension provision to which they are entitled under the trust deed.

[1] *Icarus (Hertford) v. Driscoll* [1990] P.L.R. 1; *ITN v. Ward* [1997] P.L.R. 131.

[2] Under Pensions Act 1995, ss.69–71.

[3] In connection with a necessary reduction of surplus (see *post*, p. 527), a distribution of assets to the employer when a scheme is being wound up (see *post*, p. 536), and the contracting-out of a relevant employment between April 6, 1997 and April 5, 1999.

[4] Pensions Act 1995, s.68.

[5] A purpose quite distinct from that mentioned in the text is to extend, with the consent of the employer, the class of persons who may receive death in service benefits.

[6] See *ante*, p. 514.

[7] See *ante*, p. 518.

[8] See *post*, p. 534.

of appointment, has to be exercised in the manner envisaged by its terms;[9] in particular, when the consent of the employer is necessary it must be obtained in the prescribed way. The employer must always act in accordance with the "*Imperial*" duty of good faith which has already been considered.[10] The trustees must exercise their own discretion rather than simply following the suggestions of the employer;[11] they cannot validly make an amendment which reduces rights to present or future pensions which have already accrued and cannot generally make one which reduces the future accrual of benefits. Further, both employer and trustees must use the power of amendment for the purpose for which it was conferred; in the absence of contrary indication, this is to promote the purposes of the scheme, whether those purposes are expressly stated in the trust deed or not. However, it is accepted that these purposes are not immutable and may change over time as the pension scheme itself evolves.[12]

Amendments were successfully challenged on the ground that they did not promote the purposes of the scheme in *Re Courage Group's Pension Schemes*.[13] The employer was part of a group which had been taken over by a purchaser who intended in due course to sell off the different parts of the group but wanted in the meantime to extract a part of the substantial surplus in the three relevant pension schemes. The amendments made for this purpose, which involved making the purchaser the employer under the schemes, were held to conflict with the purpose for which the schemes had been established, the provision of retirement benefits. This conclusion was undoubtedly assisted by a finding that the purchaser was not recognisably the successor either to the employer's business or to its workforce.[14]

Amendments must also comply with the provisions of the Pensions Act 1995,[15] under which a power "to modify the scheme"[16] cannot be exercised "in a manner which would or might affect any entitlement, or accrued right, of any member of the scheme acquired before the power is exercised"[17] unless the trustees are satisfied that, in respect of that member, either "the certification requirements" or "the consent requirements" are met (where the power is being exercised by the employer, the trustees must have approved its exercise on this basis). The certification requirements are satisfied if an actuary has first certified to the trustees that the amendment would not adversely affect the entitlements or accrued rights acquired by the member before the power of amendment is exercised.[18] The consent requirements are satisfied if

---

[9] See *ante*, p. 212.

[10] See *ante*, p. 517. This is also the case when, rarely, the employer can require the trustees to exercise the power.

[11] Save, rarely, when the employer can require them to exercise the power; his ability to do so is now further restricted by Pensions Act 1995, s.67, discussed *infra* in the text.

[12] *Re Courage Group's Pension Schemes* [1987] 1 W.L.R. 495.

[13] [1987] 1 W.L.R. 495.

[14] See also *Harwood-Smart v. Caws* [2000] P.L.R. 101; *BEST v. Stuart* [2001] P.L.R. 283,

[15] Pensions Act 1995, s.67; see Schaffer [1999] British Pensions Lawyer 3.

[16] This expression may not actually be limited to formal amendments of the trust deed, although this is not relevant for present purposes.

[17] The precise scope of "entitlement" and "accrued right" is not entirely clear, in particular whether rights whose exercise requires the employer's consent, future statutory increases to deferred pensions, and modifications affecting the security of benefits are included.

[18] Pensions Act 1995, s.67(4)(a).

the member has consented in writing.[19] For this purpose, member includes anyone entitled or prospectively entitled to a payment under the scheme.

An amendment can also be successfully challenged if its terms fail to comply with any restrictions written into the power of amendment by the trust deed; these tend to be substantial. Whether or not the terms fail to comply is entirely a matter of construction of the provisions of the power of amendment in question.[20] It is therefore appropriate only to set out a number of principles which apply irrelevant of the construction adopted.

1.  It has been held[21] that, unless a power of amendment is specifically included in the provisions of the trust deed governing winding up, that power cannot be exercised after the winding up has commenced, although this is apparently possible during the period of any notice given by the employer to the trustees to wind up the scheme.[22]

2.  A provision permitting retrospective amendments is valid but, in the absence of any such provision, an amendment would be unlikely to be permitted to have retrospective effect[23] unless that effect was entirely uncontroversial, such as to enable retrospective compliance with some new statutory requirement.

3.  A provision permitting the amendment of the power of amendment itself is valid, although an increase in the restrictions on that power could never be justified[24] and the removal of existing restrictions on it will not be easy to justify either unless they are purely formal. In the absence of any such provision, such an amendment will not be possible.

4.  Where the power of amendment requires the consent of the members to any or to specific types of amendments, this can be treated as having been given one month after the second of two notifications at least two months apart sent to a member's last known address.[25] This rule does not apply to the types of amendments which must comply with the provisions of the Pensions Act 1995, where the only substitute for written consent is the actuary's certification.

The types of difficulties of construction with which the courts have to grapple are well illustrated by the facts of *National Grid Co. v. Mayes*,[26] the only case concerning powers of amendment which has so far reached the House of

---

[19] *ibid.* s.67(4)(b).

[20] For the extent to which the courts do or should adopt particular principles of construction and, in particular the question whether they should be pro-employer or pro-beneficiary, see Nobles, *Pensions, Employment and the Law* (1993) Chap. 2; McAllister 11 Superannuation (2000) 73.

[21] *Thrells Ltd. (1974) Pension Scheme v. Lomas* [1992] P.L.R. 149, confirming the earlier unreported decision in *Re ABC Television* (1973), in Ellison, *op.cit.*, Sources p. 28.

[22] *Municipal Mutual v. Harrop* [1998] P.L.R. 149.

[23] An amendment retrospectively taking away vested rights was disallowed in *Municipal Mutual v. Harrop* [1998] P.L.R. 149.

[24] Because the trustees would thereby be fettering their own discretion.

[25] Pensions Act 1995, s.67(6).

[26] [2001] 1 W.L.R. 864.

Lords. Since the case also concerns the treatment of surplus, it is best considered in the discussion of that topic which immediately follows.

### 5. The Treatment of Surplus[27]

The question of what should be done about a surplus which has arisen in a pension trust arises in three situations.

1. Whenever an obligatory three-yearly actuarial valuation shows that an exempt approved scheme has a surplus of assets over liabilities which exceeds the statutory limit of 105 per cent[28] under the prescribed actuarial assumptions,[29] immediate steps have to be taken to eradicate the resulting excessive statutory surplus or Inland Revenue approval of the scheme will be withdrawn with extremely adverse retrospective fiscal consequences. There are basically three permissible ways of achieving this:[30]

   (a) permitting the employer and/or the employee to stop or to reduce their contributions to the scheme for up to five years[31] (this is known as a "contributions holiday");
   (b) paying the whole or part of the surplus to the employer; and
   (c) enhancing the existing benefits provided by the scheme or creating new ones (this can of course potentially benefit both past and present employees).

   It is apparent that in such circumstances the interests of the employer and the past and present employees will almost inevitably be diametrically opposed, as will the interests of the past employees and the present employees *inter se* if both are not treated equally (something which will is not only unlikely but will of course also be an indirect consequence of any reduction of employee contributions).

2. When an actuarial valuation shows a surplus which does not amount to an excessive statutory surplus but is nevertheless substantially in excess of what is needed fully to fund the scheme,[32] the trustees or the employer will generally have a power under the trust deed to dispose of some or all of this surplus (in the unlikely event that there is neither any such power nor any possibility of adding one by means of

---

[27] See Pollard 17 T.L.I. (2003) 2.

[28] Income and Corporation Taxes Act 1988, Sched. 22; Pension Scheme Surpluses (Valuation) Regulations 1987 (S.I. 1987/412), referring to the previous legislation in Finance Act 1986, Sched. 12.

[29] These are generally regarded as rather "conservative" and it is therefore possible for there to be a very substantial surplus in the fund when it is valued in accordance with the actuary's normal assumptions and criteria without there being any statutory surplus at all; for a scheme to have an excessive statutory surplus, it would have to have a valuation of around 200% of the minimum funding requirement.

[30] The legislation actually states these three as five (Income and Corporation Taxes Act 1988, Sched. 22, para.3(3)).

[31] If the surplus has not been eradicated by then, a further period can be added but the entire decision making process has to be gone through again (in practice there will have been a further actuarial review after the first three of the five years anyway).

[32] For a final salary scheme, this will effectively now be the minimum funding requirement.

the power of amendment, nothing will be able to be done at all). However, unless this power is mandatory, it will not have to be exercised; consequently, in this situation there is in effect a possibility additional to such of the three possibilities set out above as are conferred by the power, the possibility of leaving the surplus in the scheme to constitute a reserve. The trustees will have an obvious interest in this being done, thus adding a further element to the potential conflicts of interest mentioned above.

The surpluses produced in pension schemes during the 1980s were often so substantial that they became an important element in take-overs, leading to subsequent disputes as to what was to happen to the surpluses between the employees and whoever took over the employer. In present financial conditions, a purchaser of a business is more likely to be concerned about inheriting a deficit in its pension scheme than about having the opportunity of extracting a surplus. However, even today, enough pension schemes are still in surplus for disputes of this kind between employers and employees to remain a possibility.

3.   Where a surplus arises as a result of the winding up of a pension scheme, steps also have to be taken to deal with this surplus. In this situation, which will be dealt with separately at the end of this chapter,[33] the only two of the possibilities mentioned so far which are feasible are the second and third ones set out above.

All three of these situations can theoretically arise both in final salary schemes and in money purchase schemes.[34] In practice, however, surpluses in money purchase schemes have always been less likely than in final salary schemes because of the lower level of employer contributions and, even if such a surplus had to be eradicated while a scheme was still on-going, there would be little or no potential for the sort of conflicts of interest referred to above. All the pensioners would already have their annuities and so would effectively be out of the picture and the fact that the employer and the employees tend to contribute equal amounts to money purchase schemes would remove any conceivable justification for any payment being made to the employer. Consequently, in practice, the trustees would have no option but to give both employer and employees a contributions holiday until the desired amount of surplus had been used up.

On the other hand, when a surplus in a final salary scheme is to be reduced while the scheme is still on-going, both the employer and its past and present employees are likely to take the view that the surplus belongs to them; the employer will do so on the basis that the pension fund is a security provided for the protection of those employees and that it is therefore entitled to any surplus over and above the security which is necessary, while the employees will do so on the basis that the fund constitutes part of their emoluments Neither of these views constitutes the whole truth but each has a point in relation to a final salary scheme: on the one hand, the open-ended commit-

---

[33] *Post*, p. 540.
[34] See Pollard 17 T.L.I. (2003) 2.

ment under which the employer has to make up any deficit while the scheme is on-going must give it at least some rights to any surplus in such a scheme; on the other hand, the beneficiaries are entitled not only to their fixed rights under the scheme but also to unquantifiable expectations of enhanced benefits. The trustees may well adopt yet a third view, that the surplus is a necessary reserve against the results of over-optimism by the scheme's actuary or underperformance by the scheme's investments. In reality, as Vinelott J. said in *Taylor v. Lucas Pensions Trust*,[35] the surplus of an occupational pension trust "does not in any intelligible sense belong to anyone".

Because of the improbability of excessive statutory surpluses arising, disputes have invariably concerned the second situation referred to above and have often been between the employees and employers who have just taken over the business. The latter of course want the whole of the available surplus paid to them, but the past and present employees understandably want at least part of it to be utilised for their own benefit. The employees' challenge to such an employer succeeded in *Re Courage Pension Schemes*,[36] for the reasons discussed in the previous part of this section.[37] However, Millett J. drew a clear distinction between the two possible methods of enabling the employer to benefit from a surplus. He rejected a contention that the employees were entitled as of right to a contributions holiday when the available surplus permitted this, taking the view that any surplus in a final salary scheme arose primarily from the employer and so it was the latter who should be primarily entitled to any contributions holiday. On the other hand, he stated that, where the employer was instead seeking a payment out of the scheme, it could be anticipated that the employer would be influenced by the desire to maintain good industrial relations with its workforce while the trustees could and should press for enhanced benefits for both present and past employees.

The Pensions Act 1995 has now provided[38] that any power to return assets to the employer must be exercised by the trustees, even if the trust deed confers it on someone else, and can be exercised only if the trustees are satisfied that this is in the interests of the beneficiaries and if there has been limited price indexation of all pensions payable under the scheme. The trustees must notify all the members on two occasions of the proposed method of reducing or distributing the surplus and invite representations not earlier than two months after the first notice; the second notice must be given after the last date for making representations and no payment can be made pursuant to it for a further three months. If OPRA considers, as a result of written representations by a member or from any other source, that there is sufficient doubt as to whether all these requirements have been met, OPRA will notify the trustees that no payment should be made until it is satisfied that this is indeed the case; in all other cases the trustees must obtain confirmation from OPRA before making the payment that its approval is not necessary.

This statutory intervention has, however, done little to resolve the outcome of disputes as to the destination of surplus, which still primarily depend on the terms of the pension trust in question. As Knox J. said in *L.R.T. Pension*

---

[35] [1994] O.P.L.R. 29.
[36] [1987] 1 W.L.R. 498.
[37] An amendment which was necessary in order to make the purchaser of the group the new employer under the schemes was held to be impermissible.
[38] Pension Act 1995, s. 37.

*Fund Trustee Co. v. Hatt*,[39] quoting the words of Cooke P. in a New Zealand decision,[40] "Considerations of the merits are of little importance. What must be decisive are the terms of the trusts constituted by the particular scheme." This is what has also emerged from *National Grid Co. v. Mayes*;[41] although this case went to the House of Lords, the best summary of the current law in this respect was made by the Court of Appeal:[42] "The solution lies within the terms of the scheme itself, and not within a world populated by competing philosophies as to the true nature and ownership of actuarial surplus."

Consequently, in any individual case, what is necessary is to establish which of the possible methods of dealing with a surplus is permitted by the deed of trust and, in so far as the desired method is not, whether the necessary permission can be inserted be the use of the power of amendment. Everything therefore depends on the terms of the scheme, properly construed, and on any statutory provisions which override them. In the latter respect, in addition to the provisions of the Pensions Act 1995 which have already been mentioned, OPRA has a statutory power to override the prohibitions on the return of any surplus to the employer which are found in many older schemes because the Inland Revenue at one time required such prohibitions as a condition of approval.[43]

The principal issues of construction are usually whether or not the method which has been or is to be used to deal with the surplus is permitted by the provisions of the trust deed governing the treatment of surplus and/or whether or not that method is prohibited by any other provision of the trust deed. Given the nature of issues of this type,[44] it is appropriate only to state the following general propositions:

1.  Giving the employer a contributions holiday does not amount to a payment of surplus to the employer and so neither breaches a provision of the trust prohibiting the payment of surplus to the employer or, more significantly, triggers the provisions of the Pensions Act 1995[45] that the power being used must be exercised by the trustees and then only when there has first been limited price indexation of all pensions payable under the scheme.

2.  Where the trust deed permits the payment of surplus to the employer, that is not outside the purposes of the pension scheme.[46] However, where the treatment of surplus requires the consent of the employer, it is appropriate for the trustees not simply to do what the employer wants but to bargain with the employer on behalf of the past and present employees for benefit improvements.[47]

---

[39] [1993] P.L.R. 227.
[40] *U.E.B. Industries v. Brabant* [1991] P.L.R. 109 (Court of Appeal of New Zealand).
[41] [2001] 1 W.L.R. 864.
[42] [1999] P.L.R. 37.
[43] Now in Pensions Act 1995, s.69 (first introduced in 1973).
[44] For the extent to which the courts do or should adopt particular principles of construction and, in particular the question of whether they should be pro-employer or pro-beneficiary, see Pollard 17 T.L.I. (2003) 2.
[45] Pensions Act 1995, s. 37.
[46] *National Grid Co. v. Mayes* [2001] 1 W.L.R. 864.
[47] *Re Courage Group's Pension Schemes* [1987] 1 W.L.R. 495.

3. Leaving a surplus in a pension scheme is a permitted use of that surplus unless the trust deed specifically mandates or requires surplus to be used for something else, such as the enhancement of benefits.

The types of difficulties of construction with which the courts have to grapple are well illustrated by the facts of *National Grid Co. v. Mayes*,[48] the only case concerning either powers of amendment or the treatment of surplus which has so far reached the House of Lords. The two employers each had both a power to deal with surplus, which simply stated that the employers "shall make arrangements, certified by the actuary as reasonable, to deal with the surplus", and a power of amendment, which prohibited amendments "making any moneys ... payable to" the employers. Both employers used about one-third of the surpluses to enhance benefits[49] and the remainder to extinguish debts which they owed to their respective pension schemes in respect of the sums necessary in order to fund additional pension payments to employees who had been made redundant or had retired early. The questions which arose were, first, whether this cancellation of debts was permitted by the power to deal with the surplus and, secondly, whether it amounted to the making of payments to the employers.

The Pensions Ombudsman held, first, that cancellation of debts did amount to payments to the employers and, secondly, that the wording of the power of amendment led to the conclusion that the power to deal with the surplus did not permit payments to the employers; the debts could not therefore be cancelled. Robert Walker J.[50] disagreed with the second conclusion and held that the debts could be cancelled because the power to deal with the surplus was wholly unrestricted and was not in any way affected by the other provisions of the trust deed such as the power of amendment; he therefore did not have to consider the first conclusion. The Court of Appeal[51] agreed with the Pensions Ombudsman, and not with Robert Walker J., as to the second conclusion and so held that the debts could not be cancelled. But they disagreed with the first conclusion of the Pensions Ombudsman and stated that the cancellation of debts did not amount to payments to the employers. Consequently, the power of amendment could be used to amend the power to deal with the surplus retrospectively[52] and the employers duly used their respective powers to do so before the hearing of their appeal to the House of Lords.

The House of Lords held that, taking into account the fiscal origin of prohibitions of the type found in the power of amendment, the cancellation of debts did not amount to payments to the employers; an amendment to permit such a process would therefore not be prohibited by the power of amendment. This meant that the debts could be cancelled whether or not this was per-

---

[48] [2001] 1 W.L.R. 864.

[49] In both cases by increasing death in service benefits and spouses' pensions and, in one case, by also reducing employee contributions by 50% for three years and increasing by 10% the lump sum benefits of deferred members. Since employer contributions were twice employee contributions, this reflected the proportion of the surplus produced by the employees' contributions.

[50] [1997] P.L.R. 157.

[51] [2002] I.C.R. 174.

[52] This was permitted by the wording of the power of amendment.

mitted by the power to deal with the surplus since, if it was not, that power could be amended anyway.[53] But the House went on to consider whether or not this was in fact permitted by that power and concluded that it was; no amendment was therefore actually necessary and it was up to the employers whether or not they chose to embody the arrangements which they had made into a formal amendment.

When a power of this kind is being exercised by the employer, it can have regard to its own financial and other interests but only to the extent that it can do so without breaching the "*Imperial*" obligation of good faith to its employees[54] which has already been considered.[55] When, on the other hand, the power is being exercised by the trustees, as will now always be the case if any payment is to be made to the employer,[56] they are under no obligation to act impartially as between the different categories of members, deferred members and pensioners. In *Edge v. Pensions Ombudsman*,[57] the trustees decided to use surplus to credit additional service to those members in employment on a particular date and to reduce the contributions of both employers and employees from a date six months earlier; no additional service was credited either to the pensioners or to the deferred members or to a number of employees who were to be made redundant during the six-month period. The trustees explained to one of the latter that their decision had been taken in order to encourage all employees to become and remain members of the pension scheme and to support the employers in providing continued employment for their current employees. The Pensions Ombudsman set aside the trustees' decision on the grounds that the trustees had breached their duty of impartiality and had not acted in the best interests of all the beneficiaries. His decision was reversed by the Court of Appeal, who held that the duty to act impartially was no more than the ordinary duty imposed on any holder of a discretionary power, namely to exercise the power for the purposes for which it is given, giving proper consideration to the matters which are relevant and excluding from consideration matters which are irrelevant. Provided the trustees complied with that duty, they were entitled to reach a decision which appeared to prefer the claims of some beneficiaries over others.

### III. INTERESTS UNDER PENSION TRUSTS AND THIRD PARTIES

Because the purpose of a pension scheme is to provide an income on retirement, the Pensions Act 1995 provides that accrued rights thereunder cannot, generally speaking, be dealt with by the beneficiary by way of assignment, surrender or charge;[58] this does not of course affect assignments or surrenders

---

[53] The House of Lords also rejected an argument by the employees that, if an amendment was needed, it would under Pensions Act 1995, s.37 (*supra*) have to make the power exercisable by the trustees and not by the employers because cancellation of debts would amount to payment to the employees for the purposes of that provision. The House held that the provision only applies to funds which have actually been paid into a pension trust, not sums owing to that trust.

[54] The obligation laid down in *Imperial Group Pension Trust v. Imperial Tobacco* [1991] 1 W.L.R. 589.

[55] See *ante*, p. 517.

[56] By virtue of Pension Act 1995, s.37, *supra*.

[57] [2000] Ch. 602.

[58] *ibid.* s.91(1).

in favour of the beneficiary's surviving spouse and dependants after his death. However, in two situations, on bankruptcy and on divorce, third parties may wish to assert a claim to the interest of a beneficiary under a pension trust.[59]

## 1. *The Position on Bankruptcy*

It is not the policy of the insolvency legislation to deprive a bankrupt beneficiary of a pension scheme of the provision which he has made for his retirement and consequently the basic rule has generally been that his accrued rights are not available to his creditors.[60] Whether that necessarily meant that he would nevertheless be entitled to his present or future benefits under any occupational pension scheme of which he was a member used to depend on the rules of the scheme in question; many schemes contain provisions forfeiting a beneficiary's rights in the event of his bankruptcy to which the courts used to give effect,[61] a possibility which the Pensions Act 1995[62] expressly confirmed. Further, the basic rule did not anyway apply to benefits to which the bankrupt beneficiary of a personal pension scheme or a retirement annuity policy was entitled and these benefits vested directly in his trustee in bankruptcy.[63]

However, the Welfare Reform and Pensions Act 1999 now expressly provides[64] that any rights which a bankrupt may have under any exempt approved pension scheme, whether occupational, personal or stakeholder, are excluded from the bankrupt's estate when a bankruptcy order is made on or after 29 May, 2000. Any provision in a pension trust deed providing for forfeiture in the event of bankruptcy will therefore be ineffective in respect of bankruptcies on or after that date. Only the benefits to which a bankrupt is entitled under an unauthorised pension scheme will now vest in his trustee in bankruptcy and even in that respect the Secretary of State has been given power to make regulations to govern certain situations.[65]

The Welfare Reform and Pensions Act 1999 has not affected other provisions of the Pensions Act 1995,[66] which permit pension schemes to contain provisions for outright forfeitures of benefits in a number of other situations: first, where prior to the pension becoming payable, a beneficiary is convicted of treason or of offences under the Official Secrets Acts; secondly, where a beneficiary has failed to claim a pension within the appropriate limitation period or within six years; and, thirdly, in respect of any monetary obligations incurred by the beneficiary to the employer arising out of any criminal, neg-

---

[59] See Miller [2001] P.C.B. 46.
[60] *ibid.* s.91(3).
[61] Thus in *Re Scientific Investment Pension Plan Trust* [1999] Ch. 53 Rattee J. upheld a rule which provided that, in the event of any assignment or anything happening which would vest the beneficiary's property in someone else, his benefits would be forfeited but the trustees should have power in the event of hardship to apply them for the benefit of his dependants. Although this case concerned a bankruptcy in 1992, the result would still have been the same under Pensions Act 1995, s.92.
[62] Pensions Act 1995, s.92.
[63] *Re Landau* [1997] 3 All E.R. 322.
[64] Welfare Reform and Pensions Act 1999, s.11.
[65] *ibid.* s.12(2). The situations envisaged are where the bankrupt either makes an agreement with his trustee in bankruptcy or applies to the court.
[66] Pensions Act 1995 ss. 92, 93.

ligent or fraudulent act or omission. Provisions of this type will clearly continue to be upheld.

Nevertheless, despite these general rules, it would be wholly inappropriate if a beneficiary who anticipated that he was in some danger of becoming bankrupt was allowed to deprive his creditors of assets by making additional voluntary contributions to an existing occupational pension scheme. The Pensions Act 1995[67] has therefore inserted into the Insolvency Act 1986 provisions relating to the setting aside of such contributions made within the five years immediately prior to the bankruptcy similar to the provisions relating to the setting aside of settlements made during the same period which have already been considered;[68] the criterion is whether the contributions were excessive and unfairly prejudicial to the creditors, a question to which the intentions of the beneficiary in making them will clearly be particularly relevant.

## 2. *The Position on Divorce*

The two most valuable assets of most married couples are likely to be their matrimonial home and their pension rights. The courts have long had[69] an absolute discretion to vary matrimonial property rights at the termination of marriage and among the matters to which they must have regard are the value to either party of any pension which he or she will lose the chance of acquiring as a result of the divorce. The discretion of the courts includes the ability to make what are known as deferred lump sum orders and such orders have been made requiring one spouse to pay to the other one half of whatever lump sum he becomes entitled to receive from a pension trust on his retirement.[70] However, the courts generally considered pension entitlements as being too far in the future or too speculative to be the subject of specific orders and, in so far as they took pension rights into account at all, they generally limited themselves to offsetting likely pension rights against the other property of the former spouses.

The courts nevertheless could, and still can, order the payment of pensions as well as lump sums, in the relatively rare situation where the pension trust in question can be held to constitute a marriage settlement. This is only likely where a private pension scheme has been set up for both spouses by one of them or by a company of which the latter is the alter ego. This was indeed what had happened in *Brooks v. Brooks*,[71] where such a settlement was found to have been created by virtue of the fact that the husband had power under a pension scheme set up for him by his company to elect to provide a pension for a spouse out of the fund; the House of Lords therefore varied the pension trust to provide his wife with both an immediate pension and a deferred pension payable from the husband's death. But Lord Nicholls emphasised in his speech that this procedure would not work where persons other than the spouses were beneficiaries of the pension trust in question and specifically

---

[67] *ibid.* s.95.
[68] See *ante*, p. 255.
[69] Under what is now Matrimonial Causes Act 1973, s. 25
[70] See the authorities referred to in *SRJ v. DWJ (Financial Provision)* [1999] 2 F.L.R. 176, although no such order was made in that case.
[71] [1996] A.C. 375.

stated that legislation would be necessary to enable the courts "to split pension rights on divorce in the more usual case of a multi-member scheme where the wife has no earnings of her own from the same employer".[72]

This was the only basis on which the courts could order the payment of pensions, as distinct from lump sums, until the Pensions Act 1995[73] inserted new provisions into the Matrimonial Causes Act 1973[74] to enable the court, when making a financial provision order, to divert all or part of the benefits (whether lump sum or periodical payments) payable to one of the former spouses under an occupational or a private pension scheme to the other former spouse as and when they become payable under the scheme. This process was originally known as earmarking; since the coming into force of the Welfare Reform and Pensions Act 1999, it has instead been known as attachment, by which name it will be referred to here.

The judgments in the only two reported decisions on attachment[75] and the lack of any others suggest that the legislation is not proving easy to apply. The matter is complicated by the court's statutory obligation to consider whether it would be appropriate to make what is known as a clean break and its power to bring one about; attaching of future, as distinct from present, pension rights is clearly inconsistent with a clean-break. Further, although these two decisions were not clean break cases, no orders attaching future pension payments were made there either; it was said[76] that the courts would be in just as effective a position jurisdictionally to deal with the matter at the time of retirement and would then be far better informed. This suggests that attaching pension payments is only likely even in non-clean break cases when a divorce occurs very close to retirement age. On the other hand, it is obviously possible to attach any lump sum payable on retirement,[77] since this could be done, although not formally by way of attachment, even before the Pensions Act 1995. If this is done, it will generally be necessary also to attach the quite different death-in-service benefits which will be paid if the beneficiary dies before reaching retirement age,[78] usually a lump sum which the trustees have discretion as to how to distribute with, sometimes, a power of nomination given to the deceased beneficiary.

The Family Law Act 1996 subsequently enacted provisions envisaging a rather different process, the splitting of pensions, on divorce but these provisions have not been brought into force. Instead the Finance Act 1999 and the Welfare Reform and Pensions Act 1999 have inserted further provisions into the Matrimonial Causes Act 1973, introducing what is effectively the same thing but which is instead known as pension sharing on divorce; these provisions affected divorce proceedings commenced after December 1, 2000. All existing Inland Revenue approved schemes are now obliged, as a condition of continued Inland Revenue approval, to amend their rules so as to enable

---

[72] [1996] A.C. 375 at 396.
[73] Pensions Act 1995, s.166.
[74] Matrimonial Causes Act 1973, ss.25B, 25C & 25D.
[75] *T v. T (Financial Relief: Pensions)* [1998] 1 F.L.R. 1072; *Burrow v. Burrow* [1999] 1 F.L.R. 508.
[76] By Singer J. in *T v. T (Financial Relief: Pensions)* [1998] 1 F.L.R. 1072.
[77] This was done in *Burrow v. Burrow* [1999] 1 F.L.R. 508.
[78] The court was prepared to do this in both *T v. T (Financial Relief: Pensions)* [1998] 1 F.L.R. 1072 and *Burrow v. Burrow* [1999] 1 F.L.R. 508 but in the event did not regard this as actually necessary.

pension sharing to be introduced; this has applied to all schemes seeking approval or continued approval since May 10, 2000.

Under the new provisions inserted into the Matrimonial Causes Act 1973,[79] a pension sharing order can provide that a specific percentage of one party's pension rights, including SERPS or S2P rights but not the basic State pension, is subject to pension sharing. The former spouse acquiring the rights has a choice between becoming a member of the other spouse's pension scheme (although this is necessarily the only option in the case of unfunded schemes) and taking a transfer out into a personal pension scheme or stakeholder scheme of his or her own choice. Statutory instruments have laid down how benefits under pension schemes are to be valued and provide for a uniform measure of valuation for all types of pensions, which is known as the Cash Equivalent Transfer Value ("the CETV"). The pension provider or the State is obliged to provide information to enable this to be done. It is the appropriate percentage of the CETV which is awarded. Death benefits, discretionary benefits, future expectations and non United Kingdom pensions are excluded from the CETV, which values the pension on the assumption that the service of the member of any relevant schemes terminates at the valuation date, thus also excluding future service. However, that does not prevent the court from taking into account likely future service when assessing what percentage of the CETV to award.

Attachment continues alongside pension sharing and is brought into line with it by having to be expressed as a percentage of the CETV but it is not possible to make an attachment and a pension sharing order in respect of the same pension scheme. It is not considered likely that this will increase the overall number of attachment orders made; pension sharing is clearly likely to predominate. The courts will obviously also at least consider continuing to offset pension benefits against the other assets of the former spouses rather than making pension sharing orders. It also remains to be seen what use the courts will make of the CETV where a significant part of the pension in question has been "earned" prior to the marriage in question. In a pre-attachment case,[80] which concerned a doctor of 41 who had belonged to the National Health Service Pension Scheme for 13 years, it was said that, "in deciding what weight to give to pension rights it is more important ... to look at the value of what has been earned during cohabitation than to look at the prospective value of what may be earned over the course of the 25 or 30 years between separation and retirement age". The position will become clearer once reported decisions on pension sharing begin to emerge.

## IV. WINDING UP PENSION SCHEMES

### 1. *How are Pension Schemes Wound Up?*

It is often necessary for pension schemes to be wound up. The two most common situations are where the employer becomes insolvent or decides to stop making contributions to the Scheme but the Rules of the Scheme can

---

[79] Matrimonial Causes Act 1973, s.24B.
[80] *H v. H* [1993] 2 F.L.R. 335.

provide for winding up in a number of further situations. Since 1997 it has also been possible for OPRA to order that a scheme should be wound up.[81] Where the employer becomes insolvent, it is the responsibility of its liquidator to ensure that there is at least one "independent trustee" and, if there is not, to appoint one;[82] although this does not displace the other trustees (unless the insolvent employer was the sole trustee), all the discretionary powers conferred on the trustees (and all fiduciary powers conferred on the employer) become exercisable only by the independent trustee so he will have the conduct of the winding up. In all other cases, the trustees will have the conduct of the winding up.

On winding up the trustees have to realise the assets of the Scheme and purchase annuities for everyone who is beneficially entitled unless any members or deferred members instead opt for a transfer into another approved pension scheme or a personal pension fund within three months of being notified what their benefits are (after that point the trustees can buy annuities without any need for their consent).[83] In the case of a money purchase scheme, the sub-fund of each member and deferred member will simply be used to purchase the necessary annuity or make the appropriate transfer (pensioners will of course already have annuities because that is the way that money purchase schemes work). In the case of a final salary scheme, annuities will have to be purchased for each pensioner and for any member or deferred member who does not opt for a transfer.

Trustees are often given an express power and now have a statutory power[84] to defer the commencement of the winding up and instead operate the scheme as a paid up scheme for a period. However, in the case of a final salary scheme, this runs the risk of favouring the interests of some members (those close to retirement who retire in the interim) at the expense of the other members because they will go into a higher priority group in the event of any shortfall; further, operating the scheme as a paid up scheme will in the event of a shortfall favour both members and pensioners at the expense of the deferred members because it will use up assets which would otherwise be available for them (in the interim the members will acquire more pensionable service, thus increasing their final benefits, and the pensioners will receive their pensions in full). It is therefore generally felt to be unwise for trustees to exercise this power, although they must at least consider whether or not to do so.

It has been held that, once winding up has commenced, the trustees no longer have the powers and discretions conferred on them by the provisions of the scheme except in so far as such powers and discretions are specifically included in the provisions governing winding up.[85] The specific decision was that a power of amendment could not be exercised after the winding up had commenced, although such a power can apparently be exercised during the period of any notice given by the employer to the trustees to wind up the

---

[81] Pensions Act 1995, s.11.
[82] *ibid.* ss.22–26; see *Icarus (Hertford) v. Driscoll* [1990] P.L.R. 1 and *Mettoy Pensions Trustees v. Evans* [1990] 1 W.L.R. 1587, *ante*, p. 210.
[83] *ibid.* s.24.
[84] *ibid.* s.38.
[85] *Thrells Ltd. (1974) Pension Scheme v. Lomas* [1992] P.L.R. 149, confirming the earlier unreported decision in *Re ABC Television* (1973), in Ellison, *op.cit.*, Sources p. 28.

scheme.[86] Any necessary amendments to powers or to the order of priorities therefore will not normally be able to made after winding up has commenced. Further, the trustees will be at risk of being impugned for fraud on a power if they make amendments immediately before that point which prejudice the interests of some particular group of beneficiaries (however, in practice, because of the statutory order of priorities considered below, the trustees can at present only effectively make amendments in respect of benefits other than SERPS equivalents which accrued to members and deferred members before April 6, 1997 and any guaranteed increases to those benefits).

## 2. *The Effect of a Shortfall*

This is only an issue in final salary schemes since in money purchase schemes each person has his own sub-fund and that is the beginning and end of his rights unless the sub-fund has been reduced by criminal conduct, in which case the employer has to make up the amount lost. Shortfalls in final salary schemes are very common because the minimum funding requirement proceeds on the basis that the scheme will continue and the costs of providing annuities is often as much as 20 per cent more than the funding notionally held for each pensioner, member and deferred member. Further, the costs of winding up a final salary scheme are very considerable because of the need to calculate the benefits of every single person; most actuaries make provision of about 4 per cent of the fund for this and include that within the minimum funding requirement but in difficult cases and, in particular where there are a large number of deferred pensioners with relatively short periods of pensionable service, the costs can be considerably higher. Unless the Scheme is in substantial surplus, shortfalls are a problem even where the employer is solvent because, although any shortfall constitutes a statutory debt[87] payable by the employer to the trustees, a shortfall for this purpose is a minimum funding requirement shortfall taking into account the likely costs of winding up the scheme rather than the cost of funding the annuities. Further, when the employer is insolvent, even that statutory debt will not be paid in full because, since it is not a preferred debt, the scheme will only receive the same number of pence in the pound as all the other general creditors of the employer. Therefore pension benefits will often not be able to be funded in full.

The provisions of the trust deed invariably provide a list of the order in which benefits are to be funded but since 1997 this has been subject to a statutory list.[88] The present order, after costs and liabilities of the scheme have been dealt with, is as follows (it was intended that this would govern winding ups which commence between April 6, 1997 and April 5, 2007 but the Government has now announced reforms which will prevent solvent employers winding up final salary schemes without providing all the necessary funding and which will, where there is a shortfall, restrict pensioners to 90% of their entitlements):

---

[86] *Municipal Mutual v. Harrop* [1998] P.L.R. 149.
[87] Pensions Act 1995, s.75(1).
[88] Contained in Pensions Act 1995, s.73 (the original form of this section has been substantially altered by the Occupational Pension Schemes (Winding Up) Regulations 1996 (S.I. 1996/3126).

(a) the benefits purchased by members or deferred members who have made additional voluntary contributions;[89]

(b) insurance policies taken out prior to April 6, 1997 in respect of any particular member whose entitlement to some payment has arisen if either the policies cannot be surrendered or the proceeds of their surrrender would not exceed the potential pension liability;

(c) pensions in payment or whose payment has been deferred because a member has continued to work after normal retirement age;

(d) ranking equally,

   (i) refunds of contributions to members with less than two years' pensionable service;
   (ii) whatever constituted the SERPS equivalent prior to April 6, 1997; and
   (iii) benefits accruing after April 5, 1997 including any pension share of those benefits given to a divorced spouse (the priority thus given to this and to category (d)(i) is very unfair since it favours short-term employees at the potential expense of long-term employees and deferred members);[90]

(e) (because the amounts necessary to fund future increases in pensions are excluded from all the categories so far except, obviously, additional voluntary contributions) the amounts necessary to fund future increases in pensions payable under (ii) and (iii) above, ranking equally as between them;

(f) (for the same reason) the amounts necessary to fund future increases in SERPS equivalents and benefits accruing after April 5, 1997;[91] and lastly

(g) everything else,[92] which is basically benefits other than SERPS equivalents which accrued before April 6, 1997 and any guaranteed increases to those benefits.

Other than additional voluntary contributions and pensions in payment or whose payment has been deferred, benefits are not funded in full at each level but are limited to the minimum funding requirement valuation. This works in respect of members and deferred members if they take transfers, assuming that there are enough assets to cover the minimum funding requirement; however, there may well not be in the light of the amount it is likely to cost to purchase the annuities for the pensioners (this is likely to cost up to 20 per cent

---

[89] Payments made by members who will not have completed enough years of service to obtain the maximum pension on their retirement in order to acquire additional years of service. Although such contributions were very common in the years when final salary schemes were in substantial surplus in order to acquire an additional proportion of any enhancement of benefits subsequently given, there is less point in making them in present circumstances; however, because of their position in the list, they are not actually at any risk.

[90] From April 6, 2007, all benefits of this type will fall into this category irrelevant of when they were earned.

[91] From April 6, 2007, this and the previous category will be combined.

[92] From April 6, 2007, there will not be "anything else" so this category will disappear.

more than the minimum funding requirement earmarked for them and so can eat into the minimum funding requirement earmarked for the members and deferred members, particularly if the scheme has a substantial proportion of pensioners). The situation can become catastrophic for members and deferred members if annuities have to be purchased for some or all of them as well, leading to substantial reductions even if the scheme in question complied with the minimum funding requirement at all times (it can of course be even worse if an employee becomes insolvent before the fund has been brought up to the minimum funding requirement). Winding up a scheme even where the employee is solvent can cause inroads to be made into benefits other than SERPS equivalents which accrued before April 6, 1997, and winding up a scheme where the employee is insolvent can deprive everyone other than pensioners (and sometimes even them) of a substantial proportion of the benefits for which they have worked throughout their working lives.

Winding up tends to take a considerable time, usually at least a year, and the trustees can face very considerable difficulties in deciding what to do in the interim in respect of early requests to refund contributions, early requests to make transfers, applications for early retirement or retirement on the grounds of incapacity, normal retirements, deaths and increases to pensions. In all cases, they will simply not know how much they can afford to pay until it is clear how many of the members and deferred members will have to be bought annuities; on the other hand, failure to comply with such requests or to commence payments of pensions and death benefits will produce a tremendous amount of aggravation so they clearly have to pay something, presumably initially only what would be payable on a worst case scenario with a further reduction to cover the possibility of the fund falling in value during winding up (it is not yet clear whether in these circumstances the statutory debt[93] can be reviewed enabling the trustees to go back to the employer and ask for a further payment).

### 3. The Effect of a Surplus

In present conditions, a surplus on a winding up is unlikely; in practice it is only feasible if, first, the pension scheme was in substantial surplus or, secondly, most of the members and deferred members take transfers rather than annuities and the proportion of pensioners is not substantial. However, a surplus can nevertheless arise both in a final salary scheme and in a money purchase scheme; what then happens to it. There are three possible situations.

1.    The trustees may have a power under the provisions of the trust deed to return the surplus to the employer. In this event, the trustees must[94] first provide for any annual increases which have not yet been funded and then consider whether to augment benefits up to Inland Revenue limits. They must then notify all the beneficiaries on two occasions of their decision in this respect and of their decision to return the surplus to the employer. If no one objects to OPRA within a specified period of at least three months from the second notice,

---

[93] Under Pensions Act 1995, s.75(1).
[94] ibid. s.76.

they can then pay the surplus to the employer; if anyone objects, they can only do so after OPRA has reached the conclusion that all the requirements of the section have been satisfied, something which will in practice also involve OPRA in deciding whether the trustees have been guilty of fraud on a power in making any of the relevant decisions.

2.    The provisions of the trust deed may prohibit the trustees from returning the surplus to the employer. In this event, the trustees must[95] provide for any annual increases which have not yet been funded and then augment benefits up to Inland Revenue limits; only then may they pay the surplus to the employer.

3.    The provisions of the trust deed may contain no provisions as to what is to happen to any surplus. This is obviously a relatively unlikely situation, particularly given the possibility of inserting a provision by use of the power of amendment before winding up commences.

This situation was, however, considered by Scott J. in *Davis v. Richards & Wallington Industries*.[96] The benefits of the employees had been augmented up to Inland Revenue limits, which in practice will be inevitable in this situation. Scott J. opined that such part of the remaining surplus as represented the employer's contributions would be held on resulting trust for the employer while such part as represented the employees' contributions would be held as *bona vacantia*. He accepted that neither the contractual relationship between employer and employees nor the fact that the employees had obtained everything for which they had contracted necessarily prevented there being a resulting trust in their favour as well. However, for two reasons he held that there was no such trust: first, because no intention could be imputed to the employees that they should receive a surplus greater than there were entitled to receive under the relevant tax legislation; and, secondly, because a resulting trust of their contributions would have been unworkable due to the need to value the benefits received by each employee in order to ascertain his entitlement to the surplus.

Subsequently, in *Air Jamaica v. Charlton*,[97] the Privy Council regarded the approach of Scott J. to the imputation of intention as erroneous, saying that it was not obvious that employees should ever be regarded as having no expectation of obtaining a return of excess contributions in the event of a surplus. But this was no more than a dictum because the Privy Council was actually considering what was to happen to the subject matter of some of the trusts of the pension scheme in question which were void for perpetuity and in such circumstances it was impossible to say that the employees had received everything for which they had contracted anyway. Nor did the valuation difficulty which Scott J. had identified apply in the light of

---

[95] *ibid.* s.77.
[96] [1990] 1 W.L.R. 1511.
[97] [1999] 1 W.L.R. 1399.

the way in which the Privy Council had construed the provisions of the scheme which was before it.

However, the rejection of *bona vacantia* by the Privy Council is clearly preferable to its adoption by Scott J., at least where a resulting trust of the employees' contributions is workable. If this is the case then, in the unlikely event that this situation recurs, it is to be hoped that there would be held to be resulting trusts of both the part of the remaining surplus which represents the employer's contributions and that part which represents the employees' contributions.

CHAPTER 13

# THE APPOINTMENT, RETIREMENT AND REMOVAL OF TRUSTEES

THE appointment and retirement of trustees is a matter of prime concern for everyone connected with the trust. Once the trust has been set up, the settlor, unless he has specially reserved powers to himself, will have handed to his trustees complete control over the property subject to the trust. The interest of the beneficiaries will only be adequately protected if the trustees are scrupulously honest, are prepared to give adequate time to the administration of the trust, have enough common sense and business acumen to do well with the trust property and are able to treat fairly beneficiaries whose interests possibly conflict, such as a tenant for life and his remainderman.[1] So far as the trustee himself is concerned, his appointment is not to be considered lightly. Unless there is a provision in the trust instrument to the contrary or the trustee is either a trust corporation or is acting as trustee in a professional capacity,[2] he will have to devote his time to the administration of the trust entirely without payment or other benefit.[3] In return for his efforts, he may well receive from the beneficiaries not gratitude but bitterness[4] and, if he is not as careful as he might be and consequently makes a mistake, he may find himself liable to make good any loss out of his own pocket.[5]

## I. TYPES OF TRUSTEE

### 1. *Ordinary Trustees*

In general, any individual, limited company or other corporation may be appointed a trustee,[6] and a limited company may act as a trustee jointly with

---

[1] The conflict of interest between tenant for life and remainderman is explained in connection with investments, see *post*, pp. 593 *et seq.*

[2] This will be the case if he acts in the course of a profession or business which consists of or includes the provision of services in connection with the managament or administration of trusts generally or in any particular respect. See Trustee Act 2000, ss.28, 29.

[3] See *post*, pp. 721 *et seq.*

[4] In *Re Londonderry's Settlement* [1965] Ch. 918, a discretionary beneficiary to whom and to whose family a total of £165,000 had been paid showed anything but gratitude to the trustees.

[5] See *post*, p. 761.

[6] See *ante*, p. 95.

an individual,[7] as well as with another limited company or other corporation.[8] Except in the case of infants,[9] there is no statutory prohibition upon the appointment of any person as a trustee; however, there are some persons who, while they have the legal capacity to be trustees, may nevertheless be so undesirable as trustees that the court will remove them if they are ever appointed. A person may be undesirable in this sense either because of a defect in his character involving financial irresponsibility, as manifested by some circumstances leading to bankruptcy,[10] or by conviction of crimes involving dishonesty,[11] or because, as a result of being appointed a trustee, he would be placed in a position where his interest as a beneficiary under the trust would conflict with his duty as a trustee. In the latter respect, however, while the appointment of a beneficiary as a sole trustee may well be undesirable, the appointment of a beneficiary as one of two or more trustees will often be advantageous, because the beneficiary will then be induced to do the best he can for the trust by his financial interest in the property as well as by his duty as trustee.

Minors are in a curious position. It is clear that a minor may be a trustee. Thus in *Re Vinogradoff*,[12] a woman transferred a holding of War Stock into the joint names of herself and her granddaughter, then aged four. There was no presumption of advancement[13] and the court decided that the granddaughter held that stock as a trustee on resulting trust.[14] But although a minor may be a trustee by implication or by operation of law, he cannot be expressly appointed as a trustee; section 20 of the Law of Property Act 1925 declares void the appointment of a minor as a trustee. If a minor is to be a trustee, he will therefore have to become one other than by express appointment.

An ordinary trustee is not normally entitled to remuneration for his services unless this is authorised by a provision in the trust instrument or the trustee is either a trust corporation or is acting as trustee in a professional capacity.[15] Remuneration is considered in detail in a later chapter.[16]

---

[7] The Bodies Corporate (Joint Tenancy) Act 1889. See *Re Thompson's Settlement Trusts* [1905] 1 Ch. 229.

[8] While it has always been possible for all the original trustees to be limited companies or other corporations and for a trust corporation to be sole trustee, in recent times it is only since January 1, 1997 that it has been possible for individual trustees to retire leaving as trustees only limited companies and/or other corporations (Trusts of Land and Appointment of Trustees Act 1996, Sched. 3, para. 3(12), (13) amending Trustee Act 1925, ss.37(1)(c), 39(1)).

[9] See Law of Property Act 1925, s.20, *infra*.

[10] *Re Barker's Trusts* (1875) 1 Ch.D. 43.

[11] *Coombe v. Brookes* (1871) L.R. 12 Eq. 61; *Re Forster* (1886) 55 L.T. 479; *Re Henderson* [1940] Ch. 764; see *post*, p. 475.

[12] [1935] W.N. 68.

[13] The woman did not stand *in loco parentis* to her granddaughter.

[14] See *ante*, p. 277.

[15] This will be the case if he acts in the course of a profession or business which consists of or includes the provision of services in connection with the managment or administration of trusts generally or in any particular respect. See Trustee Act 2000, ss.28, 29.

[16] See *post*, p. 721.

## 2. *Judicial Trustees*

A judicial trustee is a person or corporation appointed by the court to act as a trustee where the administration of the trust is intended to be subject to close supervision by the court. Such an appointment is made under the provisions of the Judicial Trustees Act 1896; it is not to be confused with the appointment of an ordinary trustee by the court. The appointment of a judicial trustee is generally made on the application of an existing trustee or beneficiary but the appointment can also be made at the instance of a person who is intending to create a trust.[17] It is also possible to appoint a judicial trustee in order to administer an estate. At one time, when there was no machinery by means of which a personal representative could retire, this provided a means of replacing one who was no longer able to act. However, the court can now appoint a replacement personal representative under section 50 of the Administration of Justice Act 1985. In an application under the 1985 Act, the court may proceed as if there had instead been an application under the 1896 Act and vice versa.[18]

The distinctive feature of a judicial trustee is that the beneficiaries are protected in the event of his default by virtue of the fact that he is usually required to give security to the court for the proper performance of his duties.[19] He is subject to close supervision by the court and special provisions govern the auditing of his accounts.[20] As a result, a judicial trustee becomes an officer of the court, so that he is able to obtain the directions of the court informally at any time.

In practice it is rare for a judicial trustee to be appointed save where complex litigation is in prospect,[21] where there has been gross mismanagement of the trust in question in the past, or where the admininstration of a trust involves problems of extraordinary complexity or difficulty.[22]

A judicial trustee may always charge for his services[23] and is paid from the trust funds.

### 3. *Trust Corporations*

**(A) Definition**

It has already been seen[24] that, in principle, any company as well as any individual can be appointed as a trustee. However, a company which is

---

[17] Judicial Trustees Act 1896, s.1(1).

[18] Administration of Justice Act 1985, s.50(4); Judicial Trustees Act 1896, s.1(7).

[19] Judicial Trustees Act 1896, s.4(1); Judicial Trustee Rules 1983, r.6.

[20] Judicial Trustees Act 1896, ss.1(6), 4(1); Administration of Justice Act 1982, s.57; *Re Ridsdel* [1947] Ch. 597.

[21] See *Re Diplock* [1948] Ch. 465, affirmed *sub nom. Minister of Health v. Simpson* [1951] A.C. 251.

[22] *Re Chisholm* (1898) 43 S.J. 43.

[23] Judicial Trustees Act 1896, ss.1(5), 4(1); Judicial Trustee Rules 1983, r.11.

[24] See *ante*, p. 543.

appointed a trustee is not by virtue of that fact alone a trust corporation. This term is applied only to a body corporate, such as a bank or insurance company, which undertakes the business of acting as a trustee and which fulfils certain conditions.[25] The basic conditions are:[26]

(a) Its constitution must authorise it to undertake the business of acting as a trustee and of acting as a personal representative.

(b) It must have an issued capital of not less than £250,000, of which not less than £100,000 must have been paid up in cash.

(c) The company must be incorporated either in the United Kingdom or some other European Union country.

(d) The company must have a place of business in the United Kingdom, no matter where it is incorporated.

The second of these conditions, which was, at the time when it was originally imposed, intended to afford a considerable measure of protection to beneficiaries, is now totally inadequate for this purpose. The value of the assets in any one trust may exceed several times the amount of the minimum required paid up capital. Further, the test relates to the amount of the issued share capital of the company, not its asset value. Thus, provided that a company has actually issued shares to the extent of £250,000, it is still be eligible to be a trust corporation even if it has by some act of imprudence managed to lose all its shareholders' funds.

In addition to commercial companies which carry on the business of acting as trustees, a number of other bodies also rank as trust corporations. They are given this status so that they can take advantage of the privileges given to trust corporations.[27] The following persons and bodies are included in the definition of trust corporation:

(a) Any body corporate which is appointed by the court to be a trustee in any particular case.[28]

(b) Certain bodies which are incorporated to act as trustees of charitable trusts.[29]

---

[25] The path to the definition is tortuous: first, certain bodies are entitled to act as custodian trustee (see *post*, p. 549) by virtue of the Public Trustee Rules 1912, as amended; secondly, the Public Trustee Rules 1912 were made under the power conferred by the Public Trustee Act 1906; and, thirdly, the Trustee Act 1925, s.68(18) provides that the definition of a "trust corporation" for the purposes of the Act includes any corporation entitled to act as a custodian trustee under the rules made under the Public Trustee Act 1906.

[26] The Public Trustee (Custodian Trustee) Rules 1975 (S.I. 1975 No. 1189). The rules were made to implement the EEC Council Directive 73/183/EEC.

[27] See *post*, p. 547.

[28] Trustee Act 1925, s.68(18).

[29] The incorporation must be by Special Act, or Royal Charter, or under the Charitable Trustees Incorporation Act 1872; Public Trustee Rules 1912, r.30(c), (d), as substituted.

    (c)   Certain public officers, such as the Public Trustee,[30] the Treasury Solicitor, and the Official Solicitor.[31]

    (d)   Major local authorities[32] and certain public authorities, such as the Gas Council and Regional Hospital Boards.[33]

## (B) Ability to Act

A trust corporation can act in the administration of any trust[34] unless the trust instrument forbids its employment.

## (C) Privileges

The general principle is that, whenever statutory provisions require an act to be done by two private trustees, that act can be done by a sole trustee where that trustee is a trust corporation. It follows that the main privileges of a trust corporation are as follows:

    (a)   A trust corporation can by itself give a good receipt for capital money under a trust of land[35] or a settlement under the Settled Land Act 1925.[36]

    (b)   A trust corporation can by itself exercise various powers of management, such as the apportionment of blended funds, accepting compositions and effecting compromises.[37]

    (c)   Where a private trustee acts jointly with a trust corporation and the private trustee wishes to delegate the performance of his duties, he may delegate them to the trust corporation.[38] He cannot, however, delegate his powers to his co-trustee if the co-trustee is a private trustee permanently, unless he is a trustee-beneficiary of a trust of land.

    (d)   A private trustee may be discharged without a fresh trustee being appointed in his place where a trust corporation will be left to perform the trusts.[39]

As a result of these provisions, it is common to find a trust corporation acting as the sole trustee of a trust, despite the fact that it can act jointly with a private trustee.

## (D) Remuneration

Since the enactment of the Trustee Act 2000, a trust corporation has been able

---

[30] Trustee Act 1925, s.68(18). See also the Public Trustee and Administration of Funds Act 1986, which confers on the Public Trustee all the functions of the Judge of the Court of Protection under the Mental Health Act 1983, Pt. VII.

[31] Law of Property (Amendment) Act 1926, s.3(1).

[32] The Public Trustee Rules 1912, r.30(g); Local Government Act 1972, s.241.

[33] The Public Trustee Rules 1912, r.30(e), (f).

[34] *Re Cherry's Trusts* [1914] 1 Ch. 83.

[35] Trustee Act 1925, s.14(2), as amended by Trusts of Land and Appointment of Trustees Act 1996, Sched. 3, para. 3(3).

[36] Settled Land Act 1925, ss.94, 95.

[37] Trustee Act 1925, s.19.

[38] s.25(1), (2), substituted by the Powers of Attorney Act 1971. See *post*, p. 570.

[39] See *post*, p. 566.

to charge "reasonable remuneration" out of the trust funds for any services which it provides to or on behalf of a private trust;[40] this is defined as "such remuneration as is reasonable in the circumstances for the provision of those services to or on behalf of that trust by that trustee".[41] Prior to this legislation, a trust corporation was in the same position as an ordinary trustee and was only entitled to remuneration where there was a provision to that effect in the trust instrument; this meant that in practice a trust corporation would not agree to act as an original trustee until express arrangements had been made for its remuneration. It is obviously likely that trust corporations will continue to insist on such express arrangements in order to avoid any dispute as to what constitutes "reasonable remuneration".[42] It remains to be seen what attitude the courts now adopt when appointing a trust corporation to be a trustee, usually of course as a replacement trustee; they remain entitled to fix its remuneration,[43] but may now prefer to leave the trust corporation to claim the reasonable remuneration to which it is entitled under the 2000 Act.

### 4. The Public Trustee

The Public Trustee is a corporation sole which was established by the Public Trustee Act 1906. His main function is to administer private trusts, particularly small trusts, although he may also be appointed a judicial[44] or custodian trustee,[45] and may be appointed to administer the property of a convicted criminal.[46] His functions were extended by the Public Trustee and Administration of Funds Act 1986, which confers on him all the functions of the Judge of the Court of Protection in relation to the property and affairs of mental patients under Part VII of the Mental Health Act 1983.[47] He may not act as the trustee of a religious or a charitable trust[48] and may only carry on a business owned by a trust for the purpose of winding it up.[49] Although the Public Trustee is a public officer, he can only act in the administration of any trust if he has been appointed to do so in the same way as a private individual. He may also refuse to accept any trust for any reason other than the smallness of the trust property. He may act either alone or jointly with other trustees. However, he is able to act alone notwithstanding any normal requirement for a plurality of trustees to act in, for example, the case of an overreaching conveyance.[50]

As he is a corporation sole, the Public Trustee never dies. This means that where he is the sole trustee, it is never necessary for a new trustee to be

---

[40] Trustee Act 2000, s.29(1); this provision does not apply to charitable trusts.

[41] s.29(3).

[42] Express provisions in a trust instrument oust the provisions relating to reasonable remuneration; s.29(5).

[43] Trustee Act 1925, s.42.

[44] See ante, p. 545.

[45] See post, infra.

[46] Public Trustee Act 1906, s.5.

[47] s.3.

[48] Re Hampton (1918) 88 L.J.Ch. 103.

[49] Public Trustee Rules 1912, r.7(1),(2).

[50] Re Duxbury [1995] 1 W.L.R. 425.

appointed. A further advantage is that, if he acts improperly and loss occurs, the State makes good that loss.[51]

The Public Trustee may always charge for his services,[52] his fees being calculated not on the amount of work done but on the value of the property administered.

### 5. *Custodian Trustees*

The function of a custodian trustee, who may be the Public Trustee or any other trust corporation, is merely to hold the property of a trust, leaving the administration of the trust in the hands of managing trustees. A custodian trustee is usually appointed so that, once the trust property is vested in his name, it will not be necessary to have any further appointment of new trustees and so that he may have custody of the trust deeds and securities.

A custodian trustee may always charge for the services which he performs in that capacity.[53]

### II. THE APPOINTMENT OF TRUSTEES

Trustees may be appointed, first, on the creation of a new trust and, secondly, during the continuance of an existing trust, whether in substitution for a trustee who is retiring or who has died, or in addition to the existing trustees. In both cases, the appointment is almost always made by deed without the court becoming involved in any way but, in exceptional cases, when there is no one else able to do so, the court can make the appointment itself. Thus both appointments made outside the court and appointments made by the court itself must be considered. In some circumstances, there are restrictions on the maximum number of trustees. It is also possible for a trustee to assume office as a result of his own officious conduct.

### 1. *Appointing the Original Trustees*

When a settlor creates a trust inter vivos, he will usually appoint the first trustees of the settlement himself. If he wishes to appoint people other than himself to be the trustees, he will include a clause appointing them in the original settlement or trust deed. If, on the other hand, he wishes to appoint himself, he may make a declaration of trust to the effect that from then on he will be holding specified property on certain trusts, in which case he will then be the only trustee of the trust; alternatively, he may appoint himself and one or more other persons to be the first trustees. But, as soon as the trust has come into existence, the settlor loses his right as settlor to appoint the trustees of the settlement. He may in the trust instrument have conferred on himself (or, for that matter, on someone else) the power to appoint trustees in the future;[54] however, if he makes any future appointment under that power, he will be

---

[51] Public Trustee Act 1906, s.7.
[52] *ibid.*, s.9, as amended by the Public Trustee (Fees) Act 1957.
[53] Public Trustee Act 1906, s.2; see *post*, p. 722.
[54] See *post*, p. 551.

doing so because he has given himself that power in the trust instrument, not because he was the settlor.

Occasionally, there may be no trustees of a new trust. The trustees named in the settlement may be dead or may refuse to act, or the settlor may have forgotten to name any. If the trust instrument has given anyone a power to appoint new trustees, that power can then be used; otherwise, the appointment will have to be made by the court.[55] In so doing, the court will be giving effect to the equitable maxim that "the court will not allow a trust to fail for want of a trustee".

In practice, trusts arise most frequently as the result of a death. Where the deceased left a will, he may have expressly thereby set up a trust. Alternatively, a trust may arise by operation of law. Thus, if the deceased left a legacy to a child, the money cannot actually be paid to that child until he reaches the age of 18 because a minor cannot give a good receipt for capital money. Until then the money will have to be held upon trust for the minor. If, on the other hand, the deceased died intestate, the devolution of his property will be governed by the Administration of Estates Act 1925, as varied by subsequent statutes and statutory instruments.[56] In some circumstances, the intestate's property will have to be held on statutory trusts.[57] For example, if the deceased was worth £200,000 and left a wife and children, the wife will at present be entitled to the first £125,000;[58] the remaining £75,000[59] will be divided into two halves: one half goes to the children outright and the other half is held on trust for the wife for life, remainder to the children.[60]

It is possible where a trust is created by will to designate different persons as trustees and executors but normally the same persons are appointed to fulfil both functions. In particular, where a different person is not appointed trustee, the executor may automatically become the trustee. Whether he will in fact do so depends on the function which he is discharging at the point in time being considered. The rules which govern the time at which an executor becomes a trustee are not considered here, but it is sufficient to say that the functions of an executor (or, where there is no executor, an administrator) are:

(a)  in the case of an executor, obtaining probate of the deceased's will or, in the case of an administrator, obtaining letters of administration of the deceased's estate;

(b)  getting in the deceased's property, including any debts due to him;

(c)  paying any inheritance tax and the debts owed by the deceased;

(d)  paying any legacies;

---

[55]  *Dodkin v. Brunt* (1868) L.R. 6 Eq. 580.
[56]  Such as the Intestates' Estates Act 1952, the Family Provision Act 1966, and the Inheritance (Provision for Family and Dependents) Act 1975.
[57]  Administration of Estates Act 1925, s.46(1).
[58]  This is the fixed net sum payable under Administration of Estates Act 1925, s.55(1)(x), which is raised periodically by statutory instrument (Family Provision Act 1966, s.1; Administration of Justice Act 1977, s.28.; the current statutory instrument is Family Provision (Intestate Succession) Order 1993 (SI 1993/2906)).
[59]  Under Administration of Estates Act 1925, s.46(1), the wife would in addition receive the personal chattels of the deceased.
[60]  Administration of Estates Act 1925, s.46(1).

(e)  agreeing the distribution account with the beneficiaries; and

(f)  distributing all the property which can be immediately distributed, that is to say all the property remaining after the payment of debts and legacies, other than that which is governed by a trust or which is not immediately payable to a beneficiary because he is still under 18.

When all this has been done, in general the executor or administrator ceases to be a personal representative; if any of the deceased's property is still in his name, from then on he holds it as trustee, not as personal representative. In the case of land, however, an executor or administrator will continue to hold the property as personal representative until he assents to its vesting in himself as trustee; in the case of legal interests, the assent must be in writing.[61] In this case, therefore, the test is not one of function, but whether or not there has been an assent.

## 2. Appointing New Trustees

It is necessary to distinguish, on the one hand, the persons who are able to appoint new trustees from, on the other hand, the occasions on which they are able to do so.

**(A) The Persons who can Appoint New Trustees**
The rules relating to the appointment of new trustees are the same whether the trust was set up inter vivos or arose as the result of a death.

**(1) The order in which the rules are applied**
Where the trust instrument makes provision for the appointment of new trustees, either generally or in the specific situation which has arisen, the person or persons nominated clearly have the primary right to make any appointment. However, if reliance is placed on that power, then its terms must be strictly followed.

Where, on the other hand, the trust instrument does not make any provision for whatever situation has arisen, then new trustees may be appointed in two distinct ways which exist alongside one another: first, by virtue of the statutory power in section 36 of the Trustee Act 1925 (if there is a conflict between the provisions of the trust instrument and the statutory power, the statutory power prevails), the following persons in the following order have the right to appoint new trustees: the person or persons nominated in the trust instrument; the surviving or continuing trustees; and the personal representatives of the last or only surviving trustee (only if there is no person in any one group or if the persons in that group refuse to appoint can an appointment be made by a person in the subsequent group); and, secondly, by virtue of section 19 of the Trusts of Land and Appointment of Trustees Act 1996, which only applies where the trust instrument has made no provision for the appointment of new trustees, where all the beneficiaries are of full age and capacity and between them absolutely entitled to the trust property, they can direct the appointment of new trustees.

---

[61] *Re King's Will Trusts* [1964] Ch. 542; see *ante*, p. 31.

Additionally, in one particular situation, where a trustee is incapable by reason of mental disorder of exercising his functions as such and there is no one able and willing to exercise the statutory power contained in section 36 of the Trustee Act 1925, then by virtue of section 20 of the Trusts of Land and Appointment of Trustees Act 1996, where all the beneficiaries are of full age and capacity and between them absolutely entitled to the trust property, they can direct his replacement.

Finally, failing all else, new trustees can be appointed by the court.

### (2) Observations about the rules

The rules are applied strictly in the order set out above; thus in *Re Higginbottom*,[62] the existing trustee had the power to appoint new trustees and her right to do so was held to prevail against the wishes of a large majority of the beneficiaries who sought to appoint others.[63]

Where an appointment is made in good faith by the person entitled, the court will not interfere with the appointment even if it would have preferred someone else to have been appointed.[64]

Where two or more persons have the power of appointing new trustees, they must exercise the power jointly unless there is a provision in the trust instrument to the contrary. If they cannot agree who the new trustee shall be, they are treated as refusing to exercise their power and so that the power to appoint becomes exercisable by the persons in the next category. Thus in *Re Sheppard's Settlement Trusts*,[65] the trust instrument gave the power of appointing trustees to two persons. When they could not agree on the appointee, it was held that the power could be exercised by the continuing trustees. The position is the same if the person having the power to appoint cannot be found[66] or is incapable of making the appointment.[67]

The person who has the power of appointing new trustees may appoint a separate set of trustees for any part of the trust property which is held on trusts distinct from those on which the remainder of the trust property is held.[68] If, therefore, trustees hold three-quarters of the trust fund on trust for Andrew and his family, and one-quarter for Bernard and his family, separate trustees can be appointed for the quarter held for Bernard. While, however, the appointment is valid for all purposes connected with the administration of the trust, for certain tax purposes the original trustees will continue to be regarded as trustees.[69]

### (B) The Occasions on which Trustees may be Appointed

### (1) By the exercise of an express power in the trust instrument

Where a person is nominated in the trust instrument,[70] whether it is the settlor,

---

[62] [1892] 3 Ch. 132.
[63] See also Re *Brockbank* [1948] Ch. 206.
[64] Re *Gadd* (1883) 23 Ch.D. 134; Re *Norris* (1884) 27 Ch.D. 333; Re *Sales* (1911) 55 S.J. 838.
[65] [1888] W.N. 234.
[66] *Craddock v. Witham* [1895] W.N. 75.
[67] Re *Blake* [1887] W.N. 75.
[68] Trustee Act 1925, s.37(1)(b).
[69] *Roome v. Edwards* [1982] A.C. 279.
[70] See Re *Walker and Hughes* (1883) 24 Ch.D. 698 and Re *Sheppard's Settlement Trusts* [1888] W.N. 234.

the protector of the settlement (if there is one), or anyone else, he is usually given the power to appoint new trustees in all circumstances; he may even be given power at any time to replace all the existing trustees without having to show cause. Such a power was conferred on a protector in *Von Knieriem v. Bermuda Trust Co.*,[71] and his exercise of it was held to have been valid even though he had apparently acted more in the interests of the settlor than of the beneficiaries.

Where, however, a power is able to be exercised only in limited circumstances, that power is strictly construed. In *Re Wheeler*,[72] a person was nominated to appoint a new trustee in the place of any trustee who was "incapable" of acting. One trustee became bankrupt and so became "unfit" to act,[73] but not "incapable" of acting. It was held that the nominated person did not have a power to appoint in those circumstances because the condition was not fulfilled.[74] Further, where a power to appoint is given jointly to two or more persons, it can only be exercised by those persons. Unless, therefore, there is evidence of a contrary intention, the power will not be exercisable at all where one of the donees of the power dies, or becomes incapable of making the appointment.[75] On the other hand, where a beneficiary is nominated in the trust instrument as having power to appoint new trustees, the power of appointment is generally treated as being detached from the beneficial interest. Thus, if the beneficiary disposes of his interest then, unless there is a provision in the trust instrument to the contrary, he will still be entitled to appoint new trustees.[76]

An illogical difference exists in respect of the appointment of a new trustee between the position where an existing trustee is retiring and where an additional trustee is to be appointed without the retirement of an existing trustee. If a person who is nominated in the trust instrument to appoint new trustees has been given only the statutory power[77] rather than some broader power, he may appoint himself to be a trustee in the place of a retiring trustee but not as an additional trustee. This results from a difference of wording between the different provisions of the Trustee Act 1925. Section 36(1), which applies where a new trustee is being appointed in the place of an outgoing trustee, gives the power to the nominated person to "appoint one or more other persons (whether or not being the persons exercising the power) to be a trustee", while section 36(6), which confers the power to appoint additional trustees, gives the nominated person a power to appoint "another person or other persons to be the trustee". It is hard to imagine that this difference was intended by the legislature.

## (2) By exercise of the statutory power

Section 36(1) of the Trustee Act 1925 sets out a number of circumstances in which new trustees can be appointed by anyone nominated in the trust

[71] (1994) 1 B.O.S. 116. See *ante*, p. 192.
[72] [1896] 1 Ch. 315 (a case on Trustee Act 1893, s.10(1), re-enacted in Trustee Act 1925, s.36(1)).
[73] As to the distinction, see *post*, p. 568.
[74] See also *Turner v. Maule* (1850) 15 Jur. 761; *Re Watts' Settlement* (1851) 9 Hare 106; *Re May's Will Trusts* [1941] Ch. 109.
[75] *Re Harding* [1923] 1 Ch. 182.
[76] *Hardaker v. Moorhouse* (1884) 26 Ch.D. 417.
[77] *Re Power's Settlement Trust* [1951] Ch. 1074.

instrument for this purpose[78] and, in default, by the surviving or continuing trustees or the personal representatives of the last surviving trustee.[79] However, it must be emphasised that this provision gives rise only to a power to appoint a new trustee; it does not impose any duty so to do.

The right of a surviving or continuing trustee so to appoint under section 36(1) is, rather surprisingly, extended by virtue of section 36(8) to a trustee who has refused to act or wishes to retire if he is willing to act in exercising the powers of the section. The curious result of this is that, despite the fact that a trustee refuses to act as a trustee or that he wishes to retire, he must be allowed to join in the appointment of a new trustee if he wishes to do so. However, for the purposes of this provision, the expression "refusing or retiring trustee" is narrowly construed. In *Re Stoneham's Settlement Trusts*,[80] a new trustee was appointed in the place of another trustee who had remained out of the United Kingdom for longer than 12 months, something which justifies compulsory removal from office. When the displaced trustee returned, he applied to the court to upset the appointment on the ground that he had not participated in it. However, Danckwerts J. held that a trustee who is removed compulsorily from the trust is not a "refusing or retiring" trustee but a "removed" trustee; consequently, his participation is not necessary.

Where there are no surviving or continuing trustees and the appointment can instead be made by the personal representative of the last surviving trustee, it is necessary to distinguish between, on the one hand, the power of appointment itself and, on the other hand, the method of proving entitlement to exercise that power. The executor of the last surviving trustee has the power to appoint new trustees as soon as that last trustee dies. Accordingly, it is not necessary for him to obtain a grant of probate before exercising his power to do so.[81] However, a personal representative can only actually prove his entitlement to exercise the power by producing a grant of probate or letters of administration in respect of the estate in question.

This can cause problems in respect of overseas grants. It is the general practice of the English court only to recognise grants of probate or letters of administration which have been issued in the United Kingdom or, if issued by a court overseas, have been re-sealed by a court in the United Kingdom. The point arose in *Re Crowhurst Park*.[82] The deceased was the sole trustee of various tenancies of land in England. His widow obtained a grant of probate of his will in Jersey, but she did not obtain a grant in the United Kingdom. The widow executed a deed by which, in her capacity as the personal representative of the deceased, she purported to appoint herself as the new trustee of the trust of the land. It was held that, while she was entitled to exercise the power of appointment, she could only prove that entitlement by a grant of probate or letters of administration granted in the United Kingdom. Accordingly, the widow could not bring proceedings in respect of the tenancies until she had obtained a United Kingdom grant.

---

[78] Such a person will not need to rely on the statutory power where he has been given express power to appoint in the situation which has arisen but only in other situations not expressly envisaged by his power.

[79] *Re Shafto's Trusts* (1885) 29 Ch.D. 247.

[80] [1953] Ch. 59.

[81] *Re Parker's Trusts* [1894] 1 Ch. 707; *Re Crowhurst Park* [1974] 1 All E.R. 991 at 1001.

[82] [1974] 1 All E.R. 991.

Although the personal representatives of the last surviving trustee may therefore appoint new trustees, this is a mere power and they cannot be compelled to do so.[83] They are, however, given statutory encouragement to exercise their power; even if they intend to renounce their office as personal representatives, they are still entitled to appoint new trustees before they renounce.[84] Without the express statutory provision, the exercise of the power would be sufficient to show an acceptance of the office of personal representative.

The statutory power makes provision for the appointment of new trustees both in place of an outgoing trustee and as an additional trustee, where all the existing trustees are remaining. In both cases the appointment must be made inter vivos; it cannot be made by will.[85] The only formal requirement is that it should be made in writing; however, it is in most cases desirable that it should be made by deed.[86]

**(a) Appointing a replacement for an outgoing trustee**. Where an appointment is being made of a replacement for an outgoing trustee, the section applies in the case of any outgoing trustee, whether or not he was the original trustee of the trust and whether or not he was appointed by the court. The statutory power applies in the following situations:

*(i) Where a trustee is dead.* This includes the situation where a person nominated as a trustee dies without ever having taken up his office. This would be the case, for example, where a person who is nominated as the trustee of a will dies before the death of the testator.

*(ii) Where a trustee remains out of the United Kingdom for more than twelve months.* The period abroad must be a continuous period and a break for even a very short time, such as a week, will prevent this provision operating.[87] The motive for the absence is irrelevant,[88] so that even if the trustee has been absent because he has been imprisoned abroad, he can still be removed from his trusteeship.

In some circumstances, the trust instrument modifies the statutory provision and seeks to achieve the same broad effect by different wording. Where this is done, the provision must be carefully construed but the courts lean towards an interpretation that the period abroad must have an element of permanence. This was satisfied in *Re Earl of Stamford*,[89] where the power arose if a trustee should "be abroad" and a trustee lived in France, making only occasional visits to England.[90]

The provision is often totally inappropriate where a foreign trust is to be established or where an English trust is to be "exported".[91] In such cases, it is

---

[83] *Re Knight's Will* (1883) 26 Ch.D. 82.
[84] Trustee Act 1925, s.36(5).
[85] See *Re Parker's Trust* [1894] 1 Ch. 707.
[86] So that Trustee Act 1925, s.40 may operate; see *post*, p. 563.
[87] *Re Walker* [1910] 1 Ch. 259.
[88] *Re Stoneham* [1953] Ch. 59.
[89] [1896] 1 Ch. 288.
[90] See also *Re Moravian Society* (1858) 26 Beav. 101.
[91] See *post*, p. 867.

prudent to provide expressly that a trustee shall not be capable of being replaced merely because he is resident abroad.

*(iii) Where a trustee desires to be discharged.*	This statutory provision is wide enough to include the position where the trustee desires to be discharged from only part of the trust.[92] Thus a trustee might wish to remain a trustee of part of a trust fund which was being set aside to provide a life interest for a beneficiary, while wishing to retire as a trustee of the main fund.

*(iv) Where a trustee refuses to act.*	Logically, this provision should apply only to a person who has accepted the trusteeship and refuses to act after accepting office. Until that time, it is difficult to see how he can be said to be a "trustee". However, there is old authority on the predecessor of the section to the effect that its scope also includes a trustee who disclaims.[93]

*(v) Where a trustee is unfit to act.*	There is little authority as to the meaning of "unfitness" for the purposes of this provision but it seems clear that "unfitness" here refers not to medical infirmity but to defects of character. In the absence of authority, it is only possible to deduce the meaning of the expression from some of the circumstances in which the court will remove trustees.[94] These cases include conviction of a crime involving dishonesty,[95] and, in certain circumstances, bankruptcy. In the case of bankruptcy, the court will generally remove a trustee who has become bankrupt,[96] particularly if the beneficiaries request this to be done, if only on the ground that a person who has lost all his own money ought not to be in charge of other people's money. But as an exception to this, the court has refused to remove a trustee whose bankruptcy was due to misfortune and who was entirely free of moral blame.[97]

*(vi) Where a trustee is incapable of acting.*	Incapacity here refers to physical or mental incapacity to attend, or to attend properly, to the administration of the trust.[98] Special provisions affect mental incapacity where the trustee also has a beneficial interest in the property if he is a person whose mental illness makes him subject to the provisions of the Mental Health Act 1983. In this case, no appointment of a new trustee in his place may be made without the consent of the authority having jurisdiction over him under Part VII of the Mental Health Act 1983.[99]

---

[92] If this statutory power is excluded, a trustee cannot be discharged from part only of the fund without the intervention of the court; *Savile v. Couper* (1887) 36 Ch.D. 520; *Re Moss's Trusts* (1888) 37 Ch.D. 513.

[93] *Noble v. Meymott* (1841) 14 Beav. 471; *Re Hadley* (1851) 5 De G. & Sm. 67; *Viscountess D'Adhemar v. Bertrand* (1865) 35 Beav. 19; *Re Birchall* (1889) 40 Ch.D. 436.

[94] See *post,* p. 568.

[95] *Turner v. Maule* (1850) 15 Jur. 761; *Re Wheeler and De Rochow* [1896] 1 Ch. 315; *Re Sichel's Settlements* [1916] 1 Ch. 358.

[96] *Re Barker's Trusts* (1875) 1 Ch.D. 43.

[97] *Re Bridgman* (1860) 1 Drew. & Sm. 164.

[98] *Re Moravian Society* (1858) 26 Beav. 101; *Re Watt's Settlement* (1872) L.R. 7 Ch. 223; *Turner v. Maule* (1850) 15 Jur. 761; *Re East* (1873) 8 Ch.App. 735; *Re Lemann's Trusts* (1883) 22 Ch.D. 633; *Re Blake* [1887] W.N. 173; *Re Weston's Trusts* [1898] W.N. 151.

[99] Mental Health Act 1983, s.148, Sched. IV, para. 4(a), replacing Mental Health Act 1959, ss.149(1), 153 & Sched. VII, which in turn replaced Trustee Act 1925, s.36(9).

A person is also incapable of acting if there is any legislation in force which expressly prohibits persons in specified circumstances from holding property or acting as trustees. Such a prohibition has applied to enemy aliens in time of war.[1]

*(vii) Where a trustee is a minor.* As has been seen,[2] a minor cannot validly be expressly appointed a trustee and the provisions will only apply where the minor is a trustee under a resulting or constructive trust.

*(viii) Where section 36(3) applies.* The statutory power can also be utilised where a corporation which has been acting as a trustee is dissolved.

**(b) Appointing an additional trustee.** The statutory power to appoint additional trustees is contained in section 36(6). This provision only permits the appointment of an additional trustee where there are not more than three existing trustees. Although more than one additional trustee may be appointed at the same time, the section provides that the total number of trustees must not be increased beyond four (this restriction applies to all trusts, not only to trusts affecting land where there is always a limit of four).[3] However, the trust instrument can provide for a higher number,[4] although such a provision is ineffective when the trust affects land. The former rule that additional trustees could not be appointed under this section if any existing trustee was a trust corporation has now been abrogated.[5]

**(3) By the beneficiaries**
Where the trust instrument does not make any provision for the appointment of new trustees,[6] then in two situations the beneficiaries of the trust will have a power of appointment unless it is excluded by the settlor.[7]

The first situation exists alongside the statutory power of appointment conferred by section 36 of the Trustee Act 1925. Where all the beneficiaries of the trust are of full age and capacity and between them absolutely entitled to

---

[1] *Re Sichel's Settlements* [1916] 1 Ch. 358.
[2] See *ante*, p. 544.
[3] See *post*, p. 560.
[4] s.36(6), like all the provisions of the Trustee Act 1925, can be ousted by contrary intention by virtue of s.69(2).
[5] Trusts of Land and Appointment of Trustees Act 1996, Sched. 3, para. 3(11).
[6] The relevant legislation (Trusts of Land and Appointment of Trustees Act 1996) refers throughout to "trusts created by a disposition" and, although this must presumably include trusts created orally because of the incorporation (by virtue of s.23(2)) of the non-inclusive definition of "disposition" in the Law of Property Act 1925, s.205(1)(ii), the wording of the 1996 legislation does not always fit very easily with trusts so created.
[7] Trusts of Land and Appointment of Trustees Act 1996, s.21(5) provides that the two provisions conferring this power on the beneficiaries (ss.19 & 20) can be excluded by the trust instrument and in practice they generally are so excluded. In respect of trusts created before January 1, 1997, the provisions can be excluded by a deed executed by the settlor (or the survivor of joint settlors) but if this is not done the provisions apply to such trusts (which of course means that they necessarily apply to all trusts created by will before that date).

the trust property,[8] they have at any time and in any circumstances the power to give a written direction to the existing trustee(s) or, if there are none to the personal representatives of the last surviving trustee, to appoint as trustee(s) whatever person or persons they specify. This is a new power contained in section 19 of the Trusts of Land and Appointment of Trustees Act 1996. It can be coupled with a direction to some or all of the existing trustees to retire[9] and will have to be so coupled if its effect is that the permissible number of trustees[10] is exceeded. It is important to stress that, whereas the power given by section 36 of the Trustee Act 1925 is limited to the circumstances listed in that section, the power given by section 19 of the Trusts of Land and Appointment of Trustees Act 1996 can be exercised whenever the beneficiaries fulfil its sole precondition and as often as they like; where this provision applies, they can therefore completely frustrate the power conferred by the Trustee Act 1925.

The second situation, however, has not one but a number of preconditions. The beneficiaries must still all be of full age and capacity and between them absolutely entitled to the trust property. But they only have a power of appointment where a trustee is incapable by reason of mental disorder of exercising his functions as such and where, in addition, neither anyone with a power of appointment under the trust instrument nor the surviving trustees nor any personal representative of the last surviving trustee is able and willing to appoint a trustee in his place. If all three of these preconditions are satisfied, then, by virtue of section 20 of the Trusts of Land and Appointment of Trustees Act 1996, the beneficiaries may give a written direction to an appropriate representative of the incapable trustee (his receiver, or holder of his enduring power of attorney or person authorised for the purpose under the Mental Health Act 1983) to appoint whoever they specify in his place.

### (4) By the court

If all else fails, new trustees may be appointed by the court. Whenever it is desirable that a new trustee should be appointed and it is "inexpedient, difficult or impracticable so to do without the assistance of the court", the court may appoint a new trustee either as an additional trustee, or in substitution for an existing trustee.[11] The court will not, in the absence of exceptional circumstances, exercise its power if advantage can be taken of a provision in the trust instrument or of the statutory power.[12] Further, there appears to be no reported decision in which the court has appointed a trustee against the

---

[8] "Absolutely entitled to the trust property" would normally include the beneficiaries of a discretionary trust as a whole. However, "beneficiary" is defined in s.22(1) of the Act as "a person who under the trust has an interest in property subject to the trust". Barraclough & Matthews, *The Trusts of Land and Appointment of Trustees Act 1996* (1997) take the view that, because the House of Lords held, in *Gartside v. I.R.C.* [1968] A.C. 553 that, at least for tax purposes, an object of a discretionary trust has no interest in any part of the property, discretionary beneficiaries may not be able to utilise these powers. However, this decision does not necessarily have any effect other than for tax purposes and so the author of this edition of this work does not agree with this view; the matter obviously awaits judicial resolution.

[9] See *post*, p. 565.

[10] See *post*, p. 560.

[11] Trustee Act 1925, s.41. See also *Re Hodson's Settlement* (1851) 9 Hare 118; *Finlay v. Howard* (1842) 2 Dru. & War. 490.

[12] *Re Gibbon* (1882) 45 L.T. 756, 30 W.R. 287.

wishes of a person who has the power to appoint and who is prepared to exercise it in good faith. This is so even if the court would prefer to see someone else appointed.[13] Where the court proposes to appoint a new trustee in substitution for an existing trustee, it may do so even against the wishes of the existing trustee.[14]

In practice, this power is used mainly in the following circumstances: first, where there is doubt whether the statutory power can be exercised, for example, as to whether a trustee is in fact "unfit" to act; secondly, where there is no person capable of making an appointment; and, thirdly, where it is wished to increase the number of trustees and the statutory power under section 36 of the Trustee Act 1925 does not apply.

Occasionally, an application is made to the court for the appointment of a new trustee simply because, if a new trustee is so appointed, it cannot afterwards be alleged that the trustee was appointed in circumstances which were improper or in order to facilitate a breach of trust.[15] The court will, therefore, only exercise its power where it is clearly in the interest of the beneficiaries for it to make the appointment. An example of a case where the court refused to exercise its power is *Re Weston's Settlement*,[16] which is discussed in a later chapter.[17]

The court has a discretion as to whom it will appoint as a trustee, but the principles upon which this discretion will be exercised are as follows:

(a) If the settlor has expressly or by clear implication made known his wishes, the court will have regard to his wishes. This is particularly so if the settlor has indicated whom he does not wish to be appointed.

(b) A trustee will not be appointed to promote the interest of some of the beneficiaries in opposition to the interest of other beneficiaries.[18] The attitude of the courts has, however, changed over the last century or so in two important respects. First, the courts have gone back on their former practice of not appointing a beneficiary to be a trustee;[19] it has been realised that in some circumstances a person who has a beneficial interest may put a greater effort and enthusiasm into the administration of the trust than someone else and that the appointment of such a person as a trustee may be appropriate, particularly where there is also an independent trustee. Secondly, the courts are now much more ready than they formerly were[20] to appoint professional advisers such as a family solicitor as trustees, particularly where this is desired by the beneficiaries; this is in the light of their greater confidence in the integrity of professional advisers and the

---

[13] *Re Higginbottom* [1892] 3 Ch. 132, see *ante*, p. 552; *Re Brockbank* [1948] Ch. 206, see *ante*, p. 552.
[14] *Re Henderson* [1940] Ch. 764.
[15] See *post*, p. 761.
[16] [1969] 1 Ch. 223.
[17] See *post*, p. 884.
[18] *Re Parsons* [1940] Ch. 973.
[19] For fear that the trustee-beneficiary would be tempted to act more in his own interest than that of the other beneficiaries; see *Re Harrop's Trusts* (1883) 24 Ch.D. 717; *Re Knowles' Settled Estates* (1884) 27 Ch.D. 707.
[20] See *Re Kemp's Settled Estates* (1883) 24 Ch.D. 485; *Re Earl of Stamford* [1896] 1 Ch. 288; *Re Spencer's Settled Estates* [1903] 1 Ch. 75.

realisation of the advantage which detailed knowledge of the family circumstances brings, such persons may now be appointed.

(c) The court will have regard to whether the proposed appointment will promote the execution of the trust, or whether it will impede it.[21]

An interesting situation arises where the existing trustees have made it known that they will refuse to act with the person whom the court proposes to appoint. On the one hand, the court's dignity is involved. In *Re Tempest*,[22] Turner L.J. said:

"I think it would be going too far to say that the court ought, on that ground alone, to refuse to appoint the proposed trustee: for this would, as suggested in the argument, be to give the continuing or surviving trustee a veto upon the appointment of the new trustee. In such a case I think it must be the duty of the court to inquire and ascertain whether the objection of the surviving or continuing trustee is well founded or not, and to act or refuse to act upon it accordingly."

On the other hand, the basic object of the court's power is to promote the interests of the beneficiaries and these interests will not be protected by the existence of serious friction between the trustees. Indeed, on this ground alone the court will sometimes remove a trustee.[23]

Unless, presumably, a trustee has been guilty of serious malpractice, so that his removal is a matter of urgency, the court is reluctant to appoint new trustees in the place of existing trustees if to do so would place the existing trustees in a worse financial position. In *Re Pauling's Settlement (No.2)*,[24] it was sought to remove trustees against whom an action had been brought for breach of trust.[25] But this was resisted because they might have been able to have impounded the beneficiaries' interests[26] in the event that they were successful in an appeal in the other action. Wilberforce J. held that, even if the existing trustees were removed, they could still exercise their right to impound. As it happened, the court refused to appoint new trustees in the place of the existing trustees, *inter alia* because to have done so would have deprived them of security for the costs which would be payable to them if the appeal were successful.

### 3. Restrictions on the Numbers of Trustees

The general principle is that any number of persons may be trustees; the determining factor as to how many there should be is not a legal one but the practical one of having, on the one hand, enough trustees to be able to take advantage of various skills and experience but, on the other hand, not too

---

[21] *Re Tempest* (1866) 1 Ch.App. 485.
[22] (1866) L.R. 1 Ch.App. 485 at 490.
[23] *Re Henderson* [1940] Ch. 764.
[24] [1963] Ch. 576.
[25] This case is discussed at pp. 698 and 792.
[26] As to the circumstances in which a beneficiary's interest can be impounded, see *post*, p. 793.

many to make the working of the trust unwieldy. Nevertheless, there are certain restrictions on the numbers of trustees:

(a) The maximum number of trustees of a trust of land or of a settlement subject to the Settled Land Act 1925 is four, and if more than four persons are named, the first four named who are able and willing to act are the trustees; this is provided by section 34 of the Trustee Act 1925. This limitation does not apply in the case of land held upon trust for charitable, ecclesiastical or public purposes.[27]

(b) There need only be one trustee to hold land but, unless that trustee is a trust corporation two or more trustees are needed to give a valid receipt for capital money,[28] so that two or more trustees are in fact needed to sell land.

(c) Where, under a will or an intestacy, property is to be held for an infant and no trustees are appointed by any will, the personal representatives of the deceased may appoint trustees to hold that property on trust for the infant but the number of those trustees must not exceed four.[29] This applies whatever the nature of the property.

(d) Where an additional trustee is being appointed under the power in section 36 of the Trustee Act 1925 referred to above and all the existing trustees are remaining, the section provides that the number of trustees must not be increased to more than four in any case. However, the trust instrument can provide for a higher number,[30] although such a provision is ineffective when the trust affects land.

(e) Where a trustee wishes to retire but it is not proposed to appoint a new trustee in his place, he can only do so if a minimum of two persons or a trust corporation will remain as trustees thereafter; this is provided by section 39 of the Trustee Act 1925.[31]

In any event, a minimum of two trustees is usually desirable, in order to give the beneficiaries adequate protection. One of the basic safeguards for beneficiaries is that property must usually be under the control of at least two persons, so that it is very much more difficult for one to misappropriate the money.

### 4. Assumption of Office by Conduct

Acceptance of the office of trustee of an *inter vivos* trust is usually signified by the trustee executing the trust deed. But where a trustee does any act which amounts to performance of the trust, in that event he will be presumed to have

---

[27] Trustee Act 1925, s.34(3).

[28] Trustee Act 1925, s.14(2).

[29] Administration of Estates Act 1925, s.42.

[30] s.36(6), like all the provisions of the Trustee Act 1925, can be ousted by contrary intention by virtue of s.69(2).

[31] As amended by Trusts of Land and Appointment of Trustees Act 1996, Sched. 3, para. 3(13). See *post*, p. 566.

accepted the office of trustee as a result of his conduct. Any act, however slight, by way of performance of the terms of the trust is sufficient.[32]

### 5. Actions which Trustees should Carry Out on their Appointment

**(A) Disclosure Prior to Appointment**
It has already been seen in that a trustee should not, except with the express consent of the person setting up the trust or of all the beneficiaries, put himself in a position in which his own interests might conflict with his duties of impartiality as a trustee. As a result of this rule, it has been decided that a person who is asked to become a trustee ought before being appointed to disclose any circumstances unknown to the persons appointing him which might bring his interest and duty into conflict. In *Peyton v. Robinson*,[33] a beneficiary under a trust was indebted to the trustee personally but this fact was not known to the settlor. The terms of the trust instrument gave the trustee a discretion to make payments to this beneficiary. In exercise of this discretion, the trustee made payments; however, it was held that he could not accept repayment of his debt from the amount paid to the beneficiary. The trustee was placed in a position where his interest, to pay trust money to the beneficiary with a view to being repaid his debt, conflicted with his duty, to exercise his discretion entirely without thought for his own personal advantage.

**(B) Following Appointment**
When a person accepts a trusteeship, he should do four things: first, acquaint himself with the terms of the trust; secondly, inspect the trust instrument and any other trust deeds; thirdly, procure that all the property subject to the trust is vested in the joint names of himself and his co-trustees and that all title deeds are placed under their joint control; and, fourthly, in the case of an appointment as a new trustee of an existing trust, to investigate any suspicious circumstances which indicate a prior breach of trust, and to take action to recoup the trust fund if any breach has in fact taken place. If he fails to do these things, he may make himself liable to the beneficiaries in an action for breach of trust.

**(1) Acquainting himself with the terms of the trust**
The first duty of a trustee on appointment is to ensure that he knows and understands the terms of the trust instrument because, as is explained elsewhere,[34] if a trustee pays money to a wrong beneficiary, or pays the right beneficiary too little money, or departs in any other way without authority from the terms of the trust instrument, he thereby commits a breach of trust, however honestly he may act. Admittedly, in certain circumstances he may apply to the court for relief from liability;[35] however, even if the court grants total or partial relief, that will not alter the fact that he has committed a breach

---

[32] *Lord Montfort v. Lord Cadogan* (1816) 19 Ves. 635; *James v. Frearson* (1842) 1 Y. & C.C.C. 370. Thus a person designated a trustee should expressly announce if he does not wish to act.
[33] (1823) 1 L.J. (O.S.) Ch. 191.
[34] See *post*, p. 767.
[35] Under Trustee Act 1925, s.61, discussed *post*, p. 789.

of trust. In *Nestlé v. National Westminster Bank*,[36] the trustee bank had doubts as to the precise nature of its investment powers. The Court of Appeal described these doubts as "understandable" but held that it was "inexcusable that the bank took no step at any time to obtain legal advice as to the scope of its powers".[37] (In fact, however, the plaintiff beneficiary was unable to show that she had suffered any loss thereby so no liability was actually imposed.)

### (2) Inspection of the trust documents

The second duty of a trustee on appointment is to inspect the trust instrument in order to ascertain whether any notices have previously been given to the trustees of dealings by beneficiaries with their interests in the trust fund. A beneficiary who has an interest under a trust is usually entitled to sell, mortgage, give away or in some other manner deal with his interest in the trust fund, just as he may deal with any other property. As far as the trustees are concerned, this disposition is complete when the assignee gives notice of the disposition to the trustees.[38] Once such notice has been given, the trustees must pay to the assignee the trust money to which the beneficiary named in the trust instrument would otherwise have been entitled. If a memorandum of the transaction is endorsed on the trust instrument, this is sufficient to give the persons who are the trustees for the time being notice of the dealing by the beneficiary with his equitable interest.[39]

Furthermore, if a beneficiary should attempt to assign or charge his interest more than once, the assignee or chargee who is the first to give notice of the dealing to the trustees takes priority.[40] If, therefore, a newly appointed trustee finds on inspection of the trust instrument more than one notice of assignment, he must ascertain carefully the order in which such notices were received.

### (3) Placing the trust property under joint control

The third duty of a trustee on appointment is to ensure that all the trust property is placed in the joint names of himself and his co-trustees. As soon as he is appointed he becomes responsible with his co-trustees for what happens to the trust property, and if he negligently allows property to remain in the names of others and loss occurs, he may be liable to make good the loss to the beneficiaries out of his own pocket.[41] The property may be placed in the name of the new trustee, jointly with the continuing trustees, by the mode of transfer appropriate to the type of property.[42] The appropriate mode of transfer in respect of the major types of property is:

(a)  unregistered freehold land        conveyance

(b)  unregistered leasehold land       assignment

---

[36] [1993] 1 W.L.R. 1260.
[37] *ibid.* at 1265, per Dillon L.J.
[38] By virtue of the rule in *Dearle v. Hall* (1828) 3 Russ. 1.
[39] Law of Property Act 1925, s.137.
[40] *Dearle v. Hall* (1828) 3 Russ. 1.
[41] See *post*, p. 767.
[42] The use of the appropriate mode of transfer is also discussed in connection with whether a trust is completely constituted; see *ante*, p. 136.

| | | |
|---|---|---|
| (c) | registered freehold or leasehold land | transfer and subsequent registration of the transfer at the Land Registry |
| (d) | bearer stocks and shares | delivery |
| (e) | other stocks and shares | transfer and subsequent registration of the transfer by the company or authority concerned |
| (f) | debts and other choses in action | assignment (plus notice to the other party in order to secure priority) |
| (g) | indorsable negotiable instruments payable to bearer | delivery and indorsement |
| (h) | personal chattels | either assignment or physical delivery |

However, these formalities can sometimes be avoided by virtue of section 40 of the Trustee Act 1925, when a person is appointed a new trustee, or retires from trusteeship, and the appointment or retirement, as the case may be, is effected by deed (the section does not, however, apply where property is held by a personal representative[43] because, in this case, there is not an existing trust). Section 40 provides that, unless the deed contains a provision to the contrary, it automatically vests the trust property in the new or remaining trustees as joint tenants. The section applies to all types of trust property with the following exceptions: first, mortgages of land, when a formal transfer of mortgage is required; secondly, leasehold land where the lease provides that before any assignment the permission of the landlord must be obtained and the landlord's permission has not been obtained before the deed of appointment or retirement has been executed (the reason for this exception is to prevent an unwitting breach of covenant under the lease, so giving rise to a possible claim for forfeiture); thirdly, stocks and shares, where a formal transfer has to be registered by the company; fourthly, registered land, in respect of which, although no transfer is actually necessary,[44] the deed of appointment or retirement has to be registered so that the proprietorship register is brought up to date. The first three of these exceptions arise by virtue of section 40(4) of the Trustee Act 1925 and the fourth arises by virtue of section 27 of the Land Registration Act 2002.

Further, section 40 of the Trustee Act 1925 obviously cannot apply to "bearer" securities, in respect of which difficulties sometimes arise. "Bearer" securities are issued securities that are not registered in the name of anyone. The issuing company pays dividends to whoever at the time when the dividend is payable is able to produce to the company the bearer certificate, or any coupons attached to it. By definition bearer securities cannot be placed in the names of the trustees. However, section 18 of the Trustee Act 2002 provides that the trustees must appoint a custodian of any bearer securities unless the

---

[43] See *ante*, p. 31.
[44] Although this is formally the case, for practical purposes a transfer is desirable since, if one is not executed, the Land Registry may insist on retaining the deed of appointment or retirement, or at the very least on being supplied with a certified copy of it.

trust already has a custodian or they are exempted from complying with this requirement by the trust instrument or any statutory provision. Prior to this Act, trustees were obliged to deposit bearer securities with a bank and, in *Lewis v. Nobbs*,[45] where one trustee allowed bearer securities to remain in the hands of his co-trustee, who misappropriated them, it was held that the trustee was guilty of a breach of trust for having allowed the securities to remain under the control of the other so that they could be so misappropriated. Even today, all title deeds to trust property should be deposited with a bank or agent to be held to the order of all trustees.[46]

**(4) Investigating previous breaches of trust**
The final duty on a trustee on appointment is to consider the possibility that there have been previous breaches of trust. A new trustee is not expected to act like a bloodhound straining to sniff out some breach of trust; in the absence of suspicious circumstances he may assume that the previous trustees have properly discharged their duties.[47] But the new trustee must inquire into any circumstances which might suggest that a breach of trust has been committed; if, as a result of the fact that he has not inquired into such circumstances, the trust fund suffers loss, he may find himself liable. In such circumstances, he will be liable not because he participated in the original breach of trust but because he himself has committed a breach of trust in not making sufficient inquiry.[48] The most obvious circumstances which would put a new trustee on inquiry is if the trust fund is materially less at the time of his appointment than it was at some previous point of time. There may be many bona fide explanations of this but the new trustee must inquire and, if appropriate, take action.

### III. THE RETIREMENT OF TRUSTEES

### 1. *The Circumstances in which Trustees Must Retire*

A trustee must retire from his office if the beneficiaries are able to give him and do give him a direction so to do under section 19 of the Trusts of Land and Appointment 1996. Where a trust instrument does not make any provision for the appointment of new trustees and all the beneficiaries of the trust are of full age and capacity and between them absolutely entitled to the trust property,[49] then, unless their power so to do has been excluded by the settlor,[50] the beneficiaries have at any time and in any circumstances the power to give a written direction to any existing trustee requiring him to retire. However, he is

---

[45] (1878) 8 Ch.D. 591.
[46] See *post*, p. 764.
[47] *Re Straham* (1856) 8 De G.M. & G. 291.
[48] *Harvey v. Olliver* (1887) 57 L.T. 239.
[49] See *ante*, fn. 8.
[50] See *ante*, fn. 7.

only obliged to execute the necessary deed of retirement if three further conditions are satisfied: first, there will be a sufficient number of trustees left thereafter;[51] secondly, either a replacement is to be appointed[52] or the continuing trustees consent; and, thirdly, "reasonable arrangements have been made for the protection of any rights of his in connection with the trust".[53]

### 2. *The Circumstances in Which Trustees May Retire*

A trustee may retire from his office in any of four ways:

(a) by taking advantage of any power in the trust instrument;

(b) by taking advantage of the powers in the Trustee Act 1925, namely

    (i)   section 36, where a new trustee is being appointed in his place; or

    (ii)  section 39, where no new trustee is being appointed;

(c) by obtaining the consent of all beneficiaries, who must be sui juris and between them absolutely entitled to the whole beneficial interest; or

(d) by obtaining the consent of the court.

If the trust instrument makes provision for a trustee to retire, then a trustee can take advantage of this power, even though it is wider than the statutory power. In fact, however, the statutory power in sections 36 and 39 of the Trustee Act 1925 is so wide that specific provisions are not now normally included in trust instruments. Retirement when coupled with the appointment of a new trustee has already been considered but by section 39 a trustee can retire even where no new trustee is being appointed in his place. Under this section,[54] a trustee may retire if:

(a) after his retirement there will remain as trustees a minimum of two persons or a trust corporation; and

(b) he obtains the consent to his retirement of the remaining trustees; and

(c) he obtains the consent of anyone named in the trust instrument as having the power to appoint new trustees; and

(d) the retirement is by deed.

However, none of these conditions applies if one of the remaining trustees is

---

[51] Two persons or a trust corporation.

[52] Such a trustee will obviously normally be appointed by the beneficiaries, also pursuant to Trusts of Land and Appointment of Trustees Act 1996, s.19; see *ante*, p. 557. However, this is not actually necessary so the replacement trustee could equally be appointed by whoever has the statutory power of appointment under Trustee Act 1925, s.36.

[53] It is not entirely clear what this means. The "reasonable arrangements" can hardly be intended to replace the indemnity and the lien on the trust property which Trustee Act 1925, s.30(2) confers on any retiring trustee (see *post*, p. 618); presumably this therefore enables a trustee who is forced to retire to claim more security than he would otherwise have been able to.

[54] As amended by Trusts of Land and Appointment of Trustees Act 1996, Sched. 3, para. 3(13).

the Public Trustee.[55] The requirement that two persons or a trust corporation shall remain as trustees applies to all trusts; it has no connection whatever with the fact that the presence of at least two trustees or a trust corporation is necessary in order for a valid receipt to be given for capital payments arising under a trust of land or a settlement under the Settled Land Act 1925.[56]

Provided the conditions of section 39 are fulfilled, the retirement will be effective but if the trustee has retired in order to procure or facilitate a breach of trust, he may nevertheless remain liable for any such breach.[57]

As a last resort, if none of these cases applies, a trustee may apply to the court to be discharged as a trustee. The court will usually discharge a trustee provided that there is at least one other trustee who continues or some suitable new trustee can be found; however, the trustee who wishes to retire will usually be ordered to pay the costs of the application unless he can show that the circumstances have materially altered since he accepted the trusteeship.[58]

There is one important difference between the scope of section 36 and that of section 39. As has been seen,[59] under section 36 a trustee can retire from part only of the trusts but under section 39 the trustee can retire only from the whole of the trusts.

Whether these conditions can be overridden by the express provisions of the settlement is not entirely clear. It is questionable as a matter of principle whether a statutory power of this type should be able to be ousted, a view which appeared to be confirmed by Warner J. in *Mettoy Pension Trustees v. Evans*,[60] when he stated that there was a doubt as to whether the purported retirement of two individual trustees had left the remaining trustee company as sole trustee of the scheme. However, in *L.R.T. Pension Trust Co. v. Hatt*,[61] Knox J. in effect decided that it was possible to exclude the now abrogated requirement for either two individuals or a trust corporation to continue as trustees;[62] although his specific decision is no longer of any relevance, his approach must constitute the law at present. It remains to be seen which of the two approaches will be adopted in future decisions.

There is, however, no doubt at all that a retirement which does not comply with these requirements is invalid and that the trustee in question will consequently remain in office.[63]

### 3. *Release of Retiring Trustees*

When trustees retire they sometimes request a formal release of any liability arising from the trusteeship. If trustees retire in favour of new trustees, they

---

[55] Public Trustee Act 1906, s.6.

[56] See *ante*, p. 560.

[57] See *post*, p. 762.

[58] The court has expressed its disapproval of applications being made to the court for the appointment of a new trustee where advantage could be taken of the statutory power, and doubtless it would be equally disapproving if applications were made to it for retirement when advantage could be taken of the statutory power.

[59] See *ante*, p. 565.

[60] [1990] 1 W.L.R. 1587 at 1607; see Jacobs (1986) 1 Trust Law & Practice 95.

[61] [1993] P.L.R. 227.

[62] As a result of Trusts of Land and Appointment of Trustees Act 1996, Sched. 3, para. 3(13), the requirement is now only for two "persons" or a trust corporation.

[63] *Mettoy Pension Trustees v. Evans* [1990] 1 W.L.R. 1587.

are not entitled to such a release unless the trust instrument contains a provision to that effect, something which trusts instruments in many off-shore
jurisdictions habitually do. However, it seems that, if a trust is actually being
wound up, its retiring trustees are entitled to such a release.[64] Either way,
however, a release is only effective to the extent that the beneficiaries are in
possession of all the relevant facts at the time when they execute it.

## IV. THE REMOVAL OF TRUSTEES

### 1. When may a Trustee be Removed from Office

A trustee may be removed from his office:

(a)  under a power contained in the trust instrument;

(b)  under the statutory power contained in section 36 of the Trustee Act
1925;

(c)  in effect as a result of the beneficiaries directing him to retire under
section 19 of the Trusts of Land and Appointment of Trustees Act
1996; or

(d)  by the court.

Powers of removing trustees contained in the trust instrument are strictly
construed; consequently, if it is desired to take advantage of any such power, it
must be clear that the circumstances envisaged by such power have actually
arisen.[65]

The power of removal of trustees under section 36 of the Trustee Act 1925
when a new trustee is being appointed has been dealt with above. The circumstances are, it will be recalled:

(a)  where the trustee remains out of the United Kingdom for more than
12 months consecutively;

(b)  where he refuses to act;

(c)  where he is unfit to act; or

(d)  where he is incapable of acting.[66]

The circumstances in which the beneficiaries can direct a trustee to retire
under section 19 of the Trusts of Land and Appointment of Trustees Act 1996
have already been considered; although such a direction will have the effect of
removing the trustee in question, he will technically have retired rather than
been removed.

The final method, removal by the court, presents rather more difficulty. The

[64] *Tiger v. Barclays Bank* [1951] 2 K.B. 556.
[65] *London and County Banking Co. v. Goddard* [1897] 1 Ch. 642. Such a power was of course exercised
in *Von Knieriem v. Bermuda Trust Co.* (1994) 1 B.O.S. 116. See *ante*, pp. 192, 555.
[66] *Re Lemann's Trust* (1883) 22 Ch.D. 633.

court's primary concern is to protect and enhance the interests of the beneficiaries. Thus where the trustee is convicted of dishonesty or, by becoming bankrupt or otherwise,[67] shows that he is not fit to be in charge of other people's property, the court will remove him.[68] Nevertheless, removal by the court does involve, at least to the outside world, some degree of moral stigma and difficulties arise where an application is made to remove a trustee, not because he has done anything wrong, but because he cannot agree with or work with his co-trustees.

The position was considered by the Privy Council in *Letterstedt v. Broers*,[69] where Lord Blackburn observed:

"In exercising so delicate a jurisdiction as that of removing trustees, their Lordships do not venture to lay down any general rule beyond the very broad principle that their main guide must be the welfare of the beneficiaries. Probably it is not possible to lay down any more definite rule in a matter so essentially dependent on details often of great nicety."

Mere friction between trustee and beneficiary is not an adequate ground but if there were a permanent condition of hostility between one trustee and the other trustees, the court would probably remove him. In *Re Wrightson*,[70] Warrington J. said: "You must find something which induces the court to think either that the trust property will not be safe or that the trust will not be properly executed in the interests of the beneficiaries." A permanent condition of hostility between trustees would probably be a sufficient deterrent to efficient administration of the trust for the court to exercise its powers.

It is difficult to appeal successfully against an order by an inferior court ordering the removal of a trustee. Thus, in *Re Edwards' Will Trusts*,[71] where Megarry V.-C. had removed a trustee without giving any reasons for so doing, the Court of Appeal refused to interfere with his decision.

### 2. *Protection of Purchasers where a Trustee has been Removed*

Some of the grounds for the removal of a trustee under section 36 of the Trustee Act 1925 and his replacement by a new trustee are that the trustee has remained out of the United Kingdom for more than 12 months, that he refuses to act, or that he is unfit to act. These grounds can give rise to dispute. Thus a displaced trustee could argue that he was not in fact unfit to act so that his purported removal was ineffective. In the absence of a provision to the contrary, a purchaser from the new trustees would not obtain a good title in the event that the purported removal was ineffective. However, purchasers of land in this position will be protected by section 38 of the Trustee Act 1925, which provides that a statement in a deed of appointment that a trustee:

(a)   has remained out of the United Kingdom for more than 12 months; or

---

[67] *Re Lemann's Trust* (1883) 22 Ch.D. 633; *Re Phelps' Settlement Trust* (1885) 55 L.J.Ch. 465 (intellectual decay).
[68] See the cases discussed *ante*, p. 555.
[69] (1884) 9 App.Cas. 371 at 382. See also *Earl of Portsmouth v. Fellows* (1820) 5 Madd. 450.
[70] [1908] 1 Ch. 789 at 803.
[71] [1981] 2 All E.R. 941.

    (b)  refuses to act; or

    (c)  is incapable of acting; or

    (d)  is unfit to act

"shall, in favour of a purchaser of a legal estate, be conclusive evidence of the matter stated". Because it is "conclusive" evidence, a purchaser need not look behind the statement.[72] Further, in favour of a purchaser, an appointment of trustees which depends on such a statement being true and any express or implied vesting declaration are also valid.[73] However, section 38 only applies in the case of land and no protection is conferred by the inclusion of such a statement in other circumstances.

    Although the section gives protection to purchasers, it does not affect the position of a person who has not in fact ceased to be a trustee. If, therefore, a person is purportedly removed as a trustee on the ground that he is unfit to act and another person is purportedly appointed in his stead, the person purportedly removed could apply to the court for a declaration that he continues to be a trustee. Even if such a declaration were to be made, however, it would not prejudice a purchaser of land who had relied on the statement in the instrument of appointment that the trustee had been removed on that ground.

## V. THE DELEGATION OF TRUSTEESHIP

In limited circumstances, a trustee can delegate his powers as such without himself ceasing to be a trustee. This is generally only possible for periods of up to twelve months at a time but a trustee of a trust of land who is also a beneficiary of that trust can delegate his powers as such indefinitely.

    Under section 25 of the Trustee Act 1925,[74] a trustee can, by power of attorney, delegate all or any of the trusts, powers and discretions vested in him as a trustee, whether he is a sole trustee or one of a number of trustees.[75] The delegation cannot be for a period of more than 12 months, although that period does not have to start on the date on which the power of attorney is executed;[76] there appears to be no restriction on the number of times on which a delegation can be made. It is now possible for the delegation to be in favour of anyone, even the only other trustee.[77] Before or within seven days of granting the power of attorney, the donor must[78] give written notice of the delegation to each of the other trustees and to any other person who has a power of appointing new trustees. This notice must specify the date when the power comes into operation, its duration, the donee, the reason why the power is being given, and which of the trusts, powers and discretions are being

---

[72] Contrast the position where enactments provide only for "sufficient" evidence. See for example, Administration of Estates Act 1925, s.36(7) and *Re Duce and Boots Cash Chemists (Southern) Ltd.'s Contract* [1937] Ch. 642.

[73] Trustee Act 1925, s.38(2).

[74] As substituted by Trustee Delegation Act 1999, s.5.

[75] Trustee Act 1925, s.25(1).

[76] *ibid.* s.25(2).

[77] *ibid.* s.25(3). Until the substitution by the Trustee Delegation Act 1999, delegation could not be in favour of the only other trustee.

[78] Trustee Act 1925, s.25(4).

delegated. However, even if this notice is not given, a person dealing with the donee of the power is not prejudiced. The donor remains liable for the acts or defaults of the donee as if they were his own.[79] The donee is in the same position as the donor, except that he cannot himself exercise any power of delegation under the section.

This provision is in practice rarely used. While it is useful in enabling discretions and powers to be delegated, the fact that the donor remains liable for every act or default of the donee is potentially disadvantageous to him. Trustees can collectively appoint agents to carry out their functions in the manner which will be discussed in the next chapter,[80] although such agents admittedly cannot exercise functions relating to the manner in which the assets of the trust are distributed. Trustees who have done so are only liable for the acts or defaults of an agent if they fail to exercise the statutory duty of care imposed by section 1 of the Trustee Act 2000.[81] Consequently, when the donee of a power of attorney does something which could have been done by an agent, the donor of the power is potentially liable for an act or default of the donee when he would not have been liable for the same act or default of an agent. Section 25 of the Trustee Act 1925 could therefore work in a completely unjust way, particularly since the donor is likely to have no more control over the donee than he would have over an agent. However, where only one of a number of trustees wishes to appoint someone to act on his behalf, he will have no option but to use one of the two provisions at present under discussion.

The other possibility of delegating trusteeship is under section 1 of the Trustee Delegation Act 1999. This is limited to the situation where the delegating trustee has a beneficial interest in land held by the trust and was intended principally to be utilised in cases of co-ownership of land, where all the trustees are normally also beneficiaries and, when the co-ownership is expressly created and there are no more than four co-owners, all the beneficiaries are also trustees. Such co-owners cannot only delegate without being restricted by the provisions of section 25 of the Trustee Act 1925; they can also make provision for the disposal of the land if they become mentally incapable.[82] Section 1 of the 1999 Act provides:

"(1) The donee of a power of attorney is not prevented from doing an act in relation to —

(a) land,
(b) the capital proceeds of a conveyance of land, or
(c) income from land

by reason only that the act involves the exercise of a trustee function of the donor if, at the time when the act is done, the donor has a beneficial interest in the land, proceeds or income."

A trustee function of the donor is a function which the donor has as trustee

---

[79] *ibid.* s.25(7).
[80] See *post*, p. 611.
[81] See *post*, p. 573.
[82] Because the power of attorney can be made in the form of an enduring power of attorney; see *infra.*

(either alone or jointly with any other person or persons.[83] Section 1(1) only applies in the absence of a contrary intention in the instrument creating the power of attorney or in the trust instrument[84] and where the donee of the power is not authorised to exercise the trustee function in question in some other way, such as under a provision of the trust instrument or by virtue of a power of attorney granted under section 25 of the Trustee Act 1925[85] (thus keeping the two types of powers of attorney separate). A statement by the donee of the power that the donor had the requisite beneficial interest is "conclusive evidence" in favour of a purchaser whose interest depends on the donee having had power under section 1(1) of the 1999 Act if the statement was made at the time of the act in question or within three months thereafter.[86]

Both the provisions which have been discussed enable one of two trustees to grant a power of attorney to the other and each of two or more trustees to grant powers of attorney to the same donee. The obvious risk that this poses in relation to overreaching conveyances, where a purchaser will only take free of overreachable interests if any capital money arising is paid to not less than two trustees or to a trust corporation, has been addressed by section 7 of the Trustee Delegation Act 1999, which provides that this requirement for the payment of capital money is not satisfied by a receipt being given by a person other than a trust corporation who is acting either both as a trustee and as attorney for one or more trustees or as attorney for two or more trustees. This simply means that a person who is in either of these two situations will have to exercise the power which he will normally have by virtue of being able to exercise the discretions of all the relevant trustees[87] to appoint a further trustee to join with him in receiving the capital money.

The Trustee Delegation Act 1999 also removed an anomaly created by the Enduring Powers of Attorney Act 1985, legislation which was basically enacted in order to permit the creation of what are known as enduring powers of attorney, powers which will survive the incapacity of the donor provided that they are registered with the Court of Protection once the donor has become incapable (unless and until he does so, such powers can be exercised in the same manner as any other power of attorney). Section 3(3) of the 1985 Act seemed to have given trustees a quite separate right to delegate their powers as such by enduring power of attorney which was not only not subject either to any time limit or to any obligation to notify anyone but which would also arise whether or not the donor trustee had considered the matter and so intended. This subsection has now been repealed,[88] subject to elaborate transitional provisions. Instead both the types of powers of attorney considered above can now be made in the form of and take effect as enduring powers of attorney.[89]

---

[83] Trustee Delegation Act 1999, s.1(2).
[84] *ibid.* s.1(3), (5).
[85] *ibid.* s.1(8).
[86] *ibid.* s.2.
[87] See *ante*, p. 551. He will only not have this power if the power of appointment of new trustees is vested in someone else, which is highly unlikely in the case of co-ownership trusts, which are the only circumstances in which these situations are likely to arise.
[88] Trustee Delegation Act 1999, s.4.
[89] This is specifically provided in the case of powers under Trustee Act 1925, s.25 by Trustee Delegation Act 1999, s.6 and is implicit in the wording of Trustee Delegation Act 1999, s.1.

# CHAPTER 14

# THE ADMINISTRATION OF TRUSTS

THIS Chapter is concerned with the general obligations of the trustees with regard to the trust property and various specific powers which they are given in order to facilitate its administration.

## I. THE TRUSTEES' DUTY OF CARE

The Trustee Act 2000, which came into force on February 1, 2001, enacted a number of recommendations of the Law Commission,[1] produced only after extensive consultation. Section 1 imposes on trustees the following new statutory duty of care:

> "(1) Whenever the duty under this subsection applies to a trustee, he must exercise such care and skill as is reasonable in the circumstances, having regard in particular—
>
> (a) to any special knowledge or experience that he has or holds himself out as having, and
> (b) if he acts as trustee in the course of a business or profession, to any special knowledge or experience that it is reasonable to expect of a person acting in the course of that kind of business or profession."

Under the pre-existing common law rule, unpaid trustees were bound to use only such due diligence and care in the management of the trust as an ordinary prudent man of business would use in the management of his own affairs.[2] This rule had been incorporated into a number of statutory provisions, all of which were duly repealed by the Trustee Act 2000. However, because the statutory duty of care only applies in the situations specifically listed in the Trustee Act 2000,[3] it is possible, depending on what attitude is adopted to statutory interpretation, that the common law rule may have survived, presumably unintentionally, in some of the situations not specifically included in the list.

The common law rule provided an objective standard of reference, admittedly not at all easy to apply to particular circumstances. It was however clear

---

[1] Law Com. No. 260 (1999), *Report on Trustees' Powers and Duties.*
[2] *Speight v. Gaunt* (1883) 9 App.Cas. 1.
[3] Principally in Sched. 1, to which s.2 specifically refers.

that that standard was not measured by the standard actually adopted by the trustee in question in the management of his own affairs.[4] In contrast, the criterion of the statutory duty of care is what is "reasonable in the circumstances"; two of these circumstances are specified, relating to specialist knowledge or experience which the particular trustee has, holds himself out as having or, if he is acting as trustee in the course of a business or profession, can be reasonably expected to have. Here there is clearly room for the personal characteristics of the particular trustee to be relevant since one of the specified circumstances is itself such a characteristic. So it may be that a trustee who is unintelligent or unworldly owes a lower statutory duty of care, not just than that of a trustee who is neither but also than that of the prudent man of business under the pre-existing law. The Law Commission appears to have thought that the introduction of the statutory duty of care could only increase the requisite level of care and skill,[5] but it is not obvious that this is in fact the case.

On the other hand, the two specified characteristics are undoubtedly meant to impose a higher standard of care and skill. The first, in section 1(1)(a), gives the beneficiaries the benefit not only of any special knowledge or experience that the trustee actually has but also of any which he has held himself out as having (the advantage of judging him by his own professed standards is, however, somewhat undermined by the fact that the provision does not say to whom he has to have held himself out).[6] The second, in section 1(1)(b), adds special knowledge or experience which it is reasonable to expect of a trustee acting in the course of a business or profession, whether or not he actually has it or professes it. The pre-existing law did tend to expect higher standards of trust corporations,[7] but the inclusion of professional trustees as such in this category is new; however, it is unclear whether it is reasonable to expect a solicitor acting as a trustee as part of his general practice to have the special knowledge and experience of solicitors in general or that of a solicitor specialising in trusts and estates.

The statutory duty of care applies only to the situations listed in the Trustee Act 2000, principally in Schedule 1, which also provides[8] that the statutory duty of care may be excluded "in so far as it appears from the trust instrument that the duty was not meant to apply" (however well-intended, the formulation of this provision is asking for trouble).[9] These situations are as follows:

    (a)  exercising any power of investment, including carrying out the new

---

[4] *Rae v. Meek* (1889) 14 App. Cas. 558 at 569; *Re Lord de Clifford's Estate* [1900] 2 Ch. 707 at 716.

[5] Law Com. No. 260 (1999) para. 3.24(2).

[6] It is hardly likely that he will so have held himself out to the beneficiaries, although this would clearly suffice, so presumably a holding out to the settlor or testator must be meant also to suffice.

[7] See *Bartlett v. Barclays Bank Trust Co.* [1980] Ch. 515; *Australian Securities Commission v. AS Nominees* [1996] P.L.R. 297 (Federal Court of Australia).

[8] Trustee Act 2000, Sched. 1, para. 7.

[9] It clearly goes well beyond express exclusions. Does the not uncommon provision that the trustees are to have "wholly uncontrolled discretion" in respect of, say, the exercise of a power of appointment therefore also oust the statutory duty of care in respect of administrative powers like the power of investment? Hopefully not but someone is bound to litigate this.

duties imposed by the Trustee Act 2000[10] to review investments and to obtain advice;[11]

(b) exercising any power to acquire land and any power in relation to land so acquired;[12]

(c) "entering into arrangements" to appoint agents, nominees and custodians (this peculiar formulation was intended to exclude from the scope of the statutory duty of care the decision as to whether or not to utilise such persons at all[13] and leave subject it only the decision as to exactly who to utilise);[14]

(d) exercising powers of compromise "and so on";[15]

(e) exercising a power of insurance;[16]

(f) exercising any power to agree the value of reversionary interests, to fix the value of trust property for the purpose of giving effect to the trust, and to do associated things.[17]

On the other hand, the following situations appear to be excluded from the application of the statutory duty of care.

(a) The obligation of the trustees to get in the trust property has always been absolute;[18] it was unaffected by the common law rule and is now unaffected by the statutory duty of care. This was clearly intentional and is sound as a matter of principle.

(b) The custody and management of the trust property is not specifically referred to anywhere in the list of situations subject to the statutory duty of care except in the case of land. While the Trustee Act 2000 expressly confers on trustees the powers to appoint nominees and custodians[19] to hold the trust property, no provision is made as to the nature of their liability to take care of the trust property if they choose not to do so. While all matters relating to the management of land seem within the statutory duty of care, the management of chattels is not, although that is admittedly unlikely to be particularly significant. However, the important obligation to inquire into or intervene in the affairs of any company in which the trust has a controlling or majority interest also seems to have been omitted unless it can

---

[10] *ibid.* ss. 4, 5.
[11] *ibid.* Sched. 1, para. 1.
[12] *ibid.* para. 2.
[13] Law Com. No. 260 (1999) para. 3.12; para. 3.e suggests that "perverse" decisions of this type can be attacked but it is not obvious how.
[14] *ibid.* para. 3.
[15] *ibid.* para. 4.
[16] *ibid.* para. 5.
[17] *ibid.* para. 6. This refers to the powers in Trustee Act 1925, s.22(1), (3) which confer power to do the things mentioned in the text and to "any corresponding power". The heading of the paragraph also refers to "audit" but this seems to be an error unless a power to conduct an audit can somehow be regarded as a corresponding power.
[18] See *ante*, p. 563.
[19] Trustee Act 2000, ss. 16, 17; see *post*, p. 615.

somehow be squeezed into the obligation "from time to time to review the investments of the trust and consider whether ... they should be varied". Admittedly, this was a respect in which the common law duty was more stringent anyway, at least so far as corporate trustees were concerned.[20] It will therefore not be the end of the world if this obligation is held still to be governed by this duty rather than by the statutory duty of care but this can hardly be what was intended.

(c) The issuing and defending of proceedings on behalf of the trust does not seem to be subject to the statutory duty of care either except, possibly in the case of proceedings involving land held by the trust. There is no difficulty in respect of the costs of such proceedings since, in the types of proceedings where there is any risk of the trustees being personally liable for those costs, they can protect themselves against any such liability by making an application seeking the advance approval of the court for the potential expenditure of the trust funds on the costs of the litigation;[21] if they do not do so, their liability depends on whether approval would have been given if it had been sought. But this does not cover the duty of the trustees to consider whether or not to bring proceedings of this type. It would clearly be appropriate for this to be governed by the statutory duty of care; to the extent that it is not, it must presumably still be governed by the common law rule, which again cannot possibly be what was intended

Trustees will be well advised to bear in mind constantly that at some time in the future some disgruntled beneficiary may well seek to question their actions. Thus where, for example, trustees wish to sell or lease property, they should normally take the precaution of employing a valuer and sell or lease with regard to his figures.[22] While the numerous authorities on the common law rule are obviously no longer good law, the absence as yet of any authorities on the Trustee Act 2000 means that the facts of some of the older authorities are still worth consideration. In *Ward v. Ward*,[23] the House of Lords held that a trustee had acted reasonably in not immediately issuing proceedings in the way in which he would normally have been obliged to do[24] against a beneficiary who was also a debtor to the trust; had proceedings been issued, that beneficiary would have been ruined and his children, who were also beneficiaries, would have been placed in difficult circumstances. On the other hand, in *Re Lucking's Will Trusts*,[25] a trustee was a director of a private company, in which the trust held a majority shareholding. The trustee-director allowed another director to overdraw heavily from the company by signing and returning blank cheques sent to him by the other director. When these drawings proved to be irrecoverable, the trustee-director was held liable to the

---

[20] See *Bartlett v. Barclays Bank Trust Co.* [1980] Ch. 515.
[21] See *post*, p. 620; this is generally known as an application for a "*Beddoe* Order".
[22] *Oliver v. Court* (1820) 8 Pr. 127.
[23] (1843) 2 H.L.Cas. 777.
[24] See *Re Brogden* (1888) 38 Ch.D. 546.
[25] [1968] 1 W.L.R. 866.

trust for the consequential reduction in the value of the trust shares. Much more straightforward examples of the imposition of liability, this time for failure to take action, have been on trustees who have allowed rent to fall into arrears[26] or have failed to register a transaction which needs to be registered, such as a transfer of registered land or of shares, and as a result someone else obtains priority.[27]

Occasionally, the common law rule has conflicted with the rule that a trustee must do the best he can for his beneficiaries and it is apparent that the statutory duty of care is capable of doing so also. Suppose, for example, that trustees who have put a property up for sale have received and provisionally accepted an offer for £500,000 but subsequently receive an offer for £550,000. They are under a clear obligation to consider the second offer, even if, had they been dealing with their own property, they would not have entertained that offer out of considerations of ordinary commercial morality. They still of course retain their discretion and, if there is some reason which genuinely leads them to conclude that the first offer should be accepted (if, for example, the sale to the first proposed purchaser would be completed materially earlier), they may conclude that the first offer should be accepted. But their discretion must be exercised generally in the interests of the beneficiaries[28] and, in the example given, they should accept the second offer unless there is some good reason for accepting the first.

## II. JOINT ACTS

Except in rare circumstances, an act or decision will only be effective if it is the act or decision of all the trustees. There is no question of a decision of the majority binding all the trustees[29] in the absence of an express provision to the contrary. The settlor or testator has reposed his trust in all the trustees, not just some of them; the liabilities and responsibilities are consequently those of all the trustees. Actions taken and decisions made in the administration of the trust must therefore be those of all the trustees. It may often happen that one trustee who is more enthusiastic in his duties than his co-trustee will come to be spoken of as the "acting trustee", whose decisions are merely endorsed by his co-trustee(s). But in this context, "acting trustee" is not a concept recognised by law. Each of the trustees must exercise his discretion and each is equally liable.[30]

Should a dispute arise, a trustee may be justified in concurring in an action of his co-trustee with which he is not in favour, either because he considers his co-trustee to be more experienced in, or to be more knowledgeable about, the type of transaction in hand[31] or in order to prevent a complete deadlock in the administration of the trust. Whether he is being reasonable in deferring to his co-trustee, or whether he should have stood firm and if necessary made an

---

26  *Tebbs v. Carpenter* (1816) 1 Madd. 290.
27  *Macnamara v. Carey* (1867) Ir.R. 1 Eq. 9.
28  *Buttle v. Saunders* [1950] 2 All E.R. 193.
29  *Boardman v. Phipps* [1967] 2 A.C. 46.
30  *Munch v. Cockerell* (1840) 5 Myl. & Cr. 178.
31  *Re Schneider* (1906) 22 T.L.R. 223.

application to the court, will depend on the circumstances of the particular case.

To this general rule that all the trustees must act jointly there are certain exceptions. First, the trust instrument can of course authorise individual action. Secondly, one trustee alone often has power to give a receipt for income, whether rent or dividends from shares (the latter is a necessary provision, because the articles of association of most companies provide that dividends are to be paid to the first-named registered holder of those shares). Thirdly, just as some acts can be delegated to an agent, so most of those acts can be delegated by all the trustees to one of their number. Lastly, in the case of trustees of a private trust, a majority of trustees can pay money into court[32] even if the minority objects.

Although it is not an exception to the basic principle, it is possible to achieve the practical result that not all the trustees need agree on a certain course of action if a provision to this effect is contained in the trust instrument. This can be done by imposing a primary duty on the trustees to follow a particular course of conduct but also giving them a secondary power not to do so, or to follow some other course, if they all agree. This method is adopted by the Trusts of Land and Appointment of Trustees Act 1996 in respect of land which is subject to an express trust for sale; despite the primary duty imposed on the trustees to sell the land, section 4 of that Act gives the trustees an express power to exercise a discretion to postpone sale indefinitely without being responsible for so doing. However, the trustees can only exercise their power to postpone sale if they all agree so to do; consequently, if only one of them wishes to sell, all the trustees have to comply with their duty so to do.[33] Prior to the enactment of the 1996 Act, the Law of Property Act 1925 both imposed such a duty and conferred such a power on the trustees of all jointly owned land.[34] However, such land is now instead subject to a trust of land[35]; that trust, while equally conferring on the trustees the same power to postpone sale,[36] imposes no specific duty to sell.

It should also be noted that, in some circumstances, the decision of the majority of trustees of a charity can bind all its trustees.[37]

## III. THE TRUSTEES' DISCRETIONS AND POWERS

It is an inherent part of the position of every trustee that he give due consideration to the exercise of any discretions and powers vested in him[38]; there are a wide variety of circumstances in which he will need to do so.

Trustees can of course only exercise the discretions and powers vested in them within the limits prescribed by law or by the trust instrument. Their exercise will be defective unless it is exercised with whatever formalities are

---

[32] Trustee Act 1925, s.63.
[33] Re Mayo [1943] Ch. 302.
[34] By virtue of ss.34–36 and s.25 respectively.
[35] ss.25 & 35 are repealed by Trusts of Land and Appointment of Trustees Act 1996, Sched. 4 and the effect of ss.34 & 36 is amended by Trusts of Land and Appointment of Trustees Act 1996, s.1.
[36] Trusts of Land and Appointment of Trustees Act 1996, s.4.
[37] Re Whiteley [1910] 1 Ch. 600.
[38] Generally with regard to the trustee's discretion, see ante, Chap. 6.

required by the trust instrument. In principle, the exercise of neither a discretion nor a power requires any formality but in practice, while trust instruments do not normally prescribe any formality for the exercise of discretions, they almost always prescribe some formality for the exercise of powers of appointment.[39] A discretion or power can also only be exercised within the limits prescribed by law or by the trust instrument; consequently, it must be exercised within any time limit fixed by the trust instrument and, if it can be exercised only with the consent of some person, that consent must be duly obtained. In *Breadner v. Granville-Grossman,*[40] a power of appointment was held to have been executed one day too late and its exercise was therefore ineffective; consequently, the interests of those entitled in default of exercise of the power took effect. In *Re Massingberd's Settlement,*[41] trustees were given power to vary investments with the consent of the tenant for life. They sold an authorised security and, with the consent of the tenant for life, invested the proceeds in an unauthorised one. Subsequently they realised that unauthorised investment and reinvested in an authorised one; however, this time they did not obtain the consent of the tenant for life and as a result they were held to have committed a breach of trust.

Assuming that all such limits on the trustee's discretion are observed, it is of paramount importance that the trustees should exercise their discretion as the result of an active mental process and not allow a situation to arise merely as a result of their inaction. In *Turner v. Turner,*[42] the trustees left all the decisions to the settlor (who was not a trustee) and signed the necessary documents without actually reading them. A power of appointment which they signed in this manner was held to be defective. Similarly, in *Wilson v. Turner,*[43] the trustees had a power to pay or apply income arising from the trusts to or for the maintenance of an infant beneficiary. They did not make any conscious decision whether or not to do so but merely handed over the income to the infant's father. The Court of Appeal held that their payments had been ineffective and that they had to repay the money to the trust fund. However, had the trustees actively considered the merits of the case and consciously decided to apply the income for the maintenance of the infant, their decision would have been valid and would have been upheld. The test is therefore not the consequences of the action or inaction of the holder of the discretion or power in question but the nature of his own mental processes.

However, where the trustees do consciously exercise their discretion, they derive a large measure of support from the courts. When they exercise a discretion or power, they do not have to give the objects of that power or discretion the reasons for their decisions; however, as Robert Walker J. stated in *Scott v. The National Trust,*[44] if their decision is challenged in the courts they may be compelled to do so either through the process of disclosure if there are any relevant documents or, in practical terms, as the only way of avoiding an adverse inference being drawn.

---

[39] See *ante*, p. 187.
[40] [2001] Ch. 523.
[41] (1890) 63 L.T. 296.
[42] [1984] Ch. 100.
[43] (1883) 22 Ch.D. 521.
[44] [1998] 2 All E.R. 705 at 717–719.

In *Re Beloved Wilkes' Charity*,[45] trustees had a duty from time to time to select a candidate to be sent to the University of Oxford to be trained as a minister of the Church of England; they were obliged to select any suitable candidate who came forward from certain nominated parishes but in default had a more general discretion. They decided to nominate a candidate from outside those parishes rather than one from within them. Lord Truro L.C. declined to interfere with this decision, saying:

> "It is to the discretion of the trustees that the execution of the trust is confided, that discretion being exercised with an entire absence of indirect motive, with honesty of intention, and with a fair consideration of the subject. The duty of supervision on the part of this court will thus be confined to the question of the honesty, integrity and fairness with which the deliberation has been conducted, and will not be extended to the accuracy of the conclusion arrived at."

However, if the trustees do choose to state their reasons, the court will examine them in order to ascertain whether or not the trustees have acted in error. In *Klug v. Klug*,[46] a mother who was one of a number of trustees declined to concur in the exercise of a power in favour of her daughter on the grounds that she disapproved of the latter's marriage. The court held that this was an impermissible reason; consequently she had acted dishonestly and her refusal to concur was set aside. Trustees of pensions trusts also tend, quite understandably, to give reasons for their decisions. But, as Robert Walker J. stated in *Scott v. The National Trust*,[47] the principles on which the court must proceed are the same whether or not the trustees give their reasons; it simply becomes easier for the court to examine a decision if the reasons for it have been disclosed.

In *Edge v. Pensions Ombudsman*,[48] the trustees of a pension trust had to decide how to utilise a surplus which was not needed for the provision of the benefits payable under the pension scheme. They decided to use it to credit additional service to those members in employment on a particular date and to reduce the contributions of both employers and employees from a date six months earlier; no additional service was credited either to those already receiving pensions or to a number of employees who were to be made redundant during the six-month period. The trustees explained to one of the latter that their decision had been taken in order to encourage all employees to become and remain members of the pension scheme and to support the employers in providing continued employment for their current employees. The Pensions Ombudsman set aside the trustees' decision on the grounds that the trustees had breached their duty of impartiality and had not acted in the best interests of all the beneficiaries. His decision was reversed by the Court of Appeal, who held that the duty to act impartially was no more than the ordinary duty imposed on any holder of a discretionary power, namely to exercise the power for the purposes for which it is given, giving proper consideration to the

---

[45] (1851) 3 Mac. & G. 440.
[46] [1918] 2 Ch. 67.
[47] [1998] 2 All E.R. 705 at 717–719.
[48] [2000] Ch. 602.

matters which are relevant and excluding from consideration matters which are irrelevant. Provided the trustees complied with that duty, they were entitled to reach a decision which appeared to prefer the claims of some beneficiaries over others.

Decisions can also be reviewed if trustees have exercised a discretion or power as a result of a mistake:[49] if they were mistaken in any way and there is convincing proof of what they had really intended to do, their decision will be rectifiable; if they were mistaken as to the effect of what they have done, their decision will be void *ab initio*; if they merely fail to take into account all the correct considerations, their decision may be able to be set aside, although it is at present unclear both what types of mistake will produce this effect and whether the decision is then void or voidable. It is also possible successfully to impugn their exercise of a discretion or power on the grounds that the trustees have not acted honestly and so are guilty of what is known as "fraud on a power" (this expression is used in connection with the exercise of both a power and a discretion);[50] this also renders their decision void *ab initio*.

Where trustees who have a discretion or power fail to exercise it, the position depends on whether or not they were under any obligation to exercise it. If they were not, their ability to do so will lapse after a reasonable period and cannot later be revived.[51] If, on the other hand, they were under an obligation to exercise it, their ability to do so will never lapse, but will instead be enforced. In *Re Locker's Settlement Trusts*,[52] the trustees of a discretionary trust held income subject to a positive obligation to distribute the income among such of the beneficiaries as they should determine. They failed to distribute income which had arisen during a three-year period but then some years later, wished to distribute it. On their application to the court for a declaration as to whether the discretion was still exercisable, the court held that it was because it was of an obligatory nature.

## IV. THE DUTY TO PROVIDE INFORMATION

Trustees must be prepared at all times to provide information as to the state of the trust property and to any dealings with it; they must therefore be in a position to provide any relevant accounts and, within certain limits, documents relating to actions taken in the administration of a trust.[53] Precisely who is entitled to require such trust documents has been a matter of some controversy; while there has never been any doubt about the right of beneficiaries of both fixed and discretionary trusts to do so, the position of persons who are merely potential beneficiaries of a trust by virtue of being potential objects of the exercise of a discretion or power has been more uncertain. However, the Privy Council has recently held[54] that the right to require trust documents is best approached as one aspect of the court's inherent jurisdiction to supervise

---

[49] See *ante*, p. 213.
[50] See *ante*, p. 220.
[51] *Re Allen-Meyrick's Will Trusts* [1966] 1 W.L.R. 499; *Re Gulbenkian's Settlement Trusts (No.2)* [1970] Ch. 408.
[52] [1978] 1 All E.R. 216.
[53] *Tiger v. Barclays Bank* [1952] 1 All E.R. 85.
[54] In *Schmidt v. Rosewood Trust* [2003] 2 W.L.R. 1442.

(and where appropriate intervene in) the administration of trusts and that there is no reason to distinguish either between the holders of fixed and discretionary interests or between the rights of an object of a discretionary trust and those of the object of a fiduciary power. This view is clearly likely to become generally accepted. But beneficiaries and potential beneficiaries can anyway only ask for trust documents if they are actually aware of their rights or potential rights in the first place. It is therefore necessary to commence with a consideration of the extent to which trustees must provide beneficiaries with information as to the existence of a trust in their favour.

**1.** *The duty to provide information as to the existence of a trust*
A settlor of an inter vivos trust is not obliged to notify either the trustees or the beneficiaries of its existence. Thus in *Fletcher v. Fletcher*,[55] a settlor entered into a covenant with trustees that, if either or both of his two illegitimate sons survived him, his executors should, within 12 months of his death, pay to the trustees £60,000 which was to be held on trust for such of the two as reached the age of 21. He never revealed the existence of the deed either to the trustees or to his sons; he retained the deed in his possession until his death and it was only discovered some years later among his papers. As has already been seen,[56] this did not prevent the one son who survived him and reached the age of 21 from enforcing what was held to be a completely constituted trust of the benefit of that covenant. This was of course a most unusual case and in such circumstances the trustees are under no obligation to act. However, save where an inter vivos trust is created by declaration, it will only be validly constituted once the trust property has been vested in the trustees;[57] this will in practice normally require the trustees to be parties to the trust instrument, in which case they will necessarily be aware of the trust's existence.

It is much more common for testamentary trusts to be created without either trustees or beneficiaries being aware of their existence. A testator is under no obligation whatever to inform his executors and testamentary trustees that he has nominated them to act as such and there is certainly no reason to suppose that he will inform the beneficiaries of his will of their possible future interests thereunder. Executors and testamentary trustees are under no obligation to act even if they have been informed of their appointment, never mind if they have not. If an executor agrees to act, in practice one of the first things which he will do is to send a copy of the will to each beneficiary who has rights thereunder. However, it has been held that executors are under no duty so to do,[58] although their position will clearly change once the administration of the estate is concluded if they continue to hold assets of the estate as trustees.

This is because it is clear that trustees who have agreed to act are under a duty to inform the beneficiaries of the existence and nature of their interests under the trust. This was held in *Hawkesley v. May*,[59] where the plaintiff was

---

[55] (1844) 4 Hare 67.

[56] See *ante*, p. 173.

[57] See *ante*, p. 136.

[58] *Re Lewis* (1868) 5 L.R. Eq. 545. This was a particularly strong case since the executor was entitled to the subject matter of a legacy in the event that the beneficiary in question failed to claim it and the failure to inform the latter of the existence of the legacy meant that he failed to do so prior to his death.

[59] [1956] 1 Q.B. 304.

jointly entitled with his sister to the income and capital of the trust fund at 21. When he reached that age, the trustees failed to inform him of his rights and continued accumulating the income until his sister also reached that age. Havers J. held that they had been under a duty to inform him of his interest and of his immediate entitlement to call for his share of the income. This was a fixed trust but the same principle presumably applies to discretionary trusts in favour of relatively small groups of beneficiaries. However, the position of potential members of the enormous classes of beneficiaries in favour of whom many modern discretionary trusts are created is more problematical. It is clearly impracticable to oblige or to expect trustees of this type of discretionary trust to notify every single potential member of his potential rights thereunder;[60] the most that they could conceivably be expected to do would be to advertise for potential beneficiaries to present themselves so that the trustees can comply with the duty to survey the field which, as has already been seen,[61] is imposed on them by *McPhail v. Doulton*,[62] and *Re Hay's Settlement Trusts*.[63] However, it cannot seriously be doubted that the need to compel the proper administration of trusts dictates that trustees should be obliged to give a truthful answer to any potential beneficiary who actually enquiries.[64]

A rather different aspect of the right of a beneficiary to know of the existence of his interest had to be considered in *Murphy v. Murphy*.[65] Most if not all the shares in a family company were settled on discretionary off-shore trusts by their respective owners. The plaintiff was aware that he had been specifically named as a beneficiary of two discretionary trusts, one set up by his father, who had reserved the power to appoint its trustees, and one set up by his deceased mother, who had not reserved any such power but whose estate had been administered by the father; he also thought that he was a potential beneficiary of other discretionary trusts set up by them and his brother. He therefore issued a summons to compel his father to disclose to him the names and addresses of the current trustees of all these trusts so that he could find out what had happened to the trust property and make out a case that he should receive some of the property. Neuberger J. held that no principle of equity had been invoked to suggest that the court had no power to grant such relief and ordered the father to make discovery of the information sought in respect of the trusts of which the plaintiff was an actual beneficiary, on the basis that the father must know this information.[66] However, he denied this relief in respect of all the other trusts, saying that it would be most undesirable

---

[60] See Davies (1995) 7 Bond Law Review 5, referring to the remarks of Mahoney J.A. in *Hartigan Nominees v. Rydge* (1992) 29 N.S.W.L.R. 405 at 425 and 432 (Court of Appeal of New South Wales).

[61] See *ante*, p. 73.

[62] [1971] A.C. 424.

[63] [1982] 1 W.L.R. 202, *per* Megarry V.-C. at 209–210.

[64] The Bahamas has legislated in this respect. (The Bahamas) Trustee Act 1998, s.83 provides that trustees are only obliged to inform beneficiaries of the trust's existence if they have a vested interest under the trusts although, at any time when there is no such beneficiary, they must inform at least one person who is in a position to enforce the trust. Although some of the consequences are rather absurd (default beneficiaries will have to be informed even though there is little or no likelihood that they will ever become entitled to anything), this clarification is nevertheless extremely helpful and the provision is likely to be copied widely.

[65] [1999] 1 W.L.R. 282.

[66] But he gave the father the right to adduce evidence as to any possible inconvenience and cost and to be reimbursed for the latter.

to make orders which would be likely to result in trustees being badgered with claims by large numbers of potential beneficiaries, particularly when the plaintiff, as someone who was at best only entitled to be considered as a possible additional member, was in reality in no better position than anyone else in the world who had not been specifically excluded.

## 2. The Right to Require Trust Documents

Prior to the recent decision in Schmidt v. Rosewood Trust,[67] there had never been any doubt about the right of beneficiaries of both fixed trusts and small discretionary trusts to require information as to the state of the trust property and to any dealings with it and the corresponding trust documents; nor was any distinction drawn between beneficiaries with interests in possession and those whose interests had either not yet vested or had not yet vested in possession. It had been clear since the decision in Re Londonderry's Settlement[68] that this right was not confined to beneficiaries of fixed trusts since the Court of Appeal there regarded the right as basically applicable to a discretionary trust whose beneficiaries were the members of a family,[69] although different considerations there determined the non-availability of the documents which the beneficiary wanted to see. But doubts had been expressed both as to whether the right was or should be available to every single potential member of the enormous classes of beneficiaries which many modern discretionary trusts now have[70] and as to the position of persons who are not among the actual beneficiaries of a discretionary trust but are merely among the possible objects of a power of appointment.[71] According to the Privy Council in Rosewood Trust v. Schmidt,[72] these distinctions no longer have any formal significance; the right to require information is instead now to be approached as merely one aspect of the court's inherent jurisdiction to supervise (and where appropriate intervene in) the administration of trusts; in practice, however, these distinctions will obviously remain highly relevant in the court's exercise of that inherent jurisdiction.

In Rosewood Trust v. Schmidt, the effective objects of two discretionary trusts set up in the Isle of Man were Russian businessmen associated with one of the largest privatised oil companies in Russia. They and the Royal National Lifeboat Institution were beneficiaries of both trusts, under each of which the trustees had a power to accumulate income and an overriding power of appointment in favour of the beneficiaries exercisable with the prior written consent of the protector. In the first trust, there was a provision for each beneficiary's "portion" of the trust fund to be held on his death for the persons

[67] [2003] 2 W.L.R. 1442.

[68] [1965] Ch. 918.

[69] This was subsequently confirmed in Chaine-Nickson v. Bank of Ireland [1976] Irish Reports 393 (Supreme Court of Ireland); Spellson v. George (1987) 11 N.S.W.L.R. 300 at 315–316 (Supreme Court of New South Wales).

[70] Hartigan Nominees v. Rydge (1992) 29 N.S.W.L.R. 405 (Court of Appeal of New South Wales).

[71] It had been suggested in Chaine-Nickson v. Bank of Ireland [1976] Irish Reports 393 (Supreme Court of Ireland) and in Spellson v. George (1987) 11 N.S.W.L.R. 300, 315–316 (Supreme Court of New South Wales) that there was no distinction between such persons and persons who are actually beneficiaries but this view was decisively rejected in Rosewood Trust v. Schmidt in the Court of Appeal of the Isle of Man ([2001] W.T.L.R. 1081).

[72] [2003] 2 W.L.R. 1442.

notified by him to the trustees and in default for his closest relatives. In the second trust, there was instead a power to add beneficiaries and a discretionary trust of income in favour of the beneficiaries in default of accumulation or appointment. The claimant was the son and personal representative of one of the beneficiaries, who had also been protector of the first trust. Some $US27,000,000 had been appointed out to nominee companies which were regarded as his but no beneficial interest in either trust had ever actually been appointed to him. He had however written to the trustees notifying them that the claimant was to be his successor under the first trust on his death and expressing the wish that the claimant should be given his share of the second trust.

The claimant, who had been paid the funds actually held by the nominee companies, wanted to find out whether these comprised the whole of the funds actually allocated to those companies and whether, but for possible breaches of fiduciary duty, including over-charging, more funds would have been available for allocation to his father. He therefore sought full disclosure of documents which, had he or his father been a beneficiary of the trusts, he would undoubtedly have been allowed to see under the authorities discussed above. But the trustees claimed that he was not entitled to that disclosure since he was not himself a beneficiary of either trust and his father, whose personal representative he was, had been no more than an object of the overriding powers of appointment under both trusts (in fact he himself was undoubtedly also a possible object of the power to add beneficiaries to the second trust who, in the light of his father's letter, had "exceptionally strong claims to be considered" but this added nothing).[73] This claim succeeded before the Court of Appeal of the Isle of Man,[74] who held that there is a distinction between a beneficiary of a discretionary trust and an object of a mere power of appointment, the latter being entitled only to have his case considered from time to time by the trustees, in default to seek directions from the court that they should consider his case and, if they still refused, to seek their replacement.[75] This of course meant (as the court accepted) that, towards the end of a trust period, there might be no one with both the legal standing and the economic interest to hold the trustee to account.[76]

However, the Privy Council held that there was for this purpose no formal distinction between the different types of beneficiaries and potential beneficiaries of a trust and allowed the claimant's appeal. Lord Walker stated that:

"a beneficiary's right to seek disclosure of trust documents, although

---

[73] In the Privy Council, the claimant himself claimed to be a beneficiary of the first trust as a result of the combined effect of the notification provision and the notification; however, the Privy Council held that he could not be treated as such pending resolution of the proper construction of the documents. At no stage was any point taken that his father had been a default discretionary beneficiary of income under the second trust, possibly because relatively little of the funds allocated to his father's companies had come from that trust.

[74] Technically known as "The Staff of Government Division".

[75] This is admittedly the effect of Re Manisty's Settlement [1974] Ch. 17 and Re Hay's Settlement Trusts [1982] 1 W.L.R. 202; see ante, p. 209.

[76] (The Bahamas) Trustee Act 1998, s.83(5) confines the rights to information to those beneficiaries who have to be informed of the existence of the trusts (ante, fn. 64) and thus has the same effect as the decision of the Manx court; it therefore also excludes beneficiaries with contingent or other non-vested interests.

sometimes not inappropriately described as a proprietary right, is best approached as one aspect of the court's inherent jurisdiction to supervise (and where appropriate intervene in) the administration of trusts. There is therefore in their Lordships' view no reason to draw any bright dividing-line either between transmissible and non-transmissible (that is, discretionary) interests, or between the rights of an object of a discretionary trust and those of the object of a mere power (of a fiduciary character). ... However, the recent cases also confirm that no beneficiary (and least of all a discretionary object) has any entitlement as of right to disclosure of anything which can plausibly be described as a trust document. ... Evaluation of the claims of a beneficiary (and especially of a discretionary object) may be an important part of the balancing exercise which the court ahs to perform on the materials placed before it. In many cases the court may have no difficulty in concluding that an applicant with no more than a theoretical possibility of benefit ought not to be granted any relief."

The case was sent back to the Isle of Man for this decision to be applied but Lord Walker indicated that, on the face of things, the claimant as personal representative had a powerful case for the fullest disclosure in respect of the funds actually allocated to his father's companies and in respect of his claims for breach of fiduciary duties; Lord Walker also emphasised that he personally had "exceptionally strong claims" to be considered as an object of the power to add beneficiaries to the second trust.

Although *Schmidt v. Rosewood Trust* is, as a decision of the Privy Council, not technically binding on the English courts, it is bound to be followed. However, trustees would be unwise to take too literally Lord Walker's remark that "no beneficiary (and least of all a discretionary object) has any entitlement as of right to disclosure of anything which can plausibly be described as a trust document". The immediate beneficiaries of fixed trusts and of small discretionary trusts are bound in practice to be given exactly the same trust documents as at present. Room for manoeuvre for the trustees continues to exist in relation to the beneficiaries of large discretionary trusts and potential beneficiaries of all types of trusts; in respect of the latter categories, the criteria laid down by Lord Walker are likely to restrict disclosure to those who in practical terms have a reasonable chance of receiving some part of the trust property at some point. However, the rights of default beneficiaries, the ultimate beneficiaries of discretionary trusts who, although they are necessssarily beneficiaries of fixed trusts, are only likely to take in the event of the death of all the other beneficiaries, may well now in practice be considerably restricted by these criteria.

### 3. The Nature of Trust Documents

A person who is entitled to require the trustees to show him the trust documents will be entitled to see documents of a number of different types.

### (A) Accounts and Investments

A trustee must maintain accurate accounts of the trust property. He must allow a person entitled to see trust documents, or that person's solicitor, to inspect those accounts and the vouchers supporting them and he must be prepared to give full information as to the amount of the trust fund. He is not obliged to supply copies of the accounts, or settlements of account, to the beneficiaries unless the beneficiaries themselves pay for those copies. Under the modern law, trustees will be entitled to employ agents to keep the accounts whether or not they are capable of doing so themselves.[77]

Where trust money is invested, the trustees must on request supply a person entitled to see trust documents with details of the investments, and even produce the stock or share certificates, or other deeds and documents, representing that investment. Where, however, such a person requires information as to his position under a trust, and this information cannot be supplied by the trustees without incurring expense, the trustees can pass on the expense to him. Trustees who do not keep proper accounts may be ordered to do so by the court, and may be forced to bear personally the costs of the application to the court.[78] As the trustees may at any time be called upon to give information as to the administration of a trust, it is advisable for them to keep in addition to the trust accounts a trust diary. This is a type of minute book in which decisions taken in the administration of a trust are recorded. However, in view of the fact that access is usually given to the trust diary, trustees may, in the light of the authorities discussed in the previous section of this chapter, choose to record their decisions but not the reasons for them.

It seems that the court has a discretion to withhold even documents of this kind "if the probative value is minimal and is outweighed by prejudice to the other beneficiaries or to the proper administration of the trust".[79]

## (B) Other Documents

A person entitled to see trust documents is also entitled to inspect most other documents relating to the trust.[80] However, this right will not be allowed to impinge on the rule that trustees are not obliged to give reasons for their decisions. This was the issue which *Re Londonderry's Settlement*,[81] actually had to resolve. The trustees of a settlement were to distribute the trust fund in such proportions as they thought fit among certain named persons. One of them considered that she had received too little[82] and, in order to launch an attack upon the trustees, sought to inspect numerous trust documents which would probably have indicated the reasons which led the trustees to make the distributions that they had made. The disgruntled beneficiary claimed that she had a right to inspect the documents. The trustees claimed that she had not; they could not to be compelled to give reasons for their decisions and, if the court ordered that the beneficiary was able to see the documents which she

---

[77] See *post*, p. 611. At one time this was not the case; but in *Wroe v. Seed* (1863) 4 Giff. 425 it was held that a trustee who was illiterate, and so could not keep accounts, was justified in employing an agent simply for the purpose of keeping them.

[78] See (1936) 52 L.Q.R. 365.

[79] *Lemos v. Coutts & Co. (Cayman)* (1993) 1 Butterworths Offshore Service 171 at 216; *Re Rabaiotti 1989 Settlement* [2000] J.L.R. 173, [2000] W.T.L.R. 953.

[80] The older authorities, such as *O'Rourke v. Darbishire* [1920] A.C. 581, stated that this was because, just as the beneficiaries were the equitable owners of the trust property, they were also the equitable owners of the documents which had arisen in the course of the trust administration, and often at the expense of the trust. However, this view was rejected in *Schmidt v. Rosewood Trust*.

[81] [1965] Ch. 918.

[82] She and her family had in fact received £165,000. The total amount of the trust fund is not recorded.

wished to see, the rule which enabled the trustees to keep their reasons to themselves would be defeated. The Court of Appeal held, in effect, that the rule enabling a beneficiary to inspect trust documents did not extend to documents which gave reasons for the trustees' decisions; indeed the court went so far as to order that, where a document is basically in the category of those which the beneficiary is entitled to see but also contains details of the trustees' reasons, the latter passages should be covered up when the document is produced to the beneficiary.

Although this decision is unquestionably welcome, the reasons given by the court are far from clear. The court clearly had sympathy with the trustees' contention that family strife would result if the beneficiary were given access to documents which gave their reasons for their dealings with the trust property. It may well be that the court first decided what conclusions they wanted to reach and then tried to find some reasons with which to support it. Harman L.J. considered, but did not decide, whether the documents were trust documents at all, presumably on the basis that, if they were not, the beneficiary would not have a right of access to them at all. He said:[83]

> "I would hold that, even if documents of this type ought properly to be described as trust documents, they are protected for the special reason which protects the trustees' deliberations on a discretionary matter from disclosure. If necessary, I hold that this principle overrides the ordinary rule."

Danckwerts L.J. based his decision firmly on the practical ground that, if the trustees' reasons were not protected from disclosure, it would be impossible for them to do their job. The third member of the Court of Appeal, Salmon L.J., also toyed with the idea of declaring that the documents were not trust documents but had to admit defeat.[84]

There are thus several possible reasons for the conclusion reached; however, the decision does at least clearly establish that beneficiaries do not have a right of access to documents which the trustees intend to be private and which record the reasons for their decisions. This proposition was more recently reviewed in *Wilson v. The Law Debenture Trust Corp.*[85] in the context of the discretions vested in the trustees of a pension trust, specifically in respect of a decision not to transfer a surplus in the fund to another pension scheme to which its member employees had been transferred. Despite the fact that, as has already been seen,[86] the beneficiaries of a pension fund are not volunteers, Rattee J. affirmed the applicability of the decision in *Re Londonderry's Settlement* and refused to order the trustees to reveal their reasons.[87]

All the questions considered so far had to be considered in a slightly different context, that of whether beneficiaries are entitled to see letters of wishes,

---

[83] [1965] Ch. 918 at 933.
[84] *ibid.* at 938.
[85] [1995] 2 All E.R. 337.
[86] See *ante,* p. 522.
[87] The decision has been criticised by Schaffer 8 T.L.I. 118. It may anyway in practice be indirectly undermined by the fact that the Pensions Act 1995 now requires that, at least in principle, every pension trust must have member trustees; see *ante,* p. 518.

in *Hartigan Nominees v. Rydge,*[88] a decision of the Court of Appeal of New South Wales. As has already been seen,[89] letters of wishes are documents which exist outside the formal trust documents; they set out the wishes of the settlor but are not binding on the trustees. Access was, by a majority, denied but each of the three members of court took a different view: one of the members of the majority held that letters of wishes are not trust documents and so do not fall within the basic right of access; the other member of the majority held that letters of wishes are trust documents but do not have to be disclosed because they provide insight into the trustees' reasons; and the dissentient held that letters of wishes are trust documents but should be disclosed even if they do provide insight into the trustees' reasons (in effect, therefore, rejecting *Re Londonderry's Settlement*). Different majorities therefore held that letters of wishes are trust documents and that they do not have to be disclosed on the grounds of confidentiality.

The view that letters of wishes are not trust documents and for that reason do not have to be disclosed was followed and applied by the Royal Court of Jersey in *Re Rabaiotti 1989 Settlement*[90] in relation to two settlements subject to the law of Jersey, which contains a specific statutory provision to this effect,[91] and two subject to the law of the British Virgin Islands, which does not. This seems the better view. However, the court went on to hold that it did, in all four cases, have discretion to order disclosure in appropriate circumstances and duly did so on the basis that disclosure was in the interests of the both adult beneficiaries,[92] who supported it. But it is unlikely that this discretion will be exercised very often, particularly where other beneficiaries are not in favour of disclosure.

The fact that documents which are, like those in *Re Londonderry's Settlement*, clearly trust documents do not have to be disclosed for the reasons stated in that case is, however, not necessarily the end of the matter. In that case, the beneficiary had made a direct application to inspect the documents in question. The Court of Appeal made it clear that their decision did not govern the question of whether such documents were disclosable in pending proceedings brought upon some other ground. If, for example, a beneficiary brings proceedings against the trustees for breaches of trust which involve an allegation of improper motive on the part of the trustees, it may well be that in the course of disclosure the beneficiary will be entitled to see all the trustees' documents, including those which reveal the reasons for their decisions. Robert Walker J. stated this expressly in *Scott v. National Trust*[93] and added that the trustees may in practical terms be compelled to reveal their reasons in order to avoid any adverse inference being drawn.

However, in *Murphy v. Murphy,*[94] Neuberger J. emphasised the traditional judicial reluctance to sanction proceedings brought mainly in order to try to

---

[88] (1992) 29 N.S.W.L.R. 405.
[89] See *ante*, p. 195.
[90] *Re Rabaiotti 1989 Settlement* 2000 J.L.R. 173, [2000] W.T.L.R. 953.
[91] Trusts (Jersey) Law 1984, Art. 25. See also (The Bahamas) Trustee Act 1998, s.83.
[92] One of them had been ordered by an English court to produce the documents for the purposes of his divorce; it was clearly in the interests of all the beneficiaries for the true position to be known.
[93] *Scott v. National Trust* [1998] 2 All E.R. 705.
[94] [1999] 1 W.L.R. 282.

flush out the documents in question;[95] he stated that trustees who have done nothing wrong should not be identified for the purpose of enabling a party to consider whether or not to bring proceedings of a highly speculative nature. This clearly shows that, if disclosure of documents showing reasons is some day sought in proceedings brought on some other ground, the courts will have to try to decide whether there is a genuine need for disclosure in the other proceedings or whether the latter have been brought mainly in order to try to flush out the documents in question. But dicta in *Hartigan Nominees v. Rydge*,[96] suggest that the principle that reasons should not be revealed is paramount and may not be circumvented even by the process of disclosure.[97]

## V. ADMINISTRATIVE POWERS RELATING TO TRUST PROPERTY

Part II of the Trustee Act 1925 confers general powers on trustees, particularly with regard to the administration of property. Like all the provisions of that Act, they can be increased, reduced or completely ousted by any contrary provision in the trust deed in question.[98] Under these powers, trustees may where appropriate raise money by sale or mortgage, sell trust property at auction, and insure the property. Further, although this is not actually mentioned by the statute, trustees are bound to see that trust property does not fall into decay through want of repair.[99] The following provisions require consideration.

Section 15 of the Trustee Act 1925 governs the trustees' power to compound liabilities by giving them the power to:

"(a) accept any property, real or personal, before the time at which it is made transferable or payable; or

(b) sever and apportion any blended trust funds or property; or

(c) pay or allow any debt or claim on any evidence that he or they think sufficient; or

(d) accept any composition or any security, real or personal, for any debt or for any property, real or personal, claimed; or

(e) allow any time for payment of any debt; or

(f) compromise, compound, abandon, submit to arbitration, or otherwise settle any debt, account, claim, or thing whatever relating to the testator's or intestate's estate or to the trust."

The section goes on to provide that the trustees will not be liable for any loss which occurs from the exercise of any of these powers, provided that they have discharged the statutory duty of care.[1] The consent of the beneficiaries

---

[95] A unpermissible tactic which is generally known as a "fishing expedition".
[96] (1992) 29 N.S.W.L.R. 405, *per* Mahoney J.A. at 437.
[97] (The Bahamas) Trustee Act 1998, s.83(8) specifically so provides.
[98] Trustee Act 1925, s.69(2).
[99] *Re Hotchkys* (1886) 32 Ch.D. 408.
[1] Trustee Act 1925, s. 15; Trustee Act 2000, s. 1 and Sched. 1, para. 4.

has never been necessary; it is for the trustees to decide whether they consider the compromise to be in the interest of all beneficiaries taken together and that, if they do, they have power to accept it despite the opposition of one of the beneficiaries.[2]

Section 16 of the Trustee Act 1925 governs the trustees' power to mortgage the trust property. This applies where trustees are authorised either by the general law or by the trust instrument "to pay or apply capital money subject to the trust for any purpose or in any manner". In these circumstances, the section gives the trustees power to raise the necessary money either by mortgaging or selling the trust assets. However, the section is construed narrowly and is confined to the cases where money is required either to preserve assets or to advance capital. In Re Suenson-Taylor's Settlement,[3] the trustees, who had very wide powers of investment and who, in accordance with these powers, properly held a large area of land for investment purposes, wished to borrow upon the security of that land in order to buy further land. It was held that this would be outside the power conferred by section 16. The court however observed that there could be cases where it was necessary to purchase further land in order to protect existing investments. For example, if trustees own a house, it may be appropriate to buy land which the house overlooks, in order to prevent anyone else building upon it. Such a purchase is now clearly permissible under the Trusts of Land and Appointment of Trustees Act 1996 since trustees of land now have all the powers of an absolute owner.[4] However, that does not necessarily mean that the purchase price can be raised on mortgage.

Section 19 of the Trustee Act 1925 governs the trustees' power to insure the trust property. This provision used to be less than wholly satisfactory in that trustees had power to insure the trust property only for an amount not exceeding three-quarters of its full value. However, this was remedied by the Trustee Act 2000,[5] which substituted a new provision under which the power of the trustees to insure trust property against risks of loss or damage is unrestricted both as to the risks insured and the level of cover obtained.[6] The Trustee Act 2000 also makes the power to insure subject to the statutory duty of care,[7] which trustees will inevitably breach if they do not insure adequately. The new section 19 also specifically provides that the premiums can be paid out of the trust funds, which for this purpose means any income or capital of the trust;[8] it is not stated on which premiums are primarily chargeable. If the insured assets are income producing, the premiums will obviously be primarily chargeable on that income as an expense of obtaining it. If, on the other hand, land is not income producing because it is occupied by a beneficiary, the trustees should in principle make the payment of insurance premiums a condition of occupation; they are entitled to impose such conditions under the

---

[2] Re Earl of Strafford [1979] 1 All E.R. 513.
[3] Re Suenson-Taylor's Settlement [1974] 3 All E.R. 397.
[4] Trusts of Land and Appointment of Trustees Act 1996, s.6(1).
[5] Trustee Act 2000, s.34(1).
[6] The power of bare trustees to insure is subject to any direction given by the beneficiaries; Trustee Act 1925, s.19(2)–(4).
[7] Trustee Act 2000, Sched. 1, para. 5.
[8] Trustee Act 1925, s.19(1), (5).

Trusts of Land and Appointment of Trustees Act 1996[9] where land is occupied by a beneficiary with an interest in possession; it is not clear whether they can do so when land is occupied by a beneficiary without an interest in possession. However, where trust property is not income producing for some other reason or the premiums cannot be paid in the ways envisaged above,[10] then, in the event that there is no specific provision in the trust deed (which there usually will be), the trustees will be entitled to pay insurance premiums out of capital; this is obviously preferable to leaving the property uninsured.

It should be noted that there is no statutory power to insure the life of any beneficiary, something which may in practice be desirable since any of the trust property in which a beneficiary holds an interest in possession will be subject to inheritance tax on his or her death which the trust will be primarily liable to pay.[11] Modern trust deeds however generally confer such a power expressly.[12]

In addition to the powers already referred to, the trustees have all the powers of a legal owner of the property in question and powers which can only be exercised on proof of legal ownership can only be exercised by them. In *Schalit v. Nadler*,[13] a beneficiary who was solely entitled to trust property which was leased levied distress for arrears of rent. It was held that only the trustee as legal owner could levy distress; consequently, the distress actually levied was wrongful. Similarly, only the legal owner can serve a notice to quit on a tenant.

## VI. INVESTING THE TRUST PROPERTY

### 1. The Duty of Care

**(A) The Statutory Duty of Care**
THE statutory duty of a care[14] applies to trustees exercising any power of investment.[15] Formerly the normal common law duty, to use only such due diligence and care in the management of the trust as an ordinary prudent man of business would use in the management of his own affairs,[16] was modified in the case of powers of investment so that trustees investing trust funds were to take such care as an ordinary prudent man of business would take if he were under a duty to make the investment for the benefit of other persons for whom he felt morally bound to provide.[17] This was because "business men of prudence may, and frequently do, select investments which are more or less of a

---

[9] Trusts of Land and Appointment of Trustees Act 1996, s.13(1), (3), (5).
[10] Such as the fact that a beneficiary occupying land is doing so pursuant to an express provision of the trust deed which does not permit him to be charged insurance premiums.
[11] See *post*, p. 639.
[12] See the different sets of administrative provisions set out and discussed in Kessler, *Drafting Trusts and Will Trusts* (it is particularly important always to use the most recent edition of this work; the current one is the 6th (2002) edition).
[13] [1933] 2 K.B. 79 and see *ante*, p. 18.
[14] See *ante*, p. 573.
[15] Trustee Act 2000, s.1 and Sched. 1, para. 1.
[16] *Speight v. Gaunt* (1883) 9 App.Cas. 1.
[17] *Re Whiteley* (1886) 33 Ch.D. 347 at 355, affirmed *sub nom. Learoyd v. Whiteley* (1887) 12 App. Cas. 727.

speculative character but it is the duty of a trustee to confine himself to the class of investments which are permitted by the trust and likewise to avoid all investments of that class which are attended with hazard".[18] Some of the extended elements of this test are likely to be considered relevant in deciding whether a trustee has satisfied the statutory duty of care by exercising such care and skill as is reasonable in the circumstances.

The relevant principles of course apply not just to the initial investment of the trust property but also to the variation and continuation of investments. In their consideration of the investments of the trust as a whole, Hoffmann J. made it clear in *Nestlé v. National Westminster Bank*,[19] that "modern trustees acting within their investment powers are entitled to be judged by the standards of current portfolio theory, which emphasises the risk level of the entire portfolio rather than the risk attaching to each investment taken in isolation". This view was subsequently adopted by the Treasury in a Consultation Paper on the Investment Powers of Trustees published in May 1996 and must therefore now be regarded as part of the general law.

### (B) Trusts for Persons by way of Succession

As part of the modified common law duty, trustees were also bound to make their investments in such a way that those entitled in possession obtain a reasonable income and the capital is nevertheless preserved for those entitled to it in remainder[20] and this will undoubtedly continue to be the case under the statutory duty of care. High income investments are likely to produce little, if any, capital appreciation and thus will generally benefit the tenant for life at the expense of the remaindermen, while low income investments are likely to produce more substantial capital appreciation and thus will generally benefit the remaindermen at the expense of the tenant for life. A balance must be secured so that all beneficiaries are treated equally and fairly.

In *Nestlé v. National Westminster Bank*,[21] the remainderman complained that the fund to which she became entitled when her interest vested in possession would have been worth almost four times as much had it been properly invested. The trustees had erroneously regarded their investment powers as more limited than they actually were and, as a result, had invested in a more restricted range of investments than they were actually obliged to. Further, they had failed to make sufficiently regular reviews of the fund. However, since the remainderman was unable to prove that any loss had been suffered thereby, the Court of Appeal held that she was not entitled to any compensation. The Court also emphasised that trustees are entitled to take into account the taxation position of the beneficiaries. Consequently, they had been entitled, where the tenant for life was non-resident, to purchase investments which would not be subject to deduction of income tax at source or to what is now inheritance tax on his death; further, they could take into account the relative wealth of the tenant for life and the remainderman in deciding whether to purchase high income or low income investments. However, the Court did hold that at least half of a trust fund held for persons by way of succession

---

[18] *Learoyd v. Whiteley* (1887) 12 App. Cas. 727 at 733.
[19] (1988) unreported but transcribed in (1996) 10 Trust Law International 112.
[20] *Re Whiteley* (1886) 33 Ch.D. 347 at 350.
[21] [1993] 1 W.L.R. 1260.

should be invested in "equities", ordinary shares issued by commercial companies which tend to keep pace with inflation.[22]

It therefore follows that, even if the trustees invest entirely in accordance with the powers conferred on them by statute[23] and the trust instrument[24] itself, they will not necessarily be protected from attack by the beneficiaries. Even an authorised investment may in the particular circumstances of the case be unjustified and amount to a breach of the trustees' general duties of care and impartiality. But in circumstances such as these, the onus would be on the beneficiaries to establish that the investment was imprudent and not for the trustees to show the converse.[25] As Hoffmann J. said at first instance in *Nestlé v. National Westminster Bank*:[26]

"Trustees like the Bank act for reward and therefore owe duties of professional skill, but the engagement into which they enter is not one of insurance. They do not guarantee results. Possibly for a suitable premium such a guarantee could be obtained, but I very much doubt it and the transaction would be very different from that which the Bank undertook for modest reward."

### (C) Non-Financial Considerations

Recent authorities have also considered whether trustees, in reaching their decisions as to the selection and retention of particular investments, are entitled to take into account non-financial considerations. In *Cowan v. Scargill*,[27] five of the ten trustees of a mineworkers' pension fund were appointed by the National Union of Miners. They refused to accept an investment plan submitted to the trustees by an advisory panel of experts in so far as it envisaged new or continuing investment overseas and in energies which were in direct competition with coal. Such investments were contrary to the policy of the National Union of Miners, which was understandably primarily interested in preserving the prosperity and, consequently, in ensuring the continued existence of the British coal mining industry. Their arguments were thus ideological in nature. There can be little doubt that most pension funds would indeed be benefited by the maintenance of the prosperity of the industry in question but, as Megarry V.-C. commented, the mineworkers' pension fund was in this respect unusual because of the declining nature of the coal mining industry, there being substantially more pensioners than miners so that the assets of the fund far exceeded the value of the industry. Further, overseas investments can be substantially more risky than home investments because of the possibility of exchange rate variations. However, Megarry V.-C. held that the trustees would be in breach of trust unless they accepted the investment plan submitted. Their duty was to act in the best interests of their bene-

---

[22] See *post*, pp. 606–608.
[23] See *post*, p. 597.
[24] See *post*, p. 605.
[25] *Shaw v. Cates* [1909] 1 Ch. 389 at 395.
[26] (1988), unreported except in (1996) 10 Trust Law International 112.
[27] [1985] Ch. 270. See generally Ellison (1991) 5 Trust Law International 157; Irish & Kent (1994) 8 Trust Law International 10; Lord Nicholls of Birkenhead, extra-judicially, (1995) 9 Trust Law International 10.

ficiaries[28] and, if the purpose of the trust was the provision of financial benefits, a power of investment had to be exercised so that the funds yielded the best return by way of income and capital appreciation.

> "Trustees may have strongly held social or political views. They may be firmly opposed to any investment in South Africa or other countries, or they may object to any form of investment in companies concerned with alcohol, tobacco, armaments or many other things. In the conduct of their own affairs, of course, they are free to abstain from making any such investments. Yet under a trust, if investments of this type would be more beneficial to the beneficiaries than other investments, the trustees must not refrain from making the investments by reason of the views that they hold."[29]

In exceptional cases, account could be taken of the particular inclinations of the beneficiaries but this was not relevant in the case in hand since many of the beneficiaries no longer had any financial interest in the welfare of the coal industry. The trustees were therefore pursuing union policy at the potential expense of the beneficiaries and, in the last resort, would have to be removed from office.

It is possible that the fact that the trustees so overtly based their case on ideological grounds did not favour their case. There seems no reason why trustees should not limit themselves to investments which they regard as politically and ethically "sound" provided that they have satisfied themselves that these investments are no less financially sound than those which they have rejected. What *Cowan v. Scargill* decides is that they must not fetter their discretion by deciding to exclude any particular class of investments irrelevant of their financial merits. This is confirmed by *Martin v. City of Edinburgh District Council*,[30] where a Scottish court held that a breach of duty had been committed by a local authority which, in order to oppose the regime in the then apartheid ridden South Africa, had adopted a policy of disinvesting in companies which had interests in that country without considering whether this was in the best financial interests of the beneficiaries. It is therefore clear that no investment policy, whether to prefer or whether to avoid particular classes of investments, can be adopted unless the trustees have paid the necessary attention to the financial interests of the beneficiaries.

It has also been contended that trusts for charitable purposes should not make investments in undertakings whose operations are incompatible with those purposes. In *Harries v. Church Commissioners*,[31] the Bishop of Oxford sought a declaration that in the management of their assets the Church Commissioners were obliged to have regard to the object of promoting the Christian faith through the established Church of England and were not entitled to act in a manner which would be incompatible with that object. This declaration was denied. Nicholls V.-C. held that, where charitable trustees held assets as investments, the discharge of their duty of furthering the pur-

---

[28] The Uniform Prudent Investor Act 1994, s.5 (United States of America) now similarly requires investment solely in the interest of the beneficiaries.
[29] [1985] Ch. 270 at 287–288.
[30] [1988] S.L.T. 329.
[31] [1992] 1 W.L.R. 1241.

poses of the trust would normally require them to seek the maximum return which was consistent with commercial prudence and they could not properly use such assets for non-investment purposes. The Commissioners already had a policy of excluding investments in certain business activities which might be offensive to the Church of England, such as in armaments, gambling, tobacco and newspapers and in South Africa. This was entirely proper but it would not be right for them to adopt a still more restrictive policy which would entail taking into account non-financial considerations to an extent which would give rise to a risk of significant financial detriment to the proper object of the trusts.

The cases just discussed all concerned trusts which had some public element. While the considerations expressed in the judgments clearly also apply to wholly private trusts, there is of course nothing to stop any settlor, or indeed the totality of the beneficiaries if they are all *sui juris*, from prescribing that the trustees either must make or must refrain from making investments of any particular type.

### (D) Continuing Supervision

In addition to making investments, the duties of the trustees inevitably extend to keep their investments under review. In the case of holdings in large quoted public companies, a periodic review will usually be sufficient. However, where the trustees have a majority holding or a controlling interest in a company or some other special position of influence, they will be expected to take advantage of it. If an individual shareholder in this position would require information about the company's affairs which is not generally available, the trustees will also need to obtain it. If an individual would insist on board representation, or board control, the trustees will themselves need to insist on it.

In *Bartlett v. Barclays Bank Trust Co.,*[32] the settlor settled almost the whole of the shares in a company which he had incorporated to manage his properties on trust for his wife and issue. Initially the board of the company included members of the settlor's family but that gradually changed. However, the trustees, while sending a representative to statutory meetings of the company, did not seek representation on the board. The company purchased a property opposite the Old Bailey in the City of London at a price well in excess of its investment value, in the hope that permission would be obtained for its development. Permission was not forthcoming and the company later disposed of the property at a loss. Brightman J. held that the trustees were in breach of their duty to obtain the information which, as they were majority shareholders, was available to them.

Information is not, however, an end in itself,[33] and must be used to protect the interests of the beneficiaries. If necessary, a trustee must intervene to remove directors and procure the appointment of his own nominees.[34]

Some professional trustees and trust corporations are reluctant to assume this responsibility and therefore include in their standard trust deeds a pro-

---

[32] [1980] Ch. 515.
[33] See Re Lucking's Will Trust [1968] 1 W.L.R. 866, discussed *ante*, p. 576, where the trustees had information but did not use it.
[34] [1980] Ch. 515 at 530.

vision which negatives what would otherwise be their duty to interfere in the management of companies in which they are shareholders. These provisions are not necessarily effective at all unless they also negative any power so to interfere, since the trustees could be held liable for failure to exercise what would necessarily be a fiduciary power. It remains to be seen whether they are upheld by the courts.

## 2. The Statutory Powers of Investment

### (A) The General Power of Investment

Section 3(1) of the Trustee Act 2000 confers on a trustee the power to "make any kind of investment that he could make if he were absolutely entitled to the assets of the trust"; this power is described as "the general power of investment".[35] Prior to this legislation, the statutory powers of investment of trustees[36] depended on the nature of the investment and only a specified proportion of the trust property[37] could be invested in "equities", ordinary shares issued by commercial companies. However, since the general power of investment applies to all trusts whenever created,[38] the pre-existing law is only relevant to alleged breaches of trust committed before the Trustee Act 2000 came into force on February 1, 2001.

The general power of investment is additional to any powers conferred on trustees in any other way,[39] obviously in particular by the trust instrument, but is subject to the following restrictions:

(a) the word "investment" is restricted to investment in assets from which a profit or some income is expected;

(b) the phrase "investments which he could make" is not in the form habitually used by express powers of investment, which confer the powers of an absolute beneficial owner on the trustees in question, and this may affect the position of corporate trustees, whose powers of investments of their own corporate assets are limited in some way;

(c) investments in land are not permitted other than by way of loans secured on land;[40]

(d) a trust instrument made on or after August 3, 1961[41] may restrict the general power of investment in any way; and

---

[35] Trustee Act 2000, s.3(2).
[36] Contained in the Trustee Investment Act 1961.
[37] 50% from 1961 until 1996; 75% thereafter. The assets had to be divided into two funds and the percentages were relevant only at that point or when any property was subsequently added to the settlement; once divided, the fluctuations in the value of the subject matter of the two funds were obviously not uniform.
[38] Trustee Act 2000, s.7(1).
[39] Trustee Act 2000, s.6(1)(a).
[40] Trustee Act 2000, s.3(3) which does however refer to s.8; see *post*, p. 601.
[41] The date on which the Trustee Investment Act 1961 came into force (the reason for this exclusion is that until then there were no general statutory powers of investment, merely a statutory list of permitted investments, to which trust instruments simply tended to add; this approach was incompatible with the Trustee Investment Act 1961 and remains incompatible with the Trustee Act 2000).

(e)   the general power of investment does not apply to pension trusts,[42] to unit trusts,[43] or to common investment schemes or common deposit schemes made for charitable trusts.[44]

## (B) Investment in Mortgages of Land

The Trustee Act 2000 makes it clear that investments "by way of loans secured on land" are within the general power of investment by excluding them from the prohibition on investments in land. However, trustees are not always justified in investing the trust funds in mortgages of land. They must comply with the statutory duty of care and act with impartiality. They should not therefore make this sort of investment simply for the benefit of one of the beneficiaries and certainly not for the benefit of a person who is not even a beneficiary.[45] The rule that trustees are not necessarily free from responsibility because they invest in accordance with the powers conferred on them by statute and the trust instrument[46] applies with considerable force to investments in mortgages of land and this is clearly shown by the limitations on the trustees' powers imposed by the decided cases which are obviously likely to be applied to investments in mortgages of land made pursuant to the general power of investment.

According to these authorities, trustees should, in the absence of express authority to do otherwise, invest only in first mortgages of freehold or leasehold land. The security should be a first mortgage because it is desirable that the mortgage should enjoy priority. While the Trustee Act 2000 does not prohibit investments in second mortgages, it seems consistent with the statutory duty of care for these generally to be avoided since the first mortgagee will be able to exercise his power of sale irrrelevant of the fact that this will leave nothing for the second mortgagee.[47] It used also to be said that trustees should obtain a legal mortgage rather than an equitable mortgage because otherwise their mortgage might be postponed to a subsequent legal mortgage but in practice, the possibility of protecting equitable mortgages under the provisions of the Land Registration Act 2002 and the Land Charges Act 1972 will prevent this happening and this seems to constitute sufficient protection. Trustees should however avoid what is called a contributory mortgage (that is to say, a joint loan by the trustee and other persons) because in such a case the trustee would not possess complete control.[48] On the other hand, a sub-mortgage may be quite proper,[49] for here the mortgagee will mortgage to the

---

[42] Trustee Act 2000, s.36(3). Pension trusts are governed by Pensions Act 1995, s.34(1) which enables the trustees to invest "as if they were absolutely entitled", does not exclude investment in land, but requires the preparation of written statements of the principles governing investment decisions and the obtaining of advice and is subject to rigid restrictions on the making of employer-related investments.

[43] Trustee Act 2000, s.37. Unit trusts often invest exclusively in shares of companies engaged in particular types of business or in particular jurisdictions and so such trusts necessarily have to be governed by express investment clauses.

[44] Trustee Act 2000, s.38; see *ante*, p. 497.

[45] See *Whitney v. Smith* (1869) L.R. 4 Ch. 513 at 521; *Re Walker* (1890) 62 L.T. 449.

[46] See *ante*, p. 592.

[47] *Norris v. Wright* (1851) 14 Beav. 291; *Lockhart v. Reilly* (1857) 1 De G. & J. 464.

[48] *Webb v. Jonas* (1888) 39 Ch.D. 660.

[49] *Smethurst v. Hastings* (1885) 30 Ch.D. 490.

trustee and the latter will obtain either a legal mortgage or an equitable mortgage which is capable of protection.

The Trustee Act 1925 (and its predecessors) expressly imposed various conditions, which were not affected by the Trustee Investments Act 1961, which in effect required the trustees first to have been acting upon a report as to the value of the property made by a person whom they reasonably believed to be an able practical surveyor or valuer instructed and employed independently of any owner of the property and, secondly, not to lend more than two-thirds of the value of the property as stated in that report;[50] in the event of failure to comply, they were liable only in respect of any excess over the sum properly advanced.[51] These provisions have been repealed by the Trustee Act 2000 but their general tenor must necessarily remain relevant in assessing whether or not trustees have satisfied the statutory duty of care. The trustees should therefore certainly still obtain a report as to the value of the property from an able practical surveyor or valuer instructed and employed independently of any owner of the property. However, while the precise nature of the requirements of the provisions of the Trustee Act 1925 as to their beliefs about the surveyor or valuer[52] will obviously no longer be relevant, it is likely that the trustees will still have to exercise their own judgment in deciding whether the surveyor or valuer is competent and will not be safe to trust blindly even in a nomination from their own solicitor, never mind one from the mortgagor's solicitor.[53] But there is no reason why the trustees should continue to restrict themselves rigidly to advances of two-thirds of the value of the security although an advance of more than the amount which institutional lenders are at the time prepared to consider or without the additional security which such institutional lenders would require is likely to be held to be a breach of the statutory duty of care. Further, it is most unlikely that the former restriction on the level of the trustees' liability for an excessive advance will be continued; if the trustees are held to have breached their statutory duty of care, their liability is therefore likely potentially to extend to the entire loss suffered by the trust.

### (C) The Acquisition of Land

Although trustees have long been able to invest in mortgages of land, until the enactment of the Trustee Act 2002 they had no general power to purchase

---

[50] Trustee Act 1925, s.8.

[51] Trustee Act 1925, s.9.

[52] In *Re Walker* (1890) 62 L.T. 449 at 452, Kekewich J. had held that the trustee need only believe the surveyor or valuer to be able but that the latter must in fact be employed independently of the owner of the property; although the latter point seemed to be in accordance with the natural meaning of the words in the section, it was doubted in *Re Solomon* [1912] 1 Ch. 261 at 281 by Warrington J., who seemed to think that a belief of independent employment would be sufficient.

[53] *Shaw v. Cates* [1909] 1 Ch. 389 at 404. Nor should they rely on the former statutory provision that the surveyor or valuer need not necessarily be a local man or have specialised local knowledge.

land by way of investment. Where the property settled included land,[54] there was admittedly a statutory power so to do[55] and the purchase of land could obviously also be expressly authorised by the trust instrument. But even where the purchase of land was so expressly authorised, the authorisation did not necessarily include the purchase of land for residential purposes. In *Re Power*,[56] the clause was to the effect that "all moneys required to be invested under this my will may be invested by the trustee in any manner in which he may in his absolute discretion think fit including the purchase of freehold property in England and Wales". Jenkins J. held that the trustees were not entitled to purchase a dwelling-house with vacant possession for occupation by a beneficiary; this was on the basis that "investment" entails an income yield and the purchase of a home for occupation by a beneficiary does not yield income.[57]

The latter restriction was removed by the enactment of the Trusts of Land and Appointment of Trustees Act 1996. This legislation applies to any trust of land as defined in that Act,[58] namely any trust of property which consists of or includes land[59] and any trust of the proceeds of sale of land.[60] In its original form, section 6(3) conferred on the trustees of any such trust the power to purchase a legal estate in any land in England and Wales, whether for investment, for occupation by a beneficiary or for any other reason (this subsection has now been amended in form, although not in substance, by the Trustee Act 2000). Further, section 12(1) conferred (and confers) on any beneficiary who is entitled to an interest in possession in land subject to a trust of land the right to occupy it at any time if either the purposes of the trust include making the land available for his occupation or the land is held by the trustees

---

[54] In which case the trust in question would before 1997 necessarily have been either a settlement under the Settled Land Act 1925 or a trust for sale. Since 1996 no new settlements under the Settled Land Act 1925 have been able to be created (although existing ones continue) and any such trust has been a trust of land (Trusts of Land and Appointment of Trustees Act 1996, s.1).

[55] Under Settled Land Act 1925, s.73(1)(xi), which enables capital money to be used to purchase land, although the power will be held by the tenant for life or the statutory owner rather than by the trustees. The same power was, by the now repealed Law of Property Act 1925, s.28(1), vested in trustees for sale of land, who could purchase land with the proceeds of sale provided that they had not ceased to be trustees for sale within the statutory definition contained in s.205 of the same Act (*Re Wakeman* [1945] Ch. 177) by having parted with all the land held on trust for sale.

[56] [1947] Ch. 572; *Re Wragg* [1919] 2 Ch. 58, where the land in question was to yield income, was distinguished.

[57] Trustees could only purchase land in two cases: first, if they had an express power for this purpose under the trust instrument (such powers could be drafted in such a way as to circumvent the decision in *Re Power* [1947] Ch. 572); and, secondly, if they were able to rely on a special statutory power appropriate to the circumstances of the case).

[58] This excludes settlements under the Settled Land Act 1925, which continue to be governed by s.73(1)(xi) of that Act, although such settlements irrevocably cease to be governed by that Act once all land and heirlooms held thereunder have been sold (Trusts of Land and Appointment of Trustees Act 1996, s.2(4))

[59] Trusts of Land and Appointment of Trustees Act 1996, s.1(1)(a).

[60] *ibid.* s.17(1), referring to s.17(3) under which "trust of proceeds of sale of land" means any trust of property which consists of or includes any proceeds of a disposition of land held in trust (which includes a settlement formerly subject to the Settled Land Act 1925) or any property representing such proceeds.

so as to be so available,[61] subject to the trustees' right to impose reasonable conditions on him in relation to that occupation.[62] However, where a trust was not a trust of land, which was the case where the property settled was entirely pure personalty, the basic prohibition on the purchase of land in the absence of an express power in the trust instrument continued to apply.

Section 8(1) of the Trustee Act 2000 has, however, extended to all trusts a slightly modified form of the power of investment enacted for trusts of land in the Trusts of Land and Appointment of Trustees Act 1996 (which, presumably in the interests of consistency, has been amended to provide that trustees of land can instead acquire land under the power conferred by section 8 of the Trustee Act 2000).[63] This provision[64] enables trustees to acquire freehold or leasehold land in the United Kingdom (defined for the purposes of England and Wales as a legal estate in land)[65] as an investment, for occupation by a beneficiary, or for any other reason. Trustees can also now acquire such land with mortgage finance whether or not the trust already holds any land (under the Trusts of Land and Appointment of Trustees Act 1996, this was only possible where the trust already held land). Trustees who acquire land by virtue of section 8 have all the powers of an absolute owner of the land in question.[66]

Once trustees have exercised their power under section 8, they will be trustees of land and so they will additionally have all the powers and duties conferred by the Trusts of Land and Appointment of Trustees Act 1996. Thus the trustees,[67] when considering exercising any of their functions relating to land held by them, will have, so far as practicable, to consult the beneficiaries of full age who are entitled to an interest in possession in the land and give effect to their wishes[68] in so far as this is consistent with the general interest of the trust. Further, any beneficiary who is entitled to an interest in possession will have the right to occupy the land at any time if either the purposes of the trust include making the land available for his occupation or the land is held by the trustees so as to be so available,[69] subject to the trustees' right to impose reasonable conditions on him in relation to that occupation.[70]

However, section 8 of the Trustee Act 2000 permits the purchase of land for occupation by "a beneficiary", not merely a beneficiary with an interest in

---

[61] This right does not extend to any land which is unavailable or unsuitable for his occupation (*ibid.* s.12(2)). Detailed provisions (*ibid.* s.13) govern the trustees' rights to exclude and restrict beneficiaries' rights of occupation.

[62] *ibid.* s.13(3). By s.13(5), these include the payment of outgoings and expenses and the assumption of any other obligation in relation to the land or to any activity which is or is proposed to be conducted there.

[63] Trustee Act 2000, s.40(1), Sched. 2, Pt. II, para. 45(1). This adds nothing to Trustee Act 2000, s.8.

[64] Which does not apply to settlements under the Settled Land Act 1925 or to certain types of charitable trusts (*ibid.* s.10).

[65] *ibid.* s.8(2)(a).

[66] *ibid.* s.8(3), parallelling Trusts of Land and Appointment of Trustees Act 1996, s.6(1).

[67] Trusts of Land and Appointment of Trustees Act 1996, s.11.

[68] Or in the event of dispute to the wishes of the majority by value.

[69] Trusts of Land and Appointment of Trustees Act 1996, s.12(1); this right does not extend to any land which is unavailable or unsuitable for his occupation (*ibid.* s.12(2)). Detailed provisions (*ibid.* s.13) govern the trustees' rights to exclude and restrict beneficiaries' rights of occupation.

[70] *ibid.* s.13(3). By s.13(5), these include the payment of outgoings and expenses and the assumption of any other obligation in relation to the land or to any activity which is or is proposed to be conducted there.

possession. The provision must therefore implicitly enable trustees to purchase land for occupation of land by beneficiaries who do not have an interest
in possession and, for that matter, permit land already held to be occupied by
such beneficiaries, even though they are not within the scope of the provisions
of the Trusts of Land and Appointment of Trustee Act 1996. However, trustees
who did so would have to be careful not to prejudice the interests of other
beneficiaries since this could breach their duty of impartiality. There is
therefore no obvious reason why the trustees should not permit land to be
occupied by a beneficiary of a discretionary trust where that trust is the current interest in possession, provided that, as would usually be the case, the
trustees had a discretion to pay the whole of the income of the trust to that
beneficiary anyway. However, trustees could not permit occupation by a
remainderman without prejudicing the interests of the beneficiaries with prior
interests, whether those interests (and for that matter the interest of the
remaindermen) arose under a fixed or a discretionary trust, although they
could obviously do so if those beneficiaries consented. Further, the Trustee Act
2000 does not in terms enable trustees to impose reasonable conditions in
relation to occupation by a beneficiary who does not have an interest in possession. This is presumably an oversight and might be able to be remedied by
regarding the imposition of such conditions as implicit in the power to purchase for occupation, although such an argument is hardly consistent with the
fact that an express power to impose such conditions was included in the
Trusts of Land and Appointment of Trustees Act 1996.

It is not entirely clear what reason other than investment or occupation by a
beneficiary there could be for trustees to exercise their power under section 8.
They could presumably acquire premises in the relatively unlikely event that
these were necessary for the administration of the trust and, possibly, for the
use of a company wholly owned by a beneficiary who had an interest in
possession. However, it is unlikely that the trustees would be able to acquire
land for the purposes of a business carried on by the trust itself, unless the
carrying on of that business was itself specifically authorised by the trust
instrument. This is of course a specific manifestation of the general rule that
the provisons of section 8 are not only additional to any other powers conferred on the trustees but are also subject to any restrictions imposed by the
trust instrument.[71] Any such restrictions are likely to be strictly construed and
will be particularly relevant in relation to the ability to purchase land with
mortgage finance and the right to permit occupation by beneficiaries.

### (D) Standard Investment Criteria
Section 4 of the Trustee Act 2000 lays down what it describes as standard
investment criteria. Trustees must have regard to these criteria both when
exercising the general power of investment or any other investment power,
and when carrying out the obligation which that section also imposes on them
from time to time to review the investments of the trust and consider whether
they should be varied (annual reviews will generally be sufficient[72] unless the

---

[71] Trustee Act 2000, s.9.
[72] The trustees will need to review the trust's investments towards the end of every tax year in
order to utilise the trust's annual capital gains tax exemption and will also often need to take
decisions on individual investments between reviews, particularly in the event of company
reorganisations, mergers or takeovers.

investments are of a particularly volatile type). The criteria, which are similar to requirements contained in the Trustee Investment Act 1961,[73] are:

> "(a) the suitability to the trust of investments of the same kind as any particular investment proposed to be made or retained and of that particular investment as an investment of that kind; and
> (b) the need for diversification of investments of the trust, in so far as is appropriate to the circumstances of the trust."

The sort of problem with which the trustees will be faced in relation to the first criterion is whether, and to what extent, present income should be sacrificed in the interests of future growth; in this respect, much will depend on arriving at a decision on the actual needs of the beneficiaries, the expected duration of the trust and, today, the beneficiaries' tax position. The way in which these factors have to be considered is shown by taking three examples:

(a) If trustees are holding property on trust for a minor beneficiary at the age of 18 in, say, 2008, they might invest in a government stock maturing in that year and therefore redeemable then at its highest value, just in time for the proceeds to be paid to the beneficiary with the additional advantage that the increase in its capital value will be exempt from capital gains tax[74] (increases in the capital value of most other investments will be subject to capital gains tax when the beneficiary reaches the age of 18 and becomes absolutely entitled to the trust property as against the trustees).

(b) If a very small sum is to be held for a fairly short period of, for example, between five and 10 years but the beneficiary has adequate income from other sources, National Savings Certificates might be a suitable investment; although the rate of interest is small, this interest is free of tax[75] and the capital is also exempt from capital gains tax.[76]

(c) If the beneficiary to whom the trustees are obliged to pay or in whose favour the trustees intend to exercise a discretion to pay the income of the trust has only a small total income,[77] the trustees might endeavour to invest at least part of the fund in a security which produces a high income, so far as they consider that this is consistent with their duties to the remainderman. But they should not select just any security which produces a high income, or even just any security which produces a high income and is considered particularly safe. A beneficiary with a small total income will only have to pay income tax of 10 per cent on this income (even if the trust is a discretionary trust, the balance of the overall income tax which is payable will be recoverable by him). However, the tax liability may well be higher in

---

[73] In s.6(1).
[74] Taxation of Chargeable Gains Act 1992, s.115.
[75] Income and Corporation Taxes Act 1988, s.326.
[76] Taxation of Chargeable Gains Act 1992, s.121.
[77] Of £6,575 or less (in 2003–2004, he paid income tax at 10 per cent on the first £1,960 after his personal allowance of £4,615 (and at 22 per cent above £6,575).

respect of income from foreign companies and there will certainly be no possibility of any foreign tax being recovered. Consequently, in these circumstances the trustees must look for a company which has virtually the whole of its activities in England so that the minimum amount of tax will ultimately be payable.

It is in the light of considerations of this type that the full significance of this first criterion becomes apparent.

So far as the need for diversification is concerned, diversification is not actually defined but obviously means maintaining a spread of investments. The need referred to is the reduction of risk by spreading the trust's funds across a diversified portfolio of investments. But it is in this respect particularly that "modern trustees acting within their investment powers are entitled to be judged by the standards of current portfolio theory, which emphasises the risk level of the entire portfolio rather than the risk attaching to each investment taken in isolation."[78] Circumstances of the trust which could legitimately be taken into account to reduce or remove any need for diversification would undoubtedly include the smallness of the fund or the life tenant's paramount need of income.

### (E) Advice

The provisions of the Trustee Act 2000 are also similar to the equivalent provisions of the Trustee Investment Act 1961.[79] Section 5 of the Trustee Act 2000 provides that, before exercising the general power of investment or any other investment power and before each review of the investments, the trustees "must (unless the exception applies) obtain and consider proper advice about the way in which, having regard to the standard investment criteria, the power should be exercised". The exception[80] is that the trustees need not obtain such advice if they "reasonably conclude that in all the circustances it is unnecessary or inappropriate so to do"; this would apply where the fund was small and any investment proposed was a comparatively safe one or where one or more of the trustees was competent to give the necesssary advice.

The operative words of the basic rule are "obtain and consider"; the trustees are not therefore bound to follow the advice. Proper advice is defined[81] as "the advice of a person who is reasonably believed by the trustee to be qualified to give it by his ability in and practical experience of financial and other maters relating to the proposed investment". Since the enactment of the Financial Services Act 1986 (now the Financial Services and Markets Act 2000) the adviser must now be licensed anyway although the trustees must bear in mind that not everyone licensed under that legislation will necessarily be qualified to advise as to the particular circumstances of their trust. Although written advice is not actually required, trustees will be well advised to require any advice to be put into writing and also to minute whatever decisions they take as a result of receiving it.

---

[78] *Nestlé v. National Westminster Bank* (1988) unreported but transcribed in (1996) 10 Trust Law International 112.

[79] In s.6(3), (5).

[80] Trustee Act 2000, s.5(3).

[81] *ibid.* s.5(4).

## 3. Express Investment Clauses

When statutory powers of investment were restricted, as they were until the enactment of the Trustee Act 2000, clauses in trust deeds expressly enlarging the trustee's powers of investment beyond the scope authorised by law were extremely common. Historically such clauses tended to be construed strictly.[82] It is debateable to what extent this attitude to construction was adopted in practice in the decades immediately prior to the enactment of the Trustee Act 2000 anyway but, since the enactment of that legislation, it is certainly arguable that express investment clauses should be given a liberal interpretation.

The following illustrations from the case law manifest the different approaches, one from the late nineteenth century and the others from the present day. In *Bethell v. Abraham*,[83] trustees were given power to "continue or change securities from time to time as to the majority shall seem meet". This clause was strictly construed by Jessel M.R., who held that the words related merely to determining the time at which a change of securities was to be made; they did not authorise a substantive change of investment outside the range of investments which were authorised. This case may be compared with the more recent decision in *Re Harari's Settlement Trusts*,[84] where the clause empowered the trustees to invest "in or upon such investments as to them may seem fit"; Jenkins J. held that there was no justification for implying any restriction on these words and that the trustees were consequently able to makes investments outside the range of investments which were authorised. A similarly liberal result was arrived at in *Re Peczenic's Settlement Trusts*,[85] where the trustees were authorised to make such investments in "any shares stocks property or property holding company as the trustees in their discretion shall consider to be in the best interest of" the beneficiary. Buckley J. held that the trustees were authorised to invest in anything of these types which was properly able to be treated as an investment but not to invest merely on personal security, which was clearly not within the list. These illustrations appear to manifest different attitudes to investment clauses in the modern law; however, the true position seems to be that it is entirely a question of construction of the particular investment clause before the court and that, although previous cases may be helpful, they will not necessarily be decisive.[86]

In the light of the present statutory powers of investment, use of express investment clauses is no longer as necessary. However, there is little doubt that trusts *inter vivos*, as distinct from wills, will continue to utilise one of the well-known model clauses giving the trustees even more unrestricted investment powers than the statutory powers. In particular such powers are necessary for investment in non-income producing investments and, probably, on personal credit; they are also advisable if a settlor wishes trustees to be able to retain particular investments, such as shares in his own or his family

---

[82] *Re Peczenic's Settlement Trusts* [1964] 1 W.L.R. 720 at 722.
[83] (1873) L.R. 17 Eq. 24.
[84] [1949] 1 All E.R. 430.
[85] [1964] 1 W.L.R. 720.
[86] See also, in addition to the cases cited in the text, *Re Maryon-Wilson's Estate* [1912] 1 Ch. 55; *Re McEacharn's Settlement Trusts* [1939] Ch. 858; *Re Hart's Will Trusts* [1943] 2 All E.R. 557; *Re Douglas' Will Trusts* [1959] 1 W.L.R. 744 (affirmed on another point [1959] 1 W.L.R. 1212); *Re Kob's Will Trusts* [1962] Ch. 531 (interpretation of various investment clauses).

companies, without having to be concerned about their obligation under the second of the standard investment criteria to diversify investments. The Society of Trusts and Estate Practitioners has produced a set of standard administrative provisions which can be incorporated by reference[87]; these are particularly useful for wills where tailor-made provisions are not generally necessary. The Trust Law Committee is also to produce what has been described as a new Table A of Trustees' Powers, which will presumably also be capable of being incorporated by reference. However, it must be emphasised that the statutory duty of care applies just as much to the exercise of express powers of investment as it does to the statutory powers of investment.

### 4. Types of Investment

It has already been seen that, when any investment is contemplated, the trustees will have to give due consideration to the interest of all the beneficiaries and will have to hold the balance equally between them; the trustees will also have to consider advice and comply with the standard investment criteria, particularly the need for diversification of investments. Before the trustees can adequately do any of these things, they must have some knowledge of the characteristics of the different types of investment.

**(A) Securities**
Investments in stocks, shares and bonds are colloquially termed "securities" but that term is somewhat dangerous; a "security" in this sense is not necessarily "secure".) The points to consider with any investment are, *inter alia*:

(a)  whether or not that investment is a "fixed-interest" security;

(b)  whether or not the capital value will fluctuate; and

(c)  if the capital value will fluctuate, in what way such fluctuation is likely.

If a security is a "fixed-interest" security, the amount of interest or dividend which is produced will never alter. Trustees who buy £10,000 Treasury 8.5 per cent Stock 2005 know that, whatever happens to the economic state of the nation, they will receive £850 per annum income. On the other hand, if they invest in ordinary shares of commercial companies, known as "equities", they do not know what they will receive, for this will depend entirely on the amount of the dividend which the companies in each year decide to pay. In bad years the companies may pay nothing, but in other years they may pay a larger amount than any fixed-interest security.

As regards capital value, there are only a few types of security where there will be no fluctuation. This will only occur where such securities are purchasable solely from the Government or other persons issuing them and are

---

[87] These can be found in Kessler, *Drafting Trusts and Will Trusts*, which also contains, among the administrative provisons of the precedents of different types of trusts, a rather more detailed model investment clause (it is particularly important always to use the most recent edition of this work; the current one is the 6th (2002) edition).

not bought and sold among private individuals. The best known examples are National Savings Certificates, which may be bought over the counter of the Post Office or Trustee Savings Bank, and some bonds issued by local authorities.

By contrast, the capital value of all other securities, whether of the Government, local authorities, or commercial undertakings dealt with on a stock exchange, will fluctuate. To understand the terminology used in connection with this fluctuation, it is necessary to distinguish between the nominal price of an investment and its market price. The nominal price is the value of the investment as named on its face and at which, usually, it was originally issued. The market price is the price at which that security can for the time being be purchased. Suppose that the Government issued in 2000 a new stock which carries interest at £8 per cent and that a person then purchased from the Government a holding of £100 of the stock for £100 cash. Suppose also that in 2003 someone buys that holding on the Stock Exchange for £120 cash. The purchaser would be described as buying that holding of £100 nominal stock for a market price of £120. The interest, of course, is always calculated on the nominal value and so, however much the market price alters, the amount of interest will always be the same. When a security is bought for the same amount of cash as its nominal value, as in the example just given of the purchase in 2000 of £100 nominal stock for £100, that security is said to be bought at "par".

The other term which is used in this context is "yield". This is the amount of income from a security expressed as a percentage of the market price paid for it and not of its nominal price. So if £120 cash is paid for £100 nominal £8 per cent stock, as the interest is fixed at £8 per annum the yield is:

$$\frac{8}{120} \times 100 = \text{£6.67 per annum}$$

More precisely, the "yield" as just described is the "interest only" or "flat" yield. Where an investment is purchased at less than its nominal value but will be redeemed at its nominal value, its "redemption yield" may also be calculated. Very broadly, the redemption yield measures the gain to be expected on the redemption of the security together with the income which will be derived.[88]

It must be stressed that there are many factors which will govern fluctuations of market price but, in the case of government securities, there are two in particular. First, there is the general level of interest rates obtainable elsewhere. If the normal yield at any time is £10 per cent from investments which are considered "safe", the market price of government securities is likely to be adjusted so that that security will produce a yield of about £10 per cent. If the market price were substantially higher, no one would buy the government securities since a safe £10 per cent yield could be obtained elsewhere. The second factor is whether and at what pace inflation (and so, depreciation in the purchasing power of money) is likely to occur. If a period of rapid inflation is forecast, most investors will not favour fixed-interest securities but will choose

---

[88] The redemption yield is, strictly, the amount by which the eventual capital sum which will be obtained on the redemption of the security, together with the income which will arise until redemption, has to be discounted to reduce the security to its present value.

investments from which the return is likely to increase as inflation occurs; thus lack of demand will force down the market value of the fixed-interest securities. An example is the undated 3.5 per cent War Loan stock, which during the last period at which inflation was relatively high (during 1993) had a market value in the region of £38 for each £100 nominal of stock. By 1994, inflation had fallen and so the market value had risen to £58. It was thereafter remained relatively constant (for example its market value during 1998 fluctuated between a low of £55 and a high of £60) until the substantial fall in the prices of equities which took place in 2002, as a result of which in the year to May 2003 its value fluctuated between a low of £65 and a high of £80 (at the time of writing in May 2003 its market value was £75, producing a yield of £4.67 per annum).

In the case of ordinary shares in commercial companies, the yield will also be important and this may be expected to be rather higher than from government securities A commercial undertaking cannot give the capital guarantee which the Government does and the yield is greater to compensate for this; even companies of national standing can become insolvent. But there are two other important factors which influence the capital value of ordinary shares: first, the anticipated ability of the company to pay dividends in the future at least at the rate which it has paid for them in the past; and, secondly, the company's prospects for any increased profits and growth in the future.

### (B) Land

The possible range of investments in land has already been considered.[89] Trustees can both invest in mortgages of land and acquire a legal estate in freehold or leasehold land in the United Kingdom as an investment, for occupation by a beneficiary, or for any other reason.

### (C) Bank Deposits

Bank deposits of course produce no capital appreciation, merely income, and as such are the clearest possible example of an investment which favours the tenant for life at the expense of the remaindermen; nor is the rate of interest paid usually much in excess of inflation save in the case of long fixed term deposits. Where property is held for persons by way of succession, trustees will generally be unwise to leave any more of the trust property on deposit than is likely to be necessary to cover the next few years' anticipated regular payments, such as income tax and professional fees (it is not usually desirable for a trust to have no liquid funds at all since securities may then have to be sold at disadvantageous times in order to fund regular payments of this type). In other types of trusts, such as immediate discretionary trusts, trustees will have a freer hand in this respect but bank deposits should nevertheless still be restricted to a relatively small percentage of the total trust property.

### (D) Non-Income Producing Investments

Non-income producing assets are the exact converse of bank deposits since they can produce only capital appreciation and are the clearest possible example of an investment which favours the remaindermen at the expense of the tenant for life. Such investments are not within any of the statutory powers

---

[89] See *ante*, pp. 598, 599.

of investment; this is because the legal meaning of "investment" is still its traditional meaning, namely an asset which produces income with the connotation that it is likely to produce a surplus on revenue account over the anticipated period of holding of the asset.[90] This means that such investments can only be purchased pursuant to an express investment clause.[91] When property is held for persons by way of succession, trustees will generally be unwise to invest any of the trust property in non-income producing assets except to the extent that the part of the property in question is sufficiently balanced by investments which produce a high rate of income at the expense of capital appreciation. In other types of trust, however, as a result of fiscal legislation it has become more and more prudent in many situations to reduce or eliminate income and instead to seek capital appreciation. Consequently, in general and financial usage, the word "investment" now implies any asset which will produce a good return even if that is entirely in the form of capital appreciation.

The fiscal legislation has produced the following results:[92]

(a) Income, when paid to a beneficiary, is taxable in his hands at the same rate as that at which he pays income tax[93] up to a maximum effective rate of 40 per cent[94] although the trust's administration expenses will always bear tax at the rate at which the sums in question are taxed in the hands of the trustees, which varies according to their source and the nature of the trust.

(b) Where trustees instead accumulate income, that income will be subject to income tax of 34 per cent (25 per cent in the case of company distributions).

(c) Capital gains realised by trustees are always taxable at the rate of 34 per cent; those realised by beneficiaries are taxed at the same rate as that at which they pay income tax.

(d) If the trustees instead hold an asset which never produces income, their liability is to capital gains tax only.

As a result, trustees have increasingly sought to lay out trust funds in the acquisition of non-income, or low-income, producing assets. It must be repeated that this can only be done where there is an express power to this effect in the trust instrument but, where there is such a power, the following are some of the possibilities which have recently found favour.

## (1) Non-income-bearing securities
A number of securities have been developed particularly to meet this need. Under split-level shares and units, one of the two classes carries the entitle-

---

[90] See the reasoning in Cooke v. Haddock (1960) 39 T.C. 64; Johnston v. Heath [1970] 1 W.L.R. 1567.
[91] Re Power [1947] Ch. 572.
[92] See post, pp. 629, 631.
[93] Save that income from company distributions will suffer income tax of 10 per cent (the amount retained by the company) even if the beneficiary himself is not taxable at this rate and so is not basically taxable at all.
[94] Although income from company distributions paid out to a beneficiary of a discretionary trust who pays income tax at 40 per cent will in fact bear a total of 46 per cent income tax.

ment to all income but no capital appreciation and the other class, which is what is acquired by the trust, carries entitlement to all capital appreciation but no income. Under single-premium bonds, a policy of assurance is effected with an insurance company for the payment of one premium only at the outset; on maturity (after a fixed period of years or the earlier death of the assured), the payee receives a sum equivalent to the original premium paid, together with a profit which depends on the success which the insurance company has had in the investment of its funds. In principle, the total proceeds of both securities are received as capital.

### (2) Chattels
A wide variety of chattels have been purchased by trustees as growth investments. Over the last few years trustees have invested in works of art, antique furniture, silver, silver bullion and oriental carpets. Almost invariably these are unsuitable as investments unless the trustees have considerable freedom of choice as to the time of disposal; due to the volatility of the various markets, a period of some years may have to elapse before it becomes a good time to sell.

### (3) Loans to beneficiaries
In some circumstances, it may be thought desirable that capital appreciation should accrue to a beneficiary rather than to the trustees. In such circumstances, the trustees may choose to lend trust funds to the beneficiary, interest free, perhaps securing the loan by taking a charge over the assets which the beneficiary purchases with them. On the death of the beneficiary, the loan is repaid from his estate. However, where this is done, the whole of the capital appreciation accrues to the beneficiary and not to the fund as a whole, so that this will only be proper where it is specifically authorised by the trust instrument or where all the other beneficiaries affected agree.

### 5. *Insider Dealing*

A particular problem arises with regard to "insider dealing". Part V of the Criminal Justice Act 1993 imposes wide-ranging prohibitions on insider dealing. Section 52 provides that a person will be guilty of insider dealing in three situations:

(a) if he deals in securities about which he has unpublished price-sensitive information (a person is defined as dealing in securities if he acquires or disposes of them or procures, directly or indirectly, an acquisition or disposal of the securities by an agent, nominee or other person acting at his direction);

(b) if he encourages another person to deal with the securities, knowing or having reasonable cause to believe that the acquisition or disposal would take place on a regulated market; and,

(c) if he discloses the information, other than in the course of his employment or profession, to another person.

If a person who is a director or other officer of a company and thereby obtains unpublished price-sensitive information about the company, is also a trustee of a trust which holds shares in the company, he is immediately placed in a position of conflict of duty. On the one hand, he must not contravene the Criminal Justice Act 1993, which creates criminal offences. On the other hand, he must do the best he can for the trust.

The previous legislation contained an express provision dealing with the position of such a trustee. Section 7 of the Company Securities (Insider Dealing) Act 1985 provided that a trustee who, in that capacity, dealt in securities was presumed to have done so otherwise than with a view to financial advantage (and so not to have committed an offence) if he acted on the advice of a person who appeared to him to be an appropriate person from whom to seek such advice and did not appear to him to be prohibited by the legislation from dealing in the securities. However, there was no corresponding presumption in relation to the disclosure of the information. The legislation thus appeared to suggest that, where a trustee had obtained inside information, he should obtain advice from the trust's investment advisers about that investment in question, without arousing their suspicions and without disclosing his own information, and that subsequently to act, or to join with his co-trustees in acting, on that advice would not amount to an offence.

There is no provision in the Criminal Justice Act 1993 expressly dealing with the position of trustees. However, section 53 provides that a person will not be guilty of either dealing or encouraging dealing if he shows that he would have done what he did even if he had not had the information (as in the previous legislation, the defence does not apply to disclosure). The Economic Secretary to the Treasury[95] explained in Standing Committee that this defence "allows a trustee who possesses insider information to deal in price-affected securities on the basis of independent investment advice".[96] This suggests that the protection expressly given to trustees by the Insider Dealing Act 1985 has survived, although not explicitly, in the Criminal Justice Act 1993. While the advice to a trustee in this difficult position must therefore remain the same, the fact is that, in many cases where a trustee is known to be in a position in which he is likely to be able to obtain inside information, it will be impossible for him to seek advice from the trust's investment advisers without arousing suspicion by so doing. In such circumstances, the only prudent course may well be for him to resign his trusteeship.

## VII. THE EMPLOYMENT OF AGENTS

Trustees often wish to engage other persons to assist them in the execution of their trust or the administration of the trust property. Examples are where the trustees consider it appropriate for the trust accounts and records to be kept by a solicitor or an accountant; where particular action requires special skills, such as the type of advice in relation to the investments of the trust which has already been considered; or where particular difficulties arise in the course of the administration of the trust property, as may happen when trust property is situated abroad. Any person appointed by trustees to act on their behalf in the execution of their trust is known as their "agent", although two types of

---

[95] Mr Anthony Nelson.
[96] *Hansard*, June 10, 1993, Standing Committee B, Col. 175.

agents with specific functions, nominees and custodians, are generally known by the latter names.

### 1. *The Trustees' Powers to Appoint Agents*

It is possible that the trust instrument itself may confer on the trustees an effective power for the appointment of agents. However, this is not actually necessary and so is in practice uncommon because of the existence of a general statutory power first created by the Trustee Act 1925 and now contained in the Trustee Act 2000. The powers conferred by the latter Act, which apply to all trusts whenever created,[97] are additional to any other powers to appoint agents conferred on the trustees and are subject to any restrictions or exclusions imposed by the trust instrument.[98] The Trustee Act 2000 confers both a general power to appoint agents similar in scope but different in terms from that which existed under the Trustee Act 1925 and specific powers to appoint nominees and custodians which are entirely novel and were much needed.

The statutory powers enable appointment to be made on such terms as to remuneration and other matters as the trustees may determine but these terms cannot, unless it is reasonably necessary, include either a provision permitting the agent to appoint a substitute, or any exemption clause restricting the agent's liability, or any term permitting the agent to act in circumstances which give rise to potential conflicts of interest.[99] For so long as the agent in question continues to act, the trustees must[1] keep under review the arrangements and the way in which they are working and consider in appropriate circumstances whether there is a need to exercise any power of intervention which they may have; such a power is defined[2] as including a power to give directions as well as a power to revoke the agent's appointment. If the trustees consider that there is a need to intervene, they must do so.

Trustees must exercise their powers of appointment, particularly in relation to the selection of the agent and the terms on which he is to act, and also their duty of review in accordance with the statutory duty of care.[3]

#### (A) The General Power to Appoint Agents

Section 11 of the Trustee Act 2000 confers a general authority for trustees collectively[4] to delegate their delegable functions to agents. Trustees have, as they had under the provision which this replaced,[5] the power to appoint an agent to do an act even if they could readily have done that act themselves.[6] The agent may be one of the trustees,[7] provided that he is not also a bene-

---

[97] Trustee Act 2000, s.27.
[98] *ibid.* s.26.
[99] *ibid.* ss.14, 20.
[1] *ibid.* s.22(1).
[2] *ibid.* s.22(4).
[3] *ibid.* s.1 and Sched. 1, para. 3; see *ante*, p. 573.
[4] The Trustee Act 2000 is not concerned with individual delegation, delegation by individual trustees of their functions as such. This is the subject of the Trustee Delegation Act 1999; see *ante*, p. 571.
[5] Trustee Act 1925, s.23(1).
[6] But see *ante*, p. 571.
[7] Trustee Act 2000, s.12(1).

ficiary, but may not be one of the beneficiaries, whether or not he is also a trustee.[8] Two or more persons may not be authorised to exercise the same function unless they are to do so jointly[9] but it does not matter if the agent is also the nominee and/or the custodian of the trustees.[10]

The Law Commission[11] originally proposed that a distinction should be drawn between administrative powers, which would be delegable even if they involved considerably more than merely ministerial acts, and distributive powers, which would not be delegable. However, it was wisely concluded that such a broad distinction would cause difficulties, particularly in the case of powers to appoint and replace trustees which the Law Commission considered should not be delegable in the absence of express authority in the trust instrument. Section 11 therefore contains a general power to delegate under which "the trustees of a trust may authorise any person to exercise any or all of their delegable functions as their agent".[12] This is followed by a list of delegable functions which differs depending on whether or not the trust in question is charitable.

Section 11(2) provides that, in the case of a trust which is not a charitable trust, any function is a delegable function except the following four types:

(a) "any function relating to whether or in what way any assets of the trust should be distributed" (these functions are of course true dispositive discretions or powers);

(b) "any power to decide whether any fees or other payment due to made out of the trust funds should be made out of income or capital";

(c) "any power to appoint a person to be a trustee of the trust" (it was presumably concluded that any power to remove trustees would not be likely to be vested in any or all of the existing trustees); or

(d) "any power conferred by any other enactment or the trust instrument which permits the trustees to delegate any of their functions or to appoint a person to act as a nominee or custodian".

On the other hand, section 11(3) provides that, in the case of a charitable trust, only the following functions are delegable:

(a) "any function consisting of carrying out a decision that the trustees have taken" (purely ministerial functions);

(b) "any function relating to the investment of assets subject to the trust (including, in the case of land held as an investment, managing the land and creating or disposing of an interest in the land)";

(c) "any function relating to the raising of funds for the trust otherwise than by means of profits of a trade which is an integral part of car-

---

[8] *ibid.* s.12(3).
[9] *ibid.* s.12(2).
[10] *ibid.* s.12(4).
[11] Law Com. No. 260 (1999), *Report on Trustees' Powers and Duties*, Part IV.
[12] Trustee Act 2000, s.11(1).

rying out the trust's charitable purpose" (defined[13] as a trade[14] whose profits are applied solely for the purposes of the trust where either "the trade is exercised in the course of the actual carrying out of a primary purpose of the trust" or the relevant work is mainly carried out by its beneficiaries); and

(d) "any other function prescribed by an order made by the Secretary of State" exercisable by statutory instrument subject to parliamentary review.[15]

Where an agent is authorised to exercise a function which is itself subject to specific duties or restrictions, such as the requirement to have regard to the standard investment criteria when exercising any power of investment,[16] he is subject to those duties or restrictions[17] unless the latter relate to the obtaining of advice and he is a person from whom it would be proper for that advice to have been obtained.[18] However, an agent is not obliged to carry out the consultations with beneficiaries of full age with interests in possession in land held by the trust which are envisaged by the Trusts of Land and Appointments of Land Act 1996[19]; on the other hand, the terms of any delegation of functions relating to land held by the trust must not prevent the trustees from themselves complying with their duty to carry out such consultations.[20]

Special provisions[21] apply to agents who are to exercise asset management functions, which are defined[22] as the investment of trust assets, the acquisition of trust property, the management of trust property, and the disposal of, or the creation or disposal of an interest in, trust property (this broad definition goes well beyond pure investment management). The agreement with the agent must be in, or be evidenced in, writing[23] and must include a term to the effect that the agent will secure compliance with a written policy statement, or any revisions to it, prepared in advance by the trustees giving guidance as to how the agent's functions should be exercised; the guidance must be formulated with a view to ensuring that the agent will exercise his functions in the best interests of the trust.[24] The trustees' general obligation[25] to keep under review the arrangements and the way in which they are working specifically includes[26] a duty to consider whether there is any need to revise or replace the policy statement, a duty to revise or replace it if they consider that this is necessary, and a duty to assess whether the policy statement is being complied with.

---

[13] *ibid.* s.11(4).
[14] Whether or not it is carried on in the United Kingdom.
[15] Trustee Act 2000, s.11(4).
[16] See *ante*, p. 602.
[17] Trustee Act 2000, s.13(1).
[18] *ibid.* s.13(2).
[19] *ibid.* s.13(5). Such consultations are discussed *ante*, p. 601.
[20] *ibid.* s.13(4).
[21] *ibid.* s.15.
[22] *ibid.* s.15(5).
[23] *ibid.* s.15(1).
[24] *ibid.* s.15(2)–(4).
[25] *ibid.* s.22(1).
[26] *ibid.* s.22(2).

## (B) Nominees and Custodians

Until the enactment of the Trustee Act 2000, trustees had no statutory power to appoint nominees and custodians. The lack of any such power, in the absence of any provision to this effect in the trust instrument, was extremely inconvenient in the light of modern investment practices whereby securities are almost invariably held by nominees in order to facilitate rapid sales. The Trustee Act 2000 has now conferred on trustees:

(a) a power to appoint a nominee in relation to such of the assets of the trust other than settled land as they determine and take such steps as are necessary to secure that those assets are vested in him[27];

(b) a power to appoint a custodian, defined as someone who undertakes the safe custody of assets or of any documents or records concerning them, in relation to such of the assets of the trust as they determine[28]; and,

(c) where the trust property includes bearer securities, a duty to appoint a custodian of those securities, unless the trust already has a custodian or the trustees are exempted from complying with this requirement by the trust instrument or by any statutory provision.[29]

In all three cases, the appointment must be made in, or be evidenced in writing. The person appointed must[30] either carry on a business which consists of or includes acting as a nominee or custodian, or be a body corporate controlled by the trustees, or be an incorporated solicitors practice[31] (charitable trustees must additionally act in accordance with any guidance given by the Charity Commissioners). The nominee or custodian may be any trustee who is a trust corporation or two or more trustees acting jointly (contrary to the position for agents, there is no prohibition on them also being beneficiaries). It does not matter if the person appointed is both nominee and custodian and/or also an agent of the trustees.

### 2. The Liability of Trustees for the Acts or Defaults of Agents

Prior to the enactment of the Trustee Act 2000, the law governing the liability of trustees for the acts or defaults of their agents was a matter of some controversy due to doubts as to the correct interpretation of the now repealed section 30 of the Trustee Act 1925 and due to the existence of inconsistencies between that section, no matter how it was interpreted, and the equally repealed section 23(1) of the Trustee Act 1925. However, the Trustee Act 2000 simply provides[32] that a trustee is not liable for any act or default of any agent, nominee or custodian unless he has failed to comply with the statutory duty of care applicable to him[33] "when entering into the arrangements under which

---

[27] ibid. s.16.
[28] ibid. s.17.
[29] ibid. s.18.
[30] ibid. s.19.
[31] Under Administration of Justice Act 1985, s.9.
[32] Trustee Act 2000, s.23(1).
[33] Under ibid. s.1 and Sched. 1, para. 3.

the person acts as agent, nominee or custodian" or when carrying out the duties to keep under review those arrangements and the way in which they are working which have already been considered.[34] Where, unusually,[35] the trustee has agreed a term under which the agent, nominee or custodian can appoint a substitute, the trustee will similarly not be liable for any act or default of the substitute unless he has failed to comply with the statutory duty of care applicable to him[36] "when agreeing that term" or when carrying out his duties of review.[37]

There are as yet no reported cases on these provisions but an authority on the pre-existing common law duty to use the diligence and care of an ordinary prudent man of business whose facts remain relevant is *Fry v. Tapson*.[38] Trustees were prepared to lend trust money on mortgage, as they were entitled to do; however, instead of exercising their own judgment as to the valuer to be appointed, they relied on the advice of their solicitors. The surveyor chosen in fact was the agent of the potential mortgagor and had a financial interest in the transaction being completed. The money was lent and, when loss occurred, it was held that the trustees were bound to make it good. They would not have been made liable if they had made an independent choice of the agent themselves. This is an example of a decision which the trustees ought themselves to have made, an act which could not properly be delegated, and it is inevitable that trustees who acted in this way today would be held to have breached their statutory duty of care.

## VIII. PAYMENTS TO BENEFICIARIES

The general principle is that a trustee is absolutely responsible for ensuring that the right amount is paid to the right beneficiary. In *Eaves v. Hickson*,[39] trustees were provided with a forged marriage certificate which led them to believe that certain children were legitimate and consequently beneficiaries; they therefore paid the trust funds out to them. The trustees were nevertheless held liable to make good to the rightful beneficiary so much of these funds as could not be recovered either from the children or from their father, who had provided the forged certificate. Similarly, where trustees pay trust money to the wrong beneficiary, on an erroneous but bona fide construction of the trust instrument[40] or simply because they assumed that its provisions were valid when they were in fact void for uncertainty,[41] they will be held liable to make good the loss. Where the trustees have in the particular circumstances acted honestly and reasonably and ought fairly to be excused, the court has a discretion to grant them relief,[42] but this does not alter the trustees' primary obligation of ensuring payment to the right beneficiary.

---

[34] See *ante*, p. 612.
[35] This is only possible where it is reasonably necessary; Trustee Act 2000, ss.14(2), 20(2).
[36] *ibid*. s.1 and Sched. 1, para. 3.
[37] *ibid*. s.23(2).
[38] (1884) 28 Ch.D. 268.
[39] (1861) 30 Beav. 136.
[40] *Hilliard v. Fulford* (1876) 4 Ch.D. 389.
[41] See the facts which gave rise to *Re Diplock* [1948] Ch. 465.
[42] Trustee Act 1925, s.61; see *post*, p. 789.

Where there is any doubt as to who is entitled to trust property, the trustees should apply to the court for directions in the manner discussed later in this chapter. They will then be protected if they comply with whatever directions the court gives. If the beneficiary entitled cannot be traced, the trustees may pay the money into court, and so obtain a good discharge for it. And where one of several beneficiaries cannot be traced, the court may authorise the trustees to distribute the trust fund as if the beneficiary who cannot be traced were dead.[43] Nevertheless, the court is keen to discourage trustees from making payment into court of trust money where there is no good reason for doing so; the trustees can therefore be made personally liable for the costs of the application for payment in. The power of payment into court is one of the exceptional cases in which the wishes of the majority of the trustees binds them all. The court equally discourages applications by trustees for protection where they incur no practical risk at all. Thus, in Re Pettifor,[44] Pennycuick J. said that, in normal circumstances, the court would consider it an unnecessary waste of money for trustees to come to court and ask for permission to distribute a trust fund on the basis that a woman of 70 would not have a further child.

When making distributions, trustees must remember that beneficial interests under the trust can be assigned or charged. Where an assignee makes a claim to trust property, the trustees will, before making payment, have to investigate his title to the interest assigned; however, they will be obliged to give effect to effective assignments.

Before finally distributing the trust property, the trustees must take care to discharge all its debts. In most cases of long-standing trusts, there cannot be any debts due from the trust of which the trustees are unaware. However, where there is a possibility of outstanding debts, advantage should be taken of section 27 of the Trustee Act 1925. Under this section, the trustees may advertise in the London Gazette, and usually also in another newspaper, their intention of distributing the trust fund to the beneficiaries and requiring persons interested in the trust fund to send them notice of their claim. Any such claims must be sent in within the time fixed by the notice, which must not be less than two months after it is published. At the expiration of that time, the trustees can safely distribute the trust fund after discharging only those claims of which they have notice. If a creditor subsequently comes forward, he may in appropriate circumstances be able to follow the trust property into the hands of the beneficiaries to whom it has been distributed; however, he will have no remedy against the trustees themselves.

Finally, when a trusteeship comes to an end, the trustees are entitled to put themselves into the position in which no further disputes can be raised about payments to the beneficiaries. To achieve this, they are entitled to present their final accounts to the beneficiaries and to require them to give a formal discharge from the trusteeship. If the beneficiaries refuse, the trustees may have the accounts taken in court, that is, examined by an official of the Chancery

---

[43] The so-called "Benjamin Order"; see Re Benjamin [1902] 1 Ch. 723, Re Taylor's Estate [1969] 2 Ch. 245; Re Lowe's Will Trust [1973] 1 W.L.R. 882 at 887; Re Green's Will Trust [1985] 3 All E.R. 455; Re Evans (deceased) [1999] 2 All E.R. 777.

[44] [1966] Ch. 257.

Division, at the expense of the trust fund and in that way obtain confirmation that those accounts are in order.

## IX. PAYMENT OF TRUSTEES' EXPENSES

It will be seen in a later chapter[45] that, in the absence of a provison in the trust instrument permitting a trustee to be paid for his services, only trust corporations and trustees who act in the course of a profession or busines which consists of or includes the management or administration of trusts are entitled to be paid for their services. Trustees are, however, entitled to be reimbursed all expenses which have been properly incurred (however, they are not normally entitled to interest thereon). This right of reimbursement is in respect both of money actually spent by the trustee and of liabilities which he has incurred. Thus in *Benett v. Wyndham*,[46] a trustee of an estate directed woodcutters employed on the estate to fell some trees. The woodcutters were negligent and allowed a bough to fall on a passer-by who was injured. The trustee, as legal owner of the estate, was sued and he was allowed to reimburse himself the damages out of the trust fund. However, it does not follow that a trustee will be allowed all his expenses; they must be reasonable and proper in all the circumstances. In *Malcolm v. O'Callaghan*,[47] an ingenious trustee made a number of journeys to Paris to be present at the hearing of a case in the French courts which concerned the trust, but which turned solely on a question of French law and for which the trustee's presence was in no way necessary. He was not allowed his expenses against the trust.

Trustees are obviously entitled to be reimbursed the expenses of properly taking or defending legal proceedings on behalf of the trust in the same way as other expenses. However, it is generally prudent for trustees, before taking or defending proceedings, to apply to the court for its approval in the manner discussed below. If they do not do so and the proceedings are unsuccessful, it will be up to them to prove that they had reasonable grounds for taking or defending proceedings; if they cannot prove this, they will be deprived of their costs (and for that matter may well finish up paying the costs of the other side as well).

The trustees' right of indemnity is generally against the trust property,[48] not against the beneficiaries. If, therefore, the trustees' right of indemnity exceeds the value of the trust property, they will not normally be able to claim the balance from the beneficiaries personally. The right of indemnity can, however, be enforced against a beneficiary personally in three circumstances: first, where the beneficiary in question was the creator of the trust;[49] secondly, where the trustees accepted the trust at the request of a beneficiary;[50] and, thirdly, where the trustees are nominees.[51]

---

[45] See *post*, p. 721.
[46] (1862) 4 De G. 7. & J. 259.
[47] (1835) 3 Myl. & Cr. 52.
[48] Trustee Act 2000, s.31(1).
[49] *Matthews v. Ruggles-Brise* [1911] 1 Ch. 194.
[50] *Jervis v. Wolferstan* (1874) L.R. 18 Eq. 18 at 24.
[51] *Hardoon v. Belilios* [1901] A.C. 118.

## X. APPLICATIONS TO THE COURT

There are a number of circumstances in which it is appropriate for trustees to seek the guidance of the court. Such applications to the court used to be made by way of originating summons but, since the introduction of the Civil Procedure Rules 1998, they are instead made by application under Part 23 of those Rules.

### 1. *Applications by way of Construction Summons*

One of the most common grounds on which trustees apply to the court is in order to determine the proper construction of words in a will or settlement whose meaning is uncertain; such applications have traditionally been known as a "construction summons" and this expression has survived despite the fact that what is now made is an application rather than a summons. This process requires all those persons who could conceivably be beneficiaries according to any of the possible constructions of the documents in question to be joined as defendants; they may or may not choose to take any part in the proceedings but the fact that they have been joined ensures that they will be bound by the judgment of the court whether or not they actually appear.[52]

### 2. *Applications for Directions*

Where trustees are in doubt as to the manner in which they should act, they may make an application to the court for directions. Provided that the trustees place before the court all the relevant facts and subsequently act in accordance with the court's directions, it is an established principle that they will be absolutely protected. Indeed, where a trust has a large number of beneficiaries, such an application may be necessary prior to an application being made by way of construction summons in the manner explained above so that the court can appoint a number of representative beneficiaries[53] to argue in favour of the different possible constructions of the relevant documents; the court can, if necessary, also specify the particular issues which are to be determined.[54] But this is only one of the examples of the situations in which trustees may make an application for directions.

Such an application was made in *Re Londonderry's Settlement*[55] for directions as to whether the documents sought by the beneficiary ought to be disclosed. At first instance Plowman J. decided that they ought to be. The trustees appealed, successfully in the event, but the Court of Appeal nearly refused to hear the appeal. Harman L.J. observed that it seemed to him that the appeal was "an irregularity" on the basis that "trustees seeking the protection of the court are protected by the court's order and it is not for them to appeal".[56] There is little doubt that, had the trustees acted under what turned out to be the erroneous decision of Plowman J., they would have been protected. But if they considered the decision both wrong and adverse to the interests of the

---

[52] See *Russell-Cooke Trust Co. v. Prentis* [2003] 2 All E.R. 478 at 482–483.
[53] Under Civil Procedure Rules 1998, Pt. 19.
[54] The court did both in *Russell-Cooke Trust Co. v. Prentis* [2003] 2 All E.R. 478; see at 482–483.
[55] [1965] Ch. 918.
[56] *ibid.* at 930.

beneficiaries, as they did, why should they not have been entitled to appeal? It is particularly ironic that this statement on the part of Harman L.J. should have been made in a case where, because the trustees did appeal, the law was patently improved for the benefit of all trustees. Fortunately Salmon L.J. took a different view, saying[57] that in his view the trustees were "fully justified in bringing this appeal" and that "it was their duty to bring it since they believed, rightly, that an appeal was essential for the protection of the general body of beneficiaries". What is remarkable is not that Salmon L.J. made this statement but that he had to make it in the first place.

However, his remarks unfortunately introduced a further difficulty. It might have been thought that permitting the trustees to appeal in *Re Londonderry's Settlement*,[58] would simply have established the principle that, in the event that trustees apply to the court and are given a decision which is wrong, they may appeal. But, according to Salmon L.J., they must appeal; in other words, they have a duty to do so. As a result it may one day have to be decided to what extent trustees are protected if they act in accordance with a decision of the court which they believe to be clearly wrong. The general view, encapsulated by the remarks of Harman L.J., is that they would be protected; however, this does not square with the enunciation by Salmon L.J. of a duty to appeal in such circumstances.

### 3. *Applications for a "Beddoe Order"*

One of the most important situations from the point of view of trustees in which it will be necessary for them to apply to the court is in relation to taking and defending legal proceedings on behalf of the trust. This is because of the risk that, in the event that the proceedings are unsuccessful, a challenge may be made to the propriety of their conduct with the consequential risk that they may have to pay out of their own pockets not just the costs incurred by the trust but any costs awarded by the court to the other party. Trustees will be at risk if they act without either the consent of all the beneficiaries, which is only feasible if all are ascertainable and *sui iuris*, or pursuant to the directions of the Chancery Division of the High Court. An application of this type is known as an application for a "*Beddoe* Order".[59]

Such an application is made in separate proceedings, to which all the beneficiaries, or representative beneficiaries, have to be joined; full disclosure must be made in order to enable the court to form a view on the prospects of success of the claim or defence and therefore determine what ought to be done in the best interests of the trust.[60] Where a *Beddoe* Order is obtained, the trustee

---

[57] *ibid.* at 936.

[58] [1965] Ch. 918.

[59] After the case of *Re Beddoe* [1893] 1 Ch. 547, in which the Court of Appeal deprived a trustee of the costs of an action for detinue which he had unsuccessfully defended in the Queen's Bench Division and in which an adverse order for costs had been made against him; he was allowed only what it would have cost for him to make what is now known as an Application to the Chancery Division for directions.

[60] *Weth v. The Attorney-General* [2001] W.T.L.R. 155 at 175. The court obviously does not determine the rights of anyone since the other party will not normally be either before the court or indeed aware of the application.

"is entitled to take his costs out of the trust fund on an indemnity basis unless the court otherwise orders and the court can otherwise order only on the ground that he has acted unreasonably in the prosecution or defence of the action or that he failed to make full and proper disclosure at the time when the court's directions were sought".[61] However, a trustee who does not apply for such an order will not necessarily incur personal liability for costs; "he will normally be entitled to his costs out of the trust fund if the court is satisfied that if he had applied for directions he would have been directed to prosecute or defend the proceedings."[62]

The types of proceedings in which it is appropriate for trustees to seek a *Beddoe* Order were considered by Lightman J. in *Alsop Wilkinson v. Neary*.[63] He stated that trustees may be involved in three kinds of dispute[64]:

(a) a dispute as to the trusts on which they hold the subject matter of the settlement, which he called "a trust dispute", which may be:

    (i) "friendly" litigation involving the true construction of the trust instrument or some other question arising in the course of the administration of the trust; or

    (ii) "hostile" litigation involving a challenge in whole or in part to the validity of the settlement;

(b) a dispute with one or more of the beneficiaries as to the propriety of any action which the trustees have taken or omitted to take or may or may not take in the future, which he called "a beneficiaries dispute"; and

(c) a dispute with persons, otherwise than in the capacity of beneficiaries, in respect of rights and liabilities assumed by the trustees as such in the course of administration of the trust, which he called "a third party dispute".

Lightman J. stated that, in the case of a beneficiaries dispute, given that it is ordinary hostile litigation, costs follow the event and do not come out of the trust property; no application for a *Beddoe* Order is therefore appropriate. In the case of a trust dispute, the primary duty of the trustees is to remain neutral and offer to submit to the order of the court, leaving it to the rival contenders to fight their battles, in which case they will be entitled to the costs necessarily and properly incurred in so doing out of the trust property;[65] again no application for a *Beddoe* Order is therefore appropriate. But if the trustees instead choose to take an active part in a trust dispute and win, then they may

---

[61] *McDonald v. Horn* [1994] P.L.R. 33 at 40.
[62] *ibid.*; see also *Weth v. The Attorney-General* [2001] W.T.L.R.155 at 175.
[63] [1996] 1 W.L.R. 1220.
[64] These categories were a development of the categories enunciated by Kekewich J. in *Re Buckton* [1907] 2 Ch. 406 at 413–415, which had been approved by the Court of Appeal in *McDonald v. Horn* [1995] 1 All E.R. 961, a case which actually concerned costs incurred by beneficiaries in such proceedings.
[65] This is what occurred in *Merry v. Pownall* [1895] 1 Ch. 306.

be entitled to their costs out of the trust property;[66] but, if they lose, then[67] save in exceptional circumstances,[68] they will not be entitled to their costs.[69] Consequently, trustees who choose to take an active part in a trust dispute will need to consider protecting themselves by applying for a *Beddoe* Order. They will always need to do so in the case of a third party dispute.

### 4. Applications under Section 57 of the Trustee Act 1925

When trustees wish to effect any sale, letting, charge, or any other disposition of trust property, or wish to purchase property or make an investment with trust money and have no power to do so either under the trust instrument or under the general law, they can make an application asking the court to sanction the transaction in question under section 57 of the Trustee Act 1925.[70] The court has jurisdiction to impose any conditions which it thinks fit when approving such a transaction but can only authorise a transaction which is made "in the management or administration" of the trust property. The court has power to give authority under this section only where:

(a)  the trustees propose to do an act not authorised by the general law or by the trust instrument;

(b)  that act is in the management or administration of the trust property; and

(c)  the court thinks that it is expedient to sanction it.

Section 57 is designed to ensure that the property is administered as advantageously as possible in the interests of the beneficiaries. However, the provision must be considered in conjunction with the general principle that the court will not rewrite a trust; consequently, the power will only be exercised to authorise specific dealings with trust property. In *Boardman v. Phipps*,[71] the trustees held shares in a private company and had the opportunity to acquire further shares, although such acquisition was not authorised by the trust instrument. In litigation in which one of the beneficiaries successfully impugned the subsequent purchase of the same shares by another beneficiary and the trust solicitor, Lord Denning M.R. said in the Court of Appeal[72] that the acquisition of these shares was so clearly in the interest of the beneficiaries that the proper course would have been for the trustees to have applied to the court under section 57 for power to make the purchase. However, only the briefest reference was made to this point in the subsequent appeal to the

---

[66] This is what happened in *In Re Holder, ex parte Official Receiver* (1887) 20 Q.B.D. 43) — of course, although Lightman J. did not actually say so, in normal circumstances the trustees will obtain an order for costs against the losing party.

[67] Particularly in hostile litigation.

[68] Such as those which arose in *Bullock v. Lloyd's Bank* [1955] 1 Ch. 317.

[69] Lightman J. cited *National Anti-Vivisection Society v. Duddington* (1989) *The Times* November 23, 1989, disagreeing with what had been said by Kekewich J. in *Ideal Bedding Co. v. Holland* [1907] 2 Ch. 157 as to trustees having a duty to defend the trust and a right to their costs if the court so decides.

[70] See also *post*, p. 742.

[71] [1967] 2 A.C. 46.

[72] [1965] Ch. 992 at 1020.

House of Lords,[73] because it had formed no part of the pleaded case and had not been mentioned in the argument at any stage.

Section 57 does not authorise rearrangement of beneficial interests but this can be effected in other ways, principally under the Variation of Trusts Act 1958; this possibility is considered in a later chapter.[74]

### 5. Applications as to Trusteeship

Where the intervention of the court is being sought in relation to the appointment or removal of a trustee in the manner discussed in the previous chapter,[75] that will also be done by way of application. This can be made either by one or more of the existing trustees, or by the beneficiaries, or by a statutory regulator who wishes a member of the body which it is responsible for regulating to be replaced as trustee. For example, following an intervention by The Law Society into the practice of a solicitor on the grounds of professional misconduct, an application sometimes has to be made by The Law Society for the removal and replacement of that solicitor as trustee of assets held by him on trust for his clients.[76]

A more unusual application of this type, outside the statutory framework discussed in the previous chapter, was made to the court in *Barker v. Peile*.[77] Several actions had arisen as a result of uncertainty as to who were proper beneficiaries and the court acceded to the wish of the trustee to be relieved of the liability and annoyance of being a trustee. Special circumstances must, however, exist before the court will release a trustee from his obligations in this way.

---

[73] [1967] 2 A.C. 46. Their controversial decision is analysed in detail *ante*, p. 365.
[74] See *post*, p. 741.
[75] See *ante*, pp. 558, 568.
[76] On the basis that the trusts constitute "controlled trusts" as defined by Solicitors Act 1974, s.87; see *Russell-Cooke Trust Co. v. Prentis* [2003] 2 All E.R. 478 at 482–483. No such application is necessary in respect of funds held by the solicitor in his client account on trust for his clients since on an intervention the balance of such accounts vests directly in The Law Society under Solicitors Act 1974, Sched. 1, Pt. I, para. 6 (this Schedule contains the provisions governing such interventions).
[77] (1865) 2 Dr. & Sm. 340.

CHAPTER 15

# THE TAXATION OF A TRUST

In order to appreciate the contemporary significance of a trust, it is necessary to understand the basic principles of taxation which affect trusts. On the one hand, the prime motive for the creation of the trust may be the mitigation of a family's taxation liabilities.[1] On the other hand, when a trust is already in existence, taxation considerations will weigh heavily with the trustees. These considerations may influence the way in which the trust fund is invested,[2] how the trustees deal with income,[3] and the manner in which they exercise their discretion in respect of capital in favour of beneficiaries.[4] Trustees are concerned with four main taxes:[5]

(a) Stamp duty;

(b) Income tax;

(c) Capital gains tax; and

(d) Inheritance tax.

In particular circumstances, trustees are also concerned with other types of taxation. For example, if they own land, they may be subject to council tax, but these other types of taxation are not considered in this chapter.

## I. STAMP DUTY

Stamp duty is a once-and-for-all tax payable on a variety of different transactions. Where the transaction is one which gives rise to liability to stamp duty, the duty is paid at a stamping office of the Inland Revenue and, on payment of the duty, a stamp is impressed on the document showing the amount of the duty paid. It follows that if a transaction can be effected without any document, such as a purely oral declaration of trust,[6] no question of stamp duty can arise. The possibility of electronic transfers of property, in particular, the system of electronic conveyancing which is envisaged by the Land

---

[1] See *ante*, p. 8.
[2] See, generally, *ante*, p. 592.
[3] See *post*, p. 672.
[4] See *post*, p. 693.
[5] For charitable trusts, see *ante*, p. 444.
[6] See, however, *ante*, p. 101 *et seq*.

Registration Act 2002 but is unlikely to be brought into force for some years yet, obviously casts doubt on the entire premise of stamp duty as presently constituted. The entire tax is at present under review and reforms are inevitable during the lifetime of this edition of this work.

The main inducement to pay stamp duty at present is that a document which ought to have been stamped but has not been cannot be admitted in evidence in any legal proceedings.[7] Further no registrar will register a stampable document which is unstamped because, if he does so, he renders himself liable to a fine.[8] Trustees must therefore insist that a trust deed is properly stamped, because they may at any time have to justify their position, or their acts as trustees, by production in court of that deed; however, stamping is not now normally necessary of documents which actually create trusts.

Technically, an instrument should be stamped before execution but in practice, the Inland Revenue permit stamping within 30 days of its execution without imposing any penalty.[9] Where it is not stamped within that period, the Revenue are entitled to charge, as a condition for stamping the document out of time, the amount of the duty, interest thereon from the end of the 30-day period,[10] and a penalty, which for the first year is limited to £300 but thereafter can be for the whole of the amount of the unpaid duty.[11] In some cases, even though no duty is actually payable, the legislation nevertheless requires the document to be presented for adjudication and in these cases the document is deemed not to have been properly stamped unless it contains a stamp to the effect that it has been adjudicated.[12]

There is no general principle that every document by which every transaction is effected attracts stamp duty; a document is only stampable if it comes within one of the classes of documents specifically mentioned in the Stamp Act 1891. The amount of stamp duty to be paid depends on the class of documents within which it falls; however, the sum payable will be either a fixed duty (usually £5)[13] or an *ad valorem* duty (usually a percentage of the value of the transaction). Where *ad valorem* duty is payable, in the case of shares and securities it will be charged at 50p per £100 or part of £100 (in effect a rate of 0.5 per cent); in the case of all other property, it will be charged at variable rates: in 2003–2004, transactions up to and including £60,000 were exempt; transactions between £60,001 and £250,000 were charged at £1 per £100 or part of £100; transactions between £250,001 and £500,000 at £3 per £100 or part of £100; and transactions above £500,000 were charged at £4 per £100 or part of £100. Any instrument relating to any transaction chargeable at less than the maximum rate must contain a certificate of value, stating that the transaction effected by the instrument does not form part of a larger transaction or series

---

[7] Stamp Act 1891, s.14(4). *Ram Rattam v. Parma Nand* (1945) L.R. 73 Ind.App. 28.
[8] Stamp Act 1891, s.17.
[9] *ibid.* s.15.
[10] *ibid.* s.15A.
[11] *ibid.* s.15B.
[12] *ibid.* s.12.
[13] *ibid.* s.62.

of transactions in respect of which the amount or value or the aggregate amount or value of the consideration exceeds the relevant limit.[14]

It is appropriate to consider liability to stamp duty on the inception of a trust, during the continuance of a trust, and upon its termination.

## 1. *On the Inception of a Trust*

A conveyance or transfer on sale is subject to *ad valorem* duty.[15] A voluntary disposition executed before March 26, 1985 was also subject to *ad valorem* duty "as if" it were a conveyance or transfer on sale.[16] A declaration of trust which, while not voluntary, was not for full consideration was stated to fall within this provision[17] and a voluntary declaration of trust was held to do so;[18] however, a declaration of trust in consideration of marriage was exempt.[19] Consequently, the creation *inter vivos*[20] in writing of a trust of property which could only be transferred by an instrument, such as land, shares, and securities, was subject to *ad valorem* duty, although a transfer of cash was subject only to the fixed duty of (then) 50p. However, this charge to *ad valorem* duty was abolished by the Finance Act 1985.[21] The fixed 50p duty and an adjudication stamp continued to be required until 1987 when these requirements were also removed.[22] The effect of these reforms is that a transfer of property to trustees on trust no longer attracts stamp duty of any kind save in the relatively unlikely case that consideration in money or money's worth is furnished, in which case the transaction will be a transfer on sale and will be subject to the appropriate *ad valorem* duty. However, a declaration in writing by a settlor that he is himself holding property on trust is still subject to the fixed duty (now £5). No stamp duty is ever payable in the case of conveyances, transfers or lettings to a charity.[23]

When a transfer *inter vivos* of property to trustees on trust was *prima facie* subject to *ad valorem* duty, the duty was chargeable on the document by which the beneficial interest was transferred. Many *inter vivos* settlements are created by means of two instruments, one being the trust instrument declaring the terms of the trust and the other being the conveyance or transfer transferring the legal title to the property in question to the trustees. In such a case, the former document was chargeable with the *ad valorem* duty and the latter with the fixed duty. If, therefore, the owner of shares wished to create a settlement of them, he might execute a transfer of the shares to the proposed trustees and then execute the trust instrument; only on the execution of the latter instrument was the *ad valorem* duty payable.

This fact caused a number of attempts to be made to avoid the *ad valorem*

---

[14] The initial £60,000 exemption below which no stamp duty is payable does not apply to shares and securities because it would be too easy to split larger transactions into £60,000 slices.
[15] Stamp Act 1891, Sched. 1.
[16] Finance (1909–10) Act 1910, s.74(1).
[17] *ibid.* s.74(5).
[18] *Martin v. I.R.C.* (1930) 15 A.T.C. 631.
[19] Finance Act 1963, s.64.
[20] No stamp duty is payable on either a will or a grant of representation so that no duty has ever been payable in respect of the creation of testamentary trusts.
[21] s.82.
[22] Stamp Duty (Exempt Instruments) Regulations 1987.
[23] Finance Act 1982, s.129.

duty by creating the trust merely by means of an oral declaration. In a trust of any size, however, this was not convenient because a record of the exact terms of any trust is highly desirable. Accordingly, it became common for a settlor to make an oral declaration of trust in his solicitor's office, with one of the solicitor's secretaries taking a shorthand note of what was said. This would provide a permanent record. Although this device was theoretically justifiable, its efficacy became open to some doubt in view of *Cohen and Moore v. I.R.C.*[24] In that case settlors orally declared that they would hold certain securities upon the trusts declared by a draft deed. Five weeks later, the draft deed was executed. It was held that the verbal declaration and the later deed formed one transaction, so that duty was payable.

A similar device, less open to this sort of objection, would have been for the settlor to make his declaration of trust by recording it with its complicated provisions on tape and for the tape not to be transcribed for a considerable period. A tape would almost certainly not rank as a document under the present law and so *ad valorem duty* would not be exigible.

An extension of these devices was for a three stage operation to occur; first, the settlor would transfer the property to the trustees to hold as his nominees; secondly, he would orally direct them to hold the property on the trusts of the settlement; and, thirdly, the trustees would execute declarations of their acceptance of the settlor's directions. However, this device was struck down by the House of Lords in *Grey v. I.R.C.*[25] on the grounds that the oral direction amounted to a disposition of a subsisting equitable interest and so was void under section 53(1)(c) of the Law of Property Act 1925; consequently, the written declarations of trust transferred the beneficial interests and so were subject to *ad valorem* duty.

Of course, at present none of these devices is necessary but, if *ad valorem* duty is ever reimposed on voluntary dispositions, they will once again become extremely important. However, it is questionable whether these devices would in fact survive in the light of the intervening evolution of the much more stringent attitude towards tax avoidance enunciated in *Craven v. White,*[26] where Lord Oliver stated that, if any pre-ordained series of transactions is in practice always likely to, and in fact does, take place in its pre-ordained order for the sole purpose of tax mitigation, the court can be justified in treating the series as a single composite whole.

Finally, it should be noted that no stamp duty is payable on either a will or a grant of representation so that no duty has ever been payable in respect of the creation of testamentary trusts.

Any stamp duty which is payable on the creation of a trust is the responsibility of the settlor and it is not properly payable out of the trust fund unless the trust instrument contains an express authority for the duty to be paid by the trustees.

### 2. *During the Administration of a Trust*

Where a conveyance or transfer is made without causing any change in the

---

[24] [1933] 2 K.B. 126.
[25] [1960] A.C. 1; see *ante,* p. 103.
[26] [1989] A.C. 398.

beneficial interests, that document *prima facie* attracts only the fixed £5 duty.[27] Accordingly, a deed of retirement or appointment of new trustees, or some other instrument executed in connection with such retirement or appointment, such as a transfer of shares from an old to a new trustee,[28] formerly attracted the payment of this fixed duty.[29] However, by virtue of the Stamp Duty (Exempt Instruments) Regulations 1987, the vesting of property subject to a trust in the trustees on the appointment of a new trustee or in the continuing trustees on the retirement of a trustee is exempt from the fixed £5 duty and does not have to be presented for adjudication; however a certificate should be included in, endorsed on, or attached to the instrument to the effect that it falls within the appropriate category (in the illustration given, category A) of the Schedule to the Regulations.

If the trustees in the course of administration of the trust rearrange the assets, they will be liable to stamp duty on the purchase of assets at the same rate as on a purchase by any individual. This is so notwithstanding that the value of the trust fund is not increased, for stamp duty is payable on each transaction, in this case on the purchase of shares. Stamp duty paid on such purchase documents ranks as part of the cost of the asset for capital gains tax purposes.[30]

One apparent anomaly is that, by virtue of a Practice Direction,[31] when an order is made under the Variation of Trusts Act 1958,[32] an undertaking is given to submit a duplicate of the order for adjudication. At the time when the Practice Direction was made, voluntary dispositions were subject to *ad valorem* duty. Now that this is no longer the case, there seems no good reason for the continuing requirement of adjudication, which should be declared to be redundant.

### 3. On the Termination of a Trust

In normal circumstances no *ad valorem* duty is payable on the termination of a trust, for by that time the beneficiary has become absolutely entitled beneficially with the result that the termination of the trust produces no change in the beneficial interests. The fixed £5 duty is *prima facie* payable but this requirement was in fact removed by the Stamp Duty (Exempt Instruments) Regulations 1987. If, however, the termination comes about as the result of a rearrangement of beneficial interests, the rearrangement formerly constituted a voluntary disposition of a beneficial interest and so was subject to *ad valorem* duty. Thus, in *Platt's Trustees v. I.R.C.*,[33] where a life tenant executed a deed releasing his life interest, thereby accelerating the interest in remainder and enabling distribution of the trust fund, *ad valorem* duty was held to be payable on the deed of release. However, this will clearly no longer be the case unless *ad valorem* duty is reimposed on voluntary dispositions.

---

[27] Stamp Act 1891, s.62.
[28] Stock exchange securities are excluded from the automatic vesting provisions of Trustee Act 1925, s.40; see *ante*, p. 564.
[29] Stamp Act 1891, ss.23(1), 62.
[30] See *post*, p. 633.
[31] [1966] 1 W.L.R. 345.
[32] See *post*, p. 759.
[33] (1953) 34 A.T.C. 292.

## II. INCOME TAX

For the purposes of income tax, and for that matter of capital gains tax and of inheritance tax, trustees are treated as a separate and continuing body of persons.[34] Because trustees constitute a separate body, the liability of the trust to tax is computed without taking into account the trustees' personal tax position. Because trustees constitute a continuing body, the tax liability of the trust is unaffected by any changes in the persons who are from time to time the trustees. For most taxation purposes, therefore, a trust is treated almost as if it had its own separate legal personality.

The taxation of the income of trusts is in many ways more simple than the taxation of income of private individuals, because the various allowances and reliefs which affect the computation of an individual's liability do not apply. In the case of a private individual, the effect of personal allowances is to exempt from income tax the first "slice" of his income,[35] while the next "slice" is taxable at the starting rate of 10 per cent, the next "slice" at the basic rate of 22 per cent, and the residue at the higher rate of 40 per cent[36] (special rules apply to company distributions and bank interest). None of these complications generally applies to trust income, which is chargeable at the same rate whether it is £1 per annum or £100,000 per annum. The relevant principles are as follows:

(a) The whole of the income of the trust is taxable, irrespective of its ultimate destination.[37] Thus, the income of the trust is taxable whether it is paid to beneficiaries, absorbed in administration expenses, or accumulated.

(b) At present trusts other than discretionary trusts pay income tax at 10 per cent when the tax is withheld at source from income arising from company distributions, at 20 per cent when the tax is withheld at source from income arising from bank deposits, and at 22 per cent when the tax is payable by the trustees on income from other sources.[38] The beneficiary entitled to the income has to pay the same tax as he would have had to pay had there not been a trust. This means that non-taxpayers and starting rate taxpayers will be able to recover the excess tax paid, other than the 10 per cent withheld from company distributions; basic rate taxpayers will pay no further tax (the 10 per cent and 20 per cent withheld at source are regarded as satisfying the basic rate of taxation); and higher rate taxpayers will have to pay

---

[34] The principle is assumed but not expressly enacted for the purposes of income tax.
[35] In 2003–2004, an individual was entitled to a personal allowance of £4,615; additional allowances are available to parents, to widows and widowers and pensioners, in respect of dependant relatives and in certain other circumstances. The amounts of these allowances are reviewed annually in each budget.
[36] In 2003–2004, the first £1,960 of taxable income was taxed at 10 per cent, taxable income between £1,961 and £30,500 was taxed at 22 per cent, and taxable income in excess of £30,500 at 40 per cent. The width of the bands and their thresholds are also reviewed annually in each Budget.
[37] The rate at which income tax is paid will vary according to the nature of the income and to whether the trust is discretionary or not; see *infra*.
[38] Income and Corporation Taxes Act 1988, s.686 (as amended by Finance Act 1999).

such further tax as is necessary to bring the overall tax paid up to 40 per cent.

(c) Discretionary trusts have long been used as devices to take income away from taxpayers who are liable to pay income tax at the higher rate. Consequently, the rate of income tax paid by discretionary trusts is at present in principle 34 per cent. This is indeed the rate of tax payable on income arising from all sources other than company distributions (credit being given for the 20 per cent withheld at source on income arising from bank deposits); if any part of that income is distributed to the beneficiaries rather than being accumulated, non-taxpayers, starting rate taxpayers, and basic rate taxpayers will be able to recover the excess tax paid by the trust, while higher rate taxpayers will have to pay 6 per cent further tax to bring the overall tax paid up to 40 per cent.[39]

However, income received by discretionary trusts from company distributions is instead taxed at 25 per cent (15 per cent in addition to the 10 per cent withheld at source). That is all the tax paid if the income is accumulated. But any income which is distributed to beneficiaries rather than being accumulated is subject to further tax on the distributed amount at 34 per cent, in respect of which credit is only given for the 15 per cent already paid by the trustees, not for the 10 per cent withheld at source. This does not prejudice non-taxpayers and starting rate taxpayers, who can recover any excess tax paid by the trustees (other than the 10 per cent withheld at source). But basic rate tax payers will recover only 12 per cent out of the total of 34 per cent paid by the trustees so that income from company distributions paid to them will finish up bearing tax of 29.8 per cent; higher rate tax payers will still have to pay a further 6 per cent so that income from company distributions paid to them will finish up bearing tax of 46 per cent.[40]

Since income arising from company distributions which is received directly by basic rate taxpayers and higher rate taxpayers bears only total tax of 10 per cent and 32.5 per cent respectively, this means that, when such taxpayers receive income from company distributions pursuant to a discretionary trust, that income bears more income tax than would have been the case had the assets in question not been subject to a discretionary trust in the first place (29.8 per cent rather than 10 per cent in the case of a basic rate taxpayer and 46 per cent rather than 32.5 per cent in the case of a higher rate tax payer).

It follows from these principles that all payments of income from the trust to the beneficiaries are paid from a fund which has already been taxed.

---

[39] This will not necessarily enable the recovery of all the income tax paid by the trust because any income expended on administration expenses will not be able to be distributed and so the tax paid in respect of these expenses will not be able to be recovered. However, all administration expenses now have to be set against the 20 per cent tax withheld on bank deposits and so bear tax at the lowest possible rate. See *post*, p. 631.

[40] In all cases administration expenses can be set against the 10 per cent so withheld so that they still bear tax at the lowest possible rate.

Accordingly, with each payment of income, the trustees are bound to issue to the beneficiary a certificate of the tax notionally deducted from that payment. The gross equivalent of the net payment made to the beneficiary (in other words, the net payment plus the tax already paid) is then regarded as part of the beneficiary's total income, and he may then obtain any repayment which is appropriate having regard to his total income other, as has already been said, than the 10 per cent withheld at source on company distributions.

An example may illustrate these principles. Suppose that a trust fund has an income of £6,000 per annum gross, £2,000 of which proceeds from company dividends, £2,000 from bank interest, and £2,000 from other sources (such as rent). The administration expenses are £600 and the trustees are obliged by the trust instrument to accumulate one half of the income and to distribute the other half to a beneficiary who has a fixed interest. The 10 per cent tax withheld at source on the company dividends and the 20 per cent tax withheld at source on the bank interest will be the subject of a tax credit received from the company or bank in question. The trustees will not need to take any action in respect of this income in respect of the half payable to the beneficiary with a fixed interest, although they will have to pay the further tax in respect of the half to be accumulated. However, they will be responsible for all the tax payable in respect of the income from other sources, whether it is taxable at the basic rate of 22 per cent or the discretionary trust rate of 34 per cent. The gross figures of course determine the tax liability of any beneficiary to whom income is distributed.[41] The tax payable is calculated as follows:

| | | |
|---|---:|---:|
| Gross income | | £6,000 |
| *Less:* tax at 10% withheld on company dividends of £2,000 | £200 | |
| tax at 20% withheld on bank interest of £2,000 | £400 | |
| tax at 22% on other income of £2,000 | £440 | |
| administration expenses[42] | £600 | |
| | £1,640 | £1,640 |
| | | £4,360 |
| Net income available for distribution to fixed beneficiary (50%) | | £2,180 |
| Gross income available for accumulation (50%)[43] | | £2,180 |
| *Less:* additional tax to raise to 25% on company dividends | £150 | |
| additional tax to raise to 34% on bank interest | £140 | |

---

[41] For the purposes of the example, the gross figure for dividend income will be used.
[42] Administration expenses are not liable to the higher rates of tax.
[43] The total income available for accumulation before tax is £3,000 (half the total), from which half the administration expenses has to be deducted because these expenses are not liable to the higher rates of tax. Half the tax already paid is attributed to each half of the fund.

| | | |
|---|---|---|
| additional tax to raise to 34% on other income (in each case on 50% of relevant income) | £120 | |
| | £410 | £410 |
| Net income available for accumulation | | £1,770 |

The beneficiary who receives £2,180 net is treated as having received £2,648 from which tax of £468 is treated as having been deducted.[44] Suppose that he has no significant income from other sources and, even with the trust income, his income is insufficient to absorb his personal reliefs so that he will not be liable to income tax, not even at the starting rate of 10 per cent. In these circumstances, he can make a repayment claim and recover from the Inland Revenue £378 of the tax which he has suffered (he cannot reclaim the tax withheld on the company dividends); in order to do this, he will need to produce a certificate of deduction of tax issued by the trustees. The net benefit to him will therefore be £2,558.[45] If, on the other hand, the beneficiary is already paying income tax at the higher rate of 40 per cent, he will equally have received £2,180 and be treated as having received £2,648 from which tax of £468 has been deducted. He is, however, liable to pay tax at the higher rate of 40 per cent. Therefore, his overall tax liability is £1,059.20 (40 per cent of £2,648) and he will consequently have to pay a further £591.20 (£1,059.200 less the £468 treated as having been paid by the trust). The net benefit to him will therefore only be £1,588.20.

These principles produce three general results which trustees need to bear in mind.

(a)  As the whole income of the trust is taxable, liability to tax can only be avoided if non-income-producing assets are held by the trust. An example would be for a trust to purchase pieces of silver or works of art.[46] A more prosaic example is the purchase of National Savings Certificates, which produce no income but are repayable on maturity with a capital bonus. However, such increments will be of a capital nature for all purposes, so that a life tenant will not, in general, be entitled to any part of the bonus.[47] While a trustee must keep tax

---

[44] The expenses of £300 attributable to this half of the income are deducted equally from each source of income, each of which therefore becomes £900. The credit is of 10 per cent in respect of the half of the income from the dividends (£90), of 20% in respect of the bank interest (£180), and of 22% in respect of the half of the income from other sources (£198).

[45] This figure does not equal the total income attributable to this half of the fund (£3,000) because the tax on the company dividends and the tax payable on the administration expenses cannot be recovered.

[46] Provided that the pieces of silver are sold for a figure not in excess of £6,000, no capital gains tax is payable. Trustees hope, therefore, to dispose of the silver at a profit which will attract liability neither to income tax, because the profit is not of an income nature, nor to capital gains tax.

[47] *Re Holder* (1953) Ch. 468. See however *post*, p. 671.

considerations in mind, he must also keep in mind his general obligation to balance the interests of tenant for life and remainderman.[48]

(b) Where trustees have a discretion to accumulate income, they can only accumulate out of taxed income. Accordingly, accumulation is not a method of avoiding income tax completely but, as is shown in a later chapter,[49] in some circumstances it may be appropriate to accumulate income as capital and then to make an advancement of capital.

(c) Trustees will wish to consider the likely taxation result of a distribution of income on the tax position of the beneficiary. If, as in the example given above, the personal tax position of the beneficiary is such that he can make a repayment claim, a distribution of income to him will be clearly advantageous. If, however, the beneficiary is already paying income tax at the higher rate of 40 per cent, the trustees will know that the beneficiary will also have to pay higher rate income tax on any income paid to him by the trust.

If, instead, the trustees have a discretion as to the payment of income, all the income will be taxable at 34 or 25 per cent. Consequently, most tax will be recoverable if the trustees pay as much as possible of the income to the beneficiaries with the lowest personal rate of taxation since they will be able to reclaim at least some of the tax paid by the trust on the sum actually distributed to them.[50] If, on the other hand, all the beneficiaries are paying tax at the higher rate of 40 per cent, no tax will be able to be recovered and the trustees will have to choose between accumulating the income, which will at least restrict their tax liability to the tax already paid, with a view to a subsequent capital distribution, or paying the income to one or more of the beneficiaries on the basis that they will then be responsible for paying further tax on the sum actually distributed to them.

## III. CAPITAL GAINS TAX

The object of capital gains tax is to make a charge on capital gains made either by private individuals or by any body of persons such as trustees as a result of any actual or deemed disposal of an asset *inter vivos*, whether by way of sale, exchange or gift; no charge is made on disposals *mortis causa*.[51] Capital gains tax is imposed on any increase in the value of an asset between the date of its

---

[48] In *Nestlé v. National Westminster Bank* [1993] 1 W.L.R. 1260, the remainderman accused the trustees of allowing the tax interests of the tenant for life to influence unduly their choice of investments. The judgments contain an important discussion of the criteria which trustees should follow (see *ante*, p. 593).

[49] See *post*, p. 693.

[50] The tax paid on any administration expenses will not be able to be recovered since the right of recovery is limited to the income actually received by the beneficiary.

[51] The property of a deceased person is deemed to be acquired by his personal representatives for its market value on the date of his death, thus giving the beneficiaries a "tax-free uplift" in the event that this value is superior to its acquisition value. However, the property of the deceased will of course be potentially liable to inheritance tax and any inheritance tax payable in respect of the settled assets will, in the event that it is chargeable on those assets, have the effect of reducing the "tax-free uplift".

acquisition and the date of its disposal; any decrease in the value of an asset can be set off against future capital gains.

The value of the asset at the date of its acquisition is adjusted to take account of whatever inflation occurred prior to April 6, 1998; however, in the case of an asset acquired before March 31, 1982, its acquisition value is deemed to be its market value on that date[52] so that gains made prior to that date escape tax. Capital gains made after April 5, 1998 are subject to "taper relief", that is to say the capital gain is reduced by a percentage which rises in accordance with the period after that date during which the asset in question has been owned. The percentage differs depending on whether or not the property is business assets. The maximum reduction on business assets is 75 per cent, which is obtained after only two years; the maximum reduction on other assets is only 40 per cent, which is not obtained for ten years.

Capital gains tax is payable at the same rate as income tax[53] on that part of a private individual's capital gains in each year as exceeds his annual exemption of (in 2003–2004) £7,900[54] (there are many other exemptions, including a private individual's main residence,[55] chattels worth less than £6,000,[56] and certain securities).[57] However, trusts enjoy an annual exemption of only half that of a private individual (£3,950 in 2003–2004) and since April 6, 1998 have paid capital gains tax at 34 per cent.[58]

### 1. Trusts to which the Capital Gains Tax Legislation Applies

The basic principle of the trust provisions of the capital gains tax legislation is that property is regarded as "settled property" for the purposes of the capital gains tax legislation whenever it is held on trust.[59] However, there are three situations in which trust property is instead treated as if it were vested in the beneficiaries:[60] first, where a beneficiary is absolutely entitled to the property in question as against the trustees; secondly, where a beneficiary would be absolutely entitled to the property as against the trustees were he not a minor[61] or under some other disability; and, thirdly, where two or more persons jointly are or would be, if one or more of them were not minors or under some other disability, absolutely entitled to the property as against the trustees. These exceptions are interpreted narrowly. In *Tomlinson v. Glyns Executor and Trustee Company*,[62] trustees held property in trust for such of four minor beneficiaries

---

[52] Taxation of Chargeable Gains Act 1992, s.35. From that date, there is a published indexation allowance in respect of the period until April 5, 1998. Thereafter, indexation is irrelevant to private individuals and to trusts (it remains relevant for companies); any reduction in the apparent capital gain is now instead made by means of the "tapering" relief referred to in the text. The latter was introduced by Finance Act 1998, s.119, Sched. 21.

[53] *ibid.* s.4. Hence the rate is either 10 per cent, 22 per cent or 40 per cent.

[54] *ibid.* s.3, Sched. 1 (the exemption is index-linked).

[55] *ibid.* s.222.

[56] *ibid.* s.262.

[57] *ibid.* s.115.

[58] *ibid.* s.1AA inserted by Finance Act 1998, s.120. Until then, trusts other than discretionary trusts paid capital gains tax at the basic rate of income tax (then 23 per cent).

[59] *ibid.* s.68.

[60] *ibid.* s.60.

[61] This means 18 even for a settlement created when the age of majority was 21; see *Begg-MacBrearty v. Stilwell* [1996] S.T.C. 413.

[62] [1970] Ch. 112.

as attained the age of 21 or married under that age. When the trustees disposed of certain investments at a profit, they claimed that the infant beneficiaries were together absolutely entitled to the investments as against the trustees.[63] The Court of Appeal held that their minorities were not the only reason which, at the time of the disposal of the investments, prevented the beneficiaries from being absolutely entitled; their interests were also contingent until they reached the age of 21 or married under that age.

### 2. Capital Gains on the Creation of a Settlement

The creation of a settlement constitutes a disposal of the trust property by the settlor at its market value, even if the settlement is revocable, and whether or not he or his spouse is a beneficiary.[64] If chargeable assets are settled, any chargeable gain will be made by the settlor and capital gains tax will be payable by him in respect of that gain at the same rate as that at which he pays income tax; any chargeable loss[65] will also be made by the settlor but, because he and the trustees are connected persons,[66] that loss will be deductible only from future chargeable gains arising out of subsequent disposals by the settlor to the same settlement. It used to be possible to postpone (technically, "hold over") the payment of the capital gains tax until the property was eventually sold,[67] but this is now only possible if the assets settled comprise business property[68] or if the creation of the trust involves a chargeable transfer for the purposes of inheritance tax.[69]

### 3. Capital Gains on the Disposal of Assets by the Trustees

When a trust is created, the trustees are deemed to acquire the trust property at its market value (or, if acquired before March 31, 1982, at its market value on that date). When an asset is purchased in a transaction at arm's length, the consideration, together with the expenses associated with the purchase, constitute the acquisition value.

Apart from assets which are exempt from capital gains tax, not many of which are likely to be held by trustees apart from a residential property occupied by a beneficiary as his principal residence, any disposition of an asset for a consideration in excess of its acquisition value gives rise to a chargeable gain in respect of the difference. Where the trustees incur expense such as stamp duty, legal costs and registration fees in acquiring an asset and in

---

[63] If the trustees had succeeded in their contention, there would still have been a capital gains tax liability. However, it would have been calculated according to a special basis then in force which was open only to private individuals; see Finance Act 1965, s.21.

[64] Taxation of Chargeable Gains Act 1992, s.70.

[65] For disposals since November 29, 1993 the indexation allowance has not been able to create or increase an allowable loss. Consequently losses are now only chargeable if genuinely incurred.

[66] By virtue of Taxation of Chargeable Gains Act 1992, s.18(3).

[67] Under Finance Act 1980, s.79 (repealed in 1989).

[68] Taxation of Chargeable Gains Act 1992, s.165.

[69] See post, p. 633. It is possible to create a settlement in such a way as to give rise to a very small chargeable transfer and thus enable hold over of the capital gains tax otherwise payable (see Melville v. I.R.C. [2001] S.T.C. 1271); however, this will now only work where the settled property is ultimately to be given to someone absolutely rather than, as in Melville v. I.R.C., held on discretionary trusts (this is the effect of Finance Act 2002, s. 119).

arranging for its disposal, the total of these costs is added to the acquisition value and only the difference is chargeable. As has already been seen, all capital gains made by trusts are now[70] taxable at 34 per cent.

A simple transaction, without taking account of any adjustment to the acquisition cost by virtue of inflation or taper relief, would be:

| | | |
|---|---:|---:|
| Proceeds of sale of shares | | £10,100 |
| *Less:* purchase price | £8,000 | |
| broker's commission on purchase | £100 | |
| stamp duty on purchase | £40 | |
| | £8,140 | £8,140 |
| | | £1,960 |
| *Less:* expenses of sale | | £160 |
| Chargeable gain | | £1,800 |
| Capital gains tax payable: | | |
| 34% of £1,800: | | £612 |

Of course, if this were the only chargeable gain made by the trust during the year in question, it would be within the annual exemption of, at present, £3,950. The tax shown above would therefore only be payable in full if the annual exemption had already been completely used up.

Clearly, the most usual situation in which trustees will incur this type of liability is where they switch assets in the course of the administration of the trust. Equally clearly, the existence of capital gains tax will have an inhibiting effect on such changes of assets.

### 4. *Capital Gains on the Disposal of Interests by the Beneficiaries*

The basic rule is that a disposal by a beneficiary of his beneficial interest under a settlement, whether or not for value, does not amount to a disposal for the purposes of capital gains tax.[71] A disposal other than for value does however constitute a transfer of value for the purposes of inheritance tax. However, the disposal other than for value of future interests in settled property is often crucial for inheritance tax planning precisely because it has no inheritance tax consequences; it is therefore important that such a disposal has no capital gains tax consequences either.

The protection provided by the rule is given to the original beneficiaries of the settlement and to anyone else who acquired the beneficial interest in question other than for money or money's worth (which for this purpose does not include another interest under the same settlement). However, since March 6, 1998, the rule has not applied to any settlement which has ever been non-resident,[72] nor, since March 21, 2000, has it applied to sales by beneficiaries of interests under settlements in which the settlor or the settlor's spouse has, or at any time during the previous two tax years has had, an

---

[70] Until April 5, 1998, capital gains made by trusts other than discretionary trusts were taxable only at the basic rate of income tax (then 23 per cent).

[71] Taxation of Chargeable Gains Act 1992, s.76(1).

[72] *ibid.* s. 76(1B).

interest under the settlement or under settlements whose assets were derived from such a settlor-interested settlement during the previous two tax years.[73] Where the rule does not apply, the disposal of the beneficial interest does amount to a disposal for the purposes of capital gains tax.[74]

## 5. The Exit Charge

When a beneficiary becomes absolutely entitled to an interest in possession in the whole or any part of the trust property, the trustees are deemed to have disposed of the assets in question to him at their market value at that date and he is deemed to have acquired them for their market value at that date.[75] A beneficiary will become absolutely entitled in this sense on fulfilling some contingency, such as attaining the age of 21, or on the determination of a prior interest, or when in other circumstances the trustees make a decision to pay or to transfer the asset to him. The effect of the acquisition of the beneficial interest under a settlement, which is not normally a disposal for the purposes of capital gains tax, may also, when that interest merges with some other interest under the settlement which the acquirer already has, make him absolutely entitled in this sense.[76] An immediate liability to capital gains tax will arise which is payable by the trustees; payment of the tax can be held over only in the limited circumstances already discussed. If the trustees thereafter continue to hold the assets in their name, they will do so as nominees for the beneficiary; in this case, the trust will no longer be a settlement for the purposes of the capital gains tax legislation and the property will be deemed to be held by the beneficiary so that any future liability for capital gains tax will fall on the beneficiary and not on the trustees.

Thus if shares worth £100,000 were settled on trust for the settlor's daughter contingent on her reaching the age of 21, a deemed disposal will take place when she attains that age. If the shares are then worth £120,000, capital gains tax of £6,800 (34 per cent of £20,000) will be payable by the trustees. This will also be the case if the shares were instead held on trust for such of the settlor's children as the trustees might in their absolute discretion determine and the trustees decided to allocate these shares to the settlor's daughter absolutely. If the shares are subsequently sold for £130,000, then, whether they have in the meantime been retained by the trustees or transferred to the daughter, the further capital gain of £10,000 will be attributable to the daughter and she will pay capital gains tax on that gain at the rate at which she pays income tax.

In principle, one beneficiary can become absolutely entitled as against the trustees even though there are other beneficiaries who do not do so. If property is held on trust for such of the settlor's three children as attain the age of 25 and, if more than one of them does so, in equal shares, the membership of the class will become fixed when the eldest child attains the age of 25.[77] If there are then three children, the eldest child will immediately become absolutely entitled to a one-third share in the property even though the younger children

---

[73] ibid. s.76A and Sched. 4A.
[74] The trustees are deemed to dispose of and reacquire the relevant proportion of the trust property.
[75] Taxation of Chargeable Gains Act 1992, s.71(1).
[76] ibid. s.76(2).
[77] Under the class closing rules mentioned ante, p. 248, fn. 59.

are still under 25. If the second child dies under the age of 25, the eldest child will then become absolutely entitled to a further one-sixth share (one-half of the deceased child's presumptive share) and, when the youngest child attains the age of 25, the latter will become absolutely entitled to the remaining half share of the property.[78] However, where the settled property consists of land, it seems that one beneficiary cannot become absolutely entitled if the other beneficiaries do not also do so.[79]

Special rules apply when a beneficiary becomes absolutely entitled as the result of the determination of a prior life interest because of the death of the life tenant. Although there is still a deemed disposal by the trust and a deemed acquisition by the beneficiary, no capital gains tax will be payable because of the basic principle that no charge to capital gains tax is made on disposals *mortis causa*.[80] The absolutely entitled beneficiary will therefore acquire the trust property at its market value on the date of the death of the life tenant. There may, however, be inheritance tax liability.[81] The only exception to this rule is where the settlor has held over the payment of the capital gains tax payable on the creation of the settlement; in this case, the capital gains tax becomes payable on the death of the life tenant.[82]

## 6. Where a Settlement Continues

Where on the determination of a prior interest a settlement continues without any beneficiary becoming absolutely entitled, there are no capital gains tax consequences unless the prior interest has determined because of the death of the life tenant, in which case the rules discussed immediately above apply; there will be a deemed disposal and a deemed reacquisition by the trustees, but no capital gains tax will be payable unless the settlor has held over the payment of his own capital gains tax.[83]

Thus, if property is settled on the settlor's daughter until her marriage and subject to that for the settlor's son if he attains the age of 25, the marriage of the daughter before the son has attained the age of 25 will determine her interest; however, the son is still not absolutely entitled and so there will be no deemed disposal until he reaches the age of 25, when capital gains tax will be payable. If, on the other hand, the trust is for the daughter for life and subject to that for the son if he attains the age of 25, the death of the daughter before the son has attained the age of 25 will produce a deemed disposal and reacquisition of the property by the trustees at its market value on the date of the daughter's death but, as before, no capital gains tax will actually be payable until he attains the age of 25.

## 7. Resettlements

The almost inevitable existence of overriding powers of appointment in settlements today means that the trust property can at any time be resettled by

---

[78] *Stephenson v. Barclays Bank Trust Company* [1975] S.T.C. 151; *Pexton v. Bell* [1976] 1 W.L.R. 885.
[79] *Crowe v. Appleby* [1976] 1 W.L.R. 885.
[80] Taxation of Chargeable Gains Act 1992, s.73.
[81] See *post, infra*.
[82] Taxation of Chargeable Gains Act 1992, s.74.
[83] *ibid.* s.72.

the exercise of these powers. However, while the original settlement continues, there will be no deemed disposal for the purposes of capital gains tax unless, as a result of the exercise of the powers, a beneficiary becomes absolutely beneficially entitled as against the trustees to an interest in possession, in which case the exit charge will arise in the manner already discussed.

When, on the other hand, trust property is resettled by being transferred from one settlement to another, the trustees of the second settlement (even if they are the same persons as the trustees of the original settlement) become absolutely entitled as against the original trustees and a deemed disposal for the purposes of capital gains tax will normally occur.[84] However, if a resettlement of this type occurs only as the result of the exercise by the trustees of their overriding powers of appointment under the original settlement, it seems that the exercise of such a special power of appointment will not in itself amount to a resettlement and so there will be no automatic deemed disposal of the property in question;[85] on the other hand, while the exercise of a wider power, such as a power of advancement, will not necessarily amount to a resettlement either, it will have this effect if the new settlement is complete in itself and is sufficiently separate to require no further reference back for any purpose to the original settlement.[86]

## IV. INHERITANCE TAX

Inheritance tax is governed by what is now known as the Inheritance Tax Act 1984,[87] which was subsequently substantially modified by the Finance Act 1986. It is imposed on such part of a person's estate, which for this purpose includes any property disposed of by him other than for value during the seven years immediately prior to his death, as exceeds his lifetime allowance of, at present,[88] £255,000 (the relevant figure, which is raised periodically in line with inflation is generally known as "the nil rate sum" and as comprising what is known as "the nil rate band").[89] The rate of inheritance tax has been 40 per cent for many years.[90]

Certain property is excluded from a deceased's estate for the purposes of inheritance tax.[91] On the other hand, for these purposes, his estate includes any property in which he has, or within seven years of his death has had, an interest in possession. The most straightforward example of this is where the deceased is the life tenant of a settlement, in which case the whole of the capital value of the settled property will be potentially liable to inheritance tax

---

[84] *Hoare Trustees v. Gardner* [1979] Ch. 1.
[85] *Roome v. Edwards* [1981] S.T.C. 96; *Bond v. Pickford* [1983] S.T.C. 517.
[86] *Swires v. Renton* [1991] S.T.C. 490.
[87] It was originally called the Capital Transfer Tax Act 1984 (the tax was re-christened in 1986) and the Act may be cited in either form; in this work it will be cited as the Inheritance Tax Act 1984.
[88] In 2003–2004.
[89] There are also a number of further exemptions, including small gifts of up to £3,000 per annum, gifts between spouses, gifts in consideration of marriage, gifts to charities, and gifts of agricultural or business property.
[90] This has been the case since March 15, 1988; before that there were a number of different rates.
[91] Overseas property held by a person who is not domiciled in the United Kingdom for the purposes of inheritance tax (there is a special definition); reversionary interests; and certain government securities.

on his death.[92] This is not the case where a beneficiary of a discretionary trust is only entitled to income in the event that the trustees decide to exercise a discretion in his favour; he does not have an interest in possession. But once income has been appointed to such a beneficiary, so that he will thereafter receive it each year unless and until the appointment is revoked, he will have an interest in possession in the settled property, even if the appointment is revocable; consequently, if he dies without the appointment having been revoked, the whole of the capital value of the settled property will similarly be potentially liable to inheritance tax. The same distinction now seems also to apply to the situation where a beneficiary of a discretionary trust is in occupation of the trust property.[93]

## 1. Exempt, Potentially Exempt, and Chargeable Transfers

Inheritance tax focuses around the transfer of value, something which occurs whenever a person makes a disposition as a result of which the value of his estate immediately after the disposition is less than it would have been but for the transfer; the amount by which it is less is the value transferred by the transfer.[94] A transfer of value may be exempt, potentially exempt, or chargeable.

The principal example of an exempt transfer is any transfer of any amount between spouses, whether *inter vivos* or *mortis causa*.[95] There are a number of further exemptions. Some are personal, such as gifts of up to £3,000 per donor and £250 per donee per annum, gifts in consideration of marriage of varying amounts up to £5,000,[96] and payments for the maintenance of dependants. Some arise from the nature of the property, namely if it agricultural property, business property, or woodlands. Others are institutional, including gifts to charities, gifts to certain bodies concerned with the preservation of the national heritage or of a public nature, gifts to political parties, and gifts of works of art.

A potentially exempt transfer is any transfer made *inter vivos* by a private individual after March 17, 1986.[97] If the transferor dies within three years of making the transfer, the rate of inheritance tax payable is the same as that chargeable on death; the tax is payable on the value of the property at the time of transfer or the value of the property at the date of death, whichever is the lower; there can therefore be an advantage even if the transferor does not survive for three years. If the transferor dies more than three years but less than seven years after making the transfer, the rate of inheritance tax payable is a proportion of that chargeable on death as a result of the availability of what is known as "taper relief", under which there is a reduction of 20 per cent of the tax for each year or part of a year after the first three that the

---

[92] While the tax is computed on the basis that the settled property forms part of his estate, any tax payable has to be paid by the trustees of the settlement, not by the personal representatives of the life tenant.

[93] See *I.R.C. v. Lloyds Private Banking* [1999] S.T.C. 559, although in that case the beneficiary was held to have a determinable life interest and so clearly had an interest in possession in the property in question.

[94] Inheritance Tax Act 1984, s.3.

[95] *ibid.* s.18.

[96] Depending on the relationship of the donor to the spouses (£5,000 by each parent, £2,500 by each grandparent, and £1,000 by anyone else).

[97] *ibid.* s.3A (introduced by Finance Act 1986, s.101).

transferor has survived. As before, the tax is payable on the value of the property at the time of transfer or the value of the property at the date of death, whichever is the lower. If the transferor survives for seven years after making the transfer, it then becomes an exempt transfer. However, in certain exceptional circumstances, a transfer made *inter vivos* by a private individual is immediately liable to inheritance tax, at half the rate applicable on death (such a transfer is known as an initially chargeable transfer). The tax so paid forms part of the property transferred; consequently, if the transferor pays the tax himself, the transfer must be "grossed up" for this purpose.[98] If the transferor survives seven years, no further inheritance tax is payable but, if he fails to do so, additional inheritance tax is payable in the manner already described. The principal example of an initially chargeable transfer is the creation of a discretionary trust other than an accumulation and maintenance trust.

A chargeable transfer is any transfer made *inter vivos* by a private individual which is either initially chargeable or subsequently becomes chargeable by reason of his failure to survive seven years and any transfer *mortis causa*. Inheritance tax is payable on the value of all chargeable transfers after the first £255,000[99] at 40 per cent in respect of transfers on death or within three years of death, at the appropriate proportion of 40 per cent in respect of transfers made within seven years of but more than three years before death, and at 20 per cent in respect of initially chargeable lifetime transfers. It is therefore necessary to keep a lifetime record of all transfers *inter vivos*: first, because, if any potentially exempt transfer becomes chargeable, any transfers made during the seven-year period preceding that transfer will have to be aggregated with it in order to decide the inheritance tax ultimately payable on that potentially exempt transfer; and, secondly, because any transfers made within the seven years preceding death will have to be aggregated with the estate of the transferor in order to determine the amount of inheritance tax payable in respect of his estate. The presence of potentially exempt transfers makes the calculation of the inheritance tax payable far from straightforward.

A potentially exempt transfer will take effect as a transfer of that type in the event that the transferor has reserved a benefit thereunder; this is for the somewhat obvious reason that he cannot be permitted to enjoy the advantages of making a potentially exempt transfer if he has retained enjoyment of the property in question. Where there is such a reservation of benefit, the property will be regarded as continuing to form part of the transferor's estate unless and until such time as the benefit in question ceases (from which time the seven-year period will start to run) and will be taxed accordingly on his death. The transferor will be treated as having reserved a benefit in two cases:[1] first, where the donee has not, prior to the seven-year period preceding the donor's death (or, if the donor has died within seven years of the gift, at the date of the gift), bona fide assumed the possession and enjoyment of the property; and, secondly, where, at any time during the seven years prior to the donor's death (or, if he dies within seven years of the gift, at any time after the gift), the

---

[98] *ibid.* s.7. Where tax is payable on an immediately chargeable transfer of £100,000 (it may be absorbed by the transferor's nil rate band) and is paid by the transferor in addition to rather than out of the property transferred, the "grossed up" figure will be £125,000 (because 80 per cent of this amount is £100,000), thus producing a tax liability of £25,000.
[99] In 2003–2004.
[1] Inheritance Tax Act 1984, ss.38, 39.

property is not enjoyed "to the entire exclusion, or virtually to the entire exclusion, of the donor and of any benefit to him by contract or otherwise". However, the retention of benefit rules never apply to gifts between spouses and, where property is initially given to a spouse, this exception also extends to contemporaneous gifts of subsequent interests in the same property in favour of persons other than the spouse,[2] although this extension is to be reversed by the forthcoming Finance Act (2003).

## 2. How Inheritance Tax is Calculated

Suppose that a person who has died in 2002–2003, when the nil rate band was £250,000, leaving an estate, other than that part which he has left to his spouse and which is therefore exempt from inheritance tax, of £50,000, made the following *inter vivos* transfers: eight years before his death, when the nil rate band was £150,000, a transfer of £100,000 to his son (a potentially exempt transfer); six-and-a-half years before this death, when the nil rate band was £200,000, first a transfer of £150,000 to trustees on trust for such of his grandchildren as attain the age of 21 (a potentially exempt transfer)[3] and, secondly, a transfer of £300,000 to trustees on discretionary trust for all his descendants (an initially chargeable transfer); and, in the year of his death, a transfer of £200,000 to his daughter (a potentially exempt transfer). At all times throughout this period, the only rate of inheritance tax was 40 per cent (as it has been since March 15, 1988). It is necessary to calculate the inheritance tax payable twice: first, transfer by transfer during the deceased's lifetime; and, secondly, on his death.

(a) The transfers of £100,000 and £150,000 were both potentially exempt so no inheritance tax was payable on either occasion. The transfer of £300,000 was, however, initially chargeable so inheritance tax was payable. At that time, the deceased had not used up any of his then lifetime allowance of £200,000 (the potentially exempt transfers were assumed not to be chargeable and therefore did not have to be aggregated for that purpose); consequently, the first £200,000 of the £300,000 used up that allowance so that inheritance tax was payable at 20 per cent (half the death rate) on the remaining £100,000, thus requiring the immediate payment of £20,000 (it will be presumed that the tax was paid by the trustees of the settlement out of the £300,000 settled — had it been paid by the deceased, the total amount of the transfer would have had to be "grossed up" to take account of the tax). The transfer of £200,000 was also potentially exempt so no inheritance tax was payable then either. Thus the total inheritance tax payable during the deceased's lifetime was £20,000.

(b) By the time of the deceased's death, the potentially exempt transfer of £100,000 made eight years before his death had become exempt. However, all of the other three transfers and the deceased's estate give rise to inheritance tax liabilities which need to be calculated individually in chronological order. The value of these transfers at the

---

[2] *I.R.C. v. Eversden* [2003] W.T.L.R. 893.
[3] Because this was an accumulation and maintenance trust; see *post*, p. 651.

date when they were made is deducted from the nil rate band in full, without giving any credit for any taper relief, before the liability to inheritance tax of the deceased's remaining assets is established. His personal representatives are liable to pay any inheritance tax due in respect of the property which devolves as a result of the deceased's death; any liability in respect of the *inter vivos* transfers falls primarily on the individual transferees but in default also passes to the deceased's personal representatives.

(i)  The potentially exempt transfer of £150,000 made six-and-a-half years before his death is not in fact exempt. During the seven years preceding that transfer, the deceased had made one transfer, that of £100,000. That transfer used up £100,000 of his then lifetime allowance of £200,000. Thus, £100,000 of that allowance remained at that time to offset against the transfer of £150,000. The £50,000 balance is thus liable to inheritance tax. The death rate is 40 per cent but because the deceased survived for six-and-a-half further years, there is a reduction of 80 per cent (20 per cent for each year or part of a year after the first three). Consequently, the inheritance tax payable is 20 per cent of 40 per cent of £50,000, thus £4,000.

(ii)  The initially chargeable transfer of £300,000 made six-and-a-half years before the testator's death has already suffered inheritance tax of £20,000. During the seven years preceding that transfer, the deceased had made two transfers, those of £100,000 and £150,000, which had used up all his then lifetime allowance of £200,000. Thus, the whole of the £300,000 is liable to inheritance tax. The death rate is 40 per cent but because the deceased survived for six-and-a-half further years, there is a again a reduction of 80 per cent (20 per cent for each year or part of a year after the first three). Consequently, the inheritance tax payable is 20 per cent of 40 per cent of £300,000 less the £20,000 already paid, thus £4,000.

(iii)  The potentially exempt transfer of £200,000 made in the year of the testator's death is not in fact exempt. During the seven years preceding that transfer, the deceased had made two transfers, those of £150,000 and £300,000. These used up all his then lifetime allowance of £250,000. Thus, the whole of the £200,000 is liable to inheritance tax. The death rate is 40 per cent and there is no reduction because the deceased did not survive for three years. Consequently, the inheritance tax payable is 40 per cent of £200,000, thus £80,000.

(iv)  The deceased's estate of £50,000, other than the part which he left to his spouse, which is exempt from inheritance tax, is liable to inheritance tax. During the seven years preceding his death, the deceased made three previous transfers, those of £150,000, £300,000, and £200,000. These used up all the lifetime allowance of £250,000 which he had at the time of his death. Thus, the whole of the £50,000 is liable to inheritance tax. The death rate is 40 per cent. Consequently, the inheritance tax payable is 40 per cent of £50,000, thus £12,500.

As the amount of inheritance tax payable illustrates, this is of course a splendid illustration of how not to do it! In general, the potentially exempt transfers and, preferably, also the initially chargeable transfers during any seven-year period should be restricted to the amount of the current lifetime allowance because of the risk that the transferor may die before they have become exempt, thus producing the sort of count-back and the level of inheritance tax liability evidenced in the example.

On the testator's death any potential exempt transfers and initially chargeable transfers which have not by then become exempt are the first charge on his nil rate band. Whenever they do not use up the whole of his nil rate band, it will be necessary to calculate the rate of inheritance payable on each of the relevant assets; this is known as the estate rate. Thus, if the nil rate band is £250,000 and the deceased made a potentially exempt transfer of £100,000 two years before his death, that failed potentially exempt transfer will absorb the first £100,000 of the £250,000,[4] leaving £150,000 to be set against the deceased's other assets. If he had assets of £400,000 on his death, inheritance tax of £100,000 will be payable (40 per cent of the £250,000 which remains after the nil rate band has been used up). Since a total of £100,000 is payable on assets totalling £500,000 (including the value of the failed potentially exempt transfer), the estate rate is 20 per cent. This is the percentage of tax what will be have to be borne by the subject matter of the failed potentially exempt transfer and by each of the assets in the estate.

### 3. The Liability to Inheritance Tax of Settlements

When potentially exempt transfers were introduced,[5] only one specific type of trust, an accumulation and maintenance trust, was able to take effect as such a transfer. However, potentially exempt transfers were subsequently enlarged to include settlements in which there is an interest in possession;[6] consequently, when such a settlement is created *inter vivos*, it is capable of taking effect as a potentially exempt transfer, subject of course to the rules about reservation of benefit by the settlor which have already been discussed. However, discretionary trusts (other than accumulation and maintenance trusts) can still not take effect as potentially exempt transfers and, if created *inter vivos*, are consequently still initially chargeable transfers.

### (A) Settlements in which there is an Interest in Possession

A settlement contains an interest in possession for the purposes of the inheritance tax legislation if the beneficiary whose interest is in possession has the right to receive the income of the settlement as it arises. It does not matter that the trustees have an overriding power of appointment under which they can revoke his entitlement to appoint the income to someone else; however, the fact that the trustees have an express or statutory power to accumulate the

---

[4] This will be the case even if the testator had survived for more than three years but less than seven years; while the taper relief available will reduce the tax eventually payable and therefore the estate rate, its availability does not reduce the attribution of the potentially exempt transfer to the nil rate band.

[5] By Finance Act 1986.

[6] By Finance (No.2) Act 1987.

income, whether or not that power is being exercised, prevents the settlement from having an interest in possession for this purpose.[7]

A settlement in which there is an interest in possession for the purposes of the inheritance tax legislation can take effect as a potentially exempt transfer, provided that there is no reservation of benefit by the settlor. Consequently, there is no liability to inheritance tax on the creation of the settlement although, in the event that the settlor does not survive for a further seven years, inheritance tax may nevertheless be payable on his death for the reasons and upon the bases illustrated in the previous section.

A beneficiary who has an interest in possession for the purposes of the inheritance tax legislation is regarded as being beneficially entitled to the property which forms the subject matter of the settlement — the fact that he may have no more than a life interest in that property is irrelevant for this purpose.[8] Consequently, when an interest in possession comes to an end, its beneficiary is regarded as having made a transfer of the value of his interest, no matter why it has ended; this may be as the result of a positive act by him, such as a disposal or surrender, or as the result of a positive act by the trustees, such as the exercise of an overriding power of appointment, or as the result of the interest reaching its natural limit, such as determining event or a death of a life tenant.[9]

That transfer may be exempt, potentially exempt, or chargeable. That transfer will be exempt if it falls within any of the general exemptions already mentioned (other than the small gifts exemption of £250, which does not apply to settlements)[10]; consequently, if a husband has an interest in possession under a settlement for his lifetime and the beneficiary next entitled under the settlement is his wife, no inheritance tax will be payable whether his interest passes to her as a result of a surrender *inter vivos* or as a result of his death. That transfer will be potentially exempt whenever it occurs *inter vivos*; consequently, a disposition or surrender of the interest *inter vivos* and its determination *inter vivos* as a result of the interest reaching its natural limit will all be potentially exempt transfers. If the beneficiary survives a further seven years, the transfer will become exempt; if he does not do so, the transfer will become chargeable, as will any non-exempt transfer occurring as a result of the death of the beneficiary. In these cases, the inheritance tax payable is assessed on the basis of the lifetime transfers made by the beneficiary, not those made by the settlor.[11] However, any tax due is actually payable out of the settled property and the trustees and the beneficiary's estate are jointly responsible for its payment.

There are certain special reliefs. Where the settled property reverts to the settlor or his spouse, there is, subject to certain qualifications, total relief;[12] where as a result of the transfer the beneficiary becomes entitled to some other interest in the settled property, there will be partial relief if, and to the extent to which, his new interest is worth less than his previous interest (there being a

---

[7] The authorities all concern capital transfer tax, where the same criteria applied. See particularly *Pearson v. I.R.C.* [1981] A.C. 753.
[8] Inheritance Tax Act 1984, s.49.
[9] *ibid.*, ss.51, 52.
[10] *ibid.*, s.57.
[11] *ibid.*, s.52.
[12] *ibid.*, s.54.

potentially exempt transfer to this extent) while if he becomes entitled to the settled property absolutely, there will be a potentially exempt transfer of the amount of any purchase moneys he has paid for the outstanding interests;[13] finally, where tax is payable within five years of a previous chargeable transfer, quick succession relief reduces the rate of tax.[14]

### (B) Discretionary Trusts

For the purposes of the inheritance tax legislation, a discretionary trust is any settlement in which there is no interest in possession,[15] with the exception of accumulation and maintenance trusts, which will be considered in the next section, and certain other trusts which are given special treatment (including charitable trusts, newspaper trusts, maintenance funds for historic buildings, pension trusts, trusts for the benefit of employees and disabled persons, and protective trusts).[16]

As has already been seen, the creation *inter vivos* of any discretionary trust, other than an accumulation and maintenance trust, is an initially chargeable transfer and consequently is subject to an immediate payment of inheritance tax, charged at half the death rate; thus at present[17] it will be charged at 20 per cent if, and to the extent that, the total of transfers which are neither exempt nor potentially exempt during the seven years preceding the transfer exceed the settlor's lifetime allowance. Further, in the event that the settlor dies within seven years of the transfer, the amount of inheritance tax payable may have to be reassessed if any transfer which was potentially exempt at the time of the original assessment turns out in the end not to be exempt from inheritance tax (see the example discussed in the previous part of this section). This total of transfers is deemed to be the discretionary trust's own total of transfers which will never be lost throughout its existence.

The creation *post mortem* of any discretionary trust, other again than an accumulation and maintenance trust, will similarly give rise to an immediate charge to inheritance tax to the extent that its subject matter is not absorbed within whatever remains of the deceased's lifetime allowance at the time of his death. However, the vast majority of discretionary trusts in existence today have been created precisely in order to ensure that that allowance is utilised in full. These are the so-called "nil rate band discretionary trusts", habitually contained in the wills of spouses in order to ensure that none of the lifetime allowance of the first spouse to die is wasted, as it would be if the whole of his or her property was left to the surviving spouse. Whatever remains of the lifetime allowance is left to trustees to hold on discretionary trust for, usually, the surviving spouse and children; that way the surviving spouse can, if necessary, receive the income of that trust without its capital becoming potentially liable to inheritance tax on his or her death. The state of the testator's lifetime allowance is similarly deemed to reflect the discretionary trust's own total of transfers which will never be lost throughout its existence.

Further charges to inheritance tax potentially arise under all discretionary trusts, other again than accumulation and maintenance trusts. The incidence

---

[13] *ibid.*, s.53(2).
[14] *ibid.*, s.141.
[15] *ibid.*, s.58.
[16] *ibid.*, ss.58, 86, 87, 88 & 89.
[17] In 2003–2004.

and amount of these charges depend on how long the discretionary trust in question has been in operation; the crucial dates occur at 10-year intervals from the date on which the settlement in question was originally created (not from the date on which the discretionary trust itself came into effect).[18] In chronological order, these potential further charges are as follows.

The first possibility of a further charge to inheritance tax arising is if any of the settled property ceases to be subject to the discretionary trust during the first 10-year period.[19] Property ceases to be subject to a discretionary trust not only where a capital payment is made to a beneficiary but also where the trustees, pursuant to an overriding power of appointment, appoint some or all of the property subject to the discretionary trust on an interest-in-possession trust or an accumulation and maintenance trust. The intention of this charge is to produce the appropriate proportion of the inheritance tax which would otherwise have been payable at the end of the first 10-year period in the manner explained below. The rate of tax payable is the appropriate fraction, taking into account the number of quarters which have passed since the discretionary trust came into effect, of the rate of tax which would have been payable on a hypothetical chargeable transfer of the property originally settled, taking into account the state of the settlor's lifetime allowance at the time when the settlement was originally created[20] (consequently, if two years have passed since the discretionary trust came into effect, the appropriate fraction is eight-fortieths so the rate of tax payable is eight-fortieths of the rate of tax payable on the hypothetical chargeable transfer).

The second possibility of a further charge to inheritance tax arising is on the first (and, for that matter, every subsequent) tenth anniversary of the date on which the settlement containing the discretionary trust was created. The rate of tax payable is 30 per cent of the inheritance tax which would have been payable if the property subject to the settlement on the day before the tenth anniversary in question had been transferred to the settlement at that time.[21] The tax notionally payable in respect of that notional transfer is assessed by reference to the state of the settlor's lifetime allowance at the time when the settlement was originally created and account is also taken of any settled property which has ceased to be subject to the discretionary trust during the preceding 10 years (inheritance tax will already have been potentially payable at the time when that property ceased to be subject to the trust). The tax notionally payable is assessed in the light of the nil rate band as it exists at the time of the notional transfer.

The third possibility of a further charge to inheritance tax arising is if any of the settled property ceases to be subject to the discretionary trust at any time after the first 10-year period. This charge arises in the same circumstances as during the first 10-year period and the intention of this charge is also similar, namely to produce the appropriate proportion of the inheritance tax which would have been payable at the end of the next 10-year period. This time the

---

[18] Thus if property is settled on a person for life and, subject to that, on discretionary trusts, the 10-year periods will run from the date of the settlement, not the date of the death of the life tenant, although none of the further charges to inheritance tax will actually become payable until after the life tenant's death.

[19] Inheritance Tax Act 1984, s.65.

[20] *ibid.*, s.68.

[21] *ibid.*, ss.64, 66.

rate of tax payable is the appropriate fraction of the tax paid on the last 10-year anniversary, as before taking into account the number of quarters which have passed in the current 10-year period[22] (if two years have passed since the last 10-year anniversary, the appropriate fraction is again eight-fortieths so the tax payable on the value of the property which ceases to be subject to the settlement is eight-fortieths of the rate of tax payable on the last 10-year anniversary, which was of course itself 30 per cent of the inheritance tax which would have been payable had the property then subject to the settlement been settled then).

The two relatively simple examples that follow, illustrate how these formulae work (more complex illustrations are provided in specialist works on taxation). Suppose in each case that £150,000 was settled on discretionary trusts in 1992–1993, when the lifetime allowance was £150,000; that exactly five years after the creation of the settlement, the trustees appoint an interest in possession in £100,000 to one of the beneficiaries; and that exactly 12 years after the creation of the settlement, the trustees make a similar appointment of £100,000 to another beneficiary.

In the first example, suppose that the discretionary trust was a nil rate band discretionary trust created by the will of a testator whose entire lifetime allowance of £150,000 was available to form the subject matter of the trust.

(a) No inheritance tax will be payable on the creation of the discretionary trusts settlement since its subject matter comprised the testator's lifetime allowance.

(b) Nor will any inheritance tax be payable on the appointment of £100,000 to one of the beneficiaries exactly five years after the creation of the settlement either.[23] This is because, since the rate of tax payable on the creation of the settlement was 0 per cent, the fraction of that rate which is appropriate will inevitably also be 0 per cent. In fact, for this reason, during the first 10-year period, no inheritance tax will be payable no matter how much of the £150,000 ceases to be subject to the discretionary trust during that period or at what point during that period it does so.

(c) On the tenth anniversary of the creation of the settlement in 2002–2003, inheritance tax will only be payable if the value of the property then subject to the discretionary trust, plus the value of any property which has by then ceased to be subject to the discretionary trust, exceeds the then lifetime allowance of £250,000. All that lifetime allowance is available because the whole of the testator's lifetime allowance was available on the creation of the settlement. So inheritance tax will only be payable then to the extent that the property subject to the discretionary trust has outperformed the rate of inflation, which is what is supposed to determine the annual increases to the lifetime allowance.

---

[22] Inheritance Tax Act 1984, s.69.
[23] If the property were other than money, capital gains tax would be payable if the beneficiary took absolutely.

If the value of the property subject to the settlement is in 2002–2003 £300,000,[24] the notional transfer will be of that amount. The tax notionally payable in respect of that notional transfer is assessed by reference to the state of the testator's lifetime allowance at the time when the settlement was originally created (which was intact) and of the £100,000 appointed out during the preceding 10 years. The tax notionally payable is thus 20 per cent of that part of £400,000 which exceeds the then nil rate band of £250,000, 20 per cent of £150,000, thus £30,000. The rate of tax payable on the tenth anniversary is thus 10 per cent (£30,000 divided by £300,000). The rate of inheritance tax actually payable will therefore be 30 per cent of 10 per cent, or 3 per cent. Therefore, the tax payable is 3 per cent of £150,000, thus £4,500 (this will have to be paid out of the settled property).

(d) If no inheritance tax is payable on the tenth anniversary of the creation of the settlement in 2002–2003, none will be payable on the appointment of £100,000 to one of the beneficiaries exactly twelve years after the creation of the settlement either. Only if any inheritance tax is payable on that tenth anniversary is any inheritance tax payable during the next 10-year period. If tax was then payable on the tenth anniversary, then a further eight quarters will have passed when £100,000 ceases to be subject to the settlement exactly 12 years after its creation. Consequently, the inheritance tax payable is eight-fortieths (20 per cent) of the rate of tax paid on the tenth anniversary, which was 10 per cent. Therefore, the tax payable is 20 per cent of 10 per cent, that is 2 per cent, of £100,000, thus £2,000.

All this means that a discretionary trust which is limited to the lifetime allowance of the settlor will give rise to no liability to inheritance tax whatever during the first 10-year period, even if the whole of the property ceases to be subject to the discretionary trust during that period, and will only give rise to any inheritance tax thereafter to the extent that the value of the property subject to it outperforms the rate of inflation.

Secondly, suppose the discretionary trust of £150,000 was created *inter vivos* by a settlor who had already used up all his then lifetime allowance of £150,000 in the preceding seven years and whose cumulative total stood at that £150,000 (in this event, depending on how long he survived, further inheritance tax may also have been payable on his death; this possibility is illustrated by the example which has already been discussed,[25] but it will be assumed for the purposes of the present example that this was not the case).

(a) On the creation of the settlement, inheritance tax is payable at half the death rate. Since the settlor had at the date of the settlement already used up all his then lifetime allowance of £150,000 in the preceding seven years, this tax is payable in full. Consequently, £30,000 tax (20 per cent of £150,000) is payable. It will be assumed that this is paid by the trustees (were it to be paid by the settlor, the sum settled would

---

[24] Due to capital appreciation and the accumulation of some income.
[25] See *ante*, pp. 642–644.

have to be "grossed up"). Thus only £120,000 is actually held on discretionary trust initially.

(b) On the appointment of £100,000 exactly five years after the creation of the settlement, twenty quarters have passed. Consequently, the inheritance tax payable is twenty-fortieths (50 per cent) of 30 per cent of the rate of tax payable on a hypothetical chargeable transfer of the property originally settled taking into account the state of the settlor's lifetime allowance at the date of the creation of the settlement. The latter rate is once again 20 per cent, since the settlor had already used up all his then lifetime allowance at the date of the creation of the settlement. Consequently, the overall rate of tax is 50 per cent of 30 per cent of 20 per cent, which is 3 per cent. Therefore the tax payable is 3 per cent of £100,000, thus £3,000. It will be assumed that this is paid by the beneficiary out of the £100,000 appointed to him (were it to be paid by the trustees, the sum appointed would equally have to be "grossed up").

(c) On the tenth anniversary of the creation of the settlement, if the value of the property subject to the settlement is, as before, £300,000, the notional transfer will be of that amount. The tax notionally payable in respect of that notional transfer is assessed by reference to the state of the testator's lifetime allowance at the time when the settlement was originally created (when it stood at £150,000) and of the £100,000 appointed out during the preceding 10 years. The tax notionally payable is thus 20 per cent of that part of £550,000 which exceeds the then nil rate band of £250,000, 20 per cent of £300,000, thus £60,000. The rate of tax payable on the tenth anniversary is thus 20 per cent (£60,000 divided by £300,000), which is the maximum possible. The rate of inheritance tax actually payable will therefore be 30 per cent of 20 per cent, or 6 per cent, also the maximum possible. Therefore, the tax payable is 6 per cent of £300,000, thus £18,000 (this will have to be paid out of the settled property).

(d) On the appointment of £100,000 exactly 12 years after the creation of the settlement, eight quarters have passed since the tenth anniversary of the creation of the settlement. Consequently, the inheritance tax payable is eight-fortieths (20 per cent) of the rate of tax paid on the tenth anniversary of the creation of the settlement, which was 6 per cent. Therefore, the tax payable is 20 per cent of 6 per cent, that is 1.2 per cent, of £100,000, thus £1,200. It will once again be assumed that this is paid by the beneficiary out of the £100,000 appointed to him (were it to be paid by the trustees, the sum appointed would again have to be "grossed up").

It will be seen from these examples that, apart from the inheritance tax payable on the creation of the settlement, which will be avoided if the property settled falls within the settlor's lifetime allowance and still remains within it at the date of his death, the incidence of inheritance tax is not substantial. This type of trust therefore retains some attraction for a settlor, particularly if, like all nil rate band discretionary trusts, it is limited to the settlor's lifetime allowance.

## (C) Accumulation and Maintenance Trusts

An accumulation and maintenance trust must be for the benefit of one or more persons under 25, usually, but not necessarily, the children or grandchildren of the settlor. At least one beneficiary must be alive at the date of the creation of the accumulation and maintenance trust. However, there is no requirement for any beneficiary to have been alive at the date of the creation of the settlement itself.[26] The beneficiaries must be entitled to the trust property or to an immediate vested interest in possession in its income upon reaching an age not exceeding 25; in the meantime, the income can either be accumulated or be applied for the maintenance, education or benefit of the children.[27]

Three types of accumulation and maintenance trusts are common: first, where the beneficiaries acquire interests in possession in both income and capital on attaining the age of 25 (or such lower age as is specified); secondly, where the beneficiaries acquire interests in possession only in the income on attaining the specified age and interests in possession in the capital only on attaining some greater age; and, thirdly, where the beneficiaries acquire interests in possession only in the income on attaining the specified age and never acquire interests in possession in the capital at all, these being passed down to the next generation (if in the event the beneficiaries of an accumulation and maintenance trust of the second or third type require capital to which they are not entitled under the terms of the trust, the trustees will generally be able to give them the necessary capital by exercising their overriding powers of appointment).

In all three cases, however, the accumulation and maintenance trusts (as distinct from the trusts which replace them when the beneficiaries acquire interests in possession) can only last for 25 years unless, as is usually the case, all the beneficiaries have a common grandparent. If the trust ceases to qualify as an accumulation and maintenance trust for this or any other reason, inheritance tax becomes payable as if it were a normal discretionary trust; if this occurs because the 25-year period has come to an end, the inheritance tax payable will be a swingeing 21 per cent of the capital of the trust (however, in a well-drafted accumulation and maintenance trust, this liability can be avoided by resettling the property just before the end of the 25-year period).[28]

There are no particular fiscal advantages in respect of income tax; the income of the trust is taxed at the same rate as any other discretionary trust and any income applied for the maintenance or education of a beneficiary is, provided that the trust is irrevocable, taxed as the income of the beneficiary (unless he is a minor unmarried child of the settlor, in which case it is aggregated with the income of the latter).[29] So far as capital gains tax is concerned, there is no deemed disposal when the beneficiaries obtain interests in possession in the capital provided that they do so at the same time as they obtain interests in possession in the income (there will however be a deemed

---

[26] This means that it is possible to create an accumulation and maintenance trust by the use of overriding powers of appointment in favour of a class of beneficiaries, none of whom was in existence at the date of the settlement.

[27] Inheritance Tax Act 1984, s.71. For a detailed discussion of the conditions, see *Inglewood (Lord) v. I.R.C.* [1983] 1 W.L.R. 366.

[28] If this cannot be done, it is still possible for an application to vary the trusts to be made under the Variation of Trusts Act 1958; see *post*, p. 747.

[29] Income and Corporation Taxes Act 1988, ss.663–665.

disposal if interests in possession in the capital are obtained at any later time); however, this only postpones capital gains tax — the tax is not eliminated. The principal fiscal advantages of such trusts therefore relate to inheritance tax. Accumulation and maintenance trusts are potentially exempt transfers;[30] consequently, such trusts are not liable to any of the additional charges to inheritance tax outlined in the previous section (this is why inheritance tax is payable if a discretionary trust is converted into an accumulation and main-tenance trust). Consequently, no inheritance tax will be payable at all if the settlor survives a further seven years; even if he fails to do so, inheritance tax will only be payable to the extent that his estate and the transfers made during the last seven years of his life exceed his lifetime allowance.

---

[30] Inheritance Tax Act 1984, s.3A.

# CHAPTER 16

# APPORTIONMENTS

It has already been seen[1] that a fundamental rule is that a trustee must not allow a conflict of interest to arise between his own personal position and his duties to the beneficiaries. The sister rule is that, where there is a conflict between the interests of different beneficiaries, a trustee must hold a balance between them. This is not so much because this is what the settlor actually did intend, for he may well never have given the matter any thought at all, but rather because equity presumes that this is what the settlor would have intended had he directed his mind to the point. It is therefore not necessary to find any actual evidence of intention on the part of the settlor for this principle to apply, yet on the other hand he is able to provide expressly or by implication that the principle shall not operate. Avoidance of a conflict of interest is of particular importance in relation to investments; this principle also underlies the rules governing apportionments.[2] These formal rules apply as between tenants for life and remaindermen. However, other conflicts of interest can arise. In *Lloyds Bank v. Duker*,[3] the conflict of interest was between majority and minority beneficiaries. The testator who owned 999 of the 1,000 shares of a private company, left 46/80ths of the 999 shares to his wife. It was held that the 574 shares which represented this proportion could not be transferred to her because such a majority holding would give her the control of the company and, in relation to the remaining minority shares, would be worth more than her due proportion. Consequently, the trustees were directed to sell all 999 shares and distribute the proceeds of sale in the appropriate proportions.

## I. APPORTIONMENTS BETWEEN CAPITAL AND INCOME

### 1. The Principle

Suppose that Basil settles property upon trust for Clare for life, remainder to Priscilla absolutely, and the trust property consists of: £5,000 3.5 per cent War Stock; the cow Buttercup; and the right under Basil's grandfather's will to

---

[1] See *ante*, p. 330.
[2] There have been a number of recommendations made for the reform of the subject matter of this chapter, most recently by the Trust Law Committee. However, since there is no indication that any of these recommendations is to be enacted, no further reference to them seems appropriate.
[3] [1987] 1 W.L.R. 1324.

receive £15,000 on the death of his father, Fred, who is still alive (this right is known as a reversionary interest).

If these assets are retained in their present form, the holding of War Stock will produce a steady income, and a capital sum will be available to Priscilla on the death of Clare. Buttercup, a fine milk-yielding cow, may produce at first a high income but, as she grows old and her milk production decreases, she will become less and less valuable. She may well die before Clare and, if this is the case, Clare will have derived the whole of the benefit from her and Priscilla will have had none. The case of the reversionary interest is precisely the opposite. Until Fred dies, income is paid to neither Clare nor Priscilla and, if Clare dies before Fred, she will have received no benefit at all from this asset. Equity presumes that it was not Basil's intention that the beneficiaries should be treated so haphazardly and their fortunes left so much to chance. The basic solution is, therefore, for Buttercup and the reversionary interest to be sold and the proceeds invested in authorised securities so that the income may be paid to Clare and a capital sum preserved intact for Priscilla. The rules which follow prescribe how this is to be done. However, once any necessary apportionment between capital and income according to these rules has been made, the trustees are apparently entitled to make investments which produce either high or low income depending on the relative wealth of the tenant for life and the remainderman.[4]

The rules governing the necessary sale are not, however, always easy to apply. There are three questions to consider:

(a) Is there a duty to convert a particular asset into an authorised investment?

(b) If so, does the income have to be apportioned between the date when the duty arises and the date when the conversion actually takes place?

(c) If so, how is such apportionment calculated?

These questions are progressive so that, if the answer to any one is "no", there is no need to consider the remaining questions.

### 2. Is There a Duty to Convert?

The duty to convert the trust property into authorised investments may arise in two circumstances.

First, if the trust instrument so directs. The most frequent case of an express direction to convert occurs when there is an express trust for sale but any direction to convert is for this purpose equally adequate.

Secondly, as a result of the operation of the rule in *Howe v. Lord Dartmouth*,[5] which directs that the conversion of an asset should take place where there is no express direction to this effect in the trust instrument, but only where all the following conditions are satisfied:

---

[4] *Nestlé v. National Westminster Bank* [1993] 1 W.L.R. 1260.
[5] (1802) 7 Ves. 137. For a relatively up-to-date account of the rule, see L. A. Sheridan "*Howe v. Lord Dartmouth* Re-examined" (1952) 16 Conv. (N.S.) 349.

(a) the trust was created by will;

(b) there are at least two beneficiaries, and they are entitled in succession;

(c) the property consists of residuary personalty;

(d) the asset is wasting, reversionary or of an unauthorised character; and

(e) there is no contrary intention in the will.

The rule does not apply to a settlement *inter vivos* the terms of such settlements must be observed strictly because, so it is said, the settlor knew exactly the state of the assets when the settlement was created.[6]

The only one of the five conditions listed which is likely to cause any difficulty is the question of whether or not there is a contrary intention. In *Re Sewell's Estate*,[7] the trustees were given a discretion as to what part of the testator's estate should be converted. This was held to have excluded the rule in *Howe v. Lord Dartmouth* because a discretion to convert was inconsistent with the duty to convert which the rule would impose. However, in order to exclude the rule, the power must be consciously exercised.[8] In *Alcock v. Sloper*,[9] property was left on trust for a life tenant and, after his death, on trust to be sold and the proceeds divided btween various named beneficiaries. Here too it was held that the Rule in *Howe v. Lord Dartmouth* had been excluded, because the express duty to convert on the death of the life tenant was inconsistent with an implied duty to convert on the death of the testator, which is what the rule would have imposed.

The decision in *Alcock v. Sloper*[10] must be contrasted with that in *Re Evans*,[11] where property was given to trustees on trust for a life tenant and, after her death, on trust to be divided into three equal shares and distributed to three other members of the family. It was held that *Howe v. Lord Dartmouth* did apply, because the division on the death of the life tenant could be of property in either its converted or unconverted form; consequently, the directions in the will were not inconsistent with a duty to convert implied by *Howe v. Lord Dartmouth*.

Where the settlor shows an intention that the property should be enjoyed *in specie*, this clearly negatives the rule.[12] Bennett J. took this proposition a stage further in *Re Fisher*,[13] by saying that where there is a trust for conversion with a power to postpone, the settlor thereby shows that he intends that the property may be enjoyed *in specie*, and that this also is inconsistent with the duty to convert which would be imposed by *Howe v. Lord Dartmouth*. However, in the later case of *Re Berry*,[14] Pennycuick J. refused to follow *Re Fisher*. Although the logical basis of the latter decision is clear, Pennycuick J. commented that that

[6] *Re Van Straubenzee* [1901] 2 Ch. 779, per Cozens-Hardy J. and see *Milford v. Peile* (1854) 2 W.N. 181; *Hope v. Hope* (1855) 1 Jur. (N.S.) 770.
[7] (1870) L.R. 11 Eq. 80; see also *Simpson v. Earles* (1847) 11 Jur. 921.
[8] *Re Guinness* [1966] 1 W.L.R. 1355.
[9] (1833) 2 My. & K. 699; *Daniel v. Warren* (1843) 2 Y. & Coll. C.C. 290
[10] (1833) 2 My. & K. 699.
[11] [1920] 2 Ch. 309.
[12] *Macdonald v. Irvine* (1878) 8 Ch.D. 101.
[13] [1943] Ch. 377.
[14] [1962] Ch. 97.

decision was "contrary to the whole current of authority"; it was an attempt to extend the scope of the exceptions from *Howe v. Lord Dartmouth* too far.

The cases turn on fine differences in wording and, while it may be very difficult to say on any particular set of facts whether *Howe v. Lord Dartmouth* is excluded, the rule itself is clear: has the testator made any provision which is expressly or impliedly inconsistent with a duty to convert at the date of death? If he has not done so and the other conditions listed above are fulfilled, *Howe v. Lord Dartmouth* will apply.

### 3. *Whether There is a Need to Apportion Income*

If there is a duty to convert, it will be seen below that conversion should take place either at the date of death, or as at one year from the date of death.[15] It will be obvious that in the former case there is no conceivable way of effecting actual conversion at that date while, even in the latter case, actual conversion will often be delayed. The question therefore arises whether, in the event of conversion being delayed, the tenant for life is entitled to the actual income produced by the asset until it is converted or whether he is entitled only to an apportioned part of it. The primary rule is that, if the testator has provided, expressly or by implication, that the tenant for life is to enjoy the actual income which the property produces, then that intention will prevail. Where it cannot be shown that the testator expressed any such intention, then the following rules apply.

First, where the trustees improperly postpone conversion, an apportionment will be ordered. Thus in *Wentworth v. Wentworth*,[16] the trustees had a power to postpone conversion until a certain date. The trustees improperly postponed conversion beyond that date and the Privy Council held that apportionment should be made as from that date.

Secondly, where the property in question is real property, the tenant for life is entitled to the actual income which the property produces. It will be remembered that *Howe v. Lord Dartmouth* never operates to impose a duty to convert realty so that such a duty in respect of realty can only have come into existence as the result of an express trust for conversion.

Thirdly, in the case of personalty, the tenant for life is entitled only to an apportioned part of the income, unless there is an intention that he shall enjoy the asset in specie.[17] Thus the presumption is in favour of the enjoyment of actual income in the case of realty and of only an apportioned part of the income in the case of personalty.

---

[15] See *post, infra.*
[16] [1900] A.C. 163.
[17] *Re Chaytor* [1965] 1 Ch. 233. Where there is a trust for conversion with a power to postpone, the beneficiary will only receive an apportioned part of the income; *Re Berry* [1962] Ch. 97.

## 4. How is the Apportionment Calculated?

If there is a duty to convert and if, because the property has not been converted by the due date, the income has to be apportioned until conversion takes place, how is such apportionment calculated? Where the asset concerned is a reversionary interest, the rule in Re Earl of Chesterfield's Trusts[18] applies; this is dealt with below. As regards other property which has to be converted, it is necessary first to ascertain the valuation date. At common law there was a presumption that the executor's functions in administering the estate ought to be completed within one year from the death of the testator. From this the rule evolved that, where there is no power to postpone sale, conversion ought to be effected within one year from the date of death; in this case, in order to be able to calculate the apportionment, the asset has to be valued as at one year from the date of death.[19] If, however, there is a power to postpone sale, this negatives the intention that the property should be valued as at one year from the date of death and, because a better date could not be thought of, in this case the property is valued at the date of death.[20] Thus, if there is no power to postpone sale, the valuation date is one year from the date of death but, if there is a power to postpone sale, the valuation date is the date of death.

Whichever the valuation date, the tenant for life is entitled to interest on the value of the asset as at the valuation date from the date of death until the date of actual conversion. Traditionally, the rate of interest applied has been 4 per cent,[21] but as this has sometimes been unrealistically low, it may be that the court would now adopt the rate which is equivalent to that paid on the court's short-term investment account.[22] If the actual income is larger than the apportioned figure, the balance is added to capital. If the actual income is smaller than the appropriate rate, the tenant for life receives that actual income, and is entitled to have it made up from future surpluses of income or, if there are none, from capital when the asset is sold. The deficiency cannot be made good from previous surpluses of income because these have already been notionally added to capital.

An example may help. Suppose that the copyright to a book is left upon trust for Angela for life, remainder to Mary and that the copyright is worth £1,200 at the date of death and £1,000 one year from the date of death. The copyright is eventually sold three years after the date of death and during the intervening three years the royalties actually received are: Year 1: £70; Year 2: £32; and Year 3: £48. It is necessary first to ascertain the valuation date. Where there is a power to postpone, this will be the date of death. At this date the copyright is worth £1,200 so that, if the appropriate rate of interest is 4 per cent, Angela is entitled to 4 per cent × £1,200 = £48 per annum. In Year 1 she will receive £48, the balance of £22 being added to capital. In Year 2 she will receive £32, with the right to make good the deficiency of £16 in the future. In

---

[18] (1883) 24 Ch.D. 643.
[19] Re Eaton (1894) 70 L.T. 761.
[20] Re Owen [1912] 1 Ch. 519; Re Parry [1947] Ch. 23.
[21] The actual rate of interest is in the discretion of the court, but 4 per cent is usually taken as the appropriate figure; see Re Lucas [1947] Ch. 558; Re Parry [1947] Ch. 23; Re Berry [1962] Ch. 97.
[22] See Bartlett v. Barclays Bank Trust Co. (No.2) [1980] Ch. 515 and Jaffray v. Marshall [1993] 1 W.L.R. 1285 (overruled on other grounds by the House of Lords in Target Holdings v. Redferns [1996] 1 A.C. 421); see post, p. 774. See also Re Fawcett [1940] Ch. 402; Re Parry [1947] Ch. 23.

Year 3 she will receive £48, and will be entitled to a further £16 from the proceeds of the sale of the copyright to make good the deficiency in Year 2. If, however, there is no power to postpone, the valuation date will be one year from the date of death. Angela is therefore entitled to receive 4 per cent × £1,000 = £40 per annum. In Year 1 she will receive £40, with £30 being added to capital. In Year 2 she will receive £32. In Year 3 she will receive £40, plus £8 to make good the shortfall in Year 2, thus using up all the income for that year. She will therefore need to receive no part of the proceeds of sale of the copyright.

At this point it must again be stressed that the questions posed at the beginning of this discussion (is there a duty to convert? if so, does the income have to be apportioned? if so, how is such apportionment calculated?) are progressive. Therefore it is only if there is a duty to convert that it is necessary to consider whether the income has to be apportioned and it is only if there is a duty to convert and if the income does have to be apportioned that it is necessary to make the type of calculation just considered.

### 5. *Re Earl of Chesterfield's Trusts*[23]

A special method is necessary for calculating the apportionment of reversionary interests because these do not actually produce any income until they fall into possession.

At the outset it should be noted that reversionary interests are saleable. Thus, going back to the original example,[24] one of the assets which Basil left upon trust for Clare for life, remainder to Priscilla absolutely, was the right to receive £15,000 on the death of his father, Fred, who was still alive. At Basil's death the trustees could have sold that reversionary interest. The price which would be obtained would be largely governed by Fred's age at the date of Basil's death but whatever was obtained would have been invested in authorised securities, the income paid to Clare for life, and the capital held for Priscilla.

However, it is usually economically better not to sell but rather to retain the reversionary interest until it falls into possession. If this is done, it is clearly equitable, before the money that is eventually received is invested, to pay part of the amount received to Clare as compensation for the fact that she has had no income from the asset since the trust came into operation. The rule in *Re Earl of Chesterfield's Trusts* provides that, where a reversionary interest which ought to be converted is retained until it falls into possession, part of it is to be treated as arrears of income and paid to the tenant for life and only the balance is to be regarded as capital.

The rule itself says that the proportion of the amount actually received which is to be regarded as capital is that which, if invested at 4 per cent compound interest with yearly rests, would, after allowing for the deduction of income tax at the basic rate for the time being in force, have produced the sum actually received. It remains to be decided whether 4 per cent is still the

---

[23] (1883) 24 Ch.D. 643.
[24] See *ante*, pp. 653–654.

appropriate rate of interest to be applied.[25] "Yearly rests" are the intervals at which the interest is compounded.[26]

Returning to the example, suppose that Fred lived for three-and-a-quarter years after the trust came into operation and assume that the basic rate of tax throughout that period was 25 per cent (although in recent years the basic rate has been lower, utilising a basic rate of 25% makes the mathematical calculations considerably easier and therefore more comprehensible); the trustees would find that £13,625.22 invested when the trust came into operation at 4 per cent compound interest with yearly rests would, after allowing for the deduction of tax at 25 per cent, have produced £15,000 at the date when this sum was actually received.[27] The £13,625.22 would therefore be invested by the trustees as capital, and the remaining £1,374.78 would be paid to Clare as income for the preceding three-and-a-quarter years.

The same rule applies to any other property which does not produce any income. Thus it applied in *Re Duke of Cleveland's Equity* [28] to a debt which bore no interest and was not receivable immediately. And in *Re Chance*,[29]

---

[25] See *ante*, p. 657.

[26] The calculation can be complicated, but, for those who do not have super mathematical skills, the most straightforward method of making the calculation will be to follow these steps:

1. Determine the gross rate of interest to be applied. Traditionally this has been 4% but, as has been noted, a higher rate may be appropriate.

2. Deduct the basic rate of income tax, to give a net rate of interest.

3. Calculate the amount which £100 would produce if invested for the period between the date of death and the date when the reversionary interest falls in at the net rate of interest compounded annually.

4. Multiply the amount received when the reversionary interest falls in by the following fraction:

$$\frac{100}{\text{the sum calculated by 3}} .$$

5. The product is the capital element.

6. The balance is the income element.

[27] Following the steps outlined in fn. 26, the calculation is as follows (as indicated in the text, although in recent years the basic rate has been lower (22% in 2003–2004), utilising a basic rate of 25% makes the mathematical calculations considerably easier and therefore more comprehensible):

1. Gross rate: taken as 4 per cent

2. Basic rate of income tax: taken as 25 per cent. The net rate is, therefore,

$$4 \text{ per cent} \times \frac{75}{100} = 3 \text{ per cent}$$

3. The compounded amount £110.09 is calculated as follows:

| Period | Amount on which calculated | Rate | Interest for period | Total at end of period |
|---|---|---|---|---|
| Year 1 | £100.00 | 3% | £3.00 | £103.00 |
| Year 2 | £103.00 | 3% | £3.09 | £106.09 |
| Year 3 | £106.09 | 3% | £3.18 | £109.27 |
| Last 3 months | £109.27 | 3% | £0.82 | £110.09 |

4. The capital element of the amount received, £15,000, is:

$$£15,000 \times \frac{100}{110.09} = £13,625.22$$

5. The income element is (£15,000 − £13,625.22) = £1,374.78

[28] [1895] 2 Ch. 542.

[29] [1962] Ch. 593.

compensation for the refusal of planning permission under Part I of the Town and Country Planning Act 1954[30] was held to be apportionable.

### 6. *Leaseholds*

It used to be necessary to give special consideration to leaseholds. Before 1926, a residuary gift of leaseholds was treated in the same way as any other gift of residuary personalty. From 1926 to 1996, leases with over 60 years to run were authorised investments so there was no question of any apportionment in respect of them.[31] So far as leases with less than 60 years to run, which were not authorised investments, were concerned, it was clear that, by virtue of the now repealed section 28(2) of the Law of Property Act 1925, the tenant for life was entitled to the actual income where there was an express trust for the conversion of leaseholds,[32] but it was thought in some quarters[33] that the pre-1926 position still applied where the duty to convert the leaseholds in question arose only by virtue of the Rule in *Howe v. Lord Dartmouth*.[34] Since 1997 all leaseholds have been authorised investments by virtue of section 6(3) of the Trusts of Land and Appointment of Trustees Act 1996.[35] Consequently, there is now no question of any apportionment in respect of any leasehold.

## II. OTHER APPORTIONMENTS

### 1. *The Rule in* Allhusen v. Whittell[36]

There will always be an interval of time between the date of death and the date when an asset is realised. Where a person creates a trust by will in favour of persons in succession and there are debts and liabilities to be paid, it would appear that the tenant for life will gain increasingly as that delay increases. Suppose that the gross assets of an estate held on trust for persons by way of succession amount to £20,000 and that the debts amount to £5,000. If the debts

---

[30] The Town and Country Planning Act 1947 provided, in general terms, that an owner of land could not carry out any building or other works on his land without obtaining the permission of the local authority, and without paying a "development charge". The value of land was often less after the passing of this Act than before it, and in an effort to give to the landowner compensation, it was proposed that a £300 million fund would be established, on which landowners could make a claim for the depreciation in the value of their land. The fund was, in fact, never set up and the system was changed under the Town and Country Planning Act 1954, whereby the amount of the landowner's claim, plus one-seventh of it for interest (less payments for certain events made before the 1954 Act came into force), formed what is known as an "unexpended balance of established development value". Where such a balance exists, in certain cases compensation is payable up to the amount of that balance where an application for planning permission is refused. This was the situation in *Re Chance* [1962] Ch. 593. Part of the interest of the decision lies in the fact that an unexpended balance of established development value and so of money paid under the system represents interest and the amount of that interest could be determined. Wilberforce J. however, took the whole amount of the compensation received and apportioned that.

[31] *Re Gough* [1957] Ch. 323.

[32] *Re Brooker* [1926] W.N. 93.

[33] Bailey (1930–32) 4 C.L.J. 357.

[34] (1867) L.R. 4 Eq. 295.

[35] See *ante*, p. 600.

[36] (1867) L.R. 4 Eq. 295.

are paid forthwith, the tenant for life will have the income from the remaining £15,000. If, however, the debts are not paid for a year, the tenant for life will receive the income for that year on £20,000. The essence of the rule of apportionment laid down in *Allhusen v. Whittell* is to charge the tenant for life with interest on the amount subsequently used for the payment of debts so that, broadly, the tenant for life is placed in the same position as if the debts had been paid on death.

In its modern form,[37] the rule requires a calculation of the average income of the estate from the date of death to the date of payment, taken net after deduction of income tax at the basic rate.[38] The tenant for life is charged with interest at the rate of the net average income, so that the debt once paid is regarded as being paid partly from income and partly from capital. Suppose that a debt of £500 is paid one year from the date of death, that the average income of the estate taken throughout that period is 4 per cent and that the basic rate of income tax during that year is 22 per cent. The calculation is therefore:

| | | |
|---|---|---|
| Take a basic unit of | | £100.00 |
| *Add* | | |
| Average income for one year at £4 per cent | £4.00 | |
| *Less* tax | £0.88 | |
| | £3.12 | £3.12 |
| | | £103.12 |

Each debt paid one year from death is therefore regarded as being paid in the proportion:

$$\frac{100.00}{103.12} \quad \text{from capital; and}$$

$$\frac{3.12}{103.12} \quad \text{from income.}$$

Thus, the debt of £500 will be paid:

$$\frac{100.00}{£103.12} \times £500 = £484.87 \text{ from capital; and}$$

$$\frac{3.12}{£103.12} \times £500 = £15.13 \text{ from income.}$$

This £15.13 will be charged to the tenant for life.

It is easy to appreciate the theoretical justification for this rule and it is also easy to see its practical defects. In particular, a separate calculation is necessary for each debt paid at a different time. Further, where payments are to be made a considerable time after death, as where the testator in his lifetime entered into a covenant to pay an annuity and the annuity was charged on the residue of his estate, the proportion borne by income steadily increases.[39] Except where very large debts are involved or where a very long delay occurs in payment, the trouble of making the calculation does not justify the small

---

[37] *Re McEwen* [1913] 2 Ch. 704; *Re Wills* [1915] 1 Ch. 769; *Corbett v. C.I.R.* [1938] 1 K.B. 567.
[38] *Re Oldham* (1927) 71 S.J. 491.
[39] *Re Dawson* [1906] 2 Ch. 211; *Re Perkins* [1907] 2 Ch. 596; *Re Poyser* [1910] 2 Ch. 444.

adjustment between tenant for life and remainderman; consequently it is now very common to exclude the operation of the rule.

### 2. The Rule in Re Atkinson[40]

Where an authorised mortgage forms part of the estate and, upon realisation of the security by sale, the proceeds of sale are insufficient to pay the outstanding principal and interest in full, the proceeds of sale are apportioned between the tenant for life and remainderman in the proportion which the amount due for arrears bears to the amount due in respect of principal. This is the rule in Re Atkinson,[41] and it applies to any mortgage which forms part of the assets derived from the testator or settlor and also to any authorised mortgage taken by the trustee himself.

Suppose that during his lifetime a testator made a mortgage advance of £25,000 upon the security of a house at £12 per cent interest. Suppose also that the mortgagor pays a total of only £1,200 interest in respect of the period after the death of the testator and that the property is sold for £23,000 three years after death, no part of the capital secured by the mortgage having been repaid at any point. The apportionment of the £23,000 is as follows:

| | | | |
|---|---|---|---|
| Capital outstanding | | £25,000 | |
| Interest outstanding: | | | |
| 3 Years at £12 per cent on £25,000 | £9,000 | | |
| *less*: actually paid | £1,200 | | |
| | £7,800 | £7,800 | |
| Total capital and interest due | | £32,800 | |
| | | | |
| Capital element of proceeds of sale | £25,000 / £32,800 | × £23,000 = £17,530 | |
| Income element of proceeds of sale | £7,800 / £32,800 | × £23,000 = £5,470 | |
| Total proceeds of sale | | £23,000 | |

The scope of the rule is in doubt. In principle it ought to apply whenever an asset carrying both capital and interest at a fixed rate is realised at a loss and it has been held to apply to an amount received in a liquidation on account of principal and arrears of interest due under a holding of debenture stock.[42] However, the rule is not applied where preference dividends are in arrears.[43]

The rule in Re Atkinson is applied only to a capital sum realised on the sale of a security and not to income received from the asset. Thus, if under a power contained in a mortgage the trustees take possession of the property and let it, the net rents are applied entirely in the discharge of arrears of interest and only when those arrears have been paid in full is the surplus applied as capital.[44] If there are arrears of interest outstanding at the date of death, those

---

[40] [1904] 2 Ch. 160.
[41] [1904] 2 Ch. 160.
[42] Re Walker [1936] Ch. 280; compare Re Taylor [1905] 1 Ch. 734.
[43] Re Sale [1913] 2 Ch. 697; Re Wakley [1920] 2 Ch. 205.
[44] Re Coaks [1911] 1 Ch. 171.

are paid in full in priority to the interest due to the estate from the period from the date of death to the date of extinction of the mortgage. [45]

Where trustees foreclose under a mortgage, the mortgagor then loses all title to the property and the property itself becomes an asset of the estate. Accordingly, from the date of foreclosure the tenant for life is entitled to the whole of the net rents and profits until sale;[46] but, if there are arrears of interest before foreclosure, it seems that a *Re Atkinson* apportionment will be made when the property is ultimately sold.[47]

There is no authority as to whether income tax should be deducted in making a calculation for the purposes of the rule in *Re Atkinson*. It is suggested that the appropriate method of applying the rule is first to ascertain the arrears of interest and the proportion due to income without taking into account income tax. When that proportion has been calculated, the tenant for life's entitlement should be reduced by an amount equal to income tax at the basic rate on that sum.

### III. APPORTIONMENTS RELATING TO STOCKS AND SHARES

In contrast to the Rule in *Howe v. Lord Dartmouth*, which applies to unauthorised investments, apportionments of a different type are sometimes necessary in the case of authorised investments.

#### 1. *Dividends*

The first case is of apportionment of dividends received for shares. Thus, if shares are left on trust for Peter for life, with remainder to Paul for life, it may be necessary, on the death of Peter, to apportion dividends between Peter's estate and Paul. The Apportionment Act 1870 applies to most types of periodical payment and deems them to accrue from day to day. If, therefore, Peter dies on the fifty-ninth day of a year, and the company declares a dividend amounting to £150 for that calendar year, 59/365ths of £150 will belong to Peter's estate and the balance will be payable to Paul. The period in respect of which the company in question states it is paying the dividend necessarily governs the rights of all the beneficiaries. This can produce superficially rather strange results. A company pays no dividend in 2003 and 2004 but pays a dividend in 2005 which is three times as large as normal but which is stated by the company to be in respect of 2005. If Peter as before dies on the fifty-ninth day of 2005, he will only be entitled to 59/365ths. It might have been thought more equitable in these circumstances for Peter to have received 789/1096ths (being the fraction of days for the period 2003, 2004 and 2005 for which Peter has lived) but this is not the rule.[48]

It is also necessary to make a time apportionment when there is an alteration in the class of income beneficiaries. In *Re Joel*,[49] a fund was held upon trust for the testator's grandchildren contingently on attaining the age of 21. The gift

---

[45] *ibid.*
[46] Law of Property Act 1925, s.31; *Re Horn* [1924] 2 Ch. 222.
[47] *Re Horn* [1924] 2 Ch. 222 at 226.
[48] *Re Wakley* [1920] 1 Ch. 205.
[49] [1967] Ch. 14.

carried the intermediate income, which could accordingly be utilised for the benefit of the grandchildren.[50] Goff J. held that, each time a member of the class died under 21 or a new grandchild was born, the income of the trust ought to be apportioned; that way each member of the class enjoyed only that part of the income attributable to the period during which he was alive.

However, for the purposes of taxation the rules differ from those laid down by the Apportionment Act 1870; the whole of the dividend is treated as the income of the person who is entitled to the income of the trust on the day on which the income in question is payable.[51] Suppose that one of the assets of a fund held on trust for Roger for life, with remainder to Susan for life, is a holding of shares in a company which pays dividends in respect of years ending on March 31, and that in June 2004 the company declares a dividend for the year which ended on March 31, 2004. If Roger dies on February 15, 2004, his estate will be entitled to almost all the dividend by virtue of the Apportionment Act 1870; however, the whole of the dividend will form part of Susan's taxable income for the year of assessment 2004–2005.

## 2. Scrip Dividends

Companies sometimes give shareholders a choice between receiving their dividends in cash and receiving additional shares. Dividends paid in the form of shares are known as scrip dividends. This choice does not pose any particular problems for the trustees if the value of the scrip offered is more or less the same as the cash dividend. In both cases the dividend will belong to the tenant for life and in such circumstances trustees have traditionally opted to take the dividend in cash. However, in the last few years there have been a large number of enhanced scrip dividends, under which the value of the scrip on offer can be as much as 50 per cent more than the cash dividend with, sometimes, the possibility of converting the scrip into cash by selling it on at a pre-arranged price, never as high as the value of the scrip but still substantially more than the cash dividend. Trustees are clearly under an obligation to consider whether to take up such an offer. If they decide to do so, the question arises as to whether the tenant for life is entitled to the whole of the scrip (or, where appropriate, the whole of any pre-arranged purchase price for which the trustees sell it). It was held at the end of the nineteenth century that in these circumstances an apportionment is necessary as between income and capital.[52] If this decision is still good law, the tenant for life will be entitled to no more than the amount of the cash dividend; the additional value of the scrip (or, where appropriate, of any pre-arranged price for which the trustees sell it) will therefore have to be added to the capital of the trust. If enhanced scrip dividends continue to be popular, it is likely that a test case will at some stage be necessary to establish definitively whether or not such an apportionment is indeed necessary.

---

[50] See *post*, p. 672.
[51] I.R.C. v. *Henderson's Executors* (1931) 16 T.C. 282; *Bryan v. Cassin* [1942] 2 All E.R. 262; *Wood v. Owen* [1941] 1 K.B. 92; *Potel v. I.R.C.* [1971] 2 All E.R. 504.
[52] *Re Malam* [1894] 3 Ch. 578.

### 3. *Purchases and Sales Cum and Ex Dividend*

On the face of things, an apportionment would appear to be appropriate where stocks and shares are bought and sold. There are obviously a number of factors which affect the price of stock exchange investments, such as the yield which is obtained,[53] the stability of the company concerned, the general economic condition of the country as a whole, and the future prospects of the company; however, an important short term factor is the date when the dividend is to be paid. Any example is obviously artificial but, assuming that all other factors remain constant, if a dividend of £500 is payable on both January 1 and July 1 on a holding of stock worth £20,000, on January 2 the stock is worth £20,000 but its value on June 30, the day before the payment of the next dividend, will be £20,450 (£20,000 plus the net value of the dividend, £500 less the 10% income tax retained out of the dividend).[54] If trustees purchase that stock on January 2 for £20,000 and sell it for £20,450 on June 30, does the whole of that £20,450 belong to capital or is the sum apportioned so as to attribute £20,000 to capital and £450 to income? After all, had the holding been kept for one day longer, the net payment of £450 would have been received as a dividend and treated as income. Somewhat surprisingly, there is in this case no rule providing for any apportionment and the whole amount received is deemed to be capital. The explanation for this apparently inequitable rule is that there are in practice so many factors that affect the value of shares that it is thought too difficult to lay down any set rules to govern how the apportionment is to be calculated. It has, however, been said that, in the event that the rule of non-apportionment leads to a "glaring injustice", apportionment will be ordered.[55]

### 4. *Bonus Shares*

Considerable difficulty has been caused where a company issues bonus shares. Suppose the capital of a company consists of 10,000 £1 ordinary shares and that the company has prospered and has retained accumulated profits of £5,000. If the company distributes the £5,000 to its shareholders, this sum is clearly income in the hands of any trustee shareholders. But the company may alternatively decide to retain the £5,000 permanently by using it to fund the issue of 5,000 additional shares to be distributed free to the existing shareholders in the company on the basis of one new share for each two shares already held. Are these new shares equally to be treated as income in the hands of any trustee shareholders?

The general rule is that the new shares are capital and must be held by the trustees as such; however, the tenant for life will of course obtain some benefit from them by virtue of the fact that he will be entitled to the dividends which they produce.[56]

However, where the company has no power under its articles of association to create new shares in this way and therefore ought to have distributed the

---

[53] See *ante*, p. 607.
[54] Further income tax will be payable if the holder of the stock is a discretionary trust or a higher rate tax payer but this does not affect the value of the stock.
[55] *Re MacLaren's Settlement Trusts* [1951] 2 All E.R. 414 at 420.
[56] *I.R.C. v. Blott* [1921] 2 A.C. 171.

accumulated profit in cash, the shares distributed are regarded as income; this was decided in *Bouch v. Sproule*.[57] That decision was considered by the Privy Council in *Hill v. Permanent Trustee Co. of New South Wales*,[58] where Lord Russell of Killowen laid down the following principles.[59]

(a) Where a company makes a distribution of money among its shareholders, it is not concerned at all with the way in which the shareholders deal with that money. Thus, where the shareholder is a trustee, the company is not itself concerned with whether the money is treated as capital or income.

(b) Unless a company is in liquidation, it can only make a payment by way of a return of capital under a scheme for the reduction of capital approved by the court[60] (restrictions are placed on a reduction of capital by a company so that creditors of the company are not prejudiced). In any other case, apart from liquidation, it follows that, if the company is able to distribute money, that money must be profit so far as the company is concerned.

(c) Where the shareholder is a trust, the trustees will therefore generally receive the money as income which as such will be payable to the tenant for life. This will not be the case, however, if there is some provision in the trust instrument to the contrary, or if the following principle applies.

(d) Where the company has power under its articles of association to utilise its profits by adding them to capital and issuing bonus shares representing the amount of that additional capital to its shareholders, those shares are capital.

(e) Where the company's capital is increased in this way, its assets are undiminished (for the cash never leaves its hands) whereas, if a distribution of profits is made, the company's assets are consequently diminished.[61]

To these five principles a sixth was, in effect, added by Plowman J. in *Re Outen*,[62] namely that, where under a power in its articles of association a company capitalises profits, not by using the profits to issue new shares but by issuing some other investment in the company, that other investment is capital in the hands of a shareholder who is a trustee. This case arose out of a takeover bid made in 1962 by I.C.I. for Courtaulds. The bid was resisted by the directors of Courtaulds who, in order to persuade their stockholders not to sell their stock to I.C.I., capitalised £40 million of reserves, which represented capital profits, in accordance with the company's articles of association and used this sum to make a free issue of new loan stock to their stockholders. Before the takeover battle had commenced, a testatrix had left her holding of stock to

---

[57] (1887) 12 App.Cas. 385.
[58] [1930] A.C. 720.
[59] *ibid.* at 730–732.
[60] See now Companies Act 1985, s.135.
[61] Though why this should be relevant to a trustee is difficult to understand.
[62] [1963] Ch. 291.

trustees upon trust and in due course they, along with all the other stock-holders in Courtaulds, were issued with a holding of the new loan stock. Was this to be treated as capital or as income? Plowman J. held that, although Courtauld's actions had not involved the creation of any new shares, that company had effected a capitalisation under which the assets which were its subject matter ceased to have the character of divisible profits. The company's decision to this effect was binding on its stockholders; consequently the loan stock was capital.

A further complication arises where a company gives its shareholders the option either to have bonus shares or cash. In such circumstances what is crucial is whether the company intends to make a capital distribution or whether it really intends to distribute income.[63] If the intention of the company is to make a capital distribution then, whether the trustees take the bonus shares or the cash, what is received by them will be capital (in fact the cash offer is usually inferior in value to the offer of bonus shares and so the trustees should normally take the bonus shares). If, on the other hand, the intention of the company is to distribute income, then what is received by the trustees will be income; if the trustees take the cash, this will obviously be payable to the tenant for life but, if they take the bonus shares (which is what they should normally do), it was held at the end of the nineteenth century that the tenant for life will still receive only the value of the cash offer, the remainder of the value of the shares being regarded as capital.[64]

In summary, in the ordinary case where a company issues bonus shares, the reserves or profits which are used within the company to back the bonus shares are retained by the company as long-term capital. Consequently, bonus shares are in general received by trustees as capital. Where, on the other hand, the company has no power under its articles of association to create new shares in this way, the shares distributed are received by trustees as income. This is also the case where the intention of the company was to distribute income.

### 5. Capital Profits Dividends

All forms of distribution by a company by way of money or money's worth other than the issue of bonus shares or stock consist of the company passing on to its shareholders a profit which it has received without the company itself retaining any long-term benefit from the distribution. Therefore in the ordin-ary case, such dividends are received by the trustees as income.

The best illustration of this is provided by capital profits dividends, the distribution by a company of capital profits either in cash or in some other valuable form. A series of cases were decided around 1951 in relation to a capital profit dividend declared by Thomas Tilling & Co. A substantial part of the business of this company consisted of operating buses and coaches. When this part of its business was nationalised, the company received in compen-sation some British Transport stock, which it in turn distributed among its shareholders as a capital profits dividend. Was this stock to be regarded as

---

[63] I.R.C. v. Fisher's Executors [1926] A.C. 395.
[64] Re Malam [1894] 3 Ch. 578.

capital or as income for the purposes of a trust? In *Re Sechiari*,[65] and *Re Kleinwort*,[66] it was held that trustees received the stock as income and so it belonged to the tenant for life. The position was not the same as that of bonus shares in the company making the distribution, where the increase in the number of shares entitles the holders to participate in future dividends; this was an isolated payment, complete in itself, from which no future benefit would accrue directly from the company.

Nevertheless, in *Re Kleinwort*, Vaisey J. considered that, in special circumstances, the sum received was properly apportionable between capital and income. Such circumstances would arise where the trustees had committed a breach of trust, particularly in not maintaining a balance between the conflicting interests of different beneficiaries. Thus if the trustees acted solely with the intention of benefiting the tenant for life at the expense of the remainderman by investing in shares in a company in the expectation of a capital profits distribution, they would have committed a breach of trust and the court would undoubtedly apportion the capital profits dividend between income and capital. However, in *Re Rudd*,[67] it was held that a breach of trust had not been committed merely by virtue of the fact that trustees, who foresaw the capital dividend and so could have sold the stock with a large profit for capital, did not do so; consequently, the court refused to apportion the capital profit dividend received. This decision seems to be based entirely on the motive of the trustees which involved no intention of prejudicing the remainderman. Special circumstances were, however, found to exist in *Re MacLaren*.[68] The tenant for life consented to the purchase of stock in Thomas Tilling & Co. as a capital investment after it became known that that company intended to distribute the British Transport stock among its shareholders. It was held that he had to be regarded as having consented to the British Transport stock being regarded as capital and that it therefore was to be treated as capital.

The principle just illustrated by reference to the Thomas Tilling & Co. cases applies to any case where a company makes a capital profit and distributes it either in cash or in some other valuable form. That profit will therefore in normal circumstances be received by the trustees as income and so will be payable to the tenant for life. Where the distribution is as substantial as that made by Thomas Tilling & Co., the capital value of the fund will thereby be substantially reduced; in that case, the price of the shares fell by as much as 77 per cent, amount to an enormous windfall for the tenant for life and a substantial loss for the remaindermen.

## 6. Demergers

Similar potential difficulties are caused by the recently fashionable practice of demerging companies, that is to say hiving off some composite part of the businesses of a company into a new company and issuing all the shareholders of the original company with fully paid-up shares in the new demerged

---

[65] [1950] 1 All E.R. 417.
[66] [1951] Ch. 860.
[67] [1952] 1 All E.R. 254.
[68] [1951] 2 All E.R. 414.

company. This is done by the original company transferring the part of its assets which relate to the businesses which are to be demerged to a new subsidiary company and then declaring a dividend out of distributable profits. There are two ways of proceeding after that: the "direct" method is for the original company to satisfy the dividend directly by allocating to its shareholders shares in the subsidiary company, which then becomes the demerged company; the "indirect" method is for the shares in the subsidiary company to be transferred to a quite separate company, which then satisfies the dividend indirectly by allocating its own shares to the shareholders of the original company. Both of these methods appear to amount to a capital distribution which, in accordance with the principles just discussed, appears to be received as income for the purposes of a trust and will therefore be payable to the tenant for life. In one of the largest demergers of its time, that of the bioscience activities of I.C.I. into a new company, Zeneca Group, this potentially had the effect of halving the value of the capital investment in I.C.I. of any trust which held shares in that company and of providing the tenant for life with a windfall of half the capital value of those shares.

The companies involved were sufficiently anxious about this question to arrange for a test case, Sinclair v. Lee,[69] to be brought to establish how the shares allocated in the new company would be treated for the purposes of a trust. This demerger was to be carried out by the "indirect" method. Nicholls V.-C. stated that "no one, unversed in the arcane mysteries I shall be mentioning shortly, would have any doubt over the answer. Nobody would think that the Zeneca Group shares could sensibly be regarded as income."[70] He relied on the fact that, since this demerger was to be carried out by the "indirect" method, the shares of the demerged company, Zeneca Group, would never be held or received by I.C.I.; this enabled him to distinguish the authorities discussed in the previous two sections of this chapter and he therefore held that the distribution of Zeneca Group shares would indeed be capital for the purposes of a trust.

This decision establishes that shares in a company which is demerged by the "indirect" method will be capital for the purposes of a trust. However, the decision leaves completely open the position of shares in a company which is demerged by the "direct" method. Since the ground on which Nicholls V.-C. was able to distinguish the earlier authorities applies only to "indirect" demergers, it may well be that the opposite conclusion will be reached in respect of "direct" demergers. It may be that another test case will one day have to be brought in order to resolve this question.

## 7. Taxation Considerations

The treatment of the various types of dividends, distributions, and shares which have just been considered for the general purposes of trust administration has to be distinguished from their treatment for the purposes of taxation.

Company distributions are normally paid with a tax credit of 10 per cent so that the sum actually received has in effect suffered tax of 10 per cent, which is

---

[69] [1993] Ch. 497.
[70] ibid. at 504.

regarded as satisfying the basic rate of income tax. Trustees of fixed trusts need take no further action in respect of distributions paid over to a beneficiary who has a fixed interest; the distributions are taxed as his income so, if he is a higher rate taxpayer, he has to pay a further 30 per cent tax. However, discretionary trusts pay tax at a higher rate and so a further 15 per cent tax will be payable by the trustees of these settlements to bring the rate paid up to 25 per cent; distributions to beneficiaries will involve the trustees and higher rate taxpayer beneficiaries in paying further tax (other beneficiaries will be able to reclaim tax).

Where trustees elect to take scrip dividends rather than cash and where shares are held which carry with them the right to receive bonus shares,[71] then, if the company is resident in the United Kingdom,[72] the shares received are treated as income. The usual 10 per cent tax credit will not be forthcoming from the company and so tax is payable as if a dividend had been paid of an amount which, after deducting income tax at 10 per cent, equals the value of the scrip dividend or other shares at the date of issue.[73] If the scrip dividend or shares are passed to an income beneficiary, the notional amount of the dividend is treated as part of his income for income tax purposes. If the scrip dividend or shares are retained by the trustees as an accretion to capital for a remainderman there will be no further tax liability;[74] however, if the dividend or shares are retained by the trustees of a discretionary trust, they will have to pay a further 15 per cent tax to bring the tax paid up to 25 per cent.[75] Bonus shares and capital profits dividends are treated in the same way. Where, on the other hand, the company which pays the scrip dividend or in which the shares are held which carry with them the right to receive bonus shares is resident outside the United Kingdom, the shares which are received are treated as capital for taxation purposes if they would be so treated for the purposes of trust administration.[76]

The transfer of shares in demerged companies is not a distribution and so does not give rise to any payment of income tax. However, there are potential difficulties as to precisely what the base cost of the shares is for the purposes of capital gains tax where the shares are treated as the property of a fixed interest beneficiary; this particular question awaits resolution.

## IV. APPORTIONMENTS IN RESPECT OF NATIONAL SAVINGS CERTIFICATES

It has been seen[77] that, by virtue of the Apportionment Act 1870, it may be

---

[71] That is, the terms upon which the shares are issued gives the shareholders the right to call for bonus shares.

[72] Income and Corporation Taxes Act 1988, s.349.

[73] If, therefore, an issue of scrip is made which is worth £100, the company will be treated as if it paid a dividend of £111.11 from which 10 per cent income tax had been retained (£111.11 less £11.11 tax = £100).

[74] Because, in general, income received by trustees subject to deduction of tax at source is not further taxable in their hands; see *ante*, p. 629.

[75] This is the rate of tax payable on accumulated company distributions; see *ante*, p. 630. In the example given *ante*, fn. 73, the trustees would therefore be liable to pay an additional 15% of £111.11 = £16.67.

[76] *I.R.C. v. Wright* (1926) 11 T.C. 181.

[77] See *ante*, p. 663.

necessary to apportion by time dividends or other income between the person entitled to the income before an event, such as death, and the person entitled after that event. It is, however, first necessary to establish that the amount in question is of an income nature. This problem arises in particular with the increment over the purchase price which is payable on the encashment of National Savings Certificates. In *Re Holder*,[78] the testator in his lifetime purchased National Savings Certificates for £375, which were encashed after his death for £534. Roxburgh J. held that, by virtue of the terms on which the certificates were issued by the Government, the increment up to the date of death was capital. It was conceded that the increment which arose between the date of death and the date of encashment was to be treated as income, but the point was not actually argued. Although the basis for the concession does not appear from the report of the case, it would appear to be a correct concession, following the rule in *Re Earl of Chesterfield's Trusts*.[79]

## V. APPORTIONMENT OF OUTGOINGS

Subject to contrary directions in the trust instrument, expenses which relate solely to the income of a trust, such as the cost of making an income tax return, are primarily payable out of income, and other expenses, such as the cost of appointing new trustees or of bringing legal proceedings, are payable out of capital.

Where an audit takes place, however, the trustees may apportion the cost of this between capital and income in such proportions as they think fit.[80]

## VI. EXCLUDING APPORTIONMENTS

The apportionment rules are designed to achieve fairness and in most cases it is easy to see the logic behind them. Nevertheless, it is becoming increasingly common for them to be expressly excluded. This is partly due to taxation considerations but, in the main, it is because the calculations which have to be made under some of the rules are so complicated that it is far simpler from an administrative point of view for apportionments to be excluded. Ironically, then, the long-term effect of the rules has probably been the reverse of what equity actually intended.

---

[78] [1953] Ch. 468.
[79] (1883) 24 Ch.D. 643; see *ante*, p. 658.
[80] Trustee Act 1925, s.22(4).

CHAPTER 17

# INCOME FROM THE TRUST FUND

FIVE questions have to be considered about the income from a trust fund.

(a) What is the relationship between income received by the trustees from the assets which comprise the trust fund and the income to which the beneficiaries are entitled?

(b) Which beneficial interests under the trust carry the right to income?

(c) Are the trustees entitled to retain income?

(d) How are the trustees to apply income where the beneficiary is an infant?

(e) What are the taxation consequences of entitlement to income?

## I. THE INCOME OF THE TRUST FUND

### 1. *The Accounting Period*

One of the fundamental elements in the concept of income is that of time; it is only possible to speak of the income of trustees, or indeed of any person, if the period of time which is to be considered is known. For taxation purposes, the period to be considered is, generally,[1] the fiscal year of assessment which ends on April 5. Where a trust is created (as a result of becoming completely constituted) on any date other than April 6, the first accounting period for taxation purposes will be from the date of the creation of the trust until the following April 5, and the final accounting period will from the April 6 immediately prior to the date of termination of the trust until that date.

There are, however, no corresponding statutory rules for the purposes of general trust administration. The various Trustee Acts seem to proceed on the basis that the basic accounting period will be 12 months,[2] but this is not expressly provided anywhere and so the trustees can in principle select any period which they wish.[3] In practice, however, most trustees adopt for the

---

[1] The general rule applies for income tax and capital gains tax.
[2] See, for example, Trustee Act 1925, s.22(4) authorising trustees to have the trust accounts audited once in every three "years".
[3] Unless the trust instrument itself prescribes the accounting period.

purposes of trust administration the same accounting period as that adopted for the purposes of taxation.

## 2. Gross and Net Income

The trustees may derive income from a number of sources during an accounting period. For example, they may receive company distributions such as dividends, bank deposit interest, and rent. From this gross income, the expenses of the management of the trust will be deducted in so far as those expenses are applicable to income; so will any other payments which the trustees make in the exercise of administrative powers.

However, the net income will usually only be determined at some point of time after the end of an accounting period. This is because trustees have a reasonable time[4] within which to exercise powers and discretions and they will often wish to wait until the end of an accounting period before so doing in order that they can take their decisions in the light of the amount of gross income received in the whole of that period.

## 3. Trust Management Expenses

Expenses of a recurrent nature are generally payable out of income, unless the trust instrument provides otherwise. Thus, out of income is paid council tax and rates on any land owned by the trust;[5] rent payable in respect of leasehold property owned by the trust;[6] income tax;[7] and the cost of preparation of the annual accounts and the income tax returns.[8] The expenses which are payable from capital are discussed later.[9]

Although, in general, expenses are payable either from income or from capital according to their nature, the trust instrument can direct how the expenses are to be borne[10] and, in certain instances, the trustees are given a discretion. Thus, where the trustees require the trust accounts to be audited under the statutory power so to do,[11] they have an absolute discretion to pay the fees of the auditor either from income or from capital, or partly from income and partly from capital.

## 4. Administrative Powers

In *Pearson v. I.R.C.*,[12] the House of Lords drew a distinction between administrative powers and dispositive powers. Where payments are made by the

---

[4] See, for example, *Re Gulbenkian's Settlement Trusts (No.2)* [1970] Ch. 408.
[5] *Fountaine v. Pellet* (1791) 1 Ves. Jun. 337 at 342.
[6] *Re Gjers* [1899] 2 Ch. 54; *Re Betty* [1899] 1 Ch. 821.
[7] *Re Cain's Settlement* [1919] 2 Ch. 364. Capital gains tax is of course payable out of capital.
[8] See *Shore v. Shore* (1859) 4 Drew. 501. Strictly speaking, the costs of preparation of the capital gains tax return, which forms part of the same document as the income tax return, should be charged to capital; however, unless the time spent on doing this was very substantial, in practice the entire cost is likely to be paid out of income.
[9] See *post*, p. 693.
[10] However, the court may override the direction in the trust instrument; *Re Tubbs* [1915] Ch. 137; *Re Hicklin* [1917] 2 Ch. 278.
[11] Trustee Act 1925, s.22(4).
[12] [1981] A.C. 753.

trustees out of income in the exercise of their administrative powers, these payments are treated in the same way as trust management expenses, that is to say they are deducted from the gross receipts in determining the amount of the net trust income. On the other hand, payments which are made in the exercise of a dispositive power are applications of net trust income.

There are, in many respects, no clear authority as to precisely which powers are to be regarded as administrative and which as dispositive. In the absence of authority, the following classification is suggested for present purposes; however, as will be seen in a later chapter,[13] different considerations, and therefore a slightly different classification as to which powers are and are not administrative, may be necessary when it has to be decided, as a matter of private international law, which of these powers are governed by the proper law of a trust and which are governed by a different law which has been specified as governing that trust's administration.[14] The following are classified as administrative powers for all purposes:

(a) the power to engage and pay agents and professional advisers;

(b) the power to have investments held in the name of a nominee or by a custodian and to pay the nominee or custodian;

(c) the power to insure trust assets and to pay the premiums;

(d) the power to insure the life of the settlor or any beneficiary and to pay the premiums;

(e) the power to pay taxes and duties;[15] and

(f) the power to use income to improve land.

The following can also be classified as administrative powers for present purposes, although they may not be for the purposes of private international law:

(a) the power to charge for services;

(b) the power to retain commission, brokerage, and directors' fees; and

---

[13] See *post*, p. 861.

[14] The proper law of the trust will govern the nature of the interests of the beneficiaries and the duties of the trustees towards them (including any powers which they have to determine the manner in which the income and capital of the trust is distributed and their duties to convert and apportion the trust property) and also the construction of the trust instrument (unless this has been expressly reserved to the law of some other jurisdiction). The trustees' duties to provide accounts and to give information to the beneficiaries are purely administrative, as are their powers to appoint and remove trustees and all the powers listed in the first group of powers below in the text. But a number of other powers which are, for other purposes, often classified as administrative are capable of affecting directly or indirectly the interests of the beneficiaries in the event that the provisions of the proper law and of the law specified as governing administration differ as to their existence or scope. The presence or absence of a power for the trustees to remunerate themselves (although such a power is now implied in the case of trustees acting in a professional capacity) clearly affects the income and capital available for the beneficiaries. So does the presence or absence of powers of advancement, maintenance and accumulation in the event that they are exercised. So too, to a lesser extent, do the trustees' powers of investment.

[15] As to which see *Pearson v. I.R.C.* [1981] A.C. 753 itself.

(c)   the power to advance capital.[16]

The following can be classified as dispositive powers for present purposes although it is not inconceivable that they could be classified as administrative for the purposes of private international law.[17]

(a)   The power to accumulate income.

(b)   The power to pay or apply income to or for the maintenance, education, or benefit of a beneficiary.

(c)   The power to allow a beneficiary to use trust assets (even if on the exercise of that power an interest in possession in the assets is not created).

(d)   The power to pay the premiums on a policy of assurance which is effected for the benefit of a beneficiary.

(e)   The power to pay or apply income in securing the discharge of an obligation owed by a beneficiary or in guaranteeing the performance of an obligation by a beneficiary.

### 5. Net Trust Income

The net trust income in respect of an accounting period may, therefore, be said to be the aggregate of the gross income received[18] in that period from all the trust assets, less trust management expenses paid from income either by virtue of their nature or pursuant to a provision in the trust instrument, and less any other payments made from income in the exercise of an administrative power. In the remainder of this chapter, the net trust income in this sense is referred to as the trust income.

### II. GIFTS CARRYING INCOME

Once the amount of the trust income has been ascertained, it is then necessary to determine whether any beneficiary is entitled to that income. If he is, his interest is said to carry the intermediate income. The possibilities are:

(a)   a beneficiary is entitled to the income without any further decision of the trustees being necessary (this will usually be the case where trustees hold a fund upon trust to pay the income to Adam for life, with remainder to Eve);

(b)   no person is entitled to the income, because the trustees have the power to accumulate it and do so;

---

[16] In *Inglewood (Lord) v. I.R.C.* [1983] 1 W.L.R. 866, this power was treated as "similar" to an administrative power even though its exercise unquestionably affects beneficial entitlement.

[17] By analogy with the power to advance capital listed above.

[18] In many respects it is uncertain whether, in order for an amount to be taken into account, it must actually be received by the trustees or whether the fact that it is merely receivable suffices.

(c)  a beneficiary is entitled to the income but only as a result of the trustees exercising a discretion in his favour; and

(d)  the income has not been effectively disposed of and so is held on a resulting trust either for the settlor or, in the case of a trust *post mortem*, for the deceased's residuary beneficiaries or those entitled on his intestacy.

Vested gifts carry the intermediate income[19] unless the trust instrument provides either that it is to be paid to someone else,[20] or that it is to be accumulated and added to capital. This is the case whether the trust is fixed or discretionary.[21]

The question of whether contingent gifts carry intermediate income is more complex. In the case of wills, it is largely, but not entirely, governed by section 175 of the Law of Property Act 1925. This section[22] provides that, except in so far as the testator has otherwise expressly disposed of the income, the following types of gift carry the intermediate income as from the testator's death:

(a)  contingent or future specific devises or bequests[23] of property, whether real or personal;

(b)  contingent residuary devises of freehold land;

(c)  specific or residuary devises of freehold land to trustees upon trust for persons whose interests are contingent or executory.

The position in relation to vested and contingent interests under both *inter vivos* trusts and *post mortem* trusts,[24] in so far as the latter are not governed by section 175 of the Law of Property Act 1925, is as follows:

(a)  The directions of the settlor or testator always prevail. Accordingly, if the trust instrument directs that the income is to be accumulated, that direction will prevent the gift from carrying the intermediate income.[25] Similarly, even if the gift is vested and there is a direction for the payment of the income to another, that direction will prevail and the gift will not carry the intermediate income (an example would be where property was held in trust for a minor absolutely, subject to a provision that, until he attained the age of majority, the income should be paid to his cousin). Again, if payment is expressly

---

[19]  *Re Stapleton* [1946] 1 All E.R. 323.
[20]  Thus in the case of the gift to Adam for life, with remainder to Eve, both gifts are vested but the gift to Eve does not carry the intermediate income because the trust deed provides that it is to be paid to Adam.
[21]  Thus a discretionary trust of income for such of Adam, Eve, Abel and Cain as the trustees in their absolute discretion determine with a provision for accumulation in default does not carry the intermediate income during the accumulation period; once that period has ended, the gift does carry the intermediate income.
[22]  Which applies only to wills coming into operation on or after January 1, 1926.
[23]  A "devise" is a gift of realty by will; a "bequest" is a gift of personalty by will.
[24]  In each case, when they take effect after 1925.
[25]  *Re Turner's Will Trusts* [1967] Ch. 15; *Re Ransome* [1957] Ch. 348; *Re Reade-Revell* [1930] 1 Ch. 52.

deferred until a future date, the gift will not carry the intermediate income.[26]

(b) In the absence of express directions from the settlor or testator, a vested interest will carry the intermediate income subject to just one exception, a testamentary gift of residuary personalty which is expressly deferred to a future date.[27]

(c) In the absence of express directions from the settlor, a contingent interest arising under an *inter vivos* settlement carries the intermediate income provided the contingency is attaining the age of majority or the happening of some event (usually but not necessarily his marriage) before he attains that age.

(d) In the absence of express directions from the testator, a contingent interest arising under a will carries the intermediate income if it is:

   (i)   a residuary gift of personalty[28] but not if the interest is expressly deferred to a future date;[29]
   (ii)  a residuary gift of realty[30] but not if the interest is expressly deferred to a future date;[31]
   (iii) a specific gift of personalty, other than a pecuniary legacy,[32] even if the interest is expressly deferred to a future date.[33]

(e) In the absence of express directions from the testator, a pecuniary legacy does not generally carry the intermediate income. To this general principle there are two exceptions, when the gift does carry the intermediate income, namely:

   (i)   if the gift was to an infant by his parent or by some other person who stood *in loco parentis* to him, and

      (a)   if the gift is contingent, the contingency is not the attaining of an age greater than 18,[34] and
      (b)   there is no other fund set aside for the maintenance of the infant; or[35]

   (ii)  the testator directs that the legacy to be set apart from the rest of his estate for the benefit of the legatee.[36]

---

[26] *Re Geering* [1964] Ch. 136.
[27] *Re Oliver* [1947] 2 All E.R. 162; *Re Gillett's Will Trusts* [1950] Ch. 102.
[28] *Re Adams* [1893] 1 Ch. 329 (unaffected by the 1925 legislation).
[29] *Re Geering* [1964] Ch. 136.
[30] Law of Property Act 1925, s.175.
[31] This situation is not covered by Law of Property Act 1925, s.175.
[32] There is little logic in the distinction between contingent pecuniary legacies and other contingent gifts of personalty.
[33] *Re McGeorge* [1963] Ch. 544.
[34] *Re Jones* [1932] 1 Ch. 642; Family Law Reform Act 1969, s.1.
[35] *Re West* [1913] 2 Ch. 245. This is the effect of the words in what is now section 31(3) of the Trustee Act 1925 that the section "applies to a future or contingent legacy by the parent of the legatee if and for such period as, under the general law, the legacy carries interest for the maintenance of the legatee".
[36] *Re Jones* [1932] 1 Ch. 642; Family Law Reform Act 1969, s.1.

It should be emphasised that, as has already been mentioned, where the intermediate income is not carried, it is undisposed of; consequently, it is held on resulting trust for the settlor or, in the case of a trust *post mortem*, for the deceased's residuary beneficiaries or those entitled on his intestacy.

## III. THE RETENTION OF INCOME

Where trustees do not pay out or apply all the income, they will necessarily either have accumulated it or have retained it in its character as income.

### 1. *Accumulation*

Accumulation is the conversion of what was income into capital. It occurs at the moment at which the trustees decide to accumulate the income and, while no formality is required, it is desirable as a matter of practice for the decision to accumulate to be recorded carefully in the trust's minutes. Income can only be accumulated if, first, the trust instrument contains a trust or power enabling this to be done; secondly, that trust or power is not for an excessive period; and, thirdly, the trustees decide to give effect to the trust or to exercise the power.

### 2. *A Trust or Power to Accumulate*

Trustees have no general power to accumulate income. In *Re Gourju's Will Trusts*,[37] trustees held a fund upon protective trusts;[38] the fixed interest of the principal beneficiary having come to an end, the trustees sought to accumulate the income. However, Simonds J. said:[39]

> "I come to the conclusion that the obligation of the trustees is to apply the trust income as and when they receive it for the purposes indicated in the subsection. ... Putting it in a negative way, they are not entitled, regardless of the needs of the beneficiaries, to retain in their hands the income of the trust estate."

The trust or power to accumulate may arise either by virtue of the provisions of the trust instrument or, in the case of income which is held for the benefit of a minor beneficiary, by statute[40] to the extent that that income is not used for his maintenance.

---

[37] [1943] Ch. 24.
[38] Under Trustee Act 1925, s.33; see *ante*, p. 265.
[39] [1943] Ch. 24 at 34.
[40] Trustee Act 1925, s.31.

## 3. *Excessive Powers*

Where the trust is subject to English law, a trust to accumulate can at present only be prescribed for a maximum of one of the following periods:[41]

(a) the life of the settlor;

(b) a period of 21 years from the death of the settlor;

(c) the duration of the minority or respective minorities of any person or persons living or *en ventre sa mère* at the death of the settlor;

(d) the duration of the minority or respective minorities of infant beneficiaries who, if of full age, would be entitled to the income;

(e) a term of 21 years from the creation of the settlement; and

(f) the duration of the minority or respective minorities of any person or persons in being when the settlement is created, whether or not they are beneficiaries or have any other connection with the a settlement.

The period most commonly utilised is the term of 21 years from the creation of the settlement ((e) above). However, proposed new legislation will substitute all the above six possibilities for a period of 125 years (accumulation during the infancy of a beneficiary will obviously also continue to the possible).[42] If, at the end of the prescribed period, the income is *prima facie* payable to a beneficiary who is a minor, then income can nevertheless still be accumulated, to the extent that it is not utilised for the minor's maintenance, under the statutory trust to accumulate; this is also possible if a minor becomes the beneficiary in possession at a later stage.[43] Outside the permissible accumulation periods, the income cannot be accumulated and must be distributed to someone; where no beneficiary of the trust is entitled to it, it will have to be paid to the settlor or to those entitled to his estate.

If a trust prescribes accumulation for a period which is longer than that prescribed by statute, the whole gift is void if that period is longer than the appropriate perpetuity period,[44] but if that period is less than that period, it is void only as to the excess.[45] However, where a settlor wishes income to be accumulated for a period longer than the maximum permitted by English law, this can be achieved by providing for the trust to have as its proper law the law of a jurisdiction which permits a longer period. An on-shore jurisdiction which is popular for this purpose is Northern Ireland, which permits accumulation for the entire perpetuity period;[46] virtually all off-shore jurisdictions have longer accumulation periods, usually fixed periods of years. However, few, if any, of these jurisdictions have an accumulation period longer than the

---

[41] Law of Property Act 1925, s.164; Perpetuities and Accumulations Act 1964, s.13. These periods do not apply where the settlor is a body corporate; *Re Dodwell & Co. Ltd's Trust Deed* [1978] 3 All E.R. 738.

[42] See *ante*, p. 253.

[43] Trustee Act 1925, s.31(2).

[44] See *ante*, p. 242.

[45] *Re Joel's Will Trusts* [1967] Ch. 14.

[46] For an example of the use of trusts governed by the law of Northern Ireland for this purpose, see *Vestey v. I.R.C.* [1980] A.C. 1148.

125 years envisaged by the proposed new legislation, which is also proposed as the new perpetuity period.

## 4. Exercise of Power

Trustees must exercise any discretion within a reasonable time. What is reasonable depends on the facts of each case. In *Re Gulbenkian's Settlement Trusts (No.2)*,[47] trustees learned in April 1957 of a decision[48] which cast doubt on the validity of a provision in the trust instrument and they then retained the income in their hands as income without accumulating it. The doubt as to validity was not resolved until the decision of the House of Lords in *Re Gulbenkian's Settlement Trusts*[49] in October 1968. Plowman J. held that in the circumstances the trustees' retention of the income was not unreasonable and they were therefore still able to exercise their discretion in respect of all the income which had arisen since 1957. Thus, provided that they act reasonably, trustees can clearly retain income as income for a considerable time and then accumulate it.

If the trustees are under a specific duty to accumulate income, that duty is not extinguished by lapse of time. In such circumstances, the trustees can carry out their duty long after the income has actually arisen; further, if they do not do so, the court will issue a direction to this effect.[50] If, on the other hand, the trustees have only a mere power to accumulate, that is a duty to consider whether to accumulate but without any duty to do so, their power to accumulate will be lost if they do not act within a reasonable time.[51]

## 5. The Fiscal Effect of Accumulation

Trust instruments which impose a duty or confer a power to accumulate frequently also confer a power for payments from capital to be made to beneficiaries. The trustees may thus have both a power in respect of income, under which they may either distribute income as it arises to members of a discretionary class or accumulate it, and a trust or power to distribute capital, including accumulated income, to the same persons. What difference does it make to the beneficiary whether he receives a distribution of income or capital? This is largely governed by fiscal considerations.

What is the position of trustees of a fund who receive gross income of £1,000 per annum which they have a discretion either to distribute as income or to accumulate and who are considering making some form of distribution to two of the discretionary objects, George who pays income tax at the basic rate[52] of 22 per cent,[53] and Harry who pays income tax at the top rate of 40 per cent? The trustees are themselves generally liable to pay income tax at a total rate of

---

[47] [1970] Ch. 408.
[48] *Re Gresham's Settlement* [1956] 1 W.L.R. 573, subsequently overruled.
[49] [1970] A.C. 508.
[50] *Re Locker's Settlement Trusts* [1977] 1 W.L.R. 1323; see *ante*, p. 581.
[51] *Re Gourju's Will Trusts* [1943] Ch. 24; *Re Wise* [1896] 1 Ch. 281; *Re Allen-Meyrick's Will Trusts* [1968] 1 W.L.R. 499.
[52] See *ante*, p. 629.
[53] These examples assume that the top rate of tax payable by George will not alter as a result of him receiving another £1,000 gross income.

34 per cent on any income capable of being accumulated,[54] although a different rate is payable in respect of income from company distributions. On the assumption that none of the £1,000 is income from company distributions, the tax payable will be £340, although 20 per cent will already have been retained on any bank interest.

If the trustees then distribute the net amount of £660 to one of the two potential beneficiaries as income without first accumulating it, the beneficiary is treated as having received a gross payment of £1,000, from which tax at 34 per cent has been deducted. In the case of George, his marginal rate of tax is 22 per cent so he will be able to make a claim for the repayment of the difference between the tax which he ought to have suffered on the £1,000, namely £220, and the £340 tax which the income has actually borne; in the final result, he will therefore receive £660 from the trustees and £120 by way of tax reclaim. On the other hand Harry, who is liable to tax at 40 per cent, will be required to pay to the Inland Revenue the difference between the tax which the income of £1,000 has already borne, namely £340, and the £400 which is appropriate to his own top rate. He will therefore have to pay to the Inland Revenue £60 of the £660 which he receives from the trustees.

If the trustees instead accumulate the net income of £660 and then at some later stage distribute it as a capital payment, it is treated as capital for all purposes relating to income tax; consequently, no repayment claims can be made, nor can any further liability arise. Thus, George will be worse off because he will not be able to recover the £120 from the Inland Revenue but Harry will be better off since he will not have to pay the additional tax of £60. However, such a distribution from capital which has been derived from accumulated income will be treated in the same way as any other distribution of capital and may therefore give rise to a liability to inheritance tax.[55]

## 6. Retained Income

As income can be converted into capital as a result of a decision by the trustees to accumulate it, as a matter of strict theory the income can never be accumulated in the absence of such a decision. However, if the trustees are under a duty to accumulate, the longer the period which elapses the greater will be the willingness of the courts to hold that there has been an accumulation in any event. Similarly, the courts will infer that a decision to accumulate has been made if the trustees act in a manner which indicates that income has been accumulated; this will be the case for example, where trustees complete an income tax return for the trust showing the income as having been accumulated.

## 7. Beneficial Entitlement

Special rules apply where income has been accumulated during the minority of a minor beneficiary.[56] Apart from these special rules, which will be con-

---

[54] The provision also applies to income subject to a discretion. Income and Corporation Taxes Act 1988, s.686 (as amended by Finance Act 1993).
[55] Inheritance Tax Act 1984, s.65. See *ante*, p. 646.
[56] See *post*, p. 682.

sidered below, and subject to any contrary provision in the trust instrument, income which has been accumulated will be added to capital and the beneficiary ultimately entitled to the capital will also become entitled to the accumulations. On the other hand, income which is retained by the trustees without being accumulated will belong to the beneficiary, if any, who is entitled to income.

## IV. THE MAINTENANCE OF MINOR BENEFICIARIES

### 1. The Trust Instrument Prevails

Section 31 of the Trustee Act 1925 confers upon trustees a power to apply income in the maintenance of minor beneficiaries.[57] However, it was decided in Re Turner,[58] that all the provisions of this section, irrespective of whether they are expressed as powers or as duties, are in fact only "powers conferred by this Act" for the purposes of section 69(2) of the Act (this sub-section of course provides that "the powers conferred by this Act on trustees" apply only in so far as there is no intention expressed in the trust instrument that they should not apply). Therefore, although the general principle is that the statutory powers are additional to any powers in the trust instrument, any of the statutory powers, including the power of maintenance, may be expressly excluded, or varied, under section 69(2).

The statutory power of maintenance will be excluded: first, if and to the extent that the terms of an express power of maintenance are inconsistent with the statutory power; secondly, where any other provision in the trust instrument, such as a direction to accumulate the whole of the income, is inconsistent with the statutory power; and, thirdly, where there is a provision expressly excluding the statutory power. Re Erskine's Settlement Trusts,[59] is an example of the second and third of these circumstances. The settlor created a settlement for the benefit of his grandson Richard, who became entitled to the capital of the fund upon attaining the age of 22. What was Richard's entitlement to income prior to attaining that age? The trust instrument provided that the income should be accumulated both during the lifetime of the settlor and thereafter until Richard reached the age of 22; it also provided that the statutory powers of maintenance and advancement should not apply. The provision for accumulation was in fact void,[60] but Stamp J., following Re Turner,[61] held that the statutory power of maintenance was nevertheless effectively excluded. Consequently the income remained undisposed of until Richard reached the age of 22; it therefore belonged to the settlor's estate. While it is therefore possible to exclude the statutory power, that power will only be excluded if there is a clear expression of intention to that effect. If the trust instrument is silent on the point, then the statutory power will apply.

---

[57] There is no statutory power to maintain adult beneficiaries.
[58] [1937] Ch. 15.
[59] [1971] 1 W.L.R. 162.
[60] Because it was contrary to the Law of Property Act 1925, s.164.
[61] [1937] Ch. 15.

## 2. The Statutory Power

The statutory power of maintenance is contained in section 31 of the Trustee Act 1925. This provides[62] that, where property is held upon trust for any minor, then during the minority of that person the trustees may, if in their discretion they think fit, pay the whole or part of the income to the parent or guardian of the minor beneficiary or otherwise apply it for or towards his maintenance, education, or benefit. The trustees are under a duty to accumulate the whole of the income which is not paid or applied in this way.[63]

It follows from what has been said earlier in this chapter that the trustees will have a power to maintain a minor beneficiary unless the gift to the infant beneficiary does not carry the intermediate income[64] or the power has been excluded.[65] Where the statutory power arises, it has the following noteworthy features:

(a) The statutory power applies where the interest of the beneficiary is vested and to this extent overrides the apparent provisions of the trust instrument. Where trustees hold a fund upon trust for Cedric for life, remainder to Edmund, the terms of the trust instrument would suggest that Cedric is entitled to the whole of the income. However, the effect of the application of the statutory power of maintenance, assuming that it has not been excluded, is to deprive Cedric of any right to the income while he is under the age of 18 except to the extent that the trustees decide to pay or apply the whole or any part of it for his maintenance.

(b) The statutory power also applies where the interest of the beneficiary is contingent. So where a fund is held upon trust for Fergus if he attains the age of 30, the trustees may use the whole or any part of the income for his maintenance while he is under the age of 18, provided that the gift carries the intermediate income.[66]

(c) Although the statutory power refers to vested interests, it applies also to vested interests which are defeasible. Thus it applies where a fund is held upon trust for Solly but, if he dies under the age of 30, for Holly.

(d) The statutory power only applies while the beneficiary is under the age of 18.[67]

(e) Where the statutory power has not been excluded, the trustees are under a duty to consider whether to exercise their power but are under no obligation to do so. In deciding whether, and, if so, to what extent, to exercise the power, the trustees are directed by section 31 to

---

[62] Trustee Act 1925, s.31(1).
[63] ibid. s.31(2).
[64] See ante, p. 675.
[65] See ante, p. 682.
[66] See ante, p. 675. If the gift does not carry the intermediate income, there will obviously be no income available for the trustees to use.
[67] Family Law Reform Act 1969, Sched. 3, para. 5. See post, p. 684, as to the position when the beneficiary reaches the age of 18.

have regard: first, to the age of the minor; secondly, to what other income, if any, is available for his maintenance; thirdly, to his requirements; and, fourthly, "generally to the circumstances of the case". If the trustees know that other income is available for the maintenance of the minor and the total amount available exceeds the needs of the minor, then so far as is practicable a proportionate part only of each fund should be paid or applied for his maintenance. The trustees may pay any money which they decide to use either to the minor's parent or guardian[68] or apply it directly for his maintenance, education or benefit.

(f)  The statutory power applies whatever the nature of the property.[69]

(g)  Where the statutory power is to be exercised, the trustees must exercise it positively and not merely pay out the money for the minor's maintenance without considering whether or not it is desirable for them to do so. Thus, where[70] trustees made automatic payments to a minor's father without exercising any discretion, the court ordered that the money had to be repaid by them to the trust fund. But as long as the trustees exercise their discretion in good faith, the court will not interfere with their decision.[71]

### 3. Accumulation of Surplus Income

All income which is not paid to the parent or guardian of the infant beneficiary or applied by the trustees for his maintenance, education, or benefit must be accumulated.[72] Despite the fact that, by being accumulated, the surplus income becomes capital, the trustees may nevertheless use the income accumulated in previous years as if it were the income of a later year, provided that the interest of the beneficiary in question actually continues in that later year.[73]

### 4. Income Arising After the Age of 18

There is no statutory power to maintain an adult beneficiary. The general principle is therefore that, once the beneficiary has reached the age of 18, he is thereafter entitled either to the whole of the income[74] or to none of it. It is, however, possible for the trust instrument to confer an express power to maintain in these circumstances.[75] In Re McGeorge,[76] a testator devised land to his daughter but declared that the devise should not take effect until the death of his wife. It was held that this was a "future specific devise" within section 175 of the Law of Property Act 1925 and so prima facie carried the intermediate income. The daughter was over 18 and so claimed the income of the property.

---

[68] Sowarsby v. Lacy (1819) 4 Madd. 142.
[69] Stanley v. I.R.C. [1944] K.B. 255; Re Baron Vestey [1951] Ch. 209.
[70] Wilson v. Turner (1883) 22 Ch.D. 521 and see ante, p. 187.
[71] Re Bryant [1894] 1 Ch. 324; Re Lofthouse (1885) 29 Ch.D. 921.
[72] Trustee Act 1925, s.31(2). The manner in which the accumulations are dealt with is discussed post, p. 685.
[73] ibid.
[74] Re Jones' Will Trusts [1947] Ch. 48.
[75] Re Turner [1937] Ch. 15.
[76] [1963] Ch. 544.

Her claim was unsuccessful. Cross J. held that the testator, by having deferred the enjoyment of the property until after the widow's death, had expressed the intention that the daughter should not in fact have the intermediate income; it therefore had to be accumulated.

Where, on attaining the age of 18, the beneficiary has only a contingent interest in the trust property, he would, in the absence of any other provision, have no entitlement to anything until he satisfied the contingency. However, section 31(1)(ii) of the Trustee Act 1925 has the effect of accelerating the beneficiary's interest. It provides that, once the beneficiary has attained the age of 18, the trustees shall[77] thereafter pay to the beneficiary the income from the trust fund and the income from any accumulations[78] until the contingency is either satisfied or fails.

### 5. Accumulated Income at the Age of 18

When the minor beneficiary attains the age of 18, the trustees will hold the accumulations, including income from the accumulated fund which has itself been accumulated, in accordance with any provision of the trust instrument and, if there is no such provision, either for the beneficiary absolutely or as an accretion to the capital of the trust property.[79] A beneficiary will become entitled to the accumulations in the following circumstances:

(a) in any circumstances in which the trust instrument so provides; or

(b) if during his minority his interest was according to the settlement vested and he attains the age of 18;[80] or

(c) if he attains the age of 18 and is then entitled to capital[81] (for this purpose, a beneficiary is entitled to capital if, where the property is realty, he is entitled to a fee simple absolute, a determinable fee simple, or an entailed interest[82] or if, where the property is personalty, he is entitled to the property absolutely or for an entailed interest).[83]

In any other case, the accumulations are added to the capital of the property from which they arose.[84] Where they arose from a share of a fund and that share continued to exist as a separate share, the accumulations are an accretion to that share and not to the fund as a whole.[85] This is in contrast with the position where a beneficiary dies before attaining the age of 18 (or marrying

---

[77] Despite this apparently mandatory provision, the section can be excluded; Re Turner [1937] Ch. 15.
[78] Trustee Act 1925, s.31(1)(ii).
[79] ibid. s.31(2).
[80] ibid. s.31(2)(i)(a). This also applies if he marries under the age of 18 and had a vested interest until marriage.
[81] ibid. s.31(2)(i)(b). This also applies if he marries under the age of 18.
[82] See Re Sharp's Settlement Trusts [1973] Ch. 331 at 338.
[83] ibid.
[84] Trustee Act 1925, s.32(2)(ii).
[85] Re Sharp's Settlement Trusts [1973] Ch. 331.

under that age), in which case, subject to any provision in the trust instrument, the accumulations are an accretion to the fund as a whole.[86]

This latter point arose for consideration in *Re Sharp's Settlement Trusts*.[87] A settlement had conferred a power of appointment, exercisable during the perpetuity period, over the trust property, to which in default of appointment the children of the settlor were entitled in equal shares if they attained the age of 21. The settlor had three children: Penelope, who attained her majority in 1964; Russell, who attained his majority in 1967; and Joanne, who was at all material times an infant. Income had arisen under the settlement since 1966 and the trustees had appointed it to the three children equally; it obviously had to be paid out to any child who was of age. Between 1966 and the date when Russell attained his majority in 1967, his share of accumulated income amounted to about £5,000. Between 1966 and the date of the hearing in May 1972, Joanne's share of accumulated income amounted to about £41,000 and accumulation was continuing. Did the accumulations of the income of the shares of Russell and Joanne pass to them absolutely when each attained the age of 21 or did they instead form part of the settled fund, in which case they would still be subject to the future exercise of the power of appointment? Since the fund was personalty, Pennycuick V.-C. held that Russell and Joanne were not absolutely entitled to the accumulations which were therefore subject to the power of appointment (this is admittedly anomalous;[88] had the property been realty and the interest of the beneficiaries a determinable fee,[89] they would have been entitled to the accumulations). The further question then arose as to whether the accumulations were accretions to their individual shares or accretions to the fund as a whole. Penelope argued for the latter (because she would therefore potentially become entitled to part of the income from them). However, Pennycuick V.-C. took the opposite view; thus the accumulations from Russell's share were held, with that share itself, for Russell subject to any future exercise of the power of appointment, and Joanne's share was held in the same way, contingently on her reaching the age of 21. Russell was therefore immediately entitled to the income from his share, including the income produced by the accumulations.

The manner in which trustees deal with accumulations when a beneficiary reaches the age of 18 is illustrated by the following table. For the purposes of the table, "Conditions A" means that the beneficiary had a vested interest during infancy and attains the age of 18 and "Conditions B" means that the beneficiary attains the age of 18 and then becomes entitled to the capital.

---

[86] See *Re Joel* [1967] Ch. 14; *ante*, p. 663.
[87] [1973] Ch. 331.
[88] *ibid.* at 340.
[89] Although not a fee simple subject to a condition subsequent. As to the distinction, see *Megarry's Manual of the Law of Real Property* (8th ed., 2002), pp. 51 *et seq.*

| Trust instrument provides for fund to be held for | Circumstances | Entitlement | Remarks |
|---|---|---|---|
| Andrew absolutely[90] | Andrew attains 18 | Andrew | Conditions B |
| | Andrew dies under 18 | Andrew's estate | The entitlement is by virtue of the original gift, not s.31 |
| Brian for life | Brian attains 18 | Brian | Conditions A |
| | Brian dies under 18 | Added to capital | Neither Conditions satisfied |
| Charles for life if he attains 18 | Charles attains 18 | Added to capital | Charles' interest during infancy was contingent only and he does not become entitled to the capital |
| | Charles dies under 18 | Added to capital | Neither Conditions satisfied |
| Douglas if he attains 18 | Douglas attains 18 | Douglas | Conditions B |
| | Douglas dies under 18 | Added to capital | Neither Conditions satisfied |
| Edward if he attains 30 | Edward attains 18 | Added to capital | Neither Conditions satisfied |
| | Edward dies under 18 | Added to capital | Neither Conditions satisfied |
| Frank, but if he dies under 30, for George | Frank attains 18 | Frank | Although Frank's interest was defeasible, it was vested and Conditions A is satisfied |
| | Frank dies under 18 | Added to capital | Neither Conditions satisfied |
| Henry, but if he dies under 18 for Ian | Henry attains 18 | Henry | Conditions A |
| | Henry dies under 18 | Added to capital | Neither Conditions satisfied |

It will be seen from this table: first, that where the beneficiary dies under the age of 18, the accumulations will always be added to capital, except where the property was held for a minor beneficiary absolutely (as in the case of Andrew); secondly, that where the beneficiary has a life interest which is contingent on his attaining the age of 18, or some later age, then, notwithstanding the fact that he satisfies the contingency, the accumulations are added to capital (as in the case of Charles and Edward); and, thirdly, that the

---

[90] Andrew's infancy being the only reason why he could not call for the capital to be transferred to him.

distinction between a contingent interest (as in the case of Charles and Edward) and a vested interest which is defeasible (as in the case of Frank) is crucial.

## V. TAXATION CONSEQUENCES

Section 31 of the Trustee Act 1925 and the actions taken by trustees pursuant to that section can have a considerable effect on the fiscal position of the beneficiary. In considering these fiscal consequences, two points must be kept in mind: first, that section 31 can be excluded by the trust instrument; and, secondly, that where, according to the trust instrument, a minor beneficiary has a vested life interest, section 31 converts that interest into a life interest contingent on his attaining 18 in respect of any income which is accumulated (this happens because, notwithstanding the terms of the settlement, during the minority of the beneficiary the trustees will have a power to maintain and a trust to accumulate the remaining income and the beneficiary (or his estate) will only become entitled to the accumulations if he attains the age of 18). The latter point can cause considerable confusion. In order to determine the destination of accumulations, then, whether or not a beneficiary had during his minority a vested interest, regard is paid to the terms of the trust instrument. For all other purposes, however, the nature of the beneficiary's interest is determined by the terms of the trust instrument as modified by the section itself.

### 1. *Income Tax*

It has already been seen[91] that the income tax is payable at the basic rate[92] on all income which is received by trustees, regardless of whether that income is used for the payment of trust management expenses, paid to a beneficiary, or accumulated but that, if the trustees have a discretion with regard to the distribution of income or are directed to accumulate it, they are liable to pay additional income tax[93] so as to bring the total payable up a higher flat rate.[94]

If section 31 applies, then, whether the beneficiary's interest under the terms of the trust instrument is vested or contingent, the trustees necessarily have a discretion in that they have a power to maintain; consequently, they are liable to the higher flat rate. However, there is no further liability on the beneficiary unless the income is actually paid out to him, or applied for his benefit.

There is, however, a further rule under which a beneficiary will be taxable on the whole of the net trust income if he has a vested interest in it. He is taxable according to the rate of income tax applicable to his own income but he

---

[91] See *ante*, p. 629.

[92] At present (2003–2004) the trustees have to pay 22 per cent on all income except for company distributions and bank interest, in respect of which tax is retained at source at 10 per cent and 20 per cent respectively and those retentions satisfy the basic rate of tax.

[93] The additional rate is not payable in respect of that part of the gross income which was paid out in trust management expenses, which have in the first instance to be set against income taxed at 10 per cent, then against income taxed at 20 per cent and only subsequently against income taxed at 22 per cent.

[94] At present (2003–2004) 34 per cent in respect of all income except for company distributions, which are taxable at 25 per cent; credit is given for the 20 per cent retained on bank interest, and the 10 per cent retained on company distributions.

is entitled to a credit in respect of the income tax already paid by the trustees on the trust income paid to him. Suppose, therefore, that Harry, the beneficiary of a trust, has income apart from the trust of £40,000; that the income of the trust fund is £6,000 per annum gross, £2,000 from bank interest, and £4,000 from other sources (such as rent).[95] 20 per cent tax (£400) will have been withheld at source on the bank interest. The trust administration expenses are £700. If Harry has a vested interest under the trust, his liability is as follows:

| | | |
|---|---:|---:|
| The trustees have received | £6,000 | |
| *less*: 20% tax withheld on bank interest of £2,000 | £400 | |
| leaving | £5,600 | |
| from which they have paid trust management expenses of | £700 | |
| leaving net income paid to Harry of | £4,900 | |
| This is treated as a gross sum of | £5,250 | |
| from which income tax[96] has been retained of | £350 | |
| | £4,900 | |
| So Harry's trust income is: the amount paid to him | £4,900 | |
| and the tax retained on that amount | £350 | |
| | £5,250 | £5,250 |
| which is added to his other income of | | £40,000 |
| making a total income of | | £45,250 |
| On the "slice" of income between £40,000 and £45,250 the present rate of income tax[97] is 40%, producing a total liability of (40% × £5,250.00) | | £2,100 |
| The appropriate part of the retentions at source was | | £350 |
| So Harry has a further liability of | | £1,750 |

If the facts are varied so that Harry will only receive any income if the trustees exercise a discretion in his favour, either because the trust is a discretionary trust anyway or because he is a minor and section 31 applies, then the trustees can choose either to accumulate the income or to pay it to Harry. If they choose to accumulate the whole of the income, the total tax liability will be imposed on the trustees, as follows:

| | | |
|---|---:|---:|
| The trustees have received | £6,000 | |
| *less*: 20% tax withheld on bank interest of £2,000 | £400 | |
| leaving | £5,600 | |
| from which they have paid trust management expenses of | £700 | |
| leaving net income to be accumulated of | £4,900 | £4,900 |

---

[95] In practice, the trust would be likely also to have some income from company distributions but the different tax treatment of this source of income would make the example excessively complicated if any income from it were included.

[96] In effect, the £400 tax retained out of the trust income is attributed: as to
700/5600 × 400 = £50.00 to trust management expenses
4900/5600 × 400 = £350.00 to income paid to Harry.

[97] For 2003–2004.

| | | |
|---|---:|---:|
| *less:* tax at the flat rate of 34%[98] | £1,666 | |
| discounting the 20% retained at source on that part of the gross income of the trust of £6,000 not used in the payment of management expenses, which as seen above was £350 | £350 | |
| so the tax payable by the trustees is | £1,316 | £1,316 |
| So the net income accumulated is | | £3,584 |

If the trustees instead choose to pay the whole of the income to Harry, the total amount of tax payable will be the same as if Harry had had a vested interest.[99] The position will be:

| | | |
|---|---:|---:|
| Harry's trust income is: | | |
| the net income available for accumulation paid to him | £3,584 | |
| and the tax retained at source | £350 | |
| and the tax paid by the trustees | £1,316 | |
| | £5,250 | £5,250 |
| which is added to his other income of | £40,000 | |
| making a total income as before of | £45,250 | |
| On the "slice" of income between £40,000 and £45,250 the present rate of income tax is 40%, producing a total liability as before of (40% × £5,250.00) | £2,100 | |
| *less:* the appropriate part of the retentions at source | £350 | |
| the tax paid by the trustees | £1,316 | |
| So Harry has a further liability of | £434 | |

The income will be treated as that of Harry, during Harry's minority: first, if he is absolutely entitled to both capital and income, so that his infancy is the sole reason why he cannot call for the capital to be transferred to him, and either he, if he lives, or his estate, if he does not, will be entitled to the accumulations;[1] and, secondly, if, according to the terms of the trust instrument, Harry is entitled to the whole of the income, section 31 therefore being excluded, so that the trustees do not have power to accumulate any part of it. In all other circumstances, only that income which is actually paid to Harry or applied for his benefit, is treated as his for the purposes of income tax.[2] The remainder of the income, which is accumulated, is taxable in the hands of the trustees at the higher flat rate of, at present, 34 per cent.

### 2. Inheritance Tax

It has already been explained[3] that the relevant legislation[4] divides settled property into two main categories, according to whether or not there is, at the

---

[98] If any part of the income was from company distributions, then only a total of 25 per cent income tax would be payable on that income; 10 per cent retained and 15 per cent by the trustees; see *ante,* p. 630.

[99] This would not be the case if any part of the income was from company distributions, because then a total of 46% would be paid on that income rather than 40%; see *ante,* p. 630.

[1] *Roberts v. Hanks* (1926) 10 T.C. 351; *Edwardes-Jones v. Down* (1936) 20 T.C. 279.

[2] *Stanley v. I.R.C.* [1944] K.B. 255.

[3] See *ante,* p. 644.

[4] Finance (No.2) Act 1987.

time being considered, an interest in possession in that property. A beneficiary has an interest in possession if he is entitled to the trust income without the need for any further decision of the trustees to that effect.[5] Subject to certain limited exceptions, a charge to inheritance tax arises whenever an interest in possession terminates.[6]

In general, if there is no interest in possession in settled property and one then arises, there is a charge to inheritance tax at that time.[7] However, special inheritance tax privileges are given to one type of discretionary trust known as an "accumulation and maintenance settlement". Such settlements are governed by section 71 of the Inheritance Tax Act 1984, which was drafted with section 31 of the Trustee Act 1925 in mind. Section 71 of the 1984 Act provides that a settlement is an accumulation and maintenance settlement at any given time at which:[8] first, there is no interest in possession; secondly, the income is applied for the maintenance, education or benefit of a beneficiary and, to the extent that it is not so applied, it is to be accumulated; and, thirdly, it can be said that one or more beneficiaries will, on attaining a specified age not exceeding 25, become beneficially entitled either to the settled property itself or to an interest in possession in that property. Where the conditions for an accumulation and maintenance settlement are satisfied, the trust is not subject to what would otherwise be a potential charge to inheritance tax on every tenth anniversary of the date of its creation[9] and there is no charge to inheritance tax on the first occasion when each beneficiary becomes entitled either to an interest in possession in the settled property or to the settled property itself.[10]

The following table[11] illustrates the interaction of section 31 of the Trustee Act and the inheritance tax provisions. In the table, "I.H.T." means Inheritance Tax, "Acc. & Mtce" means an accumulation and maintenance settlement, "I.I.P." means interest in possession, and "D.T." means a discretionary trust other than an accumulation and maintenance settlement.

---

[5] *Pearson v. I.R.C.* [1981] A.C. 753; see *ante*, p. 673.
[6] Inheritance Tax Act 1984, ss.51, 52.
[7] *ibid.*, s.65.
[8] Only the basic conditions are given in the text; certain further ancillary conditions must also be satisfied. See Inheritance Tax Act 1984, s.65.
[9] By virtue of Inheritance Tax Act 1984, ss.64, 66.
[10] *ibid.*, s.65.
[11] There is no need to try to memorise this table. It is intended to show how it is necessary to consider, first, the terms of the trust instrument; secondly, whether the gift carries the intermediate income; and, thirdly, whether s.31 is or is not excluded.

| Trust instrument provides for | Section 31 Applies | | | Section 31 Excluded | | |
|---|---|---|---|---|---|---|
| | I.H.T. category during minority | Whether charge to tax on death under age 18 | I.H.T. effect on attaining 18 | I.H.T. category during minority | Whether charge to tax on death under age 18 | I.H.T. effect on attaining 18 |
| Andrew absolutely | Personal | Yes | Continues to be personal | Personal | Yes | Continues to be personal |
| Brian for life | Acc. & Mtce[1] | No | Brian becomes entitled to I.I.P | I.I.P. | Yes | I.I.P continues |
| Charles for life if he attains 18 | Acc. & Mtce[2] | No | Charles becomes entitled to I.I.P. | (i) I.I.P. if gift carries intermediate income<br>(ii) D.T. otherwise | Yes<br>No | I.I.P. continues<br>I.I.P. arises, if gift then carries intermediate income; and charge to tax |
| Douglas absolutely if he attains 18 | Acc. & Mtce[3] | No | Personal | (i) I.I.P. if gift carries intermediate income<br>(ii) D.T. otherwise | Yes<br>No | Personal<br>No charge to tax<br>Personal<br>Charge to tax |
| Edward if he attains 30 | (i) Acc. & Mtce[4] if gift carries intermediate income<br>(ii) D.T. otherwise | No | (i) I.I.P. if gift carries intermediate income<br>(ii) D.T. otherwise | (i) I.I.P. if gift carries intermediate income<br>(ii) D.T. otherwise | Yes<br>No | I.I.P. if gift continues to carry the intermediate income<br>(i) I.I.P. arises if gift begins to carry intermediate income. Charge to tax<br>(ii) Otherwise D.T. continues |
| Frank, but if he dies under 30, for George | Acc. & Mtce if gift carries intermediate income | No | I.I.P. if gift carries intermediate income. No charge to tax | I.I.P. if gift carries intermediate income | Yes | If gift carries intermediate income, I.I.P. contines |
| Henry, but if he dies under 18, for Ian | Acc. & Mtce if gift carries intermediate income | No | Personal. No charge to tax | I.I.P. if gift carries intermediate income<br>D.T. if gift does not carry intermediate income | Yes<br>No | Personal. No charge to tax if gift has carried intermediate income.<br>Charge to tax |

(1) The apparent interest in possession of Brian is removed by s.31.
(2) The conditions for an accumulation and maintenance settlement are prima facie satisfied because Charles will become entitled at an age not exceeding 25.
(3) Provided that the gift carries the intermediate income.
(4) The vested defeasible interest of Edward is converted by s.31.

CHAPTER 18

# APPLICATIONS OF TRUST CAPITAL

In general, entitlement to capital will depend, in the case of a fixed trust, on the terms of the trust instrument or, in the case of a discretionary trust, on the decision of the trustees. However, as in the same way as in the case of entitlement to income, the quantum of capital which is available for beneficiaries will be determined after the payment of those costs and expenses which are attributable to capital.[1] Further, even in the case of a fixed trust, the trustees may take decisions which have the effect of altering the time at which a beneficiary will take capital or the quantum of his entitlement.

The main powers which are capable of affecting the time and the quantum of entitlement to capital are powers of advancement, powers of appointment, and powers of appropriation. Powers of appointment have already been considered.[2] This chapter will, after dealing with expenses payable from capital, be concerned primarily with the powers of advancement and powers of appropriation.

## I. Expenses From Capital

It has already been seen[3] that, in general, recurrent expenses are payable out of the income of the trust fund. This is partly because of the recurrent nature of these expenses and partly because such expenses are generally incurred primarily for the benefit of the beneficiary who is entitled to income. The corollary of this is that, in principle, the capital of the trust fund has generally to bear expenses which constitute capital expenditure on one or more assets of the trust or which apply to the trust as a whole because these expenses can consequently be said to be for the benefit of all the beneficiaries.

Examples of expenses which are treated as capital expenditure on a trust asset are sums applied in discharging mortgage debts,[4] and sums applied in improving land and buildings.[5] Where a building is purchased by the trustees when it is in a derelict state, the cost of putting it into good condition at the outset will be treated as if it were part of the purchase price and so will be chargeable to capital.[6] On the other hand, ordinary repairs are, in principle,

---

[1] As to net income, see *ante*, p. 675.
[2] See *ante*, p. 182.
[3] See *ante*, p. 673.
[4] *Whitbread v. Smith* (1854) 3 De G.M. & G. 727; *Marshall v. Crowther* (1874) 2 Ch.D. 199.
[5] *Earl of Cowley v. Wellesley* (1866) L.R. 1 Eq. 656; *Re Walker's Settled Estate* [1894] 1 Ch. 189.
[6] *Re Courtier* (1886) Ch.D. 136.

payable out of income. However, where the repairs can be said to be for the benefit of all beneficiaries, in certain circumstances the trustees and the court have a statutory power to direct that the whole or part of the cost is to be borne by capital.[7] It can also be expressly provided by the trust instrument that the trustees have a discretion over when the cost of such repairs should be charged to income or to capital.[8] Where any such power exists, it must be exercised in such a way that the costs in question will be borne equitably between the beneficiaries with different interests.[9]

The second category of expenses which are borne by capital covers those items relating to the trust as a whole and which can be said to be for the benefit of all the beneficiaries. Examples are the costs of appointing new trustees,[10] of making changes in investments, of obtaining legal advice as to the extent of the trustees' powers,[11] and of taking or defending court proceedings for the protection of the trust assets.[12]

## II. ADVANCEMENTS

### 1. The Concept

An advancement essentially consists of the payment or the application of a capital sum in order to establish a person in life or to make permanent provision for him.[13] An advancement is often of an amount which, in the light of the circumstances of the recipient, is large; where a payment is large in this sense, there is a presumption that it is made by way of advancement.[14] However, it is not now generally necessary to consider in relation to the administration of trusts[15] whether or not a payment is, strictly speaking, by way of advancement; this is because the trustees now usually have a power to apply capital for the advancement or other benefit of a beneficiary, either under the statutory power considered below or under an express power in the trust instrument.

### 2. The Statutory Power

The statutory power of advancement is contained in section 32 of the Trustee Act 1925. This section gives trustees a power to pay or apply capital for the

---

[7] Under the Settled Land and Trustee Acts (Courts' General Powers) Act 1943 and Emergency Powers (Miscellaneous Provisions) Act 1953.

[8] See Paragraphs 1.4 and 1.5 of the Precedents for Administrative Provisions set out and discussed in Kessler, *Drafting Trusts and Will Trusts* (it is particularly important always to use the most recent edition of this work; the current one is the 6th (2002) edition).

[9] *Re Lord De Tabley* (1896) 75 L.T. 328; *Re Earl of Stamford and Warrington* [1916] 1 Ch. 404.

[10] *Re Fulham* (1850) 15 Jur. 69; *Re Fellows' Settlement* (1856) 2 Jur. (N.S.) 62.

[11] *Poole v. Pass* (1839) 1 Beav. 600.

[12] *Re Earl of Berkeley's Will Trusts* (1874) 10 Ch. App. 56; *Re Earl De La Warr's Estates* (1881) 16 Ch.D. 587; *Stott v. Milne* (1884) 25 Ch.D. 710.

[13] *Boyd v. Boyd* (1867) L.R. 4 Eq. 305; *Taylor v. Taylor* (1875) L.R. 20 Eq. 155; *Re Hayward* [1957] Ch. 528; *Hardy v. Shaw* [1975] 2 All E.R. 1052.

[14] *Taylor v. Taylor* (1875) L.R. 20 Eq. 155 at 157; *Hardy v. Shaw* [1975] 2 All E.R. 1052 at 1056.

[15] The situation is different in the administration of estates; see Administration of Estates Act 1925, s.46(1).

benefit of any beneficiary who is interested in the capital of the trust fund, whether his interest is vested or contingent, and whether or not it is liable to be defeated by the exercise of a power. Exercise of the power of advancement always has one and may have two important effects.

(a) The beneficiary who receives the advancement inevitably obtains a capital benefit from the trust earlier than he would otherwise have done. If trustees hold a fund on trust for Gerald for life, with remainder to Harry, and are able to pay part of the fund to Harry during the lifetime of Gerald,[16] Harry will takes the benefit of that part at that time, rather than having to wait until the death of Gerald.

(b) The beneficiary who receives the advancement may well receive a capital benefit from the trust which he otherwise might not have received at all. If trustees hold a fund on trust for Ian if he attains the age of 30 but, if he dies under that age, for John and pay part of the trust fund to Ian when he is aged 22, the subsequent death of Ian at the age of 25 means that he has obtained a capital benefit for which in the event he never actually qualified.

## (A) The Extent of the Statutory Power

Under the statutory power, the trustees can make payments by way of advancement or benefit to the same beneficiary on more than one occasion, provided that the total which is paid or applied does not exceed one half of the presumptive or vested share of the beneficiary.[17] It was decided in *The Marquess of Abergavenny v. Ram*[18] that, if the trustees ever advance to a beneficiary the whole of the permissible half of his presumptive or vested share, their power of advancement in favour of that beneficiary is thereby exhausted and no further advancement can be made to him even if the value of the remaining trust assets subsequently appreciates.[19] If the trustees of a trust out of which there have been no previous advancements made an advancement of £25,000 in 1998 to its sole contingent beneficiary when the value of the trust fund was £50,000 but by 2004 the value of the unadvanced half has risen to £80,000, they will have fully exhausted their power in 1998 and can make no further advancement in 2004. If, on the other hand, they only advanced £24,000 in 1998, so that their power was not fully exhausted, in 2004 they could advance the further sum of £28,000[20] (although it would again be better to advance only a lessser sum of (say) £27,000 so as to leave room for further advancements in the future).

---

[16] The consent of Gerald will be necessary, see *post*, p. 696.
[17] Trustee Act 1925, s.32(1), proviso (a).
[18] [1981] 1 W.L.R. 843.
[19] The decision was on a provision of the Marquess of Abergavenny's Estate Act 1946 but it is equally applicable to s.32 of the Trustee Act 1925.
[20] The calculation is:

| | |
|---|---|
| Value of fund in 2004 | 80,000 |
| Add: amount previously advanced | £24,000 |
| | £104,000 |
| One half of that | £52,000 |
| *less*: amount previously advanced | £24,000 |
| Maximum further advance | £28,000 |

### (B) Bringing Advancements into Account

If, after a beneficiary has received an advancement, he is or becomes absolutely and indefeasibly entitled to the trust property or to a share in it, he must bring into account the amount of his advancement.[21] Suppose that trustees who hold a fund upon trust for James and John in equal shares if and when they attain the age of 30 paid £20,000 by way of advancement to James when he was aged 26; if, by the time when the fund is distributed to James and John, it is worth £100,000, the amounts which they will receive are:

| | |
|---|---|
| Value of fund | £100,000 |
| Amount advanced | £20,000 |
| Total | £120,000 |

*Entitlement*

| | James | John |
|---|---|---|
| ½ × £120,000 | £60,000 | £60,000 |
| *less*: advancement | £20,000 | — |
| Net entitlement | £40,000 | £60,000 |

When an advancement was not made in cash but in specie, the amount to be brought into account is the value of the asset at the time when the beneficiary becomes absolutely and indefeasibly entitled to his share.[22]

However, if the beneficiary who received the advancement had only a contingent or defeasible interest and never becomes absolutely and indefeasibly entitled, the amount advanced to him cannot be clawed-back. Consequently, the trustees can, by making an advancement to a contingent beneficiary, partially defeat the interests of other beneficiaries.

### (C) The Possible Need for Consents

Where the making of an advancement will prejudice the interest of a prior beneficiary, the advance can only be made if that beneficiary is of full age and consents in writing to it. Thus if £100,000 is settled upon trust for Mary for life, with remainder to Derek, the statutory power, if applicable, will enable the trustees to advance up to £50,000 to Derek but only if Mary consents. If Mary does consent and an advancement of the full £50,000 is made, thereafter her income will be that produced by the remaining £50,000 and not, as previously, by £100,000. It should be noted that a person on whom property is settled on protective trusts will not normally forfeit his life interest by consenting to an advancement.[23]

### (D) The Nature of Property which can be Advanced

The statutory power of advancement applies only to money or securities or to land which is the subject matter of a trust of land. It therefore does not apply to capital money arising under a settlement subject to the Settled Land Act 1925.[24]

---

[21] Trustee Act 1925, s.32(1), proviso (b).

[22] See *Hardy v. Shaw* [1975] 2 All E.R. 1052.

[23] See *ante*, p. 269.

[24] Trustee Act 1925, s.32(2) (substituted by Trusts of Land and Appointment of Trustees Act 1996 Sched. 3, para. 3(8)). No further settlements under the Settled Land Act can now be created.

## 3. Exclusion, Extension and Replacement of the Statutory Power

The statutory power will apply even where there is no mention of it in the trust instrument. However, the power is one which falls within the scope of section 69(2) of the Trustee Act 1925;[25] consequently, the settlor or testator can exclude or extend or completely replace that power in the trust instrument. Thus, in *Re Evans's Settlement*,[26] Stamp J. held that, where the trust instrument provided that the trustees could advance up to £5,000, this by implication excluded the statutory power of advancing up to one-half of the prospective interest. Further, in *I.R.C. v. Bernstein*,[27] where there was a direction to accumulate income during the settlor's lifetime, the Court of Appeal held that this was a sufficient indication that the settlor did not intend the statutory power of advancement to apply. However, in practice it is more likely that the statutory power will be extended or completely replaced. The most usual extensions give the trustees a power to advance up to the whole and not merely one half of the beneficiary's share, extend the power to the subject matter of settlements under the Settled Land Act 1925, and, in some cases, do away with the need to obtain the consent of beneficiaries with prior interests. But it is now more common completely to replace the statutory power by conferring on the trustees a totally unfettered power to make advancements as part of their overriding power of appointment.[28]

## 4. The Purpose of an Advancement

It has already been seen[29] that a power of advancement had originally to relate to some substantial preferment in life. Examples were the purchasing of a commission in the Army[30] (the modern equivalent would be purchasing a partnership in a business or practice), the purchasing or furnishing of a house,[31] or even establishing the husband of a daughter in business.[32] It has also been seen that the need for a substantial preferment of this kind has been modified by the extension of the statutory power of advancement to payments which produce "benefit", a word of wide import. However, the trustees must nevertheless still consider whether a particular advancement is or is not for the benefit of the beneficiary in question. In *Lowther v. Bentinck*,[33] it was held that the payment of his debts was not as such for the benefit of a beneficiary, though in special circumstances a payment to a beneficiary which enabled him to discharge his debts might be a benefit for this purpose.[34] And it is extremely clear that the trustees must not make an advancement which will benefit

---

[25] See *ante*, p. 682.
[26] [1967] 1 W.L.R. 1294.
[27] [1960] Ch. 444.
[28] See the overriding powers of appointment in the different precedents set out and discussed in Kessler, *Drafting Trusts and Will Trusts* (it is particularly important always to use the most recent edition of this work; the current one is the 6th (2002) edition).
[29] See *ante*, p. 694.
[30] *Lawrie v. Bankes* (1857) 4 Kay & J. 142.
[31] *Perry v. Perry* (1870) 18 W.R. 482.
[32] *Re Kershaw's Trust* (1868) L.R. 6 Eq. 322.
[33] (1875) L.R. 19 Eq. 166.
[34] See *Re The Esteem Settlement* [2002] W.T.L.R. 337 (Jersey Court of Appeal).

themselves. In *Molyneux v. Fletcher*,[35] the trustees made an advance to a beneficiary to enable her to pay the debts which her father owed to one of the trustees; this was held to be an improper exercise of the power of advancement.

In most cases the "benefit" for which an advancement is made is some form of material benefit. In some circumstances, however, the court will authorise an advancement to be made for the moral, and not necessarily material, benefit of the beneficiary. In *Re Clore*,[36] a beneficiary who was entitled to an interest in a trust fund of considerable value felt a moral obligation to make payments to charity. Pennycuick J. authorised an advancement to enable him to do so on the apparent basis that, since the beneficiary felt that he was subject to this obligation, the payment by the trustees was only relieving him of a financial obligation which he would otherwise have sought to meet from his personal funds. The judge made it clear, however, that the beneficiary must genuinely feel the moral obligation himself; the trustees were not at liberty to make payments in satisfaction of what they considered to be the beneficiary's moral obligations if the beneficiary did not himself share their view. Further, with the possible exception of relatively small amounts, it is considered prudent for trustees to seek the prior sanction of the court before making advancements of this nature.

Just as trustees cannot properly make an advancement in order to benefit themselves,[37] they cannot make an advancement with a view to benefiting some other person other than the beneficiary. In *Re Pauling's Settlement Trusts*,[38] the bankers Coutts & Co. were trustees of a fund for a wife for her life, with remainder to her children. The trust instrument contained an express power for the trustees to advance to the children up to one-half of their share with the consent of the wife. The husband of the life tenant, who was the father of the children, regularly lived beyond his means and therefore sought to obtain part of the trust moneys. A series of advancements were made, nominally to the children. However, the money advanced was used for the benefit of the father or the family in general; the proceeds of one advance were used to purchase a house for the father in the Isle of Man and the proceeds of another one were used to discharge a loan incurred by the mother. Counsel had advised the trustees that, so far as they were concerned, they were advancing the money to the children for their own absolute use and that what the latter then did with the money was not the trustees' concern. This view was unanimously rejected by the Court of Appeal, who considered that:

"the power [of advancement] can be exercised only if it is for the benefit of the child or remoter issue to be advanced or, as was said during argument, it is thought to be 'a good thing' for the advanced person to have a share of capital before his or her due time. ... [A] power of advancement [can] be exercised only if there is some good reason for it. That good reason must be beneficial to the person to be advanced; [the

---

[35] [1898] 1 Q.B. 648.
[36] [1966] 1 W.L.R. 955.
[37] *Molyneux v. Fletcher* [1898] 1 Q.B. 648.
[38] [1964] Ch. 303.

power] cannot be exercised capriciously or with some other benefit in view."[39]

In their consideration of the circumstances in which an advancement could properly be made, the Court of Appeal drew a distinction between the situation where the beneficiary applies for an advancement for a particular purpose and the situation where the trustees themselves stipulate the purpose to which the advancement is to be put. As Willmer L.J. said:

"if the trustees make the advance for a particular purpose which they state, they can quite properly pay it over to the advancee if they reasonably think they can trust him or her to carry out the prescribed purpose. What they cannot do is to prescribe a particular purpose and then raise and pay the money over to the advancee, leaving him or her entirely free, legally and morally, to apply it for that purpose or to spend it in any way he or she chooses. ... This much is plain, that if such misapplication [of the money advanced] came to [the trustees'] notice, they could not safely make further advances for particular purposes without making sure that the money was in fact applied to that purpose, since the advancee would have shown him or herself quite irresponsible."[40]

The court expressly left open the question whether, in the event that money advanced for a particular purpose was used for something quite different, that money could be recovered by the trustees. This possibility apart, the trustees certainly have no legal control over the money once they have paid it to the beneficiary; consequently, they must take pains to ensure that the beneficiary is under a moral obligation to apply the money to the purpose intended.

### 5. Adult Beneficiaries

While, as has already been seen,[41] the statutory power of maintenance applies only to minor beneficiaries, the statutory power of advancement can be exercised in favour of beneficiaries of any age.[42]

### 6. Fiscal Considerations

Where an advancement is made, there is a potential liability both to capital gains tax and to inheritance tax.

If the advancement is made in cash, there can be no liability to capital gains tax in respect of the advancement itself although, if the trustees disposed of chargeable assets in order to produce funds with which to make the advancement, a liability to capital gains tax in respect of that disposal may have arisen according to general principles.[43] If, however, the advancement is made in specie then, at the time when the trustees decide to make the

---

[39] ibid. at 333.
[40] ibid. at 334, 335.
[41] See ante, p. 682.
[42] In Hardy v. Shaw [1975] 2 All E.R. 1052 there was an advancement, in the strict sense of the expression, in favour of persons who were middle-aged.
[43] See ante, p. 633.

advancement, they will be deemed to have disposed of the asset at its market value at that time and then immediately to have re-acquired it at that value as nominees for the beneficiary.[44] If the asset has risen in value since it was acquired, the same capital gains tax will be payable as if the asset had actually been sold for that value. However, provided that the beneficiary is resident in the United Kingdom, the trustees and the beneficiary can elect for "hold-over" relief to apply if, first, the assets settled comprise business assets[45] or if, secondly, the creation of the trust involves a chargeable transfer for the purposes of inheritance tax.[46]

With regard to inheritance tax, if the advancement is to a beneficiary who immediately before the advancement had an interest in possession, there will be no liability to inheritance tax by virtue of that advancement.[47] In every other case there will be a potential liability,[48] although in the case of small advancements, its amount may be reduced by the use of the annual exemption[49] of the beneficiary who has the interest in possession.[50]

## III. ADVANCEMENTS INTO SETTLEMENT

### 1. Generally

Originally, an advancement necessarily consisted of an outright payment of money or the transfer of an asset to a beneficiary. However, during the twentieth century,[51] it became established that a power of advancement could, in principle, be exercised so that the money or property was not transferred outright but became held on new trusts for the benefit of the beneficiary in question.[52] This is usually done in one of three ways.

(a) If the beneficiary is *sui juris*, the trustees may make an outright payment to him, thereby putting him into the position in which he can himself creating a new settlement.[53]

(b) The trustees may exercise a power given to them in the trust instrument in order to declare that thenceforth they will hold a part

---

[44] Taxation of Chargeable Gains Act 1992, s.71(1).
[45] *ibid.* s.165.
[46] See *ante*, p. 635.
[47] Finance Act 1975, Sched. 5, para. 4(3).
[48] *ibid.*, para.4(2). The transfer may of course be exempt, potentially exempt or chargeable.
[49] For 2003–2004, this is £3,000.
[50] Even if the transfer is chargeable, no tax will actually be payable to the extent that its value falls within the beneficiary's nil rate band.
[51] Following certain decisions at the end of the nineteenth century.
[52] The principle has long been established. See *Re Halstead's Will Trusts* [1937] 2 All E.R. 570; *Re Moxon's Will Trusts* [1958] 1 W.L.R. 165; *Re Ropner's Settlement Trusts* [1956] 1 W.L.R. 902; *Re Wills' Will Trusts* [1959] Ch. 1; *Re Abraham's Will Trusts* [1969] 1 Ch. 463; *Re Hastings-Bass (dec'd.)* [1975] Ch. 25; *Pilkington v. I.R.C.* [1964] A.C. 612.
[53] In *Roper-Curzon v. Roper-Curzon* (1871) L.R. 11 Eq. 452, where it was necessary for the court to give its sanction to an advancement, it refused to give that sanction unless the beneficiary resettled the amount to be advanced.

of trust fund on separate trusts for the benefit of one or more of the beneficiaries.[54]

(c) A new settlement may be created, either by the trustees or by some other person, usually with a nominal sum of money, so that a convenient "vehicle" can be established. The trustees of the existing settlement then transfer the amount to be advanced to the trustees of the new settlement as an addition to the funds of that settlement to be held on the trusts declared by it.[55]

It will be apparent that the trustees of the original settlement may, but not necessarily will, be the trustees of new settlement created with the advanced fund. Whichever method is used, some aspects of the passing of funds from an existing settlement into a new settlement require consideration.

### 2. Is the Proposed Advance for the Benefit of the Beneficiary?

Any advancement, whether outright or into settlement, must be for the benefit of the beneficiary to be advanced. The following principles are established by the authorities.

In general, "benefit" means direct financial benefit, so that it is unlikely that there will have been a valid exercise of the power of advancement if the quantum of the beneficiary's interest is reduced. This point is most likely to arise where the trustees wish to make a settled advance on protective trusts for the beneficiary in question. In *Re Morris*,[56] Jenkins L.J. laid down the principle that a "power of advancement is a purely ancillary power, enabling the trustee to anticipate by means of an advance under it the date of actual enjoyment by a beneficiary and it can only affect the destination of the fund indirectly in the event of the person advanced failing to attain a vested interest". He therefore held that an advancement into settlement on protective trusts was not valid because it altered the beneficial interests. However,[57] some advancements on protective trusts can nevertheless be held to be for the direct financial benefit of the beneficiary, provided that they comply with the remaining requirements.

An advancement on settlement will be for the benefit of the beneficiary if a fiscal liability which would otherwise arise in respect of the funds held for the beneficiary is mitigated.[58] The position was summarised by Viscount Radcliffe in *Pilkington v. I.R.C.*,[59] when he said that "if the advantage of preserving the funds of a beneficiary from the incidence of [tax][60] is not an advantage personal to that beneficiary, I do not see what is". If, in order to effect the fiscal mitigation, it is necessary for the beneficiary not to take any, or any direct, financial interest in the advanced fund, the advancement may still be proper.

---

[54] See *Hoare Trustees v. Gardner* [1978] 1 All E.R. 791.
[55] See *Hart v. Briscoe* [1978] 1 All E.R. 791; *Pilkington v. I.R.C.* [1964] A.C. 612.
[56] [1951] 2 All E.R. 528.
[57] See *post, infra.*
[58] *Re Ropner's Settlement Trusts* [1956] 3 All E.R. 332; *Re Meux* [1958] Ch. 154; *Re Wills' Will Trusts* [1959] Ch. 1.
[59] [1964] A.C. 612 at 640.
[60] The tax in question was estate duty.

*Re Clore's Settlement Trusts,*[61] which has already been mentioned,[62] concerned a transfer of funds into a charitable settlement under which the beneficiary took no beneficial interest.[63]

In determining whether an advancement into settlement is for the benefit of a beneficiary, all the terms of the instrument which constitutes the new settlement, not merely those under which the trustees are in practice likely to act, must be considered. In *Re Hunter's Will Trusts,*[64] a testator settled property upon trust for his sister for life, with remainder to her children with "such provision for their respective advancement maintenance and education" as the sister should by will appoint; one of the sister's sons was financially unstable and in fact became bankrupt shortly after she made her will. In an attempt to enable her son to enjoy the benefit of part of the trust property, she purported to appoint that property upon protective trusts for him. Cross J. held the trust invalid, following the dictum of Jenkins L.J. in *Re Morris*[65] that protective trusts should not be regarded

> "merely as a device to enable a forfeiting life-tenant to enjoy the income notwithstanding purported alienation and so forth or the event of his or her bankruptcy, and that the discretionary trust should be regarded merely as machinery to that end and not as really designed to confer any beneficial interest on the issue nominally included in it. The validity or otherwise of the discretionary trust declared in the event of forfeiture must, in my view, be determined by reference to what the trustees are empowered to do under such a trust, and not by reference to what they would in fact be likely to do, or be expected to do, under it."

A beneficiary may derive a benefit from knowing that financial provision is being made for his wife and children. So, in *Re Halsted's Will Trusts,*[66] Farwell J. held that trustees could in the exercise of a power of advancement for a beneficiary properly settle funds on trust for the beneficiary, his wife and his children. Nor is there any necessary connection between "benefit" and "need". Thus, an advancement of funds may be valid if the trustees consider that it is for the benefit of the beneficiary, irrespective of his needs.[67]

### 3. *The Benefit of the Other Beneficiaries under the Advancement*

Property will only be settled if at least one person other than the beneficiary receiving the advancement has some interest therein, either vested or contingent. The fact that one or more other persons will or might benefit does not

---

[61] [1966] 1 W.L.R. 955.
[62] See *ante*, p. 698.
[63] The decision may depend on its particular facts.
[64] [1963] Ch. 372.
[65] [1951] 2 All E.R. 528.
[66] [1937] 2 All E.R. 570.
[67] In *Re Pilkington's Will Trusts* [1961] Ch. 466 the Court of Appeal had held that there could only be a valid advancement into settlement where the benefit to be conferred was related to the real or personal needs of the beneficiary. This was rejected by the House of Lords in *Pilkington v. I.R.C.* [1964] A.C. 612.

in itself make an advancement into settlement defective. This is one of the several points which the House of Lords decided in *Pilkington v. I.R.C.*[68]

A testator set up a will trust under which the trustees were directed to hold the trust fund on trust, broadly, for the benefit of the testator's nephew Richard for life, with remainder to such of Richard's children as he should appoint, or, in default of appointment, for all of his children in equal shares. Richard had three children, all born after the death of the testator, one of whom was his daughter Penelope. When Penelope was still very young, the trustees wished to advance funds into a new settlement for her benefit. What was proposed was the creation of a settlement under which the income would be accumulated or used for Penelope's maintenance until she reached the age of 21. Penelope was to be entitled to income on attaining that age and to the capital on attaining the age of 30; if she died under the age of 30, other members of the family were to benefit. One-half of Penelope's share under the original settlement was to be transferred to the trustees of the proposed new settlement. The House of Lords held that, in principle,[69] this would be within the trustees' power of advancement, notwithstanding the fact that other members of the family might benefit instead of or as well as Penelope.

### 4. *Can Dispositive Discretions be Conferred under the New Settlement?*

In *Re Wills' Will Trusts*,[70] Upjohn J. said that "a settlement created in exercise of the power of advancement cannot in general delegate any powers or discretions, at any rate in relation to beneficial interests, to any trustees or other persons, and in so far as the settlement purports to do so, it is pro tanto invalid". These remarks have given rise to the view that an advance into a discretionary settlement would be unauthorised; they have also given rise to the view that, if there is an effective advancement into a settlement on protective trusts, the discretionary trusts which would normally arise on the termination of the principal beneficiary's life interest would also be ineffective. Both the dictum of Upjohn J. and the views to which it has given rise follow from the maxim *delegatus non potest delegare*. However, the better view seems to be that discretions can be conferred on the trustees of the new settlement. In the first place, in *Pilkington v. I.R.C.*,[71] Viscount Radcliffe said:

> "I am unconvinced by the argument that the trustees would be improperly delegating their trust by allowing the money raised to pass over to new trustees under a settlement conferring new powers on the latter. In fact I think the whole issue of delegation is here beside the mark. The law is not that trustees cannot delegate: it is that trustees cannot delegate unless they have authority to do so. If the power of advancement which they possess is so read as to allow them to raise money for the purpose of having it settled[72] then they do have the necessary authority to let the money pass out of the old settlement into the new trusts. No question of delegation of their powers or trust arises."

---

[68] [1964] A.C. 612.
[69] The actual appointment was void because it contravened the rule against perpetuities.
[70] [1959] Ch. 1 at 13.
[71] [1964] A.C. 612 at 639.
[72] Which was how the power was read by the House of Lords.

This seems to mean that, provided that the power in the original settlement is sufficiently wide, the advancement can properly be made into a new settlement which does confer dispositive powers on its trustees and, further, that the statutory power, or an express power with similar effect, will be construed as being sufficiently wide. Modern overriding powers of appointment generally expressly permit the conferring of dispositive powers on both trustees of new settlements and others.[73]

Secondly, where there is an advancement into settlement, the principle of *delegatus non potest delegare* is rarely observed in its entirety. It is clear that, even when the original settlement does not give its trustees any general right to confer dispositive powers on the trustees of a new settlement, powers of advancement can nevertheless be conferred.[74] It has of course already been seen[75] that, while a power of advancement may conceptually be regarded as nothing more than a power to bring forward the date at which a beneficiary begins to enjoy the benefit of the trust property,[76] the exercise of such a power may well nevertheless alter the ultimate beneficial enjoyment of the funds advanced.

Thirdly, if in appropriate circumstances[77] there can be a valid advancement into a settlement under which the beneficiary whose interest is being advanced takes no interest whatever in the sum advanced, it would be quite absurd if there could not be a valid advance into a settlement under which he was a discretionary beneficiary.[78]

While it is therefore thought that there is no fundamental objection to a new settlement conferring dispositive powers on its trustees, it is nevertheless still necessary in any particular case to show that the creation of the new settlement is for the benefit of the beneficiary whose interest is being advanced.

## 5. What Perpetuity Period Applies to the New Settlement?

Where the trustees of an existing settlement make an advance into a new settlement, for the purposes of the rules against perpetuities the trustees are treated as if they had exercised a special power of appointment. Accordingly, the interests limited by the new settlement, when read back into the original settlement, must comply with the rule against perpetuities as it applied to the original settlement. It was on this ground that the House of Lords held that the proposed appointment in *Pilkington v. I.R.C.*[79] would have been void.

The Perpetuities and Accumulations Act 1964 will therefore only apply to the advancement if the original settlement itself was made after July 15, 1964;[80] this is why the pre-existing rules must even today still govern many

---

[73] See the overriding powers of appointment in the different precedents set out and discussed in Kessler, *Drafting Trusts and Will Trusts* (it is particularly important always to use the most recent edition of this work; the current one is the 6th (2002) edition).

[74] *Re Mewburn* [1934] Ch. 112; *Re Morris* [1951] 2 All E.R. 528; *Re Hunter's Will Trusts* [1963] Ch. 372.

[75] See *ante*, p. 693.

[76] *Re Morris* [1951] 2 All E.R. 528; see *ante*, p. 700.

[77] As in *Re Clore's Settlement Trust* [1966] 1 W.L.R. 955; see *ante*, p. 698.

[78] Although the issues of benefit and delegation are separate, much greater tax mitigation may be achieved by using discretionary, rather than fixed, trusts.

[79] [1964] A.C. 612; see *ante*, p. 701.

[80] s.15(4) will apply to exclude the Act in the case of original settlements made before that date.

advancements — powers of advancement can be exercised at any time until a beneficiary obtains an absolute vested interest in possession, which may not occur for well over fifty years. However, where the 1964 Act does apply, the interests under the new settlement will be treated as valid until, if at all, it becomes established that those interests will in fact vest outside the perpetuity period.[81] But under the proposed new legislation, all special powers, whenever created, will be permitted the new 125-year fixed period measured from the date of the original creation of the power (this is one of only two provisions of that legislation which will affect gifts which have already come into effect).

If some of the interests purportedly created by the new settlement fall foul of the applicable rule against perpetuities, the result of the advancement will depend on whether the provisions of the new settlement which are effective will, when taken by themselves, be for the benefit of the beneficiary whose interest is being advanced and will not have an effect totally different from what the trustees intended. This is shown by the decision in Re Hastings-Bass (deceased),[82] where trustees transferred from an existing settlement the sum of £50,000 to be held upon the trusts of a new settlement by way of advancement for the primary benefit of one particular beneficiary, William. However, the trustees had misunderstood the effect of the new settlement, under which the life interest conferred on William was valid but all of the remaining beneficial interest were void for perpetuity.

The first question was whether an exercise of the statutory power of advancement could be valid when its effect was to give the beneficiary whose interest was being advanced, in this case William, only an interest in income and no interest in capital. The court held that this was a sufficient "application" of the funds and that the appointment was not necessarily defective on that ground.

The second question was of more general application. Was the purported exercise of the power effective when the trustees did not fully appreciate the effects of the new settlement and so could not take into account all the relevant circumstances? The court held that, where trustees purport to exercise a power in good faith, then, even if the effect of that purported exercise is different from that intended by the trustees, the court would only interfere with the purported exercise in two circumstances. First, the court would interfere if the result actually achieved was not authorised by the trustees' power. Secondly, the court would interfere if it was clear that the trustees would not have acted as they did had they not taken into account considerations which they ought not to have taken into account or if they had not failed to take into account considerations which they ought to have taken into account (there has since been considerable controversy both as to the correct formulation of this particular principle, which has become known as the Rule in Re Hastings-Bass (deceased), and as to the circumstances which will bring that Rule into operation[83] but this is not relevant for present purposes). In this case, the effect of conferring an effective life interest on William was to achieve a substantial saving of estate duty.[84] It was likely, therefore, that the trustees would have

---

[81] s.3; see ante, p. 242.
[82] [1975] Ch. 25.
[83] See ante, p. 215.
[84] The inheritance tax rules are different; consequently no tax would be saved if the facts recurred at the present time.

acted broadly as they had even if they had appreciated the true effect of the advancement; consequently, the court held that the exercise of their power was valid. If, however, it had been held that the trustees would not have acted as they had if they had appreciated the true effect of the advancement, the purported exercise of their power would have been void.[85]

### 6. Fiscal Considerations

Just as a liability to capital gains tax may arise in the case of an ordinary advancement,[86] so it may arise in the case of an advance into settlement. The capital gains tax legislation treats most settlements as if they are each separate legal persons. Thus, if an asset is transferred from one settlement to another settlement, that asset is deemed to have been disposed of by the trustees of the transferring settlement and to have been acquired by the trustees of the acquiring settlement. However, the capital gains tax legislation does not actually prescribe any rules for determining precisely what constitutes a separate settlement. Particular difficulties arise where the trustees of a settlement declare that they will themselves henceforth by way of advancement hold part of the trust fund on separate trusts for the benefit of one of the beneficiaries; when will that part of the trust fund become subject to a new settlement and when will it remain within the original settlement? In *Roome v. Edwards*,[87] Lord Wilberforce said "Since 'settlement' and 'trusts' are legal terms, which are also used by businessmen or laymen in a business or practical sense, I think that the question whether a particular set of facts amounts to a settlement should be approached by asking what a person, with a knowledge of the legal context of the word under established doctrine and applying this knowledge in a practical and commonsense manner to the facts under examination, would conclude."

If the resettlement occurs only as the result of the exercise by the trustees of their powers under the original settlement, it seems that the exercise of a special power of appointment will not amount to a resettlement so that there will be no consequential deemed disposal of the property in question;[88] on the other hand, while the exercise of a wider power, such as a power of advancement, will not necessarily amount to a resettlement, it will have this effect if the new settlement is complete in itself and is sufficiently separate to require no further reference back for any purpose to the original settlement.[89] If there is such a resettlement, the trustees of the original settlement are deemed to dispose of all the assets which become subject to the new settlement at their market value at the time and the assets are then reacquired at that value. However, if the acquiring settlement is resident in the United Kingdom, hold-over relief is available in the circumstances already discussed: if, first, the assets settled comprise business assets[90] or if, secondly, the creation of the trust involves a chargeable transfer for the purposes of inheritance tax.[91]

---

[85] *Re Abraham's Will Trust* [1969] 1 Ch. 463 but see now *ante*, p. 219.
[86] See *ante*, p. 699.
[87] [1981] 1 All E.R. 736 at 739.
[88] *Roome v. Edwards* [1981] 1 All E.R. 736; *Bond v. Pickford* [1983] S.T.C. 517.
[89] *Swires v. Renton* [1991] S.T.C. 490.
[90] Taxation of Chargeable Gains Act 1992, s.165.
[91] See *ante*, p. 635.

There may also be a liability to inheritance tax if there was an interest in possession under the original settlement and the same beneficiary does not have an immediate interest in possession under the new settlement.[92] There will not usually be a liability if there was no interest in possession either under the original or the new settlement[93] but in other cases there usually will be.

## IV. OTHER APPLICATIONS OF CAPITAL

In some cases, the available powers of maintenance and advancement, whether they are the statutory powers or are contained in the trust instrument, will not be sufficient for a beneficiary's needs. Where this is the case, there are four other possibilities:

(a) maintenance out of capital;

(b) an application to the court under section 53 of the Trustee Act 1925;

(c) an application to the court under its inherent jurisdiction; and

(d) an application to the court to vary the trust (this is considered in a later chapter).[94]

### 1. Maintenance out of Capital

Although, in principle, income is to be used for the maintenance of a beneficiary,[95] it is just about possible that the trustees can use capital for this purpose.

Section 31 of the Trustee Act 1925 clearly envisages that only income will be used for maintenance and it was said, in a note to the old case of *Barlow v. Grant*,[96] that "the court will not permit executors and trustees to break in upon the capital of infants' legacies without the sanction of the court, and the court itself, though it will break in upon the capital for the purpose of advancement, will rarely do so for maintenance". But, no matter how rarely a court will exercise its power to use capital for an infant's maintenance, it undoubtedly does have such a power. Lord Alvanley L.C. said in *Lee v. Brown*,[97] that "[t]he principle is now established that if an executor does without application what the court would have approved, he shall not be called to account, and forced to undo that merely because it was done without application". The precise extent of this dictum (the case actually concerned an advancement) is not entirely clear but it is just about possible that a trustee who had maintained out of capital would not be called upon to make good the capital if the court would itself have ordered maintenance out of capital.

However, quite apart from the doubtful legality of such a course of conduct, there would today be fiscal disadvantages in following it; in respect of every

---

[92] Inheritance Tax Act 1984, ss.51, 52.
[93] *ibid.*, s.81; however, for tax purposes the property remains comprised in the first settlement.
[94] See *post*, p. 747.
[95] See *ante*, p. 682.
[96] (1684) 1 Vern. 255.
[97] (1798) 4 Ves. 362.

£1 taken out of capital for this purpose, the trustees would today have to deduct income tax at the basic rate and pay it over to the Revenue.[98] In contrast, no income tax is payable where an advancement of capital is made; thus, by making an advancement, the result of a purported maintenance out of capital can be achieved much more advantageously.

## 2. Section 53 of the Trustee Act 1925

This section provides that, where a minor is beneficially entitled to any property, the court may, "with a view to the application of the capital or income thereof for the maintenance, education, or benefit of the" minor, make an order appointing a person to convey the minor's interest on his behalf. This section is chiefly used where the minor's interest is small and produces very little income and where, if the interest were sold, the proceeds could be used for the minor's maintenance or benefit.[99] It was however pointed out in *Re Meux*,[1] that this section does not give the court power to dispose of the minor's interest whenever it is merely for the minor's benefit; there must be "a view to the application" of the capital or income for the maintenance, education or benefit of the minor. It therefore seems that it must be intended to apply the capital or income in some way for the benefit of the minor. In *Re Heyworth's Contingent Reversionary Interest*,[2] the court refused to give its consent under section 53 to a proposal merely to sell the minor's interest and hand over a cash sum without there being any clear idea as to what was to happen to that money thereafter. On the other hand, where what is proposed is to resettle the money and the transaction as a whole is for the minor's benefit, the court has held that the fact that there was to be a resettlement was a sufficient "application" to come within this section.[3]

An example of the use of this power can be seen in *Re Bristol's Settled Estates*.[4] There were two tenants in fee tail of settled land, the Marquis of Bath and his infant son, Lord Jermyn. The estate was a large one and in order to save estate duty it was, in essence, proposed that the existing settlement should be terminated, part of the property paid absolutely to the Marquis of Bath, and the remaining part resettled. Provided the Marquis lived for a period of five years (and an insurance policy was to be taken out to cover the possibility of him failing to do so), both he and the ultimate beneficiaries would gain by the arrangement, the only loser being the Inland Revenue. Before the scheme could be put into operation, it was necessary for the estates in fee tail to be "barred" by being converted into estates in fee simple. The Marquis of Bath was entitled to carry out this process in respect of his own estate in fee tail and, had Lord Jermyn not been a minor, he could have done the same with the consent of his father, who was (in the original sense of the expression) the protector of the settlement.[5] The court made an order under

---

[98] See *ante*, p. 629.
[99] *Ex parte Green* (1820) 1 Jac. & W. 253; *Ex parte Chambers* (1829) 1 Russ. & M. 577; *Ex parte Swift* (1828) 1 Russ. & M. 575.
[1] [1958] Ch. 154.
[2] [1956] Ch. 364.
[3] *Re Meux* [1958] Ch. 154.
[4] [1965] 1 W.L.R. 469.
[5] For the original and the modern sense of this expression, see *ante*, p. 190, fn. 75.

section 53 appointing a named person to execute with the consent of the Marquis of Bath an assurance on behalf of Lord Jermyn "barring" his estate in fee tail; that way the capital and income could, under the proposed scheme, be appointed for his benefit.[6]

Schemes for raising money for the education of a minor, or to provide him with a house, or to purchase a share in a partnership for him clearly also fall within the terms of section 53 of the Trustee Act 1925.[7]

### 3. The Inherent Jurisdiction of the Court

In limited circumstances the court has an inherent jurisdiction (quite apart from the Variation of Trusts Act 1958)[8] to modify the terms of the trust. One of the occasions in which it will do so is where a settlor or testator has made some provision for a family but has postponed the enjoyment for example, by directing accumulation of the income for a set period. Where this has been done, the trustees cannot themselves use the income to maintain a minor but the court will assume from the fact that the settlor has made provision for the family that he did not intend to leave the minor children inadequately provided for. The court has, therefore, in some cases directed that the income (or some part of it) is not to be accumulated but is instead to be used for the maintenance of the minor.[9]

### V. APPROPRIATION

Appropriation occurs when trustees effectively set aside part of the trust property and earmark it for a specific purpose. For the purposes of trust law generally, the effect of appropriation is that beneficiaries who have an interest in the appropriated fund have no rights in respect of the non-appropriated property and the beneficiaries of the non-appropriated property have no rights in respect of the appropriated fund. The position is, generally speaking, as follows:

(a) Trustees do not have any general power to appropriate.

(b) The trust instrument may direct appropriation or confer on the trustees a power to appropriate.

(c) If the trust instrument directs that different property to be held on different trusts, that will be treated as an implied direction to appropriate.[10] If, therefore, the trust instrument directs one quarter of the trust property to be held on trust for Pinky for life, with

---

[6] See also Re Lansdowne's Will Trusts [1967] Ch. 603.

[7] Re Baron Vestey's Settlement [1951] Ch. 209.

[8] See post, p. 747, as to the circumstances in which the court may vary beneficial interests in this and other cases.

[9] Havelock v. Havelock (1881) 17 Ch.D. 807; Re Collins (1886) 32 Ch.D. 229; Revel v. Watkinson (1748) 1 Ves. Sen. 93; Re Walker [1901] 1 Ch. 879; Greenwell v. Greenwell (1800) 5 Ves. 194; Cavendish v. Mercer (1776) 5 Ves. 195; Errat v. Barlow (1807) 14 Ves. 202.

[10] Fraser v. Murdoch (1881) 6 App. Cas. 855; Re Walker (1890) 62 L.T. 449; Re Nicholson [1939] 3 All E.R. 832.

remainder to her issue, and the other three quarters to be held on trust for Perky for life with remainder to her issue, then separate funds should be appropriated.

(d) It seems that, if property is held on express trust for sale, the trustees have an implied power to appropriate unless there is a direction to the contrary in the trust instrument.[11]

(e) A mere power to appropriate, whether express or implied, will require the consent of any adult beneficiaries affected, although not of minor or unborn beneficiaries. However, the power may go beyond one merely to appropriate, in which case it will be a power to appropriate without any consent being required. In any event, consents are not required where the trust instrument directs appropriation.

(f) Personal representatives are given a statutory power of appropriation,[12] but this does not apply to trustees.

---

[11] *Re Nickels* [1898] 1 Ch. 630; *Re Brooks* (1897) 76 L.T. 771.
[12] By Administration of Estates Act 1925, s.41.

CHAPTER 19

# THE POSITION OF A BENEFICIARY UNDER A TRUST

In general terms, as long as a trust is being properly administered and is continuing, a beneficiary has no right to interfere in its administration but has passively to wait to receive the benefits to which he is entitled under the trust. If, however, the trust is not being properly administered, the beneficiary can take steps to compel its proper administration, and in any case may take certain action to preserve his position. Ultimately, however, the destiny of the trust may well lie in the beneficiary's own hands since, if various conditions are fulfilled, he can bring the trust to an end even if this appears contrary to the wording of the trust instrument.

## I. THE BENEFICIARY'S RIGHT TO INFORMATION

A beneficiary will obviously not be able to do anything unless he actually knows that he is a beneficiary in the first place. It has already been seen[1] that, while executors are under no duty to inform the beneficiaries of a will of their rights thereunder,[2] trustees of both testamentary and *inter vivos* fixed trusts who have agreed to act are under a duty to inform the beneficiaries of the existence and nature of their interests under the trust.[3] The same principle presumably applies to discretionary trusts in favour of relatively small groups of beneficiaries. However, it is clearly impracticable to oblige or to expect trustees of the many modern discretionary trusts which have enormous classes of beneficiaries to notify every single potential member of his potential rights thereunder;[4] the most that they could conceivably be expected to do would be to advertise for potential beneficiaries to present themselves. But it cannot seriously be doubted that the need to compel the proper administration of trusts dictates that trustees should be obliged to give a truthful answer to any potential beneficiary who actually enquiries. Where a beneficiary knows that he is a beneficiary or a potential beneficiary of a discretionary trust but does not know the identity of the current trustees, he is able to oblige the

---

[1] See *ante*, p. 582.
[2] *Re Lewis* (1868) 5 L.R. Eq. 545. This was a particularly strong case since the executor was entitled to the subject matter of a legacy in the event that the beneficiary in question failed to claim it and the failure to inform the latter of the existence of the legacy meant that he failed to do so prior to his death.
[3] *Hawkesley v. May* [1956] 1 Q.B. 304.
[4] See Davies (1995) 7 Bond Law Review 5, referring to the remarks of Mahoney J.A. in *Hartigan Nominees v. Rydge* (1992) 29 N.S.W.L.R. 405 at 425 & 432 (Court of Appeal of New South Wales).

settlor to disclose this information to him;[5] however, this right does not extend to trusts of which he merely suspects that he is a beneficiary or potential beneficiary.

When a beneficiary is or has become aware that he is a beneficiary or potential beneficiary, it has also already been seen[6] that there has until recently never been any doubt about the right of beneficiaries of both fixed trusts and small discretionary trusts to require information as to the state of the trust property and to any dealings with it and sight of the corresponding trust documents; nor was any distinction drawn between beneficiaries with interests in possession and those whose interests had either not yet vested or had not yet vested in possession.[7] Doubts had, however, been expressed both as to whether the right was or should be available to every single potential member of the enormous classes of beneficiaries which many modern discretionary trusts now have[8] and as to the position of persons who are not among the actual beneficiaries of a discretionary trust but are merely among the possible objects of a power of appointment. However, according to the Privy Council in *Rosewood Trust v. Schmidt*,[9] these distinctions no longer have any formal significance; the right to require information is instead now to be approached as merely one aspect of the court's inherent jurisdiction to supervise (and where appropriate intervene in) the administration of trusts. In practice, however, these distinctions will obviously remain highly relevant in the court's exercise of that inherent jurisdiction. The immediate beneficiaries of fixed trusts and of small discretionary trusts are bound in practice to be given exactly the same trust documents as hitherto. But disclosure to the beneficiaries of large discretionary trusts and potential beneficiaries of all types of trusts is likely to be restricted to those who in practical terms have a reasonable chance of receiving some part of the trust property at some point. This means that the rights of default beneficiaries, the ultimate beneficiaries of discretionary trusts who, although they are necesssarily beneficiaries of fixed trusts, are only likely to take in the event of the death of all the other beneficiaries, may well now in practice be considerably restricted.

## II. THE CONTROL OF TRUSTEES' DISCRETIONS

Two fundamental principles govern the control of trustees by beneficiaries. First, so long as the trust continues, decisions which have to be made in the administration of the trust are to be made by the trustees alone. Secondly, all the beneficiaries under the trust, if they are *sui juris* and between them absolutely entitled to the trust property, may bring the trust to an end.[10]

The court is jealous to preserve the trustees' powers, largely because the main function of trustees is to control the trust as a whole and the right to exercise all the decisions necessary goes to the root of trusteeship. Thus, even where it has power to do so under the Variation of Trusts Act 1958, the court

---

[5] *Murphy v. Murphy* [1999] 1 W.L.R. 282.
[6] See *ante*, p. 584.
[7] *Re Londonderry's Settlement* [1965] Ch. 918.
[8] *Hartigan Nominees v. Rydge* (1992) 29 N.S.W.L.R. 405 (Court of Appeal of New South Wales).
[9] [2003] 2 W.L.R. 1142.
[10] See *post*, p. 717.

will not approve an arrangement which could override the discretionary powers which the trustees intend to exercise.[11] The leading case is *Re Brockbank*,[12] although the actual decision in that case has been abrogated by statute. It was seen in an earlier chapter[13] that, where the trust instrument does not expressly confer the power to appoint new trustees on anyone, then the existing trustee or trustees are given that power by section 36 of the Trustee Act 1925. In *Re Brockbank*, the beneficiaries, who were all *sui juris* and were between them absolutely entitled to the whole of the beneficial interest under the trust, wished to appoint a new trustee against the wishes of the existing trustee. It was held that the appointment of new trustees was a power given to the existing trustees and this power could not be exercised by the beneficiaries. This principle survives in relation to powers in general; however, where section 19 of the Trusts of Land and Appointment of Trustees Act 1996 applies to the trust in question (which it will do unless it has been excluded by the settlor),[14] beneficiaries who are *sui juris* and between them absolutely entitled to the whole of the beneficial interest under the trust are now entitled to require the trustees to retire and to appoint the new trustees nominated by the beneficiaries.

It has also been suggested,[15] probably correctly, that, while the beneficiaries cannot generally speaking cut down the trustees' powers, they can add to them. It must be stressed that this right, if it exists, is only to add to the powers of trustees, not to their duties; their existing discretions are therefore preserved intact but are enlarged.

The main areas in which beneficiaries are likely to seek to control the trustees' discretions are with regard to investments and in respect of the exercise of their discretions under discretionary trusts. In both respects the trustees' position is essentially the same. They must take note of any representations made to them, for these representations may properly affect the exercise of their discretion. Thus, if one of the beneficiaries passes to the trustees confidential information that shares in a particular company are likely to improve rapidly, the trustees must give full consideration to that information in reaching their decision as to whether or not to buy. But the decision must be theirs, for they are the persons who can best judge the interests of all the beneficiaries and it will be them, not the beneficiary in question, who will be ultimately answerable for the decision reached.

To the general rule that the trustees should listen, but must alone make the decisions, there are certain exceptions.

(a) The trustees' discretions may be limited by contract; thus, where a person acts as nominee for another, the terms of the arrangement between them may require the trustee-nominee to act in accordance with the directions of the beneficiary.

(b) The trustees' discretions may be limited by the terms of the trust instrument itself; the usual form of this limitation is to require the

---

[11] *Re Steed's Will Trusts* [1960] Ch. 407, also discussed *post*, p. 751.
[12] [1948] Ch. 206.
[13] See *ante*, p. 551.
[14] It is usually so excluded.
[15] Underhill & Hayton, *Law of Trusts and Trustees* (16th ed., 2003), p. 735.

consent of a beneficiary or other person to the sale of a particular asset but there is no reason in principle why their discretions should not be restricted in some other way.

(c) In the case of trusts of land, the trustees' discretions are, unusually, restricted by statute, the Trusts of Land and Appointment of Trustees Act 1996. This provides that, subject to any contrary provision in the trust instrument,[16] trustees of land are under an obligation, when exercising any of their functions relating to land which is subject to the trust,[17] to consult, so far as is practicable, the beneficiaries of full age entitled to interests in possession in the land.[18] The trustees must, so far as is consistent with the general interests of the trust, give effect to the wishes of those beneficiaries or, in the event that they are not all in agreement, to the wishes of the majority by value.[19] Obligations of this type were first introduced by the Law of Property Act 1925,[20] but only in the context of the statutory trusts for sale implied by that statute in the case of co-ownership, a situation in which the trustees will also normally be the beneficiaries anyway, unless there are more than four beneficiaries;[21] consequently, this was more a matter for land law than for the law of trusts.[22] But the Trusts of Land and Appointment of Trustees Act 1996 modified the obligation to consult in respect of the trusts implied in the case of co-ownership and, more significantly for present purposes, extended it to all trustees of land; however, the obligation is of course limited to the exercise of functions relating to land and so does not apply to any pure personalty which the trustees of land are also holding on trust. Further, even when the obligation to consult arises, the trustees are not actually obliged to follow the wishes of the beneficiaries, nor need a purchaser be concerned to see that the trustees have complied with the obligation.[23]

(d) There is also a further exception of somewhat uncertain extent, which arises from the decision of the Court of Appeal in *Butt v. Kelson*.[24] The trustees of a trust held a large proportion of the shares in a private limited company, of which they were also directors by virtue of their trust shareholding. The question arose as to how far the beneficiaries could control the votes of the trustees both as directors and as shareholders. It was held that the trustees' votes as directors could not be controlled by the beneficiaries, while their votes as share-

---

[16] Trusts of Land and Appointment of Trustees Act 1996, s.11(2)(a).
[17] Other than their right to compel absolutely entitled beneficiaries to take a conveyance of the legal title; *ibid.* s.11(2)(c).
[18] Other than persons who are merely annuitants; *ibid.* s.22(3).
[19] *ibid.* s.11(1).
[20] Law of Property Act 1925, s.26(3) (now repealed).
[21] In which case only four of them will be able to be trustees; see Trustee Act 1925, s.34, *ante* p. 561.
[22] There was no such obligation in the case of express trusts for sale of land and, in the case of settlements under the Settled Land Act 1925, the functions in question were vested in the beneficiary of full age entitled to the interest in possession for the time being anyway.
[23] Trusts of Land and Appointment of Trustees Act 1996, s.16(1); this was also the case under Law of Property Act 1925, s.26.
[24] [1952] Ch. 197.

holders could be controlled. The apparent inconsistency of this curious result may be explained by the fact that under company law, directors have duties to all the shareholders, not only to those shareholders, if any, whom they represent; it would therefore have been inconsistent with this obligation if the trustees had been compelled to vote as directors solely in accordance with the wishes of the beneficiaries. On the other hand, their votes as shareholders were not subject to this conflict of duty. That does not alter the fact that at first sight it seems that the manner in which the voting power was to be exercised should have been a matter for the trustees' discretion, exercisable by them free from any interference by the beneficiaries. *Butt v. Kelson* was on this ground criticised by Upjohn J. in *Re Whichelow*[25] as being inconsistent with the principle laid down in *Re Brockbank*. It is, however, possible to regard a right to vote in a company as a property right and for special considerations to apply to such votes. Nevertheless, *Butt v. Kelson* is probably incorrect in so far as it allows beneficiaries to control the votes of trustee-shareholders and should not be extended.

### III. THE RIGHT TO COMPEL DUE ADMINISTRATION

Whether or not a beneficiary suspects that there has been any improper conduct on the part of the trustees, he may nevertheless insist that the accounts of the trust are audited by any solicitor or accountant who is acceptable to the trustees. If agreement cannot be reached as to the identity of the auditor, the audit is carried out by the Public Trustee. Unless special circumstances exist, the audit cannot be carried out more than once in every three years; a beneficiary who does require more frequent audits will therefore be ordered personally to pay the costs.[26] Although this is not particularly relevant for present purposes, the position is exactly the same where the trustee requires an audit to be carried out.

Where the beneficiary thinks that the trust is not being properly administered, where there is some point of doubt relating to the administration of the trust, and in certain other circumstances, he may have recourse to the court. There are two possibilities: first, by issuing an application to the court for the determination of a specific question or questions (such applications used to be made by way of originating summons but, since the introduction of the Civil Procedure Rules 1998, they are instead made by application under Part 23 of those Rules); and, secondly, by issuing proceedings for the general administration of the trust. It is preferable that the former method is used whenever possible, because it is cheaper, quicker and simpler than the latter method.

The following are examples of the circumstances in which it may be appropriate for the beneficiaries to apply to the court (the circumstances in which it may be appropriate for the trustees to apply to the court, some of

---

[25] [1954] 1 W.L.R. 5.
[26] Trustee Act 1925, s.22(4); Public Trustee Act 1906, s.13(5).

which are comparable and some of which are quite distinct, have already been considered):[27]

(a) The court may be asked to approve a specific transaction for which permission is not given by the general law or by the trust instrument but which is thought to be in the interests of the beneficiaries as a whole[28] (in most cases, of course, this type of application will be made by the trustees).[29]

(b) The court may be asked to direct the trustees to do a particular act which they ought to do or to refrain from doing a particular act which they ought not to do. The act referred to must be one which the trustees are under a definite obligation to do or not to do; it is not appropriate for a beneficiary to question by this means an act in respect of which the trustees have a discretion.[30]

(c) The court may be asked to direct the payment of money in the hands of the trustees into court.[31]

(d) The court may be asked to construe the provisions of the trust instrument or to ascertain the class(es) of beneficiaries (again, in most cases this type of application will be made by the trustees).[32]

(e) The court may be asked to determine any other specific question which arises in the course of the administration of a trust.

It is not generally appropriate for the beneficiaries to make an application to the court in this way where its subject-matter will involve third parties or in any action against trustees for breach of trust where the facts are in dispute.

It will be seen that almost all the specific questions which arise in the administration of a trust can be dealt with by issuing an application to the court in this manner. Consequently, the alternative of issuing proceedings for the general administration of a trust, which is intended to lead to the court itself becoming responsible for the entire administration of the trust, is usually only necessary in three situations: first, where there have been constant disputes between the trustees; secondly, where the circumstances of the trust give rise to recurring difficulties which would require frequent single applications to the court; and, thirdly, where clear *prima facie* doubts exist as to the bona fides of the trustees.

## IV. THE RIGHT TO ENFORCE CLAIMS

As part of his right to compel the due administration of the trust, a beneficiary can apply to the court if the trustees fail to take any action necessary to pre-

---

[27] See *ante*, p. 619.
[28] See *Boardman v. Phipps* [1967] 2 A.C. 46 (which was, at least in the opinion of the court, an example of the circumstances where an application should have been made); see *ante*, p. 622.
[29] See *ante*, p. 622.
[30] *Syffolk v. Lawrence* (1884) 32 W.R. 899.
[31] As to the circumstances in which money is payable into court, see Trustee Act. 1925, s.63.
[32] See *ante*, p. 619.

serve the trust property.[33] A cause of action against a third party can itself be an item of trust property and the court may either direct the trustees to enforce that claim or allow the beneficiary to sue the third party directly for the benefit of the trust, where necessary using the name of the trustees.[34] Alternatively, a beneficiary can sue the trustees, making those who are alleged to be under obligations to the trust co-defendents.

In *Wills v. Cooke*,[35] the trust property included a farm which was subject to a tenancy. The trustees had retained solicitors to advise them with regard to the administration of the trust but, it was alleged, the solicitors had failed to advise the trustees to take action to increase the rent in accordance with the Agricultural Holdings Act 1948. One of the beneficiaries sued the solicitors directly, claiming that the trustees had a right of action against them and that that right was an item of trust property. On what is now known as an interim application, Slade J. held that that right might be an item of trust property and that the statement of claim should not be struck out. He also said, however, that the right would not have been an item of trust property if the trustees had entered into the contract with the solicitors solely for their own protection and benefit.

## V. THE RIGHT TO TERMINATE A TRUST

If there is only one beneficiary under a trust who is *sui juris*, or if there are two or more beneficiaries and they are all *sui juris* and all in agreement, he or they can bring the trust to an end irrespective of the wishes of the trustees or of the creator of the trust. This is what is known as the Rule in *Saunders v. Vautier*,[36] and has two underlying bases.

1.  Equity regards the role of the trustees as primarily that of holding the balance between various beneficiaries with conflicting interests; where all the beneficiaries are of the same mind, the basic reason for the trustees' existence has therefore disappeared. If, on the other hand, the beneficiaries still want the trust to continue, it has already been seen that they cannot generally speaking control the trustees' discretions; either the trust must be terminated or the trustees must be allowed to carry on with their task.

2.  Secondly, a voluntary trust is in equity the equivalent of a gift at common law[37] so that, as a general principle, once a trust has been created, the settlor has no longer any control over it; after all, if he had made instead an outright gift of property to the beneficiaries, he would thereafter have had no control over what his donees subsequently did with that property. Thus, if all the beneficiaries are *sui juris* and between them entitled to the whole of the beneficial interest

---

[33] *Fletcher v. Fletcher* (1844) 4 Hare 67.
[34] As in *Foley v. Burnell* (1783) 1 Bro. C.C. 274, a case of trespass to trust land.
[35] (1979) Law Soc. Gaz., July 11, 1979.
[36] (1841) Cr. & Ph. 240. See also *Josselyn v. Josselyn* (1837) 9 Sim. 63; *Gosling v. Gosling* (1859) Johns. 265; *Wharton v. Masterman* [1895] A.C. 186; *Re Johnston* [1894] 3 Ch. 204; *Re Smith* [1928] Ch. 915; *Re Lord Nunburnholme* [1911] 2 Ch. 510; *Berry v. Green* [1938] A.C. 575.
[37] *Re Bowden* [1936] Ch. 71.

in the trust property, the settlor's provisions as expressed in the trust instrument will not prevent those beneficiaries from bringing the trust to an end.

In *Saunders v. Vautier* itself, a trustee held a sum of money upon trust to accumulate the income until a specified date, and then to pay it to the nominated beneficiary. The beneficiary reached the age of 21, then the age of majority, and so became *sui juris*, before the date specified for payment to him. He successfully claimed that the capital and accumulated income to date should be paid over to him immediately. However, if the trust instrument had instead provided that the beneficiary would not obtain a vested interest unless and until he survived to the specified date, then he would not have been able to invoke the Rule without the concurrence of the person entitled in default of his attaining that age.[38] Similarly, in *Tod v. Barton*,[39] property had been left to charity subject to the payment of an annuity of £20,000 a year to the testator's son from the age of 65 (he was about 50 at the time of the testator's death). The charity and the son agreed that the son should receive an immediate payment of £164,000 rather than the annuity and, despite a challenge by the testator's widow,[40] this agreement was upheld under the Rule in *Saunders v. Vautier*.

The Rule can also be utilised in a number of further situations.

1. The beneficiaries of a trust can break it before they have all fulfilled a contingency provided that they are all *sui juris*. If property is held on trust for such of two beneficiaries as attain the age of 25, then the two of them can agree to bring about the termination of the trust as soon as one has attained the age of 25 and the other has attained the age of 18; this is because, even if the younger beneficiary dies without attaining the age of 25, his potential share will then go to the older beneficiary and so between them they are the only persons who can conceivably ever become entitled to the trust property.

2. Beneficiaries who are entitled by way of succession can also break the trust. If property is held on trust for Andrew for life, remainder to Brian for life, remainder to Charles absolutely, the three of them can bring the trust to an end if they are all alive and *sui juris* and they all join in.

3. The beneficiaries of a discretionary trust can also break that trust in certain circumstances. If property is held on trust for such of David, Edward and Francis as the trustees in their absolute discretion decide, none of the three has any actual right to anything. Nevertheless, if there is no gift over in the event that the trustees fail to exercise their discretion, then the three of them can still bring the trust to an end if they are all alive and *sui juris* and they all join in.

---

[38] *Gosling v. Gosling* (1859) Johns. 265; *Re Lord Nunburnholme* [1912] 1 Ch. 489.
[39] [2002] 4 I.T.E.L.R. 715.
[40] The challenge was made on the grounds that the testator's will was not, as it expressly provided, subject to English law but subject to the law of the jurisdiction where he had died domiciled, Texas, where beneficiaries can only terminate a trust once all its purposes have been fulfilled or become illegal or impossible to fulfil (*Lanius v. Fletcher* (1907) 101 S.W. 1076; *Frost National Bank v. Newton* (1977) 554 S.W. 2d 149). This challenge is considered *post*, p. 856.

However, today the vast majority of discretionary trusts are subject to overriding powers of appointment and as a result have default beneficiaries, whose existence is sufficient to prevent the Rule being applied.

Whenever a trust is brought to an end under the Rule in *Saunders v. Vautier*, the beneficiaries can compel the trustees to convey the property to whoever they direct[41] and, if the trustees refuse, they will personally have to pay the cost of the beneficiaries' application to the court for a direction to this effect. This of course means that the beneficiaries can bring the trust to an end and compel the trustees to transfer the property to their own chosen trustees on the same trusts. This enables the beneficiaries to overcome the actual decision in *Re Brockbank*;[42] however, as has already been seen,[43] use of the Rule in *Saunders v. Vautier* for this purpose will now only be necessary if the settlor has excluded section 19 of the Trusts of Land and Appointment of Trustees Act 1996.

It should also be noted that, if a beneficial interest under a trust is sold, the purchaser stands in the same position as the vendor and, if the vendor could have brought the trust to an end, the purchaser will be able to do so if he is *sui juris*. But if the beneficial interest is question is merely mortgaged, the mortgagee cannot bring the trust to an end for so long as the beneficiary still has a right under the mortgage to have his beneficial interest redeemed upon payment of the amount secured.[44]

However, exercising the Rule in *Saunders v. Vautier* and bringing a trust to an end may have negative consequences of a fiscal nature; this is because there will often be a liability both to capital gains tax and to inheritance tax on the termination of a trust.

1.  If a trust is terminated and the trustees sell the investments comprising the trust fund, they will be liable to capital gains tax on any increase in value which has accrued while the investments have been subject to the trust. If they instead distribute the assets *in specie*, the beneficiaries will become absolutely entitled to the assets as against the trustees,[45] and in principle a liability to capital gains tax will again arise as if the trustees had disposed of the assets on the open market for their full value at the time when the beneficiaries became entitled.[46] However, if the beneficiaries are resident in the United Kingdom, they can claim holdover relief if the assets in question comprise business assets[47] or if the vesting of the property in the beneficiaries involves a chargeable transfer for the purposes of inheritance tax. When this relief is available, the beneficiaries are treated for capital gains tax purposes[48] as acquiring the assets at their base cost to the

---

41  *Re Marshall* [1914] 1 Ch. 192; *Re Sandeman's Will Trusts* [1937] 1 All E.R. 368.
42  [1948] Ch. 206; see *ante*, p. 713.
43  See *ante*, p. 713.
44  This is the conclusion derived from *Re Bell* [1896] 1 Ch. 1.
45  This concept was considered *ante*, p. 637.
46  Taxation of Chargeable Gains Act 1992, s.71(1).
47  *ibid.* s.165.
48  See *ante*, p. 637.

trustees. By claiming this relief, the liability for the tax is deferred until the beneficiaries actually dispose of the assets themselves.

2.   The position with regard to inheritance tax is more complicated. Suppose that a fund of £100,000 is held upon trust for Elizabeth for life with remainder to Angela and it is agreed to bring the trust to an end by paying £40,000 to Elizabeth and £60,000 to Angela. It has already been seen[49] that, where a beneficiary has an interest in possession in settled property, he is treated for inheritance tax purposes as if he was beneficially entitled to the settled property itself.[50] Accordingly, immediately before the termination Elizabeth would be treated for inheritance tax purposes as being beneficially entitled to £100,000, whereas after the termination she would only be entitled to the actual sum of £40,000 paid to her. There would therefore be a potentially exempt transfer by Elizabeth of £60,000.[51] So far as Angela is concerned, she has given up a reversionary interest in a fund of £100,000 in order to obtain an immediate outright payment of £60,000. However, there will be no liability to inheritance tax on her because usually[52] no inheritance tax is payable where a person disposes of a reversionary interest.[53]

---

[49] See *ante*, p. 639.
[50] Inheritance Tax Act 1984, s.49.
[51] No inheritance tax would be payable if Elizabeth survived for a further seven years. If she failed to do so, the tax payable would be calculated by reference to her lifetime transfers.
[52] The rule under discussion does not apply where the person disposing of the reversionary interest acquired it for value, or was himself the settlor: Inheritance Tax Act 1984, s.48(1).
[53] *ibid.* ss.47, 48(1).

CHAPTER 20

# TRUSTEES' REMUNERATION AND BENEFITS

---

UNTIL the enactment of the Trustee Act 2000, the basic principle was that the office of trustee was gratuitous, that is to say that its duties had to be performed by the trustee without remuneration or profit. The development of this rule was due in part to the fact that trustees were often members of the family and persons of substance, who were prepared to act as trustees as part of the general obligations of kinship. In more recent years, however, it has become recognised that the management of money and assets is an activity which requires skill, aptitude, and often considerable technical support. Accordingly, it became, and still is, very common for trustees to be either professional advisers, such as solicitors and accountants, who act as part of their ordinary professional practice, or banks and similar trust companies; such trustees are generally prepared to act only if given adequate recompense. This caused no difficulty when such persons were to be the original trustees of an *inter vivos* trust, since an appropriate charging clause could be inserted in the trust deed. However, very real difficulties arose if a will trust or an *inter vivos* trust did not contain an appropriate provision since this would generally preclude such persons from acting either as trustees of the will trust or as replacement trustees of the *inter vivos* trust.

The answer provided by the Trustee Act 2000[1] is to permit trust corporations and trustees other than sole trustees or charitable trustees who are "acting in a professional capacity" to receive "reasonable remuneration". The legislation also provides that such trustees can charge "reasonable remuneration" or charge the remuneration to which they are entitled under an express charging clause despite the fact that the services which they are providing "are capable of being provided by a lay trustee". Where the appointment of professional trustees is envisaged when the trust instrument is being drawn up, express charging clauses will undoubtedly continue to be utilised in order to avoid any difficulties about the definitions of "acting in a professional capacity" and "reasonable remuneration". However, the legislation has resolved the difficulties which formerly arose when there was no such charging clause. But the basic principle that the office of trustee is gratuitous continues to apply to trustees who are neither trust corporations nor "acting in a professional capacity".

Whatever the position regarding remuneration, however, a trustee is always

---

[1] Trustee Act 2000, ss.28, 29.

entitled to reimburse himself for his expenses. This right has already been considered.[2]

## I. MODERN COMMERCIAL REMUNERATION TERMS

Throughout this chapter, it will be helpful to keep in mind what types of remuneration a professional trustee or a commercial trust company may wish to obtain. The main items are as follows:

(a) fees for acting as a trustee, including the actual day to day administration of the trust;

(b) fees for acting as a director where the trust property includes shares in a company and the trustees act as directors of that company;

(c) commissions customarily paid by third parties in respect of business transacted on behalf of the trust (insurance companies and brokers both habitually pay commission to those who place business with them); and

(d) profits made by the trustee from services performed for the trust as its customer (a banker trustee will wish to retain for itself its ordinary commercial profit derived from acting as banker).

The remainder of this chapter considers the extent to which a trustee can achieve these objectives.

## II. EXPRESS CHARGING CLAUSES

### 1. The Nature and Effect of Charging Clauses

The creator of any trust can authorise the trustees to be paid for their services and this is in practice what is invariably done when a professional person is appointed as the original trustee of an *inter vivos* trust. Such express charging clauses are generally also inserted in *inter vivos* trusts even where the original trustees are not to be professional persons and are included in virtually all professionally drawn wills because in such circumstances it is obviously less clear when the will is drawn up whether or not professional trustees will prove to be necessary. Express charging clauses have traditionally been construed strictly as against the trustee and this general practice will undoubtedly continue. However, the Trustee Act 2000 has now provided that trust corporations and trustees who are "acting in a professional capacity" are, in the absence of any contrary provision in an express charging clause, to be treated as being entitled to the remuneration envisaged by that clause despite the fact that the services which they are providing "are capable of being provided by a lay trustee"[3] (this provision applies to trustees of charitable trusts only where

---

[2] See *ante*, p. 618.
[3] Trustee Act 2000, s.28(1), (2). A lay trustee is defined in s.28(6) as a trustee who is not a trust corporation and "does not act in a professional capacity".

they are not sole trustees and to the extent that a majority of the other trustees have agreed that it should be applicable).[4]

Where what is envisaged is a professional person acting as trustee, express charging clauses have long been expressed in something like the following form (it is considered likely that this sort of formulation will continue to be used despite the welcome reform thus made by the Trustee Act 2000):

> "Any trustee for the time being who is a solicitor accountant or other person engaged in any profession shall be entitled to charge and be paid all usual professional or other charges for business transacted, time expended and acts done by him or any partner of his in connection with these trusts including business and acts which a trustee not being engaged in a profession or business could have done personally."

However, it has been held that a clause in this form does not permit a trust corporation to charge[4A]: this requires a reference to trust corporations.

Provided that the express charging clause in question is sufficiently wide, a trustee is entitled to engage a company which he controls to carry out work on behalf of the trust and to pay that company for so doing. In *Re Orwell's Will Trusts*,[5] the will of the author George Orwell contained a clause authorising the trustee[6] of a trust created thereby to charge for services performed by him or by his company.[7] Vinelott J. held that the company could be paid and that the trustee need not account to the trust for the remuneration which he himself had received from the company.[8] On the other hand, he stated that "it has been said that a wider form of charging clause entitling a solicitor trustee to charge for such matters ought not to be included except under express instructions given by the client himself with full knowledge of its effect". It may be that not only this wider form of charging clause but also the fact that it will now enable the trustees to charge for services capable of being provided by a lay trustee should be specifically drawn to the attention of the client in this way.

Under this form of charging clause, the trustee cannot charge exactly what he likes. Where he is a solicitor presenting bills as such, the beneficiaries can insist on having his charges taxed, that is assessed by an officer of the court. A solicitor will normally charge by the hour. However, professionals other than solicitors generally charge on the basis of the value of the assets being administered or dealt with (the *ad valorem* fees charged by the Public Trustee are set out below).[9] Provided that such fees are the normal charges of the professional in question, they will be within the type of charging clause set out above. However, whether or not a trustee is a solicitor, if he takes from the trust fund an amount in excess of the amount to which the beneficiaries consider that he

---

[4] *ibid.* s.28(3).

[4A] *Re Cooper* (1939) 160 L.T. 453.

[5] [1982] 1 W.L.R. 1337.

[6] The case concerned the literary executor of the will who, for the purposes of remuneration, was held to be in the same position as a trustee.

[7] The clause authorised the trustee to charge for work done by him "or his firm'". Although the expression "firm" generally denotes an unincorporated partnership, the court held that for the purposes of this clause the expression extended to a private company.

[8] Compare *Re Gee* [1948] 1 All E.R. 498; see *post*, p. 736.

[9] See *post*, p. 725.

is entitled, they may bring an action against him for breach of trust,[10] although this is obviously more difficult where his charges are on *ad valorem* basis.

However, the remuneration payable need not actually be the trustee's normal professional charges. It may be expressed to be a fixed amount (the position where trustees who have agreed a fixed level of remuneration subsequently wish to increase it is considered below).[11] Less commonly, it may be expressed to be the income from some proportion or part of the estate[12] or even part of the capital by virtue of the exercise of a power of appointment.[13] Since this is what the trust instrument has provided, there seems no reason why the beneficiaries should be able to object to this, provided of course that the trustee actually fulfils his functions as such.

## 2. The Risks of Charging Clauses

Charging clauses in an *inter vivos* trust are normally effective; the only possible risk for a professional trustee is the relatively unlikely possibility of the trust being set aside for one of the reasons discussed in Chapter 7,[14] in which case there will of course be no trust property out of which his fees can be paid. This risk is very much more substantial in relation to charging clauses in a will because of the possibility of the will being void or the estate having insufficient funds to pay the remuneration.

If the will turns out to be void, the charging clause will obviously be void as well; a professional executor who has begun to administer the estate under the impression that he is to receive his normal fees will not be able to charge and will have to return any fees which he has already been paid. Thus in *Gray v. Richards Butler*,[15] executors obtained a grant of probate in respect of what was thought to be the testatrix's last will. This nominated as executor one of the partners in the defendant firm of solicitors; pursuant to a charging clause, he paid his firm more than £25,000 for work done in the administration of the estate. When the will was subsequently held to be void because the two witnesses had not both witnessed it at the same time, the grant of probate was set aside and a grant was instead made to the plaintiff, who had been nominated as executor under the testatrix's previous will. He successfully claimed that the defendant solicitors were liable to repay this sum to the estate. However, the court exercised its inherent jurisdiction[16] to enable the solicitors to charge for such of their work as could properly have been undertaken for the purposes of the earlier will.[17]

Further, even when the will is valid, there may be no assets available out of which the remuneration can be paid. Prior to the enactment of the Trustee Act 2000, an express charging clause ranked only as a pecuniary legacy; consequently, if the estate in question was insolvent or was exhausted by specific

---

[10] *Re Wells* [1962] 1 W.L.R. 784.
[11] See *post*, p. 730.
[12] *Public Trustee v. I.R.C.* [1960] A.C. 398.
[13] *Re Beatty's Will Trusts* [1990] 1 W.L.R. 1503.
[14] See *ante*, pp. 255 *et seq.*
[15] (1996) [2001] W.T.L.R. 625.
[16] See *post*, p. 730.
[17] The court did not specify what work fell into this category but an obvious example would have been the preparation of the inheritance tax return, which would on the facts have been in exactly the same form no matter which of the two wills was effective.

gifts, there would be no assets available out of which the trustees' remuneration could be paid and, if the estate was insufficient to pay all the pecuniary legacies, the fees payable would abate in the same proportions as those legacies.[18] This of course meant that a professional executor who had administered the estate under the impression that he was to receive his normal fees might find himself deprived of some or all of them because the estate turned out to be subject to some unexpected claim which had priority over his. However, the Trustee Act 2000 has provided[19] that any payments to which a trustee is entitled should be regarded as remuneration for services. Consequently, such payments now[20] constitute an expense of administering the estate and therefore enjoy priority over the interests of all the beneficiaries of the will. It is therefore only in the event that the estate is insolvent that a professional trustee will be at risk and even then any payments to which he is entitled will rank equally with the sums owed to the unsecured creditors of the estate.[21]

### 3. The ad valorem Fees Charged by the Public Trustee

As an illustration of fees charged on an *ad valorem* basis, the following fees are what the Public Trustee is at present charging,[22] in all cases subject to the addition of Value Added Tax at the rate in force when the fee becomes due (17.5 per cent in 2003–2004).

### (A) Executorship Fee
When the Public Trustee act as an executor or administrator under a will or intestacy, an executorship fee is charged calculated on the gross capital value of the estate; this covers all work done during the executorship or administration period except for the same activity fees as those mentioned in (B)(1) below.

| | |
|---|---|
| On the first £50,000 | 7.7 per cent |
| On the excess over £50,000 up to £75,000 | 6.0 per cent |
| On the excess over £75,000 up to £100,000 | 3.0 per cent |
| On the excess over £100,000 | 2.0 per cent |
| Minimum fee £770. | |

Where the Public Trustee is acting as personal representative of a deceased statutory owner or tenant for life under the Settled Land Act 1925, the fee is a fixed £150 (because of course the assets in question will not form part of the deceased's estate except for the purposes of inheritance tax).

---

[18] *Re White* [1898] 2 Ch. 217.
[19] Trustee Act 2000, s.28(4)(b).
[20] In respect of deaths occurring on or after February 1, 2001.
[21] Trustee Act 2000, s.28(4)(a) also removes another trap for professional trustees by providing that the fact that either they or their spouses have attested the will no longer prevents them from claiming their remuneration.
[22] As at April 1, 2003 (the percentages charged have recently increased substantially; compare those set out in the previous (7th) edition of this work, p. 644). The basic legislation is the Public Trustee (Fees) Act 1957; Public Trustee (Fees) Orders are made from time to time under that legislation.

## (B) Trusts

### (1) Acceptance fee

This is due when the Public Trustee is appointed as original trustee of a new settlement or as trustee of an existing will or settlement. The fee is one-half of the rate shown in the table above with a minimum fee of £550.

However, when the Public Trustee is appointed under a declaration of trust to carry out investment portfolio management or by the Supreme Court under a Standard Trusts Order or as trustee of a minor's legacy, the rates and minimum fee are lower: 1.25 per cent on the first £50,000 and 0.5 per cent on any excess over £50,000, the minimum fee being £175.

### (2) Administration fee

This is due annually on April 1 each year on the net capital value of funds under administration: the valuation date is whichever of the following dates most recently precedes the date on which the fee is payable: July 1, 1987, in the case of any estate or trust in which the Public Trustee was acting on that day; September 30, 1991, in the case of any estate or trust in which the Public Trustee was acting on that day; and, in any other case, the date of the acceptance of the trust by the Public Trustee or such convenient date as he may select.

| | |
|---|---|
| On the first £30,000 | 2.25 per cent |
| On the excess over £30,000 up to £150,000 | 1.75 per cent |
| On the excess over £150,000 up to £375,000 | 1.25 per cent |
| On the excess over £375,000 up to £2,500,000 | 0.75 per cent |
| On any excess over £2,500,000 | 0.25 per cent |
| Minimum fee £60 | |

### (3) Activity fees

An income collection fee is charged of 5 per cent on the gross amount of the income actually received by the Public Trustee. There is no fee on income paid direct from source to a beneficiary.

A reasonable additional fee may be charged according to the work involved for various matters including: dealing with a business, dealing with assets outside the United Kingdom, dealing with freehold or leasehold property or a mortgage, and for duties of an unusual, complex or exacting nature. When acting as a tax agent, the charges are commensurate with the work involved.

### (4) Withdrawal fee

A withdrawal fee is due on the retirement from the trusteeship of the Public Trustee or on the distribution or withdrawal of trust property. In the case of retirement, it is charged at a percentage rate twice the effective rate of the administration fee due on the April 1 prior to retirement (no withdrawal fee is charged where the total value of the trust does not exceed £10,000); in the case of distribution or withdrawal, it is charged at a percentage rate four times the effective rate of the administration fee due on the April 1 prior to the distribution; in each case, there is a maximum percentage rate of 7.5 per cent.

When the Public Trustee is appointed under a declaration of trust to carry out investment portfolio management or by the Supreme Court under a Standard Trusts Order or as trustee of a minor's legacy, the rates are as above but there is no maximum percentage rate; in these circumstances, no withdrawal fee is charged where funds are withdrawn for transfer to an executorship or to a new trusteeship accepted by the Public Trustee.

## III. No Express Charging Clause

Where there is no express charging clause, the statutory charging provisions of the Trustee Act 2000 come into play. These distinguish between a trust corporation, a trustee "acting in a professional capacity", and a lay trustee; reference is also made to charitable trustees and sole trustees, who can obviously fall into in any of the three basic categories. There is a quite separate statutory definition of a trust corporation,[23] while the Trustee Act 2000 unhelpfully defines[24] a lay trustee as a trustee who is not a trust corporation and "does not act in a professional capacity"; the crucial definition is therefore that of "acting in a professional capacity", which is provided by section 28(5) of the Trustee Act 2000:

> "a trustee acts in a professional capacity if he acts in the course of a profession or business which consists of or includes the provision of services in connection with —
>
> (a) the management or administration of trusts generally or a particular kind of trust, or
> (b) any particular aspect of the management or administration of trusts generally or a particular kind of trust,
>
> and the services he provides to or on behalf of the trust fall within that description."

This definition is obviously intended to cover all cases where a professional person habitually acts as a trustee as part of his business; in particular, it does not appear to matter that the part of the person's business which consists of or includes the provision of the services in question is minimal provided, presumably, that he is providing these services for at least one trust other than the trust in respect of which he is endeavouring to charge. But the definition does not, unlike express charging clauses, the overwhelming majority of which are of the type set out above, cover a person who has not taken on a trusteeship as part of his business, even if he is a professional person with considerable expertise such as a practising Chancery barrister, an accountant or a surveyor. Such persons are, for the purposes of the Trustee Act 2000, just as much lay trustees as non professionals.

It should also be remembered that the provisions of the Trustee Act 2000 governing remuneration do not enable remuneration to be claimed in respect of work done before February 1, 2001, the day on which the Trustee Act 2000 came into force.

---

[23] See *ante*, p. 545.
[24] Trustee Act 2000, s.28(6).

## 1. *Trust Corporations*

As has already been seen,[25] a company which is appointed a trustee is not by virtue of that fact alone a trust corporation. This term is applied only to a body corporate, such as a bank or insurance company, which undertakes the business of acting as a trustee and which fulfils certain conditions. Where a trust instrument contains no express charging clause, a trust corporation can now charge "reasonable remuneration" out of the trust funds for any services which it provides to or on behalf of a private trust;[26] this is defined as "such remuneration as is reasonable in the circumstances for the provision of those services to or on behalf of that trust by that trustee".[27] This remuneration can be claimed even in respect of services which were capable of being provided by a lay trustee.[28]

Prior to this legislation, trust corporations other than the Public Trustee, which has always been entitled to charge,[29] were automatically entitled to charge only if they were acting as judicial trustees.[30] Otherwise, a trust corporation was in the same position as an ordinary trustee and was only entitled to remuneration pursuant to an express charging clause; this meant that in practice a trust corporation would not agree to act as an original trustee unless an express charging clause provided for its remuneration. This remains the position for trust corporations which are trustees of charitable trusts; such trustees cannot claim reasonable remuneration[31] and, although the Secretary of State may by regulations make provision for the remuneration of trustees of charitable trusts who are trust corporations,[32] no such regulations have yet been made.

It is obviously likely that trust corporations who are trustees of private trusts will continue to insist on express charging clauses where they are in a position to do so; this will almost inevitably be the case where they are original trustees of *inter vivos* trusts or where they have been involved in the preparation of the will which creates testamentary trusts of which they are appointed trustees. They are likely to so insist in order to avoid any future disputes with the beneficiaries as to exactly what constitutes "reasonable remuneration" — express charging clauses oust the provisions relating to reasonable remuneration.[33]

It remains to be seen what attitude the courts will now adopt when appointing a trust corporation to be a trustee, usually of course as a replacement trustee; the courts remain entitled to fix its remuneration,[34] but may instead now prefer to leave the trust corporation to claim the reasonable remuneration to which it is entitled under the Trustee Act 2000. Until the attitude of the courts becomes clear, trust corporations who indicate their

---

[25] See *ante*, p. 545.
[26] Trustee Act 2000, s.29(1); this provision does not apply to charitable trusts.
[27] *ibid*. s.29(3).
[28] *ibid*. s.29(4).
[29] Public Trustee Act 1906, s.9; Administration of Justice Act 1965, s.2; Public Trustee (Fees) Act 1957.
[30] Judicial Trustees Act 1896, ss.1(5), 4(1).
[31] Trustee Act 2000, s.29(1) does not apply to charitable trusts.
[32] *ibid*. s.30(1).
[33] Trustee Act 2000, s.29(5).
[34] Trustee Act 1925, s.42.

willingness to be appointed as replacement trustees[35] of trusts which do not have an adequate express charging clause would therefore be well advised to make that willingness expressly conditional on the court fixing their remuneration in accordance with their standard fees as charged from time to time.

## 2. Trustees Acting in a Professional Capacity

Where a trust instrument contains no express charging clause, a trustee who is acting in a professional capacity and is not either a trust corporation or a charitable trust or a sole trustee is entitled to receive reasonable remuneration out of the trust funds for any services which he provides to or on behalf of the trust provided that each other trustee has agreed in writing that he may be remunerated for his services.[36] A trust corporation is excluded because it is in fact in a better position in that it does not need to seek the agreement of anyone. The prohibition on sole trustees is obviously in order to prevent a trustee from agreeing to pay himself and can be readily circumvented when the power of appointing new trustees is in the sole trustee.[37] Trustees acting in a professional capacity who are trustees of charitable trusts cannot claim reasonable remuneration[38] and, although the Secretary of State may by regulations make provision for the remuneration of trustees of charitable trusts who are trust corporations,[39] no such regulations have yet been made.

While trustees who are acting in a professional capacity will certainly be protected by this provision where they are original trustees or where the original trustees were also acting in this capacity, lay trusts of a small trust who appoint a professional trustee for the first time may still be subject to criticism by virtue of the fact that his appointment has unduly increased the costs of administering the trust running and some of this criticism may rub off on the professional trustee if he continues to act and charge irrespective of the financial position of the trust. Nor is it clear whether the other trustees either can or should make an irrevocable agreement that a trustee acting in a professional capacity should be remunerated indefinitely. It may be that, at least in the case of small trusts, the trustees should agree to this only on the basis that this should be reviewed from time to time; however, it does not necessarily follow that a professional trustee will agree to be appointed on that basis.

As in the case of trust corporations, it is obviously likely that trustees of private trusts who are acting in a professional capacity will continue to insist on express charging clauses where they are in a position to do so; this will almost inevitably be the case where they are original trustees of *inter vivos* trusts or where they have been involved in the preparation of the will which creates testamentary trusts of which they are appointed trustees. They are likely to so insist in order to avoid any future disputes with the beneficiaries as

---

[35] In practice, they will have to do so in a letter signed by their officers which will be put before the court when the application is made for their appointment.

[36] Trustee Act 2000, s.29(2).

[37] As it will be in the absence of contrary provision in the trust instrument; see *ante*, p. 551.

[38] Trustee Act 2000, s.29(1) does not apply to charitable trusts.

[39] *ibid.* s.30(1).

to exactly what constitutes "reasonable remuneration" — express charging clauses oust the provisions relating to reasonable remuneration.[40]

### 3. Lay Trustees

The position of lay trustees is not affected by the Trustee Act 2000. They are still not entitled to claim any salary or remuneration for carrying out their trusteeship;[41] this is the case even where the trustee in question devotes a considerable amount of time and trouble to managing a business belonging to the trust. In Barrett v. Hartley,[42] a trustee had managed a business for six years with such success that a large profit accrued to the beneficiaries; however, his subsequent claim for remuneration was unsuccessful on the grounds that his efforts were merely part of the duties imposed upon him as a result of his acceptance of the trusteeship. The rule has always been harsh and is now also somewhat illogical in the light of the unlimited power of trustees to appoint agents to act on their behalf and to pay those agents out of the trust funds for so doing;[43] in these circumstances, why should a trustee not be paid if he instead does the work himself, as the settlor presumably intended at the time of his appointment? The general rule denying remuneration was established in the eighteenth century, a time when agents could be employed only in very limited circumstances and it is arguable that both rules should have been changed at the same time. However, after very full consultation, the Law Commission decided that the right to charge "reasonable remuneration" introduced in the Trustee Act 2000 should not be extended to lay trustees and no further review of the position is now likely.

### IV. OTHER SITUATIONS WHERE A TRUSTEE CAN CHARGE

There are a number of other situations where a trustee can charge. These apply both where a trustee is not able to charge at all and where the remuneration provided for by an express charging clause turns out to be inadequate.

### 1. Authorisation from the Court

The court may, under its inherent jurisdiction, first, authorise a trustee to be remunerated where there is no charging clause;[44] secondly, authorise a trustee to retain remuneration which he has already received;[45] and, thirdly, authorise a trustee to charge more than he agreed to receive when he accepted appointment.[46]

In some of the older cases, the courts were not averse to allowing the trustee

---

[40] Trustee Act 2000, s.29(5).
[41] Robinson v. Pett (1734) 3 P. Wms. 249; Re Thorpe [1891] 2 Ch. 360; Re Barker (1886) 34 Ch.D. 77.
[42] [1866] L.R. 2 Eq. 789.
[43] See ante, p. 611.
[44] Bainbridge v. Blair (1845) 8 Beav. 558; Re Freeman's Settlement Trusts (1887) 37 Ch.D. 148; Re Masters [1953] 1 All E.R. 19; Re Worthington (dec'd) [1954] 1 All E.R. 677.
[45] Forster v. Ridley (1864) 4 De G.J. & Sm. 452.
[46] Re Duke of Norfolk's Settlement Trusts [1982] Ch. 61.

reasonable remuneration. In *Brown v. Litton,*[47] the captain of a merchant ship took with him on a voyage a sum of money to use in trade. During the voyage he died and his mate, on assuming command of the vessel, took possession of the money and with it made considerable profits in trade. The mate was ordered to account for his profits but Harcourt L.K. nevertheless held him to be entitled to a fair remuneration, which was to be fixed by the court, for his trouble. This attitude was also adopted recently in *Gray v. Richards Butler,*[48] where the firm of a solicitor-executor had carried out work pursuant to a charging clause in respect of what was thought to be the testatrix's last will but which turned out to be void. The firm was held liable to repay the fees received to the estate but the court exercised its inherent jurisdiction to enable it to charge for such of their work as could properly have been undertaken for the purposes of the earlier will.[49]

However, the recent policy of the courts has generally been to authorise the receipt of remuneration by a trustee only where his services have been of exceptional benefit to the trust.[50] Thus remuneration or increased remuneration in respect of future work will be ordered only if the court considers that, having regard to the nature of the trust, the experience and skill of a particular trustee is of great importance for the interests of the beneficiaries, while remuneration will be authorised in respect of work already done only if the work in question was wholly outside what could have been anticipated at the time of appointment.

In *Foster v. Spencer,*[51] substantial remuneration for their past work was awarded to two of the trustees of a moribund cricket club who had over a twenty year period had to engage in repeated administrative procedures and various types of legal proceedings in order successfully to bring about a sale of the club's ground;[52] however, it was held that the remaining task of determining the beneficial interests and dealing with the proceeds of sale was insufficiently onerous to justify an order for future remuneration. On the other hand, future remuneration was ordered in *Re Duke of Norfolk's Settlement Trusts,*[53] where a trust company accepted the trusteeship of a discretionary trust on the basis that it would receive a low fixed annual fee. It became involved in an extensive re-development programme in the Strand and applied both for special remuneration in respect of the re-development, which was granted,[54] and for an increase in the ordinary standard of remuneration. The Court of Appeal held that it could authorise an increase in the agreed level

---

[47] (1711) 1 P.Wms. 140.
[48] (1996) [2001] W.T.L.R. 625.
[49] The court did not specify what work fell into this category but an obvious example would have been the preparation of the inheritance tax return, which would on the facts have been in exactly the same form no matter which of the two wills was effective.
[50] See, for example, *Protheroe v. Protheroe* [1968] 1 W.L.R. 519, ante p. 360, where the trustee was only entitled to reimbursement of his actual expenses.
[51] [1996] 2 All E.R. 672.
[52] One of the trustees, a chartered surveyor who had been principally engaged in dealing with the planning authorities and the prospective purchasers, was awarded 5 per cent commission on the purchase price while the other, who lived near the ground and had had to bear the brunt of dealing with squatters, the neighbours and the municipal authorities, was awarded £5,000 per annum for the most crucial 10-year period.
[53] [1982] Ch. 61.
[54] At first instance ([1979] Ch. 37), and not reversed by the Court of Appeal.

of remuneration, but it would only do so if the experience and skill of the trustee made it in the interest of the beneficiaries to do so. The Court of Appeal also held that it was relevant to take into account remuneration charged by other trust companies although it is not yet clear how much reliance can actually be placed on that.

The inherent jurisdiction has also been used to award remuneration to those guilty of a breach of fiduciary duty or of undue influence where their conduct has produced a substantial benefit for the other party; however, none of the relevant authorities actually concern express trustees, as distinct from constructive trustees, and such situations are fortunately uncommon.

In *Boardman v. Phipps*,[55] Boardman was the solicitor to the trustees of a will, who held among other assets 8,000 out of an issued 30,000 shares in a private company. Boardman, thinking there was considerable scope for making a profit, considered with the trustees whether they should acquire the remaining shares in the company but the trustees refused, partly because under the terms of the trust instrument they had no power to acquire additional shares in the company.[56] Boardman, with the benefit of knowledge which he had gained as a result of representing the trust, then fought, on behalf of himself and one of the beneficiaries, a lengthy takeover battle for control of the company. As Wilberforce J. observed at first instance, "it is interesting, and at times fascinating to watch, through the long correspondence that has been put in [evidence], the manner in which [Boardman] drives [the chairman of the company] from one prepared position to another until the fruit is ready to drop into his hand."[57] Eventually the fruit did indeed drop. Boardman and the beneficiary acquired virtually all the shares in the company other than those held by the trust and, having gained control of the company, were able to dispose of some of the assets and to make a capital distribution to all the shareholders, obviously including the trust. The trust benefitted to the tune of £47,000 and Boardman and the beneficiary obtained £75,000, which one of the other beneficiaries subsequently claimed.

It was held on the facts that Boardman would not have been able to have conducted these negotiations without the knowledge which he had gained while representing the trust and, controversially,[58] that he and the beneficiary were liable as constructive trustees to account for their profit. Both the Court of Appeal and the House of Lords,[59] however, considered that Boardman was "a man of conspicuous ability, of great energy, clarity of mind and persistence with a flair for negotiation" and, although he and his associate were nevertheless made to disgorge their profit, he was allowed "generous remuneration" because he had exceptional abilities in this respect, and had exercised them for the benefit of the trust. In other words, the average trustee, and even the average professional trustee, would not have been able to have achieved the results which Boardman had achieved

*Boardman v. Phipps* was a case in which remuneration was awarded to a person who had committed a breach of fiduciary duty. In *O'Sullivan v. Man-*

---

[55] [1967] 2 A.C. 46: see *ante*, p. 365.
[56] The Court of Appeal said that application should have been made to the court for permission to purchase these shares.
[57] [1965] Ch. 922 at 1014.
[58] See *ante*, p. 365.
[59] Upholding Wilberforce J.

*agement Agency and Music,*[60] remuneration was ordered even in favour of a fiduciary who had been guilty of undue influence. A fiduciary agent, whose contract with the singer Gilbert O'Sullivan was set aside for undue influence, was held to be entitled to remuneration, together with a reasonable sum by way of profit, on the basis that he had contributed significantly to the performer's success. This decision was subsequently applied in *Badfinger Music v. Evans,*[61] where a former member of a rock group which had broken up in very acrimonious circumstances had retained some tapes of a live concert which, after a considerable amount of essential remixing and remastering, he succeeded in releasing in a form which achieved a commercial success. He did not dispute that he was in a fiduciary relationship with the other members of the group or that they were entitled to share in the profit. The question was whether he was entitled to remuneration for the work which he had done. This was not a case where a fiduciary had, as in *Boardman v. Phipps,* acted honestly and openly in the best interests of his principal, although there was no doubt that his work had ultimately benefited the others. However, the judge[62] held that he could award remuneration despite a lack of honesty and openness and did so because the work done was not only of a special character calling for the exercise of a particular kind of professional skill but also could realistically only have been done by the fiduciary.

On the other hand, in *Guinness v. Saunders,*[63] a claim for remuneration by a director who had acted in good faith but in a situation where there was a clear conflict between his interest and his duty was denied by the House of Lords; indeed the House of Lords doubted whether such remuneration would ever be ordered in favour of a director.[64] Lord Goff felt that the jurisdiction could not be exercised where it would encourage trustees to put themselves into a situation of conflict; in this respect, however, his statement does not appear consistent with the authorities already discussed.

## 2. Agreement with All Beneficiaries

If the beneficiaries of a trust are all *sui juris* and between them absolutely entitled to the whole of the beneficial interest under the trust, they can validly agree with the trustees that they shall be paid. Such agreements are construed strictly, in the same way as provisions for payment in the trust instrument.[65] Where all the beneficiaries do not agree, or some are not *sui juris*, individual beneficiaries can agree with a trustee for his remuneration but that agreement obviously binds only the individual beneficiary on a personal basis and not the trust property as such.

---

[60] [1985] Q.B. 428.
[61] [2001] W.T.L.R. 1.
[62] Lord Goldsmith Q.C., sitting as a Deputy Judge of the Chancery Division.
[63] [1990] 2 A.C. 663.
[64] On the grounds that this would constitute interference by the court in the administration of the company's affairs.
[65] It seems that the agreement has to be concluded with the beneficiaries before the trustee takes up his office; *Douglas v. Archbutt* (1858) 2 De G. & J. 148; *Re Sherwood* (1840) 3 Beav. 338. This appears to be contrary to principle.

### 3. Custodian Trustees

A custodian trustee is entitled to charge fees equivalent to those which the Public Trustee could charge for acting as a custodian trustee.[66] However, this only enables the custodian trustee to charge for the services which he performs in that capacity. In *Forster v. Williams Deacon's Bank*,[67] an attempt was made to use the device of custodian trusteeship to overcome the absence of a charging clause in the trust instrument. In that case Williams Deacon's Bank had been appointed both managing trustee and custodian trustee. It was appreciated that the bank could not charge as managing trustee but it was anticipated that it could derive its remuneration from its capacity as a custodian trustee. The Court of Appeal rejected the device, however, holding that the deed merely constituted the bank the sole trustee and so the inability to charge remained. A similar attempt in a later case was held to be totally ineffective.[68] However, if the same situation recurred today, it is obviously likely that the custodian trustee in this situation would be able to charge reasonable remuneration under the Trustee Act 2000.

The fact that a validly appointed custodian trustee may always charge for his services as such does not entitle him to profit in other ways from the trust either. Thus in *Re Brooke Bond*,[69] an insurance company was a custodian trustee under the trust deed securing the pension scheme of Brooke Bond & Co. Under the terms of the trust deed the managing trustees were entitled to effect with any insurance company a policy assuring the payment of the pensions under the scheme. The managing trustees proposed to effect the policy with the custodian trustee. Cross J. held that the custodian trustee could not, without the authority of the court, contract with the managing trustee for its own benefit; however, when an application was made for the sanction of the court in this respect,[70] the managing trustees were authorised to effect the policy with the custodian trustee on the basis that the latter need not account for its profit on condition that the terms of the policy were approved by an independent actuary.

### 4. The Rule in Cradock v. Piper

Prior to the enactment of the Trustee Act 2000, a solicitor trustee, like any other trustee, could not, in the absence of an express charging clause or authorisation from the court, pay either himself or another member of his firm for work done for the trust[71] save where he could properly employ an outside solicitor in which case he might employ and pay another member of his firm provided that it had been expressly agreed that the solicitor-trustee would not take any share in the profits.[72] The so-called Rule in *Cradock v. Piper*[73] is, or was, a curious exception to this principle; it establishes that, where a solicitor-trustee

---

[66] Public Trustee Act 1906, s.4.
[67] [1935] Ch. 359.
[68] *Arning v. James* [1936] Ch. 158.
[69] [1963] Ch. 357.
[70] In the manner envisaged *ante*, p. 622.
[71] *Christophers v. White* (1847) 10 Beav. 523.
[72] *Clack v. Carlon* (1866) 30 L.J. Ch. 639.
[73] (1850) 1 Mac. & G. 664.

acts as a solicitor for himself and his co-trustees in litigation relating to the trust and the costs of acting for both of them do not exceed the expense which would have been incurred if he had been acting for the co-trustees alone, then he may be paid his usual costs.

The Rule in *Cradock v. Piper* became firmly established[74] but, despite some feeble attempts at justification made by the court,[75] was always quite illogical. If it is proper for a solicitor to be paid his usual fees for litigation, why is it not proper for him to be paid his usual fees for non-litigious work? However, in the absence of an express charging clause, a solicitor-trustee will now almost always be able to claim reasonable remuneration under the Trustee Act 2000. Consequently, the Rule survives only to the extent that an express charging clause is construed as being too narrow to entitle a solicitor to pay either himself or another member of his firm for work done for the trust; in these admittedly unlikely circumstances, he will nevertheless be able to recover the costs of engaging in litigation on behalf of the trust if he can satisfy the conditions of the Rule.

## 5. *Trust Property Abroad*

Where the trust property is situated abroad and the law of the country where the property is situated allows the trustees to be remunerated, the trustees appear to be entitled to retain that remuneration. In *Re Northcote*,[76] English executors had to get in assets of the deceased in America. To do so they had to obtain a grant of probate in the State of New York, under the law of which they were entitled to a commission on the value of the assets. They deducted this for themselves and the English court held they need not account for it to the trust. However, while lay executors could undoubtedly still rely on this decision, it is probable that professional trustees who did not have the benefit of an express charging clause would be limited to the reasonable remuneration to which they are entitled under the Trustee Act 2000.

## V. DIRECTORS' FEES

The second type of remuneration which a trustee may seek to retain is fees paid to him as a director of a company in which the trust fund is invested. Three questions arise:

(a) whether the trustee-director is in principle liable to account for his director's fees;

(b) whether there are any exceptions to the basic principle; and

(c) how, when the trustee-director does have to account, should the fees be treated in the administration of the trust.

---

[74] *Broughton v. Broughton* (1855) 5 De G.M. & G. 160; *Lincoln v. Windsor* (1851) 9 Hare 158; *Re Baker* (1886) 24 Ch.D. 77.

[75] See *Re Corsellis* (1887) 34 Ch.D. 675 at 682.

[76] [1949] 1 All E.R. 442.

## 1. Liability in Principle to Account

There are two preliminary points. First, in the case of private companies, the articles of association often endeavour to prevent the directors from acting contrary to the interests of shareholders by providing that any person who becomes a director must himself hold, or must within a short specified time acquire, a number of shares in that company. In this way it is hoped that, as the director will wish to advance the value of his own shares, he will also be acting in the interests of the other shareholders. Secondly, by section 360 of the Companies Act 1985,[77] a company is not allowed to take notice of the fact that shares might be held upon trust and, as far as the company is concerned, it deals with trustees who are registered holders of shares in exactly the same way as shareholders who are beneficially entitled. It will therefore be apparent that directors can use shares which they hold as trustees as their share qualification; if they do so, will they be allowed to keep their directors' fees?

In *Re Francis*,[78] under the articles of association of a company, the holders of a specified number of shares were entitled to vote themselves into directorships. Trustees held sufficient shares on behalf of their trust and duly procured their appointment as directors. Kekewich J., following the general principle that a trustee cannot profit from his trusteeship, held that they had to account to the trust for their fees. This case, however, was not even cited in *Re Dover Coalfield Extension*,[79] which introduced new considerations. The company Dover Coalfield Extension held shares in the Consolidated Kent Collieries Corporation, with whom they did business. In order to protect the interests of the former company, one of its directors was appointed a director of the latter company; as such, he had a contract which governed the services which he was to perform and also regulated his remuneration. However, all directors were required to acquire 1,000 shares within one month of appointment. Dover Coalfield Extension therefore transferred to him this number of shares, which he held upon trust for that company. It was not disputed that he had to account for the dividends on those shares and he did in fact do so; however, he claimed that he did not have to account for his directors' fees. The Court of Appeal held that, even though he could not have continued in office without the shares, he could retain his fees; he had been appointed a director by an independent board of directors before he had acquired the shares and his directorship did not therefore automatically flow from his trusteeship.

In *Re Macadam*,[80] following *Re Francis*,[81] trustees who by virtue of the trust shareholding were able to elect themselves directorships and did in fact do so were held liable to account for their fees. However, this decision was distinguished in *Re Gee*,[82] where Harman J. said that in some circumstances, even where a trustee is able through his voting rights to compel his appointment as director, he is nevertheless entitled to retain his fees, if his appointment was in fact independent of his trust shareholding. He reviewed the previous cases and concluded that the test was whether the trustee has used powers vested in

---

[77] Replacing provisions of previous Acts.
[78] (1905) 74 L.J. Ch. 198.
[79] [1908] 1 Ch. 65.
[80] [1946] Ch. 73.
[81] (1905) 74 L.J. Ch. 198.
[82] [1948] Ch. 284.

him as trustee to procure his appointment as a director. To be liable to account the trustee therefore, first, must have powers vested in him as trustee and, secondly, must have utilised those powers to procure his appointment as director.

If any of these elements is missing, the trustee-director may retain his fees, as in *Re Dover Coalfield Extension*, where the trustee has his directorship first and, although he has powers as trustee, does not use those powers to procure his appointment as a director. Similarly, if the trustee-director has a majority shareholding in a company beneficially, as well as a minority holding as trustee, and votes himself into a directorship, his directorship will be the result of his beneficial voting power and not his voting power as trustee. Similarly, where others hold the majority shareholding, the trustee has a minority shareholding, and he is appointed a director by the votes of the others, although he has powers as trustee he will not have used those powers to procure his appointment. The court will consider all the circumstances to see whether or not the appointment was truly independent of the voting powers held as trustee.

In *Re Orwell's Will Trusts*,[83] the facts of which have already been considered,[84] Vinelott J. distinguished *Re Gee*. He held that, while the general rule is that a trustee must account for any benefit, such as remuneration, which he obtains from a company as a result of his position as a trustee, this rule does not apply if the company was properly entitled to be paid from the trust fund and there is no other nexus between the company with which the trustee is connected and the trust fund.

## 2. Exceptions to the Basic Principle

Where a trustee-director is, in principle, not entitled to retain his director's fees, there are two circumstances in which, nevertheless, he may do so.

1. The settlor can include an effective power in the trust instrument authorising the retention of directors' fees. This power may be express or implied. So in *Re Llewellin*,[85] where the testator had expressly provided that the trustees could use the trust shares to acquire directorships, it was held that he had also impliedly authorised them to retain their directors' fees.

2. The court can authorise a trustee-director to retain his director's fees. In deciding whether to exercise this power, it will consider the extent of the skill and effort which has been applied. The general rule is that a trustee is expected to exercise in the discharge of his trusteeship the effort and skill which a prudent man of business would in general undertake in the management of his own investments. A trustee-director is expected to exercise the same standard when acting as a director. So, in *Re Keeler's Settlement Trusts*,[86] the court directed that an inquiry should be held as to the extent to which trustee-directors had

---

[83] [1982] 1 W.L.R. 1337.
[84] See *ante*, p. 723.
[85] [1949] Ch. 225.
[86] [1981] Ch. 156.

exerted effort and skill above that standard and held that they could retain their directors' fees, but to that extent only.

### 3. The Manner in which Forfeited Fees should be Applied

Where a trustee-director is obliged to account for his directors' fees and does so, it seems that, notwithstanding the revenue character of those sums so far as the company is concerned, in the administration of the trust they are to be treated as an addition to the settled property and added to capital.[87]

## VI. COMMISSIONS

The third category of payment which a trustee may seek to retain is commissions paid by third parties.

### 1. The General Rule

The general rule is that the trustee is accountable for commissions which he receives in respect of trust business.[88] The test is not whether the trust has suffered a loss but whether the trustee has made a profit. Thus, in *Williams v. Barton*,[89] the trustee was a stockbrokers' clerk who was paid commission earned on business introduced by him to his firm. He arranged for his firm to value the trust assets and was duly paid his commission. It was held that he had to account for that commission. There was no suggestion that the valuation of the trust assets was improper or unnecessary but nevertheless the trustee was not entitled to make a profit from it. Had this not been the case, the trustee might have been tempted to have the assets valued more frequently than was in fact necessary.

### 2. Exceptions

The trust instrument can, and often does, empower trustees to retain commissions. The court undoubtedly also has power to authorise this but there does not seem to be any reported case in which it has exercised this power. Furthermore, the rule does not apply where the recipient of the commission is discharging a duty imposed by statute and in so doing does not act harshly or oppressively. So in *Swain v. The Law Society*,[90] the House of Lords held that The Law Society was entitled to retain the equivalent of commission paid in respect of the compulsory insurance against professional negligence which solicitors are obliged to maintain.[91] The Law Society was required to apply that commission for the benefit of the profession as a whole.

---

[87] *Re Francis* (1905) 74 L.J. Ch. 198.
[88] This question is discussed more fully *ante*, p. 340.
[89] [1927] 2 Ch. 9.
[90] [1983] A.C. 598; see *ante*, p. 330.
[91] Solicitors Act 1974, s.37. At that time they had to insure through The Law Society but this is no longer the case.

## VII. Commercial Profits

The last category of benefit which, in ordinary circumstances, a trustee may seek to keep is profits derived by him in carrying on a business, where the trust is a customer of that business. As in the case of commissions, it seems that the general rule is that the trustee is liable to account for his profit.[92] However, the trust instrument can empower trustees to retain their profit. So in *Re Sykes*,[93] two brothers who were wine merchants were appointed as trustees of a will under which one of the assets of the trust was a public house. Under the terms of the will, they were authorised to supply wine to the public house and they were held entitled to their usual profit for doing so. Similarly, in *Space Investments v. Canadian Imperial Bank of Commerce*,[94] a bank trustee was entitled under a settlement to deposit trust funds with itself on a normal commercial basis; it was held that no breach of trust had been committed by the bank in so doing and that the position of the trust was no better than any other depositor or general creditor, even when the bank went into liquidation. The court also has power to authorise trustees to retain a commercial profit.

## VIII. Other Financial Benefits

Finally, quite apart from the specific examples already considered, there is anyway a general rule that a trustee is not to be entitled to profit in any way from his trusteeship unless he is authorised to do so by the trust instrument or by the court.

An extreme, if unusual, example is *Sugden v. Crossland*,[95] where a person was anxious to become a trustee of a will. He therefore paid the existing trustee £75 to retire and to appoint him in his place. It was held that the retirement and appointment was ineffective and also that the £75 so paid belonged to the trust. Similarly in *Webb v. Earl of Shaftesbury*,[96] Lord Eldon L.C. held that trustees were not entitled to exercise sporting rights over land held by them as trustees. He held that either the rights should be let for the benefit of the beneficiaries or, if they could not be let, should be held for the heirs of the settlor on a resulting trust. The trustees could not themselves derive any benefit.

In view of the above, it hardly needs to be said that, quite apart from the rules relating to investments,[97] a trustee must not use trust moneys in his own trade or business. If he does so, he will be liable to account for the profit he makes or, at the beneficiaries' option, the sum invested with compound interest.[98] The rule applies not only to profits which are made at the expense of the trust but also to profits which are made without any loss to the trust at all

---

[92] *Re Sykes* [1909] 2 Ch. 241.
[93] [1909] 2 Ch. 241.
[94] [1986] 1 W.L.R. 1072. (Privy Council on appeal from The Bahamas).
[95] (1856) 3 Sm. & G. 192.
[96] (1802) 7 Ves. 480.
[97] See *ante*, p. 592.
[98] See *post*, p. 773.

but which are derived by virtue of the trusteeship. This principle has already been considered.[99]

---

[99] See *ante*, p. 355.

# CHAPTER 21

# VARIATION OF TRUSTS

IF all the beneficiaries of a trust are *sui juris* and absolutely entitled they can, if they think fit, terminate the trust and if they so choose, set up new trusts in respect of the trust property.[1] But if they are not all so qualified, it is necessary for an application to be made to the court for a variation of the trusts. It is important to make a distinction for this purpose between two classes of variation by the court: first, variations concerned with the management or administration of the trusts; and, secondly, variation of the beneficial interests arising under the trusts.

## I. MANAGEMENT AND ADMINISTRATIVE VARIATIONS

### 1. *The Inherent Jurisdiction of the Court*

The court has always had an inherent jurisdiction to sanction a departure from the terms of a trust but it is now clearly established that this jurisdiction applies only to the management or administration of the trust. It therefore does not apply to any rearrangement of the rights of the beneficiaries to the beneficial interests themselves,[2] with the sole exceptions of cases of "maintenance"[3] and "compromise",[4] assuming that the latter amounts to a variation in the true sense of the word.[5]

The inherent jurisdiction, although still somewhat nebulous, was defined by Romer L.J. in *Re New*[6] to cover an "emergency" which has arisen in the administration of the trust, that is to say something for which no provision is made in the trust and which could not have been foreseen or anticipated by the settlor of the trust. The inherent jurisdiction is, therefore, of distinctly limited scope. In *Re New* itself the trustees of shares in a company were authorised by the court as a matter of emergency to concur in a scheme under which shares were to be exchanged for more realisable shares in a new

---

[1] See *ante*, p. 717.
[2] *Chapman v. Chapman* [1954] A.C. 428 at 454, 455.
[3] See *post*, p. 745.
[4] See *post*, p. 745.
[5] This is perhaps doubtful because it seems that the court's sanction to a compromise of disputed rights (which is what "compromise" in this context means) does not result in a variation of the beneficial trusts but only brings to an end any dispute about them. See *post*, p. 745, for further discussion of "compromise" in this sense.
[6] [1910] 2 Ch. 524.

company. The sanction of the court was required because the trustees had no power of investment in the new shares under the terms of the trust instrument. This was in the circumstances a transaction analogous to the "salvage" of the trust property.[7]

## 2. Section 57 of the Trustee Act 1925

One of the reasons why the inherent jurisdiction is so nebulous is that it has been largely superseded by section 57 of the Trustee Act 1925, which is based on a concept wider than that of "emergency". The basis of the section is instead expediency. It provides in effect that the court may empower trustees (but not trustees under the Settled Land Act 1925)[8] to perform any act relating to the management or administration of the trust property which is not authorised by the trust instrument when in the opinion of the court it is expedient. The ambit of the section was considered by the Court of Appeal in the conjoined appeals in *Re Downshire's Settled Estates; Re Chapman's Settlement Trusts* and *Re Blackwell's Settlement Trusts.*[9] According to Lord Evershed M.R. and Romer L.J. in a joint judgment:

> "The object of section 57 was to secure that trust property should be managed as advantageously as possible in the interests of the beneficiaries, and, with that object in view, to authorise specific dealings with the property which the court might have felt itself unable to sanction under the inherent jurisdiction, either because there was no actual 'emergency' or because of inability to show that the position which called for intervention was one which the creator of the trust could not reasonably have foreseen but it was no part of the legislative aim to disturb the rule that the court will not rewrite a trust."[10]

Moreover, the court must be satisfied that the proposed transaction is for the benefit of the trust as a whole and not simply for one of its beneficiaries.[11]

The section does not, therefore, confer on the court any general jurisdiction to vary beneficial interests; it is limited to the managerial supervision and control of trust property by the trustees and cannot be stretched further than that.

Subject to this decisive limitation, however, it is an overriding provision which is to be read into every trust.[12] It has been used for a number of purposes: to authorise the partitioning of land where the necessary consent could not be obtained,[13] to authorise the sale of a reversionary interest which the

---

[7] The principle was applied in *Re Tollemache* [1903] 1 Ch. 955.

[8] Trustee Act 1925, s.57(4).

[9] [1953] Ch. 218 (Denning L.J. dissented). On appeal to the House of Lords *sub nom. Chapman v. Chapman* [1954] A.C. 429, it was conceded that s.57 did not apply. In the House of Lords, the statement of law in the Court of Appeal regarding s.57 was neither approved or disapproved and is therefore still good law.

[10] *ibid.*

[11] *Re Craven's Estate (No.2)* [1937] Ch. 431.

[12] *Re Mair* [1935] Ch. 562.

[13] *Re Thomas* [1930] 1 Ch. 194.

trustees had no power to sell until it fell into possession,[14] and to blend two charitable funds into one.[15] The section has also been used to extend trustees' investment powers,[16] most recently in *Mason v. Farbrother*[17] and *Anker-Petersen v. Anker-Petersen*.[18] It used to be thought that applications for this purpose were better made under the Variation of Trusts Act 1958.[19] However, *Anker-Petersen v. Anker-Petersen* has now established that, provided the beneficial interests are not also affected by the proposed extension of the trustees' investment powers, section 57 of the Trustee Act 1925 should be used in preference to the Variation of Trusts Act 1958.

## II. VARIATION OF BENEFICIAL INTERESTS

The rules already discussed relate only to variations relating to the management and administration of the trust. Variation of the beneficial interests of a trust obviously involves a much more drastic rewriting of its provisions.

### 1. *Section 64 of the Settled Land Act 1925*

This section provides that the court may sanction any transaction affecting or concerning the settled land or any part thereof or any other land (not being a transaction otherwise authorised by the Settled Land Act 1925 or by the terms of the settlement) which in the opinion of the court would be for the benefit of the settled land, or any part thereof, or the persons interested under the settlement.[20] Furthermore, the word "transaction" is widely defined so as to include a "compromise or other dealing or other arrangement".[21] It is now clear that, as the majority of the Court of Appeal held in *Re Downshire's Settled Estates*,[22] the section confers a more ample jurisdiction than that conferred by section 57 of the Trustee Act 1925.[23] It is not in any sense restricted to steps of a purely administrative character and therefore enables the beneficial interests under the settlement to be remoulded.[24]

A relatively recent example of the utilisation of this jurisdiction, which is likely to become progressively less significant now that the Trusts of Land and

---

[14] *Re Cockerell's Settlement Trusts* [1956] Ch. 372; compare *Re Heyworth's Contingent Reversionary Interest* [1956] Ch. 364.

[15] *Re Shipwrecked Fishermen and Mariners' Benevolent Fund* [1959] Ch. 220.

[16] *Re Brassey's Settlement* [1955] 1 W.L.R. 192; *Re Shipwrecked Fishermen and Mariners' Benevolent Fund* [1959] Ch. 220, not following *Re Royal Society's Charitable Trusts* [1956] Ch. 87.

[17] [1983] 2 All E.R. 1078.

[18] (1990) [2000] W.T.L.R. 581.

[19] See *post*, p. 747 and *Re Coates' Will Trusts* [1959] 1 W.L.R. 375; *Re Byng's Will Trusts* [1959] 2 All E.R. 54 at 57. In *Mason v. Farbrother* [1983] 2 All E.R. 1078, it was held that this was not possible because the parties were not fully representative.

[20] s.64(1). The powers have been extended by the Settled Land and Trustee Acts (Court's General Powers) Act 1943, s.1 as amended by the Emergency Laws (Miscellaneous Provisions) Act 1953, s.9.

[21] s.64(2); *Raikes v. Lygon* [1988] 1 W.L.R. 281.

[22] [1953] Ch. 218.

[23] See *ante*, p. 742.

[24] *Raikes v. Lygon* [1988] 1 W.L.R. 281.

Appointment of Trustees Act 1996[25] has prohibited the creation of any more settlements under the Settled Land Act 1925, is *Hambro v. Duke of Marlborough*.[26] The Blenheim Estate is held by the successive Dukes of Marlborough for an estate in fee tail which is, by Act of Parliament, "unbarrable", that is to say incapable of being converted into an estate in fee simple. The Duke and the trustees of what was then a settlement under the Settled Land Act 1925 considered that the Duke's heir apparent, the Marquis of Blandford, would be incapable of managing the estate if and when he succeeded his father because of what were referred to as his "unbusinesslike habits and the lack of responsibility shown by him". They proposed to seek approval for the Duke to convey the estate to the trustees of a new settlement on trust for sale[27] to pay the income to the Duke for life, subject to that for the Marquis of Blandford on protective trusts, and subject to that on the trusts of the pre-existing settlement. The matter came before Morritt J. on the preliminary issue as to whether such a conveyance, which would clearly vary the Marquis of Blandford's existing beneficial interest, would be a "transaction" which the court could sanction under section 64. This question was answered in the affirmative and approval was subsequently given.[28]

The section used also to apply to land held on trust for sale,[29] but this is now no longer the case following the Trusts of Land and Appointment of Trustees Act 1996.

## 2. Section 24 of the Matrimonial Causes Act 1973

Under this Act, which replaced earlier longstanding legislation, the Family Division of the High Court has a wide jurisdiction, after pronouncing a decree of divorce or nullity of marriage, to vary the trusts contained in any ante-nuptial or post-nuptial settlement which has been made for the benefit of the parties to the marriage or the children of that marriage.[30] It is clearly established that the jurisdiction extends to a rearrangement of beneficial interests and the fact that a saving of inheritance tax or other taxes will result will have no bearing on the exercise of this jurisdiction.[31] A recent extremely significant application of this jurisdiction is the decision of the House of Lords in *Brooks v. Brooks*[32] that a pension scheme of which a former husband was the sole member could be varied to provide an immediate annuity and an eventual

---

[25] s.2(1). Existing settlements will continue only for as long as any land or heirlooms remain subject thereto.

[26] [1994] Ch. 158.

[27] Thus bringing to an end the settlement under the Settled Land Act 1925 pursuant to s.1(7). The new settlement, to which the estate was presumably conveyed following the subsequent approval of the scheme, must now be a trust of land as a result of Trusts of Land and Appointment of Trustees Act 1996, s.1(2)(a).

[28] See *The Times* July 23, 1994.

[29] Danckwerts J. so interpreted Law of Property Act 1925, s.28 in *Re Simmons* [1956] Ch. 125 but this section has now been repealed by Trusts of Land and Appointment of Trustees Act 1996, Sched. 4.

[30] Matrimonial Causes Act 1973, s.24.

[31] See *Thomson v. Thomson and Whitmee* [1956] P. 384.

[32] [1996] 1 A.C. 375.

pension for the former wife. This decision has already been considered in detail in Chapter 12 on Pension Trusts.[33]

## 3. Section 96(3) of the Mental Health Act 1983

This provision gives the Court of Protection power to make a settlement of the property of the patient and subsequently to vary it if any material fact was not initially disclosed, or there has been a substantial change in circumstances.

## 4. Maintenance

The position here is, and has long been, that where a testator or settlor has made a settlement in such a way, which is particularly capable of occurring where the trusts provide primarily for income to be accumulated, that the immediate beneficiaries have no funds out of which they can be maintained, the court will assume that the intention to provide sensibly for the family is so paramount that it will order maintenance in disregard of the trusts.[34] Any such order for maintenance will obviously result in a variation of the beneficial interests. Moreover, the jurisdiction is not restricted to cases of "emergency",[35] nor is it dependent on the beneficiaries in question being infants.[36]

## 5. Compromise

It has long been clearly established that the court may sanction on behalf of an infant or unborn person a "compromise" proposed by those persons beneficially interested in the trusts who are *sui juris*, thus protecting the trustees from subsequent liability to the infant or unborn person. This is, like the power to award maintenance,[37] part of the inherent jurisdiction of the court and, where applicable, clearly also enables beneficial interests to be varied.

In conjoined appeals in *Re Downshire Settled Estates; Re Chapman's Settlement Trusts* and *Re Blackwell's Settlement Trusts*,[38] the Court of Appeal had to consider the important question of what amounts to a "compromise" for this purpose. The majority of the court, Lord Evershed M.R. and Romer L.J., held that the word "compromise" should not be construed narrowly so as to be confined to a compromise of disputed rights but covered any arrangement between a tenant for life and the remaindermen. The arrangements proposed in *Re Downshire Settled Estates* and *Re Blackwell's Settlement Trusts* were duly held to be in the nature of a compromise in this wider sense of the word and were accordingly sanctioned. But the majority refused to sanction the arrangement proposed in *Re Chapman's Settlement Trusts*, because they involved no compromise — even in this extended sense the court was merely being asked to destroy trusts which had been expressly created. Denning L.J.

---

[33] See *ante*, p. 534.
[34] *Re Downshire Settled Estates* [1953] Ch. 218 at 238, *per* Evershed M.R. and Romer L.J., considered in *Chapman v. Chapman* [1954] A.C. 429 at 445, 455–457, 469, 471: see *post*, p. 746. See also *Re Collins* (1886) 32 Ch.D. 229 at 232; *Havelock v. Havelock* (1881) 17 Ch.D. 807.
[35] See *ante*, p. 741 and *Hayley v. Bannister* (1820) 4 Madd. 275.
[36] *Revel v. Watkinson* (1748) 1 Ves.Sen. 93.
[37] See *ante*, p. 741.
[38] [1953] Ch. 218.

however, dissented on the basis of a broad principle that the court had the power to deal with the property and interests of infants or other persons under disability in a manner not authorised by the trust whenever the court was satisfied that what was proposed was most advantageous for them, provided that everyone of full age also agreed. He was therefore prepared to give the inherent jurisdiction of the court a very wide scope indeed.

However, when an appeal from the decision of the Court of Appeal was taken to the House of Lords in *Chapman v. Chapman*,[39] the House of Lords not only unanimously affirmed the decision of the Court of Appeal but, by a majority, adopted a considerably narrower meaning of "compromise" than that adopted by Lord Evershed M.R. and Romer L.J. The latter had shown that the inherent jurisdiction was limited to some degree by holding that the word "compromise", however widely construed, would not cover every kind of arrangement. But the majority of the House of Lords (Lord Simonds, Lord Morton and Lord Asquith) stated that the power of the court to sanction a compromise in a suit to which a person, such as an infant or unborn person, was not a party did not extend to cases where there was no real dispute between the parties. Lord Cohen alone was prepared to accept that the jurisdiction of the court extended to "compromises" in the wider sense accepted by the majority of the Court of Appeal. This decision clearly established that a "compromise" means a compromise of a disputed right and this is as far as the inherent jurisdiction of the court goes.[40] This decision led directly to the enactment of the Variation of Trusts Act 1958.[41]

It was therefore clear that in *Re Downshire Settled Estates* and *Re Blackwell's Settlement Trusts* the Court of Appeal had gone too far in giving the word "compromise" an unnatural meaning, although that did not mean that those cases had actually been wrongly decided.[42] However, a number of schemes had been approved in the Chancery Division prior to the decision of the House of Lords on the basis of the wider principle upheld by the majority of the Court of Appeal which could not possibly be so justified and the orders made therein had accordingly been made without any jurisdiction.[43] Further, it immediately became fashionable to scrutinise settlements with a view to finding a provision of sufficient ambiguity or uncertainty in its effect on the beneficial interests to form a peg on which to hand a compromise of a "genuine" dispute, a clearly undesirable development susceptible of bringing the law into disrepute.

This bizarre situation clearly could not last for long so the Law Reform Committee was invited in 1957 to consider the position. They reached the

---

[39] [1954] A.C. 429.
[40] It was subsequently held not to include a compromise of a simulated dispute (*Re Powell-Cotton's Resettlement* [1956] 1 W.L.R. 23) or a variation of the existing investment powers (*Mason v. Farbrother* [1983] 2 All E.R. 1078).
[41] See *post*, p. 747.
[42] They could probably have been justified under Settled Land Act 1925, s.64: see *ante*, p. 743.
[43] See *Re Leeds (Duke) and Re The Coal Acts 1938 to 1943* [1947] Ch. 525. *Re Downshire Settled Estates* and *Re Blackwell's Settlement Trusts* [1953] Ch. 218 may also be taken to be overruled on this point, although these decisions could probably be justified under Settled Land Act 1925, s.64; see *ante*, p. 743.

conclusion that the result produced by *Chapman v. Chapman* was most unsatisfactory. It was pointed out that on the grant of a decree of divorce or nullity
the court had the power to sanction variations in the marriage settlement even
if these were designed to produce a saving in estate duty or tax. The Committee fairly inquired why an infant whose parents were happily married
should be in a worse position than an infant whose parents had just divorced.
The recommendations of the Committee were accordingly given legislative
effect in the Variation of Trusts Act 1958.

## 6. The Variation of Trusts Act 1958[44]

The principal motive for the invocation of the inherent jurisdiction of the court
to vary beneficial interests on the basis of a "compromise" was in order to
minimise fiscal liabilities which would be incurred if the trust remained
unaltered. The old-fashioned settlement with its succession of limited interests
had, in particular, fallen out of favour because on the death of each limited
owner estate duty (the predecessor of inheritance tax) was leviable on the
value of the whole settled funds. A great deal of ingenuity had been and for
that matter still is devoted to the formulation of schemes dividing up the trust
funds between those interested in capital and income respectively in such a
way that such fiscal liabilities were minimised.

### (A) Permissible Motives[45]
These schemes formerly presented to the court for its sanction under the head
of "compromise" are therefore now presented to the court under the Variation
of Trusts Act 1958. Although Lord Morton said in *Chapman v. Chapman*,[46] that,
if the court had power to approve and did approve schemes for the purpose of
avoiding taxation, "the way would be open for a most undignified game of
chess between the Chancery Division and the legislature", the plain fact
remains that very many applications under the Act have been made successfully for this very purpose alone.[47]

　　Yet despite these realities, echoes of judicial repugnance towards tax
avoidance can still occasionally be heard and it is arguable, if only faintly, as a
result of the controversial decision in *Re Weston's Settlements*,[48] that certain
forms of tax avoidance may still be regarded as illegitimate. In this case the
applicants applied for an order for approval of an arrangement by which
property settled on English trusts should be freed from those trusts and settled
on a Jersey settlement. The purpose of the exercise was to avoid a heavy
liability to capital gains tax and estate duty.[49] Stamp J. said at first instance: "I

---

[44] For a detailed discussion of the relevant case law, see Harris (1969) 33 Conv. (N.S.) 113, 183.
[45] See also *post*, p. 883.
[46] See *ante*, p. 746.
[47] See *Re Norfolk's Will Trusts* (1966) *The Times*, March 23, 1966 (the purpose was to reduce duty on estates worth £3 million).
[48] [1969] 1 Ch. 223; see *post*, p. 884 for further discussion of this decision.
[49] Approximately £160,000.

am not persuaded that this application represents more than a cheap exercise in tax avoidance which I ought not to sanction, as distinct from a legitimate avoidance of liability to taxation."[50] The Court of Appeal, however, tended to place emphasis on other factors (not that Stamp J. ignored them). As is shown in a later chapter,[51] the primary basis of the Court of Appeal decision appears to have been that no administrative benefits would accrue in transferring the settlement to Jersey because the family had been living in Jersey for only a few months and probably would not stay there. There was also doubt as to the competence of the Jersey courts to administer trusts.[52] And finally the element of moral or social benefit was stressed. In the words of Lord Denning M.R.:

> "There are many things in life more worthwhile than money. One of these things is to be brought up in this our England which is still 'the envy of less happier lands'. I do not believe that it is for the benefit of children to be uprooted from England and transported to another country simply to avoid tax. Children are like trees: they grow stronger with firm roots."[53]

The result of this case can be justified on the grounds just mentioned. But to introduce notions of "legitimate" and "illegitimate" tax avoidance seems to be not only uncontrollably vague but also wholly unworkable.[54]

**(B) The General Scheme of the Act**
The Variation of Trusts Act 1958, which came into force on July 23, 1958, applies to trusts of real and personal property, whether the trusts arise before or after the passing of the Act, under any will, settlement or other disposition.[55] The court may, if it thinks fit, by order approve an arrangement varying or revoking all or any of the trusts, or enlarging the powers of the trustees to manage or administer any of the trust property, on behalf of four classes of beneficiaries or potential beneficiaries. These are as follows:

(a) by virtue of section 1(1)(a), persons having, directly or indirectly, a vested or contingent interest who by reason of infancy or other incapacity are incapable of assenting;

(b) by virtue of section 1(1)(b), persons, whether ascertained or not, who may become, directly or indirectly, entitled to an interest at a future date or on the happening of a future event, if they then answer a specified description or qualify as members of a specified class, but

---

[50] [1969] 1 Ch. 223 at 234.
[51] See *post*, p. 884.
[52] [1969] 1 Ch. 223 at 223 *per* Stamp J. (Chancery Division), at 247 *per* Harman L.J. (Court of Appeal); this doubt has certainly since been favourably resolved, see *post*, p. 884.
[53] [1969] 1 Ch. 223 at 245; see *post*, p. 884.
[54] The scheme was one of "tax avoidance", not "tax evasion". The latter amounts to a criminal offence and clearly a scheme which "evaded" tax could not be sanctioned. But to take advantage of the existing tax laws for a person's own benefit and thereby "avoid" tax is generally regarded as a legitimate exercise; see also Bretten [1968] 32 Conv. (N.S.) 194; Harris [1969] 33 Conv. (N.S.) 183 at 191.
[55] s.1(1).

not including such persons if the future event had happened at the date of application to the court;[56]

(c) by virtue of section 1(1)(c), persons unborn;

(d) by virtue of section 1(1)(d), persons who will be interested as discretionary beneficiaries under protective trusts[57] if the interest of the principal beneficiary thereunder should fail or determine.[58]

The court can only approve the arrangement on behalf of the persons listed in the first three classes if it is for their benefit. But the potential benefit of the persons listed in the final class does not need to be considered.[59] Further, if a beneficiary falls both within this final class and within one of the other classes, then because the four classes are alternatives, it is only necessary to apply for approval on the basis of his membership of the final class and so no benefit needs to be established.[60]

The Act thus largely gives to the court the jurisdiction for which Denning L.J. had contended in *Re Chapman's Settlement Trust*.[61] It has commendably done away with the hair-splitting technicalities involved in the precise nature of a "compromise" and has attracted a great many applications to the court since it was passed. However, it must be emphasised that, although the jurisdiction is wide in many respects, it is nevertheless limited in that it only empowers the court to authorise arrangements on behalf of the persons designated in the Act, as if they were all ascertained and *sui juris*. It does not enable the court to override any objection, no matter how unreasonable, or dispense with the consent, even if unreasonably withheld, of any beneficiary who is in fact ascertained and *sui juris*. In such circumstances, the Act simply cannot be invoked.

**(C) The Trusts to which the Act Applies**
While, by virtue of section 1(1), the Act applies where "property, whether real or personal, is held on trusts arising under any will, settlement or other disposition", it nevertheless does not apply to every type of trust. *Allen v. Dis-*

---

[56] For decisions on the meaning of this paragraph, see *Re Suffert's Settlement* [1961] Ch. 1; *Re Moncrieff's Settlement Trusts* [1962] 1 W.L.R. 1344. Briefly, if the class in question is, for example, the statutory next-of-kin of a living person, then the latter is treated as having died at the date of application to the court and the next-of-kin consequently become notionally ascertainable. Since the "future event", the death of that person, has notionally happened, a member of the class of next-of-kin who is in existence cannot be bound by an order for variation without his consent (see *Re Suffert's Settlement* [1961] Ch. 1). Further, persons who have contingent interests, however remote, are already entitled; they are not persons who "may become entitled". Consequently, in *Knocker v. Youille* [1986] 1 W.L.R. 934, it was held that consent could not be given on behalf of a very numerous class of contingently entitled beneficiaries, whose approval it was not practicable to obtain.

[57] See *ante*, p. 265.

[58] s.1(1); see also s.1(2), which defines "protective trusts" as the trusts specified in Trustee Act 1925, s.33(1)(i), (ii) or "any like trusts". For the meaning of this last expression, see *Re Wallace's Settlement* [1968] 1 W.L.R. 711 at 716, *per* Megarry J.: "The word 'like' requires not identity but similarity and similarity in substance suffices without the need for similarity in form or detail or wording." See also *Gibbon v. Mitchell* [1990] 1 W.L.R. 1304.

[59] s.1(1), proviso; see also *post*, p. 754.

[60] *Re Turner's Will Trusts* [1960] Ch. 122.

[61] [1953] Ch. 218. In *Re Chapman's Settlement Trusts (No.2)* [1959] 1 W.L.R. 372, an application to create substantially the same scheme was granted under the Variation of Trusts Act 1958.

*tillers Co. (Biochemicals)*,[62] arose as a sequel to proceedings which had been commenced on behalf of children who were alleged to have been born with physical deformities as a result of their mothers having taken the drug thalidomide during pregnancy. These proceedings had been settled on the basis that the manufacturers of the drug paid into court nearly £6 million on terms that various sums should be paid out or applied "in such manner as the judge may direct to or for the benefit of each [deformed] child". An application was consequently made under the Variation of Trusts Act 1958 for the payment of money out of court to be held by trustees on the terms of a draft which was submitted to the court for approval. Under the terms on which the original proceedings had been settled, each child was entitled to payment on attaining the age of majority, whereas under the proposed draft, the trustees were to be empowered to defer the date upon which the child would be entitled. The court held that it had no jurisdiction under the Act to approve the "variation" of the terms upon which the money had been paid into court. Eveleigh J.[63] said[64] that the terms upon which the money had been paid into court was not:

"a trust of the kind referred to in the 1958 Act. The Act contemplates a situation where a beneficial interest is created which did not previously exist and probably one which is related to at least one other beneficial interest."

Similarly, in *Mason v. Farbrother*,[65] an application under the 1958 Act for the variation of the existing investment powers of a pension fund was not pursued because of doubts about whether the parties were truly representative of the classes of beneficiaries whom they purported to represent.

The jurisdiction conferred by the Act may also now be confined to trusts governed by English law. Prior to the enactment of the Recognition of Trusts Act 1987, the English courts asserted jurisdiction to vary trusts governed by any law provided, of course, that they had jurisdiction over their trustees. Thus, in *Re Ker's Settlement Trusts*,[66] the court made an order varying the trusts of a settlement whose proper law was that of Northern Ireland and a similar order was made in *Re Paget's Settlement*,[67] in respect of a settlement whose proper law was believed to be that of New York. However, as will be seen in Chapter 23,[68] the Hague Convention on the Law applicable to Trusts and their Recognition confers exclusive jurisdiction to vary trusts on the courts of the jurisdiction of their proper law. Now that this convention has been incorporated into English law by the Recognition of Trusts Act 1987, it is therefore considered unlikely that English courts still have any jurisdiction to make orders under the Variation of Trusts Act 1958 to vary any trust whose proper law is not English law. This seems to be the case even if the trustees of such a trust are personally susceptible to the jurisdiction of the English courts.

---

[62] [1974] 2 All E.R. 365.
[63] As he said in the judgment, "a common lawyer with this problem" of what constitutes a trust.
[64] [1974] 2 All E.R. 365 at 374.
[65] [1983] 2 All E.R. 1078.
[66] [1963] Ch. 553.
[67] [1965] 1 W.L.R. 1046.
[68] See *post*, p. 859.

## (D) Specific Considerations for the Court

### (1) Benefit

The only essential guidance specifically provided in the Act as to the principles on which the exercise of the jurisdiction is based is that, with the exception of discretionary beneficiaries under protective trusts, the arrangement proposed should be for the benefit of the persons designated in the Act[69] on whose behalf its approval is sought. A definite benefit, even if it is not purely financial, must be conferred on such persons. In *Re Van Gruisen's Will Trusts*,[70] it was shown that the provisions for infants and unborn persons were, from an actuarial point of view, more beneficial to them under the proposed arrangement than under the trusts of the will. The arrangement was therefore approved but Ungoed-Thomas J. sounded a warning note by saying:

> "The court is not merely concerned with the actuarial calculation ... the court is also concerned whether the arrangement as a whole in all the circumstances, is such that it is proper to approve it. The court's concern involves, *inter alia*, a practical and businesslike consideration of the arrangement, including the total amount of the advantages which the various parties obtain and their bargaining strength."

Similar reasoning was applied in the earlier decision of *Re Clitheroe's Settlement Trusts*,[71] where the arrangement was designed to exclude any future wife from the class of objects of an immediate discretionary trust,[72] but in compensation, gave her the benefit of a covenant by the settlor to pay the trustees an annual sum for her benefit. Danckwerts J. sanctioned the arrangements in principle but required evidence to show that it was in fact for the benefit of a future wife.

The rule that a "benefit" is all-important has caused some, though admittedly very few, applications to fail. Thus in *Re Steed's Will Trusts*,[73] the Court of Appeal refused to sanction a variation sought by the beneficiary enabling her to take the whole beneficial interest because it did not take sufficient account of a "spectral spouse" whom the trusts were also designed to benefit and whom the beneficiary in question might conceivably marry. Again, in *Re Tinker's Settlement*,[74] Russell J. declined to accept the argument that it was for the benefit of unborn persons as members of a family viewed as a whole that something should be done which, although reasonable and fair, was to their financial detriment.

The same test was applied in *Re T.'s Settlement Trusts*,[75] although in this case

---

[69] s.1(1), proviso.

[70] [1964] 1 W.L.R. 449.

[71] [1959] 1 W.L.R. 1159.

[72] It was not a protective trust, so the proviso to s.1(1) did not apply.

[73] [1960] Ch. 407. See also *Re Cohen's Settlement Trusts* [1965] 1 W.L.R. 1229 (it was proposed to substitute June 14, 1973 in lieu of the applicant's death as the date when the persons to take were to receive the capital of the settled funds; Stamp J. refused the application on behalf of unborn beneficiaries because it could happen (even if it was a remote eventuality) that the applicant might survive the proposed date and under the arrangement such persons would have no interest in the fund, whereas they would have under the original settlement).

[74] [1960] 1 W.L.R. 1011.

[75] [1964] Ch. 158. The primary ground for the decision of Wilberforce J. is discussed *post*, p. 756.

this does not appear to have been the primary reason for the decision of Wilberforce J. to refuse to approve a proposed arrangement to transfer an minor female's share of settled funds to trustees to hold on protective trusts for her lifetime, with remainders over. The minor would otherwise have become absolutely entitled in possession to the funds on attaining 21 and the arrangement had been devised because she had shown herself to be irresponsible in matters of money. A secondary reason for this refusal was that the proposals were not confined simply to dealing in a beneficial way with the special requirements of the minor. Another proposal for variation was later approved. This was to the effect that the minor's right to capital should be deferred for a time, she being given a protected life interest in the meantime.

It must, however, be admitted that these authorities do not appear to be entirely consistent with the decision of Danckwerts J. in *Re Cohen's Will Trusts*.[76] It was contended that in the admittedly unlikely event of one of the testator's children predeceasing his widow, who was then aged nearly 80, the proposed arrangement would not be advantageous to his grandchildren, some of whom were minor. However, Danckwerts J. held that risk of some kind was inherent in every application under the Act and, since this risk was one which it would be reasonable for an adult to run, the court would run it on behalf of the minors.

This sort of attitude is clearly sound when a risk is non-existent. Indeed in such cases it may not even be necessary to apply to the court. Thus it has been held[77] that trustees can properly, and with complete safety, deal with their funds on the basis that a woman of 70 will not have a further child and in such circumstances an application under the Act is inappropriate: "the Act is concerned to vary trusts applicable in events which will or may happen and not to cover impossible contingencies".[78] But where there is an identifiable risk, the more general attitude is to require it to be covered by insurance. This is particularly appropriate if the risk is that a beneficiary will die within a short time of the variation being made. In such circumstances, when the proposed variation is, when viewed broadly, for the financial benefit of the beneficiaries, the court will generally require the life of that beneficiary to be insured, even if the premiums have to be paid for out of income and are in that sense at the expense of a minor beneficiary.[79]

Finally, it should be emphasised that the wishes of the settlor[79A] or testator do not prevent the court from concluding that an arrangement confers benefit. In *Goulding v. James*,[80] the testatrix left her residuary estate to her daughter for life, remainder to her 32 year old grandson at the age of 40 absolutely, remainder to any of her great-grandchildren living at her grandson's death. An arrangement was proposed whereby 45 per cent was to be held for each of the daughter and the grandson absolutely, with the remaining 10 per cent held for the as yet unborn grandchildren, who even if born obviously only had a

---

[76] [1959] 1 W.L.R. 865; compare *Re Cohen's Settlement Trusts* [1965] 1 W.L.R. 1229 (which concerned a completely different family), see *ante*, fn. 73).

[77] *Re Pettifor's Will Trusts* [1966] Ch. 257.

[78] *ibid.* at 260, 261. See also *Re Westminster Bank Ltd's Declaration of Trust* [1963] 1 W.L.R. 820, where an order was made under the Variation of Trusts Act 1958 in respect of a woman aged 50.

[79] For an example, see *Re Robinson's Settlement Trusts* [1976] 3 All E.R. 61.

[79A] Who, if alive, has to be made a party to the application unde the Rules of Court.

[80] [1997] 2 All E.R. 239.

somewhat limited chance of receiving anything under the existing trusts.[81] Laddie J. refused to approve this on the grounds that the testatrix had, on the evidence, wished to prevent her daughter from having any access to capital because she did not trust her son-in-law and wished to defer her grandson's interest until the age of 40 because he had not yet "settled down".[82] This decision was reversed by the Court of Appeal. Mummery L.J. held that "the intentions and wishes of [the testatrix], expressed externally to her will in relation to the adult beneficiaries and an adult non-beneficiary, had little, if any, relevance or weight to the issue of approval on behalf of the future unborn great grandchildren, whose interest in residue was multiplied five-fold under the proposed arrangement".[83] Sir Ralph Gibson went even further, saying that it was not clear to him "why evidence of the intention of the testator can be of any relevance whatever if it does no more than explain why the testator gave the interests set out in the will and the nature and degree of feeling with which such provisions were selected".[84]

The authorities considered thus far have, like the immense majority of all applications under the Act, been concerned exclusively with financial benefit; this is a mundane consideration admitting of reasonable proof. But it has been clearly established that this is not necessarily the only consideration to be taken into account by the court. Thus in *Re T.'s Settlement Trusts*,[85] the judge approved the alternative scheme of variation because on the special facts of the case the evidence showed that the minor beneficiary was irresponsible and immature "there appears to me to be a definite benefit for this infant for a period during which it is to be hoped that independence may bring her into maturity and responsibility to be protected against creditors".[86] This decision was followed by Megarry J. in *Re Holt's Settlement*,[87] where he said in relation to an arrangement postponing the vesting of interests in children from the age of 21 to 30: "The word 'benefit' in the proviso to section 1 of the Act of 1958 is plainly not confined to financial benefit, but may extend to moral or social benefit".[88] This approach was confirmed by the decision of the Court of Appeal in *Re Weston's Settlement*,[89] where it was decided that it was for the benefit of children to be educated in England rather than in Jersey.

An even broader view of "benefit" in this context was taken in *Re Remnant's Settlement Trusts*,[90] where Pennycuick J. approved an arrangement deleting forfeiture clauses depriving certain children of their interests if they practised Roman Catholicism or married a Roman Catholic. This appears to have been on the basis that such provisions might operate as a deterrent to them in the

---

[81] The actuarial valuation of their contingent interest was only 1.85 per cent.
[82] [1996] 4 All E.R. 853.
[83] [1997] 2 All E.R. 239 at 251–252.
[84] *ibid.* at 252.
[85] [1964] Ch. 158.
[86] *ibid.* at 162.
[87] [1969] 1 Ch. 100.
[88] *ibid.* at 121.
[89] [1969] 1 Ch. 223; for further discussion of this case, see *post*, p. 884. See also *Re C.L.* [1969] 1 Ch. 587 (mental patient surrendered his protected life interest and contingent interest in remainder; Cross J. held that it was for the patient's benefit because in all probability it was what he would have done if of sound mind).
[90] [1970] Ch. 560; compare *Re Tinker's Settlement* [1960] 1 W.L.R. 1011.

selection of a husband and might also be a source of possible family dissension.

It is also clear that an arrangement which results in improvement in the general administration of the trust may also be a "benefit" within the meaning of the Act. As will be seen in a later chapter,[91] it is on this ground that the courts have approved applications for the export of trusts to countries abroad where the beneficiaries are resident.

### (2) The position of discretionary beneficiaries under protective trusts

It has already been stated that it is unnecessary to establish that an arrangement confers any benefit on discretionary beneficiaries under protective trusts.[92] Nevertheless, their interests cannot be simply ignored. As Wilberforce J. held in *Re Burney's Settlement Trusts*,[93] in approving an arrangement varying discretionary trusts, the discretionary power conferred on the court still has to be judicially exercised and it is incumbent on the applicant to make out a case for interfering with protective trusts. Indeed, the basic principle had been stated earlier, more generally, by Lord Evershed M.R. in *Re Steed's Will Trusts*,[94] where he said that "the court is bound to look at the scheme as a whole and when it does so, to consider, as surely it must, what really was the intention of the benefactor". The requirements were spelt out in *Re Baker's Settlement Trusts*,[95] where Ungoed-Thomas J. said that where property was held on protective trusts for the benefit of the applicant and an application was made to vary those trusts, evidence (including in this case that of the financial position of the applicant and her husband) should be laid before the court to show to what extent the protective trusts continued to serve any useful purpose.

### (3) Fraud and public policy

Obviously a variation which is fraudulent or contrary to public policy will not be sanctioned.

Fraud has only arisen in connection with the doctrine of fraud on a power. In *Re Robertson's Will Trusts*,[96] the applicant had exercised a special power of appointment in favour of his children as a preliminary to the proposed arrangement. His purpose and intention in making the appointment was to benefit his children and not himself. Later he was advised that his financial position would in fact be improved if the appointment were made and the scheme approved. But Russell J. held that to suppose his original purpose and intention had been changed or added to was unjustified. It followed that there was no fraud on the power, though, if there had been, the court would not have been able to approve the scheme.

However, subsequent case law appears to indicate a certain conflict as to the precise principles to be applied. In *Re Wallace's Settlement*,[97] Megarry J. said that the fact that protected life tenants had executed appointments in favour of

---

[91] See *post*, p. 883.
[92] s.1(1), proviso.
[93] [1961] 1 W.L.R. 545.
[94] [1960] Ch. 407 at 421.
[95] [1964] 1 W.L.R. 336.
[96] [1960] 1 W.L.R. 1050.
[97] [1968] 1 W.L.R. 711.

their children in itself raised a case for inquiry because the life tenants benefited by the arrangement however, on the evidence he was satisfied that there was no fraud on the power because the benefit to the life tenants was not substantial and they had intended to make the appointment before the arrangement was approved. On the other hand, in *Re Brook's Settlement*,[98] Stamp J. adopted a rather different approach. He held that the exercise of a special power of appointment amounted to a fraud on the power and he was unable to approve the variation. Here one of the purposes of the appointment (by a protected life tenant in favour of his children from which he would also benefit from a division of the capital) was to enable the life tenant to obtain what he could not otherwise get, namely capital rather than income. This was enough to invalidate the appointment. The important feature of *Re Brook's Settlement* is that the judge emphasised that the question is whether the purpose of the appointment amounted to a fraud, not, as was apparently suggested in *Re Wallace's Settlement*, the effect of the appointment on the financial position of the appointor. It is thought that *Re Brook's Settlement* applies the correct principle.

The difficulties that may thus arise as a result of a fraud on the power, however inadvertent, may in some circumstances be avoided by releasing the power. No question of a fraud on a power normally arises on a mere release. It has been held that, provided that the power in question can be released,[99] the court will approve an arrangement varying a settlement even though the objects of the power are ignored.[1] There appears to be some doubt as to whether the release should be effected by deed, or whether it can be inferred from the facts. The latter would seem to be sufficient.[2]

Even if the power cannot be released (if for example, it was given to the donee as trustee)[3], it still seems possible to apply to the court for an arrangement extinguishing the power because this amounts to varying or revoking a trust within section 1 of the Act. But because the power is not of itself capable of release, the court is likely to impose conditions on the release. Thus in Re *Drewe's Settlement*,[4] Stamp J. in approving an arrangement insisted that such a power could only be effected by deed and with the consent of the trustees.

The only reported case in which considerations of public policy have arisen is *Re Michelham's Will Trusts*,[5] where they were neatly sidestepped by Buckley J. Approval was sought to an arrangement whereby trust property was transferred to the applicants absolutely. The efficacy of the scheme depended on their continuing to remain unmarried. Insurance policies were therefore to be effected which would ensure that, if either did in fact marry, certain sums would become available to replace the funds thus transferred. The policies included a stipulation that the insurers should be indemnified by a Swiss bank if the policy moneys became payable. The bank proposed to give the indem-

---

[98] [1968] 1 W.L.R. 1661.
[99] See *Re Wills's Trust Deeds* [1964] Ch. 219; see *ante*, p. 225 and see Hawkins (1968) 84 L.Q.R. 64.
[1] *Re Christie-Miller's Settlement* [1961] 1 W.L.R. 462; *Re Courtland's Settlement* [1965] 1 W.L.R. 1385; *Re Ball's Settlement* [1968] 1 W.L.R. 899.
[2] In *Re Ball's Settlement* [1968] 1 W.L.R. 462 Megarry J. insisted on a formal release but in *Re Christie-Miller's Settlement* [1965] 1 W.L.R. 462 and *Re Courtland's Settlement* [1965] 1 W.L.R. 1385 an inferred release was regarded as sufficient.
[3] See *ante*, p. 226.
[4] [1966] 1 W.L.R. 1518.
[5] [1964] Ch. 550.

nity on terms that it, in turn, should be indemnified by one or other of the applicants if the moneys became payable. The judge, in approving the arrangement, held that, although the counter-indemnities given by the applicants to the bank ought to be regarded as tending to discourage the applicants from marrying, that would not affect its validity. This was so because if the counter-indemnities were unenforceable by the bank on grounds of public policy, something which was a question of Swiss law, that fact alone would not relieve the bank from its obligation to indemnify the insurers.

### (4) Perpetuity

The Perpetuities and Accumulations Act 1964[6] applies only to instruments taking effect after the commencement of the Act.[7] How far do provisions of this type affect variations made under the Act of 1958? In *Re Holt's Settlement*,[8] Megarry J. held that an arrangement (taken with the court order)[9] as an "instrument" for this purpose, with the result that provisions deriving their validity from the 1964 Act might be included in the arrangement and that this would apply not only to trusts created since the commencement of the 1964 Act but also to those created before this date.[10]

However, the difficulty does remain as to whether the instrument must take effect as a "disposition". The 1964 Act tends to suggest that this is necessary.[11] The point did not arise in *Re Holt's Settlement* because the applicant there surrendered a life interest and this clearly amounted to a "disposition". It seems, however, that if the arrangement does not involve a disposition, then the benefits of the 1964 Act cannot be utilised in respect of subsequent variations of the original trusts.[12]

### (5) The precise meaning of "arrangement"

There is no doubt that this term has been widely construed to cover many classes of variation. As Lord Evershed M.R. said in *Re Steed's Will Trusts*,[13] "it is deliberately used in the widest possible sense to cover any proposal which any person may put forward for varying or revoking trusts". It need not, therefore, necessarily be *inter partes*. Views of the trustees are relevant but not conclusive and, if necessary, will be overridden.[14]

The wide meaning thus attached to an arrangement was, however, modified in *Re T.'s Settlement Trusts*,[15] whose facts have already been considered. Here Wilberforce J. refused, as the primary ground for his decision, to sanction the arrangement initially proposed because it amounted to a completely new settlement and that was beyond the jurisdiction conferred by the Act. If this

---

[6] See *ante*, p. 238. The proposed new legislation on perpetuities contains a similar provision.
[7] s.15(5).
[8] [1969] 1 Ch. 100.
[9] See *post*, p. 759.
[10] The same principle was applied but no reasons were given in *Re Lloyd's Settlement* [1967] 2 W.L.R. 1078 in relation to s.13 and to the accumulation periods.
[11] See ss.1, 3(5).
[12] See *Re Holmden's Settlement* [1968] A.C. 685, where it was suggested that a mere alteration of the period for which discretionary trusts should continue was not a "disposition".
[13] [1960] Ch. 407 at 751.
[14] *ibid.* at 420.
[15] [1964] Ch. 158; see *ante*, p. 751.

represents the true position there are limits to the conception of an "arrangement", although this does appear to be an unjustified abridgment of the court's jurisdiction.

Nevertheless subsequent case law does seem to have accepted the distinction between "variation" and "resettlement". In *Re Ball's Settlement*,[16] Megarry J. laid down the following test:

"If an arrangement changes the whole substratum of the trust, it may well be that it cannot be regarded as merely varying that trust. But if an arrangement, while leaving the substratum effectuates the purpose by other means, it may still be possible to regard that arrangement as merely varying the original trusts, even though the means employed are wholly different and even though the form is completely changed."

However, he actually held that, although the arrangement sought rescinded all beneficial and administrative trusts of the settlement and substituted new provisions, he could approve it because it preserved the "general drift" of the old trusts. The fact remains that a pedantic distinction has grown up between "variation" and "resettlement" for which there appears to be neither any sanction in the words of the Act nor any practical justification.

### (E) Investment Clauses

Prior to the enactment of the now repealed Trustee Investments Act 1961,[17] the Variation of Trusts Act 1958 was frequently used to increase the then very restricted statutory powers of investment of trustees. The Act of 1961 itself expressly preserved the discretion of the court under the Act of 1958 to extend these powers. The question was whether this entitled trustees to obtain under the Act of 1958 more extensive investment powers than those conferred by the Act of 1961. The answer in most of the reported cases was initially negative. Thus in *Re Cooper's Settlement*,[18] Buckley J. held that the court had to be satisfied that there were "special circumstances" in which the trustees should be given wider powers than the "normally appropriate" powers indicated by the Act of 1961. The fact that the extension of investment powers proposed was part of an arrangement to vary beneficial interests was specifically rejected as amounting in itself to a special circumstance justifying a departure from the scope of the statutory scheme. A similar decision was reached in *Re Kolb's Will Trusts*,[19] where it was held that the powers conferred by the Act of 1961 to invest in equities could not be extended. Only in *Re University of London Charitable Trusts*[20] were sufficient special circumstances found to enable the range of permissible investments to be extended beyond those permitted by the Act of 1961. This remained the position until the courts came to recognise that the Trustee Investments Act 1961 had itself become outdated[20A]; they then once again became readily prepared to authorise extensions of trustees' investment powers.

---

[16] [1968] 1 W.L.R. 899. See also *Re Holt's Settlement* [1969] 1 Ch. 100 at 117.
[17] s.15; see *ante*, p. 597.
[18] [1962] Ch. 826.
[19] [1961] 1 W.L.R. 1471. See also *Re Clarke's Will Trusts* [1961] 1 W.L.R. 1471.
[20] [1964] Ch. 282.
[20A] *Trustees of the British Museum v. Attorney-General* [1984] 1 W.L.R. 418.

Despite the fact that the provisions of the Trustee Investment Act 1961 have now been replaced by the general power of investment conferred on trustees by section 3 of the Trustee Act 2000,[21] extensions of investment powers may still be sought in at least two situations: first, where the trust instrument has cut down the statutory power of investment[22]; and, secondly, when the trustees wish to enlarge that power to include types of investments which are not within the general power of investment, the most obvious example being non-income producing investments.[23] Where variations of this type can be shown to be for the benefit of the beneficiaries (which will of course be considerably easier in the first case than in the second case), there seems no reason why applications of this type should not succeed. However, *Anker-Petersen v. Anker-Petersen*[24] has now established that, provided the beneficial interests are not also affected by the proposed extension of the trustees' investment powers, section 57 of the Trustee Act 1925 should be used in order to obtain such extensions rather than the Variation of Trusts Act 1958.

### (F) Procedure and Formalities

#### (1) Form of application

An application should normally be made by a life-tenant or other person entitled to the income of the trust funds. It should only be made by the trustees, as Russell J. said in *Re Druce's Settlement Trusts*,[25] where "they are satisfied that the proposals are beneficial to the persons interested and have a good prospect of being approved by the court, and further, that if they do not make the application no one else will". As these principles were satisfied in this case, the application by the trustees was held to be proper.

In the ordinary way the trustees will be respondents, as will be all the existing beneficiaries, adult and minor, the settlor, and the Attorney-General[26] if the existing settlement contains a charitable trust. It is, moreover, the duty of persons appointed as litigation friends for a minor to take proper legal advice and apprise themselves fully of the nature of the application and the manner in which the beneficial interest of the infant is proposed to be affected.[27] At the same time it is recognised that there is a limit to the necessity for joinder of parties. So it seems unnecessary, for reasons of practicality and expense, to join persons who are merely potential members of a class. Thus, it has been held that it is unnecessary to join persons who are only interested as the objects of a power which may never be exercised.[28] And the same view has been applied to persons interested under protective trusts which it is proposed to vary; as Wilberforce J. said in *Re Munro's Settlement Trusts*,[29] the court looks *prima facie* to the trustees as watchdogs to see that interested parties' interests are protected.

---

[21] See *ante*, p. 597.
[22] See *ante*, p. 605.
[23] See *ante*, p. 608.
[24] (1990) [2000] W.T.L.R. 581.
[25] [1962] 1 W.L.R. 363.
[26] See *Re Longman's Settlement Trusts* [1962] 1 W.L.R. 455.
[27] *Re Whittall* [1973] 1 W.L.R. 1027.
[28] *Re Christie-Miller's Settlement* [1961] 1 W.L.R. 462.
[29] [1963] 1 W.L.R. 145; compare *Re Courtland's Settlement* [1965] 1 W.L.R. 1385.

## (2) Combined applications

Under section 53 of the Trustee Act 1925,[30] the court has power to make vesting orders in relation to a minor's beneficial interest. In some cases it may prove necessary to combine an application under this section with one under the Variation of Trusts Act 1958. This happened in Re Bristol's Settled Estates,[31] where Buckley J. authorised the execution of a disentailing assurance on behalf of an infant tenant in tail in remainder so that the property could be dealt with for his benefit under a proposed "arrangement" which the judge also approved.

## (3) The effect of a variation

It now seems to be established that it is the arrangement itself and not the order of the court which effects the variation.[32] But it seems necessary to regard the order of the court and the arrangement as having been made at the same time.[33] The arrangement will, however, be embodied in, or referred to in, the order and, where this causes a disposition of beneficial interests, stamp duty was formerly payable (such voluntary dispositions are no longer subject thereto). In Thorn v. I.R.C.,[34] Walton J. had to consider the nature of the disposition affected. A trust fund was held upon protective trusts for the settlor's wife for life, with remainder to the settlor's daughter for life, and ultimately for the children and remoter issue of the daughter. An order had been made under the Variation of Trusts Act approving a variation on behalf of the unborn and unascertained issue of the daughter. The trustees contended that in giving its approval the court, in effect, dealt with the interest of each unborn or unascertained person. Each interest, looked at separately, would have had almost no value. However, Walton J. held that the order affected the disposition of the totality of the separate interests which therefore fell to be valued as a composite whole. This decision will once again become important if ad valorem duty is ever reimposed on voluntary dispositions.

A further question is whether the trusts are effectively varied by the arrangement when the court order is made even though the arrangement does not comply with section 53(1)(c) of the Law of Property Act 1925. This requires that the disposition of an equitable interest should be in writing.[35] In Re Holt's Settlement,[36] Megarry J. answered this question in the affirmative. In coming to this conclusion, he relied on Oughtred v. I.R.C.,[37] on the basis that the arrangement amounted to a specifically enforceable oral contract and so gave rise to a constructive trust; this meant that the requirements of section 53(1)(c) could therefore be ignored because of section 53(2) which exempts con-

---

[30] See ante, p. 708.
[31] [1965] 1 W.L.R. 469; see also Re Lansdowne's Will Trusts [1967] Ch. 603.
[32] Re Holt's Settlement [1969] 1 Ch. 100. See also Re Holmden's Settlement [1968] A.C. 685 at 701, 705, 713; Spens v. I.R.C. [1970] 1 W.L.R. 1173 at 1183, 1184. Megarry J. in Re Holt's Settlement followed Re Joseph's Will Trusts [1959] 1 W.L.R. 1019, not Re Hambledon's Will Trusts [1960] 1 W.L.R. 82, which had held that the court order effected the variation.
[33] Re Holt's Settlement [1969] 1 Ch. 100 at 115. The main reason for this requirement seems to be that decisions made on the basis of Re Hambledon's Will Trusts [1960] 1 W.L.R. 82 would have been made without jurisdiction.
[34] [1976] 2 All E.R. 622.
[35] For further discussion of this section and the authorities, see ante, p. 97.
[36] [1969] 1 Ch. 100.
[37] [1960] A.C. 206; see ante, p. 111.

structive trusts from them. In the House of Lords in *Oughtred v. I.R.C.*, this view was in fact adopted only by Lord Radcliffe, who was dissenting on the main issue, to which this point was, in the view of the majority, irrelevant.[38] However, Lord Radcliffe's view has since been expressly confirmed by the Court of Appeal in *Neville v. Wilson*,[39] so that the decision of Megarry J. now clearly constitutes the law. However, a variation will only take effect without formality on this basis where the subject matter of the trusts which have been varied is entirely pure personalty because all contracts for the sale of land are now required to be in writing.[40]

---

[38] See *ante*, p. 111.
[39] [1997] Ch. 144; see *ante*, p. 112.
[40] Under the Law of Property (Miscellaneous Provisions) Act 1989, s.2.

# CHAPTER 22

# BREACH OF TRUST

A breach of trust occurs if a trustee does any act which he ought not to do, or fails to do any act which he ought to do with regard to the administration of the trust, or with regard to the beneficial interests arising under the trust. It would be undesirable to attempt an exhaustive list of circumstances in which a breach of trust can be committed, but the following are examples:

(a) investment of trust moneys in unauthorised investments;

(b) taking a profit from the trust not authorised by the trust instrument or by the court;

(c) manipulating the investments to benefit one beneficiary at the expense of another;

(d) negligently allowing trust property to remain under the control of one trustee only;

(e) paying trust property to the wrong person;

(f) purchasing trust property without authority; and

(g) failing to exercise a proper discretion with regard to trust decisions.

Where there is an allegation of breach of trust, the following questions have to be considered:

(a) whether a breach of trust been committed;

(b) whether the proposed defendant is liable;

(c) what the *prima facie* measure of liability is;

(d) whether there is any right to contribution or indemnity;

(e) whether the proposed claimant is in time to sue; and

(f) whether the proposed defendant may be relieved from liability by the court or otherwise.

A consideration of these questions should be sufficient to ensure that no relevant point is overlooked when looking at the position from the point of view of the trustees. However, when looked at the position from the point of view of the beneficiaries, it is also necessary to ask whether they can take any action against third parties if sufficient redress cannot be obtained from the trustees. Their possibilities are:

(a) a personal claim against a third party;

(b) a legal proprietary claim in respect of the trust property; and

(c) an equitable proprietary claim in respect of the trust property.

The two types of proprietary claims can be brought against the trustees as well as against third parties and often are when one or more of the trustees is insolvent.

## I. THE LIABILITY OF A TRUSTEE FOR HIS OWN ACTS

There will usually be little difficulty in ascertaining whether a breach of trust has been committed by a trustee during his trusteeship. Complications sometimes arise, however, in respect of acts done at the beginning and end of a trusteeship.

On appointment, a trustee should take certain steps. He should inspect the trust instrument to ascertain the terms of the trust and to see whether any notices have been indorsed on it. He should ensure that all the trust property is transferred into his name jointly with the other trustees, for he may be liable if he allows the property to remain in the hands of another.[1] He may wish to go through the trust papers in order to familiarise himself with the circumstances of the trust. If in the course of doing so, or for that matter in any other way, he learns that a breach of trust has been committed, he must obtain satisfaction from the person responsible. Should the new trustee not do so, he will himself be liable for breach of trust for his own omission; the only exception to this principle is if the new trustee is reasonably satisfied that it would be useless to institute proceedings because for example, the former trustee cannot be found, or is destitute.[2] On the other hand, unless a new trustee does acquire knowledge that a breach of trust has been committed or there are sufficient suspicious circumstances to place him on enquiry, he may assume that there have been no previous breaches of trust.[3]

When a trustee retires from a trust, in principle he remains liable for breaches of trust committed during his trusteeship and his estate will be held liable if he has died by the time that the breaches come to light. He will only be relieved from liability if and to the extent that he may have been released by the continuing trustees or by the beneficiaries but, in the latter case, only where they were in possession of the relevant facts at the time of the release.

A breach of trust sometimes occurs shortly after the retirement of a trustee. In such circumstances, the retiring trustee will be liable if he contemplated that a breach of trust would occur and he retired with the intention of facilitating it or if, believing that it would occur, he retired to avoid being involved in it. In

---

[1] He will only be liable if loss is caused as a result of the property being left in the hands of others; *Re Miller's Deed Trusts* (1978) Law Society Gazette, May 3, 1978.
[2] *Re Forest of Dean Coal Co.* [1878] 10 Ch.D. 450.
[3] *Re Stratham* [1856] 8 De G.M. & G. 291.

such circumstances, he will be liable because his motive in retiring was to enable the breach of trust to occur. If he merely realised that his retirement would facilitate the breach of trust, he will not be liable just for that reason,[4] but he will be liable if, in addition to realising that his retirement would facilitate the breach, he foresaw, or ought reasonably to have foreseen, that such a breach would in fact take place. In this case he will have failed in his duty to prevent a breach of trust occurring. It follows that, if the retiring trustee did not foresee what would happen and the remaining trustees have simply taken advantage of his absence to perpetrate the breach, he will not himself have failed in any of his duties and so will not be liable.[5] Apart from this, a trustee is not liable for breaches of trust which occur after his retirement.

## II. THE LIABILITY OF A TRUSTEE FOR THE ACTS OF HIS CO-TRUSTEES

A trustee can never be liable for the acts of his co-trustees as such but he will be liable where a breach of trust is committed by his co-trustees if he himself has breached the statutory duty of care imposed by the Trustee Act 2000.[6] Until 1926 the position was governed by the general common law rule that unpaid trustees were bound to use only such due diligence and care in the management of the trust as an ordinary prudent man of business would use in the management of his own affairs;[7] however, after 1925, the position was held instead to be governed by the now repealed section 30 of the Trustee Act 1925,[8] under which a trustee was only liable for losses which occurred "through his own wilful default". The statutory duty of care clearly gives rise to liability for conduct less than wilful default and it is therefore likely that a trustee will now be liable for a breach of trust arising through the act or default of his co-trustee in the same circumstances as he would have been before 1926, that is to say:

(a) where the trustee leaves a matter in the hands of his co-trustee without inquiry;[9]

(b) where he stands by while a breach of trust of which he is aware is being committed;[10]

---

[4] *Head v. Gould* [1898] 2 Ch. 250.
[5] *ibid.*
[6] See *ante*, p. 573.
[7] *Speight v. Gaunt* (1883) 9 App.Cas. 1.
[8] See *Re Vickery* [1931] 1 Ch. 572.
[9] *Chambers* v. *Minchin* (1802) 7 Ves. 186; *Shipbrook v. Hinchinbrook* (1810) 16 Ves. 477; *Hanbury v. Kirkland* (1829) 3 Sim. 265; *Broadhurst v. Balguy* (1841) 1 Y. & C.C.C. 16; *Thompson v. Finch* (1865) 8 De G.M. & G. 560; *Mendes v. Guedalla* (1862) 8 Jur. 878; *Hale v. Adams* (1873) 21 W.R. 400; *Wynee v. Tempest* (1897) 13 T.L.R. 360; *Re Second East Dulwich Building Society* (1899) 68 L.J.Ch. 196.
[10] In *Styles v. Guy* (1849) 1 Mac. & G. 422 at 433, Lord Cottenham stated that it is the duty of executors and trustees "to watch over, and if necessary, to correct, the conduct of each other". See also *Booth v. Booth* (1838) 1 Beav. 125; *Gough v. Smith* [1872] W.N. 18.

(c) where he allows trust funds to remain in the sole control of his co-trustee;[11] and

(d) where, on becoming aware of a breach of trust committed or contemplated by his co-trustee, he takes no steps to obtain redress.[12]

The circumstances in which a trustee is liable for the acts or defaults of his agents, as distinct from of his co-trustees, have already been considered.[13]

### III. THE MEASURE OF LIABILITY

What is the measure of liability of a trustee who has committed a breach of trust? Leaving on one side the situation where the beneficiary seeks the imposition of a constructive trust on property which the trustee has himself obtained as a result of his breach of trust,[14] what the beneficiary will be seeking is an award of equitable compensation under *Nocton v. Lord Ashburton*;[15] the effect of that decision is that equitable compensation is available whether or not there has been a misappropriation of trust property.[16]

The primary means by which a beneficiary who is the victim of a breach of trust can obtain equitable compensation for that breach is by requiring the trustee to comply with his obligation to account for his stewardship.[17] This involves the trustee rendering an account of what he has done with the trust property which has been in his hands. If the beneficiary is dissatisfied with what the trustee has done, then he has the right to "surcharge" or "falsify" the account rendered. If the trustee has negligently failed to obtain all the income or capital that he should have done for the benefit of the trust, the beneficiary will surcharge the account, in other words claim a sum additional to the amount which the trustee actually obtained; in these circumstances, the excess is calculated on what is known as a footing of wilful default, in other words by reference to the specific amount of the loss occasioned by the trustee's lack of skill and care. If, on the other hand, the trustee has made an unauthorised disbursement, the beneficiary has the option of falsifying the account in that respect, in other words of disallowing the expenditure in question; in that case,

---

[11] *English v. Willats* (1831) 1 L.J.Ch. 84; *Ex parte Booth* (1831) Mont. 248; *Child v. Giblett* (1834) 3 L.J.Ch. 124; *Hewitt v. Foster* (1843) 6 Beav. 259; *Wiglesworth v. Wiglesworth* (1852) 16 Beav. 269; *Byass v. Gates* (1854) 2 W.R. 487; *Trutch v. Lamprell* (1855) 20 Beav. 116; *Cowell v. Gatcombe* (1859) 27 Beav. 568; *William v. Higgins* (1868) 17 L.T. 525; *Rodbard v. Cooke* (1877) 25 W.R. 555; *Lewis v. Nobbs* (1878) 8 Ch.D. 591.

[12] *Boadman v. Mosman* (1779) 1 Bro.C.C. 68; *Wilkins v. Hogg* (1861) 8 Jur.(N.S.) 25 at 26, *per* Lord Westbury.

[13] See *ante*, p. 611.

[14] This type of claim was considered in chap. 10.

[15] [1914] A.C. 932, see *ante*, p. 338.

[16] Equitable compensation had always been available when there had been a misappropriation of trust property and in this respect the House of Lords did no more than reaffirm the continued existence of equity's jurisdiction to award it, then thought in some quarters to have been extinguished due to the very wide interpretation which was being given to *Derry v. Peek* (1889) 14 App.Cas. 337. However, the House of Lords went considerably further than this and upheld the existence of the same jurisdiction when there had been no misappropriation of trust property but merely a breach of fiduciary duty (in that case the fact that the defendant solicitor had failed adequately to disclose a conflict of interest).

[17] See Lord Millett, extrajudicially, (1998) 114 L.Q.R. 214.

the trustee will then be treated as if he was still holding on trust the sum paid away and, once the account has been taken,[18] will be obliged to reimburse that sum to the trust.[19] However, where the disbursement was an unauthorised investment which has subsequently appreciated in value, it will not be in the interests of the beneficiary to falsify the account; he will therefore instead normally accept the unauthorised investment as part of the trust property and, in such circumstances, he is said to affirm or adopt the transaction. Whenever an account is surcharged or falsified, "the obligation of a defaulting trustee [to compensate the trust fund for such a loss] is essentially one of effecting restitution to the estate. The obligation is of a personal character and its extent is not to be limited by common law principles governing the remoteness of damage."[20]

However, the taking of an account will not necessarily or usually be appropriate where there has been neither a failure to obtain nor a misapplication of trust property. This will be the case where for example, the breach of trust complained of relates to a conflict of interest and duty. In *Nocton v. Lord Ashburton*[21] itself, a solicitor was found to be in breach of fiduciary duty as a result of his failure adequately to disclose to his client a conflict of interest and duty arising out of the fact that he was interested in the proceeds of the investment in respect of which he was advising the client; when the investment proved to be unsuccessful, equitable compensation was awarded in respect of the client's loss. In *Longstaff v. Birtles*,[22] a solicitor who had been representing a client in connection with the purchase of a hotel suggested to the client, after he had decided not to proceed, that he should instead invest in a different hotel owned by a partnership of which the solicitor was a member; the solicitor disclosed all the facts but his failure to insist that the client obtained independent legal advice was held to place him in a conflict of interest and duty and he was held liable to compensate the client for the losses arising out of his investment. A different conflict, one of interest and interest, potentially arises where a solicitor is representing more than one party to a transaction, typically both a purchaser and his mortgagee; in such circumstances, the solicitor will have committed a breach of fiduciary duty if he intentionally prefers the interests of one of his clients to those of the other.[23] However, it must always be remembered that, as the Court of Appeal emphasised in *Bristol and West Building Society v. Mothew*,[24] not every breach of duty by a fiduciary is a breach of fiduciary duty; the fiduciary's liability will be merely contractual or tortious unless he has preferred the interests of either himself or someone else to those of his principal.

In circumstances where there has been a breach of fiduciary duty of one of these types, there will normally be nothing that can be surcharged or falsified and the quantum of recovery will therefore have to be established in some

---

[18] The obligation to reimburse the trust does not arise as soon as the unauthorised disbursement has been made but only when the beneficiary elects to falsify it; until then, the trustee does not know whether or not the beneficiary will choose to do so.

[19] *Clough v. Bond* (1838) 3 My. & Cr. 490 at 496–497, *per* Lord Cottenham L.C.

[20] *Re Dawson* [1966] 2 N.S.W.L.R. 211 at 214 (Supreme Court of New South Wales).

[21] [1914] A.C. 932, see *ante*, p. 338.

[22] [2002] 1 W.L.R. 470.

[23] Such breaches of fiduciary duty were held to have arisen in *Nationwide Building Society v. Balmer Radmore* [1999] Lloyds Rep. P.N. 241.

[24] [1998] Ch. 1.

other way. Exactly how has been a matter of considerable debate but the general view is that in these circumstances it is appropriate to apply common law principles of remoteness of damages to the assessment of equitable compensation. This was the approach adopted by Lord Browne-Wilkinson in *Target Holdings v. Redferns*,[25] when he applied the "but for" test of causation to the assessment of equitable compensation; although, as will be seen later on,[26] this was a case in which an account could appropriately have been taken, the beneficiary did not seek one. Lord Browne-Wilkinson's decision and the Commonwealth authorities on which he relied[27] were subsequently applied by Hobhouse L.J. in *Swindle v. Harrison*,[28] where a solicitor had failed to disclose all the facts of a loan transaction between himself and his client; the client had suffered no loss as a result of the solicitor's breach of duty so no equitable compensation was awarded. Further, it was subsequently held in *Nationwide Building Society v. Balmer Radmore*[29] that a fiduciary who is liable for breach of fiduciary duty is entitled to prove that his principal's loss would have occurred, in whole or in part, irrespective of his breach of fiduciary duty[30] and, in the event that he can prove this, he will not be responsible for the loss, or the part of the loss, in question.[31]

It should be added that equitable compensation is not awarded in order to punish the trustee; however, if he has been fraudulent or has otherwise behaved particularly badly, the court will reflect its displeasure by increasing the amount of interest payable by the trustee above that which he would otherwise have been ordered to pay.[32]

The following examples illustrate these principles. All are concerned with the *prima facie* liability of the trustee and do not take into account the possibility of some protection or relief being given to the trustee in the manner which will be discussed later on.[33]

---

[25] [1996] 1 A.C. 421.
[26] See *post*, p. 768.
[27] *Re Dawson* [1966] N.S.W.L.R. 211 (Supreme Court of New South Wales); *Canson Enterprises v. Boughton & Co.* (1991) 85 D.L.R.(4th) 129 (Supreme Court of Canada).
[28] [1997] 4 All E.R. 705 at 727–728.
[29] [1999] Lloyds Rep. P.N. 241 at 272–279.
[30] *Brickenden v. London Loan Savings Company* [1934] 3 D.L.R. 465 (Privy Council on appeal from Canada) had established that the principal is entitled to be put back into the position in which he was prior to the breach of fiduciary duty even if his loss or some part of it would have occurred even if there had been no breach of fiduciary duty; this view had subsequently been adopted in Australia (*Gemstone Corporation of Australia v. Grasso* (1994) 13 A.C.S.R. 695 (Supreme Court of South Australia)). But Blackburne J. preferred the more recent Canadian authorities (*Commerce Trust Co. v. Berk* (1989) 68 O.R.(2d.) 257 (Ontario Court of Appeal); *Hodgkinson v. Simms* (1994) 117 D.L.R. (4th) 161 (Supreme Court of Canada)) and the New Zealand authorities (*Everist v. McEvedy* [1996] 3 N.Z.L.R. 349 (High Court of New Zealand), applying *Haira v. Burbery Mortgage Finance and Savings* [1995] 3 N.Z.L.R. 396 (New Zealand Court of Appeal)).
[31] Blackburne J. rejected (*ibid.* pp. 279–282) the further contention that the fiduciary should be entitled to rely on the contributory negligence of his principal in the way that he can in New Zealand (*Day v. Mead* [1987] 2 N.Z.L.R. 443 at 451 (New Zealand Court of Appeal)) and in Canada (*Canson Enterprises v. Boughton & Co.* (1991) 85 D.L.R. (4th) 129 at 151–152 (Supreme Court of Canada)).
[32] See *post*, pp. 773–775.
[33] See *post*, pp. 785–794.

## 1. *Improper Payments of Trusts Money*

Where the trustees make an improper payment of trust money, the beneficiaries are clearly entitled to falsify the disbursement made; consequently, the trustees are clearly liable to make good to the trust fund that amount, so that the income or capital sum wrongly paid, together with interest thereon,[34] can be paid out to the correct beneficiary.

An unusual illustration of the operation of this principle is provided by *Target Holdings v. Redferns*.[35] The plaintiff had agreed to lend £1,525,000 on the security of two properties which were in fact being acquired for £775,000 but, as a result of the interposition of two intermediate purchasers, appeared to be being purchased for £2,000,000. The defendant solicitors, who were acting in the normal way both for the purchasers and for the plaintiff mortgagee, were holding the mortgage advance on trust for the plaintiff with authority to release it to the vendor only upon receipt of the duly executed conveyances and mortgages of the properties. However, they released the funds to the intermediate purchasers several days before the execution of these documents. The plaintiff nevertheless obtained, admittedly after the release of the funds, the mortgage securities which it had instructed the defendants to obtain. However, those securities proved to be insufficient and the plaintiff failed to recover more than £1,000,000 of the sum advanced; this loss would of course have been incurred even if the defendants had complied with their instructions.

The plaintiff sought reconstitution of the trust fund. On an application for summary judgment, the Court of Appeal[36] held that the obligation of a trustee who had committed a breach of trust was to put the trust fund in the same position as it would have been if no breach had taken place. Where the breach consisted in the wrongful payment of trust moneys to a stranger, there was an immediate loss which the trustee was immediately liable to reimburse; it was not necessary for there to be any inquiry as to whether the loss would have occurred if there had been no breach of trust. Summary judgment was therefore ordered. However, this decision was reversed by the House of Lords. Lord Browne-Wilkinson held that there was only any obligation to reimburse the trust fund at all when the trust in question was ongoing rather than where the beneficiary was, like the plaintiff, absolutely entitled; further, even when such an obligation arose, it was not possible to "stop the clock" at the moment when the wrongful payment occurred and ignore all subsequent events. He therefore held that the liability of a trustee to pay equitable compensation was subject to a "but for" test of causation. The defendants would consequently only be liable if it could be shown that the transaction would not have proceeded and the plaintiff's loss would therefore not have been incurred but for the payment by the defendants to the intermediate purchasers in breach of trust.[37] The defendants were therefore given leave to defend the action; however, because of the high probability that the test of causation would be

---

[34] For the rate of interest, see *post*, pp. 773–775. See generally *Youyang v. Minter Ellison Morris Fletcher* [2003] W.T.L.R. 751.
[35] [1996] 1 A.C. 421. This case is analysed in detail in *Trends in Contemporary Trust Law* (ed. Oakley, 1996), p. 217.
[36] [1994] 1 W.L.R. 1089.
[37] This had been able to be shown in *Alliance & Leicester Buidling Society v. Edgestop* (1991) unreported.

satisfied, they were ordered to pay £1,000,000 into court as a condition of being allowed to do so. The case was subsequently settled without proceeding to trial on the basis that the plaintiff received the £1,000,000.

It has been contended[38] that this case would have been more appropriately decided on the basis of the defendant trustees' obligation to account. The plaintiff had authorised a payment only in exchange for the mortgage securities; consequently, it was entitled to "falsify" the defendants' account in respect of the payments to the intermediate purchasers since those mortgages had not yet been executed. Had an account been taken at that stage, the plaintiff would undoubtedly have been entitled to reimbursement of the whole sum paid away and could clearly have obtained summary judgment for that sum. However, the defendants had subsequently complied with their instructions by obtaining the mortgage securities, something which they were at that stage still authorised to do; this transformed their unauthorised payment into an authorised one. Consequently, nothing would be found to be due to the plaintiff on any subsequent taking of an account, which would thus have produced exactly the same result as that arrived at by the House of Lords. This analysis cannot be faulted but that does not alter the fact that no account was actually sought in the proceedings. This was because the plaintiff initially brought only proceedings for professional negligence; it was only in the course of the trial at first instance that the plaintiff became aware of the payment to the intermediate purchasers and the consequential breach of trust. The decision of the House of Lords therefore remains a perfectly acceptable authority on the measure of equitable compensation available where no account is taken. However, the taking of an account is obviously the more appropriate method by which to proceed when trust funds have been paid to the wrong person. It is therefore inevitable that an account will normally be the means by which beneficiaries proceed in cases of this kind.

### 2. Failure Properly to Invest the Trust Property

**(A) Investment in Unauthorised Investments**
Where trustees invest the trust funds in unauthorised investments, the beneficiaries have the right to falsify the disbursement and require the trustees to replace the funds wrongfully invested. In such circumstances, the trustees will in effect have to sell the unauthorised investments and make good whatever loss results.[39] On the other hand, where the unauthorised investment has made a profit, it will not be in the interests of the beneficiaries to falsify the account and, provided that they are all ascertained and *sui juris*, they will therefore be able to adopt the unauthorised investment and take the profit. Where they do so, they clearly should not be entitled also to claim the difference between the value of the improper investment and any higher amount that would have been obtained by an authorised investment. However, there is in fact a conflict of authority on this point.[40]

Unusually, in *Vyse v. Foster*,[41] the unauthorised investment consisted of an

---

[38] By Lord Millett, extra-judicially, in (1998) L.Q.R. 214.
[39] *Re Salmon* (1889) 42 Ch.D. 351.
[40] The conclusion suggested in the text was adopted in *Thornton v. Stokill* (1855) 1 Jur. 151 but in *Re Lake* [1903] 1 K.B. 439 the beneficiaries were held to be entitled to the additional amount as well.
[41] (1872) L.R. 8 Ch. 309, affirmed (1874) L.R. 7 H.L. 318.

unauthorised improvement to other trust property; in such circumstances, the beneficiaries will in effect have no option but to adopt the investment. Trustees who held land and money upon a common trust expended, without authority, some of the money on erecting a bungalow on the land at a cost of £1,600; this benefited the trust by more than the £1,600 expended. An attempt was made to say that not only were the trustees liable to reimburse the £1,600 because this expenditure was unauthorised but the beneficiaries were also entitled to the benefit of the bungalow because it was an accretion to the trust property. The Court of Appeal and House of Lords rejected this argument and it is only surprising that it was accepted at first instance. However, had the erection of the bungalow benefited the trust by less than the cost of erecting it, the beneficiaries could undoubtedly have surcharged the disbursement and recovered the difference.

If trustees instead sell an authorised investment and reinvest the proceeds in an unauthorised one, the beneficiaries have the same choice as to whether to falsify or to adopt the unauthorised investment. If it is falsified, that is likely to be because it has resulted in a loss. In such circumstances, the beneficiaries have a further choice. They can compel the trustees either to make good the difference between the sale price of the authorised investment and the proceeds of sale of the unauthorised investment, or to repurchase for the trust the authorised security, taking credit for the proceeds of sale of the unauthorised security. Suppose, therefore, that the trustees sell an authorised investment, 4,000 shares, for £100,000 and reinvest that £100,000 in an unauthorised investment such as some gold bars.[42] If a year later the gold bars are sold at a loss for £80,000, the beneficiaries have a choice. They can compel the trustees to pay to the trust fund £100,000, the proceeds of the shares, less the £80,000 which the trustees will already have paid in from the sale of the gold bars. Alternatively, they can compel the trustees to purchase for the trust 4,000 shares in the company in question, however much they might then cost; if the shares have doubled in price, the trustees will therefore have to pay £200,000 for them but can utilise as part of that sum the £80,000 received from the sale of the gold bars.

This relatively unobjectionable principle was taken a stage further in *Re Massingberd*.[43] In that case the trustees sold Consols and reinvested in an unauthorised security. The unauthorised security was in due course sold without loss but by this time the price of Consols had risen. The court held that the trustees should place the beneficiaries in the same position as they would have been had no sale taken place with the result that they had themselves to pay the increase in the price of the Consols.

Where an unauthorised investment is falsified, the trustees are not entitled to take into account any loss which would have been sustained if they had strictly performed the trust.[44] Suppose, therefore, that trustees are directed to invest in one particular investment. They make that investment but later improperly sell it for £100,000 and invest that sum in another investment. The latter declines in value and is sold for £80,000 but the investment which the

---

[42] In the absence of express authorisation in the trust instrument, these will not be an authorised investment because they are not income-producing.

[43] (1890) 63 L.T. 296.

[44] *Shepherd v. Mouls* (1845) 4 Hare 500 at 504; *Watts v. Girdlestone* (1843) 6 Beav. 188; *Byrchall v. Bradford* (1822) 6 Madd. 235.

trustees were directed to make has also declined since they sold it and its
market price is only £70,000. If the beneficiaries falsify the account, the trustees
are liable to make good, at the option of the beneficiaries, the difference
between £80,000 and £100,000 and they are not excused from liability by virtue
of the fact that, if the investment which they had been directed to make had
been retained, the holding would have been worth only £70,000. This is
because the effect of falsifying the investment is that the trustees are treated as
having held £100,000 on trust for the beneficiaries at all times.

Finally, it should be noted that, where a trust is for persons by way of
succession, an unauthorised investment which yields a very high income will
have benefited the income beneficiary at the expense of the remaindermen.
Consequently, whether the investment is falsified or adopted, it will be
necessary for the income actually obtained to be apportioned between the
income beneficiary and the remaindermen; the income beneficiary will be
entitled to interest at the ordinary rate and the balance of the income will then
be added to the trust fund as capital.[45]

### (B) Leaving Trust Property Uninvested

The Trustee Act 1925[46] gave trustees the power to pay trust money into a bank
while an investment was being sought. This provision was necessary then
because of the very restricted powers of investment which trustees had under
that Act; however, it is no longer necessary now that the Trustee Act 2000 has
conferred a general power of investment on trustees[47] and has consequently
been repealed. However, it was never thought that this provision of the
Trustee Act 1925 had affected the cases decided before 1926 to the effect that
moneys must not be left uninvested for an unreasonable time[48] and this is
clearly the case under the general power of investment. Where leaving trust
property uninvested is held to amount to a breach of the statutory duty of
care,[49] the beneficiaries will be entitled to the following equitable compensation (this will not be an appropriate case for the taking of an account). If the
trustees ought to have invested in a range of investments, as will usually be
the case, their liability is limited to making good the difference between any
interest actually received and the rate of interest fixed by the court.[50] The
trustees are not liable for any capital loss, because it is impossible to ascertain
it.[51] If, on the other hand, the trustees ought to have invested in one specified
security only but did not do so, in the event that its price rises they can be
compelled to purchase such an amount of that specified security as they could
have purchased with the trust fund at the proper time.

Trustees may erroneously regard their investment powers as more limited
than they actually are and, as a result invest in a more restricted range of
investments than they were actually obliged to. This occurred in *Nestlé v.
National Westminster Bank*.[52] The Court of Appeal held that a beneficiary who

---

[45] *Re Emmet's Estate* (1881) 17 Ch.D. 142. As to the "ordinary" rate of interest, see *post*, p. 773.
[46] Trustee Act 1925, s.11(1).
[47] Trustee Act 2000, s.3(1); *ante*, p. 592.
[48] *Cann v. Cann* (1884) 33 W.R. 40.
[49] See *ante*, p. 573.
[50] As to which, see *post*, p. 773.
[51] *Shepherd v. Mouls* (1845) 4 Hare 500 at 504.
[52] [1993] 1 W.L.R. 1260.

could prove that loss had been suffered thereby could obtain equitable compensation. However, save in extreme cases (the court used as an example the investment of the entire trust fund in fixed interest securities when the trustees had power to invest in equities), such a loss will be extremely difficult to prove and could not be established in that case.

### (D) Use by Trustees of the Trust Funds for their Personal Purposes

If the trustees use the trust money for their personal purposes, the beneficiaries will clearly be entitled to falsify these disbursements. The trustees will consequently be liable to pay back the amount used, or the value[53] of any property improperly sold to provide the funds which the trustees have used.

Special rules apply as to interest.[54] However, rather than receiving interest, the beneficiaries can instead require the trustees to pay over the actual profit which they have received.[55] Further, if a trustee has mixed the trust money with his own money and invested the whole in something which is still identifiable, the beneficiaries will normally be able to maintain an equitable proprietary claim[56] and recover, at their election,[57] either the amount of the trust money invested or a proportional share of whatever profit has been made;[58] they will obviously do the former if the investment has fallen in value and the latter if it has risen in value.

### 3. How Losses are to be Assessed

### (A) The Date at which Losses are to be Assessed

Where a trustee improperly deals with an asset which thereby ceases to be under his control, it is necessary to determine the date at which the loss to the trust fund is to be measured. Previously, when the values of many assets were more stable than at the present time, the loss was ascertained at the date when proceedings were commenced. Thus in Re Massingberd,[59] where trustees improperly sold Consols, the Court of Appeal ordered them to pay the cost of replacing the Consols as at the date of the writ. Much more recently, in Re Bell's Indenture,[60] Vinelott J. said that this was incorrect, and that the general principle was that the loss should be ascertained at the date of judgment. Subsequently, in Jaffray v. Marshall,[61] it was held that this question had not actually had to be decided in either of these cases which were therefore of no assistance; however, the conclusion actually reached in this case, that where

---

[53] Ascertained as at the date of judgment.
[54] See post, p. 773.
[55] Newman v. Bennett (1784) 1 Bro.C.C. 359; Ex parte Watson (1814) 2 V. & B. 414; Walker v. Woodward (1826) 1 Russ. 107 at 111; Att-Gen. v. Solly (1829) 2 Sim 518; Wedderburn v. Wedderburn (1838) 4 My. & Cr. 41 at 46; Jones v. Foxall (1852) 15 Beav. 388; Williams v. Powell (1852) 15 Beav. 388; Macdonald v. Richardson (1858) 1 Giff. 81; Townend v. Townend (1859) 1 Giff. 201; Re Davis [1902] 2 Ch. 314.
[56] See post, pp. 807–838.
[57] Foskett v. McKeown [2001] 1 A.C. 102 at 131 per Lord Millett
[58] In Foskett v. McKeown [2001] 1 A.C. 102, the beneficiaries recovered the proportion of the proceeds of a life insurance policy corresponding to the proportion of the premiums paid with their funds.
[59] (1890) 63 L.T. 296.
[60] [1980] 1 W.L.R. 1217 at 1233.
[61] [1993] 1 W.L.R. 1285.

there had been a continuing breach of trust, the trustees were liable to compensate the trust at the highest intermediate value of the property between the date of breach and the date of judgment, was clearly inconsistent with the subsequent decision in *Target Holdings v. Redferns*[62] and the House of Lords duly held that *Jaffray v. Marshall* had been wrongly decided. The law is thus uncertain at present; however, the view of Vinelott J. seems preferable.

Once established, the liability of a defaulting trustee to make restitution continues until restitution is actually made; this is the case even if the settlement has in the meantime come to an end. In *Bartlett v. Barclays Bank Trust Co.*,[63] a trust company had permitted a company in which the trust had a controlling interest to engage in two hazardous property speculations and was consequently held liable to compensate the trust for the loss which had ensued from the fall in the value of the shares in the company. The trust did not actually sell the shares until after the company had disposed of all its speculative investments; this was four years after three of the beneficiaries had became absolutely entitled to their shares and were therefore in control of their own destiny. It was nevertheless held in *Bartlett v. Barclays Bank Trust Co. (No.2)*,[64] that the loss suffered by the beneficiaries was to be assessed at the time when the shares were finally sold.

Whatever the general rule about the date at which losses have to be assessed actually is, it is at least clear that, if the trustees improperly dispose of an asset which, had they not disposed of it then, would have been properly disposed of at a later date, the loss is to be ascertained at that later date and not at any date thereafter. In *Re Bell's Indenture*,[65] the court was concerned with a marriage settlement made in 1907 and a voluntary settlement made in 1930, which had a common trustee who was also a common beneficiary. In 1947, the trustees of the marriage settlement improperly sold a farm for £8,200 to the trustees of the voluntary settlement. In 1949 the latter properly sold the farm to a third party for £12,400. If the trustees of the marriage settlement had not sold the farm in 1947, they would undoubtedly have done so when the trustees of the voluntary settlement did in 1949. Vinelott J. held that the liability of the trustees of the marriage settlement was to be limited to the value of the farm in 1949. He also held that their liability was not affected by the fact that, if they had sold in 1949, they would probably have reinvested the proceeds of sale in another farm, because it was impossible to determine how any such other farm would have appreciated or depreciated.

### (B) The Absence of any Allowance in respect of Tax
Where a trustee takes trust moneys and applies them for his own purposes, he is liable to restore the moneys which he has taken and is not allowed to benefit from any reduction in the liability to tax which ensues from the misapplication.[66] A further point which arose in *Re Bell's Indenture*[67] was that, if the trustees of the marriage settlement had not improperly sold the farm in 1947 but had instead retained it until 1949, sold it then and reinvested the proceeds

---

[62] [1996] 1 A.C. 421.
[63] [1980] Ch. 515.
[64] *ibid.*
[65] [1980] 1 W.L.R. 1217.
[66] Thus, the rule in *British Transport Commission v. Gourley* [1956] A.C. 185 does not apply.
[67] [1980] 1 W.L.R. 1217; see *ante*, p. 771.

of sale, the value of the trust fund would have been much greater than it actually was. This would in turn have given rise to greater liabilities to estate duty[68] on the deaths of the successive income beneficiaries. It was held that the defaulting trustee was not entitled to reduce the amount which he had to pay to make good the breach of trust by the amount of that tax saving. This decision was followed in *Bartlett v. Barclays Bank Trust Co. (No.2)*.[69] Had the trustee in that case not permitted the company to engage in loss-making speculative property investments, the company would have made larger dividend payments. This would have increased the income and with it the income tax liability of the beneficiaries. Similarly, if the company had not sustained losses, the shares could have been sold for a higher price, which would probably have increased the liability of the beneficiaries to capital gains tax. Brightman J. however held that the trustees were liable to make good the gross loss and could not take into account the tax savings which had occurred, even though this produced "a somewhat unjust bias"[70] against the trustees.

### (C) The Incidence of Interest

Where a trustee has misapplied trust funds, he is liable not only to replace those funds, but also to pay interest thereon. A trustee is similarly liable to pay interest where income is lost as a result of his failure to make an investment.[71] In such circumstances, two questions arise: first, at what rate is the interest to be calculated; and, secondly, whether the interest is to be simple or compounded and, if the latter, at what frequency.[72] The approach of the courts, particularly with regard to the rate of interest, has changed in recent years. The present position appears to be as follows.

Although in the nineteenth century the ordinary interest rate was 4 per cent,[73] this is now accepted to be totally out of line with modern rates and the general rule is instead now broadly for the payment of the current commercial rate of interest. This has sometimes been taken to be 1 per cent above what used to be called the minimum lending rate (long since re-christened the base rate).[74] However, an alternative practice[75] has been to take the rate allowed from time to time on the court's short term investment account.[76] This rate, which is generally in line with that offered on National Savings investments, is varied from time to time by statutory instrument. Changes are usually made towards the beginning of a calendar year and, because they tend to be made much less frequently than changes in base rate, calculation of the interest

---

[68] The forerunner of inheritance tax, under which this would also be the case; see *ante*, p. 633.
[69] [1980] Ch. 515.
[70] *ibid.* at 538.
[71] *Stafford v. Fiddon* (1857) 23 Beav. 386.
[72] The differences are striking. On £10,000, 10 per cent simple interest for 10 years will amount to £10,000, 10 per cent interest compounded yearly will amount to £15,937 and 10 per cent interest compounded half-yearly will amount to £16,533.
[73] *Att.-Gen. v. Alford* (1855) 4 De G.M. & G. 843; *Fletcher v. Green* (1864) 33 Beav. 426.
[74] *Wallersteiner v. Moir (No.2)* [1975] Q.B. 373; *Belmont Finance Corporation v. Williams Furniture (No.2)* [1980] 1 All E.R. 393; *Guardian Ocean Cargoes v. Banco do Brasil (No.3)* [1992] 2 Lloyd's Rep. 193.
[75] *Bartlett v. Barclays Bank Trust Co (No.2)* [1980] Ch. 515; *Jaffray v. Marshall* [1993] 1 W.L.R. 1285 (overruled on other grounds by the House of Lords in *Target Holdings v. Redferns* [1996] 1 A.C. 421); *Mathew v. T. M. Sutton* [1994] 1 W.L.R. 1455.
[76] Established under s.6(1) of the Administration of Justice Act 1965.

payable is more straightforward. If a trustee uses trust money for his own purposes, he will be ordered to pay a higher rate where it can reasonably be concluded that he would have realised a higher rate.[77] This is the case even in the absence of any evidence that the trustee did in fact derive a higher rate.

Simple interest is the general rule in the absence of special circumstances.[78] However, the court has a discretion to order a trustee to pay compound interest. He will be ordered to pay interest compounded annually if he was under an obligation to accumulate the trust income.[79] If, however, he should have invested the fund in a specified investment and accumulated the income from that investment, then the interest must be compounded at the same intervals as interest or dividends would have been received on that investment.[80] A trustee will also be ordered to pay interest compounded annually if he has used trust money in his own business,[81] or for his own commercial purposes, but probably not if he has used it in his professional practice.[82] Although the purpose of ordering a trustee to pay compound rather than simple interest has been stated[83] not to be to punish the trustee, compounding does appear to have been used for this purpose in certain cases of active and deliberate fraud or misconduct.[84]

Where a trustee pays interest, it seems that it is for the court to decide whether or not the income beneficiaries are entitled to receive the whole of that interest. In *Bartlett v. Barclays Bank Trust Co. (No.2)*[85] Brightman J. said:

"To some extent the high interest rates payable on money lent reflect and compensate for the continual erosion in the value of money by reason of galloping inflation. It seems to me arguable, therefore, that if a high rate of interest is payable in such circumstances, a proportion of that interest should be added to capital in order to help maintain the value of the corpus of the trust estate. It may be, therefore, that there will have to be some adjustment as between life tenant and remainderman."

This approach, which reflects that adopted where there is an unauthorised investment in a high income producing security, was applied in *Jaffray v. Marshall*,[86] in which judicial notice was taken of the fact that high rates of interest contain a large element which merely preserves capital values (which

---

[77] *Att.-Gen. v. Alford* (1855) De G.M. & G. 852; *Mathew v. T. M. Sutton* [1994] 1 W.L.R. 1455.
[78] *Stafford v. Fiddon* (1857) 23 Beav. 386; *Burdick v. Garrick* (1870) 5 Ch. App. 233; *Vyse v. Foster* (1874) L.R. 7 H.L. 318; *Belmont Finance Corporation v. Williams Furniture (No.2)* [1970] 1 All E.R. 393. This was the basis on which the lower courts held the local authority liable to pay compound interest in *Westdeutsche Landesbank Girozentrale v. Islington L.B.C.* [1994] 4 All E.R. 890 (Hobhouse J.), [1994] 1 W.L.R. 938, CA. However, the House of Lords [1996] A.C. 669 held that the local authority was not a trustee and so this basis did not apply; the House also held, by a majority, that there was no equitable jurisdiction to order the payment of compound interest on a purely common law claim.
[79] *Raphael v. Boehm* (1805) 11 Ves. 92; *Re Barclay* [1899] 1 Ch. 674.
[80] *Re Emmet's Estate* (1881) 17 Ch.D. 142; *Gilroy v. Stephens* (1882) 30 W.R. 745.
[81] *Wallersteiner v. Moir (No.2)* [1975] Q.B. 373; *Guardian Ocean Cargoes v. Banco do Brasil (No.3)* [1992] 2 Lloyd's Rep. 193.
[82] *Burdick v. Garrick* (1870) 5 Ch. App. 233; *Hale v. Sheldrake* (1889) 60 L.T. 292.
[83] By Lord Hatherley in *Burdick v. Garrick* (1870) 5 Ch. App. 233.
[84] Such as *Jones v. Foxall* (1852) 15 Beav. 388; *Gordon v. Gonda* [1955] 1 W.L.R. 885.
[85] [1980] Ch. 515 at 538.
[86] [1993] 1 W.L.R. 1285.

should belong to the remaindermen) while, in times when inflation was at a less high level, the rate of return needed to preserve capital was not as high. Since the period in question was of the latter kind, the interest (at the short term investment account rate) was apportioned equally between the tenant for life and the remainderman. It is to be hoped that the overruling of this decision on other grounds by the House of Lords in *Target Holdings v. Redferns*[87] does not prevent these helpful observations from being applied in future similar cases.

## (D) The Right to Set-Off

If a trustee commits more than one breach of trust, he cannot set off a gain made in one transaction against a loss suffered in another. However, each transaction is considered as a whole. In *Fletcher v. Green*,[88] trustees made an authorised investment on mortgage. The property was in due course sold at a loss and the proceeds were paid into court. The court authorities invested the money in Consols, which rose in price. It was held that the trustees could offset the gain in the Consols against the loss on the mortgage as both were incidents in the same transaction. On the other hand, in *Dimes v. Scott*,[89] trustees committed a breach of trust in that they ought to have sold an unauthorised investment and invested the proceeds in Consols. Much later on, part of the unauthorised investment was sold and the proceeds were then invested in Consols. By that time the market price of Consols had fallen considerably from the price at which they had been standing when the investment should have been made. The trustees sought to offset the gain made by virtue of the fact that they had thus been able to buy a larger quantity of Consols against the loss which had been suffered on the sale of the unauthorised investment. It was held that they could not do so for these were two distinct transactions, not one; the breach of trust was in not realising the unauthorised investment while the gain arose from the authorised investment being at an unusually low figure. *Dimes v. Scott* was followed in *Wiles v. Gresham*,[90] where trustees of a marriage settlement committed a breach of trust by negligently failing to recover from the husband the sum of £2,000 which he had covenanted to pay to them. They then committed a further breach of trust by investing some of the other trust funds in the purchase of land without having any authority so to do. However, the husband considerably improved the land so purchased by the use of his own funds and it consequently became worth considerably more than the trustees had paid for it. When a claim was made against them for failure to recover the £2,000, the trustees sought to set off the profit which had fortuitously been made on their unauthorised investment in the land; they also were held to be unable to do so because the two transactions were distinct. Both decisions, particularly that in *Dimes v. Scott*, are on the harsh side and it may be that if similar facts recurred today the court might strive to reach different conclusions.

While the rule established by these authorities is entirely clear, namely that a gain can only be set off against a loss if both occur in the same transaction, it is

[87] [1996] 1 A.C. 421.
[88] (1864) 33 Beav. 426.
[89] (1828) 4 Russ. 195.
[90] (1854) 2 Drew. 258; 24 L.J.Ch. 264.

not always easy to decide whether two or more events are stages in the same transaction or separate transactions. The test seems to be whether all the individual steps taken in pursuance of a common policy can be treated as one "transaction" for this purpose. Thus, in *Bartlett v. Barclays Bank Trust Co.*,[91] where the trustee allowed the company to embark on two speculative property developments as part of the company's policy of seeking to increase the cash funds available to it, the trustee was allowed to offset the profit from one development against the loss arising from the other.

## IV. THE POSITION OF TRUSTEES *INTER SE*

Trustees are under a duty to act jointly; therefore they only have the authority to act individually if the trust instrument so provides. Decisions of trustees must usually be unanimous and, with very limited exceptions, there is no question of a vote of the majority binding them all.[92] They are also under an obligation to ensure that all the trust property and investments are placed in the names of all the trustees. In principle, each trustee therefore takes an equal part in the administration of the trust and has an equal say in what happens to the trust property. Thus, if a breach of trust has been committed, each trustee should be equally liable. However, the wronged beneficiary is not obliged to sue every single trustee; he can of course do so but is just as entitled to sue only one or two of them. For this reason the liability of trustees is joint and several.

Prior to relatively recent legislation, the Civil Liability (Contribution) Act 1978, there was a absolute right of contribution as between the different trustees if an action was successfully brought against only one or some of them. Thus any trustee who was successfully sued had an absolute right of contribution against any trustee who had not been sued so that in the end each trustee would have contributed equally to the compensation paid to the beneficiary; the only exception to this was where the trustees had acted fraudulently.[93] The Civil Liability (Contribution) Act 1978 makes matters rather more flexible by giving the court power to award, in favour of one trustee against another, contribution of such amount as is found to be just and equitable, having regard to the extent of the responsibility of the other trustee for the loss.[94] This principle extends beyond express trustees to constructive trustees and to persons who are liable for dishonest assistance. Thus, in *Dubai Aluminium Co. v. Salaam*,[95] a firm of solicitors who had settled proceedings in which it was claimed that they were vicariously liable for the alleged dishonest assistance of their senior partner in a fraudulent breach of trust, were held able to recover contribution from the persons who had actually benefitted from the breach of trust.[96]

---

[91] [1980] Ch. 515. See also *ante*, p. 596.
[92] See *ante*, p. 577.
[93] *Bahin v. Hughes* (1886) 31 Ch.D. 390.
[94] ss.1(1), 2(1).
[95] [2002] 3 W.L.R. 1913.
[96] Controversially, they were awarded a contribution of 100 per cent on the basis that this still left the contributers with some of the benefits of the breach of trust following their own settlement with the claimant.

However, despite the principle of contribution, the trustee who is originally sued may nevertheless sometimes find himself in a very difficult position. Suppose that there are three trustees, Timothy, Titus and Tom, who commit a breach of trust involving the loss of £30,000. A beneficiary who chooses to sue Timothy alone has the right to recover the entire £30,000 from Timothy, the latter's right of contribution being completely irrelevant. Timothy can of course claim £10,000 from each of Titus and Tom but, if Titus has disappeared and Tom has gone bankrupt, Timothy's claim will remain unsatisfied; he will thus have paid out £30,000 without recovering any of it.

The Civil Liability (Contribution) Act 1978 has also made more flexible the circumstances in which a trustee who is successfully sued can claim a complete indemnity from one or more of his co-trustees. However, the three specific circumstances in which such a complete indemnity was available prior to the enactment of that legislation are all still thought to survive. These were, first, where the breach of trust was committed on the advice of a solicitor-trustee; secondly, where one trustee alone had benefited from the breach of trust; and, thirdly, where one of the trustees was also a beneficiary.

Where one of the trustees was a solicitor and the breach of trust was committed solely in reliance on his advice, then the solicitor-trustee was obliged to indemnify his co-trustees.[97] It was not sufficient to show merely that one of the trustees at the time of the breach was a solicitor: it had to be shown that the other trustees were relying entirely on his advice. Thus in *Head v. Gould*,[98] Miss Head and a solicitor, Mr Gould, were the trustees of a settlement. They sold a house forming part of the trust property and, instead of reinvesting the proceeds, in breach of trust paid the proceeds to the life tenant, Miss Head's mother. Following a successful action by the remainderman against the two trustees, Miss Head unsuccessfully sought to be indemnified by Mr Gould. Kekewich J. found that she had not relied on Mr Gould but had actively urged him to commit the breach. Where the basic rule applied because the breach of trust was committed principally on the advice of the solicitor-trustee, in order successfully to resist a claim by his co-trustee for indemnity it was for the solicitor-trustee to show that his co-trustee was in full possession of all the relevant facts and made an independent judgment. In *Re Partington*,[99] which concerned improper investments, Stirling J. said: "I have got to consider the question, has [the solicitor] communicated what he did to [the co-trustee] in such a way as to enable her to exercise her judgment upon the investments, and to make them, really and in truth, her act as well as his own?" The judge found in favour of the co-trustee, who was therefore entitled to an indemnity.

The situation where one trustee alone has benefited from the breach was considered in *Bahin v. Hughes*.[1] Cotton L.J. refused to limit the circumstances in which an indemnity would be ordered, saying "I think it wrong to lay down any limitation of the circumstances under which one trustee would be held liable to the others for indemnity, both having been held liable to the *cestui que trust* but so far as cases have gone at present, relief has only been granted against a trustee who has himself got the benefit of the breach of trust, or

---

[97] *Lockhart v. Reilly* (1856) 25 L.J.Ch. 697.
[98] [1898] 2 Ch. 250.
[99] (1887) 57 L.T. 654.
[1] (1886) 31 Ch.D. 390.

between whom and his co-trustees there has existed a relation which will
justify the court in treating him as solely liable for the breach of trust." In that
case there were two trustees, one of whom was content to leave the administration of the trust to the other. The latter acted honestly but made an
improper investment which resulted in a loss. The passive trustee unsuccessfully claimed an indemnity. It is by no means clear how far this dictum of
Cotton L.J. was intended to go.

The situation where a trustee is also a beneficiary was considered in *Chillingworth v. Chambers*.[2] It was held that a trustee who was also a beneficiary
and who had participated in a breach of trust must indemnify his co-trustee to
the extent of his beneficial interest. However, this only applied if the trustee-
beneficiary had, as between himself and his co-trustees, exclusively benefited
from the breach of trust. Suppose that Abraham and Ambrose were the
trustees of a trust, in which Ambrose had a beneficial interest worth £5,000 but
in which Abraham had no interest. If the trustees were to invest in unauthorised securities in order to obtain a higher income and Ambrose, but
obviously not Abraham, enjoyed the benefit of that higher income but the
investment ultimately produced a capital loss of £8,000, Ambrose would be
liable to indemnify Abraham to the extent of £5,000, leaving the remaining
liability of £3,000 to be shared by them equally. It is not clear whether, for the
rule in *Chillingworth v. Chambers* to apply, it is necessary for the trustee-beneficiary actually to receive a benefit from the breach, or whether it is sufficient
if the breach was committed with the intention to give him a benefit; the latter
view seems preferable.


## V. LIMITATION OF ACTIONS

On the assumption that a breach of trust has been committed which has
caused some loss, the further question arises as to whether the beneficiaries are
in time to sue. The history of limitation of actions in respect of breaches of trust
has been highly complicated; however the position is now governed by the
Limitation Act 1980, coupled with the application in certain respects of the
equitable doctrine of laches (laches occurs where a wronged person has
delayed so long in bringing his action that he is deemed by his conduct to have
waived his claim). Two distinct situations have to be considered.

### 1. Where there is No Statutory Period of Limitation

Section 21(1) of the Limitation Act 1980 provides that there shall be no statutory period of limitation in respect of an action by a beneficiary under a trust
if the action is one:

"(a) in respect of any fraud or fraudulent breach of trust to which the
      trustee was a party or privy, or
 (b) to recover from the trustee trust property or the proceeds thereof
      in the possession of the trustee, or previously received by the
      trustee and converted to his use."

---

[2] [1896] 1 Ch. 685.

Paragraph (a) has recently been considered on two occasions by the Court of Appeal. In *Armitage v. Nurse*,[3] the paragraph was held to be "limited to cases of fraud or fraudulent breach of trust properly so called, that is to say to cases involving dishonesty". It follows that, whenever trustees have, in this sense, committed fraud or have retained any of the capital of the trust, there is no question of any defence under the statute. Thus, in *Re Howlett*,[4] where a trustee occupied property belonging to the trust, he was held to be outside the scope of the 1980 Act and have no limitation defence. Likewise, in *Wassell v. Leggatt*,[5] where a husband forcibly took property belonging to his wife, thereby becoming a trustee of it for her, and kept it until his death, his executors were held to be unable to plead limitation. In *Paragon Finance v. D.B. Thakerar & Co.*,[6] the court had to consider whether paragraph (a) is restricted to fraudulent breaches of existing trusts, as in *Wassell v. Leggatt*, or whether it also applies to situations where the fraudulent act in question is the reason for the existence of the trust, in other words where the trust in question is a constructive trust which has only arisen because of the fraud of the constructive trustee. The expression "trust" in the Limitation Act 1980 does extend to constructive trusts.[7] However, the Court of Appeal held that this does no more than apply paragraph (a) to fraudulent breaches of already existing constructive trusts. Consequently, paragraph (a) does not apply to situations where the fraudulent act in question is the reason for the existence of the trust. Millett L.J. referred to *Taylor v. Davies*,[8] where this conclusion had been reached in respect of a similar Canadian statute, and said:[9]

"the distinction drawn in *Taylor v. Davies* ... marks a real difference between trustees (whether or not expressly appointed as such) who commit a breach of trust (however created) and persons who are not trustees at all but who are described as trustees for the purpose of enabling equitable relief to be granted against them. Actions founded on tort are barred after six years, and there is no exception for actions founded on fraud, though the start of the limitation period may be deferred in such cases. There is no logical basis for distinguishing between an action for damages for fraud at common law and the corresponding claim in equity for 'an account as constructive trustee' founded on the same fraud. Section 21 of the 1980 Act can sensibly be limited to wrongs cognisable by equity in the exercise of its exclusive jurisdiction. It makes no sense to extend it to the exercise of its concurrent jurisdiction."

Paragraph (b) provides that no statutory period will run in respect of trust property in the possession of the trustee or received by him himself. However, in this respect, a special rule applies where the trustee is also a beneficiary. If the trustee distributed the trust fund honestly and reasonably but made an

---

[3] [1998] Ch. 241 at 260 *per* Millett L.J.
[4] [1949] Ch. 767.
[5] [1896] 1 Ch. 554; see also *Re Tufnell* (1902) 18 T.L.R. 705; *Re Eyre-Williams* [1923] 2 Ch. 533.
[6] [1999] 1 All E.R. 400.
[7] Because the definitions section of the Limitation Act 1980, (s.38) incorporates the definition of trust in the definitions section of the Trustee Act 1925 (s.68).
[8] [1920] A.C. 636 at 652–653 (Privy Council on appeal from Canada).
[9] [1999] 1 All E.R. 400 at 413–414. Compare *James v. Williams* [2000] Ch. 1.

over-distribution to himself, the statutory period discussed below applies to the extent of his own share but only to that extent;[10] no limitation period is applicable to any excess in his hands over his own entitlement.

However, where there is no statutory period of limitation, the trustee can nevertheless raise the defence of laches. To establish this defence, it is necessary to show that the beneficiary has known of the breach of trust for a substantial period of time and has acquiesced in it. There are no fixed rules as to the period of time which must elapse; it must in the particular case be sufficiently long to enable the court to impute acquiescence. Similarly, if the beneficiaries clearly acquiesce after only a fairly short time, that will be a sufficient defence. The essence of the defence is therefore acquiescence on the part of the beneficiary when he has full knowledge of the facts. Consequently, it is generally considered that delay in taking action is merely evidence of acquiescence,[11] although it has also been suggested that such delay may in itself constitute a separate defence quite apart from any acquiescence.[12]

Although in general no statutory period will run where the trustee has himself received trust property, a special rule applies where the trustee is also a beneficiary. If the trustee distributed the trust fund honestly and reasonably, but made an over-distribution to himself, the statutory period applies to the extent of his own share, but the excess is subject only to the doctrine of laches.[13]

## 2. Where there is a Statutory Period of Limitation

### (A) The General Position

Section 21(3) of the Limitation Act 1980, which applies both to express trustees of private trusts[14] and to resulting and constructive trustees,[15] provides that actions to recover trust property or in respect of breaches of trust must be brought within six years from the date on which the right of action accrued. In the case of breaches of trust, this is the date on which the breach in question occurred, not the date when the loss was sustained.[16] Suppose that a beneficiary knows that the trustees invest in unauthorised investments and that at first the investments do well but later lead to losses; even though the losses may not be sustained for several years, the limitation period runs from when

---

[10] Limitation Act 1980, s.21(2).

[11] *Morse v. Royal* (1806) 12 Ves. 355; *Life Association of Scotland v. Siddal* (1861) 3 De G.F. & J. 58.

[12] *Re Sharpe* [1892] 1 Ch. 154 at 168, *per* Lindley L.J. See also *Smith v. Clay* (1767) 3 Bro.C.C. 639N. Laches was held to be a defence in *Nelson v. Rye* [1996] 1 W.L.R. 1378; however, in *Paragon Finance v. D.B. Thackerar & Co.* [1999] 1 All E.R. 400 at 415–416, it was held that that case had been wrongly decided in that there was an applicable limitation period so that laches was not in fact needed as a defence.

[13] Limitation Act 1980, s.21(2).

[14] The section does not apply to an action by the Attorney-General against the trustee of charitable trusts which in this sense have no beneficiaries; *Att.-Gen. v. Cocke* [1988] Ch. 414.

[15] s.21(3) only applies where the action is against a "trustee" and not where the action is against someone who, although in a fiduciary capacity, is not a trustee. In *Tito v. Waddell (No.2)* [1977] Ch. 106 (see *ante*, p. 18) the Crown was held not to be in a fiduciary position. However, Megarry V.-C. said (at 249) that, even if the Crown had been in a fiduciary position, it would not have been a trustee; consequently, the claim would not have been barred by the predecessor of s.21(3) (Limitation Act 1939, s.19(2)). The doctrine of laches therefore applied but was no bar in that case because it had not been pleaded.

[16] *Re Somerset* [1894] 1 Ch. 231.

the unauthorised investment was made. In *Re Swain*,[17] trustees were under an obligation to convert the deceased's assets into authorised investments but in breach of trust continued to carry on the deceased's business until the youngest beneficiary attained the age of 21. When, eight years later, one of the other beneficiaries sought to make the trustees liable for the loss caused through carrying on the business, they were held entitled to plead limitation.

However, where a beneficiary has a future interest, a proviso to section 21(3) specifically states that, for the purposes of the Limitation Act 1980, his right of action is deemed not to have accrued until his interest falls into possession; therefore time does not start to run against him until then. This does not actually prevent the beneficiary from suing before this point if he wishes to do so. Consequently, a remainderman can take action in respect of a breach of trust at any time during the subsistence of a prior life interest, or within six years from becoming entitled to an interest in possession. This is the case even where the breach of trust consists of an improper advance to the remainderman during the lifetime of the tenant for life, something which can only be done with the tenant for life's consent. Both these latter points emerge from the decision of Wilberforce J. in *Re Pauling's Settlement Trusts*, his decision in this respect being simply affirmed by the Court of Appeal.[18] In that case improper advancements had been made in respect of the interests of minor beneficiaries and the trustees pleaded, among other defences, that the period of limitation ran in their favour from the time when the advancements were made. In rejecting this defence, Wilberforce J. held that the interests of the minors in respect of which the advancements had been made were future interests within the terms of the proviso to section 21(3) and that, if such an improper advancement was made while this was the case, that did not start the limitation period running; since the advancements were improper, they did not bind the minor beneficiaries at all. The latter could, therefore, sue at the time when they ought to have received the whole of their share, namely when their interests vested in possession.

However, the operation of the proviso to section 21(3) is restricted by section 21(4), which provides that, where limitation can be pleaded against any particular beneficiary, he cannot benefit from an action brought by a beneficiary against whom limitation cannot be pleaded.[19] Suppose that trustees who hold investments upon trust for Daphne for life, with remainder to Chloe, sell one of those investments and improperly hand over the proceeds to Daphne's daughter, who is not a beneficiary at all. In the absence of fraudulent concealment, Daphne will be debarred from suing after six years. Chloe is obviously entitled to wait until Daphne's death before suing but is not obliged to. If she does sue before then, she can compel the trustees to make good the capital loss. Assuming they do so, they can themselves retain the income from that property during the lifetime of Daphne; this is on the basis that Daphne, by not suing, has in effect consented to the breach of trust and so the trustees, having repaired the breach, are entitled to the income which she would otherwise have received.[20]

---

[17] [1891] 3 Ch. 233.
[18] [1964] Ch. 303.
[19] *Re Somerset* (1894) 1 Ch. 231.
[20] *Fletcher v. Collis* [1905] 2 Ch. 24.

The precise meaning of "future interest" in the context of this proviso also had to be considered by the Court of Appeal in *Armitage v. Nurse*.[21] Trustees held income upon trust to accumulate it until the beneficiary in question reached the age of 25[22] subject to a power to pay it to her or apply it for her benefit. The Court of Appeal held that, while she was under the age of 25, she had a future interest for the purposes of the proviso, rejecting an argument by the trustees that the fact that she was entitled to see the trust documents was sufficient to give her an interest in possession under the trust. Millett L.J. held that the rationale of the proviso was that a beneficiary "should not be compelled to litigate (at considerable personal expense) in respect of an injury to an interest which he may never live to enjoy" and went on to say that "similar reasoning would apply to exclude a person who is merely the object of a discretionary trust or power which may never be exercised in his favour".[23] While it is clearly appropriate that a beneficiary of a fixed trust with a future interest should, when his interest vests in possession, be able to impeach any breaches of trusts committed at any time since the trust was originally created, it is superficially rather startling that a discretionary beneficiary or the object of a power to whom no income is appointed until (say) 20 years after the creation of the trust may at that point maintain an action for any breach of trust which has occurred during the previous 20 years. However, there seems no way of avoiding this conclusion since the wording of the statute provides no obvious means of distinguishing between the two cases.

This rationale enunciated by Millett L.J. may be extremely significant when the as yet unanswered question of how this proviso operates in the case of pension trusts has to be decided. Is the interest of a beneficiary of a pension trust a future interest in this sense until he becomes entitled to receive his pension? He will obviously not live to enjoy his pension if he dies before retirement age. On the other hand, his death before that time will inevitably lead to some form of payment being made, usually of both a lump sum death benefit and a pension for his surviving spouse and other dependants; he therefore certainly has an interest worth defending in the intervening period. The contention that his interest is indeed a future interest until he becomes entitled to his pension has been pleaded in a number of pension trust cases but does not appear yet to have been argued in court. If it is upheld, then the liability of the trustees of pension trusts for breach of trust will be to all intents and purposes indefinite. However, in that event, they will obtain at least some protection from section 21(4).

### (B) Cases of Fraud

It has already been stated that there is no statutory period of limitation in respect of a fraudulent breach of trust. However, it is possible for a non-fraudulent breach of trust to have been committed which is subsequently concealed by fraud. Special provision is therefore made for actions based on fraud and for rights of actions concealed by fraud. Section 32 of the 1980 Act (which is of general application and is not confined to actions for breach of

---

[21] [1998] Ch. 241.

[22] She then acquired an absolute interest in the income but did not become entitled to the capital until she reached the age of 40.

[23] [1998] Ch. 241 at 261.

trust) provides that, where an action is based upon the fraud of the defendant or his agent and where a right of action is concealed by fraud, "the period of limitation shall not begin to run until the plaintiff has discovered the fraud ... or could with reasonable diligence have discovered it". For the purposes of this section, "fraud" is wider than the type of conduct which would give rise to an independent action. In *Beaman v. A.R.T.S.*,[24] Lord Greene M.R. pointed out that the fraudulent conduct "may acquire its character as such from the very manner in which that act is performed".

The scope of section 32 is illustrated by *Eddis v. Chichester Constable*.[25] One of the assets of the trust was a painting of St John the Baptist by Caravaggio. The painting was normally hung in a stately home where the life tenant lived but in 1950 he lent it for an exhibition at Burlington House. During that exhibition, he sold it to a consortium of art dealers, who subsequently sold it to an art gallery in Kansas City. The life tenant obviously had no title to the painting and, when the trustees discovered the loss of painting in 1963, they brought an action for breach of trust against the estate of the life tenant, who had by then died, and an action for conversion against the purchasers. The normal six-year limitation period for both of these actions was held not to apply. Lord Denning M.R. said:[26]

"one thing is quite clear: the right of action was 'concealed by the fraud' of the [life tenant]. I do not know that he did anything actively to deceive the trustees, but that does not matter. His wrongful sale of the heirloom was enough. It was a fraud and by saying nothing about it, he concealed the fraud."

However, in *Paragon Finance v. D.B. Thakerar & Co.*,[27] the Court of Appeal emphasised that the question of whether section 32 will apply is determined not by whether the claimant should have discovered the fraud sooner but whether he could with reasonable diligence have done so; in this respect the burden of proof is on him to show that he could not have discovered the fraud without exceptional measures which he could not reasonably have been expected to take. In this context the fact that the applicable period of limitation is six years is irrelevant.[28]

### (C) Actions for an Account

Section 23 of the Limitation Act 1980 provides that "an action for an account shall not be brought after the expiration of any time limit under this Act which is applicable to the claim which is the basis of the duty to account". The section clearly prevents any action for an account being brought in respect of a breach of trust which is already statute-barred, even though a separate provision for

---

[24] [1949] 1 K.B. 550.
[25] [1969] 2 Ch. 345. The decision concerned the predecessor of the Limitation Act 1980, s.32, the Limitation Act 1939, s.26.
[26] *ibid.* at 356.
[27] [1999] 1 All E.R. 400 at 418.
[28] In this case, where the claimant was a mortgage lender, the court suggested that "the test was how a person carrying on a business of the relevant kind would act if he had adequate but not unlimited staff and resources and were motivated by a reasonable but not excessive sense of urgency". However, this is obviously not an appropriate test for a claimant who is a beneficiary under a trust.

this purpose hardly seems necessary. Until recently it was difficult to see what further purpose the section served. In *Attorney-General v. Cocke*,[29] the Attorney-General brought an action against the executors and trustees of an estate held on charitable trusts, seeking accounts and enquiries as to the estate. Section 21(3) of the Limitation Act 1980 was clearly inapplicable: first, because the action was being brought by the Attorney-General and not by a beneficiary and, secondly, because the claim was neither to recover trust property nor in respect of any breach of trust. Harman J. held that all fiduciaries were under a permanent duty to account arising out of their fiduciary relationships; such claims were not subject to any period of limitation under the Act and so there was no time limit to which section 23 could apply in respect of such a claim.

However in *Paragon Finance v. D. B. Thakerar & Co.*,[30] Millett L.J. held that "an action for an account brought by a principal against his agent is barred by the statutes of limitation unless the agent is more than a mere agent but is a trustee of the money which he received". This makes it clear that the purpose of section 23 is to protect fiduciaries who are not trustees from any additional liability to account; thus an agent who collects money on behalf of his principal without being under any obligation to segregate it will, in the event that an action under the contract of agency becomes statute barred, not be under any additional liability to account.


**(D) Actions for Breach of Fiduciary Duty**
Section 21 of the Limitation Act 1980 is limited to actions in respect of trust property. It therefore does not apply to actions for breaches of fiduciary duty where there has been neither a failure to obtain nor a misapplication of trust property but where the breach complained of relates to a conflict of interest and duty or of interest and interest.[31] While breaches of duty by a fiduciary which are not breaches of fiduciary duty of course sound only in tort or in contract[32] and are therefore governed by the provisions of the Limitation Act 1980 appropriate to such causes of action,[33] that Act contains no specific provision applying to claims for breaches of fiduciary duty arising out of the fiduciary preferring the interests of either himself or someone else to those of his principal. It was therefore contended in *Cia. de Seguros Imperio v. Heath (REBX)*[34] that there was no statutory period of limitation for such claims. However, the Court of Appeal rejected this contention. Section 36(1) of the Limitation Act 1980 provides that the time limits which apply to actions in tort and contract do not apply to any claim for "equitable relief, except in so far as any such time limit may be applied by the court by analogy in like manner as the corresponding time limit under any enactment repealed by the Limitation Act 1939 was applied before 1 July 1940". This provision had previously been

---

[29] [1988] Ch. 414. This decision was applied in *Nelson v. Rye* [1996] 1 W.L.R. 1378.
[30] [1999] 1 All E.R. 400 at 415–416. Millett L.J. stated that *Nelson v. Rye* [1996] 1 W.L.R. 1378 had been wrongly decided.
[31] See *ante*, p. 765.
[32] *Bristol and West Building Society v. Mothew* [1998] Ch. 1.
[33] Limitation Act 1980, s.2 (tort) and s.4 (contract).
[34] [2001] 1 W.L.R. 112

considered in *Coulthard v. Disco Mix Club*,[35] where the judge[36] summarised the authorities prior to July 1, 1940 as follows:

"First, where the court of equity was simply exercising a concurrent jurisdiction giving the same relief as was available in the court of law the statute of limitation would be applied. But secondly, even if the relief afforded by the court of equity was wider than that available at law the court of equity would apply the statute by analogy where there was 'correspondence' between the remedies available at law or in equity."

The Court of Appeal held that there was the necessary "correspondence" between actions for breach of fiduciary duty of this type and actions for breach of contract; consequently, the court would have applied the contractual time limit to such actions for breach of fiduciary duty before July 1, 1940. Therefore, the period of limitation for such claims is still the six year period which applies to actions for breach of contract.

### (E) "Liability for Dishonest Assistance"

In *Dubai Aluminium Co. v. Salaam*,[37] Lord Millett said that a person who is held liable for dishonest assistance "is not in fact a trustee at all, even though he may be liable to account as if he were. ... I think that we should now discard the words 'accountable as constructive trustee' in this context and substitute the words 'accountable in equity'." This terminology is clearly preferable but means that, for the purposes of limitation, liability for dishonest assistance does not fit into any of the categories discussed so far. However, in *Coulthard v. Disco Mix Club*,[38] it was held that such a claim for the imposition of accessory liability could not have a longer limitation period than that appropriate to the claim against whoever benefitted from the dishonest assistance in question. This in practice means that the period of limitation for such claims will be the six-year period provided for by section 21(3) of the Limitation Act 1980.

### VI. RELIEF OR EXEMPTION FROM PRIMA FACIE LIABILITY

Even if an action for breach of trust can *prima facie* be brought against a trustee, it may nevertheless be possible for him to claim total or partial relief. He may be able to do so:

(a) by virtue of a provision in the trust instrument;

(b) by means of an application to the court;

(c) by virtue of an act of the beneficiaries, either their concurrence in or their waiver of the breach; or

(d) by virtue of an indemnity obtainable from one or more of the beneficiaries.

---

[35] [2000] 1 W.L.R. 707 at 730.
[36] Jules Sher Q.C., sitting as a Deputy Judge of the Chancery Division.
[37] [2002] 3 W.L.R. 1913 at 1945.
[38] [2000] 1 W.L.R. 707 at 730.

1. *Provisions in Trust Instruments*

It has already been seen that a trust instrument can authorise a large number of acts which a trustee would not otherwise be able to do. If the trustee acts in accordance with such authorisation, he is of course not guilty of a breach of trust in the first place. However, even when a trustee has committed a breach of trust, the provisions of the trust instrument may nevertheless be effective to relieve him from liability if they include what is generally known as a trustee exemption clause.

There are some restrictions on the types of breaches of trust in respect of which liability can be excluded by a trustee exemption clause.

1.  In principle, the fundamental obligation of a trustee to account to his beneficiary cannot be excluded by a trustee exemption clause. This is part of the "irreducible core of obligations owed by the trustees to the beneficiaries and enforceable by them which is fundamental to the concept of a trust".[39] Thus, a provision in a trust agreement respecting an employee pension plan which prohibited any action against the trustees except by the employer-settlors was held to be unenforceable and did not deprive the court of jurisdiction to hear proceedings brought by the employees against the trustee.[40] However, it has been held that in special circumstances minimal accountability may subsist for a period[41] although possibly not in respect of the whole of the trust property.[42] Nor has any challenge ever been made to clauses providing that trustees have no duty or power either to inquire into or interfere with the running of companies in which the trust has a controlling shareholding unless they acquire actual knowledge of dishonesty or mental incapacity.[43]

2.  Trustee exemption clauses do not purport to exclude liability for dishonest and fraudulent breaches of trust and it follows from the

---

[39] *Armitage v. Nurse* [1998] Ch. 241 at 253 *per* Millett L.J. However, a custodian trustee appointed under the Public Trustee Act 1906 is not liable for breach of trust where he follows the instructions of the managing trustee.

[40] *Jones v. Shipping Federation of British Columbia* (1963) 37 D.L.R. (2d) 273 (Supreme Court of British Columbia).

[41] In *Hayim v. Citibank* [1987] A.C. 730 (Privy Council on appeal from Hong Kong), the testator directed that, in respect of a house forming part of his estate, which he left on trust for sale with power to postpone sale and which was occupied by his elderly brother and sister (92 and 87 years old at the date of his death), his executor and trustee should "have no responsibility or duty with respect to such property ... and my executor's and trustee's only duty and responsibility with respect thereto shall arise upon its receipt of proceeds of said residence or upon the death of the survivor of my said brother and my said sister, whichever shall first occur". The object of the exercise was clearly to prevent the brother and sister being cast on the mercy of the beneficiaries while at the same time avoiding them having a life interest in the property and so incurring a second liability to estate duty on the death of the survivor. The Privy Council upheld the validity of the clause, emphasising that it could only be used for the purpose for which it had been inserted in the will; had the trustee sought to obtain any personal advantage by its utilisation, it would have been void. The beneficiaries' action against the trustees for having failed to sell the property at the top of the market was therefore unsuccessful.

[42] The house in *Hayim v. Citibank* formed only a small part of the testator's estate.

[43] See Hayton in *Trends in Contemporary Trust Law* (ed. Oakley, 1996) 47.

decision of the Court of Appeal in *Armitage v. Nurse*,[44] that they could not validly do so. In this connection, it is significant that in *Walker v. Stones*[45] it was held that a solicitor-trustee will be dishonest and so not within the scope of a trustee exemption clause if an honest belief, though actually held, is so unreasonable that, by any objective standard, no reasonable solicitor-trustee could have thought that what he did or agreed to do was for the benefit of the beneficiaries.

3. Statute prohibits trust instruments from exempting from liability for negligence trustees of debentures,[46] managers or trustees of unit trusts,[47] and, in respect of investment functions only, trustees of pension trusts.[48] Similar non-statutory restrictions have been introduced by the securities regulatory authorities, who have the sanction of withdrawing licences; thus the Securities and Investment Board prohibited custodian trustees from exempting themselves from liability in contracts entered into as from February 2, 1998 and the Investment Management Regulatory Organisation has prohibited investment managers licensed by them from exempting themselves from liability to their private clients.

Otherwise it also follows from *Armitage v. Nurse*[49] that there are at present no restrictions on the contents of trustee exemption clauses. In particular it appears that liability for wilful default, defined in *Re Vickery*[50] as "consciousness of committing a wrong or recklessness as to whether or not a wrong was being committed", can be excluded. However, clauses in common use of the type set out below do not purport to do so:

"In the professional execution of the trusts hereof no trustee shall be liable for any loss to the trust property arising by reason of any improper investment made in good faith or by reason of any mistake or omission made in good faith by any trustee hereof or by reason of any other matter of thing except wilful and individual fraud or wrongdoing on the part of the trustee who is sought to be made liable."

In *Armitage v. Nurse*, the clause did purport to exclude liability for wilful default: "No trustee shall be liable for any loss or damage which may happen to [the] fund or any part therefor or the income thereof at any time or from any cause whatsoever unless such loss or damage shall be caused by his own actual fraud". The court construed this clause as excluding any liability for breach of trust in the absence of dishonesty, which was held to mean "at the minimum an intention on the part of the trustee to pursue a particular course of action, either knowing that it is contrary to the interests of the beneficiaries

---

[44] [1998] Ch. 241; see *infra*.
[45] [2000] 4 All E.R. 412. This decision is subject to an appeal to the House of Lords.
[46] Companies Act 1985, s.192.
[47] Financial Services Act 1986, s.84.
[48] Pensions Act 1995, s.33.
[49] [1998] Ch. 241.
[50] [1931] 1 Ch. 572. This was a decision on the meaning of this phrase in the now repealed Trustee Act 1925, s.30(1) and in that respect, but not more generally, was highly controversial.

or being recklessly indifferent whether it is contrary to their interests or not"[51] ("fraud" in the longer clause set out above would clearly be construed in the same way). The beneficiary contended[52] that clauses of this type were void, either for repugnancy or as contrary to public policy, in that they therefore excluded liability for gross negligence, a position which has been adopted by the legislature in some other jurisdictions.[53] However, the court held that this proposition was not supported by any English authority and, further, that "English lawyers have always had a healthy disrespect" for the distinction between negligence and gross negligence,[54] a distinction which is of course a necessary consequence of not permitting liability for gross negligence to be excluded. Exemption clauses of this kind are therefore valid, at least for the moment. However, the court "acknowledged that the view is widely held that these clauses have gone too far"[55] but held that only Parliament could deny them effect.

It is now clear that some form of legislative intervention will indeed occur since the Law Commission published a Consultation Paper in January 2003.[56] The period for consultation had only just finished when this edition had to go to press but the provisional view of the Law Commission was that professional trustees should no longer be able to exclude liability for negligence or be permitted to claim indemnity from the trust fund in respect of negligent breaches of trust. Any legislation enacted would affect existing trusts but only in respect of breaches of trust committed after that legislation came into force.[57] Thus lay trustees would still be able to continue to exempt themselves for liability for breach of trust up to and including wilful default. These proposals seem consistent with the distinction drawn by the Trustee Act 2000 between professional and lay trustees in the context of remuneration and it is hoped that they are enacted.

Two further aspects of trustee exemption clauses, which will not be affected by the Law Commission's proposals, have also recently had to be considered by the Court of Appeal. In *Bogg v. Raper*,[58] the Court of Appeal rejected an argument by the beneficiaries of a will which contained a clause almost identical with the one set out above that the solicitor-executor who had drawn up the will had been in a fiduciary relationship with the testator and, by obtaining the benefit of exemption from the consequences of his own future negligence, was obtaining a benefit at the testator's expense; consequently he could not rely on the clause unless he could show that the testator had

---

[51] [1998] Ch. 241 at 251.
[52] Relying on the view taken by Matthews [1989] Conv. 42.
[53] In Guernsey (Guernsey) Trusts Law 1988 s.34(7)) and Jersey (Trusts (Jersey) Law 1984 Art.26(9)). The Turks and Caicos Islands have gone even further and do not permit liability even for negligence to be excluded ((Turks & Caicos Islands) Trusts Ordinance 1990 s.29(10)).
[54] [1998] Ch. 241 at 254.
[55] *ibid.* at 256.
[56] Law Commission Consultation Paper No. 171
[57] This is what was done by the Jersey legislation.
[58] (1998) 1 I.T.E.L.R. 267.

received independent legal advice.[59] In *Wight v. Olswang*,[60] the court had to consider an argument that a rather different type of clause, providing that "Every discretion or power hereby or by law conferred on the Trustees shall be an absolute and uncontrolled discretion or power and no Trustee shall be held liable for any loss or damage accruing as a result of the Trustees concurring or failing to concur in the exercise of any such discretion or power", excluded liability for loss arising out of the exercise or non-exercise by the trustees of all powers and discretions, whether dispositive or administrative (this was crucial since it was a failure to sell trust investments at the right time which the beneficiaries were principally complaining about). However, the Court of Appeal, reversing Ferris J., held that the clause only prevented the court from interfering with the exercise of any discretion or power merely because it considered the trustees' grounds as unreasonable or would not have exercised the discretion or power in the same way; it did not actually confer any exemption on trustees who had committed a breach of trust. Consequently, such clauses cannot really be regarded as trustee exemption clauses.

## 2. Applications to the Court

It has already been seen[61] that the court has power to sanction in advance, on an application by the trustees for directions, acts of a wide variety of types even if those acts would otherwise be breaches of trust. Where no such application to the court has been made prior to the act being carried out, the court also has, by virtue of section 61 of the Trustee Act 1925, a discretion to grant relief. This section provides that, if it appears to the court that a trustee is or may be personally liable for any breach of trust but has acted honestly and reasonably and ought fairly to be excused for the breach of trust or for omitting to obtain the directions of the court in the matter in which he committed such breach, then the court may relieve him either wholly or partially from personal liability. Thus the trustee must, first, have acted honestly; secondly, have acted reasonably; and, thirdly, ought fairly to be excused.

"Honestly" here means in good faith. "Reasonably" is a question of fact which depends on the circumstances of each case. It does not follow that, whenever it is shown that a trustee has acted honestly and reasonably, he will automatically be excused; these conditions are a prerequisite of the court having discretion to grant relief, not a ground for the exercise of that discretion. The courts have consistently refused to lay down any rules[62] but there have been numerous applications under the section, and under the provisions

---

[59] Millett L.J. rejected this argument: first, because the exemption clause applied not just to the solicitor in question but to all possible trustees of the will; secondly, because it limited liability rather than conferring a benefit; thirdly, because the duty of the solicitor was to advise the testator on the terms on which his executors and/or trustees might properly accept office and so he could tell the testator that he would not accept office without such a clause; and, fourthly and in any event, any complaint that the solicitor was accepting a benefit under a will which he had prepared was a ground for opposing probate and, even if the grant of probate were now revoked for this reason, the solicitor would be able to rely on the exemption clause in respect of anything which he had done in the interim.
[60] (1999) 3 I.T.E.L.R. 352.
[61] See *ante*, p. 622.
[62] *Re Turner* [1897] 1 Ch. 536; *Re Kay* [1897] 2 Ch. 518 at 524.

which it replaced. A typical case where relief was granted was *Re Kay*,[63] where the applicant was an executor and trustee of a will of a testator who left over £22,000 with apparent liabilities of only about £100. Before advertising for claims, the executor paid to the widow a legacy of £300 and only afterwards learned that the liabilities of the estate exceeded its value. Relief was granted on the basis that it was reasonable for the executor to have assumed that with an estate of this size its liabilities would not be anywhere its total value, so that he could safely pay the legacy.

Difficulties sometimes arise where a trustee has taken legal advice which turns out to be wrong. Although it may appear hard on the trustee, the fact that he has taken and has followed legal advice does not automatically excuse him from liability. Where the advice given to a trustee by his solicitor is wrong, he should basically sue his solicitor; where he does not seek to recover the loss in this way (assuming the solicitor is in fact potentially liable for negligence), the court will generally not excuse him. In *National Trustee Co. of Australia v. General Finance Co. of Australia*,[64] trustees followed wrong advice given by their solicitors and it was held that in the special circumstances they should not be granted relief. In this connection, relevant factors are the value of the trust property, the appropriateness of the level of advice obtained in the light of that value,[65] and whether the trustees are lay or professional. In *National Trustee Co. of Australia v. General Finance Co. of Australia* the court clearly took into account the fact that the trustees were paid. But the fact that trustees are professional does not automatically disqualify them from relief. In *Re Pauling's Settlement Trusts*,[66] the Court of Appeal held that relief under section 61 of the Trustee Act 1925 can be granted to a paid trustee if the circumstances are appropriate and a degree of relief was indeed granted in that case to paid trustees who were bankers. However, in its judgment the Court of Appeal stated that "Where a banker undertakes to act as a paid trustee of a settlement created by a customer, and so deliberately places itself in a position where its duty as trustee conflicts with its interest as a banker, we think that the court should be very slow to relieve such a trustee under the provisions of the section."[67]

Two particular aspects of the section were considered in *Re Rosenthal*.[68] The testator devised his house to his sister and left the remainder of his estate to his widow. The estate duty payable in respect of the house should have been paid by the sister, but the executors, who for this purpose were treated as trustees,[69]

---

[63] [1897] 2 Ch. 518.
[64] [1905] A.C. 373.
[65] If the property is of low value, trustees would probably be acting reasonably in taking merely the advice of a solicitor, whereas if the trust fund were very large, only the advice of a Queen's Counsel might be sufficient.
[66] [1964] Ch. 303.
[67] See also *Re Windsor Steam Coal Company* (1901) [1929] 1 Ch. 151 and *Re Waterman's Will Trusts* [1952] 2 All E.R. 1054. In *Re Cooper (No.2)* (1978) 21 O.R. (2d) 579 (Ontario), the two trustees were the senior partner in a trustee law firm and one of his junior partners. The whole of the conduct of the administration was left in the hands of the senior partner, who stole Can$180,000 and was sentenced to seven and a half years imprisonment. The court found that the junior partner had no reason to suspect the fraud of his senior partner, and that he had acted honestly and reasonably. It therefore granted him relief under the Ontario equivalent of s.61.
[68] *Re Rosenthal* [1972] 1 W.L.R. 1273.
[69] One of the persons appointed as an executor had purported to resign from his office by means of the appointment of new trustees. This was probably invalid but the so-called new trustees were treated by the judge as trustees for the purposes of the case.

transferred the house to the sister without making any arrangements with her to secure the payment of the duty.[70] They improperly paid £270 out of the residue on account of this liability and a further £1,500 plus interest was still outstanding. One of the trustees, who was a solicitor and who was acting in connection with the administration of the estate, claimed to be entitled to rely on section 61. Plowman J. rejected this contention on two grounds. First, although the trustee had acted honestly in paying the £270, he had not acted reasonably and had not shown that he ought fairly to be excused; in this respect, Plowman J. took account of the fact that he was a professional trustee,[71] for which reason he appears to have adopted a more stringent approach. Secondly, in respect of the question of whether section 61 could apply to an anticipated breach of trust, the future payment of the further sum due out of the residue, the solicitor was in effect seeking a declaration that he was entitled to take this sum from residue; Plowman J. held that relief could not be given under the section in respect of a breach of trust which had not yet occurred.

### 3. Acts of the Beneficiaries

A beneficiary who has once agreed to, or concurred in, a breach of trust cannot afterwards sue the trustees in respect of it. This applies only if three conditions are satisfied:

(a) that the beneficiary was of full age and sound mind at the time when he agreed or concurred;

(b) that he had full knowledge of all relevant facts and of the legal effect of his agreement or concurrence; and

(c) that he was an entirely free agent and was not under any undue influence.

A good example of the working of this rule is *Nail v. Punter*.[72] Trustees held stock on trust for a married woman for life, with remainder to such person as she should by will appoint. During her lifetime, the woman's husband persuaded the trustees to sell the stock and pay him the proceeds. She then brought an action against the trustees but died before it was concluded, having by her will appointed the stock to her husband. The husband endeavoured to claim the same remedy as his wife had sought. But, since he had become a beneficiary by virtue of the exercise of the power of appointment, it was held that he could not succeed because he had been a party to the breach.

A trustee is also protected from action if the beneficiaries subsequently learn of the breach and either acquiesce in it or give the trustee a release. The same three conditions apply. Releases are generally granted formally by deed but an informal release, if supported by consideration, will be effective. In *Ghost v. Waller*,[73] part of the trust property was lost through a breach of trust. The beneficiary agreed by letter through her solicitors that, in consideration of the

---

[70] The liability of the sister arose under the Finance Act 1894, s.9(1). See *Re the Countess of Oxford* [1896] 1 Ch. 257.
[71] [1972] 1 W.L.R. 1273 at 1278.
[72] (1832) 5 Sim. 555.
[73] (1846) 9 Beav. 497.

trustees undertaking to assist in recovering part of the loss, she would "give up all claims if she has any against her trustees for negligence". This was held to be an effective release.

Neither a formal nor an informal release will be effective if the beneficiary was not in full possession of the facts. In *Thompson v. Eastwood*,[74] the beneficiary was entitled to a legacy under a will. The trustee denied the beneficiary's right to that legacy on the grounds of alleged illegality and the dispute was settled on the payment by the trustee of a smaller sum than that to which the beneficiary was entitled. A formal deed of release was executed but, when the beneficiary discovered the true position, he was held entitled to claim the full legacy, despite the deed of release, and despite the fact that over 25 years had passed since the breach.

In *Re Pauling's Settlement Trusts*,[75] the bank Coutts & Co. was trustee of a fund for a mother for life, remainder to her children. The trustee had an express power, which would anyway have been implied by statute, to advance to each child up to half his share of the capital provided that the mother consented. The father habitually lived beyond his means and persuaded the bank to make a series of advances to which the mother consented. These, although nominally for the benefit of the child in question, as they were required to be, were in fact used for the benefit of the father or the family as a whole. The children now sought to recover from the bank the sums advanced.

As has already been seen,[76] the bank's attempt to rely on limitation failed because of the proviso to what is now section 21(3) of the Limitation Act 1980; the children's interests were future interests until the death of the mother; she was still alive so time had not yet even started running against them. The bank's attempt to rely on section 61 of the Trustee Act 1925 succeeded only to the very limited extent that, in respect of one clearly improper advance, the bank had been lulled into a false sense of security by a letter from the solicitors of the two children in question stating that it was satisfactory; it was therefore relieved to the extent that the children had at the time benefited from it. The defence which is relevant for present purposes was a contention that each advance had been made at a time when the beneficiary in question was over the age of majority (then 21) and had consented to the improper advances being made. It is clear that, had those consents been effective, the beneficiaries could not afterwards have succeeded in an action against the trustees. The Court of Appeal actually held that the children had not been fully aware of the nature of their rights at the time of these consents. This was enough to dispose of the defence but the court went on to consider the impact of undue influence. The presumption of undue influence which arises where an infant makes a gift to a parent[77] continues for a short time — the exact period is undefined and depends on the circumstances of each case — after the infant has attained his majority.[78] The court found that the presumption arose in respect of a series of advances in favour of a daughter just over the age of majority. This raised the question of what for the purposes of any liability of the trustees is the effect on

---

[74] (1877) 2 App.Cas. 215 and see *Re Freeston's Charity* [1978] 1 W.L.R. 741 (no acquiescence in a breach of a charitable trust).
[75] [1964] Ch. 303, and see *ante*, p. 698.
[76] See *ante*, p. 781.
[77] *Huguenin v. Baseley* (1807) 14 Ves. 273.
[78] See *Lancashire Looms v. Black* [1943] 1 K.B. 380.

an advancement which favours a parent and not a child of a consent given by that child which may be the result of undue influence. The Court of Appeal said: "Without expressing a final opinion, we think that the true view may be that a trustee carrying out a transaction in breach of trust may be liable if he knew, or ought to have known, that the beneficiary was acting under the undue influence of another, or may be presumed to have done so, but will not be liable if it cannot be established that he so knew or ought to have known."

A trustee who is asked to commit a breach of trust for the benefit of a parent on the basis of consent by a beneficiary just turned 18 ought, therefore, to satisfy himself that the child is emancipated from the parent.

### 4. Indemnities Obtainable from Beneficiaries

It has already been shown that, subject to the conditions just mentioned, a beneficiary who with full knowledge concurs in a breach of trust cannot afterwards sue his trustees. This does not, however, affect the right of other beneficiaries to take action and if such action is taken the trustee may be able to claim an indemnity out of the beneficial interest of the beneficiary who has concurred in the breach. In particular, if the beneficiary who has concurred in the breach of trust is the tenant for life and the trustee repairs the breach at the behest of the remainderman, he is entitled to the income which the tenant for life would otherwise have received during the remainder of his lifetime.[79] Outside this special situation, there are two rules which overlap:

1.  Under its inherent jurisdiction, the court has power to order a beneficiary to give the trustee an indemnity if he instigated,[80] or requested,[81] a breach of trust with the intention of obtaining a personal benefit (whether or not such personal benefit was in fact received) or if he concurred in a breach of trust and actually derived a personal benefit from it.[82]

2.  Under section 62 of the Trustee Act 1925, the court may impound the interest of a beneficiary in the trust fund if he instigates or requests or consents in writing to a breach of trust by the trustee. Where the section applies, the court has a discretion whether to impound, and, if so, whether to impound the whole or only part of the beneficiary's interest.

Section 62 applies irrespective of personal benefit, or of a motive for personal benefit. On the other hand, it only applies in the case of mere consent to a breach of trust if such consent was in writing, whereas the inherent jurisdiction of the court can be utilised whether or not the consent is in writing. The court will not exercise either power to impound the beneficiary's interest unless the trustee can show that the beneficiary fully appreciated that the proposed action would constitute a breach of trust.

---

[79] *Fletcher v. Collis* [1905] 2 Ch. 24.
[80] *Trafford v. Boehm* (1746) 3 Atk. 440.
[81] *Fuller v. Knight* (1843) 6 Beav. 205.
[82] *Montford v. Cadogan* (1816) 19 Ves. 635.

As the result of a fairly robust construction, it was held in *Re Pauling's Settlement (No.2)*,[83] that the power under section 62 can be exercised in favour of a person who is not a trustee at the time when the breach of trust occurred. In coming to this decision, Wilberforce J. was clearly influenced by the consideration that, if the section only applied to persons who were trustees at the time of the application, the court might be loath to remove trustees before such application has been made, even if in the other circumstances of the case their removal was desirable.

Where a beneficiary unsuccessfully brings proceedings against a trustee alleging breach of trust, the trustee will be entitled to take his costs out of the trust fund and only if that is insufficient will an order be made against the beneficiary personally.[84]

## VII. PERSONAL CLAIMS AGAINST THIRD PARTIES

So far this chapter has been concerned with personal actions for breach of trust against the trustees who have committed those breaches. From the point of view of the beneficiaries, such claims may be inadequate and clearly will be if the trustees are insolvent. In these circumstances, the beneficiaries may additionally make either a personal claim against any third parties who have received the trust property in breach of trust or a legal or equitable proprietary claim in respect of the trust property against such third parties or against the trustees. This section is concerned with personal claims against third parties; the following two sections are concerned with legal and equitable proprietary claims.

In the leading case of *Re Diplock*,[85] Caleb Diplock by his will directed his executors to apply his residuary estate "for such charitable institution or institutions or other charitable or benevolent object or objects" as they should in their absolute discretion think fit. His executors distributed the residue, which amounted to over £200,000, among 139 charities. Subsequently, the testator's next-of-kin challenged the validity of the bequest. The House of Lords eventually held, in *Chichester Diocesan Fund and Board of Finance v. Simpson*,[86] that the bequest was invalid. *Re Diplock* was concerned with the next-of-kin's subsequent claims to recover the money from the executors and the charities which had received it.

The claims of the next-of-kin against the executors were eventually compromised, with the approval of the court. But actions continued for the considerable balance of the funds distributed against the charities, who had used the money paid to them for a variety of purposes. In the majority of cases, the cheques sent to them had been paid into their general accounts at the bank. Some of such accounts were in credit, while some were overdrawn on either a secured or an unsecured basis. In a few cases payment had been made into a special account, in others it had been earmarked for some designated purpose, while in others the money had been spent on altering or enlarging existing

---

[83] [1963] Ch. 576.

[84] *Re Spurling's Will Trusts* [1966] 1 W.L.R. 920.

[85] [1948] Ch. 465, affirmed by the House of Lords *sub nom. Ministry of Health v. Simpson* [1951] A.C. 251.

[86] [1944] A.C. 341 and see *ante*, p. 477.

buildings owned by the charity. The next-of-kin based their claim to recover the money on both personal and proprietary claims, both of which succeeded. The personal claims were brought against the charities on the basis of the "equity" which the next-of-kin had to recover the money; they contended that any unpaid creditor, legatee or next-of-kin possessed such an "equity" as against an overpaid beneficiary or stranger to the estate. In respect of personal claims of this type, Re Diplock remains the principal authority. The proprietary claims, which will be discussed later on, were to follow identifiable assets into the hands of the charities on the basis that the charities were innocent volunteers who had received assets paid away in breach of trust. In respect of proprietary claims, Re Diplock is only one of a number of leading authorities.

## 1. The Moral Claim of the Charities

In Re Diplock the charities contended that, notwithstanding the formal invalidity of the bequest, it at any rate had to be presumed that Caleb Diplock had intended them to enjoy the residuary estate in preference to his blood relations and that it therefore did not lie in the mouths of the next-of-kin to allege any "unconscientiousness" on the part of those whose claim was in accordance with the wishes of the testator, however ineffectually those wishes had been expressed. However, this argument, based as it was on the proposition that the conscience of the recipients should be in some degree affected by their retention of the moneys, was rejected as wholly untenable; the Court of Appeal held that "it is impossible to contend that a disposition which according to the general law of the land is held to be entirely invalid can yet confer upon those who, ex hypothesi, have improperly participated under the disposition some moral or equitable right to retain what they have received against those whom the law declares to be properly entitled".[87]

## 2. The Recipients' Notice of the Invalidity of the Gift

The next-of-kin contended that, since the letter which accompanied all the executors' payments to the charities set out, admittedly not entirely accurately, the terms of the gift in Caleb Diplock's will, the charities had been given notice of the invalidity of the trusts, or at least were put on enquiry as to their validity; on this basis the charities would have been constructive trustees of the moneys received for the next-of-kin on the basis that they had received these moneys with notice that they had been paid to them in breach of trust (the type of liability which has since become known as "liability for knowing receipt").[88] The Court of Appeal also rejected this argument, holding that "persons in the position of the [charities], themselves unversed in the law, are entitled in such circumstances as these to assume that the executors are properly administering the estate".[89]

---

[87] [1948] Ch. 465 at 476.
[88] See ante, p. 390.
[89] [1948] Ch. 465 at 478–479.

3. *The Equitable Right of Recovery of the Next-of-Kin*

The further contention of the next-of-kin, which the Court of Appeal subjected to an exhaustive analysis, was that, in the words of the court, "apart from any notice which the [charities] may have had of the true effect of the testator's will, they had in truth no right to receive any of the moneys paid to them and that ... the unpaid next-of-kin had a direct claim, recognised and established by the courts of equity, to recovery from the [charities] of the sums improperly paid to the [charities] and properly belonging to the next-of-kin."

### (A) Mistake of Law

At first instance,[90] Wynn-Parry J. had come to the conclusion that an unpaid beneficiary could only sue the wrongly paid recipient in equity when the payment had been made under a mistake of fact, whereas in this case the mistake had been one of law. The Court of Appeal acknowledged that the mistake was one of law and that, as Wynn-Parry J. had held, common law claims for money had and received would not lie where money had been paid under a mistake of law (this was the certainly the law then, although this is no longer the case).[91] However, the Court of Appeal held that such common law claims were in no sense derived from equity but had developed entirely independently of equity.[92] The court took the view that there was no "necessity in logic for the claim as being clothed, as it were, with all the attributes or limitations appropriate to the common law action for money had and received"[93] and went on to consider the relevant authorities dating back as far as the days of Bridgman L.K. and Finch L.K. (afterwards Lord Nottingham L.C.) to see what principles had been established by them.[94] Having done so, the court rejected the contention that in equity the mistake under which the payment is made must be one of fact. As Lord Simonds said[95] in the House of Lords, where the decision was affirmed:

> "It would be a strange thing if the Court of Chancery having taken upon itself to see that the assets of a deceased person were duly administered was deterred from doing justice to the creditor, legatee or next-of-kin because the executor had done him wrong under a mistake of law. If in truth this were so, I think that the father of Equity would not recognise his own child."

---

[90] [1947] Ch. 716.

[91] The general prohibition on the recovery of money paid under a mistake of law was rejected by the House of Lords in *Kleinworth Benson v. Lincoln City Council* [1999] 2 A.C. 349.

[92] [1948] Ch. 465 at 480.

[93] *ibid.* at 481.

[94] *ibid.* at 482. The cases cited and discussed at length included *Nelthrop v. Hill* (1669) 1 Ch.Cas. 135; *Grove v. Banson* (1669) 1 Ch.Cas. 148 at 148; *Chamberlain v. Chamberlain* (1675) 1 Ch.Cas. 256; *Noel v. Robinson* (1682) 1 Vern. 90; *Anon.* (1682) 1 Vern. 162; *Newman v. Barton* (1690) 2 Vern. 205; *Anon.* (1718) 1 P.Wms. 495; *Orr v. Kaines* (1750) 2 Ves.Sen. 194; *Walcot v. Hall* (1788) 2 Bro.C.C. 304; *Gillespie v. Alexander* (1827) 3 Russ. 130; *Greig v. Somerville* (1830) 1 Russ. & My. 338; *David v. Frowd* (1833) 1 My. & K. 200; *Sawyer v. Birchmore* (1836) 1 Keen 391; *Thomas v. Griffith* (1860) 2 Giff. 504; *Fenwick v. Clarke* (1862) 4 De G.F. & J. 240; *Peterson v. Peterson* (1866) L.R. 3 Eq. 111; *Rogers v. Ingham* (1876) 3 Ch.D. 351; *Re Robinson* [1911] 1 Ch. 502; *Re Hatch* [1919] 1 Ch. 351; *Re Rivers* [1920] 1 Ch. 320; *Re Mason* [1928] Ch. 385, [1929] 1 Ch. 1; *Re Blake* [1932] 1 Ch. 54.

[95] *Ministry of Health v. Simpson* [1951] A.C. 251 at 270.

Further, the underpaid creditor, legatee or next-of-kin will necessarily not himself be a party to the wrongful payment; only the executor will be responsible for that. As Lord Simonds said, it is therefore difficult to see what relevance the distinction between mistake of fact and law can have to such a situation (as has already been mentioned, the distinction is now no longer relevant at common law either).[96]

**(B) Administration of the Estate by the Court**
Wynn-Parry J. had also held that it was necessary that for the personal claim to lie there had to be or had to have been administration of the estate by the court. However, the Court of Appeal, after analysing the authorities,[97] came to the conclusion that they wholly negatived any such requirement.[98] Admittedly if the court had administered the estate, there would be every reason why equity should come to the rescue of an underpaid legatee if a wrong payment had been made; but there seemed no reason why such an administration should be essential.

**(C) Strangers to the Estate**
The authorities already referred to[99] also established that it is irrelevant to the applicability of the remedy that the original recipient had no title at all and was a stranger to the estate.[1] Many of these authorities were undoubtedly concerned with providing equality between the original recipient and other persons having a title similar to that of the recipient, such as next-of-kin, but that was not a reason why the remedy should not also be applied against a stranger even though the effect of the refund would actually be to dispossess the stranger rather than to produce equality.

**(D) The "Conscience" of the Recipient**
The charities had contended that the conscience of the recipient, on which equity must necessarily fasten in order to grant a remedy, was not affected in circumstances such as these. But the Court of Appeal decided that it is *prima facie* at least a sufficient circumstance that the charities had received some share of the estate to which they were not entitled.[2] As Leach M.R. had said long before in *David v. Frowd*,[3] "a party claiming under such circumstances has no great reason to complain that he is called upon to replace what he has received against his right".

**(E) The Conditions for the Application of the Equitable Remedy**
The discussion so far has shown that *Re Diplock* established, first, that an equitable remedy is available equally to an underpaid creditor, legatee or next-of-kin and, secondly, that a claim by the next-of-kin will not be liable to be defeated merely because of the absence of any administration by the court or because the mistake under which the original payment was made was one of

---

[96] *Kleinworth Benson v. Lincoln City Council* [1999] 2 A.C. 349.
[97] See the authorities cited *ante*, fn. 94.
[98] [1948] Ch. 465 at 489.
[99] See the authorities cited *ante*, fn. 94.
[1] [1948] Ch. 465 at 502.
[2] *ibid.* at 503.
[3] (1883) 1 My. & K 200 at 211.

law rather than fact or because the original recipient had no title at all and was a stranger to the estate.[4] However, there is one important qualification that must be fulfilled before a claim by an underpaid beneficiary can succeed. This was stated by the Court of Appeal in Re Diplock as follows:[5]

> "Since the original wrong payment was attributable to the blunder of the personal representatives, the right of the unpaid beneficiary is in the first instance against the wrongdoing executor or administrator and the beneficiary's direct claim in equity against those overpaid or wrongly paid should be limited to the amount which he cannot recover from the party responsible. In some cases the amount will be the whole amount of the payment wrongly made, e.g. where the executor or administrator is shown to be wholly without assets or is protected from attack by having acted under an order of the court."[6]

In Re Diplock the claims of the next-of-kin against the executors or their estates had already been compromised. Accordingly it was held that the amount recovered from the executors should be apportioned among the charities in proportion to the money the latter had wrongly received. This meant that the maximum recoverable from an individual charity by the next-of-kin would be rateably reduced.[7]

**(F) The Absence of any Liability for Interest**
The Court of Appeal held that the recipients were only liable for the principal sum claimed and not for any interest.[8]

#### 4. Possible Limitations of the Personal Claim

Re Diplock was a claim in respect of the administration of an estate and was dealt with by the Court of Appeal and by the House of Lords[9] strictly on that basis. It is not, therefore, so clearly established that the principles laid down will apply with equal force between beneficiaries under an inter vivos trust, although there seems no cogent reason why they should not do. In Butler v. Broadhead,[10] the plaintiffs had purchased land from a company in the course of being wound up. Some years later, it transpired that the company had had no title to the land and so the plaintiffs, having been deprived of it, attempted to utilise the personal claim in Re Diplock in order to claim against the contributories of the company, to whom its surplus assets had been distributed when the winding up had been concluded. They argued that such a personal claim was limited to the administration of estates; however, Templeman J. did not dismiss the claim on this ground but rather on the ground that it was

---

[4] [1948] Ch. 465 at 502.
[5] ibid. at 503.
[6] For early authority for this proposition, see Orr v. Kaines (1750) 2 Ves. Sen. 195; Hodges v. Waddington (1684) 2 Vent. 360.
[7] [1948] Ch. 465 at 506.
[8] The relevant authority is Gittins v. Steele (1818) 1 Swanst. 200.
[9] sub nom. Ministry of Health v. Simpson [1951] A.C. 251.
[10] [1975] Ch. 97.

barred by the Companies Act 1948[11] (it was assumed that the plaintiffs had failed to respond to the liquidator's advertisement seeking claims by the creditors of the company). This decision suggests that there is no reason in principle why the personal claim should not apply to *inter vivos* trusts. Subsequently, in *Re J. Leslie Engineers Company*,[12] Oliver J. accepted the theoretical availability of such a claim to the liquidator of a company who was attempting to recover payments made to a creditor by a director after the liquidation had commenced; however, he denied the claim because the creditor had given value and the liquidator had not exhausted his remedies against the director. These decisions suggest that, in an appropriate case, the personal claim could be applied at least to *inter vivos* trusts and possibly also to companies in liquidation.

A further limitation of the personal claim has presumably been created by the recognition by the House of Lords in *Lipkin Gorman v. Karpnale*,[13] of a general defence of change of position. It was the issue of whether or not there was such a defence that formed the subject matter of the appeal to the House of Lords[14] against the decision of the Court of Appeal in *Re Diplock*. At that stage, the House of Lords had refused to recognise any such defence, a decision which produced very considerable hardship for those charities who had used the funds to improve their buildings and, consequently, provoked very considerable criticism. This relatively new defence will be considered in detail in the final section of this chapter.[15] However, now that it has been established, the personal claim which succeeded in *Re Diplock* will be able to operate in a much more reasonable manner. Consequently, there seems no reason whatever why it should not now be extended to inter vivos trusts and perhaps also to companies in liquidation.

The extension of the remedy to *inter vivos* trusts is also what is in effect being proposed by those who advocate the replacement of the present rules governing "liability for knowing receipt" by the introduction of a universal principle of strict liability for receipt of trust property transferred in breach of trust. As has already been seen,[16] the most significant advocate of this view has been Lord Nicholls of Birkenhead, writing extrajudicially,[17] but Lord Millett's subsequent support for this view in *Twinsectra v. Yardley*[18] shows that a future reform of the law in accordance with that proposal certainly cannot be discounted; whether this reform could actually be effected by the judiciary or only by the legislature is unclear. However, for the reasons which have already been stated,[19] this reform is not the preferred option of this work.

---

[11] Now Companies Act 1985, s.557.
[12] [1976] 1 W.L.R. 292.
[13] [1991] 2 A.C. 548.
[14] *sub nom. Ministry of Health v. Simpson* [1951] A.C. 251.
[15] See *post*, p. 833.
[16] See *ante*, p. 403.
[17] In *Restitution – Past, Present and Future* (ed. Cornish, 1998) 231. See also Birks [1993] L.M.C.L.Q. 218; Harpum in *Frontiers of Liability* (ed. Birks, 1993) 9.
[18] [2002] 2 A.C. 164 at 194.
[19] See *ante*, p. 404.

## VIII. LEGAL PROPRIETARY CLAIMS[20]

Proprietary claims have important advantages over any personal claim. If the claimant can identify his property in the hands of the defendant, he will generally[21] be entitled to recover that property in full in priority to the claims of the general creditors of the defendant.[22] He will also normally be able to take advantage of any increase in the value of the property.[23] Further, he will also be able to claim the income or fruits of the property from the date when it reached the hands of the defendant, either the income or fruits actually produced or, if the property in question is or becomes money, interest on that money[24] (the earliest date from which the payment of interest will be awarded in a personal claim is from the date when the claim form was issued[25] and, in many cases, the payment of interest will only be ordered as from the date of judgment).[26]

Before any proprietary claim can be brought, the claimant must identify his property in the hands of the defendant. The terminology which is at present fashionable is to describe this process of identification as "following and tracing" and to distinguish both from the proprietary claim itself. However, until relatively recently, the expression "tracing" was utilised to describe both the process of identification and the proprietary claim itself. The principal protagonist in this terminological change has been Lord Millett. In *Foskett v. McKeown*,[27] he defined "following" and "tracing" in this way:

> "These are both exercises in locating assets which are or may be taken to represent an asset belonging to the plaintiffs and to which they assert ownership. The processes of following and tracing are, however, distinct. Following is the process of following the same asset as it moves from hand to hand. Tracing is the process of identifying a new asset as the substitute for the old. Where one asset is exchanged for another, a claimant can elect whether to follow the original asset into the hands of the new owner or to trace its value into the new asset in the hands of the same owner. In practice his choice is often dictated by the circumstances."

Later in the same speech[28] he distinguished between the processes of identi-

---

[20] The best short discussion of proprietary claims is found in Goff & Jones, *The Law of Restitution* (6th ed. 2002), pp. 79–119. See also Birks, *An Introduction to the Law of Restitution* (1989), pp. 358–401. Smith, *The Law of Tracing* (1997) is devoted entirely to this subject.

[21] This always occurs in the case of equitable proprietary claims but not always in the case of legal proprietary claims; see *post*, p. 801.

[22] Insolvency Act 1986, s.283; *Chase Manhattan Bank v. Israel-British Bank (London)* [1981] Ch. 105 (which concerned an equitable proprietary claim).

[23] *Re Tilley's Will Trusts* [1967] Ch. 1179; *Papamichael v. National WestminsterBank* [2003] 1 Lloyd's Rep. 341 (both equitable proprietary claims; see *post*, p. 807).

[24] In the case of an equitable proprietary claim, that interest will be compound interest; see *Westdeutsche Landesbank Girozentrale v. Islington L.B.C.* [1996] A.C. 669

[25] *Jaffray v. Marshall* [1993] 1 W.L.R. 1285 (overruled by the House of Lords on other grounds in *Target Holdings v. Redferns* [1996] 1 A.C. 421).

[26] *Re Diplock* [1948] Ch. 465.

[27] [2001] 1 A.C. 102 at 127.

[28] *ibid.* at 128.

fication and the proprietary claim itself, in this respect repeating his own earlier judicial[29] and extra-judicial[30] observations:

"Tracing is thus neither a claim nor a remedy. It is merely the process by which a claimant demonstrates what has happened to his property, identifies its proceeds and the persons who have handled or received them, and justifies his claim that the proceeds can properly be regarded as representing his property. Tracing is also distinct from claiming. It identifies the traceable proceeds of the claimant's property. It enables the claimant to substitute the traceable proceeds for the original asset as the subject matter of his claim. But it does not affect or establish his claim. That will depend on a number of factors including the nature of his interest in the original asset. He will normally be able to maintain the same claim to the substituted asset as he could have maintained to the original asset. If he held only a security interest in the original asset, he cannot claim more than a security interest in its proceeds. But his claim may also be exposed to potential defences as a result of intervening transactions."

This chapter will use the expressions "following" and "tracing" in the way in which Lord Millett has defined them and will use the expression "proprietary claim" to denote the substantive claim which is being brought by the claimant. However, it must be borne in mind that most of the authorities utilise the expression "tracing" to denote all of these things.

This section has been headed "legal proprietary claims" because the attitudes of the common law and of equity not only to following and tracing but also to proprietary claims have always been quite distinct and, despite judicial statements that one set of rules is enough,[31] for the moment they remain quite distinct. For this and other reasons, it is therefore necessary to consider legal and equitable proprietary claims separately.

### 1. The Nature of Legal Proprietary Claims

A person who seeks to assert a proprietary claim at law will use the action appropriate to the type of property which he is claiming. If he is claiming land, he will use the action for the recovery of land; he merely needs to show a better title than the other party and, if he can do so, he will not be defeated by the defence of bona fide purchase for value without notice although his action may become statute-barred as a result of the other party's adverse possession. A successful claim will produce an order for the specific recovery of the land so that a legal proprietary right to land is indeed a right *in rem*. If the claim is instead for specific chattels, the claimant will use a tortious action for conversion under the Torts (Interference with Goods) Act 1977.[32] Bona fide pur-

---

[29] In *Boscawen v. Bajwa* [1996] 1 W.L.R. 328 at 334.
[30] (1998) 110 L.Q.R. 399.
[31] See *Foskett v. McKeown* [2001] 1 A.C. 102 at 128, *per* Lord Millett. In *Banque Belge pour l'Etranger v. Hambrouck* [1921] 1 K.B. 321, Atkin L.J. went so far as to say that the rules of tracing at law and equity were in fact the same but this view is generally regarded more as an expression of hope than as a statement of reality.
[32] Torts (Interference with Goods) Act 1977, s.1.

chase for value without notice will now[33] only be a defence to such a claim if the purchaser is protected by the provisions of the Sale of Goods Act 1979.[34] However, a successful claimant is not entitled to specific recovery of the chattel, although the court has a discretion to so order.[35] Thus a legal proprietary right to chattels will only rarely amount to a right *in rem*. Finally, if the claim is for a chose in action or money, the claimant will only be able to use the action for money had and received, which imposes only a personal liability on the defendant. Bona fide purchase for value without notice will apparently be a defence to such a claim.[36] Thus, a legal proprietary right to property of this type will never amount to a right *in rem*. However, all the legal proprietary rights mentioned are now presumably subject to the defence of change of position, which will be discussed in detail at the end of the next section of this chapter.

### 2. Who can Bring a Legal Proprietary Claim?

Only the legal owner of property is entitled to bring a proprietary claim at common law. This was specifically held by the Court of Appeal in *MCC Proceeds v. Lehman Brothers International (Europe)*,[37] where they rejected a claim by the beneficiaries of a bare trust to bring an action of conversion in respect of share certificates which their trustee had in breach of trust pledged to the defendant. As in that case and in cases such as *Re Diplock*, this requirement will generally prevent the beneficiaries of a trust from taking advantage of any potential legal proprietary claim to the trust property; the legal owner of property subject to a trust is the trustees who in such cases will themselves have been responsible for the property reaching the hands of the defendant and so are prevented from reclaiming it by the principle of non-derogation from grant. It is only where the trustees have themselves been defrauded by the potential defendant to a legal proprietary claim that such a claim is likely to be available to a trust.

### 3. What Property can be the Subject Matter of a Legal Proprietary Claim?

#### (A) Property in its Original Form
Where the property which is the subject matter of the claim remains in its original form, the legal owner will, subject to the defences mentioned above, be able to follow it into the hands of anyone in the world, bring the appropriate legal proprietary claim and obtain the appropriate remedy.

Difficulties may arise, however, when chattels are intermingled with other

---

[33] It was formerly also a defence if the property had been purchased in market overt but this defence was removed by Sale of Goods (Amendment) Act 1994, which repealed Sale of Goods Act 1979, s.22(1).

[34] Sale of Goods Act 1979, s.23. See also Consumer Credit Act 1974, Sched. IV, Pt I, para. 22.

[35] Torts (Interference with Goods) Act 1977, s.3.

[36] There is no justification in principle for this view but it must follow from *Liplin Gorman v. Karpnale* [1991] 2 A.C. 548, where the plaintiff solicitors would not have been able to recover funds abstracted from their client account from the casino where those funds had been gambled and lost had the casino been able successfully to plead bona fide purchase for value without notice (it was unable to do so because of the nature of gaming contracts). See Halliwell [1992] Conv. 124.

[37] [1998] 4 All E.R. 675.

chattels of the same nature so that it cannot precisely be ascertained which belong to the claimant.[38] In these circumstances, it seems that a tortious action will still be available despite the mixing. This follows from *Jackson v. Anderson*,[39] where it was held that an action of conversion could be maintained against someone who had mixed the plaintiff's gold coins in a barrelful of the same description. So far as ownership of the intermingled chattels is concerned, this has traditionally depended on whether the mixing was accidental or deliberate.

If chattels are mixed accidentally so that they cannot be separated or identified, then the original owners are treated as tenants in common of the whole in proportion to their contributions. This was held in *Spence v. Union Marine Insurance Co.*,[40] where bales of wool belonging to different owners became indistinguishable as the result of a shipwreck.

On the other hand, it has been stated[41] that, where a person deliberately mixed the property of another with his own, then the whole must be taken to be the property of the other unless and until the mixer unmixes the chattels. This principle was applied by a Canadian court in *Jones v. De Marchant*,[42] where a wife was held to be the owner of a fur coat which her husband had had made up out of 18 beaver skins belonging to her and four skins of his own and had then given to his mistress. The result of this case would undoubtedly still be the same today but, in so far as the principle concerns fungibles, it has now been described as no longer appropriate given the availability of modern and sophisticated methods of measurement. This was in *Indian Oil Corp. v. Greenstone Shipping Co.*,[43] where the owners of a vessel had mixed with their own crude oil a cargo of crude oil which they were shipping. The owners of the cargo claimed the whole of the crude oil. However, since it was possible to determine exactly the amounts of oil belonging to each party, it was held that the mixture was held in common and that the owners of the cargo were entitled to receive a quantity of the mixed oil equal to that which had gone into the mixture, any doubts being resolved in their favour, together with damages for any loss which they had suffered. While this view seems a more appropriate way of dealing with fungibles in modern conditions, it remains to be seen which way the conflict of authority thus produced is finally resolved.

Legal proprietary claims to money, on the other hand, suffer from the difficulty that money has no earmark (it is rare for a note to be taken of the numbers of banknotes and there is no way of doing so in the case of coins). Further, since money is the universal medium of exchange, the transferor of money normally makes that money the property of the transferee. However, if a claimant can identify money in the hands of another as belonging to him (as would be the case where bank notes of known serial numbers were stolen and

---

[38] See Pearce 40 Conveyancer (N.S.) (1976) 277.
[39] (1811) 4 Taunt. 24.
[40] (1868) L.R. 3 C.P. 427.
[41] *Spence v. Union Marine Insurance Co.* (1868) L.R. 3 C.P. 427 at 437–438; *Sandeman & Sons v. Tyzack and Branfoot Steamship Co.* [1913] A.C. 680 at 695, *per* Lord Moulton. This is also the rule in equity; see *Lupton v. White* (1808) 15 Ves. 432; *Foskett v. McKeown* [2001] 1 A.C. 102 at 133, *per* Lord Millett.
[42] (1916) 28 D.L.R. 561.
[43] [1987] 2 Lloyd's Rep. 286.

found in the possession of the thief), then that money could be recovered by an action for money had and received.

## (B) Property which is Identifiable Despite a Change of Form

Provided that property or its product has at all times remained identifiable, it can be traced ar law despite a change of form and anything into which it is turned can be recovered. *Jackson v. Anderson,*[44] *Spence v. Union Marine Insurance Co.,*[45] and *Indian Oil Corp. v. Greenstone Shipping Co.*[46] are all still applicable for this purpose. In *Taylor v. Plumer,*[47] the defendant had given his stockbroker a draft for £22,000 to be disbursed on Exchequer Bills. The stockbroker, having cashed the draft and used £6,500 for this purpose, paid for certain American securities which he had already agreed to purchase and also obtained some bullion with a draft which he had exchanged for cash. He then attempted to flee the country but was intercepted by the defendant at Falmouth and surrendered to him the securities and the bullion. His trustee in bankruptcy tried to recover these assets or their value from the defendant on the basis that the latter's title could not survive these transactions; had he succeeded, the defendant would have had to take his turn with the general creditors. However, Lord Ellenborough C.J. held that the defendant could at all times have traced the product of his draft into the hands of the stockbroker and brought a proprietary claim against him in respect of the assets in his hands; this was because the product of the defendant's original draft had at all times been completely identifiable. This meant that the defendant could still claim the assets in priority to the general creditors. Lord Ellenborough stated that only when property had been turned into money and mixed with other money did the right to trace and bring a legal proprietary claim in respect of it disappear.

Although it has been contended[48] that this decision is no authority for a legal proprietary claim surviving a change of form of the property unless the nature of the transaction by which the change of form occurs is such as to vest title in the new form of the property in the claimant, *Taylor v. Plumer* has been repeatedly followed. In *Re J. Leslie Engineers Co.,*[49] the liquidator of a company was held entitled to trace at law a cheque drawn on the company account to cash into the postal orders which had been purchased with the cash and sent to the defendant. Similarly, in *Lipkin Gorman v. Karpnale,*[50] the House of Lords held that the plaintiff firm of solicitors could trace at law its right of action against its bankers in respect of the credit balance of its client account into the funds drawn in cash from the account by one of its partners and exchanged for gaming chips at the defendant's casino. In *Trustee of the Property of F. C. Jones & Sons (a Firm) v. Jones,*[51] the Court of Appeal held that the trustee in bankruptcy of a partnership could trace cheques totalling £11,700 which one of the part-

---

[44] (1811) 4 Taunt. 24.
[45] (1868) L.R. 3 C.P. 427.
[46] [1987] 2 Lloyd's Rep. 286.
[47] (1815) 3 M. & S. 562.
[48] By Khurshid & Matthews (1979) 95 L.Q.R. 78, who argue that the references in *Taylor v. Plumer* to the right of the defendant to trace were to tracing in equity, rather than to tracing at law. This argument is convincing historically and there is much to be said for it as a matter of principle; however, it is inconsistent with the authorities in which *Taylor v. Plumer* has been applied.
[49] [1976] 1 W.L.R. 292.
[50] [1991] 2 A.C. 548.
[51] [1997] Ch. 159.

ners had after the act of bankruptcy drawn on the partnership account in favour of his wife; she had paid the cheques into a new account which she opened with commodity brokers and then, having traded profitably with this account, paid the commodity broker's cheque for the profit into another new account with a bank; the trustee in bankruptcy had at all times been the legal owner of the money, had at all times been able to identify it, and so could claim not only the £11,700 and interest thereon but also the profit made with it.

Further, *Taylor v. Plumer* was, if anything, extended in *Banque Belge pour l'Etranger v. Hambrouck*,[52] where the Court of Appeal emphasised that it is not the mere payment of money into a bank account which matters but the identifiability of the property. The defendant had fraudulently obtained £6,000 from the plaintiff bank by drawing cheques on his employers in favour of himself. He paid these cheques into his own account with another bank, an account into which no other substantial sums were ever paid. From this account, he drew out cash which he paid over to his mistress in consideration for the continuance of their relationship; she paid these sums into a deposit account, whose outstanding balance was successfully claimed by the plaintiff. The majority of the Court of Appeal[53] held that the plaintiff was entitled at law to trace the money through the defendant's bank account into the hands of the mistress because it was possible to distinguish the money at every stage; the fact that, to all intents and purposes, no other sums had been paid into the defendant's account meant that the funds abstracted from the plaintiff had never lost their identity.[54]

**(C) Property which is No Longer Identifiable Following a Change of Form**
Where property is no longer identifiable following a change of form, it cannot be traced at law. Property is usually no longer identifiable because it or its product has been turned into money and mixed with other money. Payment into a mixed fund or through an inter-bank clearing system will clearly prevent a legal proprietary claim while, as *Banque Belge pour l'Etranger v. Hambrouck* clearly illustrates, payment into an unmixed bank account (other than through such a clearing system) will not. However, it is not at present entirely clear whether legal proprietary claims are limited to physical substitutions (where, as in all the cases discussed in the previous paragraph, cash is withdrawn from one bank account and used to acquire some other asset, including a credit balance in another bank account) or also extend to other forms of transfer, such as an electronic transfer from one bank account to another where the funds have not had to pass through an inter-bank clearing system.

In *Agip (Africa) v. Jackson*,[55] the name of the payee on a payment order issued by the plaintiff was fraudulently altered and the sum in question was transferred by the plaintiff's bank in Tunis through its correspondent bank in New York and then, presumably through the New York clearing system, to an account at Lloyds Bank in London in the name of a shell English company controlled by the defendants, a firm of accountants from the Isle of Man. The

---

[52] [1921] 1 K.B. 321.
[53] Bankes and Atkin L.JJ. Scrutton L.J. held that the plaintiff was entitled only to trace in equity.
[54] Atkin L.J. went so far as to say that it was possible to trace at law even into a mixed fund. However, this view is generally regarded more as an expression of hope than as a statement of reality.
[55] [1990] Ch. 265.

plaintiff subsequently claimed to be entitled to trace this payment through the account of the shell company into an account of the defendants in the Isle of Man, to which it had subsequently been transferred. The shell company's account had contained no other funds at the relevant time so there would have been no difficulty about tracing the funds from that account to the account of the defendants. However, Millett J. held that the funds could not be traced at law into the account of the shell company. Given that the money had been transmitted by telegraphic transfer and had almost certainly passed through the New York clearing system:

> "nothing passed between Tunisia and London but a stream of electrons. It is not possible to treat the money received by Lloyds Bank in London or its correspondent bank in New York as representing the proceeds of the payment order or of any other physical asset previously in its hands and delivered by it in exchange for the money."[56]

Millett J. thus seems to have restricted legal proprietary claims to cases of physical substitutions; however, in the Court of Appeal,[57] Fox L.J., while affirming the judgment of Millett J., placed a greater emphasis on the clearing system limitation. The view of Millett J. was subsequently reiterated in *Bank Tejerat v. Hong Kong and Shanghai Building Corp.*,[58] where Tuckey J. refused a legal proprietary claim to funds which had been the subject of telex instructions.

These decisions emphasise the restrictions of proprietary claims at law. However, they do not necessarily mean that payments made by cheque can never be traced at law; indeed the decision in *Trustee of the Property of F.C. Jones & Sons (a Firm) v. Jones*,[59] where cheques were traced at law, suggests quite the opposite. Consequently, where both payer and payee have their accounts at the same branch, it will clearly be possible to trace the payment at law from one account to another and this will almost certainly also be possible where the accounts are at different branches of the same bank. However, it is obviously likely that the intervention of any inter-bank clearing system will cause the funds to lose their identity and be prevented from being traced at law despite the existence of the original cheque, simply because no funds may actually have been transferred from the payer's bank to the payee's bank on the day in question (this will depend on the overall balance of cleared transactions between the two banks on that day). Whether or not this is actually the case, these restrictions on legal proprietary claims are clearly highly inconvenient; however, the difficulties have been substantially alleviated by the intervention of equity.

---

[56] [1990] Ch. 265 at 286.
[57] [1991] Ch. 547.
[58] [1995] 1 Lloyd's Rep. 239.
[59] [1997] Ch. 159.

## IX. EQUITABLE PROPRIETARY CLAIMS

A person who seeks to assert an equitable proprietary claim will be relying on the existence of an equitable proprietary interest in the property in question which he will be endeavouring to enforce against the defendant. However, no such claim will be able to be made successfully against a defendant who is a bona fide purchaser for value of a legal estate in the property without notice of the interest of the claimant (or any statutory equivalent); such a person inevitably takes the property free of such an equitable proprietary interest. Nor should such a claim be able to be made successfully against any defendant who is able to invoke the recently recognised defence of change of position. There are also some further defences open only to innocent volunteers.

### 1. The Consequences of a Successful Equitable Proprietary Claim

The consequences of a successful equitable proprietary claim are normally that the defendant will thereafter be bound by the equitable interest of the claimant and will therefore be treated as a trustee of the property in question for him. This trust is often said to be a constructive trust; this expression is not inaccurate but it is potentially confusing.[60] It does not mean that the defendant will automatically be regarded as having been subject to all the obligations of a trustee from the moment when he originally received the property in question; that will only be the case if "liability for knowing receipt" is also imposed on him under the rules which were discussed in Chapter 10.[61] However, he will certainly be subject to such obligations thereafter and, if he does not comply with them, "liability for inconsistent dealing" will be imposed on him.[62] If the claimant is able to show that any particular item of property in the hands of the defendant is, in equity, either entirely his own property or entirely the product of his own property, then he will obviously be able to call for that property to be transferred to him.[63] If, on the other hand, he is able to show that any particular item of property in the hands of the defendant is only partially the product of his own property, then he will have an election between a lien or charge over it for the amount of his contribution to that property or, if it has gone up in value, for a beneficial interest in proportion to his contribution to it. This was specifically held by Lord Millett in *Foskett v. McKeown*.[64] In all cases, he will enjoy the rights appropriate to the holder of such an interest in the type of property in question.[65] In all cases, his equitable proprietary right will amount to as much of a right *in rem* as any other proprietary right, something which is of course dependant on that right being enforceable against the defendant in the first place.

However, treating the defendant as a trustee is not the only possible con-

---

[60] See Lord Millett, extra-judicially, (1998) 114 L.Q.R. 399.
[61] See *ante*, p. 370.
[62] See *ante*, p. 405. *Sheridan v. Joyce* [1844] 1 Jo. & Lat. 41 (Court of Chancery of Ireland).
[63] *Foskett v. McKeown* [2001] 1 A.C. 102 at 130, *per* Lord Millett, who went on to say that the claimant could instead "bring a personal claim against the trustee for breach of trust and enforce an equitable lien or charge on the proceeds to secure restoration of the trust fund".
[64] [2001] 1 A.C. 102 at 131.
[65] Thus if it is land he will enjoy the same rights as any other beneficiary under a trust of land (see Trusts of Land and Appointment of Trustees Act 1996).

sequence of a successful equitable proprietary claim. The claimant can alternatively be subrogated to rights which a third party has against the defendant. This happened in *Boscawen v. Bajwa*.[66] The Abbey National Building Society had agreed to make a mortgage advance to fund the purchase of a property belonging to the defendant. The purchasers' solicitors, who were as usual acting both for the building society and for the purchasers, transferred the amount advanced to the defendant's solicitors who used them to pay off the defendant's mortgage with the Halifax Building Society. However, although the defendant had executed an undated transfer in favour of the purchasers, a small outstanding balance of the price was never paid to him so this transfer was never dated or registered; the purchasers therefore never acquired legal title to the property. To make matters worse, the contract between the defendant and the purchasers did not comply with the necessary formalities[67] and so was void; consequently, the purchasers had never acquired any equitable interest in the property either. The Abbey National therefore had no valid mortgage over the defendant's property yet their money had been used to pay off his mortgage. Various creditors of the defendant then obtained a charging order over the property and sought an order for sale. The Abbey National was able to comply with the requirements for an equitable proprietary claim and was able to demonstrate that its funds had in fact been used to discharge the mortgage. The Court of Appeal said this:[68]

"If the plaintiff succeeds in tracing his property, whether in its original or in some changed form, into the hands of the defendant, and overcomes any defences which are put forward on the defendant's behalf, he is entitled to a remedy. The remedy will be fashioned to the circumstances. The plaintiff will generally be entitled to a personal remedy; if he seeks a proprietary remedy he must usually prove that the property to which he lays claim is still in the ownership of the defendant. If he succeeds in doing this the court will treat the defendant as holding the property on a constructive trust for the plaintiff and will order the defendant to transfer it in specie to the plaintiff. But this is only one of the proprietary remedies which are available to a court of equity. If the plaintiff's money has been applied by the defendant, for example, not in the acquisition of a landed property but in its improvement, then the court may treat the land as charged with the payment to the plaintiff of a sum representing the amount by which the value of the defendant's land has been enhanced by the use of the plaintiff's money. And if the plaintiff's money has been used to discharge a mortgage on the defendant's land, then the court may achieve a similar result by treating the land as subject to a charge by way of subrogation in favour of the plaintiff."

The Abbey National was therefore held to be entitled to be subrogated to the mortgage security of the Halifax which had been paid off with its money and therefore enjoyed priority over the plaintiffs' charging order. The facts of this

---

[66] [1996] 1 W.L.R. 328.
[67] For failure to comply with the Law of Property (Miscellaneous Provisions) Act 1989, s.2.
[68] [1996] 1 W.L.R. 328 at 334–335, *per* Millett L.J. In this passage, the references to the plaintiff are to the claimant in an equitable proprietary claim, not to the plaintiffs in *Boscawen v. Bajwa*.

case were very peculiar and it is not often that a claimant will need to have recourse to subrogation in order to enforce an equitable proprietary claim. However, there seems no reason why he should not be able to do so in the sort of circumstances which occurred in *Boscawen v. Bajwa*.

## 2. What are the Prerequisites of an Equitable Proprietary Claim?

### (A) An Equitable Proprietary Interest

It is hardly necessary to state that an equitable proprietary claim can only be pursued if the claimant has an equitable proprietary interest in the property in question Although it is generally said that a claimant is able to trace an equitable proprietary interest into its product only if he can point to the existence of a fiduciary relationship, the converse is not true. Thus the fact that funds have been deposited with a fiduciary agent pursuant to a contract of loan does not entitle the depositor to bring an equitable proprietary claim; he has retained no proprietary interest in the funds deposited.[69] Nor does an agent who is retained to collect rents or other moneys on behalf of his principal automatically become a trustee of them for the latter; this will only be the case if he did or should have segregated the sums.[70]

### (B) A Fiduciary Relationship

As has already been mentioned, it is generally said that a claimant is able to trace an equitable proprietary interest into its product only if he can point to the existence of a fiduciary relationship. In *Agip (Africa) v. Jackson*,[71] Millett J. held that:

"the only restriction on the ability of equity to follow assets is the requirement that there must be some fiduciary relationship which permits the assistance of equity to be invoked. The requirement has been widely condemned and depends on authority rather than principle."

Historically there was no such requirement. In *Re Hallett's Estate*,[72] the defendant solicitor sold bonds belonging partly to his own marriage settlement and partly to a client and mixed the proceeds with his own funds in a bank account. The beneficiaries of the marriage settlement could clearly point to the existence of a fiduciary relationship but the client was also permitted to maintain an equitable proprietary claim on the basis that she was the legal and beneficial owner of the property which she had deposited with the defendant. Similarly, in *Banque Belge pour l'Etranger v. Hambrouck*,[73] Scrutton L.J., who had doubted the availability of a legal proprietary claim, held that the plaintiff had an equitable proprietary claim and both the other members of the court stated that, had they not held the plaintiff to have a legal proprietary claim, they also would have permitted an equitable proprietary claim. None of the members of

---

[69] *Daly v. The Sydney Stock Exchange* (1986) 160 C.L.R. 371 (High Court of Australia).
[70] *Cohen v. Cohen* (1929) 42 C.L.R. 91 (High Court of Australia). However, any failure to segregate means that no priority will be able to be obtained unless the whereabouts of the funds can actually be established.
[71] [1990] Ch. 265.
[72] (1880) 13 Ch.D. 696. See [1975] C.L.P. 64.
[73] [1921] 1 K.B. 321.

the court stated any requirement for the existence of a fiduciary relationship as a prerequisite to an equitable proprietary claim. There is, of course, no doubt whatever that the necessary fiduciary relationship could have been found in both these cases had it been necessary. As Millett J. went on to say in *Agip (Africa) v. Jackson*, "the requirement may be circumvented since it is not necessary that the fund to be traced should have been the subject of fiduciary obligations before it got into the wrong hands; it is sufficient that the payment to the defendant itself gives rise to a fiduciary relationship." Both the defaulting solicitor in *Re Hallett's Estate* and the fraudulent employee in *Banque Belge pour l'Etranger v. Hambrouck* could undoubtedly have been held to be constructive trustees of, respectively, the proceeds of the bonds and the proceeds of the cheques. The significant fact is that none of the judges felt it necessary to look for and find such a fiduciary relationship.

However, it is generally thought that in *Re Diplock*,[74] the Court of Appeal interpreted the decision of the House of Lords in *Sinclair v. Brougham*[75] as establishing, in the words of Goulding J. in *Chase Manhattan Bank v. Israel-British Bank (London)*,[76] "that an initial fiduciary relationship is a necessary foundation of the equitable right of tracing". It is questionable both whether this was really the opinion of the Court of Appeal in *Re Diplock* and whether *Sinclair v. Brougham* imposed any such requirement. As will be seen later on, the actual decision reached in *Sinclair v. Brougham* itself has now been overruled by the House of Lords in *Westdeutsche Landesbank Girozentrale v. Islington L.B.C.*[77] However, the House did not consider the fiduciary relationship requirement, Lord Browne-Wilkinson merely saying the House "should not be taken to be casting any doubt on the principles of tracing as established in *Re Diplock*".[78]

In *Sinclair v. Brougham*,[79] the House of Lords had had to look for and find a fiduciary relationship, wrongfully as it has now been held, because that was the only way of establishing that the depositors in an *ultra vires* banking business had an equitable proprietary interest in the funds of the building society which had been running it. This does not, however, of itself necessarily mean that a fiduciary relationship is required where the claimant has a pre-existing equitable proprietary right. Indeed, in *Re Diplock*,[80] the Court of Appeal did no more than state that "equity may operate on the conscience not merely of those who acquire a legal title in breach of some trust, express or constructive, or of some other fiduciary obligation, but of volunteers provided that as a result of what has gone before some equitable proprietary interest has been created and attaches to the property in the hands of the volunteer." It is not obvious that this passage has the effect of requiring a fiduciary relationship where the claimant already has a pre-existing equitable proprietary

---

[74] [1948] Ch. 465.
[75] [1914] A.C. 398.
[76] [1981] Ch. 105.
[77] [1996] A.C. 669.
[78] *ibid.* at 714. This may well have been a reference to the mixed fund rules established in *Re Diplock* (see *post*, pp. 831–832) rather than to its supposed enunciation of a fiduciary relationship requirement.
[79] [1914] A.C. 398.
[80] [1948] Ch. 465 at 530.

interest. However, that is the way in which it has always been subsequently interpreted, both at first instance[81] and in the Court of Appeal.[82] Whether or not such a requirement exists is not purely a technical issue. Even though the courts have on occasions strained the concept of fiduciary relationship to its limits, if not well beyond them, in order to satisfy this requirement, an absolute legal and beneficial owner of property cannot possibly point to any such relationship and so, according to the present understanding of the law, is therefore apparently not entitled to maintain an equitable proprietary claim. Consequently, if the property of such a person is stolen and its product is mixed with other money in a bank account, the victim of the theft will prima facie not be entitled to maintain a proprietary claim either at law (because of the mixing) or in equity (because of the absence of a fiduciary relationship). This ridiculous anomaly could be rectified in any of the following ways.

1. The requirement for the existence of a fiduciary relationship could be abolished. A challenge to the existence of this requirement has often been advocated but is realistically only possible in the House of Lords. It is thought that the House of Lords would if necessary abolish this requirement but this certainly cannot be assumed.

2. The thief could be held to hold the stolen property on resulting trust for his victim, thus providing both the fiduciary relationship and the equitable proprietary interest necessary for an equitable proprietary claim. Such a conclusion was reached by the High Court of Australia in *Black v. S. Freeman & Co.,*[83] a decision which was cited with approval by Lord Templeman in *Lipkin Gorman v. Karpnale,*[84] although the House of Lords was not considering any equitable proprietary claim. The difficulty about this view is that, since a thief does not acquire title to the stolen property, it is not easy to see exactly what he would actually be holding on trust.

3. The thief could be held to hold the stolen property on constructive trust for his victim as a result of his fraudulent conduct, thus equally providing both the fiduciary relationship and the equitable proprietary interest necessary for an equitable proprietary claim. In *Westdeutsche Landesbank Girozentrale v. Islington L.B.C.*[85] Lord Browne-Wilkinson specifically envisaged this possibility and in *Twinsectra v. Yardley*[86] the Court of Appeal held that a constructive trust existed for this reason (this question was not considered on the subsequent

---

[81] In *Agip (Africa) v. Jackson* [1990] Ch. 265 and in *Box v. Barclays Bank* [1998] Lloyd's Rep. Bank. 185. In the latter case Ferris J. denied the plaintiffs an equitable proprietary claim specifically because there was no fiduciary relationship (they had deposited money with a person running an unlicensed deposit taking business, a transaction which was classified as creating nothing more than a debtor-creditor relationship).

[82] In *Aluminium Industrie Vaassen v. Romalpa Aluminium* [1976] 1 W.L.R. 676 and in *Agip (Africa) v. Jackson* [1991] Ch. 547.

[83] [1910] 12 C.L.R. 105.

[84] [1992] 2 A.C. 548.

[85] [1996] A.C. 669 at 715–716.

[86] [2000] W.T.L.R. 527 at 567–568.

appeal to the House of Lords).[87] While there is obviously not the slightest difficulty about imposing a constructive trust on this ground,[88] exactly the same difficulty arises as to what the thief would be holding on trust.

4.  Alternatively, the thief could be held to hold the stolen property on constructive trust for his victim as a result of his fraudulent conduct in the way just envisaged but if he steals money or if and when he turns other types of stolen property into money. Since money is the universal medium of exchange, it becomes his property and so can certainly become the subject matter of a trust without any of the difficulties referred to above (this argument was deployed in the House of Lords in *Twinsectra v. Yardley* in order to justify the conclusion reached by the Court of Appeal but in the event the House did not need to consider it).[89]

It is suggested that this fourth possibility should be adopted in appropriate circumstances unless and until the unnecessary requirement for a fiduciary relationship is abolished.

### 3. When will these Prerequisites be Satisfied?

**(A) Express Trusts**
It is obvious that these requirements will be satisfied where the person against whom the equitable proprietary claim is being brought is an express trustee of the property in question and it was held in *Re Diplock*[90] that these requirements will also be satisfied where the property in question was originally subject to an express trust, even though the equitable proprietary claim is in fact being brought against a subsequent holder of that property. This was the case in *Foskett v. McKeown*,[91] where funds had been provided by a number of potential purchasers of plots of land in Portugal and were held on express trust to be used to make the payments necessary to bring about a transfer of the plot in question to its purchaser or, in the event that this did not happen within two years, to be returned to that purchaser. Some of the funds were misappropriated and used to pay the premiums on a life insurance policy and the purchasers were held to be entitled to bring an equitable proprietary claim against the trustees of that policy.[92]

**(B) Resulting Trusts**
These requirements will equally be satisfied where the person against whom the equitable proprietary claim is being brought is a resulting trustee of any of the traditional types.[93] They will also be satisfied in the event that a resulting

---

[87] [2002] 2 A.C. 162.
[88] See *ante*, p. 410.
[89] Given that the House of Lords upheld the existence of a *Quistclose* trust, there was no need for any constructive trust and so the House did not hear argument on whether or not one had arisen.
[90] [1948] Ch. 465.
[91] [2001] 1 A.C. 102.
[92] *ibid.* at 108, *per* Lord Browne-Wilkinson.
[93] See *ante*, Chap. 9.

trust arises as a result of a transaction which is void or voidable; since the controversial question of whether any such trust can arise involves issues of both resulting and constructive trusts, it is considered below.

### (C) Constructive Trusts

These requirements will again be satisfied where, as in *Attorney-General for Hong Kong v. Reid*,[94] the person against whom the equitable proprietary claim is being brought has been held to be a constructive trustee of the property in question; this will clearly be the case even where, as in *Agip (Africa) v. Jackson*,[95] the property in question became subject to a constructive trust only as a result of an improper disposition of that property, if in other words, the act which has given rise to the equitable proprietary claim itself brought about the imposition of the constructive trust. They will also be satisfied in the event that a constructive trust arises as a result of a transaction which is void or voidable; for the reason stated above, this is considered below.

### (D) Void, Voidable or Mistaken Transactions

Whether these requirements are also satisfied in the case of transactions which are void, voidable, or mistaken is more controversial. It has on occasion been held, or stated, that the recipient of property transferred pursuant to such a transaction holds that property either on resulting trust or on constructive trust for the transferor, thus providing him with both the existing prerequisites of an equitable proprietary claim, namely an equitable proprietary interest and a fiduciary relationship.

Where a transfer of property is void *ab initio* for some reason such as illegality, mistake or lack of capacity of the transferor, no title will generally have passed to the transferee; in that case the transferor will not need any trust as a prerequisite of asserting his title. Only where title has nevertheless passed to the transferee because the property in question was or has subsequently been turned into money is a trust necessary. In such circumstances, a constructive trust will be imposed where the money has been obtained as the result of a crime[96] and as a result of fraud[97] or undue influence;[98] in this event, an equitable proprietary claim will obviously be available to the victim of the crime, fraud or undue influence.

However, neither a resulting trust nor a constructive trust can arise where title has passed to the transferee under a transaction which is within the capacity of the transferor but beyond the capacity of the transferee. A trust was held to arise in *Sinclair v. Brougham*,[99] which concerned the liquidation of a building society in the course of which it became apparent that a banking business which it had been running was in fact *ultra vires*. When a question of priorities arose as between the shareholders of the society and the depositors

---

[94] [1993] A.C. 713.
[95] [1990] Ch. 265; [1991] Ch. 547.
[96] See *ante*, p. 407.
[97] See *ante*, p. 410.
[98] See *ante*, p. 412.
[99] [1914] A.C. 398.

in the banking business,[1] a majority of the House of Lords[2] held that the depositors did indeed have an equitable proprietary interest arising under a trust. However, this decision was overruled by the majority of the House of Lords in *Westdeutsche Landesbank Girozentrale v. Islington L.B.C.*[3] The parties had entered into an interest rate swap agreement, under which each agreed to pay to the other during a period of five years at six-monthly intervals an amount calculated by reference to the interest which would have accrued over the previous six-monthly period on a notional principal sum, the interest rate being fixed in the case of the bank and floating in the case of the local authority. However, during the five year period, such agreements were held[4] to be *ultra vires* local authorities and consequently void. The bank sought to recover the sums which it had paid to the local authority. In the lower courts,[5] it succeeded both at common law under an action for money had and received and on the basis of an equitable proprietary claim in accordance with *Sinclair v. Brougham*. However, the House of Lords held that, where title has passed to the transferee under a transaction which is within the capacity of the transferor but beyond the capacity of the transferee, the transferor retains no equitable proprietary interest therein either under a resulting or a constructive trust. Consequently, the bank was not entitled to an equitable proprietary claim.[6]

Controversy therefore remains only in respect of transfers of property which are voidable. In *El Ajou v. Dollar Land Holdings*,[7] the plaintiff had been induced to purchase shares by fraudulent misrepresentations and was seeking to impose "liability for knowing receipt" on the defendant, into whose hands the purchase moneys had come for value but, as the Court of Appeal subsequently held,[8] with sufficient knowledge of the fraud for the imposition of such liability. Millett J. held that persons who had been induced by fraudulent misrepresentations to purchase shares were "entitled to rescind the transaction and revest the equitable title to the purchase money in themselves, at least to the extent necessary to support an equitable tracing claim", stating that "the trust which is operating in these cases is not some new model remedial constructive trust, but an old fashioned institutional resulting trust".[9] (The judge has confirmed this view extra-judicially,[10] stating that, "where the plaintiff pays away his money by a valid payment, fully intending to part with the beneficial interest to the recipient, but his intention is vitiated by some factor such as fraud, misrepresentation, mistake and so on ..., the beneficial interest

---

[1] Both had agreed that the outside creditors should be paid off first.
[2] Viscount Haldane L.C. and Lord Atkinson held that the trust in question was "a resulting trust, not of an active character", while Lord Parker of Waddington held that it was a constructive trust. Lord Sumner upheld the existence of a trust but did not indicate with which of these two views he agreed. Lord Dunedin reached the same result without recourse to an equitable proprietary claim.
[3] [1996] A.C. 669.
[4] By the House of Lords in *Hazell v. Hammersmith and Fulham L.B.C.* [1992] A.C. 1.
[5] [1994] 4 All E.R. 890 (Hobhouse J.), [1994] 1 W.L.R. 938 (Court of Appeal).
[6] Consequently the bank was not entitled to compound interest on the sum, which the local authority accepted in the House of Lords that it was liable to repay at common law with simple interest thereon.
[7] [1993] 3 All E.R. 717, affirmed by the Court of Appeal without discussion of this particular point [1994] 2 All E.R. 685. See *ante*, p. 393.
[8] [1994] 2 All E.R. 685, reversing Millett J. on this point.
[9] [1993] 3 All E.R. 717 at 734.
[10] 114 L.Q.R. (1998) 399 at 416.

passes, but the plaintiff has the right to elect whether to affirm the transaction or rescind it. If he elects to rescind it, it is usually assumed that the beneficial title revests in the plaintiff, and the authorities suggest that it does so retrospectively.") No equitable proprietary claim was being brought in this case and it is questionable whether the plaintiff should have been held entitled to follow his funds into the hands of the defendant,[11] even to the extent necessary to support the imposition of "liability for knowing receipt",[12] never mind to the extent necessary to support an equitable proprietary claim. But that fact does not of itself affect the validity of the proposition enunciated by Lord Millett.

Earlier, in *Chase Manhattan Bank v. Israel-British Bank (London)*,[13] the plaintiff New York bank had, as the result of a clerical error, made twice rather than once a payment of US$2,000,000 to another New York bank for the credit of the defendant London bank, which subsequently became insolvent. The plaintiff duly proved in the liquidation in respect of the second payment made under a mistake of fact but this gave no priority over the other creditors of the defendant. The plaintiff therefore also claimed to be entitled to an equitable proprietary claim against the defendant. The legal effects of the mistaken payment had to be determined in accordance with the law of the State of New York, where a payment under a mistake of fact of money which the payee cannot conscientiously withhold gives rise to the imposition of a constructive trust. Goulding J. held, rather unexpectedly, that this was "also in accord with the general principles of equity as applied in England".[14] He justified this conclusion on the grounds that "a person who pays money to another under a factual mistake retains an equitable property in it and the conscience of that other is subjected to a fiduciary duty to respect his proprietary right".[15] This decision seems highly questionable. It is not obvious how either an equitable proprietary interest or a fiduciary duty could conceivably have arisen as the result of a payment made through a third party bank intended to be in settlement of a commercial debt.

The decision in *Chase Manhattan Bank v. Israel-British Bank (London)* was expressly applied in the Court of Appeal of New Zealand in *Liggett v. Kensington*.[16] A gold dealer had offered its purchasers the option of leaving their bullion in its custody on their behalf as "non-allocated bullion". Purchasers who did so were issued with a certificate of ownership and were entitled to

---

[11] The victims' funds had, prior to their investment in the joint venture, been moved through several civil law jurisdictions which do not recognise the existence of trusts and at one point a substantial sum had been sent from Geneva to Panama, where it had disappeared for a short time prior to the reappearance of a roughly similar sum in Geneva. Millett J. held that the property could be traced despite the passage of the funds through the civil law jurisdictions and that, notwithstanding their brief disappearance in Panama, there was sufficient evidence to conclude that the victims' funds had indeed been used to make this investment. Although Millett J. indicated the contrary, no equitable proprietary claim could possibly have survived the disappearance of the funds in Panama and it is not easy to see how such a claim could have survived the passage of the funds through the civil law jurisdictions either.

[12] If, for the purposes of knowing receipt, actual receipt is indeed determined in the same way as in legal and equitable proprietary claims, then this case was wrongly decided. Nor does it seem appropriate that actual receipt should be determined in any different way for the purposes of knowing receipt.

[13] [1981] Ch. 105.

[14] *ibid.* at 118.

[15] *ibid.* at 119.

[16] [1993] 1 N.Z.L.R. 257.

take physical possession of their bullion on seven days' notice. The gold dealer subsequently became insolvent and the question arose as to whether these purchasers were entitled to an equitable proprietary claim in priority not only to its general creditors but also to a debenture holder. As has already been seen,[17] the majority of the Court of Appeal of New Zealand held that the gold dealer was in a fiduciary relationship with the purchasers, breach of which led to the imposition of a constructive trust and thus in turn to the purchasers having an equitable proprietary interest in the purchase moneys and their product, the remaining bullion. Cooke P., however, also held, applying *Chase Manhattan Bank v. Israel-British Bank (London)*, that the mistaken belief of the purchasers that they were acquiring gold, not merely contractual rights, meant that they had throughout retained an equitable proprietary interest in the purchase moneys. However, when this case reached the Privy Council under the name of *Re Goldcorp Exchange*,[18] this decision was reversed. Lord Mustill held that there was no fiduciary relationship between the gold dealer and the purchasers so that no equitable proprietary interest could arise in that way. Further, in relation to the claim based on the retention by the purchasers of an equitable proprietary interest in the purchase money, Lord Mustill held that, whether this claim was based on mistake, misrepresentation or a total failure of consideration, the purchasers had at no time sought to rescind their contracts with the gold dealer on any of these grounds but had, on the contrary, "throughout the proceedings asserted various forms of proprietary interest in the bullion, all of them derived in one way or another from the contracts of sale". This stance was "wholly inconsistent with the notion that the contracts were and are so ineffectual that the customers are entitled to get their money back".[19] This of course meant that the Board did not have to consider the validity of the principle enunciated by Goulding J. in *Chase Manhattan Bank v. Israel-British Bank (London)* but Lord Mustill[20] declined to express an opinion as to whether or not that case was correctly decided.

His clear doubts in this respect were confirmed by Lord Browne-Wilkinson in *Westdeutsche Landesbank Girozentale v. Islington L.B.C.*[21] who specifically held that he did not accept the reasoning of Goulding J. Lord Millett has also stated, extra-judicially,[22] that he considers that *Chase Manhattan Bank v. Israel-British Bank* was wrongly decided. Unfortunately, however, in *Westdeutsche Landesbank Girozentale v. Islington L.B.C.*, Lord Browne-Wilkinson went on to say that *Chase Manhattan Bank v. Israel-British Bank (London)* nevertheless "may well have been rightly decided" on the basis that "although the mere receipt of the moneys, in ignorance of the mistake, gives rise to no trust, the retention of the moneys after the recipient bank learned of the mistake may well have given rise to a constructive trust".[23] Lord Browne-Wilkinson did not specify the basis of the imposition of such a constructive trust but this would pre-

---

[17] See *ante*, pp. 334–336.
[18] [1995] 1 A.C. 74.
[19] *ibid.* at 102.
[20] *ibid.* at 103.
[21] [1996] A.C. 669 at 715.
[22] 114 L.Q.R. [1998] 399 at 412–413.
[23] *ibid.* at 715.

sumably have been a remedial constructive trust of the type which he envisaged later in his speech.[24]

All these issues arose in the Commercial Court in *Papamichael v. National Westminster Bank*.[25] The claimant's husband deposited 2 billion Greek drachmas of the claimant's money with the bank; it was, as intended by everyone involved, converted into dollars, producing about US$6.5 million. The claimant thought that the dollars had been placed on fixed-term deposit with the bank. However, unknown to her, her husband had fraudulently arranged for the dollars to be used as security for the operation by the bank of a foreign exchange margin account for his benefit. This account traded unsuccessfully and most of the dollars were lost. It was held that the claimant was entitled to the recovery of the 2 billion drachmas from the bank on the basis that she had been under a mistake of fact as to what would happen to that sum once it had been paid to the bank. However, because the drachma had depreciated by about 20 per cent as against the dollar during what she thought was the term of the fixed deposit, she was interested in recovering the US$6.5 million instead. This was only possible if the bank held the dollars on some form of trust for her, in which case the bank was potentially liable to account to the claimant for the whole of the dollars because it had dishonestly assisted in a breach of those trusts.[26]

A trust was held to arise (and so "liability for dishonest assistance" was duly imposed on the bank) for three different reasons, two of which are relevant for present purposes. The judge[27] held[28] that such a trust arose because the husband had obtained the dollars as a result of fraudulent conduct of which the bank was aware; in this respect, the judge held that Lord Millett's statement in *El Ajou v. Dollar Land Holdings*[29] that "the trust which is operating in these cases is ... an old fashioned institutional resulting trust"[30] was "all very well, but Lord Browne-Wilkinson was specific in saying [in *Westdeutsche Landesbank Girozentale v. Islington L.B.C.*] that what was being imposed was an institutional constructive trust not a resulting trust". He also held[31] that such a trust arose because the bank had received the dollars with knowledge of the claimant's mistake; in this respect, he relied on the explanation given by Lord Browne-Wilkinson of the decision in *Chase Manhattan Bank v. Israel-British Bank*, but to do so was, as a matter of precedent, clearly wrong because of the repeated statements in the Court of Appeal[32] that the remedial constructive trust does not form part of English law and that the contention that it should be adopted by English law can only be maintained in the House of Lords. The judge therefore proceeded on the basis that both these trusts were constructive trusts rather than resulting trusts. However, he gave the bank leave to appeal to the Court of Appeal.

---

[24] *ibid.* at 716. See *ante*, pp. 325–328.
[25] [2003] 1 Lloyd's Rep. 341.
[26] See *ante*, p. 374.
[27] Judge Chambers Q.C., sitting as a Judge of the Commercial Court.
[28] [2003] 1 Lloyd's Rep. 341 at p. 373.
[29] [1993] 3 All E.R. 717, affirmed by the Court of Appeal without discussion of this particular point [1994] 2 All E.R. 685. See *ante*, p. 393.
[30] [1993] 3 All E.R. 717 at 734.
[31] [2003] 1 Lloyd's Rep. 341 at 371.
[32] Most recently in *Twinsectra v. Yardley* [1999] Lloyd's Rep. Bank 438 and *Bank of Credit and Commerce International (Overseas) v. Akindele* [2001] Ch. 437.

For the moment, there is both some doubt about the proper classification of trusts which arise as a result of fraudulent conduct (although their classification does not, of course, affect the availability of an equitable proprietary claim in appropriate circumstances) and as to whether a trust arises at all where there has been a mistaken payment. In the latter respect, it is suggested that the view expressed extra-judicially by Lord Millett is correct and that *Chase Manhattan Bank v. Israel-British Bank (London)* was both wrongly reasoned and wrongly decided; if this is the case, an equitable proprietary claim will not be available to the transferor of property under a transaction which was mistaken but it would be optimistic to suggest that this conclusion represents the law at present. Further developments are inevitable, either when *Papamichael v. National Westminster Bank* reaches the Court of Appeal or when the House of Lords is called upon to decide, as it will undoubtedly have to do one day soon, "whether English law should follow the United States and Canada by adopting the remedial constructive trust".[33]

### 4. What Property can be the Subject Matter of an Equitable Proprietary Claim?

From its earliest days, equity has always been prepared to permit a beneficiary of a trust to enforce that trust against every transferee of the trust property save where the latter can show that he is a bona fide purchaser of a legal interest in that property for value without notice (or a statutory equivalent) or, today, can make out a defence of change of position. There seems no reason why such a claim should ever have been confined to the trust property in its original form for, otherwise, any alteration in the form of the trust property would have defeated the interests of the beneficiaries. Thus, equity was prepared to allow a beneficiary to trace the trust property into its product.[34] However, at this stage equity, like the common law, only permitted an equitable proprietary claim so long as the property or its product remained identifiable; consequently, the payment of the property or its product into a mixed fund was at this stage as fatal to an equitable proprietary claim as it was (and still is) to a legal proprietary claim. However, in 1852 in *Pennell v. Deffell*,[35] the Court of Appeal in Chancery held that the fact that property had become unidentifiable in a mixed fund was no bar to an equitable proprietary claim. The fact that it is thus possible to trace in equity property which has been mixed with the property of another has made equitable proprietary claims attractive to the suppliers of goods to manufacturers. They have sought, by means of what are known as retention of title clauses, to ensure that title to the goods which they have supplied does not pass to the manufacturers until the goods have been paid for. This has meant that the rules of tracing property in equity have had to be applied in a commercial context very different from the trust context in which they were originally developed.

### (A) Property in its Original Form
Where the claimant has an equitable proprietary interest in property which is

---

[33] These are the words of Lord Browne-Wilkinson in *Westdeutsche Landesbank Girozentale v. Islington L.B.C.* [1996] A.C. 669 at 716.
[34] See *Ryall v. Ryall* (1739) 1 Atk. 59 and the other authorities cited in [1975] C.L.P. 64.
[35] (1853) De M. & G. 372.

still in its original form, he will be able to follow that property into the hands of anyone except a bona fide purchaser of a legal interest in that property for value without notice (or a statutory equivalent) or, today, able to make out a defence of change of position. In such circumstances, the claimant will often be able to compel the holder of the legal title to bring a legal proprietary claim. Thus, if property is stolen from a trust, the trustee will have the right to trace that property at law and the beneficiary will have the right to trace that property in equity. In such circumstances, because of the absence of a defence of bona fide purchase for value without notice at law, the beneficiary will be better advised to compel the trustee to trace the property or its product at law. However, this will not be possible where, as in Re Diplock,[36] the trustee has himself disposed of the property in question since he will be estopped from bringing a legal proprietary claim by the principle of non-derogation from grant. Nor will it be possible where the claimant is seeking to follow the property into the hands of someone who has acquired the property by operation of law, such as personal representatives who have acquired the property as a result of the trustee's death or a trustee in bankruptcy who has acquired it as a result of his insolvency. Where it is thus not possible for the claimant to trace the property at law, or he chooses not to do so, he will nevertheless be able to follow it in equity and call for it to be transferred to him.

## (B) Property which is Identifiable Despite a Change of Form

Where the claimant has an equitable proprietary interest in property which is still identifiable despite a change in form, he will similarly often be able to compel the holder of the legal title to bring a legal proprietary claim. However, where this is not possible for one of the reasons stated above, or where the claimant chooses not to do so, he will be able to trace the property in equity. He will then be entitled to elect between calling for the property or its product to be transferred to him or taking a charge over that property to the extent of his contribution to its acquisition. This was stated by Jessel M.R. in Re Hallett's Estate[37] and was confirmed by the House of Lords in Foskett v. McKeown.[38]

Foskett v. McKeown[39] was a case where the change of form of the property was the result of a disposition of trust property in breach of trust. The deceased took out a life insurance policy for £1,000,000 and paid the first two annual premiums out of his own funds. However, subsequent annual premiums were paid in breach of trust[40] out of funds which were held on express trust for the claimants.[41] The deceased subsequently settled the life policy on trust for his mother and his children. Following the death of the deceased, the claimants wished to trace the premiums paid with their funds into the proceeds of the life policy and to recover from its trustees the proportion of those proceeds appropriate to the proportion of the premiums paid with their funds.

---

[36] [1948] Ch. 465.
[37] (1880) 13 Ch.D. 676 at 709.
[38] [2001] 1 A.C. 102 at 131, per Lord Millett.
[39] [2001] 1 A.C. 102.
[40] The fourth and fifth annual premiums were certainly so paid; the source of the funds which had paid the third annual premium awaited determination at trial.
[41] See ante, p. 812.

The Court of Appeal[42] held, by a majority, that their rights were limited to following their funds into the premiums which they had been used to pay and to recovering the amount of those premiums with interest. Scott V.-C. held[43] that the payment of the later premiums was more akin to an improvement of existing property and had not in fact improved that property because, in the event, the £1,000,000 would have been paid out whether or not the later premiums had been paid.[44] Hobhouse L.J. similarly held[45] that the payment of the later premiums had not benefited the mother and children and had not affected the latter's right to the proceeds. But the House of Lords, by a bare majority, preferred the approach manifested in the dissenting judgment of Morritt L.J.; they rejected the improvement analogy[46] and held that the payment of the later premiums had benefited the mother and children at the time when they had been paid[47] and that was all that mattered; the fact that with the benefit of hindsight their payment had been unnecessary was irrelevant.[48] Consequently, the claimants were held to be able to trace into the proceeds of the policy.

*Russell-Cooke Trust Company v. Prentis*[49] was a case where the property in its changed form was in the hands of a successor trustee. The defendant solicitors ran an investment scheme whereby clients placed funds in the firm's client account with a view to those funds being combined and invested in short term interest only loans secured against immovable property by way of registered first charges. Some of these charges were taken in the name of the firm which therefore held them on resulting trust for the investors. When The Law Society subsequently became suspicious about the honesty of the firm and intervened in its practice, the claimant trustee company was appointed trustee of these resulting trusts. The trust company sought the directions of the court by means of an application to which representative investors were joined as defendants and was directed to distribute the proceeds of the loans to the investors in proportion to their contributions to the sums lent. The principal issue in this litigation which is relevant for present purposes was the determination of which investors' funds had been invested in which loan but there was not the slightest doubt about the right of the investors to trace their funds into their product in the hands of the replacement trustee.

*Aluminium Industrie Vaassen v. Romalpa Aluminium*[50] was a case in which a claimant with the benefit of what is known as a retention of title clause chose not to exercise a legal proprietary claim. A company selling aluminium foil was, under the terms of the contract of sale, expressed to remain the owner of the foil until such time as the purchaser had paid the purchase price in full (it was also provided that the vendor would become owner of any new objects

---

[42] [1998] Ch. 265.
[43] *ibid.* p. 278.
[44] If no further premiums had been paid after the first two, the policy would have been converted into a paid up policy and the later premiums would, in effect, have been deducted from the sum assured.
[45] [1998] Ch. 265 at 291.
[46] [2001] 1 A.C. 102, *per* Lord Browne-Wilkinson at 110, *per* Lord Millett at 137.
[47] Because it was likely that the assured would live long enough for the later premiums to be required to preserve the cover.
[48] [2001] 1 A.C. 102, *per* Lord Browne-Wilkinson at 111, *per* Lord Millett at 139.
[49] [2003] 2 All E.R. 478.
[50] [1976] 1 W.L.R. 676.

made as a result of mixing the foil with other materials). This did not prevent
the purchaser from giving a good title to third parties but, as between vendor
and purchaser, the goods remained the property of the vendor. The purchaser
went into liquidation owing substantial sums in respect of unpaid foil. The
vendor claimed to be entitled to such foil as remained in the possession of the
purchaser and to the proceeds of sale of unmixed foil sold to third parties
which had been paid by them to the receiver and had been placed by him in a
separate bank account. Once it had been held that the terms of the contract
were indeed as has been stated (this was in fact disputed by the purchaser),
the vendor was clearly entitled to the foil which was still in the possession of
the purchaser (the nature of this claim was not discussed at all but the vendor,
as legal owner of the foil, was clearly entitled to recover this property at law).
However the vendor's claim to the proceeds of sale of the unmixed foil sold to
third parties was based on *Re Hallett's Estate*.[51] The Court of Appeal held that
the purchaser held the foil as a fiduciary agent of the vendor. Consequently,
the vendor was entitled to trace the foil in equity into its product, the proceeds
of sale.[52]

**(C) Property which is No Longer Identifiable Following a Change of Form**
It has already been seen that, where property is no longer identifiable following a change of form, this is usually because it or its product has been
turned into money and mixed with other money. In such circumstances, if the
mixed fund has subsequently remained intact, the claimant will clearly be
entitled to a lien or charge on the mixed fund for the amount of his property
and, presumably, in the event that any interest has been earned, to the part of
the interest earned in respect of his property. (In practice, however, it is likely
that sums will have been withdrawn from the mixed fund, in which case the
result appears to depend on whether the mixing was authorised or unauthorised. If it was authorised, the claimant will inevitably be entitled to the
appropriate proportion of the mixed fund or its product. If, on the other hand,
the mixing was unauthorised, it is necessary to have recourse to a series of
presumptions in order to establish whether such withdrawals have been made
from the mixed funds rateably or from one or more of its component parts.
These rules will be considered in detail later on.)
   In the same way, at least in principle, a claimant who can show that his
property has been mixed with other property to form a new object should be
entitled to trace his property in equity into its product, provided that he can
show the necessary fiduciary relationship. This has indeed been attempted in a
number of cases concerning retention of title clauses. If, as in *Aluminium
Industrie Vaassen v. Romalpa Aluminium*,[53] such a claimant can show both the

---

[51] (1880) 13 Ch.D. 696.
[52] Given that neither the foil nor its proceeds of sale had ever become unidentifiable by being
mixed with other property, there seems no reason why the vendor should not equally have been
able to trace the proceeds of sale at law. However, this decision establishes that a vendor with
the benefit of a retention of title clause will be able to recover the product of the property subject
to it by means of an equitable proprietary claim, provided that the necessary fiduciary relationship had been established (this has not been possible in a number of subsequent cases
concerning retention of title clauses and, consequently, the vendors have necessarily had to
trace at law; see *Clough Mill v. Martin* [1985] 1 W.L.R. 111 and *Hendy Lennox (Industrial Engines)
v. Grahame Puttick* [1984] 1 W.L.R. 485).
[53] [1976] 1 W.L.R. 676.

necessary fiduciary relationship and a clear intention that any such new objects should become the property of the vendor in whole or in part, such a claim should in principle be able to succeed (no such claim was in fact brought in that case but in *Bordon (U.K.) v. Scottish Timber Products*,[54] the formulation used was described as "presumably effective" for this purpose). However, for a variety of reasons, such claims as have been brought have been unsuccessful. It has sometimes[55] been held that the terms of the contract have not had the effect of giving the vendor any proprietary interest in the new object; it has sometimes[56] been held that there has been no sufficient fiduciary relationship; and it has sometimes[57] been held that any interest created in the new object amounts to a charge which should have been registered under what is now the Companies Act 1985[58] and in default is consequently void for non-registration.

## (1) Identifiability

A claim to trace property in equity into a mixed fund has traditionally presupposed that the claimant can actually identify his property or its product in that fund, if necessary with the aid of the various rules and presumptions as to withdrawals to which reference has already been made. Thus, in *Re Hallett's Estate*,[59] the Court of Appeal held that the priority given to the claimants was limited to the extent that they were able to identify the product of their property in the mixed fund. However, in recent years, there have been some indications that the courts may be prepared to relax this requirement of identifiability.

In *Space Investments v. Canadian Imperial Bank of Commerce Trust Company*,[60] the trust instrument authorised the trustee, a bank, to deposit trust funds with itself; it did so but subsequently went into liquidation. A person who deposits money with a bank necessarily makes the bank absolute legal and beneficial owner thereof; were this not the case, the bank would have considerable difficulty in earning the interest payable to the depositor since it would be unable to utilise the funds other than in accordance with the relevant rules governing trust investments and would certainly not be able to use the funds to make unsecured loans. The Privy Council[61] therefore held that, since the mixing of the trust funds with the trustee's own funds had been entirely lawful, the beneficiaries had retained no proprietary interest in the funds deposited and so could not bring an equitable proprietary claim; they were therefore no more than general creditors of the bank. However, Lord Templeman emphasised that, if the mixing had been carried out without such an express authorisation, it would have been unlawful. In such circumstances, he stated that the beneficiaries would have been allowed "to trace the trust money to all the assets of the bank and to recover the trust money by an equitable charge over all the

---

[54] [1981] Ch. 25.
[55] In *Borden (U.K.) v. Scottish Timber Products* [1981] Ch. 25 and *Re Peachdart* [1984] Ch. 131.
[56] In *Re Bond Worth* [1980] Ch. 228; *Re Andrabell* [1984] 3 All E.R. 407; *Hendy Lennox (Industrial Engines) v. Grahame Puttick* [1984] 1 W.L.R. 485.
[57] In *Re Bond Worth* [1980] Ch. 228; *Re Peachdart* [1984] Ch. 131; *Re Weldtech Equipment* [1991] B.C.C. 16; *Compaq Computer v. Abercorn Group* [1991] B.C.C. 484.
[58] Companies Act 1985, ss.395–404.
[59] (1880) 13 Ch.D. 696.
[60] [1986] 1 W.L.R. 1072.
[61] On an appeal from the Court of Appeal of The Bahamas.

assets of the bank".[62] In this hypothetical situation, it is inconceivable that the trust would have been able to identify its own funds within the general assets of the bank. Consequently, if the trust would indeed have been entitled to trace, then the rights to persons entitled to trace property in equity into a mixed fund are considerably wider than has previously been held. Giving such a claimant an equitable charge over all the assets of the bank converts him to all intents and purposes into a debenture holder since he obtains priority over the general creditors even in respect of assets which were not the product of the mixed fund. This seems wholly unfair to the general creditors.[63]

Lord Templeman's remarks have been considered in two decisions concerning payments into funds which subsequently became overdrawn, something which has traditionally been fatal to the right to trace in equity. In *Re Goldcorp Exchange*,[64] the Court of Appeal of New Zealand[65] applied Lord Templeman's remarks to this situation but the Privy Council, having held that the purchasers had no equitable proprietary interest at all, did not need to consider them. Lord Mustill, having referred with approval to the traditional rule, expressed the view that "the law relating to the creation and tracing of equitable proprietary interests is still in a state of development";[66] however, he concluded that it was not "necessary or appropriate to consider the scope and ambit of the observations in *Space Investments* or their application to trustees other than bank trustees".[67] A similar approach was taken by the Court of Appeal in *Bishopsgate Investment Management v. Homan*,[68] where it was argued that the traditional rule should, on the strength of Lord Templeman's remarks, be overruled. The Court of Appeal rejected this argument, classifying the remarks as dicta, and holding that their extension to this situation had been rejected in *Re Goldcorp Exchange*; the traditional rule was therefore applied. In neither of these two decisions was a view expressed as to the situation specifically envisaged by Lord Templeman, where a bank trustee has unlawfully deposited with itself trust funds which can no longer be identified. However, the reliance placed in both cases on the traditional rules governing mixed funds suggests that these rules are likely to be followed in preference to the view expressed by Lord Templeman. It is hoped that this proves to be the case.

## (2) Authorised mixing
In the relatively unlikely situation where the mixing of trust property with the property of another has been specifically authorised by the trust instrument and the mixing occurs in precisely the manner envisaged, then the beneficiaries will inevitably be entitled to the appropriate proportion of the mixed fund. This somewhat obvious proposition does not appear to have been the subject of any English authority but was upheld in New South Wales in *Hagan*

---

[62] [1986] 1 W.L.R. 1072 at 1074.
[63] See Goode (1987) 103 L.Q.R. 433. An equally unorthodox, but this time excessively narrow, view of equitable tracing claims of this type was taken in *Re Att.-Gen.'s Reference (No.1) 1985* [1986] Q.B. 491. However, this view was based on *Lister & Co. v. Stubbs* (1890) 45 Ch.D. 1 and therefore presumably cannot survive the criticism of that decision by the Privy Council in *Att.-Gen. for Hong Kong v. Reid* [1994] 1 A.C. 324, see *ante*, p. 344.
[64] [1995] 1 A.C. 74. Lord Templeman was a member of the Board.
[65] [1993] 1 N.Z.L.R. 257.
[66] [1995] 1 A.C. 74 at 109.
[67] *ibid.* at 110.
[68] [1995] Ch. 211.

*v. Waterhouse.*[69] Following the death of their father, three brothers carried on the family bookmaking business as general partners. One having died, the other two, who were his executors and trustees, continued the partnership business and therefore necessarily mixed the assets of the estate with their own. Kearney J. held that this mixing had been authorised by the terms of the will and that, quite irrespective of the presumptions which apply where mixing is unauthorised, the estate was therefore entitled to a one-third interest in the income of the bookmaking business and the substantial investments which it had been used to purchased.

### (3) Unauthorised mixing

It is much more likely that any mixing which has occurred will have been unauthorised, either because it was not authorised at all or because it has not been carried out in the manner envisaged. Where this occurs and sums have subsequently been withdrawn from the mixed fund, it has traditionally been necessary to have recourse to a series of presumptions in order to establish whether such withdrawals have been made from the mixed funds rateably or from one or more of its component parts; the presumptions differ depending on whether the mixed fund consists of funds of the claimant and funds of a fiduciary, of funds of two claimants both entitled to trace in equity into the mixed fund, or of funds of the claimant and funds of an innocent volunteer (it is obviously also possible for a mixed fund to consist of the funds of two claimants and the funds of a fiduciary or of the funds of two claimants and the funds of an innocent volunteer; in these circumstances, the situation is resolved by treating the two claimants as one and ascertaining first what they together can recover out of the mixed fund and then what part of this sum can be recovered by each individual claimant).

### (a) Unauthorised mixing of funds of the claimant and funds of a fiduciary.

The traditional rules governing tracing into an unauthorised mixed fund consisting of funds of the claimant and funds of a fiduciary are based on the decision of the Court of Appeal in *Re Hallett's Estate.*[70] The defendant solicitor sold bonds belonging partly to his own marriage settlement and partly to a client and mixed the proceeds with his own funds in a bank account. Subsequently, he made various withdrawals from the mixed fund, which on his death was insufficient to satisfy all the claims thereon. The Court of Appeal, having held unanimously that both the beneficiaries and the client were entitled to bring equitable proprietary claims,[71] held by a majority,[72] that

---

[69] (1991) 34 N.S.W.L.R. 308.
[70] (1880) 13 Ch.D. 696.
[71] See *ante*, p. 809.
[72] Thesiger L.J. dissented, holding that payments out of the mixed fund should, in accordance with the decision of the Court of Appeal in Chancery in *Pennell v. Deffell* (1853) De M. & G. 372, be governed by the Rule in *Clayton's Case* (*Devaynes v. Noble, Clayton's Case* (1816) 1 Mer. 572); (see *post*, p. 828).

the funds drawn out must be debited to Hallett's share of the mixed fund on the basis that, where a man does an act which may be rightfully performed, he cannot be heard to say that that act was intentionally and in fact done wrongfully. The balance left in the mixed fund was sufficient to satisfy both claims so that it was not necessary to decide any question of priorities as between them.[73] The presumption, therefore, is that a fiduciary draws his own funds out first and so any balance left in the mixed fund represents the property of the claimant. His claim to that balance is of course limited to the amount of his funds which were originally mixed (together with, presumably, any interest which has been earned in respect of the part of the funds which is his property). This principle is not limited to funds but also extends to other assets which are mixed such as shares.

However, the claimant cannot normally assert a proprietary claim to further sums or property which become part of the mixed assets after the original mixing. In *James Roscoe (Bolton) v. Winder*,[74] the balance of the mixed fund fell to £25 as a result of repeated dissipation by the fiduciary. However, at his death the fund contained a balance of £358. Sarjant J. held the beneficiaries entitled to trace only £25; the sums which had been paid in after the balance feel to that amount went to the general creditors, with whom the beneficiaries could of course prove for the residue of their claim. This conclusion was approved and applied both by the Privy Council in *Re Goldcorp Exchange*[75] and by the Court of Appeal in *Bishopsgate Investment Management v. Homan*,[76] both of which concerned mixed funds which subsequently became overdrawn, thus barring any equitable proprietary claim completely. However, in the latter case, Dillon L.J.,[77] but not Leggatt L.J.,[78] was prepared to envisage the possibility of tracing funds through an overdrawn account where misappropriated funds are paid into the account in order to reduce the overdraft and so make finance available within the overdraft limits for the purchase of some particular asset. Provided that the link between the reduction of the overdraft and this subsequent purchase can be genuinely established, there seems no reason why this limited modification of the basic rule should not be adopted.

If the balance of the mixed fund is insufficient fully to discharge the liability of the fiduciary to the claimant, the latter can nevertheless trace the withdrawals into any identifiable product of the mixed fund and claim an equitable charge over that product. In *Re Oatway*,[79] a trustee, having mixed the trust money with his own, first withdrew sums which he invested and later withdrew and dissipated the remainder. His trustee in bankruptcy suggested that, according to *Re Hallett's Estate*, what he had first withdrawn was his own money; consequently, the investments belonged to him and it was the trust money which had been dissipated. This unmeritorious claim was predictably rejected; Joyce J. held that the beneficiaries were entitled to the investments on

---

[73] Had this not been the case, priorities as between the two claimants would have been determined by the Rule in *Clayton's Case* (see *post*, p. 828), as had indeed been held by Fry J. at first instance.
[74] [1915] 1 Ch. 62.
[75] [1995] 1 A.C. 74.
[76] [1995] Ch. 211.
[77] *ibid.* at 216–217.
[78] *ibid.* at 222.
[79] [1903] 2 Ch. 356.

the basis that their claim must be satisfied from any identifiable part of the mixed fund or its product before the trustee could assert any claim thereto.

In *Bishopsgate Investment Management v. Homan*,[80] Dillon L.J. was also prepared[81] to countenance the possibility of what Vinelott J. at first instance had called "backwards tracing". This novel concept envisages a situation where a fiduciary acquires an asset with borrowed money and it can be inferred that the borrowing was subsequently repaid by funds misappropriated from the claimant; in such circumstances, the claimant can apparently recover the asset even though it was acquired prior to the misappropriation in question. However, this seems contrary to the nature of proprietary claims; indeed Leggatt L.J. explicitly rejected "backwards tracing", holding that "there can be no equitable remedy against an asset acquired before misappropriation of money takes place, since *ex hypothesi* it cannot be followed into something which existed and so had been acquired before the money was received and therefore without its aid".[82] This view seems preferable. Indeed it was approved by two of the members of the Court of Appeal in *Foskett v. McKeown*,[83] however, the third member of the court[84] wished "to make it clear that I regard the point as still open and, in particular, that I do not regard the fact that an asset is paid for out of borrowed money with the borrowing subsequently repaid out of trust money as being necessarily fatal to an equitable tracing claim by the trust beneficiaries". The point was not considered on the subsequent appeal to the House of Lords so the availability of "backwards tracing" therefore clearly still awaits definitive resolution.

The precise scope of this right to trace the withdrawals from the mixed fund into their product was for long not entirely clear. In *Re Hallett's Estate*,[85] Jessel M.R. stated that, where a claimant was seeking to trace into property which was the product of a mixed fund containing funds of the claimant and funds of a fiduciary, the only remedy available to him was to take a charge over that property for the amount of his property which was laid out in its acquisition. On this basis, the claimant's right to trace was limited to his original contribution to the purchase price of the property and did not extend to any increase in its value. This view was followed[86] but different views were also

---

[80] [1995] Ch. 211.

[81] *ibid.* at 216–217.

[82] *ibid.* at 221.

[83] [1998] Ch. 265, *per* Hobhouse L.J. (one of the majority on the main issue) at 289, *per* Morritt L.J. (dissenting on the main issue) at 296. This was an appeal against an order for summary judgment so it was not possible to reach a conclusion on whether the facts necessary to give rise to the possibility of "backwards tracing" had actually occurred.

[84] Scott V.-C. (the other member of the majority on the main issue) at 283–284. Scott V.-C. referred to Smith [1995] C.L.J. 290, who is in favour not just of "backwards tracing" but of general tracing into the payment of a debt.

[85] (1880) 13 Ch.D. 696 at 709.

[86] In *Re Oatway* [1903] 2 Ch. 356.

expressed[87] which have now been definitively upheld by the House of Lords. In *Foskett v. McKeown*,[88] Lord Millett said:

"Accordingly, I would state the basic rule as follows. where a trustee wrongfully uses trust money to provide part of the costs of acquiring an asset, the beneficiary is entitled *at his option* either to claim a proportionate share of the asset or to enforce a lien upon it to secure his personal claim against the trustee for the amount of the misapplied money. It does not matter whether the trustee mixed the trust money with his own in a single fund before using it to acquire the asset, or made separate payments (whether simultaneously or sequentially) out of the differently owned funds to acquire a single asset."

The claimant therefore now clearly has a choice between taking a charge on the property for the amount of his funds which were invested in that property (which will be to his advantage if its value has fallen) or claiming an interest in the property in proportion to his contribution to its purchase (which will be to his advantage if its value has risen).

A further question, on which there is no direct authority, is whether a claimant can elect to recover an asset which is the product of the mixed fund rather than taking any balance of the mixed fund to which he is entitled. It will be of interest for him so to do if that asset has increased in value or if any part of the mixed fund to which he is *prima facie* entitled has subsequently been invested in some other asset which has fallen in value. This situation has never arisen in any of the authorities since in no case have there been both a credit balance in the mixed fund and assets purchased with funds withdrawn from it. However, the observations of all the judges, particularly those of Jessel M.R. in *Re Hallett's Estate*, indicate the mixed fund as the recourse primarily available to the claimant. The interests of the claimant and of the general creditors of the fiduciary are very evenly balanced where any part of the mixed fund to which the claimant is *prima facie* entitled has subsequently been invested in some other asset which has fallen in value. However, on the grounds of simplicity and consistency, it is suggested that the claimant must take any balance of the mixed fund to which he is entitled before proceeding to follow the withdrawals from the mixed fund into their product.

Finally, it must be emphasised that all the rules which have been discussed

---

[87] In *Re Tilley's Will Trusts* [1967] Ch. 1179 at 1189 where Ungoed-Thomas J. regarded as good law a concession that, where property is the product of a mixed fund, the claimant has the right to "require the asset to be treated as trust property with regard to that proportion of it which the trust moneys contributed to its purchase". However, on the facts, he held that trust funds which an executrix who was also tenant for life had paid into her own bank account and used as part payment for two houses had not in fact been invested in those two properties since the use by the tenant for life of the estate's funds had merely prevented her from having to use more extensive overdraft facilities, which were clearly available to her; hence the remaindermen were entitled only to the funds of the estate which had been mixed together with interest thereon. It is questionable whether it should in fact be open to a fiduciary who has committed a clear breach of trust by mixing trust funds with his own successfully to contend that any profits so made were not actually due to the use of the trust funds; while *Re Tilley's Will Trusts* clearly establishes that such a contention is possible, the opposite view has been taken in other jurisdictions (in Australia in *Scott v. Scott* (1963) 36 A.L.J.R. 345 and in the United States of America in *Primeau v. Granfield* (1911) 184 Fed. 480).

[88] [2001] 1 A.C. 102 at 131.

are no more than presumptions. Consequently, these presumptions can be rebutted in any given case if either the claimant or the fiduciary is able to establish to the satisfaction of the court that any particular withdrawal was intended to be made from some specific part of the mixed fund or that any subsequent payment back into the mixed fund was intended to replace a previous withdrawal.

**(b) Unauthorised mixing of funds of two claimants**. Where an unauthorised mixed fund consists of the funds of two claimants, both of whom are entitled to trace in equity into the mixed fund, withdrawals from the mixed fund are presumed to be made rateably from the funds held by each claimant. Since each claimant necessarily has an equitable proprietary interest in his part of the funds which have been mixed, the attribution of profits and losses rateably between them is entirely in accordance with principle. However, in the event that the mixed fund in question is an active unbroken bank account (the only relevant example is a current, but not a deposit, account), then the presumption that withdrawals from the mixed fund are presumed to be made rateably is displaced by a principle enunciated by Grant M.R. in *Devaynes v. Noble, Clayton's Case*,[89] which is generally known as the Rule in *Clayton's Case*. In such an account,

> "there is no room for any other appropriation than that which arises from the order in which the receipts and payments take place, and are carried into the account. Presumably, it is the sum first paid in, that is first drawn out. It is the first item on the debit side of the account, that is discharged, or reduced, by the first item on the credit side. The appropriation is made by the very act of setting the two items against each other. Upon that principle, all accounts current are settled, and particularly cash accounts."[90]

*Devaynes v. Noble* did not concern a tracing claim but rather a question as to the appropriation of payments. The Rule in *Clayton's Case* was, however, applied to equitable tracing claims in the first case in which tracing was permitted in equity into a mixed fund, *Pennell v. Deffell*[91] in 1852. As has already been seen, the Court of Appeal decided by a majority in *Re Hallett's Estate*[92] that the Rule should no longer apply to mixed funds containing funds of a claimant and funds of a fiduciary. However, had any question of priorities between the two claimants in *Re Hallett's Estate* had to be determined, there is no doubt that the Rule in *Clayton's Case* would have been applied for this purpose, as it had indeed been applied by Fry J. at first instance; this was expressly recognised by

---

[89] (1817) 1 Mer. 572.
[90] *ibid.* at 608–609.
[91] (1853) De M. & G. 372.
[92] (1880) 13 Ch.D. 696.

all three members of the court.[93] The same conclusion was reached in *Hancock v. Smith*.[94]

However, the Rule in *Clayton's Case* is no longer automatically applied. In *Barlow Clowes International v. Vaughan*,[95] Woolf L.J. said that there were three possible solutions: apart from applying the Rule in *Clayton's Case*, these were: "the rolling charge or North American solution ... [which] involves treating credits to a bank account made at different times and from different sources as a blend or cocktail with the result that when a withdrawal is made from the account it is treated as a withdrawal in the same proportions as the different interests in the account ... bear to each other at the moment before the withdrawal is made";[96] and "the *pari passu ex post facto* solution ... [which] involves establishing the total quantum of the assets available and sharing them on a proportionate basis among all the investors who could be said to have contributed to the acquisition of those assets, ignoring the dates on which they made their investment".[97]

The Court of Appeal nevertheless confirmed that the Rule in *Clayton's Case* provided a convenient method of determining competing claims where the funds of several beneficiaries had been blended in one account and there was a deficiency or where there had been a wrongful mixing of different sums of trust money in a single account. However, they held that, where its application would be impracticable or would result in injustice between the investors, because a relatively small number of investors would obtain most of the funds, or would be contrary to the express or implied intention of the investors, the rule would not be applied if a preferable alternative method of distribution was available. The case concerned the rights of the various subscribers to a collective investment scheme, under which their money would be mixed together and invested through a common fund, to the assets which remained available for distribution. The Court of Appeal held that, because of the shared misfortunes of these investors, they would be presumed not to have intended the Rule in *Clayton's Case* to apply and the court should therefore adopt whichever of the possible alternatives was more satisfactory; because of the complications of applying the North American solution, the *pari passu ex post facto* solution was therefore applied.

Subsequently, in *Russell-Cooke Trust Company v. Prentis*,[98] Lindsay J. restricted the application of the Rule in *Clayton's Case* still further. As has already been seen,[99] this case concerned an investment scheme whereby clients placed funds in a solicitor's client account with a view to those funds being combined and invested in short term interest only loans secured against immovable property by way of registered first charges. When The Law Society subsequently intervened, some of the clients' funds had not yet been invested and

---

[93] Jessel M.R. and Baggallay L.J., who had held that the Rule in *Clayton's Case* did not apply to a mixed fund consisting of funds of a claimant and funds of a fiduciary, agreed with Thesiger L.J., who had taken the opposite view, that the Rule in *Clayton's Case* clearly applied to mixed funds consisting of funds of two claimants.

[94] (1889) 41 Ch.D. 456, per Lord Halsbury L.C. and Cotton L.J. (Fry L.J. did not deal with the point).

[95] [1992] 4 All E.R. 22.

[96] *ibid.* at 35.

[97] *ibid.* at 36.

[98] [2003] 2 All E.R. 478.

[99] See *ante*, p. 820.

so were still in the client account; however, this account contained insufficient to repay all the funds in full.[1] All three possible solutions were put before the court. Lindsay J. held[2] that the Rule in *Clayton's Case* "can be displaced by even a slight counterweight. Indeed, in terms of its actual application between beneficiaries who have in any sense met a shared misfortune, it might be more accurate to refer to the exception that is, rather than the rule, in *Clayton's Case*." He went on to hold that the prime reason to apply the North American solution falls away when *Clayton's Case* is not being applied in any event. He therefore adopted the pari passu ex post facto solution on the basis that it is "the system least unfairly distributing loss on an account that should have been dealt with in accordance with" the rules governing solicitors' client accounts.

Consequently, although *Barlow Clowes International v. Vaughan*[3] clearly did not affect the prima facie applicability of the Rule in *Clayton's Case* to mixed funds consisting of the funds of a small number of claimants,[4] *Russell-Cooke Trust Company v. Prentis*[5] is likely to prevent the Rule applying whenever the mixed fund has fallen in value as the result of unprofitable investment or dissipation simply because the beneficiaries will have "met a shared misfortune". It also seems to follow from that decision that in such circumstances the *pari passu ex post facto* solution will virtually always be applied. This development is most welcome and it is to be hoped that the Rule in *Clayton's Case* will one day also be effectively abrogated in the relatively unlikely situation where a mixed fund of this type has made a profit.[6]

---

[1] Funds of different clients in the same client account are not treated as mixed funds because they have to be dealt with according to the strict rules governing solicitors' client accounts. However, when there is a shortfall as a result of non-compliance with those rules, the funds necessarily have to be treated as mixed funds.

[2] [2003] 2 All E.R. 478 at 495.

[3] [1992] 4 All E.R. 22.

[4] This was despite the fact that its applicability in this situation is just as capable of enabling a relatively small number of investors to obtain most of the funds as when it is applied to common funds in collective investment schemes. Suppose that a trustee mixes the funds of two trusts in a current banking account, paying in £2,000 of the funds of Trust A on one day and £1,000 of the funds of Trust B on the following day. If on the third day he withdraws £2,000 from the mixed fund and invests it in securities, those securities will have been purchased entirely with the funds of Trust A. If on the fourth day he withdraws £700 from the mixed fund and loses this sum gambling at a casino, the entire loss will fall on Trust B, whose only right will be to the £300 left in the account. (Were, on the other hand, the mixed fund a deposit account, both profits and losses would be shared rateably; Trust A and Trust B would respectively be entitled to two-thirds and one-third of the securities and £200 and £100 of the balance of the mixed fund.) It is not obvious why this result is any more absurd than it would have been to have permitted the later investors in a collective investment scheme to have recovered almost all their investment and the earlier investors to have recovered almost none of theirs (the consequence of the application of the Rule in *Clayton's Case* which induced the Court of Appeal to find the implied intention necessary to displace it in *Barlow Clowes International v. Vaughan*).

[5] [2003] 2 All E.R. 478.

[6] There has been no reported case in which this has ever happened but examiners like questions in which the first withdrawal from the mixed fund referred to in the example above is invested in a painting which turns out to be an "Old Master" worth many times the sum paid for it while the second withdrawal is still dissipated. It is not immediately obvious that this can be described as "shared misfortune" and, if it cannot, in such circumstances the Rule in *Clayton's Case* would appear to be applicable so that Trust A makes an enormous profit while Trust B still bears all the loss. And where Trust A's investment made an enormous profit while Trust B's investment produced a more normal one or broke even, there could not really be said to have been any misfortune at all.

(c) **Unauthorised mixing of funds of the claimant and funds of an innocent volunteer.** Where an unauthorised mixed fund consists of the funds of a claimant and the funds of an innocent volunteer, withdrawals from the mixed fund are presumed to be made in exactly the same way as withdrawals from a mixed fund consisting of the funds of two claimants. In other words, withdrawals are presumed to be made rateably unless the mixed fund in question is an active unbroken bank account; in that case the Rule in *Clayton's Case* has been held to apply[7] but it is now probable that one of the other two solutions reviewed in *Barlow Clowes International v. Vaughan*[8] and *Russell-Cooke Trust Company v. Prentis*[9] will be applied instead.

However, while the basic attribution of profits and losses rateably is entirely in accordance with principle in the case of a mixed fund consisting of the funds of two claimants who both have equitable proprietary interests, it is highly questionable in the case of a mixed fund consisting of the funds of a claimant and the funds of an innocent volunteer. The claimant necessarily has an equitable proprietary interest in the mixed fund; if he did not, he would not be entitled to trace in equity. How can an innocent volunteer resist a claim by the holder of an equitable proprietary interest to recover his property? What defence, other than the defence of change of position, can an innocent volunteer possibly have to an equitable proprietary claim? In principle, the claimant should be able to recover his funds in full out of the mixed fund quite irrelevant of what withdrawals have been made from that fund by the innocent volunteer.

However, this is clearly not the law. In *Re Diplock*,[10] Lord Greene M.R. held that the positions of the claimant and the innocent volunteer were equivalent.

"This burden on the conscience of the volunteer is not such as to compel him to treat the claim of the equitable owner as paramount. That would be to treat the volunteer as strictly as if he himself stood in a fiduciary relationship to the equitable owner which ex hypothesi he does not. The volunteer is under no greater duty of conscience to recognise the interest of the equitable owner than that which lies upon a person having an equitable interest in one of two trust funds of 'money' which have become mixed towards the equitable owner of the other. Such a person is not in conscience bound to give precedence to the equitable owner of the other of the two funds."

He therefore relied on *Sinclair v. Brougham*[11] as authority for the attribution of profits and losses rateably in mixed funds consisting of funds of a claimant and funds of an innocent volunteer. However, the analogy with *Sinclair v. Brougham* (which has now of course been overruled anyway)[12] is in fact unsound. The House of Lords indeed held that the shareholders and the depositors in the ultra vires banking business should share the remaining assets rateably but the depositors were held to be entitled to trace in equity by

---

[7] *Re Diplock* [1948] Ch. 465 (in respect of the claim against the National Institute for the Deaf).
[8] [1992] 4 All E.R. 22.
[9] [2003] 2 All E.R. 478.
[10] *ibid.* at 524.
[11] [1914] A.C. 398.
[12] By the House of Lords in *Westdeutsche Landesbank Girozentrale v. Islington L.B.C.* [1996] A.C. 669.

virtue of the existence of a trust in their favour. Therefore both they and the shareholders in fact had proprietary interests. This was not the case in *Re Diplock*, where only the claimants had an equitable proprietary interest.

It is of course highly unlikely, given the decision in *Re Diplock*, that an innocent volunteer will ever be held liable for the whole of the losses suffered by a mixed fund. It seems generally to be accepted that, subject to the effect of the possible operation of the Rule in *Clayton's Case*, at present losses should be attributed rateably between the claimant and the innocent volunteer. Profits are also attributed rateably at present, subject to the defence of change of position, which operates in an exceptionally favourable way in favour of an innocent volunteer. As will be seen later on, both these propositions are demonstrated by the decision of the Court of Appeal in *Foskett v. McKeown*[13] (the point did not arise in the House of Lords).[14] However, prior to this decision it had been suggested that, provided that the claimant was in a position to recover his original contribution to the mixed fund in full by means of a charge on the mixed fund or on the property which constituted its product, the innocent volunteer should be entitled to retain the benefit of any improvements which he had made or profits which he had obtained.[15] This suggestion is now unlikely to be taken up; what is surprising is the fact that it was ever made — depriving the holder of an equitable proprietary interest of profits while retaining his rateable liability for losses does not seem very consistent with the nature of an equitable proprietary claim. But suggestions of this type clearly demonstrate that the leniency shown at present towards innocent volunteers is more likely to be amplified than taken away.

## 5. When will Priority be Lost?

No equitable proprietary claim can succeed if the property in question has simply disappeared as a result of dissipation. If for example, funds which are susceptible of being traced are expended on a case of wine which is then consumed, no proprietary claim will be able to be brought against the person who has expended the funds (nor will any proprietary claim be able to be brought against the vendor of the wine, who will be a bona fide purchaser for value without notice). The disappearance of the property is not, formally, a defence to an equitable proprietary claim but its effect is the same as if it were a defence. Quite apart from this situation, there are of course a number of formal defences which can be made out to an equitable proprietary claim.

### (A) Where a Recipient has Taken Free of the Interest of the Claimant

It is, of course, axiomatic that no equitable proprietary interest can survive the bona fide purchase for value of a legal estate or interest in the property in question to a person who has no notice of any kind of the equitable proprietary interest in question (or, in the case of registered land, the bona fide purchase for value of any interest by virtue of a duly registered disposition). Thus, if shares which are subject to a trust are sold by the trustees to a bona fide purchaser for value who has no notice of the interests of the beneficiaries, the

---

[13] [1998] Ch. 265; see *post*, p. 837.
[14] [2001] 1 A.C. 102.
[15] See Hayton (1990) 106 L.Q.R. 87 at 100.

latter cannot pursue any equitable proprietary claim against the purchaser; their only possible proprietary claim will be to attempt to trace into the proceeds of sale.

On the other hand, an equitable proprietary interest will normally enjoy priority over any subsequent holder of the property who has acquired only an equitable, rather than a legal interest therein. This is the case except that "where the merits are unequal and favour the later interest, as for instance where the owner of the later equitable interest is led by conduct on the part of the owner of the earlier interest to acquire the later interest in the belief or on the supposition that the earlier interest did not then exist, priority will be accorded to the later interest".[16] Save in the relatively unlikely event of this exception applying, there is no doubt whatever that a beneficiary of an express or resulting trust will, by virtue of this rule, enjoy priority over the holder of any later equitable interest in the property in question. So will a beneficiary of a constructive trust, once the existence of that trust has actually been upheld by the court in question. What is less clear is the position of a potential beneficiary of a constructive trust, someone who is entitled to seek the imposition of a constructive trust but who has not yet obtained the necessary court order; this depends on whether his interest prior to the court order is classified as a full equitable interest, in which case he will enjoy the same priority, or a mere equity, in which case a bona fide purchaser for value of any later equitable interest without notice will take free.[17] In principle, it is suggested that his interest should be classified as a full equitable interest, giving him the same priority, but the matter awaits decision.[18]


**(B) Where there has been a Change of Position**
English law has traditionally denied any general defence of change of position[19] although in Re Diplock,[20] the Court of Appeal held that innocent volunteers could rely on two limited (and controversial) manifestations of this defence as against equitable proprietary claims. However, in Lipkin Gorman v. Karpnale,[21] the House of Lords upheld for the first time the existence of such a defence. All the members of the House of Lords agreed that, on the facts, the defendant casino could invoke the defence of change of position against the claim by the plaintiff solicitors to recover funds which had been stolen from its client account and subsequently lost at the casino but only to the extent that the casino had paid out winnings to the gambler. However, the House took considerable care not to pre-empt the subsequent development of the defence. Lord Bridge stated[22] that "in expressly acknowledging the availability of this

---

[16] Heid v. Reliance Finance Corporation (1983) 154 C.L.R. 326 at 339, per Mason & Deane JJ. (High Court of Australia). The facts of this case provided a good example of the operation of this exception.

[17] Latec Investments v. Hotel Terrigal (1965) 113 C.L.R. 265 (High Court of Australia).

[18] The only relevant authority is Re Jonton [1992] 1 Qd.R. 105 (Supreme Court of Queensland) where the conclusion suggested in the text was reached; however, this case cannot be regarded as decisive since the holder of the later interest would, if necessary, almost certainly have been held to have constructive notice anyway.

[19] See particularly Ministry of Health v. Simpson [1951] A.C. 251.

[20] [1948] Ch. 465 at 546–548.

[21] [1991] 2 A.C. 548.

[22] ibid. at 558.

defence for the first time it would be unwise to attempt to define its scope in abstract terms". Lord Goff said this:[23]

"I am most anxious that, in recognising this defence to actions of restitution, nothing should be said at this stage to inhibit the development of the defence on a case by case basis, in the usual way. It is, of course, plain that the defence is not open to one who has changed his position in bad faith, as where the defendant has paid away the money with knowledge of the facts entitling the plaintiff to restitution and it is commonly accepted that the defence should not be open to a wrongdoer. These are matters which can, in due course, be considered in depth in cases where they arise for consideration. It is not appropriate in the present case to identify all those actions in restitution to which change of position may be a defence. At present I do not wish to state the principle any less broadly than this: that the defence is available to a person whose position has so changed that it would be inequitable in all the circumstances to require him to make restitution, or alternatively to make restitution in full. I wish to stress, however, that the mere fact that the defendant has spent the money, in whole or in part, does not of itself render it inequitable that he should be called upon to repay, because the expenditure might in any event have been incurred by him in the ordinary course of things.

"I wish to add two further footnotes. The defence of change of position is akin to the defence of bona fide purchase but we cannot simply say that bona fide purchase is a species of change of position. This is because change of position will only avail a defendant to the extent that his position has been changed whereas, where bona fide purchase is invoked, no inquiry is made (in most cases) into the adequacy of the consideration. Even so, the recognition of change of position as a defence should be doubly beneficial. It will enable a more generous approach to be taken of the recognition of the right of restitution, in the knowledge that the defence is, in appropriate cases, available and, while recognising the different functions of property at law and in equity, there may also in due course develop a more consistent approach to tracing claims, in which common defences are recognised as available to such claims, whether advanced at law or in equity."

It is clear from the final passage of this quotation that Lord Goff envisaged the application of the defence of change of position to both legal and equitable proprietary claims and that he did not regard this defence as supplanting the defence of bona fide purchase for value without notice. However, in *Foskett v. McKeown*,[24] Lord Millett stated that the only defence to an equitable proprietary claim is bona fide purchase of a legal estate for value without notice, from which it must obviously follow that change of position is not a defence to such a claim. This seems consistent neither with Lord Goff's remarks nor with the earlier remarks of Lord Millett in *Boscawen v. Bajwa*;[25] nor is there any reason in principle why change of position should not be a defence to a proprietary

---

[23] *ibid.* at 579–580.
[24] [2001] 1 A.C. 102 at 129.
[25] [1996] 1 W.L.R. 328 at 334–335.

claim. Whether or not the defence is actually available must obviously await a case in which this question has to be decided. Given the uncertainty, the subsequent development of the defence must clearly be considered here, albeit briefly.

In *Lipkin Gorman v. Karpnale*, only Lord Templeman[26] added to Lord Goff's broad statement of principle by way of illustration of circumstances in which the defence of change of position would be available. He envisaged a situation in which a donee of stolen money has expended it:

"in reliance on the validity of the gift before he receives notice of the victim's claim for restitution. Thus if the donee spent £20,000 in the purchase of a motor car which he would not have purchased but for the gift, it seems to me that the donee has altered his position on the faith of the gift and has only been unjustly enriched to the extent of the second hand value of the motor car at the date when the victim of the theft seeks restitution. If the donee spends the £20,000 on a trip round the world, which he would not have undertaken without the gift, it seems to me that the donee has altered his position on the faith of the gift and that he is not unjustly enriched when the victim of the faith seeks restitution."

Subsequent authorities have established that there must be some causal link between the receipt of the claimant's property and the change of position by the defendant; the fact that the defendant's general financial position has worsened since the receipt is not in itself sufficient.[27] However, it does now appear also to suffice if the defendant relied on the validity of a void transaction rather than an actual receipt of property.[28] Nor does it now seem to matter that the change of position involved the defendant passing up an opportunity to earn income or acquire assets rather than engaging in outright expenditure.[29] The most difficult question concerns the requirement of good faith. The Privy Council has held[30] that mere negligence on the part of the recipient is not sufficient to deprive him of the defence of change of position. On the other hand, lack of good faith is not limited to subjective dishonesty in the sense identified in *Twinsectra v. Yardley*,[31] but also extends to "failure to act in a commercially acceptable way and sharp practice of a kind that falls short of outright dishonesty".[32] It has also been stated that constructive notice of the true facts ought to amount to a lack of good faith for this purpose[33] although

---

[26] [1991] 2 A.C. 548 at 560.
[27] *Scottish Equitable v. Derby* [2001] 3 All E.R. 818.
[28] *Dextra Bank & Trust Co. v. Bank of Jamaica* [2002] 1 All E.R. (Comm.) 193 at 215 (Privy Council on appeal from Jamaica); *Scottish Equitable v. Derby* [2001] 3 All E.R. 818 at 827. The opposite view appears to have been expressed earlier in *National Westminster Bank v. Somer International (U.K.)* [2002] Q.B. 1286.
[29] This seems to follow from *Dextra Bank & Trust Co. v. Bank of Jamaica* [2002] 1 All E.R. (Comm.) 193 at 215 (Privy Council on appeal from Jamaica) but the opposite view was taken in *South Metropolitan B.C. v. Svenska International* [1995] 1 All E.R. 545.
[30] *Dextra Bank & Trust Co. v. Bank of Jamaica* [2002] 1 All E.R. (Comm.) 193 at 207 (Privy Council on appeal from Jamaica).
[31] [2002] 2 A.C. 164; see *ante*, p. 382.
[32] *Niru Battery Manufacturing Co. v. Milestone Trading* [2002] 2 All E.R. (Comm.) 705, para. 135.
[33] *Papamichael v. National Westminster Bank* [2003] 1 Lloyd's Rep. 341 at 369, citing *Re Montagu* [1987] 1 Ch. 264 (see *ante*, p. 398).

the judge in question[34] was "content to proceed upon the basis of a requirement of actual knowledge ... which would include wilfully and recklessly failing to make such inquiries as an honest and reasonable man would make".[35]

Applying these authorities to legal and equitable proprietary claims on the assumption that the defence of change of position is available in such claims, there will have to have been a receipt of property for such a proprietary claim to be available in the first place and it is obviously unlikely that any defendant will have passed up an opportunity to earn income or acquire assets in reliance on such a receipt. It is clear that a defaulting fiduciary will never himself be able to utilise the defence of change of position since he will necessarily have actual knowledge of the true facts and so cannot possibly be held to have acted in good faith. On the other hand, a person other than a fiduciary who has received property in good faith and subsequently engaged in some expenditure which he would not otherwise have made will be entitled to invoke the defence of change of position to the extent that he is worse off as a result of the transaction. At law, if a person purchases stolen property in good faith and subsequently sells it on at a loss, he will be entitled to invoke the defence of change of position to the extent of his loss on the sale and repurchase. In equity, if an innocent volunteer receives in good faith property transferred to him in breach of trust, he will be able to invoke the defence of change of position to the extent that he has spent the property or its product in ways which have provided no lasting benefit to him, provided that he would not have engaged in the expenditure in question in any event. Thus a charity which, as in *Re Diplock*, receives in good faith a payment which has been made in breach of trust, will be able to invoke the defence of change of position to the extent that it discharges unsecured debts[36] or spends the funds on improvements to its properties which increases their value by less than the amount expended. A private individual will additionally be able to invoke the defence to the extent that he has spent the sum received on some item of one-off expenditure, such as a holiday, which he would not otherwise have made. The effect of the defence of change of position on proprietary claims therefore seems likely to be confined to cases of resales at a loss and of one-off non-productive expenditure.

### (C) Where a Proprietary Claim would be Inequitable

In *Re Diplock*,[37] the Court of Appeal held that it would be inequitable for a claimant to maintain an equitable proprietary claim where an innocent volunteer had used the claimant's property either to alter or improve his land or to pay off his debts. If the defence of change of position does now apply to equitable proprietary claims, these further defences must have been subsumed within it to the extent that the expenditure has produced no lasting benefit for

---

[34] Judge Chambers Q.C., sitting as a Judge of the High Court.

[35] [2003] 1 Lloyd's Rep. 341 at 369. This apparent recourse to the categories of knowledge identified by Peter Gibson J. in *Baden v. Société Générale* (1983) [1993] 1 W.L.R. 509N at 575–576 is not of course consistent with the recent authorities on "liability for dishonest assistance" and "liability for knowing receipt"; see *ante*, pp. 380, 395.

[36] Unless Smith [1995] C.L.J. 290 is right in his contention that the proceeds of unsecured debts can be traced.

[37] [1948] Ch. 465 at 546–548.

the innocent volunteer and would not have been engaged in but for the receipt of the claimant's property. However, the defences enunciated by the Court of Appeal are not limited to this situation. The court clearly envisaged that improvements made to land would constitute a complete defence whether or not the value of the land had thereby increased in value. If it has indeed increased in value, there seems no reason why the claimant should not be entitled to obtain a charge over the land for the amount by which its value has increased. Further, although it is of course axiomatic that the payment of unsecured debts prevents any subsequent equitable proprietary claim (because the discharged creditor will be a bona fide purchaser for value without notice), there seems no reason why secured debts should be treated in the same way. If secured debts of an innocent volunteer are discharged by the use of the funds of the claimant, why should the claimant not be subrogated to the security discharged with his money and be entitled to enforce that security against the innocent volunteer?[38]

Some of these aspects of the decision of the Court of Appeal in Re Diplock were approved and applied in somewhat different circumstances by Scott V.-C. in the Court of Appeal in Foskett v. McKeown.[39] It has already been seen[40] that the majority of the Court of Appeal restricted the claimants' equitable proprietary claim to the recovery of the premiums on the life insurance policy which had been paid with their funds and interest thereon and were subsequently reversed by the House of Lords, where the point at present under discussion was not considered. Scott V.-C. proceeded on the basis that the claimants' funds had been used to improve an asset which was already[41] vested in the defendants, who were of course innocent volunteers. He consequently stated that, even if the improvements had conferred any benefit on the defendants (in fact both he and Hobhouse L.J. held that this was not the case),[42] the claimants could not, in accordance with Re Diplock,[43] have traced their funds into the asset so improved.[44] This clearly indicates that the defences enunciated by the Court of Appeal in Re Diplock have survived the enunciation of the general defence of change of position and extend well beyond the scope of that general defence.

**(D) Where Compensation has been Recovered from the Offending Fiduciary**
It has already been seen[45] that any personal claim available against an innocent volunteer will be reduced to the extent that compensation can be obtained from any fiduciary responsible for having made any relevant disposition of trust property in breach of trust. In Re Diplock,[46] the Court of Appeal took the view that "prima facie and subject to discussion" any equitable proprietary claim should similarly be reduced by any amounts which the claimant had recovered from any fiduciary responsible for having made such a disposition.

---

[38] See Goff & Jones, The Law of Restitution (6th ed., 2002), p. 111.
[39] [1998] Ch. 265.
[40] See ante, p. 819.
[41] At any rate by the time of the payment of the fourth and fifth years' premiums.
[42] [1998] Ch. 265 at 282, per Scott V.-C.; at 291–292, per Hobhouse L.J.
[43] [1948] Ch. 465.
[44] [1998] Ch. 265 at 278.
[45] See ante, p. 797.
[46] [1948] Ch. 465 at 556.

The court did not actually suggest that it was necessary for the claimant to sue any such fiduciary prior to embarking on an equitable proprietary claim, merely that if any compensation had been recovered it should constitute a rateable bar to any such equitable proprietary claim.[47] It is, frankly, difficult to see why the existence of a personal liability should constitute a bar to a proprietary claim.[48] However, if it is ever held that it is in fact necessary for such a claimant to sue any fiduciary first, it is to be hoped that the fiduciary will be subrogated to that part of the claim "which represents the difference between the total of the sum recovered from the [fiduciary] and the volunteer and the loss suffered by [the claimant]".[49] It would in fact be preferable to require the claimant to proceed against the innocent volunteer before suing the fiduciary, who would then be liable only for any amount which cannot be recovered from the innocent volunteer; however, such a solution could only be imposed by statute.[50]

---

[47] *Re J. Leslie Engineers* [1976] 1 W.L.R. 292.
[48] The argument that it should was specifically rejected in *Hagan v. Waterhouse* (1991) 34 N.S.W.L.R. 308 at 369–370, *per* Kearney J. (Supreme Court of New South Wales).
[49] Goff & Jones, *The Law of Restitution* (6th ed., 2002), p. 115.
[50] As in New Zealand (Administration Act 1952, s.30B(5)) and in Western Australia (Trustee Act 1962, s.65(7)). However, Queensland has gone even further than the Court of Appeal in *Re Diplock* and prohibits, except by leave of the court, any claim against any transferee of trust property transferred in breach of trust until the claimant has exhausted his remedies against the fiduciary responsible (Trusts Act 1973, s.109(2); see Lee (1981) 1 O.J.L.S. 414).

CHAPTER 23

# TRUSTS IN THE CONFLICT OF LAWS

THE rules of the conflict of laws, often also known and described throughout this chapter as the rules of private international law, determine the jurisdiction by whose laws any legal relationship is governed. Its rules are relevant whenever a legal relationship, be it a contract, a tort, a marriage, a trust or an inheritance, has an international element. Taking an admittedly artificial example from outside the law of trusts, suppose that a Frenchman and a German make a contract for the sale and purchase of shares in a Spanish company on board a ship flying the Liberian flag which at that time happens to be moored in the Port of Amsterdam, Holland; the law of any one of the five jurisdictions mentioned could govern that contract in the event that the parties do not expressly provide what law is to constitute what is known as the proper law of the contract, which does not actually have to be any of those five (many commercial contracts, particularly shipping contracts, provide that they are to be governed by English law even though none of the parties or the subject matter of the contract has ever had any connection with the United Kingdom). In the context of trust law, if an English settlor creates a trust whose trustees are two Canadians who live and work in Bermuda, whose beneficiaries live either in Florida or in California, and whose assets consist of shares in companies constituted in various tax havens and land in other jurisdictions scattered around the world, there are an equally large number of possible jurisdictions by whose law that trust may be governed and which therefore constitute what is known as the applicable law of the trust. That is not to say that any necessary proceedings have to be brought in the jurisdiction whose law constitutes the proper law of the contract or the applicable law of the trust in question; there are a variety of reasons why those proceedings may be brought elsewhere. In such circumstances, while that other jurisdiction will have to apply the proper or applicable law when determining questions of substance, all questions of procedure will be governed by its own law, by what is known as the law of the forum, the jurisdiction in which any proceedings are being brought.

An additional complication is that countries often contain more than one jurisdiction. The United Kingdom has six: England and Wales,[1] Scotland, Northern Ireland, Guernsey, Jersey and the Isle of Man, to which have to be added the separate jurisdictions of each of its dependant territories such as

---

[1] Throughout this chapter, references to "England" and "English law" therefore mean "England and Wales" and "the law of England and Wales". This is in the interests of brevity and no disrespect is thereby intended to the inhabitants of the Principality of Wales.

The Cayman Islands and Gibraltar (to mention two which are important tax havens and so are relevant to the law of trusts). Federal countries, such as the United States of America, Australia and Canada, have as many jurisdictions as there are individual states, provinces or territories plus, in each case, an additional federal jurisdiction whose rules, which are admittedly unlikely to be applicable to many matters in which private international law is relevant, apply to the entire country. Even some basically unitary countries, such as Spain, have distinct rules governing such matters as matrimonial property regimes and rights of inheritance which apply in different parts of that country.

The situation is complicated still further by the fact that the application of the rules of private international law of different jurisdictions not infrequently produces different answers to the question of which jurisdiction's laws govern the transaction in question. This is because the common law jurisdictions, such as England and its former colonies, tend to determine the applicable law by the use of connecting factors which differ in almost every respect from those utilised by civil law jurisdictions such as those of mainland Europe. The common law jurisdictions tend to utilise connecting factors such as the domicile of the persons involved (a highly technical concept[2]) and the location of any relevant assets, whereas the civil law jurisdictions tend instead to utilise connecting factors such as habitual residence and nationality (in the case of a United Kingdom national, nationality presumably means the United Kingdom jurisdiction with which he has the closest connection[3]). Even worse, some but by no means all jurisdictions accept a reference back to their own law where the law which they regard as prima facie applicable so dictates and some common law jurisdictions also accept a reference on to the law of a third jurisdiction (both types of reference are technically known as *"renvoi"*). All this means that the law applicable to any given transaction is likely to differ depending on which jurisdiction's courts have to decide the question. Consequences of this type can only be avoided if the different rules adopted by the common law and the civil law jurisdictions can be synthesised in an international convention; this obviously involves both groups of jurisdictions

---

[2] Domicile has nothing to do with habitual residence. A person's domicile of origin is the jurisdiction in which one of his parents (usually his father) was domiciled at the time of his birth. He will only be held to have given up that domicile of origin in favour of a domicile of choice if he goes to another jurisdiction with the intention of remaining there permanently (this is a question of fact, often an extremely difficult one); however, once he has obtained a domicile of choice, he can give that up simply by leaving the jurisdiction in question. If his departure does not result in him obtaining a further domicile of choice elsewhere, his domicile of origin revives. See Collier, *Conflict of Laws* (3rd ed., 2002) pp. 37–60.

[3] This at least was what was held in the highly criticised but undoubtedly pragmatic decision in *Re O'Keefe* [1940] Ch. 124. This case is a good illustration what can actually happen in practice. The question was what law governed the intestate succession to the movable property of a U.K. national who had died with a domicile of choice in Italy. The English court initially applied Italian law on the grounds that the relevant connecting factor under English private international law was domicile. However, the relevant connecting factor under Italian private international law was nationality. The English court therefore accepted Italian law's reference back to U.K. law under the doctrine of *"renvoi"* (discussed in the next sentence of the text) and then decided that in this case United Kingdom law meant Irish law (which was duly applied) on the grounds that the deceased's domicile of origin had been what is now the Republic of Ireland (part of the U.K. at the time of her birth); it made no difference that she had only ever paid one short visit there. See Collier, *Conflict of Laws* (3rd ed., 2002) pp. 23–24.

giving way in substantial respects. The effect of such a convention will be that those states who sign and ratify it will then all apply the same rules to the same legal transaction.

Fortunately, the law of trusts is governed by such a convention, The Hague Convention on the Law Applicable to Trusts and their Recognition ("the Hague Convention"), which was incorporated into English law by the Recognition of Trusts Act 1987. This now largely governs the question of which jurisdiction is the applicable law of the trust; that law will determine at the very least the nature of the interests of the beneficiaries under the trust and the duties owed by the trustees to them (it is, however, possible for the trust instrument to provide for other questions to be governed by the law of some other jurisdiction). The incorporation of the Hague Convention into English law certainly means that it is no longer necessary (if indeed it ever was) for the student of the English law of trusts to master the intricacies of doctrines of private international law such as domicile and *renvoi*. Nor need such a student try to work out what would happen if proceedings were brought in the courts of any jurisdiction other than England, although this is obviously relevant to anyone setting up a trust governed by the law of some other jurisdiction. This chapter, after a brief discussion of the situations in which the rules of private international law governing trusts may be relevant, therefore needs to consider only two questions: first, in what circumstances an English court has jurisdiction to hear trust proceedings and, secondly, which jurisdiction's rules of substantive law it will apply when doing so. It cannot be emphasised too often that these two questions are wholly independent of one another[4] and must therefore always be considered separately.

In this and the following chapter, a trust whose applicable law is English law will be described as "an English trust", a trust whose applicable law is not English law will be described as "a foreign trust" and a trust whose applicable law is that of another specific jurisdiction will be described as, for example, "a Jersey trust".

## I. Situations Where Private International Law is Relevant

There are four principal situations in which the rules of private international law governing trusts are relevant in the English courts.

### 1. *Proceedings in England by the Beneficiaries of a Foreign Trust*

The most straightforward situation in which the rules of private international law governing trusts are relevant in the English courts are where the beneficiaries of a trust which is (or may be) a foreign trust bring proceedings against their trustees for breach of trust in England on the basis that either the trustees themselves or some part of the trust property are physically present in this jurisdiction.

An example is the leading case of *Chellaram v. Chellaram*.[5] The settlors of the

---

[4] The distinction emerges clearly in *Macmillan v. Bishopsgate Trust (No.3)* [1995] 1 W.L.R. 978 at 989.

[5] [1985] Ch. 409; *(No.2)* [2002] 3 All E.R. 17; see *post*, p. 858.

discretionary trusts in question were almost certainly domiciled in India at the time of the settlements, which were drawn up in India in English form and executed by them respectively in Singapore and in Lagos. Two of the original trustees were permanently resident in England and the third had a United Kingdom passport and spent some months each year here in a house of his ownership. The trust property was shares in Bermudan companies whose assets were situated in many parts of the world but not in India. Some of the beneficiaries brought proceedings in England seeking the removal of the then trustees, who were all born and domiciled in India but were not all resident there and all of whom visited London on a regular basis; all the trustees entered an appearance but subsequently sought a stay on the basis that England was not the most appropriate forum.[6] However, even on the basis that the trusts were Indian trusts, the court was held to have jurisdiction over those particular proceedings. But, in subsequent proceedings for breach of trust by effectively the same beneficiaries many years later, the trusts were held to be Bermudan trusts; since none of the then trustees had entered an appearance or was domiciled here, the court was held not to have jurisdiction and service out of the jurisdiction on the trustees was set aside. The court held that, even if it had had jurisdiction and the trusts had been English trusts, India not England would have been the most appropriate forum.

### 2. Where a Foreign Trust is relevant in Other Types of Proceedings

The rules of private international law can also be relevant where the nature, beneficial interests, and assets of a foreign trust affect other types of proceedings in respect of which the English courts clearly have jurisdiction.

A straightforward illustration is where the trustees and/or a beneficiary of a foreign trust have brought proceedings in England in which the nature of the foreign trust or the rights of its beneficiaries are relevant. In *Neumann v. Azon Anstalt*,[7] a Liechtenstein company which was the tenant of a flat in London declared a trust of that flat in favour of its occupier in order to enable the company to obtain a new lease to which it was entitled if the beneficiary had occupied the flat as his only or principal home for three out of the previous ten years and if the trust was actually valid; the latter question turned on whether the trust was an English trust, in which case it was clearly valid, or a Liechtenstein trust, in which case it was arguably invalid on the basis that the Liechtenstein trust legislation only envisages trusts created by transfer. It was held[8] that the trust was a Liechtenstein trust[9] and that Liechtenstein law does indeed only envisage trusts created by transfer; the trust was therefore invalid and the claim for a new lease failed.

---

[6] In technical terms, that England was not the *forum conveniens*.
[7] (2001) unreported. The author of this edition was junior counsel for the landlord.
[8] By Judge Levy Q.C. in the Central London County Court.
[9] Because in the absence of an express clause selecting an applicable law other than Liechtenstein law, a trust created by a Liechtenstein company was, as a matter of Liechtenstein law, necessarily a Liechtenstein trust.

Foreign trusts can also be relevant to proceedings for the reallocation of property following a divorce. One of the former spouses may claim assets to which the respondent former spouse is entitled under a foreign trust. Such claims have been successful in the past[10] but since the incorporation of the Hague Convention into English law it is questionable whether the English courts still have jurisdiction over foreign trusts in this respect.[11] There will be no difficulty in practice where the trustees of the foreign trust are within the English jurisdiction or can be controlled by a respondent who is himself within the English jurisdiction; in such circumstances the trustees or the respondent will be susceptible to the personal jurisdiction of the English courts. It may be[12] that the English courts will assert jurisdiction over the foreign trust by asserting that the question is governed by the law of the forum or by relying on Article 15 of the Hague Convention;[13] in policy terms, this could be justified on the grounds that otherwise putting assets in a foreign trust would be far too easy a way of protecting them from potential claims by former spouses. However, in *Compass Trustees v. McBarnett*,[14] the Royal Court of Jersey was asked to vary a Jersey trust pursuant to a judgment of the Family Division of the English High Court which held that such a variation was necessary but could only be done by the Jersey court. Given that both spouses had submitted to the jurisdiction of the English court, the Royal Court of Jersey duly made the variation as a matter of comity.[15] The history of this litigation suggests both that the English courts may well no longer regard themselves as having jurisdiction over foreign trusts in family proceedings and that a foreign court may not make the order desired by the English court if the defendant has not appeared in the English proceedings; further, a foreign court which is, unlike the Royal Court of Jersey, outside the United Kingdom may not feel obliged to act as a matter of comity at all.

In the past English courts have also been prepared to make orders under the Variation of Trusts Act 1958[16] in respect of foreign trusts but it is extremely doubtful whether the English courts still have jurisdiction in such proceedings following incorporation of the Hague Convention into English law;[17] even if they do, in the light of *Compass Trustees v. McBarnett*,[18] they may well now not feel inclined to make such orders and the courts of the foreign jurisdiction may well decline to enforce them.

---

[10] Claims to vary pre-nuptial or post-nuptial settlements of property abroad governed by foreign law with exclusively foreign trustees were successfully made in *Nunneley v. Nunneley* (1890) 15 P.D. 186, *Forsyth v. Forsyth* [1891] P. 363, and *Goff v. Goff* [1934] P. 107. More recently, claims for the reallocation of property on divorce were successfully made in *Browne v. Browne* [1989] 1 F.L.R. 291 (Jersey discretionary trust, Liechtenstein trust), *E v. E (Financial Provision)* [1990] 2 F.L.R. 233 (Guernsey discretionary trust), and *T v. T* [1996] 2 F.L.R. 357 (Jersey discretionary trust); however, in these proceedings no reference was made to the Recognition of Trusts Act 1987.

[11] It has been argued in unreported proceedings that the English courts no longer have jurisdiction to make orders governing such trusts but such arguments have not yet been the subject of a reasoned judgment.

[12] This is the view taken by Dicey & Morris, *The Conflict of Laws* (13th ed., 2000), p. 1093.

[13] See *post*, p. 859.

[14] [2003] W.T.L.R. 461.

[15] Reliance was placed on the earlier decision of that court in *Lane v. Lane* 1985 6 J.L.R. 48.

[16] *Re Ker's Settlement* [1963] Ch. 553; *Re Paget's Settlement* [1965] 1 W.L.R. 1046.

[17] See *post*, p. 859.

[18] [2003] W.T.L.R. 461.

### 3. Proceedings to Set Aside an English Trust

The rules of private international law can also be relevant where proceedings are brought in the English courts to set aside an English trust created by a settlor who is domiciled or habitually resident outside the United Kingdom. Such proceedings may be brought on a number of grounds: first, on the grounds that the creation of the trust amounted to a fraud on the settlor's creditors under foreign legislation analogous to the English legislation which has already been considered;[19] secondly, on the grounds that its creation breached the terms of his matrimonial property regime (this would, for example, be the case if a person married under French law settled property on his spouse);[20] or, thirdly, on the grounds that its creation deprived his forcible heirs of their rights (the civil law systems of continental Europe require that a substantial percentage (generally at least two-thirds) of the deceased's lifetime assets passes to any descendants and sometimes that, in default of descendants, a lower percentage passes to any ascendants, subject in both cases to provision for surviving spouses; the Muslim legal systems have similar provisions limited to the assets held at the time of death).

### 4. Dispositions of Trust Property in Breach of Trust

Finally, the rules of private international law can also be relevant where the assets of an English trust have been disposed of in breach of trust to persons in other jurisdictions or the assets of a foreign trust have been disposed of in breach of trust to persons in England and the beneficiaries are trying to maintain equitable proprietary claims or to impose "liability for knowing receipt" or "liability for dishonest assistance".

In this respect, it can sometimes be difficult to determine whether assets were actually subject to a foreign trust in the first place. In *Kuwait Oil Tanker Company v. Al Bader*,[21] it had to be decided whether the directors and other officers of companies incorporated in non common law jurisdictions can be regarded as owing fiduciary duties to those companies. The defendants were various officers of the plaintiff Kuwaiti company who had interposed offshore companies between the plaintiff and the owners of ships which it had chartered and, by the use of back to back charterparties, had creamed off the difference between the rates of hire paid by the plaintiff and the rates of hire received by the owners. The plaintiff contended that the defendants were constructive trustees, first, because they had obtained property from the plaintiff by fraud and, secondly, because they had obtained property in breach of their fiduciary duties to the plaintiff; both contentions succeeded.[22] In *Arab Monetary Fund v. Hashim (No. 8)*,[23] Chadwick J. had held that in such circumstances what the English court has to do is to decide whether the duties

---

[19] See *ante*, p. 255.
[20] Under French law (*Code Civile*, Art. 1096) all gifts between spouses are void so a settlement by one spouse of property on trust for the other spouse would also be void.
[21] (2000) *The Times* May 30, 2000.
[22] The defendants had been held liable for conspiracy so the existence of a constructive trust was relevant only to the question of whether or not the plaintiff was entitled to compound interest (see *Westdeutsche Landesbank Girozentrale v. Islington L.B.C.* [1996] A.C. 669).
[23] (June 13, 1994) unreported (there are several unreported judgments in this interminable case).

which arise under the relevant foreign law are capable of being classified by the English court as fiduciary. Both Moore-Bick J. and the Court of Appeal held that exactly the same attitude should be adopted in deciding whether a person is a constructive trustee of property which he has received. Under Kuwaiti law, anyone who receives property in bad faith is obliged to return both that property and its fruits; consequently, the defendants were held to be constructive trustees of the proceeds of their fraud. Similarly, their relationship to the plaintiff under Kuwaiti law was clearly classifiable by an English court as fiduciary and so they were held to be constructive trustees on this ground as well.

Where there is a trust, there is no difficulty about either equitable proprietary claims or claims to impose liability for knowing receipt where the claims are being brought against a person to whom the property subject to the trust was directly transferred. Assuming that that person is susceptible to the jurisdiction of the English courts in the first place, English law will clearly apply to the claims against him because he can be shown to have received the property in question. This was also held by Chadwick J. in *Arab Monetary Fund v. Hashim (No.8).*[24] Difficulties do however arise where either of these types of claim is being brought against someone to whom the original recipient has transferred the trust property on, the principal problem being that of determining by what law the second or subsequent transfer is governed. There is also some controversy as to what law governs liability for dishonest assistance.

For the purposes of an equitable proprietary claim against a subsequent recipient of the trust property, it appears that the effect of a transfer of that property between persons who are both in a jurisdiction other than England will be governed by the law of that jurisdiction. This seems to follow from the judgments of the members of the Court of Appeal in *MacMillan v. Bishopsgate Trust (No.3).*[25] Consequently, such a claim will only be able to be maintained against the later recipient if under the law of that jurisdiction the equitable interests of the beneficiaries continue to affect the property transferred to him. If they do not, as would be the case where, for example, funds were transferred to a Swiss bank,[26] then the beneficiaries will be unable to demonstrate that any of their property ever reached the hands of the recipient and so will not possibly be able to maintain an equitable proprietary claim in respect of it.

For identical reasons, the result ought to be exactly the same in the case of a claim to impose liability for knowing receipt against a subsequent recipient. However, the rules by which English law traces property into its product

---

[24] *ibid.* ("liability for knowing receipt").

[25] *MacMillan v. Bishopsgate Trust (No.3)* [1995] 1 W.L.R. 978 (Millett J.), [1996] 1 W.L.R. 387 (Court of Appeal). The conclusion in the text seems to follow from the statements in the Court of Appeal at 399, *per* Staughton L.J., at 410, *per* Auld L.J., and at 424, *per* Aldous L.J., each of whom held that the effect of such transfers was governed by the law of the place where it took place. At first instance, Millett J. reached the same conclusion for a different reason, namely that this was the place where the enrichment of the recipient took place.

[26] Under Swiss law deposits in banks become the property of the depositee and no proprietary interest in the depositor or anyone claiming through him can survive. See *Arab Monetary Bank v. Hashim (No.8)* (June 13, 1994) unreported, transcript at 316.

appear to be more flexible in cases of this kind,[27] although they certainly should not be! If such rules are classified as procedural rather than substantive (which they could conceivably be[28]) and so apply irrelevant of where any transfer took place, then the beneficiaries may nevertheless be able to demonstrate that the recipient actually received their property. It is to be hoped that this latter view is not adopted.

Liability for dishonest assistance is less straightforward. Although this liability has been held[29] to be a matter "relating to tort, delict or quasi delict" for the purposes of the allocation of jurisdiction as between European countries,[30] it has been held by the Court of Appeal[31] not to be tortious for the purpose of service of proceedings out of the jurisdiction, although the rules have now been changed[32] to permit service out of the jurisdiction in such cases. Liability for dishonest assistance has also been held not to be tortious for the purposes of the rules of private international law — this was in *Arab Monetary Fund v. Hashim (No.9)*.[33] The judge in question, Chadwick J., then stated that whether or not a person can be held liable for dishonest assistance "where the fault alleged lies wholly in things done or not done in a foreign jurisdiction ... is a question to which the authorities provide no ready answer".[34] However, he went on to hold that the matter was governed by a rule of private international law which at one time used to govern liability for tort[35] but has long since ceased to do so.[36] On this basis, liability depends, first, on whether the alleged accessory is liable under English law and, secondly, on whether he is exempted from liability under the law of the jurisdiction where the assistance took place. Only if he is both liable under English law and not exempted by the law of the other jurisdiction, will he be liable for dishonest assistance. This decision was criticised[37] on the basis that it seems at best an unsatisfactory half way house first to hold that liability for dishonest assistance is not tortious for the purposes of private international law and then to return to and adopt as of general application an abrogated rule of private international law on tort which has long since been rejected by the House of Lords. However, the decision was subsequently followed and applied by Rix J. in *Dubai Aluminium Co. v. Salaam*[38] (the point did not arise on appeal) and both at first instance and

---

[27] *El Ajou v. Dollar Land Holdings* [1993] 3 All E.R. 717 at 736, *per* Millett J.; see *ante*, p. 393.
[28] This point was left open by Millett J. (it did not have to be decided because in that case the property had been received here). The point also arose, and was again left open, in *Chase Manhattan Bank v. Israel-British Bank (London)* [1981] Ch. 105 at 127.
[29] In *Casio Computer v. Sayo* [2001] I.L.Pr. 594.
[30] Then under the Brussels and Lugano Conventions, art. 5(3); since March 1, 2002, also under Council Regulation (E.C.) 44/2001, art. 5(3); *post*, p. 853.
[31] In *Metall & Rohstoff v. Donaldson Lufkin & Jenrette* [1990] 1 Q.B. 391 at 474.
[32] Civil Procedure Rules 1998 Part 6.20, paras. 14, 15; see *post*, p. 853.
[33] (October 11, 1994) unreported, transcript at 22–23.
[34] *ibid.* at 24.
[35] The principle enunciated in *The Halley* (1868) L.R. 2 P.C. 193 (a decision of the Privy Council but, because it was on appeal from the Court of Admiralty, an English precedent).
[36] It was rejected by the House of Lords in *Boys v. Chaplain* [1971] A.C. 356, where a different rule was adopted. This has in turn been replaced by yet a further rule contained in Private International Law (Miscellaneous Provisions) Act 1995.
[37] In the 7th edition of this work, p. 748.
[38] [1999] 1 Lloyd's Rep. 415 at 452.

in the Court of Appeal in *Grupo Torras v. Al-Sabah*.[39] Consequently, this view must clearly now be regarded as constituting English law.

## II. The Jurisdiction of the English Courts

The rules governing the jurisdiction of the English courts differ depending on the applicability of the European legislation which governs the allocation of jurisdiction between the courts of the various countries who are bound by it. Prior to March 1, 2002, the relevant legislation was the Brussels and Lugano Conventions but now[40] the Brussels Convention applies only as between Denmark and the remaining members of the European Union[41] and the Lugano Convention applies only as between all the members of the European Union and Iceland, Norway, Poland and Switzerland;[42] as between the members of the European Union other than Denmark, the relevant legislation is now Council Regulation (E.C.) 44/2001 ("the Council Regulation"), which came into force on March 1, 2002 (the legislation will collectively be described as "the European Conventions"). The Brussels and Lugano Conventions were incorporated into English law by the Civil Jurisdiction and Judgments Acts of 1982 and 1991 respectively, which have been modified to incorporate the Council Regulation by statutory instrument.[43] The situation where the European Conventions do not apply will be considered first.

### 1. *Jurisdiction when the Applicable Law is Specified*

Most well-drawn trust instruments today contain a clause specifying the applicable law of the trust, which will govern all questions concerning that trust unless any of them is stated to be governed by the law of some other jurisdiction. Where English law is specified as the applicable law of a trust, there can be no doubt whatever that the English courts have jurisdiction over all questions concerning that trust (other of course than any which is stated to be governed by the law of another jurisdiction). Indeed, many trust instruments contain a further clause specifically conferring that jurisdiction on the courts in question. It is of course theoretically possible for a trust to contain both a clause specifying English law as the applicable law of the trust and a clause giving jurisdiction over all questions concerning the trust to some other jurisdiction. The latter clause would presumably have to be upheld in proceedings between the trustees and the settlor, all of whom would obviously have agreed to it by executing the trust instrument. However, the most likely parties to any proceedings are the trustees and the beneficiaries and it is improbable that the latter will have executed the trust instrument. In such circumstances, it is inconceivable that the English courts would decline jurisdiction to hear proceedings brought by any beneficiary of a trust who had

---

[39] [1999] C.L.C. 1469 (Mance L.J., sitting in the Commercial Court), [2001] Lloyd's Rep. Bank 36 (C.A.).

[40] In May 2003.

[41] Guernsey, Jersey and the Isle of Man are not members of the European Union.

[42] And any other country who accedes to the Lugano Convention; it is envisaged that the Czech Republic and Hungary will do so.

[43] S.I. 2001/3929.

not executed the trust instrument where English law was specified as the applicable law.

As has just been indicated, a trust instrument can also specify that some questions concerning its trusts are to be governed by the law of some jurisdiction other than that of its applicable law. The administration of a trust is what is most often excluded from the ambit of its applicable law, although in this and in all other cases it is usually prudent also to define extremely precisely exactly what has been so excluded. Many modern trust instruments expressly envisage the possibility of the applicable law and the law governing the administration of the trust being different by referring to them in separate clauses, even if both are initially to be governed by the law of the same jurisdiction (this is in order to enable the two to be separated later under the change of law clauses which such instruments tend also to contain). It is also not uncommon to specify that the trust instrument should be construed in accordance with the law of a particular jurisdiction, usually that of the jurisdiction in which it is being drawn up; this can be advantageous since it enables technical expressions such as "issue" to be given the meaning which the draftsman intended them to have and permits presumptions which the draftsman will consciously or unconsciously have had in mind to be carried into effect. If the law chosen to govern the construction of the trust instrument or the administration of the trust or anything else is English law, there is equally no doubt that the English courts have jurisdiction in that respect.

However, the fact that a court has jurisdiction by virtue of an express provision of the trust instrument in question does not mean that it will necessarily exercise it. It may nevertheless decline to hear the proceedings under what is known as the doctrine of forum *non conveniens* if it is satisfied that the courts of another jurisdiction constitute a more appropriate forum. In *Chellaram v. Chellaram (No.2)*,[44] the facts of which have already been considered,[45] it was held that, on the hypotheses that, contrary to earlier findings, the the court had jurisdiction and the trusts were English trusts, England was not an appropriate forum.[46] The *forum conveniens* was India: first, there were already proceedings there between the same parties involving other trusts and an Indian court was far better equipped to understand the intricacies of the parties' family relationships; and, secondly, several of the most important witnesses were there and the only important witnesses who were non-compellable there were English solicitors who would in practice attend if asked to do so by their clients.

### 2. Jurisdiction when the Applicable Law is not Specified

Where a trust instrument contains no clause specifying the applicable law, the English courts will equally have jurisdiction where all the relevant parties and the relevant property are habitually physically within their jurisdiction; such trusts will inevitably be held to be subject to English law anyway. Further, in relation to proprietary claims, the English courts are likely to assume jurisdiction if only the property and none of the parties is within the jurisdiction

---

[44] [2002] 3 All E.R. 17.
[45] See *ante*, p. 841.
[46] [2002] 3 All E.R. 17 at 50.

in this sense. It is also possible for defendants outside the jurisdiction to submit to the jurisdiction of the English courts by giving someone within the jurisdiction authority to accept service on their behalf.[47] The crucial question is obviously in what other circumstances the English courts will assume jurisdiction.

The basic rule is that the physical presence of the defendant within the jurisdiction, no matter how fleeting it may be, is sufficient to confer jurisdiction on the English courts even if the proper law of the trust is not English law. In *Ewing v. Orr-Ewing*,[48] an order was sought by an English minor beneficiary against English and Scottish executors, all of whom were regarded as having been properly served,[49] for the administration by the English court of both the English and Scottish assets of the estate of a Scottish domiciliary. Part of the assets had originally been within the jurisdiction but had been removed to Scotland by the time that the action commenced. The House of Lords made the order sought. In *Cook Industries v. Galligher*,[50] an order was sought by and granted to the plaintiff, a New York creditor under a New York judgment, for the inspection of a property in France which the defendant, an American who lived in England for approximately six months a year, was alleged to hold on trust for the plaintiff's judgment debtor. These, and other authorities not involving trusts, were relied on by Millett J. in *El Ajou v. Dollar Land Holdings*[51] in support of the proposition that "liability for knowing receipt" could be imposed on an English company in respect of assets which it had knowingly received abroad.[52] Similarly, in *Chellaram v. Chellaram*,[53] whose facts have already been considered,[54] all the trustees had been served in England, some as a result of having submitted to the jurisdiction, so the English court clearly had jurisdiction.

Further, jurisdiction can also arise as a result of service of the proceedings on defendants who are out of the jurisdiction; whether or not service out of the jurisdiction is possible is determined as at the date of the proceedings rather than as at the date when the cause of action arose.[55] The leave of the court is usually, but not always, required.[56] It is not required for service out of the jurisdiction in certain circumstances covered by the European Conventions.[57] It is always available for service out of the jurisdiction of any claim against a

---

[47] As some of the trustees had in *Chellaram v. Chellaram* [1985] Ch. 409.
[48] (1883) 9 App.Cas. 34.
[49] The Scottish executors seem to have been served in Scotland without any special leave of the court but no objection was taken.
[50] [1979] Ch. 439.
[51] [1993] 3 All E.R. 717 at 737.
[52] This proposition does not form part of his ratio since the company had actually received the assets in England. Millett J. was using this proposition based on hypothetical facts in order to establish that, if the company was potentially liable for knowing receipt if the assets had been received abroad, it was *a fortiori* potentially liable if they had been received in England.
[53] [1985] Ch. 409.
[54] *ante*, p. 841.
[55] *Chellaram v. Chellaram (No.2)* [2002] 3 All E.R. 17 at 46.
[56] Civil Procedure Rules 1998, Part 6, Sect. III. This was formerly governed by Rules of the Supreme Court, Ord. 11.
[57] See *post*, p. 853.

defendant domiciled in the jurisdiction.[58] Otherwise the relevant situations in which leave can be granted for service out of the jurisdiction are:

(a) where "the whole subject-matter of the claim is property located within the jurisdiction"[59] (in *Banca Carige v. Banco Nacional*,[60] Lightman J. confirmed that this provision extended to all property within the jurisdiction, including shares in an English company and held that leave could in principle be given to an Italian bank to serve out of the jurisdiction in respect of a challenge under the Insolvency Act 1986 to a sale of such shares by the former national bank of Cuba to its successor[61]);

(b) in respect of claims "made for any remedy which might be obtained in proceedings to execute the trusts of a written instrument where (a) the trusts ought to be executed according to English law; and (b) the person on whom the claim form is to be served is a trustee of the trusts";[62]

(c) where "a claim is made for a remedy against the defendant as constructive trustee where the defendant's alleged liability arises out of acts committed within the jurisdiction";[63] and

(d) where "a claim is made for restitution where the defendant's alleged liability arises out of acts committed within the jurisdiction".[64]

Where a court has jurisdiction under these rules, then, just as in the situation where a court has jurisdiction by virtue of an express provision of the trust instrument in question, it may also decline to hear the proceedings under the doctrine of *forum non conveniens*. An example of a situation where a court might well decline jurisdiction in proceedings involving a trust would be where the trustees had been served on a casual visit to the jurisdiction in question and had no assets within it, none of the trust property was within the

---

[58] Civil Procedure Rules 1998, Part 6.20, para. 1; this was also the case under Rules of the Supreme Court, Ord. 11.

[59] Civil Procedure Rules 1998, Part 6.20, para. 10. This is broader than Rules of the Supreme Court, Ord. 11, r. 1(1)(g), which applied only where the whole subject-matter of the action was land within the jurisdiction.

[60] [2001] 3 All E.R. 923 at pp.937–938.

[61] In the light of the facts, leave was not actually granted.

[62] Civil Procedure Rules 1998, Part 6.20, para. 11. Effectively the same provision was included in Rules of the Supreme Court, Ord. 11, r. 1(1)(j).

[63] Civil Procedure Rules 1998, Part 6.20, para. 14; this provision will presumably cover "liability for dishonest assistance" despite the view that this does not lead to the imposition of a construction trust (see *ante*, p. 374). A similar provision was included in Rules of the Supreme Court, Ord. 11, r.1(1)(t), which was added in 1990 as a result of the decision in *Metall & Rohstoff v. Donaldson Lufkin & Jenrette* [1990] 1 Q.B. 391 at 474; this certainly covered "liability for dishonest assistance". Under that provision, provided that at least some of the acts which gave rise to the claim occurred within the jurisdiction, it did not appear to matter that others and the acquisition of any knowledge necessary for liability, occurred elsewhere (dicta in *SC Technologies v. Guerin* [1992] 1 Lloyd's Rep. 430, confirmed by dicta in *Polly Peck International v. Nadir* (1993) *The Times* March 22, 1993).

[64] Civil Procedure Rules 1998, Part 6.20, para. 15; no similar provision was included in Rules of the Supreme Court, Ord. 11. If para. 14 above does not cover "liability for dishonest assistance", this paragraph may do so.

jurisdiction, and it was clear that the judgment of the court in question would not be enforced in the jurisdiction(s) where the trustees and the trust property were physically present; in such circumstances, the latter jurisdiction(s) would clearly constitute a more appropriate forum.

### 3. Jurisdiction when the European Conventions Apply

The rules discussed so far do not, however, apply when the proceedings in question fall within the scope of the European Conventions. The countries who are bound by the relevant legislation ("European Convention States") have already been considered.[65] But, by virtue of Article 1,[66] the European Conventions never apply to, among other things, revenue, customs or administrative matters, or the status or legal capacity of natural persons, rights in property arising out of a matrimonial relationship, wills and succession, or to bankruptcy. Consequently, they do not apply to claims concerning trusts in favour of individual creditors, testamentary trusts and ante-nuptial or post-nuptial settlements or to claims to set aside a trust on the grounds that its creation amounted to a fraud on the settlor's creditors, or breached the terms of his matrimonial property regime, or deprived his forcible heirs of their rights. Such claims are therefore still governed by the rules which have already been considered.

Article 3 of the European Conventions[67] prohibits the exercise of jurisdiction on the basis of the temporary physical presence of the defendant or of his property within a particular jurisdiction. Article 2[68] provides that a person who has his domicile (which means a habitual residence, not the technical English private international law concept of domicile) in a European Convention State can only be sued in the courts of that state; the only exception is where the European Conventions confer jurisdiction on the courts of another European Convention State.[69] A court must decline jurisdiction where a defendant is sued other than in accordance with these provisions.[70] When proceedings involving the same cause of action and the same parties are brought in more than one European Convention State (such a situation is possible because most of the provisions of the European Conventions do not confer exclusive jurisdiction), any court other than the court where the proceedings started first must stay its proceedings while the jurisdiction of the court where the proceedings started first is established and, if it is established, must decline jurisdiction in favour of that court.[71] When proceedings in different European Convention States are related, in that it is expedient to hear and determine them together, any court other than the court where the proceedings started first may similarly first stay the proceedings and then decline jurisdiction.[72]

---

[65] See *ante*, p. 847.
[66] Both of the Brussels and Lugano Conventions and the Council Regulation.
[67] Both of the Brussels and Lugano Conventions and the Council Regulation; the provisions are not in the same form.
[68] Both of the Brussels and Lugano Conventions and the Council Regulation.
[69] Article 3 of both the Brussels and Lugano Conventions and the Council Regulation.
[70] Brussels and Lugano Conventions, Arts. 19, 20; Council Regulation, Arts. 25, 26.
[71] Brussels and Lugano Conventions, Arts. 21, 23; Council Regulation, Arts. 27, 29.
[72] Brussels and Lugano Conventions, Art. 22; Council Regulation, Art. 28.

As a general rule, proceedings brought pursuant to the European Conventions cannot be stayed on the ground of *forum non conveniens*. This was held by the Commercial Court in *Grupo Torras v. Al-Sabah*,[73] a case which concerned a gigantic corporate fraud whereby the Spanish company which ran the Kuwaiti Investment Office in that jurisdiction was defrauded by its directors of some US$750,000,000. Claims were brought in England seeking to impose liability for conspiracy, knowing receipt and dishonest assistance both on the directors and on many of those who had assisted in spiriting away the funds. The jurisdictional point was heard as a preliminary issue with only the company and its directors represented. Mance J. rejected a contention of the directors that the Spanish courts had exclusive jurisdiction because the case principally concerned the validity of decisions of the organs of the Spanish company; he then held that the English proceedings had in fact started first and could not be stayed on the grounds of *forum non conveniens*; the latter point was not considered in the subsequent appeal to the Court of Appeal.[74]

However, it has now been held in *Ace Insurance v. Zurich Insurance Company*,[75] that an action in respect of which a court has jurisdiction under the European Conventions can, contrary to the general rule, be stayed on the grounds of *forum non conveniens* where the alternative forum is not a European Convention State; the judge therefore stayed proceedings under a re-insurance contract to which both parties were domiciled in European Convention States in favour of later proceedings brought in Texas by the defendant to the English proceedings (Texas was a more appropriate forum because its courts had exclusive jurisdiction over the original insurance contract). This principle, if upheld, is clearly capable of applying to proceedings involving trusts whose applicable law is that of a non-European Convention State (as every offshore trust jurisdiction obviously is) even if both trustees and beneficiaries are here.

The relevant provision of the European Conventions governing proceedings involving trusts is Article 5(6):[76] a person with a domicile (which again means a habitual residence, not the technical English private international law concept of domicile) in a European Convention State may be sued in another convention state if he is "settlor, trustee or beneficiary of a trust created by the operation of a statute, or by a written instrument, or created orally and evidenced in writing, in the courts of the [European Convention State] in which the trust is domiciled" (this jurisdiction is not exclusive). Because trusts do not have legal personality and cannot really be said to have a habitual residence and because the United Kingdom is not a sole jurisdiction, specific provision has had to be made as to when and where a trust is domiciled in the United Kingdom; a trust is domiciled in the United Kingdom if it is domiciled in any part of the United Kingdom and is domiciled in a part of the United Kingdom "if and only if the system of law of that part is the system of law with which the trust has its closest and most real connection".[77] This system seems likely to be that of the applicable law of the trust, even if neither the trustees nor the trust property are physically present in that jurisdiction.

The rule established by Article 5(6) is overridden where any jurisdiction has

---

[73] [1995] 1 Lloyd's Rep. 374.
[74] [1996] 1 Lloyd's Rep. 7.
[75] [2001] 1 All E.R. (Comm.) 802.
[76] Both of the Brussels and Lugano Conventions and of the Council Regulation.
[77] Civil Jurisdiction and Judgments Act 1982, s.45.

been the subject of a choice of law clause in a trust instrument.[78] In this case exclusive jurisdiction is conferred on the jurisdiction so selected. There are, however, two exceptions to both Article 5(6) and the provision by which it is overridden. Where proceedings relate to the title to immovable property or to a leasehold interest in that property, the courts of the state where the immovable property is situated have exclusive jurisdiction.[79] This provision was applied in Re Hayward (dec'd),[80] where a trustee in bankruptcy was trying to assert in an English court a claim to an undivided one half share of a property in Spain which had belonged to the bankrupt but which had since been transferred by his widow into, and registered in the name of, the other co-owner; the claim was struck out for lack of jurisdiction. However, this provision does not prevent the English courts from having jurisdiction over proceedings relating to purely beneficial interests in such property. Thus in Webb v. Webb,[81] the European Court of Justice held that the English courts were entitled to exercise jurisdiction over proceedings in which the plaintiff was claiming that the defendant, his son, was holding land in France on resulting trust for him. These proceedings did not concern the legal title to the land in question and consequently the English courts were held to be able to exercise jurisdiction by virtue of the physical presence of the son in England. This jurisdiction was held not to be restricted to declaring the existence of the beneficial interest in question but also to extend to ordering the execution by the son of the notarial conveyance necessary under French law to transfer title to the land to his father. Webb v. Webb was applied in Ashurst v. Pollard,[82] where the Court of Appeal held that the trustee in bankruptcy of an English bankrupt was entitled to claim and the bankrupt was obliged to transfer to him an interest held by the bankrupt in immovable property situated in Portugal.

These provisions of the European Conventions are also reflected in the rules governing service out of the jurisdiction.[83] No leave is required for service out of the jurisdiction against a defendant in another European Convention State in three alternative circumstances provided that no proceedings between the parties in respect of the claim are already pending in any other European Convention State: first, where the subject matter of the dispute is English immovable property; secondly, where the defendant is domiciled in the United Kingdom (this again means a habitual residence, not the technical English private international law concept of domicile); and, thirdly, where the defendant is a party to an agreement conferring exclusive jurisdiction on the English courts (this last exception would presumably apply to proceedings between a settlor and his trustees where the trust deed conferred such jurisdiction on the English courts, although such proceedings are relatively unlikely).

---

[78] Brussels and Lugano Conventions, Art. 17; Council Regulation, Art. 23.
[79] Brussels and Lugano Conventions, Art. 16(1)(a); Council Regulation, Art. 22(1).
[80] [1997] 1 All E.R. 32.
[81] Webb v. Webb [1994] Q.B. 696
[82] [2001] 2 All E.R. 75.
[83] Civil Procedure Rules 1998, Part 6.19, repeating earlier provisions in the Rules of the Supreme Court.

### III. WHAT LAW WILL THE ENGLISH COURTS APPLY?

As has already been mentioned, the rules of English law governing the applicable law of a trust are now contained in the Hague Convention, incorporated into English law by the Recognition of Trusts Act 1987.[84] As the title of the Hague Convention suggests, it actually had two broad purposes: that of determining the law by which different aspects of trusts are governed and of enabling the recognition of trusts in jurisdictions where the trust concept is unknown; indeed it was the authorities of the latter jurisdictions who suggested to the Hague Secretariat that a convention should be prepared. The sort of potential problems which the provision of such recognition was intended to resolve have already been considered.[85] This chapter is only concerned with the determination of the law by which trusts are governed.

The Recognition of Trusts Act 1987 "is obscure as to its retrospective effect".[86] Article 22 of the Hague Convention provides that it "applies to trusts regardless of the date on which they were created" while section 1(5) of the Recognition of Trusts Act 1987 provides that "Article 22 shall not be construed as affecting the law to be applied in relation to anything done or omitted before the coming into force of this Act". In *Re Carapiet's Trusts,*[87] the settlement had been created before the coming into force of the Act but the provisions under review only became operative afterwards on the death of the life tenant. Whether the Hague Convention applied was not decided because all parties agreed that the applicable law was the same at common law as under the Hague Convention. However, section 1(5) can only disapply the Hague Convention in actions for breach of trust and not many breaches of trust committed before the Recognition of Trusts Act 1987 are now likely to come before the courts. The Hague Convention will therefore clearly apply to all other trust proceedings, no matter when the trust in question was created.

### 1. *Situations where the Applicable Law is Irrelevant*

Preliminary issues concerning the question of whether a trust has actually been created are not governed by its proper law but by whatever system of law governs the capacity of the settlor to create the trust and the means by which the trust property is vested in the trustees. This is expressly provided by Article 4 of the Hague Convention and would be the case even if the Convention contained no such provision. The Hague Convention does not as such deal with trusts created by declaration or orally (see Article 3) but section 1(2) of the Recognition of Trusts Act 1987 applies it to all English trusts however created. There is, however, no reason why a civil law jurisdiction which had ratified the Hague Convention could not restrict its recognition of trusts to trusts created by transfer and/or in writing if it chose to do so. This would be particularly likely if that jurisdiction had itself enacted legislation envisaging

---

[84] See Hayton (1987) 36 I.C.L.Q. 260 (Prof. Hayton was the head of the U.K. delegation to the body which produced the Convention and is therefore uniquely qualified to comment on its background and provisions); see also generally Harris, *The Hague Trusts Convention* (2002).

[85] See *ante*, p. 14.

[86] *Re Carapiet's Trusts* [2002] W.T.L.R. 989 at 993.

[87] [2002] W.T.L.R. 989 at 993.

only the creation of such trusts; an English court has held[88] that a Liechtenstein trust can only be created by transfer (however, Lichtenstein has not ratified the Hague Convention).

Under English law a minor, that is anyone under 18, has the capacity neither to create a trust nor to transfer property to its trustees and, in the admittedly unlikely event that he purported to do so, the property would remain vested in whoever had previously held it and no trust would have been created because it would not have become completely constituted; the fact that the trust instrument provided that the applicable law was that of some jurisdiction where the law was in some way different[89] would have no effect whatever, at least in an English court. Similarly, transfers of property to trustees can be set aside under the Insolvency Act 1986, the Matrimonial Causes Act 1973 and the Inheritance (Provision for Family and Dependants) Act 1975 notwithstanding the fact that the trust in question is a foreign trust.

Further, an English trust will be invalid if its foreign settlor lacked capacity to create it under his own personal law. In *Neumann v. Azon Anstalt*[90] a Liechtenstein company which was the tenant of a flat in London declared a trust of that flat in favour of its occupier in order to enable the company to obtain a new lease to which it was entitled if the beneficiary had occupied the flat as his only or principal home for three out of the previous ten years and if the trust was actually valid. The trust declared was in English law form but did not contain an express choice of law clause. In the absence of such a clause Liechtenstein law provides that the proper law will be that of the jurisdiction where the trustees (or a majority of the trustees) are domiciled or resident; a Liechtenstein company is necessarily both domiciled and resident in Liechtenstein. The judge[91] held that, if the trust was indeed an English trust, it was invalid because, in the absence of a choice of law clause, the Liechtenstein company did not have the capacity to create an English trust.[92] Similar questions of capacity also arise where foreign settlors transfer property to the trustees of an English trust in breach of the rules of their matrimonial property regime or of their home jurisdiction's forcible heirship provisions.[93] Whether the English trust is valid will depend on whether the relevant foreign law makes the transfer by the foreign settlor void, thus affecting his capacity and rendering the English trust void, or merely voidable, in which case his capa-

---

[88] In *Neumann v. Azon Anstalt* (2001) unreported.
[89] Because the age of majority was lower there. It is difficult to think of any jurisdiction where this is the case; however, if a 19 year old person from Jersey (where the age of majority is 20) tried to create a trust, the fact that it was expressly subject to English law would not make it valid in Jersey; nor, if he purported to transfer English land vested in him to the trustees of the English trust, would the transfer be held to be effective even in an English court if its validity was subsequently challenged (by the minor's parents or guardian, or indeed by himself immediately after he obtained the age of majority).
[90] (2001) unreported.
[91] Judge Levy Q.C. in the Central London County Court.
[92] The judge went on to hold that, on the alternative hypothesis that the trust was a Liechtenstein trust, it was also invalid because Liechtenstein law does not envisage the creation of trusts by declaration, only by transfer.
[93] The ability to impeach such transactions does of course depend on the property in question still being within the reach of those seeking to set the transfers aside. It will not be if it is in the control of trustees of another jurisdiction which does not recognise and enforce the judgments of courts in the jurisdiction where any such transfer is set aside; this is the case in many off shore trust jurisdictions.

city will not be affected and the English trust will be valid. In the case of French law, the settlement of property by a person married under French law on trust for his spouse would be wholly void from the outset,[94] while a settlement of property on trust by a person habitually resident in France which left insufficient assets for his forcible heirs would be merely voidable and would only be able to be avoided in the event that there were still insufficient assets to fund their percentage of his lifetime assets on his death.[95]

Nor is the applicable law of the trust likely to be applied if the trust created is contrary to English public policy. If English land were settled on a form of trust which is prohibited by English law but permitted by the law of the jurisdiction whose law was chosen as its applicable law, such as a trust for the settlor for life or until bankruptcy[96] or on trusts which can last for ever and so blatantly infringe the rule against perpetuities,[97] an English court would be highly likely to apply English law and declare the trust to be void (it would of course have jurisdiction so to do because the subject matter was land within the jurisdiction). This would also be the case with movable property which was actually within the jurisdiction at the time of the proceedings. It is less certain how the English courts would react to the various types of purpose trusts which have recently become fashionable in many off-shore trust jurisdictions[98] which are contrary to the rules of English trust law because they have no beneficiaries or to the more extreme trusts (or so-called trusts) which deprive their beneficiaries of any right to enforce them.[99]

### 2. What is the Applicable Law?

Article 6(1) of the Hague Convention provides that:

> "A trust shall be governed by the law chosen by the settlor. The choice must be express or be implied in the terms of the instrument creating or the writing evidencing the trust, interpreted, if necessary, in the light of the circumstances of the case."

The only restriction placed by Article 6 on the settlor's choice is the requirement that the law chosen "provides for trusts or the category of trust involved"; if it does not do so, Article 6 does not apply to the trust in question, and the applicable law is determined by recourse to Article 7.

It was held in Tod v. Barton[1] that Article 6 contemplates two different situations: first, where there is an express choice of applicable law; and, secondly, where there is an implied choice of applicable law. Only in the second of those two situations can recourse be had to the circumstances of the case.

---

[94] Code Civile, Art. 1096.
[95] Code Civile, Art. 1097.
[96] Permitted in The Cook Islands.
[97] Permitted in The Cayman Islands. However, it is unlikely that there would be any difficulty about perpetuity and accumulation periods which are merely longer than the maximum period at present permitted by English law, which the proposed new legislation will extend anyway; most off-shore trusts jurisdictions at present have longer perpetuity periods than the present English law and even Northern Ireland has a longer accumulation period.
[98] Pioneered by Bermuda but now relatively common.
[99] This is now permitted in The Cayman Islands.
[1] (2002) 4 I.T.E.L.R. 715, paras. 32–35.

Consequently in *Tod v. Barton*, where the testator had expressly chosen English law, there was held to be no legal basis for the argument that in the circumstances of the case that choice could and should be disregarded (the circumstances in question were that under English law the testator's provision that his son could not take the annuity given to him by the will until he attained the age of 65 could be and was circumvented by recourse to the Rule in *Saunders v. Vautier*,[2] something which would not have been possible under the law of the testator's last domicile[3]). Where there is no express choice of applicable law, the settlor will be found to have made an implied choice if the trust instrument contains other references to a particular jurisdiction. In *Tod v. Barton*, had the testator not made an express choice of applicable law, he would have been held to have made an implied choice by virtue of the fact that the will contained a provision restricting the gift over to educational purposes which were charitable according to English law. The circumstances of the case referred to would not have prevented this conclusion, which indicates that recourse to such circumstances will only be necessary if the provisions of the trust instrument are much less clear. It must also follow that the factors which determine the applicable law in default of an express or implied choice do not constitute relevant circumstances of the case either.

Where there is no express or implied choice of applicable law, the Hague Convention provides in Article 7:

"Where no applicable law has been chosen, a trust shall be governed by the law with which it is most closely connected.

"In ascertaining the law with which a trust is most closely connected reference shall be made in particular to —

    (a) the place of the administration of the trust designated by the settlor;
    (b) the situs of the assets of the trust;
    (c) the place of residence or business of the trustee;
    (d) the objects of the trust and the places where they are to be fulfilled."

The delegations negotiating the terms of the Hague Convention decided to restrict themselves to these four factors. The need for both common law and civil law jurisdictions to make concessions meant the former had to accept the absence of domicile and the latter the absence of nationality, factors which are generally all important in these respective jurisdictions; these factors must presumably therefore be disregarded. However, as the wording of Article 7

---

[2] (1841) Cr. & P. 240; see *ante*, p. 717. The son and the Royal Chemical Society, which was otherwise entitled to the testator's residuary estate, agreed that the son should receive an immediate payment of £164,000 rather than the annuity.

[3] The testator had died domiciled in Texas, where beneficiaries can only terminate a trust once all its purposes have been fulfilled or become illegal or impossible to fulfil (*Lanius v. Fletcher* (1907) 101 S.W. 1076, *Frost National Bank v. Newton* (1977) 554 S.W. 2d 149).

itself recognises, the four factors actually listed do not constitute an exclusive list. Admittedly, the actual language of the trust instrument, and in particular any references which it may make to the law or the specific statutory provisions of any particular jurisdiction, will point towards an implied choice of applicable law under Article 6 rather than constitute an additional factor under Article 7. But the habitual residence of persons other than the trustee may be significant. The habitual residence of the testator will clearly be a key factor in testamentary trusts, although the habitual residence of the settlor will obviously be less relevant in inter vivos trusts if different from the place of residence or business of the trustee. However, the extent to which the habitual residence of the beneficiaries should be relevant, if different from the place of residence or business of the trustee (which it always will be in the case of an off-shore trust), is much more questionable.

In *Tod v. Barton*,[4] it was held that recourse to Article 7 would also have led to the conclusion that the applicable law was English law; the situs of the assets and the place where the trust was to be fulfilled were in England, as was the residence of one of the trustees, and the fact that the testator and the other trustee were resident and domiciled in Texas would not have displaced English law as the law with which the trust was most closely connected.

In *Re Carapiet's Trusts*,[5] the settlor was born in Iraq and as a result of successive marriages acquired British nationality and an Indian domicile. The settlement had been made in England, where the settlor was apparently then resident, as a result of litigation in India between her and the Armenian Patriarch of Jerusalem; the settlor had been given special permission to remove the assets from India to England. The trustee was an English bank and the settled property was held on trust for the settlor for life and subject to that to apply the income in accordance with the directions of the Armenian Patriarch for the education and advancement in life of Armenian children. Jacob J. held that this was an Article 7 case and that English law was the applicable law; it was abundantly clear from the transfer of the assets to England and the appointment of an English trustee that the settlor had wanted the trust controlled from England.

In *Chellaram v. Chellaram (No.2)*,[6] the facts of which have already been considered,[7] there was initially no express choice of an applicable law but the court upheld the validity of a decision of the trustees to change the applicable law to Bermudan law. Had it been necessary to apply Article 7, the court would have held Indian law to be the applicable law because the trusts had been drafted in India by Indian lawyers for a family of Indian origin with strong Indian ties and it was very doubtful that English law would have been the applicable law merely because two of the original trustees were in London and it was contemplated but not required that the trusts would, at least initially, be administered in London.

If whatever factors are decided to be relevant in any given case point towards the law of two different jurisdictions, one under which the trust

---

[4] (2002) 4 I.T.E.L.R. 715, para. 36.
[5] [2002] W.T.L.R. 989.
[6] [2002] 3 All E.R. 17 at 49–50.
[7] See *ante*, p. 841.

would be valid and one under which it would be void, English law at least would be likely to opt for the jurisdiction in which it is valid.[8]

### 3. What is the scope of the Applicable Law?

Article 8 of the Hague Convention provides that the applicable law shall govern "the validity of the trust, its construction, its effect, and the administration of the trust" (although this is subject to Article 9 which permits "a severable aspect of the trust, particularly matters of administration" to be governed by a different law; this possibility is considered below). There then follows a non-exhaustive list of what the applicable law will govern. This contains nearly everything which could be expected. The only significant omission appears to be powers vested in persons other than the trustee such as the settlor or a protector. However, it cannot seriously be contended that these would not be governed by the applicable law (unless, of course, their subject matter related to "a severable aspect ... governed by a different law").

The inclusion in the list of what the applicable law will govern of "(h) the variation or termination of the trust" leads to the conclusion that, as has already been mentioned,[9] the English courts no longer have the jurisdiction which they have previously arrogated[10] to approve applications under the Variation of Trusts Act 1958[11] in respect of foreign trusts; even if they do, they may well now[12] not feel inclined to make such orders and the courts of the foreign jurisdiction in question may well decline to enforce them.

On the face of things, paragraph (h) also applies to claims for the variation of a trust in proceedings for the reallocation of property following a divorce in which one of the former spouses claims assets to which the respondent former spouse is entitled under a foreign trust. Although such claims have been successful in the past,[13] on the face of things the English courts no longer have jurisdiction over foreign trusts in this respect either.[14] This will not cause any difficulty in practice where the trustees of the foreign trust are within the

---

[8]  In accordance with the decision of the majority of the Court of Appeal in *Re Baden's Deed Trusts* [1969] 2 Ch. 126, see *ante* p. 208, that, where the considerations were evenly balanced in arriving at one or other conclusion, the court was at liberty to lean towards the conclusion which might effectuate rather than frustrate the settlor's intentions (the point did not arise on the subsequent appeal to the House of Lords (*McPhail v. Doulton* [1971] A.C. 424)). This case concerned a private trust but the existence of a similar attitude towards charitable trusts was confirmed by the House of Lords in *I.R.C. v. McMullen* [1981] A.C. 1, see *ante*, p. 444, although the House did not need to resort to it in that case.

[9]  See *ante*, p. 843.

[10]  *Re Ker's Settlement* [1963] Ch. 553; *Re Paget's Settlement* [1965] 1 W.L.R. 1046.

[11]  See *ante*, p. 747.

[12]  In the light of *Compass Trustees v. McBarnett* [2003] W.T.L.R. 461, discussed in the text *infra*.

[13]  Claims to vary pre-nuptial or post-nuptial settlements of property governed by foreign law with exclusively foreign trustees were successfully made in *Nunneley v. Nunneley* (1890) 15 P.D. 186, *Forsyth v. Forsyth* [1891] P. 363, and *Goff v. Goff* [1934] P. 107. More recently, claims for the reallocation of property on divorce were successfully made in *Browne v. Browne* [1989] 1 F.L.R. 291 (Jersey discretionary trust, Liechtenstein trust), *E v. E (Financial Provision)* [1990] 2 F.L.R. 233 (Guernsey discretionary trust), and *T v. T* [1996] 2 F.L.R. 357 (Jersey discretionary trust); however, in these proceedings no reference was made to the Recognition of Trusts Act 1987.

[14]  It has been argued in unreported proceedings that the English courts no longer have jurisdiction to make orders governing such trusts but such arguments have not yet been the subject of a reasoned judgment.

English jurisdiction or can be controlled by a respondent who is himself within the English jurisdiction; in such circumstances the trustees or the respondent will be susceptible to the personal jurisdiction of the English courts. It may be[15] that, despite paragraph (h), the English courts will assert jurisdiction over the foreign trust by asserting that the question is governed by the law of the forum or by relying on Article 15 of the Hague Convention;[16] in policy terms, this could be justified on the grounds that otherwise putting assets in a foreign trust would be far too easy a way of protecting them from potential claims by former spouses. However, in *Compass Trustees v. McBarnett*,[17] the Royal Court of Jersey was asked to vary a Jersey trust pursuant to a judgment of the Family Division of the English High Court which held that such a variation was necessary but could only be done by the Jersey court. Given that both spouses had submitted to the jurisdiction of the English court, the Royal Court of Jersey duly made the variation as a matter of comity.[18] The history of this litigation suggests both that the English courts may well no longer regard themselves as having jurisdiction over foreign trusts in family proceedings and that a foreign court may not make the order desired by the English court if the defendant has not appeared in the English proceedings; further, a foreign court which, unlike the Royal Court of Jersey, is outside the United Kingdom may not feel obliged to act as a matter of comity at all.

Where a settlement takes advantage of Article 9 of the Hague Convention to provide that a severable aspect of the trust is to be governed by a different law (and most precedents now envisage this being done by providing both separate choice of law clauses for the applicable law and the law governing the administration of the trust and for the two to be independently changed), considerable difficulties can be encountered in determining precisely what is to be governed by the law of which jurisdiction unless the trust instrument has defined extremely precisely what is to be regarded as constituting whatever has been excluded from the ambit of its applicable law.

The applicable law will govern at the very least the nature of the interests of its beneficiaries and the duties of the trustees towards them; this was specifically stated in *Chellaram v. Chellaram*.[19] It will also govern all other questions concerning the trust other than any which has been stated to be governed by the law of some other jurisdiction so, in the event that it cannot be decided whether or not the trust instrument has provided for a severable aspect of the trust is to be governed by a different law, the applicable law will apply. The construction of the trust instrument and the administration of the trust are what are most commonly excluded from the ambit of its applicable law. There is no difficulty in defining the scope of the former exclusion but very considerable difficulties can be encountered in defining precisely what constitutes administration in the absence of an express definition. Prior to the incorporation of the Hague Convention into English law, Dicey & Morris,[20] the leading practitioners' text, drew a distinction between, on the one hand, the validity, interpretation and effect of a trust and, on the other hand, its

---

[15] This is the view taken by Dicey & Morris, *The Conflict of Laws* (13th ed., 2000), p. 1093.
[16] See *post*, p. 864.
[17] [2003] W.T.L.R. 461.
[18] Reliance was placed on the earlier decision of that court in *Lane v. Lane* 1985 6 J.L.R. 48.
[19] [1985] Ch. 409 at 432.
[20] *Conflict of Laws* (10th ed., 1980), Rules 120 & 121.

administration; the former were said to be governed by its applicable law and the latter was said to be governed by the law of its place of administration. This distinction was rejected by Scott J. in *Chellaram v. Chellaram*,[21] who expressed the view that all four were governed by its applicable law.[22] However, that does not answer the question of what is to be regarded as administration when the settlor has stated that administration is to be governed by a law other than the proper law without defining what he means by administration.

It has already been stated that the proper law of the trust will at the very least govern the nature of the interests of the beneficiaries and the duties of the trustees towards them (the latter will clearly include any powers which they have to determine the manner in which the income and capital of the trust is distributed and their duties to convert and apportion the trust property). The proper law will also undoubtedly govern the construction of the trust instrument if this has not been expressly reserved to the law of some other jurisdiction. At the other extreme, there can be no doubt that the trustees' duties to provide accounts and to give information to the beneficiaries are purely administrative; so are some of their powers, such as the power to appoint and remove trustees, to appoint agents, and to insure. But a number of other powers which are, for other purposes, often classified as administrative are capable of affecting directly or indirectly the interests of the beneficiaries in the event that the provisions of the proper law and of the law specified as governing administration differ as to their existence or scope. The presence or absence of a power for the trustees to remunerate themselves clearly affects the income and capital available for the beneficiaries. So does the presence or absence of powers of advancement, maintenance and accumulation in the event that they are exercised. So too, to a lesser extent, do the trustees' powers of investment. And where powers exercisable by persons other than the trustees, such as the settlor or the protector, fit in is anyone's guess; the law applicable will presumably (or at any rate should) be determined by the nature of the power in question. There therefore seems no sensible way of drawing a line in the absence of a precise definition in the trust instrument and it is consequently impossible to predict what would happen in the event that an English court had to decide by which law such powers were governed.

Such a situation would open the way for the court to ignore the provisions of the trust instrument completely and simply apply English law. Indeed, this is precisely what Scott J. did in *Chellaram v. Chellaram*,[23] which was admittedly decided before the incorporation of the Hague Convention into English law. In this case, the facts of which have already been considered,[24] the beneficiaries were seeking the removal and replacement of the trustees. Scott J. was prepared to apply the provisions of English law to this question even if both the applicable law and the law under which the trust was being administered turned out to be Indian law. He said this:[25]

---

[21] [1985] Ch. 409 at 432.
[22] The current edition of Dicey & Morris (13th ed., 2000) Rule 151 (p. 1087) states the law in accordance with the Hague Convention.
[23] [1985] Ch. 409.
[24] See *ante*, p. 841.
[25] [1985] Ch. 409 at 432–433.

"The function of English courts in trust litigation is to enforce or protect the rights of the beneficiaries which bind the conscience of the trustee defendants. The identification and extent of those rights is a matter for the [applicable] law of the settlement, but the manner of enforcement is, in my view, a matter of machinery which, under English domestic law, can be exercised by English courts where necessary in order to enable the rights of beneficiaries to be enforced or protected. . . . Accordingly, except where rights conferred by the settlement are under consideration, the removal of trustees and the appointment of new ones are not, in my judgment, a matter to be governed by the [applicable] law of the settlement. Nor, in my opinion, is it a matter to be governed by the law of the place where the administration of the settlement has taken place. It is, in my judgment, a matter to be governed by the law of the country whose courts have assumed jurisdiction to administer the trusts of the settlement in question."

The last sentence of this passage suggests, without actually stating, that English law was applicable simply because it was the law of the forum. If English domestic law is indeed applicable whenever it is necessary to protect the interests of the beneficiaries, then the possibilities for its application are infinite. It is of course possible that this approach would be held no longer to be appropriate in the light of the subsequent incorporation of the Hague Convention into English law. But in the event that this approach is still applicable, it is at least theoretically possible that the provisions of the Hague Convention could be ignored in any proceedings brought by beneficiaries against trustees to enforce their interests in which the English courts have jurisdiction; such a contention could obviously most easily be made in a case where, as in *Chelleram v. Chellaram*, the beneficiaries were seeking a change of trustees.

### 4. *Changing the Applicable Law*

Article 10 of the Hague Convention deals with changes of the applicable law (or for that matter of any other governing law) by providing that the question of whether such a change is possible shall be determined by "the law applicable to the validity of the trust". This presumably means the applicable law but it would be more helpful if the Hague Convention actually said so specifically. Such changes of governing law will require, at least under English law, either a provision in the trust instrument expressly permitting this[26] or the agreement of all the beneficiaries which, if any of them is not *sui juris*, will require an order of the court under the Variation of Trusts Act 1958.[27] That a change of governing law is not otherwise possible seems to have been confirmed by the courts of The Cayman Islands in *Wahr-Hansen v. Bridge Trust Co.*,[28] which concerned a change of applicable law from the law of The

---

[26] This follows from the authorities listed *post*, fn. 28.
[27] See *ante*, p. 747.
[28] 1997 C.I.L.R. 527 (Court of Appeal); the question was discussed more fully at first instance *sub nom. Bridge Trust Co. v. Attorney-General* 1996 C.I.L.R. 52 but did not arise on the further appeal to the Privy Council *sub nom. Attorney-General of the Cayman Islands v. Wahr-Hansen* [2001] 1 A.C. 75.

Bahamas to the law of The Cayman Islands pursuant to a clause expressly permitting such a change.[29]

A change of the applicable law of a trust away from English law will often take place as part of an arrangement by which a trust changes its fiscal status from a resident to a non-resident trust,[30] in which case the latter change will produce a deemed disposal for the purposes of capital gains tax.[31] Where a trust remains resident for fiscal purposes despite a change of applicable law, there will nevertheless be a deemed disposal for the purposes of capital gains tax where the change of applicable law is made pursuant to the agreement of the beneficiaries; this is because for at least for a moment of time the beneficiaries will be absolutely entitled to the trust property as against the trustees.[32] However, it is not thought that a deemed disposal would be a consequence of a change of applicable law pursuant to an express provision in the trust instrument.

Surprisingly Article 10, unlike the provisions governing the choice of the original applicable law, does not restrict changes of applicable law to changes to jurisdictions whose laws "provide for trusts or the category of trusts involved". A change to a jurisdiction which did not recognise trusts could lead to the settlor being regarded as absolutely entitled to the trust property or as being entitled to revoke the trusts in favour of himself; this could have disastrous fiscal consequences,[33] as could a change to a jurisdiction which recognised trusts but only of a type which English law regarded as void for public policy. Presumably, the Convention assumes that the trustees will be sensible! However, serious consideration should be given by draftsmen to restricting the scope of clauses permitting a change of law to, at the very least, jurisdictions which recognise trusts. The relevant Cayman Islands legislation requires any new applicable law to recognise both the validity of the trust and the respective interests of the beneficiaries. However, it may be that this is implied at common law anyway since in *Bridge Trust Co. v. Attorney-General*[34] the Chief Justice of The Cayman Islands held that at common law[35] a change of applicable law will not be recognised unless the new applicable law chosen

---

[29] The plaintiffs contended that the change of applicable law was ineffective because, as the Privy Council subsequently held, the entire trust was void and so the clause permitting a change of applicable law was void as well. However, at first instance, it was held that all that was necessary was that Bahamian law recognised the possibility of a change in the proper law and that, given that it did, the change of law was therefore valid because it satisfied the legislation of The Cayman Islands governing changes of applicable law. While it must admittedly be possible for such a clause permitting a change of applicable law to survive the invalidity of one or more of the individual provisions of the trust, it is hard to see how such a clause can continue to exist, like the grin of the Cheshire Cat, in a trust which has been declared to be entirely void. However, the Court of Appeal confirmed the decision at first instance in this respect and the point was not pursued further.

[30] See *post*, p. 881.

[31] See *post*, p. 879.

[32] See *ante*, p. 637.

[33] Because the settlor would under English law be regarded as being beneficially entitled to the trust property and, if he was subject to English taxation, would therefore become liable to income tax and capital gains tax on its assets. This would also stop any seven year period running for the purposes of inheritance tax.

[34] 1996 C.I.L.R. 52 (the question did not arise on appeal; see fn. 28 above).

[35] This was what applied in The Bahamas, the jurisdiction from which the applicable law was being changed, at the relevant time.

recognises both the validity of the trusts and the original interests of the beneficiaries.

### 6. Mandatory Provisions of the Hague Convention

The Hague Convention describes Articles 15 and 16 as mandatory provisions. Article 15 provides that the Hague Convention "does not prevent the application of provisions of the law designated by the conflicts rules of the forum, in so far as those provisions cannot be derogated from by voluntary act" referring in particular to, among other things,[36] "(a) the protection of minors and incapable parties (b) the personal and proprietary effects of marriage; (c) succession rights, testate and intestate, especially the indefeasible share of spouses and relatives ... (e) the protection of creditors in matters of insolvency".

In *Tod v. Barton*,[37] it was contended that Article 15 required the court to apply the rules of private international law relating to succession and, therefore, the law of the testator's domicile, Texas, which would have prevented the beneficiaries agreeing to exercise the Rule in *Saunders v. Vautier*[38] and so frustrating his wishes.[39] Lawrence Collins J. rejected this argument, holding that "the purpose of article 15 is to preserve the mandatory effect of the rules of the law designated by the conflict of laws rules for matters other than trusts". He gave as an example the rule of English law that succession to personal property is governed by the law of the deceased's domicile at the date of his death, saying that, if the law of that domicile contains forcible heirship provisions, those provisions must be given effect to notwithstanding the creation of a trust which purports to override them. But in *Tod v. Barton* the testator's domicile was relevant only for the purposes of determining the essential validity of his will. Given that it was valid and had been carried into effect, no rule of English private international law referred the validity of the agreement to vary it to Texan law.

This decision indicates that Article 15 might be a means by which English law could justify a decision to avoid a foreign trust made in fraud of creditors, spouses, and dependants[40] and/or the continuation of the jurisdiction to order the reallocation, following divorce, of property held under a foreign trust not subject to English law.[41] However, English courts may well be rather wary about declaring that any of the rules of English law "cannot be derogated from by voluntary act", since such declarations might have all sorts of implications in other situations.

Article 16 (the second paragraph of which does not form part of English law) similarly provides that "those provisions of the law of the forum which must be applied even to international situations, irrespective of" its rules of private international law are also applicable despite the provisions of the

---

[36] Those not listed are not relevant to English law, although "(d) the transfer of title to property ..." may well confirm the conclusions which have already been expressed (*ante*, p. 844) about the limitations on equitable proprietary claims and "liability for knowing receipt".

[37] (2002) 4 I.T.E.L.R. 715, paras. 39–42.

[38] (1841) Cr. & P. 240; see *ante*, p. 717.

[39] See *ante*, p. 857.

[40] See *ante*, p. 855.

[41] See *ante*, p. 859.

Hague Convention. The only obvious situation to which this would apply (and this is fairly far-fetched) would be if the trustees of a foreign trust brought in an English court proceedings which were connected in some way with assets whose sale, purchase or ownership was permitted by its applicable law but prohibited by English law (examples would be arms, drugs, classical architectural artefacts, and protected species).

## IV. The Enforcement By English Courts of Foreign Trusts Judgments

Any judgment in proceedings involving a trust given by a court which has jurisdiction under the European Conventions[42] will be automatically recognised and enforced by the English courts[43] unless it falls foul of a further provision of the European Conventions[44] for one of the following reasons:

(a) because it is contrary to public policy;

(b) because judgment was given in default of appearance in circumstances where the defendant was not properly served in sufficient time to prepare his defence;

(c) if the judgment cannot be reconciled with a judgment already given by an English court in a dispute between the same parties;

(d) (only under the Council Regulation) if the judgment cannot be reconciled with an earlier judgment already given in any country (whether a European Convention State or not) involving the same cause of action and between the same parties and that earlier judgment is entitled to be recognised by the English court;

(e) (only under the Brussels and Lugano Conventions), if the judgment was given pursuant to a rule of private international law as to capacity, matrimonial property rights, or succession which produced a result different from that which would have been reached under English private international law.

Any judgment in proceedings not subject to the European Conventions will also be recognised and enforced if it is within any bilateral or multi-lateral convention for the enforcement of judgments between the state where the judgment was given and the United Kingdom and is duly registered in the High Court of England and Wales. If no such convention is applicable, then the foreign judgment will not be recognised or enforced by the English courts; it will merely create an obligation binding on the defendant which the successful claimant will have to enforce by bringing a separate action in the English courts.[45] This is still the position where a successful claimant in any of

---

[42] See *ante*, p. 847.
[43] Brussels and Lugano Conventions, Arts. 26 & 31; Council Regulation, Arts. 33 & 38.
[44] Brussels and Lugano Conventions, Art. 27; Council Regulation, Art. 34.
[45] Since he will normally be able to obtain summary judgment, this is not usually any slower than the process of registering a judgment under a bilateral or multi-lateral convention.

the jurisdictions of the United States of America seeks to enforce his judgment in the English courts.[46]

---

[46] And of course vice-versa.

CHAPTER 24

# EXPORTING TRUSTS

## I. MOTIVES

A person may wish to create a new trust abroad or to export an existing trust for a variety of reasons. Generally, these are one or more of the following.

1. The beneficiaries or a majority of them are resident abroad or are intending to reside abroad and it will be most convenient for the trust to be administered in the country in which they are resident.[1]

2. There is a widespread fear that future United Kingdom legislation might aim to achieve a more even distribution of wealth among members of the community and that this can only be achieved by, in effect, confiscating part of the assets of those who are thought to be wealthy. A wealth tax is only one form which such legislation might take. It is not appropriate to comment here on the ethics or political wisdom of any such measures but man is an essentially greedy animal and, having acquired assets, will usually go to great lengths to retain them. Some people think, not always correctly, that if assets are transferred abroad and held by trustees, then they will be safe from the tax gatherer's prying eyes and preying hands, particularly if the transferor does not retain any legal entitlement to them.

3. From time to time, although admittedly not at present, there is an associated fear that, as a currency, sterling may not be stable and that the value and security of wealth may be enhanced if it is held abroad.

4. A settlor may occasionally wish to take advantage of foreign rules of law. Some of these rules have been considered in the previous chapter. Although it is not "foreign" in the fiscal sense, a particular example is Northern Ireland where it is possible to direct accumulation for much longer than it is at present in England and Wales, although this will change if the present proposals for reform of the law governing accumulations are enacted.[2] Many off-shore jurisdictions, which certainly are "foreign" in the fiscal sense, permit types of purpose trusts which are void under English law. However, advan-

---

[1] This was the reason for the approval of the court given in *Re Seale's Marriage Settlement* [1961] Ch. 574 and in *Re Windeatt's Will Trusts* [1969] 1 W.L.R. 692; see *post*, p. 883. See also *Re Whitehead's Will Trusts* [1971] 1 W.L.R. 833, *post*, p. 886.
[2] See *ante*, p. 253.

tage can only be taken of rules of these types if the applicable law of the trust, determined in the manner also considered in the previous chapter, is the law of the jurisdiction whose trust law contains them. The settlor of a newly created trust can of course select whatever applicable law he wishes. However, a pre-existing trust will only be able to change its applicable law to that of a foreign jurisdiction if the trust instrument contains a clause expressly permitting this or all the beneficiaries agree (which, if any of them is not *sui juris*, will require an order of the court under the Variation of Trusts Act 1958).

5.   Lastly, and predominantly, settlors and beneficiaries wish to reduce their fiscal liabilities and to ensure so far as possible that funds are protected from the admittedly increasingly unlikely possibility of any re-introduction of United Kingdom exchange control.

This chapter is concerned entirely with the extent to which the final two objectives can effectively be achieved. It examines the main aspects of the law which apply when a person resident in the United Kingdom wishes to create a new trust abroad or when an existing trust whose applicable law is English law is transferred abroad[3] (in this chapter, a trust whose applicable law is English law will be described as "an English trust", a trust whose applicable law is not or is no longer English law will be described as "a foreign trust"[4] and a trust whose applicable law is that of another specific jurisdiction will be described as, for example, "a Jersey trust").

## II. THE LEGACY OF EXCHANGE CONTROL

United Kingdom exchange control legislation was suspended in 1979.[5] That legislation had been intended to conserve the United Kingdom's gold and

---

[3] There is nothing to stop a trust whose applicable law and/or place of administration is already that of an off-shore jurisdiction from being exported to another off-shore jurisdiction. This is unlikely to have any fiscal consequences so there are only likely to be two possible reasons for this, either in order to take advantage of new or more favourable rules of trust law created in that other jurisdiction or because of anxieties about the stability of the existing off-shore jurisdiction. Trusts in some off-shore jurisdictions habitually contain what are known as "flee clauses", change of applicable law clauses which are drafted in such a way that they operate automatically, that is to say, without the trustees needing to take any action, in the event of certain things happening. When such a clause is triggered, the applicable law and also the site where the trust is being administered, if different, are automatically changed to that of another jurisdiction and trustees from that jurisdiction are automatically appointed in place of the pre-existing trustees. Some of the triggering events are of a political nature, such as the election of an unfriendly government (which obviously has to be defined) or a *coup d'état*. Other types of flee clauses attempt to oust the jurisdiction of the courts of the applicable law by providing for any attempt by the courts of that jurisdiction to assert control over the affairs of the trust to be a triggering event. It is questionable whether the latter type of flee clauses work and whether any type of flee clause is valid; see McCall [1995] P.C.B. 419.

[4] This expression obviously includes trusts governed by the law of anywhere other than England and Wales and therefore trusts governed by the law of Scotland, Northern Ireland, the Channel Islands, the Isle of Man and all other dependencies of the United Kingdom. However, for fiscal purposes, trusts governed by the law of Scotland and Northern Ireland are treated in the same way as English trusts and not in the same way as other foreign trusts.

[5] With effect from October 24, 1979.

foreign currency resources and to assist the balance of payments by restricting the outflow of funds from the United Kingdom. While the legislation was in operation, a person resident in the United Kingdom[6] who wished to purchase an investment or other asset abroad[7] had, very broadly, to do so in one of three ways.

1. With currency purchased through the official foreign exchange market. This was controlled strictly by the Bank of England, acting as the exchange control authority. In principle, the Bank of England gave permission for the use of foreign currency purchased at the official rate of exchange only where the investment was likely directly to promote United Kingdom exports, or where it promised an early benefit to the balance of payments. Permission was not generally given for personal investment.

2. With "investment currency". After the introduction of exchange control, persons who were resident in the United Kingdom and who had foreign currency securities[8] were obliged, when they sold them, to sell them through controlled channels and receive the proceeds of sale in sterling. Those proceeds of sale, known as investment currency, were available for sale to other United Kingdom residents but, because of the shortage of investment currency, at a premium which was often in excess of 40 per cent. This applied even where an investor who was resident in the United Kingdom wished to sell one foreign currency security and to re-invest the proceeds in another such security.

3. With the proceeds of foreign currency borrowings. These were sums borrowed abroad in a currency other than sterling. Such foreign currency borrowing required the permission of the Bank of England, which was not generally granted to private investors.

A further restriction was that, whenever foreign currency securities were purchased, irrespective of the source of the funds, the certificates of the securities had to be held by depositories designated by the Bank of England.[9] Furthermore, there was a general prohibition on maintaining foreign currency bank accounts.

While exchange control was in force, an individual who wished to invest abroad was therefore subject to numerous restrictions and almost invariably substantial extra cost. Further, there was always the risk that in acute national financial circumstances the Government would take action to compel the foreign currency securities held by the designated depositories to be realised. In 1979, the legislation was suspended but not repealed.[10] The general view,

---

[6] Or in the other Scheduled Territories, namely the Channel Islands, the Isle of Man, the Republic of Ireland and Gibraltar.
[7] Outside the Scheduled Territories. A special relaxation applied in the case of investment in other members of what was then known as the European Economic Community.
[8] That was securities denominated or payable in any currency other than sterling.
[9] Most banks and practising solicitors were so designated.
[10] By the Exchange Control (General Exemption) Order 1979 (S.I. 1979 No.1660) and the Exchange Control (Revocation) (No. 2) Direction 1979 (S.I. 1979 No.1162).

admittedly not universally held, is that it could be brought back into operation again merely by the Treasury laying a Statutory Instrument before Parliament.[11] However, it has to be admitted that, even on the assumption that the legislation could be brought back into operation so easily, the chances of any reintroduction are negligible for both political and practical reasons. It would be politically impossible to impose exchange control between the United Kingdom and the other members of the European Union and no such reintroduction is really necessary anyway in the light of the ever-increasing facilities for the interchange of information between member countries; the Inland Revenue can find out about any assets held openly by any United Kingdom tax-payer in any other member country. Further, although exchange control could certainly be reintroduced between the United Kingdom and countries who are not members of the European Union, far too many assets are far too long gone to have any chance of being discovered unless their owners wished voluntarily to repatriate them or to declare their existence; any legislation requiring them to do either of these things would, frankly, have about as much chance of success as the prohibition legislation in the United States of America in the first half of the twentieth century.

That does not alter the fact that since 1979, and particularly in the first decade thereafter, many individuals resident in the United Kingdom have created trusts with a view to enabling their funds to be free of any reintroduction of exchange control. The strategy was and is based on the premise that, where the trustees are resident abroad and the investments are situated abroad, the trustees will not themselves be subject to United Kingdom exchange control legislation and the beneficiary, not having the power to control the trustees, will himself not be able to procure that the funds are brought within the scope of the control. In the jargon of the 1980s, such non-resident trustees are said to be "non-compellable". There can therefore be no doubt that the fear that exchange control might be re-introduced has been and to a very much lesser extent still is a powerful stimulus to the formation of new off-shore trusts.

Trusts which already existed during the period of exchange control were, on the other hand, classified either as resident or as non-resident. Their classification depended entirely on the residential status of the creator of the trust at the time of its creation, the settlor in the case of an *inter vivos* trust and the deceased at the date of his death in the case of a will trust. Where a trust was resident, there was no restriction on the appointment of non-resident trustees as such but the assets could only be transferred to them with the consent of the Bank of England, which unsurprisingly was sparingly given. Permission was generally refused unless it could be shown that all the possible beneficiaries were themselves non-resident. On the other hand, there were very few onerous restrictions on trusts which had throughout their existence been non-resident or which had been made non-resident before the original introduction of exchange control.[12] Consequently, once exchange control had been suspended, there was every reason to make existing trusts non-resident and to take the assets abroad while there was no restriction on so doing.

---

[11] Under the Exchange Control Act 1947.
[12] By the Defence (Finance) Regulations 1939, issued under the Emergency Powers (Defence) Acts.

## III. TAXATION

### 1. *Taxation Generally*

In order to determine the taxation advantages of a trust which is for the time being non-resident,[13] it is necessary to consider the taxation liability of both the settlor, the trustees and the beneficiaries.

### 2. *Income Tax*

**(A) The Settlor**
It is extremely unlikely that a resident settlor of a non-resident trust would make himself a beneficiary of that trust but, in the event that he were to do so, his position would be the same as that of any other beneficiary. However if, as is obviously more likely, his unmarried infant children are beneficiaries, then, in the highly unlikely event that any income is actually paid to and applied for their benefit, that income will be treated as the settlor's income for the purposes of income tax.[14] This rule applies to all trusts, whether resident or non-resident; it is, however, hard to imagine that any settlor would be likely to set up a non-resident trust with a view to receiving income from it for his unmarried infant children.

**(B) The Trustees**
An underlying principle of United Kingdom income tax law is that a person is liable to income tax on his total world-wide income if he is resident here but, if he is not resident here, is liable to income tax only on income which is derived from a source in the United Kingdom.

It therefore follows that non-resident trustees will not be liable to income tax in respect of income derived from sources outside the United Kingdom; consequently, they will be wholly free of United Kingdom income tax if all the investments are made abroad. However, they will be liable to income tax in respect of income derived from sources within the United Kingdom to the same extent as trustees who are resident here. It has already been seen[15] that, in principle, this liability will be, in the case of fixed trusts, to income tax of 22 per cent (10 per cent in the case of company distributions and 20 per cent in the case of bank interest) and, in the case of accumulation and discretionary settlements, to income tax of 34 per cent except in the case of accumulated company dividends, on which 25 per cent is payable).[16]

---

[13] For the sake of simplicity, in this chapter the expression "non-resident" is used to mean both non-resident in the strict sense and non-ordinarily resident.
[14] Income and Corporation Taxes Act 1988, s.660B.
[15] See *ante*, p. 629.
[16] See *ante*, pp. 629–630.

## (C) The Beneficiaries

### (1) Actual income

Where a beneficiary is entitled to receive income from a foreign trust, he is liable to income tax on that income whether or not he actually physically receives it.[17] This is so irrespective of the jurisdiction in which the trust assets are situated. No income tax saving is effected, therefore, where the beneficiary is actually entitled to the income.

### (2) Other benefits from income

Were there no other provision, the beneficiaries would therefore escape liability if income were accumulated abroad and either retained abroad or subsequently paid to them as capital. To counter this, there are two far-reaching anti-avoidance provisions.

**(a) Section 739 of the Income and Corporation Taxes Act 1988.** This provision applies where all the following requirements are satisfied:

1. An asset[18] is transferred to a person abroad.[19] This requirement is satisfied even if the asset has not been transferred from the United Kingdom. So, if Andrew, a resident of, say, South Africa, offers to make a gift of R20,000 to Bertram, who is a United Kingdom resident, but Bertram directs Andrew to pay that sum to trustees on his behalf in Guernsey,[20] the payment of that sum will constitute a transfer of an asset for this purpose. In *I.R.C. v. Brackett*,[21] the taxpayer entered into a contract of employment with a Jersey company and was held to be caught by the section because the rights created by the contract were assets transferred to a person abroad.

2. By virtue of, or as a consequence of, that transfer, the income is either directly or indirectly[22] payable to a person or company resident abroad.[23] There is no requirement that that person should have been non-resident at the time of the transfer.[24]

3. Either the transferor or his spouse is a United Kingdom resident[25] and

---

[17] Liability is deferred if it is impossible to remit the income to the U.K.; Income and Corporation Taxes Act 1988, s.418. If the person entitled to the income is resident but not domiciled in the U.K., foreign income is only liable to U.K. income tax if remitted to the U.K.

[18] The expression includes money and property or rights of any kind.

[19] That is to say out of Great Britain and Northern Ireland.

[20] Which is "abroad" for this purpose.

[21] [1986] S.T.C. 521.

[22] This follows from the application of the general principle to a transfer by "an associated operation". s.739 defines "associated operation" in relation to any transfer as "an operation of any kind effected by any person in relation to any of the assets transferred or any assets representing, whether directly or indirectly, any of the assets transferred, or to the income arising from any such assets, or to any assets representing, whether directly or indirectly, the accumulations of income arising from any such assets".

[23] For this purpose, "income" does not include a director's remuneration.

[24] *Congreve v. I.R.C.* [1948] 1 All E.R. 948.

[25] *Vestey v. I.R.C.* [1980] A.C. 1148.

enjoys, or has power to enjoy, that income; the definition of "power to enjoy" is very wide indeed.[26]

4. In respect of income arising on or before November 25, 1996, either the transferor or his spouse was at the time of the transfer a United Kingdom resident[27] (in respect of income arising thereafter, it does not matter where the transferor or his spouse were resident at the time of the transfer).[28]

Where the section applies, the income arising abroad is treated for income tax purposes as the income of the United Kingdom resident with the power to enjoy it to the extent that the foreign resident does not actually distribute it to anyone else.

Section 741 establishes two exceptions to Section 739:

1. Where the Board of Inland Revenue is satisfied that tax avoidance was not the purpose or one of the purposes for which the transfer was effected. The House of Lords has held that taking advantage of an offer of freedom from tax which the legislation has specifically made does not constitute tax avoidance for the purpose of this exception, stating that "tax avoidance within the meaning of section 741 is a course of action designed to conflict with or defeat the evident intention of Parliament".[29] This exception is therefore likely to prove much more useful than was previously thought.[30]

2. Where the transfer was part of a bona fide commercial transaction and not designed for the purpose of avoiding tax. The precise scope

---

[26] s.742(2) provides that for the purposes of the section an individual is deemed to have power to enjoy the income of a person resident or domiciled out of the U.K. if:

"(a) the income is in fact so dealt with by any person as to be calculated, at some point of time, and whether in the form of income or not, to enure for the benefit of the individual, or

(b) the receipt or accrual of the income operates to increase the value to the individual of any assets held by him for his benefit, or

(c) the individual receives or is entitled to receive, at any time, any benefit provided or to be provided out of that income or out of moneys which are or will be available for the purpose by reason of the effect or successive effects of the associated operations on that income and on any assets which directly or indirectly represent that income, or

(d) the individual has power, by means of the exercise of any power of appointment or power of revocation or otherwise, to obtain for himself, whether with or without the consent of any other person, the beneficial enjoyment of the income, or may, in the event of the exercise of any power vested in any other person, become entitled to the beneficial enjoyment of the income, or

(e) the individual is able in any manner whatsoever, and whether directly or indirectly, to control the application of the income."

Even this is extended by s.742(3).

[27] I.R.C. v. Willoughby [1997] 1 W.L.R. 1071.
[28] Finance Act 1997, s.81.
[29] I.R.C. v. Willoughby [1997] 1 W.L.R. 1071 at 1079, per Lord Nolan.
[30] Earlier editions of this work described this exception, clearly wrongly, as "more apparent than real" (5th ed., p. 431; 6th ed., p. 564). Precisely how the "evident intention" of Parliament will be established of course remains to be seen.

of the phrase "bona fide commercial" has been the subject of some dispute[31] and awaits a definitive interpretation.[32]

Nevertheless in most cases where a United Kingdom resident forms a trust abroad and places money or other assets in that trust under which he or his spouse is a beneficiary, section 739 will apply and there will be no saving of income tax. Indeed, the liability incurred can be greater than if the income had arisen within the United Kingdom. In *Lord Chetwode v. I.R.C.*,[33] Lord Chetwode created a settlement in the Bahamas, which owned the entire share capital of a Bahamian investment company. It was held that he was assessable on the whole[34] of the income of the investment company and that he could not even deduct the expenses of the management of that company in computing the amount of income to be brought into account for tax.

**(b) Section 740 of the Income and Corporation Taxes Act 1988.** The provision just considered, section 739, applies only where the transfer of assets was made by the taxpayer or his spouse. Section 740 applies where an individual who is resident in the United Kingdom can benefit under a foreign trust but was not a settlor in relation to it. If, therefore, Edward creates a non-resident discretionary settlement under which he and his son Frank are discretionary beneficiaries and both are residents, during Edward's lifetime section 739 will apply. Frank will be liable on general principles to income tax on any income which he actually receives but, provided he took no part in setting up the arrangements, he will only be liable, if at all, under section 740 in respect of income which he does not actually receive. During Edward's lifetime, Frank will not be taxed under section 740 in respect of income on which Edward is taxed under section 739. But after Edward's death Frank is clearly potentially liable under section 740.

Under section 740, it is necessary to calculate all the income of a foreign trust which arose after March 9, 1981 directly or indirectly from a transfer of assets and which can be used for providing a benefit for an individual who is resident in the United Kingdom. Thus, in the example, income which is accumulated on which Edward is not taxed under section 739 is relevant income for this purpose because it is capable of providing a benefit for Frank at some time in the future. A running notional record is kept of this income but no liability arises at that stage. When, however, the individual receives a benefit from the trust which is not taxable as ordinary income, the value of that benefit is treated as forming part of his income for the year in which he actually receives it. Thus, if the trustees made a discretionary capital payment to Frank, he will be subject to income tax on it to the extent that it is covered by income which has already arisen to the trustees on which tax has not yet been paid.

In summary, therefore, the general position is that:

---

[31] See, in the context of a different statutory provision, *I.R.C. v. Goodwin* [1976] 1 W.L.R. 191.

[32] The point was specifically left open in *I.R.C. v. Willoughby* [1997] 1 W.L.R. 1071 at 1081, *per* Lord Nolan.

[33] [1977] 1 All E.R. 638.

[34] In practice, the Revenue do allow a very limited deduction from the gross income in respect of the costs of collecting that income.

(a) a beneficiary resident in the United Kingdom will be liable to income tax on the actual income which he receives or to which he is entitled;

(b) the settlor and his spouse[35] will, if resident in the United Kingdom, be liable to income tax on income retained within the trust unless it cannot be applied for his or her benefit, this liability being to tax when the income arises; and

(c) other beneficiaries resident in the United Kingdom will only be liable to income tax on income retained within the trust when they actually receive benefit from it.

Non-resident trusts are, therefore, a useful means by which the liability to income tax can be deferred.

### 3. Capital Gains Tax

For capital gains tax purposes, a trust will, in principle, only be regarded as non-resident if both the following conditions are fulfilled:

(a) the general administration of the trust is ordinarily carried on outside the United Kingdom (there is no definition of precisely what this means but the general administration of the trust is probably regarded as ordinarily carried on in the place where the trustees habitually meet or, if the trust is large enough to have its own secretariat, in the place where that secretariat is situated); and

(b) the majority of the trustees are not resident or ordinarily resident in the United Kingdom.[36]

These requirements can be satisfied despite the fact that the settlor was resident in the United Kingdom at the time when the trust was created.

However, a trust will also be regarded as non-resident if all the following three conditions are satisfied:

(a) all the trust property is derived from a person who is not domiciled or resident in the United Kingdom;

(b) some or all of the trustees are individuals or companies whose business consists of or includes the management of trusts or of acting as trustees; and

(c) a majority of the trustees are either such persons, or persons who are actually non-resident.[37]

Trusts who satisfy these three requirements are regarded as being non-resident even if their general administration is actually carried on in the United Kingdom.

---

[35] Which for this purpose includes his widow.
[36] Taxation of Chargeable Gains Act 1992, s.69(1).
[37] *ibid.* s.69(2).

**(A) The Settlor**

A settlor of any non-resident trust who in any year is both domiciled and resident in the United Kingdom will be personally liable to capital gains tax on all gains realised by the trust which would have been taxable if the trust had been resident where a "defined person" benefits or will or may become entitled to a benefit in either the income or the capital of the trust.[38] A "defined person" is the settlor, the settlor's spouse, any child or the spouse of any child of either the settlor or the settlor's spouse, and companies controlled by any such person.[39] In the case of trusts which are created or receive further property or go "off-shore" on or after March 17, 1998, the list also includes any grandchild or the spouse of any grandchild of either the settlor or the settlor's spouse.[40] From the same date, these liabilities also apply to the settlors of trusts created before March 19, 1991,[41] which were formerly exempt.[42] To make matters still worse, although any capital gains had the benefit of the same indexation as resident individuals and trusts until April 5, 1998, they do not have the benefit of the taper relief enjoyed by residents after that date,[43] no matter how long the trustees retain the property in question.

This is an absolutely lethal provision, particularly because it includes children and step-children (and now grandchildren and step-grandchildren) of any age. However, some alleviation is provided by the fact that it only applies where the settlor is both domiciled and resident in the year in question. Settlors of off-shore trusts can therefore avoid liability either by leaving the trust property in the form of assets such as cash which are not liable to capital gains tax in the first place or by becoming non-resident themselves before substantial capital gains are realised, although they will have to be non-resident for five years if they were resident for four of the seven years prior to their departure.[44] Further, many trusts which are created, as distinct from transferred, off-shore are purportedly created by non-resident settlors who, for a consideration, settle a nominal amount of their own money; the real trust property then reaches the hands of the trustees by a route which can best be described as circuitous (this was admittedly easier to achieve when it was considerably easier to deposit large amounts of cash and considerably more difficult to follow bank transfers than it has now become).[45] Settlements with genuine off-shore settlors are of course outside the scope of this provision altogether.

**(B) The Trustees**

In common with non-resident individuals, non-resident trustees are not

---

[38] *ibid.* s.86.
[39] *ibid.* Sched. 5, para. 2(3).
[40] Finance Act 1998, s.130.
[41] *ibid.* s.132.
[42] Taxation of Chargeable Gains Act 1992, Sched. 5, para. 9. The subsequent addition of property or of a "defined person" as a beneficiary destroyed the exemption.
[43] See *ante*, p. 634.
[44] Taxation of Chargeable Gains Act 1992, ss.10A, 86A.
[45] For this reason the extension to non-resident trusts created before March 19, 1991 (which were formerly exempt trusts) is unlikely to have much impact.

chargeable to capital gains tax in respect of gains arising on the disposal of assets, even if the assets are situated in the United Kingdom.[46]

## (C) The Beneficiaries

The liability of the beneficiaries of non-resident trusts to capital gains tax depended until March 16, 1998 on whether the trust in question was what was known[47] as a section 87 trust[48] and or a fully foreign trust.[49] However, in respect of capital gains arising on or after March 17, 1998 all non-resident trusts are subject to the regime which formerly applied only to section 87 trusts.

The provisions of section 87 of the Taxation of Chargeable Gains Act 1992, which now apply to all capital gains realised by non-resident trusts, are similar to those of section 740 of the Income and Corporation Taxes Act 1988.[50] A notional record is maintained of all gains which accrue to the trustees after March 9, 1981. These are known as "trust gains". When the trustees make a capital payment to a beneficiary,[51] that payment is treated as representing a capital gain to the extent of the available trust gains. Suppose, therefore, that the trustees realise the following gains, and make the following capital payments:

| Year of assessment | Gains | Capital Payment |
| --- | --- | --- |
| 2000/2001 | nil | £8,000 to Andrew |
| 2001/2002 | £20,000 | nil |
| 2002/2003 | £20,000 | £15,000 to Brian |
| 2003/2004 | £20,000 | £50,000 to Charles |
| 2004/2005 | £20,000 | nil |

---

[46] Taxation of Chargeable Gains Act 1992, s.2(1). There is, however, a liability if a non-resident, whether an individual or a trustee, carries on a trade in the U.K. and disposes of trading assets (*ibid.* s.10(1)).

[47] Colloquially, not by statute.

[48] "Section 87" trusts, that is trusts which were within section 87 of the Taxation of Chargeable Gains Act 1992, were trusts in which, during the year of assessment being considered:
  (a) the trustees were non-resident;
  (b) if the trust was created *inter vivos*, and the settlor was still alive, the settlor
    (i) was domiciled and resident in the United Kingdom at the time when the settlement was created; or
    (ii) was domiciled and resident in the United Kingdom in the year of assessment being considered; or
  (c) if the settlement was created *inter vivos* and the settlor was dead, he was domiciled and resident in the United Kingdom when the settlement was created; or
  (d) if the settlement was created by will, the testator was domiciled and resident in the United Kingdom at the date of his death.

[49] A "fully foreign trust" was one which was non-resident and which was outside the scope of s.87. No liability attached to beneficiaries, even if resident in the U.K., in respect of gains realised by the trustees of a fully non-resident trust. This was so whether or not the trustees made capital payments to the beneficiaries. However, where a beneficiary became absolutely entitled to assets as against the trustees of a fully foreign trust, he would in general be treated as acquiring those assets at a nil base cost and so he would be taxable on the whole of the proceeds of sale when he disposed of them. This regime does not apply to any capital gains realised by a non-resident trust on or after March 17, 1998. However, beneficiaries who became absolutely entitled to assets as against the trustees of a fully foreign trust before that date will still be taxable on the whole of the proceeds of sale when they dispose of them.

[50] See *ante*, p. 874.

[51] Whether resident or non-resident.

The trust gains for 2000/2001 are nil. Of the gains realised in 2001/2002, £8,000 are attributed to Andrew for 2001/2002, and the balance of £12,000 is carried forward to 2002/2003. The trust gains for 2002/2003 are (a) the balance brought forward from 1996/1997, £12,000, and (b) the gains arising in the year, £20,000, less (c) £15,000 which is attributed to Brian. The balance of £17,000 is carried forward. In 2003/2004 the trust gains total £37,000[52] so that £37,000 is attributed to Charles for 2003/2004. The remaining £13,000 which Charles has received in that year will have the gains for 2004/2005 attributed to it. If any of Andrew, Brian or Charles is domiciled and resident in the United Kingdom in the year in which any of these gains is attributed to a capital payment made to him, he will have to pay the appropriate capital gains tax on the gain in question in accordance with the normal rules; thus, he can deduct from the attributed gain any losses and his annual exemption and he will be taxed on the balance at the same rate as that at which he pays income tax. As before, although any capital gains had the benefit of the same indexation as resident individuals and trusts until April 5, 1998, they do not have the benefit of the taper relief enjoyed by residents after that date,[53] no matter how long the trustees retain the property in question. However, no capital gains tax will be payable by any beneficiary who is not domiciled and resident in the United Kingdom in the year in question.

Further, in addition to the basic capital gains tax payable in the manner illustrated in this example, beneficiaries who receive capital payments after April 5, 1992 and are liable to pay capital gains tax because they are domiciled and resident in the United Kingdom also have to pay a supplementary interest charge of 10 per cent per annum of the tax actually payable in respect of any period up to six years during which payment of capital gains tax has been deferred.[54] In the example above, the capital payment to Andrew is not liable to this interest charge because no capital gains tax was actually deferred. However, the capital payments made to Brian and Charles will be liable to this payment. Of the £15,000 attributed to Brian in 2002/2003, £12,000 was brought forward from 2001/2002; if he is domiciled and resident in the United Kingdom in 2002/2003, he will therefore have to pay an extra 10 per cent of the tax due in respect of that £12,000 by way of interest (no interest will be payable in respect of the other £3,000 since that gain arose in the year in which he received the capital payment). In the same way, Charles will, if domiciled and resident in the United Kingdom in 2003/2004, have to pay an extra 10 per cent of the tax due in respect of £17,000 of the £37,000 attributed to him in 2003/2004 by way of interest.

The provisions seem complicated but their effect is that no liability can attach to a resident beneficiary until he actually receives a capital payment. Accordingly, deferment of capital gains tax can be achieved merely by retaining all capital within the trust, although such deferment will of course now be liable to an interest payment of 10 per cent per annum of the tax due in respect of any gains during the six years prior to the receipt of a capital payment by a resident beneficiary.

---

[52] That is to say, £17,000 brought forward from 2002/2003 and the £20,000 which arises in 2004/2005.
[53] See *ante*, p. 634.
[54] Taxation of Chargeable Gains Act 1992, ss.91–97.

It is obviously possible for the same capital payment to be capable of being treated both as the income of the beneficiary under section 740 of the Income and Corporation Taxes Act 1988 for the purposes of income tax and as representing a capital gain by that beneficiary to the extent of the available trust gains under section 87 of the Taxation of Chargeable Gains Act 1992 for the purpose of capital gains tax. In such circumstances, the treatment of the payment as income enjoys priority over its treatment as representing a capital gain.

Finally, it should be noted that dispositions of beneficial interests by the beneficiaries of non-resident trusts give rise to a chargeable gain and, therefore, to a potential liability to capital gains tax. The exemption given to resident trusts by section 76 of the Taxation of Chargeable Gains Act 1992[55] does not apply.[56]

## (D) Exporting Trusts

Since March 19, 1991, the exportation of a trust has constituted a deemed disposal by the trustees[57] similar to that which occurs when a beneficiary becomes absolutely entitled to the whole or any part of the trust property.[58] The deemed disposal is said to take place immediately before the trustees cease to become resident in the United Kingdom. Consequently, it is the retiring United Kingdom trustees who make the disposal and become primarily liable for the tax. This obviously means that exporting a trust involves the payment of capital gains tax on all gains made prior to export. Subsequent capital gains realised before March 17, 1998 escaped tax to the extent that the trust when exported did not become a section 87 trust (which it usually would have anyway).[59] Otherwise capital gains tax will be payable if any capital payments are made to beneficiaries who are domiciled and resident in the United Kingdom. The introduction of this exit charge has made exporting trusts considerably less attractive than hitherto. Nevertheless, provided that the settlor does not himself become liable to tax on the capital gains realised by the trust, there is still some merit in hiving off and exporting those assets in a trust which are likely to make substantial capital gains in the future and there is everything to be said for hiving off and exporting those assets in a trust which are actually showing a capital loss.

## 4. Inheritance Tax

Where settled property is situated in the United Kingdom, inheritance tax will in any event be payable by the settlor, the trustees and the beneficiaries according to the ordinary rules already discussed, which depend on whether or not there is an interest in possession in that property.[60]

Where settled property is situated outside the United Kingdom, that property is "excluded property" for inheritance tax purposes if, but only if, the settlor was domiciled outside the United Kingdom at the time when the set-

---

[55] See *ante*, p. 636.
[56] *ibid*. s.76(1A), (1B).
[57] *ibid*. s.80(2).
[58] See *ante*, p. 637.
[59] Because of the domiciliary and residential status of the settlor; see *ante*, fn. 48.
[60] See *ante*, pp. 639, 644.

tlement was made.[61] If property is excluded property, there will be no liability upon the coming to an end of an interest in possession, or upon any of the occasions on which inheritance tax is normally payable in the case of a discretionary trust, such as the making of a capital distribution out of the settled property, or the decennial anniversaries of the creation of the settlement.

The settlor will be treated as being domiciled in some part of the United Kingdom at the time when the settlement was created if:

(a) he would have been treated as so domiciled according to the general law; or

(b) he would have been treated as so domiciled according to the general law at any time within three years prior to the creation of the settlement[62]; or

(c) he had been resident in the United Kingdom for at least 17 out of the 20 years ending with that in which the settlement was made.[63]

The last two categories only have full application where the property became settled after December 9, 1974.

Where, at the time when a settlement was made, the settlor was domiciled in some part of the United Kingdom, that settlement will, in principle, be permanently within the purview of inheritance tax. Strictly, inheritance tax will be payable even if the settlor, trustees, and all possible beneficiaries are resident outside the United Kingdom, and all the settled property is situated outside the United Kingdom. Realistically, however, the Inland Revenue will only have any chance of collecting any inheritance tax due if on his death the settlor left assets in the United Kingdom in respect of which a grant of representation is necessary; otherwise, the Inland Revenue are unlikely even to discover that he has died, never mind have any assets against which to charge the tax. This is one of a number of examples of circumstances in which, following the export of a settlement, the parties are content to rely on the rule that one state will not enforce the tax laws of another; in other words, although inheritance tax may be payable, the parties will so conduct themselves that the tax cannot in practice be recovered.

In other circumstances it may be possible to rely on a specific exemption which applies to Government securities. Most United Kingdom Government securities issued before March 18, 1977[64] are exempt from all United Kingdom taxation, including inheritance tax,[65] while they are in the beneficial ownership of persons who are neither domiciled,[66] nor ordinarily resident in the United Kingdom. This exemption applies to settled property where a person who is neither domiciled nor resident in the United Kingdom has an interest in

---

[61] Inheritance Tax Act 1984, s.6(1).
[62] *ibid.* s.267(1)(a).
[63] *ibid.* s.267(1)(b); for this purpose, domicile has its normal meaning and s.267 does not apply to treat the person in question as domiciled (s.267(2)).
[64] *ibid.* s.6(2).
[65] But the specific requirements for obtaining the exemption which are set out in the inheritance tax legislation must be satisfied; *Van Ernst & Cie S.A. v. I.R.C.* [1980] 1 All E.R. 677.
[66] "Domiciled" here has its ordinary, and not its extended, meaning.

possession in the securities.[67] If there is no interest in possession in the securities, the exemption only applies if it can be shown that all known persons for whose benefit the settled property or its income has been or might be applied are neither domiciled nor ordinarily resident in the United Kingdom.[68] Anti-avoidance provisions prevent exempt securities from being channelled from a trust with resident discretionary beneficiaries to one without any.[69] It follows that where for example, a fund is held upon trust for Andrew for life, with remainder to Hamish, inheritance tax will be avoided if, at the death of Andrew, he is neither domiciled nor resident in the United Kingdom and the fund is invested in exempt Government securities.

However, the liability to inheritance tax does not generally depend on the residential status of the trust. If the settlement was created by a non-domiciled settlor and the property is situated abroad, the excluded property rules apply whether the trust is resident or non-resident. If the trust property consists of exempt British Government securities and the beneficiaries are non-domiciled and non-resident, the exemption will also apply whether the trust is resident or non-resident. Exporting a trust will, therefore, neither mitigate nor exacerbate the liability to inheritance tax.

### 5. *Taxation Summary*

The preceding parts of this chapter have attempted briefly to describe the effect of highly complex legislation. It will have been seen that if a new non-resident trust is created, or if an existing resident trust is exported:

(a) there will be no income tax saving in respect of income received, or receivable by a resident beneficiary;

(b) liability to income tax on accumulated or withheld income may be deferred until the benefit of it is received by a resident beneficiary;

(c) provided that the settlor does not become liable to tax on the capital gains realised by the non-resident trust, the liability of a resident beneficiary to capital gains tax will be deferred until a capital payment is received subject to the payment of interest in respect of the period of deferment, but only after the exit charge has been paid, thus restricting benefit to subsequent capital gains; and

(d) liability to inheritance tax will be the same as if the trust had remained resident.

### IV. HOW TRUSTS ARE EXPORTED

The incidence of the taxes to which the settlor, the trustees and the beneficiaries of a non-resident trust are potentially liable does not in any case depend on the identity of the applicable law of the trust in question. The applicable law of any newly-created non-resident trust will almost inevitably

---

[67] Inheritance Tax Act 1984, s.48(4).
[68] *ibid.*
[69] *ibid.* s.48(5).

not be English law. However, it is highly likely that the proper law of any existing resident trust which is exported will be English law. Any change in that applicable law will require either the existence of a provision in the trust instrument expressly permitting this, or the agreement of all the beneficiaries which, if any of the beneficiaries is not *sui juris*, will require an order of the court under the Variation of Trusts Act 1958.[70] But not only is such a change of applicable law not necessary in order to export a trust; it will not of itself achieve the fiscal advantages which have already been considered. None of these can be obtained unless the trustees also become non-resident; further, capital gains tax advantages can only, generally speaking, be obtained if the general administration of the trust is thereafter ordinarily carried on outside the United Kingdom.[71]

A change in the applicable law may be desirable for other reasons, such as a wish to take advantage of what are perceived as the more favourable provisions of the trust law of some other jurisdiction[72] or simply a wish to have the trust property administered in accordance with the trust law of the jurisdiction where it or the administration of the trust is to be situated.[73] More fundamental changes to the existing trust instrument may also be necessary to take account of differences between English trust law and the new proper law. Indeed, if a trust is to be exported to a jurisdiction which does not recognise trusts or does not recognise them in the form known to English law, the beneficial interests may have to be completely recast. Most modern trust deeds contain what are known as overriding powers of appointment, permitting the trustees and/or the settlor and/or the protector to revoke all the existing beneficial interests and declare new ones; however, the standard forms of this power can probably only be used to declare new "trusts" in the sense in which that term is understood by English law. It may be that wider powers including a provision to declare new beneficial interests as nearly as possible equating to trusts under English law may become common.

Where a change of applicable law or some more fundamental change to the existing trust instrument is either desirable or necessary for one of the reasons referred to in the previous paragraph, then whether or not that is possible will be determined by the provisions of the trust instrument and/or the agreement of the beneficiaries and/or the court. However, whether or not this is the case, it will undoubtedly be necessary for the trust to acquire non-resident trustees. Where no other changes are desirable and/or possible, this is all that will be necessary. In principle, and very much in theory, the existing trustees (or one or more of them) could themselves simply emigrate. This is obviously possible where the existing trustees include the settlor and/or the beneficiaries but is almost inconceivable in the case of professional trustees and corporate trustees could not emigrate even if they wanted to. In practice, therefore, it is almost inevitable that it will be necessary to replace at least some of the existing resident trustees by non-resident trustees.

Superficially, this process appears quite straightforward. Whoever has the power to appoint new trustees to the trust in question[74] can simply appoint

---

[70] See *ante*, p. 862.
[71] See *ante*, p. 875.
[72] See *ante*, p. 867.
[73] *ibid.*
[74] See *ante*, p. 551.

new non-resident trustees and the existing trustees can then retire with the trust property being simultaneously transferred to the new trustees or being left to vest in them automatically.[75] Unfortunately, however, as the next two sections of this chapter demonstrate, this apparently straightforward process is not always as simple as it seems.

## V. WHEN NON-RESIDENT TRUSTEES MAY BE APPOINTED

There are no statutory provisions referring specifically to the appointment of non-resident, as distinct from resident, trustees, probably because the possibility would not even have occurred to anyone for most of the nineteenth century and certainly did not become at all common until long after the Trustee Act 1925 was enacted. Such rules as have been developed have therefore had to be developed by the courts.

The English courts undoubtedly have power to appoint non-resident trustees of a settlement whose proper law is English law[76] and also have power to approve an arrangement under the Variation of Trusts Act 1958 by which non-resident trustees are appointed and the trust is consequently exported.[77] This power will be exercised if the court considers that such an appointment is in the interest of the beneficiaries.

It will usually be in the interest of the beneficiaries for the trust to be administered and for the trustees to be resident in the same territory as that in which the beneficiaries, or a majority of them, reside. *Re Seale's Marriage Settlement*,[78] was concerned with a marriage settlement made in 1931 at a time when the husband and wife were domiciled in England. The husband and wife subsequently emigrated to Canada with their children and at the date of the hearing in 1961 had been living in Canada for some years and were domiciled there. Buckley J. found as a fact that they intended to continue to reside there. They wanted to export the trust to Quebec in two stages: first, by the appointment of a Canadian trust corporation as trustee of the marriage settlement with the consequential discharge of the English trustees; and, secondly, by the property subject to the marriage settlement being transferred to the Canadian corporation as trustee of a new Quebec settlement. The new settlement followed as closely as possible the terms of the English settlement but could not include certain protective life interests which were not recognised by the law of Quebec. Buckley J. was satisfied that it was to the advantage of all the beneficiaries for the settlement to be exported and he approved the arrangements. This decision was followed in *Re Windeatt's Will Trusts*.[79] The testator, who died domiciled in England, created a will trust for the benefit principally of his daughter and her children. The daughter and her children had lived in Jersey for 19 years prior to the application and were held to be permanently resident there. Pennycuick J. approved an arrangement for

---

[75] See *ante*, p. 563.
[76] *Meinertzhagen v. Davis* (1844) 1 Coll.N.C. 355; *Re Long's Settlement* (1869) 17 W.R. 218; *Re Seale's Marriage Settlement* [1961] Ch. 574; *Re Whitehead's Will Trusts* [1971] 1 W.L.R. 833.
[77] *Re Seale's Marriage Settlement* [1961] Ch. 574; *Re Windeatt's Will Trusts* [1969] 1 W.L.R. 692; *Re Whitehead's Will Trusts* [1971] 1 W.L.R. 833.
[78] [1961] Ch. 574.
[79] [1969] 1 W.L.R. 692.

two Jersey residents to be appointed as trustees and for the trust assets to be transferred to them.

In certain circumstances it will also be in the interests of the beneficiaries for non-resident trustees to be appointed even if the beneficiaries are resident in a jurisdiction different from that in which the trustees are resident. It may be in the interests of the beneficiaries for the trust to be exported from the United Kingdom so that it may cease to be liable to United Kingdom taxation but not appropriate for the trust to be exported to the jurisdiction in which the beneficiaries are resident if that jurisdiction does not recognise, or is not fully acquainted with, the concept of a trust; in such circumstances, it may clearly be appropriate for the trust to be exported to a territory which does recognise trusts. In *Re Chamberlain*,[80] some of the beneficiaries of a trust subject to English law were resident in France and the others were resident in Indonesia; neither of these jurisdictions recognised trusts and so the court approved an arrangement to export the trust to Guernsey by the appointment of trustees resident there.

On the other hand, the court will not approve the appointment of non-resident trustees if they are resident in a territory which may be reluctant to enforce the trust. If all the trustees are non-resident and the assets are situated abroad, the court will be incapable of protecting the beneficiaries and it will therefore wish to be satisfied that, in the case of any maladministration, the beneficiaries will be given protection by the local law. This was a factor which influenced the Court of Appeal in *Re Weston's Settlement*[81] to refuse to appoint non-resident trustees, although, as will be seen later on, this was not the principal reason for their decision. The basis of this conclusion was the fact that at that time there was no equivalent of the Trustee Act 1925 in Jersey and no *inter vivos* settlement had ever had to be enforced by the courts of Jersey. While this general principle is unquestionably sound, the particular objection to Jersey appears to have been misconceived and Pennycuick J. subsequently approved the exportation of trusts to Jersey in both *Re Windeatt's Will Trusts*[82] and *Re Whitehead's Will Trusts*.[83] It should be added that comprehensive trust legislation was enacted in Jersey in 1984.[84]

Whether the court will approve exportation where the beneficiaries are all resident in England and the principal purpose is the mitigation of fiscal liabilities is much less clear. In principle, in view of the attitude which the court has taken in the case of applications to mitigate such liabilities in other circumstances,[85] there should be no insuperable objection to the export of a trust in these circumstances. However, some doubts were cast on this conclusion by the decision in *Re Weston's Settlements*,[86] where there were admittedly three different grounds on which approval was denied.

The settlor had in 1964 transferred a total of 500,000 shares in The Stanley Weston Group to the trustees of two settlements for the benefit of his two sons.

---

[80] [1976] N.L.J. 1934.
[81] [1969] 1 Ch. 223, discussed in detail *ante* p. 747; *post, infra.*
[82] [1969] 1 W.L.R. 692; see *ante*, p. 883.
[83] [1971] 1 W.L.R. 833; see *post*, p. 886.
[84] Trusts (Jersey) Law 1984.
[85] See for example *Pilkington v. I.R.C.* [1964] A.C. 612, *ante*, p. 703 and decisions on the Variation of Trusts Act 1958, *ante*, p. 747.
[86] [1969] 1 Ch. 223; see also *ante*, p. 747.

In the very next year, the legislature introduced, for the first time, a capital gains tax, something which neither the settlor nor his advisers had anticipated. The shares rose in value and, by the time of the hearing at first instance in 1968, they were pregnant with a liability to capital gains tax of £163,000. The settlor lived in England until 1967. Having in the first half of that year made three visits of a few days each to Jersey, he then purchased a house there, in which he lived from August 1967. In November 1967 an application was made to the court for the appointment as trustees of the two settlements of two professional men in Jersey of impeccable standing and the approval of an arrangement under which the property subject to the settlements could be transferred to settlements in identical terms subject to the law of Jersey. It was hoped that the property subject to the settlements would thereby avoid capital gains tax[87] and also estate duty.[88]

Both Stamp J. and the Court of Appeal refused to sanction the arrangement. They were influenced by two main factors.[89] First, there was clearly some doubt whether the settlor and his children, the main beneficiaries, would live in Jersey permanently, particularly as they had only been there for a few months prior to the date of the hearing; that was insufficient to show any settled intention to remain and the court was clearly worried about the possibility that, following the approval of the arrangement and a sale of the shares free of capital gains tax, the beneficiaries would return to England.[90] Secondly, as has already been mentioned in a previous chapter,[91] this was, according to Stamp J., "a cheap exercise in tax avoidance" which ought not to be sanctioned,[92] a view also taken in the Court of Appeal by Harman L.J., who described it as "an essay in tax avoidance naked and unashamed".[93]

It is, frankly, somewhat surprising that this seems to have disturbed the court in the light of the fact that numerous applications under the Variation of Trusts Act 1958 have had as their main, if not their only, motive the minimisation of fiscal liabilities.[94] It is impossible to avoid wondering whether the court was influenced by the feeling that the settlor, who was the son of a Russian immigrant who had built up his fortune in England during the 1939–45 war, should not be permitted to escape the tax liabilities to which he would normally have been subject. With the benefit of hindsight, it seems that the trustees were unfortunately advised and that the arrangement would have been approved if it had been made a few years later, when it could have been shown that the beneficiaries had genuinely settled in Jersey. However, in *Re Windeatt's Will Trusts*,[95] Pennycuick J. expressed himself to be "in the most complete agreement" with the decision in *Re Weston's Settlements* and in *Richard v. MacKay*[96] Millett J. said that the court was unlikely to appoint non-

---

[87] The exportation of the trust would now of course amount to a deemed disposal and so capital gains tax would be payable; see *ante*, p. 879.
[88] Now replaced by inheritance tax.
[89] A third one, whether the courts of Jersey would enforce the trust, has already been considered; see *ante*, p. 884.
[90] [1969] 1 Ch. 223 at 245, 246, *per* Lord Denning M.R.
[91] See *ante*, p. 747.
[92] [1969] 1 Ch. 223 at 234.
[93] *ibid.* at 246.
[94] See *ante*, p. 747.
[95] [1969] 1 W.L.R. 692 at 696.
[96] (1987) unreported; see (1997) 11 Trust Law International 22 and *post*, p. 887.

resident trustees "where the scheme is nothing more than a device to avoid tax and has no advantages of any kind". However, since neither of these decisions involved any tax avoidance whatever, it remains to be seen what view is adopted when the question actually has to be decided; facts such as those in *Re Weston's Settlements* are obviously unlikely to recur. Provided that the scheme is not entirely motivated by tax avoidance, the practical answer for trustees in this position is probably to make the appointment themselves, assuming of course that they have power to do so, in the way envisaged in *Re Beatty (deceased) (No.2)*,[97] which is discussed below.[98]

The authorities considered so far have concerned the question of when the courts will appoint non-resident trustees. It is now necessary to consider whether, and if so when, resident trustees who have adequate powers for the purpose under the trust instrument or the Trustee Act 1925 can themselves do so.

It has long been clear that, where the court would itself be prepared to appoint non-resident trustees, resident trustees with the power to do so can make an effective appointment without the intervention of the court. In *Re Whitehead's Will Trusts*,[99] the main beneficiary had emigrated to Jersey in 1959 and was found to be permanently resident there.[1] In 1969 the trustees, who were resident in the United Kingdom, executed a deed under section 36 of the Trustee Act 1925[2] appointing persons resident in Jersey as new trustees and retiring from the trusts. However, since the resident trustees wished to be fully protected, the deed of retirement and appointment was made conditional upon the principal beneficiary obtaining from the court a declaration that the resident trustees were effectively discharged. Pennycuick V.-C. duly made the declaration sought.

However, two further questions arise: first, are the trustees only protected if a declaration of this sort is obtained; and, secondly, can the trustees also exercise their own powers in circumstances where the courts would not themselves appoint non-resident trustees? In *Re Whitehead's Will Trusts*,[3] where a declaration was of course obtained, Pennycuick V.-C. said:[4]

"the law has been quite well established for upwards of a century that there is no absolute bar to the appointment of persons resident abroad as trustees of an English trust. I say 'no absolute bar', in the sense that such an appointment would be prohibited by law and would consequently be invalid. On the other hand, apart from exceptional circumstances, it is not proper to make such an appointment, that is to say, the court would not, apart from exceptional circumstances, make such an appointment, nor would it be right for the donees of the power to make such an appointment out of court. If they did, presumably the court would be likely to interfere at the instance of the beneficiaries. There do, however, exist exceptional circumstances in which such an appointment can properly be

---

[97] (1991) unreported; see (1997) 11 Trust Law International 7.
[98] See *post*, pp. 887–888.
[99] [1971] 1 W.L.R. 833.
[1] *ibid.* at 838.
[2] See *ante*, p. 551.
[3] [1971] 1 W.L.R. 833.
[4] *ibid.* at 837.

made. The most obvious exceptional circumstances are those [which actually occurred in that case] in which the beneficiaries have settled permanently in some country outside the United Kingdom and what is proposed to be done is to appoint new trustees in that country."

However, this view has subsequently been rejected in two unreported decisions. In *Richard v. MacKay*,[5] trustees sought a declaration that they were entitled to exercise a power undoubtedly vested in them to transfer about a quarter of the assets of an accumulation and maintenance trust for the benefit of the settlor's children to a new trust which the settlor proposed to create in Bermuda. The settlor, his Malaysian wife, and the children were all resident in the United Kingdom but they had substantial contacts with the Far East both of a financial and of a family nature and there was a real possibility that the children, and indeed their mother in the event of early widowhood, would decide to settle in the Far East. The trust's assets were invested all over the world and the principal motive was flexibility and diversification rather than any immediate tax advantage. Millett J. referred to the observations of Pennycuick V.-C. set out above and said:

"In my judgment, the language of Sir John Pennycuick, which is narrowly drawn, is too restrictive for the circumstances of the present day if, at least, it is intended to lay down any rule of practice. Nor, in my view, is it accurate to equate the approach that the court adopts in the exercise of its own discretion with the approach which it adopts when asked to authorise the trustees to exercise theirs.

"Where the court is invited to exercise an original discretion of its own, the court will require to be satisfied that the discretion should be exercised in the manner proposed. The applicants must make out a positive case for the exercise of the discretion, and the court is unlikely to assist them where the scheme is nothing more than a device to avoid tax and has no advantages of any kind.

"Where, however, the transaction is proposed to be carried out by the trustees in exercise of their own discretion, entirely out of court, the trustees retaining their discretion and merely seeking the authorisation of the court for their own protection, then, in my judgment, the question that the court asks itself is quite different. It is concerned to ensure that the proposed exercise of the trustees' power is lawful and within the power and that it does not infringe the trustees' duty to act as ordinary, reasonable and prudent trustees might act, but it requires only to be satisfied that the trustees can properly form the view that the proposed transaction is for the benefit of beneficiaries or the trust estate.

"In my judgment, where the trustees retain their discretion, as they do in the present case, the court should need to be satisfied only that the proposed transaction is not so inappropriate that no reasonable trustee could entertain it."

He therefore made the declaration sought. His views were subsequently approved and applied by Vinelott J. in another unreported case, *Re Beatty*

---

[5] (1987) unreported; see (1997) 11 Trust Law International 22.

*(deceased) (No.2)*,[6] where a similar declaration was sought by the trustees of the will of a testatrix who had died domiciled and resident in the United Kingdom; they wished to appoint replacement trustees resident in Jersey and transfer to them an absolutely enormous residuary estate, held in more or less equal shares for one resident beneficiary, one non-resident beneficiary, and one beneficiary who was about to become non-resident, in order to avoid a deemed disposal for the purposes of capital gains tax which would arise when the latter two obtained interests in possession.[7]

The trustees can therefore certainly exercise their own powers to appoint non-resident trustees in circumstances where the courts would not themselves do so provided that the proposed transaction is not so inappropriate that no reasonable trustee could entertain it. Given that this is now clearly the law, there cannot possibly be any formal need for the trustees to go to the court for a declaration in every case, although they might well feel that it was prudent for them to do so in a case with facts as extreme as those in *Re Weston's Settlements*![8] However, where they do not seek a declaration, then for the reasons stated in the next section they may also be well-advised to seek adequate indemnities from the non-resident trustees or the beneficiaries.

## VI. EXPORTING PART OF THE TRUST

*Richard v. MacKay*[9] was a case in which non-resident trustees were appointed of part, but not the whole, of the trust fund. Provided that the circumstances are appropriate for the appointment of non-resident trustees in the first place, there is obviously no fundamental objection to this. Indeed, section 37(1)(b) of the Trustee Act 1925 provides that a separate set of trustees may be appointed for any part of the trust property held on trusts distinct from those relating to any other part of the trust property; this provision clearly covers the situation where separate trustees are appointed even although there is no alteration to the trustees of the remainder of the trust fund.

However, as the trustees in *Roome v. Edwards*[10] found out, there are major risks in so doing. This case concerned a marriage settlement created in 1944; in 1955, a power of appointment was exercised in respect of a comparatively small part of the trust fund, whereby that part was thereafter to be held on trust to accumulate the income until a daughter of the marriage reached the age of 25 and then to transfer the capital of that part to her. The appointed fund was, from 1955 onwards, administered as if it were a trust separate from the main fund. One of the assets of the main trust appreciated very substantially in value and with a view to saving capital gains tax the main fund, but not the 1955 fund, was exported by means of the retirement of the resident trustees and the appointment of trustees resident in the Cayman Islands. The capital gain was realised shortly thereafter and the Inland Revenue claimed the capital gains tax from the trustees of the 1955 fund, who were still resident.

---

[6] (1991) unreported; see (1997) 11 Trust Law International 7.
[7] Fortunately for the beneficiaries, judgment in this case was given just 19 days before the exportation itself became a deemed disposal; see *ante*, p. 879.
[8] [1969] 1 Ch. 223.
[9] (1987) unreported; see (1997) 11 Trust Law International 22.
[10] [1981] 1 All E.R. 736.

The House of Lords held that the 1955 fund and the main fund still comprised only one settlement for the purposes of capital gains tax; consequently, the claim succeeded by virtue of the fact that, where part of the property comprised in a settlement is vested in one set of trustees and part in another, they are to be treated as together constituting and acting on behalf of a single body of trustees. The resident trustees of the 1955 fund were therefore liable to pay the tax on the gain realised by the non-resident trustees of the main fund. Lord Roskill gave a clear warning:[11]

"Persons, whether professional men or not, who accept appointment as trustees of settlements such as these are clearly at risk under the [1992] Act and have only themselves to blame if they accept the obligations of trustees in these circumstances without ensuring that they are sufficiently and effectively protected whether by their beneficiaries or otherwise for fiscal or other liabilities which may fall on them personally as a result of the obligations which they had felt able to assume."

Not only are there therefore particular risks in the export of part rather than the whole of a trust but the decision in *Roome v. Edwards* reinforces the view that, whenever resident trustees retire in favour of non-resident trustees without the intervention of the court, they should always seek adequate indemnities.

---

[11] *ibid.* at 744.

# INDEX

[*All references are to page number*]